SOCIAL THEORY

SIXTH EDITION

SOCIAL THEORY

The Multicultural, Global,
and Classic Readings

EDITED WITH COMMENTARIES BY

CHARLES LEMERT

WESTVIEW
PRESS

Westview Press was founded in 1975 in Boulder, Colorado, by notable publisher and intellectual Fred Praeger. Westview Press continues to publish scholarly titles and high-quality undergraduate- and graduate-level textbooks in core social science disciplines. With books developed, written, and edited with the needs of serious nonfiction readers, professors, and students in mind, Westview Press honors its long history of publishing books that matter.

Every effort has been made to secure required permissions for all text, images, maps, and other art reprinted in this volume.

Westview Press books are available at special discounts for bulk purchases in the United States by corporations, institutions, and other organizations. For more information, please contact the Special Markets Department at 2300 Chestnut Street, Suite 200, Philadelphia, PA 19103, or call (800) 810-4145, ext. 5000, or e-mail special. markets@perseusbooks.com.

Names: Lemert, Charles C., 1937- author.
Title: Social theory : the multicultural, global, and classic readings /
   Charles Lemert.
Description: Sixth Edition. | Boulder : Westview Press, 2016. | Revised
   edition of Social theory, 2013.
Identifiers: LCCN 2016015315 (print) | LCCN 2016016941 (ebook) | ISBN
   9780813350028 (hardcover) | ISBN 9780813350448 (ebook)
Subjects: LCSH: Sociology. | Sociology--History.
Classification: LCC HM585 .L3936 2016 (print) | LCC HM585 (ebook) | DDC
   301--dc23
LC record available at https://lccn.loc.gov/2016015315

10 9 8 7 6 5 4 3 2 1

In loving memory of
Florence Brown Lyons (1915?–1995),
who taught me to think and feel about these things,
and thus to read and speak of them

Contents

PART TWO

Social Theories and World Conflict: 1919–1945

Charles Lemert, 149

PART THREE

The Golden Moment: 1945–1963
Charles Lemert, 215

PART FOUR

Will the Center Hold? 1963–1979

Charles Lemert, 287

PART FIVE

After Modernity: 1979–2001

Charles Lemert, 343

PART SIX

Global Realities in an Uncertain Future
Charles Lemert, 443

Preface/2016 Edition

When a book enjoys nearly a quarter-century of life, as this one has, it becomes a kind of monument to the time covered. The problem with historical time is that it has its own mysterious manners, too often changing its direction in ways few saw coming. When this book first appeared in 1994 no one had the kind of lightweight personal computers that today seem to be everywhere. No one, except science fiction readers, could have then imagined the global smart phone that today links anyone anywhere to others elsewhere. More importantly, who then could have imagined the attacks on the World Trade Towers on September 11, 2001. Nor, even after 9/11, was it thinkable that the world would become involved in wars in the Middle East, Central Asia, and North Africa that would tear apart the then seeming stable global order. A good quarter-century ago the then long-enduring modern world order started to come undone in the wake of the collapse of the Cold War. Ever after, the spiral spins faster and faster.

In the past few years, the vicious atrocities of the Islamic State in Iraq and Syria make Osama bin Laden's Taliban seem tame by the contrast. Even in the allegedly civil sphere, political leaders use violent gestures and language to intimidate their opponents. A president of Russia invades neighbors in an effort to turn back the clock to the worst days of the Cold War. American police officers shoot and kill with impunity, actions vaguely warranted by the fact the United States is unable or unwilling to limit the sale of the weapons of war used to kill the innocent. As I write, one grand old American political party is campaigning for the nation's highest office as though the civil sphere were a playground if not a gangland.

If this, and more, take place in the wider global sphere, then it should be expected that the vibrations will resonate in the quieter realm of social thought. *Social Theory*, now in its 6th edition, has not only lived during these events, it has also come into its own in a time when the very meaning of "social theory" has taken on a broader meaning. It wasn't all that long ago in the second half of the twentieth century that social thinkers were more likely to identify what they did as, say, sociological or literary theory, feminist or critical race theories. Though this narrower disciplinary names still have a currency, more and more their proponents are likely to view what they do in the broader sense of *social* theory. For one instance, critical race theory began and was once mostly confined to legal studies. Now, through the work of writers like Kimberlé Williams Crenshaw, whose essay on *intersectionality* is included in this edition, is a thoroughly social theorist of the kind that enjoys a close kinship to Patricia Hill Collins's *matrix of domination*. Collins herself would once have been judged to be a black feminist theorist. Today she is well known as a major social theorist and past-president of the American Sociological Association.

One of the seldom recognized consequences of this new recognition of social theory's pervasive value is the realization that social theory has long been, and still is, a normal practical work of writers and thinkers who are not necessarily academics. One of the sad attitudes of many in sociology, my field, is the claim that sociology must never be mere journalism as if to say that those who dig deeper into the facts in order to report important public stories are somehow less serious than academics. The truth is that a great deal of journalism, but also literary non-fiction, even fiction on occasion, is very often both more true and more readable than academic social science. Paul Krugman, the *New York Times* columnist, is an excellent reporter on the global economic situation not because he is a Princeton professor and Nobel Prize winner but because over time he has learned to write out of his academic knowledge in a way that makes sense to a general public.

In this edition of *Social Theory*, I defend the claim that good social theory works at the limits of traditional common sense and academic formalism. This is not an insistence that academics know nothing. I am an academic and some people, it seems, think I know at least something—otherwise they wouldn't read this book. But in this day, more than any before it, social theorists can relax into the realization what we do, whatever our calling in life, is the practical work of trying to understand, even to explain, the world as it is. One consequence of my claim is that the sixth edition of the book includes a new concluding section, *Social Theory at the Limit of the Social*. Here readers will find selections from, among others, writers like Oliver Sacks, Eula Biss, and Ta-Nehisi Coates who have written seriously for the general reader. Then too there are academics who have written at the limits of their disciplinary fields—Robert Pogue Harrison on the dead and Owen Fiss on the limits of the normal understanding of constitutional law; and, too, Marilynne Robinson who, though known for her brilliant fiction is able to write convincingly about the fears that shake ordinary lives in our day.

There are other additions to the earlier sections of the book meant to account for changes of another sort. Harriet Martineau the earliest feminist theorist is here at this late date because her omission previously was a mistake more obvious now that the long history of feminist social theory is better known. Likewise John Stuart Mill is added because his classic book *On Liberty* represents the most coherent essay on liberal theory as it came to be in the nineteenth century. In the 1990s many social theorists assumed that liberalism was dead. A quarter-century later this is far from the case even if the bastardized liberal ideas in neoliberalism are a curse to real economic freedom. Readers will find, if they look closely, that some authors in previous editions have been dropped for the reason that their theories have not endured the test of time. These have been replaced by selections that, even if written some time ago, seem ever more current today. Then too, writers who were introduced in recent editions remain in place even though the day of their original popularity is long past. Bruno Latour, Achille Mbembe, Giorgio Agamben, Gilles Deleuze, and Slavoj Žižek remain, notwithstanding the fact that some finding their writing difficult, even obscure. They are trying to say something of special social importance, often in a manner meant to reflect their view of the times.

There is a cautionary note in all this. We who are older and believe we have figured the hard stuff out, should remember that social theory is first and foremost an attempt to explain or describe social riddles that occur in daily life before anyone bothers to make a theory of them. The young, even the young who are genuinely busy in their lives, understand a text we might find too hard because they are living the reality.

Social Theory as Practical Theories of Unsettled Worlds

When do very big things in life start to change? This is surely one of the more gripping questions anyone can ask. What were the first signs that the love of your life was about to leave? Or when do kids begin to realize that their parents are going to split up? Or, in the larger frame of human events, when exactly did Rome start to decline, or capitalism begin to change how business is done, or the British first realize they were losing their empire, or the telephone first become a cellular body part? Whether the questions are personal or global, people have good reason to wonder when changes of all kinds got under way. Perhaps we worry about this because we want to know why things must change. In the absence of good answers to the why, we settle for a when.

No question is more basic to social science than "why?"; and none is harder to answer than the why of social changes. It is likely that there would be no social science at all without ordinary people asking why things are as they are. Why do apples, ripe but unpicked, fall to the ground? Gravity is the answer everywhere except in outer space. But "gravity" is merely a name for less than self-evident laws of nature. Why, for another example, do people in large groups get along as well as they do? This, it turns out, is a question still more difficult to answer because, as anyone honest with herself knows, to live with others is to be impressed by how impossible they are and how little they respect our perfect social manners. Social scientists would be more than pleased were they able to agree on a term like "gravity" that would explain why, in spite of the countless troubles and conflicts of social life, people in groups do as well together as they do. That it happens, we know. How things happen as they did or do is hard to know because social things are tricky, even devious. If *how* people live together changes, then *why* they get along more than you would suppose also changes.

Hence, asking *when* important social relations and structures begin to change is a central question of any social science. We want to know the *why*, we are dimly aware of the *how*, but we will settle for the *when*. None of the three types of questions is easily answered but at least the when question has the merit of being as common to everyday life as it is to academic social science.

Herein is found the special role of social theory. The first duty of social theorists is to ask fresh why questions. Knowing when the love of one's life may have decided to quit the relationship is some solace to the jilted lover. Was it at that party when she seemed so happy to see that new guy? Is she with him now? Popular music, from country to rap, would be more bereft of coherent lyrics than already they are if it were it not for the devastations love can visit upon the young at heart. At the other extreme, social studies might not have become sciences if people had not wondered, from the start, just when this modern world came into its own, thus to change how people lived together. Anyone who loses a love may doubt his or her self-worth. The people who lose their traditional ways may wonder what will become of them without the old, familiar ways.

Social theories are often able to propose a why, sometimes a how, and even a when to solve these mysteries. Still, when social theories suggest answers to any or all of these questions, they usually start arguments that can last for years to come. The lover who loses out usually gets over it. Social theorists never get over the whys and wherefores they are obliged to ask, even when they admit that answers are hard to come by.

Social theory is the art, if not always the science, of asking the right questions at the risk of irritating the hell out of those who, in their own minds, have already settled the matter. *Social Theory* is a collection of readings that is not meant to be an answer book so much as a compendium of the struggles of modern social theory to ask and answer the why, how, and when of the unthinkable nature of social worlds. The answers once thought convincing may still be. When it comes to social theory, few answers are completely right or wrong, which gives them a good shelf life and makes them worth reading even today. To be a social thinker, if not a professional theorist, is to live with uncertainty—in respect to which the most certain social thing in the modern world is that sooner or later everything changes. This may sound a bit daunting, but when you stop to think about it, most things in life that we consider absolutely certain are not. In life with others the important thing is to accept the changes that cannot be prevented, and to understand them. The social theories you will read here are more than that, to be sure, but they are at least that, which is what makes them interesting, even exciting.

Teaching and Reading Social Theory

If, as I think, social theory is inherently exciting because, when it is good, it tries to identify and explain the big questions that all individuals and collectivities must face, then what might be the corollary to this assumption in respect to reading it? I have already stated my first assumption, learned slowly over the years of teaching the subject while also writing it as best I can. The single most touching letter I have received from a reader of this book was written by a woman in midlife, with kids still at home, working a full-time job, attending a community college in Florida. She claimed that what she read in the book changed her life. She didn't say which texts had this effect, nor did she explain how she found time to read amid all else she was dealing with in life. But it was a sincere message that, over the years, has been repeated many times by others. Let all teachers remember that much of what Karl Marx wrote was written *for* the working class, or that Max Weber's famous essays on science and politics as vocations were given as public lectures, or that Èmile Durkheim was the leading public intellectual of his day, or that no one was more influential in the development of American public education than John Dewey. On it goes. So rule number one is: *Don't be afraid!*

When it comes to teaching, I am sure that some teachers look at this book and say, "interesting stuff but the selections are way too short for what I do." A few have said just this to me; to which I reply, "fair enough." On the other hand, one thing I have learned both as an editor and teacher is that it is amazing how quickly it is possible to go to the core of an argument if that is what you are required to do. I do not claim to have gotten this right in every case. A few times I've gotten it quite wrong and have tried to correct the selections when the time came. I do not claim any special genius at this. If there is a skill here it is to take seriously the practice of Ralph Waldo Emerson who, in his day, read nearly everything (almost literally), but who claimed that he *never* read any book from cover to cover. He was a philosopher. Nonfiction works are easier to treat this way. I would not recommend this approach for the reading of fiction. But for social theories, like philosophies and similar writings, there is wisdom in Emerson's method. There is always a core idea and, in my experience, only the very best have more than one of them, revised and elaborated on. Some of my friends and colleagues in the field will think ill of me for saying it, but Marx's *Capital* is the only classical book of social theory that has quite a few ideas. Happily, they are all in a single section near the start of the argument. By the time he gets to the long chapters on the working day, a good reader will have already gotten his point. By contrast, there are few books, still read today, that are very long but with not much more one than one idea. Durkheim's *Elementary Forms of the Religious Life* is an example—though quickly I add what an idea it was to conclude that Kant's theory of knowledge was wrong because knowledge belongs to the collective life, not the categories of mental life.

It may seem either a conceit or foolishness on my part to suggest that shorter selections can often get at the heart of a social theory (the conceit being that I have been able to do this well). Teachers who do not want to teach shorter selections from a big book are not wrong to think this way. A good many of them (myself included) get around the problem by assigning whole books to provide what *Social Theory* does not or cannot. I have regularly assigned the whole of Weber's *Protestant Ethic and the Spirit of Capitalism* (while excusing college students from responsibility for the footnotes, which constitute more than half the book's mass). Why this book? One reason is that I love the challenge of encouraging students to learn to follow a long and sometimes wayward argument that covers what, to them, can be weirdly obscure subjects like *extra ecclesium nulla salus*. But also because, Emerson notwithstanding, I do believe that reading books is important and that everyone should do it often. I happen also to think that Weber's book is one of the few from which it is very difficult to snatch a few pages to make the main points.

This brings me to another generic point that, to me, has never been more important than now: *Read!* We all know that not many kids today read books. This does not mean they are stupid. But it does mean that when they become students pursuing higher degrees, they are often ill equipped to do the work. Social theory and other kinds of writing can be difficult if readers have not spent a lifetime facing the daunting task of reading long and complicated books, whether fiction or nonfiction. I am not actually a gifted reader. I grew up in a home without books. My wife, on the other hand, has been reading since she was a child when she locked herself in the only family bathroom to read *War and Peace*. I am seventy-five and that book is still on my list. Very long. I have tried to read Dickens's *Bleak House*. It drives me crazy. Last summer I gave up. At my age, I must save time for *War and Peace*. On the other hand, Dickens's *Great Expectations* is also long and I could hardly put it down. Tastes are always involved in what one reads. In school, teachers usually determine what is required according to their own tastes. But students and other readers just getting into the habit serve themselves very well if they take what is required then follow it by spending time in a good library wandering through undiscovered stacks. If you browse, you will find all manner of mysteries.

One Sunday, as my wife and I rode the E train uptown, I read. Having lost interest in the subway ads for hemorrhoid laser surgeries, I had brought along a collection of Raymond Carver's short stories, *What We Talk About When We Talk About Love.* I finished the first story in the few stops between Canal Street and Penn Station. I paused only a moment. My wife said, "Amazing, isn't it?" I just nodded. It was.

Later, while we were walking in the park, on the East Side just north of the zoo, a jogger lunged toward us at a good pace. His stride was strong but broken. He was crippled. Cerebral palsy, we thought, saying little else. After, we took the shortcut to the Westside. Soon, he came again, having already circled most of the six-mile circuit. Then, my wife said, "I've seen him running here for years. Think of what it takes." I did. I imagined a solitary life, ordered around chaotic limbs, a life he ran with dignity among hundreds of beautiful bodies on roller blades. She had her thoughts, too. We said a little, but less than you would suppose.

Reading is like that. A relatively few abstracted marks or events evoke worlds others already know. But how does it work? When I was a little boy, I asked such a question about the radio. How was it that, each weekday evening at 6:15, I could tune in to *Tom Mix* on the Magnavox console in the safe, far corner of the living room? Though I have since learned many theories about reading, I still do not understand either it or the radio. Somehow, something is broadcast in the air. We get it. Others do, too, even those with whom we share no intimacies at all. In a blurb on the back of the book of stories I read on the subway, Frank Kermode says, "Carver's fiction is so spare in manner that it takes a time before one realizes how completely a whole culture and a whole moral condition is represented by even the most seemingly slight sketch." Though Raymond Carver was among the masters of this sort of writing, much the same can be said of all writing. It succeeds at whatever it does in spite of the sparseness of its means relative to the worlds evoked.

The difference between reading and radio listening, though, is that reading seems to have become an activity of no necessary limits. Among the people I talk to, it is common to refer to the analysis of many different sorts of situations as a "reading." I once heard a little story in which the term was used in such a way. At a dinner party some time ago, a guest had delivered a crude ethnic insult that angered and embarrassed most of those at the table. In a response calculated to set things straight without disrupting the dinner, the hostess gave him what the teller of the story described as "a postmodern reading of the anti-Semitism in his remark." Apparently, that reading did little of its intended good. The old insult was still raw. Just the same, in this case a "reading" is a vastly more complex communication than whatever it was that allowed my wife to understand what I was feeling about a story we had both read and a jogging man we saw. If "reading" is an activity inclusive not just of books and events in the park but even of delicate retorts to gratuitous insults, then it is possible that there is no end to what reading might be. Nor should there be.

However it works, reading does seem to be an accurate way to describe what happens when different people discover a similar sense in an event as spare as that of a handicapped man running well. In the same way that there is not an infinite number of meanings to be derived from a written text like one of Carver's short stories, neither is it that the true nature of that man's world is likely to be much different from what most people might imagine. Different, surely, but certainly not random. Otherwise, nothing we read would make sense. However it works, reading cannot work all too differently from the radio. Somehow, in Kermode's words, "a whole culture" is out there. Reading is what is done with it in order to make worlds for ourselves.

Reading, in this expanded sense, is the natural corollary to social theory. If the least common denominator of social theory is telling one's world into being, then reading must be the means by which others recognize that story as somehow familiar to them. Many will disagree with this view. One of the anonymous academic readers of this book was particularly irritated at my suggestion that scientific social theory is no different from the theories people produce in ordinary life. There is a difference, of course. But, however people may cherish and defend that difference, I do not think that professional social theories are degraded in any way by enjoying common ground with ordinary human activity. On the contrary.

I would not say that social theory is nothing but reading, of course. But, in my experience writing books and essays, I have learned a lesson that works very well in my teaching. It seems certain that one of the best ways to read difficult material is to force oneself (or be forced) to write about it. Several years ago, I picked up a tip from Audrey Sprenger, perhaps the best teacher I have ever known, who assigned to her students what she called "close readings," by which she meant for students to write short essays that closely interpret a text. Invariably, some of my own students will call these "closed" readings, either as a joke or because, unconsciously, the stuff seems closed to them. Yet, even when they do not quite understand the material very well, the work of trying to say something about it usually pays off in the long run. I ask students to write one of these a week. They are never graded or returned. The point is to get them engaged as writers. Sometimes, what they write is awful. But, by the end of a semester, when they do these short essays, they have the makings of a substantial essay. They like it and the serious students never complain. So my second rule is: *Read and write 'til you drop.*

We who make a life out of writing social theory are also teachers. So far as I know it is impossible to be a social theorist without a day job, and teaching is the one most of us have. In my experience, there are few things more interesting than listening to a really first-rate scholar talk about teaching and its effect on research. It happened to me not long ago at Yale when Peter Bearman, a distinguished sociologist at Columbia, spoke to faculty and students. Bearman generally does highly mathematical sociology, but, on this occasion, he spoke of writing an ethnography. I don't recall the last time I was so well taught by a serious scholar talking about teaching. Experiences like these remind those who read and write social theory that the point of it all in the long run is to *teach* it.

It is not—nor should it be—just the teachers who teach. Students, it is well known, are really good at this sort of thing. I learned this when I happened on the practice of organizing students into groups assigned to read a list of theories together *and* write a joint paper they present to the class as a whole. At first, they hate this assignment, if only because it takes time and trouble to meet with others outside of class. Of course, there are always free riders who try to get away with doing very little. It turns out that I seldom have to deal with this problem because their fellow group members are often more punitive than I would be. This is because, I assume, they form a social bond of a temporary kind with fellow group members. More often than not, they produce very good social theory that sparks excellent discussion. Many report that they actually have fun.

So, if my first rule of reading social theory is *Don't be afraid*, and the second is *Read and write until you are blue in the face*; my third rule is *Have fun!* Truth be told, I have had quite a lot of it reading, thinking about, writing, and then teaching social theory; and I am not alone.

—Charles Lemert, New Haven

Acknowledgments 2016 Edition

Over five previous editions since 1993, the book has benefited from the generous work of many excellent editors at Westview. In fact, over the course of now six editions there have been, if memory serves, eleven different editors. Such is the way of book publishing these days. I have thank them all along the way of the editions they helped bring to life. For this, the sixth edition, I thank Grace Fujimoto who stepped in early in the process in spite of the fact that she at the time had many other editorial duties at Westview. She has been a supportive as well as meticulous production editor. Yet, I cannot fail to say that the book would not have come to be without its original editor, Dean Birkenkamp. Since 1993 we have become friends. He remains one of academic publishing's most imaginative editors.

Between the first and second editions, Florence Brown Lyons died. The dedication of the first gave her much pleasure. The subsequent dedications to her memory give me pleasure of another kind, though one chastened by her absence.

Between the second and third editions, we lost Matthew to a suicide I have come to accept and even to respect. I miss him still and will until whatever comes next. In this same time, Anna came to Geri, Noah, and me. As this new editions appears Anna is on her way to college. Noah married Adrienne. Geri and I continue to keep our happy life going.

Over the years, many colleagues, students, teachers, friends, and strangers have contributed to my understanding of what the book required and how, over time, it needed to change or remain as it was. I have thanked them in the previous editions. The list by now would be so long as to risk mockery of the gratitude I feel. I think of them often, always with thanksgiving. For this edition I thank Raymond Gunn who, on a warm summer morning on my front porch, forced me to rethink how this book could better treat race theorists and their affines. At every turn, I've done my best.

Charles Lemert
January 19, 2016

Introduction—Social Theory: Its Uses and Pleasures

CHARLES LEMERT

Social theory is a basic survival skill. This may surprise those who believe it to be a special activity of experts of a certain kind. True, there are professional social theorists, usually academics. But this fact does not exclude my belief that social theory is something done necessarily, and often well, by people with no particular professional credential. When it is done well, by whomever, it can be a source of uncommon pleasure.

When, many years ago, my now-adult son Noah was in elementary school, he came home one day with questions that led to some good social theory. After Noah had spent his first two school years in an informal, somewhat countercultural school, we moved. He was then enrolled in a more traditional public school. Thus began a more lively and sociologically interesting line of dinner table talk. He observed, for example, that when his class marched from its classroom to the lunchroom, the boys were told to form one line, the girls another. The march itself was under a code of silence. Having grown accustomed to schools with few rules of any sort, my son found this strange. At dinner, he reported this exotic practice with the ironic question, "What was this for? Do they think we are going to attack the girls?" He was perhaps seven at the time.

Later, in junior high school, he began to figure this out. After some years of close observation, Noah determined that schools impose arbitrary social rules, like walking silently in sex-segregated lines, because they are institutions concerned as much with civil discipline and authority as with learning. He used his own words, but he had developed a social theory congruent to his earlier questions. This he enjoyed because he felt the power of being able to say something persuasive about the world he was then just beginning to engage with the quiet rebellion of a young man in the making.

Most people—whatever their social class, age, gender, race, or sexual orientation—develop a good enough repertoire of social theories of this sort. Usually, one suspects, these theories come into some focus in childhood and early adolescence, often in reply to innocent questions about daily social practices. When such theories are stated, very often in ordinary language, innocence is already lost. The world as it is comes into being.

In *There Are No Children Here* (1991), Alex Kotlowitz tells the story of two boys trying to survive in one of Chicago's most dangerous public housing projects. I read the book a good many years ago; the boys are now grown up like my son. Lafeyette, then age ten, said: "If I grow up, I want to be a bus driver." The "if" suggests one of the reasons Kotlowitz took the book's title from an observation by Lafeyette's mother: "But you know, there are no children here. They've seen too much to be children." This, too, is a social theory. The boy and his mother both put into plain words the social world of the uncounted thousands of urban children whose lullaby is gunfire. If not pleasure, there must at least be some satisfaction in knowing and being able to describe one's place in a world. If you cannot say it, how can you deal with it? Between the experiences of the middle-class, white boy (my son) and a welfare-class, Black boy (Lafeyette), there is common ground. Both knew they knew something important about their social worlds, and they knew what they knew because they could put it into words.

Thus considered, social theory is the normal accomplishment of socially adept human creatures figuring out what other creatures of the same sort are doing with, to, or around them. Such theories are everywhere, though they are not easy to come by. David Bradley, in his classic novel *The Chaneysville Incident* (1981), explains why:

> The key to the understanding of any society lies in the observation and analysis of the insignificant and the mundane. For one of the primary functions of societal institutions is to conceal the basic nature of the society, so that the individuals that make up the power structure can pursue the business of consolidating and increasing their power untroubled by the minor carpings of a dissatisfied peasantry. Societal institutions act as fig leaves for each other's nakedness.... And so, when seeking to understand the culture or the history of a people, do not look at the precepts of the religion, the form of the government, the curricula of the schools, or the operations of businesses; flush the johns.

Bradley then put into words what his readers all know but never have reason to say: the toilets on buses are foul, while those on airplanes are neat and well supplied, and it is no accident that poor people ride buses, while the less poor fly. It is, thus, a plausibly coherent social theory to say that such a society considers its poor filth, yet wishes to disguise this unpleasant attitude.

Social theory, Bradley might suggest, is about the mundane and the concealed—those hidden aspects of social life we sometimes encounter in the ordinary course of daily life. We don't always see them, thus we aren't always in a position to speak of them, for at least the following reasons: (1) The powers-that-be want them concealed (Bradley's idea). (2) Either the empowered or the weak may resist talking about them because they are too threatening (Kotlowitz's implicit idea that some people deny the reality of urban life because it's too much to deal with). Or (3) people need time and experience to learn how to put into words the reality they live with (but not everyone has the time to do this). Social theories don't just occur to us. Some we never get. Others come in time. Some we have to work to get at. But they are there to be known and said.

It could therefore be said that an individual survives in society to the extent he or she can say plausibly coherent things about that society. Our ability to endure, and on occasion to enjoy, the worlds of irrational lunch-line rules, of crack wars in the hallways, of clean airplane restrooms and much more depends on our knowing something about *why* things are as they are. And we only *know* such things well enough when we can talk about them.

Professional social theorists may find this too simple a definition of their stock-in-trade. Presumably, no one likes the idea that what he or she does for a living is but a specialized version of what any person on the street can do. Yet the evidence supports the idea that there is at best a difference of degree, not of kind, between practical and professional theories of social life. Professional social theorists, if they are honest, must admit that they encounter this truth whenever they teach students who invariably say in introductory courses, "Interesting stuff, but it sounds like jargon for what everyone knows." The comeback to the wisdom of these students should be: "Perhaps, but can they all *say* it?" Though professional social theorists sometimes get carried away with *how* they say what they know about the social world, they at least are skilled at coming up with something coherent to say.

From this uneasy balance of trade between practical and professional social theorists, I draw the justification for this collection of readings in social theory. Everyone can do it. Everyone should do more of it. Responsible practical members of society presumably would live better— with more power, perhaps more pleasure—if they could produce more social theories, that is, if they could use their already considerable practical sociologies to greater advantage. One of the ways lay members can learn to say more about their social worlds is to pay attention to what professional social theorists have said and are saying. This is not because the professionals are more likely to be right—only because they are more practiced.

The Origins of Social Theory

The surprising thing is that professional social theorists have not been practicing their trade for very long, at least not in great numbers. In fact, professional social theory has been around only for the past several hundred years, roughly since the beginning of modern times. Though it has been argued that earlier peoples did a type of social theory (the Greeks are usually cited in this regard), social theory as we know it really began only in the eighteenth century in the various expressions of Enlightenment culture. It did not become a popular activity among the urban intelligentsia until the middle of the nineteenth century, when there first were relatively free and open social spaces. The development of civil society in the eighteenth century, mostly in European (and a few North American) urban centers, permitted enough freedom of expression to encourage independent thinking. These were the circumstances in which a critical mass of literate citizens began to pose the questions that social theory tries to answer.

It is even possible to say that the foundational categories with which social theory first began were themselves an attempt to account for what was then a striking difference between modern societies and the preceding traditional ones. The modern/traditional dichotomy became, therefore, a technical expression with innumerable variations. Max Weber wrote of a rational, future-oriented ethic as the distinctive feature of modern, capitalist societies and distinguished this ethic from traditionalism. Èmile Durkheim wrote of different types of moral cohesiveness, the modern being a more complicated social division of labor in which individuals tended to become lost without the more immediate social controls of traditional societies. Karl Marx, of course, wrote of the uniquely subtle forms of alienation under the capitalist mode of production in which despotism, slavery, and feudal domination were replaced by less overt, but still exploitative, aggressions against the human spirit. Though these three, and many other nineteenth-century social theorists, held sharply different views on the actual state of the modern world, all began their social theories with an explicit theory of the modern world's differences from the traditional.

In the briefest of terms, they all believed what no thinking person could deny: beginning with the cultural, political, and economic revolutions of the late eighteenth and nineteenth centuries, fewer and fewer people could avoid the responsibility to have something to say about the new society. This was not just because the society was new and changing. More importantly, it was because this society demanded, in effect, that its more urbanized and literate citizens participate. Little in early or later modernity was settled. Little remained the same for any period of time. As a result, in a world where change was everywhere, those who desired to have a public life and to participate in the economic and political activities of the new times had to make up their own minds about what was going on.

The contrast with the immediately preceding period must have been quite compelling, perhaps shocking. Few of us who live in the Europeanized, Northern world today have any inkling of what the change must have meant. Even those who come from rural areas can only catch a glimpse. I once lived in rural southern Illinois. On a Sunday's drive, one could visit small villages like Buncombe (pop. 850), where the boarded-up general store and the peeling paint told of the effect of the new Wal-Mart outlet in Carbondale, twelve miles to the north. There, the traditional rural world was still passing away. But today's passings of the pre-modern order in rural Illinois or Nebraska are but occasional glimpses of the early modern experience when *everywhere* the old life was disappearing.

Today, we can only imagine, at some remove, the traditional world that the early social theorists saw fading. Consider a passage from R. W. Southern's *The Making of the Middle Ages* (1953):

> By the thirteenth century . . . the main features of village life were established as they were to exist for another five hundred years. Materially, there was probably remarkably little difference between the life of the peasant in the thirteenth century and the village before it was transformed by modern mechanisms: the produce of the land had

increased sixfold or tenfold during these centuries, but very little of this increase went into the pocket or stomach of the individual peasant. Compared with the rest of the community, he remained immune from new wants, or the means of satisfying them. Everywhere the peasant kept himself alive on a diet whose scarcity and monotony was broken only by intermittent feastings, at harvest time, at pig-killing time, and when people got married or died. There were great differences in the fortunes of individual peasants: families rose and fell, holdings grew and withered away again, following laws similar to those which governed the rise and fall of kingdoms. Over the fortunes of all, high and low, there presided the unpredictable factors of marriage and childbirth. The rules of succession, infinitely various and complicated, often modified, but with the general authority of centuries of growth behind them, were the framework within which the pattern of village—as of national—life was woven.

Since R. W. Southern wrote these words in 1953, social historians have learned a great deal more about the underlying strains and potential for rebellion and change in the traditional medieval world. Just the same, one can take this view of village life as a fair guide to the traditional, pre-modern world. Yes, there was change. But change was a "rise and fall" of fortune. Everything social was pressed under the "general authority of centuries of growth." For at least five hundred years, social life in these villages remained much the same. Hence, we have Max Weber's eloquent definition of traditional values as those adhering to the "eternal yesterday."

By contrast, read the description of modern life written in 1903 by a friend of Weber's, Georg Simmel, in "The Metropolis and Mental Life" (1903):

> The psychological foundation, upon which the metropolitan individual is erected, is the intensification of emotional life due to the swift and continuous shift of external and internal stimuli. Man is a creature whose existence is dependent on differences, i.e., his mind is stimulated by the difference between present impressions and those which have preceded. Lasting impressions, the slightness in their differences, the habituated regularity of their course and contrast between them, consume, so to speak, less mental energy than the rapid telescoping of changing images, pronounced differences within what is grasped at a single glance, and the unexpectedness of violent stimuli. To the extent that the metropolis creates these psychological conditions—with every crossing of the street, with the tempo and multiplicity of economic, occupational, and social life—it creates in the sensory foundations of mental life, and the degree of awareness necessitated by our organization as creatures dependent on differences, a deep contrast with these lower, more habitual, more smoothly flowing rhythms of the sensory-mental phase of small town and rural existence.

Hardly anyone who lives in or has recently visited a modern metropolis could fail to understand intuitively what Simmel meant by the psychological individual who, even on crossing an urban street, must react differently from—and thus become some other sort of human individual than—a rural cousin or an ancestor in an early thirteenth-century village. But what is most interesting is that it would have been impossible for Simmel merely to describe the metropolitan mental life. He had to produce a theory. The passage is, of course, a sometimes abstract but clear enough social theory, not just of urban mentality but also of modern life itself. Few people in those earliest decades of the new urban society, even as late as 1903 when Simmel wrote, could have spoken of the new life without comparing it somehow to the traditional or the rural. This necessity was the first condition of social theory.

Thus, we may say that the first professional theorists were individuals who could not have done social theory without the new society. At the same time, they were individuals who, having begun to think of that society, could not help but think about it theoretically. It was as though the open space and rapid pace of the new world meant one could best embrace it not with any act of the will or reflex of feeling but only with a theory. The first form of that theory was comparative. Simmel and the others writing a century and more ago thought of the modern social world in comparison to the traditional.

Today, these are no longer the necessary conditions for doing social theory. The social worlds in which people must now do their theories are sharply different from those in the late nineteenth century. Still, always in the background somewhere is that foundational condition of social theory: it would not have come into its own, certainly not as a professional activity, had it not been for the new modern society that encouraged and even required thoughtful talk about what was going on.

Thinking an Earlier New World Order

Today's changed conditions for doing social theory have disturbed the original balance of trade between lay and expert social theorists. Were we to compare, say, the end of the nineteenth century to the end of the twentieth, we would soon find two major differences in the circumstances affecting who thinks about social life and how they think. First, the number of people with ready access to a culture supportive of critical thinking has increased dramatically, especially after the hold of the European powers lost control on their colonies in the 1950s and 1960s. Second, the people normally engaged in critical social thinking today are no longer necessarily identified with a dominant class of bourgeois intellectuals. Many of the new social theorists do not consider themselves bourgeois (even if they are), and many are visibly not anything like the white, male advocates of European culture who wrote the first, best-known social theories.

[margin handwriting: hard to compare social theories from 100's of yrs ago... so much has changed]

These two differences—one of number, another of kind—make social theory today an enterprise largely, but not entirely, different from that in the nineteenth century. Among the more salient differences is that today's social theory is produced in more intimate intercourse with the lives of people who are not at all professional in the subject. Hence, the balance is different. At the end of the nineteenth century, social theory was chiefly done by experts; today, even the experts pay closer attention to what some call everyday-life social theory.

Alvin W. Gouldner, a social theorist who wrote in the period when these differences became evident, would have referred to these as cultures of critical discourse—cultures that encourage large numbers of people to think critically about the social world *and* that provide these people with the tools with which to do the thinking. Gouldner himself thought of this change in what turned out to be overly general terms. He assumed there was one culture of critical discourse and that it was ready-made within the culture of modern life. In one important sense, Gouldner was correct. Modern life, in contrast to the traditional, *did* seem to encourage critical thinking. This was, in effect, the main point of the Enlightenment—the idea that, in Immanuel Kant's famous definition, modern, enlightened people would "dare to know." Daring to know and daring to use that knowledge are attitudes toward life and the world that could only arise among people willing to break with tradition, thereby looking to new, future possibilities. In this sense, modernity was a culture of critical thinking and thus of social theory. Just the same, the present social world encourages a state of mind more complicated than an essential and universal humanistic attitude of critical reasoning. Increasingly in the last generation, the world seems to engender any number of different cultures, many of which, in turn, encourage critical social theories—theories that may each be in a different voice.

Very often, these differences are subtle, barely detectable. My son and Lafeyette were about the same age when each put into words a shrewd diagnosis of his worldly circumstances. On the surface, both boys might seem to have been producing social ideas appropriate to a certain level of male psychological development. On close inspection (whatever developmental psychology might teach us about when children can formulate cognitive or moral objects), the differences between the theories of the two boys are there to be seen. The white, middle-class boy who diagnoses the duplicitous and confusing functions of his school does so in a gesture of prowess. What *[margin handwriting: skill]* he discovers and says about this aspect of his world is, to be sure, armament against a sometimes

[handwritten marginalia: the boys grew up completely dif. lives → they view the future differently]

[handwritten: Noah]

frightening, often goofy social arrangement. Yes, even members of the middle class have reason to fear the world. Some individuals make the journey to adult life with ease, some with great pain. And a few do not make it at all. But most do, somehow.

Lafeyette's real world was different. He said "if I grow up" in recognition of the harsh world in which he lived. By the time he met Kotlowitz, Lafeyette had witnessed the murder of other children not much older than he. Like the middle-class boy in a safer, suburban life, he was a shrewd observer. Yet Lafeyette was expressing something that went well beyond keen observational sense. He was putting into words what every Black, male child growing up in urban projects knows to be true: Poor Black boys do not always grow up. Boys like my son can be enrolled in countercultural schools or private schools where, on occasion, the rules make more sense. They might have options.

But boys like Lafeyette, whatever their options, cannot escape the simple, hard facts of their social situation. Their odds are different, and the difference is a complex result of powerful social forces that go well beyond anything Lafeyette and his brother and their mates could hope to manage. He was not using the technical language of social theory, but he was saying that he recognized the meaning of being poor, Black, male, American. These four social forces—class, race, gender, nationality—form a matrix that defines, and limits, at an early age, what and who boys like Lafeyette can be. Some may outrun the limits; some grow up; some grow up whole and well. But boys born into Lafeyette's social circumstances must, somehow, figure out who they are and what they want to be in relation to the limiting condition "*If* I grow up." This makes his theory of his world different from my son's.

But what about this is new? Surely this is not the only world in which a generation of children, even a generation of children of a specific race and gender, has been under threat of extinction. No, but it may be a time when the culture in which children grow up believes that a person's social identity is fixed somehow in relation to the particulars of his or her life. The children themselves cannot be expected to grasp such abstractions, but a child like Lafeyette must, it seems, understand his concrete difference from others. "If I grow up, I want to be a bus driver." Lafeyette understood, and answered, the question asked of all children. The "if" was local knowledge of his reality.

The world today, early in the twenty-first century, is less dominated than it once was by a single, unified dream of how things should be. People living in areas influenced by modern European culture have always exaggerated the truth of their dream. For several centuries, they and quite a few others were persuaded that theirs was also the world's dream. European modernity's idea of human history moving progressively toward a better world—one in which life everywhere would be more and more like life in some European or North American metropolis—was an ideology of global proportions and quite a successful one. But today, boys like Lafeyette are not alone in refusing to be taken in by such promises. Whatever is noble in it, the dream of one world or one America getting better all the time does not speak to them.

This is the big and recent change in social theory. The new social theories are no longer beholden to the West's ideology of human history. At the beginning, the classic social theorists accepted with modest reluctance the idea that European culture was the future for humankind. The great ones had their reservations, true. Still, Marx's *Manifesto* began with a famous line about the specter haunting Europe then quickly shifted to a discussion of "the history of all hitherto existing society," which turned out to be a history of the West. Durkheim, likewise, wrote humbly of the foundations of knowledge in the most elementary and non-European religious societies; yet his primary scientific and political preoccupations were to explain and develop a thoroughly modern society, of which Third Republic France was the ideal.

Weber, too, was restrained and judicious in his scholarly studies of non-Western religions, but his most famous book, *The Protestant Ethic and the Spirit of Capitalism,* has contributed mightily to the myth of the superiority of Western rationality over Eastern traditionalism. Certainly, Weber's doubts about the future of the West were severe—but not because he preferred some other civilization. He was vexed because he believed in the West. These three men, along with Sigmund Freud, are usually considered the greatest of the original social theorists, and surely their greatness is due in some part to their intuitive sense that something was wrong with the West's dream of having discovered the final solution to humanity's problem. Others before them (like Auguste Comte) and after them (like Talcott Parsons) dreamed the dream with much less caution.

Until the past generation, most of the recognized experts in social theory took for granted the parochial idea that the culture of a relatively small number of white people in the North explained the "is and ought" of the world. Because the modern culture that invented social theory also invented the various myths of the inherent superiority of the West, one can easily see the limitations built into the classic versions of the best-known social theories in the last century and a half. It is tempting to conclude that just as the late nineteenth century required its version of critical social theory to account for the startling emergence of the modern, so the late twentieth century required some other sort of social theory to reckon with the disturbances in the culture and political economy of the European and American spheres of influence. This is why the changes in social theory could first be detected with the rebellions and revolutions in European and American societies that began in the 1960s. If social theory, whether lay or expert, is a theory of a kind of world, then the type of theory must change as the world turns. *constantly changing*

At the very end of the twentieth century, hardly any public issue was more controversial than this, particularly in the United States. There are those who still insist that, whatever has changed, America and the world can still be unified around the original Western ideas that Arthur Schlesinger described as "still a good answer—still the best hope" in *The Disuniting of America* (1991). Schlesinger—white, male, Harvard, liberal, intellectual, historian—is the most persuasive of those in this camp. Against them are others who say, "Enough. Whatever is useful in these ideas, they don't speak to me." Audre Lorde—Black, feminist, lesbian, poet and social theorist—put this opposing view sharply in an often-quoted line: "The master's tools will never dismantle the master's house." Between these two views, there is more than enough controversy to go around. Even now, well into the twenty-first century, the controversies over America's place in the world continues as a prominent political sloganeering, of which the most famous is, 'We'll make America great again!', against which serious public figures and academic theorists have taken very strong exception.

In large part, the controversy is between two different types of social theorists *and* over how social theory ought be done. It involves who has the right to say what about the social world. As the world turns more and more into an information age of uncertain globalizing effects, hardly anyone can refuse to say something about the social world. Social theory, thus, becomes ever more a virtual imperative of life in the global society. This is an odd turn. The change in social theory has brought social theory back full circle to at least one important aspect of its origins. Though the first social theorists were bourgeois intellectuals, they were also, for the most part, public figures. Marx stirred the masses, wrote for newspapers, and roused the suspicion of the authorities. In Paris a generation later, the public took note of what Durkheim had to say on any number of topics, from the innocence of Captain Alfred Dreyfus to the reform of French schools. At about the same time, Weber's public lectures were packed, and the early recruits of the Chicago School of sociology were reformers, journalists, settlement house workers, and clergy. Then, social theory was a public activity. Now, after a long exile in the guise of an academic science, social theory is slowly working its way back into the public sphere—as provocateur of social conscience, as object of ridicule and controversy, as source of new thinking about the social world.

The reason for this is clear. Everyone, from the politician to the common man or woman, is aware that there seems to be something different in the world, something that can reasonably be called a new world order. Few can define it. No one can be certain what it is. Some do not believe in it. Some consider it their best hope in a long while. Yet whatever one thinks, the changes in the world between the mid-1960s and the early 1990s seem gradually to have cumulated to the point where now hardly anyone refuses to speak of them. *new century*

What is meant by the new world order? What place will it allow for the old ways? What new demands will it put before human beings? Questions like these nag at us, whatever our politics or ethics or situation in life. In this respect, the end of the twentieth century is a time much like the end of the nineteenth. We are asked what to make of the new order. We are asked to think about the world in terms different from, and more serious than, those used before. This is why *lots of new changes*

social theory has changed. This is why having something different to say about the world is of broad human interest—even, and especially, to those with no particular professional investment in social theory. Social theory has come back to its roots.

The New Social Theories, the Multicultural, and Beyond

It would not be very far wrong to say that social theory sets root only in the soil of social disruption. This seems to be equally true for both practical and professional social theories. The evidence is reasonably clear.

Social theories arose in their classic form when Europe was most disrupted by the uncertain progress of the modern world. Marx and Engels wrote their *Manifesto* on the eve of the 1848 revolutions. Marx's *Capital* was written during the flood and ebb of economic confusion in the two decades that followed. Durkheim wrote during the bouleversements caused by France's attempts, during the Third Republic, to conclude its century-long revolution by founding a thoroughly modern social order. Weber and Simmel wrote during the social conflicts caused by Germany's transition from the traditionalism under Otto von Bismarck's reign to its role as a world industrial power under the ineffectual principles of the Weimar Republic. Each of these men, in their personal lives as in their published theories, reflected the tensions of their times.

Tensions expressed in the master concepts of the great white men—Marx's alienation, Weber's iron cage, Durkheim's anomie—were felt throughout their societies. What they sensed through the veil of their bourgeois culture was confirmed in other writings, repressed until recently, by social theorists who experienced more directly the brutalities visited on ordinary people for reason of their race or gender—and more. Charlotte Perkins Gilman's "The Yellow Wallpaper" (1892), now understood to be a classic of feminist writing, is witness to more than the oppressive attitudes of the men in her life. Though fiction, it documented the way in which the female character's insanity was not a wholly inappropriate reaction to the modern world. Gilman's fictional character was modeled on her own experiences during a rest cure for a mental disorder, after the leading (male) specialist on "the nervous disorders of women" had prescribed complete abandonment of all work. Gilman's then-husband enforced this cure, which only deepened her distress. The wallpaper in the room to which she was confined became a projective field for her character's (and her own) experiences of the world:

> He thought I was asleep first, but I wasn't, and lay there for hours trying to decide whether that front pattern and the back pattern really did move together or separately.
>
> On a pattern like this, by daylight, there is a lack of sequence, a defiance of law, that is a constant irritant to a normal mind.
>
> The color is hideous enough, and unreliable enough, and infuriating enough, but the pattern is torturing.

How different is this from the madness Max Weber saw in the superficially rational patterns of modern life? He spoke of this in the closing words of *The Protestant Ethic and the Spirit of Capitalism (1905)*: "Specialists without spirit, sensualists without heart; this nullity imagines that it has attained a level of civilization never before achieved." Was not his image of the iron cage of the modern world Weber's figure for the odd, disturbing effect of a world in which the rational front pattern moved irregularly against an irrational back pattern, in such defiance of reason that the normal mind was unsettled?

And what of W. E. B. Du Bois's now-famous figure of the "twoness" haunting and defining the American Negro? In *The Souls of Black Folk* (1903), Du Bois spoke of the social experience of his race in words that described what had to have been a widespread, if not universal, social experience of the earlier moderns—of a social world divided within, and against, itself:

> It is a peculiar sensation, this double-consciousness, this sense of always looking at one's self through the eyes of others, of measuring one's soul by the tape of a world that looks

on in amused contempt and pity. One ever feels his twoness—an American, a Negro; two souls, two thoughts, two unreconciled strivings; two warring ideas in one dark body, whose dogged strength alone keeps it from being torn asunder.

Du Bois, like Gilman, wrote in the more autobiographical languages that gave them access to the conditions and dreams of ordinary life. Anna Julia Cooper—writer, early Black feminist, and educator—used the same languages. In *A Voice from the South* (published, like "The Yellow Wallpaper," in 1892), Cooper spoke of the "colored woman's office," of the Black woman's responsibility to redeem America and the West by showing the moral path beyond the limitations of race and gender—a path between the good race-men (who could not understand women) and the good white feminists (who could not understand Blacks). Cooper, in her way, wrote of a double-consciousness, or perhaps a multiple consciousness, that was incumbent upon American Black women, who bore the several obligations of race and gender.

Writers like these, some only now coming into the public eye, help us see the deep, mysterious ties that bind all people thinking about their social worlds in times of change and turmoil. In many ways, the writings of Du Bois (especially his more personal books, *The Souls of Black Folk* and *Dusk of Dawn*) are near-perfect repositories of the struggles of early modern social thinkers. They provide today's readers access to the trained thought of expert social theorists shaken by reverberations of the suffering and desires of ordinary folk. Du Bois's concept of double-consciousness could be said to be one of those rare ideas that entered both theoretical literature and the popular imagination because it resonated finely with both. This was its power. As the passage just quoted suggests, Du Bois, though trained at Harvard and educated in Europe, was very much in touch with the pathos of Black Americans during his lifetime. Born just after the Civil War, he lived for ninety-five years—from Reconstruction, through Jim Crow, Booker T. Washington, the founding of the National Association for the Advancement of Colored People (NAACP), Marcus Garvey, to the civil rights movement. Du Bois died in Ghana on the morning of August 27, 1963, just as Martin Luther King, Jr. was preparing to deliver his "I Have a Dream" speech the next day in Washington, DC. In a certain sense, Du Bois's life embodied, even acted out, a good portion of the social history of race in modern America (which is why his *Dusk of Dawn* is subtitled *An Autobiography of the Race Concept*). Du Bois had been a student of both William James and Max Weber (though he was much closer to James). The formal aspect of his double-consciousness concept was reasonably close to James's idea of the social self. "A man has as many social selves," said James, "as there are individuals who recognize him and carry an image of him in their mind." Against this, compare Du Bois's "sense of always looking at one's self through the eyes of others." In addition to its apparent relation to James's social self, Du Bois's double-consciousness appeared in *The Souls of Black Folk* in 1903, one year after Charles Horton Cooley defined the looking-glass self and just over a year before Max Weber wrote of the strangely double nature of the modern world—rational, yet irrational; freedom bound by the iron cage.

Men and women, both writers and ordinary others, reflecting on their world around the end of the nineteenth century seemed to have been thinking along similar lines. Whatever the subterranean passages connecting the professional and the amateur social theories, the similarities in the separate writings of Simmel, Weber, Du Bois, Gilman, James, Cooper, and Cooley are evident—not neatly linked and certified, but present nonetheless.

Perhaps because of the social disturbances of the present time, we are only now able to appreciate the complexity of classical social theory. The great white men—Weber, Marx, Durkheim—were great social thinkers because they did not buy the official story of the modern world uncritically. They were circumspect (Durkheim), conflicted (Weber), or passionate (Marx) in their reservations about the progressive glory claimed by modern European culture and industry. In this respect, they understood quite well the underside of progress, the destruction visited on ordinary people by a changing world. They understood, if vaguely and uncertainly, that no single dream of progress for all of humanity could soothe the just (if sometimes inarticulate) complaints of those living outside the security of bourgeois society. At the same time, the voices of people like Du Bois, Cooper, and Gilman were muffled by the prejudices of the times and for that reason were necessarily truer expressions of what those less able to put their words into a public voice might have been thinking.

Thus, by juxtaposing the writings of the great official social theorists and those of the great but ignored (though now rediscovered) theorists, today's reader can begin to see the many complex sides of social theory's contributions to survival in the social world. On one side, the expert social theorists themselves are always, in some sense, conflicted because their task is to be at critical odds with the world about which they are speaking. The more disturbed the social order, as in the late nineteenth century, the more open the social theories. But on another side, one can entertain a supposition for which there is now compelling evidence: that official, professional, expert social theories (by whatever name) ought not always be considered the most articulate expressions of the social thinking of inarticulate, ordinary people. One must *never* assume that those without a public voice are inarticulate. The arrogance of intellectuals lies in the assumption that they alone know and speak the truth. Even the most radical, most passionately critical of thinkers fails to escape this arrogance for long. Marx, for one, certainly did not. The oppressed people of any social world *always* have a voice and thus something to say. For very good and sensible reasons, those in the privileged position in any society seldom hear what the oppressed say—not because they are ignorant and inarticulate (though they may be) but often because the weak have the good sense not to tell us, in so many words, what they think. The weak know very well that their truth—their understanding of social arrangements—may be a weapon for their survival if kept hidden but a cause of deepening their misery if revealed to the wrong authorities. Thus, what they know, when written, is very often hidden under pseudonyms or otherwise kept at a secretive distance from those in a position to punish.

In 1861, Harriet Jacobs published (under the name Linda Brent) *Incidents in the Life of a Slave Girl,* which included an astute analysis of the plantation household in which she had been held. The following passage is from her analysis of the household's delicate political balance. It came just after she described with analytic precision her mistress's pained restraint on hearing the slave's confession of how the master, a physician, had made sexual advances toward Harriet:

> I did as she ordered. As I went on with my account her color changed frequently, she wept, and sometimes groaned. She spoke in tones so sad, that I was touched by her grief. The tears came to my eyes; but I was soon convinced that her emotions arose from anger and wounded pride. . . . I pitied Mrs. Flint. . . . She was completely foiled and knew not how to proceed. She would gladly have had me flogged for my supposed false oath; but, as I have already stated, the doctor never allowed any one to whip me. The old sinner was politic. The application of the lash might have led to remarks that would have exposed him in the eyes of his children and grandchildren. How often did I rejoice that I lived in a town where all the inhabitants knew each other! If I had been on a remote plantation, or lost among the multitude of a crowded city, I should not be a living woman.

On the surface, the confrontation with her mistress put Harriet Jacobs at risk. Yet as the narrative suggests, she held the upper hand. Mrs. Flint was to be pitied. Harriet had the power of understanding more exactly than her mistress the complicated workings of the rural community and the power of protection it gave her. Narratives of this sort and their equivalent among women in the white community were the early resources for Anna Julia Cooper, W. E. B. Du Bois, and Charlotte Perkins Gilman. The original narratives may be described as lay social theories of a local world—the frank reflections of ordinary people forced to think through that world. The subsequent writings drew on this knowledge to fashion theories poised midway between the official theories that were salient in the eyes of the dominant culture and the reflex of pain and hope in the hearts of common, oppressed people.

This is the culture of social theory—any social world unsettled enough to disturb the natural tendency of social thought to relax, any social world that discomforts the easy acceptance of appearances as realities. Social theories, as distinct from the formal theories of social sciences and official policymaking, work in the tense, unreconciled spaces of social turmoil. Social theories require the energy and vision that come from those who are less comfortable in any society. *Social theory*, therefore, is simply a name for talk about the social world, talk rooted in the common experiences of those least able to avoid the consequences of social disruption. Were there ever a world in which all people were comfortable with whatever was, a world in which whatever appeared in daily life was a good enough reality, then social theory would slowly fade away, to be replaced by the confident pronouncements of enlightened science or well-intended policies. The most creative moments in the modern history of social theories were those when fewer and fewer of the privileged could relax as more and more of the disadvantaged could speak. The classic period of social theory, we now know, was one such moment. Not until the mid-1960s was there another quite the same.

Between the late nineteenth century and the 1960s, social theory remained more on the margins. In the interwar years, 1917 to 1945, social theory was preoccupied with the turmoil felt most acutely in the European sphere—political instability, depression, fascism, another world war. In this period, the disruption tested the ability of the West to believe in itself and to make that belief work in successful political and economic systems. Social theories of this time gave voice to the urban poor in new industrial cities, to the new marginal working class, to the dislocated in urban areas, to Jewish people suffering under Hitler, and to the first liberation movements among what were later called Third World people. These were the people whose suffering provoked social theories. Yet this period of world conflict ended in 1945 with the world order essentially the same as it had been at the end of the nineteenth century, with only one crucial difference: the Americans now reigned where once the British had.

For a moment in the 1950s and early 1960s in America, many thought they were within reach of a world order in which, indeed, one could relax in order to enjoy the benefits of an affluent society and the apparent reality of America showing just how good society could be. Then, social theory went underground. A newly confident social science dominated thinking about society, only slightly disturbed by the hedged bets of writers like Erik Erikson, Erving Goffman, and David Riesman. Riesman, principally, suggested in *The Lonely Crowd* (1950) that the old ideas of the world no longer suited as they once did. He described a change in the American and modern character from the inner-directed entrepreneur of early modernity to someone else: the other-directed conformist.

Still, this was before very many people in so comfortable a world understood the full force of what was coming. They thought the Communists were the problem. Little did they know. This was before those riding the wave of post-World War II affluence in the United States and recovery in Europe could ever have been expected to understand the final effects of the independence of India, the falling away of Europe's colonies in Africa, and the early civil rights movements in the United States. This was before even the best and brightest of liberal people could understand exactly what was happening before their eyes. In the 1950s, they were much too preoccupied with the Soviets' Sputnik, China's revolution, the Korean War, and Cuba's Fidel Castro. The real, long-lasting perturbations were just beginning to erupt nearer to home.

In late October 1960, only days before the American electorate would decide between Richard Nixon and John F. Kennedy, Martin Luther King Jr. was arrested in Georgia. His life was at risk. Taylor Branch, in *Parting the Waters* (1988), described the moment when Robert Kennedy came face to face with a reality he could not yet understand. The account began with a campaign aide's defensive report to Kennedy on King's situation:

> "They took Dr. King out of Atlanta on an old traffic charge of driving without a license. Then they sentenced him to four months on the chain gang, denied bail, and took him off in the middle of the night to the state prison. All in one day."

"How could they do that?" Kennedy asked doubtfully. "Who's the judge? You can't deny bail on a misdemeanor."

Martin [the campaign aide] decided that Kennedy may have lost sight of the essential fact that King was a Negro—a detail Southern politicians carefully avoided in their protests against interference in the King case. "Well, they just did it," said Martin. "They wanted to make an example of him as an uppity Negro…."

Kennedy paused for a number of seconds and then said, "Uh, godammit," in a weary expletive that could have cut in many directions.

Without discussion, Robert Kennedy later called the judge. King was freed from danger, and the word spread through the Black community. John Kennedy won the election by a margin attributable to his unexpected voter strength among Blacks. Whatever Robert Kennedy's motivation may have been—political, legal, moral—this was a moment of foggy recognition of the true social circumstances of others about whom he then knew little. Though, like Kennedy's expletive, the experience cut in many directions among different people, it was of a sort encountered by many people—mostly white, mostly privileged—in Europe and North America through the 1960s.

This led to the second important time of creativity in social theory. As the Golden Age of America (what Henry Luce had called "the American Century") faded, there were signs that the movement of Blacks in the American South was not an isolated, regional event provoked by the Communists. Within the decade following the Montgomery, Alabama, bus boycott of 1955–1956, the first major event in the modern civil rights movement, it had become clear that the demands of American Blacks were close in content and form to those of other previously colonized people throughout the world. It is too seldom realized that many of the important intellectual resources for the Black rebellion in the United States were of Third World origin—Gandhi, Islam, and Africa.

Between 1956 and 1966, as Blacks eventually moved away from the civil rights movements and turned to Black consciousness, whites—including early feminists, students, antiwar protesters, and gays and lesbians—began to transform the ideas and political experiences (good and bad) of the civil rights movement into their own demands for change. C. Wright Mills's vision of the sociological imagination in 1959 was a direct inspiration for the early political philosophy of the Students for a Democratic Society (SDS) as expressed in their *Port Huron Statement* in 1962. One year later, Betty Friedan's *The Feminine Mystique* took up (without acknowledgment) the ideas of Simone de Beauvoir's *The Second Sex* (1949). Friedan was read both by middle-class, white women suffering under the stultifying demands of suburban life and by younger women, often the daughters of suburban housewives, who had heard of Mary King and Casey Hayden's underground manifesto against the sexist treatment of women in the Civil Rights Movement.

Post-World War II feminism was thus born. In 1963, Blacks and whites also began to read Frantz Fanon, just one of a number of theorists critical of the colonial world. In 1964, following the march on Washington, Malcolm X delivered his stunning "Ballot or the Bullet" speech. At first, the social theories of these thinkers migrated slowly, initially among those young people already engaged in the dialogue and eventually spreading in wider and wider circles. More and more people—more and more white, middle-class people—came to that moment of recognition and turned as Robert Kennedy did—awkwardly, slowly, but definitely.

This was the beginning of the second great period in social theory, a period during which social theory itself changed. The greatest irony of the time was that the social theories of previously excluded and oppressed peoples came increasingly to the fore in large part because of the success of some very abstract philosophical doctrines taught in the most bourgeois and philosophical of world cities, Paris. The year 1966 was the year in which Stokely Carmichael is said to have first used the term Black Power. It was also the year of the first influential pronouncements of the French philosophers Jacques Derrida and Michel Foucault. Hence the irony, doctrines that are to this day virtually unintelligible (even to trained academics) were somehow part and parcel of the movement that brought lay social theories their most influential public attention.

How could this be? One explanation, not necessarily the most satisfying, is that many peo- ple who were young revolutionaries in the 1960s crossed that magical age of thirty in the 1970s. They had to find work, and in the United States and parts of Europe, the universities were then still hiring. Academic work was consistent with their earlier revolutionary thinking, and it paid the rent. The French social theorists, like a different line of German critical think- ers (of which Jürgen Habermas is the most important), were academically respectable, in part because they were difficult to understand. The appropriation of the ideas of the European thinkers thus contributed to the building of academic careers without seriously compromising political and moral ideals. One of the deepest ironies in the aftermath of the 1960s is that the students who had once rebelled against the academic establishment now moved so *directly* to enter it. In the 1990s, many of them are still part of that establishment. They teach and debate Habermas, Derrida, and Foucault or the ideas that evolved from the movements their writings encouraged. Many became deans, departmental chairs, international academic stars, editors, and worse. One might well appreciate their need to hold a job and the wider appeal of career success and fame. But even this does not explain the irony. The deeper explanation lies in the ideas themselves, the weird but true connection between a new wave of professional social theories and the real world experiences of many people who would never dream of inventing a word like deconstruction.

In 1966, in a now-famous talk at Johns Hopkins University in Baltimore, Jacques Derrida announced the beginning of poststructuralism, a theoretical movement in which the practice known as deconstructionism came to be well regarded. Also in 1966, Derrida spoke at the first international conference of academics interested in what was then considered the newest, most exciting method in humanistic studies. Although he appreciated the contributions of structural- ism, Derrida devoted his talk to the argument that even structuralism's innovative spirit did not make it different from all prior, traditional forms of thought. His principal complaint against all philosophies up to that moment was that they limited the free play of social imagination. They were, he said, methods of thinking that so revolved around a principle of the Center that the freedom to explore and affirm differences was destroyed. Derrida believed he and those who shared his ideas were living in a revolutionary moment when that principle of the Center was giving way to, of all things, language:

> This was the moment when language invaded the universal problematic, the moment when, in the absence of a center or origin, everything became discourse—provided we can agree on this word—that is to say, a system in which the central signified, the origi- nal or transcendental signified, is never absolutely present outside a system of differ- ences. The absence of the transcendental signified extends the domain and the play of signification infinitely.

Not, to be sure, the clearest of statements to the uninitiated. But certain key words are clear or clearly implied: decentering, play, differences.

Derrida's poststructuralist social theory uses these three terms in two ways. First, they propose an alternative way of thinking. Social theory, he argued, should reject overarching, limiting prin- ciples and open itself to the world of differences. Second, this was justified because only this method could make sense of the world of the mid-1960s—a world in which, in France and the United States, former colonial subjects, women, workers, and Blacks were asserting themselves by asserting their differences. It was, clearly, a time when neither the political nor the economic Cen- ter was holding against the play of cultural and political differences. Within two years, Paris and many of the Western capitals would shake with political protest. The complexity of his philosophy notwithstanding, Derrida was drawing the connection between very abstract social theory and political events in the social world. Theory, he argued, had to be decentered because the social world was decentering. Give up the West and its philosophy, he advised (though not in so many words), because the world all around—Algeria, Cuba, Vietnam, Alabama, Mississippi—was shifting rapidly out from under the sway of the cultural and political powers that had dominated the modern era.

Others, like Michel Foucault, said much the same thing. As their works were translated into the languages of the world, people coming into the universities from lives of political activism found the ideas persuasive, entirely suited to their own experiences, if not to their accustomed way of speaking. Today, the movements that Derrida and Foucault and others spawned in the mid-1960s are still at the center of controversy in the academy, though now they are widely known as postmodernism. To the amazement of those who bother to look into it, postmodernism bears a very close resemblance to other social theories rooted directly in the common language of people who are, in effect, following a lead much like that offered by Derrida. These are the theories of individuals asserting, for political and personal reasons, the authority of their previously suppressed cultures in order to define new ways of understanding themselves and their experiences without regard for the powers of the Center.

Gloria Anzaldúa, in *Borderlands/La Frontera* (1987), an autobiographically based theory of the new mestiza, described this culture rediscovering its past and present life in the cultural and political borderland between the United States and Mexico:

> The US–Mexican border *es una herida abierta* where the Third World grates against the first and bleeds. And before a scab forms it hemorrhages again, the lifeblood of two worlds merging to form a third country—a border culture. Borders are set up to define the places that are safe and unsafe, to distinguish *us* from *them*. A border is a dividing line, a narrow strip along a steep edge. . . . *Los atravesados* live here: the squint-eyed, the perverse, the queer, the troublesome, the mongrel, the mulatto, the half-breed, the half dead; in short, those who cross over go through the confines of the "normal." Gringos in the U.S. Southwest consider the inhabitants of the borderlands transgressors, aliens— whether they possess documents or not, whether they're Chicanos, Indians or Blacks. . . . The only "legitimate" inhabitants are those in power, the whites and those who align themselves with whites.

Anzaldúa claims these illegitimate people as her own. She is one of them—a people whose history reaches back before the United States appropriated these borderlands in 1848. Her theory is not really a theory in the usual sense. Its form is more in the tradition of Du Bois, Cooper, and Gilman. It transgresses the formal dependence of theory on prose. It plays with poetry, imagination, languages, and idioms. It rejects the gringo to affirm multiply cultured peoples who live and have lived against the oppressive force of American ambition.

Multiculturalism, like social theory, is a term without any definite denotation. One could say that the former term has come to represent the social theories of those who resist the usual classifications of thought and politics. Whichever terms are used, the evidence is clear that the latest period in social theory has produced theories that disturb tradition. They resist easy classification—neither lay and practical nor professional, neither poetry nor sociology, neither political nor academic, neither American nor Spanish nor African, and so on. Yet the new theories are social theories in every coherent sense of the term. They say something clear about the social world. They do so in words utterly different from anything that has gone before in the West. Oddly, however, they are not that far from the spirit and practice of social theory in its earliest days.

The longer the world lives in a multicultural environment, the more people accept, however grudgingly in some cases, that the unleashing of social differences in the arena of public politics is somehow aggravated by (perhaps even the result of) the odd shrinking of the world caused by new information technologies—not to mention the irony of globalization that the less people are able to avoid distant others, the more they must confront social differences far from their daily lives. The peoples of the many-cultured world are a long way from understanding just exactly how, and why, these technologies have *simultaneously* made us aware of our differences *and* brought us into more intimate contact with each other. Yet the inhabitants of the globalizing world, as they strain against each other in this odd mix of social distance and intimacy, realize that they—that *we*, that is—must assume, at least in spirit, the moral imperatives of the earliest days of modern social theory. Though the structures of the social world of the end of the nineteenth century were light years distant from ours today in the early twenty-first, we bear the same responsibilities as did our great-grandparents and grandparents in those days. We have no choice but to speak of our worlds, such as they are—and when we do, we become social theorists of a very practical and necessary sort.

As the worlds edged over into a new millennium, the realities of what had come to be known as globalization had set in. Yes, even practical social thinkers had to face up to cultural differences made all the more acute by the speed of telecommunications, not to mention the speed with which danger can strike near to home. September 11, 2001, and its reverberations around the world, seemed to change everything. Whether that one terrible day was the beginning of the changes is uncertain. Some say that 9/11 was but a logical conclusion of the historical contradictions and social inequalities of the modern world—aspects of modernity's uneven development that had become more abrasive in the concluding decades of the twentieth century. This question remains open and will for time to come. What is certain as the twenty-first century moves into its own is that the ways people engage with their worlds are now changed beyond what could have been imagined, even in the early days of multicultural awareness. It may well be that, though the word "multiculturalism" retains an important meaning, as a phenomenon it has outgrown its earlier forms.

As the new millennium in which we find ourselves draws toward the end of its second decade, social theory has more and more taken global reality as its primary field of reflection—so much so that some have begun to conclude that the original concept of the *social* is no longer the apt term for theories of global social things. One sign that social theory is becoming something other than what it had been in the nineteenth century is the sudden appearance after 2001 of theories of globalization. Another, less obvious, sign of the ways social theory must be more elastic than it once had been is the extent to which new social theories disturb what once were foundational ideas. Bruno Latour, for example, argues for the erasure of the classical distinction between the social world and the natural. Similarly, economist Thomas Piketty writes of capitalism in a decidedly social theoretical way, as neurologist Oliver Sacks contributed to making neuroscience a topic of broad social understanding. In these new worlds, *how* we think and *what* we think require a wide-awake ability to look to new, more global horizons.

When the worlds in which people come up against each other in a global environment are themselves moved by social forces that come from around the globe as if in an instant, then those who aim to live powerfully in such an environment must learn to think differently—to think, that is, not only in respect for the differences they encounter but also of the vast global forces that both accentuate the differences and incomprehensibly pull them together in ways that defy the older logics of causes and effects. Oddly, one of the global methods needed is the ability to put these mysteries into words.

Saying It, Reading It, and Getting By Better

When Derrida announced the beginning of his new social theory, he referred to an event in which "language entered the universal problematic." What?

Why has language become so much the preoccupation of social theorists in the last half-century? Among academic social theorists, it is normal, almost necessary, to develop a theory of language, literature, or discourse early in one's career. Other, less traditionally professorial writers—like Gloria Anzaldúa, Toni Morrison, and Audre Lorde—tend to *use* language to disturb the world. What both types of social theorists have in common is one basic idea: if our way of thinking about the world has changed, so must our way of speaking and writing. Yet the new social theorists believe that we cannot escape the languages we have. The best course, they agree, is to use language to call attention to meanings. Anzaldúa gives mestiza and borderland new meanings, just as other people have given Black, Latina, woman, African, queer, and American new political meanings.

The importance of these terms to those who define themselves in relation to them is very often beyond those who are seldom, if ever, called on to explain themselves. One of the unintended consequences of the modern world has been that the original Enlightenment principles have actually worked to better effect than the early moderns ever dreamed. At the end of the twentieth century, we live in a time of confusion wrought every bit as much by the successes of modernity as by its failures. True, by the formal measures of what was promised, the modern age has not paid off. War, poverty, human misery, and hunger recur as they always have, now alongside quite a few environmental and other miseries the modern world invented of its own accord. Cell phones, iPods, Blackberrys, and other of the ever-changing wonders of technology hardly balance this ledger. Just the same, it is unlikely that any of the bourgeois revolutionaries in the eighteenth century dreamed that human knowledge would be so widely and immediately communicated to every corner and level of global society as it is today. How could they have? Their world was so small. Kant, the author of the Enlightenment's slogan "dare to know," is also known to have been a racist by any standard. Few of the Enlightenment thinkers, political revolutionaries, or even early social theorists gave more than passing thought to the moral, political, or economic powers and rights of those outside their very narrow spheres of social experience.

Such observations may be considered cheap shots, insensitive to moral standards prevailing in the earliest days of the modern age—trendy indictments of white, middle-class males everywhere. But this is the point: It is a fact of no minor importance that, until recently, the culture to which educated people have been expected to conform was invented and sustained mostly by men who encountered little in their experience that would or could broaden their horizons. They may be excused for their original innocence, if not for their clumsy attempt to hang on even at this late moment. Thus, we can rightly conclude that the original idea of a culture in which knowledge would give human beings new power to define and move their world has enjoyed an unexpected success. Our forefathers had an excellent idea. Our criticism of them should be tempered with some forbearance. What they were not able to anticipate a century ago was that this new knowledge would be held so widely, and used so powerfully and in such alarming ways, to criticize the very world they dreamed up.

This is where language entered the universal problematic. Language is the most important weapon of the weak (to borrow a phrase from James Scott). However much people are oppressed, however much they may be systematically deprived of the means to defend themselves or attack their opponents, people can always use words. The poor, the enslaved, the depressed, the illiterate, the imprisoned, and the abused can speak. Even those so disturbed by some primeval trauma in early life so as to lose their minds in later years can speak. They may speak only to themselves or to those who own or are wise to their condition. But they can speak. They may speak in some unusual code—of dreams, of a political underground, of the gang or the cellblock, of the schizophrenic, of the therapist's office, of hushed conversations with others in like circumstance—but they do speak.

For some, this is a revolting idea. It is, indeed. Of all the available human capacities, Putting-it-into-words is the most powerful. Thinking-it, Feeling-it, or Seeing-it, by themselves, are nothing. It is only when people put what they think or sense or see into words that whatever is there to be thought, felt, or seen comes into play as a force in social life. The willingness to trust the language of things is what distinguishes social theory from seemingly similar but often quite different activities—like, say, social *science*. The attitude of science in the modern world is Seeing-it, then Thinking-it. Thus, sociologists and other academics regularly can be overheard describing their current research project in this way: "I'm *looking at* . . . such and such." The ideal of science is that of the enlightened thinker who peers sensitively and knowingly into the world in order to gather up its evidence that data, in turn, may be thought into truth.

Social theory, even in its original forms, tends to be skeptical of science's neat idea of truth—of a world offering up its evidence to the enlightened vision of the scientist. The great classic

men—Freud, Marx, Ferdinand de Saussure, even Weber in his way—w
with finding some clever way *around* science. Freud based everythin
clues to the unconscious life, clues that may appear in dreams and sn
on the couch. Saussure developed the original formal theory of th
language, the abstract system of grammars and terms that lie behind a
master of the tour de force, sought to invent a science of human things
truths of subjective meanings through the aesthetic trick of ideal types. And Ma
only good science was one that refused to take appearances for reality. The truth of the
value of labor was found not in the marketplace but in the hidden secrets of production. Hau
through the first volume of *Capital,* he said that the social theorist who hopes to uncover this
secret must leave the shop floor and the marketplace,

> this noisy sphere, where everything takes place on the surface and in the view of all men,
> and follow [Mr. Moneybags] into the hidden abode of production, on whose threshold
> there stares us in the face "No admittance except on business." Here we shall see, not
> only how capital produces, but how capital is produced. We shall at last force the secret
> of profit making.

Even Durkheim, in his last and greatest work, *Elementary Forms of the Religious Life (1912),*
seemed to set aside his earlier confident belief in scientific progress to explain that the secret of
knowledge itself was not even the mind's ability to see the world but the human being's elementary dependence on the social group.

The classic social thinkers have been used to justify various types of sociologies and other social sciences. This is good. Science is good, important in its way. Sensible social theory need not
set itself against science, from which it gathers a good bit of its descriptive information. Whether
classic or new, social theory need only accept itself for what it is—that type of social knowledge
concerned with putting into words whatever is there, especially whatever is most difficult to see
on the surface. Those well trained in social theory do this for a living. Because they devote so
much of their lives to it, they are more practiced in finding the words to say something sensible,
critical, and revolting about the social world. This, however, does not make them different from
any other social creature who, given the right degree of social disturbance and sufficient reason,
finds a way to say, "If I grow up, I want to be a bus driver." Writers like Du Bois, Gilman, Anzaldúa, and Lorde—the other, and new, social theorists—would understand Lafeyette as standing
somehow alongside the great original theorists.

The world is unevenly cruel. Whatever pleasures it offers are offered only to those who find a
way to get by in it. Many, it would seem, are given such a head start that they would apparently
have no use for social theory, no need for putting into words the deeper secrets. Yet those who
are wise know this is not true. It would be absurd to suggest that Lafeyette and my son started
from the same place, that a middle-class white boy in America suffers as much as the boy in a
city's failed project who must sleep, if at all, through threats of death. At the same time, it would
be another kind of romance to believe that relatively well-off boys with all the necessary comforts
do not struggle. The uneven cruelty of the world does not exempt any of us from the only real
universal in human experience—that we encounter limits and injuries we must overcome, that
survival is the prerequisite of pleasure.

Social theory is what we do when we find ourselves able to put into words what nobody seems
to want to talk about. When we find those words, and say them, we begin to survive. For some,
learning to survive leads to uncommon and exhilarating pleasures. For others, perhaps the greater
number of us, it leads at least to the common pleasure—a pleasure rubbed raw with what is: the
simple but necessary power of knowing that one *knows* what is there because one can *say* it.

This, whatever else, is what makes social theory worth reading.

C. L.

otes

Footnotes are seldom at the foot anymore. Usually, they are at the end and difficult to find. Sometimes, they grow out of proportion to the text at the foot of which they claim to be humbly poised. The notes in Weber's *Protestant Ethic* are longer than the book itself! Notes, thus, can discourage reading. Yet the reader rightly desires some information, even if it is difficult to know how much and where. Because most of the references in this general introduction and the section introductions are to familiar sources, often to texts appearing elsewhere in the book, notes are kept to a bare minimum and located just after the introduction.

Page 1: Kotlowitz, *There Are No Children Here* (Doubleday, 1991), x.
Page 2: Bradley, *Chaneysville Incident* (Harper & Row, 1981), 6.
Page 3: Southern, *Making of the Middle Ages* (Arrow Books, 1953), 78.
Page 4: Simmel, in *On Individuality and Social Forms* (University of Chicago Press, 1971), 235.
Page 7: Schlesinger, *Disuniting of America* (Whittle Books, 1991), 83.
Page 10: Jacobs, *Incidents in the Life of a Slave Girl* (Oxford University Press, 1988), 53.
Page 11: Branch, *Parting the Waters* (Simon and Schuster, 1988), 365.
Page 14: Anzaldúa, *Borderlands/La Frontera* (Spinsters, 1987), 3.

Quoted material not noted here is usually from a selection elsewhere in this book and acknowledged there.

PART ONE

Modernity's Classical Age: 1848–1919

A work of literature is considered a "classic" when, long after it was written, readers continue to read it. A famous example is Sophocles's dramatic telling of the story of Oedipus. This is so much a classic that one does not need to have read Sophocles, Shakespeare's *Hamlet,* or Freud to know something of the story. Most people recognize in themselves the truth told in this ancient Greek drama: that human beings are affected deeply by extreme feelings of love and hate for their parents.

In most versions of the story, Oedipus loves his mother too much. Without knowing what he is doing or who the people involved really are, Oedipus kills his father and marries his mother. He rules his land with Jocasta, his mother-wife and queen. When a plague threatens the kingdom, Oedipus learns that his land can be saved only if his father's murder is avenged—and that he himself is the murderer! He blinds himself and goes into exile. Oedipus's actual blindness represents his deeper blindness to the effects of his desires on his behavior. His fate is tragically determined not because he had forbidden feelings of love and aggression for his parents but because he acted on them without knowing what he was doing. This story is a classic because people find in it some sort of standard for normal, if confusing, human experience. In literature, a writing is classic because it still serves as a useful reference or meaningful model for stories people tell of their own lives.

Hence, a period of historical time is considered classical because people still refer back to it in order to say things about what is going on today. Generally speaking, classical ages contain a greater number of classical writings for the obvious reason that literatures express their social times. Thus, at present, when people refer to the Oedipus story, they usually have in mind Freud's version, which still conveys much of the drama of the modern world affecting people today. The Oedipus story figured prominently in one of Freud's classic writings, *The Interpretation of Dreams,* which was published in 1899. In this book, Freud made one of his most fundamental claims about dreams just after retelling the Oedipus story. Dreams, he explained, are always distorted stories of what the dreamer really wishes or feels. They can thus serve "to prevent the generation of anxiety or other forms of distressing affect."

Freud's telling of the Oedipus myth is a subject of controversy today because it is taken as a case in point for the feminist criticism that most classical writings in the social and human sciences systematically excluded and distorted women's reality. They did. In this case, Freud distorted reality by his preposterous inference from the Oedipus he saw in his patients to the claim that the major drama of early life is the little boy's desire to make love to his mother. Little girls were left out of this story, the crucial formative drama of early life. They were said to be driven by the trivial desire of envy for the visible instrument of true human development, the boys' penis. The feminist critique is to the point, but it does not destroy the classic status of Freud's writings. Feminists are among those who still find much else of interest in his ideas.

Timeline: 1821 – 1939

Social Theory		Wider World

Social Theory	Year	Wider World
		Harriet Martineau born **1802**
		John Stuart Mill born **1806**
		Simón Bolívar liberates New Granada (now Colombia, Venezuela, and Ecuador) from Spain **1819**
	1820	Napoleon Bonaparte dies **1821**
	1830	First Railroad Station in US at Baltimore **1830**
		Simon Bolivar dies **1830**
		Lowell Mills in US built **1830s**
		Cyrus McCormick invents the harvesting reaper **1831**
		Charles Darwin's Voyage on HMS Beagle **1831-1836**
Harriet Martineau, *Woman* 1837		Samuel Colt invents the Colt Revolver **1837**
		The Victorian Era begins **1837**
		Charles Dickens, *Oliver Twist* **1838**
	1840	US has 3500 miles of Railroad; 1200 factories in North **1840**
		Charles Thurber invents the typewriter **1843**
Karl Marx, *Economic and Philosophical Manuscripts* 1844		Samuel Morse invents the telegraph **1844**
		Friedrich Nietzsche born **1844**
Marx and Friedrich Engels, *The German Ideology* 1845-1846		First use of anesthesia in surgery, in Boston **1846**
		Charlotte Brönte, *Jane Eyre* **1847**
Marx and Engels, *The Manifesto of Class Struggle* 1848		Revolutions Across Europe **1848-1851**
		Women's Rights Convention, Seneca Falls NY **1848**
	1850	Five percent of British ships are steam powered **1850**
		Harriet Taylor Mill, Enfranchisement of Woman **1851**
Marx, *The Eighteenth Brumaire of Louis Bonaparte* 1852		Herman Melville, *Moby Dick* **1851**
		Auguste Comte, *Système de Politique Positive* **1851-54**
		Louis Napoleon establishes conservative control in Paris **1852**
		Harriet Beecher Stowe, *Uncle Tom's Cabin* **1852**
Marx, *On Imperialism in India* 1853		Commodore Perry in Japan, seeks opening to US trade **1853**
		London Clock Tower is built; industrial time dominates **1854**
		Bessemer Process for Steel Manufacture **1855**
		Sigmund Freud born **1856**
John Stuart Mill, *On Liberty* 1859		Charles Darwin, *Origin of the Species* **1859**
		Suez Canal built **1859-69**
	1860	American Civil War **1861-65**
		Otto von Bismarck President of Germany **1862**
		Abraham Lincoln Emancipates Slavers, **1863**
		London Underground Opens **1863**
		Max Weber born **1864**
Marx, *Capital, Vol I* 1867		W.E.B. Du Bois born **1868**
		Emile Durkheim born **1868**
		US Transcontinental Railroad completed **1869**
	1870	Franco-Prussian War ends, strengthening Bismarck **1871**
		Paris Commune crushed **1871**
		Great Depression **1873-96**
		Alexander Graham Bell invents telephone **1876**
		Light bulb invented in Canada **1879**
	1880	John D Rockefeller controls 95% of US Oil **1880**
		Afrikaners rebel against British rule **1881**
		Karl Marx dies **1883**
Engels, *The Patriarchal Family* 1884		Orient Express opens **1883**
		European powers subdivide colonies in Africa **1885**
		Leopold of Belgium controls Congo **1885**
Friedrich Nietzsche, *Peoples and Countries in Beyond Good and Evil* 1886		Karl Benz invents internal combustion engine **1885**
		Ethiopia resents Italian colonization **1885**
		George Eastman invents Kodak camera **1887**
		Hitler is born in Austria **1889**

Social Theory		Wider World
William James, *Principles of Psychology* 1890	**1890**	45% of American workers live in cities **1890**
		Economic downturn in Europe **1890**
Charlotte Perkins Gilman, *The Yellow Wallpaper* 1892		Bismarck resigns **1890**
		Zipper invented **1891**
Anna Julia Cooper, *The Colored Woman's Office* 1892		Social Democrats institute reforms in Germany **1891**
Emile Durkheim, *Division of Labor* 1893		In Cuba, Jose Marti leads revolt against Spain **1895**
Jane Addams, *The Settlement as a Factor in the Labor Movement* 1895		US Supreme Court authorizes racial segregation **1896**
Durkheim, *Sociology and Social Facts* 1897		In France, Zola takes stand in Dreyfus Affair **1897**
Durkheim, *Suicide and Modernity* 1897		Jane Addams founds Hull House **1898**
Gilman, *Women and Economics* 1898		Alfred Dreyfus pardoned **1899**
Sigmund Freud, *Interpretation of Dreams* 1900	**1900**	Friedrich Nietzsche dies **1900**
		Paper Clip invented **1900**
Charles Horton Cooley, *The Looking-Glass Self* 1902		1.5 million telephones in US **1900**
		World population 1.7 billion **1900**
Durkheim, *Notes on Occupational Groups* 1902		Queen Victoria dies **1901**
		Britain wins Boer War creates South Africa **1902**
W. E. B. Du Bois, *The Souls of Black Folk* 1903		Wright Brothers first flight **1903**
		Weber visit US, meets Du Bois **1904**
Durkheim and Marcel Mauss, *Primitive Classifications and Social Knowledge* 1903		Einstein publishes first papers on special relativity **1905**
		Weber writes voluminously, **1905-1920**
		Saussure lectures on linguistics in Geneva, **1906-1911**
Max Weber, *The Spirit of Capitalism and the Iron Cage* 1905		Run on US Banks **1907**
George Simmel, *The Stranger* 1908		Henry Ford's Model T **1907**
		First Jewish Kibbutz in Palestine **1909**
Durkheim, *Elementary Forms of the Religious Life* 1912	**1910**	In China, Qing Dynasty collapses **1911**
		Italy defeats Ottoman Turkey **1912**
		Sun Yat-sen and nationalists come to power In China **1912**
John Dewey, *Democracy and Education* 1916		Archduke Ferdinand killed; World War I begins **1914**
		Japan, Australia, Canada enter war **1914**
		Germany defeats Russians, repels French **1914**
Weber, *What Is Politics?* 1918		Germans sink Britain's Lusitania **1915**
Freud, *Remembering, Repeating, and Working-Through* 1919		Durkheim dies **1917**
	1920	In Russia, Red Army forces civil war **1919**
		Weber dies **1920**

Freud's version of Oedipus also tells the deeper story of human blindness, of the natural tendency of most human beings to resist the full truth of their lives—to deny many deep feelings of love and hate that govern them and the world. Freud's Oedipus remains a classic today because, among other reasons, people still find in it two basic truths of their lives: (1) They have very mixed and strong feelings about the people around them, and (2) therefore, they tend to distort what they say and think about the world because what they feel below the surface is far too upsetting. People are blind to their own feelings because their worlds are too much to feel.

Social Theory's Classical Age: Confusion and Doubt in a Changing World

This would also be a reasonably good description of what many bourgeois Europeans at the turn of the century were feeling (but not saying) about the modern world in which they lived. They said it was a wonderful thing, filled with hope. They felt, but resisted saying, that the modern world did a lot of harm and made them feel less than hopeful about the human condition. In other words, Freud told of Oedipus to help tell the story of dreams, which in turn helped tell the larger story of the late modern culture in which many people wanted to believe anything but the complicated reality of their worlds. Carl Schorske, in *Fin-de-siècle Vienna* (1961), explained that in his theory of dreams, "Freud gave his fellow liberals an ahistorical theory of man and society that could make bearable a political world spun out of orbit and beyond control."

This, it turns out, is a good description of the modern world in the period from the revolutions of 1848 through at least the end of World War I. Contemporaries of those who visited Freud for psychoanalytic consultation in Vienna at the end of the nineteenth century were the children or grandchildren of people whose roots were in the traditional world. People who lived in a major city like Vienna may have enjoyed much of its cultural, political, and economic abundance. But it would be hard to believe that they did not also regret what was lost in these new cities. The political revolutions in America and France at the end of the previous century promised a new and better world, as did the dramatic economic revolution that was then spreading from England across modern Europe. Democracy in politics, capitalism in the marketplace, and science in culture offered much. On the surface, everything was expected to be better. For many it was.

For many more, and even for those whose material lives were better than anything their parents ever knew, life was filled with anxiety. For one thing, the modern world brought destruction. Throughout the century, lands were taken to build the railroads that fueled the factory system. In America, native civilizations were destroyed in the name of progress. Someone *must* have given this a second thought. If not, people surely saw what was happening closer to home. After 1853, Baron Georges Haussmann, often called the first city planner, ordered the destruction of much of old Paris to build the new boulevards and monuments that today's tourists mistakenly associate with tradition. The boulevards were allegedly built to allow a straight cannon shot into the working-class quarters, where rebellions like those in 1848 were most likely to recur. In Chicago in 1871, the great fire destroyed much of the city. The fire provided occasion for the rebuilding of Chicago as a modern city. Architectural historians claim that engineering advances necessary to construct the skyscraper were developed in order to rebuild Chicago vertically. Even today, everyone who lives in a city knows that modern "progress" entails the tearing down of much that is traditional. The skyscraper became the strong symbol of modern urban power, typically built on the site of perfectly good lands and homes. What met the eye in the cities was just the surface representation of what so many people felt about the modern world. In a different political sense, many still contend that the modern world destroys the old family and small-town values, as indeed it does.

Modernity could be defined as that culture in which people are promised a better life—one day. Until then, they are expected to tolerate contradictory lives in which the benefits of modernity are not much greater than its losses, if that. In Marx's famous line, the modern world was one in which "all that is solid melts into air"—nothing was quite what it appeared to be. No future payoff was ever quite assured for the vast majority of people. The first sign of the coming good society was always, it seemed, the destruction or loss of something familiar and dear. Many people in Europe and North America in the second half of the nineteenth century lived in an oedipal state, as Freud described it: affected by strong feelings of love and anger for their world but unable to give voice to the anger for fear of "saying the wrong thing." They were expected to love a world that was killing what was dear to them.

These were the cultural conditions prevailing in the modern West from 1848 into the first quarter of the twentieth century. This was the classic age of modernity, and of social theory. Whether practical or professional, social theory became a more acutely necessary skill in this period. Practically, ordinary people, many of them new to the strange and alien city, needed to learn to introduce and explain themselves to strangers who knew nothing of their family names. Professionally, there arose for the first time a class of writers, lecturers, teachers, and public intellectuals who devoted themselves to telling, in scientific language, the story of the modern West. Among them were the classic writers of modernity's classic age.

Classic Social Theories Struggle with the Contradictions of the Modern

Karl Marx, Èmile Durkheim, Max Weber, Georg Simmel, Sigmund Freud, and others are still considered classic writers because they told the story of modernity with a subtle regard for its two sides—for the official story of progress and the good society and for the repressed story of destruction, loss, and the terror of life without meaningful traditions. Their value to present-day readers is partly evident in the very fact that they are still read. This separates them from others: those great writers of the nineteenth century who are no longer read seriously lacked the subtle grasp of both sides of the modern world. Auguste Comte is often considered to be a founding father of sociology, along with his mentor Saint-Simon. But few would read his works today in order to understand the modern world. Comte was too blind to the other side of that world. He believed too much in its progress and thus could say, in 1822: "A social system is in its decline, a new system arrived at maturity and approaching its completion—such is the fundamental character that the general progress of civilization has assigned to the present epoch." Simple, all too simple. Much the same can be said of the sociologist who has become for many the perfect illustration of the fallen classical god. Herbert Spencer, a more sober and scientific man than Comte, saw the world as progressing slowly but perfectly toward good and thus could say, in 1857: "Progress is not an accident, not a thing within human control, but a beneficent necessity."

Delicate is the line separating those no longer read and those who are. The difference is not so much in the ideas themselves as in the finer sensibilities with which certain nineteenth-century social theorists let on that they knew the world was complicated, while others did not. Èmile Durkheim, heir apparent to Comte's faith in modern science, let it be known that scientific sociology was urgently needed not just because progress was at hand but also because the lawlessness of modern society had devastating effects on the weaker, more marginal individuals. And each of the writers who are still read wrote of concepts that described the dark side of modern life—Durkheim's anomie, Marx's alienation (or estrangement), Weber's overrationalization. Even Freud, who was not considered a social theorist until recently, hardly makes sense outside the social world for which he wrote. How else are we to interpret his compelling sense of psychological life as a wild disturbance in the hostile conflict between deep, natural desires to love and kill and the prudish, censorious forces of bourgeois manners? As much as Marx and Weber, Freud described the hidden irrational forces of social life. More perhaps than they, he described how the irrational is a given in the order of human things found just below the tranquil surface of reason.

Then too among the classical social theorists, Marx in particular set his theory of political economy against the classical political economists—Adam Smith, Thomas Malthus, and David Ricardo. But Marx was not alone in seeking a more robust idea of social forces in relation to the autonomous individual. Durkheim and Weber, even Freud, along with Marx, proposed theories that served to challenge the all-but-absolutely free individual of classic economics. Modern man was to them socially determined (Durkheim and Marx), or caught in a web of social ambiguities (Weber), or irrationally driven by primordial unconscious forces (Freud). Yet, as time went by, John Stuart Mill, a theoretical heir of the classic economists, wrote in *On Liberty* (1859) of the individual in a way that took seriously the social fact that individual freedoms are socially embedded. Not long after Mill, a philosopher of quite a different temperament wrote devastatingly of European culture and its philosophies. Friedrich Nietzsche, whose appreciation for the negative side of modern society is said by some to have influenced Weber and Freud, was also able to write in *Beyond Good and Evil* (1886) with sociological sensitivity of the practical nature of social relations.

These classic writers in a classical age are considered worthwhile because people continue to struggle with the confusing effects of modern life. There are some who would say, a century after social theory's classical age, that the modern world is coming to an end. This could be. But what remains true is that a great many people still find hard reality at moral odds with the promise of progress. Those who have no experience of this contradiction would not find these classic writers interesting, just as anyone who denies his or her experience of the deeper emotional forces would find Freud's Oedipus opaque.

It must be said, however, that a work can be considered classical for reasons other than the continuing appeal of its wisdom. Classics serve less lofty social purposes as well. The process of canon formation is well understood today to be part of the social process whereby those in power (or some of those with some power) seek to perpetuate the authority of certain authors in order to enhance their own vested interests in a given view of social life.

The first condition of being read is to be published. Because publication involves commercial as well as literary judgments, decisions to publish are always and necessarily susceptible to the influence of editors, publishers, advisers, and critics whose interest in what is read is touched by an interest in the economics of literary and cultural life. Great works of literature can be excluded from an official canon for many reasons having nothing at all to do with their merit. Publishers think they won't sell. Editors think they serve no good purpose. Critics cannot understand why anyone would buy and read something by one of those people. Authors don't even try because they know what publishers will say. This is neither good nor bad. It is, however, a fact of cultural life that a literary work of great merit can be denied the status of a classic because it is excluded from the canon; conversely, a work can appear in the official canon of great writings even though it has little or no merit.

A writing that endures over time always encounters these two forces: to be classic, it must be readable to readers; to be a canonized classic, it must serve the interests of those who decide what readers will read. Great books like W. E. B. Du Bois's *The Souls of Black Folk (1903)* were virtually unknown to the dominant, mostly white, literary establishment until recently. Other books, like Èmile Durkheim's *Rules of Sociological Method (1895),* have been canonized even though no one reads them. Herein lies a particularly interesting story. Durkheim's *Rules* is a book that made little or no sense, not even to Durkheim. When he tried to demonstrate his rules in his study of suicide, he was unable to make them work. Yet the young Durkheim wrote the book specifically so that it might one day *be* a classic. *Rules* began with a familiar locution: "*Up to now* sociologists have scarcely occupied themselves with the task of characterizing and defining the method they apply to the study of social facts" (my emphasis). He then proceeded to attack the most widely known textbook on sociology, which just happened to have been Spencer's *Study of Sociology* (1873). Durkheim thus used a familiar prophetic device—"Up to now . . . / but, verily, I say unto you"— to establish his little book as a classic. He was seeking a definite canonical market position. Today, as in his day, there are those who like the idea of keeping Durkheim's book on methods in the canon, so they assign it, students buy it, publishers print it. But does anyone read it? If so, can anyone honestly make sense of it? Has anyone ever actually used those rules? Not likely.

A classic must interest readers, whether or not it is in the official canon of classic works. Conversely, canonical status does not automatically make a book a classic. This awkward relation between the classical and canonical statuses of a writing is somewhat accidental and, in retrospect, of surprising importance to social theory. Today, it is well understood that a great number of social theories written during the classic age were, directly or indirectly, excluded from the list of officially approved great works. They were, therefore, denied the public availability that would have caused them to be read as classics. Until now.

In addition to such powerful works as *The Souls of Black Folk* (1903), Charlotte Perkins Gilman's "The Yellow Wallpaper" (1892), and Anna Julia Cooper's *Voice from the South* (1892), there are thousands of essays, novels, and narratives by women, freed slaves, workers, Native Americans, and others denied privilege of place in the public culture of their times. The discovery of these writings has encouraged a rethinking not only of some of the official classics of the modern era but also of the historical period itself. Once again, in a different way, the literature reveals the times. First in importance among the earliest of feminist writers was Harriet Martineau who, as early as 1837 in the short essay *"Woman"* wrote boldly and persuasively of the "injuries suffered by women at the hands of those who hold the power."

If Marx, Weber, Durkheim, and Freud sketched theories of the contradictory nature of the modern world in the late nineteenth century, then these theories are painted in bolder, more passionate tones in the newly discovered classic texts. Du Bois wrote of the double-consciousness of American Blacks forced to live beyond the veil of racial degradations. Gilman's "The Yellow Wallpaper" similarly described a woman's double-consciousness—expected (and desiring) to please the men who would heal her, knowing the irrationality of their condescending reasonableness. Cooper gave voice to the Black women in the South who knew (and know) that they must be doubly or multiply conscious of the good men of their own race and of the good whites of their own gender. These were the experiences of people cruelly oppressed by the dominant forces of modern culture. The traditionally oppressed were to serve the market and domestic purposes of the new capitalist world in field, factory, and home. Du Bois, Gilman, Cooper, and many others gave them voice.

But one might still ask: Were these degradations a cause or an effect of modern life? Was not, at least in some degree, the ugly oppression of people part and parcel of modernity's destructive force? If possible, one also ought to see borrowings and takings, back and forth, between the literature of those excluded and of those canonized in the classical era. People on several sides of the racial, class, and gender divides experienced the split life of the modern world. On the more oppressed side, the split tore at life in cruel ways; on the other, it tugged in ways that made people crazy. But its effect was evident. As a result, it is now possible to reread certain classic texts in the process of finding new ones. Perhaps the most striking example is the unexplored relation between Du Bois and William James. Among professional social theorists, it is customary to assume a line of theoretical influence from James, through Charles Horton Cooley, to George Herbert Mead, to modern-day theories of the social self. Viewed in the cool retrospect of the history of ideas, one can read William James's ideas as fertile, philosophical statements of the logic of social life, perhaps overlooking that his theories were themselves quite confusing and contradictory. If, as James explained, an individual develops a sense of personal identity when he recognizes that "I am the same self today that I was yesterday," then how is this important state to be reconciled with the experience of also "having as many social selves as there are individuals who recognize him"? In the cool wisdom of professional theory, there are ways to ease the contradictory demands of the personal and social selves on the individual. But the very idea of a social self takes on different, more convincing meanings when it is considered in relation to the writing of James's student, Du Bois. Is the double-consciousness of the American Black the social psychology of a particular social group with its own history? Or is it a special, if extreme, case of the social psychology of modernity? The questions change one's view of the theory.

Social Theory: Remembering, Repeating and Working Through

Once the lines of canonical thinking are disturbed by such questions, theory is pushed in two directions at once: down closer to ordinary life and out from the canon of officially recognized experience. Could one, then, suggest that Gilman's mental illness was every bit as much a result of her sensitivity to modern life as of her early feminist sensibilities? Or from the other side, was she treated with well-intended condescension by her husband and her male physician because she suffered what they considered a female malady, or did they do what they did because modern culture possessed no understanding of its effects on people? Is mental exhaustion a normal response to modern life? Were those who treated women as though they had female diseases really acting through their own denial of the other side of modern society? The answers are not clear, but the questions change everything. Reading the officially excluded writers causes one to rethink not just social theories but also the idea of modern life with which people still struggle.

This is not just a matter of a canonical fair play. Nor is it something so simple as revising the list of recommended classics in an appropriate response to demands for a multicultural attitude. It is more a matter of discovering in the exclusion of certain writings a disturbing fact about the modern world: since the last century, modernity has obsessively denied its darker side. The exclusion of writings, like the oppression of people, is more than a passing aberration of an early, less-conscious time. It is a deep structural feature of the historical logic of modernity. Life in the modern world is a split life. Modern persons are torn—by their conflicting passions, by the contradictory messages of their culture, by the improbable divorce between what is promised and what is actually given. The hitherto excluded classic writers are worth reading today for a better understanding of the culture itself.

Reading authors once ignored in relation to those normally included can change one's literary and political sensitivities. If Du Bois changes what one sees in James, or even Weber, then Gilman's *Women and Economics* (1898) can alter what is found in Marx, just as Cooper's views on the moral duplicity of the post-Reconstruction South could add dimension to Durkheim's theory of modern morality. In one sense, this is not a strange process. Writings of all kinds, not just classics, are never read in isolation, as though the literary culture were not a complex field of influences. All that is changed now in reading the hitherto excluded is the way their works allow the reader to rethink the culture of exclusion, as well as the normally included classics. Both moves, taken together, enrich.

Social theories, like personal narratives, are ways of understanding social life by bringing its story out of memory, where it lies hidden and distorted. In "Remembering, Repeating, and Working-Through," Freud explained that the stories analytic patients tell in session allow them to work through the compulsion to repeat actions that prevent them from getting what they want. It might be that societies, too, must tell things through in order to move from their pasts to the present. For Freud, the idea was that the more we can tell a good listener of the story of our lives, the more we shall be able to remember and, thus remembering, to act less out of compulsion and more out of understanding. This, surely, is why Freud was so interested in his last years in the question of how a civilization recovers what it may have repressed, how it works through its compulsion to act out, rather than talk out, its aggression.

But Freud was far from the only classic social theorist to have such an idea. Marx began "The Eighteenth Brumaire of Louis Bonaparte" (1852) with the famous lines: "Hegel remarks somewhere that all great, world-historical facts and personages occur, as it were, twice. He had forgotten to add: the first time as tragedy, the second as farce." The essay following these words is, in effect, an interpretation of the revolutions of 1848 as a distorted repetition of the revolutions after 1789. It could be said that Marx's method, here and in *Capital,* was to retell the story of modern political and economic life in order to work through society's recurring tendency to act as though ownership and domination were more human than productive labor in cooperation with others.

All these classical writers told stories with such an effect. Weber's *Protestant Ethic (1905)* is more than the demonstration of an artful technique; it is the story of how the West invented itself to serve universal human truth, and then found itself apprenticed to a machine it could not control. Even Durkheim returned to the most elementary traces of human society in order to tell the truth of Knowledge—in effect, to show that science was not some essence of Being but a palpable property of social life. Du Bois, like Frederick Douglass before him, told his autobiography four different times. Du Bois was not alone in using his own story to tell social theories. Cooper and Gilman did much the same. It might even be said that people in traditionally oppressed and excluded positions base the authority of their stories about the world on what they remember and can tell about their lives.

Social theory might be thought of as remembering in order to work through the distortions of the past. The classic social theorists are worth our attention because they did just this. At a time when others continued to deny the darker side of modern life, they spoke of it without lapsing into despair. In our day, near the beginning of the twenty-first century, people across the globe, particularly in the West, need to work through their disappointment that the promises of early modernity have been paid so poorly. Social theory, beginning with these classic writings, is one of the ways this is done.

C.L.

Notes

Page 19: Freud, *Interpretation of Dreams* (Avon Books, 1965), 301.
Page 22: Schorske, *Fin-de-siècle Vienna* (Vintage, 1981), 203.
Page 23: Comte, in Gertrud Lenzer, ed., *Auguste Comte: Essential Writings* (Harpers, 1975), 9.
Page 23: Spencer, in *Illustrations of Universal Progress* (1857).
Page 24: Durkheim, *Rules of Sociological Method* (Free Press, 1982), 48.

Other quotations are from material appearing in the selections that follow.

The Two Sides of Society

Karl Marx (1818–1883) lived the life of an independent intellectual and political activist. After his studies, he worked as a journalist before leaving his native Germany in 1843, initially for Paris. There, Marx met **Friedrich Engels** (1820–1895), his life-long friend, collaborator, and benefactor. Marx's writings of this early period in Paris reflected his youthful philosophical interests in the then-popular debate over Hegel. *The Communist Manifesto,* written with Engels, appeared in 1848, on the eve of that year's revolutions. The following year, he settled in London, where he began his scholarly labors in the public reading room of the British Museum. In 1867, the first volume of *Capital* was published. It is fashionable, and plausible, to describe the ideas in *Capital* as Marx's more mature science in contrast to his more humanistic philosophy in the 1840s. In the 1860s, Marx was the dominant intellectual and political force behind the working people's movement known as the International. Marx died alone in 1883, shortly after the deaths of his daughter and wife, both named Jenny.

Marxism as a political and social philosophy took many forms with very different effects—from the bloody terror of Stalinism to the aesthetically subtle explorations of economic and cultural life by critical theorists and other students of culture today. The selections represent the full range of Marx's thinking. "Estranged Labour" is from his early, philosophical period. Readers should note that this translation often uses "estrangement" where the term "alienation" might be expected (and

vice-versa—the English terms are interchangeable). "Camera Obscura" is Marx's memorable metaphoric description of ideology's inverted relation to social reality. "Class Struggle" is from his best-known public tract, the *Manifesto,* in which he combined a commanding popular style with precise theoretical analysis. "The Eighteenth Brumaire," likewise, was a popular account of the 1851 coup in Paris, and it presented Marx's political theory through a careful, if passionate, interpretation of historical events. "The Values of Commodities" is the key section from Marx's important labor theory of value. Though it is offered as an argument in his critique of capital, the theory has been used as a general theory of value in society. (In fact, there are passages in Ferdinand de Saussure's discussion of linguistic and social value that could have been lifted from Marx.) "The Fetishism of Commodities" (1867) might be compared to "Estranged Labour" (1844) to determine how some of Marx's ideas were unchanged in his more mature writings. "Labour-Power and Capital" (1867) is one of the most powerful examples of Marx's critical and structural method. Having led the reader, in the first half of *Capital* (vol. 1), through his technical theory of the relation between labor and economic value, Marx abruptly announced that the secret of capitalist profit cannot be seen in the visible marketplace. He then turned to the hidden logic of the capitalist and capitalism. The final selection, Engels's "Patriarchal Family" (1884), is a classic source for the outlines of a materialist feminism.

Estranged Labour*
*Karl Marx (1844**)*

We have proceeded from the premises of political economy. We have accepted its language and its laws. We presupposed private property, the separation of labour, capital and land, and of wages, profit of capital and rent of land—likewise division of labour, competition, the concept of exchange-value, etc. On the basis of political economy itself, in its own words, we have shown that the worker sinks to the level of a commodity and becomes indeed the most wretched of commodities; that the wretchedness of the worker is in inverse proportion to the power and magnitude of his production; that the necessary result of competition is the accumulation of capital in a few hands, and thus the restoration of monopoly in a more terrible form; that finally the distinction between capitalist and land-rentier, like that between the tiller of the soil and the factory-worker, disappears and that the whole of society must fall apart into the two classes—the property-*owners* and the propertyless *workers*.

Political economy proceeds from the fact of private property, but it does not explain it to us. It expresses in general, abstract formulae the *material* process through which private property actually passes, and these formulae it then takes for *laws*. It does not *comprehend* these laws—i.e., it does not demonstrate how they arise from the very nature of private property. Political economy does not disclose the source of the division between labour and capital, and between capital and land. When, for example, it defines the relationship of wages to profit, it takes the interest of the capitalists to be the ultimate cause; i.e., it takes for granted what it is supposed to evolve. Similarly, competition comes in everywhere. It is explained from external circumstances. As to how far these external and apparently fortuitous circumstances are but the expression of a necessary

course of development, political economy teaches us nothing. We have seen how, to it, exchange itself appears to be a fortuitous fact. The only wheels which political economy sets in motion are *avarice* and the *war amongst the avaricious—competition*.

Precisely because political economy does not grasp the connections within the movement, it was possible to counterpose, for instance, the doctrine of competition to the doctrine of monopoly, the doctrine of craft-liberty to the doctrine of the corporation, the doctrine of the division of landed property to the doctrine of the big estate—for competition, craft-liberty and the division of landed property were explained and comprehended only as fortuitous, premeditated and violent consequences of monopoly, the corporation, and feudal property, not as their necessary, inevitable and natural consequences.

Now, therefore, we have to grasp the essential connection between private property, avarice, and the separation of labour, capital and landed property; between exchange and competition, value and the devaluation of men, monopoly and competition, etc.; the connection between this whole estrangement and the *money*-system.

Do not let us go back to a fictitious primordial condition as the political economist does, when he tries to explain. Such a primordial condition explains nothing. He merely pushes the question away into a grey nebulous distance. He assumes in the form of fact, of an event, what he is supposed to deduce—namely, the necessary relationship between two things—between, for example, division of labour and exchange. Theology in the same way explains the origin of evil by the fall of man: that is, it assumes as a fact, in historical form, what has to be explained.

We proceed from an *actual* economic fact.

The worker becomes all the poorer the more wealth he produces, the more his production increases in power and range. The worker becomes an ever cheaper commodity the more commodities he creates. With the *increasing value* of the world of things proceeds in direct proportion the *devaluation* of the world of men. Labour produces not only commodities; it produces itself and the worker as a *commodity*—and does so in the proportion in which it produces commodities generally.

This fact expresses merely that the object which labour produces—labour's product—confronts it as *something alien*, as a *power independent* of the producer. The product of labour is labour which has been congealed in an object, which has become

---

*From "Economics and Philosophical Manuscripts of 1844" in *The Marx-Engels Reader*, Second Edition by Karl Marx and Friedrich Engels, edited by Robert C. Tucker. Copyright © 1978, 1972 by W. W. Norton & Company, Inc. Used by permission of W. W. Norton & Company, Inc.

** Dates following names usually refer to the first publication of the author's text. Where a work was composed over many years, those dates are given. For example, "*Max Weber (1909–1920)*" for texts from *Economy and Society*. In general, texts are identified by the dates considered important to their historical origin or impact—whichever is more significant to their interpretation. Explanatory notes are provided as needed.

material: it is the *objectification* of labour. Labour's realization is its objectification. In the conditions dealt with by political economy this realization of labour appears as *loss of reality* for the workers; objectification as *loss of the object* and *object-bondage;* appropriation as *estrangement,* as *alienation.*

So much does labour's realization appear as loss of reality that the worker loses reality to the point of starving to death. So much does objectification appear as loss of the object that the worker is robbed of the objects most necessary not only for his life but for his work. Indeed, labour itself becomes an object which he can get hold of only with the greatest effort and with the most irregular interruptions. So much does the appropriation of the object appear as estrangement that the more objects the worker produces the fewer can he possess and the more he falls under the dominion of his product, capital.

All these consequences are contained in the definition that the worker is related to the *product of his labour* as to an *alien* object. For on this premise it is clear that the more the worker spends himself, the more powerful the alien objective world becomes which he creates over-against himself, the poorer he himself—his inner world—becomes, the less belongs to him as his own. It is the same in religion. The more man puts into God, the less he retains in himself. The worker puts his life into the object; but now his life no longer belongs to him but to the object. Hence, the greater this activity, the greater is the worker's lack of objects. Whatever the product of his labour is, he is not. Therefore the greater this product, the less is he himself. The *alienation* of the worker in his product means not only that his labour becomes an object, an *external* existence, but that it exists *outside him,* independently, as something alien to him, and that it becomes a power of its own confronting him; it means that the life which he has conferred on the object confronts him as something hostile and alien.

Let us now look more closely at the *objectification,* at the production of the worker; and therein at the *estrangement,* the *loss* of the object, his product.

The worker can create nothing without *nature,* without the *sensuous external world.* It is the material on which his labour is manifested, in which it is active, from which and by means of which it produces.

But just as nature provides labor with the *means of life* in the sense that labour cannot *live* without objects on which to operate, on the other hand, it also provides the *means of life* in the more restricted sense—i.e., the means for the physical subsistence of the *worker* himself.

Thus the more the worker by his labour *appropriates* the external world, sensuous nature, the more he deprives himself of *means of life* in the double respect: first, that the sensuous external world more and more ceases to be an object belonging to his labour—to be his labour's *means of life;* and secondly, that it more and more ceases to be *means of life* in the immediate sense, means for the physical subsistence of the worker.

Thus in this double respect the worker becomes a slave of his object, first, in that he receives an *object of labour,* i.e., in that he receives *work;* and secondly, in that he receives *means of subsistence.* Therefore, it enables him to exist, first, as a *worker;* and, second, as a *physical subject.* The extremity of this bondage is that it is only as a *worker* that he continues to maintain himself as a *physical subject,* and that it is only as a *physical subject* that he is a *worker.*

(The laws of political economy express the estrangement of the worker in his object thus: the more the worker produces, the less he has to consume; the more values he creates, the more valueless, the more unworthy he becomes; the better formed his product, the more deformed becomes the worker; the more civilized his object, the more barbarous becomes the worker; the mightier labour becomes, the more powerless becomes the worker; the more ingenious labour becomes, the duller becomes the worker and the more he becomes nature's bondsman.)

Political economy conceals the estrangement inherent in the nature of labour by not considering the direct relationship between the worker (labour) *and production.* It is true that labour produces for the rich wonderful things—but for the worker it produces privation. It produces palaces—but for the worker, hovels. It produces beauty—but for the worker, deformity. It replaces labour by machines—but some of the workers it throws back to a barbarous type of labour, and the other workers it turns into machines. It produces intelligence—but for the worker idiocy, cretinism.

The direct relationship of labour to its produce is the relationship of the worker to the objects of his production. The relationship of the man of means to the objects of production and to production itself is only a *consequence* of this first relationship—and confirms it. We shall consider this other aspect later.

When we ask, then, what is the essential relationship of labour we are asking about the relationship of the *worker* to production.

Till now we have been considering the estrangement, the alienation of the worker only in one of its aspects, i.e., the worker's *relationship to the products of his labour.* But the estrangement is manifested not only in the result but in the *act of production*—within the *producing activity* itself. How would the worker come to face the product of his activity as a stranger, were it not that in the very act of production he was estranging himself from himself? The product is after all but the summary of the activity of production. If then the product of labour is alienation, production itself must be active alienation, the alienation of activity, the activity of alienation. In the estrangement of the object of labour is merely summarized the estrangement, the alienation, in the activity of labour itself.

What, then, constitutes the alienation of labour?

First, the fact that labour is *external* to the worker, i.e., it does not belong to his essential being; that in his work, therefore, he does not affirm himself but denies himself, does not feel content but unhappy, does not develop freely his physical and mental energy but mortifies his body and ruins his mind. The worker therefore only feels himself outside his work, and in his work feels outside himself. He is at home when he is not working, and when he is working he is not at home. His labour is therefore not voluntary, but coerced; it is *forced labour*. It is therefore not the satisfaction of a need; it is merely a *means* to satisfy needs external to it. Its alien character emerges clearly in the fact that as soon as no physical or other compulsion exists, labour is shunned like the plague. External labour, labour in which man alienates himself, is a labour of self-sacrifice, of mortification. Lastly, the external character of labour for the worker appears in the fact that it is not his own, but someone else's, that it does not belong to him, that in it he belongs, not to himself, but to another. Just as in religion the spontaneous activity of the human imagination, of the human brain and the human heart, operates independently of the individual—that is, operates on him as an alien, divine or diabolical activity—in the same way the worker's activity is not his spontaneous activity. It belongs to another; it is the loss of his self.

As a result, therefore, man (the worker) no longer feels himself to be freely active in any but his animal functions—eating, drinking, procreating, or at most in his dwelling and in dressing-up, etc.; and in his human functions he no longer feels himself to be anything but an animal. What is animal becomes human and what is human becomes animal.

Certainly eating, drinking, procreating, etc., are also genuinely human functions. But in the abstraction which separates them from the sphere of all other human activity and turns them into sole and ultimate ends, they are animal.

We have considered the act of estranging practical human activity, labour, in two of its aspects. (1) The relation of the worker to the *product of labour* as an alien object exercising power over him. This relation is at the same time the relation to the sensuous external world, to the objects of nature as an alien world antagonistically opposed to him. (2) The relation of labour to the *act of production* within the *labour* process. This relation is the relation of the worker to his own activity as an alien activity not belonging to him; it is activity as suffering, strength as weakness, begetting as emasculating, the worker's *own* physical and mental energy, his personal life or what is life other than activity—as an activity which is turned against him, neither depends on nor belongs to him. Here we have *self-estrangement,* as we had previously the estrangement of the *thing*.

We have yet a third aspect of *estranged labour* to deduce from the two already considered.

Man is a species being, not only because in practice and in theory he adopts the species as his object (his own as well as those of other things), but—and this is only another way of expressing it—but also because he treats himself as the actual, living species; because he treats himself as a *universal* and therefore a free being.

The life of the species, both in man and in animals, consists physically in the fact that man (like the animal) lives on inorganic nature; and the more universal man is compared with an animal, the more universal is the sphere of inorganic nature on which he lives. Just as plants, animals, stones, the air, light, etc., constitute a part of human consciousness in the realm of theory, partly as objects of natural science, partly as objects of art—his spiritual inorganic nature, spiritual nourishment which he must first prepare to make it palatable and digestible—so too in the realm of practice they constitute a part of human life and human activity. Physically man lives only on these products of nature, whether they appear in the form of food, heating, clothes, a dwelling, or whatever it may be. The universality of man is in practice manifested precisely in the universality which makes all nature his *inorganic body*—both inasmuch as nature is (1) his direct means of life, and (2) the material, the object, and the instrument of his life-activity. Nature is man's *inorganic body*—nature, that is, in so far as it is not itself the human body. Man *lives* on nature—means that nature is his *body,* with which he must remain in continuous intercourse if he is not to die. That man's physical and spiritual life is linked to nature means simply that nature is linked to itself, for man is a part of nature.

In estranging from man (1) nature, and (2) himself, his own active functions, his life-activity, estranged labour estranges the *species* from man. It turns for him the *life of the species* into a means of individual life. First it estranges the life of the species and individual life, and secondly it makes individual life in its abstract form the purpose of the life of the species, likewise in its abstract and estranged form.

For in the first place labour, *life-activity, productive life* itself, appears to man merely as a *means* of satisfying a need—the need to maintain the physical existence. Yet the productive life is the life of the species. It is life-engendering life. The whole character of a species—its species character—is contained in the character of its life-activity; and free, conscious activity is man's species character. Life itself appears only as *a means to life.*

The animal is immediately identical with its life-activity. It does not distinguish itself from it. It is *its life-activity.* Man makes his life-activity itself the object of his will and of his consciousness. He has conscious life-activity. It is not a determination with which he directly merges. Conscious life-activity directly distinguishes man from animal life-activity. It is just because of this that he is a species being. Or it is only because he is a species being that he is a Conscious Being, i.e., that his own life is an object for him. Only because of that is his activity free activity. Estranged labour reverses this relationship, so that it is just because man is a conscious being that he makes his life-activity, his *essential* being, a mere means to his *existence.*

In creating an *objective world* by his practical activity, in *working-up* inorganic nature, man proves himself a conscious species being, i.e., as a being that treats the species as its own essential being, or that treats itself as a species being. Admittedly animals also produce. They build themselves nests, dwellings, like the bees, beavers, ants, etc. But an animal only produces what it immediately needs for itself or its young. It produces one-sidedly, whilst man produces universally. It produces only under the dominion of immediate physical need, whilst man produces even when he is free from physical need and only truly produces in freedom therefrom. An animal produces only itself, whilst man reproduces the whole of nature. An animal's product belongs immediately to its physical body, whilst man freely confronts his product. An animal forms things in accordance with the standard and the need of the species to which it belongs, whilst man knows how to produce in accordance with the standard of every species, and knows how to apply everywhere the inherent standard to the object. Man therefore also forms things in accordance with the laws of beauty.

It is just in the working-up of the objective world, therefore, that man first really proves himself to be a *species being.* This production is his active species life. Through and because of this production, nature appears as *his* work and his reality. The object of labour is, therefore, the *objectification of man's species life:* for he duplicates himself not only, as in consciousness, intellectually, but also actively, in reality, and therefore he contemplates himself in a world that he has created. In tearing away from man the object of his production, therefore, estranged labour tears from him his *species life,* his real species objectivity, and transforms his advantage over animals into the disadvantage that his inorganic body, nature, is taken from him.

Similarly, in degrading spontaneous activity, free activity, to a means, estranged labour makes man's species life a means to his physical existence.

The consciousness which man has of his species is thus transformed by estrangement in such a way that the species life becomes for him a means.

Estranged labour turns thus:

(3) *Man's species being,* both nature and his spiritual species property, into a being *alien* to him, into a *means* to his *individual existence.* It estranges man's own body from him, as it does external nature and his spiritual essence, his *human* being.

(4) An immediate consequence of the fact that man is estranged from the product of his labour, from his life-activity, from his species being is the *estrangement of man* from *man.* If a man is confronted by himself, he is confronted by the *other* man. What applies to a man's relation to his work, to the product of his labour and to himself, also holds of a man's relation to the other man, and to the other man's labour and object of labour.

In fact, the proposition that man's species nature is estranged from him means that one man is estranged from the other, as each of them is from man's essential nature.

The estrangement of man, and in fact every relationship in which man stands to himself, is first realized and expressed in the relationship in which a man stands to other men.

Hence within the relationship of estranged labour each man views the other in accordance with the standard and the position in which he finds himself as a worker.

We took our departure from a fact of political economy—the estrangement of the worker and his production. We have formulated the concept of this fact—*estranged, alienated* labour. We have analysed this concept—hence analysing merely a fact of political economy.

Let us now see, further, how in real life the concept of estranged, alienated labour must express and present itself.

If the product of labour is alien to me, if it confronts me as an alien power, to whom, then, does it belong?

If my own activity does not belong to me, if it is an alien, a coerced activity, to whom, then, does it belong?

To a being *other* than me.

Who is this being?

The *gods?* To be sure, in the earliest times the principal production (for example, the building of temples, etc., in Egypt, India and Mexico) appears to be in the service of the gods, and the product belongs to the gods. However, the gods on their own were never the lords of labour. No more was *nature.* And what a contradiction it would be if, the more man subjugated nature by his labour and the more the miracles of the gods were rendered superfluous by the miracles of industry, the more man were to renounce the joy of production and the enjoyment of the produce in favour of these powers.

The *alien* being, to whom labour and the produce of labour belongs, in whose service labour is done and for whose benefit the produce of labour is provided, can only be *man* himself.

If the product of labour does not belong to the worker, if it confronts him as an alien power, this can only be because it belongs to some *other man than the worker.* If the worker's activity is a torment to him, to another it must be *delight* and his life's joy. Not the gods, not nature, but only man himself can be this alien power over man.

We must bear in mind the above-stated proposition that man's relation to himself only becomes *objective* and *real* for him through his relation to the other man. Thus, if the product of his labour, his labour *objectified,* is for him an *alien,* hostile, powerful object independent of him, then his position towards it is such that someone else is master of this object, someone who is alien, hostile, powerful, and independent of him. If his own activity is to him an unfree activity, then he is treating it as activity performed in the service, under the dominion, the coercion and the yoke of another man.

Every self-estrangement of man from himself and from nature appears in the relation in which he places himself and nature to men other than and differenti-

ated from himself. For this reason religious self-estrangement necessarily appears in the relationship of the layman to the priest, or again to a mediator, etc., since we are here dealing with the intellectual world. In the real practical world self-estrangement can only become manifest through the real practical relationship to other men. The medium through which estrangement takes place is itself *practical.* Thus through estranged labour man not only engenders his relationship to the object and to the act of production as to powers that are alien and hostile to him; he also engenders the relationship in which other men stand to his production and to his product, and the relationship in which he stands to these other men. Just as he begets his own production as the loss of his reality, as his punishment; just as he begets his own product as a loss, as a product not belonging to him; so he begets the dominion of the one who does not produce over production and over the product. Just as he estranges from himself his own activity, so he confers to the stranger activity which is not his own.

Till now we have only considered this relationship from the standpoint of the worker and later we shall be considering it also from the standpoint of the non-worker.

Through *estranged, alienated labour,* then, the worker produces the relationship to this labour of a man alien to labour and standing outside it. The relationship of the worker to labour engenders the relation to it of the capitalist, or whatever one chooses to call the master of labour. *Private property* is thus the product, the result, the necessary consequence, of *alienated labour,* of the external relation of the worker to nature and to himself.

Camera Obscura[*]
Karl Marx (1845–1846)

The fact is, therefore, that definite individuals who are productively active in a definite way enter into these definite social and political relations. Empirical observation must in each separate instance bring out empirically, and without any mystification and speculation, the connection of the social and political structure with production. The social structure and the State are continually evolving out of the life

[*] From "The German Ideology" in *The Marx-Engels Reader,* Second Edition by Karl Marx and Friedrich Engels, edited by Robert C. Tucker. Copyright © 1978, 1972 by W. W. Norton & Company, Inc. Used by permission of W. W. Norton & Company, Inc.

process of definite individuals, but of individuals, not as they may appear in their own or other people's imagination, but as they *really* are; i.e., as they operate, produce materially, and hence as they work under definite material limits, presuppositions and conditions independent of their will.

The production of ideas, of conceptions, of consciousness, is at first directly interwoven with the material activity and the material intercourse of men, the language of real life. Conceiving, thinking, the mental intercourse of men, appear at this stage as the direct efflux of their material behaviour. The same applies to mental production as expressed in the language of politics, laws, morality, religion, metaphysics, etc., of a people. Men are the producers of their conceptions, ideas, etc.—real, active men, as they are conditioned by a definite development of their productive forces and of the intercourse corresponding to these, up to its furthest forms. Consciousness can never be anything else than conscious existence, and the existence of men is their actual life-process. If in all ideology men and their circumstances appear upside-down as in a *camera obscura,* this phenomenon arises just as much from their historical life-process as the inversion of objects on the retina does from their physical life-process.

The Manifesto of Class Struggle[*]

Karl Marx and Friedrich Engels (1848)

The history of all hitherto existing society is the history of class struggles.

Freeman and slave, patrician and plebeian, lord and serf, guild-master and journeyman, in a word, oppressor and oppressed, stood in constant opposition to one another, carried on an uninterrupted, now hidden, now open fight, a fight that each time ended, either in a revolutionary re-constitution of society at large, or in the common ruin of the contending classes.

In the earlier epochs of history, we find almost everywhere a complicated arrangement of society into various orders, a manifold gradation of social rank. In ancient Rome we have patricians, knights, plebeians, slaves; in the Middle Ages, feudal lords, vassals, guild-masters, journeymen, apprentices, serfs; in almost all of these classes, again, subordinate gradations.

[*]From "Manifesto of the Communist Party" in *The Marx-Engels Reader,* Second Edition by Karl Marx and Friedrich Engels, edited by Robert C. Tucker. Copyright © 1978, 1972 by W. W. Norton & Company, Inc. Used by permission of W. W. Norton & Company, Inc.

The modern bourgeois society that has sprouted from the ruins of feudal society has not done away with class antagonisms. It has but established new classes, new conditions of oppression, new forms of struggle in place of the old ones.

Our epoch, the epoch of the bourgeoisie, possesses, however, this distinctive feature: it has simplified the class antagonisms: Society as a whole is more and more splitting up into two great hostile camps, into two great classes directly facing each other: Bourgeoisie and Proletariat.

From the serfs of the Middle Ages sprang the chartered burghers of the earliest towns. From these burgesses the first elements of the bourgeoisie were developed.

The discovery of America, the rounding of the Cape, opened up fresh ground for the rising bourgeoisie. The East-Indian and Chinese markets, the colonisation of America, trade with the colonies, the increase in the means of exchange and in commodities generally, gave to commerce, to navigation, to industry, an impulse never before known, and thereby, to the revolutionary element in the tottering feudal society, a rapid development.

The feudal system of industry, under which industrial production was monopolised by closed guilds, now no longer sufficed for the growing wants of the new markets. The manufacturing system took its place. The guild-masters were pushed on one side by the manufacturing middle class; division of labour between the different corporate guilds vanished in the face of division of labour in each single workshop.

Meantime the markets kept ever growing, the demand ever rising. Even manufacture no longer sufficed. Thereupon, steam and machinery revolutionised industrial production. The place of manufacture was taken by the giant, Modern Industry, the place of the industrial middle class, by industrial millionaires, the leaders of whole industrial armies, the modern bourgeois.

Modern industry has established the world-market, for which the discovery of America paved the way. This market has given an immense development to commerce, to navigation, to communication by land. This development has, in its turn, reacted on the extension of industry; and in proportion as industry, commerce, navigation, railways extended, in the same proportion the bourgeoisie developed, increased its capital, and pushed into the background every class handed down from the Middle Ages.

We see, therefore, how the modern bourgeoisie is itself the product of a long course of development, of a series of revolutions in the modes of production and of exchange.

Each step in the development of the bourgeoisie was accompanied by a corresponding political advance of that class. An oppressed class under the sway of the feudal nobility, an armed and self-governing association in the mediaeval commune; here independent urban republic (as in Italy and Germany), there taxable "third estate" of the monarchy (as in France), afterwards, in the period of manufacture proper, serving either the semi-feudal or the absolute monarchy as a counterpoise against the nobility, and, in fact, corner-stone of the great monarchies in general, the bourgeoisie has at last, since the establishment of Modern Industry and of the world-market, conquered for itself, in the modern representative State, exclusive political sway. The execution of the modern State is but a committee for managing the common affairs of the whole bourgeoisie.

The bourgeoisie, historically, has played a most revolutionary part.

The bourgeoisie, wherever it has got the upper hand, has put an end to all feudal, patriarchal, idyllic relations. It has pitilessly torn asunder the motley feudal ties that bound man to his "natural superiors," and has left remaining no other nexus between man and man than naked self-interest, than callous "cash payment." It has drowned the most heavenly ecstasies of religious fervour, of chivalrous enthusiasm, of philistine sentimentalism, in the icy water of egotistical calculation. It has resolved personal worth into exchange value, and in place of the numberless indefeasible chartered freedoms, has set up that single, unconscionable freedom—Free Trade. In one word, for exploitation, veiled by religious and political illusions, it has substituted naked, shameless, direct, brutal exploitation.

The bourgeoisie has stripped of its halo every occupation hitherto honoured and looked up to with reverent awe. It has converted the physician, the lawyer, the priest, the poet, the man of science, into its paid wage-labourers.

The bourgeoisie has torn away from the family its sentimental veil, and has reduced the family relation to a mere money relation.

The bourgeoisie has disclosed how it came to pass that the brutal display of vigour in the Middle Ages, which Reactionists so much admire, found its fitting complement in the most slothful indolence. It has been the first to show what man's activity can bring about. It has accomplished wonders far surpassing Egyptian pyramids, Roman aqueducts, and Gothic cathedrals; it has conducted expeditions that put in the shade all former Exoduses of nations and crusades.

The bourgeoisie cannot exist without constantly revolutionising the instruments of production, and thereby the relations of production, and with them the whole relations of society. Conservation of the old modes of production in unaltered form, was, on the contrary, the first condition of existence for all earlier industrial classes. Constant revolutionising of production, uninterrupted disturbance of all social conditions, everlasting uncertainty and agitation distinguish the bourgeois epoch from all earlier ones. All fixed, fast-frozen relations, with their train of ancient and venerable prejudices and opinions, are swept away, all new-formed ones become antiquated before they can ossify. All that is solid melts into air, all that is holy is profaned, and man is at last compelled to face with sober senses, his real conditions of life, and his relations with his kind.

The need of a constantly expanding market for its products chases the bourgeoisie over the whole surface of the globe. It must nestle everywhere, settle everywhere, establish connexions everywhere.

The bourgeoisie has through its exploitation of the world-market given a cosmopolitan character to production and consumption in every country. To the great chagrin of Reactionists, it has drawn from under the feet of industry the national ground on which it stood. All old-established national industries have been destroyed or are daily being destroyed. They are dislodged by new industries, whose introduction becomes a life and death question for all civilised nations, by industries that no longer work up indigenous raw material, but raw material drawn from the remotest zones; industries whose products are consumed, not only at home, but in every quarter of the globe. In place of the old wants, satisfied by the productions of the country, we find new wants, requiring for their satisfaction the products of distant lands and climes. In place of the old local and national seclusion and self-sufficiency, we have intercourse in every direction, universal inter-dependence of nations. And as in material, so also in intellectual production. The intellectual creations of individual nations become common property. National one-sidedness and narrow-mindedness become more and more impossible, and from the numerous national and local literatures, there arises a world literature.

The bourgeoisie, by the rapid improvement of all instruments of production, by the immensely facilitated means of communication, draws all, even the most barbarian, nations into civilisation. The cheap prices of its commodities are the heavy artillery with which it batters down all Chinese walls, with which it forces the barbarians' intensely obstinate hatred of foreigners to capitulate. It compels all nations, on pain of extinction, to adopt the bourgeois mode of production; it compels them to introduce what it calls civilisation into their midst, *i.e.,* to become bourgeois themselves. In one word, it creates a world after its own image.

The bourgeoisie has subjected the country to the rule of the towns. It has created enormous cities, has greatly increased the urban population as compared with the rural, and has thus rescued a considerable part of the population from the idiocy of rural life. Just as it has made the country dependent on the towns, so it has made barbarian and semi-barbarian countries dependent on the civilised ones, nations of peasants on nations of bourgeois, the East on the West.

The bourgeoisie keeps more and more doing away with the scattered state of the population, of the means of production, and of property. It has agglomerated population, centralised means of production, and has concentrated property in a few hands. The necessary consequence of this was political centralisation. Independent, or but loosely connected provinces, with separate interests, laws, governments and systems of taxation, became lumped together into one nation, with one government, one code of laws, one national class-interest, one frontier and one customs-tariff.

The bourgeoisie, during its rule of scarce one hundred years, has created more massive and more colossal productive forces than have all preceding generations together. Subjection of Nature's forces to man, machinery, application of chemistry to industry and agriculture, steam-navigation, railways, electric telegraphs, clearing of whole continents for cultivation, canalisation of rivers, whole populations conjured out of the ground—what earlier century had even a presentiment that such productive forces slumbered in the lap of social labour?

We see then: the means of production and of exchange, on whose foundation the bourgeoisie built itself up, were generated in feudal society. At a certain stage in the development of these means of production and of exchange, the conditions under which feudal society produced and exchanged, the feudal organisation of agriculture and manufacturing industry, in one word, the feudal relations of property became no longer compatible with the already developed productive forces; they became so many fetters. They had to be burst asunder; they were burst asunder.

Into their place stepped free competition, accompanied by a social and political constitution adapted to it, and by the economical and political sway of the bourgeois class.

A similar movement is going on before our own eyes. Modern bourgeois society with its relations of production, of exchange and of property, a society that has conjured up such gigantic means of production and of exchange, is like the sorcerer, who is no longer able to control the powers of the nether world whom he has called up by his spells. For many a decade past the history of industry and commerce is but the history of the revolt of modern productive forces against modern conditions of production, against the property relations that are the conditions for the existence of the bourgeoisie and of its rule. It is enough to mention the commercial crises that by their periodical return put on its trial, each time more threateningly, the existence of the entire bourgeois society. In these crises a great part not only of the existing products, but also of the previously created productive forces, are periodically destroyed. In these crises there breaks out an epidemic that, in all earlier epochs, would have seemed an absurdity—the epidemic of over-production. Society suddenly finds itself put back into a state of momentary barbarism; it appears as if a famine, a universal war of devastation had cut off the supply of every means of subsistence; industry and commerce seem to be destroyed; and why? Because there is too much civilisation, too much means of subsistence, too much industry, too much commerce. The productive forces at the disposal of society no longer tend to further the development of the conditions of bourgeois property; on the contrary, they have become too powerful for these conditions, by which they are fettered, and so soon as they overcome these fetters, they bring disorder into the whole of bourgeois society, endanger the existence of bourgeois property. The conditions of bourgeois society are too narrow to comprise the wealth created by them. And how does the bourgeoisie get over these crises? On the one hand by enforced destruction of a mass of productive forces; on the other, by the conquest of new markets, and by the more thorough exploitation of the old ones. That is to say, by paving the way for more extensive and more destructive crises, and by diminishing the means whereby crises are prevented.

The weapons with which the bourgeoisie felled feudalism to the ground are now turned against the bourgeoisie itself.

But not only has the bourgeoisie forged the weapons that bring death to itself; it has also called into existence the men who are to wield those weapons—the modern working class—the proletarians.

In proportion as the bourgeoisie, *i.e.,* capital, is developed, in the same proportion is the proletariat, the modern working class, developed—a class of labourers, who live only so long as they find work, and who find work only so long as their labour increases capital. These labourers, who must sell themselves piece-meal, are a commodity, like every other article of commerce, and are consequently exposed to all the vicissitudes of competition, to all the fluctuations of the market.

Owing to the extensive use of machinery and to division of labour, the work of the proletarians has lost all individual character, and consequently, all charm for the workman. He becomes an appendage of the machine, and it is only the most simple, most monotonous, and most easily acquired knack, that is required of him. Hence, the cost of production of a workman is restricted, almost entirely, to the means of subsistence that he requires for his maintenance, and for the propagation of his race. But the price of a commodity, and therefore also of labour, is equal to its cost of production. In proportion, therefore, as the repulsiveness of the work increases, the wage decreases. Nay more, in proportion as the use of machinery and division of labour increases, in the same proportion the burden of toil also increases, whether by prolongation of the working hours, by increase of the work exacted in a given time or by increased speed of the machinery, etc.

Modern industry has converted the little workshop of the patriarchal master into the great factory of the industrial capitalist. Masses of labourers, crowded into the factory, are organised like soldiers. As privates of the industrial army they are placed under the command of a perfect hierarchy of officers and sergeants. Not only are they slaves of the bourgeois class, and of the bourgeois State; they are daily and hourly enslaved by the machine, by the over-looker, and, above all, by the individual bourgeois manufacturer himself. The more openly this despotism proclaims gain to be its end and aim, the more petty, the more hateful and the more embittering it is.

The less the skill and exertion of strength implied in manual labour, in other words, the more modern industry becomes developed, the more is the labour of men superseded by that of women. Differences of age and sex have no longer any distinctive social validity for the working class. All are instruments of labour, more or less expensive to use, according to their age and sex.

No sooner is the exploitation of the labourer by the manufacturer, so far, at an end, that he receives his wages in cash, than he is set upon by the other portions of the bourgeoisie, the landlord, the shopkeeper, the pawnbroker, etc.

The Eighteenth Brumaire of Louis Bonaparte[*]
Karl Marx (1852)

Hegel remarks somewhere that all great, world-historical facts and personages occur, as it were, twice. He has forgotten to add: the first time as tragedy, the second as farce. Caussidière for Danton, Louis Blanc for Robespierre, the Mountain of 1848 to 1851 for the Mountain of 1793 to 1795, the Nephew for the Uncle. And the same caricature occurs in the circumstances in which the second edition of the Eighteenth Brumaire is taking place.

Men make their own history, but they do not make it just as they please; they do not make it under circumstances chosen by themselves, but under circumstances directly found, given and transmitted from the past. The tradition of all the dead generations weighs like a nightmare on the brain of the living. And just when they seem engaged in revolutionising themselves and things, in creating something entirely new, precisely in such epochs of revolutionary crisis they anxiously conjure up the spirits of the past to their service and borrow from them names, battle slogans and costumes in order to present the new scene of world history in this time-honoured disguise and this borrowed language. Thus Luther donned the mask of the Apostle Paul, the Revolution of 1789 to 1814 draped itself alternately as the Roman Republic and the Roman Empire, and the Revolution of 1848 knew nothing better to do than to parody, in turn, 1789 and the revolutionary tradition of 1793 to 1795. In like manner the beginner who has learnt a new language always translates it back into his mother tongue, but he has assimilated the spirit of the new language and can produce freely in it only when he moves in it without remembering the old and forgets in it his ancestral tongue.

Consideration of this world-historical conjuring up of the dead reveals at once a salient difference. Camille Desmoulins, Danton, Robespierre, Saint-Just, Napoleon, the heroes, as well as the parties and the masses of the old French Revolution, performed the task of their time in Roman costume and with Roman

[*]From *The Marx-Engels Reader*, Second Edition, by Karl Marx and Friedrich Engels, edited by Robert C. Tucker. Copyright © 1978, 1972 by W. W. Norton & Company, Inc. Used by permission of W. W. Norton & Company, Inc.

phrases, the task of releasing and setting up modern bourgeois society. The first ones knocked the feudal basis to pieces and mowed off the feudal heads which had grown from it. The other created inside France the conditions under which free competition could first be developed, the parcelled landed property exploited, the unfettered productive power of the nation employed, and outside the French borders he everywhere swept the feudal formations away, so far as was necessary to furnish bourgeois society in France with a suitable up-to-date environment on the European Continent. The new social formation once established, the antediluvian Colossi disappeared and with them the resurrected Romans—the Brutuses, Gracchi, Publicolas, the tribunes, the senators and Caesar himself. Bourgeois society in its sober reality had begotten its true interpreters and mouthpieces in the Says, Cousins, Royer-Collards, Benjamin Constants and Guizots; its real military leaders sat behind the office desks, and the hogheaded Louis XVIII was its political chief. Wholly absorbed in the production of wealth and in the peaceful struggle of competition, it no longer comprehended that ghosts from the days of Rome had watched over its cradle. But unheroic as bourgeois society is, yet it had need of heroism, of sacrifice, of terror, of civil war and of national battles to bring it into being. And in the classically austere traditions of the Roman Republic its gladiators found the ideals and the art forms, the self-deceptions that they needed in order to conceal from themselves the bourgeois limitations of the content of their struggles and to keep their passion at the height of the great historical tragedy. Similarly, at another stage of development, a century earlier, Cromwell and the English people had borrowed speech, passions and illusions from the Old Testament for their bourgeois revolution. When the real aim had been achieved, when the bourgeois transformation of English society had been accomplished, Locke supplanted Habakkuk.

The awakening of the dead in those revolutions therefore served the purpose of glorifying the new struggles, not of parodying the old; of magnifying the given tasks in imagination, not of taking flight from their solution in reality; of finding once more the spirit of revolution, not of making its ghost walk again.

From 1848 to 1851 only the ghost of the old revolution walked, from Marrast, the *republicain en gants jaunes* [Republican in yellow gloves], who disguised himself as the old Bailly, to the adventurer who hides his trivially repulsive features under the iron death mask of Napoleon. An entire people, which had imagined that by a revolution it had increased its power of action, suddenly finds itself set back into a dead epoch and, in order that no doubt as to the relapse may be possible, the old data again arise, the old chronology, the old names, the old edicts, which have long become a subject of antiquarian erudition, and the old henchmen, who had long seemed dead and decayed. The nation appears to itself like that mad Englishman in Bedlam, who fancies that he lives in the times of the ancient Pharaohs and daily bemoans the hard labour that he must perform in the Ethiopian mines as a gold digger, immured in this subterranean prison, a dimly burning lamp fastened to his head, the overseer of the slaves behind him with a long whip, and at the exits a confused mass of barbarian mercenaries, who understand neither the forced labourers in the mines nor one another, since they have no common speech. "And all this is expected of me," groans the mad Englishman, "of me, a free-born Briton, in order to make gold for the old Pharaohs." "In order to pay the debts of the Bonaparte family," sighs the French nation. The Englishman, so long as he was in his right mind, could not get rid of the fixed idea of making gold. The French, so long as they were engaged in revolution, could not get rid of the memory of Napoleon, as the election of December 10, 1848, proved. From the perils of revolution their longings went back to the flesh-pots of Egypt, and December 2, 1851, was the answer. They have not only a caricature of the old Napoleon, they have the old Napoleon himself, caricatured as he would inevitably appear in the middle of the nineteenth century.

The social revolution of the nineteenth century cannot draw its poetry from the past, but only from the future. It cannot begin with itself, before it has stripped off all superstition in regard to the past. Earlier revolutions required world-historical recollections in order to drug themselves concerning their own content. To arrive at its content, the revolution of the nineteenth century must let the dead bury their dead. There the phrase went beyond the content; here the content goes beyond the phrase.

The February Revolution was a sudden attack, a taking of the old society by *surprise,* and the people proclaimed this unhoped for *stroke* as a world-historic deed, opening the new epoch. On December 2 the February Revolution is conjured away by a card-sharper's trick, and what seems overthrown is no longer the monarchy; it is the liberal concessions that were wrung from it by century-long struggles. Instead of *society* having conquered a new content for itself, the *state* only appears to have returned to its oldest form, to the shamelessly simple domination of the sabre and the cowl. This is the answer to the *coup de main* of February 1848, given by the *coup de tête* of December 1851. Easy come, easy go. Meanwhile the interval has not passed by unused. During the years 1848 to 1851 French society has made up, and that by an abbreviated, because revolutionary, method, for the studies and experiences which, in a regular, so to speak, text-book development would have had to precede the February Revolution, if the latter was to be more than disturbance of the surface. Society now seems to have fallen back behind its point of departure; it has in truth first to create for itself the revolutionary point of departure, the situation, the relationships, the conditions, under which modern revolution alone becomes serious.

Bourgeois revolutions, like those of the eighteenth century, storm more swiftly from success to success; their dramatic effects outdo each other; men and things seem set in sparkling brilliants; ecstasy is the everyday spirit; but they are short lived; soon they have attained their zenith, and a long depression lays hold of society before it learns soberly to assimilate the results of its storm and stress period. Proletarian revolutions, on the other hand, like those of the nineteenth century, criticise themselves constantly, interrupt themselves continually in their own course, come back to the apparently accomplished in order to begin it afresh, deride with unmerciful thoroughness the inadequacies, weaknesses and paltrinesses of their first attempts, seem to throw down their adversary only in order that he may draw new strength from the earth and rise again more gigantic before them, recoil ever and anon from the indefinite prodigiousness of their own aims, until the situation has been created which makes all turning back impossible. . . .

The French bourgeoisie offered resistance to the domination of the working proletariat; it has brought the *lumpenproletariat* to domination, with the chief of the Society of December 10 at the head. The bourgeoisie kept France in breathless fear of the future terrors of red anarchy; Bonaparte discounted this future for it when, on December 4, he had the eminent bourgeois of the Boulevard Montmartre and the Boulevard des Italiens shot down at their windows by the army of order, whose enthusiasm was inspired by liquor. It apotheosised the sword; the sword rules it. It destroyed the revolutionary press; its own press has been destroyed. It placed public meetings under police supervision; its salons are under the supervision of the police. It disbanded the democratic National Guard; its own National Guard has been disbanded. It imposed the state of siege; the state of

siege has been imposed on it. It supplanted the juries by military commissions; its juries are supplanted by military commissions; it subjected public education to the priests; the priests subject it to their own education. It transported people without trial; it is transported without trial. It suppressed every stirring in society by means of the state power; every stirring in its society is repressed by means of the state power. Out of enthusiasm for its purse, it rebelled against its own politicians and men of letters; its politicians and men of letters are swept aside, but its purse is plundered now that its mouth has been gagged and its pen broken. The bourgeoisie never wearied of crying out to the revolution what Saint Arsenius cried out to the Christians: "*Fuge, tace, quiesce!*" Flee, be silent, keep quiet! Bonaparte cries to the bourgeoisie: "*Fuge, tace, quiesce!*" Flee, be silent, keep quiet!

The French bourgeoisie had long since found the solution to Napoleon's dilemma: "*Dans cinquante ans l'Europe sera républicaine ou cosaque*" ["Within fifty years Europe will be republican or Cossack"]. It had found the solution to it in the "*république cosaque.*" No Circe, by means of black magic, has distorted that work of art, the bourgeois republic, into a monstrous shape. That republic has nothing but the semblance of respectability. The present-day France was contained in a finished state within the parliamentary republic. It only required a bayonet thrust for the bubble to burst and the monster to spring forth before our eyes. . . .

Why did not the Paris proletariat rise in revolt after December?

The overthrow of the bourgeoisie had as yet only been decreed; the decree had not been carried out. Any serious insurrection of the proletariat would at once have put fresh life into the bourgeoisie, would have reconciled it with the army and would have ensured a second June defeat for the workers. . . .

But the revolution is thorough-going. It is still in process of passing through purgatory. It does its work methodically. By December 2, 1851, it had completed one half of its preparatory work; it is now completing the other half. First it perfected the parliamentary power, in order to be able to overthrow it. Now that it has attained this, it perfects the *executive power*, reduces it to its purest expression, isolates it, sets it up against itself as the sole target, in order to concentrate all its forces of destruction against it. And when it has done this second half of its preliminary work, Europe will leap from her seat and exultantly exclaim: Well grubbed, old mole!

This executive power with its enormous bureaucratic and military organisation, with its artificial state machinery embracing wide strata, with a host of officials numbering half a million, besides an army of another half million, this appalling parasitic growth, which enmeshes the body of French society like a net and chokes all its pores, sprang up in the days of the absolute monarchy, with the decay of the feudal system, which it helped to hasten. The seigniorial privileges of the landowners and towns became transformed into so many attributes of the state power, the feudal dignitaries into paid officials and the motley pattern of conflicting mediaeval plenary powers into the regulated plan of a state authority, whose work is divided and centralised as in a factory. The first French Revolution, with its task of breaking all local, territorial, urban and provincial independent powers in order to create the bourgeois unity of the nation, was bound to develop what the absolute monarchy had begun—centralisation, but at the same time the extent, the attributes and the agents of governmental authority. Napoleon perfected this state machinery. The Legitimist monarchy and the July monarchy added nothing but a greater division of labour, growing in the same measure that the division of labour within bourgeois society created new groups of interests, and, therefore, new material for state administration. Every *common* interest was straightaway severed from society, counter-posed to it as a higher, *general* interest, snatched from the self-activity of society's members and made an object of governmental activity from the bridge, the school-house and the communal property of a village community to the railways, the national wealth and the national university of France. The parliamentary republic, finally, in its struggle against the revolution, found itself compelled to strengthen, along with the repressive measures, the resources and centralisation of governmental power. All the revolutions perfected this machine instead of smashing it. The parties that contended in turn for domination regarded the possession of this huge state edifice as the principal spoils of the victor.

But under the absolute monarchy, during the first revolution, and under Napoleon, bureaucracy was only the means of preparing the class rule of the bourgeoisie. Under the Restoration, under Louis Philippe and under the parliamentary republic, it was the instrument of the ruling class, however much it strove for power of its own.

Only under the second Bonaparte does the state seem to have made itself completely independent. As against bourgeois society, the state machine has consolidated its position so thoroughly that the chief of the Society of December 10 suffices for its head, an adventurer blown in from abroad, elevated on the shield by a drunken soldiery, which he has bought with liquor and sausages, and which he must continually ply with sausage anew. Hence the downcast despair, the feeling of most dreadful humiliation and degradation that oppresses the breast of France and makes her catch her breath. She feels herself dishonoured.

Capital and the Values of Commodities[*]
Karl Marx (1867)

The Two Factors of a Commodity: Use-Value and Value (The Substance of Value and the Magnitude of Value)

The wealth of those societies in which the capitalist mode of production prevails, presents itself as "an immense accumulation of commodities," its unit being a single commodity. Our investigation must therefore begin with the analysis of a commodity.

A commodity is, in the first place, an object outside us, a thing that by its properties satisfies human wants of some sort or another. The nature of such wants, whether, for instance, they spring from the stomach or from fancy, makes no difference. Neither are we here concerned to know how the object satisfies these wants, whether directly as means of subsistence, or indirectly as means of production.

Every useful thing, as iron, paper, &c., may be looked at from the two points of view of quality and quantity. It is an assemblage of many properties, and may therefore be of use in various ways. To discover the various uses of things is the work of history. So also is the establishment of socially-recognised standards of measure for the quantities of these useful objects. The diversity of these measures has its origin partly in the diverse nature of the objects to be measured, partly in convention.

The utility of a thing makes it a use-value. But this utility is not a thing of air. Being limited by the physical properties of the commodity, it has no existence apart from that commodity. A commodity, such as iron, corn, or a diamond, is therefore, so far as it is a material thing, a use-value, something useful. This property of a commodity is independent of the amount of labour required to appropriate its

---

[*] From Capital, Vol. I in *The Marx-Engels Reader*, Second Edition by Karl Marx and Friedrich Engels, edited by Robert C. Tucker. Copyright © 1978, 1972 by W. W. Norton & Company, Inc. Used by permission of W. W. Norton & Company, Inc.

useful qualities. When treating of use-value, we always assume to be dealing with definite quantities, such as dozens of watches, yards of linen, or tons of iron. The use-values of commodities furnish the material for a special study, that of the commercial knowledge of commodities. Use-values become a reality only by use or consumption: they also constitute the substance of all wealth, whatever may be the social form of that wealth. In the form of society we are about to consider, they are, in addition, the material depositories of exchange-value.

Exchange-value, at first sight, presents itself as a quantitative relation, as the proportion in which values in use of one sort are exchanged for those of another sort, a relation constantly changing with time and place. Hence exchange-value appears to be something accidental and purely relative, and consequently an intrinsic value, *i.e.,* an exchange-value that is inseparably connected with, inherent in commodities, seems a contradiction in terms. Let us consider the matter a little more closely.

A given commodity, *e.g.,* a quarter of wheat is exchanged for x blacking, y silk, or z gold, &c.—in short, for other commodities in the most different proportions. Instead of one exchange-value, the wheat has, therefore, a great many. But since x blacking, y silk, or z gold, &c., each represent the exchange-value of one quarter of wheat, x blacking, y silk, z gold, &c., must, as exchange-values, be replaceable by each other, or equal to each other. Therefore, first: the valid exchange-values of a given commodity express something equal; secondly, exchange-value, generally, is only the mode of expression, the phenomenal form, of something contained in it, yet distinguishable from it.

Let us take two commodities, *e.g.,* corn and iron. The proportions in which they are exchangeable, whatever those proportions may be, can always be represented by an equation in which a given quantity of corn is equated to some quantity of iron: *e.g.,* 1 quarter corn = x cwt. iron. What does this equation tell us? It tells us that in two different things— in 1 quarter of corn and x cwt. of iron, there exists in equal quantities something common to both. The two things must therefore be equal to a third, which in itself is neither the one nor the other. Each of them, so far as it is exchange-value, must therefore be reducible to this third.

A simple geometrical illustration will make this clear. In order to calculate and compare the areas of rectilinear figures, we decompose them into triangles. But the area of the triangle itself is expressed by something totally different from its visible figure, namely, by half the product of the base into the altitude. In the same way the exchange-values of commodities must be capable of being expressed in terms of something common to them all, of which thing they represent a greater or less quantity.

This common "something" cannot be either a geometrical, a chemical, or any other natural property of commodities. Such properties claim our attention only in so far as they affect the utility of those commodities, make them use-values. But the exchange of commodities is evidently an act characterised by a total abstraction from use-value. Then one use-value is just as good as another, provided only it be present in sufficient quantity. Or, as old Barbon says, "one sort of wares are as good as another, if the values be equal. There is no difference or distinction in things of equal value. . . . An hundred pounds' worth of lead or iron, is of as great value as one hundred pounds' worth of silver or gold." As use-values, commodities are, above all, of different qualities, but as exchange-values they are merely different quantities, and consequently do not contain an atom of use-value.

If then we leave out of consideration the use-value of commodities, they have only one common property left, that of being products of labour. But even the product of labour itself has undergone a change in our hands. If we make abstraction from its use-value, we make abstraction at the same time from the material elements and shapes that make the product a use-value; we see in it no longer a table, a house, yarn, or any other useful thing. Its existence as a material thing is put out of sight. Neither can it any longer be regarded as the product of the labour of the joiner, the mason, the spinner, or of any other definite kind of productive labour. Along with the useful qualities of the products themselves, we put out of sight both the useful character of the various kinds of labour embodied in them, and the concrete forms of that labour; there is nothing left but what is common to them all; all are reduced to one and the same sort of labour, human labour in the abstract.

Let us now consider the residue of each of these products; it consists of the same unsubstantial reality in each, a mere congelation of homogeneous human labour, of labour-power expended without regard to the mode of its expenditure. All that these things now tell us is, that human labour-power has been expended in their production, that human labour is embodied in them. When looked at as crystals of this social substance, common to them all, they are—Values.

We have seen that when commodities are exchanged, their exchange-value manifests itself as something totally independent of their use-value. But if we abstract from their use-value, there remains their Value as defined above. Therefore, the common substance that manifests itself in the exchange-value of commodities, whenever they are exchanged, is their value. The progress of our investigation will show that exchange-value is the only form in which the value of commodities can manifest itself or be expressed. For the present, however, we have to consider the nature of value independently of this, its form.

A use-value, or useful article, therefore, has value only because human labour in the abstract has been embodied or materialised in it. How, then, is the magnitude of this value to be measured? Plainly, by the quantity of the value-creating substance, the labour, contained in the article. The quantity of labour, however, is measured by its duration, and labour-time in its turn finds its standard in weeks, days, and hours.

Some people might think that if the value of a commodity is determined by the quantity of labour spent on it, the more idle and unskillful the labourer, the more valuable would his commodity be, because more time would be required in its production. The labour, however, that forms the substance of value, is homogeneous human labour, expenditure of one uniform labour-power. The total labour-power of society, which is embodied in the sum total of the values of all commodities produced by that society, counts here as one homogeneous mass of human labour-power, composed though it be of innumerable individual units. Each of these units is the same as any other, so far as it has the character of the average labour-power of society, and takes effect as such; that is, so far as it requires for producing a commodity no more time than is needed on an average, no more than is socially necessary. The labour-time socially necessary is that required to produce an article under the normal conditions of production, and with the average degree of skill and intensity prevalent at the time. The introduction of power-looms into England probably reduced by one-half the labour required to weave a given quantity of yarn into cloth. The hand-loom weavers, as a matter of fact, continued to require the same time as before; but for all that, the product of one hour of their labour represented after the change only half an hour's social labour, and consequently fell to one-half its former value.

We see then that that which determines the magnitude of the value of any article is the amount of labour socially necessary, or the labour-time socially necessary for its production. Each individual commodity, in this connexion, is to be considered as an average sample of its class. Commodities, therefore, in which equal quantities of labour are embodied, or which can be produced in the same time, have the same value. The value of one commodity is to the value of any other, as the labour-time necessary for the production of the one is to that necessary for the production of the other. "As values, all commodities are only definite masses of congealed labour-time."

The value of a commodity would therefore remain constant, if the labour-time required for its production also remained constant. But the latter changes with every variation in the productiveness of labour. This productiveness is determined by various circumstances, amongst others, by the average amount of skill of the workmen, the state of science, and the degree of its practical application, the social organisation of production, the extent and capabilities of the means of production, and by physical conditions. For example, the same amount of labour in favourable seasons is embodied in 8 bushels of corn, and in unfavourable, only in four. The same labour extracts from rich mines more metal than from poor mines. Diamonds are of very rare occurrence on the earth's surface, and hence their discovery costs, on an average, a great deal of labour-time. Consequently much labour is represented in a small compass. Jacob doubts whether gold has ever been paid for at its full value. This applies still more to diamonds. According to Eschwege, the total produce of the Brazilian diamond mines for the eighty years, ending in 1823, had not realised the price of one-and-a-half years' average produce of the sugar and coffee plantations of the same country, although the diamonds cost much more labour, and therefore represented more value. With richer mines, the same quantity of labour would embody itself in more diamonds, and their value would fall. If we could succeed at a small expenditure of labour, in converting carbon into diamonds, their value might fall below that of bricks. In general, the greater the productiveness of labour, the less is the labour-time required for the production of an article, the less is the amount of labour crystallised in that article, and the less is its value; and *vice versa,* the less the productiveness of labour, the greater is the labour-time required for the production of an article, and the greater is its value. The value of a commodity, therefore, varies directly as the quantity, and inversely as the productiveness, of the labour incorporated in it.

A thing can be a use-value, without having value. This is the case whenever its utility to man is not due to labour. Such are air, virgin soil, natural meadows, &c. A thing can be useful, and the product of human labour, without being a commodity. Whoever directly satisfies his wants with the produce of his own labour, creates, indeed, use-values, but no commodities. In order to produce the latter, he must not only produce use-values, but use-values for others, social use-values. (And not only for others, without more. The mediaeval peasant produced quit-rent-corn for his feudal lord and tithe-corn for his parson. But neither the quit-rent-corn nor the tithe-corn became commodities by reason of the fact that they had been produced for others. To become a commodity a product must be transferred to another, whom it will serve as a use-value, by means of an exchange.) Lastly nothing can have value, without being an object of utility. If the thing is useless, so is the labour contained in it; the labour does not count as labour, and therefore creates no value.

Capital's Two-Fold Nature: How Commodities Embody Human Labor

At first sight a commodity presented itself to us as a complex of two things—use-value and exchange-value. Later on, we saw also that labour, too, possesses the same two-fold nature; for, so far as it finds expression in value, it does not possess the same characteristics that belong to it as a creator of use-values. I was the first to point out and to examine critically this two-fold nature of the labour contained in commodities. As this point is the pivot on which a clear comprehension of Political Economy turns, we must go more into detail.

Let us take two commodities such as a coat and 10 yards of linen, and let the former be double the value of the latter, so that, if 10 yards of linen = W, the coat = 2W.

The coat is a use-value that satisfies a particular want. Its existence is the result of a special sort of productive activity, the nature of which is determined by its aim, mode of operation, subject, means, and result. The labour, whose utility is thus represented by the value in use of its product, or which manifests itself by making its product a use-value, we call useful labour. In this connexion we consider only its useful effect.

As the coat and the linen are two qualitatively different use-values, so also are the two forms of labour that produce them, tailoring and weaving. Were these two objects not qualitatively different, not produced respectively by labour of different quality, they could not stand to each other in the relation of commodities. Coats are not exchanged for coats, one use-value is not exchanged for another of the same kind.

To all the different varieties of values in use there correspond as many different kinds of useful labour, classified according to the order, genus, species, and variety to which they belong in the social division of labour. This division of labour is a necessary condition for the production of commodities, but it does not follow, conversely, that the production of commodities is a necessary condition for the division of labour. In the primitive Indian community there is social division of labour, without production of commodities. Or, to take an example nearer home, in every factory the labour is divided according to a system, but this division is not brought about by the operatives mutually exchanging their individual products. Only such products can become commodities with regard to each other, as result from different kinds of labour, each kind being carried on independently and for the account of private individuals.

To resume, then: In the use-value of each commodity there is contained useful labour, *i.e.*, productive activity of a definite kind and exercised with a definite aim. Use-values cannot confront each other as commodities, unless the useful labour embodied in them is qualitatively different in each of them. In a community, the produce of which in general takes the form of commodities, *i.e.*, in a community of commodity producers, this qualitative difference between the useful forms of labour that are carried on independently by individual producers, each on their own account, develops into a complex system, a social division of labour.

Anyhow, whether the coat be worn by the tailor or by his customer, in either case it operates as a use-value. Nor is the relation between the coat and the labour that produced it altered by the circumstance that tailoring may have become a special trade, an independent branch of the social division of labour. Wherever the want of clothing forced them to it, the human race made clothes for thousands of years, without a single man becoming a tailor. But coats and linen, like every other element of material wealth that is not the spontaneous produce of Nature, must invariably owe their existence to a special productive activity, exercised with a definite aim, an activity that appropriates particular nature-given materials to particular human wants. So far therefore as labour is a creator of use-value, is useful labour, it is a necessary condition, independent of all forms of society, for the existence of the human race; it is an eternal nature-imposed necessity, without which there can be no material exchanges between man and Nature, and therefore no life.

The use-values, coat, linen, &c., *i.e.*, the bodies of commodities, are combinations of two elements—matter and labour. If we take away the useful labour expended upon them, a material substratum is always left, which is furnished by Nature without the help of man. The latter can work only as Nature does, that is by changing the form of matter. Nay more, in this work of changing the form he is constantly helped by natural forces. We see, then, that labour is not the only source of material wealth, of use-values produced by labour. As William Petty puts it, labour is its father and the earth its mother.

Let us now pass from the commodity considered as a use-value to the value of commodities.

By our assumption, the coat is worth twice as much as the linen. But this is a mere quantitative difference, which for the present does not concern us. We bear in mind, however, that if the value of the coat is double that of 10 yds. of linen, 20 yds. of linen must have the same value as one coat. So far as they are values, the coat and the linen are things of a like substance, objective expressions of essentially identical labour. But tailoring and weaving are, qualitatively, different kinds of labour. There are, however, states of society in which one and the same man does tailoring and weaving alternately, in which case these two forms of labour are mere modifications of the labour of the same individual, and no special and fixed functions of different persons; just as the coat which our tailor makes one day, and the trousers which he makes another day, imply only a variation in the labour of one and the same individual. Moreover, we see at a glance that, in our capitalist society, a given portion of human labour is, in accordance with the varying demand, at one time supplied in the form of tailoring, at another in the form of weaving. This change may possibly not take place without friction, but take place it must.

Productive activity, if we leave out of sight its special form, viz., the useful character of the labour, is nothing but the expenditure of human labour-power. Tailoring and weaving, though qualitatively different productive activities, are each a productive expenditure of human brains, nerves, and muscles, and in this sense are human labour. They are but two different modes of expending human labour-power. Of course, this labour-power, which remains the same under all

its modifications, must have attained a certain pitch of development before it can be expended in a multiplicity of modes. But the value of a commodity represents human labour in the abstract, the expenditure of human labour in general. And just as in society, a general or a banker plays a great part, but mere man, on the other hand, a very shabby part, so here with human labour. It is the expenditure of simple labour-power, *i.e.*, of the labour-power which, on an average, apart from any special development, exists in the organism of every ordinary individual. Simple average labour, it is true, varies in character in different countries and at different times, but in a particular society it is given. Skilled labour counts only as simple labour intensified, or rather, as multiplied simple labour, a given quantity of skilled being considered equal to a greater quantity of simple labour. Experience shows that this reduction is constantly being made. A commodity may be the product of the most skilled labour, but its value, by equating it to the product of simple unskilled labour, represents a definite quantity of the latter labour alone. The different proportions in which different sorts of labour are reduced to unskilled labour as their standard, are established by a social process that goes on behind the backs of the producers, and, consequently, appear to be fixed by custom. For simplicity's sake we shall henceforth account every kind of labour to be unskilled, simple labour; by this we do no more than save ourselves the trouble of making the reduction.

Just as, therefore, in viewing the coat and linen as values, we abstract from their different use-values, so it is with the labour represented by those values: we disregard the difference between its useful forms, weaving and tailoring. As the use-values, coat and linen, are combinations of special productive activities with cloth and yarn, while the values, coat and linen, are, on the other hand, mere homogeneous congelations of undifferentiated labour, so the labour embodied in these latter values does not count by virtue of its productive relation to cloth and yarn, but only as being expenditure of human labour-power. Tailoring and weaving are necessary factors in the creation of the use-values, coat and linen, precisely because these two kinds of labour are of different qualities, but only in so far as abstraction is made from their special qualities, only in so far as both possess the same quality of being human labour, do tailoring and weaving form the substance of the values of the same article.

Coats and linen, however, are not merely values, but values of definite magnitude, and according to our assumption, the coat is worth twice as much as the ten yards of linen. Whence this difference in their values? It is owing to the fact that the linen contains only half as much labour as the coat, and consequently, that in the production of the latter, labour-power must have been expended during twice the time necessary for the production of the former.

While, therefore, with reference to use-value, the labour contained in a commodity counts only qualitatively, with reference to value it counts only quantitatively, and must first be reduced to human labour pure and simple. In the former case, it is a question of How and What, in the latter of How much? How long a time? Since the magnitude of the value of a commodity represents only the quantity of labour embodied in it, it follows that all commodities, when taken in certain proportions, must be equal in value.

If the productive power of all the different sorts of useful labour required for the production of a coat remains unchanged, the sum of the values of the coats produced increases with their number. If one coat represents x days' labour, two coats represent 2x days' labour, and so on. But assume that the duration of the labour necessary for the production of a coat becomes doubled or halved. In the first case, one coat is worth as much as two coats were before; in the second case, two coats are only worth as much as one was before, although in both cases one coat renders the same service as before, and the useful labour embodied in it remains of the same quality. But the quantity of labour spent on its production has altered.

An increase in the quantity of use-values is an increase of material wealth. With two coats two men can be clothed, with one coat only one man. Nevertheless, an increased quantity of material wealth may correspond to a simultaneous fall in the magnitude of its value. This antagonistic movement has its origin in the two-fold character of labour. Productive power has reference, of course, only to labour of some useful concrete form, the efficacy of any special productive activity during a given time being dependent on its productiveness. Useful labour becomes, therefore, a more or less abundant source of products, in proportion to the rise or fall of its productiveness. On the other hand, no change in this productiveness affects the labour represented by value. Since productive power is an attribute of the concrete useful forms of labour, of course it can no longer have any bearing on that labour, so soon as we make abstraction from those concrete useful forms. However then productive power may vary, the same labour, exercised during equal periods of time, always yields equal amounts of value. But it will yield, during equal periods of time, different quantities of values in use; more, if the productive power rise, fewer, if it fall. The same change in productive power, which increases the fruitfulness of labour, and, in consequence, the quantity of use-values produced by that labour, will diminish the total value of this increased quality of use-values, provided such change shorten the total labour-time necessary for their production; and *vice versa*.

On the one hand all labour is, speaking physiologically, an expenditure of human labour-power, and in its character of identical abstract human labour, it creates and forms the value of commodities. On the other hand, all labour is the expenditure of human labour-power in a special form and with a definite aim, and in this, its character of concrete useful labour, it produces use-values.

The Form of Value or Exchange-Value

Commodities come into the world in the shape of use-values, articles, or goods, such as iron, linen, corn, &c. This is their plain, homely, bodily form. They are, however, commodities, only because they are something two-fold, both objects of utility, and, at the same time, depositories of value. They manifest themselves therefore as commodities, or have the form of commodities, only in so far as they have two forms, a physical or natural form and a value-form.

The reality of the value of commodities differs in this respect from Dame Quickly, that we don't know "where to have it." The value of commodities is the very opposite of the coarse materiality of their substance, not an atom of matter enters into its composition. Turn and examine a single commodity, by itself, as we will, yet in so far as it remains an object of value, it seems impossible to grasp it. If, however, we bear in mind that the value of commodities has a purely social reality, and that they acquire this reality only in so far as they are expressions or embodiments of one identical social substance, viz., human labour, it follows as a matter of course, that value can only manifest itself in the social relation of commodity to commodity. In fact we started from exchange-value, or the exchange relation of commodities, in order to get at the value that lies hidden behind it. We must now return to this form under which value first appeared to us.

Every one knows, if he knows nothing else, that commodities have a value-form common to them all, and presenting a marked contrast with the varied bodily forms of their use-values. I mean their money-form. Here, however, a task is set us, the performance of which has never yet even been attempted by *bourgeois* economy, the task of tracing the genesis of this money-form, of developing the expression of value implied in the value-relation of commodities, from its simplest, almost imperceptible outline, to the dazzling money-form. By doing this we shall, at the same time, solve the riddle presented by money.

The simplest value-relation is evidently that of one commodity to some one other commodity of a different kind. Hence the relation between the values of two commodities supplies us with the simplest expression of the value of a single commodity.

Elementary or Accidental Form of Value:

x commodity A = y commodity B, or
x commodity A is worth y commodity B.
20 yards of linen = 1 coat, or
20 yards of linen are worth 1 coat.

The Two Poles of the Expression of Value: Relative Form and Equivalent Form

The whole mystery of the form of value lies hidden in this elementary form. Its analysis, therefore, is our real difficulty.

Here two different kinds of commodities (in our example the linen and the coat), evidently play two different parts. The linen expresses its value in the coat; the coat serves as the material in which that value is expressed. The former plays an active, the latter a passive, part. The value of the linen is represented as relative value, or appears in relative form. The coat officiates as equivalent, or appears in equivalent form.

The relative form and the equivalent form are two intimately connected, mutually dependent and inseparable elements of the expression of value; but, at the same time, are mutually exclusive, antagonistic extremes—*i.e.,* poles of the same expression. They are allotted respectively to the two different commodities brought into relation by that expression. It is not possible to express the value of linen in linen. 20 yards of linen = 20 yards of linen is no expression of value. On the contrary, such an equation merely says that 20 yards of linen are nothing else than 20 yards of linen, a definite quantity of the use-value linen. The value of the linen can therefore be expressed only relatively—*i.e.,* in some other commodity. The relative form of the value of the linen pre-supposes, therefore, the presence of some other commodity—here the coat—under the form of an equivalent. On the other hand, the commodity that figures as the equivalent cannot at the same time assume the relative form. That second commodity is not the one whose value is expressed. Its function is merely to serve as the material in which the value of the first commodity is expressed.

No doubt, the expression 20 yards of linen = 1 coat, or 20 yards of linen are worth 1 coat, implies the opposite relation: 1 coat = 20 yards of linen, or 1 coat is worth 20 yards of linen. But, in that case, I must reverse the equation, in order to express the value of the coat relatively; and, so soon as I do that, the linen becomes the equivalent instead of the coat. A single commodity cannot, therefore, simultaneously assume, in the same expression of value, both forms. The very polarity of these forms makes them mutually exclusive.

Whether, then, a commodity assumes the relative form, or the opposite equivalent form, depends entirely upon its accidental position in the expression of value—that is, upon whether it is the commodity whose value is being expressed or the commodity in which value is being expressed.

Capital and the Fetishism of Commodities[*]
Karl Marx (1867)

A commodity appears, at first sight, a very trivial thing, and easily understood. Its analysis shows that it is, in reality, a very queer thing, abounding in metaphysical subtleties and theological niceties. So far as it is a value in use, there is nothing mysterious about it, whether we consider it from the point of view that by its properties it is capable of satisfying human wants, or from the point that those properties are the product of human labour. It is as clear as noon-day, that man, by his industry, changes the forms of the materials furnished by Nature, in such a way as to make them useful to him. The form of wood, for instance, is altered, by making a table out of it. Yet, for all that, the table continues to be that common, every-day thing, wood. But, so soon as it steps forth as a commodity, it is changed into something transcendent. It not only stands with its feet

---

[*] From Capital, Vol. I in The Marx-Engels Reader, Second Edition, by Karl Marx and Friedrich Engels, edited by Robert C. Tucker. Copyright © 1978, 1972 by W. W. Norton & Company, Inc. Used by permission of W. W. Norton & Company, Inc.

on the ground, but, in relation to all other commodities, it stands on its head, and evolves out of its wooden brain grotesque ideas, far more wonderful than "table-turning" ever was.

The mystical character of commodities does not originate, therefore, in their use-value. Just as little does it proceed from the nature of the determining factors of value. For, in the first place, however varied the useful kinds of labour, or productive activities, may be, it is a physiological fact, that they are functions of the human organism, and that each such function, whatever may be its nature or form, is essentially the expenditure of human brain, nerves, muscles, &c. Secondly, with regard to that which forms the groundwork for the quantitative determination of value, namely, the duration of that expenditure, or the quantity of labour, it is quite clear that there is a palpable difference between its quantity and quality. In all states of society, the labour-time that it costs to produce the means of subsistence, must necessarily be an object of interest to mankind, though not of equal interest in different stages of development. And lastly, from the moment that men in any way work for one another, their labour assumes a social form.

Whence, then, arises the enigmatical character of the product of labour, so soon as it assumes the form of commodities? Clearly from this form itself. The equality of all sorts of human labour is expressed objectively by their products all being equally valued; the measure of the expenditure of labour-power by the duration of that expenditure, takes the form of the quantity of value of the products of labour; and finally, the mutual relations of the producers, within which the social character of their labour affirms itself, take the form of a social relation between the products.

A commodity is therefore a mysterious thing, simply because in it the social character of men's labour appears to them as an objective character stamped upon the product of that labour; because the relation of the producers to the sum total of their own labour is presented to them as a social relation, existing not between themselves, but between the products of their labour. This is the reason why the products of labour become commodities, social things whose qualities are at the same time perceptible and imperceptible by the senses. In the same way the light from an object is perceived by us not as the subjective excitation of our optic nerve, but as the objective form of something outside the eye itself. But, in the act of seeing, there is at all events, an actual passage of light from one thing to another, from the external object to the eye. There is a physical relation between physical things. But it is different with commodities. There, the existence of the things *qua* commodities, and the value-relation between the products of labour which stamps them as commodities, have absolutely no connexion with their physical properties and with the material relations arising therefrom. There it is a definite social relation between men, that assumes, in their eyes, the fantastic form of a relation between things. In order, therefore, to find an analogy, we must have recourse to the mist-enveloped regions of the religious world. In that world the productions of the human brain appear as independent beings endowed with life, and entering into relation both with one another and the human race. So it is in the world of commodities with the products of men's hands. This I call the Fetishism which attaches itself to the products of labour, so soon as they are produced as commodities, and which is therefore inseparable from the production of commodities.

This Fetishism of commodities has its origin, as the foregoing analysis has already shown, in the peculiar social character of the labour that produces them.

As a general rule, articles of utility become commodities, only because they are products of the labour of private individuals or groups of individuals who carry on their work independently of each other. The sum total of the labour of all these private individuals forms the aggregate labour of society. Since the producers do not come into social contact with each other until they exchange their products, the specific social character of each producer's labour does not show itself except in the act of exchange. In other words, the labour of the individual asserts itself as a part of the labour of society, only by means of the relations which the act of exchange establishes directly between the products, and indirectly, through them, between the producers. To the latter, therefore, the relations connecting the labour of one individual with that of the rest appear, not as direct social relations between individuals at work, but as what they really are, material relations between persons and social relations between things. It is only by being exchanged that the products of labour acquire, as values, one uniform social status, distinct from their varied forms of existence as objects of utility. This division of a product into a useful thing and a value becomes practically important, only when exchange has acquired such an extension that useful articles are produced for the purpose of being exchanged, and their character as values has therefore to be taken into account, beforehand, during production. From this moment the labour of the individual producer acquires socially a two-fold character. On the one hand, it must, as a definite useful kind of labour, satisfy a definite social want, and thus hold its place as part and parcel of the collective labour of all, as a branch of a social division of labour that has sprung up spontaneously. On the other hand, it can satisfy the manifold wants of the individual producer himself, only in so far as the mutual exchangeability of all kinds of useful private labour is an established social fact, and therefore the private useful labour of each producer ranks on an equality with that of all others. The equalisation of the most different kinds of labour can be the result only of an abstraction from their inequalities, or of reducing them to their common denominator, viz., expenditure of human labour-power or human labour in the abstract. The two-fold social character of the labour of the individual appears to him, when reflected in his brain, only under those forms which are impressed upon that labour in every-day practice by the exchange of products. In this way, the character that his own labour possesses of being socially useful takes the form of the condition, that the product must be not only useful, but useful for others, and the social character that his particular labour has of being the equal of all other particular kinds of labour, takes the form that all the physically different articles that are the products of labour, have one common quality, viz., that of having value.

Hence, when we bring the products of our labour into relation with each other as values, it is not because we see in these articles the material receptacles of homogeneous human labour. Quite the contrary: whenever, by an exchange, we equate as values our different products, by that very act, we also equate, as human labour, the different kinds of labour expended upon them. We are not aware of this, nevertheless we do it. Value, therefore, does not stalk about with a label describing what it is. It is value, rather, that converts every product into a social hieroglyphic. Later on, we try to decipher the hieroglyphic, to get behind the secret of our own social products; for to stamp an object of utility as a value, is just as much a social product as language. The recent scientific discovery, that the products of labour, so far as they are values, are but material expressions of the human labour spent in their production, marks, indeed, an epoch in the history of the development of the human race, but, by no means, dissipates the mist through which the social character of

labour appears to us to be an objective character of the products themselves. The fact, that in the particular form of production with which we are dealing, viz., the production of commodities, the specific social character of private labour carried on independently, consists in the equality of every kind of that labour, by virtue of its being human labour, which character, therefore, assumes in the product the form of value—this fact appears to the producers, notwithstanding the discovery above referred to, to be just as real and final, as the fact, that, after the discovery by science of the component gases of air, the atmosphere itself remained unaltered.

Labour-Power and Capital*
Karl Marx (1867)

The change of value that occurs in the case of money intended to be converted into capital, cannot take place in the money itself, since in its function of means of purchase and of payment, it does no more than realise the price of the commodity it buys or pays for; and, as hard cash, it is value petrified, never varying. Just as little can it originate in the second act of circulation, the re-sale of the commodity, which does not more than transform the article from its bodily form back again into its money-form. The change must, therefore, take place in the commodity bought by the first act, M—C, but not in its value, for equivalents are exchanged, and the commodity is paid for at its full value. We are, therefore, forced to the conclusion that the change originates in the use-value, as such, of the commodity, *i.e.,* in its consumption. In order to be able to extract value from the consumption of a commodity, our friend, Moneybags, must be so lucky as to find, within the sphere of circulation, in the market, a commodity, whose use-value possesses the peculiar property of being a source of value, whose actual consumption, therefore, is itself an embodiment of labour, and consequently, a creation of value. The possessor of money does find on the market such a special commodity in capacity for labour or labour-power.

By labour-power or capacity for labour is to be understood the aggregate of those mental and physical capabilities existing in a human being, which he

---

*From Capital, Vol. I in *The Marx-Engels Reader*, Second Edition, by Karl Marx and Friedrich Engels, edited by Robert C. Tucker. Copyright © 1978, 1972 by W. W. Norton & Company, Inc. Used by permission of W. W. Norton & Company, Inc.

exercises whenever he produces a use-value of any description.

But in order that our owner of money may be able to find labour-power offered for sale as a commodity, various conditions must first be fulfilled. The exchange of commodities of itself implies no other relations of dependence than those which result from its own nature. On this assumption, labour-power can appear upon the market as a commodity, only if, and so far as, its possessor, the individual whose labour-power it is, offers it for sale, or sells it, as a commodity. In order that he may be able to do this, he must have it at his disposal, must be the untrammelled owner of his capacity for labour, *i.e.,* of his person. He and the owner of money meet in the market, and deal with each other as on the basis of equal rights, with this difference alone, that one is buyer, the other seller; both, therefore, equal in the eyes of the law. The continuance of this relation demands that the owner of the labour-power should sell it only for a definite period, for if he were to sell it rump and stump, once for all, he would be selling himself, converting himself from a free man into a slave, from an owner of a commodity into a commodity. He must constantly look upon his labour-power as his own property, his own commodity, and this he can only do by placing it at the disposal of the buyer temporarily, for a definite period of time. By this means alone can he avoid renouncing his rights of ownership over it.

The second essential condition to the owner of money finding labour-power in the market as a commodity is this—that the labourer instead of being in the position to sell commodities in which his labour is incorporated, must be obliged to offer for sale as a commodity that very labour-power, which exists only in his living self.

In order that a man may be able to sell commodities other than labour-power, he must of course have the means of production, as raw material, implements, &c. No boots can be made without leather. He requires also the means of subsistence. Nobody—not even "a musician of the future"—can live upon future products, or upon use-values in an unfinished state; and ever since the first moment of his appearance on the world's stage, man always has been, and must still be a consumer, both before and while he is producing. In a society where all products assume the form of commodities, these commodities must be sold after they have been produced; it is only after their sale that they can serve in satisfying the requirements of their producer. The time necessary for their sale is superadded to that necessary for their production.

For the conversion of his money into capital, therefore, the owner of money must meet in the market with the free labourer, free in the double sense, that as a free man he can dispose of his labour-power as his own commodity, and that on the other hand he has no other commodity for sale, is short of everything necessary for the realisation of his labour-power.

The question why this free labourer confronts him in the market, has no interest for the owner of money, who regards the labour-market as a branch of the general market for commodities. And for the present it interests us just as little. We cling to the fact theoretically, as he does practically. One thing, however, is clear—Nature does not produce on the one side owners of money or commodities, and on the other men possessing nothing but their own labour-power. This relation has no natural basis, neither is its social basis one that is common to all historical periods. It is clearly the result of a past historical development, the product of many economic revolutions, of the extinction of a whole series of older forms of social production.

So, too, the economic categories, already discussed by us, bear the stamp of history. Definite historical conditions are necessary that a product may become a commodity. It must not be produced as the immediate means of subsistence of the producer himself. Had we gone further, and inquired under what circumstances all, or even the majority of products take the form of commodities, we should have found that this can only happen with production of a very specific kind, capitalist production. Such an inquiry, however, would have been foreign to the analysis of commodities. Production and circulation of commodities can take place, although the great mass of the objects produced are intended for the immediate requirements of their producers, are not turned into commodities, and consequently social production is not yet by a long way dominated in its length and breadth by exchange-value. The appearance of products as commodities pre-supposes such a development of the social division of labour, that the separation of use-value from exchange-value, a separation which first begins with barter, must already have been completed. But such a degree of development is common to many forms of society, which in other respects present the most varying historical features. On the other hand, if we consider money, its existence implies a definite stage in the exchange of commodities. The particular functions of money which it performs, either as the mere equivalent of commodities, or as means of circulation, or means of payment, as hoard or as universal money, point, according to the extent and relative preponderance of the one function or the other, to very different stages in the process of social production. Yet we know by experience that a circulation of commodities relatively primitive, suffices for the production of all these forms. Otherwise with capital. The historical conditions of its existence are by no means given with the mere circulation of money and commodities. It can spring into life, only when the owner of the means of production and subsistence meets in the market with the free labourer selling his labour-power. And this one historical condition comprises a world's history. Capital, therefore, announces from its first appearance a new epoch in the process of social production.

We must now examine more closely this peculiar commodity, labour-power. Like all others it has a value. How is that value determined?

The value of labour-power is determined, as in the case of every other commodity, by the labour-time necessary for the production, and consequently also the reproduction, of this special article. So far as it has value, it represents no more than a definite quantity of the average labour of society incorporated in it. Labour-power exists only as a capacity, or power of the living individual. Its production consequently presupposes his existence. Given the individual, the production of labour-power consists in his reproduction of himself or his maintenance. For his maintenance he requires a given quantity of the means of subsistence. Therefore the labour-time requisite for the production of labour-power reduces itself to that necessary for the production of those means of subsistence; in other words, the value of labour-power is the value of the means of subsistence necessary for the maintenance of the labourer. Labour-power, however, becomes a reality only by its exercise; it sets itself in action only by working. But thereby a definite quantity of human muscle, nerve, brain, &c., is wasted, and these require to be restored. This increased expenditure demands a larger income. If the owner of labour-power works to-day, to-morrow he must again be able to repeat the same process in the same conditions as regards health and strength. His means of subsistence must therefore be sufficient to maintain him in his normal state as a labouring individual. His natural wants, such as food, clothing, fuel, and

housing, vary according to the climatic and other physical conditions of his country. On the other hand, the number and extent of his so-called necessary wants, as also the modes of satisfying them, are themselves the product of historical development, and depend therefore to a great extent on the degree of civilization of a country, more particularly on the conditions under which, and consequently on the habits and degree of comfort in which, the class of free labourers has been formed. In contradistinction therefore to the case of other commodities, there enters into the determination of the value of labour-power a historical and moral element. Nevertheless, in a given country, at a given period, the average quantity of the means of subsistence necessary for the labourer is practically known.

The owner of labour-power is mortal. If then his appearance in the market is to be continuous, and the continuous conversion of money into capital assumes this, the seller of labour-power must perpetuate himself, "in the way that every living individual perpetuates himself, by procreation." The labour-power withdrawn from the market by wear and tear and death, must be continually replaced by, at the very least, an equal amount of fresh labour-power. Hence the sum of the means of subsistence necessary for the production of labour-power must include the means necessary for the labourer's substitutes, *i.e.,* his children, in order that this race of peculiar commodity-owners may perpetuate its appearance in the market.

In order to modify the human organism, so that it may acquire skill and handiness in a given branch of industry, and become labour-power of a special kind, a special education or training is requisite, and this, on its part, costs an equivalent in commodities of a greater or less amount. This amount varies according to the more or less complicated character of the labour-power. The expenses of this education (excessively small in the case of ordinary labour-power), enter pro tanto into the total value spent in its production.

The value of labour-power resolves itself into the value of a definite quantity of the means of subsistence. It therefore varies with the value of these means or with the quantity of labour requisite for their production.

Some of the means of subsistence, such as food and fuel, are consumed daily, and a fresh supply must be provided daily. Others such as clothes and furniture last for longer periods and require to be replaced only at longer intervals. One article must be bought or paid for daily, another weekly, another quarterly, and so on. But in whatever way the sum total of these outlays may be spread over the year, they must be covered by the average income, taking one day with another. If the total of the commodities required daily for the production of labour-power = A, and those required weekly = B, and those required quarterly = C, and so on, the daily average of these commodities = (365A + 52B + 4C + &c.)/365. Suppose that in this mass of commodities requisite for the average day there are embodied six hours of social labour, then there is incorporated daily in labour-power half a day's average social labour, in other words, half a day's labour is requisite for the daily production of labour-power. This quantity of labour forms the value of a day's labour-power or the value of the labour-power daily reproduced. If half a day's average social labour is incorporated in three shillings, then three shillings is the price corresponding to the value of a day's labour-power. If its owner therefore offers it for sale at three shillings a day, its selling price is equal to its value, and according to our supposition, our friend Moneybags, who is intent upon converting his three shillings into capital, pays this value.

The minimum limit of the value of labour-power is determined by the value of the commodities, without the daily supply of which the labourer cannot renew his vital energy, consequently by the value of those means of subsistence that are physically indispensable. If the price of labour-power fall to this minimum, it falls below its value, since under such circumstances it can be maintained and developed only in a crippled state. But the value of every commodity is determined by the labour-time requisite to turn it out so as to be normal quality.

It is a very cheap sort of sentimentality which declares this method of determining the value of labour-power, a method prescribed by the very nature of the case, to be a brutal method, and which wails with Rossi that, "To comprehend capacity for labour (*puissance de travail*) at the same time that we make abstraction from the means of subsistence of the labourers during the process of production, is to comprehend a phantom (*être de raison*). When we speak of labour, or capacity for labour, we speak at the same time of the labourer and his means of subsistence, of labourer and wages." When we speak of capacity for labour, we do not speak of labour, any more than when we speak of capacity for digestion, we speak of digestion. The latter process requires something more than a good stomach. When we speak of capacity for labour, we do not abstract from the necessary means

of subsistence. On the contrary, their value is expressed in its value. If his capacity for labour remains unsold, the labourer derives no benefit from it, but rather he will feel it to be a cruel nature-imposed necessity that this capacity has cost for its production a definite amount of the means of subsistence and that it will continue to do so for its reproduction. He will then agree with Sismondi: "that capacity for labour . . . is nothing unless it is sold."

One consequence of the peculiar nature of labour-power as a commodity is, that its use-value does not, on the conclusion of the contract between the buyer and seller, immediately pass into the hands of the former. Its value, like that of every other commodity, is already fixed before it goes into circulation, since a definite quantity of social labour has been spent upon it; but its use-value consists in the subsequent exercise of its force. The alienation of labour-power and its actual appropriation by the buyer, its employment as a use-value, are separated by an interval of time. But in those cases in which the formal alienation by sale of the use-value of a commodity is not simultaneous with its actual delivery to the buyer, the money of the latter usually functions as means of payment. In every country in which the capitalist mode of production reigns, it is the custom not to pay for labour-power before it has been exercised for the period fixed by the contract, as for example, the end of each week. In all cases, therefore, the use-value of the labour-power is advanced to the capitalist: the labourer allows the buyer to consume it before he receives payment of the price; he everywhere gives credit to the capitalist. That this credit is no mere fiction, is shown not only by the occasional loss of wages on the bankruptcy of the capitalist, but also by a series of more enduring consequences. Nevertheless, whether money serves as means of purchase or as a means of payment, this makes no alteration in the nature of the exchange of commodities. The price of the labour-power is fixed by the contract, although it is not realised till later, like the rent of a house. The labour-power is sold, although it is only paid for at a later period. It will, therefore, be useful, for a clear comprehension of the relation of the parties, to assume provisionally, that the possessor of labour-power, on the occasion of each sale, immediately receives the price stipulated to be paid for it.

We now know how the value paid by the purchaser to the possessor of the peculiar commodity, labour-power, is determined. The use-value which the former gets in exchange, manifests itself only in the actual usufruct, in the consumption of the labour-power. The money-owner buys everything necessary for this purpose, such as raw material, in the market, and pays for it at its full value. The consumption of labour-power is at one and the same time the production of commodities and of surplus-value. The consumption of labour-power is completed, as in the case of every other commodity, outside the limits of the market or of the sphere of circulation. Accompanied by Mr. Moneybags and by the possessor of labour-power, we therefore take leave for a time of this noisy sphere, where everything takes place on the surface and in view of all men, and follow them both into the hidden abode of production, on whose threshold there stares us in the face "No admittance except on business." Here we shall see, not only how capital produces, but how capital is produced. We shall at last force the secret of profit making.

This sphere that we are deserting, within whose boundaries the sale and purchase of labour-power goes on, is in fact a very Eden of the innate rights of man. There alone rule Freedom, Equality, Property and Bentham. Freedom, because both buyer and seller of a commodity, say of labour-power, are constrained only by their own free will. They contract as free agents, and the agreement they come to, is but the form in which they give legal expression to their common will. Equality, because each enters into relation with the other, as with a simple owner of commodities, and they exchange equivalent for equivalent. Property, because each disposes only of what is his own. And Bentham, because each looks only to himself. The only force that brings them together and puts them in relation with each other, is the selfishness, the gain and the private interests of each. Each looks to himself only, and no one troubles himself about the rest, and just because they do so, do they all, in accordance with the preestablished harmony of things, or under the auspices of an all-shrewd providence, work together to their mutual advantage, for the common weal and in the interest of all.

The Patriarchal Family[*]
Friedrich Engels (1884)

The pairing family, itself too weak and unstable to make an independent household necessary, or even desirable, did not by any means dissolve the commu-

* From *The Marx-Engels Reader*, Second Edition, by Karl Marx and Friedrich Engels, edited by Robert C. Tucker. Copyright © 1978, 1972 by W. W. Norton & Company, Inc. Used by permission of W. W. Norton & Company, Inc.

nistic household transmitted from earlier times. But the communistic household implies the supremacy of women in the house, just as the exclusive recognition of a natural mother, because of the impossibility of determining the natural father with certainty, signifies high esteem for the women, that is, for the mothers. That woman was the slave of man at the commencement of society is one of the most absurd notions that have come down to us from the period of Enlightenment of the eighteenth century. Woman occupied not only a free but also a highly respected position among all savages and all barbarians of the lower and middle stages and partly even of the upper stage. Let Arthur Wright, missionary for many years among the Seneca Iroquois, testify what her place still was in the pairing family: "As to their family system, when occupying the old long houses [communistic households embracing several families] . . . it is probable that some one clan [gens] predominated, the women taking husbands from other clans [gentes]. . . . Usually the female portion ruled the house; the stores were in common; but woe to the luckless husband or lover who was too shiftless to do his share of the providing. No matter how many children or whatever goods he might have in the house, he might at any time be ordered to pack up his blanket and budge; and after such orders it would not be healthful for him to attempt to disobey. The house would be too hot for him; and he had to retreat to his own clan [gens]; or, as was often done, go and start a new matrimonial alliance in some other. The women were the great power among the clans [gentes], as everywhere else. They did not hesitate, when occasion required, to knock off the horns, as it was technically called, from the head of the chief and send him back to the ranks of the warriors." . . .

As wealth increased, it, on the one hand, gave the man a more important status in the family than the woman, and, on the other hand, created a stimulus to utilise this strengthened position in order to overthrow the traditional order of inheritance in favour of his children. But this was impossible as long as descent according to mother right prevailed. This had, therefore, to be overthrown, and it was overthrown; and it was not so difficult to do this as it appears to us now. For this revolution—one of the most decisive ever experienced by mankind—need not have disturbed one single living member of a gens. All the members could remain what they were previously. The simple decision sufficed that in the future the descendants of the male members should remain in the gens, but that those of the females

[handwritten: take fathers last name?]

were to be excluded from the gens and transferred to that of their father. The reckoning of descent through the female line and the right of inheritance through the mother were hereby overthrown and male lineage and right of inheritance from the father instituted. We know nothing as to how and when this revolution was effected among the civilised peoples. It falls entirely within prehistoric times. That it was actually *effected* is more than proved by the abundant traces of mother right which have been collected, especially by Bachofen. How easily it is accomplished can be seen from a whole number of Indian tribes, among whom it has only recently taken place and is still proceeding, partly under the influence of increasing wealth and changed methods of life (transplantation from the forests to the prairies), and partly under the moral influence of civilisation and the missionaries. Of eight Missouri tribes, six have male and two still retain the female lineage and female inheritance line. Among the Shawnees, Miamis and Delawares it has become the custom to transfer the children to the father's gens by giving them one of the gentile names obtaining therein, in order that they may inherit from him. "Innate human causuistry to seek to change things by changing their names! And to find loopholes for breaking through tradition within tradition itself, wherever a direct interest provided a sufficient motive!" (Marx) As a consequence, hopeless confusion arose; and matters could only be straightened out, and partly were straightened out, by the transition to father right. "This appears altogether to be the most natural transition." (Marx) As for what the experts on comparative law have to tell us regarding the ways and means by which this transition was effected among the civilised peoples of the Old World—almost mere hypotheses, of course—see M. Kovalevsky, *Outline of the Origin and Evolution of the Family and Property,* Stockholm, 1890.

The overthrow of mother right was the *world-historic defeat of the female sex.* The man seized the reins in the house also, the woman was degraded, enthralled, the slave of the man's lust, a mere instrument for breeding children. This lowered position of women, especially manifest among the Greeks of the Heroic and still more of the Classical Age, has become gradually embellished and dissembled and, in part, clothed in a milder form, but by no means abolished. . . .

Slavery was the first form of exploitation, peculiar to the world of antiquity; it was followed by serfdom in the Middle Ages, and by wage labour in modern times. These are the three great forms of servitude, characteristic of the three great epochs of civilisation; open, and, latterly, disguised slavery, are its steady companions.

The stage of commodity production, with which civilisation began, is marked economically by the introduction of 1) metal money and, thus, of money capital, interest and usury; 2) the merchants acting as middlemen between producers; 3) private ownership of land and mortgage; 4) slave labour as the prevailing form of production. The form of the family corresponding to civilisation and under it becoming the definitely prevailing form is monogamy, the supremacy of the man over the woman, and the individual family as the economic unit of society. The cohesive force of civilised society is the state, which in all typical periods is exclusively the state of the ruling class, and in all cases remains essentially a machine for keeping down the oppressed, exploited class. Other marks of civilisation are: on the one hand fixation of the contrast between town and country as the basis of the entire division of social labour; on the other hand, the introduction of wills, by which the property holder is able to dispose of his property even after his death. This institution, which was a direct blow at the old gentile constitution, was unknown in Athens until the time of Solon; in Rome it was introduced very early, but we do not know when. Among the Germans it was introduced by the priests in order that the good honest German might without hindrance bequeath his property to the Church. *[handwritten: all about a will]*

With this constitution as its foundation civilisation has accomplished things with which the old gentile society was totally unable to cope. But it accomplished them by playing on the most sordid instincts and passions of man, and by developing them at the expense of all his other faculties. Naked greed has been the moving spirit of civilisation from the first day of its existence to the present time; wealth, more wealth and wealth again; wealth, not of society, but of this shabby individual was its sole and determining aim. If, in the pursuit of this aim, the increasing development of science and repeated periods of the fullest blooming of art fell into its lap, it was only because without them the ample present-day achievements in the accumulation of wealth would have been impossible.

Since the exploitation of one class by another is the basis of civilisation, its whole development moves in a continuous contradiction. Every advance in production is at the same time a retrogression in the condition of the oppressed class, that is, of the great majority. What is a boon for the one is necessarily a bane for the other; each new emancipation of one class always means a new oppression of another class. The most striking proof of this is furnished by the introduction of machinery, the effects of which are well known today. And while among barbarians, as we have seen, hardly any distinction could be made between rights and duties, civilisation makes the difference and antithesis between these two plain even to the dullest mind by assigning to one class pretty nearly all the rights and to the other class pretty nearly all the duties.

But this is not as it ought to be. What is good for the ruling class should be good for the whole of the society with which the ruling class identifies itself. Therefore, the more civilisation advances, the more it is compelled to cover the ills it necessarily creates with the cloak of love, to embellish them, or to deny their existence; in short, to introduce conventional hypocrisy—unknown both in previous forms of society and even in the earliest stages of civilisation—that culminates in the declaration: The exploiting class exploits the oppressed class solely and exclusively in the interest of the exploited class itself; and if the latter fails to appreciate this, and even becomes rebellious, it thereby shows the basest ingratitude to its benefactors, the exploiters. *True*

John Stuart Mill (1806–1873) was born in London the son of James Mill, a philosopher and co-founder of classic economics. The father famously had his son studying Greek at age three, then Latin at age eight, when the boy was already reading Greek classic literature in the original. John Stuart Mill grew to become a prominent philosopher with strong utilitarian convictions drawn from his childhood education with his father and his father's friend, Jeremy Bentham. Like his mentors, the younger Mill was a rationalist. Still, in time he was also influenced by other European traditions of culture and thought, including romanticism. The latter may have been a cause of John Stuart Mill's more robust and, some would say, balanced approach to the question of the primacy of the enlightened individual in social and economic philosophy. While he wrote works like *A System of Logic* (1843) and *Principles of Political Economy* (1848), he also wrote *On the Subjection of Women* (1869) and *On Liberty* (1859), from which the

selection is taken. *On Liberty* is sometimes compared to Marx's *Manifesto of the Communist Party* as one of the two most important short essays in mid-nineteenth century social thought. Mill of course was philosophically the opposite of Marx, yet the comparison stands on the fact that *On Liberty* is relatively free of dogma and rich in social theoretical subtlety. "Of Society and the Individual" is a particularly good illustration of the extent to which Mill's commitments to the rational individual are tempered by a sensible appreciation of the extent to which liberty is also a social thing.

Of Society and the Individual*
John Stuart Mill (1859)

What, then, is the rightful limit to the sovereignty of the individual over himself? Where does the authority of society begin? How much of human life should be assigned to individuality, and how much to society?

Each will receive its proper share, if each has that which more particularly concerns it. To individuality should belong the part of life in which it is chiefly the individual that is interested; to society, the part which chiefly interests society.

Though society is not founded on a contract, and though no good purpose is answered by inventing a contract in order to deduce social obligations from it, every one who receives the protection of society owes a return for the benefit, and the fact of living in society renders it indispensable that each should be bound to observe a certain line of conduct towards the rest. This conduct consists, first, in not injuring the interests of one another; or rather certain interests which, either by express legal provision or by tacit understanding, ought to be considered as rights; and secondly, in each person's bearing his share (to be fixed on some equitable principle) of the labours and sacrifices incurred for defending the society or its members from injury and molestation. These conditions society is justified in enforcing, at all costs to those who endeavour to withhold fulfilment. Nor is this all that society may do. The acts of an individual may be hurtful to others, or wanting in due consideration for their welfare, without going the length of violating any of their constituted rights. The offender

*John Stewart Mill, *On Liberty*. London: The Walter Scott Publishing Co., Ltd. Originally published 1859. pp. 140–144

may then be justly punished by opinion though not by law. As soon as any part of a person's conduct affects prejudicially the interests of others, society has jurisdiction over it, and the question whether the general welfare will or will not be promoted by interfering with it, becomes open to discussion. But there is no room for entertaining any such question when a person's conduct affects the interests of no persons besides himself, or needs not affect them unless they like (all the persons concerned being of full age, and the ordinary amount of understanding). In all such cases there should be perfect freedom, legal and social, to do the action and stand the consequences.

It would be a great misunderstanding of this doctrine, to suppose that it is one of selfish indifference, which pretends that human beings have no business with each other's conduct in life, and that they should not concern themselves about the well-doing or well-being of one another, unless their own interest is involved. Instead of any diminution, there is need of a great increase of disinterested exertion to promote the good of others. But disinterested benevolence can find other instruments to persuade people to their good, than whips and scourges, either of the literal or the metaphorical sort. I am the last person to undervalue the self-regarding virtues; they are only second in importance, if even second, to the social. It is equally the business of education to cultivate both. But even education works by conviction and persuasion as well as by compulsion, and it is by the former only that, when the period of education is past, the self-regarding virtues should be inculcated. Human beings owe to each other help to distinguish the better from the worse, and encouragement to choose the former and avoid the latter. They should be for ever stimulating each other to increased exercise of their higher faculties, and increased direction of their feelings and aims towards wise instead of foolish, elevating instead of degrading, objects and contemplations. But neither one person, nor any number of persons, is warranted in saying to another human creature of ripe years, that he shall not do with his life for his own benefit what he chooses to do with it. He is the person most interested in his own well-being: the interest which any other person, except in cases of strong personal attachment, can have in it, is trifling, compared with that which he himself has; the interest which society has in him individually (except as to his conduct to others) is fractional, and altogether indirect: while, with respect to his own feelings and circumstances, the most ordinary man or woman has means of knowledge immeasurably surpassing those that can be possessed by any one else. The interference of society to overrule his judgment and purposes in what only regards himself, must be grounded on general presumptions; which may be altogether wrong, and even if right, are as likely as not to be misapplied to individual cases, by persons no better acquainted with the circumstances of such cases than those are who look at them merely from without. In this department, therefore, of human affairs, Individuality has its proper field of action. In the conduct of human beings towards one another, it is necessary that general rules should for the most part be observed, in order that people may know what they have to expect; but in each person's own concerns, his individual spontaneity is entitled to free exercise. Considerations to aid his judgment, exhortations to strengthen his will, may be offered to him, even obtruded on him, by others; but he himself is the final judge. All errors which he is likely to commit against advice and warning, are far outweighed by the evil of allowing others to constrain him to what they deem his good.

Jane Addams (1860–1935) was born in Cedarville, Illinois, and grew to world fame as the founder, in 1889, of Hull House in Chicago. As an early leader of the settlement house movement in the United States, Addams was an exemplary practical social theorist of the rights and needs of the poor, especially women. Though Addams lectured around the world and published voluminously, her lifelong service to the poor of Chicago was the ultimate authority for her social theory. Among her writings were *Democracy and Social Ethics* (1902), *Twenty Years at Hull-House* (1912), and *The Long Road of Woman's Memory* (1916). The selection following is from an essay published in 1895. It demonstrates Addams's practical approach to questions of economic and social injustice that concerned other social theorists of the time. The suggestion that the settlement house must serve as the moral conscience of the labor movement seems to soften the archaic use of "man" throughout and to imply the then-widespread belief that morality was a special province of women. Yet, it is hard to miss the tough-minded social criticism in her thinking. Addams was awarded the Nobel Peace Prize in 1931.

union?

The Settlement as a Factor in the Labor Movement[*]
Jane Addams (1895)

One man or group of men sometimes reveal to their contemporaries a higher conscience by simply incorporating into the deed what has been before but a philosophic proposition. By this deed the common code of ethics is stretched to a higher point.

Such an act of moral significance, for instance, was John Burns's loyalty to the dockers' strike of East London. "The injury to one" did at last actually "become the concern of all"; and henceforth the man who does not share that concern drops below the standard ethics of his day. The proposition which workingmen had long quoted was at last incarnated by a mechanic, who took his position so intelligently that he carried with him the best men in England, and set the public conscience. Other men became ashamed of a wrong to which before they had been easily indifferent.

When the social conscience, if one may use the expression, has been thus strikingly formulated, it is not so hard for others to follow. They do it weakly and stumblingly perhaps; but they yet see a glimmer of light of which the first man could not be sure, and they have a code of ethics upon which the first man was vague. They are also conscious of the backing of a large share of the community who before this expression knew not the compunction of their own hearts. A settlement accepts the ethics of its contemporaries that the sharing of the life of the poor is essential to the understanding and bettering of that life; but by its very existence it adopts this modern code somewhat formally. The social injury of the meanest man not only becomes its concern, but by virtue of its very locality it has put itself into a position to see, as no one but a neighbor can see, the stress and need of those who bear the brunt of the social injury. A settlement has not only taken a pledge towards those thus injured, but it is placed where the motive-power for the fulfilment of such a pledge is constantly renewed. Propinquity is an unceasing factor in its existence.

A review of the sewing-trades, as seen from a settlement, will be sufficient to illustrate this position.

Hull-House is situated in the midst of the sweaters' district of Chicago. The residents came to the district with the general belief that organization for

* Excerpt from Jean Bethke Elshtain, ed., *The Jane Addams Reader* (New York: Basic Books, 2002), pp. 46–49. Reprinted with permission of Basic Books, a member of the Perseus Books Group.

workingpeople was a necessity. They would doubtless have said that the discovery of the power to combine was the distinguishing discovery of our time; that we are using this force somewhat awkwardly, as men use that which is newly discovered. In social and political affairs the power to combine often works harm; but it is already operating to such an extent in commercial affairs, that the manufacturer who does not combine with others of his branch is in constant danger of failure; that a railroad cannot be successfully projected unless the interests of parallel roads are consulted; and that working-people likewise cannot be successful until they, too, learn skillfully to avail themselves of this power.

This was to the residents, as to many people, an accepted proposition, but not a working formula. It had not the driving force of a conviction. The residents have lived for five years in a neighborhood largely given over to the sewing-trades, which is an industry totally disorganized. Having observed the workers in this trade as compared to those in organized trades, they have gradually discovered that lack of organization in a trade tends to the industrial helplessness of the workers in that trade. If in all departments of social, political, and commercial life, isolation is a blunder, and results in dreariness and apathy, then in industrial affairs isolation is a social crime; for it there tends to extermination.

This process of extermination entails starvation and suffering, and the desperate moral disintegration which inevitably follows in their train, until the need of organization in industry gradually assumes a moral aspect. The conviction arrived at entails a social obligation.

No trades are so overcrowded as the sewing-trades; for the needle has ever been the refuge of the unskilled woman. The wages paid throughout the manufacture of clothing are less than those in any other trade. In order to meet the requirements of the workers, lack of skill and absence of orderly life, the work has been so subdivided that almost no skill is required after the garment leaves the cutter. It is given practically to the one who is at hand when it is ready, and who does it for the least money. This subdivision and low wage have gone so far, that the woman who does home finishing alone cannot possibly gain by it a living wage. The residents of Hull-House have carefully investigated many cases, and are ready to assert that the Italian widow who finishes the cheapest goods, although she sews from six in the morning until eleven at night, can only get enough to keep her children clothed and fed; while for her rent and fuel she must always depend upon charity or the hospitality of her countrymen. If the American sewing-woman, supporting herself alone, lives on bread and butter and tea, she finds a Bohemian woman next door whose diet of black bread and coffee enables her to undercut. She competes with a wife who is eager to have home finishing that she may add something to the family comfort; or with a daughter who takes it that she may buy a wedding outfit.

The Hebrew tailor, the man with a family to support, who, but for this competition of unskilled women and girls, might earn a wage upon which a family could subsist, is obliged, in order to support them at all, to put his little children at work as soon as they can sew on buttons.

It does not help his industrial situation that the woman and girl who have brought it about have accepted the lower wages in order to buy comforts for an invalid child, or to add to the earnings of an aged father. The mother who sews on a gross of buttons for seven cents, in order to buy a blue ribbon with which to tie up her little daughter's hair, or the mother who finishes a dozen vests for five cents, with which to buy her children a loaf of bread, commits unwittingly a crime against her fellow-workers, although our hearts may thrill with admiration for her heroism, and ache with pity over her misery.

The maternal instinct and family affection is woman's most holy attribute; but if she enters industrial life, that is not enough. She must supplement her family conscience by a social and an industrial conscience. She must widen her family affection to embrace the children of the community. She is working havoc in the sewing-trades, because with the meagre equipment, sufficient for family life she has entered industrial life.

Have we any right to place before untrained women the alternative of seeing their little children suffer, or of complicating the industrial condition until all the children of the community are suffering? We know of course what their decision would be. But the residents of a settlement are not put to this hard choice, although it is often difficult to urge organization when they are flying to the immediate relief of the underfed children in the neighborhood.

If the settlement, then, is convinced that in industrial affairs lack of organization tends to the helplessness of the isolated worker, and is a menace to the entire community, then it is bound to pledge itself to industrial organization, and to look about it for the lines upon which to work. And at this point the settlement enters into what is more technically known as the labor movement.

The labor movement may be called a concerted effort among the workers in all trades to obtain a more equitable distribution of the product, and to secure a more orderly existence for the laborers. How may the settlement be of value to this effort?

If the design of the settlement is not so much the initiation of new measures, but fraternal co-operation with all good which it finds in its neighborhood, then the most obvious line of action will be organization through the trades-unions, a movement already well established.

The trades-unions say to each workingman, "Associate yourself with the fellow-workers in your trade. Let your trade organization federate with the allied trades, and they, in turn, with the National and International Federation, until working-people become a solid body, ready for concerted action. It is the only possible way to prevent cuts in the rate of wages, and to regulate the hours of work. Capital is organized, and has influence with which to secure legislation in its behalf. We are scattered and feeble because we do not work together."

Trades-unionism, in spite of the many pits into which it has fallen, has the ring of altruism about it. It is clearly the duty of the settlement to keep it to its best ideal.

Harriet Martineau (1802–1876) was born in Norwich, England to a family of means and a brood of eight children. In part because Victorian culture relegated girls and women to the domestic sphere, Harriet was self-educated. Her learning was however broad and well formed such that, in time, when the family fell on hard times, Harriet turned to a career as a writer. Once again contrary to the norm of the day, she was sufficiently successful to be able to support her family. The Martineau family was formed in the tradition of English Dissenters, which set Harriet toward Unitarian, hence rational, religious conviction. Her early books in the 1830s included popular writings that explained the conditions appertaining to then-current ideas of the political-economists (of whom, according to Alan Sica, she had no primary knowledge). *Illustrations of Political Economy* (1834), for example, was a nine-volume collection of short fictions meant to introduce readers to then-contemporary political and economic realities. The book was a best seller, the income from which paid for an extended stay in the United States, which in turn formed the basis for another popular work, *Society in America* (1837). These and other works led to her reputation as the first woman sociologist. Though her practical sociology did not hold up to that of Charlotte Perkins Gilman at the end of that century, Martineau is certainly a pioneer of feminist thinking on the Women Question (her phrase). Her feminism was not a focus of any book-length writing, as it would be in Harriet Taylor Mill's *Enfranchisement of Women* (1851). Martineau's feminist ideas are dispersed through many other of her books and essays, of which the selection is an instance.

Woman[*]

Harriet Martineau (1837)

If a test of civilisation be sought, none can be so sure as the condition of that half of society over which the other half has power,—from the exercise of the right of the strongest. Tried by this test, the American civilisation appears to be of a lower order than might have been expected from some other symptoms of its social state. The Americans have, in the treatment of women, fallen below, not only their own democratic principles, but the practice of some parts of the Old World.

The unconsciousness of both parties as to the injuries suffered by women at the hands of those who hold the power is a sufficient proof of the low degree of civilisation in this important particular at which they rest. While woman's intellect is confined, her morals crushed, her health ruined, her weaknesses encouraged, and her strength punished, she is told that her lot is cast in the paradise of women: and there is no country in the world where there is so much boasting of the "chivalrous" treatment she enjoys. That is to say,—she has the best place in stage-coaches: when there are not chairs enough for everybody, the gentlemen stand: she hears oratorical flourishes on public occasions about wives and home, and apostrophes to woman: her husband's hair stands on end at the idea of her working, and he toils to indulge her with money: she has liberty to get her brain turned by religious excitements, that her attention may be diverted from morals, politics, and philosophy; and, especially, her morals are guarded by the strictest observance of propriety in

her presence. In short, indulgence is given her as a substitute for justice. Her case differs from that of the slave, as to the principle, just so far as this; that the indulgence is large and universal, instead of petty and capricious. In both cases, justice is denied on no better plea than the right of the strongest. In both cases, the acquiescence of the many, and the burning discontent of the few, of the oppressed testify, the one to the actual degradation of the class, and the other to its fitness for the enjoyment of human rights.

The intellect of woman is confined. I met with immediate proof of this. Within ten days of my landing, I encountered three outrageous pedants, among the ladies; and in my progress through the country I met with a greater variety and extent of female pedantry than the experience of a lifetime in Europe would afford. I could fill the remainder of my volume with sketches: but I forbear, through respect even for this very pedantry. Where intellect has a fair chance, there is no pedantry, among men or women. It is the result of an intellect which cannot be wholly passive, but must demonstrate some force, and does so through the medium of narrow morals. Pedantry indicates the first struggle of intellect with its restraints; and it is therefore a hopeful symptom.

The intellect of woman is confined by an unjustifiable restriction of both methods of education,—by express teaching, and by the discipline of circumstance. The former, though prior in the chronology of each individual, is a direct consequence of the latter, as regards the whole of the sex. As women have none of the objects in life for which an enlarged education is considered requisite, the education is not given. Female education in America is much what it is in England. There is a profession of some things being taught which are supposed necessary because everybody learns them. They serve to fill up time, to occupy attention harmlessly, to improve conversation, and to make women something like companions to their husbands, and able to teach their children somewhat. But what is given is, for the most part, passively received; and what is obtained is, chiefly, by means of the memory. There is rarely or never a careful ordering of influences for the promotion of clear intellectual activity. Such activity, when it exceeds that which is necessary to make the work of the teacher easy, is feared and repressed. This is natural enough, as long as women are excluded from the objects for which men are trained. While there are natural rights which women may not use, just claims which are not to be listened to, large objects which may not be approached, even in imagination,

---

* Martineau, Harriet. From *Society in America*, Volume III, Part III, Chapter II, "Woman." London: Saunders and Otley, 1837, pp. 105-106.

intellectual activity is dangerous: or, as the phrase is, unfit. Accordingly, marriage is the only object left open to woman. Philosophy she may pursue only fancifully, and under pain of ridicule: science only as a pastime, and under a similar penalty. Art is declared to be left open: but the necessary learning, and, yet more, the indispensable experience of reality, are denied to her. Literature is also said to be permitted: but under what penalties and restrictions?

Èmile Durkheim (1858–1917) was born in Lorraine in rural eastern France. His father and forefathers for generations were rabbis. Though Durkheim abandoned these roots in a provincial religious community, he devoted his intellectual life to studying, teaching, and advancing the sociology of moral life. After a brilliant student career at the École Normale Supérieure in Paris, Durkheim taught in Bordeaux. In the 1890s, he wrote *Division of Labor* (his doctoral thesis), *Rules of Sociological Method* (1895), and *Suicide* (1897). Though *Suicide* was meant, at least in part, to illustrate Durkheim's sociological method, it was every bit as much a social theory of the disorder of modern life. Here is where he refined his famous concept "anomie," introduced in *Division of Labor* when Durkheim first compared the moral order of traditional and modern societies. In 1902, he was called to the Sorbonne in Paris, where he founded academic sociology in France and, just as importantly, influenced the future course of French public education through his teaching. Durkheim the sociologist was also a prominent public figure in Third Republic France. His sociological vision of the moral needs of modern society formed the basis of his political contributions to his native land. Some consider his last book, *The Elementary Forms of the Religious Life* (1912), a classic source for modern cultural studies. Durkheim was just fifty-nine when he died in 1917, seemingly from the emotional effects of his son's death two years earlier.

In "Mechanical and Organic Solidarity" (1893) Durkheim famously states an early version of his idea that the social division of labor determines the individual's fate. "Anomie and the Modern Division of Labor" (1902) is Durkheim's recommendation for stronger occupational groups, like unions, to counter the effects of anomie in modern life. The selection plainly states Durkheim's critique of modern society. "Sociology and Social Facts" (1897) is a defense of sociology as Durkheim understood it. The argument

that social facts are things is the scientific corollary to Durkheim's moral argument that society is a reality in its own right and thus must be morally powerful in order to guide the individual. "Suicide and Modernity" (1897)—from Durkheim's brilliant statistical study, *Suicide*—reveals both the precision of his scientific mind and his deep preoccupation with the effects of anomie on the modern individual. Durkheim's studies of religion were foundations for his lifelong conviction that society itself is the source of knowledge, including scientific knowledge. In "Primitive Classifications and Social Knowledge" (1903), written with Marcel Mauss, Durkheim examines the social organization of two tribal societies (the Sioux and the Wotjobaluk) in order to show that their bizarre methods for classifying the world were, in fact, sophisticated representations of the social order they experienced and lived by. From this, he argues that logical thought, whether tribal or modern, originates in the social experience of the group. "The Cultural Logic of Collective Representations" is from the conclusion to *Elementary Forms of the Religious Life* (1912). Durkheim's ideas on religion, knowledge, and society are an implicit attack on the arrogance of Western culture's claim that modern science contains the essential truths of human life.

Mechanical and Organic Solidarity[*]
Èmile Durkheim (1893)

If there is one rule of conduct which is incontestable, it is that which orders us to realize in ourselves the essential traits of the collective type. Among lower peoples, this reaches its greatest rigor. There, one's first duty is to resemble everybody else, not to have anything personal about one's beliefs or actions. In more advanced societies, required likenesses are less numerous; the absences of some likenesses, however, is still a sign of moral failure. Of course, crime falls into fewer different categories; but today, as heretofore, if a criminal is the object of reprobation, it is because he is unlike us. Likewise, in lesser degree, acts simply immoral and prohibited as such are those which evince dissemblances less profound but nevertheless considered serious. Is this not the case with the rule which common morality expresses when it orders a man to be a man in every sense of the word, which is to say, to have all the ideas and sentiments which go to make up a human conscience? No doubt, if this formula is taken literally, the man prescribed would be man in general and not one of some particular social species. But, in reality, this human conscience that we must integrally realize is nothing else than the collective conscience of the group of which we are a part. For what can it be composed of, if not the ideas and sentiments to which we are most attached? Where can we find the traits of our model, if not within us and around us? If we believe that this collective ideal is that of all humanity, that is because it has become so abstract and general that it appears fitting for all men indiscriminately. But, really, every people makes for itself some particular conception of this type which pertains to its personal temperament. Each represents it in its own image. Even the moralist who thinks he can, through thought, overcome the influence of transient ideas, cannot do so, for he is impregnated with them, and no matter what he does, he finds these precepts in the body of his deductions. That is why each nation has its own school of moral philosophy conforming to its character.

On the other hand, we have shown that this rule had as its function the prevention of all agitation of the common conscience, and, consequently, of social solidarity, and that it could accomplish this role only by having a moral character. It is impossible for offenses against the most fundamental collective sentiments to be tolerated without the disintegration of society, and it is necessary to combat them with the aid of the particularly energetic reaction which attaches to moral rules.

But the contrary rule, which orders us to specialize, has exactly the same function. It also is necessary for the cohesion of societies, at least at a certain period in their evolution. Of course, its solidarity is different from the preceding, but though it is different, it is no less indispensable. Higher societies can maintain themselves in equilibrium only if labor is divided; the attraction of like for like less and less suffices to produce this result. If, then, the moral character of the first of these rules is necessary to the playing of its role, it is no less necessary to the second. They both correspond to the same social need, but satisfy the need differently, because the conditions of existence in the societies themselves differ. Consequently, without speculating concerning the first principle of ethics, we can induce the moral value of one from the moral value of the other. If, from certain points of view, there is a real antagonism between them, that is not because they serve different ends. On the contrary, it is because they lead to the same end, but through opposed means. Accordingly, there is no necessity for choosing between them once for all nor of condemning one in the name of the other. What is necessary is to give each, at each moment in history, the place that is fitting to it.

Perhaps we can even generalize further in this matter.

The requirements of our subject have obliged us to classify moral rules and to review the principal types. We are thus in a better position than we were in the beginning to see, or at least to conjecture, not only upon the external sign, but also upon the internal character which is common to all of them and which can serve to define them. We have put them into two groups: rules with repressive sanctions, which may be diffuse or organized, and rules with restitutive sanctions. We have seen that the first of these express the conditions of the solidarity, *sui generis*, which comes from resemblances, and to which we have given the name mechanical; the second, the conditions of negative solidarity and organic solidarity. We can thus say that, in general, the characteristic of moral rules is that they enunciate the fundamental conditions of social solidarity. Law and morality are the totality of ties which bind each of us to society, which make a unitary, coherent aggregate of the mass of individuals. Everything which is a source of solidarity is moral, everything which forces man to take account of other men is moral, everything which forces him to regulate his conduct through something other than the striving of his ego is moral, and morality is as solid as these ties are numerous and strong. We can see how inexact it is to define it, as is often done, through liberty. It rather consists in a state of dependence. Far from serving to emancipate the individual, or disengaging him from the environment which surrounds him, it has, on the contrary, the function of making him an integral part of a whole, and, consequently, of depriving him of some liberty of movement. We sometimes, it is true, come across people not without nobility who find the idea of such dependence intolerable. But that is because they do not perceive the source from which their own morality flows, since these sources are very deep. Conscience is a bad judge of what goes on in the depths of a person, because it does not penetrate to them.

Society is not, then, as has often been thought, a stranger to the moral world, or something which has only secondary repercussions upon it. It is, on the contrary, the necessary condition of its existence. It is not a simple juxtaposition of individuals who bring an intrinsic morality with them, but rather man is a moral being only because he lives in society, since morality consists in being solidary with a group and varying with this solidarity. Let all social life disappear, and moral life will disappear with it, since it would no longer have any objective. The state of nature of the philosophers of the eighteenth century, if not immoral, is, at least, *amoral*. Rousseau himself recognized this. Through this, however, we do not come upon the formula which expresses morality as a function of social interest. To be sure, society cannot exist if its parts are not solidary, but solidarity is only one of its conditions of existence. There are many others which are no less necessary and which are not moral. Moreover, it can happen that, in the system of ties which make up morality, there are some which are not useful in themselves or which have power without any relation to their degree of utility. The idea of utility does not enter as an essential element in our definition.

As for what is called individual morality, if we understand by that a totality of duties of which the individual would, at the same time, be subject and object, and which would link him only to himself, and which would, consequently, exist even if he were solitary—that is an abstract conception which has no relation to reality. Morality, in all its forms, is never met with except in society. It never varies except in relation to social conditions. To ask what it would be if societies did not exist is thus to depart from facts and enter the domain of gratuitous hypotheses and unverifiable flights of the imagination. The duties of the individual towards himself are, in reality, duties towards society. They correspond to certain collective sentiments which he cannot offend, whether the offended and the offender are one and the same person, or whether they are distinct. Today, for example, there is in all healthy consciences a very lively sense of respect for human dignity, to which we are supposed to conform as much in our relations with ourselves as in our relations with others, and this constitutes the essential quality of what is called individual morality. Every act which contravenes this is censured, even when the agent and the sufferer are the same person. That is why, according to the Kantian formula, which is to say, in ourselves as in those like us. The sentiment of which it is the

object is not less offended in one case than in the other.

But not only does the division of labor present the character by which we have defined morality; it more and more tends to become the essential condition of social solidarity. As we advance in the evolutionary scale, the ties which bind the individual to his family, to his native soil, to traditions which the past has given to him, to collective group usages, become loose. More mobile, he changes his environment more easily, leaves his people to go elsewhere to live a more autonomous existence, to a greater extent forms his own ideas and sentiments. Of course, the whole common conscience does not, on this account, pass out of existence. At least there will always remain this cult of personality, of individual dignity of which we have just been speaking, and which, today, is the rallying-point of so many people. But how little a thing it is when one contemplates the ever increasing extent of social life, and, consequently, of individual consciences! For, as they become more voluminous, as intelligence becomes richer, activity more varied, in order for morality to remain constant, that is to say, in order for the individual to remain attached to the group with a force equal to that of yesterday, the ties which bind him to it must become stronger and more numerous. If, then, he formed no others than those which come from resemblances, the effacement of the segmental type would be accompanied by a systematic debasement of morality. Man would no longer be sufficiently obligated; he would no longer feel about and above him this salutary pressure of society which moderates his egoism and makes him a moral being. This is what gives moral value to the division of labor. Through it, the individual becomes cognizant of his dependence upon society; from it come the forces which keep him in check and restrain him. In short, since the division of labor becomes the chief source of social solidarity, it becomes, at the same time, the foundation of the moral order.

We can then say that, in higher societies, our duty is not to spread our activity over a large surface, but to concentrate and specialize it. We must contract our horizon, choose a definite task and immerse ourselves in it completely, instead of trying to make ourselves a sort of creative masterpiece, quite complete, which contains its worth in itself and not in the services that it renders. Finally, this specialization ought to be pushed as far as the elevation of the social type, without assigning any other limit to it. No doubt, we ought so to work as to realize in ourselves the collective type as it exists. There are common sentiments, common ideas, without which, as has been said, one is not a man. The rule which orders us to specialize remains limited by the contrary rule. Our conclusion is not that it is good to press specialization as far as possible, but as far as necessary. As for the part that is to be played by these two opposing necessities, that is determined by experience and cannot be calculated *a priori*. It is enough for us to have shown that the second is not of a different nature from the first, but that it also is moral, and that, moreover, this duty becomes ever more important and pressing, because the general qualities which are in question suffice less and less to socialize the individual.

It is not without reason that public sentiment reproves an ever more pronounced tendency on the part of dilettantes and even others to be taken up with an exclusively general culture and refuse to take any part in occupational organization. That is because they are not sufficiently attached to society, or, if one wishes, society is not sufficiently attached to them, and they escape it. Precisely because they feel its effect neither with vivacity nor with the continuity that is necessary, they have no cognizance of all the obligations their positions as social beings demand of them. The general ideal to which they are attached being, for the reasons we have spoken of, formal and shifting, it cannot take them out of themselves. We do not cling to very much when we have no very determined objective, and, consequently, we cannot very well elevate ourselves beyond a more or less refined egoism. On the contrary, he who gives himself over to a definite task is, at every moment, struck by the sentiment of common solidarity in the thousand duties of occupational morality.

Anomie and the Modern Division of Labor*
Èmile Durkheim (1902)

We repeatedly insist in the course of this book upon the state of juridical and moral anomie in which economic life actually is found. Indeed, in the economic order, occupational ethics exist only in the most rudimentary state. There is a professional ethic of the

* Reprinted with the permission of The Free Press, a Division of Simon & Schuster, Inc., from DIVISION OF LABOR IN SOCIETY by Èmile Durkheim. Translated from the French by George Simpson, Ph.D.. Copyright © 1947, 1964 by The Free Press. All rights reserved.

lawyer and the judge, the soldier and the priest, etc. But if one attempted to fix in a little more precise language the current ideas on what ought to be the relations of employer and employee, of worker and manager, of tradesmen in competition, to themselves or to the public, what indecisive formulas would be obtained! Some generalizations, without point, about the faithfulness and devotion workers of all sorts owe to those who employ them, about the moderation with which employers must use their economic advantages, a certain reprobation of all competition too openly dishonest, for all untempered exploitation of the consumer; that is about all the moral conscience of these trades contains. Moreover, most of these precepts are devoid of all juridical character, they are sanctioned only by opinion, not by law; and it is well known how indulgent opinion is concerning the manner in which these vague obligations are fulfilled. The most blameworthy acts are so often absolved by success that the boundary between what is permitted and what is prohibited, what is just and what is unjust, has nothing fixed about it, but seems susceptible to almost arbitrary change by individuals. An ethic so unprecise and inconsistent cannot constitute a discipline. The result is that all this sphere of collective life is, in large part, freed from the moderating action of regulation.

It is this anomic state that is the cause, as we shall show, of the incessantly recurrent conflicts, and the multifarious disorders of which the economic world exhibits so sad a spectacle. For, as nothing restrains the active forces and assigns them limits they are bound to respect, they tend to develop haphazardly, and come into collision with one another, battling and weakening themselves. To be sure, the strongest succeed in completely demolishing the weakest, or in subordinating them. But if the conquered, for a time, must suffer subordination under compulsion, they do not consent to it, and consequently this cannot constitute a stable equilibrium. Truces, arrived at after violence, are never anything but provisional, and satisfy no one. Human passions stop only before a moral power they respect. If all authority of this kind is wanting, the law of the strongest prevails, and latent or active, the state of war is necessarily chronic.

That such anarchy is an unhealthy phenomenon is quite evident, since it runs counter to the aim of society, which is to suppress, or at least to moderate, war among men, subordinating the law of the strongest to a higher law. To justify this chaotic state, we vainly praise its encouragement of individual liberty.

Nothing is falser than this antagonism too often presented between legal authority and individual liberty. Quite on the contrary, liberty (we mean genuine liberty, which it is society's duty to have respected) is itself the product of regulation. I can be free only to the extent that others are forbidden to profit from their physical, economic, or other superiority to the detriment of my liberty. But only social rules can prevent abuses of power. It is now known what complicated regulation is needed to assure individuals the economic independence without which their liberty is only nominal.

But what brings about the exceptional gravity of this state, nowadays particularly, is the heretofore unknown development that economic functions have experienced for about two centuries. Whereas formerly they played only a secondary role, they are now of the first importance. We are far from the time when they were disdainfully abandoned to the inferior classes. In the face of the economic, the administrative, military, and religious functions become steadily less important. Only the scientific functions seem to dispute their place, and even science has scarcely any prestige save to the extent that it can serve practical occupations, which are largely economic. That is why it can be said, with some justice, that society is, or tends to be, essentially industrial. A form of activity which has assumed such a place in social life evidently cannot remain in this unruly state without resulting in the most profound disasters. It is a notable source of general demoralization. For, precisely because the economic functions today concern the greatest number of citizens, there are a multitude of individuals whose lives are passed almost entirely in the industrial and commercial world. From this, it follows that as that world is only feebly ruled by morality, the greatest part of their existence takes place outside the moral sphere. Now, for the sentiment of duty to be fixed strongly in us, the circumstances in which we live must keep us awake. Naturally, we are not inclined to thwart and restrain ourselves; if, then, we are not invited, at each moment, to exercise this restraint without which there is no ethic, how can we learn the habit? If in the task that occupies almost all our time we follow no other rule than that of our well-understood interest, how can we learn to depend upon disinterestedness, on self-forgetfulness, on sacrifice? In this way, the absence of all economic discipline cannot fail to extend its effects beyond the economic world, and consequently weaken public morality.

But, the evil observed, what is its cause and what can be its remedy?

Sociology and Social Facts[*]
Èmile Durkheim (1897)

Sociology has been in vogue for some time. Today this word, little known and almost discredited a decade ago, is in common use. Representatives of the new science are increasing in number and there is something like a public feeling favorable to it. Much is expected of it. It must be confessed, however, that results up to the present time are not really proportionate to the number of publications nor the interest which they arouse. The progress of a science is proven by the progress toward solution of the problems it treats. It is said to be advancing when laws hitherto unknown are discovered, or when at least new facts are acquired modifying the formulation of these problems even though not furnishing a final solution. Unfortunately, there is good reason why sociology does not appear in this light, and this is because the problems it proposes are not usually clear-cut. It is still in the stage of system-building and philosophical syntheses. Instead of attempting to cast light on a limited portion of the social field, it prefers brilliant generalities reflecting all sorts of questions to definite treatment of any one. Such a method may indeed momentarily satisfy public curiosity by offering it so-called illumination on all sorts of subjects, but it can achieve nothing objective. Brief studies and hasty intuitions are not enough for the discovery of the laws of so complex a reality. And, above all, such large and abrupt generalizations are not capable of any sort of proof. All that is accomplished is the occasional citation of some favorable examples illustrative of the hypothesis considered, but an illustration is not a proof. Besides, when so many various matters are dealt with, none is competently treated and only casual sources can be employed, with no means to make a critical estimate of them. Works of pure sociology are accordingly of little use to whoever insists on treating only definite questions, for most of them belong to

*Reprinted with the permission of The Free Press, a Division of Simon & Schuster, Inc., from SUICIDE: A STUDY IN SOCIOLOGY by Èmile Durkheim, translated by John A. Spaulding and George Simpson. Copyright © 1951 by The Free Press; copyright renewed (c) 1979 by The Free Press. All rights reserved.

no particular branch of research and in addition lack really authoritative documentation.

Believers in the future of the science must, of course, be anxious to put an end to this state of affairs. If it should continue, sociology would soon relapse into its old discredit and only the enemies of reason could rejoice at this. The human mind would suffer a grievous setback if this segment of reality which alone has so far denied or defied it should escape it even temporarily. There is nothing necessarily discouraging in the incompleteness of the results thus far obtained. They should arouse new efforts, not surrender. A science so recent cannot be criticized for errors and probings if it sees to it that their recurrence is avoided. Sociology should, then, renounce none of its aims; but, on the other hand, if it is to satisfy the hopes placed in it, it must try to become more than a new sort of philosophical literature. Instead of contenting himself with metaphysical reflection on social themes, the sociologist must take as the object of his research groups of facts clearly circumscribed, capable of ready definition, with definite limits, and adhere strictly to them. Such auxiliary subjects as history, ethnography and statistics are indispensable. The only danger is that their findings may never really be related to the subject he seeks to embrace; for, carefully as he may delimit this subject, it is so rich and varied that it contains inexhaustible and unsuspected tributary fields. But this is not conclusive. If he proceeds accordingly, even though his factual resources are incomplete and his formulae too narrow, he will have nevertheless performed a useful task for future continuation. Conceptions with some objective foundation are not restricted to the personality of their author. They have an impersonal quality which others may take up and pursue; they are transmissible. This makes possible some continuity in scientific labor—continuity upon which progress depends.

It is in this spirit that the work here presented has been conceived. Suicide has been chosen as its subject, among the various subjects that we have had occasion to study in our teaching career, because few are more accurately to be defined and because it seemed to us particularly timely; its limits have even required study in a preliminary work. On the other hand, by such concentration, real laws are discoverable which demonstrate the possibility of sociology better than any dialectical argument. The ones we hope to have demonstrated will appear. Of course we must have made more than one error, must have overextended the facts observed in our

inductions. But at least each proposition carries its proofs with it and we have tried to make them as numerous as possible. Most of all, we have striven in each case to separate the argument and interpretation from the facts interpreted. Thus the reader can judge what is relevant in our explanations without being confused.

Moreover, by thus restricting the research, one is by no means deprived of broad views and general insights. On the contrary, we think we have established a certain number of propositions concerning marriage, widowhood, family life, religious society, etc., which, if we are not mistaken, are more instructive than the common theories of moralists as to the nature of these conditions or institutions. There will even emerge from our study some suggestions concerning the causes of the general contemporary maladjustment being undergone by European societies and concerning remedies which may relieve it. One must not believe that a general condition can only be explained with the aid of generalities. It may appertain to specific causes which can only be determined if carefully studied through no less definite manifestations expressive of them. Suicide as it exists today is precisely one of the forms through which the collective affection from which we suffer is transmitted; thus it will aid us to understand this.

Finally, in the course of this work, but in a concrete and specific form, will appear the chief methodological problems elsewhere stated and examined by us in greater detail [in *The Rules of Sociological Method*]. Indeed, among these questions there is one to which the following work makes a contribution too important for us to fail to call it immediately to the attention of the reader.

Sociological method as we practice it rests wholly on the basic principle that social facts must be studied as things, that is, as realities external to the individual. There is no principle for which we have received more criticism; but none is more fundamental. Indubitably for sociology to be possible, it must above all have an object all its own. It must take cognizance of a reality which is not in the domain of other sciences. But if no reality exists outside of individual consciousness, it wholly lacks any material of its own. In that case, the only possible subject of observation is the mental states of the individual, since nothing else exists. That, however, is the field of psychology. From this point of view the essence of marriage, for example, or the family, or religion, consists of individual needs to which these institutions supposedly correspond: paternal affection, filial love, sexual desire, the so-called religious instinct, etc. These institutions themselves, with their varied and complex historical forms, become negligible and of little significance. Being superficial, contingent expressions of the general characteristics of the nature of the individual, they are but one of its aspects and call for no special investigation. Of course, it may occasionally be interesting to see how these eternal sentiments of humanity have been outwardly manifested at different times in history; but as all such manifestations are imperfect, not much importance may be attached to them. Indeed, in certain respects, they are better disregarded to permit more attention to the original source whence flows all their meaning and which they imperfectly reflect. On the pretext of giving the science a more solid foundation by establishing it upon the psychological constitution of the individual, it is thus robbed of the only object proper to it. *It is not realized that there can be no sociology unless societies exist, and that societies cannot exist if there are only individuals.* Moreover, this view is not the least of the causes which maintain the taste for vague generalities in sociology. How can it be important to define the concrete forms of social life, if they are thought to have only a borrowed existence? *Valuable*

But it seems hardly possible to us that there will not emerge, on the contrary, from every page of this book, so to speak, the impression that the individual is dominated by a moral reality greater than himself: namely, collective reality. When each people is seen to have its own suicide-rate, more constant than that of general mortality, that its growth is in accordance with a coefficient of acceleration characteristic of each society; when it appears that the variations through which it passes at different times of the day, month, year, merely reflect the rhythm of social life; and that marriage, divorce, the family, religious society, the army, etc., affect it in accordance with definite laws, some of which may even be numerically expressed—these states and institutions will no longer be regarded simply as characterless, ineffective ideological arrangements. Rather they will be felt to be real, living, active forces which, because of the way they determine the individual, prove their independence of him; which, if the individual enters as an element in the combination whence these forces ensue, at least control him once they are formed. Thus it will appear more clearly why sociology can and must be objective, since it deals with realities as definite and substantial as those of the psychologist or the biologist.

Something greater than the individual

Suicide and Modernity[*]
Èmile Durkheim (1897)

Some needs are not necessary

No living being can be happy or even exist unless his needs are sufficiently proportioned to his means. In other words, if his needs require more than can be granted, or even merely something of a different sort, they will be under continual friction and can only function painfully. Movements incapable of production without pain tend not to be reproduced. Unsatisfied tendencies atrophy, and as the impulse to live is merely the result of all the rest, it is bound to weaken as the others relax. *No limit on needs*

In the animal, at least in a normal condition, this equilibrium is established with automatic spontaneity because the animal depends on purely material conditions. All the organism needs is that the supplies of substance and energy constantly employed in the vital process should be periodically renewed by equivalent quantities; that replacement be equivalent to use. When the void created by existence in its own resources is filled, the animal, satisfied, asks nothing further. Its power of reflection is not sufficiently developed to imagine other ends than those implicit in its physical nature. On the other hand, as the work demanded of each organ itself depends on the general state of vital energy and the needs of organic equilibrium, use is regulated in turn by replacement and the balance is automatic. The limits of one are those of the other; both are fundamental to the constitution of the existence in question, which cannot exceed them.

This is not the case with man, because most of his needs are not dependent on his body or not to the same degree. Strictly speaking, we may consider that the quantity of material supplies necessary to the physical maintenance of a human life is subject to computation, though this be less exact than in the preceding case and a wider margin left for the free combinations of the will; for beyond the indispensable minimum which satisfies nature when instinctive, a more awakened reflection suggests better conditions, seemingly desirable ends craving fulfillment. Such appetites, however, admittedly sooner or later reach a limit which they cannot pass. But how determine the quantity of well-being, comfort or

[*] Reprinted with the permission of The Free Press, a Division of Simon & Schuster, Inc., from SUICIDE: A STUDY IN SOCIOLOGY by Èmile Durkheim, translated by John A. Spaulding and George Simpson. Copyright © 1951 by The Free Press; copyright renewed (c) 1979 by The Free Press. All rights reserved.

unlimited ability to get more needs

luxury legitimately to be craved by a human being? Nothing appears in man's organic nor in his psychological constitution which sets a limit to such tendencies. The functioning of individual life does not require them to cease at one point rather than at another; the proof being that they have constantly increased since the beginnings of history, receiving more and more complete satisfaction, yet with no weakening of average health. Above all, how establish their proper variation with different conditions of life, occupations, relative importance of services, etc.? In no society are they equally satisfied in the different stages of the social hierarchy. Yet human nature is substantially the same among all men, in its essential qualities. It is not human nature which can assign the variable limits necessary to our needs. They are thus unlimited so far as they depend on the individual alone. Irrespective of any external regulatory force, our capacity for feeling is in itself an insatiable and bottomless abyss.

But if nothing external can restrain this capacity, it can only be a source of torment to itself. Unlimited desires are insatiable by definition and insatiability is rightly considered a sign of morbidity. Being unlimited, they constantly and infinitely surpass the means at their command; they cannot be quenched. Inextinguishable thirst is constantly renewed torture. It has been claimed, indeed, the human activity naturally aspires beyond assignable limits and sets itself unattainable goals. But how can such an undetermined state be any more reconciled with the conditions of mental life than with the demands of physical life? All man's pleasure in acting, moving and exerting himself implies the sense that his efforts are not in vain and that by walking he has advanced. However, one does not advance when one walks toward no goal, or—which is the same thing—when his goal is infinity. Since the distance between us and it is always the same, whatever road we take, we might as well have made the motions without progress from the spot. Even our glances behind and our feeling of pride at the distance covered can cause only deceptive satisfaction, since the remaining distance is not proportionately reduced. To pursue a goal which is by definition unattainable is to condemn oneself to a state of perpetual unhappiness. Of course, man may hope contrary to all reason, and hope has its pleasures even when unreasonable. It may sustain him for a time; but it cannot survive the repeated disappointments of experience indefinitely. What more can the future offer him than the past, since he can never reach a tenable condition nor

even approach the glimpsed ideal? Thus, the more one has, the more one wants, since satisfactions received only stimulate instead of filling needs. Shall action as such be considered agreeable? First, only on condition of blindness to its uselessness. Secondly, for this pleasure to be felt and to temper and half veil the accompanying painful unrest, such unending motion must at least always be easy and unhampered. If it is interfered with only restlessness is left, with the lack of ease which it, itself, entails. But it would be a miracle if no insurmountable obstacle were ever encountered. Our thread of life on these conditions is pretty thin, breakable at any instant.

To achieve any other result, the passions first must be limited. Only then can they be harmonized with the faculties and satisfied. But since the individual has no way of limiting them, this must be done by some force exterior to him. A regulative force must play the same role for moral needs which the organism plays for physical needs. This means that the force can only be moral. The awakening of conscience interrupted the state of equilibrium of the animal's dormant existence; only conscience, therefore, can furnish the means to re-establish it. Physical restraint would be ineffective; hearts cannot be touched by physio-chemical forces. So far as the appetites are not automatically restrained by physiological mechanisms, they can be halted only by a limit that they recognize as just. Men would never consent to restrict their desires if they felt justified in passing the assigned limit. But, for reasons given above, they cannot assign themselves this law of justice. So they must receive it from an authority which they respect, to which they yield spontaneously. Either directly and as a whole, or through the agency of one of its organs, society alone can play this moderating role; for it is the only moral power superior to the individual, the authority of which he accepts. It alone has the power necessary to stipulate law and to set the point beyond which the passions must not go. Finally, it alone can estimate the reward to be prospectively offered to every class of human functionary, in the name of the common interest.

As a matter of fact, at every moment of history there is a dim perception, in the moral consciousness of societies, of the respective value of different social services, the relative reward due to each, and the consequent degree of comfort appropriate on the average to workers in each occupation. The different functions are graded in public opinion and a certain coefficient of well-being assigned to each, according to its place in the hierarchy. According to accepted ideas, for example, a certain way of living is considered the upper limit to which a workman may aspire in his efforts to improve his existence, and there is another limit below which he is not willingly permitted to fall unless he has seriously demeaned himself. Both differ for city and country workers, for the domestic servant and the day-laborer, for the business clerk and the official, etc. Likewise the man of wealth is reproved if he lives the life of a poor man, but also if he seeks the refinements of luxury overmuch. Economists may protest in vain; public feeling will always be scandalized if an individual spends too much wealth for wholly superfluous use, and it even seems that this severity relaxes only in times of moral disturbance. A genuine regimen exists, therefore, although not always legally formulated, which fixes with relative precision the maximum degree of ease of living to which each social class may legitimately aspire. However, there is nothing immutable about such a scale. It changes with the increase or decrease of collective revenue and the changes occurring in the moral ideas of society. Thus what appears luxury to one period no longer does so to another; and the well-being which for long periods was granted to a class only by exception and supererogation, finally appears strictly necessary and equitable.

Under this pressure, each in his sphere vaguely realizes the extreme limit set to his ambitions and aspires to nothing beyond. At least if he respects regulations and is docile to collective authority, that is, has a wholesome moral constitution, he feels that it is not well to ask more. Thus, an end and goal are set to the passions. Truly, there is nothing rigid nor absolute about such determination. The economic ideal assigned each class of citizens is itself confined to certain limits, within which the desires have free range. But it is not infinite. This relative limitation and the moderation it involves, make men contented with their lot while stimulating them moderately to improve it; and this average contentment causes the feeling of calm, active happiness, the pleasure in existing and living which characterizes health for societies as well as for individuals. Each person is then at least, generally speaking, in harmony with his condition, and desires only what he may legitimately hope for as the normal reward of his activity. Besides, this does not condemn man to a sort of immobility. He may seek to give beauty to his life; but his attempts in this direction may fail without causing him to despair. For, loving what he has and not fixing his desire solely on what he lacks, his wishes and hopes may fail of what he has happened to aspire to, without his

being wholly destitute. He has the essentials. The equilibrium of his happiness is secure because it is defined, and a few mishaps cannot disconcert him.

But it would be of little use for everyone to recognize the justice of the hierarchy of functions established by public opinion, if he did not also consider the distribution of these functions just. The workman is not in harmony with his social position if he is not convinced that he has his desserts. If he feels justified in occupying another, what he has would not satisfy him. So it is not enough for the average level of needs for each social condition to be regulated by public opinion, but another, more precise rule, must fix the way in which these conditions are open to individuals. There is no society in which such regulation does not exist. It varies with times and places. Once it regarded birth as the almost exclusive principle of social classification; today it recognizes no other inherent inequality than hereditary fortune and merit. But in all these various forms its object is unchanged. It is also only possible, everywhere, as a restriction upon individuals imposed by superior authority, that is, by collective authority. For it can be established only by requiring of one or another group of men, usually of all, sacrifices and concessions in the name of the public interest.

Some, to be sure, have thought that this moral pressure would become unnecessary if men's economic circumstances were only no longer determined by heredity. If inheritance were abolished, the argument runs, if everyone began life with equal resources and if the competitive struggle were fought out on a basis of perfect equality, no one could think its results unjust. Each would instinctively feel that things are as they should be.

Truly, the nearer this ideal equality were approached, the less social restraint will be necessary. But it is only a matter of degree. One sort of heredity will always exist, that of natural talent. Intelligence, taste, scientific, artistic, literary or industrial ability, courage and manual dexterity are gifts received by each of us at birth, as the heir to wealth receives his capital or as the nobleman formerly received his title and function. A moral discipline will therefore still be required to make those less favored by nature accept the lesser advantages which they owe to the chance of birth. Shall it be demanded that all have an equal share and that no advantage be given those more useful and deserving? But then there would have to be a discipline far stronger to make these accept a treatment merely equal to that of the mediocre and incapable.

But like the one first mentioned, this discipline can be useful only if considered just by the peoples subject to it. When it is maintained only by custom and force, peace and harmony are illusory; the spirit of unrest and discontent are latent; appetites superficially restrained are ready to revolt. This happened in Rome and Greece when the faiths underlying the old organization of the patricians and plebeians were shaken, and in our modern societies when aristocratic prejudices began to lose their old ascendancy. But this state of upheaval is exceptional; it occurs only when society is passing through some abnormal crisis. In normal conditions the collective order is regarded as just by the great majority of persons. Therefore, when we say that an authority is necessary to impose this order on individuals, we certainly do not mean that violence is the only means of establishing it. Since this regulation is meant to restrain individual passions, it must come from a power which dominates individuals; but this power must also be obeyed through respect, not fear.

It is not true, then, that human activity can be released from all restraint. Nothing in the world can enjoy such a privilege. All existence being a part of the universe is relative to the remainder; its nature and method of manifestation accordingly depend not only on itself but on other beings, who consequently restrain and regulate it. Here there are only differences of degree and form between the mineral realm and the thinking person. Man's characteristic privilege is that the bond he accepts is not physical but moral; that is, social. He is governed not by a material environment brutally imposed on him, but by a conscience superior to his own, the superiority of which he feels. Because the greater, better part of his existence transcends the body, he escapes the body's yoke, but is subject to that of society.

But when society is disturbed by some painful crisis or by beneficent but abrupt transitions, it is momentarily incapable of exercising this influence; thence come the sudden rises in the curve of suicides which we have pointed out above.

In the case of economic disasters, indeed, something like a declassification occurs which suddenly casts certain individuals into a lower state than their previous once. Then they must reduce their requirements, restrain their needs, learn greater self-control. All the advantages of social influence are lost so far as they are concerned; their moral education has to be recommenced. But society cannot adjust them instantaneously to this new life and teach them to practice the increased self-repression to which they are unaccustomed. So they are not adjusted to the condition forced on them, and its very prospect is intolerable; hence the suffering which detaches them from a reduced existence even before they have made trial of it.

It is the same if the source of the crisis is an abrupt growth of power and wealth. Then, truly, as the conditions of life are changed, the standard according to which needs were regulated can no longer remain the same; for it varies with social resources, since it largely determines the share of each class of producers. The scale is upset; but a new scale cannot be immediately improvised. Time is required for the public conscience to reclassify men and things. So long as the social forces thus freed have not regained equilibrium, their respective values are unknown and so all regulation is lacking for a time. The limits are unknown between the possible and the impossible, what is just and what is unjust, legitimate claims and hopes and those which are immoderate. Consequently, there is no restraint upon aspirations. If the disturbance is profound, it affects even the principles controlling the distribution of men among various occupations. Since the relations between various parts of society are necessarily modified, the ideas expressing these relations must change. Some particular class especially favored by the crisis is no longer resigned to its former lot, and, on the other hand, the example of its greater good fortune arouses all sorts of jealousy below and about it. Appetites, not being controlled by a public opinion become disoriented, no longer recognize the limits proper to them. Besides, they are at the same time seized by a sort of natural erethism simply by the greater intensity of public life. With increased prosperity desires increase. At the very moment when traditional rules have lost their authority, the richer prize offered these appetites stimulates them and makes them more exigent and impatient of control. The state of de-regulation or anomie is thus further heightened by passions being less disciplined, precisely when they need more disciplining.

But then their very demands make fulfillment impossible. Overweening ambition always exceeds the results obtained, great as they may be, since there is no warning to pause here. Nothing gives satisfaction and all this agitation is uninterruptedly maintained without appeasement. Above all, since this race for an unattainable goal can give no other pleasure but that of the race itself, if it is one, once it is interrupted the participants are left empty-handed. At the same time the struggle grows more violent and painful, both from being less controlled and because competition is greater. All classes contend among themselves because no established classification any longer exists. Effort grows, just when it becomes less productive. How could the desire to live not be weakened under such conditions?

This explanation is confirmed by the remarkable immunity of poor countries. Poverty protects against suicide because it is a restraint in itself. No matter how one acts, desires have to depend upon resources to some extent; actual possessions are partly the criterion of those aspired to. So the less one has the less he is tempted to extend the range of his needs indefinitely. Lack of power, compelling moderation, accustoms men to it, while nothing excites envy if no one has superfluity. Wealth, on the other hand, by the power it bestows, deceives us into believing that we depend on ourselves only. Reducing the resistance we encounter from objects, it suggests the possibility of unlimited success against them. The less limited one feels, the more intolerable all limitation appears. Not without reason, therefore, have so many religions dwelt on the advantages and moral value of poverty. It is actually the best school for teaching self-restraint. Forcing us to constant self-discipline, it prepares us to accept collective discipline with equanimity, while wealth, exalting the individual, may always arouse the spirit of rebellion which is the very source of immorality. This, of course, is no reason why humanity should not improve its material condition. But though the moral danger involved in every growth of prosperity is not irremediable, it should not be forgotten.

If anomie never appeared except, as in the above instances, in intermittent spurts and acute crisis, it might cause the social suicide-rate to vary from time to time, but it would not be a regular, constant factor. In one sphere of social life, however—the sphere of trade and industry—it is actually in a chronic state.

For a whole century, economic progress has mainly consisted in freeing industrial relations from all regulation. Until very recently, it was the function of a whole system of moral forces to exert this discipline. First, the influence of religion was felt alike by workers and masters, the poor and the rich. It consoled the former and taught them contentment with their lot by informing them of the providential nature of the social order, that the share of each class was assigned by God himself, and by holding out the hope for just compensation in a world to come in return for the inequalities of this world. It governed the latter, recalling that worldly interests are not man's entire lot, that they must be subordinate to other and higher interests, and that they should therefore not be pursued without rule or measure. Temporal power, in turn, restrained the scope of economic functions by its supremacy over them and by the relatively subordinate role it assigned them. Finally, within the business world proper, the occupational groups by regulating salaries, the price of products and production itself, indirectly fixed the average level of income on which needs are partially based by the very force of circumstances. However, we do not mean to propose this organization as a model. Clearly it would be inadequate to existing societies without great changes. What we stress is its existence, the fact of its useful influence, and that nothing today has come to take its place.

Actually, religion has lost most of its power. And government, instead of regulating economic life, has become its tool and servant. The most opposite schools, orthodox economists and extreme socialists, unite to reduce government to the role of a more or less passive intermediary among the various social functions. The former wish to make it simply the guardian of individual contracts; the latter leave it the task of doing the collective bookkeeping, that is, of recording the demands of consumers, transmitting them to producers, inventorying the total revenue and distributing it according to a fixed formula. But both refuse it any power to subordinate other social organs to itself and to make them converge toward one dominant aim. On both sides nations are declared to have the single or chief purpose of achieving industrial prosperity; such is the implication of the dogma of economic materialism, the basis of both apparently opposed systems. And as these theories merely express the state of opinion, industry, instead of being still regarded as a means to an end transcending itself, has become the supreme end of individuals and societies alike. Thereupon the appetites thus excited have become freed of any limiting authority. By sanctifying them, so to speak, this apotheosis of well-being has placed them above all human law. Their restraint seems like a sort of sacrilege. For this reason, even the purely utilitarian regulation of them exercised by the industrial world itself through the medium of occupational groups has been unable to persist. Ultimately, this liberation of desires has been made worse by the very development of industry and the almost infinite extension of the market. So long as the producer could gain his profits only in his immediate neighborhood, the restricted amount of possible gain could not much overexcite ambition. Now that he may assume to have almost the entire world as his customer, how could passions accept their former confinement in the face of such limitless prospects?

Such is the source of the excitement predominating in this part of society, and which has thence extended to the other parts. There, the state of crisis and anomie is constant and, so to speak, normal. From top to bottom of the ladder, greed is aroused without knowing where to find ultimate foothold. Nothing can calm it, since its goal is far beyond all it can attain. Reality seems valueless by comparison with the dreams of fevered imaginations; reality is therefore abandoned, but so too is possibility abandoned when it in turn becomes reality. A thirst arises for novelties, unfamiliar pleasures, nameless sensations, all of which lose their savor once known. Henceforth one has no strength to endure the least reverse. The whole fever subsides and the sterility of all the tumult is apparent, and it is seen that all these new sensations in their infinite quantity cannot form a solid foundation of happiness to support one during days of trial. The wise man, knowing how to enjoy achieved results without having constantly to replace them with others, finds in them an attachment to life in the hour of difficulty. But the man who has always pinned all his hopes on the future and lived with his eyes fixed upon it, has nothing in the past as a comfort against the present's afflictions, for the past was nothing to him but a series of hastily experienced stages. What blinded him to himself was his expectation always to find further on the happiness he had so far missed. Now he is stopped in his tracks; from now on nothing remains behind or ahead of him to fix his gaze upon. Weariness alone, moreover, is enough to bring disillusionment, for he cannot in the end escape the futility of an endless pursuit.

We may even wonder if this moral state is not principally what makes economic catastrophes of our day so fertile in suicides. In societies where a man is subjected to a healthy discipline, he submits more readily to the blows of chance. The necessary effort for sustaining a little more discomfort costs him relatively little, since he is used to discomfort and constraint. But when every constraint is hateful in itself, how can closer constraint not seem intoler-

able? There is no tendency to resignation in the feverish impatience of men's lives. When there is no other aim but to outstrip constantly the point arrived at, how painful to be thrown back! Now this very lack of organization characterizing our economic condition throws the door wide to every sort of adventure. Since imagination is hungry for novelty, and ungoverned, it gropes at random. Setbacks necessarily increase with risks and thus crises multiply, just when they are becoming more destructive.

Yet these dispositions are so inbred that society has grown to accept them and is accustomed to think them normal. It is everlastingly repeated that it is man's nature to be eternally dissatisfied, constantly to advance, without relief or rest, toward an indefinite goal. The longing for infinity is daily represented as a mark of moral distinction, whereas it can only appear within unregulated consciences which elevate to a rule the lack of rule from which they suffer. The doctrine of the most ruthless and swift progress has become an article of faith. But other theories appear parallel with those praising the advantages of instability, which, generalizing the situation that gives them birth, declare life evil, claim that it is richer in grief than in pleasure and that it attracts men only by false claims. Since this disorder is greatest in the economic world, it has most victims there.

Industrial and commercial functions are really among the occupations which furnish the greatest number of suicides. (see Table [1]) Almost on a level with the liberal professions, they sometimes surpass them; they are especially more afflicted than agriculture, where the old regulative forces still make their appearance felt most and where the fever of business has least penetrated. Here is best recalled what was once the general constitution of the economic order. And the divergence would be yet greater if, among the suicides of industry, employers were distinguished from workmen, for the former are probably most stricken by the state of anomie. The enormous rate of those with independent means (720 per million) sufficiently shows that the possessors of most comfort suffer most. Everything that enforces subordination attenuates the effects of this state. At least the horizon of the lower classes is limited by those above them, and for this same reason their desires are more modest. Those who have only empty space above them are almost inevitably lost in it, if no force restrains them.

Anomie, therefore, is a regular and specific factor in suicide in our modern societies; one of the springs from which the annual contingent feeds. So we have here a new type to distinguish from the others. It differs from them in its dependence, not on the way in which individuals are attached to society, but on how it regulates them. Egoistic suicide results from man's no longer finding a basis for existence in life; altruistic suicide, because this basis for existence appears to man situated beyond life itself. The third sort of suicide, the existence of which has just been shown, results from man's activity's lacking regulation and his consequent sufferings. By virtue of its origin we shall assign this last variety the name of *anomic suicide*.

Certainly, this and egoistic suicide have kindred ties. Both spring from society's insufficient presence in individuals. But the sphere of its absence is not the same in both cases. In egoistic suicide it is deficient in truly collective activity, thus depriving the latter of object and meaning. In anomic suicide, society's influence is lacking in the basically individual passions, thus leaving them without a check-rein. In spite of their relationship, therefore, the two types are independent of each other. We may offer society everything social in us, and still be unable to control our desires; one may live in an anomic state without being egoistic, and vice versa. These two sorts of suicide therefore do not draw their chief recruits from the same social environments; one has its principal field among intellectual careers, the world of thought—the other, the industrial or commercial world.

Primitive Classifications and Social Knowledge*
Èmile Durkheim and Marcel Mauss (1903)

The foregoing permits the conclusion that the Zuñi system is really a development and a complication of the Australian system. But what finally demonstrates the reality of this relationship is that it is possible to discover the intermediate stages connecting these extremes, and thus to discern how the one developed from the other.

The Omaha tribe of the Sioux, described by Dorsey, are precisely in this mixed position: the classification of things by clans is still very clear, and was formerly even clearer, but the systematic idea of regions is only in process of formation.

The tribe is divided into two moieties, each containing five clans. These clans are recruited by exclusively patrilineal descent; which is to say that totemic organization, properly speaking, and the cult of the totem are in decline. Each of these is sub-divided in its turn into sub-clans which themselves are sometimes further sub-divided. Dorsey does not say that everything in the world is divided among these different groups. But if the classification is not exhaustive, and perhaps never really was, certainly it must

---

*Republished with permission of University of Chicago Press, from *Primitive Classifications*, by Èmile Durkheim and Marcel Mauss, pp. 55-62, 87-88. Copyright 1963, University of Chicago Press; permission conveyed through Copyright Clearance Center, Inc.

TABLE [1] Suicides per Million Persons of Different Occupations

	Trade	Transportation	Industry	Agriculture	Liberal[a] Professions
France (1878–87)[b]	440	.....	340	240	300
Switzerland (1876)	664	1,514	577	304	558
Italy (1866–76)	277	152.6	80.4	26.7	618[c]
Prussia (1883–90)	754	.....	456	315	832
Bavaria (1884–91)	465	.....	369	153	454
Belgium (1886–90)	421	.....	160	160	100
Wurttemberg (1873–78)	273	.....	190	206	...
Saxony (1878)		341.59[d]		71.17	...

[a]When statistics distinguish several different sorts of liberal occupations, we show as a specimen the one in which the suicide-rate is highest.

[b]From 1826 to 1880 economic functions seem less affected but were occupational statistics very accurate?

[c]This figure is reached only by men of letters.

[d]Figure represents Trade, Transportation and Industry combined for Saxony.

have been very comprehensive, at least in the past. This is shown by a study of the only complete clan which has been preserved for us; this is the Chatada clan, which is part of the first moiety. We shall leave on one side other accounts which are probably mutilated, and which in any case give us the same phenomena but with a lesser degree of complication.

The meaning of the word used to designate this clan is uncertain; but we have a fairly full list of the things which are connected with it. It comprises four sub-clans, which are themselves segmented.

The first sub-clan is that of the black bear. It comprises the black bear, the raccoon, the grizzly bear, and the porcupine, which seem to be totems of the segments.

The second is "they who do not eat (small) birds." Under it come: (1) hawks; (2) blackbirds, which are themselves divided into those with white heads, red heads, and yellow heads, and those with red wings; (3) grey blackbirds, or "Thunder people," who in turn are sub-divided into meadow larks and prairie chickens; and (4) owls, themselves divided into large, medium and small.

The third sub-clan is that of the eagle; it comprises in the first place three kinds of eagle; and a fourth segment which is called "Workers" and appears not to be related to a particular order of things.

Lastly, the fourth sub-clan is that of the turtle. It is related to the fog, which its members have the power to stop. Four particular species of the same animal are subsumed under the genus turtle.

Since we may justifiably believe that this case was not unique, and that many other clans must have possessed similar divisions and sub-divisions, it is not a bold supposition that the system of classification still to be observed among the Omaha was once more complex than it is today. Now besides this distribution of things, analogous to that reported from Australia, we can see the apparition, though in a rudimentary form, of notions of orientation.

When the tribe camps, the encampment is made in a circular form; and within this circle each particular group has a fixed place. The two moieties are respectively to the right and the left of the route followed by the tribe, the ascription of sides being made with reference to the point of departure. Within the semicircle occupied by each moiety, the clans, in their turn, are clearly localized with respect to each other, and the same is the case with the sub-clans. The places thus assigned to them depend less on their relationships to each other than on their social functions, and consequently on the nature of the

things subordinate to them and over which their influence is thought to be exercised. Thus in each moiety there is a clan which stands in a special relationship to thunder and war; one is the elk clan, the other that of the Ictasandas. They are placed facing each other at the camp entrance, more ritual than real, which they guard, and it is by relation to them that the other clans are disposed, still according to the same principle. Things are thus distributed in this way within the camp at the same time as the social groups to which they are attributed. Space is shared among the clans, and among beings, events, etc. which belong to these clans. But it is clear that what is divided in this way is not cosmic space, but only the space occupied by the tribe. Clans and things are orientated, not yet according to the cardinal points, but with reference to the centre of the camp. The divisions do not correspond to the quarters properly speaking, but to ahead and behind, right and left, with respect to this central point. Moreover, these particular divisions are attributed to the clans, rather than the clans being attributed to them as is the case among the Zuñi.

In other Sioux tribes the idea of orientation becomes more distinct. Like the Omaha, the Osage Indians are divided into two moieties, one situated to the right, the other to the left; but whereas among the former the functions of the two moieties merged at certain points (we have seen that each had a clan of war and the thunder), here they are clearly distinguished. One half of the tribe is in charge of war, the other of peace. This necessarily results in a more exact localization of things. We find the same organization among the Kansa Indians. Moreover, each of the clans and sub-clans stand in a definite relation to the four cardinal points. Lastly, among the Ponka we can go still further. As among the previous tribes, the circle formed by the tribe is divided into two equal halves corresponding to the two moieties. On the other hand, each moiety comprises four clans, but these are quite naturally reducible to two pairs; for the same characteristic element is attributed to two clans at the same time. From this results the following disposition of people and things. The circle is divided into four parts. In the first, to the left of the entrance, are two fire clans (or thunder clans); in the part situated at the back, two wind clans; in the first to the right, two water clans; and beyond, two earth clans. Each of the four elements is thus localized exactly in one of the four arcs of the total circumference. Given this, it is only necessary for the axis of this circumference to coincide with one of the two axes of the compass for clans and things to be oriented with relation to the cardinal points. And we know that in these tribes the entrance to the camp generally faces west.

But this orientation (which is partly hypothetical) remains indirect. The secondary groups of the tribe, together with everything subject to them, are situated in quarters of the camp which are more or less clearly oriented; but in not one of these cases is it reported that the clan stands in a particular relationship to any part of space in general. It is still a question of tribal space alone; so we continue to be fairly far from the Zuñi situation. To get close to this we have to leave America and return to Australia. We shall find in an Australian tribe a part of what we lack among the Sioux, which is a new and particularly decisive proof that the differences between what we have so far called the American system and the Australian system are not matters of simply local causes and are in no way irreducible.

This tribe is the Wotjobaluk, which we have already examined. It is true that Howitt, to whom we owe our information, does not say that the cardinal points play any part in the classification of things; and we have no reason at all to suspect the exactitude of his observations on this point. But as far as the clans are concerned there is no doubt at all; each of them is connected with a particular spatial region which is entirely its own. And this time it is not a question of a quarter of the camp, but of a delimited portion of the horizon in general. Each clan can thus be situated on the compass-card. The relation between the clan and its spatial region is so intimate that its members must be buried in the direction thus determined. For example, a Wartwut, hot wind, is buried "with the head a little to the west of north, that is, in the direction from which the hot wind blows in their country." The sun-people are buried in the direction of the sunrise, and so on for the others.

This division into spatial regions is so closely linked to the essence of the social organization of this tribe that Howitt sees it as a "mechanical method used by the Wotjobaluk to preserve and explain a record of their classes and totems, and of their relation to those and to each other." Two clans cannot be related without being *ipso facto* connected with two neighbouring regions in space. This is shown in Figure [1], which Howitt constructed according to statements made by a highly intelligent native. The latter, in order to describe the organization of the tribe, began by laying a stick pointing exactly to the east, since Ngaui, the sun, is the principal totem and all the others are determined in relation to it. In other words, it is the clan of the sun and the east-west orientation which must have provided the general orientation of the two moieties Krokitch and Gamutch, the former being situated above the east-west line, the other below. In fact, it can be seen from the Figure that the Gamutch moiety is situated entirely to the south, the other almost entirely to the north. A single Krokitch clan, No. 9, crosses over the east-west line, and we have every reason to believe that this anomaly is due to an error of observation or to a more or less late alteration in the original system. This would give us a moiety of the north and a moiety of the south, completely analogous to such as we have seen in other societies. The north-south line is fixed very exactly in the northern part by the pelican clan of Krokitch moiety, and in the southern part by the clan bearing the same name in Gamutch moiety. There are thus four sectors in which the other clans are located. As among the Omaha, the order in which they are arranged expresses relations of kinship between their totems. The spaces separating the clans bear the names of their primary clans, of which the others are segments. Thus clans 1 and 2 are described as "men of the sun"; the space between them is "wholly" of the white cockatoo. Since the white cockatoo is a synonym of the sun, as we have already shown, we may say that the whole of the sector between the east and the north is that of the sun. Similarly, the clans from 4 to 9, i.e. those going from north to west, are all segments of the pelican clan of the first moiety. It may be seen with what regularity, then, that things are oriented. . . .

Primitive classifications are therefore not singular or exceptional, having no analogy with those employed by more civilized peoples; on the contrary, they seem to be connected, with no break in continuity, to the first scientific classifications. In fact, however different they may be in certain respects from the latter, they nevertheless have all their essential characteristics. First of all, like all sophisticated classifications, they are systems of hierarchized notions. Things are not simply arranged by them in the form of isolated groups, but these groups stand in fixed relationships to each other and together form a single whole. Moreover, these systems, like those of science, have a purely speculative purpose. Their object is not to facilitate action, but to advance understanding, to make intelligible the relations which exist between things. Given certain concepts which are considered to be fundamental, the mind feels the

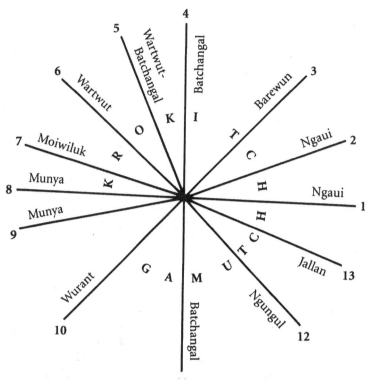

FIGURE [1] The following, so far as can be established, are the translations of the native terms designating the clans: 1 and 2 (Ngaui) mean "sun"; 3 (Barewun), "cave" (?); 4 and 11 (Batchangal), "pelican"; 5 (Wartwut-Batchangal), "hot wind-pelican"; 6 (Wartwut), "hot wind"; 7 (Moi), "carpet snake"; 8 and 9 (Munya), "kangaroo" (?); 10 (Wurant), "black cockatoo"; 12 (Ngungul), "sea"; 13 (Jallan), "death-adder."

need to connect to them the ideas which it forms about other things. Such classifications are thus intended, above all, to connect ideas, to unify knowledge; as such, they may be said without inexactitude to be scientific, and to constitute a first philosophy of nature. The Australian does not divide the universe between the totems of his tribe with a view to regulating his conduct or even to justify his practice; it is because, the idea of the totem being cardinal for him, he is under a necessity to place everything else that he knows in relation to it. We may therefore think that the conditions on which these very ancient classifications depend may have played an important part in the genesis of the classificatory function in general.

This is how it is that the idea of a logical classification was so hard to form, as we showed at the beginning of this work. It is because a logical classification is a classification of concepts. Now a concept is the notion of a clearly determined group of things; its limits may be marked precisely. Emotion, on the contrary, is something essentially fluid and inconsistent. Its contagious influence spreads far beyond its point of origin, extending to everything about it, so that it is not possible to say where its power of propagation ends. States of an emotional nature necessarily possess the same characteristic. It is not possible to say where they begin or where they end; they lose themselves in each other, and mingle their properties in such a way that they cannot be rigorously categorized. From another point of view, in order to be able to mark out the limits of a class, it is necessary to have analysed the characteristics by which the things assembled in this class are recognized and by which they are distinguished. Now emotion is naturally refractory to analysis, or at least lends itself uneasily to it, because it is too complex. Above all when it has a collective origin it defies critical and rational examination. The pressure exerted by the group on each of its members does not permit individuals to judge freely the notions which society itself has elaborated and in which it has placed something of its personality. Such constructs are sacred for individuals. Thus the history of scientific classification is, in the last analysis, the history of the stages by which this element of social affectivity has progressively weakened, leaving more and more room for the reflective thought of individuals. But it is not the case that these remote influences which we have just studied have ceased to be felt today. They have left behind them an effect which survives and which is always present; it is the very cadre of all classification, it is the ensemble of mental habits by virtue of which we conceive things and facts in the form of co-ordinated or hierarchized groups.

This example shows what light sociology throws on the genesis, and consequently the functioning, of logical operations. What we have tried to do for classification might equally be attempted for the other functions or fundamental notions of the understanding. We have already had occasion to mention, in passing, how even ideas so abstract as those of time and space are, at each point in their history, closely connected with the corresponding social organization. The same method could help us likewise to understand the manner in which the ideas of cause, substance, and the different modes of reasoning, etc. were formed. As soon as they are posed in sociological terms, all these questions, so long debated by metaphysicians and psychologists, will at last be liberated from the tautologies in which they have languished. At least, this is a new way which deserves to be tried.

The Cultural Logic of Collective Representations[*]
Èmile Durkheim (1912)

The fundamental categories of thought, and consequently of science, are of religious origin. We have seen that the same is true for magic and consequently for the different processes which have issued from it. On the other hand, it has long been known that up until a relatively advanced moment of evolution, moral and legal rules have been indistinguishable from ritual prescriptions. In summing up, then, it may be said that nearly all the great social institutions have been born in religion. Now in order that these principal aspects of the collective life may have commenced by being only varied aspects of the religious

life, it is obviously necessary that the religious life be the eminent form and, as it were, the concentrated expression of the whole collective life. If religion has given birth to all that is essential in society, it is because the idea of society is the soul of religion.

Religious forces are therefore human forces, moral forces. It is true that since collective sentiments can become conscious of themselves only by fixing themselves upon external objects, they have not been able to take form without adopting some of their characteristics from other things: they have thus acquired a sort of physical nature; in this way they have come to mix themselves with the life of the material world, and then have considered themselves capable of explaining what passes there. But when they are considered only from this point of view and this role, only their most superficial aspect is seen. In reality, the essential elements of which these collective sentiments are made have been borrowed by the understanding. It ordinarily seems that they should have a human character only when they are conceived under human forms; but even the most impersonal and the most anonymous are nothing else than objectified sentiments.

It is only by regarding religion from this angle that it is possible to see its real significance. If we stick closely to appearances, rites often give the effect of purely manual operations: they are anointings, washings, meals. To consecrate something, it is put in contact with a source of religious energy, just as to-day a body is put in contact with a source of heat or electricity to warm or electrize it; the two processes employed are not essentially different. Thus understood, religious technique seems to be a sort of mystic mechanics. But these material manoeuvres are only the external envelope under which the mental operations are hidden. Finally, there is no question of exercising a physical constraint upon blind and, incidentally, imaginary forces, but rather of reaching individual consciousnesses of giving them a direction and of disciplining them. It is sometimes said that inferior religions are materialistic. Such an expression is inexact. All religions, even the crudest, are in a sense spiritualistic: for the powers they put in play are before all spiritual, and also their principal object is to act upon the moral life. Thus it is seen that whatever has been done in the name of religion cannot have been done in vain: for it is necessarily the society that did it, and it is humanity that has reaped the fruits. . . .

Men alone have the faculty of conceiving the ideal, of adding something to the real. Now where

[*]From THE ELEMENTARY FORMS OF THE RELIGIOUS LIFE by Èmile Durkheim, translated by Joseph Ward Swain (London: George Allen & Unwin Ltd., 1913).

does this singular privilege come from? Before making it an initial fact or a mysterious virtue which escapes science, we must be sure that it does not depend upon empirically determinable conditions.

The explanation of religion which we have proposed has precisely this advantage, that it gives an answer to this question. For our definition of the sacred is that it is something added to and above the real: now the ideal answers to this same definition; we cannot explain one without explaining the other. In fact, we have seen that if collective life awakens religious thought on reaching a certain degree of intensity, it is because it brings about a state of effervescence which changes the conditions of psychic activity. Vital energies are over-excited, passions more active, sensations stronger; there are even some which are produced only at this moment. A man does not recognize himself; he feels himself transformed and consequently he transforms the environment which surrounds him. In order to account for the very particular impressions which he receives, he attributes to the things with which he is in most direct contact properties which they have not, exceptional powers and virtues which the objects of every-day experience do not possess. In a word, above the real world where his profane life passes he has placed another which, in one sense, does not exist except in thought, but to which he attributes a higher sort of dignity than to the first. Thus, from a double point of view it is an ideal world.

The formation of the ideal world is therefore not an irreducible fact which escapes science; it depends upon conditions which observation can touch; it is a natural product of social life. For a society to become conscious of itself and maintain at the necessary degree of intensity the sentiments which it thus attains, it must assemble and concentrate itself. Now this concentration brings about an exaltation of the mental life which takes form in a group of ideal conceptions where is portrayed the new life thus awakened; they correspond to this new set of psychical forces which is added to those which we have at our disposition for the daily tasks of existence. A society can neither create itself nor recreate itself without at the same time creating an ideal. This creation is not a sort of work of supererogation for it, by which it would complete itself, being already formed; it is the act by which it is periodically made and remade. Therefore when some oppose the ideal society to the real society, like two antagonists which would lead us in opposite directions, they materialize and oppose abstractions. The ideal society is not outside of the real society; it is a

part of it. Far from being divided between them as between two poles which mutually repel each other, we cannot hold to one without holding to the other. For a society is not made up merely of the mass of individuals who compose it, the ground which they occupy, the things which they use and the movements which they perform, but above all is the idea which it forms of itself. It is undoubtedly true that it hesitates over the manner in which it ought to conceive itself; it feels itself drawn in divergent directions. But these conflicts which break forth are not between the ideal and reality, but between two different ideals, that of yesterday and that of to-day, that which has the authority of tradition and that which has the hope of the future. There is surely a place for investigating whence these ideals evolve; but whatever solution may be given to this problem, it still remains that all passes in the world of the ideal.

Thus the collective ideal which religion expresses is far from being due to a vague innate power of the individual, but it is rather at the school of collective life that the individual has learned to idealize. It is in assimilating the ideals elaborated by society that he has become capable of conceiving the ideal. It is society which, by leading him within its sphere of action, has made him acquire the need of raising himself above the world of experience and has at the same time furnished him with the means of conceiving another. For society has constructed this new world in constructing itself, since it is society which this expresses. Thus both with the individual and in the group, the faculty of idealizing has nothing mysterious about it. It is not a sort of luxury which a man could get along without, but a condition of his very existence. He could not be a social being, that is to say, he could not be a man, if he had not acquired it. It is true that in incarnating themselves in individuals, collective ideals tend to individualize themselves. Each understands them after his own fashion and marks them with his own stamp; he suppresses certain elements and adds others. Thus the personal ideal disengages itself from the social ideal in proportion as the individual personality develops itself and becomes an autonomous source of action. But if we wish to understand this aptitude, so singular in appearance, of living outside of reality, it is enough to connect it with the social conditions upon which it depends.

Therefore it is necessary to avoid seeing in this theory of religion a simple restatement of historical materialism: that would be misunderstanding our thought to an extreme degree. In showing that religion is something essentially social, we do not mean to say that it confines itself to translating into another language the material forms of society and its immediate vital necessities. It is true that we take it as evident that social life depends upon its material foundation and bears its mark, just as the mental life of an individual depends upon his nervous system and in fact his whole organism. But collective consciousness is something more than a mere epiphenomenon of its morphological basis, just as individual consciousness is something more than a simple efflorescence of the nervous system. In order that the former may appear, a synthesis *sui generis* of particular consciousnesses is required. Now this synthesis has the effect of disengaging a whole world of sentiments, ideas and images which, once born, obey laws all their own. They attract each other, repel each other, unite, divide themselves, and multiply, though these combinations are not commanded and necessitated by the condition of the underlying reality. The life thus brought into being even enjoys so great an independence that it sometimes indulges in manifestations with no purpose or utility of any sort, for the mere pleasure of affirming itself. We have shown that this is often precisely the case with ritual activity and mythological thought. . . .

The nature of the concept . . . bespeaks its origin. If it is common to all, it is the work of the community. Since it bears the mark of no particular mind, it is clear that it was elaborated by a unique intelligence, where all others meet each other, and after a fashion, come to nourish themselves. If it has more stability than sensations or images, it is because the collective representations are more stable than the individual ones; for while an individual is conscious even of the slight changes which take place in his environment, only events of a greater gravity can succeed in affecting the mental status of a society. Every time that we are in the presence of a *type* of thought or action which is imposed uniformly upon particular wills or intelligences, this pressure exercised over the individual betrays the intervention of the group. Also, as we have already said, the concepts with which we ordinarily think are those of our vocabulary. Now it is unquestionable that language, and consequently the system of concepts which it translates, is the product of a collective elaboration. What it expresses is the manner in which society as a whole represents the facts of experience. The ideas which correspond to the diverse elements of language are thus collective representations....

It may be objected that we show the concept in one of its aspects only, and that its unique role is not the assuring of a harmony among minds, but also, and to a greater extent, their harmony with the nature of things. It seems as though it had a reason for existence only on condition of being true, that is to say, objective, and as though its impersonality were only a consequence of its objectivity. It is in regard to things, thought of as adequately as possible, that minds ought to communicate. Nor do we deny that the evolution of concepts has been partially in this direction. The concept which was first held as true because it was collective tends to be no longer collective except on condition of being held as true: we demand its credentials of it before according it our confidence. But we must not lose sight of the fact that even to-day the great majority of the concepts which we use are not methodically constituted; we get them from language, that is to say, from common experience, without submitting them to any criticism. The scientifically elaborated and criticized concepts are always in the very slight minority. Also, between them and those which draw all their authority from the fact that they are collective, there are only differences of degree. A collective representation presents guarantees of objectivity by the fact that it is collective: for it is not without sufficient reason that it has been able to generalize and maintain itself with persistence. If it were out of accord with the nature of things, it would never have been able to acquire an extended and prolonged empire over intellects. At bottom, the confidence inspired by scientific concepts is due to the fact that they can be methodically controlled. But a collective representation is necessarily submitted to a control that is repeated indefinitely; the men who accept it verify it by their own experience. Therefore, it could not be wholly inadequate for its subject. It is true that it may express this by means of imperfect symbols; but scientific symbols themselves are never more than approximative. It is precisely this principle which is at the basis of the method which we follow in the study of religious phenomena: we take it as an axiom that religious beliefs, howsoever strange their appearance may be at times, contain a truth which must be discovered. . . .

Undoubtedly it will be easily understood that since they are themselves concepts, they are the work of the group. It can even be said that there are no other concepts which present to an equal degree the signs by which a collective representation is recognized. In fact, their stability and impersonality are such that they have often passed as being absolutely universal and immutable. Also, as they express the fundamental conditions for an agreement between minds, it seems evident that they have been elaborated by society.

But the problem concerning them is more complex, for they are social in another sense and, as it were, in the second degree. They not only come from society, but the things which they express are of a social nature. Not only is it society which has founded them, but their contents are the different aspects of the social being; the category of class was at first indistinct from the concept of the human group; it is the rhythm of social life which is at the basis of the category of time; the territory occupied by the society furnished the material for the category of space; it is the collective force which was the prototype of the concept of efficient force, an essential element in the category of causality. However, the categories are not made to be applied only to the social realm; they reach out to all reality. Then how is it that they have taken from society the models upon which they have been constructed?

It is because they are the pre-eminent concepts, which have a preponderating part in our knowledge. In fact, the function of the categories is to dominate and envelop all the other concepts; they are permanent moulds for the mental life. Now for them to embrace such an object, they must be founded upon a reality of equal amplitude.

Undoubtedly the relations which they express exist in an implicit way in individual consciousness. The individual lives in time, and, as we have said, he has a certain sense of temporal orientation. He is situated at a determined point in space, and it has even been held, and sustained with good reasons, that all sensations have something special about them. He has a feeling of resemblances; similar representations are brought together and the new representation formed by their union has a sort of generic character. We also have the sensation of a certain regularity in the order of the succession of phenomena; even an animal is not incapable of this. However, all these relations are strictly personal for the individual who recognizes them, and consequently the notion of them which he may have can in no case go beyond his own narrow horizon. The generic images which are formed in my consciousness by the fusion of similar images represent only the objects which I have perceived directly; there is nothing there which could give me the idea of a class, that is to say, of a mould including the *whole* group of all possible objects which satisfy the same

condition. Also, it would be necessary to have the idea of group in the first place, and the mere observations of our interior life could never awaken that in us. But, above all, there is no individual experience, howsoever extended and prolonged it may be, which could give a suspicion of the existence of a whole class which would embrace every single being, and to which other classes are only co-ordinated or subordinated species. This idea of *all*, which is at the basis of the classifications which we have just cited, could not have come from the individual himself, who is only a part in relation to the whole and who never attains more than an infinitesimal fraction of reality. And yet there is perhaps no other category of greater importance; for as the role of the categories is to envelop all the other concepts, the category *par excellence* would seem to be this very concept of *totality.* The theorists of knowledge ordinarily postulate it as if it came of itself, while it really surpasses the contents of each individual consciousness taken alone to an infinite degree.

For the same reasons, the space which I know by my senses, of which I am the centre and where everything is disposed in relation to me, could not be space in general, which contains all extensions and where these are co-ordinated by personal guide-lines which are common to everybody. In the same way, the concrete duration which I feel passing within me and with me could not give me the idea of time in general: the first expresses only the rhythm of my individual life; the second should correspond to the rhythm of a life which is not that of any individual in particular, but in which all participate. In the same way, finally, the regularities which I am able to conceive in the manner in which my sensations succeed one another may well have a value for me; they explain how it comes about that when I am given the first of two phenomena whose concurrence I have observed, I tend to expect the other. But this personal state of expectation could not be confounded with the conception of a universal order of succession which imposes itself upon all minds and all events.

Since the world expressed by the entire system of concepts is the one that society regards, society alone can furnish the most general notions with which it should be represented. Such an object can be embraced only by a subject which contains all the individual subjects within it. Since the universe does not exist except in so far as it is thought of, and since it is not completely thought of except by society, it takes a place in this latter; it becomes a part of society's interior life, while this is the totality, outside of which nothing exists. The concept of totality is only the abstract form of the concept of society: it is the whole which includes all things, the supreme class which embraces all other classes. Such is the final principle upon which repose all these primitive classifications where beings from every realm are placed and classified in social forms, exactly like men. But if the world is inside of society, the space which this latter occupies becomes confounded with space in general. In fact, we have seen how each thing has its assigned place in social space, and the degree to which this space in general differs from the concrete expanses which we perceive is well shown by the fact that this localization is wholly ideal and in no way resembles what it would have been if it had been dictated to us by sensuous experience alone. For the same reason, the rhythm of collective life dominates and embraces the varied rhythms of all the elementary lives from which it results; consequently the time which it expresses dominates and embraces all particular durations. It is time in general. For a long time the history of the world has been only another aspect of the history of society. The one commences with the other; the periods of the first are determined by the periods of the second. This impersonal and total duration is measured, and the guide-lines in relation to which it is divided and organized are fixed by the movements of concentration or dispersion of society; or, more generally, the periodical necessities for a collective renewal. If these critical instants are generally attached to some material phenomenon, such as the regular recurrence of such or such a star or the alternation of the seasons, it is because objective signs are necessary to make this essentially social organization intelligible to all. In the same way, finally, the causal relation, from the moment when it is collectively stated by the group, becomes independent of every individual consciousness; it rises above all particular minds and events. It is a law whose value depends upon no person. We have already shown how it is clearly thus that it seems to have originated.

Another reason explains why the constituent elements of the categories should have been taken from social life: it is because the relations which they express could not have been learned except in and through society. If they are in a sense immanent in the life of an individual, he has neither a reason nor the means for learning them, reflecting upon them and forming them into distinct ideas. In order to orient himself personally in space and to know at what moments he should satisfy his various organic needs, he has no need of making, once and for all, a conceptual representation of time and space. Many animals are able to find the road which leads to places with which they are familiar; they come back at a proper moment without knowing any of the categories; sensations are enough to direct them automatically. They would also be enough for men, if their sensations had to satisfy only individual needs. To recognize the fact that one thing resembles another which we have already experienced, it is in no way necessary that we arrange them all in groups and species: the way in which similar images call up each other and unite is enough to give the feeling of resemblance. The impression that a certain thing has already been seen or experienced implies no classification. To recognize the things which we should seek or from which we should flee, it would not be necessary to attach the effects of the two to their causes by a logical bond, if individual conveniences were the only ones in question. Purely empirical sequences and strong connections between the concrete representations would be as sure guides for the will. Not only is it true that the animal has no others, but also our own personal conduct frequently supposes nothing more. The prudent man is the one who has a very clear sensation of what must be done, but which he would ordinarily be quite incapable of stating as a general law.

It is a different matter with society. This is possible only when the individuals and things which compose it are divided into certain groups, that is to say, classified, and when these groups are classified in relation to each other. Society supposes a self-conscious organization which is nothing other than a classification. This organization of society naturally extends itself to the place which this occupies. To avoid all collisions, it is necessary that each particular group have a determined portion of space assigned to it: in other terms, it is necessary that space in general be divided, differentiated, arranged, and that these divisions and arrangements be known to everybody. On the other hand, every summons to a celebration, a hunt or a military expedition implies fixed and established dates, and consequently that a common time is agreed upon, which everybody conceives in the same fashion. Finally, the co-operation of many persons with the same end in view is possible only when they are in agreement as to the relation which exists between this end and the means of attaining it, that is to say, when the same causal relation is admitted by all the co-operators in the enterprise. It is not surprising, therefore, that social time, social space, social classes and causality should be the basis of the corresponding categories, since it is under their social forms that these different relations were first grasped with a certain clarity by the human intellect.

In summing up, then, we must say that society is not at all the illogical or a-logical, incoherent and fantastic being which it has too often been considered. Quite on the contrary, the collective consciousness is the highest form of the psychic life, since it is the consciousness of the consciousnesses. Being placed outside of and above individual and local contingencies, it sees things only in their permanent and essential aspects, which it crystallizes into communicable ideas. At the same time that it sees from above, it sees farther; at every moment of time, it embraces all known reality; that is why it alone can furnish the mind with the moulds which are applicable to the totality of things and which make it possible to think of them. It does not create these moulds artificially; it finds them within itself; it does nothing but become conscious of them. They translate the ways of being which are found in all the stages of reality but which appear in their full clarity only at the summit, because the extreme complexity of the psychic life which passes there necessitates a greater development of consciousness. Attributing social origins to logical thought is not debasing it or diminishing its value or reducing it to nothing more than a system of artificial combinations; on the contrary, it is relating it to a cause which implies it naturally. But this is not saying that the ideas elaborated in this way are at once adequate for their object. If society is something universal in relation to the individual, it is none the less an individuality itself, which has its own personal physiognomy and its idiosyncrasies; it is a particular subject and consequently particularizes whatever it thinks of. Therefore collective representations also contain subjective elements, and these must be progressively rooted out, if we are to approach reality more closely. But howsoever crude these may have been at the beginning, the fact remains that with them the germ of a new mentality was given, to which the individual could never have raised himself by his own efforts: by them the way was opened to a stable, impersonal and organized thought which then had nothing to do except to develop its nature. . . .

Thus sociology appears destined to open a new way to the science of man. Up to the present, thinkers were placed before this double alternative: either

explain the superior and specific faculties of men by connecting them to the inferior forms of his being, the reason to the senses, or the mind to matter, which is equivalent to denying their uniqueness; or else attach them to some super-experimental reality which was postulated, but whose existence could be established by no observation. What put them in this difficulty was the fact that the individual passed as being the *finis natur*—the ultimate creation of nature; it seemed that there was nothing beyond him, or at least nothing that science could touch. But from the moment when it is recognized that above the individual there is society, and that this is not a nominal being created by reason, but a system of active forces, a new manner of explaining men becomes possible. To conserve his distinctive traits it is no longer necessary to put them outside experience. At least, before going to this last extremity, it would be well to see if that which surpasses the individual, though it is within him, does not come from this super-individual reality which we experience in society. To be sure, it cannot be said at present to what point these explanations may be able to reach, and whether or not they are of a nature to resolve all the problems. But it is equally impossible to mark in advance a limit beyond which they cannot go. What must be done is to try the hypothesis and submit it as methodically as possible to the control of facts. This is what we have tried to do.

Friedrich Nietzsche (1844–1900) was born in a small town near Leipzig. His father, who had been mentally ill, died in 1848 and two years later his older brother died. This left the boy to grow up in a household of women and girls. He entered boarding school in 1858 where his native brilliance was recognized. Yet, he was in ill health for one or another reasons most of his life. So much so that after graduate studies in Bonn and a distinguished teaching and writing career at the University of Basel in Switzerland, he was forced to retire in 1878 in his mid-40s to live on as an independent scholar. A profound mental collapse in 1889 ended his productive writing life. From Nietzsche's earliest great book, *Human All to Human* (1878), through *The Gay Science* (1882), *Thus Spoke Zarathustra* (1883), *On the Genealogy of Morality* (1887) to *Twilight of the Idols*, *The Antichrist*, and *Ecce Homo* (all three in 1888), he was a literary fountain of contrarian, superbly and powerful expressed, radical ideas directed generally at the pretenses of European culture. The selection from *Beyond Good and Evil* (1886) is, at once, an illustration of Nietzsche's biting criticism of modern Europe and his social theoretical sensibilities.

Peoples and Countries*
Friedrich Nietzsche (1886)

We "good Europeans," we also have hours when we allow ourselves a warm-hearted patriotism, a plunge and relapse into old loves and narrow views—I have just given an example of it—hours of national excitement, of patriotic anguish, and all other sorts of old-fashioned floods of sentiment. Duller spirits may perhaps only get done with what confines its operations in us to hours and plays itself out in hours—in a considerable time: some in half a year, others in half a lifetime, according to the speed and strength with which they digest and "change their material." Indeed, I could think of sluggish, hesitating races, which even in our rapidly moving Europe, would require half a century ere they could surmount such atavistic attacks of patriotism and soil-attachment, and return once more to reason, that is to say, to "good Europeanism." And while digressing on this possibility, I happen to become an ear-witness of a conversation between two old patriots—they were evidently both hard of hearing and consequently spoke all the louder. "HE has as much, and knows as much, philosophy as a peasant or a corps-student," said the one—"he is still innocent. But what does that matter nowadays! It is the age of the masses: they lie on their belly before everything that is massive. And so also in politics. A statesman who rears up for them a new Tower of Babel, some monstrosity of empire and power, they call 'great'—what does it matter that we more prudent and conservative ones do not meanwhile give up the old belief that it is only the great thought that gives greatness to an action or affair. Supposing a statesman were to bring his people into the position of being obliged henceforth to practise 'high politics,' for which they were by nature badly endowed and prepared, so that they would have to sacrifice their old and reliable virtues, out of love to a new and doubtful mediocrity;—supposing a statesman were to condemn his people generally to 'practise politics,' when they have hitherto had something better to do and think about, and when in the depths of their souls they have been unable to free themselves from a prudent loathing of the restlessness, emptiness, and noisy wranglings of the essentially politics-practising nations;—supposing such a statesman were to stimulate the slumbering passions and avidities of his people, were to make a stigma out of their former diffidence and delight in aloofness, an offence out of their exoticism and hidden permanency, were to depreciate their most radical proclivities, subvert their consciences, make their minds narrow, and their tastes 'national'—what! a statesman who should do all this, which his people would have to do penance for throughout their whole future, if they had a future, such a statesman would be GREAT, would he?"—"Undoubtedly!" replied the other old patriot vehemently, "otherwise he COULD NOT have done it! It was mad perhaps to wish such a thing! But perhaps everything great has been just as mad at its commencement!"—"Misuse of words!" cried his interlocutor, contradictorily—"strong! strong! Strong and mad! NOT great!"—The old men had obviously become heated as they thus shouted their "truths" in each other's faces, but I, in my happiness and apartness, considered how soon a stronger one may become master of the strong, and also that there is a compensation for the intellectual superficialising of a nation—namely, in the deepening of another.

Whether we call it "civilization," or "humanising," or "progress," which now distinguishes the European, whether we call it simply, without praise or blame, by the political formula the DEMOCRATIC movement in Europe—behind all the moral and political foregrounds pointed to by such formulas, an immense PHYSIOLOGICAL PROCESS goes on, which is ever extending the process of the assimilation of Europeans, their increasing detachment from the conditions under which, climatically and hereditarily, united races originate, their increasing independence of every definite milieu, that for centuries would fain inscribe itself with equal demands on soul and body,—that is to say, the slow emergence of an essentially SUPER-NATIONAL and nomadic species of man, who possesses, physiologically speaking, a maximum of the art and power of adaptation as his typical distinction. This process of the EVOLVING EUROPEAN, which can be retarded in its TEMPO by great relapses, but will perhaps just gain and

---

*Friedrich Nietzsche, "Peoples and Countries," *Beyond Good and Evil: Prelude to a Philosophy of the Future*, New York: The Macmillan Company, 1907. Helen Zimmern, translator.

grow thereby in vehemence and depth—the still-raging storm and stress of "national sentiment" pertains to it, and also the anarchism which is appearing at present—this process will probably arrive at results on which its naive propagators and panegyrists, the apostles of "modern ideas," would least care to reckon. The same new conditions under which on an average a levelling and mediocrising of man will take place—a useful, industrious, variously serviceable, and clever gregarious man— are in the highest degree suitable to give rise to exceptional men of the most dangerous and attractive qualities. For, while the capacity for adaptation, which is every day trying changing conditions, and begins a new work with every generation, almost with every decade, makes the POWERFULNESS of the type impossible; while the collective impression of such future Europeans will probably be that of numerous, talkative, weak-willed, and very handy workmen who REQUIRE a master, a commander, as they require their daily bread; while, therefore, the democratising of Europe will tend to the production of a type prepared for SLAVERY in the most subtle sense of the term: the STRONG man will necessarily in individual and exceptional cases, become stronger and richer than he has perhaps ever been before—owing to the unprejudicedness of his schooling, owing to the immense variety of practice, art, and disguise. I meant to say that the democratising of Europe is at the same time an involuntary arrangement for the rearing of TYRANTS—taking the word in all its meanings, even in its most spiritual sense.

Max Weber (1864–1920) was the ideal-type of the German university scholar. Master of several fields, Weber wrote classic works on music, economic and legal history, religion, and sociology. He was a founder of German academic sociology even though a debilitating mental breakdown ultimately forced him to abandon his own professorship. Weber's best-known book, *The Protestant Ethic and the Spirit of Capitalism,* appeared in 1905, just as he emerged from illness to enter the most productive period of his scholarly life. The book ended with his famous image of the iron cage of rationality, his most telling indictment of the dehumanizing effects of the modern world's overly rationalized social order. Today, Weber is still a source of original ideas in political

theory, cultural and religious studies, and the sociologies of organizations and law, among other fields. His lasting importance as a social theorist is due, in large part, to the complexity of his thought. He sought to found a formal science that was also sensitive to subjective meaning in human life. He described the orderly evolution of capitalism and modern bureaucracy, yet he could bring to his scientific descriptions a powerful moral concern for the human spirit. In 1918, in Munich, he delivered his public lectures on *Politics as a Vocation* and *Science as a Vocation,* which together demonstrate Weber's grasp of the complex demands of the scientific life in politically troubled times. He was first and foremost a scientist, yet he was active in German public life. He died in 1920 in his fifty-sixth year, leaving his wife, Marianne, who had participated with him in the intellectual world centered in their home in Heidelberg.

"The Spirit of Capitalism and the Iron Cage" comprises two parts of Weber's *Protestant Ethic.* The "spirit of capitalism" is Weber's most famous ideal type (a unique feature of his method). It is used here to present the ethical orientation, or disposition, of the modern capitalist. The iron cage metaphor at the end of *Protestant Ethic* is the best-known expression of Weber's doubts about the modern world, which are developed, in more technical terms, in his analysis of "The Bureaucratic Machine." The fragment "What Is Politics?" from Weber's *Politics as a Vocation,* outlines his theory of social domination, which is still used in contemporary critical theories. "The Types of Legitimate Domination" (1909–1920) illustrates the breadth of Weber's theory. Here, he touched on legal, political, and sociological insights to formulate his important theory of traditional, modern, and charismatic authority. At the same time, these selections show the extent to which his sociology attempted to solve the riddle of social life that becomes acute in the modern world: Why do people agree to obey authority? "Class, Status, Party," (1909–1920) though difficult in places, is worth reading because it is one of Weber's most succinct attempts to supplement Marx's class analysis by demonstrating the importance of status groups—as well as political parties and class position—in determining how social power is distributed in modern societies. This selection, in particular, was an important model for C. Wright Mills's critique of post–World War II American society, *The Power Elite* (1956).

The Spirit of Capitalism and the Iron Cage[*]
Max Weber (1905)

In the title of this study is used the somewhat pretentious phrase, the *spirit* of capitalism. What is to be understood by it? The attempt to give anything like a definition of it brings out certain difficulties which are in the very nature of this type of investigation.

If any object can be found to which this term can be applied with any understandable meaning, it can only be an historical individual, i.e. a complex of elements associated in historical reality which we unite into a conceptual whole from the standpoint of their cultural significance.

Such an historical concept, however, since it refers in its content to a phenomenon significant for its unique individuality, cannot be defined according to the formula *genus proximum, differentia specifica*, but it must be gradually put together out of the individual parts which are taken from historical reality to make it up. Thus the final and definitive concept cannot stand at the beginning of the investigation, but must come at the end. We must, in other words, work out in the course of the discussion, as its most important result, the best conceptual formulation of what we here understand by the spirit of capitalism, that is the best from the point of view which interests us here. This point of view (the one of which we shall speak later) is, further, by no means the only possible one from which the historical phenomena we are investigating can be analysed. Other standpoints would, for this as for every historical phenomenon, yield other characteristics as the essential ones. The result is that it is by no means necessary to understand by the spirit of capitalism only what it will come to mean to *us* for the purposes of our analysis. This is a necessary result of the nature of historical concepts which attempt for their methodological purposes not to grasp historical reality in abstract general formulae, but in concrete genetic sets of relations which are inevitably of a specifically unique and individual character.

Thus, if we try to determine the object, the analysis and historical explanation of which we are attempting, it cannot be in the form of a conceptual definition, but at least in the beginning only a provisional description of what is here meant by the spirit of capitalism. Such a description is, however, indispensable in order clearly to understand the object of the investigation. For this purpose we turn to a document of that spirit which contains what we are looking for in almost classical purity, and at the same time has the advantage of being free from all direct relationship to religion, being thus, for our purposes, free of preconceptions.

Remember, that *time* is money. [*even today*] He that can earn ten shillings a day by his labour, and goes abroad, or sits idle, one half of that day, though he spends but sixpence during his diversion or idleness, ought not to reckon *that* the only expense; he has really spent, or rather thrown away, five shillings besides.

Remember, that *credit* is money. If a man lets his money lie in my hands after it is due, he gives me the interest, or so much as I can make of it during that time. This amounts to a considerable sum where a man has good and large credit, and makes good use of it.

Remember, that money is of the prolific, generating nature. Money can beget money, and its offspring can beget more, and so on. Five shillings turned is six, turned again it is seven and threepence, and so on, till it becomes a hundred pounds. The more there is of it, the more it produces every turning, so that the profits rise quicker and quicker. He that kills a breeding-sow, destroys all her offspring to the thousandth generation. He that murders a crown, destroys all that it might have produced, even scores of pounds.

Remember this saying, *The good paymaster is lord of another man's purse.* He that is known to pay punctually and exactly to the time he promises, may at any time, and on any occasion, raise all the money his friends can spare. This is sometimes of great use. After industry and frugality, nothing contributes more to the raising of a young man in the world than punctuality and justice in all his dealings; therefore never keep borrowed money an hour beyond the time you promised, lest a disappointment shut up your friend's purse for ever.

The most trifling actions that affect a man's credit are to be regarded. The sound of your hammer at five in the morning, or eight

[*] Excerpt from Weber, Max, *Protestant Ethic & the Spirit of Capitalism*, 1st Edition, © 1977. Reprinted by permission of Pearson Education, Inc., Upper Saddle River, New Jersey, and by permission of Taylor & Francis Group UK.

at night, heard by a creditor, makes him easy six months longer; but if he sees you at a billiard-table, or hears your voice at a tavern, when you should be at work, he sends for his money the next day; demands it, before he can receive it, in a lump.

It shows, besides, that you are mindful of what you owe; it makes you appear a careful as well as an honest man, and that still increases your credit.

Beware of thinking all you own that you possess, and of living accordingly. It is a mistake that many people who have credit fall into. To prevent this, keep an exact account for some time both of your expenses and your income. If you take the pains at first to mention particulars, it will have this good effect: you will discover how wonderfully small, trifling expenses mount up to large sums, and will discern what might have been, and may for the future be saved, without occasioning any great inconvenience.

For six pounds a year you may have the use of one hundred pounds, provided you are a man of known prudence and honesty.

He that spends a groat a day idly, spends idly above six pounds a year, which is the price for the use of one hundred pounds.

He that wastes idly a groat's worth of his time per day, one day with another, wastes the privilege of using one hundred pounds each day.

He that idly loses five shillings' worth of time, loses five shillings, and might as prudently throw five shillings into the sea.

He that loses five shillings, not only loses that sum, but all the advantage that might be made by turning it in dealing, which by the time that a young man becomes old, will amount to a considerable sum of money.

It is Benjamin Franklin who preaches to us in these sentences, the same which Ferdinand Kurnberger satirizes in his clever and malicious *Picture of American Culture* as the supposed confession of faith of the Yankee. That it is the spirit of capitalism which here speaks in characteristic fashion, no one will doubt, however little we may wish to claim that everything which could be understood as pertaining to that spirit is contained in it. Let us pause a moment to consider this passage, the philosophy of which Kurnberger sums up in the words, "They make tallow out of cattle and money out of men." The peculiarity of this philosophy of avarice appears to be the ideal of the honest man of recognized credit, and above all the idea of a duty of the individual toward the increase of his capital, which is assumed as an end in itself. Truly what is here preached is not simply a means of making one's way in the world, but a peculiar ethic. The infraction of its rules is treated not as foolishness but as forgetfulness of duty. That is the essence of the matter. It is not mere business astuteness, that sort of thing is common enough, it is an ethos. *This* is the quality which interests us. . . .

In fact, the *summum bonum* of this ethic, the earning of more and more money, combined with the strict avoidance of all spontaneous enjoyment of life, is above all completely devoid of any eudaemonistic, not to say hedonistic, admixture. It is thought of so purely as an end in itself, that from the point of view of the happiness of, or utility to, the single individual, it appears entirely transcendental and absolutely irrational. Man is dominated by the making of money, by acquisition as the ultimate purpose of his life. Economic acquisition is no longer subordinated to man as the means for the satisfaction of his material needs. This reversal of what we should call the natural relationship, so irrational from a naive point of view, is evidently as definitely a leading principle of capitalism as it is foreign to all peoples not under capitalistic influence. At the same time it expresses a type of feeling which is closely connected with certain religious ideas. If we thus ask, *why* should "money be made out of men," Benjamin Franklin himself, although he was a colourless deist, answers in his autobiography with a quotation from the Bible, which his strict Calvinistic father drummed into him again and again in his youth: "Seest thou a man diligent in his business? He shall stand before kings" (Prov. xxii. 29). The earning of money within the modern economic order is, so long as it is done legally, the result and the expression of virtue and proficiency in a calling; and this virtue and proficiency are, as it is now not difficult to see, the real Alpha and Omega of Franklin's ethic, as expressed in the passages we have quoted, as well as in all his works without exception.

And in truth this peculiar idea, so familiar to us to-day, but in reality so little a matter of course, of one's duty in a calling, is what is most characteristic of the social ethic of capitalistic culture, and is in a sense the fundamental basis of it. It is an obligation which the individual is supposed to feel and does feel

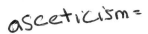
asceticism =

towards the content of his professional activity, no matter in what it consists, in particular no matter whether it appears on the surface as a utilization of his personal powers, or only of his material possessions (as capital). . . .

One of the fundamental elements of the spirit of modern capitalism, and not only of that but of all modern culture: rational conduct on the basis of the idea of the calling, was born—that is what this discussion has sought to demonstrate—from the spirit of Christian asceticism. One has only to re-read the passage from Franklin, quoted at the beginning of this essay, in order to see that the essential elements of the attitude which was there called the spirit of capitalism are the same as what we have just shown to be the content of the Puritan worldly asceticism, only without the religious basis, which by Franklin's time had died away. The idea that modern labour has an ascetic character is of course not new. Limitation to specialized work, with a renunciation of the Faustian universality of man which it involves, is a condition of any valuable work in the modern world; hence deeds and renunciation inevitably condition each other to-day. This fundamentally ascetic trait of middle-class life, if it attempts to be a way of life at all, and not simply the absence of any, was what Goethe wanted to teach, at the height of his wisdom, in the *Wanderjahren,* and in the end which he gave to the life of his *Faust.* For him the realization meant a renunciation, a departure from an age of full and beautiful humanity, which can no more be repeated in the course of our cultural development than can the flower of the Athenian culture of antiquity.

The Puritan wanted to work in a calling; we are forced to do so. For when asceticism was carried out of monastic cells into everyday life, and began to dominate worldly morality, it did its part in building the tremendous cosmos of the modern economic order. This order is now bound to the technical and economic conditions of machine production which to-day determine the lives of all the individuals who are born into this mechanism, not only those directly concerned with economic acquisition, with irresistible force. Perhaps it will so determine them until the last ton of fossilized coal is burnt. In Baxter's view the care for external goods should only lie on the shoulders of the "saint like a light cloak, which can be thrown aside at any moment." But fate decreed that the cloak should become an iron cage.

Since asceticism undertook to remodel the world and to work out its ideals in the world, material goods have gained an increasing and finally an inexorable power over the lives of men as at no previous period in history. To-day the spirit of religious asceticism—whether finally, who knows?—has escaped from the cage. But victorious capitalism, since it rests on mechanical foundations, needs its support no longer. The rosy blush of its laughing heir, the Enlightenment, seems also to be irretrievably fading, and the idea of duty in one's calling prowls about in our lives like the ghost of dead religious beliefs. Where the fulfilment of the calling cannot directly be related to the highest spiritual and cultural values, or when, on the other hand, it need not be felt simply as economic compulsion, the individual generally abandons the attempt to justify it at all. In the field of its highest development, in the United States, the pursuit of wealth, stripped of its religious and ethical meaning, tends to become associated with purely mundane passions, which often actually give it the character of sport. *who can make more*

No one knows who will live in this cage in the future, or whether at the end of this tremendous development entirely new prophets will arise, or there will be a great rebirth of old ideas and ideals, or, if neither, mechanized petrification, embellished with a sort of convulsive self-importance. For of the last stage of this cultural development, it might well be truly said: "Specialists without spirit, sensualists without heart; this nullity imagines that it has attained a level of civilization never before achieved."

But this brings us to the world of judgments of value and of faith, with which this purely historical discussion need not be burdened. The next task would be rather to show the significance of ascetic rationalism, which has only been touched in the foregoing sketch, for the content of practical social ethics, thus for the types of organization and the functions of social groups from the conventicle to the State. Then its relations to humanistic rationalism, its ideals of life and cultural influence; further to the development of philosophical and scientific empiricism, to technical development and to spiritual ideals would have to be analysed. Then its historical development from the mediaeval beginnings of worldly asceticism to its dissolution into pure utilitarianism would have to be traced out through all the areas of ascetic religion. Only then could the quantitative cultural significance of ascetic Protestantism in its relation to the other plastic elements of modern culture be estimated.

Here we have only attempted to trace the fact and the direction of its influence to their motives in one, though a very important point. But it would also further be necessary to investigate how Protestant Asceticism was in turn influenced in its development and its character by the totality of social conditions, especially economic. The modern man is in general, even with the best will, unable to give religious ideas a significance for culture and national character which they deserve. But it is, of course, not my aim to substitute for a one-sided materialistic an equally one-sided spiritualistic causal interpretation of culture and of history. Each is equally possible, but each, if it does not serve as the preparation, but as the conclusion of an investigation, accomplishes equally little in the interest of historical truth.

The Bureaucratic Machine[*]
Max Weber (1909–1920)

Characteristics of Bureaucracy

Modern officialdom functions in the following specific manner:

I. There is the principle of fixed and official jurisdictional areas, which are generally ordered by rules, that is, by laws or administrative regulations.

1. The regular activities required for the purposes of the bureaucratically governed structure are distributed in a fixed way as official duties.

2. The authority to give the commands required for the discharge of these duties is distributed in a stable way and is strictly delimited by rules concerning the coercive means, physical, sacerdotal, or otherwise, which may be placed at the disposal of officials.

3. Methodical provision is made for the regular and continuous fulfilment of these duties and for the execution of the corresponding rights; only persons who have the generally regulated qualifications to serve are employed.

In public and lawful government these three elements constitute "bureaucratic authority." In private economic domination, they constitute bureaucratic "management." Bureaucracy, thus understood, is fully developed in political and ecclesiastical communities only in the modern state, and, in the

*FROM MAX WEBER: ESSAYS IN SOCIOLOGY translated by Gerth & Wright Mills (1946) 4539w from Chp. "Bureaucratic" & Chp. "Politics as a Vocation" pp. 195-198, 224-230. © 1946, 1958, 1973 by H. H. Gerth and C. Wright Mills. By permission of Oxford University Press, USA.

private economy, only in the most advanced institutions of capitalism. Permanent and public office authority, with fixed jurisdiction, is not the historical rule but rather the exception. This is so even in large political structures such as those of the ancient Orient, the Germanic and Mongolian empires of conquest, or of many feudal structures of state. In all these cases, the ruler executes the most important measures through personal trustees, table-companions, or court-servants. Their commissions and authority are not precisely delimited and are temporarily called into being for each case.

II. The principles of office hierarchy and of levels of graded authority mean a firmly ordered system of super- and subordination in which there is a supervision of the lower offices by the higher ones. Such a system offers the governed the possibility of appealing the decision of a lower office to its higher authority, in a definitely regulated manner. With the full development of the bureaucratic type, the office hierarchy is monocratically organized. The principle of hierarchical office authority is found in all bureaucratic structures: in state and ecclesiastical structures as well as in large party organizations and private enterprises. It does not matter for the character of bureaucracy whether its authority is called "private" or "public."

When the principle of jurisdictional "competency" is fully carried through, hierarchical subordination—at least in public office—does not meant that the "higher" authority is simply authorized to take over the business of the "lower." Indeed, the opposite is the rule. Once established and having fulfilled its task, an office tends to continue in existence and be held by another incumbent.

III. The management of the modern office is based upon written documents ("the files"), which are preserved in their original or draught form. There is, therefore, a staff of subaltern officials and scribes of all sorts. The body of officials actively engaged in a "public" office, along with the respective apparatus of material implements and the files, make up a "bureau." In private enterprise, "the bureau" is often called "the office."

In principle, the modern organization of the civil service separates the bureau from the private domicile of the official, and, in general, bureaucracy segregates official activity as something distinct from the sphere of private life. Public monies and equipment are divorced from the private property of the official. This condition is everywhere the product of a long development. Nowadays, it is found in public as well as in private enterprises; in the latter, the principle extends even to the leading entrepreneur. In principle, the executive office is separated from the household, business from private correspondence, and business assets from private fortunes. The more consistently the modern type of business management has been carried through the more are these separations the case. The beginnings of this process are to be found as early as the Middle Ages.

It is the peculiarity of the modern entrepreneur that he conducts himself as the "first official" of his enterprise, in the very same way in which the ruler of a specifically modern bureaucratic state spoke of himself as "the first servant" of the state. The idea that the bureau activities of the state are intrinsically different in character from the management of private economic offices is a continental European notion and, by way of contrast, is totally foreign to the American way.

IV. Office management, at least all specialized office management—and such management is distinctly modern—usually presupposes thorough and expert training. This increasingly holds for the modern executive and employee of private enterprises, in the same manner as it holds for the state official.

V. When the office is fully developed, official activity demands the full working capacity of the official, irrespective of the fact that his obligatory time in the bureau may be firmly delimited. In the normal case, this is only the product of a long development, in the public as well as in the private office. Formerly, in all cases, the normal state of affairs was reversed: official business was discharged as a secondary activity.

VI. The management of the office follows general rules, which are more or less stable, more or less exhaustive, and which can be learned. Knowledge of these rules represents a special technical learning which the officials possess. It involves jurisprudence, or administrative or business management.

The reduction of modern office management to rules is deeply embedded in its very nature. The theory of modern public administration, for instance, assumes that the authority to order certain matters by decree—which has been legally granted to public authorities—does not entitle the bureau to regulate the matter by commands given for each case, but only to regulate the matter abstractly. This stands in extreme contrast to the regulation of all relationships through individual privileges and bestowals of favor, which is absolutely dominant in patrimonialism, at least in so far as such relationships are not fixed by sacred tradition. . . .

The Leveling of Social Differences

Bureaucratic organization has usually come into power on the basis of a leveling of economic and social differences. This leveling has been at least relative, and has concerned the significance of social and economic differences for the assumption of administrative functions.

Bureaucracy inevitably accompanies modern *mass democracy* in contrast to the democratic self-government of small homogeneous units. This results from the characteristic principle of bureaucracy: the abstract regularity of the execution of authority, which is a result of the demand for "equality before the law" in the personal and functional sense—hence, of the horror of "privilege," and the principled rejection of doing business "from case to case." Such regularity also follows from the social preconditions of the origin of bureaucracies. The non-bureaucratic administration of any large social structure rests in some way upon the fact that existing social, material, or honorific preferences and ranks are connected with administrative functions and duties. This usually means that a direct or indirect economic exploitation or a "social" exploitation of position, which every sort of administrative activity gives to its bearers, is equivalent to the assumption of administrative functions.

Bureaucratization and democratization within the administration of the state therefore signify and increase the cash expenditures of the public treasury. And this is the case in spite of the fact that bureaucratic administration is usually more "economical" in character than other forms of administration. Until recent times—at least from the point of view of the treasury—the cheapest way of satisfying the need for administration was to leave almost the entire local administration and lower judicature to the landlords of Eastern Prussia. The same fact applies to the administration of sheriffs in England. Mass democracy makes a clean sweep of the feudal, patrimonial, and—at least in intent—the plutocratic privileges in administration. Unavoidably it puts paid professional labor in place of the historically inherited avocational administration by notables.

This not only applies to structures of the state. For it is no accident that in their own organizations, the democratic mass parties have completely broken with traditional notable rule based upon personal relationships and personal esteem. Yet such personal structures frequently continue among the old conservative as well as the old liberal parties. Democratic mass parties are bureaucratically organized under the leadership of party officials, professional party and trade union secretaries, et cetera. In Germany, for instance, this has happened in the Social Democratic party and in the agrarian mass-movement; and in England, for the first time, in the caucus democracy of Gladstone-Chamberlain, which was originally organized in Birmingham and since the 1870's has spread. In the United States, both parties since Jackson's administration have developed bureaucratically. In France, however, attempts to organize disciplined political parties on the basis of an election system that would compel bureaucratic organization have repeatedly failed. The resistance of local circles of notables against the ultimately unavoidable bureaucratization of the parties, which would encompass the entire country and break their influence, could not be overcome. Every advance of the simple election techniques, for instance the system of proportional elections, which calculates with figures, means a strict and interlocal bureaucratic organization of the parties and therewith an increasing domination of party bureaucracy and discipline, as well as the elimination of the local circles of notables—at least this holds for great states.

The progress of bureaucratization in the state administration itself is a parallel phenomenon of democracy, as is quite obvious in France, North America, and now in England. Of course one must always remember that the term "democratization" can be misleading. The *demos* itself, in the sense of an inarticulate mass, never "governs" larger associations; rather, it is governed, and its existence only changes the way in which the executive leaders are selected and the measure of influence which the *demos*, or better, which social circles from its midst are able to exert upon the content and the direction of administrative activities by supplementing what is called "public opinion." "Democratization," in the sense here intended, does not necessarily mean an increasingly active share of the governed in the authority of the social structure. This may be a result of democratization, but it is not necessarily the case.

We must expressly recall at this point that the political concept of democracy, deduced from the "equal rights" of the governed, includes these postulates: (1) prevention of the development of a closed status group of officials in the interest of a universal accessibility of office, and (2) minimization of the authority of officialdom in the interest of expanding the sphere of influence of "public opinion" as far as practicable. Hence, wherever possible, political democracy strives to shorten the term of office by election and recall and by not binding the candidate to a special expertness. Thereby democracy inevitably comes into conflict with the bureaucratic tendencies which, by its fight against notable rule, democracy has produced. The generally loose term "democratization" cannot be used here, in so far as it is understood to mean the minimization of the civil servants' ruling power in favor of the greatest possible "direct" rule of the *demos,* which in practice means the respective party leaders of the *demos.* The most decisive thing here—indeed it is rather exclusively so—is the *leveling of the governed* in opposition to the ruling and bureaucratically articulated group, which in its turn may occupy a quite autocratic position, both in fact and in form.

In Russia, the destruction of the position of the old landed nobility through the regulation of the Mjeshtshitelstvo (rank order) and the permeation of the old nobility by an office nobility were characteristic transitional phenomena in the development of bureaucracy. In China, the estimation of rank and the qualification for office according to the number of examinations passed mean something similar, but they have had consequences which, in theory at least, are still sharper. In France, the Revolution and still more Bonapartism have made the bureaucracy all-powerful. In the Catholic Church, first the feudal and then all independent local intermediary powers were eliminated. This was begun by Gregory VII and continued through the Council of Trent, the Vatican Council, and it was completed by the edicts of Pius X. The transformation of these local powers into pure functionaries of the central authority were connected with the constant increase in the factual significance of the formally quite dependent chaplains, a process which above all was based on the political party organization of Catholicism. Hence this process meant an advance of bureaucracy and at the same time of "passive democratization," as it were, that is, the leveling of the governed. The substitution of the bureaucratic army for the self-equipped army of notables is everywhere a process of "passive" democratization, in the sense in which every establishment of an absolute military monarchy in the place of a feudal state or of a republic of notables is. This has held, in principle, even for the development of the state in Egypt in spite of all the peculiarities involved. Under the Roman principate the bureaucratization of the provincial administration in the field of tax collection, for instance, went hand in hand with the elimination of the plutocracy of a capitalist class, which, under the Republic, had been all-powerful. Ancient capitalism itself was finally eliminated with this stroke.

It is obvious that almost always economic conditions of some sort play their part in such "democratizing" developments. Very frequently we meet with the influence of an economically determined origin of new classes, whether plutocratic, petty bourgeois, or proletarian in character. Such classes may call on the aid of, or they may only call to life or recall to life, a political power, no matter whether it is of legitimate or of Caesarist stamp. They may do so in order to attain economic or social advantages by political assistance. On the other hand, there are equally possible and historically documented cases in which initiative came "from on high" and was of a purely political nature and drew advantages from political constellations, especially in foreign affairs. Such leadership exploited economic and social antagonisms as well as class interests merely as a means for their own purpose of gaining purely political power. For this reason, political authority has thrown the antagonistic classes out of their almost always unstable equilibrium and called their latent interest conflicts into battle. It seems hardly possible to give a general statement of this.

The extent and direction of the course along which economic influences have moved, as well as the nature in which political power relations exert influence, vary widely. In Hellenic Antiquity, the transition to disciplined combat by Hoplites, and in Athens, the increasing importance of the navy laid the foundation for the conquest of political power by the strata on whose shoulders the military burden rested. In Rome, however, the same development shook the rule of the office nobility only temporarily and seemingly. Although the modern mass army has everywhere been a means of breaking the power of notables, by itself it has in no way served as a leverage for active, but rather for merely passive, democratization. One contributing factor, however, has been the fact that the ancient citizen army rested economically upon self-equipment, whereas the modern army rests upon the bureaucratic procurement of requirements.

The advance of the bureaucratic structure rests upon "technical" superiority. This fact leads here, as in the whole field of technique, to the following: the advance has been realized most slowly where older structural forms have been technically well developed and functionally adjusted to the requirements at hand. This was the case, for instance, in the administration of notables in England and hence England was the slowest of all countries to succumb to bureaucratization or, indeed, is still only partly in the process of doing so. The same general phenomenon exists when highly developed systems of gaslight or of steam railroads with large and fixed capital offer stronger obstacles to electrification than in completely new areas which are opened up for electrification.

The Permanent Character of the Bureaucratic Machine

Once it is fully established, bureaucracy is among those social structures which are the hardest to destroy. Bureaucracy is *the* means of carrying "community action" over into rationally ordered "societal action." Therefore, as an instrument for "societalizing" relations of power, bureaucracy has been and is a power instrument of the first order—for the one who controls the bureaucratic apparatus.

Under otherwise equal conditions, a "societal action," which is methodically ordered and led, is superior to every resistance of "mass" or even of "communal action." And where the bureaucratization of administration has been completely carried through, a form of power relation is established that is practically unshatterable.

The individual bureaucrat cannot squirm out of the apparatus in which he is harnessed. In contrast to the honorific or avocational "notable," the professional bureaucrat is chained to his activity by his entire material and ideal existence. In the great majority of cases, he is only a single cog in an ever-moving mechanism which prescribes to him an essentially fixed route of march. The official is entrusted with specialized tasks and normally the mechanism cannot be put into motion or arrested by him, but only from the very top. The individual bureaucrat is thus forged to the community of all the functionaries who are integrated into the mechanism. They have a common interest in seeing that the mechanism continues its functions and that the societally exercised authority carries on.

The ruled, for their part, cannot dispense with or replace the bureaucratic apparatus of authority once it exists. For this bureaucracy rests upon expert training, a functional specialization of work, and an attitude set for habitual and virtuoso-like mastery of single yet methodically integrated functions. If the official stops working, or if his work is forcefully interrupted, chaos results, and it is difficult to improvise replacements from among the governed who are fit to master such chaos. This holds for public administration as well as for private economic management. More and more the material fate of the masses depends upon the steady and correct functioning of the increasingly bureaucratic organizations of private capitalism. The idea of eliminating these organizations becomes more and more utopian.

The discipline of officialdom refers to the attitude-set of the official for precise obedience within his *habitual* activity, in public as well as in private organizations. This discipline increasingly becomes the basis of all order, however great the practical importance of administration on the basis of the filed documents may be. The naive idea of Bakuninism of destroying the basis of "acquired rights" and "domination" by destroying public documents overlooks the settled orientation of *man* for keeping to the habitual rules and regulations that continue to exist independently of the documents. Every reorganization of beaten or dissolved troops, as well as the restoration of administrative orders destroyed by revolt, panic, or other catastrophes, is realized by appealing to the trained orientation of obedient compliance to such orders. Such compliance has been conditioned into the officials, on the one hand, and, on the other hand, into the governed. If such an appeal is successful it brings, as it were, the disturbed mechanism into gear again.

The objective indispensability of the once-existing apparatus, with its peculiar, "impersonal" character, means that the mechanism—in contrast to feudal orders based upon personal piety—is easily made to work for anybody who knows how to gain control over it. A rationally ordered system of officials continues to function smoothly after the enemy has occupied the area; he merely needs to change the top officials. This body of officials continues to operate because it is to the vital interest of everyone concerned, including above all the enemy.

During the course of his long years in power, Bismarck brought his ministerial colleagues into unconditional bureaucratic dependence by eliminating all independent statesmen. Upon his retirement, he saw to his surprise that they continued to manage their offices unconcerned and undismayed, as if he had not been the master mind and creator of these creatures, but rather as if some single figure had been exchanged for some other figure in the bureaucratic machine. With all the changes of masters in France since the time of the First Empire, the power machine has remained essentially the same. Such a machine makes "revolution," in the sense of the forceful creation of entirely new formations of authority, technically more and more impossible, especially when the apparatus controls the modern means of communication (telegraph, et cetera) and also by virtue of its internal rationalized structure. In classic fashion, France has demonstrated how this process has substituted *coups d'état* for "revolutions": all successful transformations in France have amounted to *coups d'état*.

What Is Politics?[*]
Max Weber (1918)

This lecture, which I give at your request, will necessarily disappoint you in a number of ways. You will naturally expect me to take a position on actual problems of the day. But that will be the case only in a purely formal way and toward the end, when I shall raise certain questions concerning the significance of political action in the whole way of life. In today's lecture, all questions that refer to what policy and what content one should give one's political activity must be eliminated. For such questions have nothing to do with the general question of what politics as a vocation means and what it can mean. Now to our subject matter.

What do we understand by politics? The concept is extremely broad and comprises any kind of *independent* leadership in action. One speaks of the currency policy of the banks, of the discounting policy of the Reichsbank, of the strike policy of a trade union; one may speak of the educational policy of a municipality or a township, of the policy of the president of a voluntary association, and, finally, even of the policy of a prudent wife who seeks to guide her husband. Tonight, our reflections are, of course, not based upon such a broad concept. We wish to understand by politics only the leadership, or the influencing of the leadership, of a *political* association, hence today, of a *state*.

But what is a "political" association from the sociological point of view? What is a "state"? Sociologically, the state cannot be defined in terms of its ends. There is scarcely any task that some political association has not taken in hand, and there is no

[*]FROM MAX WEBER: ESSAYS IN SOCIOLOGY translated by Gerth & Wright Mills (1946) 4539w from Chp. "Bureaucratic" & Chp. "Politics as a Vocation" pp. 77-79. © 1946, 1958, 1973 by H. H. Gerth and C. Wright Mills. By permission of Oxford University Press, USA.

task that one could say has always been exclusive and peculiar to those associations which are designated as political ones: today the state, or historically, those associations which have been the predecessors of the modern state. Ultimately, one can define the modern state sociologically only in terms of the specific *means* peculiar to it, as to every political association, namely, the use of physical force.

"Every state is founded on force," said Trotsky at Brest-Litovsk. That is indeed right. If no social institutions existed which knew the use of violence, then the concept of "state" would be eliminated, and a condition would emerge that could be designated as "anarchy," in the specific sense of this word. Of course, force is certainly not the normal or the only means of the state—nobody says that—but force is a means specific to the state. Today the relation between the state and violence is an especially intimate one. In the past, the most varied institutions—beginning with the sib—have known the use of physical force as quite normal. Today, however, we have to say that a state is a human community that (successfully) claims the *monopoly of the legitimate use of physical force* within a given territory. Note that "territory" is one of the characteristics of the state. Specifically, at the present time, the right to use physical force is ascribed to other institutions or to individuals only to the extent to which the state permits it. The state is considered the sole source of the "right" to use violence. Hence, "politics" for us means striving to share power or striving to influence the distribution of power, either among states or among groups within a state.

This corresponds essentially to ordinary usage. When a question is said to be a "political" question, when a cabinet minister or an official is said to be a "political" official, or when a decision is said to be "politically" determined, what is always meant is that interests in the distribution, maintenance, or transfer of power are decisive for answering the questions and determining the decision or the official's sphere of activity. He who is active in politics strives for power either as a means in serving other aims, ideal or egoistic, or as "power for power's sake," that is, in order to enjoy the prestige-feeling that power gives.

Like the political institutions historically preceding it, the state is a relation of men dominating men, a relation supported by means of legitimate (i.e., considered to be legitimate) violence. If the state is to exist, the dominated must obey the authority claimed by the powers that be. When and why do men obey? Upon what inner justifications and upon what external means does this domination rest?

To begin with, in principle, there are three inner justifications, hence basic *legitimations* of domination.

First, the authority of the "eternal yesterday," i.e. of the mores sanctified through the unimaginably ancient recognition and habitual orientation to conform. This is "traditional" domination exercised by the patriarch and the patrimonial prince of yore.

There is the authority of the extraordinary and personal *gift of grace* (charisma), the absolutely personal devotion and personal confidence in revelation, heroism, or other qualities of individual leadership. This is "charismatic" domination, as exercised by the prophet or—in the field of politics—by the elected war lord, the plebiscitarian ruler, the great demagogue, or the political party leader.

Finally, there is domination by virtue of "legality," by virtue of the belief in the validity of legal statute and functional "competence" based on rationally created *rules*. In this case, obedience is expected in discharging statutory obligations. This is domination as exercised by the modern "servant of the state" and by all those bearers of power who in this respect resemble him.

It is understood that, in reality, obedience is determined by highly robust motives of fear and hope—fear of the vengeance of magical powers or of the power-holder, hope for reward in this world or in the beyond—and besides all this, by interests of the most varied sort. Of this we shall speak presently. However, in asking for the "legitimations" of this obedience, one meets with these three "pure" types: "traditional," "charismatic," and "legal."

These conceptions of legitimacy and their inner justifications are of very great significance for the structure of domination. To be sure, the pure types are rarely found in reality. But today we cannot deal with the highly complex variants, transitions, and combinations of these pure types, which problems belong to "political science." Here we are interested above all in the second of these types: domination by virtue of the devotion of those who obey the purely personal "charisma" of the "leader." For this is the root of the idea of a *calling* in its highest expression.

The Types of Legitimate Domination[*]
Max Weber (1909–1920)

Domination and Legitimacy

Domination was defined above as the probability that certain specific commands (or all commands) will be obeyed by a given group of persons. It thus does not include every mode of exercising "power" or "influence" over other persons. Domination ("authority") in this sense may be based on the most diverse motives of compliance: all the way from simple habituation to the most purely rational calculation of advantage. Hence every genuine form of domination implies a minimum of voluntary compliance, that is, an *interest* (based on ulterior motives or genuine acceptance) in obedience.

Not every case of domination makes use of economic means; still less does it always have economic objectives. However, normally the rule over a considerable number of persons requires a staff, that is, a *special* group which can normally be trusted to execute the general policy as well as the specific commands. The members of the administrative staff may be bound to obedience to their superior (or superiors) by custom, by affectual ties, by a purely material complex of interests, or by ideal (*wertrationale*) motives. The quality of these motives largely determines the type of domination. *Purely* material interests and calculations of advantages as the basis of solidarity between the chief and his administrative staff result, in this as in other connexions, in a relatively unstable situation. Normally other elements, affectual and ideal, supplement such interests. In certain exceptional cases the former alone may be decisive. In everyday life these relationships, like others, are governed by custom and material calculation of advantage. But custom, personal advantage, purely affectual or ideal motives of solidarity, do not form a sufficiently reliable basis for a given domination. In addition there is normally a further element, the belief in *legitimacy*.

Experience shows that in no instance does domination voluntarily limit itself to the appeal to material or affectual or ideal motives as a basis for its continuance. In addition every such system attempts to establish and to cultivate the belief in its legitimacy. But according to the kind of legitimacy

[*]From *Economy and Society* by Max Weber, edited by Guenther Roth and Claus Wittich, © 1978 by the Regents of the University of California. Published by the University of California Press.

which is claimed, the type of obedience, the kind of administrative staff developed to guarantee it, and the mode of exercising authority, will all differ fundamentally. Equally fundamental is the variation in effect. Hence, it is useful to classify the types of domination according to the kind of claim to legitimacy typically made by each. In doing this, it is best to start from modern and therefore more familiar examples.

1. The choice of this rather than some other basis of classification can only be justified by its results. The fact that certain other typical criteria of variation are thereby neglected for the time being and can only be introduced at a later stage is not a decisive difficulty. The legitimacy of a system of control has far more than a merely "ideal" significance, if only because it has very definite relations to the legitimacy of property.

2. Not every claim which is protected by custom or law should be spoken of as involving a relation of authority. Otherwise the worker, in his claim for fulfilment of the wage contract, would be exercising authority over his employer because his claim can, on occasion, be enforced by order of a court. Actually his formal status is that of party to a contractual relationship with his employer, in which he has certain "rights" to receive payments. At the same time the concept of an authority relationship (*Herrschaftsverhältnis*) naturally does not exclude the possibility that it has originated in a formally free contract. This is true of the *authority* of the employer over the worker as manifested in the former's rules and instructions regarding the work process; and also of the *authority* of a feudal lord over a vassal who has freely entered into the relation of fealty. That subjection to military discipline is formally "involuntary" while that to the discipline of the factory is voluntary does not alter the fact that the latter is also a case of subjection to *authority*. The position of a bureaucratic official is also entered into by contract and can be freely resigned, and even the status of "subject" can often be freely entered into and (in certain circumstances) freely repudiated. Only in the limiting case of the slave is formal subjection to authority absolutely involuntary.

On the other hand, we shall not speak of formal domination if a monopolistic position permits a person to exert economic power, that is, to dictate the terms of exchange to contractual partners. Taken by itself, this does not constitute authority any more than any other kind of influence which is derived from some kind of superiority, as by virtue of erotic attractiveness, skill in sport or in discussion. Even if a big bank is in a position to force other banks into a cartel arrangement, this will not alone be sufficient to justify calling it an authority. But if there is an immediate relation of command and obedience such that the management of the first bank can give orders to the others with the claim that they shall, and the probability that they will, be obeyed regardless of particular content, and if their carrying out is supervised, it is another matter. Naturally, here as everywhere the transitions are gradual; there are all sorts of intermediate steps between mere indebtedness and debt slavery. Even the position of a "salon" can come very close to the borderline of authoritarian domination and yet not necessarily constitute "authority." Sharp differentiation in concrete fact is often impossible, but this makes clarity in the analytical distinctions all the more important.

3. Naturally, the legitimacy of a system of domination may be treated sociologically only as the probability that to a relevant degree the appropriate attitudes will exist, and the corresponding practical conduct ensue. It is by no means true that every case of submissiveness to persons in positions of power is primarily (or even at all) oriented to this belief. Loyalty may be hypocritically simulated by individuals or by whole groups on purely opportunistic grounds, or carried out in practice for reasons of material self-interest. Or people may submit from individual weakness and helplessness because there is no acceptable alternative. But these considerations are not decisive for the classification of types of domination. What is important is the fact that in a given case the particular claim to legitimacy is to a significant degree and according to its type treated as "valid"; that this fact confirms the position of the persons claiming authority and that it helps to determine the choice of means of its exercise.

Furthermore, a system of domination may—as often occurs in practice—be so completely protected, on the one hand by the obvious community of interests between the chief and his administrative staff (bodyguards, Pretorians, "red" or "white" guards) as opposed to the subjects, on the other hand by the helplessness of the latter, that it can afford to drop even the pretense of a claim to legitimacy. But even then the mode of legitimation of the relation between chief and his staff may vary widely according to the type of basis of the relation of the authority between them, and, as will be shown, this variation is highly significant for the structure of domination.

4. "Obedience" will be taken to mean that the action of the person obeying follows in essentials such a course that the content of the command may be taken to have become the basis of action for its own sake. Furthermore, the fact that it is so taken is referable only to the formal obligation, without regard to the actor's own attitude to the value or lack of value of the content of the command as such.

5. Subjectively, the causal sequence may vary, especially as between "intuition" and "sympathetic agreement." This distinction is not, however, significant for the present classification of types of authority.

6. The scope of determination of social relationships and cultural phenomena by virtue of domination is considerably broader than appears at first sight. For instance, the authority exercised in the schools has much to do with the determination of the forms of speech and of written language which are regarded as orthodox. Dialects used as the "chancellery language" of autocephalous political units, hence of their rulers, have often become orthodox forms of speech and writing and have even led to the formation of separate "nations" (for instance, the separation of Holland from Germany). The rule by parents and the school, however, extends far beyond the determination of such cultural patterns, which are perhaps only apparently formal, to the formation of the young, and hence of human beings generally.

7. The fact that the chief and his administrative staff often appear formally as servants or agents of those they rule, naturally does nothing whatever to disprove the quality of dominance. There will be occasion later to speak of the substantive features of so-called "democracy." But a certain minimum of assured power to issue commands, thus of domination, must be provided for in nearly every conceivable case.

The Three Pure Types of Authority

There are three pure types of legitimate domination. The validity of the claims to legitimacy may be based on:

1. Rational grounds—resting on a belief in the legality of enacted rules and the right of those elevated to authority under such rules to issue commands (legal authority).

2. Traditional grounds—resting on an established belief in the sanctity of immemorial traditions and the legitimacy of those exercising authority under them (traditional authority); or finally,

3. Charismatic grounds—resting on devotion to the exceptional sanctity, heroism or exemplary character of an individual person, and of the normative patterns or order revealed or ordained by him (charismatic authority).

In the case of legal authority, obedience is owed to the legally established impersonal order. It extends to the persons exercising the authority of office under it by virtue of the formal legality of their commands and only within the scope of authority of the office. In the case of traditional authority, obedience is owed to the *person* of the chief who occupies the traditionally sanctioned position of authority and who is (within its sphere) bound by tradition. But here the obligation of obedience is a matter of personal loyalty within the area of accustomed obligations. In the case of charismatic authority, it is the charismatically qualified leader as such who is obeyed by virtue of personal trust in his revelation, his heroism or his exemplary qualities so far as they fall within the scope of the individual's belief in his charisma.

Class, Status, Party*
Max Weber (1909–1920)

Economically Determined Power and the Status Order

The structure of every legal order directly influences the distribution of power, economic or otherwise, within its respective community. This is true of all legal orders and not only that of the state. In general, we understand by "power" the chance of a man or a number of men to realize their own will in a social action even against the resistance of others who are participating in the action.

"Economically conditioned" power is not, of course, identical with "power" as such. On the contrary, the emergence of economic power may be the consequence of power existing on other grounds. Man does not strive for power only in order to enrich himself economically. Power, including economic power, may be valued for its own sake. Very frequently the striving for power is also conditioned by the social honor it entails. Not all power, however, entails social honor: The typical American

---

*From *Economy and Society* by Max Weber, edited by Guenther Roth and Claus Wittich, © 1978 by the Regents of the University of California. Published by the University of California Press.

Boss, as well as the typical big speculator, deliberately relinquishes social honor. Quite generally, "mere economic" power, and especially "naked" money power, is by no means a recognized basis of social honor. Nor is power the only basis of social honor. Indeed, social honor, or prestige, may even be the basis of economic power, and very frequently has been. Power, as well as honor, may be guaranteed by the legal order, but, at least normally, it is not their primary source. The legal order is rather an additional factor that enhances the chance to hold power or honor; but it can not always secure them.

The way in which social honor is distributed in a community between typical groups participating in this distribution we call the "status order." The social order and the economic order are related in a similar manner to the legal order. However, the economic order merely defines the way in which economic goods and services are distributed and used. Of course, the status order is strongly influenced by it, and in turn reacts upon it.

Now: "classes," "status groups," and "parties" are phenomena of the distribution of power within a community.

Determination of Class Situation by Market Situation

In our terminology, "classes" are not communities; they merely represent possible, and frequent, bases for social action. We may speak of a "class" when (1) a number of people have in common a specific causal component of their life chances, insofar as (2) this component is represented exclusively by economic interests in the possession of goods and opportunities for income, and (3) is represented under the conditions of the commodity or labor markets. This is "class situation."

It is the most elemental economic fact that the way in which the disposition over material property is distributed among a plurality of people, meeting competitively in the market for the purpose of exchange, in itself creates specific life chances. The mode of distribution, in accord with the law of marginal utility, excludes the non-wealthy from competing for highly valued goods; it favors the owners and, in fact, gives to them a monopoly to acquire such goods. Other things being equal, the mode of distribution monopolizes the opportunities for profitable deals for all those who, provided with goods, do not necessarily have to exchange them. It increases, at least generally, their power in the price struggle with those who, being propertyless, have nothing to offer but their labor or the resulting products, and who are compelled to get rid of these products in order to subsist at all. The mode of distribution gives to the propertied a monopoly on the possibility of transferring property from the sphere of use as "wealth" to the sphere of "capital," that is, it gives them the entrepreneurial function and all chances to share directly or indirectly in returns on capital. All this holds true within the area in which pure market conditions prevail. "Property" and "lack of property" are, therefore, the basic categories of all class situations. It does not matter whether these two categories become effective in the competitive struggles of the consumers or of the producers.

Within these categories, however, class situations are further differentiated: on the one hand, according to the kind of property that is usable for returns; and, on the other hand, according to the kind of services that can be offered in the market. Ownership of dwellings; workshops; warehouses; stores; agriculturally usable land in large or small holdings—a quantitative difference with possibly qualitative consequences; ownership of mines; cattle; men (slaves); disposition over mobile instruments of production, or capital goods of all sorts, especially money or objects that can easily be exchanged for money; disposition over products of one's own labor or of others' labor differing according to their various distances from consumability; disposition over transferrable monopolies of any kind—all these distinctions differentiate the class situations of the propertied just as does the "meaning" which they can give to the use of property, especially to property which has money equivalence. Accordingly, the propertied, for instance, may belong to the class of rentiers or the class of entrepreneurs.

Those who have no property but who offer services are differentiated just as much according to their kinds of services as according to the way in which they make use of these services, in a continuous or discontinuous relation to a recipient. But always this is the generic connotation of the concept of class: that the kind of chance in the *market* is the decisive moment which presents a common condition for the individual's fate. Class situation is, in this sense, ultimately market situation. The effect of naked possession *per se,* which among cattle breeders gives the non-owning slave or serf into the power of the cattle owner, is only a fore-runner of real "class" formation. However, in the cattle loan and in the naked severity of the law of debts in such communities for the first time mere "possession" as such emerges as decisive for the fate of the individual; this is much in contrast to crop-raising communities, which are based on labor. The creditor-debtor relation becomes the basis of "class situations" first in the cities, where a "credit market," however primitive, with rates of interest increasing according to the extent of dearth and factual monopolization of lending in the hands of a plutocracy could develop. Therewith "class struggles" begin.

Those men whose fate is not determined by the chance of using goods or services for themselves on the market, e.g., slaves, are not, however, a class in the technical sense of the term. They are, rather, a status group.

Social Action Flowing from Class Interest

According to our terminology, the factor that creates "class" is unambiguously economic interest, and indeed, only those interests involved in the existence of the market. Nevertheless, the concept of class-interest is an ambiguous one: even as an empirical concept it is ambiguous as soon as one understands by it something other than the factual direction of interests following with a certain probability from the class situation for a certain average of those people subjected to the class situation. The class situation and other circumstances remaining the same, the direction in which the individual worker, for instance, is likely to pursue his interests may vary widely, according to whether he is constitutionally qualified for the task at hand to a high, to an average, or to a low degree. In the same way, the direction of interests may vary according to whether or not social action of a larger or smaller portion of those commonly affected by the class situation, or even an association among them, e.g., a trade union, has grown out of the class situation, from which the individual may expect promising results for himself. The emergence of an association or even of mere social action from a common class situation is by no means a universal phenomenon.

The class situation may be restricted in its efforts to the generation of essentially *similar* reactions, that is to say, within our terminology, of "mass behavior." However, it may not even have this result. Furthermore, often merely amorphous social action emerges. For example, the "grumbling" of workers known in ancient Oriental ethics: The moral disapproval of the work-master's conduct, which in its practical significance was probably equivalent to an increasingly typical phenomenon of precisely the latest industrial development, namely, the slowdown of laborers by virtue of tacit agreement. The degree in which "social action" and possibly associations emerge from the mass behavior of the members of a class is linked to general cultural conditions, especially to those of an intellectual sort. It is also linked to the extent of the contrasts that have already evolved, and is especially linked to the transparency of the connections between the causes and the consequences of the class situation. For however different life chances may be, this fact in itself, according to all experience, by no means gives birth to "class action" (social action by the members of a class). For that, the real conditions and the results of the class situation must be distinctly recognizable. For only then the contrast of life chances can be felt not as an absolutely given fact to be accepted, but as a resultant from either (1) the given distribution of property, or (2) the structure of the concrete economic order. It is only then that people may react against the class structure not only through acts of intermittent and irrational protest, but in the form of rational association. There have been "class situations" of the first category (1), of a specifically naked and transparent sort, in the urban centers of Antiquity and during the Middle Ages; especially then when great fortunes were accumulated by factually monopolized trading in local industrial products or in foodstuffs; furthermore, under certain conditions, in the rural economy of the most diverse periods, when agriculture was increasingly exploited in a profit-making manner. The most important historical example of the second category (2) is the class situation of the modern proletariat.

Types of Class Struggle

Thus every class may be the carrier of any one of the innumerable possible forms of class action, but this is not necessarily so. In any case, a class does not in itself constitute a group (*Gemeinschaft*). To treat "class" conceptually as being equivalent to "group" leads to distortion. That men in the same class situation regularly react in mass actions to such tangible situations as economic ones in the direction of those interests that are most adequate to their average number is an important and after all simple fact for the understanding of historical events. However, this fact must not lead to that kind of pseudo-scientific operation with the concepts of class and class

interests which is so frequent these days and which has found its most classic expression in the statement of a talented author, that the individual may be in error concerning his interests but that the class is infallible about its interests.

If classes as such are not groups, nevertheless class situations emerge only on the basis of social action. However, social action that brings forth class situations is not basically action among members of the identical class; it is an action among members of different classes. Social actions that directly determine the class situation of the worker and the entrepreneur are: the labor market, the commodities market, and the capitalistic enterprise. But, in its turn, the existence of a capitalistic enterprise presupposes that a very specific kind of social action exists to protect the possession of goods *per se,* and especially the power of individuals to dispose, in principle freely, over the means of production: a certain kind of legal order. Each kind of class situation, and above all when it rests upon the power of property *per se,* will become most clearly efficacious when all other determinants of reciprocal relations are, as far as possible, eliminated in their significance. It is in this way that the use of the power of property in the market obtains its most sovereign importance.

Now status groups hinder the strict carrying through of the sheer market principle. In the present context they are of interest only from this one point of view. Before we briefly consider them, note that not much of a general nature can be said about the more specific kinds of antagonism between classes (in our meaning of the term). The great shift, which has been going on continuously in the past, and up to our times, may be summarized, although at a cost of some precision: the struggle in which class situations are effective has progressively shifted from consumption credit toward, first, competitive struggles in the commodity market and then toward wage disputes on the labor market. The class struggles of Antiquity—to the extent that they were genuine class struggles and not struggles between status groups— were initially carried on by peasants and perhaps also artisans threatened by debt bondage and struggling against urban creditors. For debt bondage is the normal result of the differentiation of wealth in commercial cities, especially in seaport cities. A similar situation has existed among cattle breeders. Debt relationships as such produced class action up to the days of Catilina. Along with this, and with an increase in provision of grain for the city by transporting it from the outside, the struggle over the means of sustenance emerged. It centered in the first place around the provision of bread and determination of the price of bread. It lasted throughout Antiquity and the entire Middle Ages. The propertyless flocked together against those who actually and supposedly were interested in the dearth of bread. This fight spread until it involved all those commodities essential to the way of life and to handicraft production. There were only incipient discussions of wage disputes in Antiquity and in the Middle Ages. But they have been slowly increasing up into modern times. In the earlier periods they were completely secondary to slave rebellions as well as to conflicts in the commodity market.

The propertyless of Antiquity and of the Middle Ages protested against monopolies, pre-emption, forestalling, and the withholding of goods from the market in order to raise prices. Today the central issue is the determination of the price of labor. The transition is represented by the fight for access to the market and for the determination of the price of products. Such fights went on between merchants and workers in the putting-out system of domestic handicraft during the transition to modern times. Since it is quite a general phenomenon we must mention here that the class antagonisms that are conditioned through the market situations are usually most bitter between those who actually and directly participate as opponents in price wars. It is not the rentier, the share-holder, and the banker who suffer the ill will of the worker, but almost exclusively the manufacturer and the business executives who are the direct opponents of workers in wage conflicts. This is so in spite of the fact that it is precisely the cash boxes of the rentier, the share-holder, and the banker into which the more or less unearned gains flow, rather than into the pockets of the manufacturers or of the business executives. This simple state of affairs has very frequently been decisive for the role the class situation has played in the formation of political parties. For example, it has made possible the varieties of patriarchal socialism and the frequent attempts—formerly, at least—of threatened status groups to form alliances with the proletariat against the bourgeoisie.

Status Honor

In contrast to classes, *Stande* (*status groups*) are normally groups. They are, however, often of an amorphous kind. In contrast to the purely economically determined "class situation," we wish to designate as *status situation* every typical component of the life of men that is determined by a specific, positive or negative, social estimation of *honor*. This honor may be connected with any quality shared by a plurality, and, of course, it can be knit to a class situation: class distinctions are linked in the most varied ways with status distinctions. Property as such is not always recognized as a status qualification, but in the long run it is, and with extraordinary regularity. In the subsistence economy of neighborhood associations, it is often simply the richest who is the "chieftain." However, this often is only an honorific preference. For example, in the so-called pure modern democracy, that is, one devoid of any expressly ordered status privileges for individuals, it may be that only the families coming under approximately the same tax class dance with one another. This example is reported of certain smaller Swiss cities. But status honor need not necessarily be linked with a class situation. On the contrary, it normally stands in sharp opposition to the pretensions of sheer property.

Both propertied and propertyless people can belong to the same status group, and frequently they do with very tangible consequences. This equality of social esteem may, however, in the long run become quite precarious. The equality of status among American gentlemen, for instance, is expressed by the fact that outside the subordination determined by the different functions of business, it would be considered strictly repugnant—wherever the old tradition still prevails—if even the richest boss, while playing billiards or cards in his club would not treat his clerk as in every sense fully his equal in birthright, but would bestow upon him the condescending status-conscious "benevolence" which the German boss can never dissever from his attitude. This is one of the most important reasons why in America the German clubs have never been able to attain the attraction that the American clubs have.

In content, status honor is normally expressed by the fact that above all else a specific *style of life* is expected from all those who wish to belong to the circle. Linked with this expectation are restrictions on social intercourse (that is, intercourse which is not subservient to economic or any other purposes). These restrictions may confine normal marriages to within the status circle and may lead to complete endogamous closure. Whenever this is not a mere individual and socially irrelevant imitation of another style of life, but consensual action of this closing character, the status development is under way.

(margin, handwritten, rotated) Birth Rights.

In its characteristic form, stratification by status groups on the basis of conventional styles of life evolves at the present time in the United States out of the traditional democracy. For example, only the resident of a certain street ("the Street") is considered as belonging to "society," is qualified for social intercourse, and is visited and invited. Above all, this differentiation evolves in such a way as to make for strict submission to the fashion that is dominant at a given time in society. This submission to fashion also exists among men in America to a degree unknown in Germany; it appears as an indication of the fact that a given man puts forward a *claim* to qualify as a gentleman. This submission decides, at least *prima facie*, that he will be treated as such. And this recognition becomes just as important for his employment chances in swank establishments, and above all, for social intercourse and marriage with "esteemed" families, as the qualification for dueling among Germans. As for the rest, status honor is usurped by certain families resident for a long time, and, of course, correspondingly wealthy, or by the actual or alleged descendants of the "Indian Princess" Pocahontas, of the Pilgrim fathers, or of the Knickerbockers, the members of almost inaccessible sects and all sort of circles setting themselves apart by means of any other characteristics and badges. In this case stratification is purely conventional and rests largely on usurpation (as does almost all status honor in its beginning). But the road to legal privilege, positive or negative, is easily traveled as soon as a certain stratification of the social order has in fact been "lived in" and has achieved stability by virtue of a stable distribution of economic power.

Ethnic Segregation and Caste

Where the consequences have been realized to their full extent, the status group evolves into a closed caste. Status distinctions are then guaranteed not merely by conventions and laws, but also by religious sanctions. This occurs in such a way that every physical contact with a member of any caste that is considered to be lower by the members of a higher caste is considered as making for a ritualistic impurity and a stigma which must be expiated by a religious act. In addition, individual castes develop quite distinct cults and gods.

In general, however, the status structure reaches such extreme consequences only where there are underlying differences which are held to be "ethnic." The caste is, indeed, the normal form in which ethnic communities that believe in blood relationship and exclude exogamous marriage and social intercourse usually associate with one another. As mentioned before, such a caste situation is part of the phenomenon of pariah peoples and is found all over the world. These people form communities, acquire specific occupational traditions of handicrafts or of other arts, and cultivate a belief in their ethnic community. They live in a diaspora strictly segregated from all personal intercourse, except that of an unavoidable sort, and their situation is legally precarious. Yet, by virtue of their economic indispensability, they are tolerated, indeed frequently privileged, and they live interspersed in the political communities. The Jews are the most impressive historical example.

A status segregation grown into a caste differs in its structure from a mere ethnic segregation: the caste structure transforms the horizontal and unconnected coexistences of ethnically segregated groups into a vertical social system of super- and subordination. Correctly formulated: a comprehensive association integrates the ethnically divided communities into one political unit. They differ precisely in this way: ethnic coexistence, based on mutual repulsion and disdain, allows each ethnic community to consider its own honor as the highest one; the caste structure brings about a social subordination and an acknowledgement of "more honor" in favor of the privileged caste and status groups. This is due to the fact that in the caste structure ethnic distinctions as such have become "functional" distinctions within the political association (warriors, priests, artisans that are politically important for war and for building, and so on). But even pariah peoples who are most despised (for example, the Jews) are usually apt to continue cultivating the belief in their own specific "honor," a belief that is equally peculiar to ethnic and to status groups.

However, with the negatively privileged status groups the sense of dignity takes a specific deviation. A sense of dignity is the precipitation in individuals of social honor and of conventional demands which a positively privileged status group raises for the deportment of its members. The sense of dignity that characterizes positively privileged status groups is naturally related to their "being" which does not transcend itself, that is, it is related to their "beauty and excellence" (*kalokagauia*). Their kingdom is "of this world." They live for the present and by exploiting their great past. The sense of dignity of the negatively privileged strata naturally refers to a future lying beyond the present, whether it is of this life or of another. In other words, it must be nurtured by the belief in a providential mission and by a belief in a specific honor before God. The chosen people's dignity is nurtured by a belief either that in the beyond "the last will be the first," or that in this life a Messiah will appear to bring forth into the light of the world which has cast them out the hidden honor of the pariah people. This simple state of affairs, and not the resentment which is so strongly emphasized in Nietzsche's much-admired construction in the *Genealogy of Morals,* is the source of the religiosity cultivated by pariah status groups; moreover, resentment applies only to a limited extent; for one of Nietzsche's main examples, Buddhism, it is not at all applicable.

For the rest, the development of status groups from ethnic segregations is by no means the normal phenomenon. On the contrary. Since objective "racial differences" are by no means behind every subjective sentiment of an ethnic community, the question of an ultimately racial foundation of status structure is rightly a question of the concrete individual case. Very frequently a status group is instrumental in the production of a thoroughbred anthropological type. Certainly status groups are to a high degree effective in producing extreme types, for they select personally qualified individuals (e.g. the knighthood selects those who are fit for warfare, physically and psychically). But individual selection is far from being the only, or the predominant, way in which status groups are formed: political membership or class situation has at all times been at least as frequently decisive. And today the class situation is by far the predominant factor. After all, the possibility of a style of life expected for members of a status group is usually conditioned economically.

Status Privileges

For all practical purposes, stratification by status goes hand in hand with a monopolization of ideal and material goods or opportunities, in a manner we have come to know as typical. Besides the specific status honor, which always rests upon distance and exclusiveness, honorific preferences may consist of the privilege of wearing special costumes, of eating special dishes taboo to others, of carrying arms—which is most obvious in its consequences—the right to be a dilettante, for example, to play certain musical instruments. However, material monopolies provide the most effective motives for the exclusiveness of a status group; although, in themselves, they are rarely sufficient, almost always they come into play to some extent. Within a status circle there is

the question of intermarriage: the interest of the families in the monopolization of potential bridegrooms is at least of equal importance and is parallel to the interest in the monopolization of daughters. The daughters of the members must be provided for. With an increased closure of the status group, the conventional preferential opportunities for special employment grow into a legal monopoly of special offices for the members. Certain goods become objects for monopolization by status groups, typically, entailed estates, and frequently also the possession of serfs or bondsmen and, finally, special trades. This monopolization occurs positively when the status group is exclusively entitled to own and to manage them; and negatively when, in order to maintain its specific way of life, the status group must *not* own and manage them. For the decisive role of a style of life in status honor means that status groups are the specific bearers of all conventions. In whatever way it may be manifest, all stylization of life either originates in status groups or is at least conserved by them. Even if the principles of status conventions differ greatly, they reveal certain typical traits, especially among the most privileged strata. Quite generally, among privileged status groups there is a status disqualification that operates against the performance of common physical labor. This disqualification is now "setting in" in America against the old tradition of esteem for labor. Very frequently every rational economic pursuit, and especially entrepreneurial activity, is looked upon as a disqualification of status. Artistic and literary activity is also considered degrading work as soon as it is exploited for income, or at least when it is connected with hard physical exertion. An example is the sculptor working like a mason in his dusty smock as over against the painter in his salon-like studio and those forms of musical practice that are acceptable to the status group.

Economic Conditions and Effects of Status Stratification

The frequent disqualification of the gainfully employed as such is a direct result of the principle of status stratification, and of course, of this principle's opposition to a distribution of power which is regulated exclusively through the market. These two factors operate along with various individual ones, which will be touched upon below.

We have seen above that the market and its processes knows no personal distinctions: "functional" interests dominate it. It knows nothing of honor.

The status order means precisely the reverse: stratification in terms of honor and styles of life peculiar to status groups as such. The status order would be threatened at its very root if mere economic acquisition and naked economic power still bearing the stigma of its extra-status origin could bestow upon anyone who has won them the same or ever greater honor as the vested interests claim for themselves. After all, given equality of status honor, property *per se* represents an addition even if it is not overtly acknowledged to be such. Therefore all groups having interest in the status order react with special sharpness precisely against the pretensions of purely economic acquisition. In most cases they react the more vigorously the more they feel themselves threatened. Calderon's respectful treatment of the peasant, for instance, as opposed to Shakespeare's simultaneous ostensible disdain of the *canaille* illustrates the different way in which a firmly structured status order reacts as compared with a status order that has become economically precarious. This is an example of a state of affairs that recurs everywhere. Precisely because of the rigorous reactions against the claims of property *per se,* the "parvenu" is never accepted, personally and without reservation, by the privileged status groups, no matter how completely his style of life has been adjusted to theirs. They will only accept his descendants who have been educated in the conventions of their status group and who have never besmirched its honor by their own economic labor.

As to the general *effect* of the status order, only one consequence can be stated, but it is a very important one: the hindrance of the free development of the market. This occurs first for those goods that status groups directly withhold from free exchange by monopolization, which may be effected either legally or conventionally. For example, in many Hellenic cities during the "status era" and also originally in Rome, the inherited estate (as shown by the old formula for placing spendthrifts under a guardian) was monopolized, as were the estates of knights, peasants, priests, and especially the clientele of the craft and merchant guilds. The market is restricted, and the power of naked property *per se,* which gives its stamp to class formation, is pushed into the background. The results of this process can be most varied. Of course, they do not necessarily weaken the contrasts in the economic situation. Frequently they strengthen these contrasts, and in any case, where stratification by status permeates a community as strongly as was the case in all political communities

of Antiquity and of the Middle Ages, one can never speak of a genuinely free market competition as we understand it today. There are wider effects than this direct exclusion of special goods from the market. From the conflict between the status order and the purely economic order mentioned above, it follows that in most instances the notion of honor peculiar to status absolutely abhors that which is essential to the market: hard bargaining. Honor abhors hard bargaining among peers and occasionally it taboos it for the members of a status group in general. Therefore, everywhere some status groups, and usually the most influential, consider almost any kind of overt participation in economic acquisition as absolutely stigmatizing.

With some over-simplification, one might thus say that classes are stratified according to their relations to the production and acquisition of goods; whereas status groups are stratified according to the principles of their *consumption* of goods as represented by special styles of life.

An "occupational status group," too, is a status group proper. For normally, it successfully claims social honor only by virtue of the special style of life which may be determined by it. The differences between classes and status groups frequently overlap. It is precisely those status communities most strictly segregated in terms of honor (viz. the Indian castes) who today show, although within very rigid limits, a relatively high degree of indifference to pecuniary income. However, the Brahmins seek such income in many different ways.

As to the general economic conditions making for the predominance of stratification by status, only the following can be said. When the bases of the acquisition and distribution of goods are relatively stable, stratification by status is favored. Every technological repercussion and economic transformation threatens stratification by status and pushes the class situation into the foreground. Epochs and countries in which the naked class situation is of predominant significance are regularly the periods of technical and economic transformations. And every slowing down of the change in economic stratification leads, in due course, to the growth of status structures and makes for a resuscitation of the important role of social honor.

Parties

Whereas the genuine place of classes is within the economic order, the place of status groups is within the social order, that is, within the sphere of the distribution of honor. From within these spheres, classes and status groups influence one another and the legal order and are in turn influenced by it. *"Parties"* reside in the sphere of power. Their action is oriented toward the acquisition of social power, that is to say, toward influencing social action no matter what its content may be. In principle, parties may exist in a social club as well as in a state. As over against the actions of classes and status groups, for which this is not necessarily the case, party-oriented social action always involves association. For it is always directed toward a goal which is striven for in a planned manner. This goal may be a cause (the party may aim at realizing a program for ideal or material purposes), or the goal may be personal (sinecures, power, and from these, honor for the leader and the followers of the party). Usually the party aims at all these simultaneously. Parties are, therefore, only possible within groups that have an associated character, that is, some rational order and a staff of persons available who are ready to enforce it. For parties aim precisely at influencing this staff, and if possible, to recruit from it party members.

In any individual case, parties may represent interests determined through class situation or status situation, and they may recruit their following respectively from one or the other. But they need be neither purely class nor purely status parties; in fact, they are more likely to be mixed types, and sometimes they are neither. They may represent ephemeral or enduring structures. Their means of attaining power may be quite varied, ranging from naked violence of any sort to canvassing for votes with coarse or subtle means: money, social influence, the force of speech, suggestion, clumsy hoax, and so on to the rougher or more artful tactics of obstruction in parliamentary bodies.

The sociological structure of parties differs in a basic way according to the kind of social action which they struggle to influence; that means, they differ according to whether or not the community is stratified by status or by classes. Above all else, they vary according to the structure of domination. For their leaders normally deal with its conquest. In our general terminology, parties are not only products of modern forms of domination. We shall also designate as parties the ancient and medieval ones, despite the fact that they differ basically from modern parties. Since a party always struggles for political control (*Herrschaft*), its organization too is frequently strict and "authoritarian." Because of these variations between the forms of domination, it is impossible to say anything about the structure of parties without discussing them first. Therefore, we shall now turn to this central phenomenon of all social organization.

Before we do this, we should add one more general observation about classes, status groups and parties: The fact that they presuppose a larger association, especially the framework of a polity, does not mean that they are confined to it. On the contrary, at all times it has been the order of the day that such association (even when it aims at the use of military force in common) reaches beyond the state boundaries. This can be seen in the [interlocal] solidarity of interests of oligarchs and democrats in Hellas, of Guelphs and Ghibellines in the Middle Ages, and with the Calvinist party during the age of religious struggles; and all the way up to the solidarity of landlords (International Congresses of Agriculture), princes (Holy Alliance, Karlsbad Decrees [of 1819]), socialist workers, conservatives (the longing of Prussian conservatives for Russian intervention in 1850). But their aim is not necessarily the establishment of a new territorial dominion. In the main they aim to influence the existing polity.

Sigmund Freud (1856–1939) lived to see the full effects of modern culture in the twentieth century: two world wars, economic depression, Hitler, and a great deal more. In his last writings, particularly *Civilization and Its Discontents* (1930), Freud addressed his social concerns directly. Most of his writings, however, especially those following *Interpretation of Dreams* (1900), were devoted to the scientific and popular advancement of psychoanalysis. Like the other classic social theorists, he was a broadly educated man. His study of Sophocles' *Oedipus, the King* was just one of the many references he made to literature and the arts. He began his career in the 1880s as a medical doctor specializing in neurology. Before settling into life and marriage (to Martha Bernays in 1886, he spent about four months in Paris, from October 1885 to January 1886. There, influenced deeply by Jean-Martin Charcot's clinical work on hypnosis, Freud began to think independently on the effects of unconscious life. Once his study of dreams established the general principles of psychoanalysis, Freud was irreversibly involved as the leader of the psychoanalytic movement. The path was not easy. He quarreled with members of the school (notably the Swiss analyst Carl Jung). He was not able to stop smoking, which aggravated the pain caused by his palate cancer. It seems, also, that he had his own trouble separating from his mother. Just the same, it was Freud's undeniable humanity as well as his prodigious learning and creativity that gave rise to psychoanalysis. Today, psychoanalytic thought serves equally the psychotherapists and social theorists who recognize the power of unconscious desire to shape personal, cultural, and political life.

The first selections, "The Psychical Apparatus and the Theory of Instincts" and "Dream-Work and Interpretation," outline Freud's famous three-part division of the psyche, his mature theory of the instincts, and his view of dreams. Though his thinking changed over the years, these selections (from one of Freud's last works, left incomplete at his death) summarize the essentials of the theories. "Oedipus, the Child" is a text from his earliest work on dreams. It represents one of his many references to versions of Sophocles' *Oedipus*. "Remembering, Repeating, and Working-Through" (1919) is one of Freud's numerous clinical writings, intended to instruct analysts in his therapeutic technique. "The Return of the Repressed in Social Life" (from *Moses and Monotheism*, 1937–1939) and "Civilization and the Individual" (from *Civilization and Its Discontents*, 1930) are also late works, written during the period when he was most concerned to use his theory to reflect on Western civilization. Both show his attempt to link psychological theory to social life. The latter clearly indicates his reservations toward the alleged superiority of Western civilization. Indeed, the last sentence, added with Hitler in mind, reveals his concerns for the very future of that civilization.

The Psychical Apparatus and the Theory of Instincts[*]
Sigmund Freud (1900–1939)

Psycho-analysis makes a basic assumption, the discussion of which is reserved to philosophical thought but

[*] From AN OUTLINE OF PSYCHO-ANALYSIS by Sigmund Freud, translated by James Strachey. Copyright 1949 by W. W. Norton & Company, Inc. Copyright (c) 1969 by The Institute of Psycho-Analysis and Alix Strachey. Used by permission W. W. Norton & Company, Inc. From *The Standard Edition of the Complete Psychological Works of Sigmund Freud*, translated and edited by James Strachey, published by the Hogarth Press. Reprinted by permission of The Random House Group Ltd., and by permission of The Marsh Agency Ltd on behalf of Sigmund Freud Copyrights. Copyright © 1949 by W. W. Norton & Company, Inc. Used by permission of W. W. Norton & Company, Inc.

the justification for which lies in its results. We know two kinds of things about what we call our psyche (or mental life): firstly, its bodily organ and scene of action, the brain (or nervous system) and, on the other hand, our acts of consciousness, which are immediate data and cannot be further explained by any sort of description. Everything that lies between is unknown to us, and the data do not include any direct relation between these two terminal points of our knowledge. If it existed, it would at the most afford an exact localization of the processes of consciousness and would give us no help towards understanding them.

Our two hypotheses start out from these ends or beginnings of our knowledge. The first is concerned with localization. We assume that mental life is the function of an apparatus to which we ascribe the characteristics of being extended in space and of being made up of several portions—which we imagine, that is, as resembling a telescope or microscope or something of the kind. Notwithstanding some earlier attempts in the same direction, the consistent working-out of a conception such as this is a scientific novelty.

We have arrived at our knowledge of this psychical apparatus by studying the individual development of human beings. To the oldest of these psychical provinces or agencies we give the name of *id*. It contains everything that is inherited, that is present at birth, that is laid down in the constitution—above all, therefore, the instincts, which originate from the somatic organization and which find a first psychical expression here [in the id] in forms unknown to us.

Under the influence of the real external world around us, one portion of the id has undergone a special development. From what was originally a cortical layer, equipped with the organs for receiving stimuli and with arrangements for acting as a protective shield against stimuli, a special organization has arisen which henceforward acts as an intermediary between the id and the external world. To this region of our mind we have given the name of *ego*.

Here are the principal characteristics of the ego. In consequence of the pre-established connection between sense perception and muscular action, the ego has voluntary movement at its command. It has the task of self-preservation. As regards *external* events, it performs that task by becoming aware of stimuli, by storing up experiences about them (in the memory), by avoiding excessively strong stimuli (through flight), by dealing with moderate stimuli (through adaptation) and finally by learning to bring about expedient changes in the external world to its own advantage (through activity). As regards *internal* events, in relation to the id, it performs that task by gaining control over the demands of the instincts, by deciding whether they are to be allowed satisfaction, by postponing that satisfaction to times and circumstances favourable in the external world or by suppressing their excitations entirely. It is guided in its activity by consideration of the tensions produced by stimuli, whether these tensions are present in it or introduced into it. The raising of these tensions is in general felt as *unpleasure* and their lowering as *pleasure*. It is probable, however, that what is felt as pleasure or unpleasure is not the *absolute* height of this tension but something in the rhythm of the changes in them. The ego strives after pleasure and seeks to avoid unpleasure. An increase in unpleasure that is expected and foreseen is met by a *signal of anxiety;* the occasion of such an increase, whether it threatens from without or within, is known as a *danger*. From time to time the ego gives up its connection with the external world and withdraws into the state of sleep, in which it makes far-reaching changes in its organization. It is to be inferred from the state of sleep that this organization consists in a particular distribution of mental energy.

The long period of childhood, during which the growing human being lives in dependence on his parents, leaves behind it as a precipitate the formation in his ego of a special agency in which this parental influence is prolonged. It has received the name of *super-ego*. In so far as this super-ego is differentiated from the ego or is opposed to it, it constitutes a third power which the ego must take into account.

An action by the ego is as it should be if it satisfies simultaneously the demands of the id, of the super-ego and of reality—that is to say, if it is able to reconcile their demands with one another. The details of the relation between the ego and the super-ego become completely intelligible when they are traced back to the child's attitude to its parents. This parental influence of course includes in its operation not only the personalities of the actual parents but also the family, racial and national traditions handed on through them, as well as the demands of the immediate social *milieu* which they represent. In the same way, the super-ego, in the course of an individual's development, receives contributions from later successors and substitutes of his parents, such as teachers and models in public life of admired social ideals. It will be observed that,

for all their fundamental difference, the id and the super-ego have one thing in common: they both represent the influences of the past—the id the influence of heredity, the super-ego the influence, essentially, of what is taken over from other people—whereas the ego is principally determined by the individual's own experience, that is by accidental and contemporary events.

This general schematic picture of a psychical apparatus may be supposed to apply as well to the higher animals which resemble man mentally. A super-ego must be presumed to be present wherever, as is the case with man, there is a long period of dependence in childhood. A distinction between ego and id is an unavoidable assumption. Animal psychology has not yet taken in hand the interesting problem which is here presented. . . .

The Theory of the Instincts

The power of the id expresses the true purpose of the individual organism's life. This consists in the satisfaction of its innate needs. No such purpose as that of keeping itself alive or of protecting itself from dangers by means of anxiety can be attributed to the id. That is the task of the ego, whose business it also is to discover the most favourable and least perilous method of obtaining satisfaction, taking the external world into account. The super-ego may bring fresh needs to the fore, but its main function remains the limitation of satisfactions.

The forces which we assume to exist behind the tensions caused by the needs of the id are called *instincts*. They represent the somatic demands upon the mind. Though they are the ultimate cause of all activity, they are of a conservative nature; the state, whatever it may be, which an organism has reached gives rise to a tendency to re-establish that state so soon as it has been abandoned. It is thus possible to distinguish an indeterminate number of instincts, and in common practice this is in fact done. For us, however, the important question arises whether it may not be possible to trace all these numerous instincts back to a few basic ones. We have found that instincts can change their aim (by displacement) and also that they can replace one another—the energy of one instinct passing over to another. This latter process is still insufficiently understood. After long hesitancies and vacillations we have decided to assume the existence of only two basic instincts, *Eros* and *the destructive instinct*. (The contrast between the instincts of self-preservation and the preservation of the species, as well as the contrast between ego-love and object-love, fall within Eros.) The aim of the first of these basic instincts is to establish ever greater unities and to preserve them thus—in short, to bind together; the aim of the second is, on the contrary, to undo connections and so to destroy things. In the case of the destructive instinct we may suppose that its final aim is to lead what is living into an inorganic state. For this reason we also call it the *death instinct*. If we assume that living things came later than inanimate ones and arose from them, then the death instinct fits in with the formula we have proposed to the effect that instincts tend towards a return to an earlier state. In the case of Eros (or the love instinct) we cannot apply this formula. To do so would presuppose that living substance was once a unity which had later been torn apart and was now striving towards reunion.

In biological functions the two basic instincts operate against each other or combine with each other. Thus, the act of eating is a destruction of the object with the final aim of incorporating it, and the sexual act is an act of aggression with the purpose of the most intimate union. This concurrent and mutually opposing action of the two basic instincts gives rise to the whole variegation of the phenomena of life. The analogy of our two basic instincts extends from the sphere of living things to the pair of opposing forces—attraction and repulsion—which rule in the inorganic world.

Modifications in the proportions of the fusion between the instincts have the most tangible results. A surplus of sexual aggressiveness will turn a lover into a sex-murderer, while a sharp diminution in the aggressive factor will make him bashful or impotent.

There can be no question of restricting one or the other of the basic instincts to one of the provinces of the mind. They must necessarily be met with everywhere. We may picture an initial state as one in which the total available energy of Eros, which henceforward we shall speak of as "libido," is present in the still undifferentiated ego-id and serves to neutralize the destructive tendencies which are simultaneously present. (We are without a term analogous to "libido" for describing the energy of the destructive instinct.) At a later stage it becomes relatively easy for us to follow the vicissitudes of the libido, but this is more difficult with the destructive instinct.

So long as that instinct operates internally, as a death instinct, it remains silent; it only comes to our notice when it is diverted outwards as an instinct of destruction. It seems to be essential for the preservation of the individual that this diversion should occur; the muscular apparatus serves this purpose. When the super-ego is established, considerable amounts of the aggressive instinct are fixated in the interior of the ego and operate there self-destructively. This is one of the dangers to health by which human beings are faced on their path to cultural development. Holding back aggressiveness is in general unhealthy and leads to illness (to mortification). A person in a fit of rage will often demonstrate how the transition from aggressiveness that has been prevented to self-destructiveness is brought about by diverting the aggressiveness against himself: he tears his hair or beats his face with his fists, though he would evidently have preferred to apply this treatment to someone else. Some portion of self-destructiveness remains within, whatever the circumstances; till at last it succeeds in killing the individual, not, perhaps, until his libido has been used up or fixated in a disadvantageous way. Thus it may in general be suspected that the *individual* dies of his internal conflicts but that the *species* dies of its unsuccessful struggle against the external world if the latter changes in a fashion which cannot be adequately dealt with by the adaptations which the species has acquired.

It is hard to say anything of the behavior of the libido in the id and in the super-ego. All that we know about it relates to the ego, in which at first the whole available quota of libido is stored up. We call this state absolute, primary *narcissism*. It lasts till the ego begins to cathect the ideas of objects with libido, to transform narcissistic libido into object-libido. Throughout the whole of life the ego remains the great reservoir from which libidinal cathexes are sent out to objects and into which they are also once more withdrawn, just as an amoeba behaves with its pseudopodia. It is only when a person is completely in love that the main quota of libido is transferred on to the object and the object to some extent takes the place of the ego. A characteristic of the libido which is important in life is its *mobility*, the facility with which it passes from one object to another. This must be contrasted with the *fixation* of the libido to particular objects, which often persists throughout life.

There can be no question but that the libido has somatic sources, that it streams to the ego from various organs and parts of the body. This is most clearly seen in the case of that portion of the libido which, from its instinctual aim, is described as sexual excitation. The most prominent of the parts of the body from which this libido arises are known by the name of "*erotogenic zones*," though in fact the whole body is an erotogenic zone of this kind. The greater part of what we know about Eros—that is to say, about its exponent, the libido—has been gained from a study of the sexual function, which, indeed, on the prevailing view, even if not according to our theory, coincides with Eros. We have been able to form a picture of the way in which the sexual urge, which is destined to exercise a decisive influence on our life, gradually develops out of successive contributions from a number of component instincts, which represent particular erotogenic zones.

Dream-Work and Interpretation[*]
Sigmund Freud (1900–1939)

An investigation of normal, stable states, in which the frontiers of the ego are safeguarded against the id by resistances (anti-cathexes) and have held firm, and in which the super-ego is not distinguished from the ego, because they work together harmoniously—an investigation of that kind would teach us little. The only thing that can help us are states of conflict and uproar, when the contents of the unconscious id have a prospect of forcing their way into the ego and into consciousness and the ego puts itself once more on the defensive against this invasion. It is only under these conditions that we can make such observations as will confirm or correct our statements about the two partners. Now, our nightly sleep is precisely a state of this sort, and for that reason psychical activity during sleep, which we perceive as dreams, is our most favourable object of study. In that way, too, we avoid the familiar reproach that we base our constructions of normal mental life on pathological findings; for dreams are regular events in the life of a normal person, however much their characteristics may differ from the productions of our waking life. Dreams, as everyone knows, may be

*From AN OUTLINE OF PSYCHO-ANALYSIS by Sigmund Freud, translated by James Strachey. Copyright 1949 by W. W. Norton & Company, Inc. Copyright © 1969 by The Institute of Psycho-Analysis and Alix Strachey. Used by permission W. W. Norton & Company, Inc. From *The Standard Edition of the Complete Psychological Works of Sigmund Freud*, translated and edited by James Strachey, published by the Hogarth Press. Reprinted by permission of The Random House Group Ltd., and by permission of The Marsh Agency Ltd on behalf of Sigmund Freud Copyrights.

confused, unintelligible or positively nonsensical, what they say may contradict all that we know of reality, and we behave in them like insane people, since, so long as we are dreaming, we attribute objective reality to the contents of the dream.

We find our way to the understanding ("interpretation") of a dream by assuming that what we recollect as the dream after we have woken up is not the true dream-process but only a *façade* behind which that process lies concealed. Here we have our distinction between the *manifest* content of a dream and the *latent* dream-thoughts. The process which produces the former out of the latter is described as the *dream-work*. The study of the dream-work teaches us by an excellent example the way in which unconscious material from the id (originally unconscious and repressed unconscious alike) forces its way into the ego, becomes preconscious and, as a result of the ego's opposition, undergoes the changes which we know as *dream-distortion*. There are no features of a dream which cannot be explained in this way.

It is best to begin by pointing out that the formation of a dream can be provoked in two different ways. Either, on the one hand, an instinctual impulse which is ordinarily suppressed (an unconscious wish) finds enough strength during sleep to make itself felt by the ego, or, on the other hand, an urge left over from waking life, a preconscious train of thought with all the conflicting impulses attached to it, finds reinforcement during sleep from an unconscious element. In short, dreams may arise either from the id or from the ego. The mechanism of dream-formation is in both cases the same and so also is the necessary dynamic precondition. The ego gives evidence of its original derivation from the id by occasionally ceasing its functions and allowing a reversion to an earlier state of things. This is logically brought about by its breaking off its relations with the external world and withdrawing its cathexes from the sense organs. We are justified in saying that there arises at birth an instinct to return to the intra-uterine life that has been abandoned—an instinct to sleep. Sleep is a return of this kind to the womb. Since the waking ego governs motility, that function is paralysed in sleep, and accordingly a good part of the inhibitions imposed on the unconscious id become superfluous. The withdrawal or reduction of these "anticathexes" thus allows the id what is now a harmless amount of liberty.

The evidence of the share taken by the unconscious id in the formation of dreams is abundant and convincing. (*a*) Memory is far more comprehensive in dreams than in waking life. Dreams bring up recollections which the dreamer has forgotten, which are inaccessible to him when he is awake. (*b*) Dreams make an unrestricted use of linguistic symbols, the meaning of which is for the most part unknown to the dreamer. Our experience, however, enables us to confirm their sense. They probably originate from earlier phases in the development of speech. (*c*) Memory very often reproduces in dreams impressions from the dreamer's early childhood of which we can definitely assert not only that they had been forgotten but that they had become unconscious owing to repression. That explains the help—usually indispensable—given us by dreams in the attempts we make during the analytic treatment of neuroses to reconstruct the dreamer's early life. (*d*) Furthermore, dreams bring to light material which cannot have originated either from the dreamer's adult life or from his forgotten childhood. We are obliged to regard it as part of the *archaic heritage* which a child brings with him into the world, before any experience of his own, influenced by the experiences of his ancestors. We find the counterpart of this phylogenetic material in the earliest human legends and in surviving customs. Thus dreams constitute a source of human prehistory which is not to be despised.

But what makes dreams so invaluable in giving us insight is the circumstance that, when the unconscious material makes its way into the ego, it brings its own modes of working along with it. This means that the preconscious thoughts in which the unconscious material has found its expression are handled in the course of the dream-work as though they were unconscious portions of the id; and, in the case of the alternative method of dream-formation, the preconscious thoughts which have obtained reinforcement from an unconscious instinctual impulse are brought down to the unconscious state. It is only in this way that we learn the laws which govern the passage of events in the unconscious and the respects in which they differ from the rules that are familiar to us in waking thought. Thus the dream-work is essentially an instance of the unconscious working-over of preconscious thought-processes. To take an analogy from history: invading conquerors govern a conquered country, not according to the judicial system which they find in force there, but according to their own. It is, however, an unmistakable fact that the outcome of the dream-work is a compromise. The ego-organization is not yet paralysed, and its influence is to be seen in the distortion imposed on the unconscious material and in what are often very ineffective attempts at giving the total result a form not too unacceptable to the ego (*secondary revision*). In our analogy this would be an expression of the continued resistance of the defeated people.

The laws that govern the passage of events in the unconscious, which come to light in this manner, are remarkable enough and suffice to explain most of what seems strange to us about dreams. Above all there is a striking tendency to *condensation,* an inclination to form fresh unities out of elements which in our waking thought we should certainly have kept separate. As a consequence of this, a single element of the manifest dream often stands for a whole number of latent dream-thoughts as though it were a combined allusion to all of them; and in general the compass of the manifest dream is extraordinarily small in comparison with the wealth of material from which it has sprung. Another peculiarity of the dream-work, not entirely independent of the former one, is the ease with which psychical intensities (cathexes) are *displaced* from one element to another, so that it often happens that an element which was of little importance in the dream-thoughts appears as the clearest and accordingly most important feature of the manifest dream, and, *vice versa,* that essential elements of the dream-thoughts are represented in the manifest dream only by slight allusions. Moreover, as a rule the existence of quite insignificant points in common between two elements is enough to allow the dream-work to replace one by the other in all further operations. It will easily be imagined how greatly these mechanisms of condensation and displacement can increase the difficulty of interpreting a dream and of revealing the relations between the manifest dream and the latent dream-thoughts. From the evidence of the existence of these two tendencies to condensation and displacement our theory infers that in the unconscious id the energy is in a freely mobile state and that the id sets more store by the possibility of discharging quantities of excitation than by any other consideration; and our theory makes use of these two peculiarities in defining the character of the primary process we have attributed to the id.

The study of the dream-work has taught us many other characteristics of the processes in the unconscious which are as remarkable as they are important; but we must only mention a few of them here. The governing rules of logic carry no weight in the unconscious; it might be called the Realm of the Illogical. Urges with contrary aims exist side by side in the unconscious without any need arising for an adjustment between them. Either they have no influence whatever on each other, or, if they have, no decision is reached, but a compromise comes about which is nonsensical since it embraces mutually incompatible details. With this is connected the fact that contraries are not kept apart but treated as though they were identical, so that in the manifest dream any element may also have the meaning of its opposite. Certain philologists have found that the same held good in the most ancient languages and that contraries such as "strong-weak," "light-dark" and "high-deep" were originally expressed by the same roots, until two different modifications of the primitive word distinguished between the two meanings. Residues of this original double meaning seem to have survived even in a highly developed language like Latin in its use of words such as "*altus*" ("high" and "deep") and "*sacer*" ("sacred" and "infamous").

In view of the complication and ambiguity of the relations between the manifest dream and the latent content lying behind it, it is of course justifiable to ask how it is at all possible to deduce the one from the other and whether all we have to go on is a lucky guess, assisted perhaps by a translation of the symbols that occur in the manifest dream. It may be said in reply that in the great majority of cases the problem can be satisfactorily solved, but only with the help of the associations provided by the dreamer himself to the elements of the manifest content. Any other procedure is arbitrary and can yield no certain result. But the dreamer's associations bring to light intermediate links which we can insert in the gap between the two [between the manifest and latent content] and by aid of which we can reinstate the latent content of the dream and "interpret" it. It is not to be wondered at if this work of interpretation (acting in a direction opposite to the dream-work) fails occasionally to arrive at complete certainty.

It remains for us to give a dynamic explanation of why the sleeping ego takes on the task of the dream-work at all. The explanation is fortunately easy to find. With the help of the unconscious, every dream that is in process of formation makes a demand upon the ego—for the satisfaction of an instinct, if the dream originates from the id; for the solution of a conflict, the removal of a doubt or the forming of an intention, if the dream originates from a residue of preconscious activity in waking life. The sleeping ego, however, is focused on the wish to maintain sleep; it feels this demand as a disturbance and seeks to get rid of the disturbance. The ego succeeds in doing this by what appears to be an act of compli-

ance: it meets the demand with what is in the circumstances a harmless *fulfilment of a wish* and so gets rid of it. This replacement of the demand by the fulfilment of a wish remains the essential function of the dream-work. It may perhaps be worth while to illustrate this by three simple examples—a hunger dream, a dream of convenience and a dream prompted by sexual desire. A need for food makes itself felt in a dreamer during his sleep: he has a dream of a delicious meal and sleeps on. The choice, of course, was open to him either of waking up and eating something or of continuing his sleep. He decided in favour of the latter and satisfied his hunger by means of the dream—for the time being, at all events, for if his hunger had persisted he would have had to wake up nevertheless. Here is the second example. A sleeper had to wake up so as to be in time for his work at the hospital. But he slept on, and had a dream that he was already at the hospital—but as a patient, who has no need to get up. Or again, a desire becomes active during the night for the enjoyment of a forbidden sexual object, the wife of a friend of the sleeper. He has a dream of sexual intercourse—not, indeed, with this person but with someone else of the same name to whom he is in fact indifferent; or his struggle against the desire may find expression in his mistress remaining altogether anonymous.

Naturally, every case is not so simple. Especially in dreams which have originated from undealt-with residues of the previous day, and which have only obtained an unconscious reinforcement during the state of sleep, it is often no easy task to uncover the unconscious motive force and its wish-fulfilment; but we may assume that it is always there. The thesis that dreams are the fulfilments of wishes will easily arouse scepticism when it is remembered how many dreams have an actually distressing content or even wake the dreamer in anxiety, quite apart from the numerous dreams without any definite feeling-tone. But the objection based on anxiety dreams cannot be sustained against analysis. It must not be forgotten that dreams are invariably the product of a conflict, that they are a kind of compromise-structure. Something that is a satisfaction for the unconscious id may for that very reason be a cause of anxiety for the ego.

As the dream-work proceeds, sometimes the unconscious will press forward more successfully and sometimes the ego will defend itself with greater energy. Anxiety dreams are mostly those whose content has undergone the least distortion. If the demand made by the unconscious is too great for the sleeping ego to be in a position to fend it off by the means at its disposal, it abandons the wish to sleep and returns to waking life. We shall be taking every experience into account if we say that a dream is invariably an *attempt* to get rid of a disturbance of sleep by means of a wishfulfilment, so that the dream is a guardian of sleep. The attempt may succeed more or less completely; it may also fail, and in that case the sleeper wakes up, apparently woken precisely by the dream. So, too, there are occasions when that excellent fellow the night-watchman, whose business it is to guard the little township's sleep, has no alternative but to sound the alarm and waken the sleeping townspeople.

Oedipus, the Child[*]
Sigmund Freud (1900)

In my experience, which is already extensive, the chief part in the mental lives of all children who later become psychoneurotics is played by their parents. Being in love with the one parent and hating the other are among the essential constituents of the stock of psychical impulses which is formed at that time and which is of such importance in determining the symptoms of the later neurosis. It is not my belief, however, that psychoneurotics differ sharply in this respect from other human beings who remain normal—that they are able, that is, to create something absolutely new and peculiar to themselves. It is far more probable—and this is confirmed by occasional observations on normal children—that they are only distinguished by exhibiting on a magnified scale feelings of love and hatred to their parents which occur less obviously and less intensely in the minds of most children.

This discovery is confirmed by a legend that has come down to us from classical antiquity: a legend whose profound and universal power to move can only be understood if the hypothesis I have put forward in regard to the psychology of children has an equally universal validity. What I have in mind is the legend of King Oedipus and Sophocles' drama which bears his name.

Oedipus, son of Laïus, King of Thebes, and of Jocasta, was exposed as an infant because an oracle

---

[*]Excerpt from James Strachey, ed. and trans., *The Interpretation of Dreams* (New York: Avon Books, 1965), pp. 294–301. Reprinted with permission of Basic Books, a member of the Perseus Books Group.

had warned Laïus that the still unborn child would be his father's murderer. The child was rescued, and grew up as a prince in an alien court, until, in doubts as to his origin, he too questioned the oracle and was warned to avoid his home since he was destined to murder his father and take his mother in marriage. On the road leading away from what he believed was his home, he met King Laïus and slew him in a sudden quarrel. He came next to Thebes and solved the riddle set him by the Sphinx who barred his way. Out of gratitude the Thebans made him their king and gave him Jocasta's hand in marriage. He reigned long in peace and honour, and she who, unknown to him, was his mother bore him two sons and two daughters. Then at last a plague broke out and the Thebans made enquiry once more of the oracle. It is at this point that Sophocles' tragedy opens. The messengers bring back the reply that the plague will cease when the murderer of Laïus has been driven from the land.

> But he, where is he? Where shall now be read
> The fading record of this ancient guilt?

The action of the play consists in nothing other than the process of revealing, with cunning delays and ever-mounting excitement—a process that can be likened to the work of a psycho-analysis—that Oedipus himself is the murderer of Laïus, but further that he is the son of the murdered man and of Jocasta. Appalled at the abomination which he has unwittingly perpetrated, Oedipus blinds himself and forsakes his home. The oracle has been fulfilled.

Oedipus Rex is what is known as a tragedy of destiny. Its tragic effect is said to lie in the contrast between the supreme will of the gods and the vain attempts of mankind to escape the evil that threatens them. The lesson which, it is said, the deeply moved spectator should learn from the tragedy is submission to the divine will and realization of his own impotence. Modern dramatists have accordingly tried to achieve a similar tragic effect by weaving the same contrast into a plot invented by themselves. But the spectators have looked on unmoved while a curse or an oracle was fulfilled in spite of all the efforts of some innocent man: later tragedies of destiny have failed in their effect.

If *Oedipus Rex* moves a modern audience no less than it did the contemporary Greek one, the explanation can only be that its effect does not lie in the contrast between destiny and human will, but is to be looked for in the particular nature of the material on which that contrast is exemplified. There must be something which makes a voice within us ready to recognize the compelling force of destiny in the *Oedipus,* while we can dismiss as merely arbitrary such dispositions as are laid down in [Grillparzer's] *Die Ahnfrau* or other modern tragedies of destiny. And a factor of this kind is in fact involved in the story of King Oedipus. His destiny moves us only because it might have been ours—because the oracle laid the same curse upon us before our birth as upon him. It is the fate of all of us, perhaps, to direct our first sexual impulse towards our mother and our first hatred and our first murderous wish against our father. Our dreams convince us that that is so. King Oedipus, who slew his father Laïus and married his mother Jocasta, merely shows us the fulfilment of our own childhood wishes. But, more fortunate than he, we have meanwhile succeeded, in so far as we have not become psychoneurotics, in detaching our sexual impulses from our mothers and in forgetting our jealousy of our fathers. Here is one in whom these primaeval wishes of our childhood have been fulfilled, and we shrink back from him with the whole force of the repression by which those wishes have since that time been held down within us. While the poet, as he unravels the past, brings to light the guilt of Oedipus, he is at the same time compelling us to recognize our own inner minds, in which those same impulses, though suppressed, are still to be found. The contrast with which the closing Chorus leaves us confronted—

> . . . Fix on Oedipus your eyes,
>   Who resolved the dark enigma, noblest champion and most wise.
>   Like a star has envied fortune mounted beaming far and wide:
>   Now he sinks in seas of anguish, whelmed beneath a raging tide . . .

—strikes as a warning at ourselves and our pride, at us who since our childhood have grown so wise and so mighty in our own eyes. Like Oedipus, we live in ignorance of these wishes, repugnant to morality, which have been forced upon us by Nature, and after their revelation we may all of us well seek to close our eyes to the scenes of our childhood.

There is an unmistakable indication in the text of Sophocles' tragedy itself that the legend of Oedipus sprang from some primaeval dream-material which had as its content the distressing disturbance of a child's relation to his parents owing to the first stirrings of sexuality. At a point when Oedipus, though he is not yet enlightened, has begun to feel troubled by his recollection of the oracle, Jocasta consoles him by referring to a dream which many people dream, though, as she thinks, it has no meaning:

> Many a man ere now in dreams hath lain
>   With her who bare him. He hath least annoy
>   Who with such omens troubleth not his mind.

Today, just as then, many men dream of having sexual relations with their mothers, and speak of the fact with indignation and astonishment. It is clearly the key to the tragedy and the complement to the dream of the dreamer's father being dead. The story of Oedipus is the reaction of the imagination to these two typical dreams. And just as these dreams, when dreamt by adults, are accompanied by feelings of repulsion, so too the legend must include horror and self-punishment. Its further modification originates once again in a misconceived secondary revision of the material, which has sought to exploit it for theological purposes. The attempt to harmonize divine omnipotence with human responsibility must naturally fail in connection with this subject-matter just as with any other.

Another of the great creations of tragic poetry, Shakespeare's *Hamlet,* has its roots in the same soil as *Oedipus Rex.* But the changed treatment of the same material reveals the whole difference in the mental life of these two widely separated epochs of civilization: the secular advance of repression in the emotional life of mankind. In the *Oedipus* the child's wishful phantasy that underlies it is brought into the open and realized as it would be in a dream. In *Hamlet* it remains repressed; and—just as in the case of a neurosis—we only learn of its existence from its inhibiting consequences. Strangely enough, the overwhelming effect produced by the more modern tragedy has turned out to be compatible with the fact that people have remained completely in the dark as to the hero's character. The play is built up on Hamlet's hesitations over fulfilling the task of revenge that is assigned to him; but its text offers no reasons or motives for these hesitations and an immense variety of attempts at interpreting them have failed to produce a result. According to the view which was originated by Goethe and is still the prevailing one today, Hamlet represents the type of man whose power of direct action is paralysed by an excessive development of his intellect. (He is "sicklied o'er with the pale cast of thought.") According to another view, the dramatist has tried to portray a pathologically irresolute character which might be classed as neurasthenic. The plot of the drama shows us, however, that Hamlet is far from being represented as a person incapable of taking any action. We see him doing so on two occasions: first in a sudden outburst of temper, when he runs his sword through the eavesdropper behind the arras, and secondly in a premeditated and even crafty fashion, when, with all the callousness of a Renaissance prince, he sends the two courtiers to the death that had been planned for himself. What is it, then, that inhibits him in fulfilling the task set him by his father's ghost? The answer, once again, is that it is the peculiar nature of the task. Hamlet is able to do anything—except take vengeance on the man who did away with his father and took that father's place with his mother, the man who shows him the repressed wishes of his own childhood realized. Thus the loathing which should drive him on to revenge is replaced in him by self-reproaches, by scruples of conscience, which remind him that he himself is literally no better than the sinner whom he is to punish. Here I have translated into conscious terms what was bound to remain unconscious in Hamlet's mind; and if anyone is inclined to call him a hysteric, I can only accept the fact as one that is implied by my interpretation. The distaste for sexuality expressed by Hamlet in his conversation with Ophelia fits in very well with this: the same distaste which was destined to take possession of the poet's mind more and more during the years that followed, and which reached its extreme expression in *Timon of Athens*. For it can of course only be the poet's own mind which confronts us in Hamlet. I observe in a book on Shakespeare by Georg Brandes (1896) a statement that *Hamlet* was written immediately after the death of Shakespeare's father (in 1601), that is, under the immediate impact of his bereavement and, as we may well assume, while his childhood feelings about his father had been freshly revived. It is known, too, that Shakespeare's own son who died at an early age bore the name of "Hamnet," which is identical with "Hamlet." Just as *Hamlet* deals with the relation of a son to his parents, so *Macbeth* (written at approximately the same period) is concerned with the subject of childlessness. But just as all neurotic symptoms, and, for that matter, dreams, are capable of being "over-interpreted" and indeed need to be, if they are to be fully understood, so all genuinely creative writings are the product of more than a single motive and more than a single impulse in the poet's mind, and are open to more than a single interpretation. In what I have written I have only attempted to interpret the deepest layer of impulses in the mind of the creative writer.

I cannot leave the subject of typical dreams of the death of loved relatives, without adding a few more words to throw light on their significance for the theory of dreams in general. In these dreams we find the highly unusual condition realized of a dream-thought formed by a repressed wish entirely eluding censorship and passing into the dream without modification. There must be special factors at work to make this event possible, and I believe that the occurrence of these dreams is facilitated by two such factors. Firstly, there is no wish that seems more remote from us than this one: "we couldn't even *dream*"—so we believe—of wishing such a thing. For this reason the dream-censorship is not armed to meet such a monstrosity, just as Solon's penal code contained no punishment for parricide. Secondly, in this case the repressed and unsuspected wish is particularly often met half-way by a residue from the previous day in the form of a *worry* about the safety of the person concerned. This worry can only make its way into the dream by availing itself of the corresponding wish; while the wish can disguise itself behind the worry that has become active during the day. We may feel inclined to think that things are simpler than this and that one merely carries on during the night and in dreams with what one has been turning over in one's mind during the day; but if so we shall be leaving dreams of the death of people of whom the dreamer is fond completely in the air and without any connection with our explanation of dreams in general, and we shall thus be clinging quite unnecessarily to a riddle which is perfectly capable of solution.

It is also instructive to consider the relation of these dreams to anxiety-dreams. In the dreams we have been discussing, a repressed wish has found a means of evading censorship—and the distortion which censorship involves. The invariable concomitant is that painful feelings are experienced in the dream. In just the same way anxiety-dreams only occur if the censorship has been wholly or partly overpowered; and, on the other hand, the overpowering of the censorship is facilitated if anxiety has already been produced as an immediate sensation arising from somatic sources. We can thus plainly see the purpose for which the censorship exercises its office and brings about the distortion of dreams: it does so *in order to prevent the generation of anxiety or other forms of distressing affect.*

Remembering, Repeating, and Working-Through*
Sigmund Freud (1919)

At this point I will interpolate a few remarks which every analyst has found confirmed in his observations. Forgetting impressions, scenes or experiences nearly always reduces itself to shutting them off. When the patient talks about these "forgotten" things he seldom fails to add: "As a matter of fact I've always known it; only I've never thought of it." He often expresses disappointment at the fact that not enough things come into his head that he can call "forgotten"—that he has never thought of since they happened. Nevertheless, even this desire is fulfilled, especially in the case of conversion hysterias. "Forgetting" becomes still further restricted when we assess at their true value the screen memories which are so generally present. In some cases I have had an impression that the familiar childhood amnesia, which is theoretically so important to us, is completely counterbalanced by screen memories. Not only *some* but *all* of what is essential from childhood has been retained in these memories. It is simply a question of knowing how to extract it out of them by analysis. They represent the forgotten years of childhood as adequately as the manifest content of a dream represents the dream-thoughts.

The other group of psychical processes—phantasies, processes of reference, emotional impulses, thought-connections—which, as purely internal acts, can be contrasted with impressions and experiences, must, in their relation to forgetting and remembering, be considered separately. In these processes it particularly often happens that something is "remembered" which could never have been "forgotten" because it was never at any time noticed—was never conscious. As regards the course taken by psychical events it seems to make no difference whatever whether such a "thought-connection"

was conscious and then forgotten or whether it never managed to become conscious at all. The conviction which the patient obtains in the course of his analysis is quite independent of this kind of memory.

In the many different forms of obsessional neurosis in particular, forgetting is mostly restricted to dissolving thought-connections, failing to draw the right conclusions and isolating memories.

There is one special class of experiences of the utmost importance for which no memory can as a rule be recovered. These are experiences which occurred in very early childhood and were not understood at the time but which were *subsequently* understood and interpreted. One gains a knowledge of them through dreams and one is obliged to believe in them on the most compelling evidence provided by the fabric of the neurosis. Moreover, we can ascertain for ourselves that the patient, after his resistances have been overcome, no longer invokes the absence of any memory of them (any sense of familiarity with them) as a ground for refusing to accept them. This matter, however, calls for so much critical caution and introduces so much that is novel and startling that I shall reserve it for a separate discussion in connection with suitable material.

Under the new technique very little, and often nothing, is left of this delightfully smooth course of events. There are some cases which behave like those under the hypnotic technique up to a point and only later cease to do so; but others behave differently from the beginning. If we confine ourselves to this second type in order to bring out the difference, we may say that the patient does not *remember* anything of what he has forgotten and repressed, but *acts* it out. He reproduces it not as a memory but as an action; he *repeats* it, without, of course, knowing that he is repeating it.

For instance, the patient does not say that he remembers that he used to be defiant and critical towards his parents' authority; instead, he behaves in that way to the doctor. He does not remember how he came to a helpless and hopeless deadlock in his infantile sexual researches; but he produces a mass of confused dreams and associations, complains that he cannot succeed in anything and asserts that he is fated never to carry through what he undertakes. He does not remember having been intensely ashamed of certain sexual activities and afraid of their being found out; but he makes it clear that he is ashamed of the treatment on which he is now embarked and tries to keep it secret from everybody. And so on.

*From *The Standard Edition of the Complete Psychological Works of Sigmund Freud*, translated and edited by James Strachey, published by the Hogarth Press. Reprinted by permission of The Random House Group Ltd., and by permission of The Marsh Agency Ltd on behalf of Sigmund Freud Copyrights.

Above, the patient will *begin* his treatment with a repetition of this kind. When one has announced the fundamental rule of psycho-analysis to a patient with an eventful life-history and a long story of illness and has then asked him to say what occurs to his mind, one expects him to pour out a flood of information; but often the first thing that happens is that he has nothing to say. He is silent and declares that nothing occurs to him. This, of course, is merely a repetition of a homosexual attitude which comes to the fore as a resistance against remembering anything. As long as the patient is in the treatment he cannot escape from this compulsion to repeat; and in the end we understand that this is his way of remembering.

What interests us most of all is naturally the relation of this compulsion to repeat to the transference and to resistance. We soon perceive that the transference is itself only a piece of repetition, and that the repetition is a transference of the forgotten past not only on to the doctor but also on to all the other aspects of the current situation. We must be prepared to find, therefore, that the patient yields to the compulsion to repeat, which now replaces the impulsion to remember, not only in his personal attitude to his doctor but also in every other activity and relationship which may occupy his life at the time—if, for instance, he falls in love or undertakes a task or starts an enterprise during the treatment. The part played by resistance, too, is easily recognized. The greater the resistance, the more extensively will acting out (repetition) replace remembering. For the ideal remembering of what has been forgotten which occurs in hypnosis corresponds to a state in which resistance has been put completely on one side. If the patient starts his treatment under the auspices of a mild and unpronounced positive transference it makes it possible at first for him to unearth his memories just as he would under hypnosis, and during this time his pathological symptoms themselves are quiescent. But if, as the analysis proceeds, the transference becomes hostile or unduly intense and therefore in need of repression, remembering at once gives way to acting out. From then onwards the resistances determine the sequence of the material which is to be repeated. The patient brings out of the armoury of the past the weapons with which he defends himself against the progress of the treatment—weapons which we must wrest from him one by one.

We have learnt that the patient repeats instead of remembering, and repeats under the conditions of resistance. We may now ask what it is that he in fact repeats or acts out. The answer is that he repeats everything that has already made its way from the sources of the repressed into his manifest personality—his inhibitions and unserviceable attitudes and his pathological character-traits. He also repeats all his symptoms in the course of the treatment. And now we can see that in drawing attention to the compulsion to repeat we have acquired no new fact but only a more comprehensive view. We have only made it clear to ourselves that the patient's state of being ill cannot cease with the beginning of his analysis, and that we must treat his illness, not as an event of the past, but as a present-day force. This state of illness is brought, piece by piece, within the field and range of operation of the treatment, and while the patient experiences it as something real and contemporary, we have to do our therapeutic work on it, which consists in a large measure in tracing it back to the past.

Remembering, as it was induced in hypnosis, could not but give the impression of an experiment carried out in the laboratory. Repeating, as it is induced in analytic treatment according to the newer technique, on the other hand, implies conjuring up a piece of real life; and for that reason it cannot always be harmless and unobjectionable. This consideration opens up the whole problem of what is so often unavoidable—"deterioration during treatment."

First and foremost, the initiation of the treatment in itself brings about a change in the patient's conscious attitude to his illness. He has usually been content with lamenting it, despising it as nonsensical and under-estimating its importance; for the rest, he has extended to its manifestations the ostrich-like policy of repression which he adopted towards its origins. Thus it can happen that he does not properly know under what conditions his phobia breaks out or does not listen to the precise wording of his obsessional ideas or does not grasp the actual purpose of his obsessional impulse. The treatment, of course, is not helped by this. He must find the courage to direct his attention to the phenomena of his illness. His illness itself must no longer seem to him contemptible, but must become an enemy worthy of his mettle, a piece of his personality, which has solid ground for its existence and out of which things of value for his future life have to be derived. The way is thus paved from the beginning for a reconciliation with the repressed material which is coming to expression in his symptoms, while at the same time place is found for a certain tolerance for the state of being ill. If this new attitude towards the illness intensifies the conflicts and brings to the fore symptoms which till then had been indistinct, one can easily console the patient by pointing out that these are only necessary and temporary aggravations and that one cannot overcome an enemy who is absent or not within range. The resistance, however, may exploit the situation for its own ends and abuse the licence to be ill. It seems to say: "See what happens if I really give way to such things. Was I not right to consign them to repression?" Young and childish people in particular are inclined to make the necessity imposed by the treatment for paying attention to their illness a welcome excuse for luxuriating in their symptoms.

Further dangers arise from the fact that in the course of the treatment new and deeper-lying instinctual impulses, which had not hitherto made themselves felt, may come to be "repeated." Finally, it is possible that the patient's actions outside the transference may do him temporary harm in his ordinary life, or even have been so chosen as permanently to invalidate his prospects of recovery.

The tactics to be adopted by the physician in this situation are easily justified. For him, remembering in the old manner—reproduction in the psychical field—is the aim to which he adheres, even though he knows that such an aim cannot be achieved in the new technique. He is prepared for a perpetual struggle with his patient to keep in the psychical sphere all the impulses which the patient would like to direct into the motor sphere; and he celebrates it as a triumph for the treatment if he can bring it about that something that the patient wishes to discharge in action is disposed of through the work of remembering. If the attachment through transference has grown into something at all serviceable, the treatment is able to prevent the patient from executing any of the more important repetitive actions and to utilize his intention to do so *in statu nascendi* as material for the therapeutic work. One best protects the patient from injuries brought about through carrying out one of his impulses by making him promise not to take any important decisions affecting his life during the time of his treatment—for instance, not to choose any profession or definitive love-object—but to postpone all such plans until after his recovery.

At the same time one willingly leaves untouched as much of the patient's personal freedom as is compatible with these restrictions, nor does one hinder him from carrying out unimportant intentions, even if they are foolish; one does not forget that it is in fact only through his own experience and mishaps that a person learns sense. There are also people whom one cannot restrain from plunging into some quite undesirable project during the treatment and who only afterwards become ready for, and accessible to, analysis. Occasionally, too, it is bound to happen that the untamed instincts assert themselves before there is time to put the reins of the transference on them, or that the bonds which attach the patient to the treatment are broken by him in a repetitive action. As an extreme example of this, I may cite the case of an elderly lady who had repeatedly fled from her house and her husband in a twilight state and gone no one knew where, without ever having become conscious of her motive for decamping in this way. She came to treatment with a marked affectionate transference which grew in intensity with uncanny rapidity in the first few days; by the end of the week she had decamped from me, too, before I had had time to say anything to her which might have prevented this repetition.

The main instrument, however, for curbing the patient's compulsion to repeat and for turning it into a motive for remembering lies in the handling of the transference. We render the compulsion harmless, and indeed useful, by giving it the right to assert itself in a definite field. We admit it into the transference as a playground in which it is allowed to expand in almost complete freedom and in which it is expected to display to us everything in the way of pathogenic instincts that is hidden in the patient's mind. Provided only that the patient shows compliance enough to respect the necessary conditions of the analysis, we regularly succeed in giving all the symptoms of the illness a new transference meaning and in replacing his ordinary neurosis by a "transference-neurosis" of which he can be cured by the therapeutic work. The transference thus creates an intermediate region between illness and real life through which the transition from the one to the other is made. The new condition has taken over all the features of the illness; but it represents an artificial illness which is at every point accessible to our intervention. It is a piece of real experience, but one which has been made possible by especially favourable conditions, and it is of a provisional nature. From the repetitive reactions which are exhibited in the transference we are led along the familiar paths to the awakening of the memories, which appear without difficulty, as it were, after the resistance has been overcome.

The Return of the Repressed in Social Life*

Sigmund Freud (1937–1939)

There are a number of similar processes among those which the analytic investigation of mental life has made known to us. Some of them are termed pathological; others are counted among the varieties of the normal. This matters little, however, for the limits between the two are not strictly defined, and the mechanisms are to a certain extent the same. It is much more important whether the changes in question take place in the Ego itself or whether they confront it as alien; in the latter case they are called symptoms. From the fullness of the material at my disposal I will choose cases that concern the formation of character.

A young girl had developed into the most decided contrast to her mother; she had cultivated all the qualities she missed in her mother and avoided all those that reminded her of her mother. I may add that in former years she had identified herself with her mother—like any other female child—and had now come to oppose this identification energetically. When this girl married, however, and became a wife and mother in her turn, we are surprised to find that she became more and more like the mother towards whom she felt so inimical, until at last the mother-identification she had overcome had once more unmistakably won the day. The same thing happens with boys, and even the great Goethe, who in his *Sturm und Drang* period certainly did not respect his pedantic and stiff father very highly, developed in old age traits that belonged to his father's character. This result will stand out more strikingly where the contrast between the two persons is more pronounced. A young man, whose fate was determined by his having to grow up with a good-for-nothing father, developed at first—in spite of the father—into a capable, trustworthy, and honourable man. In the prime of life his character changed and from then on he behaved as if he had taken this same father as his example. So as not to lose the connection with our topic we must keep in mind that at the

beginning of such a process there always exists an identification with the father from early childhood days. This gets repudiated, even over-compensated, and in the end again comes to light.

It has long since become common knowledge that the experience of the first five years of childhood exert a decisive influence on our life, one which later events oppose in vain. Much could be said about how these early experiences resist all efforts of more mature years to modify them, but this would not be relevant. It may not be so well known, however, that the strongest obsessive influence derives from those experiences which the child undergoes at a time when we have reason to believe his psychical apparatus to be incompletely fitted for accepting them. The fact itself cannot be doubted, but it seems so strange that we might try to make it easier to understand by a simile; the process may be compared to a photograph, which can be developed and made into a picture after a short or long interval. Here I may point out, however, that an imaginative writer, with the boldness permitted to such writers, made this disconcerting discovery before me. E. T. A. Hoffmann used to explain the wealth of imaginative figures that offered themselves to him for his stories by the quickly changing pictures and impressions he had received during a journey in a post-chaise, lasting for several weeks, while he was still a babe at his mother's breast. What a child has experienced and not understood by the time he has reached the age of two he may never again remember, except in his dreams. Only through psychoanalytic treatment will he become aware of those events. At any time in later years, however, they may break into his life with obsessive impulsiveness, direct his actions, force him to like or dislike people, and often decide the choice of his love-object by a preference that so often cannot be rationally defended. The two points that touch on our problem are unmistakable. They are, first, the remoteness of time, which is considered here as the really decisive factor, as, for instance, in the special state of memory that in these childhood experiences we class as "unconscious." In this feature we expect to find an analogy with the state of mind that we ascribe to tradition when it is active in the mental emotional life of a people. It was not easy, it is true, to introduce the conception of the unconscious into mass psychology.

Contributions to the phenomena we are looking for are regularly made by the mechanisms that lead to a neurosis. Here also the decisive experiences in early childhood exert a lasting influence, yet in this case the stress falls not on the time, but on the process opposing that event, the reaction against it. Schematically expressed, it is thus: As a consequence of a certain experience there arises an instinctual demand which claims satisfaction. The Ego forgoes this satisfaction, either because it is paralysed by the excessiveness of the demand or because it recognizes in it a danger. The first of these reasons is the original one; both end in the avoidance of a dangerous situation. The Ego guards against this danger by repression. The excitation becomes inhibited in one way or another; the incitement, with the observations and perceptions belonging to it, is forgotten. This, however, does not bring the process to an end; either the instinct has kept its strength, or it will regain it, or it is reawakened by a new situation. It renews its claim and—since the way to normal satisfaction is barred by what we may call the scar tissue of repression—it gains at some weak point new access to a so-called substitutive satisfaction which now appears as a symptom, without the acquiescence and also without the comprehension of the Ego. All phenomena of symptom-formation can be fairly described as "the return of the repressed." The distinctive character of them, however, lies in the extensive distortion the returning elements have undergone, compared with their original form. Perhaps the objection will be raised here that in this last group of facts I have deviated too much from the similarity with tradition. I shall feel no regret, however, if this has led us nearer to the problems of instinctual renunciation.

The Historical Truth

I have made all these psychological digressions to make it more credible that the religion of Moses exercised influence on the Jewish people only when it had become a tradition. We have scarcely achieved more than a probability. Yet let us assume we have succeeded in proving this conclusively; the impression would still remain that we had satisfied only the qualitative factor of our task, not the quantitative as well. To all matters concerning the creation of a religion—and certainly to that of the Jewish one—pertains something majestic, which has not so far been covered by our explanations. Some other element should have part in it: one that has few analogies and nothing quite like it, something unique and commensurate with that which has grown out of it, something like religion itself.

Let us see if we can approach our subject from the reverse side. We understand that primitive man needs a god as creator of the world, as head of his tribe, and as one who takes care of him. This god takes his place

behind the dead fathers of whom tradition still has something to relate. Man in later times—in our time, for instance—behaves similarly. He also remains infantile and needs protection, even when he is fully grown; he feels he cannot relinquish the support of his god. So much is indisputable, but it is not so easily to be understood why there must be only one god, why just the progress from henotheism to monotheism acquires such an overwhelming significance. It is true, as I have mentioned before, that the believer participates in the greatness of his god, and the more powerful the god, the surer the protection he can bestow. The power of a god, however, need not presuppose his being an only god: many peoples only glorified their chief god the more if he ruled over a multitude of inferior gods; he was not the less great because there were other gods than he. It also meant sacrificing some of the intimate relationship if the god became universal and cared equally for all lands and peoples. One had, so to speak, to share one's god with strangers and had to compensate oneself for that by believing that one was favoured by him. The point could be made that the conception of an Only God signifies a step forward in spirituality; this point, however, cannot be estimated so very highly.

The true believer knows of a way adequately to fill in this obvious gap in motivation. He says that the idea of an Only God has had this overwhelming effect on mankind because it is part of eternal truth, which, hidden for so long, has at last come to light and has swept all before it. We have to admit that at last we have an element of an order commensurate to the greatness of the subject as well as to that of the success of its influence.

I also should like to accept this solution. However, I have my misgivings. The religious argument is based on an optimistic and idealistic premiss. The human intellect has not shown itself elsewhere to be endowed with a very good scent for truth, nor has the human mind displayed any special readiness to accept truth. On the contrary, it is the general experience that the human intellect errs very easily without our suspecting it at all, and that nothing is more readily believed than what—regardless of the truth—meets our wishes and illusions half-way. That is why our agreement needs modifying. I too should credit the believer's solution with containing the truth; it is not, however, the material truth, but a historical truth. I would claim the right to correct a certain distortion which this truth underwent on its re-emergence. That is to say, I do not believe that one supreme great God "exists" today, but I believe that in primeval times there was one person who must needs appear gigantic and who, raised to the status of a deity, returned to the memory of men.

Our supposition was that the religion of Moses was discarded and partly forgotten and that, later on, it forced itself on the notice of the people as a tradition. I make the assumption that this process was the repetition of an earlier one. When Moses gave to his people the conception of an Only God it was not an altogether new idea, for it meant the reanimation of primeval experience in the human family that had long ago faded from the conscious memory of mankind. The experience was such an important one, however, and had produced, or at least prepared, such far-reaching changes in the life of man that, I cannot help thinking, it must have left some permanent trace in the human soul—something comparable to a tradition.

The psychoanalyses of individuals have taught us that their earliest impressions, received at a time when they were hardly able to talk, manifest themselves later in an obsessive fashion, although those impressions themselves are not consciously remembered. We feel that the same must hold good for the earliest experiences of mankind. One result of this is the emergence of the conception of one great God. It must be recognized as a memory—a distorted one, it is true, but nevertheless a memory. It has an obsessive quality; it simply must be believed. As far as its distortion goes, it may be called a delusion; in so far as it brings to light something from the past, it must be called truth. The psychiatric delusion also contains a particle of truth; the patient's conviction issues from this and extends to the whole delusional fabrication surrounding it.

. . . In 1912 I tried in my book *Totem and Taboo* to reconstruct the ancient situation from which all these effects issued. In that book I made use of certain theoretical reflections of Charles Darwin, J. J. Atkinson, and especially Robertson Smith, and combined them with findings and suggestions from psychoanalytic practice. From Darwin I borrowed the hypothesis that men originally lived in small hordes; each of the hordes stood under the rule of an older male, who governed by brute force, appropriated all the females, and belaboured or killed all the young males, including his own sons. From Atkinson I received the suggestion that this patriarchal system came to an end through a rebellion of the sons, who united against the father, overpowered him, and together consumed his body. Following Robertson Smith's totem theory, I suggested that this horde, previously ruled by the father, was followed by a totemistic brother clan. In order to be able

to live in peace with one another the victorious brothers renounced the women for whose sake they had killed the father, and agreed to practise exogamy. The power of the father was broken and the families were regulated by matriarchy. The ambivalence of the sons towards the father remained in force during the whole further development. Instead of the father a certain animal was declared the totem; it stood for their ancestor and protecting spirit, and no one was allowed to hurt or kill it. Once a year, however, the whole clan assembled for a feast at which the otherwise revered totem was torn to pieces and eaten. No one was permitted to abstain from this feast; it was the solemn repetition of the father-murder, in which social order, moral laws, and religion had had their beginnings. The correspondence of the totem feast (according to Robertson Smith's description) with the Christian Communion has struck many authors before me.

I still adhere to this sequence of thought. I have often been vehemently reproached for not changing my opinions in later editions of my book, since more recent ethnologists have without exception discarded Robertson Smith's theories and have in part replaced them by others which differ extensively. I would reply that these alleged advances in science are well known to me. Yet I have not been convinced either of their correctness or of Robertson Smith's errors. Contradiction is not always refutation; a new theory does not necessarily denote progress. Above all, however, I am not an ethnologist, but a psychoanalyst. It was my good right to select from ethnological data what would serve me for my analytic work. The writings of the highly gifted Robertson Smith provided me with valuable points of contact with the psychological material of analysis and suggestions for the use of it. I cannot say the same of the work of his opponents.

Civilization and the Individual[*]
Sigmund Freud (1930)

The analogy between the process of civilization and the path of individual development may be extended

[*]From *Civilization and Its Discontents* by Sigmund Freud, translated by James Strachey. Copyright © 1961 by James Strachey, renewed 1989 by Alix Strachey. Used by permission of W. W. Norton & Company, Inc. From *The Standard Edition of the Complete Psychological Works of Sigmund Freud*, translated and edited by James Strachey, published by the Hogarth Press. Reprinted by permission of The Random House Group Ltd., and by permission of The Marsh Agency Ltd on behalf of Sigmund Freud Copyrights.

in an important respect. It can be asserted that the community, too, evolves a super-ego under whose influence cultural development proceeds. It would be a tempting task for anyone who has a knowledge of human civilizations to follow out this analogy in detail. I will confine myself to bringing forward a few striking points. The super-ego of an epoch of civilization has an origin similar to that of an individual. It is based on the impression left behind by the personalities of great leaders—men of overwhelming force of mind or men in whom one of the human impulsions has found its strongest and purest, and therefore often its most one-sided, expression. In many instances the analogy goes still further, in that during their lifetime these figures were—often enough, even if not always—mocked and maltreated by others and even despatched in a cruel fashion. In the same way, indeed, the primal father did not attain divinity until long after he had met his death by violence. The most arresting example of this fateful conjunction is to be seen in the figure of Jesus Christ—if, indeed, that figure is not a part of mythology, which called it into being from an obscure memory of that primal event. Another point of agreement between the cultural and the individual super-ego is that the former, just like the latter, sets up strict ideal demands, disobedience to which is visited with "fear of conscience." Here, indeed, we come across the remarkable circumstance that the mental processes concerned are actually more familiar to us and more accessible to consciousness as they are seen in the group than they can be in the individual man. In him, when tension arises, it is only the aggressiveness of the super-ego which, in the form of reproaches, makes itself noisily heard; its actual demands often remain unconscious in the background. If we bring them to conscious knowledge, we find that they coincide with the precepts of the prevailing cultural super-ego. At this point the two processes, that of the cultural development of the group and that of the cultural development of the individual, are, as it were, always interlocked. For that reason some of the manifestations and properties of the super-ego can be more easily detected in its behaviour in the cultural community than in the separate individual.

The cultural super-ego has developed its ideals and set up its demands. Among the latter, those which deal with the relations of human beings to one another are comprised under the heading of ethics. People have at all times set the greatest value on ethics, as though they expected that it in particular would produce especially important results. And it does in fact deal with a subject which can easily be recognized as the sorest spot in every civilization. Ethics is thus to be regarded as a therapeutic attempt—as an endeavour to achieve, by means of a command of the super-ego, something which has so far not been achieved by means of any other cultural activities. As we already know, the problem before us is how to get rid of the greatest hindrance to civilization—namely, the constitutional inclination of human beings to be aggressive towards one another; and for that very reason we are especially interested in what is probably the most recent of the cultural commands of the super-ego, the commandment to love one's neighbour as oneself. In our research into, and therapy of, a neurosis, we are led to make two reproaches against the super-ego of the individual. In the severity of its commands and prohibitions it troubles itself too little about the happiness of the ego, in that it takes insufficient account of the resistances against obeying them—of the instinctual strength of the id [in the first place], and of the difficulties presented by the real external environment [in the second]. Consequently we are very often obliged, for therapeutic purposes, to oppose the super-ego, and we endeavour to lower its demands. Exactly the same objections can be made against the ethical demands of the cultural super-ego. It, too, does not trouble itself enough about the facts of the mental constitution of human beings. It issues a command and does not ask whether it is possible for people to obey it. On the contrary, it assumes that a man's ego is psychologically capable of anything that is required of it, that his ego has unlimited mastery over his id. This is a mistake; and even in what are known as normal people the id cannot be controlled beyond certain limits. If more is demanded of a man, a revolt will be produced in him or a neurosis, or he will be made unhappy. The commandment, "Love thy neighbour as thyself," is the strongest defence against human aggressiveness and an excellent example of the unpsychological proceedings of the cultural super-ego. The commandment is impossible to fulfil; such an enormous inflation of love can only lower its value, not get rid of the difficulty. Civilization pays no attention to all this; it merely admonishes us that the harder it is to obey the precept the more meritorious it is to do so. But anyone who follows such a precept in present-day civilization only puts himself at a disadvantage *vis-à-vis* the person who disregards it. What a potent obstacle to civilization aggressiveness must be, if the defence against it can cause as much unhappiness as aggressiveness itself! "Natural" ethics, as it is called, has nothing to offer here except the narcissistic satisfaction of being able to think oneself better than others. At this point the ethics based on religion introduces its promises of a better afterlife. But so long as virtue is not rewarded here on earth, ethics will, I fancy, preach in vain. I too think it quite certain that a real change in the relations of human beings to possessions would be of more help in this direction than any ethical commands; but the recognition of this fact among socialists has been obscured and made useless for practical purposes by a fresh idealistic misconception of human nature.

I believe the line of thought which seeks to trace in the phenomena of cultural development the part played by a super-ego promises still further discoveries. I hasten to come to a close. But there is one question which I can hardly evade. If the development of civilization has such a far-reaching similarity to the development of the individual and if it employs the same methods, may we not be justified in reaching the diagnosis that, under the influence of cultural urges, some civilizations, or some epochs of civilization—possibly the whole of mankind—have become "neurotic"? An analytic dissection of such neuroses might lead to therapeutic recommendations which could lay claim to great practical interest. I would not say that an attempt of this kind to carry psycho-analysis over to the cultural community was absurd or doomed to be fruitless. But we should have to be very cautious and not forget that, after all, we are only dealing with analogies and that it is dangerous, not only with men but also with concepts, to tear them from the sphere in which they have originated and been evolved. Moreover, the diagnosis of communal neuroses is faced with a special difficulty. In an individual neurosis we take as our starting-point the contrast that distinguishes the patient from his environment, which is assumed to be "normal." For a group all of whose members are affected by one and the same disorder no such background could exist; it would have to be found elsewhere. And as regards the therapeutic application of our knowledge, what would be the use of the most correct analysis of social neuroses, since no one possesses authority to impose such a therapy upon the group? But in spite of all these difficulties, we may expect that one day someone will venture to embark upon a pathology of cultural communities.

For a wide variety of reasons, it is very far from my intention to express an opinion upon the value of human civilization. I have endeavoured to guard myself against the enthusiastic prejudice which holds that our civilization is the most precious thing that we possess or could acquire and that its path will necessarily lead to heights of unimagined perfection. I can at least listen without indignation to the critic who is of the opinion that when one surveys the aims of cultural endeavour and the means it employs, one is bound to come to the conclusion that the whole effort is not worth the trouble, and that the outcome of it can only be a state of affairs which the individual will be unable to tolerate. . . . Thus I have not the courage to rise up before my fellow-men as a prophet, and I bow to their reproach that I can offer them no consolation: for at bottom that is what they are all demanding—the wildest revolutionaries no less passionately than the most virtuous believers.

The fateful question for the human species seems to me to be whether and to what extent their cultural development will succeed in mastering the disturbance of their communal life by the human instinct of aggression and self-destruction. It may be that in this respect precisely the present time deserves a special interest. Men have gained control over the forces of nature to such an extent that with their help they would have no difficulty in exterminating one another to the last man. They know this, and hence comes a large part of their current unrest, their unhappiness and their mood of anxiety. And now it is to be expected that the other of the two "Heavenly Powers," eternal Eros, will make an effort to assert himself in the struggle with his equally immortal adversary. But who can foresee with what success and with what result?

Ferdinand de Saussure (1857–1913), a Swiss linguist, was a contemporary of Èmile Durkheim and Max Weber. His writings show signs of direct influence from Durkheim as well as Marx. Yet little is known of his direct connections to the other social theorists of his time. Though his theory of linguistics is technical and occasionally esoteric, many readers find in it the outlines of a general social theory. Saussure's theory of language as a silent reservoir of linguistic knowledges on which speakers draw was a major influence on early structuralism and post-structuralism in the two decades following World War II. One could even say that Saussure was discovered in this period, after his death, in order to serve as a classic source for social theorists interested in remaking the social and human sciences with reference to language. This notion gains some credence from the fact that his best-known book, *Course in General Linguistics* (1966), was composed by former students from notes they took in his classes in Geneva between 1906 and 1911. There were fewer public demands for Saussure's ideas during his lifetime.

The selections from *Course in General Linguistics* represent those aspects of Saussure's linguistics most frequently used in current social theory: the theory of signs, the social basis of language, and the theory of linguistic and social values. A careful reading will reveal the influences of Durkheim and Marx, which partly explain Saussure's later popularity among French structuralist social theorists.

Arbitrary Social Values and the Linguistic Sign*
Ferdinand de Saussure (1906–1911)

Sign, Signified, Signifier

Some people regard language, when reduced to its elements, as a naming-process only—a list of words, each corresponding to the thing that it names. For example:

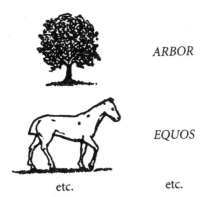

ARBOR

EQUOS

etc.   etc.

This conception is open to criticism at several points. It assumes that ready-made ideas exist before words; it does not tell us whether a name is vocal or psychological in nature (*arbor,* for instance, can be considered from either viewpoint); finally, it lets us assume that the linking of a name and a thing is a very simple operation—an assumption that is

* Saussure, Ferdinand de; Charles Bally and Albert Sechenhaye, eds., Wade Baskin, trans. *Course in General Linguistics*. New York: Philosophical Library (1966). Reprinted with permission of Philosophical Library, Inc.

anything but true. But this rather naive approach can bring us near the truth by showing us that the linguistic unit is a double entity, one formed by the associating of two terms.

We have seen in considering the speaking-circuit that both terms involved in the linguistic sign are psychological and are united in the brain by an associative bond. This point must be emphasized.

The linguistic sign unites, not a thing and a name, but a concept and a sound-image. The latter is not the material sound, a purely physical thing, but the psychological imprint of the sound, the impression that it makes on our senses. The sound-image is sensory, and if I happen to call it "material," it is only in that sense, and by way of opposing it to the other term of the association, the concept, which is generally more abstract.

The psychological character of our sound-images becomes apparent when we observe our own speech. Without moving our lips or tongue, we can talk to ourselves or recite mentally a selection of verse. Because we regard the words of our language as sound-images, we must avoid speaking of the "phonemes" that make up the words. This term, which suggests vocal activity, is applicable to the spoken word only, to the realization of the inner image in discourse. We can avoid that misunderstanding by speaking of the *sounds* and *syllables* of a word provided we remember that the names refer to the sound-image.

The linguistic sign is then a two-sided psychological entity that can be represented by the drawing:

The two elements are intimately united, and each recalls the other. Whether we try to find the meaning of the Latin word *arbor* or the word that Latin uses to designate the concept "tree," it is clear that only the associations sanctioned by that language appear to us to conform to reality, and we disregard whatever others might be imagined.

Our definition of the linguistic sign poses an important question of terminology. I call the combination of a concept and a sound-image a *sign,* but in current usage the term generally designates only a sound-image, a word, for example (*arbor,* etc.). One tends to forget that *arbor* is called a sign only because it carries the concept "tree," with the result that the idea of the sensory part implies the idea of the whole.

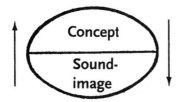

Ambiguity would disappear if the three notions involved here were designated by three names, each suggesting and opposing the others. I propose to retain the word *sign* [*signe*] to designate the whole and to replace *concept* and *sound-image* respectively by *signified* [*signifié*] and *signifier* [*signifiant*]; the last two terms have the advantage of indicating the opposition that separates them from each other and from the whole of which they are parts. As regards *sign,* if I am satisfied with it, this is simply because I do not know of any word to replace it, the ordinary language suggesting no other.

The linguistic sign, as defined, has two primordial characteristics. In enunciating them I am also positing the basic principles of any study of this type.

Principle I: The Arbitrary Nature of the Sign

The bond between the signifier and the signified is arbitrary. Since I mean by sign the whole that results from the associating of the signifier with the signified, I can simply say: *the linguistic sign is arbitrary.*

The idea of "sister" is not linked by any inner relationship to the succession of sounds *s-ö-r* which serves as its signifier in French; that it could be represented equally by just any other sequence is proved by differences among languages and by the very existence of different languages: the signified "ox" has as its signifier *b-ö-f* on one side of the border and *o-k-s* (*Ochs*) on the other.

No one disputes the principle of the arbitrary nature of the sign, but it is often easier to discover a truth than to assign to it its proper place. Principle I dominates all the linguistics of language; its consequences are numberless. It is true that not all of them are equally obvious at first glance; only after many detours does one discover them, and with them the primordial importance of the principle.

One remark in passing: when semiology becomes organized as a science, the question will arise whether or not it properly includes modes of expression based on completely natural signs, such as pantomime. Supposing that the new science welcomes them, its main concern will still be the whole group of systems grounded on the arbitrariness of the sign. In fact, every means of expression used in society is based, in principle, on collective behavior or—what amounts to the same thing—on convention. Polite formulas, for instance, though often imbued with a certain natural expressiveness (as in the case of a Chinese who greets his emperor by bowing down to the ground nine times), are nonetheless fixed by rule; it is this rule and not the intrinsic value of the gestures that obliges one to use them. Signs that are wholly arbitrary realize better than the others the ideal of the semiological process; that is why language, the most complex and universal of all systems of expression, is also the most characteristic; in this sense linguistics can become the master-pattern for all branches of semiology although language is only one particular semiological system.

The word *symbol* has been used to designate the linguistic sign, or more specifically, what is here called the signifier. Principle I in particular weighs against the use of this term. One characteristic of the symbol is that it is never wholly arbitrary; it is not empty, for there is the rudiment of a natural bond between the signifier and the signified. The symbol of justice, a pair of scales, could not be replaced by just any other symbol, such as a chariot.

The word *arbitrary* also calls for comment. The term should not imply that the choice of the signifier is left entirely to the speaker (we shall see below that the individual does not have the power to change a sign in any way once it has become established in the linguistic community); I mean that it is unmotivated, i.e. arbitrary in that it actually has no natural connection with the signified. . . .

The Sign and the Community

The signifier, though to all appearances freely chosen with respect to the idea that it represents, is fixed, not free, with respect to the linguistic community that uses it. The masses have no voice in the matter, and the signifier chosen by language could be replaced by no other. This fact, which seems to embody a contradiction, might be called colloquially "the stacked deck." We say to language: "Choose!" but we add: "It must be this sign and no other." No individual, even if he willed it, could modify in any way at all the choice that has been made; and what is more, the community itself cannot control so much as single word; it is bound to the existing language.

No longer can language be identified with a contract pure and simple, and it is precisely from this viewpoint that the linguistic sign is a particularly interesting object of study; for language furnishes the best proof that a law accepted by a community is a thing that is tolerated and not a rule to which all freely consent.

Let us first see why we cannot control the linguistic sign and then draw together the important consequences that issue from the phenomenon.

No matter what period we choose or how far back we go, language always appears as a heritage of the preceding period. We might conceive of an act by which, at a given moment, names were assigned to things and a contract was formed between concepts and sound-images; but such an act has never been recorded. The notion that things might have happened like that was prompted by our acute awareness of the arbitrary nature of the sign.

No society, in fact, knows or has ever known language other than as a product inherited from preceding generations, and one to be accepted as such. That is why the question of the origin of speech is not so important as it is generally assumed to be. The question is not even worth asking; the only real object of linguistics is the normal, regular life of an existing idiom. A particular language-state is always the product of historical forces, and these forces explain why the sign is unchangeable, i.e. why it resists any arbitrary substitution.

Nothing is explained by saying that language is something inherited and leaving it at that. Can not existing and inherited laws be modified from one moment to the next?

To meet that objection, we must put language into its social setting and frame the question just as we would for any other social institution. How are other social institutions transmitted? This more general question includes the question of immutability. We must first determine the greater or lesser amounts of freedom that the other institutions enjoy; in each instance it will be seen that a different proportion exists between fixed tradition and the free action of society. The next step is to discover why in a given category, the forces of the first type carry more weight or less weight than those of the second. Finally, coming back to language, we must ask why the historical factor of transmission dominates it entirely and prohibits any sudden widespread change.

There are many possible answers to the question. For example, one might point to the fact that succeeding generations are not superimposed on one another like the drawers of a piece of furniture, but fuse and interpenetrate, each generation embracing individuals of all ages—with the result that modifications of language are not tied to the succession of generations. One might also recall the sum of the efforts required for learning the mother language and conclude that a general change would be impossible. Again, it might be added that reflection does not enter into the active use of an idiom—speakers are largely unconscious of the laws of language; and if they are unaware of them, how could they modify them? Even if they were aware of these laws, we may be sure that their awareness would seldom lead to criticism, for people are generally satisfied with the language they have received. . . .

The linguistic sign is arbitrary; language, as defined, would therefore seem to be a system which, because it depends solely on a rational principle, is free and can be organized at will. Its social nature, considered independently, does not definitely rule out this viewpoint. Doubtless it is not on a purely logical basis that group psychology operates; one must consider everything that deflects reason in actual contacts between individuals. But the thing which keeps language from being a simple convention that can be modified at the whim of interested parties is not its social nature; it is rather the action of time combined with the social force. If time is left out, the linguistic facts are incomplete and no conclusion is possible.

If we considered language in time, without the community of speakers—imagine an isolated individual living for several centuries—we probably would notice no change; time would not influence language. Conversely, if we considered the community of speakers without considering time, we would not see the effect of the social forces that influence language. To represent the actual facts, we must then add to our first drawing a sign to indicate passage of time:

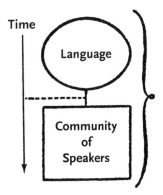

Language is no longer free, for time will allow the social forces at work on it to carry out their effects. This brings us back to the principle of continuity, which cancels freedom. But continuity necessarily implies change, varying degrees of shifts in the relationship between the signified and the signifier.

Linguistic and Social Values

Very few linguists suspect that the intervention of the factor of time creates difficulties peculiar to linguistics and opens to their science two completely divergent paths.

Most other sciences are unaffected by this radical duality; time produces no special effects in them. Astronomy has found that the stars undergo considerable changes but has not been obliged on this account to split itself into two disciplines. Geology is concerned with successions at almost every instant, but its study of strata does not thereby become a radically distinct discipline. Law has its descriptive science and its historical science; no one opposes one to the other. The political history of states is unfolded solely in time, but a historian depicting a particular period does not work apart from history. Conversely, the science of political institutions is essentially descriptive, but if the need arises it can easily deal with a historical question without disturbing its unity.

On the contrary, that duality is already forcing itself upon the economic sciences. Here, in contrast to the other sciences, political economy and economic history constitute two clearly separated disciplines within a single science; the works that have recently appeared on these subjects point up the distinction. Proceeding as they have, economists are—without being well aware of it—obeying an inner necessity. A similar necessity obliges us to divide linguistics into two parts, each with its own principle. Here as in political economy we are confronted with the notion of *value;* both sciences are concerned with *a system for equating things of different orders*—labor and wages in one and a signified and signifier in the other. . . .

To prove that language is only a system of pure values, it is enough to consider the two elements involved in its functioning: ideas and sounds.

Psychologically our thought—apart from its expression in words—is only a shapeless and indistinct mass. Philosophers and linguists have always agreed in recognizing that without the help of signs we would be unable to make a clear-cut, consistent distinction between two ideas. Without language, thought is a vague, uncharted nebula. There are no pre-existing ideas, and nothing is distinct before the appearance of language.

Against the floating realm of thought, would sounds by themselves yield predelimited entities? No more so than ideas. Phonic substance is neither more fixed nor more rigid than thought; it is not a mold into which thought must of necessity fit but a plastic substance divided in turn into distinct parts to furnish the signifiers needed by thought. The linguistic fact can therefore be pictured in its totality—i.e. language—as a series of contiguous subdivisions marked off on both the indefinite plane of jumbled ideas and the equally vague plane of sounds. . . .

Language can also be compared with a sheet of paper: thought is the front and the sound the back; one cannot cut the front without cutting the back at the same time; likewise in language, one can neither divide sound from thought nor thought from sound; the division could be accomplished only abstractedly, and the result would be either pure psychology or pure phonology.

Linguistics then works in the borderland where the elements of sound and thought combine; *their combination produces a form, not a substance.*

These views give a better understanding of what was said before about the arbitrariness of signs. Not only are the two domains that are linked by the linguistic fact shapeless and confused, but the choice of a given slice of sound to name a given idea is completely arbitrary. If this were not true, the notion of value would be compromised, for it would include an externally imposed element. But actually values remain entirely relative, and that is why the bond between the sound and the idea is radically arbitrary.

The arbitrary nature of the sign explains in turn why the social fact alone can create a linguistic system. The community is necessary if values that owe their existence solely to usage and general acceptance are to be set up; by himself the individual is incapable of fixing a single value.

In addition, the idea of value, as defined, shows that to consider a term as simply the union of a certain sound with a certain concept is grossly misleading. To define it in this way would isolate the term from its system; it would mean assuming that one can start from the terms and construct the system by adding them together when, on the contrary, it is from the interdependent whole that one must start and through analysis obtain its elements. . . .

When we speak of the value of a word, we generally think first of its property of standing for an idea, and this is in fact one side of linguistic value. But if this is true, how does *value* differ from *signification?* Might the two words be synonyms? I think not, although it is easy to confuse them, since the confusion results not so much from their similarity as from the subtlety of the distinction that they mark.

From a conceptual viewpoint, value is doubtless one element in signification, and it is difficult to see how signification can be dependent upon value and still be distinct from it. But we must clear up the issue or risk reducing language to a simple naming-process.

Let us first take signification as it is generally understood and as it was pictured. As the arrows in the drawing show, it is only the counterpart of the sound-image. Everything that occurs concerns only the sound-image and the concept when we look upon the word as independent and self-contained.

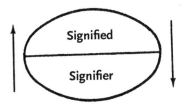

But here is the paradox: on the one hand the concept seems to be the counterpart of the sound-image, and on the other hand the sign itself is in turn the counterpart of the other signs of language.

Language is a system of interdependent terms in which the value of each term results solely from the simultaneous presence of the others, as in the diagram:

How, then can value be confused with signification, i.e. the counterpart of the sound-image? It seems impossible to liken the relations represented here by horizontal arrows to those represented above by vertical arrows. Putting it another way—and again taking up the example of the sheet of paper that is cut in two—it is clear that the observable relation between the different pieces A, B, C, D, etc. is distinct from the relation between the front and back of the same piece as in A/A, B/B, etc.

To resolve the issue, let us observe from the outset that even outside language all values are apparently governed by the same paradoxical principle. They are always composed:

1. of a *dissimilar* thing that can be *exchanged* for the thing of which the value is to be determined; and

2. of *similar* things that can be *compared* with the thing of which the value is to be determined.

Both factors are necessary for the existence of a value. To determine what a five-franc piece is worth one must therefore know: (1) that it can be exchanged for a fixed quantity of a different thing, e.g. bread; and (2) that it can be compared with a similar value of the same system, e.g. a one-franc piece, or with coins of another system (a dollar, etc.). In the same way a word can be exchanged for something dissimilar, an idea; besides, it can be compared with something of the same nature, another word. Its value is therefore not fixed so long as one simply states that it can be "exchanged" for a given concept, i.e. that it has this or that signification: one must also compare it with similar values, with other words that stand in opposition to it. Its content is really fixed only by the concurrence of everything that exists outside it. Being part of a system, it is endowed not only with a signification but also and especially with a value, and this is something quite different.

A few examples will show clearly that this is true. Modern French *mouton* can have the same signification as English *sheep* but not the same value, and this for several reasons, particularly because in speaking of a piece of meat ready to be served on the table, English uses *mutton* and not *sheep*. The difference in value between *sheep* and *mouton* is due to the fact that *sheep* has beside it a second term while the French word does not.

Within the same language, all words used to express related ideas limit each other reciprocally; synonyms like French *redouter* "dread," *craindre* "fear," and *avoir peur* "be afraid" have value only through their opposition: if *redouter* did not exist, all its content would go to its competitors. Conversely, some words are enriched through contact with others: e.g. the new element introduced in *décrépit* (un vieillard *décrépit*) results from the co-existence of *décrépi* (un mur *décrépi*). The value of just any term is accordingly determined by its environment; it is impossible to fix even the value of the word signifying "sun" without first considering its surroundings: in some languages it is not possible to say "sit in the *sun*."

Everything said about words applies to any term of language, e.g. to grammatical entities. The value of a French plural does not coincide with that of a Sanskrit plural even though their signification is usually identical; Sanskrit has three numbers instead of two (*my eyes, my ears, my arms, my legs,* etc. are dual); it would be wrong to attribute the same value to the plural in Sanskrit and in French; its value clearly depends on what is outside and around it.

If words stood for pre-existing concepts, they would all have exact equivalents in meaning from one language to the next; but this is not true. French uses *louer* (*une maison*) "let (a house)" indifferently to mean both "pay for" and "receive payment for," whereas German uses two words, *mieten* and *vermieten;* there is obviously no exact correspondence of values. The German verbs *schätzen* and *urteilen* share a number of significations, but that correspondence does not hold at several points.

Inflection offers some particularly striking examples. Distinctions of time, which are so familiar to us, are unknown in certain languages. Hebrew does not recognize even the fundamental distinctions between the past, present, and future. Proto-Germanic has no special form for the future; to say that the future is expressed by the present is wrong, for the value of the present is not the same in Germanic as in languages that have a future along with the present. The Slavic languages regularly single out two aspects of the verb: the perfective represents action as a point, complete in its totality; the imperfective represents it as taking place, and on the line of time. The categories are difficult for a Frenchman to understand, for they are unknown in French; if they were predetermined, this would not be true. Instead of pre-existing ideas then, we find in all the foregoing examples *values* emanating from the system. When they are said to correspond to concepts, it is understood that the concepts are purely differential and defined not by their positive content but negatively by their relations with the other terms of the system. Their most precise characteristic is in being what the others are not.

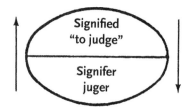

Now the real interpretation of the diagram of the signal becomes apparent. This means that in French the concept "to judge" is linked to the sound-image *juger;* in short, it symbolizes signification. But it is quite clear that initially the concept is nothing, that is only a value determined by its relations with other similar values, and that without them the signification would not exist. If I state simply that a word

signifies something when I have in mind the associating of a sound-image with a concept, I am making a statement that may suggest what actually happens, but by no means am I expressing the linguistic fact in its essence and fullness.

John Dewey (1859–1952) was of solid, if liberal, New England stock. After receiving his undergraduate degree at the University of Vermont, he was drawn to teaching, then to the study of philosophy—two subjects, among the many he wrote on, that would drive his intellectual life. After teaching high school, he returned to Johns Hopkins University where he completed doctoral studies. Dewey began his academic career in 1884 at the University of Michigan. He moved to the University of Chicago in 1894 where his reputation as an educator grew, in part, because he founded the University's Laboratory School. A decade later, he moved to Columbia University and Teacher's College until his retirement in 1930. Over a long academic career, he wrote voluminously on many subjects, including logic and psychology, democracy and education. He is included here, however, because of his important contributions, along with those of William James and George Herbert Mead, to pragmatism. Pragmatism, America's most distinctive philosophy, has recently enjoyed renewed attention from European social theorists, especially Jürgen Habermas. The selection is from one of Dewey's earliest and abidingly important books, *Democracy and Education* (1916).

Democracy and Education[*]
John Dewey (1916)

Every expansive era in the history of mankind has coincided with the operation of factors which have tended to eliminate distance between peoples and classes previously hemmed off from one another. Even the alleged benefits of war, so far as more than alleged, spring from the fact that conflict of peoples at least enforces intercourse between them and thus accidentally enables them to learn from one another, and thereby to expand their horizons. Travel,

[*] From *Democracy and Education* by John Dewey. Copyright © 1916 by The Macmillan Company; copyright renewed 1944 by John Dewey.

economic and commercial tendencies, have at present gone far to break down external barriers; to bring peoples and classes into closer and more perceptible connection with one another. It remains for the most part to secure the intellectual and emotional significance of this physical annihilation of space.

2. The Democratic Ideal.—The two elements in our criterion both point to democracy. The first signifies not only more numerous and more varied points of shared common interest, but greater reliance upon the recognition of mutual interests as a factor in social control. The second means not only freer interaction between social groups (once isolated so far as intention could keep up a separation) but change in social habit—its continuous readjustment through meeting the new situations produced by varied intercourse. And these two traits are precisely what characterize the democratically constituted society.

Upon the educational side, we note first that the realization of a form of social life in which interests are mutually interpenetrating, and where progress, or readjustment, is an important consideration, makes a democratic community more interested than other communities have cause to be in deliberate and systematic education. The devotion of democracy to education is a familiar fact. The superficial explanation is that a government resting upon popular suffrage cannot be successful unless those who elect and who obey their governors are educated. Since a democratic society repudiates the principle of external authority, it must find a substitute in voluntary disposition and interest; these can be created only by education. But there is a deeper explanation. A democracy is more than a form of government; it is primarily a mode of associated living, of conjoint communicated experience. The extension in space of the number of individuals who participate in an interest so that each has to refer his own action to that of others, and to consider the action of others to give point and direction to his own, is equivalent to the breaking down of those barriers of class, race, and national territory which kept men from perceiving the full import of their activity. These more numerous and more varied points of contact denote a greater diversity of stimuli to which an individual has to respond; they consequently put a premium on variation in his action. They secure a liberation of powers which remain suppressed as long as the incitations to action are partial, as they must be in a group which in its exclusiveness shuts out many interests.

The widening of the area of shared concerns, and the liberation of a greater diversity of personal capacities which characterize a democracy, are not of course the product of deliberation and conscious effort. On the contrary, they were caused by the development of modes of manufacture and commerce, travel, migration, and intercommunication which flowed from the command of science over natural energy. But after greater individualization on one hand, and a broader community of interest on the other have come into existence, it is a matter of deliberate effort to sustain and extend them. Obviously a society to which stratification into separate classes would be fatal, must see to it that intellectual opportunities are accessible to all on equable and easy terms. A society marked off into classes need be specially attentive only to the education of its ruling elements. A society which is mobile, which is full of channels for the distribution of a change occurring anywhere, must see to it that its members are educated to personal initiative and adaptability. Otherwise, they will be overwhelmed by the changes in which they are caught and whose significance or connections they do not perceive. The result will be a confusion in which a few will appropriate to themselves the results of the blind and externally directed activities of others.

Split Lives in the Modern World

William James (1842–1910) was a psychologist in the days before the boundaries between psychology and philosophy were well formed. His writings, including *Principles of Psychology* (1890), were, therefore, equally important to modern psychology's early history in the United States and to pragmatism, the most indigenous American school of philosophy. James was born into America's literary elite. His father had been an intimate of Ralph Waldo Emerson, and his brother was Henry James, the novelist. Throughout most of his adult life, William James was associated with Harvard, where the building that houses the social sciences now bears his name. The selection that follows describes his attempt to classify the dimensions of self. This is the classic formulation of the idea of a social self, described against three other parts of the self. Though this is a formal scientific exposition, its manifest confusion over the parts of self reflect the ordinary life experience of individuals who feel themselves pulled in a number of directions.

The Self and Its Selves[*]
William James (1890)

Let us begin with the Self in its widest acceptation, and follow it up to its most delicate and subtle form,

*THE WORKS OF WILLIAM JAMES: PRINCIPLES OF PSYCHOLOGY - VOLUME I, Frederick Burkhardt, General Editor and Fredson Bowers, Textual Editor, Copyright © 1981 by the President and Fellows of Harvard College. Reprinted by permission of the publisher.

advancing from the study of the empirical, as the Germans call it, to that of the pure, Ego.

The Empirical Self or Me

The Empirical Self of each of us is all that he is tempted to call by the name of *me*. But it is clear that between what a man calls *me* and what he simply calls *mine* the line is difficult to draw. We feel and act about certain things that are ours very much as we feel and act about ourselves. Our fame, our children, the work of our hands, may be as dear to us as our bodies are, and arouse the same feelings and the same acts of reprisal if attacked. And our bodies themselves, are they simply ours, or are they *us*? Certainly men have been ready to disown their very bodies and to regard them as mere vestures, or even as prisons of clay from which they should some day be glad to escape.

We see then that we are dealing with a fluctuating material; the same object being sometimes treated as a part of me, at other times as simply mine, and then again as if I had nothing to do with it at all. *In its widest possible sense,* however, *a man's Self is the sum total of all that he* CAN *call his,* not only his body and his psychic powers, but his clothes and his house, his wife and children, his ancestors and friends, his reputation and works, his lands and horses, and yacht and bank-account. All these things give him the same emotions. If they wax and prosper, he feels triumphant; if they dwindle and die away, he feels cast down—not necessarily in the same degree for each thing, but in much the same way for all. Understanding the Self in this widest sense, we may begin by dividing the history of it into three parts, relating respectively to—

1. Its constituents;
2. The feelings and emotions they arouse—*Self-feelings;*
3. The actions to which they prompt—*Self-seeking and Self-preservation.*

1. *The constituents of the Self* may be divided into two classes, those which make up respectively—
a. The material Self;
b. The social Self;
c. The spiritual Self; and
d. The pure Ego.

(*a*) The body is the innermost part of *the material Self* in each of us; and certain parts of the body seem more intimately ours than the rest. The clothes come next. The old saying that the human person is composed of three parts—soul, body and clothes—is more than a joke. We so appropriate our clothes and identify ourselves with them that there are few of us who, if asked to choose between having a beautiful body clad in raiment perpetually shabby and unclean, and having an ugly and blemished form always spotlessly attired, would not hesitate a moment before making a decisive reply. Next, our immediate family is a part of ourselves. Our father and mother, our wife and babes, are bone of our bone and flesh of our flesh. When they die, a part of our very selves is gone. If they do anything wrong, it is our shame. If they are insulted, our anger flashes forth as readily as if we stood in their place. Our home comes next. Its scenes are part of our life; its aspects awaken the tenderest feelings of affection; and we do not easily forgive the stranger who, in visiting it, finds fault with its arrangements or treats it with contempt. All these different things are the objects of instinctive preferences coupled with the most important practical interests of life. We all have a blind impulse to watch over our body, to deck it with clothing of an ornamental sort, to cherish parents, wife and babes, and to find for ourselves a home of our own which we may live in and "improve."

An equally instinctive impulse drives us to collect property; and the collections thus made become, with different degrees of intimacy, parts of our empirical selves. The parts of our wealth most intimately ours are those which are saturated with our labor. There are few men who would not feel personally annihilated if a lifelong construction of their hands or brains—say an entomological collection or an extensive work in manuscript—were suddenly swept away. The miser feels similarly towards his gold; and although it is true that a part of our depression at the loss of possessions is due to our feeling that we must now go without certain goods that we expected the possessions to bring in their train, yet in every case there remains, over and above this, a sense of the shrinkage of our personality, a partial conversion of ourselves to nothingness, which is a psychological phenomenon by itself. We are all at once assimilated to the tramps and poor devils whom we so despise, and at the same time removed farther than ever away from the happy sons of earth who lord it over land and sea and men in the full-blown lustihood that wealth and power can give, and before whom, stiffen ourselves as we will be appealing to anti-snobbish first principles, we cannot escape an emotion, open or sneaking, of respect and dread.

(*b*) A man's *Social Self* is the recognition which he gets from his mates. We are not only gregarious animals, liking to be in sight of our fellows, but we have an innate propensity to get ourselves noticed, and noticed favorably, by our kind. No more fiendish punishment could be devised, were such a thing physically possible, than that one should be turned loose in society and remain absolutely unnoticed by all the members thereof. If no one turned round when we entered, answered when we spoke, or minded what we did, but if every person we met "cut us dead," and acted as if we were non-existing things, a kind of rage and impotent despair would ere long well up in us, from which the cruellest bodily tortures would be a relief; for these would make us feel that, however bad might be our plight, we had not sunk to such a depth as to be unworthy of attention at all.

Properly speaking, *a man has as many social selves as there are individuals who recognize him* and carry an image of him in their mind. To wound any one of these his images is to wound him. But as the individuals who carry the images fall naturally into classes, we may practically say that he has as many different social selves as there are distinct *groups* of persons about whose opinion he cares. He generally shows a different side of himself to each of these different groups. Many a youth who is demure enough before his parents and teachers, swears and swaggers like a pirate among his "tough" young friends. We do not show ourselves to our children as to our club-companions, to our customers as to the laborers we employ, to our own masters and employers as to our intimate friends. From this there results what practically is a division of the man into several selves; and this may be a discordant splitting, as where one is afraid to let one set of his acquaintances know him as he is elsewhere; or it may be a perfectly harmonious division of labor, as where one tender to his children is stern to the soldiers or prisoners under his command.

The most peculiar social self which one is apt to have is in the mind of the person one is in love with. The good or bad fortunes of this self cause the most intense elation and dejection—unreasonable enough as measured by every other standard than that of the organic feeling of the individual. To his own consciousness he *is* not, so long as this particular social self fails to get recognition, and when it is recognized his contentment passes all bounds.

A man's *fame,* good or bad, and his *honor* or dishonor, are names for one of his social selves. The particular social self of a man called his honor is usually the result of one of those splittings of which we have spoken. It is his image in the eyes of his own "set," which exalts or condemns him as he conforms or not to certain requirements that may not be made of one in another walk of life. Thus a layman may abandon a city infected with cholera; but a priest or a doctor would think such an act incompatible with his honor. A soldier's honor requires him to fight or to die under circumstances where another man can apologize or run away with no stain upon his social self. A judge, a statesman, are in like manner debarred by the honor of their cloth from entering into pecuniary relations perfectly honorable to persons in private life. Nothing is commoner than to hear people discriminate between their different selves of this sort: "As a man I pity you, but as an official I must show you no mercy"; "As a politician I regard him as an ally, but as a moralist I loathe him"; etc., etc. What may be called "clubopinion" is one of the very strongest forces in life. The thief must not steal from other thieves; the gambler must pay his gambling debts, though he pay no other debts in the world. The code of honor of fashionable society has throughout history been full of permissions as well as of vetoes, the only reason for following either of which is that so we best serve one of our social selves. You must not lie in general, but you may lie as much as you please if asked about your relations with a lady; you must accept a challenge from an equal, but if challenged by an inferior you may laugh him to scorn: these are examples of what is meant.

(c) By the Spiritual Self, so far as it belongs to the Empirical Me, I mean a man's inner or subjective being, his psychic faculties or dispositions, taken concretely; not the bare principle of personal Unity, or "pure" Ego, which remains still to be discussed. These psychic dispositions are the most enduring and intimate part of the self, that which we most verily seem to be. We take a purer self-satisfaction when we think of our ability to argue and discriminate, of our moral sensibility and conscience, of our indomitable will, than when we survey any of our other possessions. Only when these are altered is a man said to be *alienatus a se.* . . .

But when I forsake such general descriptions and grapple with particulars, coming to the closest possible quarters with the facts, *it is difficult for me to detect in the activity any purely spiritual element at all. Whenever my introspective glance succeeds in turning round quickly enough to catch one of these manifestations of spontaneity in the act, all it can ever feel distinctly is some bodily process, for the most part taking place within the head.* Omitting for a moment what is obscure in these introspective results, let me try to state those particulars which to my own consciousness seem indubitable and distinct.

In the first place, the acts of attending, assenting, negating, making an effort, are felt as movements of something in the head. In many cases it is possible to describe these movements quite exactly. In attending to either an idea or a sensation belonging to a particular sense-sphere, the movement is the adjustment of the sense-organ, felt as it occurs. I cannot think in visual terms, for example, without feeling a fluctuating play of pressures, convergences, divergences, and accommodations in my eyeballs. The direction in which the object is conceived to lie determines the character of these movements, the feeling of which becomes, for my consciousness, identified with the manner in which I make myself ready to receive the visible thing. My brain appears to me as if all shot across with lines of direction, of which I have become conscious as my attention has shifted from one sense-organ to another, in passing to successive outer things, or in following trains of varying sense-ideas.

When I try to remember or reflect, the movements in question, instead of being directed towards the periphery, seem to come from the periphery inwards and feel like a sort of *withdrawal* from the outer world. As far as I can detect, these feelings are due to an actual rolling outwards and upwards of the eyeballs, such as I believe occurs in me in sleep, and is the exact opposite of their action in fixating a physical thing. In reasoning, I find that I am apt to have a kind of vaguely localized diagram in my mind, with the various fractional objects of the thought disposed at particular points thereof; and the oscillations of my attention from one of them to another are most distinctly felt as alternations of direction in movements occurring inside the head.

In consenting and negating, and in making a mental effort, the movements seem more complex, and I find them harder to describe. The opening and closing of the glottis play a great part in these operations, and, less distinctly, the movements of the soft palate, etc., shutting off the posterior nares from the mouth. My glottis is like a sensitive valve, intercepting my breath instantaneously at every mental hesitation or felt aversion to the objects of my thought, and as quickly opening, to let the air pass through my throat and nose, the moment the repugnance is overcome. The feeling of the movement of this air is, in me, one strong ingredient of the feeling of assent. The movements of the muscles of the brow and eyelids also respond very sensitively to every fluctuation in the agreeableness or disagreeableness of what comes before my mind.

In *effort* of any sort, contractions of jaw-muscles and of those of respiration are added to those of the brow and glottis, and thus the feeling passes out of the head properly so called. It passes out of the head whenever the welcoming or rejecting of the object is *strongly* felt. Then a set of feelings pour in from many bodily parts, all "expressive" of my emotion, and the head-feelings proper are swallowed up in this larger mass.

In a sense, then, it may be truly said that, in one person at least, *the "Self of selves," when carefully examined, is found to consist mainly of the collection of these peculiar motions in the head or between the head and throat.* I do not for a moment say that this is *all* it consists of, for I fully realize how desperately hard is introspection in this field. But I feel quite sure that these cephalic motions are the portions of my innermost activity of which I am *most distinctly aware.* If the dim portions which I cannot yet define should prove to be like unto these distinct portions in me, and I like other men, *it would follow that our entire feeling of spiritual activity, or what commonly passes by that name, is really a feeling of bodily activities whose exact nature is by most men overlooked. . . .*

(*d*) *The Pure ego* [is the most puzzling aspect of the self—a transitional feature from the phenomenal self and pure personal identity—CL]. Having summed up the principal results of the chapter thus far, I have said all that need be said of the constituents of the phenomenal self, and of the nature of self-regard. Our decks are consequently cleared for the struggle with that pure principle of personal identity which has met us all along our preliminary exposition, but which we have always shied from and treated as a difficulty to be postponed. Ever since Hume's time, it has been justly regarded as the most puzzling puzzle with which psychology has to deal; and whatever view one may espouse, one has to hold his position against heavy odds. If, with the Spiritualists, one contends for a substantial soul, or transcendental principle of unity, one can give no positive account of what that may be. And if, with the Humians, one deny such a principle and say that the stream of passing thoughts is all, one runs against the entire common-sense of mankind, of which the belief in a distinct principle of selfhood seems an integral part. Whatever solution be adopted in the pages to come, we may as well make up our minds in advance that it will fail to satisfy the majority of those to whom it is addressed. The best way of approaching the matter will be to take up first—

The Sense of Personal Identity

In the last chapter it was stated in as radical way as possible that the thoughts which we actually know to exist do not fly about loose, but seem each to belong to some one thinker and not to another. Each thought, out of a multitude of other thoughts of which it may think, is able to distinguish those which belong to its own Ego from those which do not. The former have a warmth and intimacy about them of which the latter are completely devoid, being merely conceived, in a cold and foreign fashion, and not appearing as blood-relatives, bringing their greetings to us from out of the past.

Now this consciousness of personal sameness may be treated either as a subjective phenomenon or as an objective deliverance, as a feeling, or as a truth. We may explain how one bit of thought can come to judge other bits to belong to the same Ego with itself; or we may criticise its judgment and decide how far it may tally with the nature of things.

As a mere subjective phenomenon the judgment presents no difficulty or mystery peculiar to itself. It belongs to the great class of judgments of sameness; and there is nothing more remarkable in making a judgment of sameness in the first person than in the second or the third. The intellectual operations seem essentially alike, whether I say "I am the same," or whether I say "the pen is the same, as yesterday." It is as easy to think this as to think the opposite and say "neither I nor the pen is the same."

This sort of *bringing of things together into the object of a single judgment* is of course essential to all thinking. The things are conjoined *in* the thought, whatever may be the relation in which they appear to the thought. The thinking them is *thinking* them together, even if only with the result of judging that they do not *belong* together. This sort of *subjective synthesis,* essential to knowledge as such (whenever it has a complex object), must not be confounded with *objective synthesis* or union instead of difference or disconnection, known among the things. The subjective synthesis is involved in thought's mere existence. Even a really disconnected world could only be *known* to be such by having its parts temporarily united in the Object of some pulse of consciousness.

The sense of personal identity is not, then, this mere synthetic form essential to all thought. It is the sense of a sameness perceived *by* thought and predicated of things *thought-about.* These things are a present self and a self of yesterday. The thought not only thinks them both, but thinks that they are identical. The psychologist, looking on and playing the critic, might prove the thought wrong, and show there was no real identity,—there might have been no yesterday, or, at any rate, no self of yesterday; or, if there were, the sameness predicated might not obtain, or might be predicated on insufficient grounds. In either case the personal identity would not exist as a *fact;* but it would exist as a *feeling* all the same; the consciousness of it by the thought would be there, and the psychologist would still have to analyze that, and show where its illusoriness lay. Let us now be the psychologist and see whether it be right or wrong when it says, *I am the same self that I was yesterday.*

William Edward Burghardt (W. E. B.) Du Bois (1868–1963) was born and grew up in Great Barrington, Massachusetts, where he experienced racial discrimination only obliquely. Yet he came to be the greatest American social theorist of race. Nearly every event in the history of race in America, from Reconstruction to the Civil Rights Movement, was influenced by his ideas or his political actions. In his youth, Du Bois studied at Fisk University, then attended Harvard, where he received his Ph.D. in 1895 after two years of study in Germany. Early in his scholarly career, he single-handedly completed the first major, and still important, empirical sociological study of Negro life in the United States, *The Philadelphia Negro* (1899). But until recently, he was largely ignored by official sociology. Eventually, his work moved beyond social science into history, fiction, and essays. A chapter in his *Souls of Black Folk* (1903) sparked his battle with Booker T. Washington, then the dominant spokesman for Negro Americans. Du Bois organized the Niagara Movement (1905–1910) in opposition to Washington, who opposed the higher education of Blacks in favor of industrial training. From the Niagara Movement came the National Association for the Advancement of Colored People (NAACP), with which Du Bois was associated during much of the rest of his active life. In the 1920s, he was locked in controversy with Marcus Garvey over their differing views of Pan-Africanism. Though Du Bois's roots were in America, he was a leader in the global Pan-African movement, and, in his last years, he was honored in China, the USSR, Africa, and Europe. In 1961, then ninety-three years old, Du Bois moved to Ghana to begin work on the *Encyclopedia Africana.* He died on the eve of the civil rights march on Washington, D.C.—August 27, 1963.

"Double-Consciousness and the Veil" is the opening chapter of *Souls of Black Folk,* in which Du Bois used poetry, autobiography, and history to make strong theoretical points. His concept of twoness, or double-consciousness, has been an enduring force in African-American social and literary theory. The book's title is meant precisely—two souls, one self. Du Bois's literary method reflected his theory, as in his practice of composing epigraphs that juxtaposed the classic literature of the West with unmarked bars of music from the American black tradition. "The Spirit of Modern Europe," published only recently, was the title of an address given in Louisville, Kentucky, in 1900, shortly after Du Bois returned from London, where he had organized and led the first international Pan-African conference. This is a clear example of what today might be called a multicultural social theory. Du Bois understated his attack on Europe's narrow cultural logic in order to define the global interests (and responsibilities) of the civilizations of Africa and other societies across the world.

Double-Consciousness and the Veil[*]

W. E. B. Du Bois (1903)

O water, voice of my heart, crying in the
    sand,
All night long crying with a mournful cry,
As I lie and listen, and cannot understand
The voice of my heart in my side or the voice
    of the sea,
O water, crying for rest, is it I, is it I?
All night long the water is crying to me.
Unresting water, there shall never be rest
Till the last moon droop and the last tide fail,
And the fire of the end begin to burn in the
    west;
And the heart shall be weary and wonder and
    cry like the sea,
All life long crying without avail,
As the water all night long is crying to me.
               —*Arthur Symons*

Between me and the other world there is ever an unasked question: unasked by some through feelings of delicacy; by others through the difficulty of rightly framing it. All, nevertheless, flutter round it. They approach me in a half-hesitant sort of way, eye me curiously or compassionately, and then, instead of saying directly, How does it feel to be a problem? they say, I know an excellent colored man in my town; or, I fought at Mechanicsville; or, Do not these Southern outrages make your blood boil? At these I smile, or am interested, or reduce the boiling to a simmer, as the occasion may require. To the real question, How does it feel to be a problem? I answer seldom a word.

And yet, being a problem is a strange experience,—peculiar even for one who has never been anything else, save perhaps in babyhood and in Europe. It is in the early days of rollicking boyhood that the revelation first bursts upon one, all in a day, as it were. I remember well when the shadow swept across me. I was a little thing, away up in the hills of New England, where the dark Housatonic winds between Hoosac and Taghkanic to the sea. In a wee wooden schoolhouse, something put it into the boys' and girls' heads to buy gorgeous visiting-cards—ten cents a package—and exchange. The exchange was merry, till one girl, a tall newcomer, refused my card,—refused it peremptorily, with a glance. Then it dawned upon me with a certain suddenness that I was different from the others; or like, mayhap, in heart and life and longing, but shut out from their world by a vast veil. I had thereafter no desire to tear down that veil, to creep through; I held all beyond it in common contempt, and lived above it in a region of blue sky and great wandering shadows. That sky was bluest when I could beat my mates at examination-time, or beat them at a foot-race, or even beat their stringy heads. Alas, with the years all this fine contempt began to fade; for the words I longed for, and all their dazzling opportunities, were theirs, not mine. But they should not keep these prizes, I said; some, all, I would wrest from them. Just how I would do it I could never decide: by reading law, by healing the sick, by telling the wonderful tales that swam in my head,—some way. With other black boys the strife was not so fiercely sunny: their youth shrunk into tasteless sycophancy, or into silent hatred of the pale world about them and mocking distrust of everything white; or wasted itself in a bitter cry. Why did God make me an outcast and a stranger in mine own house? The shades of the prison-house closed round about us all: walls strait and stubborn to the whitest, but relentlessly narrow, tall, and unscalable to sons of night who must plod darkly on in resignation, or beat unavailing palms against the stone, or steadily, half hopelessly, watch the streak of blue above.

After the Egyptian and Indian, the Greek and Roman, the Teuton and Mongolian, the negro is a sort of seventh son, born with a veil, and gifted with second-sight in this American world,—a world which yields him no true self-consciousness, but only lets him see himself through the revelation of the other world. It is a peculiar sensation, this double-consciousness, this sense of always looking at one's self through the eyes of others, of measuring one's soul by the tape of a world that looks on in amused contempt and pity. One ever feels his twoness,—an American, a Negro; two souls, two thoughts, two unreconciled strivings; two warring ideals in one dark body, whose dogged strength alone keeps it from being torn asunder.

The history of the American Negro is the history of this strife,—this longing to attain self-conscious manhood, to merge his double self into a better and

---

[*] Excerpt from *The Souls of Black Folk* (New York: A. C. McClurg & Co., 1904), pp. 1–9.

truer self. In this merging he wishes neither of the older selves to be lost. He would not Africanize America, for America has too much to teach the world and Africa. He would not bleach his Negro soul in a flood of white Americanism, for he knows that Negro blood has a message for the world. He simply wishes to make it possible for a man to be both a Negro and an American, without being cursed and spit upon by his fellows, without having the doors of Opportunity closed roughly in his face.

This, then, is the end of his striving: to be a co-worker in the kingdom of culture, to escape both death and isolation, to husband and use his best powers and his latent genius. These powers of body and mind have in the past been strangely wasted, dispersed, or forgotten. The shadow of a mighty Negro past flits through the tale of Ethiopia the Shadowy and of Egypt the Sphinx. Through history, the powers of single black men flash here and there like falling stars, and die sometimes before the world has rightly gauged their brightness. Here in America, in the few days since Emancipation, the black man's turning hither and thither in hesitant and doubtful striving has often made his very strength to lose effectiveness, to seem like absence of power, like weakness. And yet it is not weakness,—it is the contradiction of double aims. The double-aimed struggle of the black artisan—on the one hand to escape white contempt for a nation of mere hewers of wood and drawers of water, and on the other hand to plough and nail and dig for a poverty-stricken horde—could only result in making him a poor craftsman, for he had but half a heart in either cause. By the poverty and ignorance of his people, the Negro minister or doctor was tempted toward quackery and demagogy; and by the criticism of the other world, toward ideals that made him ashamed of his lowly tasks. The would-be black *savant* was confronted by the paradox that the knowledge of his people needed was a twice-told tale to his white neighbors, while the knowledge which would teach the white world was Greek to his own flesh and blood. The innate love of harmony and beauty that set the ruder souls of his people a-dancing and a-singing raised but confusion and doubt in the soul of the black artist; for the beauty revealed to him was the soul-beauty of a race which his larger audience despised, and he could not articulate the message of another people. This waste of double aims, this seeking to satisfy two unreconciled ideals, has wrought sad havoc with the courage and faith and deeds of ten thousand thousand people,—has sent them

often wooing false gods and invoking false means of salvation, and at times has even seemed about to make them ashamed of themselves.

Away back in the days of bondage they thought to see in one divine event the end of all doubt and disappointment; few men ever worshipped Freedom with half such unquestioning faith as did the American Negro for two centuries. To him, so far as he thought and dreamed, slavery was indeed the sum of all villainies, the cause of all sorrow, the root of all prejudice; Emancipation was the key to a promised land of sweeter beauty than ever stretched before the eyes of wearied Israelites. In song and exhortation swelled one refrain—Liberty; in his tears and curses the God he implored had Freedom in his right hand. At last it came,—suddenly, fearfully, like a dream. With one wild carnival of blood and passion came the message in his own plaintive cadences:—

"Shout, O children!
Shout, you're free!
For God has bought your liberty!"

Years have passed away since then,—ten, twenty, forty; forty years of national life, forty years of renewal and development, and yet the swarthy spectre sits in its accustomed seat at the Nation's feast. In vain do we cry to this our vastest social problem:—

"Take any shape but that, and my firm nerves
Shall never tremble!"

The Nation has not yet found peace from its sins; the freedman has not yet found in freedom his promised land. Whatever of good may have come in these years of change, the shadow of a deep disappointment rests upon the Negro people,—a disappointment all the more bitter because the unattained ideal was unbounded save by the simple ignorance of a lowly people.

The first decade was merely a prolongation of the vain search for freedom, the boon that seemed ever barely to elude their grasp,—like a tantalizing will-o'-the-wisp, maddening and misleading the headless host. The holocaust of war, the terrors of the Ku-Klux Klan, the lies of carpet-baggers, the disorganization of industry, and the contradictory advice of friends and foes, left the bewildered serf with no new watchword beyond the old cry for freedom. As the time flew, however, he began to grasp a new idea. The ideal of liberty demanded for its attainment powerful means, and these the Fifteenth Amendment gave him. The ballot, which before he had looked upon as a visible sign of freedom, he now regarded as the chief means of gaining and perfecting the liberty with which war had partially endowed him. And why not? Had not votes made war and emancipated millions? Had not votes enfranchised the freedmen? Was anything impossible to a power that had done all this? A million black men started with renewed zeal to vote themselves into the kingdom. So the decade flew away, the revolution of 1876 came, and left the half-free serf weary, wondering, but still inspired. Slowly but steadily, in the following years, a new vision began gradually to replace the dream of political power,—a powerful movement, the rise of another ideal to guide the unguided, another pillar of fire by night after a clouded day. It was the ideal of "book-learning"; the curiosity, born of compulsory ignorance, to know and test the power of the cabalistic letters of the white man, the longing to know. Here at last seemed to have been discovered the mountain path to Canaan; longer than the highway of Emancipation and law, steep and rugged, but straight, leading to heights high enough to overlook life.

Up the new path the advance guard toiled, slowly, heavily, doggedly; only those who have watched and guided the faltering feet, the misty minds, the dull understandings, of the dark pupils of these schools know how faithfully, how piteously, this people strove to learn. It was weary work. The cold statistician wrote down the inches of progress here and there, noted also where here and there a foot had slipped or some one had fallen. To the tired climbers, the horizon was ever dark, the mists were often cold, the Canaan was always dim and far away. If, however, the vistas disclosed as yet no goal, no resting-place, little but flattery and criticism, the journey at least gave leisure for reflection and self-examination; it changed the child of Emancipation to the youth with dawning self-consciousness, self-realization, self-respect. In those sombre forests of his striving his own soul rose before him, and he saw himself,—darkly as through a veil; and yet he saw in himself some faint revelation of his power, of his mission. He began to have a dim feeling that, to attain his place in the world, he must be himself, and not another. For the first time he sought to analyze the burden he bore upon his back, that dead-weight of social degradation partially masked behind a half-named Negro problem. He felt his poverty; without a cent, without a home, without land, tools, or savings, he had entered into competition with rich, landed, skilled neighbors. To be a poor

man is hard, but to be a poor race in a land of dollars is the very bottom of hardships. He felt the weight of his ignorance,—not simply of letters, but of life, of business, of the humanities; the accumulated sloth and shirking and awkwardness of decades and centuries shackled his hands and feet. Nor was his burden all poverty and ignorance. The red stain of bastardy, which two centuries of systematic legal defilement of Negro women had stamped upon his race, meant not only the loss of ancient African chastity, but also the hereditary weight of a mass of corruption from white adulterers, threatening almost the obliteration of the Negro home.

A people thus handicapped ought not to be asked to race with the world, but rather allowed to give all its time and thought to its own social problems. But alas! while sociologists gleefully count his bastards and his prostitutes, the very soul of the toiling, sweating black man is darkened by the shadow of a vast despair. Men call the shadow prejudice, and learnedly explain it as the natural defence of culture against barbarism, learning against ignorance, purity against crime, the "higher" against the "lower" races. To which the Negro cries Amen! and swears that to so much of this strange prejudice as is founded on just homage to civilization, culture, righteousness, and progress, he humbly bows and meekly does obeisance. But before that nameless prejudice that leaps beyond all this he stands helpless, dismayed, and well-nigh speechless; before that personal disrespect and mockery, the ridicule and systematic humiliation, the distortion of fact and wanton license of fancy, the cynical ignoring of the better and the boisterous welcoming of the worse, the all-pervading desire to inculcate disdain for everything black, from Toussaint to the devil,—before this there rises a sickening despair that would disarm and discourage any nation save that black host to whom "discouragement" is an unwritten word.

But the facing of so vast a prejudice could not but bring the inevitable self-questioning, self-disparagement, and lowering of ideals which ever accompany repression and breed in an atmosphere of contempt and hate. Whisperings and portents came borne upon the four winds: Lo! we are diseased and dying, cried the dark hosts; we cannot write, our voting is vain; what need of education, since we must always cook and serve? And the Nation echoed and enforced this self-criticism, saying: Be content to be servants, and nothing more; what need of higher culture for half-men? Away with the black man's ballot, by force or fraud,—and behold the suicide of a race! Nevertheless, out of the evil came something of good,—the more careful adjustment of education to real life, the clearer perception of the Negroes' social responsibilities, and the sobering realization of the meaning of progress.

So dawned the time of *Sturm und Drang:* storm and stress to-day rocks our little boat on the mad waters of the world-sea; there is within and without the sound of conflict, the burning of body and rending of soul; inspiration strives with doubt, and faith with vain questionings. The bright ideals of the past,— physical freedom, political power, the training of brains and the training of hands,—all these in turn have waxed and waned, until even the last grows dim and overcast. Are they all wrong,—all false? No, not that, but each alone was over-simple and incomplete,—the dreams of a credulous race-childhood, or the fond imaginings of the other world which does not know and does not want to know our power. To be really true, all these ideals must be melted and welded into one. The training of the schools we need to-day more than ever,—the training of deft hands, quick eyes and ears, and above all the broader, deeper, higher culture of gifted minds and pure hearts. The power of the ballot we need in sheer self-defence,— else what shall save us from a second slavery? Freedom, too, the long-sought, we still seek,—the freedom of life and limb, the freedom to work and think, the freedom to love and aspire. Work, culture, liberty,—all these we need, not singly but together, not successively but together, each growing and aiding each, and all striving toward that vaster ideal that swims before the Negro people, the ideal of human brotherhood, gained through the unifying ideal of Race; the ideal of fostering and developing the traits and talents of the Negro, not in opposition to or contempt for other races, but rather in large conformity to the greater ideals of the American Republic, in order that some day on American soil two world-races may give each to each those characteristics both so sadly lack. We the darker ones come even now not altogether empty-handed: there are to-day no truer exponents of the pure human spirit of the Declaration of Independence than the American Negroes; there is no true American music but the wild sweet melodies of the Negro slave; the American fairy tales and folklore are Indian and African; and, all in all, we black men seem the sole oasis of simple faith and reverence in a dusty desert of dollars and smartness. Will America be poorer if she replace her brutal dyspeptic blundering with light-hearted but determined Negro humility? or her coarse and cruel wit with loving jovial good-humor? or her vulgar music with the soul of the Sorrow Songs?

Merely a concrete test of the underlying principles of the great republic is the Negro Problem, and the spiritual striving of the freedmen's sons is the travail of souls whose burden is almost beyond the measure of their strength, but who bear it in the name of an historic race, in the name of this the land of their fathers' fathers, and in the name of human opportunity.

Charlotte Perkins Gilman (1860–1935) is best known today for "The Yellow Wallpaper" (1892), the fictionalized account of her nervous breakdown, which was the most acute in the two years following April 1886. At that time, she was married to Charles Walter Stetson, who colluded in a treatment plan that called for her to withdraw from all intellectual labors. Charlotte eventually worked her way out of the illness by resuming her intellectual life. After her first marriage ended more or less amicably, she moved to California, where she rebuilt a life with her daughter. In these years, she earned her livelihood in large part through public lectures. Her feminism was undoubtedly shaped by these early experiences. While living the life of a public intellectual, reformer, and feminist, Charlotte Perkins Gilman wrote important scholarly works, including publications in academic journals such as the *American Journal of Sociology*. Her principal writings in social theory developed a sophisticated feminist interpretation of the effects and relations among economic life, the family, and gender roles. *Women and Economics* (1898) was widely read in its day. Other books, along with scholarly articles, brought her a degree of recognition from the literary and academic establishment; these include *The Home* (1903) and *Human Work* (1904). For seven years, beginning in 1909, she organized, edited, and wrote every word (including advertising copy) for *Forerunner*, a monthly magazine. By her own estimate, the total words involved equaled that of four major books each year. Indeed, her literary output—scholarly works, essays, lectures, fiction—was prodigious. After the *Forerunner* years, Gilman's influence lessened. Yet she continued to write and live with purpose and courage—after 1922, in Norwich, Connecticut. She took her own life in 1935, saying, "I have preferred chloroform to cancer."

The selection from "The Yellow Wallpaper" illustrates Gilman's ability to use fiction to rivet the reader's attention on what amounts to an implicit social theory of gender relations. Her utopian novel, *Herland* (1915), extends this method into a more complete feminist statement. The "Women and Economics" selection stands up well against more recent analyses of the family wage system and "second-shift" labor demands whereby a society's economic interests are served at a cost to women.

The Yellow Wallpaper*
Charlotte Perkins Gilman (1892)

It is very seldom that mere ordinary people like John and myself secure ancestral halls for the summer.

A colonial mansion, a hereditary estate, I would say a haunted house and reach the height of romantic felicity—but that would be asking too much of fate!

Still I will proudly declare that there is something queer about it.

Else, why should it be let so cheaply? And why have stood so long untenanted?

John laughs at me, of course, but one expects that.

John is practical in the extreme. He has no patience with faith, an intense horror of superstition, and he scoffs openly at any talk of things not to be felt and seen and put down in figures.

John is a physician, and *perhaps*—(I would not say it to a living soul, of course, but this is dead paper and a great relief to my mind)—*perhaps* that is one reason I do not get well faster.

You see, he does not believe I am sick! And what can one do?

If a physician of high standing, and one's own husband, assures friends and relatives that there is really nothing the matter with one but temporary nervous depression—a slight hysterical tendency—what is one to do?

My brother is also a physician, and also of high standing, and he says the same thing.

So I take phosphates or phosphites—whichever it is—and tonics, and air and exercise, and journeys, and am absolutely forbidden to "work" until I am well again.

Personally, I disagree with their ideas.

Personally, I believe that congenial work, with excitement and change, would do me good.

But what is one to do?

I did write for a while in spite of them; but it *does* exhaust me a good deal—having to be so sly about it, or else meet with heavy opposition.

I sometimes fancy that in my condition, if I had less opposition and more society and stimulus—but John says the very worst thing I can do is to think about my condition, and I confess it always makes me feel bad.

So I will let it alone and talk about the house.

The most beautiful place! It is quite alone, standing well back from the road, quite three miles from the village. It makes me think of English places that you read about, for there are hedges and walls and gates that lock, and lots of separate little houses for the gardeners and people.

There is a *delicious* garden! I never saw such a garden—large and shady, full of box-bordered paths, and lined with long grape-covered arbors with seats under them.

There were greenhouses, but they are all broken now.

There was some legal trouble, I believe, something about the heirs and co-heirs; anyhow, the place has been empty for years.

That spoils my ghostliness, I am afraid, but I don't care—there is something strange about the house—I can feel it.

I even said so to John one moonlight evening, but he said what I felt was a draught, and shut the window.

I get unreasonably angry with John sometimes. I'm sure I never used to be so sensitive. I think it is due to this nervous condition.

But John says if I feel so I shall neglect proper self-control; so I take pains to control myself—before him, at least, and that makes me very tired.

I don't like our room a bit. I wanted one downstairs that opened onto the piazza and had roses all over the window, and such pretty old-fashioned chintz hangings! But John would not hear of it.

He said there was only one window and not room for two beds, and no near room for him if he took another.

He is very careful and loving, and hardly lets me stir without special direction.

I have a schedule prescription for each hour in the day; he takes all care from me, and so I feel basely ungrateful not to value it more.

*Gilman, Charlotte Perkins. *The Yellow Wall Paper*. Boston, MA: Small, Maynard & Company, 1901. Print.

He said he came here solely on my account, that I was to have perfect rest and all the air I could get. "Your exercise depends on your strength, my dear," said he, "and your food somewhat on your appetite; but air you can absorb all the time." So we took the nursery at the top of the house.

It is a big, airy room, the whole floor nearly, with windows that look all ways, and air and sunshine galore. It was nursery first, and then playroom and gymnasium, I should judge, for the windows are barred for little children, and there are rings and things in the walls.

The paint and paper look as if a boys' school had used it. It is stripped off—the paper—in great patches all around the head of my bed, about as far as I can reach, and in a great place on the other side of the room low down. I never saw a worse paper in my life. One of those sprawling, flamboyant patterns committing every artistic sin.

It is dull enough to confuse the eye in following, pronounced enough constantly to irritate and provoke study, and when you follow the lame uncertain curves for a little distance they suddenly commit suicide—plunge off at outrageous angles, destroy themselves in unheard-of contradictions.

The color is repellant, almost revolting: a smouldering unclean yellow, strangely faded by the slow-turning sunlight. It is a dull yet lurid orange in some places, a sickly sulphur tint in others.

No wonder the children hated it! I should hate it myself if I had to live in this room long.

There comes John, and I must put this away—he hates to have me write a word....

Women and Economics[*]
Charlotte Perkins Gilman (1898)

The economic status of the human race in any nation, at any time, is governed mainly by the activities of the male: the female obtains her share in the racial advance only through him.

Studied individually, the facts are even more plainly visible, more open and familiar. From the day laborer to the millionaire, the wife's worn dress or flashing jewels, her low roof or her lordly one, her weary feet or her rich equipage,—these speak of the economic ability of the husband. The comfort, the luxury, the necessities of life itself, which the woman receives, are obtained by the husband, and given her

by him. And, when the woman, left alone with no man to "support" her, tries to meet her own economic necessities, the difficulties which confront her prove conclusively what the general economic status of the woman is. None can deny these patent facts,—that the economic status of women generally depends upon that of men generally, and that the economic status of women individually depends upon that of men individually, those men to whom they are related. But we are instantly confronted by the commonly received opinion that, although it must be admitted that men make and distribute the wealth of the world, yet women earn their share of it as wives. This assumes either that the husband is in the position of employer and the wife as employee, or that marriage is a "partnership," and the wife an equal factor with the husband in producing wealth.

Economic independence is a relative condition at best. In the broadest sense, all living things are economically dependent upon others,—the animals upon the vegetables, and man upon both. In a narrower sense, all social life is economically interdependent, man producing collectively what he could by no possibility produce separately. But, in the closest interpretation, individual economic independence among human beings means that the individual pays for what he gets, works for what he gets, gives to the other an equivalent for what the other gives him. I depend on the shoemaker for shoes, and the tailor for coats; but, if I give the shoemaker and the tailor enough of my own labor as a house-builder to pay for the shoes and coats they give me, I retain my personal independence. I have not taken of their product, and given nothing of mine. As long as what I get is obtained by what I give, I am economically independent.

Women consume economic goods. What economic product do they give in exchange for what they consume? The claim that marriage is a partnership, in which the two persons married produce wealth which neither of them, separately, could produce, will not bear examination. A man happy and comfortable can produce more than one unhappy and uncomfortable, but this is as true of a father or son as of a husband. To take from a man any of the conditions which make him happy and strong is to cripple his industry, generally speaking. But those relatives who make him happy are not therefore his business partners, and entitled to share his income.

Grateful return for happiness conferred is not the method of exchange in a partnership. The comfort a man takes with his wife is not in the nature of a

[*]Gilman, Charlotte Perkins. *Women and Economics*. Boston, MA: Small, Maynard & Company, 1898. Print.

business partnership, nor are her frugality and industry. A housekeeper, in her place, might be as frugal, as industrious, but would not therefore be a partner. Man and wife are partners truly in their mutual obligation to their children,—their common love, duty, and service. But a manufacturer who marries, or a doctor, or a lawyer, does not take a partner in his business, when he takes a partner in parenthood, unless his wife is also a manufacturer, a doctor, or a lawyer. In his business, she cannot even advise wisely without training and experience. To love her husband, the composer, does not enable her to compose; and the loss of a man's wife, though it may break his heart, does not cripple his business, unless his mind is affected by grief. She is in no sense a business partner, unless she contributes capital or experience or labor, as a man would in like relation. Most men would hesitate very seriously before entering a business partnership with any woman, wife or not.

If the wife is not, then, truly a business partner, in what way does she earn from her husband the food, clothing, and shelter she receives at his hands? By house service, it will be instantly replied. This is the general misty idea upon the subject,—that women earn all they get, and more, by house service. Here we come to a very practical and definite economic ground. Although not producers of wealth, women serve in the final processes of preparation and distribution. Their labor in the household has a genuine economic value.

For a certain percentage of persons to serve other persons, in order that the ones so served may produce more, is a contribution not to be overlooked. The labor of women in the house, certainly, enables men to produce more wealth than they otherwise could; and in this way women are economic factors in society. But so are horses. The labor of horses enables men to produce more wealth than they otherwise could. The horse is an economic factor in society. But the horse is not economically independent, nor is the woman. If a man plus a valet can perform more useful service than he could minus a valet, then the valet is performing useful service. But, if the valet is the property of the man, is obliged to perform this service, and is not paid for it, he is not economically independent.

The labor which the wife performs in the household is given as part of her functional duty, not as employment. The wife of the poor man, who works hard in a small house, doing all the work for the family, or the wife of the rich man, who wisely and gracefully manages a large house and administers its functions, each is entitled to fair pay for services rendered.

To take this ground and hold it honestly, wives, as earners through domestic service, are entitled to the wages of cooks, housemaids, nursemaids, seamstresses, or housekeepers, and to no more. This would of course reduce the spending money of the wives of the rich, and put it out of the power of the poor man to "support" a wife at all, unless, indeed, the poor man faced the situation fully, paid his wife her wages as house servant, and then she and he combined their funds in the support of their children. He would be keeping a servant: she would be helping keep the family. But nowhere on earth would there be "a rich woman" by these means. Even the highest class of private housekeeper, useful as her services are, does not accumulate a fortune. She does not buy diamonds and sables and keep a carriage.

But the salient fact in this discussion is that, whatever the economic value of the domestic industry of women is, they do not get it. The women who do the most work get the least money, the women who have the most money do the least work. Their labor is neither given nor taken as a factor in economic exchange. It is held to be their duty as women to do this work; and their economic status bears no relation to their domestic labors, unless an inverse one. Moreover, if they were thus fairly paid,—given what they earned, and no more,—all women working in this way would be reduced to the economic status of the house servant. Few women—or men either—care to face this condition. The ground that women earn their living by domestic labor is instantly forsaken, and we are told that they obtain their livelihood as mothers. This is a peculiar position. We speak of it commonly enough, and often with deep feeling, but without due analysis.

In treating of an economic exchange, asking what return in goods or labor women make for the goods and labor given them,—either to the race collectively or to their husbands individually,—what payment women make for their clothes and shoes and furniture and food and shelter, we are told that the duties and services of the mother entitle her to support.

If this is so, if motherhood is an exchangeable commodity given by women in payment for clothes and food, then we must of course find some relation between the quantity or quality of the motherhood and the quantity and quality of the pay. This being true, then the women who are not mothers have no economic status at all; and the economic status of those who are must be shown to be relative to their motherhood. This is obviously absurd. The childless wife has as much money as the mother of many,—more; for the children of the latter consume what would otherwise be hers; and the inefficient mother is no less provided for than the efficient one. Visibly, and upon the face of it, women are not maintained in economic prosperity proportioned to their motherhood. Motherhood bears no relation to their economic status. Among primitive races, it is true,—in the patriarchal period, for instance,—there was some truth in this position. Women being of no value whatever save as bearers of children, their favor and indulgence did bear direct relation to maternity; and they had reason to exult on more grounds than one when they could boast a son. To-day, however, the maintenance of the woman is not conditioned upon this. A man is not allowed to discard his wife because she is barren. The claim of motherhood as a factor in economic exchange is false to-day. But suppose it were true. Are we willing to hold this ground, even in theory? Are we willing to consider motherhood as a business, a form of commercial exchange? Are the cares and duties of the mother, her travail and her love, commodities to be exchanged for bread?

It is revolting so to consider them; and, if we dare face our own thoughts, and force them to their logical conclusion, we shall see that nothing could be more repugnant to human feeling, or more socially and individually injurious, than to make motherhood a trade. Driven off these alleged grounds of women's economic independence; shown that women, as a class, neither produce nor distribute wealth; that women, as individuals, labor mainly as house servants, are not paid as such, and would not be satisfied with such an economic status if they were so paid; that wives are not business partners or co-producers of wealth with their husbands, unless they actually practise the same profession; that they are not salaried as mothers, and that it would be unspeakably degrading if they were,—what remains to those who deny that women are supported by men? This (and a most amusing position it is),—that the function of maternity unfits a woman for economic production, and, therefore, it is right that she should be supported by her husband.

The ground is taken that the human female is not economically independent, that she is fed by the male of her species. In denial of this, it is first alleged that she is economically independent,—that she does support herself by her own industry in the house. It being shown that there is no relation between the economic status of woman and the labor she performs in the home, it is then alleged that not as house servant, but as mother, does woman earn her living. It being shown that the economic status of woman bears no relation to her motherhood, either in quantity or quality, it is then alleged that motherhood renders a woman unfit for economic production, and that, therefore, it is right that she be supported by her husband. Before going farther, let us seize upon this admission,—that she *is* supported by her husband.

Without going into either the ethics or the necessities of the case, we have reached so much common ground: the female of genus homo is supported by the male. Whereas, in other species of animals, male and female alike graze and browse, hunt and kill, climb, swim, dig, run, and fly for their livings, in our species the female does not seek her own living in the specific activities of our race, but is fed by the male.

Now as to the alleged necessity. Because of her maternal duties, the human female is said to be unable to get her own living. As the maternal duties of other females do not unfit them for getting their own living and also the livings of their young, it would seem that the human maternal duties require the segregation of the entire energies of the mother to the service of the child during her entire adult life, or so large a proportion of them that not enough remains to devote to the individual interests of the mother.

Such a condition, did it exist, would of course excuse and justify the pitiful dependence of the human female, and her support by the male. As the queen bee, modified entirely to maternity, is supported, not by the male, to be sure, but by her co-workers, the "old maids," the barren working bees, who labor so patiently and lovingly in their branch of the maternal duties of the hive, so would the human female, modified entirely to maternity, become unfit for any other exertion, and a helpless dependant.

Is this the condition of human motherhood? Does the human mother, by her motherhood, thereby lose control of brain and body, lose power and skill and desire for any other work? Do we see before us the human race, with all its females segregated entirely to the uses of motherhood, consecrated, set apart, specially developed, spending every power of their nature on the service of their children?

We do not. We see the human mother worked far harder than a mare, laboring her life long in the service, not of her children only, but of men; husbands, brothers, fathers, whatever male relatives she has; for mother and sister also; for the church a little, if she is allowed; for society, if she is able; for charity and education and reform,—working in many ways that are not the ways of motherhood.

It is not motherhood that keeps the housewife on her feet from dawn till dark; it is house service, not child service. Women work longer and harder than most men, and not solely in maternal duties. The savage mother carries the burdens, and does all menial service for the tribe. The peasant mother toils in the fields, and the workingman's wife in the home. Many mothers, even now, are wage-earners for the family, as well as bearers and rearers of it. And the women who are not so occupied, the women who belong to rich men,—here perhaps is the exhaustive devotion to maternity which is supposed to justify an admitted economic dependence. But we do not find it even among these. Women of ease and wealth provide for their children better care than the poor woman can; but they do not spend more time upon it themselves, nor more care and effort. They have other occupation.

In spite of her supposed segregation to maternal duties, the human female, the world over, works at extra-maternal duties for hours enough to provide her with an independent living, and then is denied independence on the ground that motherhood prevents her working!...

Anna Julia Cooper (1858–1964) was born in North Carolina, the daughter of Hannah Stanley Haywood, a slave, and her owner. After being widowed as a young woman, Cooper attended Oberlin College, where she was a classmate of Mary Church Terrell, another important black feminist of the classic age. Most of her career was devoted to teaching, principally at Washington, D.C.'s M Street School. She served the students at M Street off and on from 1887 until her retirement. In 1906, she was forced out of her position as principal of M Street by agents of Booker T. Washington, who favored industrial training over classical education for blacks. Cooper, who had helped students gain admission to the best universities, was considered too similar in her views to Washington's chief opponent, W. E. B. Du Bois.

Anna Julia Cooper's *A Voice from the South* (1892) was her most important book. Yet after returning to M Street in 1910, she lived a life of varied accomplishments as writer, lecturer, settlement house founder, adoptive mother (at age fifty-seven) of five children, translator, college president, and scholar (she received her Ph.D. from the Sorbonne at age sixty-seven). Today, she is recognized as a major figure in the tradition of black feminist social theory. She died in Washington, D.C., in 1964, having lived from the days of slavery and emancipation to the modern Civil Rights Movement.

"The Colored Women's Office" represents Cooper's principal contribution to black feminist social theory. In these selections from *A Voice from the South*, she argues that moral progress depends on the only person able to understand the deep connections of race and gender in America—the black woman.

The Colored Woman's Office[*]
Anna Julia Cooper (1892)

Now the fundamental agency under God in the regeneration, the re-training of the race, as well as the ground work and starting point of its progress upward, must be the *black woman.*

With all the wrongs and neglects of her past, with all the weakness, the debasement, the moral thralldom of her present, the black woman of to-day stands mute and wondering at the Herculean task devolving upon her. But the cycles wait for her. No other hand can move the lever. She must be loosed from her bands and set to work.

Our meager and superficial results from past efforts prove their futility; and every attempt to elevate the Negro, whether undertaken by himself or through the philanthropy of others, cannot but prove abortive unless so directed as to utilize the indispensable agency of an elevated and trained womanhood.

A race cannot be purified from without. Preachers and teachers are helps, and stimulants and conditions as necessary as the gracious rain and sunshine are to plant growth. But what are rain and dew and sunshine and cloud if there be no life in the plant germ? We must go to the root and see that that is sound and healthy and vigorous; and not deceive ourselves with waxen flowers and painted leaves of mock chlorophyll.

We too often mistake individuals' honor for race development and so are ready to substitute

---

*A VOICE FROM THE SOUTH by Cooper (1988) 3518w from pp.28-31, 94-101, 134-135, 140-145. © 1988 by Oxford University Press, Inc. By permission of Oxford University Press, USA.

pretty accomplishments for sound sense and earnest purpose.

A stream cannot rise higher than its source. The atmosphere of homes is no rarer and purer and sweeter than are the mothers in those homes. A race is but a total of families. The nation is the aggregate of its homes. As the whole is sum of all its parts, so the character of the parts will determine the characteristics of the whole. These are all axioms and so evident that it seems gratuitous to remark it; and yet, unless I am greatly mistaken, most of the unsatisfaction from our past results arises from just such a radical and palpable error, as much almost on our own part as on that of our benevolent white friends.

The Negro is constitutionally hopeful and proverbially irrepressible; and naturally stands in danger of being dazzled by the shimmer and tinsel of superficials. We often mistake foliage for fruit and overestimate or wrongly estimate brilliant results.

The late Martin R. Delany, who was an unadulterated black man, used to say when honors of state fell upon him, that when he entered the council of kings the black race entered with him; meaning, I suppose, that there was no discounting his race identity and attributing his achievements to some admixture of Saxon blood. But our present record of eminent men, when placed beside the actual status of the race in America to-day, proves that no man can represent the race. Whatever the attainments of the individual may be, unless his home has moved on *pari passu,* he can never be regarded as identical with or representative of the whole.

Not by pointing to sun-bathed mountain tops do we prove that Phoebus warms the valleys. We must point to homes, average homes, homes of the rank and file of horny handed toiling men and women of the South (where the masses are) lighted and cheered by the good, the beautiful, and the true,—then and not till then will the whole plateau be lifted into the sunlight.

Only the Black Woman can say "when and where I enter, in the quiet, undisputed dignity of my womanhood, without violence and without suing or special patronage, then and there the whole *Negro race enters with me.*" Is it not evident then that as individual workers for this race we must address ourselves with no half-hearted zeal to this feature of our mission. The need is felt and must be recognized by all. There is a call for workers, for missionaries, for men and women with the double consecration of a fundamental love of humanity and a desire for its melioration through the Gospel; but

superadded to this we demand an intelligent and sympathetic comprehension of the interests and special needs of the Negro. . . .

I would eliminate also from the discussion all uncharitable reflections upon the orderly execution of laws existing in certain states of this Union, requiring persons known to be colored to ride in one car, and persons supposed to be white in another. A good citizen may use his influence to have existing laws and statutes changed or modified, but a public servant must not be blamed for obeying orders. A railroad conductor is not asked to dictate measures, nor to make and pass laws. His bread and butter are conditioned on his managing his part of the machinery as he is told to do. If, therefore, I found myself in that compartment of a train designated by the sovereign law of the state for presumable Caucasians, and for colored persons only when traveling in the capacity of nurses and maids, should a conductor inform me, as a gentleman might, that I had made a mistake, and offer to show me the proper car for black ladies; I might wonder at the expensive arrangements of the company and of the state in providing special and separate accommodations for the transportation of the various hues of humanity, but I certainly could not take it as a want of courtesy on the conductor's part that he gave the information. It is true, public sentiment precedes and begets all laws, good or bad; and on the ground I have taken, our women are to be credited largely as teachers and moulders of public sentiment. But when a law has passed and received the sanction of the land, there is nothing for our officials to do but enforce it till repealed; and I for one, as a loyal American citizen, will give those officials cheerful support and ready sympathy in the discharge of their duty. But when a great burly six feet of masculinity with sloping shoulders and unkempt beard swaggers in, and, throwing a roll of tobacco into one corner of his jaw, growls out at me over the paper I am reading, "Here gurl," (I am past thirty) "you better git out 'n dis kyar 'f yer don't, I'll put yer out,"—my mental annotation is *Here's an American citizen who has been badly trained. He is sadly lacking in both "sweetness" and "light";* and when in the same section of our enlightened and progressive country, I see from the car window, working on private estates, convicts from the state penitentiary, among them squads of boys from fourteen to eighteen years of age in a chain-gang, their feet chained together and heavy blocks attached—not in 1850, but in 1890, '91 and '92, I make a note on the flyleaf of my memorandum, *The women in this section should organize a Society for the Prevention of Cruelty to Human Beings, and disseminate civilizing tracts, and send throughout the region apostles of anti-barbarism for the propagation of humane and enlightened ideas.* And when farther on in the same section our train stops at a dilapidated station, rendered yet more unsightly by dozens of loafers with their hands in their pockets while a productive soil and inviting climate beckon in vain to industry; and when, looking a little more closely, I see two dingy little rooms with "FOR LADIES" swinging over one and "FOR COLORED PEOPLE" over the other; while wondering under which head I come, I notice a little way off the only hotel proprietor of the place whittling a pine stick as he sits with one leg thrown across an empty goods box; and as my eye falls on a sample room next door which seems to be driving the only wide-awake and popular business of the commonwealth, I cannot help ejaculating under my breath, "What a field for the missionary woman." I know that if by any fatality I should be obliged to lie over at that station, and, driven by hunger, should be compelled to seek refreshments or the bare necessaries of life at the only public accommodation in the town, that same stick-whittler would coolly inform me, without looking up from his pine splinter, "We doan ucommodate no niggers hyur." And yet we are so scandalized at Russia's barbarity and cruelty to the Jews! We pay a man a thousand dollars a night just to make us weep, by a recital of such heathenish inhumanity as is practiced on Sclavonic soil.

A recent writer on Eastern nations says: "If we take through the earth's temperate zone, a belt of country whose northern and southern edges are determined by certain limiting isotherms, not more than half the width of the zone apart, we shall find that we have included in a relatively small extent of surface almost all the nations of note in the world, past or present. Now, if we examine this belt and compare the different parts of it with one another, we shall be struck by a remarkable fact. *The peoples inhabiting it grow steadily more personal as we go west.* So unmistakable is this gradation, that one is almost tempted to ascribe it to cosmical rather than to human causes. It is as marked as the change in color of the human complexion observable along any meridian, which ranges from black at the equator to blonde toward the pole. In like manner the sense of self grows more intense as we follow in the wake of the setting sun, and fades steadily as we advance into the dawn. America, Europe, the Levant, India, Japan, each is less personal than the one before. . . .

That politeness should be one of the most marked results of impersonality may appear surprising, yet a slight examination will show it to be a fact. Considered *a priori,* the connection is not far to seek. Impersonality by lessening the interest in one's self, induces one to take an interest in others. Looked at *a posteriori,* we find that where the one trait exists the other is most developed, while an absence of the second seems to prevent the full growth of the first. This is true both in general and in detail. *Courtesy increases as we travel eastward round the world, coincidently with a decrease in the sense of self.* Asia is more courteous than Europe, Europe than America. Particular races show the same concomitance of characteristics. France, the most impersonal nation of Europe, is at the same time the most polite." And by inference, Americans, the most personal, are the least courteous nation on the globe.

The Black Woman had reached this same conclusion by an entirely different route; but it is gratifying to vanity, nevertheless, to find one's self sustained by both science and philosophy in a conviction, wrought in by hard experience, and yet too apparently audacious to be entertained even as a stealthy surmise. In fact the Black Woman was emboldened some time since by a well put and timely article from an Editor's Drawer on the "Mannerless Sex," to give the world the benefit of some of her experience with the "*Mannerless Race*"; but since Mr. Lowell shows so conclusively that the entire Land of the West is a *mannerless continent,* I have determined to plead with our women, the mannerless sex on this mannerless continent, to institute a reform by placing immediately in our national curricula a department for teaching good manners.

Now, am I right in holding the American Woman responsible? Is it true that the exponents of woman's advancement, the leaders in woman's thought, the preachers and teachers of all woman's reforms, can teach this nation to be courteous, to be pitiful, having compassion one of another, not rendering evil for inoffensiveness, and railing in proportion to the improbability of being struck back; but contrariwise, being *all* of one mind, to love as brethren?

I think so.

It may require some heroic measures, and like all revolutions will call for a determined front and a courageous, unwavering, stalwart heart on the part of the leaders of the reform.

The "*all*" will inevitably stick in the throat of the Southern woman. She must be allowed, please, to except the "darkey" from the "all"; it is too bitter a pill with black people in it. You must get the Revised Version to put it, "*love all white people* as brethren." She really could not enter any society on earth, or in heaven above, or in—the waters under the earth, on such unpalatable conditions.

The Black Woman has tried to understand the Southern woman's difficulties; to put herself in her place, and to be as fair, as charitable, and as free from prejudice in judging her antipathies, as she would have others in regard to her own. She has honestly weighed the apparently sincere excuse, "But you must remember that these people were once our slaves"; and that other, "But civility towards the Negroes will bring us on *social equality* with them." . . .

The colored woman of to-day occupies, one may say, a unique position in this country. In a period of itself transitional and unsettled, her status seems one of the least ascertainable and definitive of all the forces which make for our civilization. She is confronted by both a woman question and a race problem, and is as yet an unknown or an unacknowledged factor in both. While the women of the white race can with calm assurance enter upon the work they feel by nature appointed to do, while their men give loyal support and appreciative countenance to their efforts, recognizing in most avenues of usefulness the propriety and the need of woman's distinctive co-operation, the colored woman too often finds herself hampered and shamed by a less liberal sentiment and a more conservative attitude on the part of those for whose opinion she cares most. That this is not universally true I am glad to admit. There are to be found both intensely conservative white men and exceedingly liberal colored men. But as far as my experience goes the average man of our race is less frequently ready to admit the actual need among the sturdier forces of the world for woman's help or influence. That great social and economic questions await her interference, that she could throw any light on problems of national import, that her intermeddling could improve the management of school systems, or elevate the tone of public institutions, or humanize and sanctify the far reaching influence of prisons and reformatories and improve the treatment of lunatics and imbeciles,—that she has a word worth hearing on mooted questions in political economy, that she could contribute a suggestion on the relations of labor and capital, or offer a thought on honest money and honorable trade, I fear the majority of "Americans of the colored variety" are not yet prepared to concede. . . .

Not unfelt, then, if unproclaimed has been the work and influence of the colored women of America. Our list of chieftains in the service, though not long, is not inferior in strength and excellence, I dare believe, to any similar list which this country can produce.

Among the pioneers, Frances Watkins Harper could sing with prophetic exaltation in the darkest days, when as yet there was not a rift in the clouds overhanging her people:

"Yes, Ethiopia shall stretch
Her bleeding hands abroad;
Her cry of agony shall reach the burning
   throne of God.
Redeemed from dust and freed from chains
Her sons shall lift their eyes,
From cloud-capt hills and verdant plains
Shall shouts of triumph rise."

Among preachers of righteousness, an unanswerable silencer of cavilers and objectors, was Sojourner Truth, that unique and rugged genius who seemed carved out without hand or chisel from the solid mountain mass; and in pleasing contrast, Amanda Smith, sweetest of natural singers and pleaders in dulcet tones for the things of God and of His Christ.

Sarah Woodson Early and Martha Briggs, planting and watering in the school room, and giving off from their matchless and irresistible personality an impetus and inspiration which can never die so long as there lives and breathes a remote descendant of their disciples and friends.

Charlotte Fortin Grimke, the gentle spirit whose verses and life link her so beautifully with America's great Quaker poet and loving reformer.

Hallie Quinn Brown, charming reader, earnest, effective lecturer and devoted worker of unflagging zeal and unquestioned power.

Fannie Jackson Coppin, the teacher and organizer, pre-eminent among women of whatever country or race in constructive and executive force.

These women represent all shades of belief and as many departments of activity; but they have one thing in common—their sympathy with the oppressed race in America and the consecration of their several talents in whatever line to the work of its deliverance and development.

Fifty years ago woman's activity according to orthodox definitions was on a pretty clearly cut "sphere," including primarily the kitchen and the nursery, and rescued from the barrenness of prison bars by the womanly mania for adorning every discoverable bit of china or canvass with forlorn looking cranes balanced idiotically on one foot. The woman of to-day finds herself in the presence of responsibilities which ramify through the profoundest and most varied interests of her country and race. Not one of the issues of this plodding, toiling, sinning, repenting, falling, aspiring humanity can afford to shut her out, or can deny the reality of her influence. No plan for renovating society, no scheme for purifying politics, no reform in church or in state, no moral, social, or economic question, no movement upward or downward in the human plane is lost on her. A man once said when told his house was afire: "Go tell my wife; I never meddle with household affairs." But no woman can possibly put herself or her sex outside any of the interests that affect humanity. All departments in the new era are to be hers, in the sense that her interests are in all and through all; and it is incumbent on her to keep intelligently and sympathetically *en rapport* with all the great movements of her time, that she may know on which side to throw the weight of her influence. She stands now at the gateway of this new era of American civilization. In her hands must be moulded the strength, the wit, the statesmanship, the morality, all the psychic force, the social and economic intercourse of that era. To be alive at such an epoch is a privilege, to be a woman then is sublime.

In this last decade of our century, changes of such moment are in progress, such new and alluring vistas are opening out before us, such original and radical suggestions for the adjustment of labor and capital, of government and the governed, of the family, the church and the state, that to be a possible factor though an infinitesimal in such a movement is pregnant with hope and weighty with responsibility. To be a woman in such an age carries with it a privilege and an opportunity never implied before. But to be a woman of the Negro race in America, and to be able to grasp the deep significance of the possibilities of the crisis, is to have a heritage, it seems to me, unique in the ages. In the first place, the race is young and full of the elasticity and hopefulness of youth. All its achievements are before it. It does not look on the masterly triumphs of nineteenth century civilization with that *blase* world-weary look which characterizes the old washed out and worn out races which have already, so to speak, seen their best days.

Said a European writer recently: "Except the Sclavonic, the Negro is the only original and distinctive genius which has yet to come to growth—and the feeling is to cherish and develop it."

Everything to this race is new and strange and inspiring. There is a quickening of its pulses and a glowing of its self-consciousness. Aha, I can rival that! I can aspire to that! I can honor my name and vindicate my race! Something like this, it strikes me, is the enthusiasm which stirs the genius of young Africa in America; and the memory of past oppression and the fact of present attempted repression only serve to gather momentum for its irrepressible powers. Then again, a race in such a stage of growth is peculiarly sensitive to impressions. Not the photographer's sensitized plate is more delicately impressionable to outer influences than is this high strung people here on the threshold of a career.

What a responsibility then to have the sole management of the primal lights and shadows! Such is the colored woman's office. She must stamp weal or woe on the coming history of this people. May she see her opportunity and vindicate her high prerogative.

Georg Simmel (1858–1918), though he never enjoyed a significant position in a university, was a founder (with Weber and Ferdinand Toennies) of the German Sociological Society. Simmel was a regular participant in Max and Marianne Weber's Heidelberg circle of intellectual friends. He was esteemed by many of the luminaries of German intellectual life, including Edmund Husserl and Heinrich Rickert. Yet he lived the life of an independent bourgeois intellectual, which earned him the respect denied by the university establishment. Today, his writings are read for their unusual theoretical insight into the inner workings of life in the modern world. The following selection illustrates Simmel's simple style and disarming ability to describe an important character in all social groups: the stranger—a character who became all the more important in the modern world, especially when viewed from the perspective of Europe's stranger within, the Jew.

The Stranger*
Georg Simmel (1908)

If wandering, considered as a state of detachment from every given point in space, is the conceptual opposite of attachment to any point, then the sociological form of "the stranger" presents the synthesis, as it were, of both of these properties. (This is another indication that spatial relations not only are determining conditions of relationships among men, but are also symbolic of those relationships.) The stranger will thus not be considered here in the usual sense of the term, as the wanderer who comes today and goes tomorrow, but rather as the man who comes today and stays tomorrow—the potential wanderer, so to speak, who, although he has gone no further, has not quite got over the freedom of coming and going. He is fixed within a certain spatial circle—or within a group whose boundaries are analogous to spatial boundaries—but his position within it is fundamentally affected by the fact that he does not belong in it initially and that he brings qualities into it that are not, and cannot be, indigenous to it.

In the case of the stranger, the union of closeness and remoteness involved in every human relationship is patterned in a way that may be succinctly formulated as follows: the distance within this relation indicates that one who is close by is remote, but his strangeness indicates that one who is remote is near. The state of being a stranger is of course a completely positive relation; it is a specific form of interaction. The inhabitants of Sirius are not exactly strangers to us, at least not in the sociological sense of the word as we are considering it. In that sense they do not exist for us at all; they are beyond being far and near. The stranger is an element of the group itself, not unlike the poor and sundry "inner enemies"—an element whose membership within the group involves both being outside it and confronting it.

The following statements about the stranger are intended to suggest how factors of repulsion and distance work to create a form of being together, a form of union based on interaction.

In the whole history of economic activity the stranger makes his appearance everywhere as a trader, and the trader makes his as a stranger. As long as production for one's own needs is the general rule, or

products are exchanged within a relatively small circle, there is no need for a middleman within the group. A trader is required only for goods produced outside the group. Unless there are people who wander out into foreign lands to buy these necessities, in which case they are themselves "strange" merchants in this other region, the trader *must* be a stranger; there is no opportunity for anyone else to make a living at it.

This position of the stranger stands out more sharply if, instead of leaving the place of his activity, he settles down there. In innumerable cases even this is possible only if he can live by trade as a middleman. Any closed economic group where land and handicrafts have been apportioned in a way that satisfies local demands will still support a livelihood for the trader. For trade alone makes possible unlimited combinations, and through it intelligence is constantly extended and applied in new areas, something that is much harder for the primary producer with his more limited mobility and his dependence on a circle of customers that can be expanded only very slowly. Trade can always absorb more men than can primary production. It is therefore the most suitable activity for the stranger, who intrudes as a supernumerary, so to speak, into a group in which all the economic positions are already occupied. The classic example of this is the history of European Jews. The stranger is by his very nature no owner of land—land not only in the physical sense but also metaphorically as a vital substance which is fixed, if not in space, then at least in an ideal position within the social environment.

Although in the sphere of intimate personal relations the stranger may be attractive and meaningful in many ways, so long as he is regarded as a stranger he is no "landowner" in the eyes of the other. Restriction to intermediary trade and often (as though sublimated from it) to pure finance gives the stranger the specific character of *mobility.* The appearance of this mobility within a bounded group occasions that synthesis of nearness and remoteness which constitutes the formal position of the stranger. The purely mobile person comes incidentally into contact with *every* single element but is not bound up organically, through established ties of kinship, locality, or occupation, with any single one.

Another expression of this constellation is to be found in the objectivity of the stranger. Because he is not bound by roots to the particular constituents and partisan dispositions of the group, he confronts all of these with a distinctly "objective" attitude, an attitude that does not signify mere detachment and nonparticipation, but is a distinct structure composed of remoteness and nearness, indifference and involvement. I refer to my analysis of the dominating positions gained by aliens, in the discussion of superordination and subordination, typified by the practice in certain Italian cities of recruiting their judges from outside, because no native was free from entanglement in family interests and factionalism.

Connected with the characteristic of objectivity is a phenomenon that is found chiefly, though not exclusively, in the stranger who moves on. This is that he often receives the most surprising revelations and confidences, at times reminiscent of a confessional, about matters which are kept carefully hidden from everybody with whom one is close. Objectivity is by no means nonparticipation, a condition that is altogether outside the distinction between subjective and objective orientations. It is rather a positive and definite kind of participation, in the same way that the objectivity of a theoretical observation clearly does not mean that the mind is a passive tabula rasa on which things inscribe their qualities, but rather signifies the full activity of a mind working according to its own laws, under conditions that exclude accidental distortions and emphases whose individual and subjective differences would produce quite different pictures of the same object.

Objectivity can also be defined as freedom. The objective man is not bound by ties which could prejudice his perception, his understanding, and his assessment of data. This freedom, which permits the stranger to experience and treat even his close relationships as though from a bird's-eye view, contains many dangerous possibilities. From earliest times, in uprisings of all sorts the attacked party has claimed that there has been incitement from the outside, by foreign emissaries and agitators. Insofar as this has happened, it represents an exaggeration of the specific role of the stranger: he is the freer man, practically and theoretically; he examines conditions with less prejudice; he assesses them against standards that are more general and more objective; and his actions are not confined by custom, piety, or precedent.

Finally, the proportion of nearness and remoteness which gives the stranger the character of objectivity also finds practical expression in the more *abstract* nature of the relation to him. That is, with the stranger one has only certain *more general* qualities in common, whereas the relation with organically connected persons is based on the similarity of just those specific traits which differentiate them from the merely universal. In fact, all personal relations whatsoever can be analyzed in terms of this scheme. They are not determined only by the existence of certain common characteristics which the individuals share in addition to their individual differences, which either influence the relationship or remain outside of it. Rather, the kind of effect which that commonality has on the relation essentially depends on whether it exists only among the participants themselves, and thus, although general within the relation, is specific and incomparable with respect to all those on the outside, or whether the participants feel that what they have in common is so only because it is common to a group, a type, or mankind in general. In the latter case, the effect of the common features becomes attenuated in proportion to the size of the group bearing the same characteristics. The commonality provides a basis for unifying the members, to be sure; but it does not specifically direct *these* particular persons to one another. A similarity so widely shared could just as easily unite each person with every possible other. This, too, is evidently a way in which a relationship includes both nearness and remoteness simultaneously. To the extent to which the similarities assume a universal nature, the warmth of the connection based on them will acquire an element of coolness, a sense of the contingent nature of precisely *this* relation—the connecting forces have lost their specific, centripetal character.

In relation to the stranger, it seems to me, this constellation assumes an extraordinary preponderance in principle over the individual elements peculiar to the relation in question. The stranger is close to us insofar as we feel between him and ourselves similarities of nationality or social position, of occupation or of general human nature. He is far from us insofar as these similarities extend beyond him and us, and connect us only because they connect a great many people.

A trace of strangeness in this sense easily enters even the most intimate relationships. In the stage of first passion, erotic relations strongly reject any thought of generalization. A love such as this has never existed before; there is nothing to compare either with the person one loves or with our feelings for that person. An estrangement is wont to set in (whether as cause or effect is hard to decide) at the moment when this feeling of uniqueness disappears from the relationship. A skepticism regarding the intrinsic value of the relationship and its value for us adheres to the very thought that in this relation, after all, one is only fulfilling a general human destiny, that one has had an experience that has occurred a thousand times before, and that, if one had not accidentally met this precise person, someone else would have acquired the same meaning for us.

Something of this feeling is probably not absent in any relation, be it ever so close, because that which is common to two is perhaps never common *only* to them but belongs to a general conception which includes much else besides, many *possibilities* of similarities. No matter how few of these possibilities are realized and how often we may forget about them, here and there, nevertheless, they crowd in like shadows between men, like a mist eluding every designation, which must congeal into solid corporeality for it to be called jealousy. Perhaps this is in many cases a more general, at least more insurmountable, strangeness than that due to differences and obscurities. It is strangeness caused by the fact that similarity, harmony, and closeness are accompanied by the feeling that they are actually not the exclusive property of this particular relation, but stem from a more general one—a relation that potentially includes us and an indeterminate number of others, and therefore prevents that relation which alone was experienced from having an inner and exclusive necessity.

On the other hand, there is a sort of "strangeness" in which this very connection on the basis of a general quality embracing the parties is precluded. The relation of the Greeks to the barbarians is a typical example; so are all the cases in which the general characteristics one takes as peculiarly and merely human are disallowed to the other. But here the expression "the stranger" no longer has any positive meaning. The relation with him is a non-relation; he is not what we have been discussing here: the stranger as a member of the group itself.

As such, the stranger is near and far *at the same time,* as in any relationship based on merely universal human similarities. Between these two factors of nearness and distance, however, a peculiar tension arises, since the consciousness of having only the absolutely general in common has exactly the effect of putting a special emphasis on that which is not common. For a stranger to the country, the city, the race, and so on, what is stressed is again nothing individual, but alien origin, a quality which he has, or could have, in common with many other strangers. For this reason strangers are not really perceived as individuals, but as strangers of a certain type. Their remoteness is no less general than their nearness.

This form appears, for example, in so special a case as the tax levied on Jews in Frankfurt and elsewhere during the Middle Ages. Whereas the tax paid by Christian citizens varied according to their wealth at any given time, for every single Jew the tax was fixed once and for all. This amount was fixed because the Jew had his social position as a *Jew,* not as the bearer of certain objective contents. With respect to taxes every other citizen was regarded as possessor of a certain amount of wealth, and his tax could follow the fluctuations of his fortune. But the Jew as taxpayer was first of all a Jew, and thus his fiscal position contained an invariable element. This appears most forcefully, of course, once the differing circumstances of individual Jews are no longer considered, limited though this consideration is by fixed assessments, and all strangers pay exactly the same head tax.

Despite his being inorganically appended to it, the stranger is still an organic member of the group. Its unified life includes the specific conditioning of this element. Only we do not know how to designate the characteristic unity of this position otherwise than by saying that it is put together of certain amounts of nearness and of remoteness. Although both these qualities are found to some extent in all relationships, a special proportion and reciprocal tension between them produce the specific form of the relation to the "stranger."

Charles Horton Cooley (1864–1929) grew up at the University of Michigan, where his father taught law. There, he eventually became a presence in his own right, ascending after his studies to a professorship. From that position, he played a part in the early development of sociology in the United States. His books include *Human Nature and the Social Order* (1902), *Social Organization* (1909), and *Social Process* (1918). The following short selection presents his most famous concept, the looking-glass self, which still comes to mind when social theorists reconsider the social self.

The Looking-Glass Self*
Charles Horton Cooley (1902)

I remarked above that we think of the body as "I" when it comes to have social function or significance, as when we say "I am looking well to-day," or "I am taller than you are." We bring it into the social world, for the time being, and for that reason put

*From *Human Nature and the Social Order* by Charles Horton Cooley. Copyright © 1902, 1922 by Charles Scribner's Sons; copyright renewed 1930 by Elsie Cooley.

our self-consciousness into it. Now it is curious, though natural, that in precisely the same way we may call any inanimate object "I" with which we are identifying our will and purpose. This is notable in games, like golf or croquet, where the ball is the embodiment of the player's fortunes. You will hear a man say, "I am in the long grass down by the third tee," or "I am in position for the middle arch." So a boy flying a kite will say "I am higher than you," or one shooting at a mark will declare that he is just below the bullseye.

In a very large and interesting class of cases the social reference takes the form of a somewhat definite imagination of how one's self—that is any idea he appropriates—appears in a particular mind, and the kind of self-feeling one has is determined by the attitude toward this attributed to that other mind. A social self of this sort might be called the reflected or looking-glass self:

"Each to each a looking-glass

Reflects the other that doth pass."

As we see our face, figure, and dress in the glass, and are interested in them because they are ours, and pleased or otherwise with them according as they do or do not answer to what we should like them to be;

so in imagination we perceive in another's mind some thought of our appearance, manners, aims, deeds, character, friends, and so on, and are variously affected by it.

A self-idea of this sort seems to have three principal elements: the imagination of our appearance to the other person; the imagination of his judgment of that appearance, and some sort of self-feeling, such as pride or mortification. The comparison with a looking-glass hardly suggests the second element, the imagined judgment, which is quite essential. The thing that moves us to pride or shame is not the mere mechanical reflection of ourselves, but an imputed sentiment, the imagined effect of this reflection upon another's mind. This is evident from the fact that the character and weight of that other, in whose mind we see ourselves, makes all the difference with our feeling. We are ashamed to seem evasive in the presence of a straightforward man, cowardly in the presence of a brave one, gross in the eyes of a refined one, and so on. We always imagine, and in imagining share, the judgments of the other mind. A man will boast to one person of an action— say some sharp transaction in trade—which he would be ashamed to own to another.

PART TWO

Social Theories and World Cc
1919–1945

If the prevailing attitude in the West's classical age was denial, then in the interwar years, it was shock. The world wars, the Holocaust, failure in the capitalist world-system, fascism, Hitler, Stalin—these were not supposed to be. It was not that the nineteenth century had been free of war, economic trouble, or political terror—hardly. But in the popular imagination, these horrors were expected to loosen their hold as time went by. That was the promise of modern society. Progress! Everything was Progress.

The very foundations of modern culture in the European world, including North America, were inspiring because they were so simple: *Man, freed from political tyranny, if he dare think for himself, will know the Truth. What is the Truth? Simply that Man, enlightened and free, will make the world better.* Though these exact words were said by no one in particular, the idea they express was everywhere from the eighteenth century well into the twentieth. You can find it in Kant and the *philosophes* in France; in and behind the American Declaration of Independence, the French Declaration of the Rights of Man, and *The Communist Manifesto*; in Adam Smith and the political economists; in the framers of early American political consciousness—Thomas Paine, Thomas Jefferson, and many others; among those, like Herbert Spencer, who applied Darwinian principles to modern society as John Dewey applied pragmatism to education in democracies; and, of course, in the writings of all the classic social theorists. Everywhere.

This new culture also inspired the practical thinking of the masses. Some picked it up from intellectual and political leaders. Others just caught it from the air of the times. In fact, few of the dramatic political or economic events in the hundred years following 1776 would have been possible without a prior conversion to this new faith by great numbers of people. One does not need to be a historian of the nineteenth century to imagine what poor and working people, as well as the bourgeoisie, must have felt in those days. Who among those who stormed the Bastille on July 14, 1789, would dare to stand against the weight of traditional authority if he did not believe truth was on his side? Who among those who migrated in the 1830s from the agrarian countryside to new industrial centers in the north of England could possibly abandon family roots in the raising of sheep's wool for the cotton-weaving factory if they did not believe in a better life? Who in the United States of the 1860s would leave her roots in the East to join a frontiersman in the Indian territories if she did not somehow believe in Progress? Who among the millions of European immigrants to Chicago, to the plains of the Northwest Territories, and to the factories of the Northeast could separate themselves from everything held dear for centuries were it not for trust in this doctrine? *Daring now to think for ourselves, let us seek a better world.* This was the popular foundation of modern culture. Deep in its intellectual bowels—below its new philosophies, its brilliant technologies, its wonderful sciences—modernity preached this simple, compelling faith. Progress was Truth.

Social Theory

Wider World

1917

Thomas and Florian Znaniecki, *The Polish Peasant in Europe and America* 1918-1920

In Russia, Romanovs deposed; Bolsheviks win control of government **1917**
Lenin's 1902 *What is to be done?* comes into play **1917**
US enters war; German submarines fail to turn war **1917**
Lukács joins Hungarian Communist Party, **1918**
Red Army engages civil war in Russia **1919**
Dissatisfaction with Versailles Treaty; Keynes quits as British delegate **1919**
Ottoman Empire dissolves **1919**

1920

John Maynard Keynes, *The Economic Consequences of the Peace: The Psychology of Modern Society* 1920

Max Weber, *Economy and Society* 1922

Georg Lukács, *History of Class Consciousness* 1922

Starvation in Russia; Bolsheviks turn back opposition **1920**
Gandhi assumes leadership of the Indian National Congress **1921**
In Italy, Mussolini publishes *Fascist Manifesto* **1921**
Max Weber's key works collected and published posthumously **1922**
First radio station in Britain; first ttrans-Atlantic radio fax **1922**
Gandhi arrested by British in India; imprisoned **1922**
Italian tanks press into Libya; Mussolini becomes Italian prime minister **1922**
Harvard limits Jewish applicants **1922**
Bolsheviks win Russian civil war; USSR established **1922**
Hitler imprisoned for role in Beer Hall Putsch; writes *Mein Kampf* **1923**
Lenin dies **1924**
Ho Chi Minh begins revolutionary activity in Vietnam **1924**

1925

Louis Wirth, *The Ghetto* 1928
Erich Fromm, *Psychoanalysis and Sociology* 1929
Virginia Woolf, *A Room of One's Own* 1929

US transcontinental radio network **1925**
F. Scott Fitzgerald's *The Great Gatsby* **1925**
Gramsci imprisoned by Fascists in Italy **1926**
Charles Lindbergh's solo flight from US to France **1927**
Al Capone virtually controls Chicago **1927**
Mohandas Karamchand Gandhi, *Autobiography or the Story of My Experiments with Truth* **1927**
Chinese Nationalists under Chiang Kai-shek control Beijing **1928**
G. H. Mead begins lectures on self theory, University of Chicago **1929**
US Stock Market Crashes **1929**
Edwin Hubble asserts galaxies moving from each other **1929**

1930

Karl Mannheim, *Ideology and Utopia* 1929-1931
Antonio Gramsci, *Prison Notebooks* 1929-1936
Freud, *Civilization and Its Discontents* 1930

Reinhold Niebuhr, *Moral Man and Immoral Society* 1932

George Herbert Mead, *Mind, Self, and Society* 1934

Economic crisis in Germany **1930**
Gandhi leads Salt March against British taxes **1930**
Nazi's gain seats in Reichstag **1930**
Frank Whittle patents jet engine **1930**
Chrysler Building opens, world's tallest **1930**
Gold standard abandoned **1930**
Stalin presses 25m peasants to factory labor **1931**
Japanese occupy Manchuria **1931**
Empire State Building replaces Chrysler Building as world's tallest **1931**
Roosevelt elected US President **1932**
Erskine Caldwell, *Tobacco Road*; Aldous Huxley, *Brave New World* **1932**
Unemployment in Germany at record level **1932**
Hitler becomes German Chancellor; Heinrich Himmler opens Dachau **1933**
Prohibition ends in US **1933**
...Japan withdraws from League of Nations **1933**
Gertrude Stein, *Autobiography of Alice B. Toklas* **1933**
W.E.B. Du Bois quits NAACP in dispute over segregation policies **1934**
Elijah Muhammad leads Nation of Islam **1934**
Heinrich Himmler controls Gestapo **1934**
Germany leaves League of Nations, USSR joins **1934**
Chinese Communist Long March begins **1934**

Social Theory | | Wider World

Social Theory	Year	Wider World
W.E.B. Du Bois, *Black Reconstruction: the Racial Wage* 1935	**1935**	Mao leads Chinese Communist Party 1935
		Count Basie's orchestra 1935
		Marx Brothers *A Night at the Opera* 1935
Walter Benjamin, *Art in an Age of Mechanical Reproduction: War and Fascism* 1936		Hitler advances U-Boat program; announces Jews no longer citizens 1935
		Charlie Chaplin's film, *Modern Times* 1935
		Margaret Mitchell, *Gone with the Wind* 1936
		Spanish Civil War begins 1936
		Hitler and Mussolini form Axis 1936
		Roosevelt wins reelection 1936
Talcott Parsons, *The Structure of Social Action: The Unit Act* 1937		Joe Louis becomes World Heavyweight Champion 1937
		First can of Spam sold 1937
Mao Tse-tung, *Identity, Struggle, Contradiction* 1937		John Steinbeck's novel *Of Mice and Men* 1937
		Pablo Picasso's painting *Guernica* 1937
		Thornton Wilder's play *Our Town* 1938
Robert K. Merton, *Social Structure and Anomie* 1938		Sergei Eisenstein's film *Alexander Nevsky* 1938
		Kristallnacht 1938
		Freud dies 1939
Freud, *Moses and Monotheism* 1939		John Steinbeck publishes *Grapes of Wrath* 1939
		Igor Sikorsky's first helicopter 1939
		Einstein warns FDR on atom bomb 1939
		Britain and France declare war on Germany 1939
		Warsaw falls to Germany 1939
		Russia invades Poland from the East, 1939
	1940	Benjamin commits suicide rather than return to Germany 1940
		Earnest Hemingway, *For Whom the Bell Tolls* 1940
		Winston Churchill becomes Prime Minister 1940
		Paris falls to Germans 1940
		FDR wins third term 1940
		Pearl Harbor; US enters WWII 1941
		Charles de Gaulle forms French government in exile 1941
		Gandhi advances rebellion against British Rule 1942
		US defeats Japanese fleet at Midway 1942
Max Horkheimer and Theodore Adorno, *The Culture Industry as Deception* 1944		Russian army stops Germans at Stalingrad 1942
		Allied bombing of Berlin begins 1943
		Aaron Copeland's ballet *Appalachian Spring* 1944
		Allies invade Normandy 1944
Gunnar Myrdal, *American Dilemma: The Negro Problem as a Moral Issue* 1944		Paris liberated 1944
		General Douglas MacArthur reinvades Philippines 1944
		FDR elected to fourth term 1944
	1945	Tennessee Williams play *The Glass Menagerie* 1945
		Roosevelt, Churchill, Stalin meet at Yalta 1945
		US takes Iwo Jima 1945
		Dietrich Bonhoeffer hung by Nazis 1945
		President Roosevelt dies 1945
		Hitler commits suicide; Germany surrenders 1945
		Atom bombs destroy Hiroshima and Nagasaki; Japan surrenders; 1945
Martin Heidegger, *The Question Concerning Technology* 1949		

In the 1890s, this idea predominated. The prevailing mood was expectation, and hope was strong even though the reality of life in the West had been hard. Thousands had died in revolutions that compromised original principles. Millions were degraded and exploited in the industrial centers. Women and children, as well as frontiersmen, died in the Western territories, as they did in industrial neighborhoods. Immigrants from Europe and Asia encountered miseries only marginally less acute than those they had left behind. There was no reason whatsoever to believe that life in Europe and the United States was dramatically better, or worse, for the masses than at an earlier, or later, time.

Yet at the end of the nineteenth century, people continued to look ahead, believing in Progress. The classical social theorists, many of them then at the height of their powers, were no exceptions. Yes, they understood the dark sides of modern life. But for the most part, they also shared this popular faith. Durkheim's social theory of moral life was intended to serve the modern future of France. Most of Weber's basic ideas were defined against his desire to explain the modernizing world. Whatever was wrong with it, he believed in the superiority of the rational West. The followers of Marx, an increasingly contentious lot by the 1890s, still shared his elemental faith that a final, ultimate stage of economic history was within reach. Even Freud seemed to believe that the Truth was strong enough to combat the irrational forces at war in the unconscious souls of modern people. In fact, even those who had no good reason to trust the promises of Western culture seemed to believe. In the 1890s, Frederick Douglass, Anna Julia Cooper, and W. E. B. Du Bois were chief among American Blacks who knew better than to trust the preachings, yet they, too, believed—in knowledge, in freedom, in Progress. In 1892, Cooper said, "There can be no doubt that here in America is the arena in which the next triumph of civilization is to be won."

One of Max Weber's most enduring insights came from his attempt to answer one question: Why do people obey authority? His answer: human beings have an inner need for meaning. They will obey if the authority makes sense of their lives. In other words, people want value in return for obedience. They are, in this sense, ethical. Thus, as he explained in *The Protestant Ethic*, modern culture arose when an increasing number of people accepted the idea that meaning lay in the future, not the past. The ethical disposition of people who caught the spirit of capitalism was: Think about future goals; calculate everything to achieve those goals. In order to revolt, migrate, or brave the seas and frontiers, one had to have this ethical attitude in nearly the same measure as did the early capitalist entrepreneurs. A culture of Progress is a culture that encourages people to turn from the past, toward the future—to change their orientation in time's space. Belief in one's own rational abilities encourages a readiness to marshal energies and resources, and marshaling draws, in turn, on the storehouse of reasonable calculations.

What, precisely, are the means to this end? This was the ethical question that moved so many people through the nineteenth century. Trust that the answer would be evident and available was what enticed them to overlook the dark miseries all around. There is, however, a serious risk taken by those whose ethic is Progress itself. The ethical promise must eventually be kept. The payoff need not be immediate, perhaps not even in one's own time. But at least one must be able to picture the day when the children or their children will have a better life. Throughout the nineteenth century, up to World War I, enough was gained by enough people to support the doctrine that held its own well into the twentieth century.

The Dark Side of Modernity after the War of 1914

But in the quarter century between the world wars, from 1914 to 1945, the world's events disturbed confidence in the original, uncomplicated version of this faith in Progress. The shock experienced in this period stemmed, in part, from the realization that what some had been saying all along had to be taken seriously. In the 1890s, all the classic social theorists understood that something was wrong—exploitation, estrangement, anomie, the bureaucratic machine, the veil, the irrational instincts. Yet none of them ever seemed to doubt that good knowledge would ultimately triumph, that moral progress would win the day. Among the canonical writers, only Weber was unready to believe that hope would overcome his gloom. He left the question open. Among the marginalized writers of the time, only Friedrich Nietzsche took serious measure of this prospect. Only he thought deeply enough about modern culture's one-sided faith in its Truth to consider the idea that the modern world was not itself an end. In 1887 in *Genealogy of Morals*, Nietzsche said:

> What would our existence amount to were it not for this, that the will to truth has been forced to examine itself? It is by this dawning self-consciousness of the will to truth that ethics must now perish. This is the great spectacle of a hundred acts that will occupy Europe for the next two centuries, the most terrible and problematical but also the most hopeful of spectacles. . . .

Were the events between the two wars that spectacle?

How can it be said, even by Nietzsche, that the political and economic crises that led to war, Hitler, and depression were theatrical displays? In what ways were they even unusual? Had not the Europeans passed the nineteenth century continuing to colonize Africa and Asia, while the Americans openly did to African slaves and their own native people something like what Hitler would do to Jewish people? Was not social evil just as evenly distributed across the nineteenth century as the twentieth? Yes, but. A spectacle, like any drama on whatever stage, depends entirely on the expectations of the audience drawn into it. The plays of Sophocles and Shakespeare pack dramatic punch into the surprise of feeling oneself not much less blind than Oedipus or Hamlet. One is led to expect something else, for dramatic surprise always works in relation to what went before. World history is no different. Thus, the spectacle of the nineteenth century was that of man's fresh hopes rising above evil to meet tomorrow's dawn. For European people, at home or abroad in America, the spectacle of the twentieth century was staged against that of the nineteenth. Dawn's light was dim. Instead of spring, winter lingered. Those expecting a day, clear and warm, eventually had to reconsider the holding power of night, cold and dark.

It would be a fruitless, and inhumane, exercise to calculate a coefficient of the actual horrors of the two centuries. How exactly could one sum up the balance between the economic miseries of the new working classes in nineteenth-century industrial capitalism against the sorrows of those who lost their fortunes in the Great Depression of the twentieth century? What possible formula would one use to compare the horror wrought by Hitler against the Jews or the Soviet people in the 1930s and 1940s against the nightmare of Africans, among other peoples, enslaved and murdered throughout the nineteenth century and before? How exactly does one measure what Andrew Jackson did to the Cherokee nation in the 1830s against what Stalin did a century later? What is the worth of saying that so many more Americans died in the Civil War than in either of the two world wars? The calculation itself is cruel.

What matters to people trying to understand their worlds is beyond any calculus. They ask deeper questions: Will the present evil be overcome? What does it mean that such evil is still present after all these years? For many people through the end of the nineteenth century, it seemed right to expect if not an end to evil at least a lessening of it. This was Progress. For their counterparts in the period after 1919, this expectation seemed fragile, if not false. This, it might be said, was when the culture of the nineteenth century faded and that of the twentieth emerged. Much had to be rethought.

In social theory, what had to be rethought was the relation of the human individual to the forces of modern life. The earlier version of this moral riddle was now too simple. The forces of the modern world had to be considered against the complicated power of the state as an agent of power in world politics. The state was no longer some vague aspect of the invisible hand of modern Progress. Its capacity for good and evil became evident in this period. Against such a world, the enlightened individual could no longer be left to his or her own devices. Social theory had to adjust its assumptions.

John Maynard Keynes, as much as anyone, addressed the issue at just the proper moment. In 1919, having seen the irrelevance of nineteenth-century doctrine to the Versailles Peace Conference, he wrote:

> I seek only to point out that the principle of accumulation based on inequality was a vital part of the pre-war order of Society and of progress as we then understood it, and to emphasize that this principle depended on unstable psychological conditions, which it may be impossible to recreate. . . . The bluff is discovered; the laboring classes may be no longer willing to forego so largely, and the capitalist classes, no longer confident of the future, may seek to enjoy more fully their liberties of consumption so long as they last, and thus precipitate the hour of their confiscation.

This sober critique of the culture of Progress was the perfect requisite to Keynes's economic philosophy. The individualism of the previous centuries could not possibly account for the economic and social needs of the twentieth century. Political control had to be exerted in the marketplace. Smith's invisible hand magically guiding the enlightened individual had to be replaced by the hand of the state defining market and fiscal reality. Conservatives, to this day, hate Keynes's economics, just as much for his devastating attack on the simple pieties of the nineteenth century as for the welfare state that was later justified by his ideas. Apart from his influence as an economist, Keynes was an important social theorist because he was one of the first to reassess nineteenth-century laissez-faire philosophies. After him, many came to the conclusion that the rights of individuals could no longer be accorded the unexamined privilege of being the exclusive first concerns of government.

The prior assumption of all nineteenth-century laissez-faire doctrines was no longer obvious. The social world was not moving necessarily toward Progress. As a result, one of the dominant issues in social theory between the wars was how to rethink the relation of the individual to society. In one sense, this was but a variant of the original philosophical concerns of modern culture—a question of many forms: How does the subject know the objective world? How are individual rights protected against civil authorities? How is moral action responsible to, or constrained by, the social group? How is social order maintained against the demands for political and social freedom? These were the classic formulations through the end of the nineteenth century. In the period of world crisis in the twentieth century, these older questions took on a special urgency. In the process, the questions changed in ways suited to the times and in ways that would endure long after the end of World War II: How is the action of society derived from individual agents? How is the social self both an individual and a social thing? And most urgent of all, is the modern democratic state an agent of good or of evil in the lives of individuals? Though the issue necessarily had to be stated in different ways according to different specific concerns, all the questions still boiled down to a refinement of the question asked by most classic social theorists: What, precisely, is the fate of the individual in the modern world?

The crucial difference in the interwar period was that conflicts within and between world states eroded the manifest plausibility of doctrines of social hope. Progress was in doubt, for good reasons. The social fate of the individual—the subject, the agent of history, the moral self, whatever the name—had to be examined with new intellectual seriousness. In effect, looking back to the social theorists of the 1890s, one could say that the more sober estimates of Weber and Nietzsche won out in the interwar period. By contrast, the deeper cultural assumptions of Marx, Durkheim, Du Bois, and Cooper were too naive. Progress was their defiant position. Without anyone saying it in so many words, the classic social theorists shared some version of the earlier nineteenth-century doctrine that the individual can do what needs to be done because society inclines toward progress. Weber was one of the few to voice suspicion that the constraining force of modern society was much more than a passing stage (as Marx thought) or a sometimes unreliable source of moral guidance (as Durkheim thought). The world conflicts in the early twentieth century came so late in the long story of modern life that progress counted for a great deal less. Social anxiety deepened accordingly.

If, in economic philosophy, Keynes was the prophet of a need for serious reconsideration of state action, then, in social philosophy, the period's most distinctively new school of thought prepared a similar brief for knowledge, science, and culture. The Frankfurt Institute for Social Research (later popularly known as the German School of Critical Theory) had its roots in the political and economic realities of Germany between the wars. Among the major European powers of the twentieth century, Germany had been late to enter fully into modern politics. The extended grip of Bismarckian culture and politics through the end of the nineteenth century reinforced the hold of traditionalism in politics and, to some extent, in economics. Even though France, Great Britain, and the United States struggled in this time with the contradictions between traditionalism and modernity, the conflict was distorted in Germany. By the end of the nineteenth century, Germany was, in effect, a leading industrial power resting on a foundation that was weak in the exercise of democratic politics. The Weimar Republic that governed unsuccessfully after World War I was, at best, more of a cultural experiment. Though France's Third Republic had only marginally greater staying power in the end, at least in France there had been a century-long struggle to understand the democratic basis of the modern state. Weber surely saw the differences between traditionalism and modernity, as well as the horrors of the bureaucratic state, because of his firsthand familiarity with Germany's uncertain giant steps into the modern world. These political uncertainties, joined to the worldwide economic crises in the 1920s, gave birth to fascism. If the great island cultures of the time—Great Britain and the United States—had the easier paths of relative isolation in which to learn modernity, Germany in particular among the nation-states of continental Europe had the tougher path.

Social Theory Must Think the Demonic

Paul Tillich (1886–1965), one of the many German exiles who had been associated with the Frankfurt School, defined the demonic as the "form-destroying eruption of the good." Tillich spoke as a theologian, but, with minor translation, his idea fit the times and the German experience. Social evil in this period was, indeed, a "form-destroying eruption of the good" in modern life. The destructive side of modernity was within, and part of, its good. This is what Weber the sociologist and Nietzsche the philosopher also saw at an earlier time. At some risk, one might say that Germany, in the interwar period, acted out the evil impulses that lay hidden within the whole of modern culture. Hitler was the manifest spectacle of those impulses. He made visible modernity's worst nightmares.

The German critical theorists were deeply shaped by their direct experiences with Hitler. Yet the brilliance of their theory lay in their courageous understanding that modern society, including its culture, had to be examined critically if one were to understand modern life. If the naive assumption of the nineteenth century had been that knowledge would set men free, then the realities of the twentieth century were that knowledge, far from being the final social good, was implicated in evil. In effect, the critical theorists were forced to take up Marx's earlier materialist critique of knowledge in order to develop a more complete, positive critique of modern culture. It was no longer enough to proclaim official science and knowledge as the ideological reverse image—the camera obscura—of economic life. Knowledge, science, and culture in the interwar years were manifestly more than passive instruments of the ruling class. They were perhaps this, but more. Hitler preached an ideology that inspired followers. Yes, he could be said to have drugged a nation, but he actually induced people to believe and act in accord with his ideas. Direct experience with the power of ideas meant knowledge could be neither the passive reflex of economic power nor the primal source of enlightened action. The ideas taken to be true knowledge had a more complicated relation to economic and political power. The German critical theorists thus began a long tradition of social theory that sought to reexamine both the assumptions of the Enlightenment and those of Marx in order to rethink the political values of knowledge itself. Eventually, theorists associated with the Frankfurt tradition came to define their view of critical social theory as the basis for human liberation from social evil. Critical theory became the social theoretical tradition most invested in defining truly emancipatory knowledge—that is, social theory with the power to free people. To fulfill the promise of modern culture, that culture had to be subjected to a thorough critique. Critical theorists were, from the beginning, radical modernists, unafraid to face the worst in modern life, prepared to define its highest realistic standard for human freedom.

Among the earliest resources of the Frankfurt School were the early, more Hegelian writings of Karl Marx, many of which were just then being taken seriously. Georg Lukács was an important early influence on the critical theorists in Germany because his thinking linked these elements in Marx to a general theory of modern culture and knowledge. His precise philosophical analysis of the subject as a reified object unable to see itself except as an abstraction harkened back to Marx's thinking in the 1844 Manuscripts. It was also a telling diagnosis of modern life in 1923 when Lukács's *History and Class Consciousness* first appeared. He was, as he said, intent on writing a social theory that could diagnose "the unhistorical and antihistorical character of bourgeois thought" as the historical problem of the present.

Max Horkheimer and Theodor Adorno were first among equals in the earliest generation of the Frankfurt School in Germany. Over their years of philosophical and sociology work on many subjects, one constant theme was the failure of science and culture to resist the demonic forces that regularly disrupted and destroyed the creative promises of modern economic and social institutions. At the heart of their critical theory was a radical revision of vulgar Marxism's idea that culture, including the sciences, were mere reflections of the class interests of the bourgeoisie. Their underlying purpose was to come to more direct terms with nineteenth-century versions of the Enlightenment, which believed that science was the final key to progress and, for the most part, ignored the extent to which culture could be understood as a dialectic of the good and evil of modern order. The most famous essay among those coauthored by Horkheimer and Adorno was written in part on the basis of their experiences in exile in America. "The Culture Industry as Deception" parallels the Frankfurt tradition's critique of science to the effect that culture, which promises so much good to human society, ultimately becomes a shadow of itself by serving the commercial interests of mass society.

Just as Horkheimer and Adorno fused ideas from Marx and Weber, as well as other thinkers critical of the Enlightenment, Erich Fromm explored the relations between psychoanalysis and sociology (including Marxism). In 1929, when Fromm wrote "Psychoanalysis and Sociology," a short piece for his Frankfurt Institute colleagues, the usefulness of a method like psychoanalysis was evident. At the time, it alone among the developed human sciences took with utter seriousness the power of hidden, unconscious forces in the interplay between mental life and society. The Frankfurt school had learned the hard lessons of the Nazi regime from which they fled.

Martin Heidegger, the German philosopher known for his massive and difficult book, *Being and Time* (1927), was a slightly older contemporary of Horkheimer and Adorno. Yet, while the critical theorists left Nazi Germany, Heidegger remained and is widely, if not universally, thought to have at least passively supported Hitler's regime. That presumption of fact has not, however, prevented Heidegger from being still today one of the most influential philosophers of his time. He was not, however, a critical theorist. Yet his thinking contributed importantly to challenging the time-honored categories of modern philosophy, notably Kant's attempt to rescue the knowing subject from the uncertainties of objective knowledge. "The Age of the World Picture," taken from one of Heidegger's more accessible shorter writings, "The Question Concerning Technology" (1954), is striking as a criticism of modern culture and science as they come together to form the illusion of technological prowess.

States, Structures, and the Social Qualify the Enlightenment's Free Individual

Karl Mannheim's sociology of knowledge, decidedly more sociological thinking, is thus closer in political attitude to the Frankfurt tradition. In his own way, Mannheim illustrates the intellectual crisis of the period between the wars. After World War I, serious thinkers no longer thought of the human subject as the simple source of all knowledge, much less moral action. It was well understood, especially in Europe, that social forces were basic to the discovery and application of knowledge. Mannheim was closer to Weberian sociology than were the Frankfurt theorists; yet, like them, his experience in Germany clearly affected his classic description of ideology.

Mannheim developed Marx's critique of ideology in a different, more Weberian, direction. Like Horkheimer and Adorno, he sought to show how ideas reflect the social crises of their times without being mere inversions of the true social reality, namely, the economy. When one reads Mannheim after reading Lenin, the effect can be stunning. Even though Lenin's "What Is To Be Done?" was composed at the turn of the twentieth century from 1901 to 1902, it is the classic source for his argument that the extremes of vulgar Marxist economics prevent effective political action. The revolutionary vanguard must act in relation to the total life of the working class, not just its economic circumstances. This, of course, was a theoretical move necessary for a revolutionary theory of the socialist state. There was little in Marx's theories to guide a full social revolution, including the formation of a post-revolutionary state. Lenin's ideas, as well as his actions in the Soviet revolutionary government, demonstrated the need for a theory of governing elites. Later, Stalin's capacity for evil demonstrated the limits of Lenin's ideas. Still, the question Lenin asked was the prevailing question of the period, and his answer to it had more actual political effect than those offered by any of the others, except perhaps for Keynes.

Some would argue that it is foolishness to suggest that the Frankfurt School be read in the same context as Keynes, to say nothing of Talcott Parsons and Robert K. Merton, much less of Lenin and Mannheim. But when one keeps the focus on the social concerns of the period, their apparent differences are less acute. Parsons and Merton became the *grands hommes* of American sociology's Golden Age in the 1940s and 1950s. Parsons headed the Harvard School, Merton the Columbia School. To a very large degree, they and their students represented in this later time an exaggerated revision of the old idea that Progress could, in fact, win the day with sociology as its tool. Yet in their writings in the 1930s, both Merton and Parsons could just as properly be read as critics of the nineteenth-century theories of the social individual.

In 1937, Parsons's *Structure of Social Action* was a rethinking of those he considered the classic social theorists in order to define the terms of a truly modern sociology. The omission of Marx from Parsons's list was just one of the ways in which he took the influence of Weber in an entirely different direction from that of the German critical thinkers. Had Parsons suffered in Germany, he might have thought differently. Just the same, his technical analysis of the four elements of an action system, though abstract, is sensitive to the issues of the day. Parsons saw the individual as the unit of social analysis, but his was not the freethinking individual of the nineteenth century. The Parsonian individual was lodged in a system in which individual action was constrained not just by social conditions but also by the goals of the system itself and by the complex interrelation of its structured parts. In this early writing, Parsons's individual was defined against a very complex set of social forces. Later in his career, the individual became an even more complicated unit as Parsons introduced the idea (taken from Freud) that social actors are bearers of unconsciously introjected motivational forces. Already in 1937, the individual's relation to the social system was constrained, if dynamic; situated, though motivated. The action of the individual was seen as the action of a system, not the autonomous self.

Robert K. Merton refused to write such abstract theory. Yet his views were not that different from those of Parsons. In 1938, his "Social Structure and Anomie" gave voice to the same general concerns expressed by others in this period but in a different, more elegant tone. Merton's basic assumption was that the individual is not just *in* a structured system of action but that his or her actions may be forced *by* the demands of the system. Merton argued that when the economic system fails to provide legitimate means to earn income, and status, the cultural logic of the social system may force the individual to act in ways that are culturally logical, even if illegal. Here, Merton did several things at once. He revised Durkheim's idea of anomie in ways that allowed for the real political and economic contradictions of society. (Merton, though then a functionalist, also knew his Marx.) At the same time, he offered a shrewd description of the cultural logic of American capitalism. Always understated, Merton's text can be read as much as a critique as a defense of the American way of social life. In this famous essay, Merton stood on the shoulders of Durkheim, and of Marx and Weber.

George Herbert Mead's theory of the social self is considered a classic in American social psychology and a foundation of the school of symbolic interactionism. Thus, Mead is sometimes thought to be a social theorist of limited interest. Yet his ideas of the social self represented a major advance over those of William James and Charles Horton Cooley. With Mead, the social self was more definitely a social, as opposed to a mental, thing. "The self," he said, "is essentially a social structure, and it arises in social experience." Though Mead was developing what he called a social behaviorism, his theory had radical aspects that do not meet the eye in a first reading. For example, Mead was one of the first to work out the notion, already evident in James, that the social self was, by nature, multiple. "The multiple personality is in a certain sense normal," he said. The implication is that social selves, structured by social experience in modern society, are necessarily multiple—a thinly veiled allusion to the craziness of social life. Ideas like this linked Mead to the other social theorists of the interwar years who sought to come to terms with the individual's tortured relation to social structures. Though Mead remained a philosopher throughout his life, his ideas provided a theoretical framework for many in the Chicago School of sociology—those noted particularly for the study of the urban underworld of immigrant life, gangs, urban violence, and deviant lifestyles. Mead's view of the social self as a dynamic structure of multiple parts clearly supported the study of those forms of urban life in which deviant behavior was also seen as an adjustment to two or more worlds—the normal and the "abnormal." The parallels to Du Bois's idea of double-consciousness are apparent. Mead's theories thus linked the Chicago studies of his time to a post-World War II Chicago tradition that included Erving Goffman, perhaps the most famous exponent of the social study of normal deviance.

It is possible to interpret the interwar years in another way. From the inside, it was a period in which the hidden contradictions of modern culture broke out. It was, to be sure, a time of world conflict. But by the end of World War II, the world retained its form. The European dominance of world politics remained intact. The West, whatever its internal conflicts, remained the world's master. From the outside, however, one could begin to see in this period that the West was losing its grip on world politics. Though the Allies defeated both Germany and Japan, only a few years after World War II India won its independence and the Chinese Communists overthrew the nationalists allied with Western military and economic interests. A little over a decade later, the African colonies rejected European rule. Thus, though the Euro-American world kept its form at the end of this period, it began to lose its heart in the face of unavoidable and seemingly unresolvable dilemmas.

Signs of Changes to Come: Conflicts and the Seeds of Global Revolution

Reinhold Niebuhr was among those Americans who most clearly contended that the conflict between individual and political interests was unbridgeable. If others, like Parsons or Merton or Mead, were confident that an integrated social theory of the social individual could be constructed, Niebuhr was among those who considered this unlikely. He argued that state power is selfish and thus something entirely different from individual interests. Individual interactions can eventuate in love; state power can, at best, result in social justice. As a theologian and social ethicist, writing in 1932, Niebuhr was viewed as a radical attacking Protestant piety. It is no accident that his social theories became clear after a long tenure as pastor among the working poor in Detroit. The strangeness of urban life, particularly in the United States, bore witness to the conflicts of the twentieth century. In the working-class urban neighborhoods of Detroit and Chicago, social theorists like Niebuhr encountered not just the psychological tensions of modern life (like those described by Simmel) but also the socially structured conflicts between different people of different ethnic backgrounds.

America was trying to adjust both to new immigrant peoples and to the radically different cultures that called into question the very idea of "normal." Gunnar Myrdal's *American Dilemma* (1944) later demonstrated the structural sources of social conflict in America's long-enduring moral contradiction in its relations to the African people within its borders. If racial conflict is the most fundamental moral dilemma in the United States, then urban conflict with and among immigrant groups was the fundamental social dilemma. It was not just a matter of understanding the different habits of strangers. Far more, students of urban life in this period came to understand that the real cultural differences required a different understanding of social norms. This idea was later apparent in Merton's theory of adaptation to anomie. But earlier in the interwar period, principally in Chicago, studies of urban groups led to theories of social deviation in which behavior considered illegal or deviant by American culture at large was understood as "normal" within the social circumstances of a localized culture.

W. I. Thomas and Florian Znaniecki's *Polish Peasant* (1918–1919) was one of many books of the Chicago School that made this point. Reading the early Chicago studies today, one might not be impressed by their originality. We have grown accustomed to social differences and somewhat immune to the notion that normal social behavior is nearly impossible to define. To the more traditional Christian people of the 1920s, however, these studies of urban life must have been every bit as shocking as Niebuhr's pronouncement that Christian piety could never save the political world. One of the most famous essays to emerge from the Chicago School studies was Louis Wirth's "Urbanism as a Way of Life" (1938). It is considered a classic because Wirth (1887–1952) was among the first to argue that cities were not just densely populated ecological zones but also the spawning ground of unique ways of life. Again, this is not news today, but it was then. The differences inherent in urban life, like those inherent in America's immoral racial conflicts, were chief among the unavoidable dilemmas that were internal to the newest of Europe's nations. Wirth's first book, *The Ghetto* (1928), reflects his own German origins and very German theoretical sensibility. While his study of Jewish Ghetto is hardly a book of theory one can see in it the traces of his particular interest in Karl Mannheim, whose *Ideology and Utopia* (1929) Wirth translated and introduced.

If one reads Walter Benjamin's "Art in the Age of Mechanical Reproduction" (1936) after the writings of the American urbanists, it is possible to see a striking similarity behind the obvious differences. Benjamin was one of the Frankfurt Institute's critical theorists most respected for his brilliant studies of aesthetics. Much like the other German critical theorists (he was a close friend of Adorno's), Benjamin saw fascism as an extreme expression of modernity's doomed struggle to accommodate the expressive interests of the new urban masses with the property interests of the capitalist class. Though fascism was quite a different phenomenon, and Benjamin a different type of theorist, there is still a similarity with the Chicago School theorists. They, too, studied the new urban masses in order to understand the conflict between the interests of the social world as it was and the reality of the world as it was becoming. Benjamin recoiled from the aesthetics of war. The Chicago urbanists, being more traditionally scientific, stood back in appreciation of the new urban life. The perspectives were utterly at odds. The dilemmas were not.

Unless one was directly affected, it was possible not to see what was happening at home and abroad. Mohandas Gandhi and Mao Tse-tung are the most notable historical figures in this period who were engaged in political lives that would eventually change the world's structure. Both were self-conscious social theorists in the sense that they developed explicit social theories to organize political action. Gandhi, first in South Africa and later in India, developed the theory of forceful nonviolence that would not only change India but also affect the American Civil Rights Movement after World War II. Mao, in this period, organized the Chinese Communists he led after the war with evident references to a theory of world contradiction.

The failure to understand a contradiction played out in China is one thing. It is quite another when the contradiction is right at home. Virginia Woolf's "A Room of One's Own" (1929) began with a fictionalized account of male "horror and indignation" that a woman would transgress on man's preserve. Though a fiction, like Gilman's "The Yellow Wallpaper," Woolf's 1929 lecture became a classic source of feminist social theory because it described so powerfully one of the most ubiquitous contradictions structured into daily life in the West.

It is particularly instructive to read Antonio Gramsci alongside Virginia Woolf, on the one hand, and Karl Mannheim, on the other. Gramsci's influential development of the Marxian notion of social hegemony accounts for the ways in which intellectuals, being part of the organic process of their social classes, are very often less than likely to be free-floating critics of the social order. In this respect, his notion of the intellectual is consistent with Mannheim's sociology of knowledge. Yet, though Virginia Woolf was assaulted by the prevailing intellectual culture of her day, she managed to stand firm against it. Hence, the contradiction that Gramsci described from his prison cell that "every man is an intellectual"—from which arises the critical possibility.

C. L.

Notes

Page 152: Cooper, *A Voice from the South* (Oxford University Press, 1988), 12.

Page 153: Nietzsche, *Genealogy of Morals*, Third Essay, 27.

Page 155: I heard Tillich's line either from his lectures at Harvard early in the 1960s or from his friend (and my teacher) James Luther Adams. One of the effects of reading social theory over many years is that certain things are just there, somewhere in and between what was said or written and what is remembered. But see Tillich, *Interpretation of History* (Scribner's, 1936), 81.

Other quotations are in the selections that follow.

Action and Knowledge in a Troubled World

John Maynard Keynes (1883–1946) became the dominant economist in the West between the two world wars. While serving as a senior member of Britain's delegation to the Versailles Peace Conference in 1919, he rethought in more radical terms the ideas of Alfred Marshall, his teacher at Cambridge. Keynes resigned from the delegation and wrote *Economic Consequences of the Peace* (1920), in which he attacked the prevailing orthodoxy of political and economic thinking. "The Psychology of Modern Society" is from that book. In this selection, Keynes's radical spirit is evident in his implicit statement of purpose: to state the truth of what lay hidden in "the unconscious recess of [capitalist society's] being." Subsequently, Keynes softened somewhat his criticism of capitalism, but only to the extent of arguing for a more direct role of the state in controlling and directing economic markets. This idea influenced Franklin Roosevelt's New Deal as well as the leading social theorists of the time (most notably Talcott Parsons), and Keynes' more robustly social philosophy. Keynes, thus, was largely responsible for the post–World War II idea in the West that the state must function to regulate economic markets. Keynes's most important technical study was *The General Theory of Employment, Interest and Money* (1936). His ideas are particularly lucid examples of the social theoretical sentiments that arose between the wars: Given the global economic and political crises, social theory had to rethink the individual's relation to society and the state had to become an active player in the economic world.

The Psychology of Modern Society[*]
John Maynard Keynes (1920)

Europe was so organized socially and economically as to secure the maximum accumulation of capital. While there was some continuous improvement in the daily conditions of life of the mass of the population, Society was so framed as to throw a great part of the increased income into the control of the class least likely to consume it. The new rich of the nineteenth century were not brought up to large expenditures, and preferred the power which investment gave them to the pleasures of immediate consumption. In fact, it was precisely the *inequality* of the distribution of wealth which made possible those vast accumulations of fixed wealth and of capital improvements which distinguished that age from all others. Herein lay, in fact, the main justification of the Capitalist System. If the rich had spent their new wealth on their own enjoyments, the world would long ago have found such a régime intolerable. But like bees they saved and accumulated, not less to the advantage of the whole community because they themselves held narrower ends in prospect.

[*] Excerpt from *The Economic Consequences of the Peace* (New York: Harcourt, Brace, and Howe, 1920), pp. 18–22.

The immense accumulations of fixed capital which, to the great benefit of mankind, were built up during the half century before the war, could never have come about in a Society where wealth was divided equitably. The railways of the world, which that age built as a monument to posterity, were, not less than the Pyramids of Egypt, the work of labor which was not free to consume in immediate enjoyment the full equivalent of its efforts.

Thus this remarkable system depended for its growth on a double bluff or deception. On the one hand the laboring classes accepted from ignorance or powerlessness, or were compelled, persuaded, or cajoled by custom, convention, authority, and the well-established order of Society into accepting a situation in which they could call their own very little of the cake that they and Nature and the capitalists were co-operating to produce. And on the other hand, the capitalist classes were allowed to call the best part of the cake theirs and were theoretically free to consume it, on the tacit underlying condition that they consumed very little of it in practice. The duty of "saving" became nine-tenths of virtue and the growth of the cake the object of true religion. There grew round the non-consumption of the cake all those instincts of puritanism which in other ages has withdrawn itself from the world and has neglected the arts of production as well as those of enjoyment. And so the cake increased; but to what end was not clearly contemplated. Individuals would be exhorted not so much to abstain as to defer, and to cultivate the pleasures of security and anticipation. Saving was for old age or for your children; but this was only in theory,—the virtue of the cake was that it was never to be consumed, neither by you nor by your children after you.

In writing thus I do not necessarily disparage the practices of that generation. In the unconscious recesses of its being Society knew what it was about. The cake was really very small in proportion to the appetites of consumption, and no one, if it were shared all round, would be much the better off by the cutting of it. Society was working not for the small pleasures of today but for the future security and improvement of the race,—in fact for "progress." If only the cake were not cut but was allowed to grow in the geometrical proportion predicted by Malthus of population, but not less true of compound interest, perhaps a day might come when there would at last be enough to go round, and when posterity could enter into the enjoyment of *our* labors. In that day overwork, overcrowding, and underfeeding would have come to an end, and men, secure of the comforts and necessities of the body, could proceed to the nobler exercises of their faculties. One geometrical ratio might cancel another, and the nineteenth century was able to forget the fertility of the species in a contemplation of the dizzy virtues of compound interest.

There were two pitfalls in this prospect: lest, population still outstripping accumulation, our self-denials promote not happiness but numbers; and lest the cake be after all consumed, prematurely, in war, the consumer of all such hopes.

But these thoughts lead too far from my present purpose. I seek only to point out that the principle of accumulation based on inequality was a vital part of the pre-war order of Society and of progress as we then understood it, and to emphasize that this principle depended on unstable psychological conditions, which it may be impossible to recreate. It was not natural for a population, of whom so few enjoyed the comforts of life, to accumulate so hugely. The war has disclosed the possibility of consumption to all and the vanity of abstinence to many. Thus the bluff is discovered; the laboring classes may be no longer willing to forego so largely, and the capitalist classes, no longer confident of the future, may seek to enjoy more fully their liberties of consumption so long as they last, and thus precipitate the hour of their confiscation.

Talcott Parsons (1902–1979) is considered the founder of American sociological theory. Among his many former students, Parsons's name is a virtual synonym for theoretical brilliance; however, among a comparable number of younger sociologists, the same name is synonymous with abstract, conservative, and incomprehensible scientism. After graduating with an economics degree from Amherst College in 1924, Parsons studied in England at the London School of Economics, then at Heidelberg from 1925 to 1926. In England, Parsons studied the economics of Alfred Marshall; in Germany, he discovered the writings of Max Weber. Parsons translated *Protestant Ethic* (1905) and other works by Weber. He first taught economics at Harvard in 1927. Later, he began teaching sociology at the invitation of the Russian émigré Pitirim Sorokin (1889–1968), who was instrumental in establishing sociology's reputation at Harvard. Parsons came into his own with the publication of *The Structure of Social Action* in 1937.

This two-volume tour de force carefully analyzed those whom Parsons considered the classical social theorists (Weber, Durkheim, Marshall, and Vilfredo Pareto) in order to renew sociological theory and research. His goal was to establish a general theory of social action that encompassed all the behavioral sciences, including biology. In the 1940s, Parsons's theoretical synthesis formed the intellectual basis for Harvard's Department of Social Relations, which, in the 1950s, was considered by many the major department in the field. Parsons chaired the department from 1946 to 1956, but the experiment at synthesis collapsed when Parsons retired and times changed.

"The Unit Act of Action Systems," from *Structure of Social Action*, may be difficult reading, but it is an important sample of Parsons's theoretical intention to define the elements in a theory of social action: the actor, the actor's ends (or goals), the social situation, and the structured relation among these elements. Though this is a different sort of writing from that of Keynes (who was also an influence on Parsons) or of Lukács or the others in this period, readers should be able to see a common theoretical concern for the fate of the individual in modern, structured society.

I don't like this reading

The Unit Act of Action Systems*
Talcott Parsons (1937)

In the first chapter attention was called to the fact that in the process of scientific conceptualization concrete phenomena come to be divided into units or parts. The first salient feature of the conceptual scheme to be dealt with lies in the character of the units which it employs in making this division. The basic unit may be called the "unit act." Just as the units of a mechanical system in the classical sense, particles, can be defined only in terms of their properties, mass, velocity, location in space, direction of motion, etc., so the units of action systems also have certain basic properties without which it is not possible to conceive of the unit as "existing." Thus, to continue the analogy, the conception of a unit of matter which has mass but which cannot be located in space is, in terms of the classical mechanics, non-

sensical. It should be noted that the sense in which the unit act is here spoken of as an existent entity is not that of concrete spatiality or otherwise separate existence, but of conceivability as a unit in terms of a frame of reference. There must be a minimum number of descriptive terms applied to it, a minimum number of facts ascertainable about it, before it can be spoken of at all as a unit in a system.

In this sense then, an "act" involves logically the following: (1) It implies an agent, an "actor." (2) For purposes of definition the act must have an "end," a future state of affairs toward which the process of action is oriented. (3) It must be initiated in a "situation" of which the trends of development differ in one or more important respects from the state of affairs to which the action is oriented, the end. This situation is in turn analyzable into two elements: those over which the actor has no control, that is which he cannot alter, or prevent from being altered, in conformity with his end, and those over which he has such control. The former may be termed the "conditions" of action, the latter the "means." Finally (4) there is inherent in the conception of this unit, in its analytical uses, a certain mode of relationship between these elements. That is, in the choice of alternative means to the end, in so far as the situation allows alternatives, there is a "normative orientation" of action. Within the area of control of the actor, the means employed cannot, in general, be conceived either as chosen at random or as dependent exclusively on the conditions of action, but must in some sense be subject to the influence of an independent, determinate selective factor, a knowledge of which is necessary to the understanding of the concrete course of action. What is essential to the concept of action is that there should be a normative orientation, not that this should be of any particular type. As will be seen, the discrimination of various possible modes of normative orientation is one of the most important questions with which this study will be confronted. But before entering into the definition of any of them a few of the major implications of the basic conceptual scheme must be outlined.

The first important implication is that an act is always a process in time. The time category is basic to the scheme. The concept end always implies a future reference, to a state which is either not yet in existence, and which would not come into existence if something were not done about it by the actor or, if already existent, would not remain unchanged. This process, seen primarily in terms of its relation to ends, is variously called "attainment," "realization," and "achievement."

Second, the fact of a range of choice open to the actor with reference both to ends and to means, in combination with the concept of a normative orientation of action, implies the possibility of "error," of the failure to attain ends or to make the "right" choice of means. The various meanings of error and the various factors to which it may be attributed will form one of the major themes to be discussed.

Third, the frame of reference of the schema is subjective in a particular sense. That is, it deals with phenomena, with things and events *as they appear from the point of view of the actor* whose action is being analyzed and considered. Of course the phenomena of the "external world" play a major part in the influencing of action. But in so far as they can be utilized by this particular theoretical scheme, they must be reducible to terms which are subjective in this particular sense. This fact is of cardinal importance in understanding some of the peculiarities of the theoretical structures under consideration here. The same fact introduces a further complication which must be continually kept in mind. It may be said that all empirical science is concerned with the understanding of the phenomena of the external world. Then the facts of action are, to the scientist who studies them, facts of the external world—in this sense, objective facts. That is, the symbolic reference of the propositions the scientist calls facts is to phenomena "external" to the scientist, not to the content of his own mind. But in this particular case, unlike that of the physical sciences, the phenomena being studied have a scientifically relevant subjective aspect. That is, while the social scientist is not concerned with studying the content of his own mind, he is very much concerned with that of the minds of the persons whose action he studies. This necessitates the distinction of the objective and subjective points of view. The distinction and the relation of the two to each other are of great importance. By "objective" in this context will always be meant "from the point of view of the scientific observer of action" and by "subjective," "from the point of view of the actor."

A still further consequence follows from the "subjectivity" of the categories of the theory of action. When a biologist or a behavioristic psychologist studies a human being it is as an organism, a spatially distinguishable separate unit in the world. The unit of reference which we are considering as the actor is not this organism but an "ego" or "self." The principal importance of this consideration is that the

body of the actor forms, for him, just as much part of the situation of action as does the "external environment." Among the conditions to which his action is subject are those relating to his own body, while among the most important of the means at his disposal are the "powers" of his own body and, of course, his "mind." The analytical distinction between actor and situation quite definitely cannot be identified with the distinction in the biological sciences between organism and environment. It is not a question of distinctions of concrete "things," for the organism is a real unit. It is rather a matter of the analysis required by the categories of empirically useful theoretical systems.

A fourth implication of the schema of action should be noted. Certainly the situation of action includes parts of what is called in common-sense terms the physical environment and the biological organism—to mention only two points. With equal certainty these elements of the situation of action are capable of analysis in terms of the physical and biological sciences, and the phenomena in question are subject to analysis in terms of the units in use in those sciences. Thus a bridge may, with perfect truth, be said to consist of atoms of iron, a small amount of carbon, etc., and their constituent electrons, protons, neutrons and the like. Must the student of action, then, become a physicist, chemist, biologist in order to understand his subject? In a sense this is true, but for purposes of the theory of action it is not necessary or desirable to carry such analyses as far as science in general is capable of doing. A limit is set by the frame of reference with which the student of action is working. That is, he is interested in phenomena with an aspect not reducible to action terms only in so far as they impinge on the schema of action in a relevant way—in the role of conditions or means. So long as their properties, which are important in this context, can be accurately determined these may be taken as data without further analysis. Above all, atoms, electrons or cells are not to be regarded as units for purposes of the theory of action. Unit analysis of any phenomenon beyond the point where it constitutes an integral means or condition of action leads over into terms of another theoretical scheme. For the purposes of the theory of action the smallest conceivable concrete unit is the unit act, and while it is in turn analyzable into the elements to which reference has been made—end, means, conditions and guiding norms—further analysis of the phenomena of which these are in turn aspects is relevant to the theory of action only in so far as the units arrived at can be referred to as constituting such elements of a unit act or a system of them.

Erich Fromm (1900–1980), an early associate of the Frankfurt Institute of Social Research in the 1930s, was among those who contributed to the German critical tradition of wedding Marxism and psychoanalysis. When Fromm came to the United States, his ties with the Frankfurt School grew weak. He became a widely regarded teacher and popular writer as well as a practicing psychoanalyst. Among his most famous books are *Escape from Freedom* (1941), *Man for Himself* (1947), and *The Art of Loving* (1956). "Psychoanalysis and Sociology" was written in 1929, during his Frankfurt days. In it, he outlines the need for a unified social theory of the individual as a socialized being in a complex society.

Psychoanalysis and Sociology*
Erich Fromm (1929)

The problem of the relations between psychoanalysis and sociology, about which I will speak in the Institute's courses, has two sides. The first is the application of psychoanalysis to sociology, the second that of sociology to psychoanalysis. Of course, it is not possible even to list in a few minutes all the problems and themes that result from both sides. Therefore, I shall merely attempt to make a few fundamental remarks about the principles which seem to apply to the scientific treatment of psychoanalytic-sociological problems.

The application of psychoanalysis to sociology must definitely guard against the mistake of wanting to give psychoanalytic answers where economic, technical, or political facts provide the real and sufficient explanation of sociological questions. On the other hand, the psychoanalyst must emphasize that the subject of sociology, society, in reality consists of individuals, and that it is these human beings, rather than an abstract society as such, whose actions, thoughts, and feelings are the object of sociological research.

*Reproduced by permission of Taylor and Francis Group, LLC, a division of Informa plc, from *Critical Theory and Society: A Reader* by Erich Fromm, edited by Stephen Eric Bronner and Douglas MacKay. Copyright 1989, Psychology Press; permission conveyed through Copyright Clearance Center, Inc.

Human beings do not have one "individual psyche," which functions when a person performs as an individual and so becomes the object of psychoanalysis, contrasted to a completely separate "mass psyche" with all sorts of mass instincts, as well as vague feelings of community and solidarity, which springs into action whenever a person performs as part of mass, and for which the sociologist creates some makeshift concepts for psychoanalytical facts unknown to him. There aren't two minds within a person's head, but only one, in which the same mechanisms and laws apply whether a person performs as an individual or people appear as a society, class, community, or what have you. What psychoanalysis can bring to sociology is the knowledge—though still imperfect—of the human psychic apparatus, which is a determinant of social development alongside technical, economic, and financial factors, and deserves no less consideration than the other factors mentioned. The common task of both sciences is to investigate in what way and to what extent the psychic apparatus of the human being causally affects or determines the development or organization of society.

Let me mention here only one essential concrete problem. It is necessary to investigate what role the instinctual and the unconscious play in the organization and development of society and in individual social facts, and to what extent the changes in mankind's psychological structure, in the sense of a growing ego-organization and thus a rational ability to cope with the instinctual and natural, is a sociologically relevant factor.

Now the other side of the problem: the application of sociological approaches to psychoanalysis. However important it may be to point out to sociologists the banal fact that society consists of living people and that psychology is one of the factors affecting social development, it is equally important that psychology not underestimate the fact that the individual person in reality exists only as a socialized person. Psychoanalysis, in contrast to some other schools of psychology, can claim that it has understood this fact from the beginning. Indeed, the recognition that there is no *homo psychologicus*, no psychological Robinson Crusoe, is one of the foundations of its theory. Psychoanalysis is predominantly oriented to questions of genesis; it devotes its special interest to human childhood, and it teaches us to interpret a very essential part of the development of the human psychological apparatus on the basis of people's attachment to mother, father, siblings, in short to the family, and thus to society.

Psychoanalysis interprets the development of individuals precisely in terms of their relationship to their closest and most intimate surroundings; it considers the psychological apparatus as formed most decisively by these relationships.

Certainly, this is only a beginning, and from it a series of further important problems result, which have so far scarcely been attacked; for instance, the question of to what extent the family is itself the product of a particular social system, and how a socially conditioned change in the family as such might influence the development of the psychic apparatus of the individual. Or there is the question of what influence the growth of technology—i.e., an ever increasing gratification, or a decreasing deprivation, or the instincts—has on the psyche of the individual.

The classification from which we proceed, into problems that result from the application of psychoanalysis to sociology and of sociology to psychoanalysis, is of course only a crude one, which corresponds to practical needs. In keeping with the reciprocal interaction of person and society, there are a whole series of further problems. Some of the most important ones are precisely those where it is impossible to apply one method to the other, but where a set of facts, which are equally psychological and social in character, can be investigated by both methods and can be understood only by employing both perspectives. It is just such a problem of how much certain concerns of psychology, which are simultaneously sociological, such as religion, depend on the material development of mankind in their appearance and decline, that constitutes the subject of the latest book by Freud.

There Freud advances the idea that religion is the psychic correlative to mankind's helplessness in the face of nature. From there he opens a perspective onto a problem which may be considered one of the most important psychologic-sociological questions: What connections exist between the social, especially the economic-technical, development of humanity, and the development of the psychic apparatus, especially the ego-organization, of the human being? In short, he raises the question of the developmental history of the psyche. Psychoanalysis has so far asked and answered this question only for the individual. Freud in his latest book has extended this genetic inquiry to the psychic development of society, and has thus given important guidance to future psychoanalytic-sociological work.

In summary, I would like to say: Psychoanalysis, which interprets the human being as a socialized being, and the psychic apparatus as essentially developed and determined through the relationship of the individual to society, must consider it a duty to participate in the investigation of sociological problems to the extent the human being or his/her psyche plays any part at all. In this effort, one may quote the words, not of a psychologist, but of (Karl Marx) the greatest sociologist of all: "History does nothing, it possesses no immense wealth, it fights no battles. It is instead the human being, the real living person, who does everything, who owns everything, and who fights all battles."

Georg Lukács (1885–1971), the Hungarian Marxist philosopher, had been a visitor in Weber's Heidelberg circle before World War I. After the war, he studied at the Marx-Engels-Lenin Institute in Moscow. Lukács is considered an early contributor to the rethinking of Marx in terms suited to the twentieth century. In particular, his *History and Class Consciousness* (1923) returned explicitly to the early, somewhat Hegelian, writings of Marx in order to reformulate dialectic materialism in terms that account for the tensions within modern culture, knowledge, and literature. Yet his thinking was not so much a recovery of lost ideas as a creative reworking of Marx in light of events in the world and the history of ideas. Lukács was an important influence on the early founders of the Frankfurt Institute for Social Research and is credited with contributing to its critical theory of aesthetics. The short selection that follows, "The Irrational Chasm Between Subject and Object," is from Lukács's famous essay on reification in *History and Class Consciousness* (1923). It illustrates the ease with which he rethought the texts of what he called vulgar Marxism to formulate a social theory of modern knowledge and modern man. The individual, he suggests, is caught in a social world in which he can see himself only as an abstraction.

The Irrational Chasm Between Subject and Object[*]
Georg Lukács (1923)

. . . History must abolish itself. As Marx says of bourgeois economics: "Thus history existed once

---

[*] Lukács, Georg., History and Class Consciousness: Studies in Marxist Dialectics, pp. 157-159, © 1971 Massachusetts Institute of Technology, by permission of The MIT Press and Merlin Press Ltd.

upon a time, but it does not exist any more." And even if this antinomy assumes increasingly refined forms in later times, so that it even makes its appearance in the shape of historicism, of historical relativism, this does not affect the basic problem, the abolition of history, in the slightest.

We see the unhistorical and antihistorical character of bourgeois thought most strikingly when we consider *the problem of the present as a historical problem*. It is unnecessary to give examples here. Ever since the World War and the World Revolution the total inability of every bourgeois thinker and historian to see the world-historical events of the present as universal history must remain one of the most terrible memories of every sober observer. This complete failure has reduced otherwise meritorious historians and subtle thinkers to the pitiable or contemptible mental level of the worst kind of provincial journalism. But it cannot always be explained simply as the result of external pressures (censorship, conformity to "national" class interests, etc.). It is grounded also in a theoretical approach based upon unmediated contemplation which opens up an irrational chasm between the subject and object of knowledge, the same "dark and empty" chasm that Fichte described. This murky void was also present in our knowledge of the past, though this was obscured by the distance created by time, space and historical mediation. Here, however, it must appear fully exposed.

A fine illustration borrowed from Ernst Bloch will perhaps make this theoretical limitation clearer than a detailed analysis which in any case would not be possible here. When nature becomes landscape—e.g. in contrast to the peasant's unconscious living within nature—the artist's unmediated experience of the landscape (which has of course only achieved this immediacy after undergoing a whole series of mediations) presupposes a distance (spatial in this case) between the observer and the landscape. The observer stands outside the landscape, for were this not the case it would not be possible for nature to become a landscape at all. If he were to attempt to integrate himself and the nature immediately surrounding him in space within "nature-seen-as-landscape," without modifying his aesthetic contemplative immediacy, it would then at once become apparent that landscape only *starts* to become landscape at a definite (though of course variable) distance from the observer and that only as an observer set apart in space can he relate to nature in terms of landscape at all.

This illustration is only intended to throw light on the theoretical situation, for it is only in art that the relation to landscape is expressed in an appropriate and unproblematic way, although it must not be forgotten that even in art we find the same unbridgeable gap opening up between subject and object that we find confronting us everywhere in modern life, and that art can do no more than shape this problematic without however finding a real solution to it. But as soon as history is forced into the present—and this is inevitable as our interest in history is determined in the last analysis by our desire to understand the present—this "pernicious chasm" (to use Bloch's expression) opens up.

As a result of its incapacity to understand history, the contemplative attitude of the bourgeoisie became polarised into two extremes: on the one hand, there were the "great individuals" viewed as the autocratic makers of history, on the other hand, there were the "natural laws" of the historical environment. They both turn out to be equally impotent—whether they are separated or working together—when challenged to produce an interpretation of the present in all its radical novelty. The inner perfection of the work of art can hide this gaping abyss because in its perfected immediacy it does not allow any further questions to arise about a mediation no longer available to the point of view of contemplation. However, the present is a problem of history, a problem that refuses to be ignored and one which imperiously demands such mediation. It must be attempted. But in the course of these attempts we discover the truth of Hegel's remarks about one of the stages of self-consciousness that follow the definition of mediation already cited: "Therefore consciousness has become an enigma to itself as a result of the very experience which was to reveal its truth to itself; it does not regard the effects of its deeds as its own deeds: what happens to it is not the same experience *for it* as it is *in itself*; the transition is not merely a formal change of the same content and essence seen on the one hand as the content and essence of consciousness and on the other hand as the object or *intuited* essence of itself. *Abstract necessity*, therefore passes for the merely negative, uncomprehended *power of the universal* by which individuality is destroyed".

George Herbert Mead (1863–1931), like Durkheim and a number of other early sociologists, was born to a religious family. He grew up on the campus of Oberlin College, where Hiram Mead, his father and a Protestant minister, taught preaching. Mead's mother, Elizabeth Mead, returned to teaching after his father's early death and later became president of Mount Holyoke College. Mead studied at Harvard with William James a few years after Du Bois had finished his studies there. Like Du Bois and W. I. Thomas (and many others), Mead also studied in Germany before beginning his teaching career. In 1891, he taught philosophy at the University of Michigan, where he encountered Charles Horton Cooley and John Dewey. One year later, he joined the philosophy faculty at the new University of Chicago, whose department of sociology was just being organized. Mead had little direct contact with the sociologists, but the social justice teachings of his father influenced his association with Jane Addams's Hull House and with other progressive activists in the city. Mead's best-known book, *Mind, Self & Society*, was compiled from lecture notes for the course in social psychology that he taught until his death in 1931.

"The Self, the I, and the Me" is from the portions of that book in which Mead most precisely develops his version of the social self as a double dialogue—a dialogue with the social world, externally, and between the "I" and the "Me," internally. Mead's theory of the social self was an important advance over James and Cooley and is considered a classic source for subsequent social theories of the self, both normal and deviant.

The Self, the I, and the Me[*]
George Herbert Mead (ca. 1929)

We can distinguish very definitely between the self and the body. The body can be there and can operate in a very intelligent fashion without there being a self involved in the experience. The self has the characteristic that it is an object to itself, and that characteristic distinguishes it from other objects and from the body. It is perfectly true that the eye can see the foot, but it does not see the body as a whole. We cannot see our backs; we can feel certain portions of

them, if we are agile, but we cannot get an experience of our whole body. There are, of course, experiences which are somewhat vague and difficult of location, but the bodily experiences are for us organized about a self. The foot and hand belong to the self. We can see our feet, especially if we look at them from the wrong end of an opera glass, as strange things which we have difficulty in recognizing as our own. The parts of the body are quite distinguishable from the self. We can lose parts of the body without any serious invasion of the self. The mere ability to experience different parts of the body is not different from the experience of a table. The table presents a different feel from what the hand does when one hand feels another, but it is an experience of something with which we come definitely into contact. The body does not experience itself as a whole, in the sense in which the self in some way enters into the experience of the self.

It is the characteristic of the self as an object to itself that I want to bring out. This characteristic is represented in the word "self," which is a reflexive, and indicates that which can be both subject and object. This type of object is essentially different from other objects, and in the past it has been distinguished as conscious, a term which indicates an experience with, an experience of, one's self. It was assumed that consciousness in some way carried this capacity of being an object to itself. In giving a behavioristic statement of consciousness we have to look for some sort of experience in which the physical organism can become an object to itself.

When one is running to get away from someone who is chasing him, he is entirely occupied in this action, and his experience may be swallowed up in the objects about him, so that he has, at the time being, no consciousness of self at all. We must be, of course, very completely occupied to have that take place, but we can, I think, recognize that sort of a possible experience in which the self does not enter. We can, perhaps, get some light on that situation through those experiences in which in very intense action there appear in the experience of the individual, back of this intense action, memories and anticipations. Tolstoi as an officer in the war gives an account of having pictures of his past experience in the midst of his most intense action. There are also the pictures that flash into a person's mind when he is drowning. In such instances there is a contrast between an experience that is absolutely wound up in outside activity in which the self as an object does not enter, and an activity of memory and imagination in which the self is the principal object. The self is then entirely distinguishable from an organism that is surrounded by things and acts with reference to things, including parts of its own body. These latter may be objects like other objects, but they are just objects out there in the field, and they do not involve a self that is an object to the organism. This is, I think, frequently overlooked. It is that fact which makes our anthropomorphic reconstructions of animal life so fallacious. How can an individual get outside himself (experientially) in such a way as to become an object to himself? This is the essential psychological problem of selfhood or of self-consciousness; and its solution is to be found by referring to the process of social conduct or activity in which the given person or individual is implicated. The apparatus of reason would not be complete unless it swept itself into its own analysis of the field of experience; or unless the individual brought himself into the same experiential field as that of the other individual selves in relation to whom he acts in any given social situation. Reason cannot become impersonal unless it takes an objective, non-affective attitude toward itself; otherwise we have just consciousness, not *self*-consciousness. And it is necessary to rational conduct that the individual should thus take an objective, impersonal attitude toward himself, that he should become an object to himself. For the individual organism is obviously an essential and important fact or constituent element of the empirical situation in which it acts; and without taking objective account of itself as such, it cannot act intelligently, or rationally.

The individual experiences himself as such, not directly, but only indirectly, from the particular standpoints of other individual members of the same social group, or from the generalized standpoint of the social group as a whole to which he belongs. For he enters his own experience as a self or individual, not directly or immediately, not by becoming a subject to himself, but only in so far as he first becomes an object to himself just as other individuals are objects to him or in his experience; and he becomes an object to himself only by taking the attitudes of other individuals toward himself within a social environment or context of experience and behavior in which both he and they are involved.

The importance of what we term "communication" lies in the fact that it provides a form of behavior in which the organism or the individual may become an object to himself. It is that sort of communication which we have been discussing—not

communication in the sense of the cluck of the hen to the chickens, or the bark of a wolf to the pack, or the lowing of a cow, but communication in the sense of significant symbols, communication which is directed not only to others but also to the individual himself. So far as that type of communication is a part of behavior it at least introduces a self. Of course, one may hear without listening; one may see things that he does not realize; do things that he is not really aware of. But it is where one does respond to that which he addresses to another and where that response of his own becomes a part of his conduct, where he not only hears himself but responds to himself, talks and replies to himself as truly as the other person replies to him, that we have behavior in which the individuals become objects to themselves.

Such a self is not, I would say, primarily the physiological organism. The physiological organism is essential to it, but we are at least able to think of a self without it. Persons who believe in immortality, or believe in ghosts, or in the possibility of the self leaving the body, assume a self which is quite distinguishable from the body. How successfully they can hold these conceptions is an open question, but we do, as a fact, separate the self and the organism. It is fair to say that the beginning of the self as an object, so far as we can see, is to be found in the experiences of people that lead to the conception of a "double." Primitive people assume that there is a double, located presumably in the diaphragm, that leaves the body temporarily in sleep and completely in death. It can be enticed out of the body of one's enemy and perhaps killed. It is represented in infancy by the imaginary playmates which children set up, and through which they come to control their experiences in their play.

The self, as that which can be an object to itself, is essentially a social structure, and it arises in social experience. After a self has arisen, it in a certain sense provides for itself its social experiences, and so we can conceive of an absolutely solitary self. But it is impossible to conceive of a self arising outside of social experience. When it has arisen we can think of a person in solitary confinement for the rest of his life, but who still has himself as a companion, and is able to think and to converse with himself as he had communicated with others. That process to which I have just referred, of responding to one's self as another responds to it, taking part in one's own conversation with others, being aware of what one is saying and using that awareness of what one is saying to determine what one is going to say thereafter—that is a process with which we are all familiar. We are continually following up our own address to other persons by an understanding of what we are saying, and using that understanding in the direction of our continued speech. We are finding out what we are going to say, what we are going to do, by saying and doing, and in the process we are continually controlling the process itself. In the conversation of gestures what we say calls out a certain response in another and that in turn changes our own action, so that we shift from what we started to do because of the reply the other makes. The conversation of gestures is the beginning of communication. The individual comes to carry on a conversation of gestures with himself. He says something, and that calls out a certain reply in himself which makes him change what he was going to say. One starts to say something, we will presume an unpleasant something, but when he starts to say it he realizes it is cruel. The effect on himself of what he is saying checks him; there is here a conversation of gestures between the individual and himself. We mean by significant speech that the action is one that affects the individual himself, and that the effect upon the individual himself is part of the intelligent carrying-out of the conversation with others. Now we, so to speak, amputate that social phase and dispense with it for the time being, so that one is talking to one's self as one would talk to another person.

This process of abstraction cannot be carried on indefinitely. One inevitably seeks an audience, has to pour himself out to somebody. In reflective intelligence one thinks to act, and to act solely so that this action remains a part of a social process. Thinking becomes preparatory to social action. The very process of thinking is, of course, simply an inner conversation that goes on, but it is a conversation of gestures which in its completion implies the expression of that which one thinks to an audience. One separates the significance of what he is saying to others from the actual speech and gets it ready before saying it. He thinks it out, and perhaps writes it in the form of a book; but it is still a part of social intercourse in which one is addressing other persons and at the same time addressing one's self, and in which one controls the address to other persons by the response made to one's own gesture. That the person should be responding to himself is necessary to the self, and it is this sort of social conduct which provides behavior within which that self appears. I know of no other form of behavior than the linguistic in which the individual is an object to himself,

and, so far as I can see, the individual is not a self in the reflexive sense unless he is an object to himself. It is this fact that gives a critical importance to communication, since this is a type of behavior in which the individual does so respond to himself.

We realize in everyday conduct and experience that an individual does not mean a great deal of what he is doing and saying. We frequently say that such an individual is not himself. We come away from an interview with a realization that we have left out important things, that there are parts of the self that did not get into what was said. What determines the amount of the self that gets into communication is the social experience itself. Of course, a good deal of the self does not need to get expression. We carry on a whole series of different relationships to different people. We are one thing to one man and another thing to another. There are parts of the self which exist only for the self in relationship to itself. We divide ourselves up in all sorts of different selves with reference to our acquaintances. We discuss politics with one and religion with another. There are all sorts of different selves answering to all sorts of different social reactions. It is the social process itself that is responsible for the appearance of the self; it is not there as a self apart from this type of experience.

A multiple personality is in a certain sense normal, as I have just pointed out. There is usually an organization of the whole self with reference to the community to which we belong, and the situation in which we find ourselves. What the society is, whether we are living with people of the present, people of our own imaginations, people of the past, varies, of course, with different individuals. Normally, within the sort of community as a whole to which we belong, there is a unified self, but that may be broken up. To a person who is somewhat unstable nervously and in whom there is a line of cleavage, certain activities become impossible, and that set of activities may separate and evolve another self. Two separate "me's" and "I's," two different selves, result, and that is the condition under which there is a tendency to break up the personality. There is an account of a professor of education who disappeared, was lost to the community, and later turned up in a logging camp in the West. He freed himself of his occupation and turned to the woods where he felt, if you like, more at home. The pathological side of it was the forgetting, the leaving out of the rest of the self. This result involved getting rid of certain bodily memories which would identify the individual to himself. We often recognize the lines of cleavage that run through us. We would be glad to forget certain things, get rid of things the self is bound up with in past experiences. What we have here is a situation in which there can be different selves, and it is dependent upon the set of social reactions that is involved as to which self we are going to be. If we can forget everything involved in one set of activities, obviously we relinquish that part of the self. Take a person who is unstable, get him occupied by speech, and at the same time get his eye on something you are writing so that he is carrying on two separate lines of communication, and if you go about it in the right way you can get those two currents going so that they do not run into each other. You can get two entirely different sets of activities going on. You can bring about in that way the dissociation of a person's self. It is a process of setting up two sorts of communication which separate the behavior of the individual. For one individual it is this thing said and heard, and for the other individual there exists only that which he sees written. You must, of course, keep one experience out of the field of the other. Dissociations are apt to take place when an event leads to emotional upheavals. That which is separated goes on in its own way.

The unity and structure of the complete self reflects the unity and structure of the social process as a whole; and each of the elementary selves of which it is composed reflects the unity and structure of one of the various aspects of that process in which the individual is implicated. In other words, the various elementary selves which constitute, or are organized into, a complete self are the various aspects of the structure of that complete self answering to the various aspects of the structure of the social process as a whole; the structure of the complete self is thus a reflection of the complete social process. The organization and unification of a social group is identical with the organization and unification of any one of the selves arising within the social process in which that group is engaged, or which it is carrying on.

The phenomenon of dissociation of personality is caused by a breaking up of the complete, unitary self into the component selves of which it is composed, and which respectively correspond to different aspects of the social process in which the person is involved, and within which his complete or unitary self has arisen; these aspects being the different social groups to which he belongs within that process. . . .

Rational society, of course, is not limited to any specific set of individuals. Any person who is rational can become a part of it. The attitude of the community toward our own response is imported into ourselves in terms of the meaning of what we are doing. This occurs in its widest extent in universal discourse, in the reply which the rational world makes to our remark. The meaning is as universal as the community; it is necessarily involved in the rational character of that community; it is the response that the world made up out of rational beings inevitably makes to our own statement. We both get the object and ourselves into experience in terms of such a process; the other appears in our own experience in so far as we do take such an organized and generalized attitude.

If one meets a person on the street whom he fails to recognize, one's reaction toward him is that toward any other who is a member of the same community. He is the other, the organized, generalized other, if you like. One takes his attitude over against one's self. If he turns in one direction one is to go in another direction. One has his response as an attitude within himself. It is having that attitude within himself that makes it possible for one to be a self. That involves something beyond the mere turning to the right, as we say, instinctively, without self-consciousness. To have self-consciousness one must have the attitude of the other in one's own organism as controlling the thing that he is going to do. What appears in the immediate experience of one's self in taking that attitude is what we term the "me." It is that self which is able to maintain itself in the community, that is recognized in the community in so far as it recognizes the others. Such is the phase of the self which I have referred to as that of the "me."

Over against the "me" is the "I." The individual not only has rights, but he has duties; he is not only a citizen, a member of the community, but he is one who reacts to this community and in his reaction to it, as we have seen in the conversation of gestures, changes it. The "I" is the response of the individual to the attitude of the community as this appears in his own experience. His response to that organized attitude in turn changes it. As we have pointed out, this is a change which is not present in his own experience until after it takes place. The "I" appears in our experience in memory. It is only after we have acted that we know what we have done; it is only after we have spoken that we know what we have said. The adjustment to that organized world which is present in our own nature is one that represents the "me" and is constantly there. But if the response to it is a response which is of the nature of the conversation of gestures, if it creates a situation which is in some sense novel, if one puts up his side of the case, asserts himself over against others and insists that they take a different attitude toward himself, then there is something important occurring that is not previously present in experience.

Vladimir Ilyich Ulyanov (V. I.) Lenin (1870–1924) was the dominant force in the Russian Revolution of 1917 and the founder of Bolshevik Communism. After studying law in Saint Petersburg, he traveled throughout Russia and visited Western Europe, where he established contacts with socialist leaders. In 1895, he began organizing working people in Saint Petersburg, for which he was arrested and exiled. In exile, he wrote *The Development of Capitalism in Russia* (1899). When the revolution began in 1917, Lenin guided action while in hiding until Aleksandr Kerensky was overthrown. Later, he led the provisional Soviet government. He suffered a stroke in 1921 and died in 1924. The selection from Lenin's *What Is To Be Done?*, although composed from 1901 to 1902, more accurately belongs to the period between the wars because of its influen[...] Revolution and the dilemmas [...] Hence, the selection is [...] Lenin was in power and [...] Lenin sought to introd[...] the vanguard into the [...] mula that limited polit[...] needs of the working [...] political and economic[...] ism was the actual an[...] his ideas, Lenin shou[...] first to focus social t[...] would later put it) i[...]

What Is To Be [...]

V. I. Lenin (1917[...]

Without a revolutionary theory there can be no revolutionary movement. This cannot be insisted upon too strongly at a time when the fashionable preaching of opportunism is combined with absorption in the narrowest forms of practical activity. The importance of theory for Russian Social-Democrats is still greater for three reasons, which are often forgotten:

The first is that our party is only in the process of formation, its features are only just becoming outlined, and it has not yet completely settled its reckoning with other tendencies in revolutionary thought which threaten to divert the movement from the proper path. Indeed, in very recent times we have observed (as Axelrod long ago warned the Economists would happen) a revival of non–Social-Democratic revolutionary tendencies. Under such circumstances, what at first sight appears to be an "unimportant" mistake, may give rise to most deplorable consequences, and only the shortsighted would consider factional disputes and strict distinction of shades to be inopportune and superfluous. The fate of Russian Social-Democracy for many, many years to come may be determined by the strengthening of one or the other "shade."

The second reason is that the Social-Democratic movement is essentially an international movement. This does not mean merely that we must combat national chauvinism. It means also that a movement that is starting in a young country can be successful only on the condition that it assimilates the experi[ence of] other countries. In order to assimilate this [...] [suf]ficient merely to be ac[...] [...]y to transcribe the latest [...] [at]titude is required towards [...]y to subject it to indepen[...] [w]ho realise how much the [...]t has grown in strength will [...]ve of theoretical forces and [...] [rev]olutionary) experience is re[...]

[...] [t]hat the national tasks of Rus[...] [...] are such as have never con[...] [...] [s]ocialist party in the world. [...] [de]al with the political and organ[...] [i]n the task of emancipating the [...] the yoke of autocracy imposes [...] [...]ment, we wish merely to state [...] [van]guard can be fulfilled only by a *pa[rty]* [...] *by an advanced theory. . . .*

We have seen that the organisation of wide political agitation, and consequently, of all-sided political exposures are an absolutely necessary *and paramount* task of activity, that is, if that activity is to be truly Social-Democratic. We arrived at this conclusion *solely* on the grounds of the pressing needs of the

* Excerpt from Keith Hope, ed., *What Is To Be Done? Burning Questions of Our Movement* (New York: International Publishers, 1943 [1929]), pp. 28 and 75–78.

Antonio Gramsci bio pg 209
intellectuals & hegemony 209-210
max horkheimer & theodor adorno bio (page 173)
the culture industry as deception (pg. 173-176)

working class for political knowledge and political training. But this ground by itself is too narrow for the presentation of the question, for it ignores the general democratic tasks of Social-Democracy as a whole, and of modern, Russian Social-Democracy in particular. In order to explain the situation more concretely we shall approach the subject from an aspect that is "nearer" to the Economist, namely, from the practical aspect. "Every one agrees" that it is necessary to develop the political consciousness of the working class. But the question arises, How is that to be done? What must be done to bring this about? The economic struggle merely brings the workers "up against" questions concerning the attitude of the government towards the working class. Consequently, *however much we may try* to "give to the economic struggle itself a political character" *we shall never be able* to develop the political consciousness of the workers (to the degree of Social-Democratic consciousness) by confining ourselves to the economic struggle, for *the limits of this task are too narrow.* . . .

The workers can acquire class political consciousness *only from without*, that is, only outside of the economic struggle, outside of the sphere of relations between workers and employers. The sphere from which alone it is possible to obtain this knowledge is the sphere of relationships between *all* classes and the state and the government—the sphere of the inter-relations between *all* classes. For that reason, the reply to the question: What must be done in order that the workers may acquire political knowledge? cannot be merely the one which, in the majority of cases, the practical workers, especially those who are inclined towards Economism, usually content themselves with, i.e., "go among the workers." To bring political knowledge to the workers the Social-Democrats must *go among all classes of the population*, must despatch units of their army *in all directions.* . . .

The Social-Democrat's ideal should not be a trade-union secretary, but *a tribune of the people*, able to react to every manifestation of tyranny and oppression, no matter where it takes place, no matter what stratum or class of the people it affects; he must be able to group all these manifestations into a single picture of police violence and capitalist exploitation; he must be able to take advantage of every petty event in order to explain his Socialistic convictions and his Social-Democratic demands *to all*, in order to explain to all and every one the world historical significance of the struggle for the emancipation of the proletariat.

Max Horkheimer (1895–1973) and **Theodor Adorno** (1903–1969) are considered the founders of the German school of Critical Theory originally at the University of Frankfurt. They are among that tradition's most influential scholars. Like Horkheimer, Adorno was trained in philosophy, the arts, and literature. He was also a musicologist, which led to his famous writings on jazz and American popular culture. From 1938 to 1949, Horkheimer and Adorno, along with others who were forced to flee Nazi Germany, lived in exile in the United States. In New York City, they continued the work of Frankfurt critical studies at the Institute for Social Research (which eventually became the New School for Social Research). During these years, both men engaged in systematic research projects, of which a massive study of the effects of radio on mass culture was the most ambitious. The selection, "Culture Industry as Deception," has become a classic text in culture studies. Their deeply critical skepticism about mass culture is reflected in the title. The essay appeared in their joint book, *The Dialectic of Enlightenment* (1944), one of many efforts to reassess and renew Enlightenment values in a world devastated by the wars in Europe in the twentieth century and, of course, by Hitler's abuse of culture as a tool for the Nazi atrocities against mankind.

The Culture Industry as Deception[*]
Max Horkheimer and Theodor Adorno (1944)

Culture is a paradoxical commodity. It is so completely subject to the law of exchange that it is no longer exchanged; it is so blindly equated with use that it can no longer be used. For this reason it merges with the advertisement. The more meaningless the latter appears under monopoly, the more omnipotent culture becomes. Its motives are economic enough. That life could continue without the whole culture industry is too certain; the satiation

---

[*]Excerpt from *Dialectic of Enlightenment* by Max Horkheimer and Theodor W. Adorno, translated by Edmund Jephcott. Copyright © 1944 by Social Studies Association, NY. New edition: (c) S. Fisher Verlag GmbH, Frankfurt am Main, 1969; English trans. (c) 2002 Board of Trustees of Leland Stanford Jr. All rights reserved, Reprinted by permission of the publisher, Stanford University Press, sup.org.

and apathy it generates among consumers are too great. It can do little to combat this from its own resources. Advertising is its elixir of life. But because its product ceaselessly reduces the pleasure it promises as a commodity to that mere promise, it finally coincides with the advertisement it needs on account of its own inability to please. In the competitive society advertising performed a social service in orienting the buyer in the market, facilitating choice and helping the more efficient but unknown supplier to find customers. It did not merely cost labor time, but saved it. Today, when the free market is coming to an end, those in control of the system are entrenching themselves in advertising. It strengthens the bond which shackles consumers to the big combines. Only those who can keep paying the exorbitant fees charged by the advertising agencies, and most of all by radio itself, that is, those who are already part of the system or are co-opted into it by the decisions of banks and industrial capital, can enter the pseudomarket as sellers. The costs of advertising, which finally flow back into the pockets of the combines, spare them the troublesome task of subduing unwanted outsiders; they guarantee that the wielders of influence remain among their peers, not unlike the resolutions of economic councils which control the establishment and continuation of businesses in the totalitarian state. Advertising today is a negative principle, a blocking device: anything which does not bear its seal of approval is economically suspect. All-pervasive advertising is certainly not needed to acquaint people with the goods on offer, the varieties of which are limited in any case. It benefits the selling of goods only directly. The termination of a familiar advertising campaign by an individual firm represents a loss of prestige, and is indeed an offence against the discipline which the leading clique imposes on its members. In wartime, commodities which can no longer be supplied continue to be advertised merely as a display of industrial power. At such times the subsidizing of the ideological media is more important than the repetition of names. Through their ubiquitous use under the pressure of the system, advertising techniques have invaded the idiom, the "style" of the culture industry. So complete is their triumph that in key positions it is no longer even explicit: the imposing buildings of the big companies, floodlit advertisements in stone, are free of advertising, merely displaying the illuminated company initials on their pinnacles, with no further need of self-congratulation. By contrast, the buildings surviving from the nineteenth century, the

architecture of which still shamefully reveals their utility as consumer goods, their function as accommodation, are covered from basement to above roof level with hoardings and banners: the landscape becomes a mere background for signboards and symbols. Advertising becomes simply the art with which Goebbels presciently equated it, *l'art pour l'art*, advertising for advertising's sake, the pure representation of social power. In the influential American magazines *Life* and *Fortune* the images and texts of advertisements are, at a cursory glance, hardly distinguishable from the editorial section. The enthusiastic and unpaid picture story about the living habits and personal grooming of celebrities, which wins them new fans, is editorial, while the advertising pages rely on photographs and data so factual and lifelike that they represent the ideal of information to which the editorial section only aspires. Every film is a preview of the next, which promises yet again to unite the same heroic couple under the same exotic sun: anyone arriving late cannot tell whether he is watching the trailer or the real thing. The montage character of the culture industry, the synthetic, controlled manner in which its products are assembled—factory-like not only in the film studio but also, virtually, in the compilation of the cheap biographies, journalistic novels, and hit songs—predisposes it to advertising: the individual moment, in being detachable, replaceable, estranged even technically from any coherence of meaning, lends itself to purposes outside the work. The special effect, the trick, the isolated and repeatable individual performance have always conspired with the exhibition of commodities for advertising purposes, and today every close-up of a film actress is an advert for her name, every hit song a plug for its tune. Advertising and the culture industry are merging technically no less than economically. In both, the same thing appears in countless places, and the mechanical repetition of the same culture product is already that of the same propaganda slogan. In both, under the dictate of effectiveness, technique is becoming psychotechnique, a procedure for manipulating human beings. In both, the norms of the striking yet familiar, the easy but catchy, the worldly wise but straightforward hold good; everything is directed at overpowering a customer conceived as distracted or resistant.

Through the language they speak, the customers make their own contribution to culture as advertising. For the more completely language coincides with communication, the more words change from substantial carriers of meaning to signs devoid of qualities; the more purely and transparently they communicate what they designate, the more impenetrable they become. The demythologizing of language, as an element of the total process of enlightenment, reverts to magic. In magic word and content were at once different from each other and indissolubly linked. Concepts like melancholy, history, indeed, life, were apprehended in the word which both set them apart and preserved them. Its particular form constituted and reflected them at the same time. The trenchant distinction which declares the word itself fortuitous and its allocation to its object arbitrary does away with the superstitious commingling of word and thing. Anything in a given sequence of letters which goes beyond the correlation to the event designated is banished as unclear and as verbal metaphysics. As a result, the word, which henceforth is allowed only to designate something and not to mean it, becomes so fixated on the object that it hardens to a formula. This affects language and subject matter equally. Instead of raising a matter to the level of experience, the purified word exhibits it as a case of an abstract moment, and everything else, severed from now defunct expression by the demand for pitiless clarity, therefore withers in reality also. The outside-left in football, the blackshirt, the Hitler Youth member, and others of their kind are no more than what they are called. If, before its rationalization, the word had set free not only longing but lies, in its rationalized form it has become a straightjacket more for longing than for lies. The blindness and muteness of the data to which positivism reduces the world passes over into language itself, which is limited to registering those data. Thus relationships themselves become impenetrable, taking on an impact, a power of adhesion and repulsion which makes them resemble their extreme antithesis, spells. They act once more like the practices of a kind of sorcery, whether the name of a diva is concocted in the studio on the basis of statistical data, or welfare government is averted by the use of taboo-laden words such as "bureaucracy" and "intellectuals," or vileness exonerates itself by invoking the name of a homeland. The name, to which magic most readily attaches, is today undergoing a chemical change. It is being transformed into arbitrary, manipulable designations, the power of which, although calculable, is for that reason as willful as that of archaic names. First names, the archaic residues, have been brought up to date either by stylizing them into advertising brands—film stars' surnames have become first names—or by standardizing them collectively. By contrast, the bourgeois, family name which, instead of being a trademark, individualized its bearers by relating them to their own prehistory, sounds old-fashioned. In Americans it arouses a curious unease. To conceal the uncomfortable distance existing between particular people they call themselves Bob and Harry, like replaceable members of teams. Such forms of interaction reduce human beings to the brotherhood of the sporting public, which protects them from true fraternity. Signification, the only function of the word admitted by semantics, is consummated in the sign. Its character as sign is reinforced by the speed with which linguistic models are put into circulation from above. Whether folksongs are rightly or wrongly called upper-class culture which has come down in the world, their elements have at least taken on their popular form in a long, highly mediated process of experience. The dissemination of popular songs, by contrast, is practically instantaneous. The American term "fad" for fashions which catch on epidemically—inflamed by the action of highly concentrated economic powers—referred to this phenomenon long before totalitarian advertising bosses had laid down the general lines of culture in their countries. If the German fascists launch a word like "intolerable" [*Untragbar*] over the loudspeakers one day, the whole nation is saying "intolerable" the next. On the same pattern, the nations against which the German *Blitzkrieg* was directed have adopted it in their own jargon. The universal repetition of the term denoting such measures makes the measures, too, familiar, just as, at the time of the free market, the brand name on everyone's lips increased sales. The blind and rapidly spreading repetition of designated words links advertising to the totalitarian slogan. The layer of experience which made words human like those who spoke them has been stripped away, and in its prompt appropriation language takes on the coldness which hitherto was peculiar to billboards and the advertising sections of newspapers. Countless people use words and expressions which they either have ceased to understand at all or use only according to their behavioral functions, just as trademarks adhere all the more compulsively to their objects the less their linguistic meaning is apprehended. The Minister of Public Education speaks ignorantly of "dynamic forces," and the hit songs sing endlessly of "reverie" and "rhapsody," hitching their popularity to the magic of the incomprehensible as if to some deep intimation of a higher life. Other stereotypes, such as "memory," are still partly comprehended, but become detached from the experience which might fulfill them. They obtrude into the spoken language like enclaves. On the German radio of Flesch and Hitler they are discernible in the affected diction of the announcer, who pronounces phrases like "Goodnight, listeners," or "This is the Hitler Youth speaking," or even "the *Führer*" with an inflection which passes into the mother tongue of millions. In such turns of phrase the last bond between sedimented experience and language, which still exerted a reconciling influence in dialect in the nineteenth century, is severed. By contrast, in the hands of the editor whose supple opinions have promoted him to the status of *Schriftleiter*, German words become petrified and alien. In any word one can distinguish how far it has been disfigured by the fascist "folk" community. By now, of course, such language has become universal, totalitarian. The violence done to words is no longer audible in them. The radio announcer does not need to talk in an affected voice; indeed, he would be impossible if his tone differed from that of his designated listeners. This means, however, that the language and gestures of listeners and spectators are more deeply permeated by the patterns of the culture industry than ever before, in nuances still beyond the reach of experimental methods. Today the culture industry has taken over the civilizing inheritance of the frontier and entrepreneurial democracy, whose receptivity to intellectual deviations was never too highly developed. All are free to dance and amuse themselves, just as, since the historical neutralization of religion, they have been free to join any of the countless sects. But freedom to choose an ideology, which always reflects economic coercion, everywhere proves to be freedom to be the same. The way in which the young girl accepts and performs the obligatory date, the tone of voice used on the telephone and in the most intimate situations, the choice of words in conversation, indeed, the whole inner life compartmentalized according to the categories of vulgarized depth psychology, bears witness to the attempt to turn oneself into an apparatus meeting the requirements of success, an apparatus which, even in its unconscious impulses, conforms to the model presented by the culture industry. The most intimate reactions of human beings have become so entirely reified, even to themselves, that the idea of anything peculiar to them survives only in extreme abstraction: personality means hardly more than dazzling white teeth and freedom from body odor and emotions. That is the triumph of advertising in the culture industry: the compulsive imitation by consumers of cultural commodities which, at the same time, they recognize as false.

Martin Heidegger (1889–1976) was born in Messkirch, Germany, a small town of predominately Catholic culture. In his youth he embarked on a series of school migrations which led him to Freiberg where his reading of classical philosophy began. At the University he came under the sway of Edmund Husserl with whom he eventually became a faculty colleague at Freiburg. Husserl was a founding of the modern school of phenomenology. Heidegger no doubt drew a considerable influence from Husserl's phenomenological ideas such that, in turn, he is widely thought of as primarily a phenomenologist. There can be no doubt that Heidegger's greatest work, *Being and Time* (1927) can be interpreted in this way. Yet, this work, said by many to be the greatest philosophical treatise of the twentieth century, far transcended any one school of thought. It is difficult work that demands close and serious study, yet today it remains a classic, in some good part by its decided effect on the thinking of writers like Michel Foucault and Jacques Derrida. The selection here offered is from one of Heidegger's more readable essays, "The Question Concerning Technology," which begins with the jolting statement that "the essence of technology is by no means anything technological." The essay concludes with one of Heidegger's most famous texts, "The Age of the World Picture." Here he develops the theme that in the modern era when man became the focal figure of culture and thought, the world itself became a shadow before the inventions of man's technical ingenuity which loomed as gigantic forces – things so great as to be incalculable. Hence, the selection's influential if puzzling conclusion: "This becoming incalculable remains the invisible shadow that is cast around all things everywhere when man has been transformed into *subiectum* and the world into picture."

The Question Concerning Technology: The Age of the World Picture*

Martin Heidegger (1954)

The fundamental event of the modern age is the conquest of the world as picture. The word "picture" [*Bild*] now means the structured image [*Gebild*] that is the creature of man's producing which represents and sets before. In such producing, man contends for the position in which he can be that particular being who gives the measure and draws up the guidelines for everything that is. Because this position secures, organizes, and articulates itself as a world view, the modern relationship to that which is, is one that becomes, in its decisive unfolding, a confrontation of world views; and indeed not of random world views, but only of those that have already taken up the fundamental position of man that is most extreme, and have done so with the utmost resoluteness. For the sake of this struggle of world views and in keeping with its meaning, man brings into play his unlimited power for the calculating, planning, and molding of all things. Science as research is an absolutely necessary form of this establishing of self in the world; it is one of the pathways upon which the modern age rages toward fulfillment of its essence, with a velocity unknown to the participants. With this struggle of world views the modern age first enters into the part of its history that is the most decisive and probably the most capable of enduring.

A sign of this event is that everywhere and in the most varied forms and disguises the gigantic is making its appearance. In so doing, it evidences itself simultaneously in the tendency toward the increasingly small. We have only to think of numbers in atomic physics. The gigantic presses forward in a form that actually seems to make it disappear—in the annihilation of great distances by the airplane, in the setting before us of foreign and remote worlds in their everydayness, which is produced at random through radio by a flick of the hand. Yet we think too superficially if we suppose that the gigantic is only the endlessly extended emptiness of the purely quantitative. We think too little if we find that the gigantic, in the form of continual not-ever-having-been-here-yet, originates only in a blind mania for exaggerating

and excelling. We do not think at all if we believe we have explained this phenomenon of the gigantic with the catchword "Americanism."

The gigantic is rather that through which the quantitative becomes a special quality and thus a remarkable kind of greatness. Each historical age is not only great in a distinctive way in contrast to others; it also has, in each instance, its own concept of greatness. But as soon as the gigantic in planning and calculating and adjusting and making secure shifts over out of the quantitative and becomes a special quality, then what is gigantic, and what can seemingly always be calculated completely, becomes, precisely through this, incalculable. This becoming incalculable remains the invisible shadow that is cast around all things everywhere when man has been transformed into *subiectum* and the world into picture....

*Excerpt from pp. 134-5 (500 words) from *The Question Concerning Technology and Other Essays* by Martin Heidegger. Translated and with an Introduction by William Lovitt. English language translation copyright © 1977 by Harper & Row, Publishers, Inc. Reprinted by permission of Harper-Collins Publishers.

Karl Mannheim (1893–1947), like Georg Lukács, was a Hungarian social philosopher who had benefited from contact with Max Weber and Georg Simmel in Germany. Mannheim would become a younger member of Lukács's circle in Budapest. In 1917, he delivered a lecture to this group, the title of which suggests his broad intellectual perspective—"Soul and Culture." In 1925, Mannheim returned to a professorship in Heidelberg. Later, he taught at Frankfurt in the days of the Frankfurt Institute for Social Research. In 1933, Mannheim fled to England, where he led a productive, if more English, intellectual life until his death shortly after the end of World War II. The selection, "The Sociology of Knowledge and Ideology," comprises revised portions of Mannheim's most famous book, *Ideology and Utopia*, which was first published in Germany in 1929. The opening part of the selection ("The Sociology of Knowledge") is, however, from Mannheim's English period, during which he was drawn more toward sociology as a discipline; the latter part of the selection focuses on the theory of "ideology," stemming from Mannheim's earlier days as a general social theorist. Mannheim's *Ideology and Utopia* is considered a classic text, equally for the sociology of knowledge and for the theory of ideology as a distortion of knowledge by social and political interests.

The Sociology of Knowledge and Ideology[*]
Karl Mannheim (1929, 1936)

The Sociology of Knowledge

Philosophers have too long concerned themselves with their own thinking. When they wrote of thought, they had in mind primarily their own history, the history of philosophy, or quite special fields of knowledge such as mathematics or physics. This type of thinking is applicable only under quite special circumstances, and what can be learned by analysing it is not directly transferable to other spheres of life. Even when it is applicable, it refers only to a specific dimension of existence which does not suffice for living human beings who are seeking to comprehend and to mould their world.

Meanwhile, acting men have, for better or for worse, proceeded to develop a variety of methods for the experiential and intellectual penetration of the world in which they live, which have never been analysed with the same precision as the so-called exact modes of knowing. When, however, any human activity continues over a long period without being subjected to intellectual control or criticism it tends to get out of hand.

Hence it is to be regarded as one of the anomalies of our time that those methods of thought by means of which we arrive at our most crucial decisions, and through which we seek to diagnose and guide our political and social destiny, have remained unrecognized and therefore inaccessible to intellectual control and self-criticism. This anomaly becomes all the more monstrous when we call to mind that in modern times much more depends on the correct thinking through of a situation than was the case in earlier societies. The significance of social knowledge grows proportionately with the increasing necessity of regulatory intervention in the social process. This so-called pre-scientific inexact mode of thought, however (which, paradoxically, the logicians and philosophers also use when they have to make practical decisions), is not to be understood solely by the use of logical analysis. It constitutes a complex which

cannot be readily detached either from the psychological roots of the emotional and vital impulses which underlie it or from the situation in which it arises and which it seeks to solve.

It is the most essential task of this book to work out a suitable method for the description and analysis of this type of thought and its changes, and to formulate those problems connected with it which will both do justice to its unique character and prepare the way for its critical understanding. The method which we will seek to present is that of the sociology of knowledge.

The principal thesis of the sociology of knowledge is that there are modes of thought which cannot be adequately understood as long as their social origins are obscured. It is indeed true that only the individual is capable of thinking. There is no such metaphysical entity as a group mind which thinks over and above the heads of individuals, or whose ideas the individual merely reproduces. Nevertheless it would be false to deduce from this that all the ideas and sentiments which motivate an individual have their origin in him alone, and can be adequately explained solely on the basis of his own life-experience.

Just as it would be incorrect to attempt to derive a language merely from observing a single individual, who speaks not a language of his own but rather that of his contemporaries and predecessors who have prepared the path for him, so it is incorrect to explain the totality of an outlook only with reference to its genesis in the mind of the individual. Only in a quite limited sense does the single individual create out of himself the mode of speech and of thought we attribute to him. He speaks the language of his group; he thinks in the manner in which his group thinks. He finds at his disposal only certain words and their meanings. These not only determine to a large extent the avenues of approach to the surrounding world, but they also show at the same time from which angle and in which context of activity objects have hitherto been perceptible and accessible to the group or the individual.

The first point which we now have to emphasize is that the approach of the sociology of knowledge intentionally does not start with the single individual and his thinking in order then to proceed directly in the manner of the philosopher to the abstract heights of "thought as such." Rather, the sociology of knowledge seeks to comprehend thought in the concrete setting of an historical-social situation out of which individually differentiated

[*]Excerpt from Louis Wirth and Edward Shils, trans., Ideology and Utopia: An Introduction to the Sociology of Knowledge (New York: Harcourt Brace Jovanovich, Publishers, 1936 [1929]), pp. 1–3 and 55–59. Excerpted from *Ideology and Utopia: An Introduction to the Sociology of Knowledge* by Karl Mannheim, translated by Louis Wirth and Edward Shils.

thought only very gradually emerges. Thus, it is not men in general who think, or even isolated individuals who do the thinking, but men in certain groups who have developed a particular style of thought in an endless series of responses to certain typical situations characterizing their common position.

Strictly speaking it is incorrect to say that the single individual thinks. Rather it is more correct to insist that he participates in thinking further what other men have thought before him. He finds himself in an inherited situation with patterns of thought which are appropriate to this situation and attempts to elaborate further the inherited modes of response or to substitute others for them in order to deal more adequately with the new challenges which have arisen out of the shifts and changes in his situation. Every individual is therefore in a two-fold sense predetermined by the fact of growing up in a society: on the one hand he finds a ready-made situation and on the other he finds in that situation preformed patterns of thought and of conduct. . . .

Ideology

In order to understand the present situation of thought, it is necessary to start with the problems of "ideology." For most people, the term "ideology" is closely bound up with Marxism, and their reactions to the term are largely determined by the association. It is therefore first necessary to state that although Marxism contributed a great deal to the original statement of the problem, both the word and its meaning go farther back in history than Marxism, and ever since its time new meanings of the word have emerged, which have taken shape independently of it.

There is no better introduction to the problem than the analysis of the meaning of the term "ideology": firstly we have to disentangle all the different shades of meaning which are blended here into a pseudo-unity, and a more precise statement of the variations in the meanings of the concept, as it is used to-day, will prepare the way for its sociological and historical analysis. Such an analysis will show that in general there are two distinct and separable meanings of the term "ideology"—the particular and the total.

The particular conception of ideology is implied when the term denotes that we are sceptical of the ideas and representations advanced by our opponent. They are regarded as more or less conscious disguises of the real nature of a situation, the true recognition of which would not be in accord with his interests. These distortions range all the way from conscious lies to half-conscious and unwitting disguises; from calculated attempts to dupe others to self deception. This conception of ideology, which has only gradually become differentiated from the common-sense notion of the lie is particular in several senses. Its particularity becomes evident when it is contrasted with the more inclusive total conception of ideology. Here we refer to the ideology of an age or of a concrete historico-social group, e.g. of a class, when we are concerned with the characteristics and composition of the total structure of the mind of this epoch or of this group.

The common as well as the distinctive elements of the two concepts are readily evident. The common element in these two conceptions seems to consist in the fact that neither relies solely on what is actually said by the opponent in order to reach an understanding of his real meaning and intention. Both fall back on the subject, whether individual or group, proceeding to an understanding of what is said by the indirect method of analysing the social conditions of the individual or his group. The ideas expressed by the subject are thus regarded as functions of his existence. This means that opinions, statements, propositions, and systems of ideas are not taken at their face value but are interpreted in the light of the life-situation of the one who expresses them. It signifies further that the specific character and life-situation of the subject influence his opinions, perceptions, and interpretations.

Both these conceptions of ideology, accordingly, make these so-called "ideas" a function of him who holds them, and of his position in his social milieu. Although they have something in common, there are also significant differences between them. Of the latter we mention merely the most important:—

(*a*) Whereas the particular conception of ideology designates only a part of the opponent's assertions as ideologies—and this only with reference to their content, the total conception calls into question the opponent's total *Weltanschauung* (including his conceptual apparatus), and attempts to understand these concepts as an outgrowth of the collective life of which he partakes.

(*b*) The particular conception of "ideology" makes its analysis of ideas on a purely psychological level. If it is claimed for instance that an adversary is lying, or that he is concealing or distorting a given factual situation, it is still nevertheless assumed that both parties share common criteria of validity—it is still assumed that it is possible to refute lies and eradicate sources of error by referring to accepted criteria of objective validity common to both parties. The suspicion that one's opponent is the victim of an ideology does not go so far as to exclude him from discussion on the basis of a common theoretical frame of reference. The case is different with the total conception of ideology. When we attribute to one historical epoch one intellectual world and to ourselves another one, or if a certain historically determined social stratum thinks in categories other than our own, we refer not to the isolated cases of thought-content, but to fundamentally divergent thought-systems and to widely differing modes of experience and interpretation. We touch upon the theoretical or noological level whenever we consider not merely the content but also the form, and even the conceptual framework of a mode of thought as a function of the life-situation of a thinker. "The economic categories are only the theoretical expressions, the abstractions, of the social relations of production. . . . The same men who establish social relations conformably with their material productivity, produce also the principles, the ideas, the categories, conformably with their social relations." (Karl Marx, *The Poverty of Philosophy*.) . . . These are the two ways of analysing statements as functions of their social background; the first operates only on the psychological, the second on the noological level.

(c) Corresponding to this difference, the particular conception of ideology operates primarily with a psychology of interests, while the total conception uses a more formal functional analysis, without any reference to motivations, confining itself to an objective description of the structural differences in minds operating in different social settings. The former assumes that this or that interest is the cause of a given lie or deception. The latter presupposes simply that there is a correspondence between a given social situation and a given perspective, point of view, or apperception mass. In this case, while an analysis of constellations of interests may often be necessary it is not to establish causal connections but to characterize the total situation. Thus interest psychology tends to be displaced by an analysis of the correspondence between the situation to be known and the forms of knowledge.

Since the particular conception never actually departs from the psychological level, the point of reference in such analyses is always the individual.

This is the case even when we are dealing with groups, since all psychic phenomena must finally be reduced to the minds of individuals. The term "group ideology" occurs frequently, to be sure, in popular speech. Group existence in this sense can only mean that a group of persons, either in their immediate reactions to the same situation or as a result of direct psychic interaction, react similarly. Accordingly, conditioned by the same social situation, they are subject to the same illusions. If we confine our observations to the mental processes which take place in the individual and regard him as the only possible bearer of ideologies, we shall never grasp in its totality the structure of the intellectual world belonging to a social group in a given historical situation. Although this mental world as a whole could never come into existence without the experiences and productive responses of the different individuals, its inner structure is not to be found in a mere integration of these individual experiences. The individual members of the working-class, for instance, do not experience *all* the elements of an outlook which could be called the proletarian *Weltanschauung*. Every individual participates only in certain fragments of this thought-system, the totality of which is not in the least a mere sum of these fragmentary individual experiences. As a totality the thought-system is integrated systematically, and is no mere casual jumble of fragmentary experiences of discrete members of the group. Thus it follows that the individual can only be considered as the bearer of an ideology as long as we deal with that conception of ideology which, by definition, is directed more to detached contents than to the whole structure of thought, uncovering false ways of thought and exposing lies. As soon as the total conception of ideology is used, we attempt to reconstruct the whole outlook of a social group, and neither the concrete individuals nor the abstract sum of them can legitimately be considered as bearers of this ideological thought-system as a whole. The aim of the analysis on this level is the reconstruction of the systematic theoretical basis underlying the single judgments of the individual. Analyses of ideologies in the particular sense, making the content of individual thought largely dependent on the interests of the subject, can never achieve this basic reconstruction of the whole outlook of a social group. They can at best reveal the collective psychological aspects of ideology, or lead to some development of mass psychology, dealing either with the different behaviour of the individual in the crowd, or with the results of the mass integration of the psychic experiences of many individuals. And although the collective-psychological aspect may very often approach the problems of the total ideological analysis, it does not answer its questions exactly. It is one thing to know how far my attitudes and judgments are influenced and altered by the co-existence of other human beings, but it is another thing to know what are the theoretical implications of my mode of thought which are identical with those of my fellow members of the group or social stratum.

Robert K. Merton (1910–2003) was a student at Harvard in the days of Talcott Parsons and Pitirim A. Sorokin. It is a popular misconception that Merton had been Parsons's student; more accurately, he was the student of George Sarton, Harvard's distinguished historian of science (and father of the feminist poet and writer May Sarton). Merton's most important empirical work, *Science, Technology and Society in Seventeenth-Century England* (1938), was the first of his many contributions to the sociology of science, the field of which he was the principal founder. In this regard, Merton went beyond Mannheim's preliminary definition of the sociology of knowledge to develop a branch of social studies that flourished in an era when science and technology were considered the keys to social salvation. Merton, like Parsons, is said to be a functionalist social theorist. Unlike Parsons, and in obvious response to him, Merton is known for his attempts to define researchable theories of "the middle range" between pure abstraction and mindless empiricism. With Paul Lazarsfeld, Merton made the Columbia University Department of Sociology famous for its contributions to the empirical sociology of modern American life. From 1942 to 1971, he was associate director of Columbia's Bureau of Applied Social Research, where survey research techniques were developed.

"Social Structure and Anomie" is one of the most widely read articles in the history of sociology. First published in 1938, the article reformulates Èmile Durkheim's idea of anomie to account for the unexpected ways in which social conditions force individuals to act in socially functional, if sometimes illegal, ways. It remains one of the most important works of structural theory in Amerian sociology.

Social Structure and Anomie[*]
Robert K. Merton (1938)

Until recently, and all the more so before then, one could speak of a marked tendency in psychological and sociological theory to attribute the faulty operation of social structures to failures of social control over man's imperious biological drives. The imagery of the relations between man and society implied by this doctrine is as clear as it is questionable. In the beginning, there are man's biological impulses which seek full expression. And then, there is the social order, essentially an apparatus for the management of impulses, for the social processing of tensions, for the "renunciation of instinctual gratifications," in the words of Freud. Nonconformity with the demands of a social structure is thus assumed to be anchored in original nature. It is the biologically rooted impulses which from time to time break through social control. And by implication, conformity is the result of an utilitarian calculus or of unreasoned conditioning.

With the more recent advancement of social science, this set of conceptions has undergone basic modification. For one thing, it no longer appears so obvious that man is set against society in an unceasing war between biological impulse and social restraint. The image of man as an untamed bundle of impulses begins to look more like a caricature than a portrait. For another, sociological perspectives have increasingly entered into the analysis of behavior deviating from prescribed patterns of conduct. For whatever the role of biological impulses, there still remains the further question of why it is that the frequency of deviant behavior varies within different social structures and how it happens that the deviations have different shapes and patterns in different social structures. Today, as then, we have still much to learn about the processes through which social structures generate the circumstances in which infringement of social codes constitutes a "normal" (that is to say, an expectable) response. This chapter is an essay seeking clarification of the problem.

The framework set out in this essay is designed to provide one systematic approach to the analysis of

---

[*] Reprinted with the permission of The Free Press, a Division of Simon & Schuster, Inc., from SOCIAL THEORY AND SOCIAL STRUCTURE, Revised & Enlarged edition by Robert K. Merton. Copyright © 1967, 1968 by The Free Press; copyright renewed 1985 by Robert K. Merton. All rights reserved.

social and cultural sources of deviant behavior. Our primary aim is to discover how some *social structures exert a definite pressure upon certain persons in the society to engage in nonconforming rather than conforming conduct*. If we can locate groups peculiarly subject to such pressures, we should expect to find fairly high rates of deviant behavior in these groups, not because the human beings comprising them are compounded of distinctive biological tendencies but because they are responding normally to the social situation in which they find themselves. Our perspective is sociological. We look at variations in the *rates* of deviant behavior, not at its incidence. Should our quest be at all successful, some forms of deviant behavior will be found to be as psychologically normal as conforming behavior, and the equation of deviation and psychological abnormality will be put in question.

Patterns of Cultural Goals and Institutional Norms

Among the several elements of social and cultural structures, two are of immediate importance. These are analytically separable although they merge in concrete situations. The first consists of culturally defined goals, purposes and interests, held out as legitimate objectives for all or for diversely located members of the society. The goals are more or less integrated—the degree is a question of empirical fact—and roughly ordered in some hierarchy of value. Involving various degrees of sentiment and significance, the prevailing goals comprise a frame of aspirational reference. They are the things "worth striving for." They are a basic, though not the exclusive, component of what Linton has called "designs for group living." And though some, not all, of these cultural goals are directly related to the biological drives of man, they are not determined by them.

A second element of the cultural structure defines, regulates and controls the acceptable modes of reaching out for these goals. Every social group invariably couples its cultural objectives with regulations, rooted in the mores or institutions, of allowable procedures for moving toward these objectives. These regulatory norms are not necessarily identical with technical or efficiency norms. Many procedures which from the standpoint of particular individuals would be most efficient in securing desired values—the exercise of force, fraud, power—are ruled out of the institutional area of permitted conduct. At times, the disallowed procedures include

some which would be efficient for the group itself—e.g., historic taboos on vivisection, on medical experimentation, on the sociological analysis of "sacred" norms—since the criterion of acceptability is not technical efficiency but value-laden sentiments (supported by most members of the group or by those able to promote these sentiments through the composite use of power and propaganda). In all instances, the choice of expedients for striving toward cultural goals is limited by institutionalized norms.

Sociologists often speak of these controls as being "in the mores" or as operating through social institutions. Such elliptical statements are true enough, but they obscure the fact that culturally standardized practices are not all of a piece. They are subject to a wide gamut of control. They may represent definitely prescribed or preferential or permissive or proscribed patterns of behavior. In assessing the operation of social controls, these variations— roughly indicated by the terms *prescription, preference, permission* and *proscription*—must of course be taken into account.

To say, moreover, that cultural goals and institutionalized norms operate jointly to shape prevailing practices is not to say that they bear a constant relation to one another. The cultural emphasis placed upon certain goals varies independently of the degree of emphasis upon institutionalized means. There may develop a very heavy, at times a virtually exclusive, stress upon the value of particular goals, involving comparatively little concern with the institutionally prescribed means of striving toward these goals. The limiting case of this type is reached when the range of alternative procedures is governed only by technical rather than by institutional norms. Any and all procedures which promise attainment of the all-important goal would be permitted in this hypothetical polar case. This constitutes one type of malintegrated culture. A second polar type is found in groups where activities originally conceived as instrumental are transmuted into self-contained practices, lacking further objectives. The original purposes are forgotten and close adherence to institutionally prescribed conduct becomes a matter of ritual. Sheer conformity becomes a central value. For a time, social stability is ensured—at the expense of flexibility. Since the range of alternative behaviors permitted by the culture is severely limited, there is little basis for adapting to new conditions. There develops a tradition-bound, "sacred" society marked by neophobia. Between these extreme types are societies which maintain a rough balance between emphases upon cultural goals and institutionalized practices, and these constitute the integrated and relatively stable, though changing, societies.

An effective equilibrium between these two phases of the social structure is maintained so long as satisfactions accrue to individuals conforming to both cultural constraints, *viz.*, satisfactions from the achievement of goals and satisfactions emerging directly from the institutionally canalized modes of striving to attain them. It is reckoned in terms of the product and in terms of the process, in terms of the outcome and in terms of the activities. Thus continuing satisfactions must derive from sheer participation in a competitive order as well as from eclipsing one's competitors if the order itself is to be sustained. If concern shifts exclusively to the outcome of competition, then those who perennially suffer defeat may, understandably enough, work for a change in the rules of the game. The sacrifices occasionally—not, as Freud assumed, invariably—entailed by conformity to institutional norms must be compensated by socialized rewards. The distribution of statuses through competition must be so organized that positive incentives for adherence to status obligations are provided *for every position* within the distributive order. Otherwise, as will soon become plain, aberrant behavior ensues. It is, indeed, my central hypothesis that aberrant behavior may be regarded sociologically as a symptom of dissociation between culturally prescribed aspirations and socially structured avenues for realizing these aspirations.

Of the types of societies that result from independent variation of cultural goals and institutionalized means, we shall be primarily concerned with the first—a society in which there is an exceptionally strong emphasis upon specific goals without a corresponding emphasis upon institutional procedures. If it is not to be misunderstood, this statement must be elaborated. No society lacks norms governing conduct. But societies do differ in the degree to which the folkways, mores and institutional controls are effectively integrated with the goals which stand high in the hierarchy of cultural values. The culture may be such as to lead individuals to center their emotional convictions upon the complex of culturally acclaimed ends, with far less emotional support for prescribed methods of reaching out for these ends. With such differential emphases upon goals and institutional procedures, the latter may be so vitiated by the stress on goals as to have the behavior of many individuals limited only by considerations of technical expediency. In this context, the sole significant question becomes: Which of the available procedures is most efficient in netting the culturally approved value? The technically most effective procedure, whether culturally legitimate or not, becomes typically preferred to institutionally prescribed conduct. As this process of attenuation continues, the society becomes unstable and there develops what Durkheim called "anomie" (or normlessness).

The working of this process eventuating in anomie can be easily glimpsed in a series of familiar and instructive, though perhaps trivial, episodes. Thus, in competitive athletics, when the aim of victory is shorn of its institutional trappings and success becomes construed as "winning the game" rather than "winning under the rules of the game," a premium is implicitly set upon the use of illegitimate but technically efficient means. The star of the opposing football team is surreptitiously slugged; the wrestler incapacitates his opponent through ingenious but illicit techniques; university alumni covertly subsidize "students" whose talents are confined to the athletic field. The emphasis on the goal has so attenuated the satisfactions deriving from sheer participation in the competitive activity that only a successful outcome provides gratification. Through the same process, tension generated by the desire to win in a poker game is relieved by successfully dealing one's self four aces or, when the cult of success has truly flowered, by sagaciously shuffling the cards in a game of solitaire. The faint twinge of uneasiness in the last instance and the surreptitious nature of public delicts indicate clearly that the institutional rules of the game are *known* to those who evade them. But cultural (or idiosyncratic) exaggeration of the success-goal leads men to withdraw emotional support from the rules.

This process is of course not restricted to the realm of competitive sport, which has simply provided us with microcosmic images of the social macrocosm. The process whereby exaltation of the end generates a literal *demoralization*, i.e., a de-institutionalization, of the means occurs in many groups where the two components of the social structure are not highly integrated.

Contemporary American culture appears to approximate the polar type in which great emphasis upon certain success-goals occurs without equivalent emphasis upon institutional means. It would of course be fanciful to assert that accumulated wealth stands alone as a symbol of success just as it would be fanciful to deny that Americans assign it a place high in their scale of values. In some large measure, money has been consecrated as a value in itself, over and above its expenditure for articles of consumption or its use for the enhancement of power. "Money" is peculiarly well adapted to become a symbol of prestige. As Simmel emphasized, money is highly abstract and impersonal. However acquired, fraudulently or institutionally, it can be used to purchase the same goods and services. The anonymity of an urban society, in conjunction with these peculiarities of money, permits wealth, the sources of which may be unknown to the community in which the plutocrat lives or, if known, to become purified in the course of time, to serve as a symbol of high status. Moreover, in the American Dream there is no final stopping point. The measure of "monetary success" is conveniently indefinite and relative. At each income level, as H. F. Clark found, Americans want just about twenty-five per cent more (but of course this "just a bit more" continues to operate once it is obtained). In this flux of shifting standards, there is no stable resting point, or rather, it is the point which manages always to be "just ahead." An observer of a community in which annual salaries in six figures are not uncommon, reports the anguished words of one victim of the American Dream: "In this town, I'm snubbed socially because I only get a thousand a week. That hurts."

To say that the goal of monetary success is entrenched in American culture is only to say that Americans are bombarded on every side by precepts which affirm the right or, often, the duty of retaining the goal even in the face of repeated frustration. Prestigeful representatives of the society reinforce the cultural emphasis. The family, the school and the workplace—the major agencies shaping the personality structure and goal formation of Americans— join to provide the intensive disciplining required if an individual is to retain intact a goal that remains elusively beyond reach, if he is to be motivated by the promise of a gratification which is not redeemed. As we shall presently see, parents serve as a transmission belt for the values and goals of the groups of which they are a part—above all, of their social class or of the class with which they identify themselves. And the schools are of course the official agency for the passing on of the prevailing values, with a large proportion of the textbooks used in city schools implying or stating explicitly "that education leads to intelligence and consequently to job and money success." Central to this process of disciplining people to maintain their unfulfilled aspirations are the cultural prototypes of success, the living documents

testifying that the American Dream can be realized if one but has the requisite abilities. Consider in this connection the following excerpts from the business journal, *Nation's Business*, drawn from a large amount of comparable materials found in mass communications setting forth the values of business class culture (please see following page).

The symbolism of a commoner rising to the estate of economic royalty is woven deep in the texture of the American culture pattern, finding what is perhaps its ultimate expression in the words of one who knew whereof he spoke, Andrew Carnegie: "Be a king in your dreams. Say to yourself, 'My place is at the top.'"

Coupled with this positive emphasis upon the obligation to maintain lofty goals is a correlative emphasis upon the penalizing of those who draw in their ambitions. Americans are admonished "not to be a quitter" for in the dictionary of American culture, as in the lexicon of youth, "there is no such word as 'fail.'" The cultural manifesto is clear: one must not quit, must not cease striving, must not lessen his goals, for "not failure, but low aim, is crime."

Thus the culture enjoins the acceptance of three cultural axioms: First, all should strive for the same lofty goals since these are open to all; second, present seeming failure is but a way-station to ultimate success; and third, genuine failure consists only in the lessening or withdrawal of ambition.

In rough psychological paraphrase, these axioms represent, first, a symbolic secondary reinforcement of incentive; second, curbing the threatened extinction of a response through an associated stimulus; third, increasing the motive-strength to evoke continued responses despite the continued absence of reward.

In sociological paraphrase, these axioms represent, first, the deflection of criticism of the social structure onto one's self among those so situated in the society that they do not have full and equal access to opportunity; second, the preservation of a structure of social power by having individuals in the lower social strata identify themselves, not with their compeers, but with those at the top (whom they will ultimately join); and third, providing pressures for conformity with the cultural dictates of unslackened ambition by the threat of less than full membership in the society for those who fail to conform.

It is in these terms and through these processes that contemporary American culture continues to be characterized by a heavy emphasis on wealth as a

The Document **(Nation's Business, Vol. 27, No. 8, p. 7)**	**Its Sociological Implications**
"You have to be born to these jobs, buddy, or else have a good pull."	Here is a heretical opinion, possibly born of continued frustration, which rejects the worth of retaining an apparently unrealizable goal, and, moreover, questions the legitimacy of a social structure which provides differential access to this goal.
That's an old sedative to ambition.	The counter-attack, explicitly asserting the cultural value of retaining one's aspirations intact, of not losing "ambition."
Before listening to its seduction, ask these men:	A clear statement of the function to be served by the ensuing list of "successes." These men are living testimony that the social structure is such as to permit these aspirations to be achieved, *if one is worthy*. And correlatively, failure to reach these goals testifies only to one's own personal shortcomings. Aggression provoked by failure should therefore be directed inward and not outward, against oneself and not against a social structure which provides free and equal access to opportunity.
Elmer R. Jones, president of Well-Fargo and Col, who began life as a poor boy and left school at the fifth grade to take his first job.	Success prototype I: *All* may properly have the *same* lofty ambitions, for however lowly the starting-point, true talent can reach the very heights. Aspirations must be retained intact.
Frank C. Ball, the Mason fruit jar king of America, who rode from Buffalo to Muncie, Indiana, in a boxcar along with his brother George's horse, to start a little business in Muncie that became the biggest of its kind.	Success prototype II: Whatever the present results of one's strivings, the future is large with promise; for the common man may yet become a king. Gratifications may seem forever deferred, but they will finally be realized as one's enterprise becomes the "biggest of its kind."
J. L. Bevan, present of the Illinois Central Railroad, who at twelve was a messenger boy in the freight office at New Orleans.	Success prototype III: If the secular trends of our economy seem to give little scope to small business, then one may rise within the giant bureaucracies of private enterprise. If one can no longer be a king in a realm of his own creation, he may at least become a president in one of the economic democracies. No matter what one's present station, messenger boy or clerk, one's gaze should be fixed at the top.

basic symbol of success, without a corresponding emphasis upon the legitimate avenues on which to march toward this goal. How do individuals living in this cultural context respond? And how do our observations bear upon the doctrine that deviant behavior typically derives from biological impulses breaking through the restraints imposed by culture? What, in short, are the consequences for the behavior of people variously situated in a social structure of a culture in which the emphasis on dominant success-goals has become increasingly separated from an equivalent emphasis on institutionalized procedures for seeking these goals?

Types of Individual Adaptation

Turning from these culture patterns, we now examine types of adaptation by individuals within the culture-bearing society. Though our focus is still the cultural and social genesis of varying rates and types of deviant behavior, our perspective shifts from the plane of patterns of cultural values to the plane of types of adaptation to these values among those occupying different positions in the social structure.

We here consider five types of adaptation, as these are schematically set out in the following table, where (+) signifies "acceptance," (–) signifies "rejection," and (±) signifies "rejection of prevailing values and substitution of new values."

A Typology of Modes of Individual Adaptation

Modes of Adaptation	Culture Goals	Institutionalized Means
I. Conformity	+	+
II. Innovation	+	–
III. Ritualism	–	+
IV. Retreatism	–	–
V. Rebellion	±	±

Examination of how the social structure operates to exert pressure upon individuals for one or another of these alternative modes of behavior must be prefaced by the observation that people may shift from one alternative to another as they engage in different spheres of social activities. These categories refer to role behavior in specific types of situations, not to personality. They are types of more or less enduring response, not types of personality organization. To consider these types of adaptation in several spheres of conduct would introduce a complexity unmanageable within the confines of this chapter. For this reason, we shall be primarily concerned with economic activity in the broad sense of "the production, exchange, distribution and consumption of goods and services" in our competitive society, where wealth has taken on a highly symbolic cast.

I. Conformity

To the extent that a society is stable, adaptation type I—conformity to both cultural goals and institutionalized means—is the most common and widely diffused. Were this not so, the stability and continuity of the society could not be maintained. The mesh of expectancies constituting every social order is sustained by the modal behavior of its members representing conformity to the established, though perhaps secularly changing, culture patterns. It is, in fact, only because behavior is typically oriented toward the basic values of the society that we may speak of a human aggregate as comprising a society. Unless there is a deposit of values shared by interacting individuals, there exist social relations, if the disorderly interactions may be so called, but no society. It is thus that, at mid-century, one may refer to a Society of Nations primarily as a figure of speech or as an imagined objective, but not as a sociological reality.

Since our primary interest centers on the sources of *deviant* behavior, and since we have briefly examined the mechanisms making for conformity as the modal response in American society, little more need be said regarding this type of adaptation, at this point.

II. Innovation

Great cultural emphasis upon the success-goal invites this mode of adaptation through the use of institutionally proscribed but often effective means of attaining at least the simulacrum of success—wealth and power. This response occurs when the individual has assimilated the cultural emphasis upon the goal without equally internalizing the institutional norms governing ways and means for its attainment.

From the standpoint of psychology, great emotional investment in an objective may be expected to produce a readiness to take risks, and this attitude may be adopted by people in all social strata. From the standpoint of sociology, the question arises, which features of our social structure predispose toward this type of adaptation, thus producing greater frequencies of deviant behavior in one social stratum than in another?

On the top economic levels, the pressure toward innovation not infrequently erases the distinction between business-like strivings this side of the mores and sharp practices beyond the mores. As Veblen observed, "It is not easy in any given case—indeed it is at times impossible until the courts have spoken—to say whether it is an instance of praiseworthy salesmanship or a penitentiary offense." The history of the great American fortunes is threaded with strains toward institutionally dubious innovation as is attested by many tributes to the Robber Barons. The reluctant admiration often expressed privately, and not seldom publicly, of these "shrewd, smart and successful" men is a product of a cultural structure in which the sacrosanct goal virtually consecrates the means. This is no new phenomenon. Without assuming that Charles Dickens [in *American Notes*] was a wholly accurate observer of the American scene and with full knowledge that he was anything but impartial, we cite his perceptive remarks on the American

> love of "smart" dealing: which gilds over many a swindle and gross breach of trust; many a defalcation, public and private; and enables many a knave to hold his head up with the best, who well deserves a halter. . . . The merits of a broken speculation, or a bankruptcy, or of a successful scoundrel, are not gauged by its or his observance of the golden rule, "Do as you would be done by," but are considered with reference to their smartness. . . . The following dialogue I have held a hundred times: "Is it not a very disgraceful circumstance that such a man as So-and-so should be acquiring a large property by the most infamous and odious means, and notwithstanding all the crimes of which he has been guilty, should be tolerated and abetted by your Citizens? He is a public nuisance, is he not?" "Yes, sir." "A convicted liar?" "Yes, sir." "He has been kicked and cuffed, and caned?" "Yes, sir." "And he is utterly dishonorable, debased, and profligate?" "Yes, sir." "In the name of wonder, then, what is his merit?" "Well, sir, he is a smart man."

In this caricature of conflicting cultural values, Dickens was of course only one of many wits who mercilessly probed the consequences of the heavy emphasis on financial success. . . . But perhaps most in point here was the deployment of wit by Ambrose Bierce in a form which made it evident that *wit* had not cut away from its etymological origins and still meant the power by which one knows, learns, or thinks. In his characteristically ironical and deep-seeing essay on "crime and its correctives," Bierce begins with the observation that "Sociologists have long been debating the theory that the impulse to commit crime is a disease, and the ayes appear to have it—the disease." After this prelude, he describes the ways in which the successful rogue achieves social legitimacy, and proceeds to anatomize the discrepancies between cultural values and social relations.

> The good American is, as a rule, pretty hard on roguery, but he atones for his austerity by an amiable toleration of rogues. His only requirement is that he must personally know the rogues. We all "denounce" thieves loudly enough if we have not the honor of their acquaintance. If we have, why, that is different—unless they have the actual odor of the slum or the prison about them. We may know them guilty, but we meet them, shake hands with them, drink with them and, if they happen to be wealthy, or otherwise great, invite them to our houses, and deem it an honor to frequent theirs. We do not "approve their methods"—let that be understood; and thereby they are sufficiently punished. The notion that a knave cares a pin what is thought of his ways by one who is civil and friendly to himself appears to have been invented by a humorist. On the vaudeville stage of Mars it would probably have made his fortune.
>
> [And again:] If social recognition were denied to rogues they would be fewer by many. Some would only the more diligently cover their tracks along the devious paths of unrighteousness, but others would do so much violence to their consciences as to renounce the disadvantages of rascality for those of an honest life. An unworthy person dreads nothing so much as the withholding of an honest hand, the slow, inevitable stroke of an ignoring eye.
>
> We have rich rogues because we have "respectable" persons who are not ashamed to take them by the hand, to be seen with them, to say that they know them. In such it is treachery to censure them; to cry out when robbed by them is to turn state's evidence.
>
> One may smile upon a rascal (most of us do many times a day) if one does not know

him to be a rascal, and has not said he is; but knowing him to be, or having said he is, to smile upon him is to be a hypocrite—just a plain hypocrite or a sycophantic hypocrite, according to the station in life of the rascal smiled upon. There are more plain hypocrites than sycophantic ones, for there are more rascals of no consequence than rich and distinguished ones, though they get fewer smiles each. The American people will be plundered as long as the American character is what it is; as long as it is tolerant of successful knaves; as long as American ingenuity draws an imaginary distinction between a man's public character and his private—his commercial and his personal. In brief, the American people will be plundered as long as they deserve to be plundered. No human law can stop, none ought to stop it, for that would abrogate a higher and more salutary law: "As ye sow, ye shall reap."

Living in the age in which the American robber barons flourished, Bierce could not easily fail to observe what became later known as "white-collar crime." Nevertheless, he was aware that not all of these large and dramatic departures from institutional norms in the top economic strata are known, and possibly fewer deviations among the lesser middle classes come to light. Sutherland has repeatedly documented the prevalence of "white-collar criminality" among business men. He notes, further, that many of these crimes were not prosecuted because they were not detected or, if detected, because of "the status of the business man, the trend away from punishment, and the relatively unorganized resentment of the public against white-collar criminals." A study of some 1,700 prevalently middle-class individuals found that "off the record crimes" were common among wholly "respectable" members of society. Ninety-nine per cent of those questioned confessed to having committed one or more of 49 offenses under the penal law of the State of New York, each of these offenses being sufficiently serious to draw a maximum sentence of not less than one year. The mean number of offenses in adult years—this excludes all offenses committed before the age of sixteen—was 18 for men and 11 for women. Fully 64% of the men and 29% of the women acknowledged their guilt on one or more counts of felony which, under the laws of New York, is ground for depriving them of all rights of citizenship. One

keynote of these findings is expressed by a minister, referring to false statements he made about a commodity he sold, "I tried truth first, but it's not always successful." On the basis of these results, the authors modestly conclude that "the number of acts legally constituting crimes are far in excess of those officially reported. Unlawful behavior, far from being an abnormal social or psychological manifestation, is in truth a very common phenomenon."

But whatever the differential rates of deviant behavior in the several social strata, and we know from many sources that the official crime statistics uniformly showing higher rates in the lower strata are far from complete or reliable, it appears from our analysis that the greatest pressures toward deviation are exerted upon the lower strata. Cases in point permit us to detect the sociological mechanisms involved in producing these pressures. Several researchers have shown that specialized areas of vice and crime constitute a "normal" response to a situation where the cultural emphasis upon pecuniary success has been absorbed, but where there is little access to conventional and legitimate means for becoming successful. The occupational opportunities of people in these areas are largely confined to manual labor and the lesser white-collar jobs. Given the American stigmatization of manual labor *which has been found to hold rather uniformly in all social classes*, and the absence of realistic opportunities for advancement beyond this level, the result is a marked tendency toward deviant behavior. The status of unskilled labor and the consequent low income cannot readily *compete in terms of established standards of worth* with the promises of power and high income from organized vice, rackets and crime.

For our purposes, these situations exhibit two salient features. First, incentives for success are provided by the established values of the culture, *and* second, the avenues available for moving toward this goal are largely limited by the class structure to those of deviant behavior. It is the *combination* of the cultural emphasis and the social structure which produces intense pressure for deviation. Recourse to legitimate channels for "getting in the money" is limited by a class structure which is not fully open at each level to men of good capacity. Despite our persisting open-class-ideology, advance toward the success-goal is relatively rare and notably difficult for those armed with little formal education and few economic resources. The dominant pressure leads toward the gradual attenuation of legitimate, but by and large ineffectual, strivings and the increasing use of illegitimate, but more or less effective, expedients.

Of those located in the lower reaches of the social structure, the culture makes incompatible demands. On the one hand, they are asked to orient their conduct toward the prospect of large wealth—"Every man a king," said Marden and Carnegie and Long—and on the other, they are largely denied effective opportunities to do so institutionally. The consequence of this structural inconsistency is a high rate of deviant behavior. The equilibrium between culturally designated ends and means becomes highly unstable with progressive emphasis on attaining the prestige-laden ends by any means whatsoever. Within this context, Al Capone represents the triumph of amoral intelligence over morally prescribed "failure," when channels of vertical mobility are closed or narrowed *in a society which places a high premium on economic affluence and social ascent for* all its members.

This last qualification is of central importance. It implies that other aspects of the social structure, besides the extreme emphasis on pecuniary success, must be considered if we are to understand the social sources of deviant behavior. A high frequency of deviant behavior is not generated merely by lack of opportunity or by this exaggerated pecuniary emphasis. A comparatively rigidified class structure, a caste order, may limit opportunities far beyond the point which obtains in American society today. It is when a system of cultural values extols, virtually above all else, certain *common* success-goals *for the population at large* while the social structure rigorously restricts or completely closes access to approved modes of reaching these goals *for a considerable part of the same population*, that deviant behavior ensues on a large scale. Otherwise said, our egalitarian ideology denies by implication the existence of non-competing individuals and groups in the pursuit of pecuniary success. Instead, the same body of success-symbols is held to apply for all. Goals are held to transcend class lines, not to be bounded by them, yet the actual social organization is such that there exist class differentials in accessibility of the goals. In this setting, a cardinal American virtue, "ambition," promotes a cardinal American vice, "deviant behavior."

This theoretical analysis may help explain the varying correlations between crime and poverty. "Poverty" is not an isolated variable which operates in precisely the same fashion wherever found; it is only one in a complex of identifiably interdependent social and cultural variables. Poverty as such and consequent limitation of opportunity are not enough to produce a conspicuously high rate of criminal behavior. Even the notorious "poverty in the midst of plenty" will not necessarily lead to this result. But when poverty and associated disadvantages in competing for the culture values approved for *all* members of the society are linked with a cultural emphasis on pecuniary success as a dominant goal, high rates of criminal behavior are the normal outcome. Thus, crude (and not necessarily reliable) crime statistics suggest that poverty is less highly correlated with crime in southeastern Europe than in the United States. The economic life-chances of the poor in these European areas would seem to be even less promising than in this country, so that neither poverty nor its association with limited opportunity is sufficient to account for the varying correlations. However, when we consider the full configuration—poverty, limited opportunity and the assignment of cultural goals—there appears some basis for explaining the higher correlation between poverty and crime in our society than in others where rigidified class structure is coupled with *differential class symbols of success.*

The victims of this contradiction between the cultural emphasis on pecuniary ambition and the social bars to full opportunity are not always aware of the structural sources of their thwarted aspirations. To be sure, they are often aware of a discrepancy between individual worth and social rewards. But they do not necessarily see how this comes about.

Ritualism

As located in the typology, ritualism refers to a pattern of response in which culturally defined aspirations are abandoned while "one continues to abide almost compulsively by institutional norms." As was said when this concept was introduced, "it is something of a terminological quibble to ask whether this represents 'genuinely deviant behavior.' Since the adaptation is, in effect, an internal decision and since the overt behavior is institutionally permitted, though not culturally preferred, it is not generally considered to represent a 'social problem.' Intimates of individuals making this adaptation may pass judgment in terms of prevailing cultural emphases and may 'feel sorry for them'; they may, in the individual case, feel that 'old Jonesy is certainly in a rut.' Whether this is described as deviant behavior or no, it clearly represents a departure from the cultural model in which men are obliged to strive actively, preferably through institutionalized procedures, to move onward and upward in the social hierarchy." . . .

Retreatism

The retreatist pattern consists of the substantial abandoning both of the once-esteemed cultural goals and of institutionalized practices directed toward those goals. Approximations to this pattern have recently been identified among what has been described as "problem families"—roughly, those families who do not measure up to the normative expectations prevailing in their social environment. Further evidence of this mode of response is found among workers who develop a state of psychic passivity in response to some discernible extent of anomie.

Generally, however, retreatism seems to occur in response to acute anomie, involving an abrupt break in the familiar and accepted normative framework and in established social relations, particularly when it appears to individuals subjected to it that the condition will continue indefinitely. As Durkheim noted with characteristic insight, such disruptions may be found in the "anomie of prosperity," when Fortune smiles and many experience radical upward shifts from their accustomed status, and not only in the "anomie of depression," when Fortune frowns and apparently exits for good. Much the same anomic condition often obtains in those patterned situations which "exempt" individuals from a wide array of role-obligations, as, for example, in the case of "retirement" from the job being imposed upon people without their consent and in the case of widowhood. . . .

Rebellion

It should be plain by now that the theory under review sees the conflict between culturally defined goals and institutional norms as one *source* of anomie; it does not *equate* value-conflict and anomie. Quite the contrary: conflicts between the norms held by distinct subgroups in a society of course often result in an increased adherence to the norms prevailing in each subgroup. It is the conflict between culturally accepted values and the socially structured difficulties in living up to these values which exerts pressure toward deviant behavior and disruption of the normative system. This outcome of anomie, however, may be only a prelude to the development of new norms, and it is this response

which we have described as "rebellion" in the typology of adaptation.

When rebellion is confined to relatively small and relatively powerless elements in a community, it provides a potential for the formation of subgroups, alienated from the rest of the community but unified within themselves. This pattern is exemplified by alienated adolescents teaming up in gangs or becoming part of a youth movement with a distinctive subculture of its own. This response to anomie tends, however, to be unstable unless the new groups and norms are sufficiently insulated from the rest of the society which rejects them.

When rebellion becomes endemic in a substantial part of the society, it provides a potential for revolution, which reshapes both the normative and the social structure. It is this connection that a recent study of the changing role of the bourgeoisie in eighteenth-century France significantly extends the present theory of anomie.

William Edward Burghardt (W. E. B.) Du Bois (1868–1963) may be best known for his 1903 book, *Souls of Black Folk*, but this was not his only important work of social theory. Du Bois would live a long life filled with many political and literary involvements, all of them responding to crises of the twentieth century. It is possible that the finest of all his writings is a book written in the midst of the Great Depression of the 1930s: *Black Reconstruction* (1935). This work harkens back to the failure of the post–Civil War effort to reconstruct the South. Prior to Du Bois's book, it was typical to blame the failure of Reconstruction in 1867 on the freed blacks. Du Bois, with characteristic restraint, dismisses such a ridiculous claim with a careful socio-structural analysis of economic and political tensions between black and white workers that were provoked by the white planter class. The argument is, in effect, not a question of failure so much as structured fates determined by larger political forces. Nowhere is the brilliance of Du Bois's structural sociology better illustrated than in the idea David Roediger has called the "racial wage"—the tacit accord whereby the white planters co-opted impoverished white workers to join their segregationist practices against black workers. In the post–Civil War period, the dominant class of whites regained their control of the American South by offering poor white workers the status of being white in compensation for their economic misery. The selection is from the conclusion to *Black Reconstruction*, a book of more than 700 pages.

Black Reconstruction and the Racial Wage[*]
W. E. B. Du Bois (1935)

We see this more clearly today than the nation of 1868, or any of its leaders, could possibly envisage it; but even then, Northern industry knew that universal suffrage in the South, in the hands of Negroes just freed from slavery, and of white people still enslaved by poverty, could not stand against organized industry. They promptly calculated that the same method of controlling the labor vote would come in vogue in the South as they were already using in the North, and that the industry which used these methods must in the meantime cooperate with Northern industry; that it could not move the foundation stones upon which Northern industry was consolidating its power; that is, the tariff, the money system, the debt, and national in place of state control of industry. This would seem to be what the masters of exploitation were counting upon and it certainly came true in the bargain of 1876.

Thus by singular coincidence and for a moment, for the few years of an eternal second in a cycle of a thousand years, the orbits of two widely and utterly dissimilar economic systems coincided and the result was a revolution so vast and portentous that few minds ever fully conceived it; for the systems were these: first, that of a democracy which should by universal suffrage establish a dictatorship of the proletariat ending in industrial democracy; and the other, a system by which a little knot of masterful men would so organize capitalism as to bring under their control the natural resources, wealth and industry of a vast and rich country and through that, of the world. For a second, for a pulse of time, these orbits crossed and coincided, but their central suns were a thousand light-years apart, even though the blind and ignorant fury of the South and the complacent Philistinism of the North saw them as one.

Reconstruction was an economic revolution on a mighty scale and with world-wide reverberation. Reconstruction was not simply a fight between the white and black races in the South or between master and ex-slave. It was much more subtle; it involved more than this. There have been repeated and continued attempts to paint this era as an interlude of petty politics or nightmare of race hate instead of viewing it slowly and broadly as a tremendous series of efforts to earn a living in new and untried ways, to achieve economic security and to restore fatal losses of capital and investment. It was a vast labor movement of ignorant, earnest, and bewildered black men whose faces had been ground in the mud by their three awful centuries of degradation and who now staggered forward blindly in blood and tears amid petty division, hate and hurt, and surrounded by every disaster of war and industrial upheaval. Reconstruction was a vast labor movement of ignorant, muddled and bewildered white men who had been disinherited of land and labor and fought a long battle with sheer subsistence, hanging on the edge of poverty, eating clay and chasing slaves and now lurching up to manhood. Reconstruction was the turn of white Northern migration southward to new and sudden economic opportunity which followed the disaster and dislocation of war, and an attempt to organize capital and, labor on a new pattern and build a new economy. Finally Reconstruction was a desperate effort of a dislodged, maimed, impoverished and ruined oligarchy and monopoly to restore an anachronism in economic organization by force, fraud and slander, in defiance of law and order, and in the face of a great labor movement of white and black, and in bitter strife with a new capitalism and a new political framework.

All these contending and antagonistic groups spoke different and unknown tongues; to the Negro "Freedom" was God; to the poor white "Freedom" was nothing—he had more than he had use for; to the planter "Freedom" for the poor was laziness and for the rich, control of the poor worker; for the Northern business man "Freedom" was opportunity to get rich.

Yet, with interpretation, agreement was possible here; North and South agreed that laborers must produce profit; the poor white and the Negro wanted to get the profit arising from the laborers' toil and not to divide it with the employers and landowners. When Northern and Southern employers agreed that profit was most important and the method of getting it second, the path to understanding was clear. When white laborers were convinced that the degradation of Negro labor was more fundamental than the uplift of white labor, the end was in sight. . . .

The political success of the doctrine of racial separation, which overthrew Reconstruction by uniting the planter and the poor white, was far exceeded by its astonishing economic results. The theory of laboring class unity rests upon the assumption that laborers, despite internal jealousies, will unite because of their opposition to exploitation by the capitalists. According to this, even after a part of the poor white laboring class became identified with the planters, and eventually displaced them, their interests would be diametrically opposed to those of the mass of white labor, and of course to those of the black laborers. This would throw white and black labor into one class, and precipitate a united fight for higher wage and better working conditions.

Most persons do not realize how far this failed to work in the South, and it failed to work because the theory of race was supplemented by a carefully planned and slowly evolved method, which drove such a wedge between the white and black workers that there probably are not today in the world two groups of workers with practically identical interests who hate and fear each other so deeply and persistently and who are kept so far apart that neither sees anything of common interest.

It must be remembered that the white group of laborers, while they received a low wage, were compensated in part by a sort of public and psychological wage. They were given public deference and titles of courtesy because they were white. They were admitted freely with all classes of white people to public functions, public parks, and the best schools. The police were drawn from their ranks, and the courts, dependent upon their votes, treated them with such leniency as to encourage lawlessness. Their vote selected public officials, and while this had small effect upon the economic situation, it had great effect upon their personal treatment and the deference shown them. White schoolhouses were the best in the community, and conspicuously placed, and they cost anywhere from twice to ten times as much per capita as the colored schools. The newspapers specialized on news that flattered the poor whites and almost utterly ignored the Negro except in crime and ridicule.

On the other hand, in the same way, the Negro was subject to public insult; was afraid of mobs; was liable to the jibes of children and the unreasoning fears of white women; and was compelled almost continuously to submit to various badges of inferiority. The result of this was that the wages of both classes could be kept low, the whites fearing to be supplanted by Negro labor, the Negroes always being threatened by the substitution of white labor.

Mob violence and lynching were the inevitable result of the attitude of these two classes and for a time were a sort of permissible Roman holiday for the entertainment of vicious whites. One can see for these reasons why labor organizers and labor agitators made such small headway in the South. They were, for the most part, appealing to laborers who would rather have low wages upon which they could eke out an existence than see colored labor with a decent wage. White labor saw in every advance of Negroes a threat to their racial prerogatives, so that in many districts Negroes were afraid to build decent homes or dress well, or own carriages, bicycles or automobiles, because of possible retaliation on the part of the whites. . . .

The effect of caste on the moral integrity of the Negro race in America has thus been widely disastrous; servility and fawning, gross flattery of white folk and lying to appease and cajole them; failure to achieve dignity and self-respect and moral self-assertion, personal cowardliness and submission to insult and aggression; exaggerated and despicable humility; lack of faith of Negroes in themselves and in other Negroes and in all colored folk; inordinate admiration for the stigmata of success among white folk: wealth and arrogance, cunning dishonesty and assumptions of superiority; the exaltation of laziness and indifference as just as successful as the industry and striving which invites taxation and oppression; dull apathy and cynicism; faith in no future and the habit of moving and wandering in search of justice; a religion of prayer and submission to replace determination and effort.

These are not universal results or else the Negro long since would have dwindled and died in crime and disease. But they are so widespread as to bring inner conflict as baffling as the problems of inter-racial relations, and they hold back the moral grit and organized effort which are the only hope of survival.

On this and in spite of this comes an extraordinary record of accomplishment, a record so contradictory of what one might easily expect that many people and even the Negroes themselves are deceived by it. The real question is not so much what the Negro has done in spite of caste, as what he might have accomplished with reasonable encouragement. He has cut down his illiteracy more than two-thirds in fifty years, but with decent schools it ought to have been cut down 99 per cent. He has accumulated land and property, but has not been able to hold one-tenth of that which he has rightly earned. He has achieved success in many lines, as an inventor, scientist, scholar and writer. But most of his ability has been choked in chain-gangs and by open deliberate discrimination and conspiracies of silence. He has made a place for himself in literature and art, but the great deeps of his artistic gifts have never yet been plumbed. And yet, for all that he has accomplished not only the nation but the South itself claims credit and actually points to it as proof of the wisdom or at least the innocuousness of organized suppression! . . .

If white and black in the South were free and intelligent there would be friendship and some intermarriage and there ought to be; but none would marry where he did not wish to, and there could be no greater intermingling in the future than in the shameful past, unless this union of races proved successful and attractive.

The revolution of 1876 was, in fine, a victory for which the South has every right to hang its head. After enslaving the Negro for two and one-half centuries, it turned on his emancipation to beat a beaten man, to trade in slaves, and to kill the defenseless; to break the spirit of the black man and humiliate him into hopelessness; to establish a new dictatorship of property in the South through the color line. It was a triumph of men who in their effort to replace equality with caste and to build inordinate wealth on a foundation of abject poverty have succeeded in killing democracy, art and religion.

And yet, despite this, and despite the long step backward toward slavery that black folk have been pushed, they have made withal a brave and fine fight; a fight against ridicule and monstrous caricature, against every refinement of cruelty and gross insult, against starvation, disease and murder in every form. It has left in their soul its scars, its deep scars; but when all is said, through it all has gone a thread of brave and splendid friendship from those few and rare men and women of white skins, North and South, who have dared to know and help and love black folk.

wealth = inheritance

huge wealth gap between white ⊕ black

housing market perfect example

racism is good for the ruling class

Unavoidable Dilemmas

Reinhold Niebuhr (1892–1971), as a young man, was a Protestant minister in the reform tradition. He served a parish in an industrial area of Detroit, where his concern for social justice deepened. This experience influenced his long career as a writer and teacher of social ethics at the Union Theological Seminary in New York City (1928–1960). Niebuhr was a force in progressive politics in New York and a cofounder of the Americans for Democratic Action. His most famous book, *Moral Man and Immoral Society* (1932), was an important contribution to social theory because of its then-stunning critique of the moralistic idea that good individuals filled with love for others could change the world. Nations, he argued, are concerned with power and thus with selfish interests; in politics, one strives for justice, not love. Niebuhr's thinking in 1932 was thus in line with Keynes's insistence that the era of the autonomous individual ended with the more complex political and economic crises that developed during and after World War I. Niebuhr's writings were an important influence on Martin Luther King Jr. during his student days. King's strategy of forceful nonviolence could be said to be one part Gandhi, another Niebuhr. King certainly shared Niebuhr's idea that in the social realm, love could force justice, if not love.

Moral Man and Immoral Society [*]
Reinhold Niebuhr (1932)

The difference between the attitudes of individuals and those of groups has been frequently alluded to, the thesis being that group relations can never be as ethical as those which characterise individual relations. In dealing with the problem of social justice, it may be found that the relation of economic classes within a state is more important than international relations. But from the standpoint of analysing the ethics of group behavior, it is feasible to study the ethical attitudes of nations first; because the modern nation is the human group of strongest social cohesion, of most undisputed central authority and of most clearly defined membership. The church may have challenged its pre-eminence in the Middle Ages, and the economic class may compete with it for the loyalty of men in our own day; yet it remains, as it has been since the seventeenth century, the most absolute of all human associations.

Nations are territorial societies, the cohesive power of which is supplied by the sentiment of nationality and the authority of the state. The fact that state and nation are not synonymous and that states frequently incorporate several nationalities, indicates that the authority of government is the ultimate force of national cohesion. The fact that state and nation are roughly synonymous proves that, without the sentiment of nationality with its common language and traditions, the authority of government is usually unable to maintain national unity. The unity of Scotland and England within a single British state and the failure to maintain the same unity between England and Ireland, suggest both the possibilities and the limitations of transcending nationality in the formation of states. For our purposes we may think of state and nation as interchangeable terms, since our interest is in the moral attitudes of nations which have the apparatus of a state at their disposal, and through it are able to consolidate their social power and define their political attitudes and policies.

The selfishness of nations is proverbial. It was a dictum of George Washington that nations were not to be trusted beyond their own interest. "No state," declares a German author, "has ever entered a treaty for any other reason than self interest," and adds: "A statesman who has any other motive would deserve to be hung." "In every part of the world," said Professor Edward Dicey, "where British interests are at stake, I am in favor of advancing these interests even at the cost of war. The only qualification I admit is that the country we desire to annex or take under our protection should be calculated to confer a tangible advantage upon the British Empire." National ambitions are not always avowed as honestly as this, as we shall see later, but that is a fair statement of the actual facts, which need hardly to be elaborated for any student of history.

What is the basis and reason for the selfishness of nations? If we begin with what is least important or least distinctive of national attitudes, it must be noted that nations do not have direct contact with other national communities, with which they must form some kind of international community. They know the problems of other peoples only indirectly and at second hand. Since both sympathy and justice depend to a large degree upon the perception of need, which makes sympathy flow, and upon the understanding of competing interests, which must be resolved, it is obvious that human communities have greater difficulty than individuals in achieving ethical relationships. While rapid means of communication have increased the breadth of knowledge about world affairs among citizens of various nations, and the general advance of education has ostensibly promoted the capacity to think rationally

and justly upon the inevitable conflicts of interest between nations, there is nevertheless little hope of arriving at a perceptible increase of international morality through the growth of intelligence and the perfection of means of communication. The development of international commerce, the increased economic interdependence among the nations, and the whole apparatus of a technological civilisation, increase the problems and issues between nations much more rapidly than the intelligence to solve them can be created.

Gunnar Myrdal (1898–1987), a Swedish economist, was in many ways the world statesman of social science in the post–World War II years. Myrdal was awarded the Nobel Prize in Economics in 1974. He authored more than forty books in English and Swedish on a wide range of topics in economics, social theory, and social policy. Among them is *Asian Drama: An Inquiry into the Poverty of Nations* (1968). But Myrdal's most important contribution to social theory was *An American Dilemma* (1944)—his sensitive, though firm, critique of the social and economic bases of racial conflict in the United States. "The Negro Problem as a Moral Issue" is from the introduction to this book. Myrdal argues somewhat in the structural manner of Robert K. Merton's earlier essay on anomie that race is a moral issue arising out of American economic history but against its moralistic culture. Written near the end of the interwar period, this work provides a frank assessment of conflict structured into the culture of the rising post–World War II power.

The Negro Problem as a Moral Issue [*]
Gunnar Myrdal (1944)

There is a "Negro problem" in the United States and most Americans are aware of it, although it assumes varying forms and intensity in different regions of the country and among diverse groups of the

---

[*] Excerpt from pp. xlv–xlvii (1255 words) from AN AMERICAN DILEMMA: THE NEGRO PROBLEM AND MODERN DEMOCRACY by GUNNAR MYRDAL. Copyright (c) 1944, 1962 by Harper & Row, Publishers, Inc. Reprinted by permission of HarperCollins Publishers.

American people. Americans have to react to it, politically as citizens and, where there are Negroes present in the community, privately as neighbors.

To the great majority of white Americans the Negro problem has distinctly negative connotations. It suggests something difficult to settle and equally difficult to leave alone. It is embarrassing. It makes for moral uneasiness. The very presence of the Negro in America; his fate in this country through slavery, Civil War and Reconstruction; his recent career and his present status; his accommodation; his protest and his aspiration; in fact his entire biological, historical and social existence as a participant American represent to the ordinary white man in the North as well as in the South an anomaly in the very structure of American society. To many, this takes on the proportion of a menace—biological, economic, social, cultural, and, at times, political. This anxiety may be mingled with a feeling of individual and collective guilt. A few see the problem as a challenge to statesmanship. To all it is a trouble.

These and many other mutually inconsistent attitudes are blended into none too logical a scheme which, in turn, may be quite inconsistent with the wider personal, moral, religious, and civic sentiments and ideas of the Americans. Now and then, even the least sophisticated individual becomes aware of his own confusion and the contradiction in his attitudes. Occasionally he may recognize, even if only for a moment, the incongruence of his state of mind and find it so intolerable that the whole organization of his moral precepts is shaken. But most people, most of the time, suppress such threats to their moral integrity together with all of the confusion, the ambiguity, and inconsistency which lurks in the basement of man's soul. This, however, is rarely accomplished without mental strain. Out of the strain comes a sense of uneasiness and awkwardness which always seems attached to the Negro problem.

The strain is increased in democratic America by the freedom left open—even in the South, to a considerable extent—for the advocates of the Negro, his rights and welfare. All "pro-Negro" forces in American society, whether organized or not, and irrespective of their wide differences in both strategy and tactics, sense that this is the situation. They all work on the national conscience. They all seek to fix everybody's attention on the suppressed moral conflict. No wonder that they are often regarded as public nuisances, or worse—even when they succeed in getting grudging concessions to Negro rights and welfare.

At this point it must be observed that America, relative to all the other branches of Western civilization, is moralistic and "moral-conscious." The ordinary American is the opposite of a cynic. He is on the average more of a believer and a defender of the faith in humanity than the rest of the Occidentals. It is a relatively important matter to him to be true to his own ideals and to carry them out in actual life. We recognize the American, wherever we meet him, as a practical idealist. Compared with members of other nations of Western civilization, the ordinary American is a rationalistic being, and there are close relations between his moralism and his rationalism. Even romanticism, transcendentalism, and mysticism tend to be, in the American culture, rational, pragmatic and optimistic. American civilization early acquired a flavor of enlightenment which has affected the ordinary American's whole personality and especially his conception of how ideas and ideals ought to "click" together. He has never developed that particular brand of tired mysticism and romanticism which finds delight in the inextricable confusion in the order of things and in ineffectuality of the human mind. He finds such leanings intellectually perverse.

These generalizations might seem venturesome and questionable to the reflective American himself, who, naturally enough, has his attention directed more on the dissimilarities than on the similarities within his culture. What is common is usually not obvious, and it never becomes striking. But to the stranger it is obvious and even striking. In the social sciences, for instance, the American has, more courageously than anywhere else on the globe, started to measure, not only human intelligence, aptitudes, and personality traits, but moral leanings and the "goodness" of communities. This man is a rationalist; he wants intellectual order in his moral set-up; he wants to pursue his own inclinations into their hidden haunts; and he is likely to expose himself and his kind in a most undiplomatic manner.

In hasty strokes we are now depicting the essentials of the American *ethos*. This moralism and rationalism are to many of us—among them the author of this book—the glory of the nation, its youthful strength, perhaps the salvation of mankind. The analysis of this "American Creed" and its implications have an important place in our inquiry. While on the one hand, to such a moralistic and rationalistic being as the ordinary American, the Negro problem and his own confused and contradictory attitudes toward it must be disturbing; on the other hand, the very mass of unsettled problems in his heterogeneous and changing culture, and the inherited liberalistic trust that things will ultimately take care of themselves and get settled in one way or another, enable the ordinary American to live on happily, with recognized contradictions around him and within him, in a kind of bright fatalism which is unmatched in the rest of the Western world. This fatalism also belongs to the national ethos.

The American Negro problem is a problem in the heart of the American. It is there that the interracial tension has its focus. It is there that the decisive struggle goes on. This is the central viewpoint of this treatise. Though our study includes economic, social, and political race relations, at bottom our problem is the moral dilemma of the American—the conflict between his moral valuations on various levels of consciousness and generality. The "American Dilemma," referred to in the title of this book, is the ever-raging conflict between, on the one hand, the valuations preserved on the general plane which we shall call the "American Creed," where the American thinks, talks, and acts under the influence of high national and Christian precepts, and, on the other hand, the valuations on specific planes of individual and group living, where personal and local interests; economic, social, and sexual jealousies; considerations of community prestige and conformity; group prejudice against particular persons or types of people; and all sorts of miscellaneous wants, impulses, and habits dominate his outlook.

The American philosopher, John Dewey, whose immense influence is to be explained by his rare gift for projecting faithfully the aspirations and possibilities of the culture he was born into, in the maturity of age and wisdom has written a book on *Freedom and Culture*, in which he says:

Anything that obscures the fundamentally moral nature of the social problem is harmful, no matter whether it proceeds from the side of physical or of psychological theory. Any doctrine that eliminates or even obscures the function of choice of values and enlistment of desires and emotions in behalf of those chosen weakens personal responsibility for judgment and for action. It thus helps create the attitudes that welcome and support the totalitarian state.

William I. Thomas (1863–1947) and **Florian Znaniecki** (1882–1958) collaborated in the research and writing that led to the first truly classic work in American sociology: *The Polish Peasant in Europe and America* (1918–1919). It remains a source of ideas, a case study for methods, and a landmark study of an immigrant population during the period when America was still attempting to redefine itself in response to the influx of European workers. "Disorganization of the Polish Immigrant," from *Polish Peasant*, illustrates their sensitive use of personal documents to define the social disorganization of the Polish immigrant in relation to the conflict of Old World and New World cultures. It is empirical social theory at its best.

Though they respected each other and worked closely over a number of years, Thomas and Znaniecki came from very different backgrounds. Thomas had been born in rural Virginia to a family of modest means and grew up in the mountains of Tennessee. At the University of Tennessee, teachers inspired his love of scholarship. He studied in Germany from 1888 to 1889, after which he taught at Oberlin College. He then taught at the University of Chicago, whose department of sociology is considered the founding department of the discipline in the United States. It is said that Thomas's interest in personal documents came from the chance discovery of a personal letter in the trash in one of Chicago's Polish neighborhoods. In his subsequent work, Thomas pursued the value of personal documents in the ethnographic study of urban communities. His career was ruined when, at age fifty-five, he was dismissed from the university for morals. He continued writing and lecturing until he died in 1945.

Znaniecki was born into nobility in Poland. He studied in Warsaw, Geneva, and Paris before receiving his Ph.D. in philosophy from the University of Cracow in 1909. Znaniecki first met Thomas in Poland in 1913. They renewed their relationship when Thomas fled Europe for Chicago during World War I. Znaniecki's native knowledge of the Polish people soon led to his active role in the *Polish Peasant* project. But after the war he returned to a university position in Poland, where he would define himself as a sociologist and found the Polish Sociological Institute. In the 1930s, Znaniecki visited Columbia and eventually settled permanently in the United States after accepting a position at the University of Illinois. He was president of the American Sociological Society in 1953. Thomas, too, had been so honored in 1927 when younger members of the society pressed his candidacy, in part to rectify the injustice done him by the Chicago. Znaniecki died in 1958, eleven years after Thomas.

Disorganization of the Polish Immigrant[*]
William I. Thomas and Florian Znaniecki
(1918–1919)

There are from the sociological viewpoint two very different types of crime—crime within the individual's own group and crime committed by the individual outside of his group. What are the limits of the individual's own group in any particular case depends on the range within which the ties of active social solidarity are acknowledged by him as binding. Thus, for the savage these limits are those of his particular tribe; for the ignorant old-type peasant they practically coincide with his primary community; for the average modern civilized man they are those of his nation; for the conscious socialist they extend as far as the working class; for the practical Christian they include the whole human race; for the habitual criminal they are not much wider than his gang. Of course, in many cases the lines cannot be drawn exactly, for there may be several degrees of solidarity which the individual acknowledges and in a decreasing measure; for instance, the family, the community or acquaintance milieu, the city, and the nation are the individual's own groups. Nor are the two types of crime always sharply distinguishable in practice; there are complex intermediary types in which the characters of the two fundamental types are mixed in various proportions. . . .

When studying murder among other crimes in peasant communities in Poland, we had to deal chiefly with the first type of crime, i.e., with murder committed within the individual's own group. Indeed, murders of strangers are surprisingly rare among peasants. The reason is simple. The social contacts between the individual and the social world outside of his own community are relatively few and superficial, so that there is not much motive for violence, whereas, quite independently of any considerations of social solidarity, the peasant needs really strong motives for any abnormal acts because of the stable and regulated character of his habitual life and because of the strength of his desire for security. There were, indeed, many murders committed upon strangers during the period which we have investigated, . . . but these happened mainly in towns and were the outcome of the social conditions created by

the revolution of 1905–6 and could be adequately understood only in connection with a study of this revolution. In peasant life a murder is usually the tragic solution of some difficult social situation involving powerful individual tendencies, a set of social conditions which make it impossible for the individual to realize these tendencies without removing the person, or persons who stand in his way, and almost always the feeling that he has been wronged and that this person or persons have broken first the principle of solidarity. Greed, fear, sexual desire, jealousy, and revenge, mostly exaggerated by long brooding, constitute the usual factors of murder, and it is clear that situations giving rise to such emotions are apt to develop only within the individual's own group.

Now, from what we know already about the weakening of all social bonds and traditions among the immigrants, we can expect that here the nature of crime in general and of murder in particular must be very different. On the one hand, most of the motives which actuated the peasant in the old country either do not exist any longer or are greatly weakened, precisely because all social ties are loosened. An individual seldom, if ever, finds himself here in a situation which seems to him insoluble except through murder, for his wishes, less determined by tradition, are less exclusive; he has usually many ways of satisfying them, and no institutional bonds can hold him against his will. There is no need of recurring to violent means in order to get rid of one's undesirable family members, for one can simply desert them. A house or a sum of money which the individual may inherit after the death of his parents does not mean here even approximately as much as the smallest farm in the old country either in its bearing on the individual's social position or even from the purely economic standpoint relatively to his earning power. Sexual desire can be satisfied outside of the one legal way of marriage. Jealousy still exists but is in most cases weakened by the consciousness that it is possible to have many other men or women beside the unfaithful one. The fear of social opinion can hardly compel the average individual to murder as an alternative to some shameful disclosure, for social opinion has much less influence and can be easily avoided by moving away. The desire for revenge cannot be as deep as in the old country for here an individual has less chance to inflict a really serious wrong upon another, and, since the claims of solidarity have lost most of their old meaning, a break of solidarity is less resented as such.

---

[*] Excerpt from Eli Zaretsky, ed., *The Polish Peasant in Europe and America* by W. I. Thomas and Florian Znaniecki (Urbana: University of Illinois Press, 1984 [1918–1920]), pp. 281–290.

But if thus the tragic murder, the murder with powerful motives committed within one's own group, becomes relatively rare here for lack of motives, there is a wide field for the second type of murder, the murder without internal conflict and tragedy committed outside of the criminal's group. The immigrant gets into contact with outsiders, with people not belonging to his family, community, or even race incomparably more than he ever did, and even the members of his old community living in changed conditions and no longer constituting one coherent group often become estranged from him. His usual attitude toward this social environment is not that of mere indifference. It is essentially defensive, full of mistrust, of a vague feeling of danger, of a continual expectation of wrong or offense. Mistrust toward strangers was the habitual attitude of the peasant, developed by centuries of cultural isolation and by a subordinate social status which made the peasant community often suffer from unexpected social evils whose source it could not control. The immigrant's experiences in this country, sometimes involving exploitation, often humiliation, and always full of things and happenings and human acts whose meaning he only vaguely grasps, contribute, of course, to maintain and develop this attitude of general mistrust and his first movement is usually one of apprehension or implicit hostility. Furthermore, the nervousness brought by the unsettled conditions of life makes him easily exaggerate the slightest wrong. This is the background which helps us to understand cases like the following.

Joseph Opalski, murderer of Joseph Stanczak. Joseph Opalski had been boarding with Joseph Stanczak. Stanczak was 37 years old and had been in this country 8 years. He was born in Russian Poland and married there. He had with him in Chicago his wife and 2 children, 10 and 2 years old. From the testimony at the trial of Opalski it appeared that the relations between Mrs. Stanczak and Opalski were the common gossip of the neighborhood, "but nobody wanted to interfere with him." It was well known that Stanczak wished him to leave, "but the wife wanted him to stay. Three months ago Opalski beat him up also, cutting his head. He [Opalski] had more to say in the house than the deceased." Further trouble was expected by all concerned.

One Sunday night, August 29th, Joseph Stanczak asked his brother Feliks to stay with him all night. Whether he was actually afraid of Opalski or wished his brother's help in driving the obnoxious boarder out of the house is not clear. They were all drinking beer together. Opalski said he did not drink anything but went to bed early, though he could not sleep. After he had gone to his room, where the Stanczak boy also slept, Joseph Stanczak "made two breaks to go into the room," but was stopped by his wife, who complained that she was sick and did not want any noise. Later, about 1 a.m. Stanczak went to the saloon for more beer and his brother stepped out for a moment. Mrs. Stanczak, her woman boarder, and her brother-in-law, who lived upstairs, entered Opalski's room and begged him to leave the house because Stanczak and his brother were planning to cut him up with a knife, "they were going to show him American court." He slipped quietly out of the house. When the brothers returned they went to bed, Joseph with his wife and his brother with the woman boarder—who had a husband and 2 children in the old country and an illegitimate child here.

Opalski states in his confession: "I went over to Peter Altman's house. . . . There I put on my shoes, coat, and hat, and went back to Stanczak's and entered by the rear door. Finding the two Stanczak brothers, Joe and Feliks, I said: "If you are so strong, why, commence now." Joseph ran towards me, struck me with his fist right by my right ear. I had a file which I carried inside with me; I pulled it out of my pocket and struck Joseph on the head with it. He fell down on his side and then Feliks ran toward me and I struck him twice on the head with the file. And he staggered against the stove and called out 'Women, help!' Feliks ran into the bedroom and Joe was about to get up. When I seen him getting up, the file slipped from my hand and I grabbed the chair and beat him with it on the head. The chair broke in pieces and he fell down again. I don't know how or when the women got out but they were gone at that time. I went into the front bedroom and got my revolver, which I had bought from a pawn man a few months before. . . . I bought it with the intention of killing Joseph Stanczak after a fight I had 3 months ago.

"I then went to Joseph Polowski at 49th St. I got there about 4 a.m. His brother-in-law opened the door and I asked him if Joe Polowski was home. He answered: "Yes, he just came home a few minutes ago." He let me in and I went to bed with Joe and I told him I could not sleep at home because the two brothers were fighting. Joe Polowski got up at 5.30 a.m. and went to work and I slept until about noon. Got up and ate breakfast and left there and rode to Stephen Malecki's, 26th St. I got there about 2 p.m. I changed into my Sunday clothes and left there about 4 p.m. I went downtown to see a show on State St. I left the theater at 9 p.m. and then I came home to Peter Altman's . . . and slept in the kitchen until 8 o'clock in the morning, August 31st. Then I got my revolver and went to Joseph Stanczak's. I entered by the kitchen door and went into the bedroom where Joseph Stanczak was sleeping and fired three shots at him. He was asleep. There was nobody else in the house at the time and nobody knew my intention that I know of. . . . [Went to his friends; hid the revolver; the next day went to work. The day after] I ate my supper at Stephen Weybeck's, 26th St. They mentioned that Joseph Stanczak was dead, but I didn't answer when they told me. I went down to Stanczak's place and Josephine Stanczak and Josephine Okrasina [the woman boarder] and Binkowski [Stanczak's brother-in-law] was there. And Binkowski told me that Joseph Stanczak was dead, and I answered that his time was come. The women were in bed asleep and I went to bed and slept with little John Stanczak. And no more was said about the death. The morning of September 2nd I got up at 9.30 and went to work. I worked until 1.30 p.m. At the time I was arrested. . . . "

Q. Weren't you living with her just the same as if you were married to her?
A. No, never.
Q. Why did you do this?
A. [I] done this just because I knew that this man lived long enough. He killed one in the old country. He cut a man out there with a razor.

Q. Was this man in the old country that was killed by Joseph Stanczak a relative of yours?
A. I don't know this man at all.

—From the Records of the Cook County Criminal Court

There is a common feature in all these cases of murder of the second type. The crime is always a reaction to some present or past act of aggression. The act may be insignificant in its outward manifestation—perhaps no more than a slighting remark or an expression of boisterousness; it may be even only a reaction to the murderer's own aggressive move. Evidently, however, it is not the objective side of the act which is important, but the meaning given to it by the man who answers by a murderous attempt. Now, this meaning is clear; the aggressive act is interpreted by the individual against whom it is directed as a provocation to fight. The psychological background of this interpretation is that general mistrust toward the social environment, the vague expectation of hostility which we have above characterized.

Even so, however, this does not explain why an apparent provocation to fight should ever lead him to a murderous assault. A socially normal individual might ignore the provocation, or appeal to his social milieu for arbitration, or have recourse to law as an instrument of struggle and redress, or indulge in a fist fight, or finally, follow the traditional code of honor of European nobility and fight a regular duel. The murderous reaction implies in the immigrant a predisposition different from those which we find in any organized society. The explanation seems to lie in the fact that the murderer does not feel himself backed in his dealings with the outside world by any strong social group of his own and is not conscious of being the member of a steadily organized society. His family is too weak and scattered to give him a safe social refuge where he could obtain all the response and recognition he needs and ignore outside provocations in the feeling of his social importance and security. The new Polish-American community is not a proper arbiter in personal struggles, since it does not have any coercive power and is in general not much interested in individual needs. The American law and police system are too different from what the peasant considers proper justice to become identified in his eyes with social order; they stand usually for a power which is often incomprehensible in its impersonal, institutional character and seems arbitrary in its applications from case to case. The Polish peasant likes to appeal to law as an instrument of fight and would very frequently do so during the first period of his stay in this country if he understood the institutions. But often by the time he begins to be able to utilize these institutions he has already forgotten the tradition of going to law in personal struggles and become accustomed to the idea of self-redress.

The Polish peasant is not and cannot be exactly the same kind of man as the native American, for his character has been molded by his social milieu and his social milieu has a set of traditions, an organization, and a form and standard of living very different in their concrete complexity from those which are familiar to the American reader. Anyone whose attitudes have evolved under the influence of the rapidly changing American life, which is full of new experiences, anyone trained to look toward unfamiliar emergencies and to meet them by his own initiative, who is accustomed and ready to be influenced in behavior as much, or more, by the indirect stimulation of the written or printed word as by direct human contact, and anyone for whom the impersonal political, legal, social, and economic institutions, with their general and abstract methods of dealing with human life are as real in their practical significance as immediately responsive personalities can neither understand the Polish peasant in Poland nor deal with him as immigrant in this country unless he realizes the full meaning of the following facts.

First, the peasant was adapted to the life of a permanent agricultural community, settled for many hundreds of years in the same locality and changing so slowly that each generation adapted itself to the changes with very little effort or abstract reflection. Secondly, the peasant was not accustomed to expect unfamiliar happenings in the course of his life within his community, and if they came he relied upon his group, which not only gave him assistance, when necessary, in accordance with the principle of solidarity, but helped him regain his mental balance and recover the feeling that life in general was normal in spite of the unexpected disturbance. Further, the peasant drew all his social stimulations, checks, and suggestions from direct social contact with his milieu, and the steadiness and efficiency of his life organization depended on the continuity of his social intercourse with his own group. Finally, he was until quite recently a member of a politically and culturally passive class and did not participate consciously, even in the slightest

measure, in any of the impersonal institutions that ever existed in his country.

In view of all this it is not strange that in the different conditions which he finds in this country he becomes more or less disorganized. In fact it is surprising that there is yet so much normal life left and that as time goes on constructive forces assert themselves increasingly in Polish-American communities. This is due entirely and exclusively to the social spirit of the immigrant, to his tendency to form groups, to his traditional ability for social organization. This ability is put here to a more severe test than ever before. Scattered and isolated within a practically unknown, usually indifferent, often contemptuous, sometimes even hostile society, in poor and insecure economic conditions, with very insufficient leadership, and a partly pretentious, selfish, nationalistic . . . formulation of ideals by this leadership, these small groups of people, whose higher interests were indissolubly bound up with their old milieu and who, separated from this milieu, have lost the only real foundation of their cultural life, have already almost succeeded in uniting themselves into one cultural body and in creating institutions which are indubitably factors of progress. These institutions have not prevented a rapid demoralization of those who remain outside of their influence, for the new system is neither as rich nor as efficient in controlling the individual as was the old organization, doomed to decay in the new conditions, but this task is beyond the powers of Polish-American society as isolated from American society.

Even if the Polish-American society should maintain in general that separation which its leaders have wished, the cultural level of a *Polonia Americana* would always remain lower than that of American society, since its best men are and always will be attracted by the wider and richer field of American civilization. But as to the Polish-American institutions already created, their destruction would mean the removal of the only barrier which now stands between the mass of Polish immigrants and complete wildness. The only method which can check demoralization and make of the immigrants—and particularly of their descendants—valuable and culturally productive members of the American society, and imperceptibly and without violence lead to their real Americanization is to supplement the existing Polish-American institutions by others—many others—built on a similar foundation but in closer contact with American society.

It must be always remembered that very little can be achieved by dealing with the immigrant sporadically and individually by the case method. The Polish immigrant is an essentially social being—not "man," not "woman," not "child," in the abstract, but a group member, to be dealt with *in groups*. The only question is how to form groups, and mixed groups including a large percentage of native Americans, with really important productive purposes. There is the enormous, almost untouched field of economic cooperation. A countrywide net of thousands, hundreds of thousands of small cooperative associations, with the active participation of various nationalities, coming together on a basis of real equality and united by serious common aims would do incomparably more for economic self-dependence, for the prevention of demoralization, for the development of active solidarity, and for a genuine Americanization of the immigrant than anything that has ever been done to achieve these aims. It would, besides, contribute in a measure to the solution of many of the most difficult problems which American society itself is trying to solve at this moment.

The prevalent general social unrest and demoralization is due to the decay of the primary group organization, which gave the individual a sense of responsibility and security because he *belonged to something*. This system has given way partly to the forces making for individual efficiency, and we have developed nothing to take its place—no organization which would restore the sense of social responsibility without limiting the efficiency of the individual. This new form is apparently destined to be the cooperative society, and all immigrant groups, among them perhaps preeminently the Poles, bring to this country precisely the attitudes upon which cooperative enterprises can be built.

Louis Wirth (1897-1952) was born in rural Germany. In 1911, he and his sister migrated to live with family in Omaha, Nebraska. His higher education was at the University of Chicago where, in 1925 he earned his PhD in Sociology. His thesis advisor was Robert Park, whom he joined as a faculty colleague at Chicago in 1931. Wirth, like many of the Chicago School sociologists in that era, wrote influentially on urban life, the city, and ethnic differences. The selection from *The Ghetto* is at once a social history of ghettos through history

and a particularly acute commentary on the history and experience of Jewish people in urban ghettos.

The Significance of the Jewish Ghetto [*]
Louis Wirth (1928)

The ghetto is a chapter in the history of the Jews and of Western civilization worth the telling for its own sake. But the ghetto has a much wider significance which makes it of interest to the student of human nature and society. What we find in the ghetto is essentially the same phenomenon that we see in the social life of other minority groups who live side by side with one another, or, as often is the case, live side by side without one another. Whether it be the treatment of the Czechs in the Austrian Empire of the Hapsburgs, or Fiume in the Italian Irredenta, or the British in India, or the whites in the cities of China, or the Chinese in San Francisco, fundamentally the problem is the same, because the human nature aspects of the situations are akin to those of the ghetto.

The relations between the two groups in such instances are usually relations of externality. Problems are settled by rules and laws, not by personal contact and intimate discussion. It is because the contacts between the larger and the smaller, between the dominant and the subordinate groups, are confined to mere externals that they are able to live so close to each other at all. In such cases human groups manage to live side by side, much like plants and animals, in what is known as symbiosis. The economy that arises persists without consciousness being at all involved. But among human beings consciousness and feelings will arise, and two groups can occupy a given area without losing their separate identity because each side is permitted to live its own inner life, and each somehow fears the other or idealizes the other. This relationship has been properly described as accommodation, to distinguish it from the assimilation that takes place when two people succeed in getting under each other's skins, so to speak, and come to share each other's inner life and thus become one.

The Jews drift into the ghetto, as has already been pointed out, for the same reasons that the Italians live in Little Sicily, the Negroes in the black belt, and the Chinese in Chinatowns. The various areas that compose the urban community attract the type of population whose economic status and cultural tradition is more nearly adapted to the physical and social characteristics to be found in each. As each new increment is added to the population it does not at random locate itself just anywhere, but it brings about a resifting of the whole mass of human beings, resulting finally in the anchoring of each to a milieu that, if not most desirable, is at any rate least undesirable.

What is important in this connection is, not where each shall locate, however, but the fact that each seems to find its own separate location without the apparent design of any one. Once in the area, each group tends to reproduce the culture to which it was accustomed in its old habitat as nearly as the new conditions will permit. It is this tendency which is responsible for the abrupt transition in local atmosphere as we sometimes pass from one street to another in the patchwork of little ghettos that constitutes the great immigrant quarters of our large cities.

Unlike the ghettos of old, these new ghettos do not need a wall or gates to keep the various species of man apart. Each seeks his own habitat much like the plants and animals in the world of nature; each has its own kind of food, of family life, and of amusement.

The physical distance that separates these immigrant areas from that of the natives is at the same time a measure of the social distance between them and a means by which this social distance can be maintained. This does not so much imply mutual hostility as it implies and makes possible mutual tolerance. These segregated areas make it possible for the immigrants to avoid the ancient dictum, "When in Rome, do as the Romans do," and permits them to be themselves. But the price that is paid for this freedom and relaxation is the loss of intimate contact with the other group. Here and there an individual bridges the gulf and does fraternize with the stranger, but he does so at the risk of excommunication from his own group, without the assurance of a welcome reception in the other. And yet it is the occasional adventurer into the camp of the enemy or the stranger who is finally the agent bringing about the fusion of the two.

The ghetto illustrates another phenomenon in local community life, a phenomenon which underlies also the segregation of vice areas, of bright light centers, of bohemias and hobohemias in modern cities. If we compare the medieval town with the modern urban community we find that the two structures have something fundamental in common, namely, the segregation of the population into distinct classes and vocational groups. This process is essentially a process of competition. Basically it is akin to the competitive co-operation that underlies the plant community. It differs from the plant community in that human beings are more mobile, and through locomotion can seek those areas in which they can most satisfactorily gratify their fundamental interests and wishes.

Just as there was a natural ghetto, a voluntary ghetto, before the ghetto was decreed by law, so vice areas existed before police regulations drove the prostitutes into restricted zones, and just so business centers arose before city planners and zoning ordinances took cognizance of these specializations in the urban economy. And as the ghetto persists long after it has been abolished by law, so the red light district goes on long after a righteously indignant populace assuages its conscience with the conviction that vice has been driven out of town.

This specialization of interests and cultural types is at bottom a phase of the elementary process of the division of labor. Each area in the city is suited for some one function better than for any other. Land values, rentals, accessibility, and the attitude of its inhabitants and owners determine, in the last analysis, what type of area it shall become. The more fundamental of these factors is probably that of economic values, for the sentiments of the people tend ultimately to bow before this criterion which is the expression of the competitive process. Ultimately a city plan or any artificial regulation will be successful only to the extent to which it takes account of these factors and to the extent to which it reckons with the fact that these areas are the product of growth rather than of deliberate design.

Not only does each of these areas have its own external characteristics in the form of buildings, institutions, and general appearance, but each also has its own moral code. A population seeks an area in which it is tolerated and in which the wishes of its members can be gratified with the least amount of interference. The Bohemian drifts to the Latin Quarter because there he can be himself, express himself with the minimum of restraint. The hobo seeks the main stem, not only because its institutions and standards of living are suited to his personal requirements, but also because here he finds himself and makes his home. The immigrant drifts to the slum without even being aware of the fact that he lives in a slum.

The ghetto furthermore demonstrates the extent to which a local culture is a matter of geographical location. The anthropologists have made us familiar with the concept of the culture area by which they refer to the distribution in space of more or less integrated complexes of material or immaterial cultural traits. The persistence of traditional Jewish life seems to depend upon the favorable soil of the ghetto, upon exclusion from the disintegrating and corroding influences of other cultural areas. Once the individual is removed from the soil to which he and his institutions have been attached, he is exposed to the possibility of losing his character and disappearing as a distinct type. His institutions, too, can ill afford the strain that comes with migration to another locality. That is why the synagogue in the ghetto retains its importance in Jewish communal life which it promptly loses as soon as it migrates to *Deutschland*. Each of these areas has its own distinct types of dominant personalities which change as the local life of the group undergoes transformation. Where the Jew lives is as good an index as any other as to the kind of Jew he is.

If we knew the full life-history of a single individual in his social setting, we would probably know most of what is worth knowing about social life and human nature. If we knew the full story of the ghetto we would have a laboratory specimen for the sociologist that embodies all the concepts and the processes of his professional vocabulary. The institution of the ghetto is not only the record of a historical people; it is a manifestation of human nature and a specific social order.

The ghetto has been viewed in this study primarily as an effect of isolation. The isolation of the Jews has not been merely of a physical sort, but it has been pre-eminently of a less tangible and less visible character. It has been the type of isolation produced by absence of intercommunication through difference in language, customs, sentiments, traditions, and social forms. The ghetto as we have viewed it is not so much a physical fact as it is a state of mind. The isolation of the Jew has been akin to the type of isolation of the person who feels lonely though in the midst of a crowd.

There was a time when students of human nature assumed "that strikingly different customs have been produced by peoples with differing instincts, or with instincts of different degrees of strength or intensity." The Jews, it has been argued by some, are living a

separate secluded existence because they are haughty and clannish, and not a sociable people. They lack in the instinct of gregariousness. Fortunately, in the case of the Jews we have a long written history, which leads us to believe that there was a time, at least, when they were not clannish, when they were a people of many contacts. The attempt that so many Jews of today are making to break into the gentile world seems to be another instance to the contrary. It is probably more correct to say that the Jews became exclusive because at a certain period of their history they were excluded. Another answer would be that they were separate because they had a different cultural life from that of their neighbors.

If students of human nature have learned to be cautious about any one thing more than another in recent years, it is to be cautious about attributing the character of a people and of an individual to human nature without a scrutiny of the historical experiences of the group or the individual. It may be a platitude to say that the Jews are what their history has made them, but it is a platitude worth reiterating.

The Jews owe their survival as a separate and distinct ethnic group to their social isolation. The continuity of their particular social life and their survival as a social type depends primarily upon the continuance of this isolation, just as the distinct character of any people depends upon its exclusion from contacts with other peoples. What made the career of the Jews in European ghettos so adventurous and stormy was not the fact that they were so different from the rest of the population, but that they were so much alike. "Where racial characteristics are marked, and where the social distances that separate the races are great, it sometimes happens that the individual is not discovered at all. Under these circumstances, as Shaler points out, the stranger remains strange, a representative of his race, but not a neighbor." As the Jew leaves the ghetto his type undergoes profound transformation. He changes, not merely his dress, his facial expression, and his bearing, but he generally completely transforms his consciousness: "In the vast tide of cosmopolitan life the Jewish racial type does not so much disappear as become invisible. When he is no longer seen, anti-Semitism declines. For race prejudice is a function of visibility. The races of high visibility, to speak in naval parlance, are the natural and inevitable objects of race prejudice." In quite another way the ghetto is able to throw light on a subtle feature of isolation. The ghetto is a cultural community that expresses a common heritage, a store of common traditions and sentiments. The attitudes and sentiments in the consciousness of the Jew, and the institutions and practices in which they find their external expression, have been centered around the religious life of that people. The Jewish culture, to speak in anthropological terms, represents a synagogue complex. The Jewish community of today, like that of the medieval ghetto period, has much in common with the modern sect. "Free intercourse of opposing parties is always a menace to their morale.....The solidarity of the group, like the integrity of the individual, implies a measure at least of isolation from other groups and persons as a necessary condition of its existence." Within the sect, as the ghetto clearly shows, life becomes increasingly a matter of form. Finally the form has to be preserved at all costs, though its content has long ago evaporated.

When the ghetto walls do finally crumble, at least sufficiently to permit the escape of some of the inmates, those that get a taste of the life in the freer world outside and are lured by its color are likely to be torn by the conflicting feeling that comes to hybrids generally, physical as well as social. On the one hand there is the strange and fascinating world of man; on the other, the restricted sectarianism of a little group into which he happened to be born, of neither of which he is fully a member. He oscillates between the two until a decisive incident either throws him headlong into the activities of the outer world, where he forgets his personality and metamorphoses into a new being, or else a rebuff sends him bounding into his old familiar primary group, where life, though puny in scale; is rich and deep and warm.

This same problem is not only encountered by the individuals in their own lifetimes, but it is the problem of succeeding generations in any immigrant group. This accounts for the fact that the immigrant himself scarcely ever is fully assimilated into the new group in his own lifetime, and at the same time is seldom a criminal, but that his children do become assimilated and are at the same time giving rise to problems of disorganization and crime. The ghetto shows that what matters most in social life is not so much the "hard" facts of material existence and external forms as the subtle sentiments, the dreams and the ideals of a people.

What makes the Jewish community—composed, as it is in our metropolitan centers in America, of so many heterogeneous elements—a community is its ability to act corporately. It has a common set of attitudes and values based upon common traditions, similar experiences, and common problems. In spite of its geographical separateness it is welded into a community because of conflict and pressure from without and collective action within. The Jewish community is a cultural community. It is as near an approach to communal life as the modern city has to offer.

The anomalous status of the Jew is based upon the solidarity of his communal life and his amazing ability to act collectively. It is his historical isolation—it is the ghetto, voluntary or compulsory, medieval or modern, which not only accounts for his character, but for the fantastic conception that others have of him. The history of the Jews and the history of the ghetto are in essence a history of migrations. In the course of these migrations the Jews have developed connections which have crystallized into what seems to be an international organization. As a result the Jew appears to be not merely ubiquitous but something of a mystery. If, therefore, we have not found a solution to the so-called "Jewish problem," is it not possible that in dealing with the ghetto as a natural phenomenon, without offering an apology and without presenting a program, we have made that problem more intelligible?

Walter Benjamin (1892–1940) was one of the more mythical figures among those associated with the Frankfurt School. This is due, in part, to the acknowledged brilliance of his writings, which have enjoyed a renewed popularity among literary theorists in recent years. In addition, he died a martyr. In 1938, Benjamin refused Adorno's urging to join other members of the Frankfurt School in New York. He was committed to pursuing an intellectual and political course in Europe (Paris at the time) and was ambivalent about life in the United States. He was arrested by the collaborationist French government, but was later released from a Nazi internment camp through an international effort on his behalf. After escaping from France across the Spanish border in 1940, he became emotionally overwhelmed by a combination of ill health, the strong likelihood of arrest and repatriation into Nazi hands, and the impact of the tragedy that had befallen Europe. He committed suicide at age forty-eight. Although the selection "Art, War, and Fascism" (1936) is short, it reveals Benjamin's incisive mind at work analyzing the aesthetic perversions of fascism.

Art in an Age of Mechanical Reproduction: War and Fascism*

Walter Benjamin (1936)

Around 1900 technical reproduction had reached a standard that not only permitted it to reproduce all transmitted works of art and thus to cause the most profound change in their impact upon the public; it also had captured a place of its own among the artistic processes. For the study of this standard nothing is more revealing than the nature of the repercussions that these two different manifestations—the reproduction of works of art and the art of the film—have had on art in its traditional form.

Even the most perfect reproduction of a work of art is lacking in one element: its presence in time and space, its unique existence at the place where it happens to be. This unique existence of the work of art determined the history to which it was subject throughout the time of its existence. This includes the changes which it may have suffered in physical condition over the years as well as the various changes in its ownership. The traces of the first can be revealed only by chemical or physical analyses which it is impossible to perform on a reproduction; changes of ownership are subject to a tradition which must be traced from the situation of the original.

The presence of the original is the prerequisite to the concept of authenticity. Chemical analyses of the patina of a bronze can help to establish this, as does the proof that a given manuscript of the Middle Ages stems from an archive of the fifteenth century. The whole sphere of authenticity is outside technical—and, of course, not only technical—reproducibility. Confronted with its manual reproduction, which was usually branded as a forgery, the original preserved all its authority; not so vis-à-vis technical reproduction. The reason is twofold. First, process reproduction is more independent of the original than manual reproduction. For example, in photography, process reproduction can bring out those aspects of the original that are unattainable to the naked eye yet accessible to the lens, which is adjustable and chooses its angle at will. And photographic

reproduction, with the aid of certain processes, such as enlargement or slow motion, can capture images which escape natural vision. Secondly, technical reproduction can put the copy of the original into situations which would be out of reach for the original itself. Above all, it enables the original to meet the beholder halfway, be it in the form of a photograph or a phonograph record. The cathedral leaves its locale to be received in the studio of a lover of art; the choral production, performed in an auditorium or in the open air, resounds in the drawing room.

The situations into which the product of mechanical reproduction can be brought may not touch the actual work of art, yet the quality of its presence is always depreciated. This holds not only for the art work but also, for instance, for a landscape which passes in review before the spectator in a movie. In the case of the art object, a most sensitive nucleus—namely, its authenticity—is interfered with whereas no natural object is vulnerable on that score. The authenticity of a thing is the essence of all that is transmissible from its beginning, ranging from its substantive duration to its testimony to the history which it has experienced. Since the historical testimony rests on the authenticity, the former, too, is jeopardized by reproduction when substantive duration ceases to matter. And what is really jeopardized when the historical testimony is affected is the authority of the object….

The growing proletarianization of modern man and the increasing formation of masses are two aspects of the same process. Fascism attempts to organize the newly created proletarian masses without affecting the property structure which the masses strive to eliminate. Fascism sees its salvation in giving these masses not their right, but instead a chance to express themselves. The masses have a right to change property relations; Fascism seeks to give them an expression while preserving property. The logical result of Fascism is the introduction of aesthetics into political life. The violation of the masses, whom Fascism, with its Führer cult, forces to their knees, has its counterpart in the violation of an apparatus which is pressed into the production of ritual values.

All efforts to render politics aesthetic culminate in one thing: war. War and war only can set a goal for mass movements on the largest scale while respecting the traditional property system. This is the political formula for the situation. The technological formula may be stated as follows: Only war makes it possible to mobilize all of today's technical resources while maintaining the property system. It goes without saying that the Fascist apotheosis of war does not employ such arguments. Still, Marinetti says in his manifesto on the Ethiopian colonial war:

"For twenty-seven years we Futurists have rebelled against the branding of war as anti-aesthetic ... Accordingly we state: ... War is beautiful because it establishes man's dominion over the subjugated machinery by means of gas masks, terrifying megaphones, flame throwers, and small tanks. War is beautiful because it initiates the dreamt-of metalization of the human body. War is beautiful because it enriches a flowering meadow with the fiery orchids of machine guns. War is beautiful because it combines the gunfire, the cannonades, the cease-fire, the scents, and the stench of putrefaction into a symphony. War is beautiful because it creates new architecture, like that of the big tanks, the geometrical formation flights, the smoke spirals from burning villages, and many others ... Poets and artists of Futurism! ... remember these principles of an aesthetics of war so that your struggle for a new literature and a new graphic art ... may be illumined by them!"

This manifesto has the virtue of clarity. Its formulations deserve to be accepted by dialecticians. To the latter, the aesthetics of today's war appears as follows: If the natural utilization of productive forces is impeded by the property system, the increase in technical devices, in speed, and in the sources of energy will press for an unnatural utilization, and this is found in war. The destructiveness of war furnishes proof that society has not been mature enough to incorporate technology as its organ, that technology has not been sufficiently developed to cope with the elemental forces of society. The horrible features of imperialistic warfare are attributable to the discrepancy between the tremendous means of production and their inadequate utilization in the process of production—in other words, to unemployment and the lack of markets. Imperialistic war is a rebellion of technology which collects, in the form of "human material," the claims to which society has denied its natural material. Instead of draining rivers, society directs a human stream into a bed of trenches; instead of dropping seeds from airplanes, it drops incendiary bombs over cities; and through gas warfare the aura is abolished in a new way.

"Fiat ars—pereat mundus", says Fascism, and, as Marinetti admits, expects war to supply the artistic gratification of a sense perception that has been changed by technology. This is evidently the consummation of "l'art pour l'art. Mankind, which in Homer's time was an object of contemplation for the Olympian gods, now is one for itself. Its self-alienation has reached such a degree that it can experience its own destruction as an aesthetic pleasure of the first order. This is the situation of politics which Fascism is rendering aesthetic. Communism responds by politicizing art.

Virginia Woolf (1882–1941), the English novelist, biographer, and literary critic, is one of the most important writers of the twentieth century. Her fiction includes *The Voyage Out* (1915), *Mrs. Dalloway* (1925), and *To the Lighthouse* (1927). "A Room of One's Own" (1929) is possibly her most famous essay. As the text indicates, it began as a series of lectures on women and fiction. This essay became one of the most widely used points of reference for postwar feminism, particularly among academic and literary feminists who had to balance the demands of family and work with those of the creative life. Woolf's delicately powerful, though fictional, description of a woman's experience on the manicured lawns of Oxbridge, like the female protagonist's plight in Charlotte Gilman's "The Yellow Wallpaper" (1892), is a fictionalized but powerful attack on the not-so-subtle forces of patriarchal culture. It is theory that requires no further explanation.

A Room of One's Own*
Virginia Woolf (1929)

But, you may say, we asked you to speak about women and fiction—what has that got to do with a room of one's own? I will try to explain. When you asked me to speak about women and fiction I sat down on the banks of a river and began to wonder what the words meant. They might mean simply a few remarks about Fanny Burney; a few more about Jane Austen; a tribute to the Brontës and a sketch of Haworth Parsonage under snow; some witticisms if possible about Miss Mitford; a respectful allusion to George Eliot; a reference to Mrs. Gaskell and one would have done. But at second sight the words seemed not so simple. The title women and fiction might mean, and you may have meant it to mean, women and what they are like; or it might mean women and the fiction that they write; or it might mean women and the fiction that is written about them; or it might mean that somehow all three are inextricably mixed together and you want me to consider them in that light. But when I began to consider the subject in this last way, which seemed the most interesting, I soon saw that it had one fatal drawback. I should never be able to come to a conclusion. I should never be able to fulfil what is, I understand, the first duty of a lecturer—to hand you after an hour's discourse a nugget of pure truth to wrap up between the pages of your notebooks and keep on the mantel-piece for ever. All I could do was to offer you an opinion upon one minor point—a woman must have money and a room of her own if she is to write fiction; and that, as you will see, leaves the great problem of the true nature of woman and the true nature of fiction unsolved. I have shirked the duty of coming to a conclusion upon these two questions—women and fiction remain, so far as I am concerned, unsolved problems. But in order to make some amends I am going to do what I can to show you how I arrived at this opinion about the room and the money. I am going to develop in your presence as fully and freely as I can the train of thought which led me to think this. Perhaps if I lay bare the ideas, the prejudices, that lie behind this statement you will find that they have some bearing upon women and some upon fiction. At any rate, when a subject is highly controversial—and any question about sex is that—one cannot hope to tell the truth. One can only show how one came to hold whatever opinion one does hold. One can only give one's audience the chance of drawing their own conclusions as they observe the limitations, the prejudices, the idiosyncrasies of the speaker. Fiction here is likely to contain more truth than fact. Therefore I propose, making use of all the liberties and licences of a novelist, to tell you the story of the two days that preceded my coming here—how, bowed down by the weight of the subject which you have laid upon my shoulders, I pondered it, and made it work in and out of my daily life. I need not say that what I am about to describe has no existence; Oxbridge is an invention; so is Fernham; "I" is only a convenient term for somebody who has no real being. Lies will flow from my lips, but there may perhaps be some truth mixed up with them; it is for you to seek out this truth and to decide whether any part of it is worth keeping. If not, you will of course throw the whole of it into the wastepaper basket and forget all about it.

Here then was I (call me Mary Beton, Mary Seton, Mary Carmichael or by any name you please—it is not a matter of any importance) sitting on the banks of a river a week or two ago in fine October weather, lost in thought. That collar I have spoken of, women and fiction, the need of coming to some conclusion on a subject that raises all sorts of prejudices and passions, bowed my head to the ground. To the right and left bushes of some sort, golden and crimson, glowed with the colour, even it seemed burnt with the heat, of fire. On the further bank the willows wept in perpetual lamentation, their hair about their shoulders. The river reflected whatever it chose of sky and bridge and burning tree, and when the undergraduate had oared his boat through the reflections they closed again, completely, as if he had never been. There one might have sat the clock round lost in thought. Thought—to call it by a prouder name than it deserved—had let its line down into the stream. It swayed, minute after minute, hither and thither among the reflections and the weeds, letting the water lift it and sink it, until—you know the little tug—the sudden conglomeration of an idea at the end of one's line: and then the cautious hauling of it in, and the careful laying of it out? Alas, laid on the grass how small, how insignificant this thought of mine looked; the sort of fish that a good fisherman puts back into the water so that it may grow fatter and be one day worth cooking and eating. I will not trouble you with that thought now, though if you look carefully you may find it for yourselves in the course of what I am going to say.

But however small it was, it had, nevertheless, the mysterious property of its kind—put back into the mind, it became at once very exciting, and important; and as it darted and sank, and flashed hither and thither, set up such a wash and tumult of ideas that it was impossible to sit still. It was thus that I found myself walking with extreme rapidity across a grass plot. Instantly a man's figure rose to intercept me. Nor did I at first understand that the gesticulations of a curious-looking object, in a cut-away coat and evening shirt, were aimed at me. His face expressed horror and indignation. Instinct rather than reason came to my help; he was a Beadle; I was a woman. Thus was the turf; there was the path. Only the Fellows and Scholars are allowed here; the gravel is the place for me. Such thoughts were the work of a moment. As I regained the path the arms of the Beadle sank, his face assumed its usual repose, and though turf is better walking than gravel, no very great harm was done. The only charge I could bring against the Fellows and Scholars of whatever the college might happen to be was that in protection of their turf, which has been rolled for 300 years in succession, they had sent my little fish into hiding....

Antonio Gramsci (1891–1937) was born in Sardinia. He studied at the University of Turin, where he became active in the Italian Socialist Party. By 1924 he became a founder and leader of the Italian Communist Party. Gramsci's literary, journalistic, and political activities eventually led to his arrest in 1926. He spent most of the balance of his life in prison, where he wrote his famous *Prison Notebooks*, from which the following selections are taken. Gramsci greatly broadened Marxist thinking on the role of intellectuals in the political process and the social hegemony, both of which would influence later social and cultural theory.

Intellectuals and Hegemony*

Antonio Gramsci (1929–1936)

[handwritten: leadership or predominant influence exercised by one over another]

All men are intellectuals, one could therefore say: but not all men have in society the function of intellectuals.**

When one distinguishes between intellectuals and non-intellectuals, one is referring in reality only to the immediate social function of the professional category of the intellectuals, that is, one has in mind the direction in which their specific professional activity is weighted, whether towards intellectual elaboration or towards muscular-nervous effort. This means that, although one can speak of intellectuals, one cannot speak of non-intellectuals, because non-intellectuals do not exist. But even the relationship between efforts of intellectual-cerebral elaboration and muscular-nervous effort is not always the same, so that there are varying degrees of specific intellectual activity. There is no human activity from which every form of intellectual participation can be excluded: *homo faber* cannot be separated from *homo sapiens*. Each man, finally, outside his professional activity, carries on some form of intellectual activity, that is, he is a "philosopher," an artist, a man of taste, he participates in a particular conception of the world, has a conscious line of moral conduct, and therefore contributes to sustain a conception of the world or to modify it, that is, to bring into being new modes of thought. . . .

It is worth noting that the elaboration of intellectual strata in concrete reality does not take place on the terrain of abstract democracy but in accordance with very concrete traditional historical processes. Strata have grown up which traditionally "produce" intellectuals and these strata coincide with those which have specialised in "saving," i.e. the petty and middle landed bourgeoisie and certain strata of the petty and middle urban bourgeoisie. The varying distribution of different types of school (classical and professional) over the "economic" territory and the varying aspirations of different categories within these strata determine, or give form to, the production of various branches of intellectual specialisation. Thus in Italy the rural bourgeoisie produces in particular state functionaries and professional people, whereas the urban bourgeoisie produces technicians for industry. Consequently it is largely northern Italy which produces technicians and the South which produces functionaries and professional men.

The relationship between the intellectuals and the world of production is not as direct as it is with the fundamental social groups but is, in varying degrees, "mediated" by the whole fabric of society and by the complex of superstructures, of which the intellectuals are, precisely, the "functionaries." It should be possible both to measure the "organic quality" [*organicità*] of the various intellectual strata and their degree of connection with a fundamental social group, and to establish a gradation of their functions and of the superstructures from the bottom to the top (from the structural base upwards). What we can do,

---

* Selections from the *Prison Notebooks of Antonio Gramsci*, Q Hoare and G Nowell-Smith (eds), Lawrence and Wishart, London 1971.

** Thus, because it can happen that everyone at some time fries a couple of eggs or sews up a tear in a jacket, we do not necessarily say that everyone is a cook or a tailor.

for the moment, is to fix two major superstructural "levels": the one that can be called "civil society," that is the ensemble of organisms commonly called "private," and that of "political society" or "the State." These two levels correspond on the one hand to the function of "hegemony" which the dominant group exercises throughout society and on the other hand to that of "direct domination" or command exercised through the State and "juridical" government. The functions in question are precisely organisational and connective. The intellectuals are the dominant group's "deputies" exercising the subaltern functions of social hegemony and political government. . . .

The philosophy of praxis does not tend to leave the "simple" in their primitive philosophy of common sense, but rather to lead them to a higher conception of life. If it affirms the need for contact between intellectuals and the simple, it is not in order to restrict scientific activity and preserve unity at the low level of the masses, but precisely in order to construct an intellectual moral bloc which can make politically possible the intellectual progress of the mass and not only of small intellectual groups.

The active man-in-the-mass has a practical activity, but has no clear theoretical consciousness of his practical activity, which nonetheless involves understanding the world in so far as it transforms it. His theoretical consciousness can indeed be historically in opposition to his activity. One might also say that he has two theoretical consciousnesses (or one contradictory consciousness): one which is implicit in his activity and which in reality unites him with all his fellow-workers in the practical transformation of the real world; and one, superficially explicit or verbal, which he has inherited from the past and uncritically absorbed. But this verbal conception is not without consequences. It holds together a specific social group, it influences moral conduct and the direction of will, with varying efficacity but often powerfully enough to produce a situation in which the contradictory state of consciousness does not permit of any action, any decision or any choice, and produces a condition of moral and political passivity. Critical understanding of self takes place therefore through a struggle of political "hegemonies" and of opposing directions, first in the ethical field and then in that of politics proper, in order to arrive at the working out at a higher level of one's own conception of reality. Consciousness of being part of a particular hegemonic force (that is to say, political consciousness) is the first stage towards a further progressive self-consciousness in which theory and practice will finally be one. Thus the unity of theory and practice is not just a matter of mechanical fact, but a part of the historical process, whose elementary and primitive phase is to be found in the sense of being "different" and "apart," in an instinctive feeling of independence, and which progresses to the level of real possession of a single and coherent conception of the world. This is why it must be stressed that the political development of the concept of hegemony represents a great philosophical advance as well as a politico-practical one. For it necessarily supposes an intellectual unity and an ethic in conformity with a conception of reality that has gone beyond common sense and has become, if only within narrow limits, a critical conception.

However, in the most recent developments of the philosophy of praxis the exploration and refinement of the concept of the unity of theory and practice is still only at an early stage. There still remain residues of mechanicism, since people speak about theory as a "complement" or an "accessory" of practice, or as the handmaid of practice. It would seem right for this question too to be considered historically, as an aspect of the political question of the intellectuals. Critical self-consciousness means, historically and politically, the creation of an *élite* of intellectuals. A human mass does not "distinguish" itself, does not become independent in its own right without, in the widest sense, organising itself; and there is no organisation without intellectuals, that is without organisers and leaders, in other words, without the theoretical aspect of the theory-practice nexus being distinguished concretely by the existence of a group of people "specialised" in conceptual and philosophical elaboration of ideas. But the process of creating intellectuals is long, difficult, full of contradictions, advances and retreats, dispersals and regroupings, in which the loyalty of the masses is often sorely tried.

Mao Tse-tung [Zedong] (1893–1976) was a founding leader of the Chinese Communist Party. After completing his formal studies in 1918 at the First Teachers' Training School in Changsha, Mao began a long career as writer, teacher, journalist, political organizer, and politician. He was one of the original twelve delegates to the First Congress of the Chinese Communist Party. In 1927, he led the peasant uprising in Hunan, after which he retreated into hiding. He then led the famous "long march" to Shensi Province. Thus began his role in the long Chinese revolution that culminated in the defeat of Chiang Kai-shek in 1949. After that, Mao was chairman of the People's Republic until his death in 1976. "Identity, Struggle, Contradiction" (1937) reveals Mao the theorist at his most brilliant. Here, he joins a sharp philosophical rendering of Marxist-Leninist philosophy with his direct knowledge of China's revolutionary situation. Perhaps more than anyone, including Lenin, Mao managed to unite theory and political practice into a coherent philosophy of life. In the selection, one can see the fresh meaning given to Marx's idea of contradiction in reference to China's place in the world conflicts of the interwar period.

Identity, Struggle, Contradiction*
Mao Tse-tung (1937)

…. The contradictory aspects in every process exclude each other, struggle with each other and are opposed to each other. Such contradictory aspects are contained without exception in the processes of all things in the world and in human thought. A simple process has only one pair of opposites, while a complex process has more than one pair. Various pairs of opposites are in turn opposed to one another. In this way all things in the objective world and human thought are formed and impelled to move.

But if this is so, there is an utter lack of identity, or unity. How then can we speak of identity or unity?

The reason is that a contradictory aspect cannot exist in isolation. Without the other aspect which is opposed to it, each aspect loses the condition of its existence. Just imagine, can any of the aspects of contradictory things or of contradictory concepts in the human mind exist independently? Without life, there would be no death; without death, there would also be no life. Without "above", there would be no "below"; without "below", there would also be no "above". Without misfortune, there would be no good fortune; without good fortune, there would also be no misfortune. Without facility, there would be no difficulty; without difficulty, there would also be no facility. Without landlords, there would be no

tenant-peasants; without tenant-peasants, there would also be no landlords. Without the bourgeoisie, there would be no proletariat; without a proletariat, there would also be no bourgeoisie. Without imperialist oppression of the nations, there would be no colonies and semi-colonies; without colonies and semi-colonies, there would also be no imperialist oppression of the nations. All opposite elements are like this: because of certain conditions, they are on the one hand opposed to each other and on the other hand they are interconnected, interpenetrating, interpermeating and interdependent; this character is called identity. All contradictory aspects, because of certain conditions, are characterised by non-identity, hence they are spoken of as contradictory. But they are also characterised by identity, hence they are interconnected. When Lenin says that dialectics studies "how the opposites can be and how they become identical", he is referring to such a state of affairs. How can they be identical? Because of the condition of mutual sustenance of each other's existence. This is the first meaning of identity.

But is it enough to say merely that the contradictory aspects mutually sustain each other's existence, that is, there is identity between them and consequently they can coexist in an entity? No, it is not enough. The matter does not end with the interdependence of the two contradictory aspects for their existence; what is more important is the transformation of the contradictory things into each other. That is to say, each of the two contradictory aspects within a thing, because of certain conditions, tends to transform itself into the other, to transfer itself to the opposite position. This is the second meaning of the identity of contradiction.

Why is there also identity? You see, by means of revolution, the proletariat, once the ruled, becomes the ruler, while the bourgeoisie, originally the ruler, becomes the ruled, and is transferred to the position originally occupied by its opposite. This has already taken place in the Soviet Union and will take place throughout the world. I should like to ask: if there were no interconnection and identity of opposites under certain conditions, how could such a change take place?

The Kuomintang, which played a certain positive role at a certain stage in modern Chinese history, has, because of its inherent class nature and the temptations of imperialism (these being the conditions) become since 1927 a counterrevolutionary party; but, because of the intensification of the contradiction between China and Japan and the policy

*Excerpt from "On Contradiction," Anne Fremantle, ed., *Mao Tse-tung: An Anthology of His Writings* (New York: International Publishers, 1971), pp. 234–238.

of the united front of the Communist Party (these being the conditions), it has been compelled to agree to resist Japan. Contradictory things change into one another, hence a certain identity is implied.

The agrarian revolution we have carried out is already and will be such a process in which the land-owning landlord class becomes a class deprived of its land, while the peasants, once deprived of their land, become small holders of land. The haves and the have-nots, gain and loss, are interconnected because of certain conditions; there is identity of the two sides. Under socialism, the system of the peasants' private ownership will in turn become the public ownership of socialist agriculture; this has already taken place in the Soviet Union and will take place throughout the world. Between private property and public property there is a bridge leading from the one to the other, which in philosophy is called identity, or transformation into each other, or interpermeation.

To consolidate the dictatorship of the proletariat or the people's dictatorship is precisely to prepare the conditions for liquidating such a dictatorship and advancing to the higher stage of abolishing all state systems. To establish and develop the Communist Party is precisely to prepare the condition for abolishing the Communist Party and all party systems. To establish the revolutionary army under the leadership of the Communist Party and to carry on the revolutionary war is precisely to prepare the condition for abolishing war for ever. These contradictory things are at the same time complementary.

As everybody knows, war and peace transform themselves into each other. War is transformed into peace; for example, the First World War was transformed into the post-war peace; the civil war in China has now also ceased and internal peace has come about. Peace is transformed into war; for example, the Kuomintang-Communist co-operation of 1927 was transformed into war, and the peaceful world situation today may also be transformed into a Second World War. Why? Because in a class society such contradictory things as war and peace are characterised by identity under certain conditions.

All contradictory things are interconnected, and they not only coexist in an entity under certain conditions, but also transform themselves into each other under certain conditions—this is the whole meaning of the identity of contradictions. . . .

Why can only an egg be transformed into a chicken but not a stone? Why is there identity between war and peace and none between war and a stone? Why can human beings give birth only to human beings but not to anything else? The reason is simply that identity of contradiction exists only under certain necessary conditions. Without certain necessary conditions there can be no identity whatever.

Why is it that in Russia the bourgeois-democratic revolution of February 1917 was directly linked with the proletarian-socialist revolution of October of the same year, while in France the bourgeois revolution was not directly linked with a socialist revolution, and the Paris Commune of 1871 finally ended in failure? Why is it, on the other hand, that the nomadic system in Mongolia and Central Asia has been directly linked with socialism? Why is it that the Chinese revolution can avoid a capitalist future and can be directly linked with socialism without traversing the old historical path of the western countries, without passing through a period of bourgeois dictatorship? The reason is none other than the concrete conditions of the time. When certain necessary conditions are present, certain contradictions arise in the process of development of things and, what is more, these contradictions and all contradictions of this kind depend upon each other for existence and transform themselves into each other; otherwise nothing is possible. . . .

All processes have a beginning and an end; all processes transform themselves into their opposites. The stability of all processes is relative, but the mutability manifested in the transformation of one process into another is absolute.

The movement of all things assumes two forms: the form of relative rest and the form of conspicuous change. Both forms of movement are caused by the struggle of the two contradictory factors contained in a thing itself. When the movement of a thing assumes the first form, it only undergoes a quantitative but not a qualitative change and consequently appears in a state of seeming rest. When the movement of a thing assumes the second form it has already reached a certain culminating point of the quantitative change of the first form, caused the dissolution of the entity, produced a qualitative change, and consequently appears as conspicuous change. Such unity, solidarity, amalgamation, harmony, balance, stalemate, deadlock, rest, stability, equilibrium, coagulation, attraction, as we see in daily life, are all the appearances of things in the state of quantitative change. On the other hand, the dissolution of the entity, the breakdown of such solidarity, amalgamation, harmony, balance, stalemate, deadlock, rest, stability, equilibrium, coagulation and attraction, and the change into their opposite states, are all the appearances of things in the state of qualitative change during the transformation of one process into another. Things are always transforming themselves from the first into the second form, while the struggle within the contradictions exists in both forms and reaches its solution through the second form. We say therefore that the unity of opposites is conditional, temporary and relative, while the struggle of mutually exclusive opposites is absolute.

When we said above that because there is identity between two opposite things, the two can coexist in an entity and can also be transformed into each other, we were referring to conditionality, that is to say, under certain conditions contradictory things can be united and can also be transformed into each other, but without such conditions, they cannot become contradictory, cannot coexist, and cannot transform themselves into one another. It is because the identity of contradiction obtains only under certain conditions that we say identity is conditional, relative. Here we add: the struggle within a contradiction runs throughout a process from beginning to end and causes one process to transform itself into another, and as the struggle within the contradiction is present everywhere, we say the struggle within the contradiction is unconditional, absolute.

Conditional, relative identity, combined with unconditional, absolute struggle, constitutes the movement of opposites in all things.

We Chinese often say, "Things opposed to each other complement each other." That is to say, there is identity of opposites. This remark is dialectical, and runs counter to metaphysics. To be "opposed to each other" means the mutual exclusion or struggle of the two contradictory aspects. To "complement each other" means that under certain conditions the two contradictory aspects become united and achieve identity. Struggle resides precisely in identity; without struggle there can be no identity.

In identity there is struggle, in particularity there is universality, in individual character there is common character. To quote Lenin, "there is an absolute even *within* the relative."

PART THREE

The Golden Moment: 1945–1963

At the end of World War II, no one was left standing—except the United States. Wherever the war had been fought, there was ruin. Germany, England, Russia, Japan, France, Italy, parts of Africa, most of Europe, and much of Asia lay wasted. Their industries were either destroyed or exhausted in the war. Their economies had long since overspent real wealth. Their people were devastated, physically and spiritually. The Soviet Union alone had lost 20 million people, compared to fewer than 300,000 by the United States. Such was the magnitude of loss and confusion, everywhere but in America.

The one power still standing stood taller than before, taller than any other in the modern era. Where the war had crushed others, the USA was lifted. Before the war, the US gross national product had not yet recovered from the collapse of 1929. But in 1945, it had more than doubled pre-Depression levels. After the war, steel production alone was four times greater than during the Depression, while the other steel-producing giants (Japan, Germany, Western Europe) were crippled. By one estimate, at the end of the war, the average American enjoyed an income fifteen times greater than that of any foreigner. The United States produced half or more of the world's steel, oil, and electricity and three-quarters of the automobiles. In production sectors related to the war effort, no rivals existed. The United States possessed wealth of every kind—real capital and income, industrial capacity and know-how, spiritual self-confidence, and intellectual and technical capital developed in the war effort.

If there could be a single symbol of American might in 1945, it might be the bomb. When the United States unleashed the atomic bomb in the summer of 1945, it did more than level Hiroshima and Nagasaki. It signaled that the world had changed definitively. The older powers were lesser. The USA was greater. The political and economic globe was restructured. At that moment, only one nation had succeeded where others had tried. Only the United States was able to invent, produce, and deploy the ultimate weapon. Scientific knowledge, inventive genius, productive capacity, and moral force—no other nation but the United States could then lay claim to such wonderful national strengths—possessed all at once and demonstrated. To those who then admired America, its willingness to kill in such great numbers was, itself, a perverse sign of moral power. In 1945, it could have been said that the United States was the perfect fulfillment of the modern world. Knowledge set free was power. Power unleashed freed the world of war and evil. The bitter horror of those burned to death was, as always, the price of progress. There was only one flaw. The war had taught that it was too late to pretend the destructive side of progress would disappear. Still, millions pretended.

Timeline: 1942–1970

Social Theory		Wider World
	1942	*Yankee Doodle Dandy*, the movie; Bing Crosby records *White Christmas* **1942**
		Robert Oppenheimer leads Manhattan Project to develop atomic bomb **1942**
		Huey Newton born **1942**
Talcott Parsons, *Sex Roles in the American Kinship System* 1943		Broadway musical *Oklahoma;* Elizabeth Taylor in *Lassie Come Home* **1943**
	1945	George Orwell, *The Animal Farm* **1945**
		Karl Popper, *Open Society and Its Enemies* **1945**
Winston Churchill, *Sinews of Peace/The Iron Curtain* 1946		World War II ends **1945**
		Ho Chi Minh declares Vietnam's independence from France **1945**
Simone de Beauvoir, *The Second Sex: Woman as Other* 1949		George Kennan's *Long Telegram: The United States and the Containment of the Soviets* **1946**
		Churchill gives Iron Curtain speech in Missouri **1946**
		John Rockefeller donates land for United Nations in New York City **1946**
		Marlon Brando stars in *Street Car Named Desire* **1947**
		India wins independence from Britain **1947**
		Jackie Robinson in major league baseball at Brooklyn **1947**
		Marshall Plan for reconstruction of Europe **1948**
		Harry Truman reelected US President **1948**
		Berlin Airlift defies Soviet blockade **1948**
Jacques Lacan, *The Mirror Stage* 1949		Chiang Kai-shek's nationalists defeated; Communists control China **1949**
		NATO founded **1949**
Robert Merton, *Manifest and Latent Functions* 1949		Arthur Miller, *Death of a Salesman* **1949**
		Philip Johnson builds glass house **1949**
		Claude Levi-Strauss *Elementary Structures of Kinship* **1949**
		Indonesian independence from Dutch rule **1949**
Erik Erikson, *Youth and American Identity* 1950	**1950**	Korean War begins **1950**
		Hannah Arendt publishes *Totalitarians* **1950**
David Riesman, *The Lonely Crowd: The Other-Directed Personality* 1950		First steps toward European Economic Community **1950**
		J.D. Salinger, *Catcher in the Rye* **1951**
Edwin Lemert, *Social Pathology* 1951		Humphrey Bogart and Katherine Hepburn in *African Queen* **1951**
		Elizabeth II becomes Queen of England **1952**
		Gene Kelley stars in *Singin' in the Rain* **1952**
		Norman Vincent Peale, *Power of Positive Thinking* **1952**
		Mau Mau rebellion in Kenya **1952**
		Dwight Eisenhower elected US president **1952**
		Stalin dies **1953**
		Jonas Salk discovers vaccine against polio **1953**
		Julius and Ethel Rosenberg executed as alleged spies in US **1953**
		Arthur Miller's *The Crucible* characterizes McCarthyism as witch trials **1953**
		Korean War truce ends war **1953**
		Crick and Watson discover double helix structure of DNA **1953**
		Vietnamese end French rule with victory at Dien Bien Phu **1954**
		US Supreme Court Brown V. Education outlaws school segregation **1954**
Aimé Césaire, *Discourse on Colonialism: Between Colonizer and Colonized* 1955	**1955**	Morocco wins independence from France **1955**
		Senator Joseph McCarthy censured by US Senate **1954**
		Rosa Parks initiates Civil Rights Movement in Montgomery **1954**
		James Dean stars in *Rebel Without a Cause* **1955**
		Erving Goffman publishes *On Face-Work* **1955**
		Martin Luther King Jr leads Montgomery Bus Boycott **1955**
		First Disneyland opens **1955**
		Allen Ginsberg's *Howl!* **1956**
		Winston Churchill wins Nobel Prize for Literature **1956**
		USSR's *Sputnik*, first space satellite **1957**
		Noam Chomsky, *Syntactic Structures* **1957**

Social Theory		Wider World
Martin Luther King, Jr., *Stride Toward Freedom: Nonviolent Action* 1958	**1958**	John Kenneth Galbraith publishes *The Affluent Society* 1958
		Algerian rebels control government buildings in Algiers 1958
		Charles de Gaulle elected president of France 1958
Claude Lévi-Strauss, *The Structural Study of Myth* 1958		In China Mao declares Great Leap Forward 1958
		Fidel Castro's revolution seizes power in Cuba 1959
		Hutu violence against Tutsis in Rwanda 1959
C. Wright Mills, *The Sociological Imagination* 1959	**1960**	Beatles in Liverpool 1960
		Birth control pill 1960
Erving Goffman, *Presentation of Self in Everyday Life* 1959		Mobuto Sese Seko deposes Patrice Lumumba, takes over Congo 1960
		Nelson Mandela leads militant African National Congress 1960
Daniel Bell, *The End of Ideology in the West* 1960		John F Kennedy elected US president 1960
		Vietcong begins civil war against US backed South Vietnam 1960
W.W. Rostow, *Stages of Growth: Modernization Theory* 1960		Lumumba killed, probably by agents of Western powers 1961
		Yuri Gagarin, first astronaut; Alan Shepherd, first American astronaut 1961
Frantz Fanon, *Decolonizing, The Wretched of the Earth* 1961		Bay of Pigs invasion of Cuba fails 1961
		East Germans build Berlin Wall 1961
Students for a Democratic Society, *The Port Huron Statement* 1962		Sean Connery stars in *Dr No,* first James Bond film 1962
		Andy Warhol shows Campbell Soup Can paintings 1962
		Bob Dylan's *Blowin' in the Wind*; Rolling Stones first performance 1962
		James Baldwin's *Another Country* 1962
		First Wal-Mart store in Arkansas 1962
		Ayatollah Khomeini declares fatwa against Shah of Iran 1962
		Cuban Missile crisis 1962
Betty Friedan, *The Feminine Mystique: The Problem That Has No Name* 1963		Rachel Carson, *The Silent Spring* 1963
		Pope John 23rd dies, ending liberal period in Vatican 1963
		Martin Luther King's *I have a dream* speech 1963
		JFK assassinated in Texas; Lyndon B Johnson becomes president 1963
		Kenyan independence 1963
Roland Barthes, *Elements of Semiology* 1964		Cassius Clay becomes heavyweight champion 1964
		Nelson Mandela sentenced to life in prison 1964
	1965	Malcolm X assassinated 1965
		President Johnson escalates bombing in North Vietnam 1965
		LBJ pushes Voting Rights Act in response to March to Montgomery 1965
		Leonid Brezhnev leads USSR as General-Secretary 1966
		Mao's Red Guard and Cultural Revolution begins in China 1966
		Black Panthers founded in Oakland 1966
		Gabriel Garcia Marquéz *One Hundred Years of Solitude* 1967
		Israel captures Palestinian lands from Syria, Egypt, and Jordan 1967
		Che Guevara killed in Bolivia 1967
		Alexander Dubc˘ek leads Prague Spring 1967
		Tet Offensive turns public opinion against Vietnam War 1968
		Martin Luther King and Bobby Kennedy assassinated 1968
Louis Althusser, *Ideology and the Ideological State Apparatuses* 1969		Georges Pompidou becomes French president as de Gaulle resigns 1969
	1970	Nixon sends troop into Cambodia; anti-War Movement intensifies 1970
		Students protesting War in Vietnam killed at Kent State University 1970
		Anwar Sadat, Egypt's president upon death of Nasser 1970
Talcott Parsons, *System of Modern Societies* 1971		US invades Laos 1971
		Pentagon Papers reveal truth of US War policy in Vietnam 1971
		Bangladesh emerges as India defeats Pakistan 1971
		SALT treaty limits anti-ballistic missiles 1972

The Short American Century

This was the Golden Age of America. This was the "American Century." Everything had come together at once. It was as though all the stars and moons in the Western sky had aligned—pulling the waters high, making the land shine. In this respect, the United States finally seemed to have fulfilled the poetic prophecies of George Berkeley, in 1752:

> Westward the course of empire takes its way;
> The four first acts already past,
> A fifth shall close the drama with the day;
> Time's noblest offspring is the last.

For two centuries, Europeans in great numbers had seen in America the realization of their own dreams and cultures. From the first English settlers who had preceded Berkeley by a century, through Alexis de Tocqueville a century later and the millions of European immigrants through the nineteenth century, to the final reliance of the last European powers on the United States in the war, Europe had increasingly, if warily, looked to the West. It is easily forgotten that the United States had been, and had invented itself as, a new race of European people. The historical idealization of the West was, in part, an effort to redefine European culture to include its Western diaspora.

Thus, the triumphs of the United States at the end of World War II were, in some basic sense, a European triumph. It was at least possible to dream, even as Europe itself lay in tatters, that the original values of modern culture, born in Europe, were proven in and by the Americans. Not all Europeans liked this idea. Nor should they have. But as the summer of 1945 ended and Europeans had to look about for help to rebuild, there were not many choices. It was clear, in those months, to whom they must turn, like it or not. Americans in great numbers liked it, of course. But as Walter Russell Mead rightly says, George Berkeley's eighteenth-century vision of time's noblest offspring is better read against the words of a twentieth-century American skeptic, Robinson Jeffers:

> You making haste haste on decay; not blameworthy;
> life is good, be it stubbornly long or suddenly
> A mortal splendor: meteors are not needed less than
> mountains: shine, perishing republic.

If, at the end of the war, America seemed the splendid mountain built on the achievements of European culture, observers of the night sky might be forgiven for having failed to detect the meteors among the stars. They were there to be seen.

The brilliant Golden Age of European culture in the West was to last but a moment. American triumphs were real, but their exceptional qualities were exaggerated by the leveling of every rival. Economically, US industry was humming at full speed; the rest of the world was its marketplace. Morally, America had triumphed; others, even the Allies, were beaten down, one way or another. But these conditions were artificial and passing. In March 1946, only months after the end of the war, Winston Churchill, speaking in the heartland of America, made public the phrase that would help define Western politics for nearly half a century: the Iron Curtain. With Franklin Roosevelt dead (he died the year before), only Churchill knew as well what Stalin and the Soviets intended. The fragile partitioning of Europe at Yalta in February 1945 is often said to have come about due to FDR's mortal illness. The more likely cause was a world distracted by Hitler and war—a world that failed to realize the full implications of its own internal divisions. It was not even the deep ideological rivalry between the United States and the USSR—between, as they said, "freedom" and communism. We now know that the two Cold War powers were built on ideologies composed out of a common culture that included modernity's willful refusal to look at itself. Each system looked to the other in order to account for the evil. Neither had the courage to consider its own complicity in the destructive forces of the modern world. The Iron Curtain stretched taut between the two powers was a prophylactic against self-examination. The Soviets attacked American imperialism and promised, in Nikita Khrushchev's word, to "bury" the United States. The Americans did much the same. Just weeks before Churchill's 1946 speech, US diplomat George Kennan, in his famous long telegram from Moscow, defined the moral basis for US Cold War policy. The Soviets were possessed of a "neurotic view of world affairs" that drove their own imperialist impulses. In response, he said, the United States "must have courage and self-confidence to cling to our own methods and concepts of human society." This was on February 22, 1946—not even two years after Americans and Soviets had joined hands over Hitler's defeat.

How brief that golden moment had been. In late summer and early autumn 1945, nothing seemed impossible to the Americans. Now, they were advised to have courage enough to "cling" to their own ways. For good reason. Soon, they would learn that the Soviets, too, had the bomb. America was no longer the manifest exception. In 1948, Berlin was blockaded, cementing the Soviet hold on Eastern Europe. By the end of the decade, communist parties were organized in Western Europe, China had fallen to Mao's communist forces, and no part of the world was considered "safe" from communism. By 1950, the United States was at war again, now against communism in Korea, and Senator Joseph McCarthy had begun his crusade of domestic terror. Within a decade, in 1957, the Soviets successfully launched the first earth satellites. Sputnik seemed proof that the Soviets had surpassed the United States in the area of its greatest strength. By 1959, the year Cuba fell to Castro, Vice President Richard Nixon was in Moscow arguing with Soviet President Nikita Khrushchev that America's washing machines were the true signs of progress, that they should rather compete over the quality of their domestic economies, not their military technologies. It seemed reasonable. Today, it is evident that the Soviet system was, indeed, unable to satisfy the divergent demands of military and domestic needs. But then, at the height of the Cold War, Nixon's argument was a pathetic reminder of just how far America had fallen—and how fast.

Senator McCarthy's reign of terror lasted nearly five years. He was censured by the US Senate in 1954. Still, nothing so represents the frustrations of America in its Golden Age. Somehow—no one could quite say how—this splendid world society, the perfection of modern dreams, was unable to prevent communism from winning the world, abroad or at home. So, Americans attacked themselves. McCarthyism was able to exercise its threats at home because the Americans, like the Soviets, were unable to look honestly at themselves. When they did, they saw only the outsider lurking within, not their own capacity for destruction. Both nations were postwar states built squarely on the moral psychology of modernity: progress conquers the evil without, purifying the good intentions within. The Cold War, in its way, was no less a form destroying eruption of the good than was Hitler. We now know that as many died in Stalin's Gulags as in Hitler's Holocaust. No one has ever thought to count those who died in McCarthy's terrorism. But everyone who lived through it knew someone whose life was taken, or ruined, by the American fear of its own capacity for evil. In different ways, both systems destroyed their own to avoid facing what lay within. Today, the one has collapsed; the other struggles on, trying in its way to recapture its Golden Age.

The Cold War was a world struggle between two systems still clinging to the most elemental of nineteenth-century doctrines. Though social theorists since World War I, at least, had begun to rethink the founding ideas of modernity, the Cold War effectively wiped out much of what was gained. In the public discourse in the United States, the Cold War was seen as a struggle between the basic truths of mankind: freedom versus slavery. *Better dead than Red!* Nineteenth-century Enlightenment and Marxist philosophies had changed by the middle of the twentieth century, but in the popular mind—and to a large extent in public policy—thinking had regressed. Then popular social theory took its rawest form and must be taken seriously as such.

In some ways, the debate during and after McCarthy's "Red Scare" could hardly be considered a serious version of the original political philosophies themselves. Rather, at least in the

United States, the debate was much more the attempt of ordinary people to make some sense of the most overwhelming social fact of the day. America was supposed to have it all, but in fact, it had only a quarter section of the world's moral territory. Apart from the facts of Soviet brutality in Eastern Europe, what must have most distressed the American mind was the Socialist boast of moral superiority. Americans considered themselves exceptional, most of all because they were the moral superiors.

In 1941, Henry Luce, then publisher of *Life* and *Time* magazines, proclaimed the twentieth century the American Century. He began his editorial: "In general, the issues which the American people champion revolve around their determination to make the society of men safe for the freedom, growth and increasing satisfaction of all individual men." America served the moral good of humankind! This was 1941, before the Cold War. As Gunnar Myrdal would state in 1944, at the beginning of *An American Dilemma*, the Americans were always a moralistic people. Indeed, he argued, this is why their failures in race relations could be considered America's unique moral dilemma. Such a people were likely to be unnerved when others whom they considered bullies proclaimed themselves the true champions of the world's oppressed. Socialism's moral claims were, of course, central to Marx's social theory. But in the mid-twentieth century, they were particularly troubling to Americans who could not have missed the fact that, indeed, communism was making its deepest inroads among the poorer, most oppressed people of the world—not just in China and Cuba but also in Africa and the Middle East. In 1956, when Egypt's Abdel Nasser seized the Suez Canal, he struck at American wallets. Two years later, when he accepted a loan from the USSR for construction of the Aswan Dam, he struck their moral hearts. This was but the most dramatic of the moral and diplomatic struggles throughout the Third World in which the Communists were either winning or drawing even.

The Cold War was far from a debate over abstracts, or a debate over who had the better rockets and kitchen tools. It reflected a deep wrenching in the guts of ordinary people. In the mid-1950s in America, many men and women just settling back into a normal life had likely been born in the early 1920s and thus brought up through the Depression. Very probably, they had either fought in World War II or worked in the war effort at home. Their deepest need was to enjoy the fruits of those years of courageous suffering. People thought they had good reason to believe in the moral value of what they had done, especially in war. They believed, even more urgently, in their right to enjoy the abundant life they had earned.

The Other America and the Coming New World

In fact, many enjoyed a new life of relative luxury. Life in the 1950s was good for working and middle-class white people in the United States. But not for everyone. American Blacks returned from military service to encounter the same old story. Many suburban wives stuck out in the Levittowns and other new suburban developments, far from friends and family, wondered just what happiness really was. Yes, they had husbands and kids and those new kitchens, but something was wrong. Yet on the surface of the life photographed for *Life* and *Time* magazines, all was good. Except for those Communists. People living luxuriously middling lives could not be blamed for buying Senator McCarthy's line. He told them the Reds were right there, in their schools and churches, even in the army. The Reds were the enemy within. To people who had had enough of disruption in their personal lives, it must have seemed at least a plausible claim. Whatever they thought, they surely *felt* that what was wrong was not far away. Then, later, there was Elvis. Clearly, something was wrong indeed.

What was wrong was that the culture they had trusted to give them the good society excised a hidden tax. Everyone had to pay the price of joining the enforced silence. Evil in the world did not die with Hitler. There was enough to spare. Better to think it was the commies in the schools and churches than to face the half-truth Western culture had been built on. Progress was not a necessary condition of modern life. There was plenty of the good life to go around, but this could never suffice for a people taught that, soon enough, *all* social evil would recede. The Red Scare was real. The Soviets did intend to win. They did their own evil to their people and to those they tried to crush with tanks. But for Americans, then the standard-bearers of European culture, it was simply too much to consider the notion that social evil was deeply structured *into* the American way of life. Better to blame the Reds, or Elvis's gyrating pelvis.

In early December 1955, the civil rights struggle began in Montgomery, Alabama. The year-long Montgomery bus boycott made Martin Luther King Jr. and Rosa Parks American cultural heroes. More fundamentally, the social movements that followed Montgomery sounded an alarm that no one could fail to hear a decade later. Though it could be said that, between 1955 and 1963, the American Civil Rights Movement failed to achieve the full social equality it sought for Blacks, it cannot be denied that this was the first and most shocking of a series of events that changed, perhaps forever, how Americans thought about their society.

Through the 1950s, those Americans with a strong determination to see the best could still believe in the virtues of their way of life. One of the most remarkable passages in Ambassador Kennan's 1946 telegram conveyed the attitude perfectly:

> It was no coincidence that Marxism, which had smoldered ineffectively for half a century in Western Europe, caught hold and blazed for [the] first time in Russia. Only in this land which had never known a friendly neighbor or indeed any tolerant equilibrium of separate powers, either internal or international, could a doctrine thrive which viewed economic conflicts of society as insoluble by peaceful means.

Kennan was no McCarthy. He was a learned and cultured man. In 1946, he brought the best American wisdom to bear on the reality behind the fantasy of the Soviet menace. Still, he was absolutely sure that what set the American way apart was its capacity to solve conflict by peaceful means. This was the West's hedge against communism—again, its moral superiority. But from 1955 onward, as the struggle of American Blacks moved quickly toward open confrontation, it gradually dawned that the United States might be among those world societies unable to solve conflict by peaceful means. Here, of course, lay the power of Martin Luther King Jr.'s strategy, taken from Gandhi. The early movement used the force of nonviolence to expose the violence in the oppressor. But the movement eventually forced more than the hands of Bull Connor, Ross Barnett, and George Wallace. The Southern, white segregationists used all the violence of their disposition—hoses, arrest and detention, beatings, bombs, dogs, and murder. Then, force came from another quarter. The problem was *not* regional. When President Eisenhower, then presidents Kennedy and Johnson, reluctantly brought the force of federal law and troops down on the side of the oppressed, it was natural to hope that this would be the end of it. Again, the thought was: put the visible evil away and progress would assert its righteous way. It was not to be.

Still, this was the reasonable hope of people of goodwill in the United States and around the world when John F. Kennedy took up the reins of world power after the 1960 elections. In passing the torch to a younger and different political leader, people believed that their Golden Age would recover its luster. It seemed, as if by some improbable miracle, that JFK had brought the stars back into line. He, the Beatles, John Lennon, Pope John XXIII, and Dr. King conjured up the vision of a new day dawning. Little did anyone imagine then that Dr. King and all three Johns would be dead before their time or that the sweeping changes they represented would falter, weaken, or reverse themselves. But it is easy to see why people would go with the times. Perhaps the ugly contradictions of the 1950s—abundance marred by frustration—would be resolved. They were not.

After early gains culminating in the Civil Rights and Voting Rights acts of 1964 and 1965, the Civil Rights Movement turned in a different direction. Martin Luther King Jr. took the movement beyond the South, beyond voting rights. But when he turned his eye to broader issues of social justice in a speech accepting the Nobel Prize in late 1964, he was told to keep to his specialty. The war in Vietnam started in earnest several months later, in February 1965, just days before another hero would be assassinated. One year earlier, white people began to notice

Malcolm X, who took a very different line from King. In one of his most memorable speeches, Malcolm X declared the American Dream his American Nightmare. There were those—J. Edgar Hoover, director of the FBI, and others—who tried at that late date to explain away the Black uprisings as still another communist plot. Though the accusations did damage, they did not have the force they once had. When young people who had marched with King turned in other directions—Blacks often to Black Power, whites to the antiwar movement—the crisis spread far and wide. No one could quite be convinced, however much he or she wanted to believe it, that the world and America would have been saved from the troubles of the 1960s had the Kennedys and King not been killed.

What happened between 1963 and 1968 in the United States was but part of a world drama. What was wrong in the United States was structural, as Myrdal, Niebuhr, and others had been saying. What was wrong in the world was structural, too. In the latter years of the 1950s, beginning with the uprisings in Kenya, then Ghana's independence from Britain in 1957 and the Algerian revolt against French rule in 1958, African people threw off European colonial rule. In 1959, Fidel Castro threw out America's lackey, Fulgencio Batista—just a decade after Gandhi and Mao turned India and China away from Western control. But the most telling years were 1954 and 1955, when McCarthy was ruined and Rosa Parks refused to move any more and the French lost their colonial grip on Vietnam in a humiliating defeat at Dien Bien Phu. If only the Americans had learned the lesson from the French defeat. But then, they were still struggling with their own frustrations. They were still hoping for a return to the Golden Age. As it turned out, JFK was not the beginning of a new day but the last bright glow of a meteor falling red through thick air.

Soon after the bright days of the early 1960s in the West, a long-building global quake was beginning to make itself felt on the surface. America's ill-considered venture into Vietnam would soon emerge as a major national crisis that was anything but confined to the United States. It was in fact another warning that the world was changing even more so than it had in the troubled times of world war and economic collapse in the first half of the century. The decolonizing struggles in India and much of Africa, the Cuban rejection of American imperialism in the Caribbean, and the victory of Mao's communists over nationalism in China were numbered with the failures of Western intervention in Southeast Asia. Soon enough, it was easy to feel the global movements that by 1968 would turn back again on the core states in the West, rocking them with international as well as domestic challenges.

Affirmation and Doubt in Social Theory

Between 1945 and 1963—the Golden Age—the social theories that exerted the greatest influence fell into three categories: those affirming and developing the principles of the Golden Age; those reflecting the doubts and reservations of the time; and those openly objecting.

In the 1950s, the social sciences were brought into full partnership with the political and economic powers that were. Notwithstanding the jarring effects of the decade's contradictions, professional social scientists in all fields took up positions at or near the reins of power. These were the years when the American system of higher education grew by leaps and bounds; when the promise of a college education was seriously extended to nearly all qualified students. Following suit, European societies loosened the gates of their elite university systems to young people of working-class origins. These were the years in which, in the new universities and the research centers allied with them, the modern social sciences took the shape we recognize today. Though the emergence of the modern university goes back to the 1860s in the United States, it took a full century for that modern research university to become what it is, for better or worse, today. Only in the Golden Age was there sufficient public support for a full governmental investment in building so many costly institutions of higher learning, devoted equally to teaching the young and mastering the world through science. Between the 1940s and the 1960s, the number of Americans going to college increased at least fourfold. In 1940 the

United States spent $500 million on higher education; in 1970 the figure was nearly $16 billion! There was, obviously, a happy coincidence. Veterans returning from World War II and the Korean War used the GI Bill to pay their tuition bills. The demand for college education rose sharply. At the same time, the need for social knowledge to build the postwar society was felt to be great. In real terms, however, the actual need for college graduates was artificial. There were never enough positions in US or European economies to occupy all the newly educated elite.

The ideal of higher education as a necessity and a right was, no doubt, encouraged by the boost in intellectual self-confidence gained in the war. Many academics, like Ruth Benedict, had been active in the planning, administering, and informing of the war machine. After the war, there was a widespread and reasonable belief that scientific knowledge about social reality was much more than a nicety. It worked. So, in the 1950s, particularly in the United States, it was widely believed that social knowledge was the most powerful weapon. The social sciences stepped to the fore, for a while, as professional social theory enjoyed its own Golden Age, financed by the social hopes of most Americans. George Kennan's idea that the West—the United States—was able to solve its problems without conflict was an early version of the thinking that predominated for a short while in the late 1950s and early 1960s. Daniel Bell was one of those who eloquently defended the proposition that the West had already won the struggle with Marxism, which had somehow become synonymous with the East or at least with other-than-the-West—the "uncivilized." Proponents of the end of ideology in the West made a strong theoretical claim: ideology's day was past because social knowledge's day had come. Bell announced the day of the scholar—the man of scientific objectivity, freed from the passion of the ideologue. Though Daniel Bell, like George Kennan, was a man of superior culture and refined intellectual tastes, his vision of the end of ideology was a quite thickly veiled version of the popular view that politically passionate intellectuals were, after all, essentially Marxists—or worse. Earlier, in his 1952 campaign against Adlai Stevenson, Dwight Eisenhower had pronounced intellectuals "eggheads." Either way, among those in power in politics and the university, room had to be made for the trustworthy use of knowledge—by scientists and scholars, not intellectuals and ideologues. The line between was that between objectivity and passion.

The writings of Daniel Bell were just one example of the conviction that social science could be the basis for better explaining the social world in order to make it better. The key was keeping it all objective. W. W. Rostow's theory of modernization's five stages was the most influential applied version of this world theory. To all appearances, Rostow's analysis of human economic history is scientific economics at its best. The elaboration of Weber's ideas is obvious: Societies can be shown to move from traditionalism to a period of readiness for change. If the conditions are right, take-off, maturity, and something like old age follow. The argument was persuasive because it was logical, comprehensive, and empirically valid—or so it seemed. The idea behind it seemed self-evident in the late 1950s. Was it not obvious that there were "mature" modern societies (of which the United States was the standard) and others that were less mature, just taking off or getting ready or still stuck in tradition? As a social scientific classification, the theory was one thing. As a master philosophy of human history, it was another. It was presented and received—for the most part in its former guise—as science. Today, one wonders if no one stopped to ask how such a philosophy might look to the African colonial people then in revolt against modernized rulers. Nor, in 1966, when Rostow was one of President Lyndon Johnson's advisers, did anyone seriously wonder how an uncritical application of a philosophy that defined America as the end of history might promote the passions that led to Vietnam. The line between science and ideology, between objective truth and political passion, was blurred—and not just in the Kremlin.

Social science, in its finest hour, moved with a bold confidence. Nothing less could explain the theoretical self-confidence of Talcott Parsons, who, in the *age d'or* of sociology, felt himself utterly free to pursue his theory of the social system into every minute detail of thinkable social space. He thus felt himself authorized to say whatever followed from the theory. One measure of just how different things are today is that it would be hard to find anyone willing to make the statements Parsons made about "dependent" and "neurotic" women in his 1943 "Sex Roles" article. People still think this way, but fewer say what they think, and fewer still would make a social theory out of gratuitous observations. But Parsons was not a man of evil intent. He was writing good sociological theory, following the unchecked lead of his scientific brilliance.

One of the surest signs that science was having its way is seen in the shifts taking place in this period in European social theory. Social science, as we know it today, was very slow to develop in Europe, where the tradition of classical learning and the effects of elitism on cultural life combined with the effects of the wars to slow progress toward modern social science. Between 1945 and 1963, European social scientists were still learning from the Americans, still necessarily borrowing to pay off the deficit in cultural capital created by the wars. But in the human sciences, it was a very different story. In France, in particular, this was another *age d'or*—this one in the study of human culture. It was what one commentator has called the Age of Structuralism.

Claude Lévi-Strauss, the French anthropologist, is generally considered the founder of structuralism. Borrowing from linguistics, including the ideas of Ferdinand de Saussure and Roman Jakobson, Lévi-Strauss proposed the methods he thought would establish a science of the mind. The Swiss psychologist Jean Piaget (1896–1980) was doing something similar based on laboratory observations of small children. Piaget was one of the founders of modern developmental psychology; but Lévi-Strauss would become, as Susan Sontag put it, the intellectual hero of his day. He argued that cultural life had many of the same structural features as language. It was well known at the time that all languages were constituted as infinitely complex reservoirs of grammatical rules and semantic contents on which the speaker or writer draws while producing competent communications. Lévi-Strauss used this model of language to explain human culture. Culture was equally a vast, enduring social contract. The philosophical implication of his turn to linguistics was, in part, directed against the postwar philosophy of his day—existentialism in general, Jean-Paul Sartre (1905–1980) in particular.

Structuralism, as a political theory, rejected the notion that the meaningful life was entirely dependent on real life choices made by responsible individuals. This was equivalent to suggesting that linguistic meaning was solely derived from the existential utterances of the individual speaker. Here, the linguistic model brought home the dependence of the individual on the social group. The speaker cannot say whatever he wants because communication works both ways. He or she who must listen can understand what is said only by sharing a competent grasp of the whole of the language spoken. Therefore, structuralism in its simplest terms returned the study of culture to the issues outlined by Durkheim before World War I. The important difference was that Lévi-Strauss was able to be much more precise than Durkheim about the relation between the individual event and the total structure. His advance over Durkheim was due, in large part, to the use of a linguistics model. It may have also derived from his own look at the war years. Sartre took one turn from the Nazi occupation of France, Lévi-Strauss another. Both had their reasons. Their two philosophies vied with each other in France. But clearly the day was won, for a while, by structuralism and its variants. It was more a time for rebuilding the structure of culture. There was less evident cause to resist an occupying enemy.

Some might pause on seeing the names of Roland Barthes and Robert K. Merton in the same group. This because Merton has remained the structuralist sociologist, while Barthes changed many times over until his death in 1980. But between 1945 and 1960, when sociology came into its own in the United States and structuralism into its own in France, Merton and Barthes were not far from each other. Though in different ways, each was proposing a structural science, and each proposed to use science to uncover the latent dimensions of meaning. Merton's famous distinction between manifest and latent functions in social life is particularly interesting because it derives much more from Durkheim, even Marx, than from Freud. Barthes's outline of the structural science of human sign systems (*Elements of Semiol-*

ogy, from which the selection is taken) belies his own debt to the Durkheimian tradition through Lévi-Strauss and Saussure. Later, Barthes would evolve into one of the first public proponents of a social theory based on sexual desire. But in the early 1960s, when Barthes's essay on semiology first appeared, he, like Merton and Lévi-Strauss, was proposing a structural study of cultural systems. They all relied on variants of the principle that the latent meanings in culture could best be derived by a rigorous analysis not of their surface appearances but of their deep structural elements.

In a way, Louis Althusser was doing something similar in his structuralist attempt to revise historical materialism as a science by reconstructing the intellectual biography of Marx. Althusser took from his teacher, Gaston Bachelard, his famous idea of an epistemological break in Marx's writings. This was not so much a narrow scholarly argument as a general theoretical claim with political implications. If one could show the break in Marx between the younger philosophical Hegelian in the 1840s and the mature scientist of *Capital* in the 1860s, then it was possible to justify a post-Stalinist Marxism. Why theory? The answer for many Western European Marxists in the 1960s depended on finding some key to unraveling the various strands in the history of Marxism. The idea of a structural break in a cultural or theoretical tradition permitted the leap to a Marxism that could be pure theoretical practice. Today, this seems an entirely circuitous route to a rather straightforward position. But in the days of Althusser's prominence, it was a tricky path to tread between a Left social theory and the threat of being tainted by Stalinism. In his way, Althusser was using science to clear a legitimate place for Marxism in the Cold War era. American social theorists had no such struggle. Before McCarthyism, the revelations of Stalin's terrors early in the Soviet regime all but cleared the way of any manifest left-wing social theory. By the time Althusser developed his famous theory in "Ideology and the State Ideological Apparatuses" (1969), his structuralism was, at once, at the pinnacle of the scientific analysis of classic concepts in Marx's writings and just ready to break open the scientific structuralism that soon dissolved into post-structural social theory.

Still, all the structuralists of the time—Lévi-Strauss, Barthes, Merton, and Althusser—were, in different ways, seeking to accomplish much the same goal. They sought a new, deeper method for defining the science of social and cultural life. They had learned well the lessons of the interwar years. The individual, left alone, could not account for social action. They each pressed social theory beyond the merely visible. Surprisingly, they each were still positive in their outlook, and their method. They believed in the reasonable discovery and explanation of social facts. Others were less optimistic.

One of few positive consequences of the Nazi curse in Europe was that so many European intellectuals fled Hitler's terror to settle in the United Kingdom and the United States. Today's New School for Social Research (now regrettably named New School University) in New York City became one of the havens for European intellectuals at risk. Lévi-Strauss spent time there, where he encountered Roman Jakobson, and both of them were associated with its *École libre des hautes études*. Then too, of course, there were the German critical theorists in exile at and around the New School in New York City. Among the many enduring effects of writers like Theodor Adorno and Max Horkheimer, Erich Fromm and many others was a chastening effect on American social theory. Though the postwar home of the critical theorists would again be in Germany, they left behind in the United States important theoretical ideas. Their critique of mass culture, their method of borrowing widely and reworking traditional social theories, and perhaps most important of all their deep critique of the traditional structures of science and knowledge never after were far from left social thinking in the United States. Much later, nearer the end of the twentieth century, critical social theory would be a staple of American social criticism as, in turn, the German thinkers would borrow from traditions like pragmatism that were more indigenously American. After the brief American Century had run its course, social theory would increasingly become a North Atlantic practice as the confident American empiricism would yield, slowly but surely, to the more native European theoretical approaches.

Reservations and Objections

In America, remarkably soon after the post–World War II vision of an American century of unparalleled brilliance, there arose another, more traditional social scientific trend that was, perhaps, less severe but just as concerned as the German school. One of the first and most enduring leaders of this trend was David Riesman. His *Lonely Crowd* appeared in 1950. Already, Riesman was rethinking received wisdom about modernization. He took for granted the link between individual and social character, just as he accepted the premise that the world was moving steadily along the path of economic development. Where he differed was in his judgment about what turned out to be Rostow's fifth stage of mass consumption. Although Rostow had reservations, nothing he said ten years after *Lonely Crowd* was as deeply critical of modern America as was Reisman. Riesman believed America had lost its original character. In place of the inner-directed entrepreneur, the ideal type of modern man, instead, Riesman saw an Other-directed conformist dominating America in the postwar years. He was one of the first to force discussion of a topic well understood today. But then, in the Golden Age, it was yet another shock to have to consider, on top of everything else, that Americans had lost the very moral character that had set them apart.

About the same time, Erik Erikson's *Childhood and Society* (1950) outlined a theory of social character based on studies of the psychological development of youth. His argument that an identity crisis was developmentally necessary seemed to some to lend further support to Riesman's claims. Ten years later, when parents were repulsed by the politics and culture (to say nothing of the attire) of their children, identity crisis took on an even more explicit social importance. Edwin M. Lemert's 1951 book, *Social Pathology,* set forth the radical theory that social deviance was a consequence of the deviant's reaction to how others viewed and treated him. Lemert's social theory of identity formation was, thereby, clearly in tune with the ideas of Erving Goffman. Goffman's first writings contributed to the growing suspicion that older beliefs in the moral integrity of individuals were no longer entirely satisfactory. His first book, *Presentation of Self in Everyday Life* (1959), gave popular culture the expression "impression-management." Goffman held the view that individuals in social interactions were engaged in the artful management of what others thought of them. In contrast to Erikson and Riesman, however, Goffman said little about the personal and social politics of his times. He wrote as though suspended in some transcendent observational space. But he introduced the radical idea that, far from being inner-directed, human beings in society were by nature oriented more to social others than to pursuing the dictates of some inner moral self. With Goffman, in the 1950s, William James's ideas—that the individual has as many selves as there are individuals who recognize him—took on a different, more historically acute meaning. In the 1890s, this was an interesting idea. In the 1950s, it was a social critique.

At about the same time, in Paris, a little-known psychoanalyst, Jacques Lacan, was already rewriting traditional Freudian theories in order to establish a similar notion. The unconscious life could only be the interplay of natural desires in the discourse of the Other in the other. As with his structuralist contemporaries, Lacan saw the powerful mystery of language as the field of human action. Not an easily decoded idea, but obviously one not entirely at odds with Goffman's social theory of the self as the management of the expressive order lying between social individuals. Later, Lacan became a celebrity in the cultural Left, which had no definite shape in the 1950s.

But in 1949, the notion that seems so hard to translate from Lacan was made perfectly clear by Simone de Beauvoir. In *The Second Sex* (1949), the classic text of modern feminism, she left no doubt about the ways in which woman was Other to man, nor how the whole of Western culture had been built on and around this principle. Here, for the first time, was a feminist social theory that explained the situation of women with reference to Western civilization itself. Others, like Anna Julia Cooper and Charlotte Gilman, had begun this effort. But Simone de Beauvoir was the first to complete such a critique in the language of the culture she attacked. Not much later, Césaire and Fanon, who were among the first postcolonial writers to be read seriously in the West, did much the same with respect to the colonizing instincts of European cultures. It would be easy to overlook the fact that Martin Luther King's philosophy of nonviolence was itself borrowed from the first great social critic of Western culture in the twentieth century. Gandhi's ideal of Satyagraha, nonviolent force, was defined by his first-hand understanding of the violent impulses of the European colonialist. King's use of that theory is therefore an implicit social theory of the colonializing instincts of the white man in the United States.

By the end of the period, Fanon was already read in the United States and Europe. In 1963, the year JFK died, Betty Friedan had given words to those millions of women trapped in little suburban houses in the 1950s. She gave the problem a name. *The Feminine Mystique* (1963) immediately became the *locus classicus* of American feminism. The year before, 1962, leaders of SDS began to circulate copies of a social theory of democratic society. *The Port Huron Statement* was, in its day, the manifesto of a new political generation. Its ideal was a participatory democracy in which the social structures of political life would be consistent with, and supportive of, the deepest aspirations of the human individual. In this, the *Port Huron Statement* reflected the political and social philosophy of C. Wright Mills, who was a source of inspiration and ideas for many of those who had written the statement. In 1966 *The Black Panther Party Platform* represented a still more radical version of a new social order of freedom: "We want land, bread, housing, education, clothing, justice and peace." Though the Black Panther's terrified white liberals, they in fact wanted much the same.

In 1959, Mills's *Sociological Imagination* was the embodiment of the tensions of the age. On the one hand, he caustically denounced the pretenses of social science—mindless empiricism and abstract theorizing. To this day, his parody of Parsons remains the standard for sociological sarcasm. Yet his actual idea of the sociological imagination inspired student radicals from a place well within the culture of liberalism. Mills saw the sociologist as the new model of human liberation in that time—the individual whose sociological knowledge of the historical structures of society enhanced individual life with responsible awareness of the links between personal life and public action. Though his earlier books, particularly *Power Elite*, were sharp critical theories of American society, his ideal of the sociological imagination still held out hope that if knowledge were wrenched away from the pretenses of apolitical social science, it might find its way back as power in the lives of ordinary people.

In 1962–1963, just before the Golden Age ended, the most radical young people in the United States, in the former colonial world, and in Europe still believed in the power of knowledge. This faith would have a troubled time in the years to come.

C. L.

Notes

Page 218: The Jeffers poem, "Shine, Perishing Republic," is used by Walter Russell Mead as the theme and source of the title for his *Mortal Splendor* (Houghton Mifflin, 1987).

Page 220: The idea of linking women's experience in the suburbs to McCarthyism is from Elaine Tyler May, *Homeward Bound* (Basic Books, 1988).

Page 221: George Kennan, "Long Telegram," *National Security Archive*: Part 2 at http://nsarchive.gwu.edu/coldwar/documents/episode-1/kennan.htm

Other quoted material is from the selections following.

The Golden Age

Winston Churchill (1874–1965) was born at Blenheim Palace, Woodstock, Oxfordshire—thus, and obviously, to an aristocratic family. His younger years were given over to military service as an officer in the British army. He served in India, Sudan, and South Africa. But his true career was in politics. From 1940 to 1945, he was the Conservative Party Prime Minister of Great Britain. Churchill was, thus, with Franklin D. Roosevelt, leader of the North Atlantic forces in the Second World War against Nazi Germany. After the war, he became Leader of the Opposition upon the defeat of his Conservative Party. As he had warned of the dangers of Hitler's Germany before the war, and after he warned the West of the dangers of Stalin's Soviet Union—most famously in his Iron Curtain Speech on March 5, 1946 at Westminster College in Fulton, Missouri. The selection here is from that speech, which warned of and defined the enduring Cold War breach between the Atlantic powers and their wartime ally on the Eastern Front, the Soviet Union. Churchill continued to serve in public life, again becoming Prime Minister from 1951 to 1955. Though a stroke in 1953 slowed him, he remained a force to be reckoned with, especially as the author of a six-volume memoir and the four-volume *The History of the English-Speaking People*, which cover the long story from the Roman invasion of Britain in 55 BCE through the beginning of the First World War in 1914. In 1953 he was awarded the Nobel Prize for Literature for his writings and public oratory.

The Cold War[*]
Winston Churchill (1946)

A shadow has fallen upon the scenes so lately lighted by the Allied victory. Nobody knows what Soviet Russia and its Communist international organisation intends to do in the immediate future, or what are the limits, if any, to their expansive and proselytising tendencies. I have a strong admiration and regard for the valiant Russian people and for my wartime comrade, Marshal Stalin. There is deep sympathy and goodwill in Britain—and I doubt not here also—towards the peoples of all the Russias and a resolve to persevere through many differences and rebuffs in establishing lasting friendships. We understand the Russian need to be secure on her western frontiers by the removal of all possibility of German aggression. We welcome Russia to her rightful place among the leading nations of the world. We welcome her flag upon the seas. Above all, we welcome constant, frequent and growing contacts between the Russian people and our own people on both sides of the Atlantic. It is my duty however, for I am sure you would wish me to state the facts as I see them to you, to place before you certain facts about the present position in Europe.

From Stettin in the Baltic to Trieste in the Adriatic, an iron curtain has descended across the Continent. Behind that line lie all the capitals of the ancient states of Central and Eastern Europe.

---

[*] Courtesy of the Churchill Centre & BBC Archives.

Churchill / The Cold War | 229

Warsaw, Berlin, Prague, Vienna, Budapest, Belgrade, Bucharest and Sofia, all these famous cities and the populations around them lie in what I must call the Soviet sphere, and all are subject in one form or another, not only to Soviet influence but to a very high and, in many cases, increasing measure of control from Moscow. Athens alone—Greece with its immortal glories—is free to decide its future at an election under British, American and French observation. The Russian-dominated Polish Government has been encouraged to make enormous and wrongful inroads upon Germany, and mass expulsions of millions of Germans on a scale grievous and undreamed-of are now taking place. The Communist parties, which were very small in all these Eastern States of Europe, have been raised to pre-eminence and power far beyond their numbers and are seeking everywhere to obtain totalitarian control. Police governments are prevailing in nearly every case, and so far, except in Czechoslovakia, there is no true democracy.

Turkey and Persia are both profoundly alarmed and disturbed at the claims which are being made upon them and at the pressure being exerted by the Moscow Government. An attempt is being made by the Russians in Berlin to build up a quasi-Communist party in their zone of Occupied Germany by showing special favours to groups of left-wing German leaders. At the end of the fighting last June, the American and British Armies withdrew westwards, in accordance with an earlier agreement, to a depth at some points of 150 miles upon a front of nearly four hundred miles, in order to allow our Russian allies to occupy this vast expanse of territory which the Western Democracies had conquered.

If now the Soviet Government tries, by separate action, to build up a pro-Communist Germany in their areas, this will cause new serious difficulties in the British and American zones, and will give the defeated Germans the power of putting themselves up to auction between the Soviets and the Western Democracies. Whatever conclusions may be drawn from these facts—and facts they are—this is certainly not the Liberated Europe we fought to build up. Nor is it one which contains the essentials of permanent peace.

The safety of the world requires a new unity in Europe, from which no nation should be permanently outcast. It is from the quarrels of the strong parent races in Europe that the world wars we have witnessed, or which occurred in former times, have sprung. Twice in our own lifetime we have seen the United States, against their wishes and their traditions, against arguments, the force of which it is impossible not to comprehend, drawn by irresistible forces, into these wars in time to secure the victory of the good cause, but only after frightful slaughter and devastation had occurred. Twice the United States has had to send several millions of its young men across the Atlantic to find the war; but now war can find any nation, wherever it may dwell between dusk and dawn. Surely we should work with conscious purpose for a grand pacification of Europe, within the structure of the United Nations and in accordance with its Charter. That I feel is an open cause of policy of very great importance.

In front of the iron curtain which lies across Europe are other causes for anxiety. In Italy the Communist Party is seriously hampered by having to Support the Communist-trained Marshal Tito's claims to former Italian territory at the head of the Adriatic. Nevertheless the future of Italy hangs in the balance. Again one cannot imagine a regenerated Europe without a strong France. All my public life I have worked for a Strong France and I never lost faith in her destiny, even in the darkest hours. I will not lose faith now. However, in a great number of countries, far from the Russian frontiers and throughout the world, Communist fifth columns are established and work in complete unity and absolute obedience to the directions they receive from the Communist centre. Except in the British Commonwealth and in the United States where Communism is in its infancy, the Communist parties or fifth columns constitute a growing challenge and peril to Christian civilisation. These are sombre facts for anyone to have to recite on the morrow of a victory gained by so much splendid comradeship in arms and in the cause of freedom and democracy; but we should be most unwise not to face them squarely while time remains.

Daniel Bell (1919–2011), grew up on New York City's Lower East Side, the son of working people. He finished high school at age sixteen and entered City College, where, like many young New York intellectuals, he was part of the anti-Communist Left. After graduating from college in 1938, he studied for his Ph.D. at Columbia University, then taught briefly at the University of Chicago. From 1948 to 1958, he wrote for *Fortune* magazine while maintaining ties with the academy. In 1959, Bell joined the faculty of Harvard University, where he has remained until the present. Bell has written numerous books and articles, including *The End of Ideology* (1960), from which the selection is taken, and *The Coming Post-Industrial Society* (1973). Though Bell defends the scholar against the intellectual in "The End of Ideology in the West," many would consider him every bit the intellectual by another definition—a serious, informed, and intelligent general social theorist of modern society. Obviously, by the time he began to write for *Fortune* in 1948, Bell had already relinquished the leftism of his youth. Yet as one can see from this text, the more centrist, even conservative instincts of his adult years were still informed by, and directed against, Marxist social theory. Bell's writings are taken seriously, for good reason, by social theorists from many points in the political spectrum.

The End of Ideology in the West[*]
Daniel Bell (1960)

This age, too, can add appropriate citations—made all the more wry and bitter by the long period of bright hope that preceded it—for the two decades between 1930 and 1950 have an intensity peculiar in written history: world-wide economic depression and sharp class struggles; the rise of fascism and racial imperialism in a country that had stood at an advanced stage of human culture; the tragic self-immolation of a revolutionary generation that had proclaimed the finer ideals of man; destructive war of a breadth and scale hitherto unknown; the bureaucratized murder of millions in concentration camps and death chambers.

For the radical intellectual who had articulated the revolutionary impulses of the past century and a half, all this has meant an end to chiliastic hopes, to millenarianism, to apocalyptic thinking—and to ideology. For ideology, which once was a road to action, has come to be a dead end.

Whatever its origins among the French *philosophes*, ideology as a way of translating ideas into action was given its sharpest phrasing by the left Hegelians, by Feuerbach and by Marx. For them, the function of philosophy was to be critical, to rid the present of the past. ("The tradition of all the dead generations weighs like a nightmare on the brain of

the living," wrote Marx.) Feuerbach, the most radical of all the left Hegelians, called himself Luther II. Man would be free, he said, if we could demythologize religion. The history of all thought was a history of progressive disenchantment, and if finally, in Christianity, God had been transformed from a parochial deity to a universal abstraction, the function of criticism—using the radical tool of alienation, or self-estrangement—was to replace theology by anthropology, to substitute Man for God. Philosophy was to be directed at life, man was to be liberated from the "specter of abstractions" and extricated from the bind of the supernatural. Religion was capable only of creating "false consciousness." Philosophy would reveal "true consciousness." And by placing Man, rather than God, at the center of consciousness, Feuerbach sought to bring the "infinite into the finite."

If Feuerbach "descended into the world," Marx sought to transform it. And where Feuerbach proclaimed anthropology, Marx, reclaiming a root insight of Hegel, emphasized History and historical contexts. The world was not generic Man, but men; and of men, classes of men. Men differed because of their class position. And truths were class truths. All truths, thus, were masks, or partial truths, but the real truth was the revolutionary truth. And this real truth was rational.

Thus a dynamic was introduced into the analysis of ideology, and into the creation of a new ideology. By demythologizing religion, one recovered (from God and sin) the potential in man. By the unfolding of history, rationality was revealed. In the struggle of classes, true consciousness, rather than false consciousness, could be achieved. But if truth lay in action, one must act. The left Hegelians, said Marx, were only *littérateurs*. (For them a magazine was "practice.") For Marx, the only real action was in politics. But action, revolutionary action as Marx conceived it, was not mere social change. It was, in its way, the resumption of all the old millenarian, chiliastic ideas of the Anabaptists. It was, in its new vision, a new ideology.

Ideology is the conversion of ideas into social levers. Without irony, Max Lerner once entitled a book "Ideas Are Weapons." This is the language of ideology. It is more. It is the commitment to the consequences of ideas. . . .

A social movement can rouse people when it can do three things: simplify ideas, establish a claim to truth, and, in the union of the two, demand a commitment to action. Thus, not only does ideology

[*] Bell, Daniel. *The End of Ideology*. Glencoe, IL: Free Press, 1960. Reprinted by permission of the Estate of Daniel Bell

transform ideas, it transforms people as well. The nineteenth-century ideologies, by emphasizing inevitability and by infusing passion into their followers, could compete with religion. By identifying inevitability with progress, they linked up with the positive values of science. But more important, these ideologies were linked, too, with the rising class of intellectuals, which was seeking to assert a place in society.

The differences between the intellectual and the scholar, without being invidious, are important to understand. The scholar has a bounded field of knowledge, a tradition, and seeks to find his place in it, adding to the accumulated, tested knowledge of the past as to a mosaic. The scholar, qua scholar, is less involved with his "self." The intellectual begins with *his* experience, *his* individual perceptions of the world, *his* privileges and deprivations, and judges the world by these sensibilities. Since his own status is of high value, his judgments of the society reflect the treatment accorded him. In a business civilization, the intellectual felt that the wrong values were being honored, and rejected the society. Thus there was a "built-in" compulsion for the free-floating intellectual to become political. The ideologies, therefore, which emerged from the nineteenth century had the force of the intellectuals behind them. They embarked upon what William James called "the faith ladder," which in its vision of the future cannot distinguish possibilities from probabilities, and converts the latter into certainties.

Today, these ideologies are exhausted. The events behind this important sociological change are complex and varied. Such calamities as the Moscow Trials, the Nazi-Soviet pact, the concentration camps, the suppression of the Hungarian workers, form one chain; such social changes as the modification of capitalism, the rise of the Welfare State, another. In philosophy, one can trace the decline of simplistic, rationalistic beliefs and the emergence of new stoic-theological images of man, e.g. Freud, Tillich, Jaspers, etc. This is not to say that such ideologies as communism in France and Italy do not have a political weight, or a driving momentum from other sources. But out of all this history, one simple fact emerges: for the radical intelligentzia, the old ideologies have lost their "truth" and their power to persuade.

Few serious minds believe any longer that one can set down "blue-prints" and through "social engineering" bring about a new utopia of social harmony. At the same time, the older "counter-beliefs" have lost their intellectual force as well. Few "classic"

liberals insist that the State should play no role in the economy, and few serious conservatives, at least in England and on the Continent, believe that the Welfare State is "the road to serfdom." In the Western world, therefore, there is today a rough consensus among intellectuals on political issues: the acceptance of a Welfare State; the desirability of decentralized power; a system of mixed economy and of political pluralism. In that sense, too, the ideological age has ended.

And yet, the extraordinary fact is that while the old nineteenth-century ideologies and intellectual debates have become exhausted, the rising states of Asia and Africa are fashioning new ideologies with a different appeal for their own people. These are the ideologies of industrialization, modernization, Pan-Arabism, color, and nationalism. In the distinctive difference between the two kinds of ideologies lies the great political and social problems of the second half of the twentieth century. The ideologies of the nineteenth century were universalistic, humanistic, and fashioned by intellectuals. The mass ideologies of Asia and Africa are parochial, instrumental, and created by political leaders. The driving forces of the old ideologies were social equality and, in the largest sense, freedom. The impulsions of the new ideologies are economic development and national power.

And in this appeal, Russia and China have become models. The fascination these countries exert is no longer the old idea of the free society, but the new one of economic growth. And if this involves the wholesale coercion of the population and the rise of new elites to drive the people, the new repressions are justified on the ground that without such coercions economic advance cannot take place rapidly enough. And even for some of the liberals of the West, "economic development" has become a new ideology that washes away the memory of old disillusionments.

It is hard to quarrel with an appeal for rapid economic growth and modernization, and few can dispute the goal, as few could ever dispute an appeal for equality and freedom. But in this powerful surge— and its swiftness is amazing—any movement that instates such goals risks the sacrifice of the present generation for a future that may see only a new exploitation by a new elite. For the newly-risen countries, the debate is not over the merits of Communism—the content of that doctrine has long been forgotten by friends and foes alike. The question is an older one: whether new societies can grow by building democratic institutions and allowing people to make choices—and sacrifices—voluntarily, or whether the new elites, heady with power, will impose totalitarian means to transform their countries. Certainly in these traditional and old colonial societies where the masses are apathetic and easily manipulated, the answer lies with the intellectual classes and their conceptions of the future.

Thus one finds, at the end of the fifties, a disconcerting caesura. In the West, among the intellectuals, the old passions are spent. The new generation, with no meaningful memory of these old debates, and no secure tradition to build upon, finds itself seeking new purposes within a framework of political society that has rejected, intellectually speaking, the old apocalyptic and chiliastic visions. In the search for a "cause," there is a deep, desperate, almost pathetic anger.

W. W. Rostow (1916–2003) studied at Yale, where he received his B.A. in 1936 and his Ph.D. in 1940. He was also a Rhodes Scholar before serving in the Office of Strategic Services during World War II. From 1950 to 1961, he was professor of economic history at MIT. Rostow was special assistant to President John F. Kennedy in 1961, then served on the Policy Planning Council in the Department of State for five years. From 1966 to 1969, during the worst years of the war in Vietnam, he again served as special assistant in the White House. After his service under President Lyndon Johnson, he became professor of economics and history at the University of Texas. Rostow has written many books, including *Process of Economic Growth* (1952) and the more popular *Stages of Economic Growth: A Non-Communist Manifesto* (1960), from which the selection is taken. His superior academic credentials, along with his years of service in government, lent particular weight to his theory of economic modernization. He was one of the best and brightest to join the Kennedy administration in 1960, bringing with him a philosophy of economic history that was perfectly consistent with Kennedy's goal of reinvigorating the American Golden Age.

Modernization: Stages of Growth[*]
W. W. Rostow (1960)

The Traditional Society

First, the traditional society. A traditional society is one whose structure is developed within limited production functions, based on pre-Newtonian science and technology, and on pre-Newtonian attitudes towards the physical world. Newton is here used as a symbol for that watershed in history when men came widely to believe that the external world was subject to a few knowable laws, and was systematically capable of productive manipulation.

The conception of the traditional society is, however, in no sense static; and it would not exclude increases in output. Acreage could be expanded; some ad hoc technical innovations, often highly productive innovations, could be introduced in trade, industry and agriculture; productivity could rise with, for example, the improvement of irrigation works or the discovery and diffusion of a new crop. But the central fact about the traditional society was that a ceiling existed on the level of attainable output per head. This ceiling resulted from the fact that the potentialities which flow from modern science and technology were either not available or not regularly and systematically applied.

Both in the longer past and in recent times the story of traditional societies was thus a story of endless change. The area and volume of trade within them and between them fluctuated, for example, with the degree of political and social turbulence, the efficiency of central rule, the upkeep of the roads. Population—and, within limits, the level of life— rose and fell not only with the sequence of the harvests, but with the incidence of war and of plague. Varying degrees of manufacture developed; but, as in agriculture, the level of productivity was limited by the inaccessibility of modern science, its applications, and its frame of mind.

Generally speaking, these societies, because of the limitation on productivity, had to devote a very high proportion of their resources to agriculture; and flowing from the agricultural system there was an hierarchical social structure, with relatively narrow scope—but some scope—for vertical mobility. Family and clan connexions played a large role in social

---

[*] Rostow, Walt W. *The Stages of Economic Growth.* Cambridge University Press, 1971. Print. Copyright © 1971 Cambridge University Press. Reprinted with the permission of Cambridge University Press.

organization. The value system of these societies was generally geared to what might be called a long-run fatalism; that is, the assumption that the range of possibilities open to one's grandchildren would be just about what it had been for one's grandparents. But this long-run fatalism by no means excluded the short-run option that, within a considerable range, it was possible and legitimate for the individual to strive to improve his lot, within his lifetime. In Chinese villages, for example, there was an endless struggle to acquire or to avoid losing land, yielding a situation where land rarely remained within the same family for a century.

Although central political rule—in one form or another—often existed in traditional societies, transcending the relatively self-sufficient regions, the centre of gravity of political power generally lay in the regions, in the hands of those who owned or controlled the land. The landowner maintained fluctuating but usually profound influence over such central political power as existed, backed by its entourage of civil servants and soldiers, imbued with attitudes and controlled by interests transcending the regions.

In terms of history then, with the phrase "traditional society" we are grouping the whole pre-Newtonian world: the dynasties in China; the civilization of the Middle East and the Mediterranean; the world of medieval Europe. And to them we add the post-Newtonian societies which, for a time, remained untouched or unmoved by man's new capability for regularly manipulating his environment to his economic advantage.

To place these infinitely various, changing societies in a single category, on the ground that they all shared a ceiling on the productivity of their economic techniques, is to say very little indeed. But we are, after all, merely clearing the way in order to get at the subject of this book; that is, the post-traditional societies, in which each of the major characteristics of the traditional society was altered in such ways as to permit regular growth: its politics, social structure, and (to a degree) its values, as well as its economy.

The Preconditions for Take-Off

The second stage of growth embraces societies in the process of transition; that is, the period when the preconditions for take-off are developed; for it takes time to transform a traditional society in the ways necessary for it to exploit the fruits of modern science, to fend off diminishing returns, and thus to enjoy the blessings and choices opened up by the march of compound interest.

The preconditions for take-off were initially developed, in a clearly marked way, in Western Europe of the late seventeenth and early eighteenth centuries as the insights of modern science began to be translated into new production functions in both agriculture and industry, in a setting given dynamism by the lateral expansion of world markets and the international competition for them. But all that lies behind the break-up of the Middle Ages is relevant to the creation of the preconditions for take-off in Western Europe. Among the Western European states, Britain, favoured by geography, natural resources, trading possibilities, social and political structure, was the first to develop fully the preconditions for take-off.

The more general case in modern history, however, saw the stage of preconditions arise not endogenously but from some external intrusion by more advanced societies. These invasions—literal or figurative—shocked the traditional society and began or hastened its undoing; but they also set in motion ideas and sentiments which initiated the process by which a modern alternative to the traditional society was constructed out of the old culture.

The idea spreads not merely that economic progress is possible, but that economic progress is a necessary condition for some other purpose, judged to be good: be it national dignity, private profit, the general welfare, or a better life for the children. Education, for some at least, broadens and changes to suit the needs of modern economic activity. New types of enterprising men come forward—in the private economy, in government, or both—willing to mobilize savings and to take risks in pursuit of profit or modernization. Banks and other institutions for mobilizing capital appear. Investment increases, notably in transport, communications, and in raw materials in which other nations may have an economic interest. The scope of commerce, internal and external, widens. And, here and there, modern manufacturing enterprise appears, using the new methods. But all this activity proceeds at a limited pace within an economy and a society still mainly characterized by traditional low-productivity methods, by the old social structure and values, and by the regionally based political institutions that developed in conjunction with them.

In many recent cases, for example, the traditional society persisted side by side with modern economic activities, conducted for limited economic purposes by a colonial or quasi-colonial power.

Although the period of transition—between the traditional society and the take-off—saw major changes in both the economy itself and in the balance of social values, a decisive feature was often political. Politically, the building of an effective centralized national state—on the basis of coalitions touched with a new nationalism, in opposition to the traditional landed regional interests, the colonial power, or both, was a decisive aspect of the preconditions period; and it was, almost universally, a necessary condition for take-off.

The Take-Off

We come now to the great watershed in the life of modern societies: the third stage in this sequence, the take-off. The take-off is the interval when the old blocks and resistances to steady growth are finally overcome. The forces making for economic progress, which yielded limited bursts and enclaves of modern activity, expand and come to dominate the society. Growth becomes its normal condition. Compound interest becomes built, as it were, into its habits and institutional structure.

In Britain and the well-endowed parts of the world populated substantially from Britain (the United States, Canada etc.) the proximate stimulus for take-off was mainly (but not wholly) technological. In the more general case, the take-off awaited not only the build-up of social overhead capital and a surge of technological development in industry and agriculture, but also the emergence to political power of a group prepared to regard the modernization of the economy as serious, high-order political business.

During the take-off, the rate of effective investment and savings may rise from, say, 5% of the national income to 10% or more; although where heavy social overhead capital investment was required to create the technical preconditions for take-off the investment rate in the preconditions period could be higher than 5%, as, for example, in Canada before the 1890's and Argentina before 1914. In such cases capital imports usually formed a high proportion of total investment in the preconditions period and sometimes even during the take-off itself, as in Russia and Canada during their pre-1914 railway booms.

During the take-off new industries expand rapidly, yielding profits a large proportion of which are reinvested in new plants; and these new industries, in turn, stimulate, through their rapidly expanding requirement for factory workers, the services to support them, and for other manufactured goods, a further expansion in urban areas and in other modern industrial plants. The whole process of expansion in the modern sector yields an increase of income in the hands of those who not only save at high rates but place their savings at the disposal of those engaged in modern sector activities. The new class of entrepreneurs expands; and it directs the enlarging flows of investment in the private sector. The economy exploits hitherto unused natural resources and methods of production.

New techniques spread in agriculture as well as industry, as agriculture is commercialized, and increasing numbers of farmers are prepared to accept the new methods and the deep changes they bring to ways of life. The revolutionary changes in agricultural productivity are an essential condition for successful take-off; for modernization of a society increases radically its bill for agricultural products. In a decade or two both the basic structure of the economy and the social and political structure of the society are transformed in such a way that a steady rate of growth can be, thereafter, regularly sustained. . . .

One can approximately allocate the take-off of Britain to the two decades after 1783; France and the United States to the several decades preceding 1860; Germany, the third quarter of the nineteenth century; Japan, the fourth quarter of the nineteenth century; Russia and Canada the quarter-century or so preceding 1914; while during the 1950's India and China have, in quite different ways, launched their respective take-offs.

The Drive to Maturity

After take-off there follows a long interval of sustained if fluctuating progress, as the now regularly growing economy drives to extend modern technology over the whole front of its economic activity. Some 10–20% of the national income is steadily invested, permitting output regularly to outstrip the increase in population. The make-up of the economy changes unceasingly as technique improves, new industries accelerate, older industries level off. The economy finds its place in the international economy: goods formerly imported are produced at home; new import requirements develop, and new export commodities to match them. The society makes such terms as it will with the requirements of modern efficient production, balancing off the new against the older values and institutions, or revising the latter in such ways as to support rather than to retard the growth process.

Some sixty years after take-off begins (say, forty years after the end of take-off) what may be called maturity is generally attained. The economy, focused during the take-off around a relatively narrow complex of industry and technology, has extended its range into more refined and technologically often more complex processes; for example, there may be a shift in focus from the coal, iron, and heavy engineering industries of the railway phase to machine-tools, chemicals, and electrical equipment. This, for example, was the transition through which Germany, Britain, France, and the United States had passed by the end of the nineteenth century or shortly thereafter. . . .

Formally, we can define maturity as the stage in which an economy demonstrates the capacity to move beyond the original industries which powered its take-off and to absorb and to apply efficiently over a very wide range of its resources—if not the whole range—the most advanced fruits of (then) modern technology. This is the stage in which an economy demonstrates that it has the technological and entrepreneurial skills to produce not everything, but anything that it chooses to produce. It may lack (like contemporary Sweden and Switzerland, for example) the raw materials or other supply conditions required to produce a given type of output economically; but its dependence is a matter of economic choice or political priority rather than a technological or institutional necessity.

Historically, it would appear that something like sixty years was required to move a society from the beginning of take-off to maturity. Analytically the explanation for some such interval may lie in the powerful arithmetic of compound interest applied to the capital stock, combined with the broader consequences for a society's ability to absorb modern technology of three successive generations living under a regime where growth is the normal condition. But, clearly, no dogmatism is justified about the exact length of the interval from take-off to maturity.

The Age of High Mass-Consumption

We come now to the age of high mass-consumption, where, in time, the leading sectors shift towards durable consumers' goods and services: a phase from which Americans are beginning to emerge; whose

not unequivocal joys Western Europe and Japan are beginning energetically to probe; and with which Soviet society is engaged in an uneasy flirtation.

As societies achieved maturity in the twentieth century two things happened: real income per head rose to a point where a large number of persons gained a command over consumption which transcended basic food, shelter, and clothing; and the structure of the working force changed in ways which increased not only the proportion of urban to total population, but also the proportion of the population working in offices or in skilled factory jobs—aware of and anxious to acquire the consumption fruits of a mature economy.

In addition to these economic changes, the society ceased to accept the further extension of modern technology as an overriding objective. It is in this post-maturity stage, for example, that, through the political process, Western societies have chosen to allocate increased resources to social welfare and security. The emergence of the welfare state is one manifestation of a society's moving beyond technical maturity; but it is also at this stage that resources tend increasingly to be directed to the production of consumers' durables and to the diffusion of services on a mass basis, if consumers' sovereignty reigns. The sewing-machine, the bicycle, and then the various electric-powered household gadgets were gradually diffused. Historically, however, the decisive element has been the cheap mass automobile with its quite revolutionary effects—social as well as economic—on the life and expectations of society.

For the United States, the turning point was, perhaps, Henry Ford's moving assembly line of 1913–14; but it was in the 1920's, and again in the postwar decade, 1946–56, that this stage of growth was pressed to, virtually, its logical conclusion. In the 1950's Western Europe and Japan appear to have fully entered this phase, accounting substantially for a momentum in their economies quite unexpected in the immediate postwar years. The Soviet Union is technically ready for this stage, and, by every sign, its citizens hunger for it; but Communist leaders face difficult political and social problems of adjustment if this stage is launched.

Beyond Consumption

Beyond, it is impossible to predict, except perhaps to observe that Americans, at least, have behaved in the past decade as if diminishing relative marginal utility sets in, after a point, for durable consumers' goods;

and they have chosen, at the margin, larger families—behaviour in the pattern of Buddenbrooks dynamics. Americans have behaved as if, having been born into a system that provided economic security and high mass-consumption, they placed a lower valuation on acquiring additional increments of real income in the conventional form as opposed to the advantages and values of an enlarged family. But even in this adventure in generalization it is a shade too soon to create—on the basis of one case—a new stage-of-growth, based on babies, in succession to the age of consumers' durables: as economists might say, the income-elasticity of demand for babies may well vary from society to society. But it is true that the implications of the baby boom along with the not wholly unrelated deficit in social overhead capital are likely to dominate the American economy over the next decade rather than the further diffusion of consumers' durables.

Here then, in an impressionistic rather than an analytic way, are the stages-of-growth which can be distinguished once a traditional society begins its modernization: the transitional period when the preconditions for take-off are created generally in response to the intrusion of a foreign power, converging with certain domestic forces making for modernization; the take-off itself; the sweep into maturity generally taking up the life of about two further generations; and then, finally, if the rise of income has matched the spread of technological virtuosity (which, as we shall see, it need not immediately do) the diversion of the fully mature economy to the provision of durable consumers' goods and services (as well as the welfare state) for its increasingly urban—and then suburban—population. Beyond lies the question of whether or not secular spiritual stagnation will arise, and, if it does, how man might fend it off. . . .

A Dynamic Theory of Production

These stages are not merely descriptive. They are not merely a way of generalizing certain factual observations about the sequence of development of modern societies. They have an inner logic and continuity. They have an analytic bone-structure, rooted in a dynamic theory of production.

The classical theory of production is formulated under essentially static assumptions which freeze—or permit only once-over change—in the variables most relevant to the process of economic growth. As modern economists have sought to merge classical production theory with Keynesian income analysis they have introduced the dynamic variables: population, technology, entrepreneurship etc. But they have tended to do so in forms so rigid and general that their models cannot grip the essential phenomena of growth, as they appear to an economic historian. We require a dynamic theory of production which isolates not only the distribution of income between consumption, saving, and investment (and the balance of production between consumers and capital goods) but which focuses directly and in some detail on the composition of investment and on developments within particular sectors of the economy. . . .

And there are other decisions as well that societies have made as the choices open to them have been altered by the unfolding process of economic growth; and these broad collective decisions, determined by many factors—deep in history, culture, and the active political process—outside the market-place, have interplayed with the dynamics of market demand, risk-taking, technology and entrepreneurship, to determine the specific content of the stages of growth for each society.

How, for example, should the traditional society react to the intrusion of a more advanced power: with cohesion, promptness, and vigour, like the Japanese; by making a virtue of fecklessness, like the oppressed Irish of the eighteenth century; by slowly and reluctantly altering the traditional society, like the Chinese?

When independent modern nationhood is achieved, how should the national energies be disposed: in external aggression, to right old wrongs or to exploit newly created or perceived possibilities for enlarged national power; in completing and refining the political victory of the new national government over old regional interests; or in modernizing the economy?

Once growth is under way, with the take-off, to what extent should the requirements of diffusing modern technology and maximizing the rate of growth be moderated by the desire to increase consumption per capita and to increase welfare?

When technological maturity is reached, and the nation has at its command a modernized and differentiated industrial machine, to what ends should it be put, and in what proportions: to increase social security, through the welfare state; to expand mass-consumption into the range of durable consumers' goods and services; to increase the nation's stature and power on the world scene; or to increase leisure?

And then the question beyond, where history offers us only fragments: what to do when the increase in real income itself loses its charm? Babies, boredom, three-day week-ends, the moon, or the creation of new inner, human frontiers in substitution for the imperatives of scarcity?

Talcott Parsons (1902–1979) developed his social theory of action systems throughout his career. In "Action Systems and Social Systems," his summary of that theory as he worked it between 1961 and 1971, two of the most distinctive features of Parsons's social theory are illustrated. First, he understands the social system to be a distinct entity, different from but interdependent with three other action systems: culture, personality, and the behavioral organism. Second, Parsons makes explicit reference to Èmile Durkheim in his view that social systems are *sui generis* things in which values serve to maintain the patterned integrity of the system. Some have argued that these theoretical convictions were traceable to the Golden Age culture, in which it was widely believed America was *the* exemplification of society itself because of the power of its values.

"Sex Roles in the American Kinship System" (1943) is an illustration of Parsons's theory applied to an empirical topic. Here, Parsons demonstrates his remarkable ability to press deeper and deeper into the logic of his theoretical systems. In the 1940s and 1950s, when this essay was most widely studied, his ideas were not particularly remarkable; the family as he discussed it was taken for granted by social scientists. By the 1970s, however, feminist scholars began to use Parsons's theory as a point of protest against systematic, social scientific sexism. Today, of course, anyone can understand why feminists would object to being defined as dependent, neurotic, and compulsive, perhaps especially when these views are stated in so cool a scientific language.

Action Systems and Social Systems[*]
Talcott Parsons (1961–1971)

We consider social systems to be constituents of the more general system of action, the other primary

[*]PARSONS, TALCOTT, THE SYSTEM OF MODERN SOCIETIES, 1st, ©1971. Printed and Electronically reproduced by permission of Pearson Education, Inc., NEW YORK, NEW YORK.

constituents being cultural systems, personality systems, and behavioral organisms; all four are abstractly defined relative to the concrete behavior of social interaction. We treat the three subsystems of actions other than the social system as constituents of its environment. This usage is somewhat unfamiliar, especially for the case of the personalities of individuals. It is justified fully elsewhere, but to understand what follows it is essential to keep in mind that neither social nor personality systems are here conceived as concrete entities.

The distinctions among the four subsystems of action are functional. We draw them in terms of the four primary functions which we impute to all systems of action, namely pattern-maintenance, integration, goal-attainment, and adaptation.

An action system's primary integrative problem is the coordination of its constituent units, in the first instance human individuals, though for certain purposes collectivities may be treated as actors. Hence, we attribute primacy of integrative function to the social system.

We attribute primacy of pattern-maintenance—and of creative pattern change—to the cultural system. Whereas social systems are organized with primary reference to the articulation of social relationships, cultural systems are organized around the characteristics of complexes of symbolic meaning—the codes in terms of which they are structured, the particular clusters of symbols they employ, and the conditions of their utilization, maintenance, and change as parts of action systems.

We attribute primacy of goal-attainment to the personality of the individual. The personality system is the primary *agency* of action processes, hence of the implementation of cultural principles and requirements. On the level of reward in the motivational sense, the optimization of gratification or satisfaction to personalities is the primary goal of action.

The behavioral organism is conceived as the adaptive subsystem, the locus of the primary human facilities which underlie the other systems. It embodies a set of conditions to which action must adapt and comprises the primary mechanism of interrelation with the physical environment, especially through the input and processing of information in the central nervous system and through motor activity in coping with exigencies of the physical environment. These relationships are presented systematically in Table 1.

TABLE 1   Action

Subsystems	Primary Functions
Social	Integration
Cultural*	Pattern Maintenance*
Personality*	Goal Attainment*
Behavioral Organism*	Adaptation*

*These are the social subsystem's environment.

There are two systems of reality which are environmental to action in general and not constituents of action in our analytical sense. The first is the *physical environment*, including not only phenomena as understandable in terms of physics and chemistry, but also the world of living organisms so far as they are not integrated into action systems. The second, which we conceive to be independent of the physical environment as well as of action systems as such, we will call "*ultimate reality*," in a sense derived from traditions of philosophy. It concerns what Weber called "problem of meaning" for human action and is mediated into action primarily by the cultural system's structuring of meaningful orientations that include, but are not exhausted by, cognitive "answers."

In analyzing the interrelations among the four subsystems of action—and between these systems and the environments of action—it is essential to keep in mind the phenomenon of *interpenetration*. Perhaps the best-known case of interpenetration is the *internalization* of social objects and cultural norms into the personality of the individual. Learned content of experience, organized and stored in the memory apparatus of the organism, is another example, as is the *institutionalization* of normative components of cultural systems as constitutive structures of social systems. We hold that the boundary between any pair of action systems involves a "zone" of structured components or patterns which must be treated theoretically as *common* to *both* systems, not simply allocated to one system or the other. For example, it is untenable to say that norms of conduct derived from social experience, which both Freud (in the concept of the Superego) and Durkheim (in the concept of collective representations) treated as parts of the personality of the individual, must be *either* that *or* part of the social system.

It is by virtue of the zones of interpenetration that processes of interchange among systems can take place. This is especially true at the levels of symbolic meaning and generalized motivation. In order to "communicate" symbolically, individuals must have culturally organized common codes, such as those of language, which are also integrated into systems of their social interaction. In order to make information stored in the central nervous system utilizable for the personality, the behavioral organism must have mobilization and retrieval mechanisms which, through interpenetration, subserve motives organized at the personality level.

Thus, we conceived social systems to be "open," engaged in continual interchange of inputs and outputs with their environments. Moreover, we conceive them to be internally differentiated into various orders of subcomponents which are also continually involved in processes of interchange.

Social systems are those constituted by states and processes of social interaction among acting units. If the properties of interaction were derivable from properties of the acting units, social systems would be epiphenomenal, as much "individualistic" social theory has contended. Our position is sharply in disagreement: it derives particularly from Durkheim's statement that society—and other social systems—is a "reality *sui generis*."

The structure of social systems may be analyzed in terms of four types of independently variable components: values, norms, collectivities, and roles. Values take primacy in the pattern-maintenance functioning of social systems, for they are conceptions of desirable types of social systems that regulate the making of commitments by social units. Norms, which function primarily to integrate social systems, are specific to particular social functions and types of social situations. They include not only value components specified to appropriate levels in the structure of a social system, but also specific modes of orientation for acting under the functional and situational conditions of particular collectivities and roles. Collectivities are the type of structural component that have goal-attainment primacy. Putting aside the many instances of highly fluid group systems, such as crowds, we speak of a collectivity only where two specific criteria are fulfilled. First, there must be definite statuses of membership so that a useful distinction between members and nonmembers can generally be drawn, a criterion fulfilled by cases that vary from nuclear families to political communities. Second, there must be some differentiation among members in relation to their statuses and functions within the collectivity, so that some categories of members are expected to do certain things which are not expected of other members. A role, the type of structural component that has primacy in the adaptive function, we conceive as defining a class of individuals who, through reciprocal expectations, are involved in a particular collectivity. Hence, roles comprise the primary zones of interpenetration between the social system and the personality of the individual. A role is never idiosyncratic to a particular individual, however. A father is specific to his children in his fatherhood, but he is a father in terms of the role-structure of his society. At the same time, he also participates in various other contexts of interaction, filling, for example, an occupational role.

The reality *sui generis* of social systems may involve the independent variability of each of these types of structural components relative to the others. A generalized value-pattern does not legitimize the same norms, collectivities, or roles under all conditions, for example. Similarly, many norms regulate the action of indefinite numbers of collectivities and roles, but only specific sectors of their action. Hence a collectivity generally functions under the control of a large number of particular norms. It always involves a plurality of roles, although almost any major category of role is performed in a plurality of particular collectivities. Nevertheless, social systems are comprised of *combinations* of these structural components. To be institutionalized in a stable fashion, collectivities and roles must be "governed" by specific values and norms, whereas values and norms are themselves institutionalized only insofar as they are "implemented" by particular collectivities and roles.

Sex Roles in the American Kinship System[*]
Talcott Parsons (1943)

Much psychological research has suggested the very great importance to the individual of his affective

* Reprinted with the permission of The Free Press, a Division of Simon & Schuster, Inc., from ESSAYS IN SOCIOLOGICAL THEORY by Talcott Parsons. Copyright © 1954 by The Free Press; copyright renewed (c) 1982 by Helen W. Parsons. All rights reserved.

ties, established in early childhood, to other members of his family of orientation. When strong affective ties have been formed, it seems reasonable to believe that situational pressures which force their drastic modification will impose important strains upon the individual.

Since all known kinship systems impose an incest tabu, the transition from asexual intrafamilial relationships to the sexual relation of marriage—generally to a previously relatively unknown person—is general. But with us this transition is accompanied by a process of "emancipation" from the ties both to parents and to siblings, which is considerably more drastic than in most kinship systems, especially in that it applies to both sexes about equally, and includes emancipation from solidarity with *all* members of the family of orientation about equally, so that there is relatively little continuity *with* any kinship ties established by birth for anyone.

The effect of these factors is reinforced by two others. Since the effective kinship unit is normally the small conjugal family, the child's emotional attachments to kin are confined to relatively few persons instead of being distributed more widely. Especially important, perhaps, is the fact that no other adult woman has a role remotely similar to that of the mother. Hence the average intensity of affective involvement in family relations is likely to be high. Secondly, the child's relations outside the family are only to a small extent ascribed. Both in the play group and in the school he must to a large extent "find his own level" in competition with others. Hence the psychological significance of his security within the family is heightened.

We have then a situation where at the same time the inevitable importance of family ties is intensified and a necessity to become emancipated from them is imposed. This situation would seem to have a good deal to do with the fact that with us adolescence—and beyond—is, as has been frequently noted, a "difficult" period in the life cycle. In particular, associated with this situation is the prominence in our society of what has been called a "youth culture," a distinctive pattern of values and attitudes of the age groups between childhood and the assumption of full adult responsibilities. This youth culture, with its irresponsibility, its pleasure-seeking, its "rating and dating," and its intensification of the romantic love pattern, is not a simple matter of "apprenticeship" in adult values and responsibilities. It bears many of the marks of reaction to emotional tension and insecurity, and in all probability has among its functions that of easing the difficult process of adjustment from childhood emotional dependency to full "maturity." In it we find still a third element underlying the prominence of the romantic love complex in American society.

The emphasis which has here been placed on the multilineal symmetry of our kinship structure might be taken to imply that our society was characterized by a correspondingly striking assimilation of the roles of the sexes to each other. It is true that American society manifests a high level of the "emancipation" of women, which in important respects involves relative assimilation to masculine roles, in accessibility to occupational opportunity, in legal rights relative to property holding, and in various other respects. Undoubtedly the kinship system constitutes one of the important sets of factors underlying this emancipation since it does not, as do so many kinship systems, place a structural premium on the role of either sex in the maintenance of the continuity of kinship relations.

But the elements of sex-role assimilation in our society are conspicuously combined with elements of segregation which in many respects are even more striking than in other societies, as for instance in the matter of the much greater attention given by women to style and refinement of taste in dress and personal appearance. This and other aspects of segregation are connected with the structure of kinship, but not so much by itself as in its interrelations with the occupational system.

The members of the conjugal family in our urban society normally share a common basis of economic support in the form of money income, but this income is not derived from the co-operative efforts of the family as a unit—its principal source lies in the remuneration of occupational roles performed by individual members of the family. Status in an occupational role is generally, however, specifically segregated from kinship status—a person holds a "job" as an individual, not by virtue of his status in a family.

Among the occupational statuses of members of a family, if there is more than one, much the most important is that of the husband and father, not only because it is usually the primary source of family income, but also because it is the most important single basis of the status of the family in the community at large. To be the main "breadwinner" of his family is a primary role of the normal adult man in our society. The corollary of this role is his far smaller participation than that of his wife in the internal affairs of the household. Consequently, "housekeeping" and the care of children is still the primary functional content of the adult feminine role in the "utilitarian" division of labor. Even if the married woman has a job, it is, at least in the middle classes, in the great majority of cases not one which in status or remuneration competes closely with those held by men of her own class. Hence there is a typically asymmetrical relation of the marriage pair to the occupational structure.

This asymmetrical relation apparently both has exceedingly important positive functional significance and is at the same time an important source of strain in relation to the patterning of sex roles.

On the positive functional side, a high incidence of certain types of patterns is essential to our occupational system and to the institutional complex in such fields as property and exchange which more immediately surround this system. In relatively commonsense terms it requires scope for the valuation of personal achievement, for equality of opportunity, for mobility in response to technical requirements, for devotion to occupational goals and interests relatively unhampered by "personal" considerations. In more technical terms it requires a high incidence of technical competence, of rationality, of universalistic norms, and of functional specificity. All these are drastically different from the patterns which are dominant in the area of kinship relations, where ascription of status by birth plays a prominent part, and where roles are defined primarily in particularistic and functionally diffuse terms.

It is quite clear that the type of occupational structure which is so essential to our society requires a far-reaching structural segregation of occupational roles from the kinship roles of the *same* individuals. They must, in the occupational system, be treated primarily as individuals. This is a situation drastically different from that found in practically all non-literate societies and in many that are literate.

At the same time, it cannot be doubted that a solidary kinship unit has functional significance of the highest order, especially in relation to the socialization of individuals and to the deeper aspects of their psychological security. What would appear to have happened is a process of mutual accommodation between these two fundamental aspects of our social structure. On the one hand our kinship system is of a structural type which, broadly speaking, interferes least with the functional needs of the occupational system, above all in that it exerts *relatively* little pressure for the ascription of an individual's social status—through class affiliation, property, and of course particular "jobs"—by virtue of his kinship status. The conjugal unit can be mobile in status independently of the other kinship ties of its members, that is, those of the spouses to the members of their families of orientation.

But at the same time this small conjugal unit can be a strongly solidary unit. This is facilitated by the prevalence of the pattern that normally only *one* of its members has an occupational role which is of determinate significance for the status of the family as a whole. Minor children, that is, as a rule do not "work," and when they do, it is already a major step in the process of emancipation from the family of orientation. The wife and mother is either exclusively a "housewife" or at most has a "job" rather than a "career."

There are perhaps two primary functional aspects of this situation. In the first place, by confining the number of status-giving occupational roles of the members of the effective conjugal unit to one, it eliminates any competition for status, especially as between husband and wife, which might be disruptive of the solidarity of marriage. So long as lines of achievement are segregated and not directly comparable, there is less opportunity for jealousy, a sense of inferiority, etc., to develop. Secondly, it aids in clarity of definition of the situation by making the status of the family in the community relatively definite and unequivocal. There is much evidence that this relative definiteness of status is an important factor in psychological security.

The same structural arrangements which have this positive functional significance also give rise to important strains. What has been said above about the pressure for thoroughgoing emancipation from the family of orientation is a case in point. But in connection with the sex-role problem there is another important source of strain.

Historically, in Western culture, it may perhaps be fairly said that there has been a strong tendency to define the feminine role psychologically as one strongly marked by elements of dependency. One of the best symbols perhaps was the fact that until rather recently the married woman was not *sui juris*, could not hold property, make contracts, or sue in her own right. But in the modern American kinship system, to say nothing of other aspects of the culture and social structure, there are at least two pressures which tend to counteract this dependency and have undoubtedly played a part in the movement for feminine emancipation.

The first, already much discussed, is the multilineal symmetry of the kinship system which gives no basis of sex discrimination, and which in kinship terms favors equal rights and responsibilities for both parties to a marriage. The second is the character of the marriage relationship. Resting as it does primarily on affective attachment for the other person as a concrete human individual, a "personality," rather than on more objective considerations of status, it puts a premium on a certain kind of mutuality and equality. There is no clearly structured superordination-subordination pattern. Each is a fully responsible "partner" with a claim to a voice in decisions, to a certain human dignity, to be "taken seriously." Surely the pattern of romantic love which makes his relation to the "woman he loves" the most important single thing in a man's life, is incompatible with the view that she is an inferior creature, fit only for dependency on him.

In our society, however, occupational status has tremendous weight in the scale of prestige values. The fact that the normal married woman is debarred from testing or demonstrating her fundamental equality with her husband in competitive occupational achievement, creates a demand for a functional equivalent. At least in the middle classes, however, this cannot be found in the utilitarian functions of the role of housewife since these are treated as relatively menial functions. To be, for instance, an excellent cook, does not give a hired maid a moral claim to a higher status than that of domestic servant.

This situation helps perhaps to account for a conspicuous tendency for the feminine role to emphasize broadly humanistic rather than technically specialized achievement values. One of the key patterns is that of "good taste," in personal appearance, house furnishings, cultural things like literature and music. To a large and perhaps increasing extent the more humanistic cultural traditions and amenities of life are carried on by women. Since these things are of high intrinsic importance in the scale of values of our culture, and since by virtue of the system of occupational specialization even many highly superior men are greatly handicapped in respect to them, there is some genuine redressing of the balance between the sexes.

Robert K. Merton (1910–2003) had begun his career at Columbia by the end of World War II. Much like Talcott Parsons at Harvard, Merton sought to establish postwar sociology on a scientific basis. For Merton, this work proceeded partly through his teaching at Columbia and his leadership of the Bureau of Applied Social Research and partly through the composition of articles like the one selected here. "Manifest and Latent Functions" became the lead article in Merton's *Social Theory and Social Structure* (1949), which, for his followers, was the effective textbook (in Thomas Kuhn's sense) of modern sociology. In this, as in most of the articles in that book, Merton was part teacher and part supervisor of research—always elegantly explaining his ideas, relating them to the tradition, then carefully suggesting their value to the concrete tasks of social research. In the preface to *Social Theory and Social Structure*, Merton graciously acknowledged Parsons as his teacher and friend. Yet in the book itself, he proposed a different practical direction, if not an entirely different theoretical scheme. The side-by-side development of these two masters of sociological theory in the postwar years is a compelling story of respectful scientific cooperation across differences. The Hawthorne Western Electric study that Merton mentions in the selection was one of the first and most influential studies of early industrial sociology. It was based on observations over time of men working in close quarters wiring telephone circuit banks (once used in telephone switching stations). Merton refers to the surprising results that showed efficiency was increased primarily by latent factors that were totally unexpected when the study began.

Manifest and Latent Functions[*]
Robert K. Merton (1949)

The distinction between manifest and latent functions was devised to preclude the inadvertent confusion, often found in the sociological literature, between conscious *motivations* for social behavior and its *objective consequences*. Our scrutiny of current vocabularies of functional analysis has shown how easily, and how unfortunately, the sociologist may identify *motives* with *functions*. It was further indicated that the motive and the function vary

independently and that the failure to register this fact in an established terminology has contributed to the unwitting tendency among sociologists to confuse the subjective categories of motivation with the objective categories of function. This, then, is the central purpose of our succumbing to the not-always-commendable practice of introducing new terms into the rapidly growing technical vocabulary of sociology, a practice regarded by many laymen as an affront to their intelligence and an offense against common intelligibility.

As will be readily recognized, I have adapted the terms "manifest" and "latent" from their use in another context by Freud (although Francis Bacon had long ago spoken of "latent process" and "latent configuration" in connection with processes which are below the threshold of superficial observation).

The distinction itself has been repeatedly drawn by observers of human behavior at irregular intervals over a span of many centuries. Indeed, it would be disconcerting to find that a distinction which we have come to regard as central to functional analysis had not been made by any of that numerous company who have in effect adopted a functional orientation. We need mention only a few of those who have, in recent decades, found it necessary to distinguish in their specific interpretations of behavior between the end-in-view and the functional consequences of action.

> George H. Mead: ". . . that attitude of hostility toward the law-breaker has the unique advantage [read: latent function] of uniting all members of the community in the emotional solidarity of aggression. While the most admirable of humanitarian efforts are sure to run counter to the individual interests of very many in the community, or fail to touch the interest and imagination of the multitude and to leave the community divided or indifferent, the cry of thief or murderer is attuned to profound complexes, lying below the surface of competing individual efforts, and citizens who have [been] separated by divergent interests stand together against the common enemy."

Emile Durkheim's similar analysis of the social functions of punishment is also focused on its latent functions (consequences for the community) rather than confined to manifest functions (consequences for the criminal). . . .

W. I. Thomas and F. Znaniecki: "Although all the new [Polish peasant cooperative] institutions are thus formed with the definite purpose of satisfying certain specific needs, their social function is by no means limited to their explicit and conscious purpose . . . every one of these institutions—commune or agricultural circle, loan and savings bank, or theater—is not merely a mechanism for the management of certain values but also an association of people, each member of which is supposed to participate in the common activities as a living, concrete individual. Whatever is the predominant, official common interest upon which the institution is founded, the association as a concrete group of human personalities unofficially involves many other interests; the social contacts between its members are not limited to their common pursuit, though the latter, of course, constitutes both the main reason for which the association is formed and the most permanent bond which holds it together. Owing to this combination of an abstract political, economic, or rather rational mechanism for the satisfaction of specific needs with the concrete unity of a social group, the new institution is also the best intermediary link between the peasant primary-group and the secondary national system."

These and numerous other sociological observers have, then, from time to time distinguished between categories of subjective disposition ("needs, interests, purposes") and categories of generally unrecognized but objective functional consequences ("unique advantages," "never conscious" consequences, "unintended . . . service to society," "function not limited to conscious and explicit purpose").

Since the occasion for making the distinction arises with great frequency, and since the purpose of a conceptual scheme is to direct observations toward salient elements of a situation and to prevent the inadvertent oversight of these elements, it would seem justifiable to designate this distinction by an appropriate set of terms. This is the rationale for the distinction between manifest functions and latent functions; the first referring to those objective consequences for a specified unit (person, subgroup, social or cultural system) which contribute to its adjustment or adaptation and were so intended; the second referring to unintended and unrecognized consequences of the same order.

Purposes of the Distinction

Clarifies the analysis of seemingly irrational social patterns. In the first place, the distinction aids the sociological interpretation of many social practices which persist even though their manifest purpose is clearly not achieved. The time-worn procedure in such instances has been for diverse, particularly lay, observers to refer to these practices as "superstitions," "irrationalities," "mere inertia of tradition," *etc.* In other words, when group behavior does not—and, indeed, often cannot—attain its ostensible purpose there is an inclination to attribute its occurrence to lack of intelligence, sheer ignorance, survivals, or so-called inertia. Thus, the Hopi ceremonials designed to produce abundant rainfall may be labelled a superstitious practice of primitive folk and that is assumed to conclude the matter. It should be noted that this in no sense accounts for the group behavior. It is simply a case of name-calling; it substitutes the epithet "superstition" for an analysis of the actual role of this behavior in the life of the group. Given the concept of latent function, however, we are reminded that this behavior *may* perform a function for the group, although this function may be quite remote from the avowed purpose of the behavior.

The concept of latent function extends the observer's attention beyond the question of whether or not the behavior attains its avowed purpose. Temporarily ignoring these explicit purposes, it directs attention *toward* another range of consequences: those bearing, for example, upon the individual personalities of Hopi involved in the ceremony and upon the persistence and continuity of the larger group. Were one to confine himself to the problem of whether the manifest (purposed) function occurs, it becomes a problem, not for the sociologist, but for the meteorologist. And to be sure, our meteorologists agree that the rain ceremonial does not produce rain; but this is hardly to the point. It is merely to say that the ceremony does not have this technological use; that this purpose of the ceremony and its actual consequences do not coincide. But with the concept of latent function, we continue our inquiry, examining the consequences of the ceremony not for the rain gods or for meteorological phenomena, but for the groups which conduct the ceremony. And here it may be found, as many observers indicate, that the ceremonial does indeed have functions—but functions which are non-purposed or latent.

Ceremonials may fulfill the latent function of re-inforcing the group identity by providing a periodic occasion on which the scattered members of a group assemble to engage in a common activity. As Durkheim among others long since indicated, such ceremonials are a means by which collective expression is afforded the sentiments which, in a further analysis, are found to be a basic source of group unity. Through the systematic application of the concept of latent function, therefore, *apparently* irrational behavior may *at times* be found to be positively functional for the group. Operating with the concept of latent function, we are not too quick to conclude that if an activity of a group does not achieve its nominal purpose, then its persistence can be described only as an instance of "inertia," "survival," or "manipulation by powerful subgroups in the society."

In point of fact, some conception like that of latent function has very often, almost invariably, been employed by social scientists observing *a standardized practice designed to achieve an objective which one knows from accredited physical science cannot be thus achieved.* This would plainly be the case, for example, with Pueblo rituals dealing with rain or fertility. *But with behavior which is not directed toward a clearly unattainable objective, sociological observers are less likely to examine the collateral or latent functions of the behavior.*

Directs attention to theoretically fruitful fields of inquiry. The distinction between manifest and latent functions serves further to direct the attention of the sociologist to precisely those realms of behavior, attitude and belief where he can most fruitfully apply his special skills. For what is his task if he confines himself to the study of manifest functions? He is then concerned very largely with determining whether a practice instituted for a particular purpose does, in fact, achieve this purpose. He will then inquire, for example, whether a new system of wage-payment achieves its avowed purpose of reducing labor turnover or of increasing output. He will ask whether a propaganda campaign has indeed gained its objective of increasing "willingness to fight" or "willingness to buy war bonds," or "tolerance toward other ethnic groups." Now, these are important, and complex, types of inquiry. But, so long as sociologists *confine* themselves to the study of manifest functions, their inquiry is set for them by practical men of affairs (whether a captain of industry, a trade union leader, or, conceivably, a Navaho chieftain, is for the moment immaterial), rather than by the theoretic problems which are at the core

of the discipline. By dealing primarily with the realm of manifest functions, with the key problem of whether deliberately instituted practices of organizations succeed in achieving their objectives, the sociologist becomes converted into an industrious and skilled recorder of the altogether familiar pattern of behavior. *The terms of appraisal are fixed and limited by the question put to him by the non-theoretic men of affairs, e.g.,* has the new wage-payment program achieved such-and-such purposes?

But armed with the concept of latent function, the sociologist extends his inquiry in those very directions which promise most for the theoretic development of the discipline. He examines the familiar (or planned) social practice to ascertain the latent, and hence generally unrecognized, functions (as well, of course, as the manifest functions). He considers, for example, the consequences of the new wage plan for, say, the trade union in which the workers are organized or the consequences of a propaganda program, not only for increasing its avowed purpose of stirring up patriotic fervor, but also for making large numbers of people reluctant to speak their minds when they differ with official policies, *etc.* In short, it is suggested that the *distinctive* intellectual contributions of the sociologist are found primarily in the study of unintended consequences (among which are latent functions) of social practices, as well as in the study of anticipated consequences (among which are manifest functions).

There is some evidence that it is precisely at the point where the research attention of sociologists has shifted from the plane of manifest to the plane of latent functions that they have made their *distinctive* and major contributions. This can be extensively documented but a few passing illustrations must suffice.

The Hawthorne Western Electric Studies: As is well known, the early stages of this inquiry were concerned with the problem of the relations of "illumination to efficiency" of industrial workers. For some two and a half years, attention was focused on problems such as this: do variations in the intensity of lighting affect production? The initial results showed that within wide limits there was no uniform relation between illumination and output. Production output increased *both* in the experimental group where illumination was increased (or *decreased*) *and* in the control group where no changes in illumination were introduced. In short, the investigators confined themselves wholly to a search for the manifest functions. Lacking a concept of latent social function, no attention whatever was initially paid to the social consequences of *the experiment* for relations among members of the test and control groups or for relations between workers and the test room authorities. In other words, the investigators lacked a sociological frame of reference and operated merely as "engineers" (just as a group of meteorologists might have explored the "effects" upon rainfall of the Hopi ceremonial).

Only after continued investigation, did it occur to the research group to explore the consequences of the new "experimental situation" for the self-images and self-conceptions of the workers taking part in the experiment, for the interpersonal relations among members of the group, for the coherence and unity of the group. As Elton Mayo reports it, "The illumination fiasco had made them alert to the need that very careful records should be kept of everything that happened in the room in addition to the obvious engineering and industrial devices. Their observations therefore included not only records of industrial and engineering changes but also records of physiological or medical changes, and, *in a sense*, of social and anthropological. This last took the form of a "log" that gave as full an account as possible of the actual events of every day. . . . " In short, it was only after a long series of experiments which wholly neglected the latent social functions of the experiment (as a contrived social situation) that this distinctly sociological framework was introduced. "With this realization," the authors write, "the inquiry changed its character. No longer were the investigators interested in testing for the effects of single variables. In the place of a controlled experiment, they substituted the notion of a social situation which needed to be described and understood as a system of interdependent elements." Thereafter, as is now widely known, inquiry was directed very largely toward ferreting out the latent functions of standardized practices among the workers, of informal organization developing among workers, of workers' games instituted by "wise administrators," of large programs of worker counselling and interviewing, etc. The new conceptual scheme entirely altered the range and types of data gathered in the ensuing research.

The discovery of latent functions represents significant increments in sociological knowledge. There is another respect in which inquiry into latent functions represents a distinctive contribution of the social scientist. It is precisely the latent functions of a practice or belief which are *not* common knowledge, for these

are unintended and generally unrecognized social and psychological consequences. As a result, findings concerning latent functions represent a greater increment in knowledge than findings concerning manifest functions. They represent, also, greater departures from "common-sense" knowledge about social life. Inasmuch as the latent functions depart, more or less, from the avowed manifest functions, the research which uncovers latent functions very often produces "paradoxical" results. The seeming paradox arises from the sharp modification of a familiar popular preconception which regards a standardized practice or belief *only* in terms of its manifest functions by indicating some of its subsidiary or collateral latent functions. The introduction of the concept of latent function in social research leads to conclusions which show that "social life is not as simple as it first seems." For as long as people confine themselves to *certain* consequences (*e.g.* manifest consequences), it is comparatively simple for them to pass moral judgments upon the practice or belief in question. Moral evaluations, generally based on these manifest consequences, tend to be polarized in terms of black or white. But the perception of further (latent) consequences often complicates the picture. Problems of moral evaluation (which are not our immediate concern) and problems of social engineering (which are our concern) both take on the additional complexities usually involved in responsible social decisions.

Claude Lévi-Strauss (1908–2009) was born in Belgium. He grew up in Versailles, then studied at the University of Paris. From 1932 to 1934, he followed a normal career path for intellectual stars in France by teaching high school (*lycée*). In 1934, however, he was offered the opportunity to teach sociology at the University of São Paulo in Brazil. Though he visited Paris from time to time, he remained in Brazil until 1939. His reading and field trips to the interior led to his becoming an anthropologist. After a year's military service (1939–1940), Lévi-Strauss returned to the New World, first to Martinique and Puerto Rico, then to the New School for Social Research in New York City. He was in the United States through the war until 1947. During this period, his interest in linguistics emerged, in large part through contact with Roman Jakobson. His first major book of structural anthropology, *Les Structures élémentaires de la parenté*, appeared in French in 1949. He had returned to France the previous year, where he taught initially at what was then the École Pratique des Hautes Etudes. In 1958, he was named to a chair of social anthropology at the Collège de France, the highest academic honor his country bestows. Among his numerous books are *Tristes tropiques* (1955), which is must reading for anyone who cares about the intellectual pleasures and challenges of anthropology; *Structural Anthropology*, two volumes of collected essays; and the three-volume *Mythologiques*.

The selection, "The Structural Study of Myth," first appeared in 1955 and is generally considered the original manifesto for the structural study of culture. Here, Lévi-Strauss performs a deep structural analysis of the Oedipal myth without any explicit reference to a concept of the unconscious. Lévi-Strauss's sources were much more Durkheimian and Saussurian than Freudian. Two terms used in the selection might require some explanation. Literally, a chthonian being is one who is thought to live beneath the surface of the earth (the monsters in the third column on page 312). Thus, an autochthonous origin would be one from the soil or from beneath the earth. In the myth, monsters are considered of autochthonous origin. Thus, in the Oedipus myth, the slaying of monsters is taken as a denial of man's origins as a creature of the earth. As Lévi-Strauss shows throughout his interpretation, the method is an attempt to understand meaningful elements in their structured relation to each other. In this case, he argues that one of the natural human dilemmas resolved by the Oedipal story is concern over how we can be born both of human and of primitive natural origins. In his way, Lévi-Strauss was also dealing with existential questions.

The Structural Study of Myth[*]
Claude Lévi-Strauss (1958)

Despite some recent attempts to renew them, it seems that during the past twenty years anthropology has increasingly turned from studies in the field of religion. At the same time, and precisely because the interest of professional anthropologists has withdrawn from primitive religion, all kinds of amateurs who claim to belong to other disciplines have seized this opportunity to move in, thereby turning into their private playground what we had left as a

[*] Excerpt from Claire Jacobson and Brooke Grundfest Schoepf, trans., *Structural Anthropology, I* (New York: Basic Books, 1974), pp. 202–212.

wasteland. The prospects for the scientific study of religion have thus been undermined in two ways. . . .

Of all the chapters of religious anthropology probably none has tarried to the same extent as studies in the field of mythology. From a theoretical point of view the situation remains very much the same as it was fifty years ago, namely, chaotic. Myths are still widely interpreted in conflicting ways: as collective dreams, as the outcome of a kind of esthetic play, or as the basis of ritual. Mythological figures are considered as personified abstractions, divinized heroes, or fallen gods. Whatever the hypothesis, the choice amounts to reducing mythology either to idle play or to a crude kind of philosophic speculation.

In order to understand what a myth really is, must we choose between platitude and sophism? Some claim that human societies merely express, through their mythology, fundamental feelings common to the whole of mankind, such as love, hate, or revenge or that they try to provide some kind of explanations for phenomena which they cannot otherwise understand—astronomical, meteorological, and the like. But why should these societies do it in such elaborate and devious ways, when all of them are also acquainted with empirical explanations? On the other hand, psychoanalysts and many anthropologists have shifted the problems away from the natural or cosmological toward the sociological and psychological fields. But then the interpretation becomes too easy: If a given mythology confers prominence on a certain figure, let us say an evil grandmother, it will be claimed that in such a society grandmothers are actually evil and that mythology reflects the social structure and the social relations; but should the actual data be conflicting, it would be as readily claimed that the purpose of mythology is to provide an outlet for repressed feelings. Whatever the situation, a clever dialectic will always find a way to pretend that a meaning has been found

Mythology confronts the student with a situation which at first sight appears contradictory. On the one hand it would seem that in the course of a myth anything is likely to happen. There is no logic, no continuity. Any characteristic can be attributed to any subject; every conceivable relation can be found. With myth, everything becomes possible. But on the other hand, this apparent arbitrariness is belied by the astounding similarity between myths collected in widely different regions. Therefore the problem: If the content of a myth is contingent, how are we going to explain the fact that myths throughout the world are so similar?

It is precisely this awareness of a basic antinomy pertaining to the nature of myth that may lead us toward its solution. For the contradiction which we face is very similar to that which in earlier times brought considerable worry to the first philosophers concerned with linguistic problems; linguistics could only begin to evolve as a science after this contradiction had been overcome. Ancient philosophers reasoned about language the way we do about mythology. On the one hand, they did notice that in a given language certain sequences of sounds were associated with definite meanings, and they earnestly aimed at discovering a reason for the linkage between those *sounds* and that *meaning*. Their attempt, however, was thwarted from the very beginning by the fact that the same sounds were equally present in other languages although the meaning they conveyed was entirely different. The contradiction was surmounted only by the discovery that it is the combination of sounds, not the sounds themselves, which provides the significant data. . . .

To invite the mythologist to compare his precarious situation with that of the linguist in the prescientific stage is not enough. As a matter of fact we may thus be led only from one difficulty to another. There is a very good reason why myth cannot simply be treated as language if its specific problems are to be solved; myth *is* language: to be known, myth has to be told; it is a part of human speech. In order to preserve its specificity we must be able to show that it is both the same things as language, and also something different from it. Here, too, the past experience of linguists may help us. For language itself can be analyzed into things which are at the same time similar and yet different. This is precisely what is expressed in Saussure's distinction between *langue* and *parole*, one being the structural side of language, the other the statistical aspect of it, *langue* belonging to a reversible time, *parole* being nonreversible. If those two levels already exist in language, then a third one can conceivably be isolated.

We have distinguished *langue* and *parole* by the different time referents which they use. Keeping this in mind, we may notice that myth uses a third referent which combines the properties of the first two. On the one hand, a myth always refers to events alleged to have taken place long ago. But what gives the myth an operational value is that the specific pattern described is timeless; it explains the present and the past as well as the future. This can be made clear through a comparison between myth and what appears to have largely replaced it in modern societies, namely, politics. When the historian refers to the French Revolution, it is always as a sequence of past happenings, a non-reversible series of events the remote consequences of which may still be felt at present. But to the French politician, as well as to his followers, the French Revolution is both a sequence belonging to the past—as to the historian—and a timeless pattern which can be detected in the contemporary French social structure and which provides a clue for its interpretation, a lead from which to infer future developments. Michelet, for instance, was a politically minded historian. He describes the French Revolution thus: "That day . . . everything was possible. . . . Future became present . . . that is, no more time, a glimpse of eternity." It is that double structure, altogether historical and ahistorical, which explains how myth, while pertaining to the realm of *parole* and calling for an explanation as such, as well as to that of *langue* in which it is expressed, can also be an absolute entity on a third level which, though it remains linguistic by nature, is nevertheless distinct from the other two. . . .

Whatever our ignorance of the language and the culture of the people where it originated, a myth is still felt as a myth by any reader anywhere in the world. Its substance does not lie in its style, its original music, or its syntax, but in the *story* which it tells. Myth is language, functioning on an especially high level where meaning succeeds practically at "taking off" from the linguistic ground on which it keeps on rolling. . . .

Now for a concrete example of the method we propose. We shall use the Oedipus myth, which is well known to everyone. . . . [W]e shall not interpret the Oedipus myth in literal terms, much less offer an explanation acceptable to the specialist. We simply wish to illustrate—and without reaching any conclusions with respect to it—a certain technique, whose use is probably not legitimate in this particular instance, owing to the problematic elements indicated above. The "demonstration" should therefore be conceived, not in terms of what the scientist means by this term, but at best in terms of what is meant by the street peddler, whose aim is not to achieve a concrete result, but to explain, as succinctly as possible, the functioning of the mechanical toy which he is trying to sell to the onlookers.

The myth will be treated as an orchestra score would be if it were unwittingly considered as a unilinear series; our task is to reestablish the correct arrangement. Say, for instance, we were confronted with a sequence of the type: 1,2,4,7,8,2,3,4,6,8,1,4,

5,7,8,1,2, 5,7,3,4,5,6,8 . . . , the assignment being to put all the 1's together, all the 2's, the 3's, etc.; the result is a chart:

1	2		4			7	8
	2	3	4		6		8
1			4	5		7	8
1	2			5		7	
		3	4	5	6		8

We shall attempt to perform the same kind of operation on the Oedipus myth, trying out several arrangements of the mythemes until we find one which is in harmony with the principles enumerated above. Let us suppose, for the sake of argument, that the best arrangement is shown below (although it might certainly be improved with the help of a specialist in Greek mythology).

We thus find ourselves confronted with four vertical columns, each of which includes several relations belonging to the same bundle. Were we to *tell* the myth, we would disregard the columns and read the rows from left to right and from top to bottom. But if we want to *understand* the myth, then we will have to disregard one half of the diachronic dimension (top to bottom) and read from left to right, column after column, each one being considered as a unit.

All the relations belonging to the same column exhibit one common feature which it is our task to discover. For instance, all the events grouped in the first column on the left have something to do with blood relations which are overemphasized, that is, are more intimate than they should be. Let us say, then, that the first column has as its common feature the *overrating of blood relations*. It is obvious that the second column expressed the same thing, but inverted: *underrating of blood relations*. The third column refers to monsters being slain. As to the fourth, a few words of clarification are needed. The remarkable connotation of the surnames in Oedipus' father-line has often been noticed. However, linguists usually disregard it, since to them the only way to define the meaning of a term is to investigate all the contexts in which it appears, and personal names, precisely because they are used as such, are not accompanied by any context. With the method we propose to follow the objection disappears, since the myth itself provides its own context. The significance is no longer to be sought in the eventual meaning of each name, but in the fact that all the names have a common feature: All the hypothetical meanings (which may well remain hypothetical) refer to *difficulties in walking straight and standing upright*.

What then is the relationship between the two columns on the right? Column three refers to monsters. The dragon is a chthonian being which has to be killed in order that mankind be born from the Earth; the Sphinx is a monster unwilling to permit men to live. The last unit reproduces the first one, which has to do with the *autochthonous origin* of mankind. Since the monsters are overcome by men, we may thus say that the common feature of the third column is *denial of the autochthonous origin of man*.

This immediately helps us to understand the meaning of the fourth column. In mythology it is a universal characteristic of men born from the Earth that at the moment they emerge from the depth they either cannot walk or they walk clumsily. This is the case of the chthonian beings in the mythology of the Pueblo: Muyingwu, who leads the emergence, and the chthonian Shumaikoli are lame ("bleeding-foot," "sore-foot"). The same happens to the Koskimo of the Kwakiutl after they have been swallowed by the chthonian monster, Tsiakish: When they returned to the

Cadmos seeks his sister Europa, ravished by Zeus			Cadmos kills the dragon
		The Spartoi kill one another	
			Labdacos (Laios' father) = *lame* (?)
		Oedipus kills his father, Laios	
Oedipus marries his Mother, Jocasta			Oedipus kills the Sphinx
			Laios (Oedipus' father) = *left-sided* (?)
		Eteocles kills his brother, Polynices	
			Oedipus = *swollen-foot* (?)
Antigone buries her brother, Polynices, despite prohibition			

surface of the earth "they limped forward or tripped sideways." Thus the common feature of the fourth column is the *persistence of the autochthonous origin of man.* It follows that column four is to column three as column one is to column two. The inability to connect two kinds of relationships is overcome (or rather replaced) by the assertion that contradictory relationships are identical inasmuch as they are both self-contradictory in a similar way. Although this is still a provisional formulation of the structure of mythical thought, it is sufficient at this stage.

Turning back to the Oedipus myth, we may now see what it means. The myth has to do with the inability, for a culture which holds the belief that mankind is autochthonous (see, for instance, Pausanias, VIII, xxix, 4: plants provide a *model* for humans), to find a satisfactory transition between this theory and the knowledge that human beings are actually born from the union of man and woman. Although the problem obviously cannot be solved, the Oedipus myth provides a kind of logical tool which relates the original problem—born from one or born from two?—to the derivative problem: born from different or born from same? By a correlation of this type, the overrating of blood relations is to the underrating of blood relations as the attempt to escape autochthony is to the impossibility to succeed in it. Although experience contradicts theory, social life validates cosmology by its similarity of structure. Hence cosmology is true.

Roland Barthes (1915–1980) was one of France's most astonishing literary critics and writers. He was a prolific author, but more significantly, like other artistic masters (Matisse, for example), Barthes was constantly experimenting and changing. After completing his education in classics and French literature at the University of Paris, he taught in France, Romania, and Egypt. He then held a research post at the prestigious National Center for Scientific Research (CNRS) in Paris. After the war, his first works were concerned with the theory of writing. These became *Writing Degree Zero* (1953), which was published in English with *Elements of Semiology* (1964). One could hardly imagine two more different texts by the same author, written within a decade of each other. The earlier was a founding text of the new critical movement in France; the latter a founding text of modern semiotics. Barthes's writing evolved through a number

of phases over many topics, including popular culture (*Mythologies*, 1957), literature (*Sur Racine*, 1963), literary criticism (*Essais critiques*, 1964), and the semiotics of the fashion industry (*Système de la mode*, 1967). In 1975, he was elected to the Collège de France, where he taught both semiotics and literature. In his last decade, beginning with *The Pleasure of the Text* (1973), then *A Lover's Discourse* (1977), he became one of the first social theorists of world reputation to write frankly and powerfully about sexuality and desire in literature and social life. Barthes died tragically in a street accident in Paris.

Semiological Prospects[*]
Roland Barthes (1964)

In Saussure: The (dichotomic) concept of *language/speech* is central in Saussure[**] and was certainly a great novelty in relation to earlier linguistics which sought to find the causes of historical changes in the evolution of pronunciation, spontaneous associations and the working of analogy, and was therefore a linguistics of the individual act. In working out this famous dichotomy, Saussure started from the "multiform and heterogeneous" nature of language, which appears at first sight as an unclassifiable reality the unity of which cannot be brought to light, since it partakes at the same time of the physical, the physiological, the mental, the individual and the social. . . .

The language (langue): A language is therefore, so to speak, language minus speech: it is at the same time a social institution and a system of values. As a social institution, it is by no means an act, and it is not subject to any premeditation. It is the social part

---

[*] In Sausure, "Speech (Parole)," "The Language, Speech, & The Social Sciences," "The Garment System," and "The Food System" from *Elements Of Semiology* by Roland Barthes, translated by Annette Lavers and Colin Smith. Reprinted by permission of Farrar, Straus, and Giroux. Semiological Prospects from *Elements of Semiology* by Roland Barthes. Published by Jonathan Cape, reprinted by permission of The Random House Group Limited.

[**] The Saussurean notions of *langue* and *parole* present to the translator into English notorious difficulties, which their extension in the present work does nothing to alleviate. We have translated *langue* as "*a*" or "*the* language," except when the coupling with "speech" makes the meaning clear. *Les paroles*, whether applied to several people or to several semiotic systems, has been translated by various periphrases which we hope do not obscure the identity of meaning. (Trans.)

of language, the individual cannot by himself either create or modify it; it is essentially a collective contract which one must accept in its entirety if one wishes to communicate. Moreover, this social product is autonomous, like a game with its own rules, for it can be handled only after a period of learning. As a system of values, a language is made of a certain number of elements, each one of which is at the same time the equivalent of a given quantity of things and a term of a larger function, in which are found, in a differential order, other correlative values: from the point of view of the language, the sign is like a coin which has the value of a certain amount of goods which it allows one to buy, but also has value in relation to other coins, in a greater or lesser degree. The institutional and the systematic aspect are of course connected: it is because a language is a system of contractual values (in part arbitrary, or, more exactly, unmotivated) that it resists the modifications coming from a single individual, and is consequently a social institution.

Speech (parole): In contrast to the language, which is both institution and system, *speech* is essentially an individual act of selection and actualization; it is made in the first place of the "combination thanks to which the speaking subject can use the code of the language with a view to expressing his personal thought" (this extended speech could be called *discourse*), and secondly by the "psycho-physical mechanisms which allow him to exteriorize these combinations." It is certain that phonation, for instance, cannot be confused with the language; neither the institution nor the system are altered if the individual who resorts to them speaks loudly or softly, with slow or rapid delivery, etc. The combinative aspect of speech is of course of capital importance, for it implies that speech is constituted by the recurrence of identical signs: it is because signs are repeated in successive discourses and within one and the same discourse (although they are combined in accordance with the infinite diversity of various people's speech) that each sign becomes an element of the language; and it is because speech is essentially a combinative activity that it corresponds to an individual act and not to a pure creation.

The dialectics of language and speech: Language and speech: each of these two terms of course achieves its full definition only in the dialectical process which unites one to the other: there is no language without speech, and no speech outside language. . . . On the one hand, the language is "the

treasure deposited by the practice of speech, in the subjects belonging to the same community" and, since it is a collective summa of individual imprints, it must remain incomplete at the level of each isolated individual: a language does not exist perfectly except in the "speaking mass"; one cannot handle speech except by drawing on the language. But conversely, a language is possible only starting from speech: historically, speech phenomena always precede language phenomena (it is speech which makes language evolve), and genetically, a language is constituted in the individual through his learning from the environmental speech (one does not teach grammar and vocabulary which are, broadly speaking, the language, to babies). To sum, a language is at the same time the product and the instrument of speech: their relationship is therefore a genuinely dialectical one. . . .

The language, speech and the social sciences. The sociological scope of the *language/speech* concept is obvious. The manifest affinity of the language according to Saussure and of Durkheim's conception of a collective consciousness independent of its individual manifestations has been emphasized very early on. A direct influence of Durkheim on Saussure has even been postulated; it has been alleged that Saussure had followed very closely the debate between Durkheim and Tarde and that his conception of the language came from Durkheim while that of speech was a kind of concession to Tarde's idea on the individual element. This hypothesis has lost some of its topicality because linguistics has chiefly developed, in the Saussurean idea of the language, the "system of values" aspect, which led to acceptance of the necessity for an immanent analysis of the linguistic institution, and this immanence is inimical to sociological research. . . .

It can be seen from these brief indications how rich in extra- or meta-linguistic developments the notion *language/speech* is. We shall therefore postulate that there exists a general category *language/speech*, which embraces all the systems of signs; since there are no better ones, we shall keep the terms *language* and *speech*, even when they are applied to communications whose substance is not verbal.

The garment system: We saw that the separation between the language and speech represented the essential feature of linguistic analysis; it would therefore be futile to propose to apply this separation straightaway to systems of objects, images or behaviour patterns which have not yet been studied from a semantic point of view. We can merely, in the case of some of these hypothetical systems, foresee that certain classes of facts will belong to the category of the *language* and others to that of *speech*, and make it immediately clear that in the course of its application to semiology, Saussure's distinction is likely to undergo modifications which it will be precisely our task to note.

Let us take the garment system for instance; it is probably necessary to subdivide it into three different systems, according to which substance is used for communication.

In clothes as *written* about, that is to say described in a fashion magazine by means of articulated language, there is practically no "speech": the garment which is described never corresponds to an individual handling of the rules of fashion, it is a systematized set of signs and rules: it is a language in its pure state. According to the Saussurean schema, a language without speech would be impossible; what makes the fact acceptable here is, on the one hand, that the language of fashion does not emanate from the "speaking mass" but from a group which makes the decisions and deliberately elaborates the code, and on the other hand that the abstraction inherent in any language is here materialized as written language; fashion clothes (as written about) are the language at the level of vestimentary communication and speech at the level of verbal communication.

In clothes as *photographed* (if we suppose, to simplify matters, that there is no duplication by verbal description), the language still issues from the fashion group, but it is no longer given in a wholly abstract form, for a photographed garment is always worn by an individual woman. What is given by the fashion photograph is a semi-formalized state of the garment system: for on the one hand, the language of fashion must here be inferred from a pseudo-real garment, and on the other, the wearer of the garment (the photographed model) is, so to speak, a normative individual, chosen for her canonic generality, and who consequently represents a "speech" which is fixed and devoid of all combinative freedom.

Finally in clothes as *worn* (or real clothes), as Trubetzkoy had suggested, we again find the classic distinction between language and speech. The language, in the garment system, is made i) by the oppositions of pieces, parts of garment and "details", the variation of which entails a change in meaning (to wear a beret or a bowler hat does not have the same meaning); ii) by the rules which govern the association of the pieces among themselves, either on the length of the body or in depth. Speech, in the garment system, comprises all the phenomena of anomic fabrication (few are still left in our society) or of individual way of wearing (size of the garment, degree of cleanliness or wear, personal quirks, free association of pieces). As for the dialectic which unites here costume (the language) and clothing (speech), it does not resemble that of verbal language; true, clothing always draws on costume (except in the case of eccentricity, which, by the way, also has its signs), but costume, at least today, *precedes* clothing, since it comes from the ready-made industry, that is, from a minority group (although more anonymous than that of Haute Couture).

Louis Althusser (1918–1990) was born in Algiers. During World War II, he was imprisoned in a Nazi concentration camp. After the war, in 1948, Althusser joined the French Communist Party and taught philosophy at the École Normale Supérieure in Paris. Althusser's book of early essays, *For Marx* (1965), was a controversial text among Left social theorists due to its evident scientific Marxism—a method then consistent with both the Stalinist impulses of the French Communist Party and the new spirit of scientific structuralism in France. "Ideology and the Ideological State Apparatus," though written late in the 1960s, was forged in the intellectual developments in Paris that were at issue before the revolutionary events of 1968. It belongs, therefore, to a conjuncture wherein political and theoretical structuralism sought to account for the modern state's complicity in the shaping of popular culture. This one essay may be the most enduring of all Althusser's writings for its daring use of Jacques Lacan's psychoanalytic theories to account for the unreality of the real world ideological culture's claim to represent. Althusser's theory of the state's ideological apparatus withstood criticism, largely through its contributions to cultural studies wherein the scientific methods of structuralism gave way to a more critical view of state power and culture. Tragically, Althusser's later years were marked by debilitating mental illness that led him to murder his wife and suffer a long confinement in a mental hospital.

Ideology and the Ideological State Apparatuses[*]

Louis Althusser (1968–1969)

In order to advance the theory of the State it is indispensable to take into account not only the distinction between *State power* and *State apparatus*, but also another reality which is clearly on the side of the (repressive) State apparatus, but must not be confused with it. I shall call this reality by its concept: the *ideological State apparatuses*.

What are the ideological State apparatuses (ISAs)?

They must not be confused with the (repressive) State apparatus. Remember that in Marxist theory, the State Apparatus (SA) contains: the Government, the Administration, the Army, the Police, the Courts, the Prisons, etc., which constitute what I shall in future call the Repressive State Apparatus. Repressive suggests that the State Apparatus in question "functions by violence"—at least ultimately (since repression, e.g. administrative repression, may take non-physical forms).

I shall call Ideological State Apparatuses a certain number of realities which present themselves to the immediate observer in the form of distinct and specialized institutions. I propose an empirical list of these which will obviously have to be examined in detail, tested, corrected and reorganized. With all the reservations implied by this requirement, we can for the moment regard the following institutions as Ideological State Apparatuses (the order in which I have listed them has no particular significance):

— the religious ISA (the system of the different Churches),
— the educational ISA (the system of the different public and private "Schools"),
— the family ISA,
— the legal ISA,
— the political ISA (the political system, including the different Parties),
— the trade-union ISA,
— the communications ISA (press, radio and television, etc.),
— the cultural ISA (Literature, the Arts, sports, etc.).

I have said that the ISAs must not be confused with the (Repressive) State Apparatus. What constitutes the difference?

[*]Republished with the permission of the Monthly Review Foundation, from *Lenin & Philosophy and Other Essays*, by Louis Althusser, Ben Brewster, tr., pp. 142–144, 162, 164–165, 170–171, 173–175. Copyright 1971, Monthly Review Press; permission conveyed through Copyright Clearance Center, Inc.

As a first moment, it is clear that while there is *one* (Repressive) State Apparatus, there is a *plurality* of Ideological State Apparatuses. Even presupposing that it exists, the unity that constitutes this plurality of ISAs as a body is not immediately visible.

As a second moment, it is clear that whereas the—unified—(Repressive) State Apparatus belongs entirely to the *public* domain, much the larger part of the Ideological State Apparatuses (in their apparent dispersion) are part, on the contrary, of the *private* domain. Churches, Parties, Trade Unions, families, some schools, most newspapers, cultural ventures, etc., etc., are private.

Ideology Is a "Representation" of the Imaginary Relationship

In order to approach my central thesis on the structure and functioning of ideology, I shall first present two theses, one negative, the other positive. The first concerns the object which is "represented" in the imaginary form of ideology, the second concerns the materiality of ideology.

THESIS I: Ideology represents the imaginary relationship of individuals to their real conditions of existence.

We commonly call religious ideology, ethical ideology, legal ideology, political ideology, etc., so many "world outlooks." Of course, assuming that we do not live one of these ideologies as the truth (e.g. "believe" in God, Duty, Justice, etc. . . .), we admit that the ideology we are discussing from a critical point of view, examining it as the ethnologist examines the myths of a "primitive society," that these "world outlooks" are largely imaginary, i.e. do not "correspond to reality."

However, while admitting that they do not correspond to reality, i.e. that they constitute an illusion, we admit that they do make allusion to reality, and that they need only be "interpreted" to discover the reality of the world behind their imaginary representation of that world (ideology = *illusion/allusion*). . . .

Now I can return to a thesis which I have already advanced: it is not their real conditions of existence, their real world, that "men" "represent to themselves" in ideology, but above all it is their relation to those conditions of existence which is represented to them there. It is this relation which is at the centre of every ideological, i.e. imaginary, representation of the real world. It is this relation that contains the "cause" which has to explain the imaginary distortion of the ideological representation of the real world. Or rather, to leave aside the language of causality it is necessary to advance the thesis that it is the *imaginary nature of this relation* which underlies all the imaginary distortion that we can observe (if we do not live in its truth) in all ideology.

To speak in a Marxist language, if it is true that the representation of the real conditions of existence of the individuals occupying the posts of agents of production, exploitation, repression, ideologization and scientific practice, does in the last analysis arise from the relations of production, and from relations deriving from the relations of production, we can say the following: all ideology represents in its necessarily imaginary distortion not the existing relations of production (and the other relations that derive from them), but above all the (imaginary) relationship of individuals to the relations of production and the relations that derive from them. What is represented in ideology is therefore not the system of the real relations which govern the existence of individuals, but the imaginary relation of those individuals to the real relations in which they live.

If this is the case, the question of the "cause" of the imaginary distortion of the real relations in ideology disappears and must be replaced by a different question: why is the representation given to individuals of their (individual) relation to the social relations which govern their conditions of existence and their collective and individual life necessarily an imaginary relation? And what is the nature of this imaginariness? Posed in this way, the question explodes the solution by a "clique," by a group of individuals (Priests or Despots) who are the authors of the great ideological mystification, just as it explodes the solution by the alienated character of the real world. We shall see why later in my exposition. For the moment I shall go no further.

THESIS II: Ideology has a material existence.

I have already touched on this thesis by saying that the "ideas" or "representations," etc., which seem to make up ideology do not have an ideal (*idéale* or *idéelle*) or spiritual existence, but a material existence. I even suggested that the ideal (*idéale, idéelle*) and spiritual existence of "ideas" arises exclusively in an ideology of the "idea" and of ideology, and let me add, in an ideology of what seems to have "founded" this conception since the emergence of the sciences, i.e. what extent that it has emerged that their existence is inscribed in the actions of practices governed by rituals defined in the last instance by an ideological apparatus. It therefore appears that the subject acts insofar as he is acted by the following

system (set out in the order of its real determination): ideology existing in a material ideological apparatus, prescribing material practices governed by a material ritual, which practices exist in the material actions of a subject acting in all consciousness according to his belief.

Ideology Interpellates Individuals as Subjects

This thesis is simply a matter of making my last proposition explicit: there is no ideology except by the subject and for subjects. Meaning, there is no ideology except for concrete subjects, and this destination for ideology is only made possible by the subject: meaning, *by the category of the subject* and its functioning.

By this I mean that, even if it only appears under this name (the subject) with the rise of bourgeois ideology, above all with the rise of legal ideology, the category of the subject (which may function under other names: e.g., as the soul in Plato, as God, etc.) is the constitutive category of all ideology, whatever its determination (regional or class) and whatever its historical date—since ideology has no history.

I say: the category of the subject is constitutive of all ideology, but at the same time and immediately I add that *the category of the subject is only constitutive of all ideology insofar as all ideology has the function (which defines it) of "constituting" concrete individuals as subjects.* In the interaction of this double constitution exists the functioning of all ideology, ideology being nothing but its functioning in the material forms of existence of that functioning.

In order to grasp what follows, it is essential to realize that both he who is writing these lines and the reader who reads them are themselves subjects, and therefore ideological subjects (a tautological proposition), i.e. that the author and the reader of these lines both live "spontaneously" or "naturally" in ideology in the sense in which I have said that "man is an ideological animal by nature."

That the author, insofar as he writes the lines of a discourse which claims to be scientific, is completely absent as a "subject" from "his" scientific discourse (for all scientific discourse is by definition a subject-less discourse, there is no "Subject of science" except in an ideology of science) is a different question which I shall leave on one side for the moment. . . .

I only wish to point out that you and I are *always already* subjects, and as such constantly practice the rituals of ideological recognition, which guarantee for us that we are indeed concrete, individual, distinguishable and (naturally) irreplaceable subjects. The writing I am currently executing and the reading you are currently performing are also in this respect rituals of ideological recognition, including the "obviousness" with which the "truth" or "error" of my reflections may impose itself on you.

But to recognize that we are subjects and that we function in the practical rituals of the most elementary everyday life (the hand-shake, the fact of calling you by your name, the fact of knowing, even if I do not know what it is, that you "have" a name of your own, which means that you are recognized as a unique subject, etc.)—this recognition only gives us the "consciousness" of our incessant (eternal) practice of ideological recognition—its consciousness, i.e. its *recognition*—but in no sense does it give us the (scientific) *knowledge* of the mechanism of this recognition. Now it is this knowledge that we have to reach, if you will, while speaking in ideology, and from within ideology we have to outline a discourse which tries to break with ideology, in order to dare to be the beginning of a scientific (i.e. subject-less) discourse on ideology.

Thus in order to represent why the category of the "subject" is constitutive of ideology, which only exists by constituting concrete subjects as subjects, I shall employ a special mode of exposition: "concrete" enough to be recognized, but abstract enough to be thinkable and thought, giving rise to a knowledge.

As a first formulation I shall say: *all ideology hails or interpellates concrete individuals as concrete subjects*, by the functioning of the category of the subject.

This is a proposition which entails that we distinguish for the moment between concrete individuals on the one hand and concrete subjects on the other, although at this level concrete subjects only exist insofar as they are supported by a concrete individual.

I shall then suggest that ideology "acts" or "functions" in such a way that it "recruits" subjects among the individuals (it recruits them all), or "transforms" the individuals into subjects (it transforms them all) by that very precise operation which I have called *interpellation* or hailing, and which can be imagined along the lines of the most commonplace everyday police (or other) hailing: "Hey, you there!"

Assuming that the theoretical scene I have imagined takes place in the street, the hailed individual will turn round. By this mere one-hundred-and-eighty-degree physical conversion, he becomes a *subject*. Why? Because he has recognized that the hail was "really" addressed to him, and that "it was *really him* who was hailed" (and not someone else). Experience shows that the practical telecommunication of hailings is such that they hardly ever miss their man: verbal call or whistle, the one hailed always recognizes that it is really him who is being hailed. And yet it is a strange phenomenon, and one which cannot be explained solely by "guilt feelings," despite the large numbers who "have something on their consciences".

Naturally for the convenience and clarity of my little theoretical theatre I have had to present things in the form of a sequence, with a before and an after, and thus in the form of a temporal succession. There are individuals walking along. Somewhere (usually behind them) the hail rings out: "Hey, you there!" One individual (nine times out of ten it is the right one) turns round, believing/suspecting/knowing that it is for him, i.e. recognizing that "it really is he" who is meant by the hailing. But in reality these things happen without any succession. The existence of ideology and the hailing or interpellation of individuals as subjects are one and the same thing.

Doubts and Reservations

David Riesman (1909–2002) was educated at Harvard College, then Harvard Law School, after which he clerked for Supreme Court Justice Louis Brandeis. After practicing law, including service as deputy assistant district attorney for New York County, Riesman began teaching social science at the University of Chicago in 1946. In 1957, he joined the Department of Social Relations at Harvard. He later became a professor emeritus. In addition to his contributions to the study of American social character, Riesman was considered one of the foremost experts on higher education in the United States. The selection is from *The Lonely Crowd* (1961), which Riesman wrote with Nathan Glazer and Reuel Denney. Since its first edition in 1950, the book has been an all-time best seller among sociological studies. It remains the classic study of postwar American social life. Readers will note the references to Erich Fromm, with whom Riesman once had what he calls an unorthodox analysis. The range of Riesman's sources, from psychoanalysis to economic history, begins to explain the book's broad appeal.

Character and Society:
The Other-Directed Personality[*]
David Riesman (1950)

* Riesman, David. *The Lonely Crowd: A Study of the Changing American Character*. New Haven: Yale University Press,1969. Print. © 1969. Yale University Press. Reprinted with permission of Yale University Press.

What is the relation between social character and society? How is it that every society seems to get, more or less, the social character it "needs"? Erik H. Erikson writes, in a study of the social character of the Yurok Indians, that ". . . systems of child training . . . represent unconscious attempts at creating out of human raw material that configuration of attitudes which is (or once was) the optimum under the tribe's particular natural conditions and economic-historic necessities."

From "economic-historic necessities" to "systems of child training" is a long jump. Much of the work of students of social character has been devoted to closing the gap and showing how the satisfaction of the largest "needs" of society is prepared, in some half-mysterious way, by its most intimate practices. Erich Fromm succinctly suggests the line along which this connection between society and character training may be sought: "In order that any society may function well, its members must acquire the kind of character which makes them *want* to act in the way they *have* to act as members of the society or of a special class within it. They have to *desire* what objectively is necessary for them to do. *Outer force* is replaced by *inner compulsion*, and by the particular kind of human energy which is channeled into character traits."

Thus, the link between character and society—certainly not the only one, but one of the most significant, and the one I choose to emphasize in this discussion—is to be found in the way in which society ensures some degree of conformity from the individuals who make it up. In each society, such a mode of ensuring conformity is built into the child, and then either encouraged or frustrated in later adult experience. (No society, it would appear, is quite prescient enough to ensure that the mode of conformity it has inculcated will satisfy those subject to it in every stage of life.) I shall use the term "mode of conformity" interchangeably with the term "social character"—though certainly conformity is not all of social character: "mode of creativity" is as much a part of it. However, while societies and individuals may live well enough—if rather boringly—without creativity, it is not likely that they can live without some mode of conformity—even be it one of rebellion.

My concern in this book is with two revolutions and their relation to the "mode of conformity" or "social character" of Western man since the Middle Ages. The first of these revolutions has in the last four hundred years cut us off pretty decisively from the family- and clan-oriented traditional ways of life in which mankind has existed throughout most of history; this revolution includes the Renaissance, the Reformation, the Counter-Reformation, the Industrial Revolution, and the political revolutions of the seventeenth, eighteenth, and nineteenth centuries. This revolution is, of course, still in process, but in the most advanced countries of the world, and particularly in America, it is giving way to another sort of revolution—a whole range of social developments associated with a shift from an age of production to an age of consumption.

The first revolution we understand moderately well; it is, under various labels, in our texts and our terminology; this book has nothing new to contribute to its description, but perhaps does contribute something to its evaluation. The second revolution, which is just beginning, has interested many contemporary observers, including social scientists, philosophers, and journalists. Both description and evaluation are still highly controversial; indeed, many are still preoccupied with the first set of revolutions and have not invented the categories for discussing the second set. In this book I try to sharpen the contrast between, on the one hand, conditions and character in those social strata that are today most seriously affected by the second revolution, and, on the other hand, conditions and character in analogous strata during the earlier revolution; in this perspective, what is briefly said about the traditional and feudal societies which were overturned by the first revolution is in the nature of backdrop for these later shifts.

One of the categories I make use of is taken from demography, the science that deals with birth rates and death rates, with the absolute and relative numbers of people in a society, and their distribution by age, sex, and other variables, for I tentatively seek to link certain social and characterological developments, as cause and effect, with certain population shifts in Western society since the Middle Ages.

It seems reasonably well established, despite the absence of reliable figures for earlier centuries, that during this period the curve of population growth in the Western countries has shown an S-shape of a particular type (as other countries are drawn more closely into the net of Western civilization, their populations also show a tendency to develop along the lines of this S-shaped curve). The bottom horizontal line of the S represents a situation where the total population does not increase or does so very slowly, for the number of births equals roughly the number of deaths, and both are very high. In societies of this type, a high proportion of the population is young, life expectancy is low, and the turnover of generations is extremely rapid. Such societies are said to be in the phase of "high growth potential"; for should something happen to decrease the very high death rate (greater production of food, new sanitary measures, new knowledge of the causes of disease, and so on), a "population explosion" would result, and the population would increase very rapidly. This in effect is what happened in the West, starting with the seventeenth century. This spurt in population was most marked in Europe, and the countries settled by Europeans, in the nineteenth century. It is represented by the vertical bar of the S. Demographers call this the stage of "transitional growth," because the birth rate soon begins to follow the death rate in its decline. The rate of growth then slows down, and demographers begin to detect in the growing proportion of middle-aged and aged in the population the signs of a third stage, "incipient population decline." Societies in this stage are represented by the top horizontal bar of the S, again indicating, as in the first stage, that total population growth is small—but this time because births and deaths are low.

The S-curve is not a theory of population growth so much as an empirical description of what has happened in the West and in those parts of the world influenced by the West. After the S runs its course, what then? The developments of recent years in the United States and other Western countries do not seem to be susceptible to so simple and elegant a summing up. "Incipient population decline" has not become "population decline" itself, and the birth rate has shown an uncertain tendency to rise again, which most demographers think is temporary.

It would be very surprising if variations in the basic conditions of reproduction, livelihood, and chances for survival, that is, in the supply of and demand for human beings, with all these imply for change in the spacing of people, the size of markets, the role of children, the society's feeling of vitality or senescence, and many other intangibles, failed to influence character. My thesis is, in fact, that each of these three different phases on the population curve appears to be occupied by a society that enforces conformity and molds social character in a definably different way.

The society of high growth potential develops in its typical members a social character whose conformity is insured by their tendency to follow tradition: these I shall term *tradition-directed* people and the society in which they live *a society dependent on tradition-direction.*

The society of transitional population growth develops in its typical members a social character whose conformity is insured by their tendency to acquire early in life an internalized set of goals. These I shall term *inner-directed* people and the society in which they live *a society dependent on inner-direction.*

Finally, the society of incipient population decline develops in its typical members a social character whose conformity is insured by their tendency to be sensitized to the expectations and preferences of others. These I shall term *other-directed* people and the society in which they live one *dependent on other-direction.* . . .

A definition of other-direction. The type of character I shall describe as other-directed seems to be emerging in very recent years in the upper middle class of our larger cities: more prominently in New York than in Boston, in Los Angeles than in Spokane, in Cincinnati than Chillicothe. Yet in some respects this type is strikingly similar to the American, whom Tocqueville and other curious and astonished visitors from Europe, even before the Revolution, thought to be a new kind of man. Indeed, travelers' reports on America impress us with their unanimity. The American is said to be shallower, freer with his money, friendlier, more uncertain of himself and his values, more demanding of approval than the European. It all adds up to a pattern which, without stretching matters too far, resembles the kind of character that a number of social scientists have seen as developing in contemporary, highly industrialized, and bureaucratic America: [Erich] Fromm's "marketer," [C. Wright] Mills's "fixer," Arnold Green's "middle class male child."

It is my impression that the middle-class American of today is decisively different from those Americans of Tocqueville's writings who nevertheless strike us as so contemporary, and much of this book will be devoted to discussing these differences. It is also my impression that the conditions I believe to be responsible for otherdirection are affecting increasing numbers of people in the metropolitan centers of the advanced industrial countries. My analysis of the other-directed character is thus at once an analysis of the American and of contemporary man. Much of the time I find it hard or impossible to say where one ends and the other begins. Tentatively, I am inclined to think that the other-directed type does find itself most at home in America, due to certain unique elements in American society, such as its recruitment from Europe and its lack of any feudal past. As against this, I am also inclined to put more weight on capitalism, industrialism, and urbanization—these being international tendencies—than on any character-forming peculiarities of the American scene.

Bearing these qualifications in mind, it seems appropriate to treat contemporary metropolitan America as our illustration of a society—so far, perhaps, the only illustration—in which other-direction is the dominant mode of insuring conformity. It would be premature, however, to say that it is already the dominant mode in America as a whole. But since the other-directed types are to be found among the young, in the larger cities, and among the upper income groups, we may assume that, unless present trends are reversed, the hegemony of other-direction lies not far off.

If we wanted to cast our social character types into social class molds, we could say that inner-direction is the typical character of the "old" middle class—the banker, the tradesman, the small entrepreneur, the technically oriented engineer, etc.—while other-direction is becoming the typical character of the "new" middle class—the bureaucrat, the salaried employee in business, etc. Many of the economic factors associated with the recent growth of the "new" middle class are well known. They have been discussed by James Burnham, Colin Clark, Peter Drucker, and others. There is a decline in the numbers and in the proportion of the working population engaged in production and extraction—agriculture, heavy industry, heavy transport—and an increase in the numbers and the proportion engaged in white-collar work and the service trades. People who are literate, educated, and provided with the necessities of life by an ever more efficient machine industry and agriculture, turn increasingly to the "tertiary" economic realm. The service industries prosper among the people as a whole and no longer only in court circles.

Education, leisure, services, these go together with an increased consumption of words and images from the new mass media of communications. While societies in the phase of transitional growth step up the process of distributing words from urban centers, the flow becomes a torrent in the societies of incipient population decline. This process, while modulated by profound national and class differences, connected with differences in literacy and loquacity, takes place everywhere in the industrialized lands. Increasingly, relations with the outer world and with oneself are mediated by the flow of mass communication. For the other-directed types political events are likewise experienced through a screen of words by which the events are habitually atomized and personalized—or pseudo-personalized. For the inner-directed person who remains still extant in this period the tendency is rather to systematize and moralize this flow of words.

These developments lead, for large numbers of people, to changes in paths to success and to the requirement of more "socialized" behavior both for success and for marital and personal adaptation. Connected with such changes are changes in the family and in child-rearing practices. In the smaller families of urban life, and with the spread of "permissive" child care to ever wider strata of the population, there is a relaxation of older patterns of discipline. Under these newer patterns the peer-group (the group of one's associates of the same age and class) becomes much more important to the child, while the parents make him feel guilty not so much about violation of inner standards as about failure to be popular or otherwise to manage his relations with these other children. Moreover, the pressures of the school and the peer-group are reinforced and continued—in a manner whose inner paradoxes I shall discuss later—by the mass media: movies, radio, comics, and popular culture media generally. Under these conditions types of character emerge that we shall here term other-directed. To them much of the discussion in the ensuing chapters is devoted. *What is common to all the other-directed people is that their contemporaries are the source of direction for the individual—either those known to him or those with whom he is indirectly acquainted, through friends and through the mass media. This source is of course "internalized" in the sense that dependence on it for guidance in life is implanted early. The goals toward which the other-directed person strives shift with that guidance: it is only the process of striving itself and the process of paying close attention to the signals from others that remain unaltered throughout life.* This mode of keeping in touch with others permits a close behavioral conformity, not through drill in behavior itself, as in the tradition-directed character, but rather through an exceptional sensitivity to the actions and wishes of others. . . .

The three types compared. One way to see the structural differences that mark the three types is to see the differences in the emotional sanction or control in each type.

The tradition-directed person feels the impact of his culture as a unit, but it is nevertheless mediated through the specific, small number of individuals with whom he is in daily contact. These expect of him not so much that he be a certain type of person but that he behave in the approved way. Consequently the sanction for behavior tends to be the fear of being *shamed*.

The inner-directed person has early incorporated a psychic gyroscope which is set going by his parents and can receive signals later on from other authorities who resemble his parents. He goes through life less independent than he seems, obeying this internal piloting. Getting off course, whether in response to inner impulses or to the fluctuating voices of contemporaries, may lead to the feeling of *guilt*.

Since the direction to be taken in life has been learned in the privacy of the home from a small number of guides and since principles, rather than details of behavior, are internalized, the inner-directed person is capable of great stability. Especially so when it turns out that his fellows have gyroscopes too, spinning at the same speed and set in the same direction. But many inner-directed individuals can remain stable even when the reinforcement of social approval is not available—as in the upright life of the stock Englishman isolated in the tropics.

Contrasted with such a type as this, the other-directed person learns to respond to signals from a far wider circle than is constituted by his parents. The family is no longer a closely knit unit to which he belongs but merely part of a wider social environment to which he early becomes attentive. In these respects the other-directed person resembles the tradition-directed person: both live in a group milieu and lack the inner-directed person's capacity to go it alone. The nature of this group milieu, however, differs radically in the two cases. The other-directed person is cosmopolitan. For him the border between the familiar and the strange—a border clearly marked in the societies depending on tradition-direction—has broken down. As the family continuously absorbs the strange and reshapes itself, so the strange becomes familiar. While the inner-directed person could be "at home abroad" by virtue of his relative insensitivity to others, the other-directed person is, in a sense, at home everywhere and nowhere, capable of a rapid if sometimes superficial intimacy with and response to everyone.

The tradition-directed person takes his signals from others, but they come in a cultural monotone; he needs no complex receiving equipment to pick them up. The other-directed person must be able to receive signals from far and near; the sources are many, the changes rapid. What can be internalized, then, is not a code of behavior but the elaborate equipment needed to attend to such messages and occasionally to participate in their circulation. As against guilt-and-shame controls, though of course these survive, one prime psychological lever of the other-directed person is a diffuse *anxiety*. This control equipment, instead of being like a gyroscope, is like a radar.

Erik H. Erikson (1902–1994) was born of Danish parents in Germany. After completing school in 1927, Erikson lived in Vienna, where he taught school and began analytic training. He was analyzed by Anna Freud and finished his training in 1933. He later fled Europe for Boston, becoming that city's first child analyst. He was associated with Massachusetts General Hospital and Harvard, where he began (but never completed) doctoral studies. In 1936, Erikson taught at Yale; three years later, he moved to San Francisco, where he held a research position at the University of California at Berkeley. In 1950, he refused to sign a loyalty oath and left Berkeley. Erikson taught at Harvard for many years, retiring in 1970. He was recognized as a pioneer psychoanalyst for his clinical work, his research, and his writing. His studies of children were the basis for his contributions to the psychology of emotional development. Erikson was generally considered the founder of psychohistorical

studies and one of the few ever able to use psychology to interpret history in a way that balances the different demands of the two fields. In addition to *Childhood and Society*, published in 1950 (the same year as Riesman's *The Lonely Crowd*), his many writings include *Gandhi's Truth* (1969) and *Young Man Luther* (1958).

Youth and American Identity[*]
Erik H. Erikson (1950)

Youth

With the establishment of a good initial relationship to the world of skills and tools, and with the advent of puberty, childhood proper comes to an end. Youth begins. But in puberty and adolescence all samenesses and continuities relied on earlier are more or less questioned again, because of a rapidity of body growth which equals that of early childhood and because of the new addition of genital maturity. The growing and developing youths, faced with this physiological revolution within them, and with tangible adult tasks ahead of them, are now primarily concerned with what they appear to be in the eyes of others as compared with what they feel they are, and with the question of how to connect the roles and skills cultivated earlier with the occupational prototypes of the day. In their search for a new sense of continuity and sameness, adolescents have to refight many of the battles of earlier years, even though to do so they must artificially appoint perfectly well-meaning people to play the roles of adversaries; and they are ever ready to install lasting idols and ideals as guardians of a final identity.

The integration now taking place in the form of ego identity is, as pointed out, more than the sum of the childhood identifications. It is the accrued experience of the ego's ability to integrate all identifications with the vicissitudes of the libido, with the aptitudes developed out of endowment, and with the opportunities offered in social roles. The sense of ego identity, then, is the accrued confidence that the inner sameness and continuity prepared in the past

---

are matched by the sameness and continuity of one's meaning for others, as evidenced in the tangible promise of a "career."

The danger of this stage is role confusion. Where this is based on a strong previous doubt as to one's sexual identity, delinquent and outright psychotic episodes are not uncommon. If diagnosed and treated correctly, these incidents do not have the same fatal significance which they have at other ages. In most instances, however, it is the inability to settle on an occupational identity which disturbs individual young people. To keep themselves together they temporarily overidentify, to the point of apparent complete loss of identity, with the heroes of cliques and crowds. This initiates the stage of "falling in love," which is by no means entirely, or even primarily, a sexual matter—except where the mores demand it. To a considerable extent adolescent love is an attempt to arrive at a definition of one's identity by projecting one's diffused ego image on another and by seeing it thus reflected and gradually clarified. This is why so much of young love is conversation.

Young people can also be remarkably clannish, and cruel in their exclusion of all those who are "different," in skin color or cultural background, in tastes and gifts, and often in such petty aspects of dress and gesture as have been temporarily selected as *the* signs of an in-grouper or out-grouper. It is important to understand (which does not mean condone or participate in) such intolerance as a defense against a sense of identity confusion. For adolescents not only help one another temporarily through much discomfort by forming cliques and by stereotyping themselves, their ideals, and their enemies; they also perversely test each other's capacity to pledge fidelity. The readiness for such testing also explains the appeal which simple and cruel totalitarian doctrines have on the minds of the youth of such countries and classes as have lost or are losing their group identities (feudal, agrarian, tribal, national) and face world-wide industrialization, emancipation, and wider communication.

The adolescent mind is essentially a mind of the *moratorium*, a psychosocial stage between childhood and adulthood, and between the morality learned by the child, and the ethics to be developed by the adult. It is an ideological mind—and, indeed, it is the ideological outlook of a society that speaks most clearly to the adolescent who is eager to be affirmed by his peers, and is ready to be confirmed by rituals, creeds, and programs which at the same time define what is evil, uncanny, and inimical. In searching for the social values which guide identity, one therefore confronts the problems of *ideology* and *aristocracy*, both in their widest possible sense which connotes that within a defined world image and a predestined course of history, the best people will come to rule and rule develops the best in people. In order not to become cynically or apathetically lost, young people must somehow be able to convince themselves that those who succeed in their anticipated adult world thereby shoulder the obligation of being the best. We will discuss later the dangers which emanate from human ideals harnessed to the management of super-machines, be they guided by nationalistic or international, communist or capitalist ideologies. In the last part of this book we shall discuss the way in which the revolutions of our day attempt to solve and also to exploit the deep need of youth to redefine its identity in an industrialized world. . . .

American Identity

It is a commonplace to state that whatever one may come to consider a truly American trait can be shown to have its equally characteristic opposite. This, one suspects, is true of all "national characters," or (as I would prefer to call them) national identities—so true, in fact that one may begin rather than end with the proposition that a nation's identity is derived from the ways in which history has, as it were, counterpointed certain opposite potentialities; the ways in which it lifts this counterpoint to a unique style of civilization, or lets it disintegrate into mere contradiction.

This dynamic country subjects its inhabitants to more extreme contrasts and abrupt changes during a lifetime or a generation than is normally the case with other great nations. Most of her inhabitants are faced, in their own lives or within the orbit of their closest relatives, with alternatives presented by such polarities as: open roads of immigration and jealous islands of tradition; outgoing internationalism and defiant isolationism; boisterous competition and self-effacing co-operation; and many others. The influence of the resulting contradictory slogans on the development of an individual ego probably depends on the coincidence of nuclear ego stages with critical changes in the family's geographic and economic vicissitudes.

The process of American identity formation seems to support an individual's ego identity as long as he can preserve a certain element of deliberate tentativeness of autonomous choice. The individual must be able to convince himself that the next step is up to him and that no matter where he is staying or going he always has the choice of leaving or turning in the opposite direction if he chooses to do so. In this country the migrant does not want to be told to move on, nor the sedentary man to stay where he is; for the life style (and the family history) of each contains the opposite element as a potential alternative which he wishes to consider his most private and individual decision.

Thus the functioning American, as the heir of a history of extreme contrasts and abrupt changes, bases his final ego identity on some tentative combination of dynamic polarities such as migratory and sedentary, individualistic and standardized, competitive and co-operative, pious and freethinking, responsible and cynical, etc.

While we see extreme elaborations of one or the other of these poles in regional, occupational, and characterological types, analysis reveals that this extremeness (of rigidity or of vacillation) contains an inner defense against the always implied, deeply feared, or secretly hoped-for opposite extreme.

To leave his choices open, the American, on the whole, lives with two sets of "truths": a set of religious principles or religiously pronounced political principles of a highly puritan quality, and a set of shifting slogans, which indicate what, at a given time, one may get away with on the basis of not more than a hunch, a mood, or a notion. Thus, the same child may have been exposed in succession or alternately to sudden decisions expressing the slogans "Let's get the hell out of here" and again, "Let's stay and keep the bastards out"—to mention only two of the most sweeping ones. Without any pretense of logic or principle, slogans are convincing enough to those involved to justify action whether within or just outside of the lofty law (in so far as it happens to be enforced or forgotten, according to changing local climate). Seemingly shiftless slogans contain time and space perspectives as ingrained as those elaborated in the Sioux or Yurok system; they are experiments in collective time-space to which individual ego defenses are co-ordinated. But they change, often radically, during one and the same childhood.

A true history of the American identity would have to correlate Parrington's observations on the continuity of formulated thought with the rich history of discontinuous American slogans which pervade public opinion in corner stores and in studies, in the courts and in the daily press. For in principles and concepts too, an invigorating polarity seems to exist on the one hand between the intellectual and political aristocracy which, always mindful of precedent, guards a measure of coherent thought and indestructible spirit, and, on the other hand, a powerful mobocracy which seems to prefer changing slogans to self-perpetuating principles. This native polarity of aristocracy and mobocracy (so admirably synthesized in Franklin D. Roosevelt) pervades American democracy more effectively than the advocates and the critics of the great American middle class seem to realize. This American middle class, decried by some as embodying an ossification of all that is mercenary and philistine in this country, may represent only a transitory series of overcompensatory attempts at settling tentatively around some Main Street, fireplace, bank account, and make of car; it does not, as a class should, preclude high mobility and a cultural potential unsure of its final identity. Status expresses a different relativity in a more mobile society: it resembles an escalator more than a platform; it is a vehicle, rather than a goal.

All countries, and especially large ones, complicate their own progress in their own way with the very premises of their beginnings. We must try to formulate the way in which self-contradictions in American history may expose her youth to an emotional and political short circuit and thus endanger her dynamic potential.

Edwin M. Lemert (1912–1996) was born in Cincinnati, Ohio, to a modest bourgeois family. His father was a successful insurance agent who expected his sons to become professionals. His older brother, in fact, became a physician. The presumption was that Edwin would become a lawyer. His brother remained in Cincinnati, living out the family norm of modest upward mobility. Not Edwin. After finishing his college studies at Miami University and doctoral work at Ohio State University in 1939, Lemert quit his hometown for parts West. Thereafter, he came to be viewed as the family's black sheep. How this may have influenced his theory of social reaction theory cannot be known for certain. Edwin did not become a lawyer, but he did become his generation's most important theorist of social deviance as well as a careful student of juvenile justice and social control and, more generally, of law and jurisprudence in mid-century American society. Lemert's book, *Social Pathology* (1951), remains a classic text in the social theory of deviance. The selection here summarizes his idea that crime and deviance arise neither from personality nor biology but from social effects on the one's personality by which deviant behavior becomes a moral career crucial to the individual's sense of self. As such, Lemert's thinking was consistent with other social theories of the day in respect to the power of social conformity—Goffman, Riesman, and Erikson.

Social Pathology / Societal Reaction Theory[*]
Edwin M. Lemert (1951)

Primary and Secondary Deviation

There has been an embarrassingly large number of theories, often without any relationship to a general theory, advanced to account for various specific pathologies in human behavior. For certain types of pathology, such as alcoholism, crime, or stuttering, there are almost as many theories as there are writers on these subjects. This has been occasioned in no small way by the preoccupation with the origins of pathological behavior and by the fallacy of confusing *original* causes with *effective* causes. All such theories have elements of truth, and the divergent viewpoints they contain can be reconciled with the general theory here if it is granted that original causes or antecedents of deviant behaviors are many and diversified. This holds especially for the psychological processes leading to similar pathological behavior, but it also holds for the situational concomitants of the initial aberrant conduct. A person may come to use excessive alcohol not only for a wide variety of subjective reasons but also because of diversified situational influences, such as the death of a loved one, business failure, or participating in some sort of organized group activity calling for heavy drinking of liquor. Whatever the original reasons for violating the norms of the community, they are important only for certain research purposes, such as assessing the extent of the "social problem" at a given time or determining the requirements for a rational program of social control. From a narrower sociological viewpoint the deviations are not significant until they are organized subjectively and transformed into active

roles and become the social criteria for assigning status. The deviant individuals must react symbolically to their own behavior aberrations and fix them in their sociopsychological patterns. The deviations remain primary deviations or symptomatic and situational as long as they are rationalized or otherwise dealt with as functions of a socially acceptable role. Under such conditions normal and pathological behaviors remain strange and somewhat tensional bedfellows in the same person. Undeniably a vast amount of such segmental and partially integrated pathological behavior exists in our society and has impressed many writers in the field of social pathology.

Just how far and for how long a person may go in dissociating his sociopathic tendencies so that they are merely troublesome adjuncts of normally conceived roles is not known. Perhaps it depends upon the number of alternative definitions of the same overt behavior that he can develop; perhaps certain physiological factors (limits) are also involved. However, if the deviant acts are repetitive and have a high visibility, and if there is a severe societal reaction, which, through a process of identification is incorporated as part of the "me" of the individual, the probability is greatly increased that the integration of existing roles will be disrupted and that reorganization based upon a new role or roles will occur. (The "me" in this context is simply the subjective aspect of the societal reaction.) Reorganization may be the adoption of another normal role in which the tendencies previously defined as "pathological" are given a more acceptable social expression. The other general possibility is the assumption of a deviant role, if such exists; or, more rarely, the person may organize an aberrant sect or group in which he creates a special role of his own. *When a person begins to employ his deviant behavior or a role based upon it as a means of defense, attack, or adjustment to the overt and covert problems created by the consequent societal reaction to him, his deviation is secondary.* Objective evidences of this change will be found in the symbolic appurtenances of the new role, in clothes, speech, posture, and mannerisms, which in some cases heighten social visibility, and which in some cases serve as symbolic cues to professionalization.

Role Conceptions of the Individual Must Be Reinforced by Reactions of Others

It is seldom that one deviant act will provoke a sufficiently strong societal reaction to bring about

[*]Edwin Lemert, Social Pathology: A Systematic Approach to the Theory of Sociopathic Behavior (New York, McGraw-Hill, 1951). Reprinted by permission of the Estate of Edwin Lemert.

secondary deviation, unless in the process of intro-jection the individual imputes or projects meanings into the social situation which are not present. In this case anticipatory fears are involved. For exam-ple, in a culture where a child is taught sharp distinc-tions between "good" women and "bad" women, a single act of questionable morality might conceiv-ably have a profound meaning for the girl so indulg-ing. However, in the absence of reactions by the person's family, neighbors, or the larger community, reinforcing the tentative "bad-girl" self-definition, it is questionable whether a transition to secondary de-viation would take place. It is also doubtful whether a temporary exposure to a severe punitive reaction by the community will lead a person to identify himself with a pathological role, unless, as we have said, the experience is highly traumatic. Most frequently there is a progressive reciprocal relationship between the deviation of the individual and the societal reaction, with a compounding of the societal reaction out of the minute accretions in the deviant behavior, until a point is reached where ingrouping and outgrouping between society and the deviant is manifest.* At this point a stigmatizing of the deviant occurs in the form of name calling, labeling, or stereotyping.

The sequence of interaction leading to secondary deviation is roughly as follows: (1) primary deviation; (2) social penalties; (3) further primary deviation; (4) stronger penalties and rejections; (5) further devia-tion, perhaps with hostilities and resentment begin-ning to focus upon those doing the penalizing; (6) crisis reached in the tolerance quotient, expressed in formal action by the community stigmatizing of the deviant; (7) strengthening of the deviant conduct as a reaction to the stigmatizing and penalties; (8) ulti-mate acceptance of deviant social status and efforts at adjustment on the basis of the associated role.

As an illustration of this sequence the behavior of an errant schoolboy can be cited. For one reason or another, let us say excessive energy, the schoolboy engages in a classroom prank. He is penalized for it by the teacher. Later, due to clumsiness, he creates another disturbance and again he is reprimanded. Then, as sometimes happens, the boy is blamed for something he did not do. When the teacher uses the tag "bad boy" or "mischief maker" or other invidious terms, hostility and resentment are excited in the boy, and he may feel that he is blocked in playing the role expected of him. Thereafter, there may be a strong temptation to assume his role in the class as

defined by the teacher, particularly when he discov-ers that there are rewards as well as penalties deriving from such a role. There is, of course, no implication here that such boys go on to become delinquents or criminals, for the mischief-maker role may later be-come integrated with or retrospectively rationalized as part of a role more acceptable to school authori-ties.** If such a boy continues this unacceptable role and becomes delinquent, the process must be ac-counted for in the light of the general theory of this volume. There must be a spreading corroboration of a sociopathic self-conception and societal reinforce-ment at each step in the process.

The most significant personality changes are manifest when societal definitions and their subjec-tive counterpart become generalized. When this happens, the range of major role choices becomes narrowed to one general class.*** This was very obvious in the case of a young girl who was the daughter of a paroled convict and who was attending a small Mid-dle Western college. She continually argued with herself and with the author, in whom she had con-fided, that in reality she belonged on the "other side of the railroad tracks" and that her life could be enormously simplified by acquiescing in this verdict and living accordingly. While in her case there was a tendency to dramatize her conflicts, nevertheless there was enough societal reinforcement of her self-conception by the treatment she received in her relationship with her father and on dates with col-lege boys to lend it a painful reality. Once these boys took her home to the shoddy dwelling in a slum area where she lived with her father, who was often in a drunken condition, they abruptly stopped seeing her again or else became sexually presumptive.

Erving Goffman (1922–1982) was born in Canada and took a B.A. from the University of Toronto in 1945. He then studied at the University of Chi-cago, receiving his Ph.D. in 1953. His thesis re-search was an observational study of social networks in a small Scottish island community. This study formed the basis for his first important book, *The Presentation of Self in Everyday Life* (1956). In 1961, Goffman began teaching at the University of

---

*Mead, G., "The Psychology of Punitive Justice," *American Journal of Sociology* 23 (March 1918): 577–602.

** Evidence for fixed or inevitable sequences from predelin-quency to crime is absent. Sutherland, E. H., *Principles of Crim-inology,* 1939, 4th ed., p. 202.

*** Sutherland seems to say something of this sort in connection with the development of criminal behavior. *Ibid.,* 86.

California, Berkeley, until 1968 when he moved to the University of Pennsylvania. He died of cancer at age sixty. Goffman is noted for having been brilliantly inscrutable. He refused to write what others called theory, yet his ideas have had a major impact on social theory. He is considered a Chicago School field researcher, yet his methods were multiple and idiosyncratic. He seemed to have mastered completely the professional literature on his subjects, yet he wrote entirely from his own unique literary space. His writings include *Asylums* (1961), *Stigma* (1964), *Interaction Ritual* (1967*)*, *Gender Advertisements* (1969), and an important but not yet well-understood article, "Felicity's Condition," published posthumously in 1983. He was once called sociology's Kafka for his uncanny, and disturbing, insights into human nature. The selection is from *The Presentation of Self in Everyday Life*, his most famous book. Here Goffman offers his theory of the self as a dramatic accomplishment in ongoing social interactions that serve as a stage for the presentation.

Presentation of Self
Erving Goffman (1956)

...We come now to the basic dialectic. In their capacity as performers, individuals will be concerned with maintaining the impression that they are living up to the many standards by which they and their products are judged. Because these standards are so numerous and so pervasive, the individuals who are performers dwell more than we might think in a moral world. But, *qua* performers, individuals are concerned not with the moral issue of realizing these standards, but with the amoral issue of engineering a convincing impression that these standards are being realized. Our activity, then, is largely concerned with moral matters, but as performers we do not have a moral concern with them. As performers we are merchants of morality. Our day is given over to intimate contact with the goods we display and our

minds are filled with intimate understandings of them; but it may well be that the more attention we give to these goods, then the more distant we feel from them and from those who are believing enough to buy them. To use a different imagery, the very obligation and profitability of appearing always in a steady moral light, of being a socialized character, forces one to be the sort of person who is practiced in the ways of the stage.

Staging and the Self

The general notion that we make a presentation of ourselves to others is hardly novel; what ought to be stressed in conclusion is that the very structure of the self can be seen in terms of how we arrange for such performances in our Anglo-American society.

In this report, the individual was divided by implication into two basic parts: he was viewed as a *performer*, a harried fabricator of impressions involved in the all-too-human task of staging a performance; he was viewed as a *character*, a figure, typically a fine one, whose spirit, strength, and other sterling qualities the performance was designed to evoke. The attributes of a performer and the attributes of a character are of a different order, quite basically so, yet both sets have their meaning in terms of the show that must go on.

First, character. In our society the character one performs and one's self are somewhat equated, and this self-as-character is usually seen as something housed within the body of its possessor, especially the upper parts thereof, being a nodule, somehow, in the psychobiology of personality. I suggest that this view is an implied part of what we are all trying to present, but provides, just because of this, a bad analysis of the presentation. In this report the performed self was seen as some kind of image, usually creditable, which the individual on stage and in character effectively attempts to induce others to hold in regard to him. While this image is entertained *concerning* the individual, so that a self is imputed to him, this self itself does not derive from its possessor, but from the whole scene of his action, being generated by that attribute of local events which renders them interpretable by witnesses. A correctly staged and performed scene leads the audience to impute a self to a performed character, but this imputation—this self—is a *product* of a scene that comes off, and is not a cause of it. The self, then, as a performed character, is not an organic thing that has a specific location, whose fundamental fate is to be born, to mature, and to die; it is a dramatic effect arising diffusely from a scene that is presented, and the characteristic issue, the crucial concern, is whether it will be credited or discredited.

In analyzing the self then we are drawn from its possessor, from the person who will profit or lose most by it, for he and his body merely provide the peg on which something of collaborative manufacture will be hung for a time. And the means for producing and maintaining selves do not reside inside the peg; in fact these means are often bolted down in social establishments. There will be a back region with its tools for shaping the body, and a front region with its fixed props. There will be a team of persons whose activity on stage in conjunction with available props will constitute the scene from which the performed character s self will emerge, and another team, the audience, whose interpretive activity will be necessary for this emergence. The self is a product of all of these arrangements, and in all of its parts bears the marks of this genesis.

The whole machinery of self-production is cumbersome, of course, and sometimes breaks down, exposing its separate components: back region control; team collusion; audience tact; and so forth. But, well oiled, impressions will flow from it fast enough to put us in the grips of one of our types of reality—the performance will come off and the firm self accorded each performed character will appear to emanate intrinsically from its performer.

Let us turn now from the individual as character performed to the individual as performer. He has a capacity to learn, this being exercised in the task of training for a part. He is given to having fantasies and dreams, some that pleasurably unfold a triumphant performance, others full of anxiety and dread that nervously deal with vital discreditings in a public front region. He often manifests a gregarious desire for teammates and audiences, a tactful considerateness for their concerns; and he has a capacity for deeply felt shame, leading him to minimize the chances he takes of exposure.

These attributes of the individual *qua* performer are not merely a depicted effect of particular performances; they are psychobiological in nature, and yet they seem to arise out of intimate interaction with the contingencies of staging performances.

And now a final comment. In developing the conceptual framework employed in this report, some language of the stage was used. I spoke of performers and audiences; of routines and parts; of performances coming off or falling flat; of cues, stage settings and backstage; of dramaturgical needs, dramaturgical skills, and dramaturgical strategies. Now it should be admitted that this attempt to press a mere analogy so far was in part a rhetoric and a maneuver.

The claim that all the world's a stage is sufficiently commonplace for readers to be familiar with its limitations and tolerant of its presentation, knowing that at any time they will easily be able to demonstrate to themselves that it is not to be taken too seriously. An action staged in a theater is a relatively contrived illusion and an admitted one; unlike ordinary life, nothing real or actual can happen to the performed characters—although at another level of course something real and actual can happen to the reputation of performers *qua* professionals whose everyday job is to put on theatrical performances.

And so here the language and mask of the stage will be dropped. Scaffolds, after all, are to build other things with, and should be erected with an eye to taking them down. This report is not concerned with aspects of theater that creep into everyday life. It is concerned with the structure of social encounters—the structure of those entities in social life that come into being whenever persons enter one another's immediate physical presence. The key factor in this structure is the maintenance of a single definition of the situation, this definition having to be expressed, and this expression sustained in the face of a multitude of potential disruptions.

A character staged in a theater is not in some ways real, nor does it have the same kind of real consequences as does the thoroughly contrived character performed by a confidence man; but the *successful* staging of either of these types of false figures involves use of *real* techniques—the same techniques by which everyday persons sustain their real social situations. Those who conduct face to face interaction on a theater's stage must meet the key requirement of real situations; they must expressively sustain a definition of the situation: but this they do in circumstances that have facilitated their developing an apt terminology for the interactional tasks that all of us share....

Jacques Lacan (1901–1981) was born in Paris. After studying medicine there, he specialized in psychiatry and psychoanalysis. In 1963, he began teaching at the École Pratique des Hautes Études. He founded his own school of psychoanalysis, the

École Freudienne de Paris, which has been the major psychoanalytic school in Paris since the 1960s. It is typical of psychoanalytic training centers to combine intense clinical experience with the study and interpretation of the Freudian tradition. Lacan's school was no exception. In his lecturing and writing, Lacan sought to wrest psychoanalysis away from the traditionalists by introducing his own, quite independent, understandings of the social theories of desire, language, and literature that were coming into their own in Paris in the 1960s. "The Mirror Stage" is perhaps Lacan's most famous concept. The selection refers to a universal human experience—the one that begins in infancy when the child observes herself in a mirror and imagines herself more whole than any individual "I" (or ego) could possibly be. The concept stood behind Althusser's views on ideology among numerous other post-structuralist theories.

The Mirror Stage[*]
Jacques Lacan (1949)

The conception of the mirror stage that I introduced at our last congress, thirteen years ago, has since become more or less established in the practice of the French group. However, I think it worthwhile to bring it again to your attention, especially today, for the light it sheds on the formation of the *I* as we experience it in psychoanalysis. It is an experience that leads us to oppose any philosophy directly issuing from the *Cogito*.

Some of you may recall that this conception originated in a feature of human behaviour illuminated by a fact of comparative psychology. The child, at an age when he is for a time, however short, outdone by the chimpanzee in instrumental intelligence, can nevertheless already recognize as such his own image in a mirror. This recognition is indicated in the illuminative mimicry of the *Aha-Erlebnis*, which Köhler sees as the expression of situational apperception, an essential stage of the act of intelligence.

This act, far from exhausting itself, as in the case of the monkey, once the image has been mastered

and found empty, immediately rebounds in the case of the child in a series of gestures in which he experiences in play the relation between the movements assumed in the image and the reflected environment, and between this virtual complex and the reality it reduplicates—the child's own body, and the persons and things, around him.

This event can take place, as we have known since Baldwin, from the age of six months, and its repetition has often made me reflect upon the startling spectacle of the infant in front of the mirror. Unable as yet to walk, or even to stand up, and held tightly as he is by some support, human or artificial (what, in France, we call a "*trotte-bébé*"), he nevertheless overcomes, in a flutter of jubilant activity, the obstructions of his support and, fixing his attitude in a slightly leaning-forward position, in order to hold it in his gaze, brings back an instantaneous aspect of the image.

For me, this activity retains the meaning I have given it up to the age of eighteen months. This meaning discloses a libidinal dynamism, which has hitherto remained problematic, as well as an ontological structure of the human world that accords with my reflections on paranoiac knowledge.

We have only to understand the mirror stage *as an identification*, in the full sense that analysis gives to the term: namely, the transformation that takes place in the subject when he assumes an image—whose predestination to this phase-effect is sufficiently indicated by the use, in analytic theory, of the ancient term *imago*.

This jubilant assumption of his specular image by the child at the *infans* stage, still sunk in his motor incapacity and nursling dependence, would seem to exhibit in an exemplary situation the symbolic matrix in which the *I* is precipitated in a primordial form, before it is objectified in the dialectic of identification with the other, and before language restores to it, in the universal, its function as subject.

This form would have to be called the Ideal-I, if we wished to incorporate it into our usual register, in the sense that it will also be the source of secondary identifications, under which term I would place the functions of libidinal normalization. But the important point is that this form situates the agency of the ego, before its social determination, in a fictional direction, which will always remain irreducible for the individual alone, or rather, which will only rejoin the coming-into-being (*le devenir*) of the subject asymptotically, whatever the success of the dialectical syntheses by which he must resolve as I his discordance with his own reality.

The fact is that the total form of the body by which the subject anticipates in a mirage the maturation of his power is given to him only as *Gestalt*, that is to say, in an exteriority in which this form is certainly more constituent than constituted, but in which it appears to him above all in a contrasting size (*un relief de stature*) that fixes it and in a symmetry that inverts it, in contrast with the turbulent movements that the subject feels are animating him. Thus, this *Gestalt*—whose pregnancy should be regarded as bound up with the species, though its motor style remains scarcely recognizable—by these two aspects of its appearance, symbolizes the mental permanence of the *I*, at the same time as it prefigures its alienating destination; it is still pregnant with the correspondences that unite the *I* with the statue in which man projects himself, with the phantoms that dominate him, or with the automaton in which, in an ambiguous relation, the world of his own making tends to find completion.

Indeed, for the *imagos*—whose veiled faces it is our privilege to see in outline in our daily experience and in the penumbra of symbolic efficacity—the mirror-image would seem to be the threshold of the visible world, if we go by the mirror disposition that the *imago of one's own body* presents in hallucinations or dreams, whether it concerns its individual features, or even its infirmities, or its object-projections; or if we observe the role of the mirror apparatus in the appearances of the *double*, in which psychical realities, however heterogeneous, are manifested.

Others Object

Simone de Beauvoir (1908–1986) was born in Paris to a bourgeois family. Much of her early life was spent in rebellion against the constraints of bourgeois manners. Though her public life with Jean-Paul Sartre is often considered the symbol of that rebellion, it is much more accurate to say that, from her youth, Simone de Beauvoir focused her intelligence and energy on the problem of defining, and living, the authentic human life. This was the real-life foundation of her feminism. She and Sartre met at the École Normale Supérieure, from which both graduated with distinction in 1929. They were companions, occasional lovers, and coworkers until the last years before Sartre's death in 1980. Some are inclined to fault de Beauvoir's feminist credentials because of her relation to Sartre, to whom she seemed, at times, to have ceded too much. Their relationship was, however, complicated. Hurt ran in both directions. The important thing is that they lived an honest and engaged life of politics, letters, intimacy, and friendship. De Beauvoir wrote fiction, autobiography and memoirs, and philosophy. Her *Prime of Life* (1960) is one of the best narrative descriptions both of her relation with Sartre and of life in Paris before, during, and after World War II. *The Mandarins* (1954), one of her fictional works, won the Prix Goncourt. She and Sartre were founding editors of *Les Temps modernes*. Her most enduring philosophical work is *The Second Sex*. However history may treat the philosophy of Sartre, it is virtually certain that *Second Sex* will always be remembered as a classic of feminist social theory and, thus, of modern philosophy.

Woman as Other*
Simone de Beauvoir (1949)

… What is a woman?

Merely stating the problem suggests an immediate answer to me. It is significant that I pose it. It would never occur to a man to write a book on the singular situation of males in humanity. If I want to define myself, I first have to say, "I am a woman"; all other assertions will arise from this basic truth. A man never begins by positing himself as an individual of a certain sex: that he is a man is obvious. The categories masculine and feminine appear as symmetrical in a formal way on town hall records or identification papers. The relation of the two sexes is not that of two electrical poles: the man represents both the positive and the neuter to such an extent that in French *hommes* designates human beings, the particular meaning of the word *vir* being assimilated into the general meaning of the word "homo." Woman is the negative, to such a point that any determination is imputed to her as a limitation,

* Excerpt(s) from THE SECOND SEX by Simone de Beauvoir and translated by Constance Borde and Sheila Malovany-Chevallier, translation copyright © 2009 by Constance Borde and Sheila Malovany-Chevallier. Used by permission of Alfred A. Knopf, an imprint of the Knopf Doubleday Publishing Group, a division of Penguin Random House LLC. All rights reserved.

without reciprocity. I used to get annoyed in abstract discussions to hear men tell me: "You think such and such a thing because you're a woman." But I know my only defense is to answer, "I think it because it is true," thereby eliminating my subjectivity; it was out of the question to answer, "And you think the contrary because you are a man," because it is understood that being a man is not a particularity; a man is in his right by virtue of being a man; it is the woman who is in the wrong. In fact, just as for the ancients there was an absolute vertical that defined the oblique, there is an absolute human type that is masculine. Woman has ovaries and a uterus; such are the particular conditions that lock her in her subjectivity; some even say she thinks with her hormones. Man vainly forgets that his anatomy also includes hormones and testicles. He grasps his body as a direct and normal link with the world that he believes he apprehends in all objectivity, whereas he considers woman's body an obstacle, a prison, burdened by everything that particularizes it. "The female is female by virtue of a certain *lack* of qualities," Aristotle said. "We should regard women's nature as suffering from natural defectiveness." And Saint Thomas in his turn decreed that woman was an "incomplete man," an "incidental" being. This is what the Genesis story symbolizes, where Eve appears as if drawn from Adam's "supernumerary" bone, in Bossuet's words. Humanity is male, and man defines woman, not in herself, but in relation to himself; she is not considered an autonomous being. "Woman, the relative being," writes Michelet. Thus Monsieur Benda declares in *Le rapport d'Uriel* (Uriel's Report): "A man's body has meaning by itself, disregarding the body of the woman, whereas the woman's body seems devoid of meaning without reference to the male. Man thinks himself without woman. Woman does not think herself without man." And she is nothing other than what man decides; she is thus called "the sex," meaning that the male sees her essentially as a sexed being; for him she is sex, so she is it in the absolute. She is determined and differentiated in relation to man, while he is not in relation to her; she is the inessential in front of the essential. He is the Subject; he is the Absolute. She is the Other.

The category of *Other* is as original as consciousness itself. The duality between Self and Other can be found in the most primitive societies, in the most ancient mythologies; this division did not always fall in to the category of the division of the sexes, it was not based on any empirical given: this comes out in works like Granet's on Chinese thought, and Dumé-

zeil's on India and Rome. In couples such as Varuna–Mitra, Uranus–Zeus, Sun–Moon, Day–Night, no feminine element is involved at the outset; neither in Good–Evil, auspicious and inauspicious, left and right; God and Lucifer; alterity is the fundamental category of human thought. No group ever defines itself as One without immediately setting up the Other opposite itself. It only takes three travelers brought together by change in the same train compartment for the rest of the travelers to become vaguely hostile "others." Village people view anyone not belonging to the village as suspicious "others." For the native of a country inhabitants of other countries are viewed as "foreigners"; Jews are the "others" for anti-Semites, blacks for racist Americas, indigenous people for colonists, proletarians for the propertied classes. After studying the diverse forms of primitive society in depth, Lévi-Strauss could conclude: "The passage from the state of Nature to the state of Culture is defined by man's ability to think biological relations as systems of oppositions; dualit, alternation, opposition, and symmetry, whether occurring in defined or less clear form, are not too much phenomena to explain as fundamental and immediate givens of social reality." These phenomena could not be understood if human reality were solely a *Mitsein* based on solidarity and friendship. On the contrary, they become clear if, following Hegel, a fundamental hostility to any other consciousness is found in consciousness itself; the subject posits itself only in opposition; it asserts itself as the essential and sets up the other as inessential, as the object.

But the other consciousness has an opposing reciprocal claim: traveling, a local is shocked to realize that in neighboring countries locals view him as a foreigner; between villages, clans, nations, an classes there are wards, potlatches, agreements, treaties, and struggles that remove the absolute meaning from the idea of the *Other* and bring out its relativity; whether one likes it or not, individuals and groups have no choice but to recognize the reciprocity of their relation. How is it, then, that between the sexes this reciprocity had not been put forward, that one of the terms has been asserted as the only essential one, denying any relativity in regard to its correlative, defining the latter as pure alterity. Why do women not contest male sovereignty? No subject posits itself spontaneously and at once as the inessential from the outset; it is not the Other who, defining itself as Other, defines the One; the Other is posited as Other by the One positing itself as One. But in order for the Other not to turn into the One, the Other has to submit to this foreign point of view. Where does this submission in woman come from?

There are other cases where, for a shorter or longer time, on category has managed to dominate another absolutely. It is often numerical inequality that confers this privilege: the majority imposes its law on or persecutes the minority. But women are not a minority like American blacks, or like Jews: there are as many women as men on the earth. Often, the two opposing groups concerned were once independent of each other; either they were not aware of each other in the past, or they accepted each other's autonomy; and some historical event subordinated the weaker to the stronger: the Jewish Diaspora, slavery in America, and the colonial conquests are facts with dates. In these cases, for the oppressed there was a *before:* they share a past, a tradition, sometimes a religion, or a culture. In this sense, the parallel Bebel draws between women and the proletariat would be the best founded: proletarians are not a numerical minority either, and yet they have never formed a separate group. However, not *one* event but a whole historical development explains their existence as a class and accounts for the distribution of *these* individuals in this class. There have not always been proletarians: there have always been women; they are women in their physiological structure; as far back as history can be traced, they have always been subordinate to men; their dependence is not the consequence of an event or a becoming, it did not *happen.* Alterity here appears to be an absolute, partly because it falls outside the accidental nature of historical fact. A situation created over time can come undone at another time—blacks in Haiti for one are a good example; on the contrary, a natural condition seems to defy change. In truth, nature is no more an immutable given than is historical reality. If woman discovers herself as inessential and never turns into the essential, it is because she does not bring about this transformation herself. Proletarians say "we." So do blacks. Positing themselves as subjects, they thus transform the bourgeois or whites into "others." Women—except in certain abstract gatherings such as conferences—do not use "we"; men say "women," and women adopt this word to refer to themselves; but they do not posit themselves authentically as Subjects. The proletarians made the revolution in Russia, the blacks in Haiti, the Indo–Chinese are fighting in Indochina. Women's actions have never been more than symbolic agitation; they have won only what men have been willing to conceded to

them; they have taken nothing; they have received. It is that they lack the concrete means to organize themselves into a unit that could posit itself in opposition. They have no past, no history, no religion of their own; and unlike the proletariat, they have no solidarity of labor or interests; they even lack their own space that makes communities of American blacks, the Jews in ghettos, or the workers in Saint-Denis or Renault factories. They live dispersed among men, tied by homes, work, economic interests, and social conditions to certain men—fathers or husbands—more closely than to other women. As bourgeois women, they are in solidarity with bourgeois men and not with women proletarians; as white women, they are in solidarity with white men and not black women. The proletariat could plan to massacre the whole ruling class; a fanatic Jew or black could dream of seizing the secret of the atomic bomb and turning all of humanity entirely Jewish or entirely black: but a woman could not even dream of exterminating males. The tie that binds her to her oppressors is unlike any other. The division of the sexes is a biological given, not a moment in human history. Their opposition took shape within an original *Mitsein,* and she has not broken it. The couple is a fundamental unit with the two halves riveted to each other: cleavage of society by sex is not possible. This is the fundamental characteristic of woman: she is the Other as the heart of a whole whose two components are necessary to each other. …

Aimé Césaire (1913–2008) was born in Martinique, where he attended school. He then studied at the École Normale Supérieure in Paris before returning to Martinique. Throughout his life, Césaire has been active in political life and government in Martinique. He is known as much for his poetry and drama as for *Discourse on Colonialism* (1955), from which the selection is taken. "Between Colonizer and Colonized" represents the early thinking of social theorists in the late-colonial world: The text's systematic critique of colonialism expresses the distinctive view of the colonial subject in the colonialist's language. Albert Memmi's *The Colonizer and the Colonized* (1959) is another important example of the early social theory of those who became postcolonial subjects. One of the unique features of this perspective is that it resists categorization as either a race- or class-based point of view. Many today would consider theories written from the postcolonial point of view as those most completely sensitive to the many factors at play in the systematic oppression of people anywhere.

Between Colonizer and Colonized[*]
Aimé Césaire (1955)

But let us speak about the colonized.

I see clearly what colonization has destroyed: the wonderful Indian civilizations—neither Deterding nor Royal Dutch nor Standard Oil will ever console me for the Aztecs and the Incas.

I see clearly the civilizations, condemned to perish at a future date, into which it has introduced a principle of ruin: the South Sea islands, Nigeria, Nyasaland. I see less clearly the contributions it has made.

Security? Culture? The rule of law? In the meantime, I look around and wherever there are colonizers and colonized face to face, I see force, brutality, cruelty, sadism, conflict, and, in a parody of education, the hasty manufacture of a few thousand subordinate functionaries, "boys," artisans, office clerks, and interpreters necessary for the smooth operation of business.

I spoke of contact.

Between colonizer and colonized there is room only for forced labor, intimidation, pressure, the police, taxation, theft, rape, compulsory crops, contempt, mistrust, arrogance, self-complacency, swinishness, brainless elites, degraded masses.

No human contact, but relations of domination and submission which turn the colonizing man into a classroom monitor, an army sergeant, a prison guard, a slave driver, and the indigenous man into an instrument of production.

My turn to state an equation: colonization = "thingification."

I hear the storm. They talk to me about progress, about "achievements," diseases cured, improved standards of living.

I am talking about societies drained of their essence, cultures trampled underfoot, institutions undermined, lands confiscated, religions smashed, magnificent artistic creations destroyed, extraordinary *possibilities* wiped out.

[*]Republished with the permission of the Monthly Review Foundation, from *Discourse on Colonialism*, by Aimé Césaire, Joan Pinkham, tr, pp. 20–25. Copyright 1972, Monthly Review Press; permission conveyed through Copyright Clearance Center, Inc.

They throw facts at my head, statistics, mileages of roads, canals, and railroad tracks.

I am talking about thousands of men sacrificed to the Congo-Océan.[*]

I am talking about those who, as I write this, are digging the harbor of Abidjan by hand. I am talking about millions of men torn from their gods, their land, their habits, their life—from life, from the dance, from wisdom.

I am talking about millions of men in whom fear has been cunningly instilled, who have been taught to have an inferiority complex, to tremble, kneel, despair, and behave like flunkeys.

They dazzle me with the tonnage of cotton or cocoa that has been exported, the acreage that has been planted with olive trees or grapevines.

I am talking about natural *economies* that have been disrupted—harmonious and viable *economies* adapted to the indigenous population—about food crops destroyed, malnutrition permanently introduced, agricultural development oriented solely toward the benefit of the metropolitan countries, about the looting of products, the looting of raw materials.

They pride themselves on abuses eliminated.

I too talk about abuses, but what I say is that on the old ones—very real—they have superimposed others—very detestable. They talk to me about local tyrants brought to reason; but I note that in general the old tyrants get on very well with the new ones, and that there has been established between them, to the detriment of the people, a circuit of mutual services and complicity.

They talk to me about civilization, I talk about proletarianization and mystification.

For my part, I make a systematic defense of the non-European civilizations.

Every day that passes, every denial of justice, every beating by the police, every demand of the workers that is drowned in blood, every scandal that is hushed up, every punitive expedition, every police van, every gendarme and every militiaman, brings home to us the value of our old societies.

They were communal societies, never societies of the many for the few.

They were societies that were not only ante-capitalist, as has been said, but also *anti-capitalist*.

They were democratic societies, always.

They were cooperative societies, fraternal societies.

I make a systematic defense of the societies destroyed by imperialism.

They were the fact, they did not pretend to be the idea; despite their faults, they were neither to be hated nor condemned. They were content to be. In them, neither the word *failure* nor the word *avatar* had any meaning. They kept hope intact.

Whereas those are the only words that can, in all honesty, be applied to the European enterprises outside Europe. My only consolation is that periods of colonization pass, that nations sleep only for a time, and that peoples remain.

This being said, it seems that in certain circles they pretend to have discovered in me an "enemy of Europe" and a prophet of the return of the ante-European past.

For my part, I search in vain for the place where I could have expressed such views; where I ever underestimated the importance of Europe in the history of human thought; where I ever preached a *return* of any kind; where I ever claimed that there could be a *return*.

The truth is that I have said something very different: to wit, that the great historical tragedy of Africa has been not so much that it was too late in making contact with the rest of the world, as the manner in which that contact was brought about; that Europe began to "propagate" at a time when it had fallen into the hands of the most unscrupulous financiers and captains of industry; that it was our misfortune to encounter that particular Europe on our path, and that Europe is responsible before the human community for the highest heap of corpses in history.

In another connection, in judging colonization, I have added that Europe has gotten on very well indeed with all the local feudal lords who agreed to serve, woven a villainous complicity with them, rendered their tyranny more effective and more efficient, and that it has actually tended to prolong artificially the survival of local pasts in their most pernicious aspects.

I have said—and this is something very different—that colonialist Europe has grafted modern abuse onto ancient injustice, hateful racism onto old inequality.

That if I am attacked on the grounds of intent, I maintain that colonialist Europe is dishonest in trying to justify its colonizing activity a *posteriori* by the obvious material progress that has been achieved in certain fields under the colonial regime—since *sudden* change is always possible, in history as elsewhere; since no one knows at what stage of material development these same countries would have been if Europe had not intervened; since the technical outfitting of Africa and Asia, their administrative reorganiza-

tion, in a word, their "Europeanization," was (as is proved by the example of Japan) in no way tied to the European *occupation*; since the Europeanization of the non-European continents could have been accomplished otherwise than under the heel of Europe; since this movement of Europeanization was *in progress*; since it was even slowed down; since in any case it was distorted by the European takeover.

The proof is that at present it is the indigenous peoples of Africa and Asia who are demanding schools, and colonialist Europe which refuses them; that it is the African who is asking for ports and roads, and colonialist Europe which is niggardly on this score; that it is the colonized man who wants to move forward, and the colonizer who holds things back.

Martin Luther King, Jr. (1929–1968) was born in Atlanta, Georgia. His father, the Reverend Martin Luther King, Sr., was pastor of one of the two most prestigious black churches in that city. King, Jr., studied theology at the Crozer Theological School in Chester, Pennsylvania, then at Boston University, where he received his Ph.D. in 1955. One year earlier, he had become pastor of the Dexter Avenue Baptist Church in Montgomery, Alabama. In the events following December 1955, when Rosa Parks spontaneously refused to step to the back of the bus, King was elected leader of the Montgomery Improvement Association, which directed the yearlong, successful bus boycott. In 1957, he founded the Southern Christian Leadership Conference, which was the institutional base from which he became the leader of the early Civil Rights Movement. In 1964, King was awarded the Nobel Peace Prize.

In the mid-1960s, the movement changed. Young people shifted away from the policy of nonviolence. Whites were less welcome, and women began to protest the dominance of men in the movement. When King tried to march in the North, particularly in Chicago in 1966, the resistance was ugly, and the march unsuccessful. If the most memorable event in the movement was the march on Washington in August 1963, the last great triumph was the Selma march to Montgomery in April 1965, ten years after the movement began in the same city. King was murdered in Memphis in 1968 as he was organizing the "poor people's march" on Washington. The selection explains his nonviolent philosophy and his differing debts to Niebuhr and Gandhi (described as a recollection from his student days, probably over Christmas vacation in 1949).

The Power of Nonviolent Action[*]
Martin Luther King, Jr. (1958)

During this period I had about despaired of the power of love in solving social problems. Perhaps my faith in love was temporarily shaken by the philosophy of Nietzsche. I had been reading parts of *The Genealogy of Morals* and the whole of *The Will to Power*. Nietzsche's glorification of power—in his theory all life expressed the will to power—was an outgrowth of his contempt for ordinary morals. He attacked the whole of the Hebraic-Christian morality—with its virtues of piety and humility, its other-worldiness and its attitude toward suffering—as the glorification of weakness, as making virtues out of necessity and impotence. He looked to the development of a superman who would surpass man as man surpassed the ape.

Then one Sunday afternoon I traveled to Philadelphia to hear a sermon by Dr. Mordecai Johnson, president of Howard University. He was there to preach for the Fellowship House of Philadelphia. Dr. Johnson had just returned from a trip to India, and, to my great interest, he spoke of the life and teachings of Mahatma Gandhi. His message was so profound and electrifying that I left the meeting and bought a half-dozen books on Gandhi's life and works.

Like most people, I had heard of Gandhi, but I had never studied him seriously. As I read I became deeply fascinated by his campaigns of nonviolent resistance. I was particularly moved by the Salt March to the Sea and his numerous fasts. The whole concept of "Satyagraha" (*Satya* is truth which equals love, and *agraha* is force; "Satyagraha," therefore, means truth-force or love force) was profoundly significant to me. As I delved deeper into the philosophy of Gandhi my skepticism concerning the power of love gradually diminished, and I came to see for the first time its potency in the area of social reform. Prior to reading Gandhi, I had about concluded that the ethics of Jesus were only effective in individual relationship. The "turn the other cheek" philosophy and the "love your enemies" philosophy were only valid, I felt, when individuals were in conflict with other individuals; when racial groups and nations were in conflict a more realistic approach seemed necessary. But after reading Gandhi, I saw how utterly mistaken I was.

Gandhi was probably the first person in history to lift the love ethic of Jesus above mere interaction between individuals to a powerful and effective social force on a large scale. Love for Gandhi was a potent instrument for social and collective transformation. It was in this Gandhian emphasis on love and nonviolence that I discovered the method for social reform that I had been seeking for so many months. The intellectual and moral satisfaction that I failed to gain from the utilitarianism of Bentham and Mill, the revolutionary methods of Marx and Lenin, the social-contracts theory of Hobbes, the "back to nature" optimism of Rousseau, and the superman philosophy of Nietzsche, I found in the nonviolent resistance philosophy of Gandhi. I came to feel that this was the only morally and practically sound method open to oppressed people in their struggle for freedom.

But my intellectual odyssey to nonviolence did not end here. During my last year in theological school, I began to read the works of Reinhold Niebuhr. The prophetic and realistic elements in Niebuhr's passionate style and profound thought were appealing to me, and I became so enamored of his social ethics that I almost fell into the trap of accepting uncritically everything he wrote.

About this time I read Niebuhr's critique of the pacifist position. Niebuhr had himself once been a member of the pacifist ranks. For several years, he had been national chairman of the Fellowship of Reconciliation. His break with pacifism came in the early thirties, and the first full statement of his criticism of pacifism was in *Moral Man and Immoral Society*. Here he argued that there was no intrinsic moral difference between violent and nonviolent resistance. The social consequences of the two methods were different, he contended, but the differences were in degree rather than kind. Later Niebuhr began emphasizing the irresponsibility of relying on nonviolent resistance when there was no ground for believing that it would be successful in preventing the spread of totalitarian tyranny. It could only be successful, he argued, if the groups against whom the resistance was taking place had some degree of moral

[*]Excerpt from *Stride Toward Freedom* (New York: Harper and Bros., 1958), pp. 96–97, 213–219, and 224. Reprinted by arrangement with The Heirs to the Estate of Martin Luther King, Jr., c/o Writers House as agent for the proprietor, New York, NY. Copyright © 1958 Dr. Martin Luther King, Jr. Copyright © renewed 1986 Coretta Scott King.

conscience, as was the case in Gandhi's struggle against the British. Niebuhr's ultimate rejection of pacifism was based primarily on the doctrine of man. He argued that pacifism failed to do justice to the reformation doctrine of justification by faith, substituting for it a sectarian perfectionism which believes "that divine grace actually lifts men out of the sinful contradictions of history and establishes him above the sins of the world." . . .

Violence as a way of achieving racial justice is both impractical and immoral. It is impractical because it is a descending spiral ending in destruction for all. The old law of an eye for an eye leaves everybody blind. It is immoral because it seeks to humiliate the opponent rather than win his understanding; it seeks to annihilate rather than to convert. Violence is immoral because it thrives on hatred rather than love. It destroys community and makes brotherhood impossible. It leaves society in monologue rather than dialogue. Violence ends by defeating itself. It creates bitterness in the survivors and brutality in the destroyers. A voice echoes through time saying to every potential Peter, "Put up your sword." History is cluttered with the wreckage of nations that failed to follow this command.

If the American Negro and other victims of oppression succumb to the temptation of using violence in the struggle for freedom, future generations will be the recipients of a desolate night of bitterness, and our chief legacy to them will be an endless reign of meaningless chaos. Violence is not the way.

The third way open to oppressed people in their quest for freedom is the way of nonviolent resistance. Like the synthesis in Hegelian philosophy, the principle of nonviolent resistance seeks to reconcile the truths of two opposites—acquiescence and violence—while avoiding the extremes and immoralities of both. The nonviolent resister agrees with the person who acquiesces that one should not be physically aggressive toward his opponent; but he balances the equation by agreeing with the person of violence that evil must be resisted. He avoids the nonresistance of the former and the violent resistance of the latter. With nonviolent resistance, no individual or group need submit to any wrong, nor need anyone resort to violence in order to right a wrong.

It seems to me that this is the method that must guide the actions of the Negro in the present crisis in race relations. Through nonviolent resistance the Negro will be able to rise to the noble height of opposing the unjust system while loving the perpetrators of the system. The Negro must work passionately and unrelentingly for full stature as a citizen, but he must not use inferior methods to gain it. He must never come to terms with falsehood, malice, hate, or destruction.

Nonviolent resistance makes it possible for the Negro to remain in the South and struggle for his rights. The Negro's problem will not be solved by running away. He cannot listen to the glib suggestion of those who would urge him to migrate en masse to other sections of the country. By grasping his great opportunity in the South he can make a lasting contribution to the moral strength of the nation and set a sublime example of courage for generations yet unborn.

By nonviolent resistance, the Negro can also enlist all men of good will in his struggle for equality. The problem is not a purely racial one, with Negroes set against whites. In the end, it is not a struggle between people at all, but a tension between justice and injustice. Nonviolent resistance is not aimed against oppressors but against oppression. Under its banner consciences, not racial groups, are enlisted.

If the Negro is to achieve the goal of integration, he must organize himself into a militant and nonviolent mass movement. All three elements are indispensable. The movement for equality and justice can only be a success if it has both a mass and militant character; the barriers to be overcome require both. Nonviolence is an imperative in order to bring about ultimate community.

A mass movement of a militant quality that is not at the same time committed to nonviolence tends to generate conflict, which in turn breeds anarchy. The support of the participants and the sympathy of the uncommitted are both inhibited by the threat that bloodshed will engulf the community. This reaction in turn encourages the opposition to threaten and resort to force. When, however, the mass movement repudiates violence while moving resolutely toward its goal, its opponents are revealed as the instigators and practitioners of violence if it occurs. Then public support is magnetically attracted to the advocates of nonviolence, while those who employ violence are literally disarmed by overwhelming sentiment against their stand.

Only through a nonviolent approach can the fears of the white community be mitigated. A guilt-ridden white minority lives in fear that if the Negro should ever attain power, he would act without restraint or pity to revenge the injustices and brutality of the years. It is something like a parent who continually mistreats a son. One day that parent raises his hand to strike the son, only to discover that the son is now as tall as he is. The parent is suddenly afraid—fearful that the son will use his new physical power to repay his parent for all the blows of the past.

The Negro, once a helpless child, has now grown up politically, culturally, and economically. Many white men fear retaliation. The job of the Negro is to show them that they have nothing to fear, that the Negro understands and forgives and is ready to forget the past. He must convince the white man that all he seeks is justice, *for both himself and the white man.* A mass movement exercising nonviolence is an object lesson in power under discipline, a demonstration to the white community that if such a movement attained a degree of strength, it would use its power creatively and not vengefully.

Nonviolence can touch men where the law cannot reach them. When the law regulates behavior it plays an indirect part in molding public sentiment. The enforcement of the law is itself a form of peaceful persuasion. But the law needs help. The courts can order desegregation of the public schools. But what can be done to mitigate the fears, to disperse the hatred, violence, and irrationality gathered around school integration, to take the initiative out of the hands of racial demagogues, to release respect for the law? In the end, for laws to be obeyed, men must believe they are right.

Here nonviolence comes in as the ultimate form of persuasion. It is the method which seeks to implement the just law by appealing to the conscience of the great decent majority who through blindness, fear, pride, or irrationality have allowed their consciences to sleep.

The nonviolent resisters can summarize their message in the following simple terms: We will take direct action against injustice without waiting for other agencies to act. We will not obey unjust laws or submit to unjust practices. We will do this peacefully, openly, cheerfully because our aim is to persuade. We adopt the means of nonviolence because our end is a community at peace with itself. We will try to persuade with our words, but if our words fail, we will try to persuade with our acts. We will always be willing to talk and seek fair compromise, but we are ready to suffer when necessary and even risk our lives to become witnesses to the truth as we see it.

C. Wright Mills (1916–1962) was born in Waco, Texas. After undergraduate studies at the University of Texas, Mills did his doctoral work at the University of Wisconsin. There, he met Hans Gerth, with whom he edited, translated, and introduced *From Max Weber*, a still-important collection of Weber's writings. After teaching in what he considered a provincial exile at the University of Maryland, Mills moved to Columbia and the Bureau of Applied Social Research in 1945. His earliest days at Columbia were spent in empirical social research. Yet he never became an accepted member or even a full professor in Columbia's department. In the 1950s, Mills became much more the public intellectual, while teaching primarily undergraduates at Columbia. Works like *Power Elite, Listen Yankee! White Collar,* and *The Causes of World War Three*— all written in this period—brought him much public acclaim and informal membership in New York's Left, intellectual elite. Mills was considered arrogant by many colleagues and a hero by many of his readers. He dressed and played the part of the young intellectual radical—complete with leather jacket and motorcycle. However, he suffered from a chronic heart condition that killed him at age forty-five in 1962, the year of SDS's *Port Huron Statement.* Mills was a source of intellectual inspiration to younger radicals and social theorists because, true to his ideal of the sociological imagination, his writings based strong critical ideas on careful empirical work. He read Weber in relation to Marx *and* the American pragmatists. He sought to unite the best of European and American classical theory into a social philosophy for the New Left.

The Sociological Imagination*
C. Wright Mills (1959)

The sociological imagination enables its possessor to understand the larger historical scene in terms of its meaning for the inner life and the external career of a variety of individuals. It enables him to take into account how individuals, in the welter of their daily experience, often become falsely conscious of their social positions. Within that welter,

*THE SOCIOLOGICAL IMAGINATION by Wright Mills (1959) 2093w from pp. 5-9, 13-15. © 1959, 2000 by Oxford University Press, Inc. By permission of Oxford University Press, USA.

the framework of modern society is sought, and within that framework the psychologies of a variety of men and women are formulated. By such means the personal uneasiness of individuals is focused upon explicit troubles and the indifference of publics is transformed into involvement with public issues.

The first fruit of this imagination—and the first lesson of the social science that embodies it—is the idea that the individual can understand his own experience and gauge his own fate only by locating himself within his period, that he can know his own chances in life only by becoming aware of those of all individuals in his circumstances. In many ways it is a terrible lesson; in many ways a magnificent one. We do not know the limits of man's capacities for supreme effort or willing degradation, for agony or glee, for pleasurable brutality or the sweetness of reason. But in our time we have come to know that the limits of "human nature" are frighteningly broad. We have come to know that every individual lives, from one generation to the next, in some society; that he lives out a biography, and that he lives it out within some historical sequence. By the fact of his living he contributes, however minutely, to the shaping of this society and to the course of its history, even as he is made by society and by its historical push and shove.

The sociological imagination enables us to grasp history and biography and the relations between the two within society. That is its task and its promise. To recognize this task and this promise is the mark of the classic social analyst. It is characteristic of Herbert Spencer—turgid, polysyllabic, comprehensive; of E. A. Ross—graceful, muckraking, upright; of Auguste Comte and Emile Durkheim; of the intricate and subtle Karl Mannheim. It is the quality of all that is intellectually excellent in Karl Marx; it is the clue to Thorstein Veblen's brilliant and ironic insight, to Joseph Schumpeter's many-sided constructions of reality; it is the basis of the psychological sweep of W. E. H. Lecky no less than of the profundity and clarity of Max Weber. And it is the signal of what is best in contemporary studies of man and society.

No social study that does not come back to the problems of biography, of history and of their intersections within a society has completed its intellectual journey. Whatever the specific problems of the classic social analysts, however limited or however broad the features of social reality they have examined, those who have been imaginatively aware of

the promise of their work have consistently asked three sorts of questions:

(1) What is the structure of this particular society as a whole? What are its essential components, and how are they related to one another? How does it differ from other varieties of social order? Within it, what is the meaning of any particular feature for its continuance and for its change?

(2) Where does this society stand in human history? What are the mechanics by which it is changing? What is its place within and its meaning for the development of humanity as a whole? How does any particular feature we are examining affect, and how is it affected by, the historical period in which it moves? And this period—what are its essential features? How does it differ from other periods? What are its characteristic ways of history-making?

(3) What varieties of men and women now prevail in this society and in this period? And what varieties are coming to prevail? In what ways are they selected and formed, liberated and repressed, made sensitive and blunted? What kinds of "human nature" are revealed in the conduct and character we observe in this society in this period? And what is the meaning for "human nature" of each and every feature of the society we are examining?

Whether the point of interest is a great power state or a minor literary mood, a family, a prison, a creed—these are the kinds of questions the best social analysts have asked. They are the intellectual pivots of classic studies of man in society—and they are the questions inevitably raised by any mind possessing the sociological imagination. For that imagination is the capacity to shift from one perspective to another—from the political to the psychological; from examination of a single family to comparative assessment of the national budgets of the world; from the theological school to the military establishment; from considerations of an oil industry to studies of contemporary poetry. It is the capacity to range from the most impersonal and remote transformations to the most intimate features of the human self—and to see the relations between the two. Back of its use there is always the urge to know the social and historical meaning of the individual in the society and in the period in which he has his quality and his being.

That, in brief, is why it is by means of the sociological imagination that men now hope to grasp what is going on in the world, and to understand what is happening in themselves as minute points of the intersections of biography and history within society. In large part, contemporary man's self-conscious view of himself as at least an outsider, if not a permanent stranger, rests upon an absorbed realization of social relativity and of the transformative power of history. The sociological imagination is the most fruitful form of this self-consciousness. By its use men whose mentalities have swept only a series of limited orbits often come to feel as if suddenly awakened in a house with which they had only supposed themselves to be familiar. Correctly or incorrectly, they often come to feel that they can now provide themselves with adequate summations, cohesive assessments, comprehensive orientations. Older decisions that once appeared sound now seem to them products of a mind unaccountably dense. Their capacity for astonishment is made lively again. They acquire a new way of thinking, they experience a transvaluation of values: in a word, by their reflection and by their sensibility, they realize the cultural meaning of the social sciences.

Perhaps the most fruitful distinction with which the sociological imagination works is between "the personal troubles of milieu" and "the public issues of social structure." This distinction is an essential tool of the sociological imagination and a feature of all classic work in social science.

Troubles occur within the character of the individual and within the range of his immediate relations with others; they have to do with his self and with those limited areas of social life of which he is directly and personally aware. Accordingly, the statement and the resolution of troubles properly lie within the individual as a biographical entity and within the scope of his immediate milieu—the social setting that is directly open to his personal experience and to some extent his willful activity. A trouble is a private matter: values cherished by an individual are felt by him to be threatened.

Issues have to do with matters that transcend these local environments of the individual and the range of his inner life. They have to do with the organization of many such milieux into the institutions of an historical society as a whole, with the ways in which various milieux overlap and interpenetrate to form the larger structure of social and historical life. An issue is a public matter: some value cherished by publics is felt to be threatened. Often there is a debate about what that value really is and about what it is that really threatens it. This debate is often without focus if only because it is the very

nature of an issue, unlike even widespread trouble, that it cannot very well be defined in terms of the immediate and everyday environments of ordinary men. An issue, in fact, often involves a crisis in institutional arrangements, and often too it involves what Marxists call "contradictions" or "antagonisms." . . .

In every intellectual age some one style of reflection tends to become a common denominator of cultural life. Nowadays, it is true, many intellectual fads are widely taken up before they are dropped for new ones in the course of a year or two. Such enthusiasms may add spice to cultural play, but leave little or no intellectual trace. That is not true of such ways of thinking as "Newtonian physics" or "Darwinian biology." Each of these intellectual universes became an influence that reached far beyond any special sphere of idea and imagery. In terms of them, or in terms derived from them, unknown scholars as well as fashionable commentators came to re-focus their observations and re-formulate their concerns.

During the modern era, physical and biological science has been the major common denominator of serious reflection and popular metaphysics in Western societies. "The technique of the laboratory" has been the accepted mode of procedure and the source of intellectual security. That is one meaning of the idea of an intellectual common denominator: men can state their strongest convictions in its terms; other terms and other styles of reflection seem mere vehicles of escape and obscurity.

That a common denominator prevails does not of course mean that no other styles of thought or modes of sensibility exist. But it does mean that more general intellectual interests tend to slide into this area, to be formulated there most sharply, and when so formulated, to be thought somehow to have reached, if not a solution, at least a profitable way of being carried along.

The sociological imagination is becoming, I believe, the major common denominator of our cultural life and its signal feature. This quality of mind is found in the social and psychological sciences, but it goes far beyond these studies as we now know them. Its acquisition by individuals and by the cultural community at large is slow and often fumbling; many social scientists are themselves quite unaware of it. They do not seem to know that the use of this imagination is central to the best work that they might do, that by failing to develop and to use it they are failing to meet the cultural expectations that are coming to be demanded of them and that the classic traditions of their several disciplines make available to them.

Yet in factual and moral concerns, in literary work and in political analysis, the qualities of this imagination are regularly demanded. In a great variety of expressions, they have become central features of intellectual endeavor and cultural sensibility. Leading critics exemplify these qualities as do serious journalists—in fact the work of both is often judged in these terms. Popular categories of criticism—high, middle, and low-brow, for example—are now at least as much sociological as aesthetic. Novelists—whose serious work embodies the most widespread definitions of human reality—frequently possess this imagination, and do much to meet the demand for it. By means of it, orientation to the present as history is sought. As images of "human nature" become more problematic, an increasing need is felt to pay closer yet more imaginative attention to the social routines and catastrophes which reveal (and which shape) man's nature in this time of civil unrest and ideological conflict. Although fashion is often revealed by attempts to use it, the sociological imagination is not merely a fashion. It is a quality of mind that seems most dramatically to promise an understanding of the intimate realities of ourselves in connection with larger social realities. It is not merely one quality of mind among the contemporary range of cultural sensibilities—it is the quality whose wider and more adroit use offers the promise that all such sensibilities—and in fact, human reason itself—will come to play a greater role in human affairs.

Huey P. Newton (1942–1989) was born in Monroe, Louisiana and, oddly, was named after Louisiana's one-time, populist governor, Huey P. Long. **Bobby Seale** (1936–) was born in Liberty, Texas. As boys, both migrated with their families to Oakland, California. Seale went to Berkeley High School, but Newton went to lesser schools in Oakland, of which he said, "During those long years in Oakland public schools, I did not have one teacher who taught me anything about my own life and experience." Huey P. Newton and Bobby Seale met at Merritt College in Oakland, where both were members of the African American Association. At Merritt, Newton is known to have read the works of Marx, Fanon, Malcolm X, Mao, Durkheim, and Che Guevara. Malcolm X, who was assassinated

February 21, 1965, radicalized him and Seale. The year following, early October 1966, the two men composed the Black Panther Party Platform, the founding statement of the Party itself. This was a time when the liberal Civil Rights Movement was fading before more radical and younger Black Power groups of which the Panthers were among those who defied Martin Luther King's ideal of non-violence. The Panthers, in particular, followed Malcolm X in that they considered violence no more than self-defense "by any means necessary." The selection here from *The Black Panther Platform and Principles* makes it clear that their higher purpose was to gain the right to ordinary needs of life—land, homes, education, food, justice and peace. Still, the Panthers were implicated in the urban violence of the day. Huey P. Newton was murdered in West Oakland on August 22, 1989 by a rival for control of the streets, assassinated like his namesake. His last words were: "You can kill my body…but my soul will live forever."

Black Panther Party: What We Want[*]
Huey P. Newton and Bobby Seale (1966)

WHAT WE WANT

WHAT WE BELIEVE

Ten-Point Program

1. We want freedom. We want power to determine the destiny of our Black Community.

We believe that black people will not be free until we are able to determine our destiny.

2. We want full employment for our people.

We believe that the federal government is responsible and obligated to give every man employment or a guaranteed income. We believe that if the white American businessmen will not give full employment, then the means of production should be taken from the businessmen and placed in the community so that the people of the community can organize and employ all of its people and give a high standard of living.

3. We want an end to the robbery by the white man of our Black Community.

We believe that this racist government has robbed us and now we are demanding the overdue debt of

---

[*] Huey P. Newton, Black Panther Party Platform and Program, October 1966.

forty acres and two mules. Forty acres and two mules was promised 100 years ago as restitution for slave labor and mass murder of black people. We will accept the payment in currency which will be distributed to our many communities. The Germans are now aiding the Jews in Israel for the genocide of the Jewish people. The Germans murdered six million Jews. The American racist has taken part in the slaughter of over fifty million black people; therefore, we feel that this is a modest demand that we make.

4. We want decent housing, fit for shelter of human beings.

We believe that if the white landlords will not give decent housing to our black community, then the housing and the land should be made into cooperatives so that our community, with government aid, can build and make decent housing for its people.

5. We want education for our people that exposes the true nature of this decadent American society. We want education that teaches us our true history and our role in the present-day society.

We believe in an educational system that will give to our people a knowledge of self. If a man does not have knowledge of himself and his position in society and the world, then he has little chance to relate to anything else.

6. We want all black men to be exempt from military service.

We believe that Black people should not be forced to fight in the military service to defend a racist government that does not protect us. We will not fight and kill other people of color in the world who, like black people, are being victimized by the white racist government of America. We will protect ourselves from the force and violence of the racist police and the racist military, by whatever means necessary.

7. We want an immediate end to POLICE BRUTALITY and MURDER of black people.

We believe we can end police brutality in our black community by organizing black self-defense groups that are dedicated to defending our black community from racist police oppression and brutality. The Second Amendment to the Constitution of the United States gives a right to bear arms. We therefore believe that all black people should arm themselves for self-defense.

8. We want freedom for all black men held in federal, state, county and city prisons and jails.

We believe that all black people should be released from the many jails and prisons because they have not received a fair and impartial trial.

9. We want all black people when brought to trial to be tried in court by a jury of their peer group or people from their black communities, as defined by the Constitution of the United States.

We believe that the courts should follow the United States Constitution so that black people will receive fair trials. The 14th Amendment of the U.S. Constitution gives a man a right to be tried by his peer group.

A peer is a person from a similar economic, social, religious, geographical, environmental, historical and racial background. To do this the court will be forced to select a jury from the black community from which the black defendant came. We have been, and are being tried by all-white juries that have no understanding of the "average reasoning man" of the black community.

10. We want land, bread, housing, education, clothing, justice and peace. And as our major political objective, a United Nations-supervised plebiscite to be held throughout the black colony in which only black colonial subjects will be allowed to participate, for the purpose of determining the will of black people as to their national destiny.

When, in the course of human events, it becomes necessary for one people to dissolve the political bands which have connected them with another, and to assume, among the powers of the earth, the separate and equal station to which the laws of nature and nature's God entitle them, a decent respect to the opinions of mankind requires that they should declare the causes which impel them to the separation.

We hold these truths to be self-evident, that all men are created equal; that they are endowed by their Creator with certain unalienable rights; that among these are life, liberty, and the pursuit of happiness. That, to secure these rights, governments are instituted among men, deriving their just powers from the governed; that, whenever any form of government becomes destructive of these ends, it is the right of the people to alter or to abolish it, and to institute a new government, laying its foundation on such principles, and organizing its powers 'n such form, as to them shall seem most likely to effect their safety and happiness. Prudence, indeed, will dictate that governments long established should not be changed for light and transient causes; and, accordingly, all experience hath shown, that mankind are more disposed to suffer, while evils are sufferable, than to right themselves by abolishing the forms to which they are accustomed. But, when a long train of abuses and usurpations, pursuing invariably the same object, evinces a design to reduce them under absolute despotism, it is their right, it is their duty, to throw off such government, and to provide new guards for their future security.

RULES OF THE BLACK PANTHER PARTY

Every member of the BLACK PANTHER PARTY throughout this country of racist America must abide by these rules as functional members of this party. CENTRAL COMMITTEE members, CENTRAL STAFFS, and LOCAL STAFFS, including all captains subordinate to either national, state, and local leadership of the BLACK PANTHER PARTY will enforce these rules. Length of suspension or other disciplinary action necessary for violation of these rules will depend on national decisions by national, state or state area, and local committees and staffs where said rule or rules of the BLACK PANTHER PARTY WERE VIOLATED.

Every member of the party must know these verbatim by heart. And apply them daily. Each member must report any violation of these rules to their leadership or they are counter-revolutionary and are also subjected to suspension by the BLACK PANTHER PARTY

The Rules are:

1. No party member can have narcotics or weed in his possession while doing party work.

2. Any party member found shooting narcotics will be expelled from this party.

3. No party member can be DRUNK while doing daily party work.

4. No party member will violate rules relating to office work, general meetings of the BLACK PANTHER PARTY, and meetings of the BLACK PANTHER PARTY ANYWHERE.

5. No party member will USE, POINT, or FIRE a weapon of any kind unnecessarily or accidentally at anyone.

6. No party member can join any other army force other than the BLACK LIBERATION ARMY.

7. No party member can have a weapon in his possession while DRUNK or loaded off narcotics or weed.

8. No party member will commit any crimes against other party members or BLACK people at all, and cannot steal or take from the people, not even a needle or a piece of thread.

9. When arrested BLACK PANTHER MEMBERS will give only name, address, and will sign nothing. Legal first aid must be understood by all Party members.

10. The Ten-Point Program and platform of the BLACK PANTHER PARTY must be known and understood by each Party member.

...

8 Points of Attention
1) Speak politely.
2) Pay fairly for what you buy.
3) Return everything you borrow.
4) Pay for anything you damage.
5) Do not hit or swear at people.
6) Do not damage property or crops of the poor, oppressed masses.
7) Do not take liberties with women.
8) If we ever have to take captives do not ill-treat them.
3 Main Rules of Discipline
1) Obey orders in all your actions.
2) Do not take a single needle or a piece of thread from the poor and oppressed masses.
3) Turn in everything captured from the attacking enemy.

Betty Friedan (1921–2006) was born and grew up in Illinois, where she experienced the marginalization of being Jewish in the provincial Midwest. She felt immediately liberated on entering Smith College, where she edited the school paper. She graduated in 1942. In 1963, *Feminine Mystique* became an immediate best-seller (well over one million copies were soon sold). Three years later, Friedan founded NOW, the National Organization for Women, based on the organizational ideals of the NAACP. Although NOW was soon considered too centrist as more radical feminisms emerged, it remains a powerful force in public politics. Friedan was an influential speaker, writer, and activist on women's issues.

The Problem That Has No Name[*]
Betty Friedan (1963)

The problem lay buried, unspoken, for many years in the minds of American women. It was a strange

[*] From *The Feminine Mystique* by Betty Friedan. Copyright © 1983, 1974, 1973, 1963 by Betty Friedan. Used by permission of W. W. Norton & Company, Inc and The Orion Publishing Group, London.

stirring, a sense of dissatisfaction, a yearning that women suffered in the middle of the twentieth century in the United States. Each suburban wife struggled with it alone. As she made the beds, shopped for groceries, matched slipcover material, ate peanut butter sandwiches with her children, chauffeured Cub Scouts and Brownies, lay beside her husband at night—she was afraid to ask even of herself the silent question—"Is this all?"

For over fifteen years there was no word of this yearning in the millions of words written about women, for women, in all the columns, books and articles by experts telling women their role was to seek fulfillment as wives and mothers. Over and over women heard in voices of tradition and of Freudian sophistication that they could desire no greater destiny than to glory in their own femininity. Experts told them how to catch a man and keep him, how to breastfeed children and handle their toilet training, how to cope with sibling rivalry and adolescent rebellion; how to buy a dishwasher, bake bread, cook gourmet snails, and build a swimming pool with their own hands; how to dress, look, and act more feminine and make marriage more exciting; how to keep their husbands from dying young and their sons from growing into delinquents. They were taught to pity the neurotic, unfeminine, unhappy women who wanted to be poets or physicists or presidents. They learned that truly feminine women do not want careers, higher education, political rights—the independence and the opportunities that the old-fashioned feminists fought for. Some women, in their forties and fifties, still remembered painfully giving up those dreams, but most of the younger women no longer even thought about them. A thousand expert voices applauded their femininity, their adjustment, their new maturity. All they had to do was devote their lives from earliest girlhood to finding a husband and bearing children.

By the end of the nineteen-fifties, the average marriage age of women in America dropped to 20, and was still dropping, into the teens. Fourteen million girls were engaged by 17. The proportion of women attending college in comparison with men dropped from 47 per cent in 1920 to 35 per cent in 1958. A century earlier, women had fought for higher education; now girls went to college to get a husband. By the mid-fifties, 60 per cent dropped out of college to marry, or because they were afraid too much education would be a marriage bar. Colleges built dormitories for "married students," but the students were almost always the husbands. A new degree instituted for the wives—"Ph.T." (Putting Husband Through).

Then American girls began getting married in high school. And the women's magazines, deploring the unhappy statistics about these young marriages, urged that courses on marriage, and marriage counselors, be installed in the high schools. Girls started going steady at twelve and thirteen, in junior high. Manufacturers put out brassieres with false bosoms of foam rubber for little girls of ten. And an advertisement for a child's dress, sizes 3–6x, in the *New York Times* in the fall of 1960, said: "She Too Can Join the Man-Trap Set."

By the end of the fifties, the United States birthrate was overtaking India's. The birth-control movement, renamed Planned Parenthood, was asked to find a method whereby women who had been advised that a third or fourth baby would be born dead or defective might have it anyhow. Statisticians were especially astounded at the fantastic increase in the number of babies among college women. Where once they had two children, now they had four, five, six. Women who had once wanted careers were now making careers out of having babies. So rejoiced *Life* magazine in a 1956 paean to the movement of American women back to the home.

In a New York hospital, a woman had a nervous breakdown when she found she could not breastfeed her baby. In other hospitals, women dying of cancer refused a drug which research had proved might save their lives: its side effects were said to be unfeminine. "If I have only one life, let me live it as a blonde," a larger-than-life-sized picture of a pretty, vacuous woman proclaimed from newspaper, magazine, and drugstore ads. And across America, three out of every ten women dyed their hair blonde. They ate a chalk called Metrecal, instead of food, to shrink to the size of the thin young models. Department-store buyers reported that American women, since 1939, had become three and four sizes smaller. "Women are out to fit the clothes, instead of vice-versa," one buyer said.

Interior decorators were designing kitchens with mosaic murals and original paintings, for kitchens were once again the center of women's lives. Home sewing became a million-dollar industry. Many women no longer left their homes, except to shop, chauffeur their children, or attend a social engagement with their husbands. Girls were growing up in America without ever having jobs outside the home. In the late fifties, a sociological phenomenon was suddenly remarked: a third of American women now worked, but most were no longer young and very few were pursuing careers. They were married women who held part-time jobs, selling or secretarial, to put their husbands through school, their sons through college, or to help pay the mortgage. Or they were widows supporting families. Fewer and fewer women were entering professional work. The shortages in the nursing, social work, and teaching professions caused crises in almost every American city. Concerned over the Soviet Union's lead in the space race, scientists noted that America's greatest source of unused brain-power was women. But girls would not study physics: it was "unfeminine." A girl refused a science fellowship at Johns Hopkins to take a job in a real-estate office. All she wanted, she said, was what every other American girl wanted—to get married, have four children and live in a nice house in a nice suburb.

The suburban housewife—she was the dream image of the young American women and the envy, it was said, of women all over the world. The American housewife—freed by science and labor-saving appliances from the drudgery, the dangers of childbirth and the illnesses of her grandmother. She was healthy, beautiful, educated, concerned only about her husband, her children, her home. She had found true feminine fulfillment. As a housewife and mother, she was respected as a full and equal partner to man in his world. She was free to choose automobiles, clothes, appliances, supermarkets; she had everything that women ever dreamed of.

In the fifteen years after World War II, this mystique of feminine fulfillment became the cherished and self-perpetuating core of contemporary American culture. Millions of women lived their lives in the image of those pretty pictures of the American suburban housewife, kissing their husbands goodbye in front of the picture window, depositing their stationwagonsful of children at school, and smiling as they ran the new electric waxer over the spotless kitchen floor. They baked their own bread, sewed their own and their children's clothes, kept their new washing machines and dryers running all day. They changed the sheets on the beds twice a week instead of once, took the rug-hooking class in adult education, and pitied their poor frustrated mothers, who had dreamed of having a career. Their only dream was to be perfect wives and mothers; their highest ambition to have five children and a beautiful house, their only fight to get and keep their husbands. They had no thought for the unfeminine problems of the world outside the home; they wanted the men to make the major decisions. They gloried in their role as women, and wrote proudly on the census blank: "Occupation: housewife."

For over fifteen years, the words written for women, and the words women used when they talked to each other, while their husbands sat on the other side of the room and talked shop or politics or septic tanks, were about problems with their children, or how to keep their husbands happy, or improve their children's school, or cook chicken or make slipcovers. Nobody argued whether women were inferior or superior to men; they were simply different. Words like "emancipation" and "career" sounded strange and embarrassing; no one had used them for years. When a Frenchwoman named Simone de Beauvoir wrote a book called *The Second Sex*, an American critic commented that she obviously "didn't know what life was all about," and besides, she was talking about French women. The "woman problem" in America no longer existed.

If a woman had a problem in the 1950's and 1960's, she knew that something must be wrong with her marriage, or with herself. Other women were satisfied with their lives, she thought. What kind of a woman was she if she did not feel this mysterious fulfillment waxing the kitchen floor? She was so ashamed to admit her dissatisfaction that she never knew how many other women shared it. If she tried to tell her husband, he didn't understand what she was talking about. She did not really understand it herself. For over fifteen years women in America found it harder to talk about this problem than about sex. Even the psychoanalysts had no name for it. When a woman went to a psychiatrist for help, as many women did, she would say, "I'm so ashamed," or "I must be hopelessly neurotic." "I don't know what's wrong with women today," a suburban psychiatrist said uneasily. "I only know something is wrong because most of my patients happen to be women. And their problem isn't sexual." Most women with this problem did not go to see a psychoanalyst, however. "There's nothing wrong really," they kept telling themselves. "There isn't any problem." . . .

If I am right, the problem that has no name stirring in the minds of so many American women today is not a matter of loss of femininity or too much education, or the demands of domesticity. It is far more important than anyone recognizes. It is the key to these other new and old problems which have been torturing women and their husbands and children, and puzzling their doctors and educators for years. It may well be the key to our future as a nation and a culture. We can no longer ignore that voice within women that says: "I want something more than my husband and my children and my home."

Frantz Fanon (1925–1961) was born in Martinique. He studied medicine in France and became a psychiatrist. During the French-Algerian war, Fanon served in a hospital in Algeria—an experience that deepened his native sympathy for and understanding of those subject to colonial oppressions. He died of cancer at only thirty-six, yet his works endure. *Black Skin, White Masks* (1952) and *The Wretched of the Earth* (1961) were both among the most widely read books in Europe and the United States in the 1960s, as well as early classics in the emerging literature of the late- and postcolonial world.

Decolonizing, National Culture, and the Negro Intellectual*
Frantz Fanon (1961)

National liberation, national reawakening, restoration of the nation to the people or Commonwealth, whatever the name used, whatever the latest expression, decolonization is always a violent event. At whatever level we study it—individual encounters, a change of name for a sports club, the guest list at a cocktail party, members of a police force or the board of directors of a state or private bank—decolonization is quite simply the substitution of one "species" of mankind by another. The substitution is unconditional, absolute, total, and seamless. We could go on to portray the rise of a new nation, the establishment of a new state, its diplomatic relations and its economic and political orientation. But instead we have decided to describe the kind of tabula rasa which from the outset defines any decolonization. What is singularly important is that it starts from the very first day with the basic claims of the colonized. In actual fact, proof of success lies in a social fabric that has been changed inside out. This change is extraordinarily important because it is

*Excerpts from THE WRETCHED OF THE EARTH by Frantz Fanon, English translation copyright © 1963 by Présence Africaine. Used by permission of Grove/Atlantic, Inc. Any third party use of this material, outside of this publication, is prohibited.

desired, clamored for, and demanded. The need for this change exists in a raw, repressed, and reckless state in the lives and consciousness of colonized men and women. But the eventuality of such a change is also experienced as a terrifying future in the consciousness of another "species" of men and women: the *colons*, the colonists.

Decolonization, which sets out to change the order of the world, is clearly an agenda for total disorder. But it cannot be accomplished by the wave of a magic wand, a natural cataclysm, or a gentleman's agreement. Decolonization, we know, is an historical process: In other words, it can only be understood, it can only find its significance and become self coherent insofar as we can discern the history-making movement which gives it form and substance. Decolonization is the encounter between two congenitally antagonistic forces that in fact owe their singularity to the kind of reification secreted and nurtured by the colonial situation. Their first confrontation was colored by violence and their cohabitation—or rather the exploitation of the colonized by the colonizer—continued at the point of the bayonet and under cannon fire. The colonist and the colonized are old acquaintances. And consequently, the colonist is right when he says he "knows" them. It is the colonist who *fabricated* and *continues to fabricate* the colonized subject. The colonist derives his validity, i.e., his wealth, from the colonial system.

Decolonization never goes unnoticed, for it focuses on and fundamentally alters being, and transforms the spectator crushed to a nonessential state into a privileged actor, captured in a virtually grandiose fashion by the spotlight of History. It infuses a new rhythm, specific to a new generation of men, with a new language and a new humanity. Decolonization is truly the creation of new men. But such a creation cannot be attributed to a supernatural power: The "thing" colonized becomes a man through the very process of liberation.

Decolonization, therefore, implies the urgent need to thoroughly challenge the colonial situation. Its definition can, if we want to describe it accurately, be summed up in the well-known words: "The last shall be first." Decolonization is verification of this. At a descriptive level, therefore, any decolonization is a success.

In its bare reality, decolonization reeks of red-hot cannonballs and bloody knives. For the last can be the first only after a murderous and decisive confrontation between the two protagonists. This determination to have the last move up to the front, to have them clamber up (too quickly, say some) the famous echelons of an organized society, can only succeed by resorting to every means, including, of course, violence.

You do not disorganize a society, however primitive it may be, with such an agenda if you are not determined from the very start to smash every obstacle encountered. The colonized, who have made up their mind to make such an agenda into a driving force, have been prepared for violence from time immemorial. As soon as they are born it is obvious to them that their cramped world, riddled with taboos, can only be challenged by out-and-out violence.

The colonial world is a compartmentalized world. It is obviously as superfluous to recall the existence of "native" towns and European towns, of schools for "natives" and schools for Europeans, as it is to recall apartheid in South Africa. Yet if we penetrate inside this compartmentalization we shall at least bring to light some of its key aspects. By penetrating its geographical configuration and classification we shall be able to delineate the backbone on which the decolonized society is reorganized.

The colonized world is a world divided in two. The dividing line, the border, is represented by the barracks and the police stations. In the colonies, the official, legitimate agent, the spokesperson for the colonizer and the regime of oppression, is the police officer or the soldier. In capitalist societies, education, whether secular or religious, the teaching of moral reflexes handed down from father to son, the exemplary integrity of workers decorated after fifty years of loyal and faithful service, the fostering of love for harmony and wisdom, those aesthetic forms of respect for the status quo, instill in the exploited a mood of submission and inhibition which considerably eases the task of the agents of law and order. In capitalist countries a multitude of sermonizers, counselors, and "confusion-mongers" intervene between the exploited and the authorities. In colonial regions, however, the proximity and frequent, direct intervention by the police and the military ensure the colonized are kept under close scrutiny, and contained by rifle butts and napalm. We have seen how the government's agent uses a language of pure violence. The agent does not alleviate oppression or mask domination. He displays and demonstrates them with the clear conscience of the law enforcer, and brings violence into the homes and minds of the colonized subject. . . .

The blacks who lived in the United States, Central, and Latin America in fact needed a cultural matrix to cling to. The problem they were faced with was not basically any different from that of the Africans. The whites in America had not behaved any differently to them than the white colonizers had to the Africans. We have seen how the whites were used to putting all "Negroes" in the same basket. During the First Congress of the African Society for Culture in Paris in 1956 the black Americans spontaneously considered their problems from the same standpoint as their fellow Africans. By integrating the former slaves into African civilization the African intellectuals accorded them an acceptable civil status. But gradually the black Americans realized that their existential problems differed from those faced by the Africans. The only common denominator between the blacks from Chicago and the Nigerians or Tanganyikans was that they all defined themselves in relation to the whites. But once the initial comparisons had been made and subjective feelings had settled down, the black Americans realized that the objective problems were fundamentally different. The principle and purpose of the freedom rides whereby black and white Americans endeavor to combat racial discrimination have little in common with the heroic struggle of the Angolan people against the iniquity of Portuguese colonialism. Consequently, during the Second Congress of the African Society for Culture the black Americans decided to create the American Society for African Culture.

Negritude thus came up against its first limitation, namely, those phenomena that take into account the historicizing of men. "Negro" or "Negro-African" culture broke up because the men who set out to embody it realized that every culture is first and foremost national, and that the problems for which Richard Wright or Langston Hughes had to be on the alert were fundamentally different from those faced by Léopold Senghor or Jomo Kenyatta. Likewise certain Arab states, who had struck up the glorious hymn to an Arab renaissance, were forced to realize that their geographical position and their region's economic interdependence were more important than the revival of their past. Consequently the Arab states today are organically linked to Mediterranean societies and cultures. The reason being that these states are subject to modern pressures and new commercial channels, whereas the great trade routes of the days of Arab expansion have now disappeared. But above all there is the fact that the political regimes of certain Arab states are so heterogenous and alien to each other that any encounter, even cultural, between these states proves meaningless.

It is clear therefore that the way the cultural problem is posed in certain colonized countries can lead to serious ambiguities. Colonialism's insistence that "niggers" have no culture, and Arabs are by nature barbaric, inevitably leads to a glorification of cultural phenomena that become continental instead of national, and singularly racialized. In Africa, the reasoning of the intellectual is Black-African or Arab-Islamic. It is not specifically national. Culture is increasingly cut off from reality. It finds safe haven in a refuge of smoldering emotions and has difficulty cutting a straightforward path that would, nevertheless, be the only one likely to endow it with productiveness, homogeneity, and substance.

Though historically limited the fact remains that the actions of the colonized intellectual do much to support and justify the action of the politicians. And it is true the attitude of the colonized intellectual sometimes takes on the aspect of a cult or religion. But under closer analysis it clearly reflects he is only too aware that he is running the risk of severing the last remaining ties with his people. This stated belief in the existence of a national culture is in fact a burning, desperate return to anything. In order to secure his salvation, in order to escape the supremacy of white culture the colonized intellectual feels the need to return to his unknown roots and lose himself, come what may, among his barbaric people. Because he feels he is becoming alienated, in other words the living focus of contradictions which risk becoming insurmountable, the colonized intellectual wrenches himself from the quagmire which threatens to suck him down, and determined to believe what he finds, he accepts and ratifies it with heart and soul. He finds himself bound to answer for everything and for everyone. He not only becomes an advocate, he accepts being included with the others, and henceforth he can afford to laugh at his past cowardice.

This painful and harrowing wrench is, however, a necessity. Otherwise we will be faced with extremely serious psycho-affective mutilations: individuals without an anchorage, without borders, colorless, stateless, rootless, a body of angels. And it will come as no surprise to hear some colonized intellectuals state: "Speaking as a Senegalese and a Frenchman. . . . Speaking as an Algerian and a Frenchman." Stumbling over the need to assume two nationalities, two determinations, the intellectual who is Arab and French, or Nigerian and English, if he wants to be sincere with himself, chooses the negation of one of these two determinations. Usually, unwilling or unable to choose, these intellectuals collect all the historical determinations which have conditioned them and place themselves in a thoroughly "universal perspective."

The reason being that the colonized intellectual has thrown himself headlong into Western culture. Like adopted children who only stop investigating their new family environment once their psyche has formed a minimum core of reassurance, the colonized intellectual will endeavor to make European culture his own. Not content with knowing Rabelais or Diderot, Shakespeare or Edgar Allen Poe, he will stretch his mind until he identifies with them completely. . . .

In some cases, however, at the very moment when the nationalist parties mobilize the people in the name of national independence, the colonized intellectual rejects his accomplishments, suddenly feeling them to be alienating. But this is easier said than done. The intellectual who has slipped into Western civilization through a cultural backdoor, who has managed to embody, or rather change bodies with, European civilization, will realize that the cultural model he would like to integrate for authenticity's sake offers little in the way of figureheads capable of standing up to comparison with the many illustrious names in the civilization of the occupier. History, of course, written by and for Westerners, may periodically enhance the image of certain episodes of the African past. But faced with his country's present-day status, lucidly and "objectively" observing the reality of the continent he would like to claim as his own, the intellectual is terrified by the void, the mindlessness, and the savagery. Yet he feels he must escape this white culture. He must look elsewhere, anywhere; for lack of a cultural stimulus comparable to the glorious panorama flaunted by the colonizer, the colonized intellectual frequently lapses into heated arguments and develops a psychology dominated by an exaggerated sensibility, sensitivity, and susceptibility. This movement of withdrawal, which first of all comes from a petitio principii in his psychological mechanism and physiognomy, above all calls to mind a muscular reflex, a muscular contraction.

The foregoing is sufficient to explain the style of the colonized intellectuals who make up their mind to assert this phase of liberating consciousness. A jagged style, full of imagery, for the image is the drawbridge that lets out the unconscious forces into the surrounding meadows. An energetic style, alive with rhythms bursting with life. A colorful style too, bronzed, bathed in sunlight and harsh. This style, which Westerners once found jarring, is not, as some would have it, a racial feature, but above all reflects a single-handed combat and reveals how necessary it is for the intellectual to inflict injury on himself, to actually bleed red blood and free himself from that part of his being already contaminated by the germs of decay. A swift, painful combat where inevitably the muscle had to replace the concept.

Although this approach may take him to unusual heights in the sphere of poetry, at an existential level it has often proved a dead end. When he decides to return to the routine of daily life, after having been roused to fever pitch by rubbing shoulders with his people, whoever they were and whoever they may be, all he brings back from his adventures are terribly sterile clichés. He places emphasis on customs, traditions, and costumes, and his painful, forced search seems but a banal quest for the exotic. This is the period when the intellectuals extol every last particular of the indigenous landscape. The flowing dress of the *boubou* is regarded as sacred and shoes from Paris or Italy are shunned for Muslim slippers, *babouches*. The language of the colonizer suddenly scorches his lips. Rediscovering one's people sometimes means in this phase wanting to be a "nigger," not an exceptional "nigger," but a real "nigger," a "dirty nigger," the sort defined by the white man. Rediscovering one's people means becoming a "filthy Arab," of going as native as possible, becoming unrecognizable; it means clipping those wings which had been left to grow.

The colonized intellectual decides to draw up a list of the bad old ways characteristic of the colonial world, and hastens to recall the goodness of the people, this people who have been made guardians of truth. The scandal this approach triggers among the colonists strengthens the determination of the colonized. Once the colonists, who had relished their victory over these assimilated intellectuals, realize that these men they thought saved have begun to merge with the "nigger scum," the entire system loses its bearings. Every colonized intellectual won over, every colonized intellectual who confesses, once he decides to revert to his old ways, not only represents a setback for the colonial enterprise, but also symbolizes the pointlessness and superficiality of the work accomplished. Every colonized intellectual who crosses back over the line is a radical condemnation of the method and the regime, and the uproar it causes justifies his abdication and encourages him to persevere.

PART FOUR

Will the Center Hold? 1963–1979

Americans sometimes confuse *their* Sixties with *the* Sixties. This is not entirely unreasonable. Certainly, the American 1960s had many dramatic moments, tragic and not, that drew world attention—the civil rights march on Washington, John Kennedy's assassination, Malcolm X's, the Black Power revolts, Kwame Turé (aka, Stokely Carmichael), Huey P. Newton, Bobby Seale, Martin Luther King Jr.'s assassination, Robert Kennedy's, the student rebellions at Berkeley and Columbia, Bob Dylan, People's Park, the Chicago conspiracy trial, the antiwar movement, Jerry Rubin and Abbie Hoffman, early feminist rebellions in homes and in public, Woodstock, the Stonewall rebellion, Altamont, Kent State, and so on. These were events worthy of world attention.

But if one is to speak of "the Sixties," as if to condense a long and complex series of disjointed events into something "everyone understands," then it is necessary to speak of a world event. Because the United States was the virtual center of the world at the time of these disruptions, "the Sixties" were American in the sense that the disjointing of America was a phenomenon of world importance. This is why the whole world was watching. The world was affecting what it was watching, and being affected. The Sixties time period was a global event, first and foremost. When all was said and done, this is what underlay the question of the period.

Will the Center hold? The question was drawn from a line in William Butler Yeats's "The Second Coming." It may have been Joan Didion's widely read essay "Slouching Toward Bethlehem" that brought new meaning to this famous poem. In any case, by the spring and summer of 1968, Yeats's words expressed what many (perhaps most) people, nearly everywhere, felt:

Turning and turning in the widening gyre
The falcon cannot hear the falconer;
Things fall apart; the centre cannot hold;
Mere anarchy is loosed upon the world,
The blood-dimmed tide is loosed, and everywhere
The ceremony of innocence is drowned;
The best lack all conviction, while the worst
Are full of passionate intensity.

Those closest to the Center, either by devotion or dependence, were most struck. It was not, of course, the West's first encounter with a world spinning out of control. But for reasons then not at all obvious, the spin of political events wrenched moral culture against its grain. This time, Euro-American innocence was lost. And of all that happened, nothing disturbed the West's long dreams as much as Vietnam. Startled, people awoke confused, angry, frightened.

Timeline: 1963 – 1980

Social Theory

Herbert Marcuse, *One-Dimensional Man: Repressive Desublimation* 1964

Peter Berger and Thomas Luckmann, *Social Construction of Reality: Society as a Human Product* 1966

Jacques Derrida, *The Decentering Event in Social Thought* 1966

Harold Garfinkel, *Studies in Ethnomethodology: Reflexive Properties of Practical Sociology* 1967

C. L. R. James, *World Revolution* 1968

Clifford Geertz, *Toward an Interpretative Theory of Culture: Thick Description* 1973

Dorothy Smith, *Knowing a Society from Within: A Woman's Standpoint* 1974

Immanuel Wallerstein, *The Modern World-System*, Vol 1 1974

Pierre Bourdieu, *Outline of a Theory of Practice: Structures, Habitus, Practices* 1974

Michel Foucault, *Discipline and Punishment: Biopolitics and the Carceral Society* 1975

Nancy Chodorow, *Reproduction of Mothering* 1978

Theda Skocpol, *States and Social Revolutions* 1979

Audre Lorde, *The Master's Tools Will Never Dismantle the Master's House* 1979

Alvin W. Gouldner, *The Future of Intellectuals and the Rise of the New Class* 1979

Gilles Deleuze and Felix Guattari, *A Thousand Plateaus: The Rhizome* 1980

Wider World

1963

Cassius Clay becomes Muhammad Ali **1964**

US begins increasing number of troops to Vietnam War **1965**

US first with communication satellite in space **1965**

Stokely Carmichael popularizes Black Power **1966**

Michel Foucault *Order of Things: Archaeology of Human Sciences* **1966**

World Revolution of 1968 begins, Spring **1968**

Soviets put down Prague Spring revolution **1968**

Richard Nixon elected US President **1968**

Stonewall protests begin Gay Rights Movement in US **1969**

Woodstock festival in rural New York State **1969**

Computers in different US cities linked; Internet born **1969**

1970

Kate Millett publishes *Sexual Politics* **1970**

Michel Foucault elected to College de France **1970**

Hip-hop dancing first noticed in New York City **1971**

Francis Ford Coppola's *Godfather,* part one **1972**

First report of Watergate break-in **1972**

Richard Nixon re-elected **1972**

Paris treaty ends US combat in Vietnam **1972**

Roe V Wade secures women's right to abortion **1973**

All US troops depart Vietnam **1973**

Watergate scandal intensifies pressure on Nixon **1973**

Stephen King publishers first novel, *Carrie* **1973**

Henry Kissinger becomes US Secretary of State **1973**

Alexander Solzhenitsyn's *Gulag Archipelago* first appears in West **1973**

Erica Jong publishes *Fear of Flying* **1973**

Augusto Pinochet leads junta to control of Chile **1974**

Richard Nixon, facing impeachment, resigns **1974**

Muhammad Ali defeats George Foreman to regain title in Zaire **1974**

Chiang Kai-shek dies in Taiwan **1975**

Saigon surrenders to North Vietnam **1975**

Mozambique independence from Portugal **1975**

Jack Nicholson stars in *One Flew Over the Cuckoo's Nest* **1975**

Microsoft founded by Bill Gates and Paul Allen **1975**

Franco dies in Spain **1975**

Cuban troops invade Angola **1975**

Israeli raid on Entebbe **1976**

Mao dies; Cultural Revolution ends **1976**

Jimmy Carter elected US President **1976**

Menachem Begin leads Likud to power in Israel **1977**

Steve Biko killed in South African jail **1978**

Vietnamese invade Cambodia, end reign of Khmer Rouge **1978**

Iran's Islamic Revolution overthrows Shah **1979**

Coppola's film *Apocalypse Now* **1979**

Three Mile Island nuclear melt down **1979**

1980

Microsoft contracts with IBM for operating system **1980**

Independent Rhodesia becomes Zimbabwe **1980**

Robert Mugabe begins reign in Zimbabwe **1980**

Lech Walesa leads Solidarity Movement in Poland **1980**

Ronald Reagan elected US President **1980**

Saddam Hussein begins war with Iran **1980**

The Global Sixties Turn Against the Dominant Core

Throughout the presidency of Lyndon B. Johnson, the best and brightest Kennedy had brought to Washington were still in charge. They invented the War on Poverty, and the war in Vietnam. They managed the government, the military, the universities, and much of the culture. And as events unfolded after the death of JFK, it became clear that the brightness of men like W. W. Rostow, John Kenneth Galbraith, Robert McNamara, McGeorge Bundy, and Arthur Schlesinger Jr. was part of the problem, however good their intentions. They, more than others, directly and indirectly sponsored the war in Southeast Asia. But after it became evident that massive bombing and burning made little difference, these same men could not make up their minds. To this day, they are hated by some for not having had the political will to win; by others for having abandoned morality and good sense for getting involved in the first place. Against them, those who considered themselves the saving middle remnant of society saw the worst. Unkempt youth. Strange music. Drugs. Radical protesters. Priests pouring blood on draft files. Open disobedience of authority. Abuse of the flag. Draft dodging. On the one side, there was no compelling conviction; on the other, a dirty, drug-ridden, sexual mess—or so it seemed. Whichever way they turned, those longing for a moral Center were without comfort.

Bizarre slogans defined an unfamiliar spiritual terrain. The best could say, as they sank deeper and deeper into the jungles of Vietnam, "We had to destroy it to save it." In the technical reasoning of the best and brightest, this was logic. The best of the West was its rationality applied to the technology of war. The moral force of history was on their side. The words referred to a village in Vietnam. But many of those who heard them felt they could have been referring to the world itself.

Against the best, the worst shouted: "Hey, hey, LBJ. How many kids did you kill today?" Perhaps unwittingly, they attacked the authority of the land—a man whose persona was Authority itself—at his most vulnerable point. Whatever could have rightly been said against Lyndon Johnson, he was not a child killer. He was a schoolteacher and author of the War on Poverty—a man of compassion for the weak in mass society. Yet the passionate intensity of the slogan suggested the extent to which the Center was deteriorating. The cohesive center of social life first starts to come unglued whenever members of the same family can no longer contact one another's reality. The best and the worst were not, after all, natural enemies. They were kin. The young people who shouted in protest were the intellectual and cultural children of LBJ's best, bright administrators of the war. Literally, some of those marching in the streets could have been students of W. W. Rostow at MIT or Arthur Schlesinger and McGeorge Bundy at Harvard—special assistants to the president in the early and middle 1960s.

This was a struggle *within* the most liberal sectors of American and European culture. To this, the excluded middle responded: "America: Love It or Leave It." In the absence of an intelligent Center, the silent majority's native logic prevailed. Those who had never had any palpable contact with the centers of power and persuasion were able to assert the logic of the excluded middle. To them, America was the transcendent, self-evident Truth that required no techniques and deserved no abuse. This saving principle moved more than enough voters out of the Democratic column in 1968 to defeat presidential candidate Hubert H. Humphrey, the most thoroughly decent liberal in postwar American politics. Richard M. Nixon was elected to restore law and order. Concerning America's place in the world, he exclaimed: "We are number one! Peace with Honor!"

Political language, on all sides, had become hollow. Incantations without moral feet filled the air. The West had raised the idea of a Center to the level of historical axiom. The Sixties brought the Center down to earth, where, under mundane conditions, it had lost its power. This was a world event, something much more than yet another rejection of Euro-American authority. The entire world was implicated in the spectacle of the then-great power of the West losing its grip in the absence of a ready successor. Though the meaning of all this did not become clear for a long time, by 1968 one sensed that the West's failures in Southeast Asia belonged to some new and different series of events. They were not just rebellions but the early shifts in a reconfiguration of world power and culture. Whatever was to be was making itself evident both in the United States and in the world.

In the world, the collapse of the European colonial system and the defeat of the United States in Southeast Asia were followed in the early 1970s by the birth of the Organization of Petroleum Exporting Countries (OPEC) and the world oil crisis of 1973–1974. For the first time since World War II, the Euro-American powers faced a nonwhite, alien world adversary. This time, however, the so-called Third World forces yielded neither to Westernization nor to occupation. World politics since have been different. If America remained the world superpower, it was on terms fundamentally different from those after World War II. OPEC forced the United States to borrow. As it became a debtor nation, its moral credit, though still good, was devalued. Others—in Europe, the Middle East, the Pacific Basin—now held the better hand in world capital markets, leaving the holders of world resources (usually countries poorer in capital) with a stronger card to play. Now, regional forces like Iran, Cuba, Iraq, and Afghanistan could resist, if not deter, the power of the Center, thus weakening its might. In this sense, the world lost not just the United States as Center but also the prospect that any new Center would organize the world into a system in service to the West's interest.

New and Global Social Movements Gather Force

One of the deep structural changes provoked by the global events that came to a point of crisis in 1968 was the forceful development of what social scientists call the New Social Movements. The expression continues to resonate as a way of describing social movements based less on class or national liberation interests than on what some came to call identity politics. What New Social Movements, the concept, referred to was that more and more social groups with a history of exclusion from the rights and benefits of modern societies took to the streets to invent a new vocabulary and new ways of situating their social experiences in relation the globally dominant interests. Though the deep changes began with the decolonizing movements of the 1940s and 1950s in Africa, the Caribbean, and Asia. These were, to be sure, traditional movements aimed at national liberation. Yet, the very fact that they were all rooted in the oppressed periphery of the modern world—and, not, incidentally, non-white regions colonized by whites—they inspired comparable movements in the dominant states and cities of the wealthy capitalist world. Most prominently, the American Civil Rights Movement was directly inspired by Gandhi's political philosophy in India as, later, the World Revolution described in this section by C. L. R. James drew from African and Caribbean movements. Thus, race came to the fore as itself an organizing ideal for the racially excluded, as gender did for women, sexuality for gay and other non-heterosexual people, and culture did for the student movements, and so on through nearly every possible group with a history of marginality. Though the New Social Movements tended to be established in a given nation or region, the sources of their thinking and the reach of their ideas and programs were global and their effects reverberated across social structures, domestic and global.

In the United States, for example, the Civil Rights Movement was one thing, as was the rise of Black Power after 1966. White people, whether in the excluded middle or near the centers of power, could think of these as a problem with "those" people. But when, beginning at Berkeley in 1964, the student movement turned against the university, then against the war, then seemingly against all that was normal and sacred, it was no longer an alien force within. "They," then, were "us."

If, in the Golden Age, the university was America's most distinctive institutional promise of the good society for which the brilliant government offered to be the servant, then the postwar family was the moral basis of that ideal society. But as Elaine Tyler May shows in *Homeward Bound: American Families in the Cold War Era* (1988), the postwar American family was an unstable invention of Golden Age culture. May demonstrates that the ideal suburban family—husband, wife, kids, kitchen appliances—was, as much as anything, part of the culture's strategy of domestic containment. May's study of personal reports by suburban housewives supports her claim that the family was also a means to contain society's ambivalence toward feminine sexuality. Female sexual power was, perhaps, the domestic equivalent of international communism. If the communists threatened America's masculinity abroad, female sexual power threatened it at home. Women's power therefore had to be kept from invading the male consciousness or escaping the bounds of the domestic wage-based family. Men's fear of Woman, including fear of their own feminine urges and feelings, was considered every bit as much a threat to American character as was the prospect that women might want (as indeed they did) to keep the jobs they had held of necessity in World War II. Though Elaine Tyler May did not state it in just this way, it would seem that, deep in the recess of the cultural logic of America in the 1950s, Man felt an urgency to control *his* female desires as much as "his" woman. Somehow, American might depended more or less equally on keeping women at home, homosexuals out of the army, and the Communists behind the Iron Curtain.

The so-called American family *may* have been invented at this late day, in the 1940s and 1950s, when abundance could support it and politics required it. In any case, after 1963, these three institutions—the university, government, the family—became vectors of discontent intersecting where the Center had been. Once protest arose within and against these institutions, Yeats's beast seemed nearer. No longer could it be said that the problem was "those" people—American Blacks, the PLO, the Viet Cong, Castro, colonial rebels—all incited by the Communists.

When the rebellions in the United States turned on the university, against the government, within the families, against the prevailing culture of contained sexuality, then the rough, slouching beast threatened to be born. Vietnam was, indeed, another extravagant attack of the white world against its well-defined other. But it was *not* just another international event in a series of aggressions in world politics. Soon, it became a crisis within American moral culture and thus within the West's sense of itself. It was a crisis of many parts, each eventually turning on the other in the "widening gyre." America, like the British and other European colonizing powers, fought enemies abroad to protect the culture. This was official policy. But in Vietnam, it was never clear who the enemy was. Those with whom the United States sided were a worse lot than the communists that US troops were fighting. And, whomever they were, the enemies were nowhere to be seen after they disappeared into the jungles.

To many, there *was* no enemy. Muhammad Ali (after JFK, the man most widely recognized around the world) refused induction to fight in Vietnam, saying, "No Viet Cong ever called me Nigger." Then, American ground troops began fragging officers in the dark jungles. The unreal images near the end of the film *Apocalypse Now* were real: America had entered the Heart of Darkness. By the time of the Tet Offensive early in 1968, Vietnam no longer had much to do with the traditional principles of war and politics. It was confusion *within* the moral Center of the West. The world had somehow shifted. The new enemy was not the stealthy, yellow-skinned communists who disappeared into the jungle, who rebuilt bombed bridges within days, who refused to cower. Those people were doing nothing more than what colonial people throughout the world had been doing since the late 1940s—resisting to the point of throwing out the Euro-American colonizers. The real enemy was within—the worst who so confounded the best, giving power to the excluded middle.

Between 1963, when Kennedy died, and 1968, when the Center failed to hold, everything changed in the United States and the world. In America, what Stokely Carmichael later called Black Power made its first, noncommercial appearance before white people. One of Malcolm X's early speeches before a racially mixed audience after his departure from the nation of Islam—his famous "Ballot or the Bullet" speech of April 1964—included these chilling lines: "I'm not an American. I'm one of 22 million black people who are the victims of Americanism. . . . I see America through the eyes of the victim. I don't see any American dream. I see an American nightmare." This was less than a year after Martin Luther King Jr. roused Americans, white and Black, to a new integrated dream. Malcolm was responding to King, to the Civil Rights Movement, to the myth that the white-dominated world-system would work. If King had brought the nonviolent force of Gandhi into his dream, Malcolm brought the culturally separate and morally stern principles of other parts of the non-Western world to his. Later, after Malcolm X was killed in February 1965, the Civil Rights Movement started to dissolve. The Student Nonviolent Coordinating Committee (SNCC) eventually adopted a position on the use of force in self-defense that was not much different from Malcolm X's. Kwame Turé and H. Rap Brown, among others who spoke for Black Power, became international representatives of the rising tide of color against the Center. In time, the truth of C. L. R. James's World *Revolution: 1968*—once viewed as an intolerably radical diagnoses of the global situation—came to be a common (if not universal) way of accounting for the global *boulversements* of 1968. Immanuel Wallerstein, for one, would describe that world revolution as the beginning of the end of the modern world-system as it had been since 1500.

At the same time, the women's movement moved in two directions. It worked against the restraints and abuses women suffered within the family. Consciousness-raising groups invited women to talk and understand themselves apart from the culture of patriarchal families. Men were as unsettled and angered by the separatism of wives and lovers as whites generally were by the separatism of Blacks. The movement also worked against the dominant structures, as feminists began to organize politically. NOW (National Organization for Woman) took the centrist approach. Other groups were more radical. One heard of SCUM (Society for Cutting Up Men), WAR (Women of the American Revolution), and WITCH (an acronym with multiple definitions). WITCH and the others were not so much organizations as manifestos of a movement. "There is no 'joining' WITCH. If you are a woman and dare to look within yourself, you are a WITCH." Most men, and many righteous women, were furious. They complained about the outrages of bra-burning at the 1968 protest against the Miss America Pageant in Atlantic City. But bras were never burned. They were thrown off and out. Clearly, millions simply assumed that uncontained female breasts were incendiary to the political order. They seemed to have understood that the entrance into politics of women with a feminist consciousness would change everything. Which it did.

Outrages against the abandonment of "femininity" were, certainly, subtle displays of the deeper fear that—in addition to the risks these feminists posed for the family-wage system—their apparent refusal of the culture of contained femininity would unleash sexuality. To those who hated feminism, uncontained breasts could mean nothing *but* sex. To a culture that required the strictest possible control of sex, the very idea that there could be such a thing as sexuality was unimaginable. Sexuality means that sex was more than God's procreative will or, if you must, fucking. Sexuality means that people are sexual beings and that they draw their sense of themselves in part from their sexual lives. During this time, two words gained new meanings in Western languages: woman and gender. Woman was newly constructed in part on the understanding that a gender is not exhausted by sex. Thus, feminist consciousness constructed a new political force based on the denial of a natural essence behind the feminine. This set loose sex itself.

In June 1969, in New York's Greenwich Village, the Stonewall rebellion was the first historic, public protest of gays and lesbians against the straight world. The long-standing practice of official police abuse against gays, lesbians, and bisexuals was met with a violent revolt, setting 400 police against a crowd of 2,000 gays and their supporters. Though gay and lesbian people had been organizing politically since at least the beginning of World War II, this was the event associated with organized, public resistance to the culture's silent insistence on official heterosexuality. The appearance of a militant gay movement at more or less the same time as a militant feminism aggravated the crisis. Together, they signified that the family was not what it was supposed to be.

Actually, there had already been a storm of controversy over the family, incited by another of Washington's best and brightest. Daniel Patrick Moynihan's 1965 report on the Negro family was intelligent and well intended. But its evidence, and argument, that the problem of American Blacks was linked to the disappearance of the Black man as head of family, was read by many Blacks as white society's racist ignorance of Black life. More than a few whites read it as a confirmation of what they believed, or feared, was true of Black people: Blacks would not, or could not, sustain responsible lives necessary for good family life. Somewhere, surely, white assumptions about Black sexuality lurked not far behind.

If the family was threatened by these movements, then the civil order was threatened by another. The student protests against the university, beginning with the free speech movement at Berkeley in 1964, seemed to be the worst kind of ingratitude. The new universities had been built, at great cost, to assure the futures of the very children who now protested them. To some in the student movement, the universities were factories in the machinery of an inhumane society. After the riots at Columbia in the spring of 1968, the independent report of a commission headed by Archibald Cox of Harvard Law School came very close to agreeing.

But in the public mind, the superficial similarities between legitimate political protest on campus and the counterculture's rejection of everything accepted as decent only added to the terror. Middle-class, suburban whites in conservative Cincinnati could hardly be expected to detect the fine, but evident, line distinguishing protests at the 1968 Democratic Convention in Chicago and Woodstock the following August. Jerry Rubin, once a nice boy from Cincinnati's Walnut Hills High School, was now something beyond comprehension. Yet his book with a title that needs no explanation—*Do It!*—condensed everything objectionable about students, youth, counterculture, the new attitudes, sex, and more into one volume.

All this came to a terrible denouement on May 4, 1970, at Kent State University in Ohio. Though President Nixon had begun to withdraw troops from Vietnam, students protested the continuing war. National Guard troops, called to restore order, were commanded to fire into a crowd. Four students were killed. This time, however, white, working-class kids from the industrial belt murdered their own. Now, those on the margins of the silent middle were sucked into the vortex. No one was spared. Ten days later, two Black students were killed in a similar situation at Jackson State University in Mississippi. Naturally, the public was less anguished at the latter event. The death of Blacks was considered familiar. The political slaying of whites by whites—of "good" young people *by* good young people—was something else. It marked the full turn of that gyre set in motion when the old values that centered the world gave way.

The Kent State incident occurred five years before the final pullout from Vietnam. Watergate and the OPEC oil crisis were still to come. One could say that the 1960s began in 1955, when Rosa Parks refused to move to the back of the bus, and ended some twenty years later, with the pictures of those desperate Americans clinging to the last helicopter lifting off from the US Embassy in Saigon, leaving the Vietnamese they had intended to save to an expected slaughter. What Rosa Parks did led to events that changed the United States forever. What the war did not do in Vietnam changed America's place in the world forever. The two, and everything in between, were not unrelated.

Important to notice is that even in this brief survey of the movements in the United States, behind them all stood a decidedly global movement. The feminist and race-based movements, like the student movements, were thoroughly international. The protest against the American war in Vietnam was as well and, in the United States, it brought America into a degree of global awareness that was in a way more important than the civil rights examples. Muhammad Ali was, at the time, the most famous person in the world and not just for his athletic genius but equally for this personal protest against American war policies in Asia.

One of the strangest happenstances of the 1960s is that they also gave birth to new social theories that, at first, seemed to be about as remote from the protests and war and turmoil as anything could be. They were not.

Theories Break with Modernity

In 1966, at an international meeting of scholars on a very technical subject, Jacques Derrida made public the words already quoted in the introduction to this book:

> This was the moment when language invaded the universal problematic, the moment when, in the absence of a center or origin, everything became discourse—provided we can

agree on this word—that is to say, a system in which the central signified, is never absolutely present outside a system of differences.

In 1966 in Derrida's Paris, as in the United States where this talk was presented, events leading to the collapse of the Center two years later were well under way. Whether Derrida had them specifically in mind is hard to say, though it would seem that he did. Certainly, the movement associated with him and others, like Michel Foucault, was later connected to those events in the minds of those who found the new social theories compelling. Whatever it is that may link, in some hidden way, the abstract thinking of professional social theorists with the concrete notions of practical political people, they were indeed linked in this time. At first, the name of the theoretical movement was poststructuralism. It was initially a matter of interest only to those who customarily followed current intellectual and cultural events in France, then to a growing number of philosophers and literary theorists abroad. Eventually, under various names, it became the most current line of social thinking in the universities and colleges, especially in the United States. Not everyone was pleased.

One of the reasons so many names are used to define this strange turn in social thinking is that it seems to have been not so much a refinement of arguments within a philosophical tradition as one of a number of explorations of the idea that modern culture had its limits. In the short passage from Derrida, one should take seriously the key phrases: "absence of a center," "language invaded the universal problematic," "a system of differences." Without paying any attention to the precise theoretical argument, it is fair to say that the slogans that would define the end of modernity are suggested here: decentering, discourse, and differences. In short, this was one of the first technical summaries of what became of social theory of the world. Simply put (in my words):

In the absence of a Center (whether intellectual or political), one cannot trust reality. In the absence of a trustable reality, one can only rely on language. What a person says is sufficiently true. No one person's saying is more true. Thus, the world is a world of differences. In the absence of a Center, there is difference.

Though this attitude was initially viewed with great suspicion, it soon began to make its way into the varieties of social theories that were emerging in the late 1960s (from about 1966 to 1970). Amazingly, many of them, in spite of being at considerable odds with each other, were directly or indirectly preoccupied with language. This free talk about talk itself, much like the free speech movement at Berkeley in 1964, used and explored language in order to shock and rethink the social world. It both came out of a changing world and, in time, became part of change. If this was not the end of the old cultural order, as Derrida's line suggests, it was at least the beginning of a major withdrawal of belief in its plausibility.

Michel Foucault, if anything, came to be better known than Derrida because he wrote about historically concrete subjects—madness, prisons, hospitals, sexuality. In his inaugural address in 1970 at the Collège de France, "Discourse of Language," Foucault noted precisely the public fear of what was going on culturally and politically:

There is undoubtedly in our society, and I would not be surprised to see it in others, . . . a sort of dumb fear of these events, of this mass of spoken things, of everything that could possibly be violent, discontinuous, querulous, disordered even and perilous in it, of the incessant, disorderly buzzing of discourse.

It is not by accident that Foucault's address begins with reference to the charming myth of the West that Europe's culture is universal. This was a central theme behind all of Foucault's studies.

At about the same time, C. L. R. James, the great Caribbean writer and social theorist from Trinidad, also wrote of the importance of the Black Power movement to the freedom of the world's oppressed. Like the speeches of Martin Luther King, Jr., and Malcolm X, Black Power proponents possessed very little power in real economic, political, or military terms. It was enough for Black people, feminists, and students to say something to alarm those who felt the Center was weak. This was one of the senses in which language had invaded the universal problematic.

Elsewhere, writers as different in temperament and orientation as Alvin Gouldner, Herbert Marcuse, Harold Garfinkel, and Pierre Bourdieu wrote social theories that took well-established traditions of thought in new directions. Though they were not poststructuralists, or even necessarily critics of modernity, all went deep to the heart of modern culture's way of thinking. Gouldner, in *The Coming Crisis of Western Sociology* (1970), dared to take himself—that is, the personal life of the social theorist—seriously. Though he may not have intended it, this was a move that pushed C. Wright Mills's sociological imagination beyond the traditional categories of the subject and the object. Gouldner's reflexive sociologist was meant to transform the very idea of sociology. He was, in part, responding to the political experience of the many new students attracted to the field by the events of the Sixties. He, the reflexive sociologist, is one who transforms self in order to know the world differently and thus to change it. Though the deeper sentiments of Gouldner's theory were quite the opposite of Marcuse's skepticism, what Gouldner was trying to rethink about sociology was at least consistent with Marcuse's critique of one-dimensional man. Both sought to generate some transcendent critical attitude from which individuals could escape the mind-numbing effects of modernity. Gouldner's critiques of sociology and Marxism were similar to Marcuse's famous critique of modern culture. Both saw a world that stimulated in order to contain the best human instincts. Social science and sex had both turned against humanity. Both required liberation.

Pierre Bourdieu's idea of reflexive sociology went beyond other theories of the reflexive in his attempt to reinvent sociology without relying on modernity's epistemological doublet: subject/object. Bourdieu's famous concept *habitus* aimed for a new beginning point without subjects and objects. In this same period, Harold Garfinkel published the classic text of ethnomethodology. Again, the parallels are striking. Bourdieu wanted to convey the way in which enduring social things achieve spontaneous expression in practical life by focusing on the disposition (or *habitus*) of individuals in collective action. Garfinkel did something similar in studying ordinary people's methods (literally, ethnomethods) for constructing regularity in a world of infinite reflexivities. Though in other ways they are worlds apart, Bourdieu and Garfinkel focused social theory on the practices of everyday life, from which both sought to derive, in one way or another, the world's larger structures. Then too, Alvin Gouldner, himself a proponent of reflexive social theory, was a prophet of our current microcomputer age. Gouldner, was a new kind of Marxist sociologist, one who would rework class theory by declaring that power was passing into the hands of a new class of intellectuals with technical competence in the languages of cyber-information. Reading social theorists of the day against their times and what has happened since, it is possible to see that they were developing theories that, if taken seriously, put enormous strain on anyone's naive faith that the social world was ordered by progress from a center toward some end. This was the time when the world was taken apart without any great concern to put it back together as it had been.

Audre Lorde's well-known attack on academic thinking, including academic feminism, came near the end of this period; it could just as well be considered part of the next. Yet she was one of those voices from the margins of the academy that reminded social theorists of the origins of the new social theorists in political and cultural life. Like Derrida and Foucault in the mid-1960s, Lorde declared the need for new tools, new concepts. "The Master's Tools Will Never Dismantle the Master's House" rests on the prior assumption that the house must be dismantled. By 1979, this was no longer shocking or even surprising. Rethinking the world was increasingly what one did.

Even the Mainstream Changes Course

Just the same, there were many in this same period who still believed in the basic assumptions of modern culture, however skeptical they were. Not all social theory took on a radical critique of traditionally modern methods of social theory. Jürgen Habermas, whose ideas we will encounter in Part Five, was the most prominent of those devoted, like his predecessors in the Frankfort school, to recovering and renewing a critical theory that preserved the best of modern ideas and culture.

Strikingly, among the most enduringly important cultural theorists of this period, Clifford Geertz was at once both radical and sufficiently mainstream as to be honored across the political spectrum of social and cultural theorists. This unusual gift was due to the deep empirical work that stood behind his ideas, but also because he was able to write and think with a mild but telling irony. His concept of thick description in fieldwork was, for example, on the surface an appeal for painstaking empirical research but, underneath, it was a manifesto for symbolic interpretations of data that looked for the hidden winks (his word) that cannot be fully explained but in which are found the ambiguity of all cultural facts. His example, from the philosopher Gilbert Ryle, is that when one observes a wink, how does one know whether it is a meaningful gesture of agreement, a sarcastic brush off, or a momentary tick, or a chronic disorder of the nervous system? That question of a small event can be the key to worlds of meaning.

Others straddled the same fence but in different ways. Peter Berger and Thomas Luckmann dazzled the world of professional social theorists with *The Social Construction of Reality* (1966). Not only did the book seem to bring together all the strains of European and American theory, it also defined the outlines of a new philosophy of social reality. The social world was no longer a given, an objective imprint on subjective consciousness. It was, rather, a constructed human product. From one angle, this was radical stuff; from another, it was conservative. Berger and Luckmann still believed in, and assumed, an orderly world. In 1966, when their book first appeared, that order was much in doubt. Theirs was the most successful of a number of attempts in the mid- and late 1960s to produce a grand synthesis of social theory's essential terms. It was already too late. Most of those who wrote in the 1970s turned away from systematic theorizing toward social theories of important aspects of social life—women's reality, the world economic system, the state, and the family.

Dorothy Smith's first statements of a woman's standpoint as a critique of sociology were ignored for a long while by everyone but feminists in and outside sociology. Though she kept faith with the basic terms of modern social theory, she aimed to invert their traditional order. The woman's standpoint is not just another view on social life; it is a surer way to clear and powerful knowledge. Immanuel Wallerstein's multivolume study of the capitalist world-system first appeared in 1974, the same year as Smith's first statement of her theory of women's perspective. Just as Smith's feminist standpoint position was a forthright attack on traditional social knowledge, so Wallerstein's world-systems theory was an attack on modernization theory and, in a way, on modernity itself. Though their concerns were different, both Smith and Wallerstein could be said to have attacked the master's house with the master's tools, though this is truer in Wallerstein's case. His studies of the emergence of the capitalist world-system since the sixteenth century provided what was then the most comprehensive description of the economic and historical foundations of the modern world centered in Europe. Like Smith's feminism, Wallerstein's theory attacked by describing. One learns a great deal about patriarchically inspired sociology in reading Smith, much as one learns about the world aspirations of capitalism in reading Wallerstein. Yet neither quite escapes the criticism of participating in that which they seek to criticize. Wallerstein is sometimes called a functionalist with Marxist intents. Smith can be said to have wanted to recenter sociology in a woman's perspective and, in so doing, to keep social knowledge bound to a center. The debates on the limits of Wallerstein's theory of economic development and Smith's feminist standpoint have contributed to subsequent changes in thinking in both areas.

When it first appeared in 1979, Theda Skocpol's *States and Social Revolutions* stood out among many reconsiderations of the state as an independent force in world political action. Her theory shows a willingness both to learn from and to move beyond structuralist, Marxist, and liberal theories of political action. In this sense, Skocpol was, and is, representative of the social theory since the 1960s that brought Left-liberal concerns to academic subjects, seeking to reformulate traditional assumptions. However, her supple regard for the state's Janus-like qualities—one face turned to the world, the other to its society—somewhat contradicts her readiness to accept the available methods and terms of social science. The result is a powerful argument, certainly one richer and more compelling than the abstract Marxist theories of the state popular in the early

1970s. Yet she remains, for her own good reasons, within the language of modernity. In a similar way, Nancy Chodorow's influential discussion of mothering as a dual structure—partly fixed by early childhood experience, partly fixed by the social structure of kinship—is a radical development of the respective insights of psychoanalytic and sociological reasoning.

When Chodorow is read against the furor caused by the Moynihan report on the so-called pathology of the Negro family, and Skocpol is read in relation to Wallerstein's structural theory of world economies, it is possible to get a sense of the extent to which social theory had changed in this period. Even where belief in the categories of modern culture remained constant, the subjects selected for study reflected the conditions in the world. In those days, from the mid-1960s through their aftermath in the 1970s, it was very difficult *not* to have something to say about the world and its structures, on the one hand, and engendered personal life and its structures, on the other. Though the social theorists who began to break with modernity reached into new theoretical territory, those who did not still reflected the general conditions of the world at the time. Once the Center either failed or faltered (however one chooses to frame it), there was considerable pressure, and motivation, to have something to say about one question above all others: If the world's structures are different, how do those differences affect personal life? In one sense, this is the same question C. Wright Mills asked in 1959. But, a generation later, it was put differently. At the later time, it was harder to believe uncritically in a straightforward relation of biography and structure. Between the individual with his or her troubles and the world's structured issues, a disturbing presence had intervened. For some, it was the presence of new theoretical problems requiring the best thinking. For others, it was the presence of an *absence*—that which remained when everything moderns had believed for two centuries was in doubt. The years from about 1963 to 1979 were not, in reality, the end of anything. Yet after, some began to see them as the beginning of an end.

As things would turn out a half-century plus later, early a new century, the Golden Moment from 1945–1963 had faded and the uncertainties of the remaining years of the 1960s and the 1970s had, if not won out, at least assumed a stronger place in the considerations of social theorists. The early feminist ideas of Simone de Beauvoir developed in ways that might have both pleased and surprised her. Other early feminists, including Dorothy Smith and Betty Friedan would live well in the 2000s to witness how much ideas like theirs would influence the way people everywhere would think about their worlds. By 2004, when Derrida died, his 1966 critique of the Center would appear in retrospect to have been prophetic. The realities of globalization would include new, if not ultimate, powers arising from what had been the world's periphery. After September 11, 2001, the United States would still be the world's most powerful nation in many ways, but by then it would seem wrong to think of it as the Center. But, by far, the most enduring effects on social theory of new ideas from 1945–1963 and on through the 1970s were the startling effects of decolonizing movements. Frantz Fanon, C. L. R. James, and Aimé Césaire had substantially altered the future of social theory by inspiring a movement that brought the cultures and complaints of the people of the colonized margins into the core of the modern world. It would never be decided whether these changes ought to be called postmodern. Still, the idea that modernity had come to a time of trial would take hold after 1979.

    C. L.

Notes

Page 291: Malcolm X, "Ballot or the Bullet," *Malcolm X Speaks* (Grove Press, 1966), 26.

Page 292: The WITCH quote is from a New York Covens pamphlet in Robin Morgan, ed., *Sisterhood Is Powerful* (Vintage, 1970), 605. WITCH was an acronym of multiple definitions varying from coven to coven and issue to issue.

Other cited material is from the selections following.

Experiments at Renewal and Reconstruction

Clifford J. Geertz (1926–2006) was born in California, studied at Antioch College, then Harvard where he earned his PhD in the then famous Department of Social Relations in 1956. All three of these background facts hint at his unique contributions to social and cultural theory. As California was, even in the 1920s, the epicenter of American dreaming and popular culture, so Antioch was in his day noted for its devotion to radical thinking and innovation, so too Harvard's now defunct Social Relations program was in the 1950s at once the boldest center of interdisciplinary graduate education in the social sciences and, oddly, the center of the traditional core of social and cultural thought. Geertz was a cultural anthropologist whose theoretical innovations were well founded in years of fieldwork in Southeast Asia and North Africa. He quickly emerged by 1970 as one of the world's best respected students of culture. His achievements led to appointment to the Institute for Advanced Study at Princeton. Upon his death in 2006 the Institute's press release described his importance even at an institution noted for work in mathematics and physics: "Dr. Geertz's appointment thirty-six years ago was significant not only for the distinguished leadership it would bring to the Institute, but also because it marked the initiation of the School of Social Science, which in 1973 formally became the fourth School at the Institute." Safe to say that in the first years of his tenure at the Institute few other students of culture would be so warmly embraced by a school long committed to the traditional sciences. Among Geertz's fifty plus books and countless articles *The Interpretation of Cultures* (1973), the collection from which the selection is drawn, stands still today as required reading by anyone truly interested in cultural theory. Likewise, thick description, the selection's titular concept is likely the most widely (and erroneously) quoted concept in culture studies. Readers should read the selection closely to determine how thick description is itself an ironic concept meant to identify not the mass of descriptive data but the meaningful solitary clue hidden *among* mass of data.

Thick Description: Toward an Interpretive Theory of Culture[*]
Clifford J. Geertz (1973)

The concept of culture I espouse, and whose utility the essays below attempt to demonstrate, is essentially a semiotic one. Believing, with Max Weber, that man is an animal suspended in webs of significance he himself has spun, I take culture to be those webs, and the analysis of it to be therefore not an experimental science in search of law but an interpretive one in search of meaning. It is explication I am after, construing social expressions on their surface enigmatical. But this pronouncement, a doctrine in a clause, demands itself some explication.

---

[*] Excerpt from *The Interpretation of Cultures* by Clifford Geertz (New York: Basic Books, 1973), pp. 5–7. Reprinted with permission of Basic Books, a member of the Perseus Books Group.

Operationalism as a methodological dogma never made much sense so far as the social sciences are concerned, and except for a few rather too well-swept corners—Skinnerian behaviorism, intelligence testing, and so on—it is largely dead now. But it had, for all that, an important point to make, which, however we may feel about trying to define charisma or alienation in terms of operations, retains a certain force: if you want to understand what a science is, you should look in the first instance not at its theories or its findings, and certainly not at what its apologists say about it; you should look at what the practitioners of it do.

In anthropology, or anyway social anthropology, what the practioners do is ethnography. And it is in understanding what ethnography is, or more exactly what doing ethnography is, that a start can be made toward grasping what anthropological analysis amounts to as a form of knowledge. This, it must immediately be said, is not a matter of methods. From one point of view, that of the textbook, doing ethnography is establishing rapport, selecting informants, transcribing texts, taking genealogies, mapping fields, keeping a diary, and so on. But it is not these things, techniques and received procedures, that define the enterprise. What defines it is the kind of intellectual effort it is: an elaborate venture in, to borrow a notion from Gilbert Ryle, "thick description."

Ryle's discussion of "thick description" appears in two recent essays of his (now reprinted in the second volume of his *Collected Papers*) addressed to the general question of what, as he puts it, "*Le Penseur*" is doing: "Thinking and Reflecting" and "The Thinking of Thoughts." Consider, he says, two boys rapidly contracting the eyelids of their right eyes. In one, this is an involuntary twitch; in the other, a conspiratorial signal to a friend. The two movements are, as movements, identical; from an I-am-a-camera, "phenomenalistic" observation of them alone, one could not tell which was twitch and which was wink, or indeed whether both or either was twitch or wink. Yet the difference, however unphotographable, between a twitch and a wink is vast; as anyone unfortunate enough to have had the first taken for the second knows. The winker is communicating, and indeed communicating in a quite precise and special way: (1) deliberately, (2) to someone in particular, (3) to impart a particular message, (4) according to a socially established code, and (5) without cognizance of the rest of the company. As Ryle points out, the winker has not done two things, contracted his eyelids and winked, while the twitcher has done only one, contracted his eyelids. Contracting your eyelids on purpose when there exists a public code in which so doing counts as a conspiratorial signal *is* winking. That's all there is to it: a speck of behavior, a fleck of culture, and—*voilà!*—a gesture.

That, however, is just the beginning. Suppose, he continues, there is a third boy, who, "to give malicious amusement to his cronies," parodies the first boy's wink, as amateurish, clumsy, obvious, and so on. He, of course, does this in the same way the second boy winked and the first twitched: by contracting his right eyelids. Only this boy is neither winking nor twitching, he is parodying someone else's, as he takes it, laughable, attempt at winking. Here, too, a socially established code exists (he will "wink" laboriously, overobviously, perhaps adding a grimace—the usual artifices of the clown); and so also does a message. Only now it is not conspiracy but ridicule that is in the air. If the others think he is actually winking, his whole project misfires as completely, though with somewhat different results, as if they think he is twitching. One can go further: uncertain of his mimicking abilities, the would-be satirist may practice at home before the mirror, in which case he is not twitching, winking, or parodying, but rehearsing; though so far as what a camera, a radical behaviorist, or a believer in protocol sentences would record he is just rapidly contracting his right eyelids like all the others. Complexities are possible, if not practically without end, at least logically so. The original winker might, for example, actually have been fake-winking, say, to mislead outsiders into imagining there was a conspiracy afoot when there in fact was not, in which case our descriptions of what the parodist is parodying and the rehearser rehearsing of course shift accordingly. But the point is that between what Ryle calls the "thin description" of what the rehearser (parodist, winker, twitcher…) is doing ("rapidly contracting his right eyelids") and the "thick description" of what he is doing ("practicing a burlesque of a friend faking a wink to deceive an innocent into thinking a conspiracy is in motion") lies the object of ethnography: a stratified hierarchy of meaningful structures in terms of which twitches, winks, fake-winks, parodies, rehearsals of parodies are produced, perceived, and interpreted, and without which they would not (not even the zero-form twitches, which, *as a cultural category*, are as much nonwinks as winks are nontwitches) in fact exist, no matter what anyone did or didn't do with his eyelids.

Like so many of the little stories Oxford philosophers like to make up for themselves, all this winking, fake-winking, burlesque-fake-winking, rehearsed-burlesque-fake-winking, may seem a bit artificial. In way of adding a more empirical note, let me give, deliberately unpreceded by any prior explanatory comment at all, a not untypical excerpt from my own field journal to demonstrate that, however evened off for didactic purposes, Ryle's example presents an image only too exact of the sort of piled-up structures of inference and implication through which an ethnographer is continually trying to pick his way. ...

Culture, this acted document, thus is public, like a burlesqued wink .... Though ideational, it does not exist in someone's head; though unphysical, it is not an occult entity. The interminable, because unterminable, debate within anthropology as to whether culture is "subjective" or "objective," together with the mutual exchange of intellectual insults ("idealist!"—"materialist!"; "mentalist!"—"behaviorist!"; "impressionist!"—"positivist!") which accompanies it, is wholly misconceived. Once human behavior is seen as (most of the time; there *are* true twitches) symbolic action—action which, like phonation in speech, pigment in painting, line in writing, or sonance in music, signifies—the question as to whether culture is patterned conduct or a frame of mind, or even the two somehow mixed together, loses sense. The thing to ask about a burlesqued wink or a mock sheep raid is not what their ontological status is. It is the same as that of rocks on the one hand and dreams on the other—they are things of this world. The thing to ask is what their import is: what it is, ridicule or challenge, irony or anger, snobbery or pride, that, in their occurrence and through their agency, is getting said.

This may seem like an obvious truth, but there are a number of ways to obscure it. One is to imagine that culture is a self-contained "super-organic" reality with forces and purposes of its own; that is, to reify it. Another is to claim that it consists in the brute pattern of behavioral events we observe in fact to occur in some identifiable community or other; that is, to reduce it. But though both these confusions still exist, and doubtless will be always with us, the main source of theoretical muddlement in contemporary anthropology is a view which developed in reaction to them and is right now very widely held—namely, that, to quote Ward Goodenough, perhaps its leading proponent, "culture [is located] in the minds and hearts of men."

Variously called ethnoscience, componential analysis, or cognitive anthropology (a terminological wavering which reflects a deeper uncertainty), this school of thought holds that culture is composed of psychological structures by means of which individuals or groups of individuals guide their behavior. "A society's culture," to quote Goodenough again, this time in a passage which has become the *locus classicus* of the whole movement, "consists of whatever it is one has to know or believe in order to operate in a manner acceptable to its members." And from this view of what culture is follows a view, equally assured, of what describing it is—the writing out of systematic rules, an ethnographic algorithm, which, if followed, would make it possible so to operate, to pass (physical appearance aside) for a native. In such a way, extreme subjectivism is married to extreme formalism, with the expected result: an explosion of debate as to whether particular analyses (which come in the form of taxonomies, paradigms, tables, trees, and other ingenuities) reflect what the natives "really" think or are merely clever simulations, logically equivalent but substantively different, of what they think.

As, on first glance, this approach may look close enough to the one being developed here to be mistaken for it, it is useful to be explicit as to what divides them. If, leaving our winks and sheep behind for the moment, we take, say, a Beethoven quartet as an, admittedly rather special but, for these purposes, nicely illustrative, sample of culture, no one would, I think, identify it with its score, with the skills and knowledge needed to play it, with the understanding of it possessed by its performers or auditors, nor, to take care, *en passant*, of the reductionists and reifiers, with a particular performance of it or with some mysterious entity transcending material existence. The "no one" is perhaps too strong here, for there are always incorrigibles. But that a Beethoven quartet is a temporally developed tonal structure, a coherent sequence of modeled sound—in a word, music—and not anybody's knowledge of or belief about anything, including how to play it, is a proposition to which most people are, upon reflection, likely to assent.

To play the violin it is necessary to possess certain habits, skills, knowledge, and talents, to be in the mood to play, and (as the old joke goes) to have a violin. But violin playing is neither the habits, skills, knowledge, and so on, nor the mood, nor (the notion believers in "material culture" apparently embrace) the violin. To make a trade pact in Morocco, you have to do certain things in certain ways (among others, cut, while chanting Quranic Arabic, the throat of a lamb before the assembled, undeformed, adult male members of your tribe) and to be possessed of certain psychological characteristics (among others, a desire for distant things). But a trade pact is neither the throat cutting nor the desire, though it is real enough, as seven kinsmen of our Marmusha sheikh discovered when, on an earlier occasion, they were executed by him following the theft of one mangy, essentially valueless sheepskin from Cohen.

Culture, is public because meaning is. You can't wink (or burlesque one) without knowing what counts as winking or how, physically, to contract your eyelids, and you can't conduct a sheep raid (or mimic one) without knowing what it is to steal a sheep and how practically to go about it. But to draw from such truths the conclusion that knowing how to wink is winking and knowing how to steal a sheep is sheep raiding is to betray as deep a confusion as, taking thin descriptions for thick, to identify winking with eyelid contractions or sheep raiding with chasing woolly animals out of pastures. The cognitivist fallacy—that culture consists (to quote another spokesman for the movement, Stephen Tyler) of "mental phenomena which can [he means "should"] be analyzed by formal methods similar to those of mathematics and logic"—is as destructive of an effective use of the concept as are the behaviorist and idealist fallacies to which it is a misdrawn correction. Perhaps, as its errors are more sophisticated and its distortions subtler, it is even more so.

Peter Berger (1929–) was born in Vienna but educated, after WW II in the United States. Over his career he taught both in Germany and the US, eventually settling at Boston University where in due course he founded and still today directs the Institute on Culture, Religion and World Affairs. In addition to authoring numerous works in sociology, including *An Invitation to Sociology* (1963), Berger writes as a lay theologian, as in *A Far Glory: The Quest for Faith in an Age of Credulity* (1992).

Thomas Luckmann (1927–) was born in a small town in Slovenia outside Ljubljana. He was educated in Austria, after which he taught in New York at the New School for Social Research then in Germany at Frankfurt before moving to Konstanz until his retirement in 1994. He has written *Invisible Religion* (1967) and is the editor and coauthor of Alfred

Schutz's *Structure of the Life-world*, a systematic social theory from a phenomenological point of view. Like Berger, Luckmann remains active today and even finds time for mountaineering.

Berger and Luckmann wrote *The Social Construction of Reality* at a time when both were interested in the sociology of religion. They thus worked somewhat in the spirit of the classic social theorists, who derived much of their theoretical positions from assessments of, or reaction to, religion. Berger and Luckmann both felt that religion continued as an important force in modern life. This conviction underlay their argument that the social world was orderly, even though constructed in human process. Their book, from which the selection is taken, represents the most successful attempt since Schutz to construct an explicitly phenomenological social theory.

Society as a Human Product[*]
Peter Berger and Thomas Luckmann (1966)

It should be clear from the foregoing that the statement that man produces himself in no way implies some sort of Promethean vision of the solitary individual. Man's self-production is always, and of necessity, a social enterprise. Men *together* produce a human environment, with the totality of its socio-cultural and psychological formations. None of these formations may be understood as products of man's biological constitution, which, as indicated, provides only the outer limits for human productive activity. Just as it is impossible for man to develop as man in isolation, so it is impossible for man in isolation to produce a human environment. Solitary human being is being on the animal level (which, of course, man shares with other animals). As soon as one deserves phenomena that are specifically human, one enters the realm of the social. Man's specific humanity and his sociality are inextricably intertwined. *Homo sapiens* is always, and in the same measure, *homo socius.*

The human organism lacks the necessary biological means to provide stability for human conduct. Human existence, if it were thrown back on its organismic resources by themselves, would be existence in some sort of chaos. Such chaos is, however, empirically unavailable, even though one may theoretically conceive of it. Empirically, human existence takes place in a context of order, direction, stability. The question then arises: From what does the empirically existing stability of human order derive? An answer may be given on two levels. One may first point to the obvious fact that a given social order precedes any individual organismic development. That is, world-openness, while intrinsic to man's biological make-up, is always pre-empted by social order. One may say that the biologically intrinsic world-openness of human existence is always, and indeed must be, transformed by social order into a relative world-closedness. While this reclosure can never approximate the closedness of animal existence, if only because of its humanly produced and thus "artificial" character, it is nevertheless capable, most of the time, of providing direction and stability for the greater part of human conduct. The question may then be pushed to another level. One may ask in what manner social order itself arises.

The most general answer to this question is that social order is a human product, or, more precisely, an ongoing human production. It is produced by man in the course of his ongoing externalization. Social order is not biologically given or derived from any biological *data* in its empirical manifestations. Social order, needless to add, is also not given in man's natural environment, though particular features of this may be factors in determining certain features of a social order (for example, its economic or technological arrangements). Social order is not part of the "nature of things," and it cannot be derived from the "laws of nature." Social order exists *only* as a product of human activity. No other ontological status may be ascribed to it without hopelessly obfuscating its empirical manifestations. Both in its genesis (social order is the result of past human activity) and its existence in any instant of time (social order exists only and insofar as human activity continues to produce it) it is a human product.

While the social products of human externalization have a character *sui generis* as against both their organismic and their environmental context, it is important to stress that externalization as such is an anthropological necessity. Human being is impossible in a closed sphere of quiescent interiority. Human being must ongoingly externalize itself in activity. This anthropological necessity is grounded in man's biological equipment. The inherent instability of the human organism makes it imperative that man himself provide a stable environment for his conduct. Man himself must specialize and direct his drives. These biological facts serve as a necessary presupposition for the production of social order. In other words, although no existing social order can be derived from biological *data*, the necessity for social order as such stems from man's biological equipment.

To understand the causes, other than those posited by the biological constants, for the emergence, maintenance and transmission of a social order one must undertake an analysis that eventuates in a theory of institutionalization.

Origins of Institutionalization

All human activity is subject to habitualization. Any action that is repeated frequently becomes cast into a pattern, which can then be reproduced with an economy of effort and which, *ipso facto*, is apprehended by its performer *as* that pattern. Habitualization further implies that the action in question may be performed again in the future in the same manner and with the same economical effort. This is true of non-social as well as of social activity. Even the solitary individual on the proverbial desert island habitualizes his activity. When he wakes up in the morning and resumes his attempts to construct a canoe out of matchsticks, he may mumble to himself, "There I go again," as he starts on step one of an operating procedure consisting of, say, ten steps. In other words, even solitary man has at least the company of his operating procedures.

Habitualized actions, of course, retain their meaningful character for the individual although the meanings involved become embedded as routines in his general stock of knowledge, taken for granted by him and at hand for his projects into the future. Habitualization carries with it the important psychological gain that choices are narrowed. While in theory there may be a hundred ways to go about the project of building a canoe out of matchsticks, habitualization narrows these down to one. This frees the individual from the burden of "all those decisions," providing a psychological relief that has its basis in man's undirected instinctual structure. Habitualization provides the direction and the specialization of activity that is lacking in man's biological equipment, thus relieving the accumulation of tensions that result from undirected drives. And by providing a stable background in which human activity may proceed with a minimum of decision-making most of the time, it frees energy for such decisions as may be necessary on certain occasions. In other words, the background of habitualized activity opens up a foreground for deliberation and innovation.

In terms of the meanings bestowed by man upon his activity, habitualization makes it unnecessary for each situation to be defined anew, step by step. A large variety of situations may be subsumed under its predefinitions. The activity to be undertaken in these situations can then be anticipated. Even alternatives of conduct can be assigned standard weights.

These processes of habitualization precede any institutionalization, indeed can be made to apply to a hypothetical solitary individual detached from any social interaction. The fact that even such a solitary individual, assuming that he has been formed as a self (as we would have to assume in the case of our matchstick-canoe builder), will habitualize his activity in accordance with biographical experience of a world of social institutions preceding his solitude need not concern us at the moment. Empirically, the more important part of the habitualization of human activity is coextensive with the latter's institutionalization. The question then becomes how do institutions arise.

Institutionalization occurs whenever there is a reciprocal typification of habitualized actions by types of actors. Put differently, any such typification is an institution. What must be stressed is the reciprocity of institutional typifications and the typicality of not only the actions but also the actors in institutions. The typifications of habitualized actions that constitute institutions are always shared ones. They are *available* to all the members of the particular social group in question, and the institution itself typifies individual actors as well as individual actions. The institution posits that actions of type X will be performed by actors of type X. For example, the institution of the law posits that heads shall be chopped off in specific ways under specific circumstances, and that specific types of individuals shall do the chopping (executioners, say, or members of an impure caste, or virgins under a certain age, or those who have been designated by an oracle).

Institutions further imply historicity and control. Reciprocal typifications of actions are built up in the course of a shared history. They cannot be created instantaneously. Institutions always have a history, of which they are the products. It is impossible to

understand an institution adequately without an understanding of the historical process in which it was produced. Institutions also, by the very fact of their existence, control human conduct by setting up predefined patterns of conduct, which channel it in one direction as against the many other directions that would theoretically be possible. It is important to stress that this controlling character is inherent in institutionalization as such, prior to or apart from any mechanisms of sanctions specifically set up to support an institution. These mechanisms (the sum of which constitute what is generally called a system of social control) do, of course, exist in many institutions and in all the agglomerations of institutions that we call societies. Their controlling efficacy, however, is of a secondary or supplementary kind. As we shall see again later, the primary social control is given in the existence of an institution as such. To say that a segment of human activity has been institutionalized is already to say that this segment of human activity has been subsumed under social control. Additional control mechanisms are required only insofar as the processes of institutionalization are less than completely successful. Thus, for instance, the law may provide that anyone who breaks the incest taboo will have his head chopped off. This provision may be necessary because there have been cases when individuals offended against the taboo. It is unlikely that this sanction will have to be invoked continuously (unless the institution delineated by the incest taboo is itself in the course of disintegration, a special case that we need not elaborate here). It makes little sense, therefore, to say that human sexuality is socially controlled by beheading certain individuals. Rather, human sexuality is socially controlled by its institutionalization in the course of the particular history in question. One may add, of course, that the incest taboo itself is nothing but the negative side of an assemblage of typifications, which define in the first place which sexual conduct is incestuous and which is not.

In actual experience institutions generally manifest themselves in collectivities containing considerable numbers of people. It is theoretically important, however, to emphasize that the institutionalizing process of reciprocal typification would occur even if two individuals began to interact *de novo*. . . . *A* and *B* alone are responsible for having constructed this world. *A* and *B* remain capable of changing or abolishing it. What is more, since they themselves have shaped this world in the course of a shared biography which they can remember, the world thus shaped appears fully transparent to them. They understand the world that they themselves have made. All this changes in the process of transmission to the new generation. The objectivity of the institutional world "thickens" and "hardens," not only for the children, but (by a mirror effect) for the parents as well. The "There we go again" now becomes "This is how these things are done." A world so regarded attains a firmness in consciousness; it becomes real in an ever more massive way and it can no longer be changed so readily. For the children, especially in the early phase of their socialization into it, it becomes *the* world. For the parents, it loses its playful quality and becomes "serious." For the children, the parentally transmitted world is not fully transparent. Since they had no part in shaping it, it confronts them as a given reality that, like nature, is opaque in places at least.

Only at this point does it become possible to speak of a social world at all, in the sense of a comprehensive and given reality confronting the individual in a manner analogous to the reality of the natural world. Only in this way, *as* an objective world, can the social formations be transmitted to a new generation. In the early phases of socialization the child is quite incapable of distinguishing between the objectivity of natural phenomena and the objectivity of the social formations. To take the most important item of socialization, language appears to the child as inherent in the nature of things, and he cannot grasp the notion of its conventionality. A thing *is* what it is called, and it could not be called anything else. All institutions appear in the same way, as given, unalterable and self-evident. Even in our empirically unlikely example of parents having constructed an institutional world *de novo*, the objectivity of this world would be increased for them by the socialization of their children, because the objectivity experienced by the children would reflect back upon their own experience of this world. Empirically, of course, the institutional world transmitted by most parents already has the character of historical and objective reality. The process of transmission simply strengthens the parents' sense of reality, if only because, to put it crudely, if one says, "This is how these things are done," often enough one believes it oneself.

An institutional world, then, is experienced as an objective reality. It has a history that antedates the individual's birth and is not accessible to his biographical recollection. It was there before he was born, and it will be there after his death. This history itself, as the tradition of the existing institutions, has the character of objectivity. The individual's biography is apprehended as an episode located within the objective history of the society. The institutions, as historical and objective facticities, confront the individual as undeniable facts. The institutions are *there*, external to him, persistent in their reality, whether he likes it or not. He cannot wish them away. They resist his attempts to change or evade them. They have coercive power over him, both in themselves, by the sheer force of their facticity, and through the control mechanisms that are usually attached to the most important of them. The objective reality of institutions is not diminished if the individual does not understand their purpose or their mode of operation. He may experience large sectors of the social world as incomprehensible, perhaps oppressive in their opaqueness, but real nonetheless. Since institutions exist as external reality, the individual cannot understand them by introspection. He must "go out" and learn about them, just as he must to learn about nature. This remains true even though the social world, as a humanly produced reality, is potentially understandable in a way not possible in the case of the natural world.

It is important to keep in mind that the objectivity of the institutional world, however massive it may appear to the individual, is a humanly produced, constructed objectivity. The process by which the externalized products of human activity attain the character of objectivity is objectivation. The institutional world is objectivated human activity, and so is every single institution. In other words, despite the objectivity that marks the social world in human experience, it does not thereby acquire an ontological status apart from the human activity that produced it. The paradox that man is capable of producing a world that he then experiences as something other than a human product will concern us later on. At the moment, it is important to emphasize that the relationship between man, the producer, and the social world, his product, is and remains a dialectical one. That is, man (not, of course, in isolation but in his collectivities) and his social world interact with each other. The product acts back upon the producer. Externalization and objectivation are moments in a continuing dialectical process. The third moment in this process, which is internalization (by which the objectivated social world is retrojected into consciousness in the course of socialization), will occupy us in considerable detail later on. It is already possible, however, to see the fundamental relationship of these three dialectical moments in social reality. Each of them corresponds to an essential characterization of the social world. *Society is a* human product. *Society is an objective reality. Man is a social product.* It may also already be evident than an analysis of the social world that leaves out any one of these three moments will be distortive. One may further add that only with the transmission of the social world to a new generation (that is, internalization as effectuated in socialization) does the fundamental social dialectic appear in its totality. To repeat, only with the appearance of a new generation can one properly speak of a social world.

Dorothy Smith (1926–) studied in the 1960s at the University of California at Berkeley, from which she received her Ph.D. in sociology (1963). A citizen of Canada, Smith taught at Berkeley, the University of British Columbia, and the University of Essex before joining the Ontario Institute for Studies in Education in Toronto, Canada, in 1977. She now lives in active retirement in British Columbia. Smith is the author of numerous articles and books on such topics as the family, teaching, gender, suicide, and mental illness, in relation to which she has developed her feminist social theory. Smith's work has enjoyed renewed and enduring attention among general social theorists as well as feminist theorists. Her books include *The Conceptual Practices of Power: A Feminist Sociology of Knowledge* (1990) and *Everyday World as Problematic: A Feminist Sociology* (1987) and, more recently, *Mothering for Schooling* (2004) and *Institutional Ethnography: A Sociology for People* (2004). The selection, from an early and still widely read essay, broke new ground by exploring the unique methodological and theoretical contributions of what has come to be known as feminist standpoint theory.

Knowing a Society from Within: A Woman's Standpoint*
Dorothy Smith (1974)

Women's standpoint, as I am analyzing it here, discredits sociology's claim to constitute an objective knowledge independent of the sociologist's situation. Sociology's conceptual procedures, methods, and

*Smith, Dorothy E. *The Conceptual Practices of Power: A Feminist Sociology of Knowledge*, pp 21-27. Boston, MA: Northeastern University Press. ©1990 Dorothy E. Smith. Reprinted with permission of University Press of New England, Hanover, NH.

relevances organize its subject matter from a determinate position in society. This critical disclosure is the basis of an alternative way of thinking sociology. If sociology cannot avoid being situated, then it should take that as its beginning and build it into its methodological and theoretical strategies. As it is now, these strategies separate a sociologically constructed world from that of direct experience; it is precisely that separation that must be undone.

I am not proposing an immediate and radical transformation of the subject matter and methods of the discipline nor the junking of everything that has gone before. What I am suggesting is more in the nature of a reorganization of the relationship of sociologists to the object of our knowledge and of our problematic. This reorganization involves first placing sociologists where we are actually situated, namely, at the beginning of those acts by which we know or will come to know, and second, making our direct embodied experience of the everyday world the primary ground of our knowledge.

A sociology worked on in this way would not have as its objective a body of knowledge subsisting in and of itself; inquiry would not be justified by its contribution to the heaping up of such a body. We would reject a sociology aimed primarily at itself. We would not be interested in contributing to a body of knowledge whose uses are articulated to relations of ruling in which women participate only marginally, if at all. The professional sociologist is trained to think in the objectified modes of sociological discourse, to think sociology as it has been and is thought; that training and practice has to be discarded. Rather, as sociologists we would be constrained by the actualities of how things come about in people's direct experience, including our own. A sociology for women would offer a knowledge of the social organization and determinations of the properties and events of our directly experienced world. Its analyses would become part of our ordinary interpretations of the experienced world, just as our experience of the sun's sinking below the horizon is transformed by our knowledge that the world turns away from a sun that seems to sink.

The only way of knowing a socially constructed world is knowing it from within. We can never stand outside it. A relation in which sociological phenomena are objectified and presented as external to and independent of the observer is itself a special social practice also known from within. The relation of observer and object of observation, of sociologist to "subject," is a specialized social relationship. Even to be a stranger is to enter a world constituted from within as strange. The strangeness itself is the mode in which it is experienced.

When Jean Briggs made her ethnographic study of the ways in which an Eskimo people structure and express emotion, what she learned emerged for her in the context of the actual developing relations between her and the family with whom she lived and other members of the group. Her account situates her knowledge in the context of those relationships and in the actual sites in which the work of family subsistence was done. Affections, tensions, and quarrels, in some of which she was implicated, were the living texture in which she learned what she describes. She makes it clear how this context structured her learning and how what she learned and can speak of became observable to her.

Briggs tells us what is normally discarded in the anthropological or sociological telling. Although sociological inquiry is necessarily a social relation, we have learned to dissociate our own part in it. We recover only the object of our knowledge as if it stood all by itself. Sociology does not provide for seeing that there are always two terms to this relation. An alternative sociology must preserve in it the presence, concerns, and experience of the sociologist as knower and discoverer.

To begin from direct experience and to return to it as a constraint or "test" of the adequacy of a systematic knowledge is to begin from where we are located bodily. The actualities of our everyday world are already socially organized. Settings, equipment, environment, schedules, occasions, and so forth, as well as our enterprises and routines, are socially produced and concretely and symbolically organized prior to the moment at which we enter and at which inquiry begins. By taking up a standpoint in our original and immediate knowledge of the world, sociologists can make their discipline's socially organized properties first observable and then problematic.

When I speak of *experience* I do not use the term as a synonym for *perspective*. Nor in proposing a sociology grounded in the sociologist's actual experience am I recommending the self-indulgence of inner exploration or any other enterprise with self as sole focus and object. Such subjectivist interpretations of *experience* are themselves an aspect of that organization of consciousness that suppresses the locally situated side of the bifurcated consciousness and transports us straight into mind country, stashing away the concrete conditions and practices upon which it depends. We can never escape the circles of

our own heads if we accept that as our territory. Rather, sociologists' investigation of our directly experienced world as a problem is a mode of discovering or rediscovering the society from within. We begin from our own original but tacit knowledge and from within the acts by which we bring it into our grasp in making it observable and in understanding how it works. We aim not at a reiteration of what we already (tacitly) know, but at an exploration of what passes beyond that knowledge and is deeply implicated in how it is.

Our knowledge of the world is given to us in the modes by which we enter into relations with the object of knowledge. But in this case the object of our knowledge is or originates in the co-ordering of activities among "subjects." The constitution of an objective sociology as an authoritative version of how things are is done from a position in and as a part of the practices of ruling in our kind of society. Our training as sociologists teaches us to ignore the uneasiness at the junctures where multiple and diverse experiences are transformed into objectified forms. That juncture shows in the ordinary problems respondents have of fitting their experience of the world to the questions in the interview schedule. The sociologist who is a woman finds it hard to preserve this exclusion, for she discovers, if she will, precisely that uneasiness in her relation to her discipline as a whole. The persistence of the privileged sociological version (or versions) relies upon a substructure that has already discredited and deprived of authority to speak the voices of those who know the society differently. The objectivity of a sociological version depends upon a special relationship with others that makes it easy for sociologists to remain outside the others' experience and does not require them to recognize that experience as a valid contention.

Riding a train not long ago in Ontario I saw a family of Indians—woman, man, and three children—standing together on a spur above a river watching the train go by. I realized that I could tell this incident—the train, those five people seen on the other side of the glass—as it was, but that my description was built on my position and my interpretations. I have called them "Indians" and a family; I have said they were watching the train. My understanding has already subsumed theirs. Everything may have been quite different for them. My description is privileged to stand as what actually happened because theirs is not heard in the context in which I may speak. If we begin from the world as we actually experience it, it is at least possible to see that we are indeed located and that what we know of the other is conditional upon that location. There are and must be different experiences of the world and different bases of experience. We must not do away with them by taking advantage of our privileged speaking to construct a sociological version that we then impose upon them as their reality. We may not rewrite the other's world or impose upon it a conceptual framework that extracts from it what fits with ours. Their reality, their varieties of experience, must be an unconditional datum. It is the place from which inquiry begins.

A Bifurcation of Consciousness

My experience in the train epitomizes a sociological relation. I am already separated from the world as it is experienced by those I observe. That separation is fundamental to the character of that experience. Once I become aware of how my world is put together as a practical everyday matter and of how my relations are shaped by its concrete conditions (even in so simple a matter as that I am sitting in the train and it travels, but those people standing on the spur do not), I am led into the discovery that I cannot understand the nature of my experienced world by staying within its ordinary boundaries of assumption and knowledge. To account for that moment on the train and for the relation between the two experiences (or more) and the two positions from which those experiences begin I must posit a larger socioeconomic order in back of that moment. The coming together that makes the observation possible as well as how we were separated and drawn apart as well as how I now make use of that here—these properties are determined elsewhere than in that relation itself.

Furthermore, how our knowledge of the world is mediated to us becomes a problem of knowing how that world is organized for us prior to our participation in it. As intellectuals we ordinarily receive it as a media world, a world of texts, images, journals, books, talk, and other symbolic modes. We discard as an essential focus of our practice other ways of knowing. Accounting for that mode of knowing and the social organization that sets it up for us again leads us back into an analysis of the total socioeconomic order of which it is part. Inquiry remaining within the circumscriptions of the directly experienced cannot explore and explicate the relations organizing the everyday matrices of direct experience.

If we address the problem of the conditions as well as the perceived forms and organization of immediate experience, we should include in it the even actually happen and the ordinary material we encounter as a matter of fact: the urban renewal ect that uproots four hundred families; how it is live on welfare as an ordinary daily practice; cities as the actual physical structures in which we move; the organization of academic occasions such as that in which this chapter originated. When we examine them, we find that there are many aspects of how these things come about of which we, as sociologists, have little to say. We have a sense that the events entering our experience originate somewhere in a human intention, but we are unable to track back to find it and to find out how it got from there to here.

Or take this room in which I work or that room in which you are reading and treat that as a problem. If we think about the conditions of our activity here, we can trace how these chairs, this table, the walls, our clothing, our presence come to be here; how these places (yours and mine) are cleaned and maintained; and so forth. There are human activities, intentions, and relations that are not apparent as such in the actual material conditions of our work. The social organization of the setting is not wholly available to us in its appearance. We bypass in the immediacy of the specific practical activity a complex division of labor that is an essential precondition to it. Such preconditions are fundamentally mysterious to us and present us with problems in grasping social relations with which sociology is ill equipped to deal. We experience the world as largely incomprehensible beyond the limits of what we know in a common sense. No amount of observation of face-to-face relations, no amount of commonsense knowledge of everyday life, will take us beyond our essential ignorance of how it is put together. Our direct experience of it makes it (if we will) a problem, but it does not offer any answers. We experience a world of "appearances," the determinations of which lie beyond it.

We might think of the appearances of our direct experience as a multiplicity of surfaces, the properties and relations among which are generated by social organizations not observable in their effects. The relations underlying and generating the characteristics of our own directly experienced world bring us into unseen relations with others. Their experience is necessarily different from ours. If we would begin from our experienced world and attempt to analyze and account for how it is, we must posit others whose experience is not the same as ours.

Women's situation in sociology discloses to us a typical bifurcate structure with the abstracted,

one hand and the con-
nance routines, and so
h for granted depends
e or the other so that
in contradiction to it.
experience places us a step back,
can recognize the uneasiness that comes
from sociology's claim to be about the world we live
in, and, at the same time, its failure to account for or
even describe the actual features we experience. Yet
we cannot find the inner principle of our own activity
through exploring what is directly experienced.
We do not see how it is put together because it is
determined elsewhere. The very organization of the
world that has been assigned to us as the primary
locus of our being, shaping other projects and desires, is determined by and subordinate to the relations of society funded in a capitalist mode of
production. The aim of an alternative sociology
would be to explore and unfold the relations beyond
our direct experience that shape and determine it.
An alternative sociology would be a means to anyone
of understanding how the world comes about for us
and how it is organized so that it happens to us as it
does in our experience. An alternative sociology,
from the standpoint of women, makes the everyday
world its problematic.

Immanuel Wallerstein (1930–) was a prominent
supporter of the students during the riots at Columbia University in 1968. For many years, he has
been director of the Fernand Braudel Center and
Distinguished Professor of Sociology at the State
University of New York at Binghamton. At the
same time, he spent part of each year in Paris as
Directeur d'etudes at the Ecole des Hautes en Sciences Sociales. Since 2000, Wallerstein has been
Senior Research Scholar at Yale University. He is
also the founding editor of *Review*, a journal devoted largely to studies in world development and
world-system theory. Wallerstein is recognized the
world over as first among equals for his historically
informed and theoretically influential understanding of the global economy. His major work is *The
Modern World-System* of which, to date, there are
four volumes (1974, 1980, 1989, 2011). The selection is from the first volume of this study. It summarizes Wallerstein's now-famous argument that
the modern world-system is distinguished from
empires for its reliance on economic control of the

world order by dominating capitalist core states engaged in systemic economic and political domination of peripheral and semiperipheral world areas.
In developing these concepts, Wallerstein clearly
intended to supplant modernization theory's ideological notions of a progressively developing world
economy.

The Modern World-System[*]
Immanuel Wallerstein (1974)

In order to describe the origins and initial workings of
a world system, I have had to argue a certain conception of a world-system. A world-system is a social system, one that has boundaries, structures, member
groups, rules of legitimation, and coherence. Its life is
made up of the conflicting forces which hold it together by tension, and tear it apart as each group seeks
eternally to remold it to its advantage. It has the characteristics of an organism, in that it has a life-span
over which its characteristics change in some respects
and remain stable in others. One can define its structures as being at different times strong or weak in
terms of the internal logic of its functioning.

What characterizes a social system in my view is
the fact that life within it is largely self-contained,
and that the dynamics of its development are largely
internal. The reader may feel that the use of the term
"largely" is a case of academic weaseling. I admit I
cannot quantify it. Probably no one ever will be able
to do so, as the definition is based on a counterfactual hypothesis: If the system, for any reason, were to
be cut off from all external forces (which virtually
never happens), the definition implies that the system would continue to function substantially in the
same manner. Again, of course, substantially is difficult to convert into hard operational criteria. Nonetheless the point is an important one and key to
many parts of the empirical analyses of this book.
Perhaps we should think of self-containment as a
theoretical absolute, a sort of social vacuum, rarely
visible and even more implausible to create artificially, but still and all a socially-real asymptote, the
distance from which is somehow measurable.

[*] Wallerstein, Immanuel. *The Modern World-System: Capitalist
Agriculture and the Origins of the European World-Economy in the
Sixteenth Century*. (New York: Academic Press, Inc., 1976.) pp.
229–233 Print. Copyright Elsevier 1976, and reprinted with
permission of the publisher.

Using such a criterion, it is contended here that most entities usually described as social systems—"tribes," communities, nation-states—are not in fact total systems. Indeed, on the contrary, we are arguing that the only real social systems are, on the one hand, those relatively small, highly autonomous subsistence economies not part of some regular tribute-demanding system and, on the other hand, world-systems. These latter are to be sure distinguished from the former because they are relatively large; that is, they are in common parlance "worlds." More precisely, however, they are defined by the fact that their self-containment as an economic-material entity is based on extensive division of labor and that they contain within them a multiplicity of cultures.

It is further argued that thus far there have only existed two varieties of such world-systems: world-empires, in which there is a single political system over most of the area, however attenuated the degree of its effective control; and those systems in which such a single political system does not exist over all, or virtually all, of the space. For convenience and for want of a better term, we are using the term "world-economy" to describe the latter.

Finally, we have argued that prior to the modern era, world-economies were highly unstable structures which tended either to be converted into empires or to disintegrate. It is the peculiarity of the modern world-system that a world-economy has survived for 500 years and yet has not come to be transformed into a world-empire—a peculiarity that is the secret of its strength.

This peculiarity is the political side of the form of economic organization called capitalism. Capitalism has been able to flourish precisely because the world-economy has had within its bounds not one but a multiplicity of political systems.

I am not here arguing the classic case of capitalist ideology that capitalism is a system based on the noninterference of the state in economic affairs. Quite the contrary! Capitalism is based on the constant absorption of economic loss by political entities, while economic gain is distributed to "private" hands. What I am arguing rather is that capitalism as an economic mode is based on the fact that the economic factors operate within an arena larger than that which any political entity can totally control. This gives capitalists a freedom of maneuver that is structurally based. It has made possible the constant economic expansion of the world-system, albeit a very skewed distribution of its rewards. The only alternative world-system that could maintain a high level of productivity and change the system of distribution would involve the reintegration of the levels of political and economic decision-making. This would constitute a third possible form of world-system, a socialist world government. This is not a form that presently exists, and it was not even remotely conceivable in the sixteenth century.

The historical reasons why the European world-economy came into existence in the sixteenth century and resisted attempts to transform it into an empire have been expounded at length. We shall not review them here. It should however be noted that the size of a world-economy is a function of the state of technology, and in particular of the possibilities of transport and communication within its bounds. Since this is a constantly changing phenomenon, not always for the better, the boundaries of a world-economy are ever fluid.

We have defined a world-system as one in which there is extensive division of labor. This division is not merely functional—that is, occupational—but geographical. That is to say, the range of economic tasks is not evenly distributed throughout the world-system. In part this is the consequence of ecological considerations, to be sure. But for the most part, it is a function of the social organization of work, one which magnifies and legitimizes the ability of some groups within the system to exploit the labor of others, that is, to receive a larger share of the surplus.

While, in an empire, the political structure tends to link culture with occupation, in a world-economy the political structure tends to link culture with spatial location. The reason is that in a world-economy the first point of political pressure available to groups is the local (national) state structure. Cultural homogenization tends to serve the interests of key groups and the pressures build up to create cultural-national identities.

This is particularly the case in the advantaged areas of the world-economy—what we have called the core-states. In such states, the creation of a strong state machinery coupled with a national culture, a phenomenon often referred to as integration, serves both as a mechanism to protect disparities that have arisen within the world-system, and as an ideological mask and justification for the maintenance of these disparities.

World-economies then are divided into core-states and peripheral areas. I do not say peripheral *states* because one characteristic of a peripheral area is that the indigenous state is weak, ranging from its nonexistence (that is, a colonial situation) to one with a low degree of autonomy (that is, a neo-colonial situation).

There are also semiperipheral areas which are in between the core and the periphery on a series of dimensions, such as the complexity of economic activities, strength of the state machinery, cultural integrity, etc. Some of these areas had been core-areas of earlier versions of a given world-economy. Some had been peripheral areas that were later promoted, so to speak, as a result of the changing geopolitics of an expanding world-economy.

The semiperiphery, however, is not an artifice of statistical cutting points, nor is it a residual category. The semiperiphery is a necessary structural element in a world-economy. These areas play a role parallel to that played, *mutatis mutandis*, by middle trading groups in an empire. They are collection points of vital skills that are often politically unpopular. These middle areas (like middle groups in an empire) partially deflect the political pressures which groups primarily located in peripheral areas might otherwise direct against core-states and the groups which operate within and through their state machineries. On the other hand, the interests primarily located in the semiperiphery are located outside the political arena of the core-states, and find it difficult to pursue the ends in political coalitions that might be open to them were they in the same political arena.

The division of a world-economy involves a hierarchy of occupational tasks, in which tasks requiring higher levels of skill and greater capitalization are reserved for higher-ranking areas. Since a capitalist world-economy essentially rewards accumulated capital, including human capital, at a higher rate than "raw" labor power, the geographical maldistribution of these occupational skills involves a strong trend toward self-maintenance. The forces of the marketplace reinforce them rather than undermine them. And the absence of a central political mechanism for the world-economy makes it very difficult to intrude counteracting forces to the maldistribution of rewards.

Hence, the ongoing process of a world-economy tends to expand the economic and social gaps among its varying areas in the very process of its development. One factor that tends to mask this fact is that the process of development of a world-economy brings about technological advances which make it possible to expand the boundaries of a world-economy. In this case, particular regions of the world may change their structural role in the world-economy, to their advantage, even though the disparity of reward between different sectors of the world-economy as a whole may be simultaneously widening. It is in order to observe this crucial phenomenon clearly that we have insisted on the distinction between a peripheral area of a given world-economy and the external arena of the world-economy. The external arena of one century often becomes the periphery of the next—or its semiperiphery. But then too core-states can become semiperipheral and semiperipheral ones peripheral.

While the advantages of the core-states have not ceased to expand throughout the history of the modern world-system, the ability of a particular state to remain in the core sector is not beyond challenge. The hounds are ever to the hares for the position of top dog. Indeed, it may well be that in this kind of system it is not structurally possible to avoid, over a long period of historical time, a circulation of the elites in the sense that the particular country that is dominant at a given time tends to be replaced in this role sooner or later by another country.

We have insisted that the modern world-economy is, and only can be, a capitalist world-economy. It is for this reason that we have rejected the appellation of "feudalism" for the various forms of capitalist agriculture based on coerced labor which grow up in a world-economy. Furthermore, although this has not been discussed in this volume, it is for this same reason that we will, in future volumes, regard with great circumspection and prudence the claim that there exist in the twentieth century socialist national economies within the framework of the world-economy (as opposed to socialist movements controlling certain state-machineries within the world-economy).

If world-systems are the only real social systems (other than truly isolated subsistence economies), then it must follow that the emergence, consolidation, and political roles of classes and status groups must be appreciated as elements of this *world*-system. And in turn it follows that one of the key elements in analyzing a class or a status-group is not only the state of its self-consciousness but the geographical scope of its self-definition.

Classes always exist potentially (*an sich*). The issue is under what conditions they become class-conscious (*für sich*), that is, operate as a group in the politico-economic arenas and even to some extent as a cultural entity. Such self-consciousness is a function of conflict situations. But for upper strata open conflict, and hence overt consciousness, is always *faute de mieux*. To the extent that class boundaries are not made explicit, to that extent it is more likely that privileges be maintained.

Since in conflict situations, multiple factions tend to reduce to two by virtue of the forging of alliances, it is by definition not possible to have three or more (conscious) classes. There obviously can be a multitude of occupational interest groups which may organize themselves to operate within the social structure. But such groups are really one variety of status-groups, and indeed often overlap heavily with other kinds of status-groups such as those defined by ethnic, linguistic, or religious criteria.

To say that there cannot be three or more classes is not however to say that there are always two. There may be none, though this is rare and transitional. There may be one, and this is most common. There may be two, and this is most explosive.

We say there may be only one class, although we have also said that classes only actually exist in conflict situations, and conflicts presume two sides. There is no contradiction here. For a conflict may be defined as being between one class, which conceives of itself as the universal class, and all the other strata. This has in fact been the usual situation in the modern world-system. The capitalist class (the *bourgeoisie*) has claimed to be the universal class and sought to organize political life to pursue its objectives against two opponents. On the one hand, there were those who spoke for the maintenance of traditional rank distinctions despite the fact that these ranks might have lost their original correlation with economic function. Such elements preferred to define the social structure as a non-class structure. It was to counter this ideology that the bourgeoisie came to operate as a class conscious of itself. . . .

The European world-economy of the sixteenth century tended overall to be a one-class system. It was the dynamic forces profiting from economic expansion and the capitalist system, especially those in the core-areas, who tended to be class-conscious, that is to operate within the political arena as a group defined primarily by their common role in the economy. This common role was in fact defined somewhat broadly from a twentieth-century perspective. It included persons who were farmers, merchants, and industrialists. Individual entrepreneurs often moved back and forth between these activities in any case, or combined them. The crucial distinction was between these men, whatever their occupation, principally oriented to obtaining profit in the world market, and the others not so oriented.

The "others" fought back in terms of their status privileges—those of the traditional aristocracy, those which small farmers had derived from the feudal system, those resulting from guild monopolies that were outmoded. Under the cover of cultural similarities, one can often weld strange alliances. Those strange alliances can take a very activist form and force the political centers to take account of them. We pointed to such instances in our discussion of France. Or they can take a politically passive form that serves well the needs of the dominant forces in the world-system. The triumph of Polish Catholicism as a cultural force was a case in point.

The details of the canvas are filled in with the panoply of multiple forms of status-groups, their particular strengths and accents. But the grand sweep is in terms of the process of class formation. And in this regard, the sixteenth century was indecisive. The capitalist strata formed a class that survived and gained *droit de cité*, but did not yet triumph in the political arena.

The evolution of the state machineries reflected precisely this uncertainty. Strong states serve the interests of some groups and hurt those of others. From however the standpoint of the world-system as a whole, if there is to be a multitude of political entities (that is, if the system is not a world-empire), then it cannot be the case that all these entities be equally strong. For if they were, they would be in the position of blocking the effective operation of transnational economic entities whose locus were in another state. And obviously certain combinations of these groups control the state. It would then follow that the world division of labor would be impeded, the world-economy decline, and eventually the world-system fall apart.

It also cannot be that *no* state machinery is strong. For in such a case, the capitalist strata would have no mechanisms to protect their interests, guaranteeing their property rights, assuring various monopolies, spreading losses among the larger population, etc.

It follows then that the world-economy develops a pattern where state structures are relatively strong in the core areas and relatively weak in the periphery. Which areas play which roles is in many ways accidental. What is necessary is that in some areas the state machinery be far stronger than in others.

What do we mean by a strong state-machinery? We mean strength vis-à-vis other states within the world-economy including other core-states, and strong vis-à-vis local political units within the boundaries of the state. In effect, we mean a sovereignty that is *de facto* as well as *de jure*. We also mean a state that is strong vis-à-vis any particular social group within the state. Obviously, such groups vary in the amount of pressure they can bring to bear upon the state. And obviously certain combinations of these groups control the state. It is not that the state is a neutral arbiter. But the state is more than a simple vector of given forces, if only because many of these forces are situated in more than one state or are defined in terms that have little correlation with state boundaries.

A strong state then is a partially autonomous entity in the sense that it has a margin of action available to it wherein it reflects the compromises of multiple interests, even if the bounds of these margins are set by the existence of some groups of primordial strength. To be a partially autonomous entity, there must be a group of people whose direct interests are served by such an entity: state managers and a state bureaucracy.

Such groups emerge within the framework of a capitalist world-economy because a strong state is the best choice between difficult alternatives for the two groups that are strongest in political, economic, and military terms: the emergent capitalist strata, and the old aristocratic hierarchies.

For the former, the strong state in the form of the "absolute monarchies" was a prime customer, a guardian against local and international brigandage, a mode of social legitimation, a preemptive protection against the creation of strong state barriers elsewhere. For the latter, the strong state represented a brake on these same capitalist strata, an upholder of status conventions, a maintainer of order, a promoter of luxury.

No doubt both nobles and bourgeois found the state machineries to be a burdensome drain of funds, and a meddlesome unproductive bureaucracy. But what options did they have? Nonetheless they were always restive and the immediate politics of the world-system was made up of the pushes and pulls resulting from the efforts of both groups to insulate themselves from what seemed to them the negative effects of the state machinery.

A state machinery involves a tipping mechanism. There is a point where strength creates more strength. The tax revenue enables the state to have a larger and more efficient civil bureaucracy and army which in turn leads to greater tax revenue—a process that continues in spiral form. The tipping mechanism works in other directions too—weakness leading to greater weakness. In between these two tipping

points lies the politics of state-creation. It is in this arena that the skills of particular managerial groups make a difference. And it is because of the two tipping mechanisms that at certain points a small gap in the world-system can very rapidly become a larger one.

In those states in which the state machinery is weak, the state managers do not play the role of co-ordinating a complex industrial-commercial-agricultural mechanism. Rather they simply become one set of landlords amidst others, with little claim to legitimate authority over the whole.

These tend to be called traditional rulers. The political struggle is often phrased in terms of tradition versus change. This is of course a grossly misleading and ideological terminology. It may in fact be taken as a general sociological principle that, at any given point of time, what is thought to be traditional is of more recent origin than people generally imagine it to be, and represents primarily the conservative instincts of some group threatened with declining social status. Indeed, there seems to be nothing which emerges and evolves as quickly as a "tradition" when the need presents itself.

In a one-class system, the "traditional" is that in the name of which the "others" fight the class-conscious group. If they can encrust their values by legitimating them widely, even better by enacting them into legislative barriers, they thereby change the system in a way favorable to them.

The traditionalists may win in some states, but if a world-economy is to survive, they must lose more or less in the others. Furthermore, the gain in one region is the counterpart of the loss in another.

This is not quite a zero-sum game, but it is also inconceivable that all elements in a capitalist world-economy shift their values in a given direction simultaneously. The social system is built on having a multiplicity of value systems within it, reflecting the specific functions groups and areas play in the world division of labor.

We have not exhausted here the theoretical problems relevant to the functioning of a world-economy. We have tried only to speak to those illustrated by the early period of the world-economy in creation, to wit, sixteenth-century Europe. Many other problems emerged at later stages and will be treated, both empirically and theoretically, in later volumes.

In the sixteenth century, Europe was like a bucking bronco. The attempt of some groups to establish a world-economy based on a particular division of labor, to create national states in the core areas as politico-economic guarantors of this system, and to get the workers to pay not only the profits but the costs of maintaining the system was not easy. It was to Europe's credit that it was done, since without the thrust of the sixteenth century the modern world would not have been born and, for all its cruelties, it is better that it was born than that it had not been.

It is also to Europe's credit that it was not easy, and particularly that it was not easy because the people who paid the short-run costs screamed lustily at the unfairness of it all. The peasants and workers in Poland and England and Brazil and Mexico were all rambunctious in their various ways. As R. H. Tawney says of the agrarian disturbances of sixteenth-century England: "Such movements are a proof of blood and sinew and of a high and gallant spirit. . . . Happy the nation whose people has not forgotten how to rebel."

The mark of the modern world is the imagination of its profiteers and the counter-assertiveness of the oppressed. Exploitation and the refusal to accept exploitation as either inevitable or just constitute the continuing antinomy of the modern era, joined together in a dialectic which was far from reached its climax in the twentieth century.

Theda Skocpol (1947–) teaches at Harvard University, where she was a student in the 1970s (receiving her Ph.D. in sociology in 1975). She was initially denied tenure at Harvard on the blatantly untrue grounds that her widely acclaimed book, *States and Social Revolutions*, was not sufficiently original. Skocpol brought sex discrimination charges and fought the denial. Eventually, after much embarrassment to the Department of Sociology and to Harvard, she was awarded tenure. Some believe that the attempt to deny tenure also involved a dispute over the role of secondary analysis and historical data (as opposed to quantitative studies) in sociology. While away from Harvard, Skocpol taught at the University of Chicago. After her return to Harvard, she became the Victor S. Thomas Professor of Government and Sociology and was recognized as a faculty leader, serving a productive term as Dean of the Graduate School of Arts and Sciences. Skocpol is considered a leader in the revival of interest in the sociology of the state. She is also the author of *Protecting Soldiers and Mothers: The Political Origins of Social Policy in the United States* (1992), which, like her first book, has been widely acclaimed as a classic in political

sociology. Thereafter many notable books including, most recently *The Tea Party and the Remaking of Republican Conservativism* (2012; with Vanessa Williamson). Skocpol is one of America's most influential public social scientists.

The selection from her first book presents the key elements in Skocpol's theory of the state. She takes up and revises earlier arguments for the relative autonomy of state from class power. The subtlety of her structural interpretation is seen in the way she relates the state to the structured world-system, on the one hand, and, as she puts it, the "class-divided socioeconomic structures," on the other. The study for which she devises this theory is an attempt to explain the phenomenon of social revolution with reference to the classic revolutions in eighteenth-century France and to Russia and China in the twentieth century. She explains that in none of these cases could the revolution be accounted for without accounting for changes in state structures in relation to world events and class-based pressures from below in the societies.

The State as a Janus-Faced Structure[*]
Theda Skocpol (1979)

We can make sense of social-revolutionary transformations only if we take the state seriously as a macro-structure. The state properly conceived is no mere arena in which socioeconomic struggles are fought out. It is, rather, a set of administrative, policing, and military organizations headed, and more or less well coordinated by, an executive authority. Any state first and fundamentally extracts resources from society and deploys these to create and support coercive and administrative organizations. Of course, these basic state organizations are built up and must operate within the context of class-divided socioeconomic relations, as well as within the context of national and international economic dynamics. Moreover, coercive and administrative organizations are only parts of overall political systems. These systems also may contain institutions through which social interests are represented in state policymaking as well as institutions through which nonstate actors are mobilized to participate in policy implementa-

---

tion. Nevertheless, the administrative and coercive organizations are the basis of state power as such.

Where they exist, these fundamental state organizations are at least potentially autonomous from direct dominant-class control. The extent to which they *actually* are autonomous, and to what effect, varies from case to case. It is worth emphasizing that the actual extent and consequences of state autonomy can only be analyzed and explained in terms specific to particular types of sociopolitical systems and to particular sets of historical international circumstances. . . . Also, the likely lines of conflict between landed dominant classes and state rulers in such agrarian states [as prerevolutionary France, Russia, and China] will be indicated. There is no need to go into this discussion now. For the purposes of the argument at hand, it is enough to note that states are potentially autonomous and to explore what distinct interests they *might* pursue.

State organizations necessarily compete to some extent with the dominant class(es) in appropriating resources from the economy and society. And the objectives to which the resources, once appropriated, are devoted may very well be at variance with existing dominant-class interests. Resources may be used to strengthen the bulk and autonomy of the state itself—something necessarily threatening to the dominant class unless the greater state power is indispensably needed and actually used to support dominant-class interests. But the use of state power to support dominant-class interests is not inevitable. Indeed, attempts of state rulers merely to perform the state's "own" functions may create conflicts of interest with the dominant class. The state normally performs two basic sets of tasks: It maintains order, and it competes with other actual or potential states. As Marxists have pointed out, states usually do function to preserve existing economic and class structures, for that is normally the smoothest way to enforce order. Nevertheless, the state has its own distinct interests vis-à-vis subordinate classes. Although both the state and the dominant class(es) share a broad interest in keeping the subordinate classes in place in society and at work in the existing economy, the state's own fundamental interest in maintaining sheer physical order and political peace may lead it—especially in periods of crisis—to enforce concessions to subordinate-class demands. These concessions may be at the expense of the interests of the dominant class, but not contrary to the state's own interests in controlling the population and collecting taxes and military recruits.

Moreover, we should not forget that states also always exist in determinant geopolitical environments, in interaction with other actual or potential states. An existing economy and class structure condition and influence a given state structure and the activities of the rulers. So, too, do geopolitical environments create tasks and opportunities for states and place limits on their capacities to cope with either external or internal tasks or crises. As the German historian Otto Hintze once wrote, two phenomena above all condition "the real organization of the state. These are, first, the structure of social classes, and second, the external ordering of the states—their position relative to each other, and their over-all position in the world." Indeed, a state's involvement in an international network of states is a basis for potential autonomy of action over and against groups and economic arrangements within its jurisdiction—even including the dominant class and existing relations of production. For international military pressures and opportunities can prompt state rulers to attempt policies that conflict with, and even in extreme instances contradict, the fundamental interests of a dominant class. State rulers may, for example, undertake military adventures abroad that drain resources from economic development at home, or that have the immediate or ultimate effect of undermining the position of dominant socioeconomic interests. And, to give a different example, rulers may respond to foreign military competition or threats of conquest by attempting to impose fundamental socioeconomic reforms or by trying to reorient the course of national economic development through state intervention. Such programs may or may not be successfully implemented. But even if they are not carried through, the sheer attempt may create a contradictory clash of interests between the state and the existing dominant class.

The perspective on the state advanced here might appropriately be labeled "organizational" and "realist." In contrast to most (especially recent) Marxist theories, this view refuses to treat states as if they were mere analytic aspects of abstractly conceived modes of production, or even political aspects of concrete class relations and struggles. Rather it insists that states are actual organizations controlling (or attempting to control) territories and people. Thus the analyst of revolutions must explore not only class relations but also relations of states to one another and relations of states to dominant and subordinate classes. For the historical cases of social revolutions to be discussed in the core chapters of this book, the analysis of old-regime contradictions and the emergence of revolutionary crises will center especially upon the relationships of states to military competitors abroad and to dominant classes and existing socioeconomic structures at home. And the analysis of the emergence and structure of new regimes will focus especially on the relationships of state-building revolutionary movements to international circumstances and to those subordinate classes, invariably including the peasantry, who were key insurrectionary participants in the conflicts of the revolutions. The state organizations of both old and new regimes will have a more central and autonomous place in the analysis than they would in a straightforward Marxist explanation.

Yet not only does an organizational, realist perspective on the state entail differences from Marxist approaches, it also contrasts with non-Marxist approaches that treat the *legitimacy* of political authorities as an important explanatory concept. If state organizations cope with whatever tasks they already claim smoothly and efficiently, legitimacy—either in the sense of moral approval or in the probably much more usual sense of sheer acceptance of the status quo—will probably be accorded to the state's form and rulers by most groups in society. In any event, what matters most is always the support or acquiescence not of the popular majority of society but of the politically powerful and mobilized groups, invariably including the regime's own cadres. Loss of legitimacy, especially among these crucial groups, tends to ensue with a vengeance if and when (for reasons that are always open to sociological and historical explanation) the state fails consistently to cope with existing tasks, or proves unable to cope with new tasks suddenly thrust upon it by crisis circumstances. Even after great loss of legitimacy has occurred, a state can remain quite stable—and certainly invulnerable to internal mass-based revolts—especially if its coercive organizations remain coherent and effective. Consequently, the structure of those organizations, their place within the state apparatus as a whole, and their linkages to class forces and to politically mobilized groups in society are all important issues for the analyst of states in revolutionary situations, actual or potential. Such an analytic focus seems certain to prove more fruitful than any focus primarily or exclusively upon political legitimation. The ebbing of a regime's legitimacy in the eyes of its own cadres and other politically powerful groups may figure as a mediating variable in an analysis of

regime breakdown. But the basic causes will be found in the structure and capacities of state organizations, as these are conditioned by developments in the economy and class structure and also by developments in the international situation.

The state, in short, is fundamentally Janus-faced, with an intrinsically dual anchorage in class-divided socioeconomic structures and an international system of states. If our aim is to understand the breakdown and building-up of state organizations in revolutions, we must look not only at the activities of social groups. We must also focus upon the points of intersection between international conditions and pressures, on the one hand, and class-structured economies and politically organized interests, on the other hand. State executives and their followers will be found maneuvering to extract resources and build administrative and coercive organizations precisely at this intersection. Here, consequently, is the place to look for the political contradictions that help launch social revolutions. Here, also, will be found the forces that shape the rebuilding of state organizations within social-revolutionary crises.

Nancy Chodorow (1944–) taught at the University of California at Berkeley until retirement in 2005 after which she remains active as an author and practicing psychoanalyst. Chodorow did her doctoral studies at Brandeis University at a time when its Department of Sociology's exceptional openness encouraged the early intellectual development of many of America's most important feminist sociologists. Her use of psychoanalysis and sociology is indicative of the creative and interdisciplinary approach of many academic feminists who—especially in the 1970s and 1980s—have been required, and encouraged, to work between and on the margins of the traditional disciplines. Some would say that Chodorow's *Reproduction of Mothering* (1978), apart from its important contributions to the study of gender relations, is one of the first successfully balanced integrations of psychoanalytic and sociological perspectives. One need only compare Chodorow's work to, say, Erich Fromm's earlier, more programmatic essay on the two fields to get an idea of how her attempt to resolve a concrete problem—mothering—has led to a more complex use of ideas from both sides. Some consider Chodorow's argument a standpoint feminism. In this respect, her work is often compared to

Carol Gilligan's *In a Different Voice*. Because the selection summarizes the key theoretical points in the argument, readers can judge this for themselves. In any case, *Reproduction of Mothering* is a classic text for contemporary feminist theory as well as for the sociology of gender relations and family. Chodorow is also the author of *Feminism and Psychoanalytic Theory* (1989) and *The Power of Feelings* (1999), among other books.

Gender Personality and the Reproduction of Mothering[*]
Nancy Chodorow (1978)

In spite of the apparently close tie between women's capacities for childbearing and lactation on the one hand and their responsibilities for child care on the other, and in spite of the probable prehistoric convenience (and perhaps survival necessity) of a sexual division of labor in which women mothered, biology and instinct do not provide adequate explanations for how women come to mother. Women's mothering as a feature of social structure requires an explanation in terms of social structure. Conventional feminist and social psychological explanations for the genesis of gender roles—girls and boys are "taught" appropriate behaviors and "learn" appropriate feelings—are insufficient both empirically and methodologically to account for how women become mothers.

Methodologically, socialization theories rely inappropriately on individual intention. Ongoing social structures include the means for their own reproduction—in the regularized repetition of social processes, in the perpetuation of conditions which require members' participation, in the genesis of legitimating ideologies and institutions, and in the psychological as well as physical reproduction of people to perform necessary roles. Accounts of socialization help to explain the perpetuation of ideologies about gender roles. However, notions of appropriate behavior, like coercion, cannot in themselves produce parenting. Psychological capacities and a particular object-relational stance are central and definitional to parenting in a way that they are not to many other roles and activities.

[*] From *The Reproduction of Mothering: Psychoanalysis and the Sociology of Gender, Updated Edition* by Nancy J. Chodorow, © 1999 by the Regents of the University of California. Published by the University of California Press.

Women's mothering includes the capacities for its own reproduction. This reproduction consists in the production of women with, and men without, the particular psychological capacities and stance which go into primary parenting. Psychoanalytic theory provides us with a theory of social reproduction that explains major features of personality development and the development of psychic structure, and the differential development of gender personality in particular. Psychoanalysts argue that personality both results from and consists in the ways a child appropriates, internalizes, and organizes early experiences in their family—from the fantasies they have, the defenses they use, the ways they channel and redirect drives in this object-relational context. A person subsequently imposes this intrapsychic structure, and the fantasies, defenses, and relational modes and preoccupations which go with it, onto external social situations. This reexternalization (or mutual reexternalization) is a major constituting feature of social and interpersonal situations themselves.

Psychoanalysis, however, has not had an adequate theory of the reproduction of mothering. Because of the teleological assumption that anatomy is destiny, and that women's destiny includes primary parenting, the ontogenesis of women's mothering has been largely ignored, even while the genesis of a wide variety of related disturbances and problems has been accorded widespread clinical attention. Most psychoanalysts agree that the basis for parenting is laid for both genders in the early relationship to a primary caretaker. Beyond that, in order to explain why *women* mother, they tend to rely on vague notions of a girl's subsequent identification with her mother, which makes her and not her brother a primary parent, or on an unspecified and uninvestigated innate femaleness in girls, or on logical leaps from lactation or early vaginal sensations to caretaking abilities and commitments.

The psychoanalytic account of male and female development, when reinterpreted, gives us a developmental theory of the reproduction of women's mothering. Women's mothering reproduces itself through differing object-relational experiences and differing psychic outcomes in women and men. As a result of having been parented by a woman, women are more likely than men to seek to be mothers, that is, to relocate themselves in a primary mother-child relationship, to get gratification from the mothering relationship, and to have psychological and relational capacities for mothering.

The early relation to a primary caretaker provides in children of both genders both the basic capacity to participate in a relationship with the features of the early parent-child one, and the desire to create this intimacy. However, because women mother, the early experience and preoedipal relationship differ for boys and girls. Girls retain more concern with early childhood issues in relation to their mother, and a sense of self involved with these issues. Their attachments therefore retain more preoedipal aspects. The greater length and different nature of their preoedipal experience, and their continuing preoccupation with the issues of this period, mean that women's sense of self is continuous with others and that they retain capacities for primary identification, both of which enable them to experience the empathy and lack of reality sense needed by a cared-for infant. In men, these qualities have been curtailed, both because they are early treated as an opposite by their mother and because their later attachment to her must be repressed. The relational basis for mothering is thus extended in women, and inhibited in men, who experience themselves as more separate and distinct from others.

The different structure of the feminine and masculine oedipal triangle and process of oedipal experience that results from women's mothering contributes further to gender personality differentiation and the reproduction of women's mothering. As a result of this experience, women's inner object world, and the affects and issues associated with it, are more actively sustained and more complex than men's. This means that women define and experience themselves relationally. Their heterosexual orientation is always in internal dialogue with both oedipal and preoedipal mother-child relational issues. Thus, women's heterosexuality is triangular and requires a third person—a child—for its structural and emotional completion. For men, by contrast, the heterosexual relationship alone recreates the early bond to their mother; a child interrupts it. Men, moreover, do not define themselves in relationship and have come to suppress relational capacities and repress relational needs. This prepares them to participate in the affect-denying world of alienated work, but not to fulfill women's needs for intimacy and primary relationships.

The oedipus complex, as it emerges from the asymmetrical organization of parenting, secures a psychological taboo on parent-child incest and pushes boys and girls in the direction of extrafamilial heterosexual relationships. This is one step toward the reproduction of parenting. The creation and maintenance of the incest taboo and of heterosexuality in girls and boys are different, however. For boys, superego formation and identification with their father, rewarded by the superiority of masculinity, maintain the taboo on incest with their mother, while heterosexual orientation continues from their earliest love relation with her. For girls, creating them as heterosexual in the first place maintains the taboo. However, women's heterosexuality is not so exclusive as men's. This makes it easier for them to accept or seek a male substitute for their fathers. At the same time, in a male-dominant society, women's exclusive emotional heterosexuality is not so necessary, nor is her repression of love for her father. Men are more likely to initiate relationships, and women's economic dependence on men pushes them anyway into heterosexual marriage.

Male dominance in heterosexual couples and marriage solves the problem of women's lack of heterosexual commitment and lack of satisfaction by making women more reactive in the sexual bonding process. At the same time, contradictions in heterosexuality help to perpetuate families and parenting by ensuring that women will seek relations to children and will not find heterosexual relationships alone satisfactory. Thus, men's lack of emotional availability and women's less exclusive heterosexual commitment help ensure women's mothering.

Women's mothering, then, produces psychological self-definition and capacities appropriate to mothering in women, and curtails and inhibits these capacities and this self-definition in men. The early experience of being cared for by a woman produces a fundamental structure of expectations in women and men concerning mothers' lack of separate interests from their infants and total concern for their infants' welfare. Daughters grow up identifying with these mothers, about whom they have such expectations. This set of expectations is generalized to the assumption that women naturally take care of children of all ages and the belief that women's "maternal" qualities can and should be extended to the nonmothering work that they do. All these results of women's mothering have ensured that women will mother infants and will take continuing responsibility for children.

The reproduction of women's mothering is the basis for the reproduction of women's location and responsibilities in the domestic sphere. This mothering, and its generalization to women's structural location in the domestic sphere, links the contemporary social organization of gender and social organization of production and contributes to the reproduction of each. That women mother is a fundamental organizational feature of the sex-gender system: It is basic to the sexual division of labor and generates a psychology and ideology of male dominance as well as an ideology about women's capacities and nature. Women, as wives and mothers, contribute as well to the daily and generational reproduction, both physical and psychological, of male workers and thus to the reproduction of capitalist production.

Women's mothering also reproduces the family as it is constituted in male-dominated society. The sexual and familial division of labor in which women mother creates a sexual division of psychic organization and orientation. It produces socially gendered women and men who enter into asymmetrical heterosexual relationships; it produces men who react to, fear, and act superior to women, and who put most of their energies into the nonfamilial work world and do not parent. Finally, it produces women who turn their energies toward nurturing and caring for children—in turn reproducing the sexual and familial division of labor in which women mother.

Social reproduction is thus asymmetrical. Women in their domestic role reproduce men and children physically, psychologically, and emotionally. Women in their domestic role as houseworkers reconstitute themselves physically on a daily basis and reproduce themselves as mothers, emotionally and psychologically, in the next generation. They thus contribute to the perpetuation of their own social roles and position in the hierarchy of gender.

Institutionalized features of family structure and the social relations of reproduction reproduce themselves. A psychoanalytic investigation shows that women's mothering capacities and commitments, and the general psychological capacities and wants which are the basis of women's emotional work, are built developmentally into feminine personality. Because women are themselves mothered by women, they grow up with the relational capacities and needs, and psychological definition of self-in-relationship, which commits them to mothering. Men, because they are mothered by women, do not. Women mother daughters who, when they become women, mother.

Breaking with Modernity

Jacques Derrida (1930–2004) was born in Algiers. He studied in Paris at the École Normale Supérieure and at Harvard (1956–1957). From 1960 to 1964, he taught at the Sorbonne. The following year, he became professor of the history of philosophy at the École Normale Supérieure. Derrida lectured and taught around the world and is particularly well regarded in the United States, where he held irregular professorships at Yale, Johns Hopkins, New York University, and the University of California at Irvine. Derrida's many writings include *Speech and Phenomena and Other Essays on Husserl's Theory of Signs, Writing and Difference*, and *Of Grammatology*—all three appeared in France in 1967, the year following his famous 1966 presentation at Johns Hopkins, "Structure, Sign and Play in the Discourse of the Human Sciences." He wrote many books since, but these were the texts in which the first and clearest outlines of the much misunderstood idea of deconstruction appeared. The 1966 paper, from which the selection is taken, is sometimes considered, in retrospect, the event Derrida referred to in the work's first sentence—an event in the history of structuralism, the beginning of poststructuralism; an event in the history of world structures. Given his clear critique of the philosophy of the Center, it is unlikely that he meant that he himself caused this event. Even if he did, that is not the point. Deconstruction concerns itself with problems of this sort. Well after his death in 2004, many of Derrida's shorter writing continue to appear and he remains one of the most commented upon and influential social thinkers in recent times.

The Decentering Event in Social Thought[*]
Jacques Derrida (1966)

Perhaps something has occurred in the history of the concept of structure that could be called an "event," if this loaded word did not entail a meaning which it is precisely the function of structural—or structuralist—thought to reduce or to suspect. Let us speak of an "event," nevertheless, and let us use quotation marks to serve as a precaution. What would this event be then? Its exterior form would be that of a *rupture* and a redoubling.

It would be easy enough to show that the concept of structure and even the word "structure" itself are as old as the *epistémé*—that is to say, as old as Western science and Western philosophy—and that their roots thrust deep into the soil of ordinary language, into whose deepest recesses the *epistémé* plunges in order to gather them up and to make them part of itself in a metaphorical displacement. Nevertheless, up to the event which I wish to mark out and define, structure—or rather the structurality of structure—although it has always been at work, has always been neutralized or reduced, and this by a process of giving it a center or of referring it to a point of presence,

[*] Derrida, Jacques. *Writing and Difference.* © 1978 The University of Chicago. Reprinted with permission of University of Chicago Press.

a fixed origin. The function of this center was not only to orient, balance, and organize the structure—one cannot in fact conceive of an unorganized structure—but above all to make sure that the organizing principle of the structure would limit what we might call the play of the structure. By orienting and organizing the coherence of the system, the center of a structure permits the play of its elements inside the total form. And even today the notion of a structure lacking any center represents the unthinkable itself.

Nevertheless, the center also closes off the play which it opens up and makes possible. As center, it is the point at which the substitution of contents, elements, or terms is no longer possible. At the center, the permutation or the transformation of elements (which may of course be structures enclosed within a structure) is forbidden. At least this permutation has always remained *interdicted* (and I am using this word deliberately). Thus it has always been thought that the center, which is by definition unique, constituted that very thing within a structure which while governing the structure, escapes structurality. This is why classical thought concerning structure could say that the center is, paradoxically, *within* the structure and *outside it*. The center is at the center of the totality, and yet, since the center does not belong to the totality (is not part of the totality), the totality *has its center elsewhere*. The center is not the center. The concept of centered structure—although it represents coherence itself, the condition of the *epistémé* as philosophy or science—is contradictorily coherent. And as always, coherence in contradiction expresses the force of a desire. The concept of centered structure is in fact the concept of a play based on a fundamental ground, a play constituted on the basis of a fundamental immobility and a reassuring certitude, which itself is beyond the reach of play. And on the basis of this certitude anxiety can be mastered, for anxiety is invariably the result of a certain mode of being implicated in the game, of being caught by the game, of being as it were at stake in the game from the outset. And again on the basis of what we call the center (and which, because it can be either inside or outside, can also indifferently be called the origin or end, *arché* or *telos*), repetitions, substitutions, transformations, and permutations are always taken from a history of meaning [*sens*]—that is, in a word, a history—whose origin may always be reawakened or whose end may always be anticipated in the form of presence. This is why one perhaps could say that the movement of any archaeology, like that of any

eschatology, is an accomplice of this reduction of the structurality of structure and always attempts to conceive of structure on the basis of a full presence which is beyond play.

If this is so, the entire history of the concept of structure, before the rupture of which we are speaking, must be thought of as a series of substitutions of center for center, as a linked chain of determinations of the center. Successively, and in a regulated fashion, the center receives different forms or names. The history of metaphysics, like the history of the West, is the history of these metaphors and metonymies. Its matrix—if you will pardon me for demonstrating so little and for being so elliptical in order to come more quickly to my principal theme—is the determination of Being as *presence* in all senses of this word. It could be shown that all the names related to fundamentals, to principles, or to the center have always designated an invariable presence—*eidos, arché, telos, energeia, ousia* (essence, existence, substance, subject) *alétheia*, transcendentality, consciousness, God, man, and so forth.

The event I called a rupture, the disruption I alluded to at the beginning of this paper, presumably would have come about when the structurality of structure had to begin to be thought, that is to say, repeated, and this is why I said that this disruption was repetition in every sense of the word. Henceforth, it became necessary to think both the law which somehow governed the desire for a center in the constitution of structure, and the process of signification which orders the displacements and substitutions for this law of central presence—but a central presence which has never been itself, has always already been exiled from itself into its own substitute. The substitute does not substitute itself for anything which has somehow existed before it. Henceforth, it was necessary to begin thinking that there was no center, that the center could not be thought in the form of a present-being, that the center had no natural site, that it was not a fixed locus but a function, a sort of nonlocus in which an infinite number of sign-substitutions came into play. This was the moment when language invaded the universal problematic, the moment when, in the absence of a center or origin, everything became discourse—provided we can agree on this word—that is to say, a system in which the central signified, the original or transcendental signified, is never absolutely present outside a system of differences. The absence of the transcendental signified extends the domain and the play of signification infinitely.

Where and how does this decentering, this thinking the structurality of structure, occur? It would be somewhat naive to refer to an event, a doctrine, or an author in order to designate this occurrence. It is no doubt part of the totality of an era, our own, but still it has always already begun to proclaim itself and begun to *work*. Nevertheless, if we wished to choose several "names," as indications only, and to recall those authors in whose discourse this occurrence has kept most closely to its most radical formulation, we doubtless would have to cite the Nietzschean critique of metaphysics, the critique of the concepts of Being and truth, for which were substituted the concepts of play, interpretation, and sign (sign without present truth); the Freudian critique of self-presence, that is, the critique of consciousness, of the subject, of self-identity and of self-proximity or self-possession; and, more radically, the Heideggerean destruction of metaphysics, of onto-theology, of the determination of Being as presence. But all these destructive discourses and all their analogues are trapped in a kind of circle. This circle is unique. It describes the form of the relation between the history of metaphysics and the destruction of the history of metaphysics. There is no sense in doing without the concepts of metaphysics in order to shake metaphysics. We have no language—no syntax and no lexicon—which is foreign to this history; we can pronounce not a single destructive proposition which has not already had to slip into the form, the logic, and the implicit postulations of precisely what it seeks to contest. To take one example from many: the metaphysics of presence is shaken with the help of the concept of *sign*. But, as I suggested a moment ago, as soon as one seeks to demonstrate in this way that there is no transcendental or privileged signified and that the domain or play of signification henceforth has no limit, one must reject even the concept and word "sign" itself—which is precisely what cannot be done. For the signification "sign" has always been understood and determined, in its meaning, as sign-of, a signifier referring to a signified, a signifier different from its signified. If one erases the radical difference between signifier and signified, it is the word "signifier" itself which must be abandoned as a metaphysical concept. When Lévi-Strauss says in the preface to *The Raw and the Cooked* that he has "sought to transcend the opposition between the sensible and the intelligible by operating from the outset at the level of signs," the necessity, force, and legitimacy of his act cannot make us forget that the concept of the sign cannot in itself surpass this opposition between the sensible and the intelligible. The concept of the sign, in each of its aspects, has been determined by this opposition throughout the totality of its history. It has lived only on this opposition and its system. But we cannot do without the concept of the sign, for we cannot give up this metaphysical complicity without also giving up the critique we are directing against this complicity, or without the risk of erasing difference in the self-identity of a signified reducing its signifier into itself or, amounting to the same thing, simply expelling its signifier outside itself. For there are two heterogeneous ways of erasing the difference between the signifier and the signified: one, the classic way, consists in reducing or deriving the signifier, that is to say, ultimately in *submitting* the sign to thought; the other, the one we are using here against the first one, consists in putting into question the system in which the preceding reduction functioned: first and foremost, the opposition between the sensible and the intelligible. For the *paradox* is that the metaphysical reduction of the sign needed the opposition it was reducing. The opposition is systematic with the reduction. And what we are saying here about the sign can be extended to all the concepts and all the sentences of metaphysics, in particular to the discourse on "structure." But there are several ways of being caught in this circle. They are all more or less naïve, more or less empirical, more or less systematic, more or less close to the formulation—that is, to the formalization, of this circle. It is these differences which explain the multiplicity of destructive discourses and the disagreement between those who elaborate them. Nietzsche, Freud, and Heidegger, for example, worked within the inherited concepts of metaphysics. Since these concepts are not elements or atoms, and since they are taken from a syntax and a system, every particular borrowing brings along with it the whole of metaphysics. This is what allows these destroyers to destroy each other reciprocally—for example, Heidegger regarding Nietzsche, with as much lucidity and rigor as bad faith and misconstruction, as the last metaphysician, the last "Platonist." One could do the same for Heidegger himself, for Freud, or for a number of others. And today no exercise is more widespread.

What is the relevance of this formal schema when we turn to what are called the "human sciences"? One of them perhaps occupies a privileged place—ethnology. In fact one can assume that ethnology could have been born as a science only at the moment when a decentering had come about: at the moment when European culture—and, in consequence, the history of metaphysics and of its concepts—had been *dislocated*, driven from its locus, and forced to stop considering itself as the culture of reference. This moment is not first and foremost a moment of philosophical or scientific discourse. It is also a moment which is political, economic, technical, and so forth. One can say with total security that there is nothing fortuitous about the fact that the critique of ethnocentrism—the very condition for ethnology—should be systematically and historically contemporaneous with the destruction of the history of metaphysics. Both belong to one and the same era. Now, ethnology—like any science—comes about within the element of discourse. And it is primarily a European science employing traditional concepts, however much it may struggle against them. Consequently, whether he wants to or not—and this does not depend on a decision on his part—the ethnologist accepts into his discourse the premises of ethnocentrism at the very moment when he denounces them. This necessity is irreducible; it is not a historical contingency. We ought to consider all its implications very carefully. But if no one can escape this necessity, and if no one is therefore responsible for giving in to it, however little he may do so, this does not mean that all the ways of giving in to it are of equal pertinence. The quality and fecundity of a discourse are perhaps measured by the critical rigor with which this relation to the history of metaphysics and to inherited concepts is thought. Here it is a question both of a critical relation to the language of the social sciences and a critical responsibility of the discourse itself. It is a question of explicitly and systematically posing the problem of the status of a discourse which borrows from a heritage the resources necessary for the deconstruction of that heritage itself. A problem of *economy* and *strategy*.

Michel Foucault (1926–1984) was born in Poitiers and studied at the École Normale Supérieure, where Louis Althusser was one of his teachers. He completed his state doctorate in 1960. Foucault lived and worked outside France—in Uppsala, Warsaw, and Hamburg early in his career—and was a frequent visitor to the United States (particularly Berkeley) in his later years. From 1964 to 1968, he was head of the Department of Philosophy at the University of Clermont-Ferrand. He was on the faculty at Vincennes in Paris during the events of

1968. Foucault became professor of history and systems of thought at the Collège de France in 1970; the selection is from his inaugural address there. Foucault's first writings were on mental illness and madness in Western history. *Madness and Civilization* is the English version of his French work *Folie et deraison* (1961). Other books include *Birth of the Clinic* (1963), *The Order of Things* (1966), *The Archaeology of Knowledge* (1971), *Discipline and Punish* (1975), and the series of historical studies of sexuality written at the end of his life. The inaugural address (published with *Archaeology* in the American edition) is a broad theoretical statement, one of the very few Foucault made. After 1970, he returned to specific historical studies, each with an evident political concern. His studies of sexuality are considered important contributions to current social theories of sexuality. Foucault died of AIDS in 1984. Still, in the decades since, the originality of his thinking is evident in a continuing series of edited books, most based on his lectures at the Collège de France. Had he survived he would have no doubt advanced those ideas even more than his posthumous publications allow. Like Derrida, he remains a pivotal and still powerful voice altering how social theory must reconsider the modern age and the ubiquity of power/knowledge ever assaulting us. The selection represents one of his earliest empirical formulations of his theory of power/knowledge.

Biopolitics and the Carceral Society[*]
Michel Foucault (1975)

We have seen that, in penal justice, the prison transformed the punitive procedure into a penitentiary technique; the carceral archipelago transported this technique from the penal institution to the entire social body. With several important results.

1. This vast mechanism established a slow, continuous, imperceptible gradation that made it possible to pass naturally from disorder to offence and back from a transgression of the law to a slight departure from a rule, an average, a demand, a norm. In the classical period, despite a certain common ref-

---

erence to offence in general, the order of the crime, the order of sin and the order of bad conduct remained separate in so far as they related to separate criteria and authorities (court, penitence, confinement). Incarceration with its mechanisms of surveillance and punishment functioned, on the contrary, according to a principle of relative continuity. The continuity of the institutions themselves, which were linked to one another (public assistance with the orphanage, the reformatory, the penitentiary, the disciplinary battalion, the prison; the school with the charitable society, the workshop, the *almshouse*, the penitentiary convent; the workers' estate with the hospital and the prison). A continuity of the punitive criteria and mechanisms, which on the basis of a mere deviation gradually strengthened the rules and increased the punishment. A continuous gradation of the established, specialized and competent authorities (in the order of knowledge and in the order of power) which, without resort to arbitrariness, but strictly according to the regulations, by means of observation and assessment hierarchized, differentiated, judged, punished and moved gradually from the correction of irregularities to the punishment of crime. The "carceral" with its many diffuse or compact forms, its institutions of supervision or constraint, of discreet surveillance and insistent coercion, assured the communication of punishments according to quality and quantity; it connected in series or disposed according to subtle divisions the minor and the serious penalties, the mild and the strict forms of treatment, bad marks and light sentences. You will end up in the convict-ship, the slightest indiscipline seems to say; and the harshest of prisons says to the prisoners condemned to life: I shall note the slightest irregularity in your conduct. The generality of the punitive function that the eighteenth century sought in the "ideological" technique of representations and signs now had as its support the extension, the material framework, complex, dispersed, but coherent, of the various carceral mechanisms. As a result, a certain significant generality moved between the least irregularity and the greatest crime; it was no longer the offence, the attack on the common interest, it was the departure from the norm, the anomaly; it was this that haunted the school, the court, the asylum or the prison. It generalized in the sphere of meaning the function that the carceral generalized in the sphere of tactics. Replacing the adversary of the sovereign, the social enemy was transformed into a deviant, who brought with him the multiple danger of disorder, crime and madness. The carceral net-

work linked, through innumerable relations, the two long, multiple series of the punitive and the abnormal.

2. The carceral, with its far-reaching networks, allows the recruitment of major "delinquents." It organizes what might be called "disciplinary careers" in which, through various exclusions and rejections, a whole process is set in motion. . . .

The carceral network does not cast the unassimilable into a confused hell; there is no outside. It takes back with one hand what it seems to exclude with the other. It saves everything, including what it punishes. It is unwilling to waste even what it has decided to disqualify. In this panoptic society of which incarceration is the omnipresent armature, the delinquent is not outside the law; he is, from the very outset, in the law, at the very heart of the law, or at least in the midst of those mechanisms that transfer the individual imperceptibly from discipline to the law, from deviation to offence. Although it is true that prison punishes delinquency, delinquency is for the most part produced in and by an incarceration which, ultimately, prison perpetuates in its turn. The prison is merely the natural consequence, no more than a higher degree, of that hierarchy laid down step by step. The delinquent is an institutional product. It is no use being surprised, therefore, that in a considerable proportion of cases the biography of convicts passes through all these mechanisms and establishments, whose purpose, it is widely believed, is to lead away from prison. That one should find in them what one might call the index of an irrepressibly delinquent "character": the prisoner condemned to hard labour was meticulously produced by a childhood spent in a reformatory, according to the lines of force of the generalized carceral system. Conversely, the lyricism of marginality may find inspiration in the image of the "outlaw," the great social nomad, who prowls on the confines of a docile, frightened order. But it is not on the fringes of society and through successive exiles that criminality is born, but by means of ever more closely placed insertions, under ever more insistent surveillance, by an accumulation of disciplinary coercion. In short, the carceral archipelago assures, in the depths of the social body, the formation of delinquency on the basis of subtle illegalities, the overlapping of the latter by the former and the establishment of a specified criminality.

3. But perhaps the most important effect of the carceral system and of its extension well beyond legal imprisonment is that it succeeds in making the

power to punish natural and legitimate, in lowering at least the threshold of tolerance to penality. It tends to efface what may be exorbitant in the exercise of punishment. It does this by playing the two registers in which it is deployed—the legal register of justice and the extra-legal register of discipline—against one another. In effect, the great continuity of the carceral system throughout the law and its sentences gives a sort of legal sanction to the disciplinary mechanisms, to the decisions and judgments that they enforce. Throughout this network, which comprises so many "regional" institutions, relatively autonomous and independent, is transmitted, with the "prison-form," the model of justice itself. The regulations of the disciplinary establishments may reproduce the law, the punishments imitate the verdicts and penalties, the surveillance repeat the police model; and, above all these multiple establishments, the prison, which in relation to them is a pure form, unadulterated and unmitigated, gives them a sort of official sanction. The carceral, with its long gradation stretching from the convictship or imprisonment with hard labour to diffuse, slight limitations, communicates a type of power that the law validates and that justice uses as its favourite weapon. How could the disciplines and the power that functions in them appear arbitrary, when they merely operate the mechanisms of justice itself, even with a view to mitigating their intensity? When, by generalizing its effects and transmitting it to every level, it makes it possible to avoid its full rigour? Carceral continuity and the fusion of the prison-form make it possible to legalize, or in any case to legitimate disciplinary power, which thus avoids any element of excess or abuse it may entail.

But, conversely, the carceral pyramid gives to the power to inflict legal punishment a context in which it appears to be free of all excess and all violence. In the subtle gradation of the apparatuses of discipline and of the successive "embeddings" that they involve, the prison does not at all represent the unleashing of a different kind of power, but simply an additional degree in the intensity of a mechanism that has continued to operate since the earliest forms of legal punishment. Between the latest institution of "rehabilitation," where one is taken in order to avoid prison, and the prison where one is sent after a definable offence, the difference is (and must be) scarcely perceptible. There is a strict economy that has the effect of rendering as discreet as possible the singular power to punish. There is nothing in it now that recalls the former excess of sovereign power

when it revenged its authority on the tortured body of those about to be executed. Prison continues, on those who are entrusted to it, a work begun elsewhere, which the whole of society pursues on each individual through innumerable mechanisms of discipline. By means of a carceral continuum, the authority that sentences infiltrates all those other authorities that supervise, transform, correct, improve. It might even be said that nothing really distinguishes them any more except the singularly "dangerous" character of the delinquents, the gravity of their departures from normal behaviour and the necessary solemnity of the ritual. But, in its function, the power to punish is not essentially different from that of curing or educating. It receives from them, and from their lesser, smaller task, a sanction from below; but one that is no less important for that, since it is the sanction of technique and rationality. The carceral "naturalizes" the legal power to punish, as it "legalizes" the technical power to discipline. In thus homogenizing them, effacing what may be violent in one and arbitrary in the other, attenuating the effects of revolt that they may both arouse, thus depriving excess in either of any purpose, circulating the same calculated, mechanical and discreet methods from one to the other, the carceral makes it possible to carry out that great "economy" of power whose formula the eighteenth century had sought, when the problem of the accumulation and useful administration of men first emerged.

By operating at every level of the social body and by mingling ceaselessly the art of rectifying and the right to punish, the universality of the carceral lowers the level from which it becomes natural and acceptable to be punished. The question is often posed as to how, before and after the Revolution, a new foundation was given to the right to punish. And no doubt the answer is to be found in the theory of the contract. But it is perhaps more important to ask the reverse question: how were people made to accept the power to punish, or quite simply, when punished, tolerate being so. The theory of the contract can only answer this question by the fiction of a juridical subject giving to others the power to exercise over him the right that he himself possesses over them. It is highly probable that the great carceral continuum, which provides a communication between the power of discipline and the power of the law, and extends without interruption from the smallest coercions to the longest penal detention, constituted the technical and real, immediately material counterpart of that chimerical granting of the right to punish.

4. With this new economy of power, the carceral system, which is its basic instrument, permitted the emergence of a new form of "law": a mixture of legality and nature, prescription and constitution, the norm. This had a whole series of effects: the internal dislocation of the judicial power or at least of its functioning; an increasing difficulty in judging, as if one were ashamed to pass sentence; a furious desire on the part of the judges to judge, assess, diagnose, recognize the normal and abnormal and claim the honour of curing or rehabilitating. In view of this, it is useless to believe in the good or bad consciences of judges, or even of their unconscious. Their immense "appetite for medicine" which is constantly manifested—from their appeal to psychiatric experts, to their attention to the chatter of criminology—expresses the major fact that the power they exercise has been "denatured"; that it is at a certain level governed by laws; that at another, more fundamental level it functions as a normative power; it is the economy of power that they exercise, and not that of their scruples or their humanism, that makes them pass "therapeutic" sentences and recommend "rehabilitating" periods of imprisonment. But, conversely, if the judges accept ever more reluctantly to condemn for the sake of condemning, the activity of judging has increased precisely to the extent that the normalizing power has spread. Borne along by the omnipresence of the mechanisms of discipline, basing itself on all the carceral apparatuses, it has become one of the major functions of our society. The judges of normality are present everywhere. We are in the society of the teacher-judge, the doctor-judge, the educator-judge, the "social work-er"-judge; it is on them that the universal reign of the normative is based; and each individual, wherever he may find himself, subjects to it his body, his gestures, his behaviour, his aptitudes, his achievements. The carceral network, in its compact or disseminated forms, with its system of insertion, distribution, surveillance, observation, has been the greatest support, in modern society, of the normalizing power.

5. The carceral texture of society assures both the real capture of the body and its perpetual observation; it is, by its very nature, the apparatus of punishment that conforms most completely to the new economy of power and the instrument for the formation of knowledge that this very economy needs.

Its panoptic functioning enables it to play this double role. By virtue of its methods of fixing, dividing, recording, it has been one of the simplest, crudest, also most concrete, but perhaps most indispensable conditions for the development of this immense activity of examination that has objectified human behaviour. If, after the age of "inquisitorial" justice, we have entered the age of "examinatory" justice, if, in an even more general way, the method of examination has been able to spread so widely throughout society, and to give rise in part to the sciences of man, one of the great instruments for this has been the multiplicity and close overlapping of the various mechanisms of incarceration. I am not saying that the human sciences emerged from the prison. But, if they have been able to be formed and to produce so many profound changes in the episteme, it is because they have been conveyed by a specific and new modality of power: a certain policy of the body, a certain way of rendering the group of men docile and useful. This policy required the involvement of definite relations of knowledge in relations of power; it called for a technique of overlapping subjection and objectification; it brought with it new procedures of individualization. The carceral network constituted one of the armatures of this power-knowledge that has made the human sciences historically possible. Knowable man (soul, individuality, consciousness, conduct, whatever it is called) is the object-effect of this analytical investment, of this domination-observation.

6. This no doubt explains the extreme solidity of the prison, that slight invention that was nevertheless decried from the outset. If it had been no more than an instrument of rejection or repression in the service of a state apparatus, it would have been easier to alter its more overt forms or to find a more acceptable substitute for it. But, rooted as it was in mechanisms and strategies of power, it could meet any attempt to transform it with a great force of inertia. One fact is characteristic: when it is a question of altering the system of imprisonment, opposition does not come from the judicial institutions alone; resistance is to be found not in the prison as penal sanction, but in the prison with all its determinations, links and extrajudicial results; in the prison as the relay in a general network of disciplines and surveillances; in the prison as it functions in a panoptic régime. This does not mean that it cannot be altered, nor that it is once and for all indispensable to our kind of society.

C. L. R. James (1901–1989) was born in Trinidad. From a very young age, he was a voracious reader and keen observer of social life. Under British teachers in Trinidad, he mastered the style and substance of European culture, without letting it master him. Still in his twenties, James published two novels, *La Divinia Pastora* (1927) and *Triumph* (1929). At thirty-one, he moved to London, where he soon became a prominent intellectual figure in the Trotskyist movement. In this period, he wrote the play "Toussaint L'Ouverture," based on the great Haitian revolutionary, as well as *Black Jacobins* (1938) and *World Revolution* (1937). Thereafter, James lived and worked as a world figure—always putting himself at a principled distance from European civilization. In his writing and lecturing, he applied Marxist ideas to his vast cultural and political knowledge of Africa, America, the Caribbean, and Europe. As the selection from his essay "World Revolution: 1968" shows, James was quick to respond to world events and to frame his response in world perspective, without qualifying his radical, post-colonial ideas. Behind the lines of this essay one can sense James's broad appreciation of the historical roots of Black Power. James saw Pan-African principles partly through Marxist social theory—that is, somewhat from a European perspective, somewhat as a Black Pan-Africanist. In this sense, James was in the tradition of Du Bois. He spent the last years of his life in London, where he died in 1989 just as the Socialist states of Eastern Europe were collapsing.

World Revolution: 1968[*]

C. L. R. James (1968)

This is an analysis.

1. We take it for granted that those who are in contact with the working class or classes nearest to it, either in France *or out of France*, are engaged in maintaining and increasing contact, making the situation as clear as possible, and learning as much as they can from the response of those sections of the population they are dealing with.

2. Marxists have a special function, first of all to analyse the situation and, as a necessity for fruitful intervention, to know exactly the stage of development.

3. Three things are requisite for the Marxist to understand:

[*] Excerpted from *Speak Out*, No. 21/22 (June/July 1968b).

i. The national state must be destroyed and the only way in which that can be done is the break-up of all bourgeois institutions and their replacement by socialist institutions.

The French Revolution has shown that the mass of the population is ready to take over society and to form new institutions. (de Gaulle recognises that and that is the basis of his insistence on "participation") The decay of bourgeois institutions is proved not only by the tremendous outburst of the great body of the nation (an outburst, comprehensive as no previous revolution has been), but proved also by the fact that the bourgeoisie and the middle classes were quite powerless before the strength and the desire to break up the old state. They had very little to say and, as far as can be judged from here, were paralysed by the decay and rottenness of the capitalistic regime and the power and range of the revolt against it. I have seen no evidence that this positive necessity has been made clear in any of the statements that I have seen.

ii. The first concrete enemy is the bourgeois national state. It is absolutely impossible for a national state of any kind at this stage of the twentieth century to develop and even to maintain itself even under the most revolutionary and proletarian of governments.

Therefore, the Marxist must know and seek every possible means of making clear that the national quality of the state must be destroyed; that is to say, the revolution has got to be an international socialist revolution. To put it crudely, the appeal to the masses of the population and other countries in Europe to make their own the fate of the French Revolution must be made at all levels. As far as I can see it has not been made by any section of the revolutionary leadership. I would be glad to know that here I am wrong. The national state cannot function today. And not to know that, not to make that clear, means the destruction of the revolution.

iii. Let me try to make clear what I am trying to say. The safety of the revolution, it's completion, its ability to fight against the enormous pressures which will be placed upon it, the questions of food, finance, and possible military intervention of the counter-revolution of a certain kind, these are not questions removed from the day-to-day struggle. From the very beginning it has to be made clear that the economic relations, political relations, safeguarding of the revolution against military intervention or financial pressure, every single aspect of daily and political life now depends on the transformation of the bourgeois institutions into socialist institutions, the unleashing of the strength of the working class first of all. I am afraid I am not being as successful in saying what I want to say as I would like to be: We do not make the revolution to achieve the socialist society. The socialist society makes the revolution. I hope, however, that fellow Marxists will see what I am striving at. Today there is no period of transition from one regime to another. The establishment of the socialist regime, the power of the working class and those substantial elements in the nation who are ready to go with it, that is not something which one must look for to be achieved in the future: That is absolutely necessary now, not only for the socialist society but to maintain the ordinary necessities of life and to defend the elementary rights of all society.

4. What are the new socialist institutions?

We do not know, nobody *knows*. The working class and the general mass of the population are creating them in action. Our business is to be aware of thats to let them know that they alone can create the new institutions.

We use the highest peaks of the past as a guide. The highest peak so far reached is the instinctive action of the working class in the Hungarian Revolution.

5. Such is the rejection of the bourgeois regime by the great mass of the population that without the Communist Party the regime would have collapsed completely without the possibility of any regeneration. The connection between the policy of the Communist Party and the co-existence policy of Moscow is now a *secondary question*. It is the knowledge everywhere of this which has given to the students the leadership. One conclusion now has to be drawn, it is this:

Communist Party, Social Democratic Party, Trade Union leadership, are all bourgeois institutions. The revolution which has begun in France and which we shall see continuing everywhere over the next period, will save itself delay and temporary defeats if only

from the very beginning it recognises that all negotiations and arrangements about wages or anything, else that the revolution has to undertake, are to be undertaken by its own independent organisations. It may take some time before the French Revolution establishes this. But outside of France we can learn this. *None of the regular institutions must be allowed to enter into negotiations on behalf of any section of the revolution.* Over the next period new upheavals must understand this from the very beginning. Students will represent students and discuss with university staffs. Workers will represent workers, peasants will represent peasants. *No kind of established organisation which has been functioning in the bourgeois regime is to be accepted as a representative.* This will be difficult to establish, particularly in regard to the trade union leadership especially where it represents a majority of the organised workers. But that for the revolution of 1968 is the key point at issue. No question of anarchism arises here. The very structure of modern society prepares the working class and sections of society to undertake immediately the creation of socialist institutions.

6. To get rid of de Gaulle is now a strictly minor matter.

One can take part in elections or not take part.

The real question is the substitution of new institutions for old ones.

7. It is not for someone who is away from the centre of events to be dogmatic about what should be done. But what is urgently required is (a) the sending of representatives to countries abroad and particularly to the recently independent countries; and (b) the invitation to representatives of ail countries to come to France, to take part in what is going on, and to learn the necessities of revolutionary struggle today. The absence so far not only of intervention but of any statement by organisations in advanced countries shows their deadly recognition that they live on the surface of a similar volcano.

8. It is at this stage only that I point out the stages of the Marxist movement. Marx put forward the basic ideas in the *Communist Manifesto* after profound studies in philosophy, economics and revolutionary history, and the watching of a movement of the workers in some insignificant part of France. Then followed the Commune in 1871. It was the Commune in 1871 which gave to Lenin and the Bolsheviks indications as to be able to understand what took place in 1905. 1905 was the dress rehearsal for 1917. We have to be able first *for our own benefit* to understand what has taken place between

1917 and 1968. We need not go preaching this to the working class but the Marxists have to be quite clear as to the stage of development so as to be able to recognise, welcome and intensify the advances that are taking place instinctively in the nation *and in the world at large.* This work has to be done and only a Marxist can do it. The greatest mistake would be not to do it at all...

Herbert Marcuse (1898–1979) was born in Berlin. He studied in Germany and received a Ph.D. from Freiburg University. From 1922 to 1933, he was actively associated with the Frankfurt Institute. After emigrating from Germany for the United States in 1934, Marcuse continued his association with the Frankfurt School–in–exile in its Columbia University days. He taught at Brandeis (1954–1965) and at the University of California at San Diego (1965–1969). His books include *Eros and Civilization* (1955), *Counter-Revolution and Revolt* (1972), and *The Aesthetic Dimension* (1978). It is plain from the titles alone that Marcuse was faithful to the original theoretical interests of critical theory by working in and on the relations among Marxist theory, culture and aesthetics, and psychoanalysis. In the 1960s, Marcuse's *One-Dimensional Man* (1964), from which the selection is taken, was considered must reading by intellectually serious student radicals. His famous concept repressive desublimation refers to his argument that postwar mass culture, with its profusion of sexual provocations, serves to reinforce political repression. If people are preoccupied with unauthentic sexual stimulation, their political energy will be "desublimated"; instead of acting constructively to change the world, they remain repressed and uncritical. Obviously, Marcuse advanced the prewar thinking of critical theory toward a critical account of the "one-dimensional" nature of bourgeois life in Europe and America. His thinking could, therefore, also be considered an advance of the concerns of earlier liberal critics like David Riesman.

Repressive Desublimation of One-Dimensional Man[*]
Herbert Marcuse (1964)

Today's novel feature is the flattening out of the antagonism between culture and social reality through the obliteration of the oppositional, alien, and transcendent elements in the higher culture by virtue of which it constituted *another dimension* of reality. This liquidation of *two-dimensional* culture takes place not through the denial and rejection of the "culture values," but through their wholesale incorporation into the established order, through their reproduction and display on a massive scale.

In fact, they serve as instruments of social cohesion. The greatness of a free literature and art, the ideals of humanism, the sorrows and joys of the individual, the fulfillment of the personality are important items in the competitive struggle between East and West. They speak heavily against the present forms of communism, and they are daily administered and sold. The fact that they contradict the society which sells them does not count. Just as people know or feel that advertisements and political platforms must not be necessarily true or right, and yet hear and read them and even let themselves be guided by them, so they accept the traditional values and make them part of their mental equipment. If mass communications blend together harmoniously, and often unnoticeably, art, politics, religion, and philosophy with commercials, they bring these realms of culture to their common denominator—the commodity form. The music of the soul is also the music of salesmanship. Exchange value, not truth value counts. On it centers the rationality of the status quo, and all alien rationality is bent to it.

As the great words of freedom and fulfillment are pronounced by campaigning leaders and politicians, on the screens and radios and stages, they turn into meaningless sounds which obtain meaning only in the context of propaganda, business, discipline, and relaxation. This assimilation of the ideal with reality testifies to the extent to which the ideal has been surpassed. It is brought down from the sublimated realm of the soul or the spirit or the inner man, and

---

[*] From "One-Dimensional Man" by Herbert Marcuse. Copyright © 1964 by Herbert Marcuse. Reprinted by permission of Beacon Press, Boston. "One-Dimensional Man: Studies in the Ideology of Advanced Industrial Society" by Herbert Marcuse (London: Routledge & Kegan Paul). Copyright 1964 by Herbert Marcuse. Reproduced by permission of Taylor & Francis Books UK.

translated into operational terms and problems. Here are the progressive elements of mass culture. The perversion is indicative of the fact that advanced industrial society is confronted with the possibility of a materialization of ideals. The capabilities of this society are progressively reducing the sublimated realm in which the condition of man was represented, idealized, and indicted. Higher culture becomes part of the material culture. In this transformation, it loses the greater part of its truth. . . .

It is a rational universe which, by the mere weight and capabilities of its apparatus, blocks all escape. In its relation to the reality of daily life, the high culture of the past was many things—opposition and adornment, outcry and resignation. But it was also the appearance of the realm of freedom: the refusal to behave. Such refusal cannot be blocked without a compensation which seems more satisfying than the refusal. The conquest and unification of opposites, which finds its ideological glory in the transformation of higher into popular culture, takes place on a material ground of increased satisfaction. This is also the ground which allows a sweeping *desublimation*.

Artistic alienation is sublimation. It creates the images of conditions which are irreconcilable with the established Reality Principle but which, as cultural images, become tolerable, even edifying and useful. Now this imagery is invalidated. Its incorporation into the kitchen, the office, the shop; its commercial release for business and fun is, in a sense, desublimation—replacing mediated by immediate gratification. But it is desublimation practiced from a "position of strength" on the part of society, which can afford to grant more than before because its interests have become the innermost drives of its citizens, and because the joys which it grants promote social cohesion and contentment.

The Pleasure Principle absorbs the Reality Principle; sexuality is liberated (or rather liberalized) in socially constructive forms. This notion implies that there are repressive modes of desublimation, compared with which the sublimated drives and objectives contain more deviation, more freedom, and more refusal to heed the social taboos. It appears that such repressive desublimation is indeed operative in the sexual sphere, and here, as in the desublimation of higher culture, it operates as the by-product of the social controls of technological reality, which extend liberty while intensifying domination. The link between desublimation and technological society can

perhaps best be illuminated by discussing the change in the social use of instinctual energy.

In this society, not all the time spent on and with mechanisms is labor time (i.e., unpleasurable but necessary toil), and not all the energy saved by the machine is labor power. Mechanization has also "saved" libido, the energy of the Life Instincts—that is, has barred it from previous modes of realization. This is the kernel of truth in the romantic contrast between the modern traveler and the wandering poet or artisan, between assembly line and handicraft, town and city, factory-produced bread and the home-made loaf, the sailboat and the outboard motor, etc. True, this romantic pre-technical world was permeated with misery, toil, and filth, and these in turn were the background of all pleasure and joy. Still, there was a "landscape," a medium of libidinal experience which no longer exists.

With its disappearance (itself a historical prerequisite of progress), a whole dimension of human activity and passivity has been de-eroticized. The environment from which the individual could obtain pleasure—which he could cathect as gratifying almost as an extended zone of the body—has been rigidly reduced. Consequently, the "universe" of libidinous cathexis is likewise reduced. The effect is a localization and contraction of libido, the reduction of erotic to sexual experience and satisfaction.

For example, compare love-making in a meadow and in an automobile, on a lovers' walk outside the town walls and on a Manhattan street. In the former cases, the environment partakes of and invites libidinal cathexis and tends to be eroticized. Libido transcends beyond the immediate erotogenic zones—a process of nonrepressive sublimation. In contrast, a mechanized environment seems to block such self-transcendence of libido. Impelled in the striving to extend the field of erotic gratification, libido becomes less "polymorphous," less capable of eroticism beyond localized sexuality, and the *latter* is intensified.

Thus diminishing erotic and intensifying sexual energy, the technological reality *limits the scope of sublimation*. It also reduces the *need* for sublimation. In the mental apparatus, the tension between that which is desired and that which is permitted seems considerably lowered, and the Reality Principle no longer seems to require a sweeping and painful transformation of instinctual needs. The individual must adapt himself to a world which does not seem to demand the denial of his innermost needs—a world which is not essentially hostile.

The organism is thus being preconditioned for the spontaneous acceptance of what is offered. Inasmuch as the greater liberty involves a contraction rather than extension and development of instinctual needs, it works *for* rather than *against* the status quo of general repression—one might speak of "institutionalized desublimation." The latter appears to be a vital factor in the making of the authoritarian personality of our time.

Harold Garfinkel (1917–2011) is the inventor of the term ethnomethodology and the cofounder of the movement of that name. When it first came to public attention in the late 1960s, ethnomethodology was the brunt of dismissive jokes: a "cult," "California sociology," and the like. Such complaints were partly due to the confusion readers experienced both at Garfinkel's strange language and at his even more upsetting notion that social analysis begins with the fact that language itself is an attempt to repair the social problems created in human communication. Ethnomethodology, however, remained a steady force in social theory and made significant contributions. Most importantly, ethnomethodology has worked out an empirical method for taking seriously the complex properties of common, everyday social action. In the 1940s, Garfinkel was a student of Talcott Parsons at Harvard. It is increasingly accepted that Parsons's theory of action was nearly as important an influence on Garfinkel's thinking as the phenomenology of Alfred Schutz. Certainly, he went beyond both in inventing his version of ethnomethodology. The selection is from *Studies in Ethnomethodology*, the *locus classicus* of the movement. It includes a sample of ethnomethodological reasoning applied to empirical data through observations taken from the study of the Los Angeles Suicide Prevention Center. Garfinkel's argument that the center's work was largely an attempt to turn suicide deaths into rationally accountable—hence, normally recognizable—events suggests both ethnomethodology's unique interpretive attitude and why some find it troubling. Garfinkel was professor emeritus at UCLA.

Reflexive Properties of Practical Sociology[*]
Harold Garfinkel (1967)

Virtually unanimous agreement exists among students of practical sociological reasoning, laymen and professionals, about the properties of indexical expressions and indexical actions. Impressive agreement exists as well (1) that although indexical expressions "are of enormous utility" they are "awkward for formal discourse"; (2) that a distinction between objective expressions and indexical expressions is not only procedurally proper but unavoidable for whosoever would do science; (3) that without the distinction between objective and indexical expressions, and without the preferred use of objective expressions the victories of generalizing, rigorous, scientific inquiries—logic, mathematics, some of the physical sciences—are unintelligible, the victories would fail, and the inexact sciences would have to abandon their hopes; (4) that the exact sciences are distinguishable from the inexact sciences by the fact that in the case of the exact sciences the distinction between and substitution of objective for indexical expressions for problem formulation, methods, findings, adequate demonstration, adequate evidence and the rest is both an actual task and an actual achievement, whereas in the case of the inexact sciences the availability of the distinction and substitutability to actual tasks, practices, and results remains unrealizably programmatic; (5) that the distinction between objective and indexical expressions, insofar as the distinction consists of inquirers' tasks, ideals, norms, resources, achievements, and the rest describes the difference between sciences and arts—*e.g.,* between biochemistry and documentary filming; (6) that terms and sentences can be distinguished as one or the other in accordance with an assessment procedure that makes decidable their character as indexical or objective expressions; and (7) that in any particular case only practical difficulties prevent the substitution by an objective expression for an indexical expression.

Features of indexical expressions motivate endless methodological studies directed to their remedy. Indeed, attempts to rid the practices of a science of these nuisances lends to each science its distinctive

[*] Garfinkel, Harold. "What is Ethnomethodology." *Studies in Ethnomethodology*. Upper Saddle River, NJ: Prentice-Hall, 1967. Print. Material from "Practical Sociological Reasoning: Some Features in the Work of the Los Angeles Suicide Prevention Center," in *Essays in Self Destruction*, edited by Edwin S. Shneidman, International Science Press, 1967. Reprinted with permission of the Estate of Edwin Shneidman.

character of preoccupation and productivity with methodological issues. Research practitioners' studies of practical activities of a science, whatever their science, afford them endless occasions to deal rigorously with indexical expressions.

Areas in the social sciences where the promised distinction and promised substitutability occurs are countless. The promised distinction and substitutability are supported by and themselves support immense resources directed to developing methods for the strong analysis of practical actions and practical reasoning. Promised applications and benefits are immense.

Nevertheless, *wherever practical actions are topics of study* the promised distinction and substitutability of objective for indexical expressions remains programmatic in every *particular* case and in every *actual* occasion in which the distinction or substitutability must be demonstrated. In every actual case without exception, conditions will be cited that a competent investigator will be required to recognize, such that in *that* particular case the terms of the demonstration can be relaxed and nevertheless the demonstration be counted an adequate one.

We learn from logicians and linguists, who are in virtually unanimous agreement about them, what some of these conditions are. For "long" texts, or "long" courses of action, for events where members' actions are features of the events their actions are accomplishing, or wherever tokens are not used or are not suitable as proxies for indexical expressions, the program's claimed demonstrations are satisfied as matters of practical social management.

Under such conditions indexical expressions, by reason of their prevalence and other properties, present immense, obstinate, and irremediable nuisances to the tasks of dealing rigorously with the phenomena of structure and relevance in theories of consistency proofs and computability, and in attempts to recover actual as compared with supposed common conduct and common talk with full structural particulars. Drawing upon their experience in the uses of sample surveys, and the design and application of measurements of practical actions, statistical analyses, mathematical models, and computer simulations of social processes, professional sociologists are able to document endlessly the ways in which the programmatic distinction and substitutability is satisfied in, and depends upon, professional practices of socially managed demonstration.

In short, wherever studies of practical actions are involved, the distinction and substitutability is always accomplished *only* for all practical purposes. Thereby, the first problematic phenomenon is recommended to consist of the reflexivity of the practices and attainments of sciences in and of the organized activities of everyday life, which is an essential reflexivity.

The "Uninteresting" Essential Reflexivity of Accounts

For members engaged in practical sociological reasoning—as we shall see in later studies, for staff personnel at the Los Angeles Suicide Prevention Center, for staff users of psychiatric clinic folders at U.C.L.A., for graduate student coders of psychiatric records, for jurors, for an intersexed person managing a sex change, for professional sociological researchers—their concerns are for what is decidable "for practical purposes," "in light of this situation," "given the nature of actual circumstances," and the like. Practical circumstances and practical actions refer for them to many organizationally important and serious matters: to resources, aims, excuses, opportunities, tasks, and of course to grounds for arguing or foretelling the adequacy of procedures and of the findings they yield. One matter, however, is excluded from their interests: practical actions and practical circumstances are not in themselves *a* topic, let alone a sole topic of their inquiries; nor are their inquiries, addressed to the tasks of sociological theorizing, undertaken to formulate what these tasks consist of as practical actions. In no case is the investigation of practical actions undertaken in order that personnel might be able to recognize and describe what they are doing in the first place. Least of all are practical actions investigated in order to explain to practitioners their own talk about what they are doing. For example personnel at the Los Angeles Suicide Prevention Center found it altogether incongruous to consider seriously that they be so engaged in the work of certifying mode of death that a person seeking to commit suicide and they could concert their efforts to assure the unequivocal recognition of "what really happened."

To say they are "not interested" in the study of practical actions is not to complain, nor to point to an opportunity they miss, nor is it a disclosure of error, nor is it an ironic comment. Neither is it the case that because members are "not interested" that they are "precluded" from sociological theorizing. Nor do their inquiries preclude the use of the rule of doubt, nor are they precluded from making the organized activities of everyday life scientifically problematical, nor does the comment insinuate a difference between "basic" and "applied" interests in research and theorizing.

What does it mean then to say that they are "not interested" in studying practical actions and practical sociological reasoning? And what is the import of such a statement?

There is a feature of members' accounts that for them is of such singular and prevailing relevance that it controls other features in their specific character as recognizable, rational features of practical sociological inquiries. The feature is this. With respect to the problematic character of practical actions and to the practical adequacy of their inquiries, members take for granted that a member must at the outset "know" the settings in which he is to operate if his practices are to serve as measures to bring particular, located features of these settings to recognizable account. They treat as the most passing matter of fact that members' accounts, of every sort, in all their logical modes, with all of their uses, and for every method for their assembly are constituent features of the settings they make observable. Members know, require, count on, and make use of this reflexivity to produce, accomplish, recognize, or demonstrate rational-adequacy-for-all-practical-purposes of their procedures and findings.

Not only do members—the jurors and the others—take that reflexivity for granted, but they recognize, demonstrate, and make observable for each other the rational character of their actual, and that means their occasional, practices while respecting that reflexivity as an unalterable and unavoidable condition of their inquiries.

When I propose that members are "not interested" in studying practical actions, I do not mean that members will have none, a little, or a lot of it. That they are "not interested" has to do with reasonable practices, with plausible argument, and with reasonable findings. It has to do with treating "accountable-for-all-practical-purposes" as a discoverable matter, exclusively, only, and entirely. For members to be "interested" would consist of their undertaking to make the "reflexive" character of practical activities observable; to examine the artful practices of rational inquiry as organizational phenomena without thought for correctives or irony. Members of the Los Angeles Suicide Prevention Center are like members wherever they engage in practical sociological inquiries: though they would, they *can* have none of it.

The Analyzability of Actions-in-Context as a Practical Accomplishment

In indefinitely many ways members' inquiries are constituent features of the settings they analyze. In the same ways, their inquiries are made recognizable to members as adequate-for-all-practical-purposes. For example, at the Los Angeles Suicide Prevention Center, that deaths are made accountable-for-all-practical-purposes are practical organizational accomplishments. Organizationally, the Suicide Prevention Center consists of practical procedures for accomplishing the rational accountability of suicidal deaths as recognizable features of the settings in which that accountability occurs.

In the actual occasions of interaction that accomplishment is for members omnipresent, unproblematic, and commonplace. For members doing sociology, to make that accomplishment a topic of practical sociological inquiry seems unavoidably to require that they treat the rational properties of practical activities as "anthropologically strange." By this I mean to call attention to "reflexive" practices such as the following: that by his accounting practices the member makes familiar, commonplace activities of everyday life recognizable *as* familiar, commonplace activities; that on each occasion that an account of common activities is used, that they be recognized for "another first time"; that the member treat the processes and attainments of "imagination" as continuous with the *other* observable features of the settings in which they occur; and of proceeding in such a way that at the same time that the member "in the midst" of witnessed actual settings recognizes that witnessed settings have an *accomplished* sense, an accomplished facticity, an accomplished objectivity, an accomplished familiarity, an accomplished accountability, for the member the organizational hows of these accomplishments are unproblematic, are known vaguely, and are known only in the doing which is done skillfully, reliably, uniformly, with enormous standardization and as an unaccountable matter.

That accomplishment consists of members doing, recognizing, and using ethnographies. In unknown ways that accomplishment is for members a commonplace phenomenon. And in the unknown ways that the accomplishment is commonplace it is for our interests, an awesome phenomenon, for in its unknown ways it consists (1) of members' uses of concerted everyday activities as methods with which to recognize and demonstrate the isolatable, typical, uniform, potential repetition, connected appearance, consistency, equivalence, substitutability, directionality, anonymously describable, planful—in short, the rational properties of indexical expressions and indexical actions. (2) The phenomenon consists, too, of the analyzability of actions- in-context given that not only does no concept of context-in-general exist, but every use of "context" without exception is itself essentially indexical.

The *recognizedly* rational properties of their common sense inquiries—their recognizedly consistent, or methodic, or uniform, or planful, etc. character—are *somehow* attainments of members' concerted activities. For Suicide Prevention Center staff, for coders, for jurors the rational properties of their practical inquiries *somehow* consist in the concerted work of making evident from fragments, from proverbs, from passing remarks, from rumors, from partial descriptions, from "codified" but essentially vague catalogues of experience and the like how a person died in society, or by what criteria patients were selected for psychiatric treatment, or which among the alternative verdicts was correct. *Somehow* is the problematic crux of the matter.

What Is Ethnomethodology?

The earmark of practical sociological reasoning, wherever it occurs, is that it seeks to remedy the indexical properties of members' talk and conduct. Endless methodological studies are directed to the tasks of providing members a remedy for indexical expressions in members' abiding attempts, with rigorous uses of ideals to demonstrate the observability of organized activities in actual occasions with situated particulars of talk and conduct.

The properties of indexical expressions and indexical actions are ordered properties. These consist of organizationally demonstrable sense, or facticity, or methodic use, or agreement among "cultural colleagues." Their ordered properties consist of organizationally demonstrable rational properties of indexical expressions and indexical actions. Those ordered properties are ongoing achievements of the concerted commonplace activities of investigators. The demonstrable rationality of indexical expressions and indexical actions retains over the course of its managed production by members the character of ordinary, familiar, routinized practical circumstances. As process and attainment the produced rationality of indexical expressions consists of practical

tasks subject to every exigency of organizationally situated conduct.

I use the term "ethnomethodology" to refer to the investigation of the rational properties of indexical expressions and other practical actions as contingent ongoing accomplishments of organized artful practices of everyday life.

Alvin W. Gouldner (1920–1980) grew up in the Bronx, where he fashioned himself as a street tough, a self-image he maintained through his life. Gouldner was also a brilliant student in the New York City schools and eventually at Columbia University, where, as a student of Robert K. Merton, he did his doctoral studies in sociology. His thesis was published in two parts, *Wildcat Strike* (1954) and *Patterns of Industrial Bureaucracy* (1954). The latter became a classic in industrial sociology. Though Gouldner would later become one of the world's foremost critical interpreters of Marxism, in his early career he expressed his radical views in a more Weberian form. In the mid-1960s, Gouldner began a major multivolume rethinking of social theory, beginning with *Enter Plato* (1965). He always challenged narrow boundaries. Some classicists hated him for daring to write on the Greeks without knowledge of the ancient language. He was undaunted. *The Coming Crisis of Western Sociology* (1970), the source of the selection, appeared in 1970. In many respects, it had an influence similar to Mills's *Sociological Imagination* a decade earlier. *Crisis* was a kind of textbook for many young radicals pursuing careers in sociology as the 1960s came to an end. His ideas on reflexive sociology are clearly consistent with the New Left ideal of taking seriously the personal as well as the political. Gouldner's other books include *The Dialectic of Ideology and Technology* (1976), *The Two Marxisms* (1980), and *The Future of Intellectuals and the Rise of the New Class* (1979), from which the selection is taken. This trilogy was written at the end of his short life. To the end, Gouldner was tough-minded in keeping faith with his roots in Marxism and sociology while at the same time looking to the future. When one considers that personal computers, the Internet, and other technologies of information cultures were not widespread until the very end of the twentieth century, his analysis of technology as a social force ranks him among the most prophetic of social theorists. Underneath a rough and abrasive manner, Gouldner was a sensitive soul. These differing personal attributes contributed to his remarkable willingness to see the weakness and strength of his resources. *Crisis*, like most of what he wrote, is an attempt to define a third force in social theory—part sociology, part Marxism, part academic, part political. With Gouldner, nothing was ever simple.

The New Class as a Cultural Bourgeoisie[*]
Alvin W. Gouldner (1979)

Thesis Five: The New Class as a Cultural Bourgeoisie

5.1   The New Class and the old class are at first undifferentiated; the New Class commonly originates in classes with property advantages, that is, in the old class, or is sponsored by them. The New Class of intellectuals and intelligentsia are the relatively more *educated* counterpart—often the brothers, sisters, or children—of the old moneyed class. Thus the New Class contest sometimes has the character of *a civil war within the upper classes*. It is the differentiation of the old class into contentious factions. To understand the New Class contest it is vital to understand how the *privileged* and advantaged, not simply the suffering, come to be alienated from the very system that privileges them.

5.2   "The non-negotiable" objectives of the old moneyed class are to reproduce their capital, at a minimum, but, preferably, to make it accumulate and to appropriate profit: M-C-M', as Marx said. This is done within a structure in which all of them must compete with one another. This unrelenting competition exerts pressure to rationalize their productive and administrative efforts and unceasingly to heighten efficiency. (Marx called it, "revolutionizing" production.) But this rationalization is dependent increasingly on the efforts of the New Class intelligentsia and its expert skills. It is inherent in its structural situation, then, that the old class must bring the New Class into existence.

5.3   Much of the New Class is at first trained under the direct control of the old class' firms or enterprises. Soon, however, the old class is separated from the reproduction of the New Class by the emergence and development of a public system of education whose costs are "socialized."[30]

5.4   The more that the New Class's reproduction derives from specialized systems of public education, the more the New Class develops an ideology that stresses its *autonomy*, its separation from and presumable independence of "business" or political interests. This autonomy is said to be grounded in the specialized knowledge or cultural capital transmitted by the educational system, along with an emphasis on the obligation of educated persons to attend to the welfare of the collectivity. In other words, the *ideology* of "professionalism" emerges.[31]

5.5   Professionalism is one of the public *ideologies* of the New Class, and is the genteel subversion of the old class by the new. Professionalism is a phase in the historical development of the "collective consciousness" of the New Class. While not overtly a critique of the old class, professionalism is a tacit claim by the New Class to *technical and moral superiority* over the old class, implying that the latter lack technical credentials and are guided by motives of commercial venality. Professionalism silently installs the New Class as the paradigm of virtuous and legitimate authority, performing with technical skill and with dedicated concern for the society-at-large. Professionalism makes a focal claim for the legitimacy of the New Class which tacitly de-authorizes the old class.

On the one side, this is a bid for prestige *within* the established society; on the other, it tacitly presents the New Class as an *alternative* to the old. In asserting its own claims to authority, professionalism in effect *devalues the authority of the old class*.

5.6   The special privileges and powers of the New Class are grounded in their *individual* control of special cultures, languages, techniques, and of the skills resulting from these. The New Class is a cultural bourgeoisie who appropriates privately the advantages of an historically and collectively produced cultural capital. Let us be clear, then: the New Class is not just *like* the old class; its special culture is not just *like* capital. No metaphor is intended. The special culture of the New Class *is* a stock of capital that generates a stream of income (some of) which it appropriates privately.

5.7   The fundamental objectives of the New Class are: to increase its own share of the national product; to produce and reproduce the special social conditions enabling them to appropriate privately larger shares of the incomes produced by the special

[*] Alvin W. Gouldner, The Future of Intellectuals and the Rise of the New Class. New York: Seabury Press/Continuum, 1979.

cultures they possess; to control their work and their work settings; and to increase their political power partly in order to achieve the foregoing. The struggle of the New Class is, therefore, to *institutionalize a wage system,* i.e., a social system with a distinct principle of distributive justice: "from each according to his ability, to each according to his work," which is also the norm of "socialism." Correspondingly, the New Class may oppose other social systems and their different systems of privilege, for example, systems that allocate privileges and incomes on the basis of controlling stocks of money (i.e., old capital). The New Class, then, is prepared to be egalitarian so far as the privileges of the *old* class are concerned. That is, under certain conditions it is prepared to remove or restrict the special incomes of the old class: profits, rents, interest. The New Class is anti-egalitarian, however, in that it seeks special guild advantages— political powers and incomes—on the basis of its possession of cultural capital.

Thesis Six: The New Class as a Speech Community

6.1 The culture of critical discourse (CCD)[38] is an historically evolved set of rules, a grammar of discourse, which (1) is concerned to *justify* its assertions, but (2) whose *mode* of justification does not proceed by invoking authorities, and (3) prefers to elicit the *voluntary* consent of those addressed solely on the basis of arguments adduced. CCD is centered on a specific speech act: justification. It is a culture of discourse in which there is nothing that speakers will on principle permanently refuse to discuss or make problematic; indeed, they are even willing to talk about the value of talk itself and its possible inferiority to silence or to practice. This grammar is the deep structure of the common ideology shared by the New Class. *The shared ideology of the intellectuals and intelligentsia is thus an ideology about discourse.* Apart from and underlying the various technical languages (or sociolects) spoken by specialized professions, intellectuals and intelligentsia are commonly committed to a culture of critical discourse (CCD). CCD is the latent but mobilizable infrastructure of modern "technical" languages.

6.2 The culture of critical discourse is characterized by speech that is *relatively* more *situation-free,* more context or field "independent." This speech culture thus values expressly legislated meanings and devalues tacit, context-limited meanings. Its ideal is: "one word, one meaning," for everyone and forever.

The New Class's special speech variant also stresses the importance of particular modes of *justification,* using especially explicit and articulate rules, rather than diffuse precedents or tacit features of the speech context. The culture of critical speech requires that the validity of claims be justified without reference to the speaker's *societal position or authority.* Here, good speech is speech that can make its own principles *explicit* and is oriented to conforming with them, rather than stressing context-sensitivity and context-variability. Good speech here thus has *theoreticity.*[39]

Being pattern-and-principle-oriented, CCD implies that that which is said may *not* be correct, and may be *wrong.* It recognizes that "What Is" may be mistaken or inadequate and is therefore open to alternatives. CCD is also relatively more *reflexive,* self-monitoring, capable of more meta-communication, that is, of talk about talk; it is able to make its own speech problematic, and to edit it with respect to its lexical and grammatical features, as well as making problematic the validity of its assertions. CCD thus requires considerable "expressive discipline," not to speak of "instinctual renunciation."

6.3 Most importantly, the culture of critical speech forbids reliance upon the speaker's person, authority, or status in society to justify his claims. As a result, CCD de-authorizes all speech grounded in traditional societal authority, while it authorizes itself, the elaborated speech variant of the culture of critical discourse, as the standard of *all* "serious" speech. From now on, persons and their social positions must not be visible in their speech. Speech becomes impersonal. Speakers hide behind their speech. Speech seems to be disembodied, de-contextualized and self-grounded. (This is especially so for the speech of intellectuals and somewhat less so for technical intelligentsia who may not invoke CCD except when their paradigms break down.) The New Class becomes the guild masters of an invisible pedagogy.

6.4 The culture of critical discourse is the common ideology shared by the New Class, although technical intelligentsia sometimes keep it in latency. The skills and the social conditions required to reproduce it are among the common *interests* of the New Class. Correspondingly, it is in the common interest of the New Class to prevent or oppose all censorship of its speech variety and to install it as the standard of good speech. *The New Class thus has both a common ideology in CCD and common interests in its cultural capital.*

6.5   *Query:*   Is the New Class actually "unified" by its common rules of discourse? Are not intellectuals perpetual malcontents, eternally outside of any class? Are not technical intelligentsia (because they operate *within* "paradigms") necessarily conservative? Let us take the last question first.

Technical intelligentsia center their work on the detailed development of the paradigm dominant in their technical specialty. Where that specialty is mature, there may only be one paradigm, but often there are more. Where there are several, the technical intelligentsia face this alternative: either they abandon discussion with one another, alleging a total "incommensurability of paradigms," or they must reactivate the latent common culture of critical discourse underlying their technical language. Any problem with a paradigm, is characteristically resolved then by recourse to CCD. People must give reasons; they cannot rely upon their position in society or in their science to justify technical decisions. (In this way, they are substantially different from *bureaucrats,* even when pursuing "normal science.") And even when operating within a single paradigm, an accumulation of anomalous findings requires them to revise or abandon the paradigm, which they are able to do only by reverting once again to the culture of critical discourse.

In short, CCD is a common bond between humanistic intellectuals and technical intelligentsia, as well as among different technical intelligentsia themselves. As a language, CCD unifies in much the same way as ordinary languages, say French or German. Just as French and German are boundary-establishing, unifying elements, making it easier for members of the nation to communicate with one another, but making it harder for them to do so with people who do not speak their language, so, too, does CCD unify those who use it and establish distance between themselves and those who do not.

This does not mean, of course, that there are no significant differences between those who speak German, or CCD; it does not mean that those who speak German, or CCD, might not be seriously divided or be hostile to one another in some ways. Still, despite those divisions, there is a special solidarity brought by the sharing of a language.

Pierre Bourdieu (1930–2002) studied at the Lycée Louis le Grand in Paris then at the École Normale Supérieure, where he was a student of philosophy.

He came into sociology with the support of Raymond Aron and soon became one of the dominant forces in French sociology. At the time of his death in 2002 Bourdieu was a giant among intellectual heroes in France, and was respected the world over as a brilliant empirical researcher, inventive writer, and path-breaking social theorist of cultural politics. In 1975, he founded the journal *Actes de la récherche en sciences sociales*—in which appeared early expressions of his brilliant empirical studies of French culture Bourdieu did with coworkers like Monique de St. Martin. In 1982, Bourdieu was elected to a chair in sociology at the Collège de France. His many books include *Outline of a Theory of Practice* (1972), *Distinction* (1979), *Homo Academicus* (1984), and *The Logic of Practice* (1990). The selection is from the last of these. It presents Bourdieu's famous idea of habitus—that is, the notion that objective structures never work in the abstract but exert themselves in the habitual dispositions of individuals. In habitus, subjective consciousness meets objective reality in practical human action that is both enduring and unique. This is clearly one of the most inventive attempts to work through the dilemma of modern social theory: How do structures affect actions? A comparison with earlier thinkers reveals just how far social thinking had advanced since Niebuhr and Keynes saw, in the 1920s and 1930s, that individuals and structures were not easy companions.

Structures, Habitus, Practices[*]
Pierre Bourdieu (1974, 1980)

Objectivism constitutes the social world as a spectacle offered to an observer who takes up a "point of view" on the action and who, putting into the object the principles of his relation to the object, proceeds as if it were intended solely for knowledge and as if all the interactions within it were purely symbolic exchanges. This viewpoint is the one taken from high positions in the social structure, from which the social world is seen as a representation (as the word is used in idealist philosophy, but also as in painting) or a performance

---

[*]From *The Logic of Practice* by Pierre Bourdieu, Translated by Richard Nice. Copyright © 1989 Polity Press. All rights reserved. Used with the permission of Stanford University Press, www.sup.org. French language edition *Le Sens pratique* de Pierre Bourdieu, © 1980 by Les Editions de Minuit.

(in the theatrical or musical sense), and practices are seen as no more than the acting-out of roles, the playing of scores or the implementation of plans. The theory of practice as practice insists, contrary to positivist materialism, that the objects of knowledge are constructed, not passively recorded, and, contrary to intellectualist idealism, that the principle of this construction is the system of structured, structuring dispositions, the *habitus*, which is constituted in practice and is always oriented towards practical functions. It is possible to step down from the sovereign viewpoint from which objectivist idealism orders the world, as Marx demands in the *Theses on Feuerbach*, but without having to abandon to it the "active aspect" of apprehension of the world by reducing knowledge to a mere recording. To do this, one has to situate oneself *within* "real activity as such," that is, in the practical relation to the world, the preoccupied, active presence in the world through which the world imposes its presence, with its urgencies, its things to be done and said, things made to be said, which directly govern words and deeds without ever unfolding as a spectacle. One has to escape from the realism of the structure, to which objectivism, a necessary stage in breaking with primary experience and constructing the objective relationships, necessarily leads when it hypostatizes these relations by treating them as realities already constituted outside of the history of the group—without falling back into subjectivism, which is quite incapable of giving an account of the necessity of the social world. To do this, one has to return to practice, the site of the dialectic of the *opus operatum* and the *modus operandi*; of the objectified products and the incorporated products of historical practice; of structures and *habitus*.

The bringing to light of the presuppositions inherent in objectivist construction has paradoxically been delayed by the efforts of all those who, in linguistics as in anthropology, have sought to "correct" the structuralist model by appealing to "context" or "situation" to account for variations, exceptions and accidents (instead of making them simple variants, absorbed into the structure, as the structuralists do). They have thus avoided a radical questioning of the objectivist mode of thought, when, that is, they have not simply fallen back on to the free choice of a rootless, unattached, pure subject. Thus, the method known as "situational analysis," which consists of "observing people in a variety of social situations" in order to determine "the way in which individuals are able to exercise choices within the limits of a specified social structure" (Gluckman 1961) remains locked within the framework of the rule and the exception, which Edmund Leach (often invoked by the exponents of this method) spells out explicitly: "I postulate that structural systems in which all avenues of social action are narrowly institutionalized are impossible. In all viable systems, there must be an area where the individual is free to make choices so as to manipulate the system to his advantage."

The conditionings associated with a particular class of conditions of existence produce *habitus*, systems of durable, transposable dispositions, structured structures predisposed to function as structuring structures, that is, as principles which generate and organize practices and representations that can be objectively adapted to their outcomes without presupposing a conscious aiming at ends or an express mastery of the operations necessary in order to attain them. Objectively "regulated" and "regular" without being in any way the product of obedience to rules, they can be collectively orchestrated without being the product of the organizing action of a conductor.

It is, of course, never ruled out that the responses of the *habitus* may be accompanied by a strategic calculation tending to perform in a conscious mode the operation that the *habitus* performs quite differently, namely an estimation of chances presupposing transformation of the past effect into an expected objective. But these responses are first defined, without any calculation, in relation to objective potentialities, immediately inscribed in the present, things to do or not to do, things to say or not to say, in relation to a probable, "upcoming" future (*un à venir*), which—in contrast to the future seen as "absolute possibility" (*absolute Möglichkeit*) in Hegel's (or Sartre's) sense, projected by the pure project of a "negative freedom"—puts itself forward with an urgency and a claim to existence that excludes all deliberation. Stimuli do not exist for practice in their objective truth, as conditional, conventional triggers, acting only on condition that they encounter agents conditioned to recognize them. The practical world that is constituted in the relationship with the *habitus*, acting as a system of cognitive and motivating structures, is a world of already realized ends—procedures to follow, paths to take—and of objects endowed with a "permanent teleological character," in Husserl's phrase, tools or institutions. This is because the regularities inherent in an arbitrary condition ("arbitrary" in Saussure's and Mauss's sense) tend to appear as necessary, even natural, since they are the basis of the schemes of perception and appreciation through which they are apprehended.

If a very close correlation is regularly observed between the scientifically constructed objective probabilities (for example, the chances of access to a particular good) and agents' subjective aspirations ("motivations" and "needs"), this is not because agents consciously adjust their aspirations to an exact evaluation of their chances of success, like a gambler organizing his stakes on the basis of perfect information about his chances of winning. In reality, the dispositions durably inculcated by the possibilities and impossibilities, freedoms and necessities, opportunities and prohibitions inscribed in the objective conditions (which science apprehends through statistical regularities such as the probabilities objectively attached to a group or class) generate dispositions objectively compatible with these conditions and in a sense pre-adapted to their demands. The most improbable practices are therefore excluded, as unthinkable, by a kind of immediate submission to order that inclines agents to make a virtue of necessity, that is, to refuse what is anyway denied and to will the inevitable. The very conditions of production of the *habitus*, a virtue made of necessity, mean that the anticipations it generates tend to ignore the restriction to which the validity of calculation of probabilities is subordinated, namely that the experimental conditions should not have been modified. Unlike scientific estimations, which are corrected after each experiment according to rigorous rules of calculation, the anticipations of the *habitus*, practical hypotheses based on past experience, give disproportionate weight to early experiences. Through the economic and social necessity that they bring to bear on the relatively autonomous world of the domestic economy and family relations, or more precisely, through the specifically familial manifestations of this external necessity (forms of the division of labour between the sexes, household objects, modes of consumption, parent-child relations, etc.), the structures characterizing a determinate class of conditions of existence produce the structures of the *habitus*, which in their turn are the basis of the perception and appreciation of all subsequent experiences.

The *habitus*, a product of history, produces individual and collective practices—more history—in accordance with the schemes generated by history. It ensures the active presence of past experiences, which, deposited in each organism in the form of schemes of perception, thought and action, tend to

guarantee the "correctness" of practices and their constancy over time, more reliably than all formal rules and explicit norms. This system of dispositions—a present past that tends to perpetuate itself into the future by reactivation in similarly structured practices, an internal law through which the law of external necessities, irreducible to immediate constraints, is constantly exerted—is the principle of the continuity and regularity which objectivism sees in social practices without being able to account for it; and also of the regulated transformations that cannot be explained either by the extrinsic, instantaneous determinisms of mechanistic sociologism or by the purely internal but equally instantaneous determination of spontaneist subjectivism. Overriding the spurious opposition between the forces inscribed in an earlier state of the system, outside the body, and the internal forces arising instantaneously as motivations springing from free will, the internal dispositions—the internalization of externality—enable the external forces to exert themselves, but in accordance with the specific logic of the organisms in which they are incorporated, i.e., in a durable, systematic and non-mechanical way. As an acquired system of generative schemes, the *habitus* makes possible the free production of all the thoughts, perceptions and actions inherent in the particular conditions of its production—and only those. Through the *habitus*, the structure of which it is the product governs practice, not along the paths of a mechanical determinism, but within the constraints and limits initially set on its inventions. This infinite yet strictly limited generative capacity is difficult to understand only so long as one remains locked in the usual antinomies—which the concept of the *habitus* aims to transcend—of determinism and freedom, conditioning and creativity, consciousness and the unconscious, or the individual and society. Because the *habitus* is an infinite capacity for generating products—thoughts, perceptions, expressions and actions—whose limits are set by the historically and socially situated conditions of its production, the conditioned and conditional freedom it provides is as remote from creation of unpredictable novelty as it is from simple mechanical reproduction of the original conditioning.

Nothing is more misleading than the illusion created by hindsight in which all the traces of a life, such as the works of an artist or the events at a biography, appear as the realization of an essence that seems to preexist them. Just as a mature artistic style is not contained, like a seed, in an original inspiration but is continuously defined and redefined in the dialectic between the objectifying intention and the already objectified intention, so too the unity of meaning which, after the event, may seem to have preceded the acts and works announcing the final significance, retrospectively transforming the various stages of the temporal series into mere preparatory sketches, is constituted through the confrontation between questions that only exist in and for a mind armed with a particular type of schemes and the solutions obtained through application of these same schemes. The genesis of a system of works or practices generated by the same *habitus* (or homologous *habitus*, such as those that underlie the unity of the lifestyle of a group or a class) cannot be described either as the autonomous development of a unique and always self-identical essence, or as a continuous creation of novelty, because it arises from the necessary yet unpredictable confrontation between the *habitus* and an event that can exercise a pertinent incitement on the *habitus* only if the latter snatches it from the contingency of the accidental and constitutes it as a problem by applying to it the very principles of its solution; and also because the *habitus*, like every "art of inventing," is what makes it possible to produce an infinite number of practices that are relatively unpredictable (like the corresponding situations) but also limited in their diversity. In short, being the product of a particular class of objective regularities, the *habitus* tends to generate all the "reasonable," "common-sense," behaviours (and only these) which are possible within the limits of these regularities, and which are likely to be positively sanctioned because they are objectively adjusted to the logic characteristic of a particular field, whose objective future they anticipate. At the same time, "without violence, art or argument," it tends to exclude all "extravagances" ("not for the likes of us"), that is, all the behaviours that would be negatively sanctioned because they are incompatible with the objective conditions.

Because they tend to reproduce the regularities immanent in the conditions in which their generative principle was produced while adjusting to the demands inscribed as objective potentialities in the situation as defined by the cognitive and motivating structures that constitute the *habitus*, practices cannot be deduced either from the present conditions which may seem to have provoked them or from the past conditions which have produced the *habitus*, the durable principle of their production. They can therefore only be accounted for by relating the social conditions in which the *habitus* that generated them

was constituted, to the social conditions in which it is implemented, that is, through the scientific work of performing the interrelationship of these two states of the social world that the *habitus* performs, while concealing it, in and through practice. The "unconscious," which enables one to dispense with this interrelating, is never anything other than the forgetting of history which history itself produces by realizing the objective structures that it generates in the quasi-natures of *habitus*. . . .

The *habitus*—embodied history, internalized as a second nature and so forgotten as history—is the active presence of the whole past of which it is the product. As such, it is what gives practices their relative autonomy with respect to external determinations of the immediate present. This autonomy is that of the past, enacted and acting, which, functioning as accumulated capital, produces history on the basis of history and so ensures the permanence in change that makes the individual agent a world within the world. The *habitus* is a spontaneity without consciousness or will, opposed as much to the mechanical necessity of things without history in mechanistic theories as it is to the reflexive freedom of subjects "without inertia" in rationalist theories.

Thus the dualistic vision that recognizes only the self-transparent act of consciousness or the externally determined thing has to give way to the real logic of action, which brings together two objectifications of history, objectification in bodies and objectification in institutions or, which amounts to the same thing, two states of capital, objectified and incorporated, through which a distance is set up from necessity and its urgencies. This logic is seen in paradigmatic form in the dialectic of expressive dispositions and instituted means of expression (morphological, syntactic and lexical instruments, literary genres, etc.) which is observed in the intentionless invention of regulated improvisation. Endlessly overtaken by his own words, with which he maintains a relation of "carry and be carried," as Nicolai Hartmann put it, the virtuoso finds in his discourse the triggers for his discourse, which goes along like a train laying its own rails. In other words, being produced by a *modus operandi* which is not consciously mastered, the discourse contains an "objective intention," as the Scholastics put it, which outruns the conscious intentions of its apparent author and constantly offers new pertinent stimuli to the *modus operandi* of which it is the product and which functions as a kind of "spiritual automaton." If witticisms strike as much by their unpredictability as by their retrospective necessity, the reason is that the *trouvaille* that brings to light long buried resources presupposes a *habitus* that so perfectly possesses the objectively available means of expression that it is possessed by them, so much so that it asserts its freedom from them by realizing the rarest of the possibilities that they necessarily imply. The dialectic of the meaning of the language and the "sayings of the tribe" is a particular and particularly significant case of the dialectic between *habitus* and institutions, that is, between two modes of objectification of past history, in which there is constantly created a history that inevitably appears, like witticisms, as both original and inevitable.

This durably installed generative principle of regulated improvisations is a practical sense which reactivates the sense objectified in institutions. Produced by the work of inculcation and appropriation that is needed in order for objective structures, the products of collective history, to be reproduced in the form of the durable, adjusted dispositions that are the condition of their functioning, the *habitus*, which is constituted in the course of an individual history, imposing its particular logic on incorporation, and through which agents partake of the history objectified in institutions, is what makes it possible to inhabit institutions, to appropriate them practically, and so to keep them in activity, continuously pulling them from the state of dead letters, reviving the sense deposited in them, but at the same time imposing the revisions and transformations that reactivation entails. Or rather, the *habitus* is what enables the institution to attain full realization: it is through the capacity for incorporation, which exploits the body's readiness to take seriously the performative magic of the social, that the king, the banker or the priest are hereditary monarchy, financial capitalism or the Church made flesh. Property appropriates its owner, embodying itself in the form of a structure generating practices perfectly conforming with its logic and its demands. If one is justified in saying, with Marx, that "the lord of an entailed estate, the first-born son, belongs to the land," that "it inherits him," or that the "persons" of capitalists are the "personification" of capital, this is because the purely social and quasi-magical process of socialization, which is inaugurated by the act of marking that institutes an individual as an eldest son, an heir, a successor, a Christian, or simply as a man (as opposed to a woman), with all the corresponding privileges and obligations, and which is prolonged, strengthened and confirmed by social treatments that tend to transform instituted difference into natural distinction, produces quite real effects, durably

inscribed in the body and in belief. An institution, even an economy, is complete and fully viable only if it is durably objectified not only in things, that is, in the logic, transcending individual agents, of a particular field, but also in bodies, in durable dispositions to recognize and comply with the demands immanent in the field.

Audre Lorde (1934–1992) was born in Manhattan and graduated from Hunter College and Columbia University. She was an acclaimed poet whose poetry and other writings are classic texts to contemporary feminism, particularly to Black lesbian feminisms. Lorde traveled and lectured across the world and was a founder of the Women of Color Press. Between 1968 and 1992, Lorde published at least seventeen books of poetry, essays, and memoirs. She was the poet laureate of the State of New York in 1991. Her book of essays, *A Burst of Light*, won an American Book Award in 1989, and an earlier collection, *From the Land Where Other People Live* (1973), was nominated for a National Book Award. Lorde's last book was *Undersong: Chosen Poems, Old and New* (1992). The selection is a 1979 essay from her collection of feminist essays and talks, *Sister Outsider* (1984). Here, Lorde frames an earlier version of the fractured identities perspective as a critique of white, academic feminism. This and her famous open letter to Mary Daly of the same year are early statements of the distance women of color sometimes felt, and continue to feel, from white-dominated academic feminism. Implicitly, Lorde's argument is a critique of standpoint feminism in that she affirms that her identity is not simply that of her gender but also of her race and sexuality. Audre Lorde died in 1992, after many years struggling with cancer, about which she wrote in *Cancer Journals* (1980).

The Master's Tools Will Never Dismantle the Master's House[*]
Audre Lorde (1979)

I agreed to take part in a New York University Institute for the Humanities conference a year ago, with

---

[*]From SISTER OUTSIDER, published by Crossing Press, Random House Inc. Copyright © 1984, 2007 by Audre Lorde. Used herein by permission of the Charlotte Sheedy Literary Agency, Inc.

the understanding that I would be commenting upon papers dealing with the role of difference within the lives of American women: difference of race, sexuality, class, and age. The absence of these considerations weakens any feminist discussion of the personal and the political.

It is a particular academic arrogance to assume any discussion of feminist theory without examining our many differences, and without a significant input from poor women, Black and Third World women, and lesbians. And yet, I stand here as a Black lesbian feminist, having been invited to comment within the only panel at this conference where the input of Black feminists and lesbians is represented. What this says about the vision of this conference is sad, in a country where racism, sexism, and homophobia are inseparable. To read this program is to assume that lesbian and Black women have nothing to say about existentialism, the erotic, women's culture and silence, developing feminist theory, or heterosexuality and power. And what does it mean in personal and political terms when even the two Black women who did present here were literally found at the last hour? What does it mean when the tools of a racist patriarchy are used to examine the fruits of that same patriarchy? It means that only the most narrow perimeters of change are possible and allowable.

The absence of any consideration of lesbian consciousness or the consciousness of Third World women leaves a serious gap within this conference and within the papers presented here. For example, in a paper on material relationships between women, I was conscious of an either/or model of nurturing which totally dismissed my knowledge as a Black lesbian. In this paper there was no examination of mutuality between women, no systems of shared support, no interdependence as exists between lesbians and women-identified women. Yet it is only in the patriarchal model of nurturance that women "who attempt to emancipate themselves pay perhaps too high a price for the results," as this paper states.

For women, the need and desire to nurture each other is not pathological but redemptive, and it is within that knowledge that our real power is rediscovered. It is this real connection which is so feared by a patriarchal world. Only within a patriarchal structure is maternity the only social power open to women.

Interdependency between women is the way to a freedom which allows the *I* to *be*, not in order to be used, but in order to be creative. This is a difference between the passive *be* and the active *being*.

Advocating the mere tolerance of difference between women is the grossest reformism. It is a total denial of the creative function of difference in our lives. Difference must be not merely tolerated, but seen as a fund of necessary polarities between which our creativity can spark like a dialectic. Only then does the necessity for interdependency become unthreatening. Only within that interdependency of different strengths, acknowledged and equal, can the power to seek new ways of being in the world generate, as well as the courage and sustenance to act where there are no charters.

Within the interdependence of mutual (nondominant) differences lies that security which enables us to descend into the chaos of knowledge and return with true visions of our future, along with the concomitant power to effect those changes which can bring that future into being. Difference is that raw and powerful connection from which our personal power is forged.

As women, we have been taught either to ignore our differences, or to view them as causes for separation and suspicion rather than as forces for change. Without community there is no liberation, only the most vulnerable and temporary armistice between an individual and her oppression. But community must not mean a shedding of our differences, nor the pathetic pretense that these differences do not exist.

Those of us who stand outside the circle of this society's definition of acceptable women; those of us who have been forged in the crucibles of difference—those of us who are poor, who are lesbians, who are Black, who are older—know that *survival is not an academic skill.* It is learning how to stand alone, unpopular and sometimes reviled, and how to make common cause with those others identified as outside the structures in order to define and seek a world in which we can all flourish. It is learning how to take our differences and make them strengths. *For the master's tools will never dismantle the master's house.* They may allow us temporarily to beat him at his own game, but they will never enable us to bring about genuine change. And this fact is only threatening to those women who still define the master's house as their only source of support.

Poor women and women of Color know there is a difference between the daily manifestations of marital slavery and prostitution because it is our daughters who line 42nd Street. If white American feminist theory need not deal with the differences between us, and the resulting difference in our oppressions, then how do you deal with the fact that the women who clean your houses and tend your children while you attend conferences on feminist theory are, for the most part, poor women and women of Color? What is the theory behind racist feminism?

In a world of possibility for us all, our personal visions help lay the groundwork for political action. The failure of academic feminists to recognize difference as a crucial strength is a failure to reach beyond the first patriarchal lesson. In our world, divide and conquer must become define and empower.

Why weren't other women of Color found to participate in this conference? Why were two phone calls to me considered a consultation? Am I the only possible source of names of Black feminists? And although the Black panelist's paper ends on an important and powerful connection of love between women, what about interracial cooperation between feminists who don't love each other?

In academic feminist circles, the answer to these questions is often, "We did not know who to ask." But that is the same evasion of responsibility, the same cop-out, that keeps Black women's art out of women's exhibitions, Black women's work out of most feminist publications except for the occasional "Special Third World Women's Issue," and Black

women's texts off your reading lists. But as Adrienne Rich pointed out in a recent talk, white feminists have educated themselves about such an enormous amount over the past ten years, how come you haven't also educated yourselves about Black women and the differences between us—white and Black—when it is key to our survival as a movement?

Women of today are still being called upon to stretch across the gap of male ignorance and to educate men as to our existence and our needs. This is an old and primary tool of all oppressors to keep the oppressed occupied with the master's concerns. Now we hear that it is the task of women of Color to educate white women—in the face of tremendous resistance—as to our existence, our differences, our relative roles in our joint survival. This is a diversion of energies and a tragic repetition of racist patriarchal thought.

Simone de Beauvoir once said: "It is in the knowledge of the genuine conditions of our lives that we must draw our strength to live and our reasons for acting."

Racism and homophobia are real conditions of all our lives in this place and time. I urge each one of us here to reach down into that deep place of knowledge inside herself and touch that terror and loathing of any difference that lives there. See whose face it wears. Then the personal as the political can begin to illuminate all our choice

PART FIVE

After Modernity: 1979–2001

Each of the previous periods began with a specific year, and the meaning of each is evident: 1848, 1919, 1945, 1963. Reasonable people might disagree over whether historical periods actually began in those years. Just the same, the years are meaningful. Nothing similar could be said of 1979 or 1980 or any particular year thereabout.

The late 1970s and early 1980s were, historically speaking, a sloppy, indefinite time. Much happened, but hardly anyone today can say what it all meant. In the two years 1979 and 1980, the following notable events occurred in the United States: gasoline rationing; US inflation was 13 percent; Chrysler Corporation was bailed out by taxpayers; Tom Wolfe's *Right Stuff* was published; Christopher Lasch's *The Culture of Narcissism* became a best-seller; Francis Ford Coppola directed *Apocalypse Now*; the Three-Mile Island nuclear reactor was damaged; Walter Cronkite retired. Interesting, but hard to figure. In the world, in the same two years, the following events transpired: the Ayatollah Khomeini led a successful revolution in Iran; the Sandinistas chased Anastasio Somoza from Managua; Panama took control of the Canal Zone; Egypt and Israel entered into a peace treaty; Rhodesia became Zimbabwe; the Soviets invaded Afghanistan; Iraq invaded Iran; Mother Teresa won the Nobel Peace Prize; Leonid Brezhnev won the Lenin Peace Prize. Though the events on both lists may suggest trends developing from the events of the 1960s, no large event defined the historical moment as in 1945 or 1963 or 1968. The late 1970s and 1980s just were whatever they were.

Yet many would claim that, sometime around these years, the most momentous event of the last 500 years may have occurred: the beginning of the end of modernity itself. Or, more modestly put, around 1980 or so, people began to talk seriously about postmodernism. Why, though, is unclear. One might say, however, that the very indefiniteness of the nonevent (in contrast to the event of which Derrida spoke in 1966) is typical of postmodernism, whatever it might be or, by now, might have been.

This, of course, was not the first time social commentators spoke of a "post-something." Beginning in 1945, "postwar" meant something was changed, hopefully forever—and for the better. In the late 1950s, Daniel Bell and others who wrote of the end of ideology had in mind a new era of democratic freedoms. Later, about the time John Kenneth Galbraith wrote *The New Industrial State* (1967), many were talking seriously of a postindustrial world order. In the early 1990s, then-US President George Herbert Walker Bush and a good many European public figures spoke of a new world order. Ventures like these to define the end of one thing and the beginning of the next were, in one sense, little more than the natural tendency of modern people to feel the upward-rising trajectory of progress. Modernity's foremost logical dilemma is that it must always project a next stage (thus, a post-the-previous stage)—or it must prove that the present is, in fact, the final fulfillment of history. Because the latter is almost impossible to prove, modernity has always pressed on to the next envelope of time.

Timeline: 1976–2001

Social Theory		Wider World
Michel Foucault, *History of Sexuality I: Power as Knowledge* 1976	**1976**	Apple personal computer hits market **1976**
	1977	George Lucas releases *Star Wars* **1977** Elvis Presley dies in Memphis **1977**
	1978	Menachem Begin and Anwar Sadat win Nobel Peace Prize **1978**
Jean-François Lyotard, *The Postmodern Condition* 1979		John Lennon murdered in NYC **1980**
	1981	Deng Xiaoping assumes power in China **1981** AIDS becomes official medical term **1981** IBM personal computer with Intel chip **1981** Junta rules Argentina **1981** Sadat killed; Hosni Mubarak assumes power in Egypt **1981** Habermas, *Theory of Communicative Behavior, Vol 1* **1981**
	1982	British engage Falkland War with Argentina **1982** Israel invades Lebanon over PLO **1982** Michael Jackson's *Thriller* **1982**
	1983	Bob Hawke elected Australian PM **1983** Yamaha releases first digital synthesizer **1983** Philip Johnson's postmodern ATT building **1983** Compact disc **1983** Apple mouse **1983**
Juergen Habermas, *Theory of Communicative Behavior, Vol 2: Colonized Life-World* 1984	**1984**	Milan Kundera *Unbearable Lightness of Being* **1984** Anthony Giddens publishes *Constitution of Society* **1984** Famine in Ethiopia **1984** Madonna releases *Like a Virgin* **1984** Ronald Reagan reelected **1984**
	1985	Mikhail Gorbachev introduces liberal reforms in USSR **1985** First *Oprah Winfrey Show* **1985**
	1986	AZT, first promising drug for HIV/AIDS **1986** Chernobyl nuclear disaster in USSR **1986**
Randall Collins, *Interaction Ritual Chains* 1987 Nancy Hartsock, *A Theory of Power for Women?* 1987	**1987**	Mugabe makes himself president for life, Zimbabwe **1987** Toni Morrison's *Beloved* **1987** Palestinian Intifada against Israel; Hamas founded **1987**
Gayatri Chakravorty Spivak, *Can the Subaltern Speak?* 1988	**1988**	Cease fire in Angola; Cubans leave **1988** Osama bin Laden and Al-Qaeda in Afghanistan **1988** Soviet troops quit Afghanistan **1988** Iraq-Iran war ends **1988** Saddam Hussein kills Kurds with chemical weapons **1988** Pinochet resigns in Chile after vote **1988** George H.W. Bush elected US president **1988**

Social Theory

Trinh T. Minh-ha, *Infinite Layers/ Third World?* **1989**

Richard Rorty, *Contingency Irony, and Solidarity* **1989**

Slavoj Žizěk, *Sublime Object of Ideology: Cynicism as a Form of Ideology* **1989**

Patricia Hill Collins, *Black Feminist Thought in the Matrix of Domination* **1990**

Anthony Giddens, *Consequences of Modernity: Post-Modernity or Radicalized Modernity?* **1990**

Eve Sedgwick, *Epistemology of the Closet* **1990**

Cornel West, *The New Cultural Politics of Difference* **1990**

Judith Butler, *Imitation and Gender Insubordination* **1991**

Arlene Stein and Ken Plummer, *I Can't Even Think Straight* **1994**

Wider World

1989

Exxon Valdez oil spill in Alaska **1989**
Tiananmen Square rebellion in Beijing **1989**
Solidarity wins power in Poland **1989**
Erich Honecker resigns power in East Germany **1989**
Berlin Wall destroyed **1989**
Velvet Revolution in Czechoslovakia **1989**
Aung San Suu Kyi arrested in Burma **1989**

1990

White rule ends in South Africa **1990**
Nelson Mandela released after 26 years in prison **1990**
Boris Yelstin quits Communist Part in USSR **1990**
Germany reunified **1990**
James Coleman, *Foundations of Social Theory: The New Social Science* **1990**

1991

Jeffrey Weeks, *Against Nature: Sexual Identification Is a Strange Thing* **1991**
Nirvana and Grunge **1991**
Osama bin Laden expelled from Saudi Arabia **1991**
US Gulf War against Iraq **1991**
USSR dissolved; Gorbachev resigns **1991**
Aung San Suu Kyi wins Nobel Peace Prize **1991**

1992

Serbs and Croats at war in Bosnia **1992**
Serbs institute policy of genocide in Bosnia **1992**
Eric Clapton's *Unplugged* **1992**
Bill Clinton elected US president **1992**
Francis Fukuyama, *End of History* **1992**

1993

Whites vote to end apartheid in South Africa **1993**
Mandela and F.W. de Klerk win Nobel Peace Prize **1993**
Samuel Huntington's essay, *Clash of Civilizations* **1993**

1994

Hutu genocide against Tutsis Rwanda **1994**
Tom Hanks in *Forest Gump* **1994**
Nelson Mandela president of SA **1994**
Bill Clinton loses health care fight; and Congress **1994**
Tony Blair prime minister of UK **1994**

The Idea of the Postmodern and Its Critics

Prophecies of a postmodern time are different from an actual historical event. Claims of this kind are based on no more than the most general facts, and in the case of the vision of the postmodern, they did not propose a new era of progress. Nor did they prophesy a reversal of history's linear fortunes, a kind of progressive devolution. This does not mean that they are without merit. From time to time in the modern era, cyclical theories of the rise and fall of civilization offered this sort of interpretation. Some, even now, say that America and Europe are in decline, to be surpassed by the rising Asian powers, China, Korea, Japan and India. But these, too, are variants on the theme of modern progress; that is, when things go bad, one way to account for the absence of progress is to say it has temporarily turned back, as if to clear the way for the rise of the next, better civilization. But theories of the postmodern did not make this sort of claim.

Those who, not that long ago, were adamant postmodernists were different from even cyclical theorists. They tended to think of the postmodern as a surprising, sometimes humorous, and always disconcerting mixture of present, past, and future—as a period when cultural and spatial elements from these different times were at once coming apart and refitting themselves in new configurations. Probably the most famous architectural symbol of the postmodern is the AT&T building in midtown New York City. Physically, the building rises from a classic base of Greco-Roman arches and columns to a Chippendale pediment decorating the top of a modernist skyscraper. At least three design features, from at least as many different periods of time, seem to be saying that history is not a straight, progressive line. History is not real and simple but complicated and perverse. The Chippendale decoration is clearly a joke of some kind. Is it to say, "This building is really a piece of furniture"? Or, as some suggest, is the Chippendale design a mockery of AT&T's product—a cradle for old-fashioned telephones? Impossible to say, but it *is* a joke, even if one cannot get it. Then, of course, one must wonder why one of the world's most visibly powerful American corporations wanted a building that made a joke of the idea that history makes sense. When, in the early 1990s, AT&T sold the building to one of Japan's most visible corporations, Sony, it only added to the confusion, the joke, the disruption of normal cultural and economic sense. Since architectural monuments, musical and artistic pieces, films and philosophies, and a good many theoretical and literary documents still today toy with the comings of goings of historical time and space, it is fair to admit that postmodernism remains a plausible idea, even as the term itself has faded in popularity. At the least, it is correct to say that early in the twenty-first century global things are more than a little different from what came before and decidedly more mixed up than even the twentieth century avant-garde anticipated.

In "Post-Modernity or Radicalized Modernity?" (1990), Anthony Giddens conveys the popular impression that the postmodern is about fragmentation, the dissolution of the self, the uncertainty of any theory of knowledge. Those, like Giddens, who are skeptical of postmodernism tend to picture it just so: a kind of ongoing drama of 1968, the ever-augmenting disappearance of the Center into a sea of relativism. Some proponents of the postmodern find this impression too overwrought. They would point out, for example, that whatever is going on design-wise, the AT&T building is still a building that works, complete with restrooms, offices, real telephones, and working people. A controversy like this, one without an evidently strong solution, at least helps clarify the questions being asked: Are modern times at their end? Has the world changed, in the last generation, in such a way that the culture of the modern world that took shape in the eighteenth century is no longer viable? Is the new world order somehow different? Put this way, the debate makes better sense. Those who believe in the postmodern could argue that the world is, indeed, more fragmented, without a single powerful political and economic Center. The notion that things are progressing steadily and obviously toward some definitely better state is far from clear, they would add.

On the other side, proponents of the modern (like Jürgen Habermas or Giddens and many others) would argue: obviously, the modern world has changed since the nineteenth or even mid-twentieth century. Social life is less well tied together in the older sense: some would contend it is better integrated in other ways. Electronic media (CNN, fax machines, computer networks) are the tools of extra-governmental forces (corporations, terrorist groups, new political movements) that integrate the world in new ways. The fall of the European powers, some modernists would say, does not mean the modern world is *not* advancing. In Giddens's words, radicalized modernity "sees high modernity as a set of circumstances in which dispersal is dialectically connected to profound tendencies towards global integration." In simpler terms, other modernists believe that, as bad as things are, it is still possible to gather the world's people around common principles of human aspiration. The old Enlightenment doctrines need revision, they insist, but the principles still work.

This is obviously a point on which, despite their differences, Giddens and Habermas are both radical modernists and similarly opposed to the idea of the postmodern. In this view, the hand we've been dealt may not be great, but it is good enough to effect human liberation from all that oppresses. Modernists, and especially radical ones, tend to assume that postmodernists have given up on humanity, that their jokes and frivolity take the world too lightly. Serious modernists will refer this way to writers like Jean Baudrillard, who seem to say that the real world is no more real than Disneyland. Radical and ordinary modernists alike find this an absurdly apolitical attitude. On the other hand, postmodernists, even those who would never say that Disneyland is reality, might argue that the trouble with modernists of all kinds is that they take themselves and history far too seriously. Habermas, for notable example, is as committed today as were his predecessors among the German critical theorists early in the twentieth century to what they call the project of Enlightenment to, that is, the work of rethinking the best critical elements of modern thought. In this respect, Habermas is actually less radical than Giddens or others who, in the 1980s, rebelled against then-current postmodern ideas by putting forth their kinds of radical modernist theories in the form of New Left, Neo-Marxist, or cultural theoretical programs. Similarly, but with a very different purpose, Nancy Hartsock was among the feminists of the time who also took account of writers like Michel Foucault while resisting the temptations to dissolve modern categories of subjective action that were then, and still are, crucial to a great deal of feminist thought. By contrast, somewhat later, Arlene Stein and Ken Plummer wrote the now classic essay "I Can't Even Think Straight" (1994), a striking statement of queer theory that many rightly took as a deep rejection of modern categories for defining gender, sexuality, and knowledge itself.

Meanwhile, even among more mainstream social theorists in the last two decades of the twentieth century, there were serious and enduring revisions of categories that until then had more or less been taken for granted. Randall Collins, for example, was the most persuasive among a long list of thinkers who attempted to come to turns with what was called the Micro-Macro Link—or, the question of how large transcendent structures are to be understood in respect to smaller daily life interactions. Collins, borrowing from Erving Goffman, suggested that the link was a series of *interaction ritual chains* that are neither purely macro structures nor merely micro events. In this, his ideas were, perhaps unwittingly, remarkably parallel to proposals made earlier by Pierre Bourdieu and Anthony Giddens. Also, a decade after Collins's essay, Mustafa Emirbayer and Ann Mische interpreted the analytic components of social agency in ways that allowed for theoretical clarity as to just how agency interacts with components of larger structures.

Each point of view—whether radically modern or postmodern—has something to recommend it. It is true that modernity, whether traditional or radical, has proven itself ponderous, self-important, and largely unable to support its claims that social things are getting better. On the other hand, proponents of the postmodern seemed to be tricksters far too ready to throw out the best hopes for human freedom and fulfillment, *without* a ready explanation as to what we are to do in a fragmented world without moral centers or values of any kind. Choosing between the two alternatives is mostly a matter of taste. Pick the one that appeals to your sensibilities. This is, itself, a kind of postmodern dilemma. If one side cannot win the argument, if there is no final authority (as Richard Rorty puts it) to which we can refer to resolve the debate, then are we not in something like a postmodern time, whatever we might call it? It turns out that recognition of this dilemma is the only (admittedly weak) reason to select a date like 1979 as the beginning of a *possible* postmodern period. This was when Jean-François Lyotard, a French philosopher, and Richard Rorty, an American, published two very different books, *The Postmodern Condition* and *Philosophy and the Mirror of Nature*. For some, these books provided explanations for the commonsense experience that no one seemed to agree on what, if anything, was real—and that no one had any final argument or wonderful story to tell on which people might agree.

It is, of course, more than a little outrageous to suggest that two very technical, academic books could serve as defining moments. But because enthusiasts for the postmodern tend to be in the cultural elite (many of them are academics), this is not surprising. It would be wrong, however, to leave the impression that the idea of a postmodern condition is nothing more than the fad of certain paid social theorists. The issue of the postmodern was and remains, in large part, a debate among intellectuals. Even so, it stands for an important phase in a necessary debate about the history of the world and its culture. For every unsettling book about Disneyland that said there is no real world, one could find real world events to support the postmodern claim. Vietnam was somehow like a Francis Ford Coppola movie. Richard Nixon's Watergate was, as younger critics then said, "unreal." It was unbelievable that the Americans would become involved in Vietnam after what happened to the French—and that the Soviets would make the same unreal mistake in Afghanistan; then, decades later, that the Americans would repeat, even after they had been through a parallel failure in Vietnam. There is, if these historical instances are to be taken seriously, something about the repetition compulsion of modern states that reflects both a nostalgia for the past mixed with a vain hope about the future—a state of political mind that surely confounds a realistic attempt to come to terms with the present. There really *are* quirky buildings like the Sony, formerly AT&T, skyscraper. Popular cultures of all kinds—from rock to rap, from trash TV to Facebook and more—invited the masses into a world in which music, culture, sex, politics, everything is without any stable distinction, a world in which reality is focused on fragments not really meant to resolve themselves. Even those who say they hate hip-hop, or don't quite get it, somehow "know" what is being said—like it or not.

So, though it is a very un-postmodern thing to say, one could conclude that, whatever the cultural elite writes or produces, there is still something "out there" that corresponds to their ideas. Postmodernism—that is, the idea that we are now in a state of postmodernity—is not just an idea. It *might* be real, so to speak. Therefore, whether one believes in it or not, it is possible to reconstruct, in general terms, the historical markers (if not events) on which the belief in postmodernity is founded.

If there were or is such a thing as the postmodern, then the years 1979 and 1980 must be thought of much like the quantum rings vibrating around the unstable energy nucleus of all elemental atoms in the universe. These years are, in such a sense, arbitrary points of reference between two very extreme high-energy points: 1968, on the one hand, and 1989–1990, on the other. These were the quantum limits between the year things collapsed in the 1960s to the years the Cold War era ended around 1990 with the dramatic changes in Eastern Europe and the former Soviet Union. In 1968, while all the Western capitals were under a state of siege, the Soviets crushed the first clear signs of internal rebellion in Prague. A little more than twenty years later, Prague broke out again—in Berlin, in Moscow, in Bucharest—everywhere in the East of the West. The end of the 1960s and the end of the 1980s seem now to be defining limits in the same series of events. True, there are those in the West who claim that the fall of communism was really the triumph of the West. But the enormous financial crises within the West, from Berlin to Tokyo (not to mention the United States), make such a claim less than self-evident. That the only remaining, if flawed, superpower, the USA, is, in fact, *only* a military superpower and (at best) first among near equals economically makes the term superpower mean something different. The United States "won" its first war in Iraq with superior military technology, then struggled in a second war in Iraq and the post-9/11 war in Afghanistan—wars in which rebels in alleyways and mountain redoubts made military technology futile. In the end, winning wars is a passing state of global affairs in which not much is changed, even after all the expense, death, and destruction.

All that has come to pass since 1989-1991 and the end of the Cold War has served to undermine the culture of the West, which always defined itself against a barbarian other. Without the Communists, the West lacks a defining evil. No one has yet been able to inflate the Iraqis into a threat of sufficient scale to keep the West believing in itself. This is largely because most Western societies are dependent on world conditions. None can stand alone. The stronger economies require world labor, resources, and commodity markets. Nothing is local, or even regional. Economic growth means constantly chasing the last few remaining profit markets. Most of the American and European economies have long been forced to open their borders to foreign labor. To undercut the high wage demands of indigenous skilled workers, they all liberalized immigration laws, admitting workers who gave the word "stranger" a new meaning. In the United States since the mid-1960s, internal (or border) labor is increasingly provided by people from the Caribbean, Latin America, Mexico, Vietnam, and elsewhere in Asia. Just as Germany imported workers from Turkey, France and Britain imported them from former African or Far Eastern colonies. These workers, who built buildings, cleaned streets, guarded doorways, and the like, eventually became major forces in the host countries. It is well known that by the end of the century, the populations of most American cities will be predominantly minority. But this time the minorities are not Irish, Italian, or other European peoples. Many are from parts of the world where none of the European languages are spoken. Eventually, the United States will not be merely bilingual (English and variants of Spanish) but multilingual. This, in part, is why there has been ever since so much fear and anger over multiculturalism today.

Multiculturalism—Another Expression of the Postmodern Idea?

By the 1990s, multiculturalism had become the tagline for the then-obvious fact that the Western powers, and to an increasing extent, the rising Asian ones, could not resist the fast-flowing migration of people from overseas or, even, from their own hinterlands to the urban centers. Americans, being given to fads, have largely tried to eliminate the idea of the multicultural after the 1990s. Yet anger over immigrants who are said to be "illegal" (even as they have served the American economy very well) provoke conservatives to pursue the most regressive of social policies in the hope that immigrant peoples will go away, which they will not. Europeans tend to have embraced the concept of the multicultural longer, perhaps because of the relatively recent rise of their dependence on large numbers of immigrant workers who have become permanent residents practicing their traditional linguistic, cultural, and religious habits. Still, also in Europe, there are conservatives deeply hostile to most nonwhite immigrant workers, many of whom migrated from Europe's former colonies.

When all is said and done, it seems all but certain that what unnerves those who see a suddenly different America (or Germany, or England, or France, etc.) is that the traditionally white, European peoples who dominated throughout the modern era are no longer the only players in the cultural game. The white dominant populations invited people from abroad into their labor markets. When the multicultural populations refused to limit themselves to a host society's dirty work, the traditionally dominant peoples saw a new world—a many-cultured one that threatened because it was so at odds with their longstanding modern ideals. When the new populations stayed, then insisted they had not only rights but also viable cultural and economic terms of their own, the formerly dominant people were, at the least, less welcoming. They believed, without any real evidence, that as different people settle in, the mostly white majority would lose their advantages. The problem is that the original Euro-Americans in the West depend on the very people whose presence and practices they now despise. Let a white, middle-class visitor from Illinois try getting a cab or a bagel and coffee at three o'clock in the morning in New York City without dealing with someone who is "different."

When the world changes, it never changes in theory alone. Theories always reflect something. It is far from clear that the multiculturalization of European and North American societies means the end of the modern world. It is not even clear what it all means. But it means *something*, and this is what the supposition of a postmodern world is based on. Clearly, enough people take it with enough seriousness to fight cultural wars over it. It is a sad commentary on the liberal values of the Euro-Americans that they must struggle, often to fail, just to extend their own decent values to their new neighbors. One might even propose that whatever postmodernism turns out to be in the long run of history, the multicultural fear internal to the former colonizing societies may well have been its early warning sign.

Postmodernism can be made to look naive and foolish when it is a matter of social theorists debating Disneyland or Gaga, hip-hop or other cultural phenomena—fads, as the critics think of them. It is a more serious matter when it involves the destructive fury of right-wing talk-show hosts and camera-ready politicians directed against "those people." They may be cultural wars on the surface but they are in fact real wars in which real people get hurt. Though the epistemological meaning of "real" may be in doubt, the political and personal reality of these injuries is not. The reality of Western societies no longer dominated by the traditional European peoples, and the anger this condition inspires, points to a world newly structured since the 1960s. How much these changes derived directly from the decentering world events of the 1960s is somewhat more difficult to assess. That they seem to be connected, more or less directly, is enough to establish as fact that the mythical West, the home of Modern Times, has a different set of conditions on its hands. However the world turns out, the talk of a postmodern, multicultural world that started in earnest around 1979 is a reality that requires consideration. This is why, since then, most social theory has had something to say in support of, in opposition to, or in response to various theories of the postmodern.

New Cultural Theories After Modernity

One of the surest signs that *something* was different in the 1980s and 1990s was the variety of responses to the new cultural circumstances. Not all of them were framed as responses to postmodernity. In fact, many were outright defenses of modernity or, at least, attempts to revise its culture or philosophy. But it would be hard for anyone to identify any point on the cultural or political spectrum that was *not* affected by the controversy over the state of culture. The 1980s were when people first started to speak of the cultural wars. Even more, this was the period when "culture" superseded "politics" or, at least, when the two were thought of as so complexly related that a person's politics were assumed to be his or her culture as well. Then, in the words of Cornel West, one could speak of the "new cultural politics" or, in the phrase given currency by Henry Louis Gates Jr., of the cultural Left. In several of his writings, Gates defined the cultural Left as a loose mixture of positions drawn from feminism, poststructuralism, Marxism, African American studies and culture, and gay-lesbian studies (or, later, queer theory), among other activities more or less associated with the universities. It was to the cultural Left that a seemingly endless number of journalistic, and a few academic, books responded. The most famous was the late Alan Bloom's *Closing of the American Mind* (1987). Bloom's subtitle captures the position he took in the cultural wars: *How Higher Education Has Failed Democracy and Impoverished the Souls of Today's Students.* Thus began the cultural Right. Thereafter, William Bennett, Bill O'Reilly, Dinesh D'Souza, evangelical preachers in the lineage of Pat Robertson, and others would claim, or be given, a cultural Right identity. Between the cultural Right and the Left, virtually everyone with an academic reputation to maintain was forced for a long while to take a position, even if only to say both were ridiculous. Today, this is not so stark an opposition, if only because the divergent poles with respect to culture have themselves become more embedded in actual political movements.

What remains a curiosity to this day, and what may never be fully explained, is how exactly it happened that political struggle came to be so closely identified with a struggle over who controls the right to determine what the mainstream culture is in American society. Only one, frankly speculative, explanation is readily available: everyone (or virtually everyone) understood that the older cultural ways of modern times no longer had the power they once had. Indeed, in some quarters, traditional beliefs were becoming objects of disdain or mere shadows of what they once were. If there is any fact in all this, it is this: we do not know who will win the cultural wars, but everyone can have a position. And most do. Whenever "everyone" assumes they need a position in a debate, something is at stake, and that something is not likely to be abstract. The cultural wars are about how we are to view the world that is thought to have changed—too much for some, too little for others.

Cornel West's "The New Cultural Politics of Difference" (1990) is still one of the clearest statements of the cultural Left's interpretation of the West's cultural history—how it came to be, what it thought, and how it fell apart. And Henry Louis Gates, Jr.'s introduction to an important 1986 collection of essays, *"Race," Writing and Difference*, was itself an event in the cultural wars. Then, for the first time, most of the leading figures of the cultural Left lent their views to a special issue of an academic journal, *Critical Inquiry*; they made a statement of their understanding of the necessity of seeing world politics as defined largely by cultural differences. Gates's own introduction was one of the most important essays in the collection. He summarized in clear terms what many had understood: that the very idea of the West was founded, arbitrarily, on a massive cultural figure of speech that served to sort everything culturally European into the category of civilization and everything else into the category "Other." The West, Gates explained, just happened to be white; the Other was of color. Gates was not the first to draw this connection. But much like Derrida in 1966, Gates in 1986 was able to put the argument together at the right time with the right cultural authority. The fact that he and Cornel West are African Americans and are considered leaders in both African American studies and Black culture not only added to their public authority but also solidified the claim that the wars over culture were political.

Europeans, as in many things, were more accustomed to critical thinking about modern culture. This was in large part because Europe suffered more directly from the ravages of the Holocaust and the Nazi era. Though America joined after 1941, Europe had never really recovered fully from the discouragements of the First World War, of which the Second World War was in many ways but a continuation. As a result, a good many of Europe's twentieth century social theorists, even when in exile in the United States, directed their efforts at the failures of the modern state to assure lasting peace and prosperity. Obviously, the German critical theorists were the first European theoretical movement to engage with the terrors of Hitler, which could just as well be described as liberal rationalism gone wild and evil.

In France, a very different movement arose after WWII. Properly described, that movement began as structuralism, which was a reaction in turn to the existentialism that dominated in the mid-1940s. Where existentialism emphasized the importance of individual experience as the first instance of engagement with history, structuralism aimed to correct the argument by showing that the problems of twentieth century Europe were structural. Hitler was an individual; his movement was a terrible structure. But, just as quickly as structuralism come on the scene, there developed a poststructuralist movement. Jacques Derrida's famous 1966 paper and talk at Johns Hopkins was its point of departure. Many American social theorists in the 1980s and after began to refer to Derrida and other of the French social theorists as postmodern, a label the theorists themselves seldom considered. Of the others, the best known alongside Derrida was Michel Foucault, whose thinking in the 1970s veered sharply in the direction of culture as a mechanism of power used to control populations through a micro-power of social instruction shaping ideas with respect to sexuality, health, and family relations. In the years prior to his death in 1984, Foucault's writings on the history of sexuality were published, and almost immediately he became even more of a public media star. In short order, he would be recognized as the early inspiration of queer theory—the movement that grew out of gay and lesbian social theories to become, in effect, a challenge to the traditional social ideas of how social knowledge and power operate.

Though nothing in all this was ever simple, the reader of texts like those following would do well to keep one question in mind: What does this author believe about the Center? Authors who believe the world is, or can be, organized around one or a few cultural or political principles will move in one direction; those who don't move in another. For example, Donna Haraway's 1985 essay "The Cyborg Manifesto" belongs in the postmodern or multicultural camp. But a first reading of this essay could lead one to think of it as a kind of theater of the absurd within modernity. The writing is circular, the figure of the cyborg is duplicitous, the theory is a mixture of socialism and feminism—or neither, but rather something beyond. There are people who have read this essay time and time again without ever quite getting inside it, so to speak. Yet whatever else one concludes, it is clear that Haraway is arguing that the world is a challenging mixture of identities and realities in which the normal boundaries between human, mechanical, and natural things are utterly blurred and inverted. "The Cyborg Manifesto" was an opening in the debate over fractured identities—the idea that many people in the world do not believe their identity can be reduced to any one essence. Far from being American or European, these people are not even simply feminist, Black, lesbian, working-class, postcolonial, subaltern, or any one thing. They are, rather, varying combinations of several fracturing, yet integrating, political and cultural identities. For example, Haraway was among the first to call the attention of white, middle-class intellectuals to the importance of the figure of the "woman of color":

> "Women of color," a name contested at its origins by those whom it would incorporate, as well as a historical consciousness marking systematic breakdown of all the signs of Man in "Western" traditions, constructs a kind of postmodernist identity out of otherness, difference, specificity.

Haraway's essay first began to circulate after publication in *Socialist Review* in 1985, the year before Gates's collection was completely published. Soon after, an increasing number of members of the cultural Left began to discover other writings by women of color, some of which are represented in the selections that follow. Gloria Anzaldúa, Gayatri Chakravorty Spivak, Patricia Hill Collins, Trinh T. Minh-ha, and Paula Gunn Allen are among those whose social theoretical positions are adequately characterized by Haraway's statement. Each represents (a word that itself is open to debate) a woman-of-color position; each takes a position that sees the world, including the world of people's self-understanding, as one of multiple elements; each understands culture and politics, and thus the politics of culture, to be an ongoing process of defining and living according to one's several affinities. Eventually, by the early 1990s, queer theory came into public notice as gay and lesbian social theorists developed the importance of sexuality in political and cultural identification. Judith Butler was then and remains today prominent among theorists in this tradition. But one need only read Gloria Anzaldúa's statements on the importance of her lesbian identity to see that gay, lesbian, and bisexual identity had already been an important option, and resource, in the politics of culture. The range of these programs for construing the complex and sometimes conflicting ways that social forces can interact in the life courses of individuals and social groups were presented under a variety of names with much the same purpose. Donna Haraway referred to *fractured identities*, Patricia Hill Collins wrote of a *matrix of domination*, as Kimberlé Williams Crenshaw rethought critical race theory and legal process in respect to *intersectional oppressions*.

These writers may or may not allow themselves to be labeled postmodern. But each trades on a similar intellectual and cultural tradition, and each shares some version of the historical judgment that the world is no longer one—or even unifiable. To them, the world is many, and culture, like politics, is the differences individuals encounter whenever they step into the world as it is. Whether they are looking for bagels and coffee or for a way to explain themselves to themselves and others, people in such a world are forced to face differences. Postmodernists do not find this a tragic loss. They do not worry over the decline of the West or of America or of the

British Empire. Rather, they rejoice and occasionally make poetry or jokes about the fresh air of a world that may not, after all, be heading toward some final, progressive End.

It is sometimes difficult to distinguish postmodernists from those who might better be described as radical or Left modernists. But keeping that test question in mind, the reader can figure out which authors still somehow take a modernist, or modernist-like, position. The question, again, is: Who believes in a Center of whatever kind? Gates argued this idea (somewhat in the tradition of Du Bois's twoness theory) in *The Signifying Monkey* (1988), his book on African American literary theory. He, and more sharply Afrocentist writers like Molefi Kete Asante, drew attention to the power of language and literature as possessing a potent political power. In contrast to European beliefs about discourse, African cultures, it is now well know, believe language is not the product of the speaker so much as that of the community. In *Signifying Monkey*, Gates made references to these facts of public rhetoric. Like a good many standpoint feminisms, the emerging race theories sought to invert the world—to suggest that the traditionally white Eurocentric culture by excluding women, non-whites, and others, got the world quite wrong. Just as a standpoint feminist *might* seek to replace a patriarchal principle with Woman's perspective, then certain Afrocentrists might want to replace Eurocentric principles with a Black standpoint. Similarly, queer theorists would call into question the very principles of modern knowledge.

As it is within feminist theory, the debate over the Center is of crucial importance in framing the theoretical attitude of the social theorists. Nancy Hartsock's critique of Michel Foucault's theory of power bears some comparison to Asante's Afrocentric idea. Hartsock is respectfully critical of Foucault's view that power is dispersed throughout the micropolitics of a society and is never simply a matter of those in the ruling elite crushing the oppressed. Central to Foucault's theory of power was his prior argument that one of the ways modernity exerted its force on individuals was by shaping their subjecthood. By encouraging individuals to believe in their subjective authority, modern culture actually weakened their political convictions. Foucault was, therefore, among those who argued that a critique of modern culture also required a critique of the modernist ideal of the strong moral subject. Hartsock is among those who consider this a dangerous move. In making her case, she has authored one of the most memorable lines in recent social theory:

> Why is it just when so many of us who have been silenced begin to demand the right to name ourselves, to act as subjects rather than objects of history, that just then the concept of subjecthood becomes problematic?

Hartsock's powerful, and subtle, argument is one of the most compelling attacks on postmodernism. In effect, she says: Postmodernism may be right about the world and right about all the evils encouraged by modernist culture and philosophy, but what does it put in the place of modernity's most liberating values? Like many others on the cultural and political Left, she does not want to throw the baby out with the bathwater. This is a question that must be taken seriously, especially when it is posed by members of social groups who have, over time, been silenced. The ironic lightness of some postmodernisms can, indeed, be justification to avoid the deadly seriousness of reality. However much the world has changed, people suffer in real ways. It is said that, sometime before he died of AIDS, Michel Foucault stated that AIDS was a discursive phenomenon. There are some realities. The question is, what to make of them and how? This is what the cultural wars are about. There is no certain agreement as to how, if at all, one can settle the matter. What is indisputable is that the real-world culture wars were part and parcel of a renewed, even necessary, attention to culture as a defining, and thus powerful, feature of late-modern or postmodern societies.

There are many social theorists who find themselves in still another position on the spectrum of cultural politics—neither postmodern nor modernist in the usual sense; certainly not cultural Right but also not cultural Left. These are writers who are willing and able to respond constructively to the "Whither Postmodernism?" debate without accepting one of the obvious settled positions. If Jürgen Habermas's critical theoretical defense of modernity is the most ambitious attempt to keep modernity as a source of Left principles, then Anthony Giddens's structuration theory is one of the most imaginative attempts to stretch modernist social theory to a limit just shy of postmodernism. Somewhere between Habermas and Giddens, one might situate Jeffrey Alexander's important contribution in the defining of cultural sociology. Alexander frankly defends liberal culture in *The Civil Sphere* (2006), but he does so by means of a serious attempt to assess the prospect of the public sphere and democracy while engaging many of the themes of even poststructuralist thought—notably language or discourse and the question of evil.

In the end, wherever one stands in the cultural wars and whatever becomes of the postmodern idea, what is here to stay for the near future at least is that, as globalized technologies add to the uncertainties and possibilities that confront the remainders of the modern world, culture itself and cultural theory in particular will continue to be central to social theorists that want to come to terms with social worlds as they are.

C. L.

Note

Page 343: Bloom, *Closing of the American Mind* (Simon and Schuster, 1987).

Other quoted material is from selections following.

The Idea of the Postmodern
and Its Critics

Jean-François Lyotard (1926–1998) was born in Versailles and was educated in Paris at the prestigious Lycée Louis le Grand and the University of Paris. After completing his studies, he held a research post with France's National Center for Scientific Research, which (unlike the National Science Foundation [NSF] in the United States) frequently grants research positions to philosophers as well as scientists. He taught at Nanterre, where the events of 1968 are generally said to have started, from 1966 to 1970; he then taught at Vincennes from 1970 to 1972, before teaching at various branches of the University of Paris. At the time of his death in 1998, Lyotard was teaching at Emory University in Atlanta. Lyotard wrote numerous books, including *Economie libidinale* (1974), *Le Différend* (1983), and *Le Postmoderne expliqué aux enfants* (1986)—some of which are translated in excerpted form. He was best known, however, for the 1979 book *The Postmodern Condition*, a work commissioned by the Province of Quebec on the modest topic "A Report on Knowledge." Even though the book is small and parts of it quite straightforward philosophical discourse on discourse, *Postmodern Condition* was an immediate sensation—so much so that it could itself be considered a beginning point in the history of postmodernism, much as Derrida's 1966 lecture was the beginning of poststructuralism. The selection from that book presents Lyotard's most enduring idea—that postmodernity arises with the collapse of the grand narrative of the Enlightenment. This figure of a deflated grand narrative elegantly condenses the idea that modernity was, after all, more a narrative than the Truth; once revealed as such, modernity loses its power. No one has better captured the assumptions and language of postmodernity.

The Postmodern Condition[*]
Jean-François Lyotard (1979)

In contemporary society and culture—postindustrial society, postmodern culture—the question of the legitimation of knowledge is formulated in different terms. The grand narrative has lost its credibility, regardless of what mode of unification it uses, regardless of whether it is a speculative narrative or a narrative of emancipation.

The decline of narrative can be seen as an effect of the blossoming of techniques and technologies since the Second World War, which has shifted emphasis from the ends of action to its means; it can also be seen as an effect of the redeployment of advanced liberal capitalism after its retreat under the protection of Keynesianism during the period 1930–60, a renewal that has eliminated the communist alternative and

[*] From Geoff Bennington and Brian Massumi, trans. *The Postmodern Condition: A Report on Knowledge by Jean-François Lyotard*. (Minnesota: University of Minneapolis Press, 1984 [1979]), pp. 37–41. English translation and Foreword copyright 1984 by the University of Minnesota. French-language edition *La Condition postmoderne* de Jean-François Lyotard, © 1979 by Les Editions de Minuit.

valorized the individual enjoyment of goods and services.

Anytime we go searching for causes in this way we are bound to be disappointed. Even if we adopted one or the other of these hypotheses, we would still have to detail the correlation between the tendencies mentioned and the decline of the unifying and legitimating power of the grand narratives of speculation and emancipation.

It is, of course, understandable that both capitalist renewal and prosperity and the disorienting upsurge of technology would have an impact on the status of knowledge. But in order to understand how contemporary science could have been susceptible to those effects long before they took place, we must first locate the seeds of "delegitimation" and nihilism that were inherent in the grand narratives of the nineteenth century.

First of all, the speculative apparatus maintains an ambiguous relation to knowledge. It shows that knowledge is only worthy of that name to the extent that it reduplicates itself ("lifts itself up," *hebt sich auf*, is sublated) by citing its own statements in a second-level discourse (autonymy) that functions to legitimate them. This is as much as to say that, in its immediacy, denotative discourse bearing on a certain referent (a living organism, a chemical property, a physical phenomenon, etc.) does not really know what it thinks it knows. Positive science is not a form of knowledge. And speculation feeds on its suppression. The Hegelian speculative narrative thus harbors a certain skepticism toward positive learning, as Hegel himself admits.

A science that has not legitimated itself is not a true science; if the discourse that was meant to legitimate it seems to belong to a prescientific form of knowledge, like a "vulgar" narrative, it is demoted to the lowest rank, that of an ideology or instrument of power. And this always happens if the rules of the science game that discourse denounces as empirical are applied to science itself.

Take for example the speculative statement: "A scientific statement is knowledge if and only if it can take its place in a universal process of engendering." The question is: Is this statement knowledge as it itself defines it? Only if it can take its place in a universal process of engendering. Which it can. All it has to do is to presuppose that such a process exists (the Life of spirit) and that it is itself an expression of that process. This presupposition, in fact, is indispensable to the speculative language game. Without

it, the language of legitimation would not be legitimate; it would accompany science in a nosedive into nonsense, at least if we take idealism's word for it.

But this presupposition can also be understood in a totally different sense, one which takes us in the direction of postmodern culture: we could say, in keeping with the perspective we adopted earlier, that this presupposition defines the set of rules one must accept in order to play the speculative game. Such an appraisal assumes first that we accept that the "positive" sciences represent the general mode of knowledge and second, that we understand this language to imply certain formal and axiomatic presuppositions that it must always make explicit. This is exactly what Nietzsche is doing, though with a different terminology, when he shows that "European nihilism" resulted from the truth requirement of science being turned back against itself.

There thus arises an idea of perspective that is not far removed, at least in this respect, from the idea of language games. What we have here is a process of delegitimation fueled by the demand for legitimation itself. The "crisis" of scientific knowledge, signs of which have been accumulating since the end of the nineteenth century, is not born of a chance proliferation of sciences, itself an effect of progress in technology and the expansion of capitalism. It represents, rather, an internal erosion of the legitimacy principle of knowledge. There is erosion at work inside the speculative game, and by loosening the weave of the encyclopedic net in which each science was to find its place, it eventually sets them free.

The classical dividing lines between the various fields of science are thus called into question—disciplines disappear, overlappings occur at the borders between sciences, and from these new territories are born. The speculative hierarchy of learning gives way to an immanent and, as it were, "flat" network of areas of inquiry, the respective frontiers of which are in constant flux. The old "faculties" splinter into institutes and foundations of all kinds, and the universities lose their function of speculative legitimation. Stripped of the responsibility for research (which was stifled by the speculative narrative), they limit themselves to the transmission of what is judged to be established knowledge, and through didactics they guarantee the replication of teachers rather than the production of researchers. This is the state in which Nietzsche finds and condemns them.

The potential for erosion intrinsic to the other legitimation procedure, the emancipation apparatus flowing from the *Aufklärung* [Enlightenment], is no less extensive than the one at work within speculative discourse. But it touches a different aspect. Its distinguishing characteristic is that it grounds the legitimation of science and truth in the autonomy of interlocutors involved in ethical, social, and political praxis. As we have seen, there are immediate problems with this form of legitimation: the difference between a denotative statement with cognitive value and a prescriptive statement with practical value is one of relevance, therefore of competence. There is nothing to prove that if a statement describing a real situation is true, it follows that a prescriptive statement based upon it (the effect of which will necessarily be a modification of that reality) will be just.

Take, for example, a closed door. Between "The door is closed" and "Open the door" there is no relation of consequence as defined in propositional logic. The two statements belong to two autonomous sets of rules defining different kinds of relevance, and therefore of competence. Here, the effect of dividing reason into cognitive or theoretical reason on the one hand, and practical reason on the other, is to attack the legitimacy of the discourse of science. Not directly, but indirectly, by revealing that it is a language game with its own rules (of which the a priori conditions of knowledge in Kant provide a first glimpse) and that it has no special calling to supervise the game of praxis (nor the game of aesthetics, for that matter). The game of science is thus put on a par with the others.

If this "delegitimation" is pursued in the slightest and if its scope is widened (as Wittgenstein does in his own way, and thinkers such as Martin Buber and Emmanuel Lévinas in theirs) the road is then open for an important current of postmodernity: science plays its own game; it is incapable of legitimating the other language games. The game of prescription, for example, escapes it. But above all, it is incapable of legitimating itself, as speculation assumed it could.

The social subject itself seems to dissolve in this dissemination of language games. The social bond is linguistic, but is not woven with a single thread. It is a fabric formed by the intersection of at least two (and in reality an indeterminate number) of language games, obeying different rules. Wittgenstein writes: "Our language can be seen as an ancient city: a maze of little streets and squares, of old and new houses, and of houses with additions from various periods; and this surrounded by a multitude of new boroughs with straight regular streets and uniform houses." And to drive home that the principle of unitotality—or synthesis under the authority of a metadiscourse of knowledge—is inapplicable, he subjects the "town" of language to the old sorites paradox by asking: "how many houses or streets does it take before a town begins to be a town?"

New languages are added to the old ones, forming suburbs of the old town: "the symbolism of chemistry and the notation of the infinitesimal calculus." Thirty-five years later we can add to the list: machine languages, the matrices of game theory, new systems of musical notation, systems of notation for nondenotative forms of logic (temporal logics, deontic logics, modal logics), the language of the genetic code, graphs of phonological structures, and so on.

We may form a pessimistic impression of this splintering: nobody speaks all of those languages, they have no universal metalanguage, the project of the system-subject is a failure, the goal of emancipation has nothing to do with science, we are all stuck in the positivism of this or that discipline of learning, the learned scholars have turned into scientists, the diminished tasks of research have become compartmentalized and no one can master them all. Speculative or humanistic philosophy is forced to relinquish its legitimation duties, which explains why philosophy is facing a crisis wherever it persists in arrogating such functions and is reduced to the study of systems of logic or the history of ideas where it has been realistic enough to surrender them.

Turn-of-the-century Vienna was weaned on this pessimism: not just artists such as Musil, Kraus, Hofmannsthal, Loos, Schönberg, and Broch, but also the philosophers Mach and Wittgenstein. They carried awareness of and theoretical and artistic responsibility for delegitimation as far as it could be taken. We can say today that the mourning process has been completed. There is no need to start all over again. Wittgenstein's strength is that he did not opt for the positivism that was being developed by the Vienna Circle, but outlined in his investigation of language games a kind of legitimation not based on performativity. That is what the postmodern world is all about. Most people have lost the nostalgia for the lost narrative. It in no way follows that they are reduced to barbarity. What saves them from it is their knowledge that legitimation can only spring from their own linguistic practice and communicational interaction. Science "smiling into its beard" at every other belief has taught them the harsh austerity of realism.

Richard Rorty (1931–2007) was born in New York City then educated at Berkeley and Yale (Ph.D. in philosophy, 1956). He taught at Yale, Wellesley, Princeton, and the University of Virginia. Where Lyotard is sometimes opaque, Rorty is satisfyingly clear. Where Lyotard seems to enjoy being a postmodernist, Rorty claims nothing more than that he is a philosopher, explicitly in the modest American tradition of pragmatism. Yet differences aside, Rorty makes clear the full philosophical implications of Lyotard's dead narrative figure. In the selection, from *Contingency, Irony, and Solidarity*, Rorty discusses both his political philosophy and his two most compelling ideas: (1) that there is no longer a final authority to judge the truth of philosophical discourse, and (2) that the Plato-Kant canon is dead, leaving philosophy with literary criticism. Irony, in effect, is the philosophical attitude of postmodernity. This thinking was anticipated in Rorty's important critique of foundationalism in the philosophy of knowledge, *Philosophy and the Mirror of Nature*, which appeared in 1979, the year that Lyotard's book was published. The conjunction of these two books is one of the more or less arbitrary reasons for suggesting that, although postmodernity is an uncertain thing historically, 1979 was the year in which it became clear that the postmodern had to be taken seriously. Ironically, one could argue that neither of the two books is postmodern, strictly speaking. This is the way postmodernism is.

Private Irony and Liberal Hope[*]
Richard Rorty (1989)

All human beings carry about a set of words which they employ to justify their actions, their beliefs, and their lives. These are the words in which we formulate praise of our friends and contempt for our enemies, our long-term projects, our deepest self-doubts and our highest hopes. They are the words in which we tell, sometimes prospectively and sometimes retrospectively, the story of our lives. I shall call these words a person's "final vocabulary."

* Rorty, Richard. *Contingency, Irony, and Solidarity*. (Cambridge University Press, 1989.) pp. 73–74, 79–80, 84–85, 86–87. Print. Copyright © 1989 Cambridge University Press. Reprinted with the permission of Cambridge University Press.

It is "final" in the sense that if doubt is cast on the worth of these words, their user has no noncircular argumentative recourse. Those words are as far as he can go with language; beyond them there is only helpless passivity or a resort to force. A small part of a final vocabulary is made up of thin, flexible, and ubiquitous terms such as "true," "good," "right," and "beautiful." The larger part contains thicker, more rigid, and more parochial terms, for example, "Christ," "England," "professional standards," "decency," "kindness," "the Revolution," "the Church," "progressive," "rigorous," "creative." The more parochial terms do most of the work.

I shall define an "ironist" as someone who fulfills three conditions: (1) She has radical and continuing doubts about the final vocabulary she currently uses, because she has been impressed by other vocabularies, vocabularies taken as final by people or books she has encountered; (2) she realizes that argument phrased in her present vocabulary can neither underwrite nor dissolve these doubts; (3) insofar as she philosophizes about her situation, she does not think that her vocabulary is closer to reality than others, that it is in touch with a power not herself. Ironists who are inclined to philosophize see the choice between vocabularies as made neither within a neutral and universal metavocabulary nor by an attempt to fight one's way past appearances to the real, but simply by playing the new off against the old.

I call people of this sort "ironists" because their realization that anything can be made to look good or bad by being redescribed, and their renunciation of the attempt to formulate criteria of choice between final vocabularies, puts them in the position which Sartre called "meta-stable": never quite able to take themselves seriously because always aware that the terms in which they describe themselves are subject to change, always aware of the contingency and fragility of their final vocabularies, and thus of their selves. Such people take naturally to the line of thought developed in the first two chapters of this book. If they are also liberals—people for whom (to use Judith Shklar's definition) "cruelty is the worst thing they do"—they will take naturally to the views offered in the third chapter.

The opposite of irony is common sense. For that is the watchword of those who unselfconsciously describe everything important in terms of the final vocabulary to which they and those around them are habituated. To be commonsensical is to take for granted that statements formulated in that final vocabulary suffice to describe and judge the beliefs, actions and lives of those who employ alternative final vocabularies. . . .

We ironists treat these people not as anonymous channels for truth but as abbreviations for a certain final vocabulary and for the sorts of beliefs and desires typical of its users. The older Hegel became a name for such a vocabulary, and Kierkegaard and Nietzsche have become names for others. If we are told that the actual lives such men lived had little to do with the books and the terminology which attracted our attention to them, we brush this aside. We treat the names of such people as the names of the heroes of their own books. We do not bother to distinguish Swift from *saeva indignatio*, Hegel from Geist, Nietzsche from Zarathustra, Marcel Proust from Marcel the narrator, or Trilling from *The Liberal Imagination*. We do not care whether these writers managed to live up to their own self-images. What we want to know is whether to adopt those images—to re-create ourselves, in whole or in part, in these people's image. We go about answering this question by experimenting with the vocabularies which these people concocted. We redescribe ourselves, our situation, our past, in those terms and compare the results with alternative redescriptions which use the vocabularies of alternative figures. We ironists hope, by this continual redescription, to make the best selves for ourselves that we can.

Such comparison, such playing off of figures against each other, is the principal activity now covered by the term "literary criticism." Influential critics, the sort of critics who propose new canons—people like Arnold, Pater, Leavis, Eliot, Edmund Wilson, Lionel Trilling, Frank Kermode, Harold Bloom—are not in the business of explaining the real meaning of books, nor of evaluating something called their "literary merit." Rather, they spend their time placing books in the context of other books, figures in the context of other figures. This placing is done in the same way as we place a new friend or enemy in the context of old friends and enemies. In the course of doing so, we revise our opinions of both the old and the new. Simultaneously, we revise our own moral identity by revising our own final vocabulary. Literary criticism does for ironists what the search for universal moral principles is supposed to do for metaphysicians.

For us ironists, nothing can serve as a criticism of a final vocabulary save another such vocabulary; there is no answer to a redescription save a re-re-redescription. Since there is nothing beyond vocabularies which serves as a criterion of choice between them, criticism is a matter of looking on this picture and on that, not of comparing both pictures with the original. Nothing can serve as a criticism of a person save another person, or of a culture save an alternative culture—for persons and cultures are, for us, incarnated vocabularies. So our doubts about our own characters or our own culture can be resolved or assuaged only by enlarging our acquaintance. The easiest way of doing that is to read books, and so ironists spend more of their time placing books than in placing real live people. Ironists are afraid that they will get stuck in the vocabulary in which they were brought up if they only know the people in their own neighborhood, so they try to get acquainted with strange people (Alcibiades, Julien Sorel), strange families (the Karamazovs, the Casaubons), and strange communities (the Teutonic Knights, the Nuer, the mandarins of the Sung). . . .

The social glue holding together the ideal liberal society described in the previous chapter consists in little more than a consensus that the point of social organization is to let everybody have a chance at self-creation to the best of his or her abilities, and that that goal requires, besides peace and wealth, the standard "bourgeois freedoms." This conviction would not be based on a view about universally shared human ends, human rights, the nature of rationality, the Good for Man, nor anything else. It would be a conviction based on nothing more profound than the historical facts which suggest that without the protection of something like the institutions of bourgeois liberal society, people will be less able to work out their private salvations, create their private self-images, reweave their webs of belief and desire in the light of whatever new people and books they happen to encounter. In such an ideal society, discussion of public affairs will revolve around (1) how to balance the needs for peace, wealth, and freedom when conditions require that one of these goals be sacrificed to one of the others and (2) how to equalize opportunities for self-creation and then leave people alone to use, or neglect, their opportunities.

The suggestion that this is all the social glue liberal societies need is subject to two main objections. The first is that as a practical matter, this glue is just not thick enough—that the (predominantly) metaphysical rhetoric of public life in the democracies is essential to the continuation of free institutions. The second is that it is psychologically impossible to be a liberal ironist—to be someone for whom "cruelty is the worst thing we do," and to have no metaphysical beliefs about what all human beings have in common. . . .

If you tell someone whose life is given meaning by this hope that philosophers are waxing ironic over real essence, the objectivity of truth, and the existence of an ahistorical human nature, you are unlikely to arouse much interest, much less do any damage. The idea that liberal societies are bound together by philosophical beliefs seems to me ludicrous. What binds societies together are common vocabularies and common hopes. The vocabularies are, typically, parasitic on the hopes—in the sense that the principal function of the vocabularies is to tell stories about future outcomes which compensate for present sacrifices.

Modern, literate, secular societies depend on the existence of reasonably concrete, optimistic, and plausible *political* scenarios, as opposed to scenarios about redemption beyond the grave. To retain social hope, members of such a society need to be able to tell themselves a story about how things might get better, and to see no insuperable obstacles to this story's coming true. If social hope has become harder lately, this is not because the clerks have been committing treason but because, since the end of World War II, the course of events has made it harder to tell a convincing story of this sort. The cynical and impregnable Soviet Empire, the continuing shortsightedness and greed of the surviving democracies, and the exploding, starving populations of the Southern Hemisphere make the problems our parents faced in the 1930s—Fascism and unemployment—look almost manageable. People who try to update and rewrite the standard social democratic scenario about human equality, the scenario which their grandparents wrote around the turn of the century, are not having much success. The problems which metaphysically inclined social thinkers believe to be caused by our failure to find the right sort of theoretical glue—a philosophy which can command wide assent in an individualistic and pluralistic society—are, I think, caused by a set of historical contingencies. These contingencies are making it easy to see the last few hundred years of European and American history—centuries of increasing public hope and private ironism—as an island in time, surrounded by misery, tyranny, and chaos. As Orwell put it, "The democratic vistas seem to end in barbed wire." . . .

In the ideal liberal society, the intellectuals would still be ironists, although the nonintellectuals would not. The latter would, however, be commonsensically nominalist and historicist. So they would see themselves as contingent through and through, without feeling any particular doubts about the contingencies they happened to be. They would not be bookish, nor would they look to literary critics as moral advisers. But they would be commonsensical nonmetaphysicians, in the way in which more and more people in the rich democracies have been commonsensical nontheists. They would feel no more need to answer the questions "*Why* are you a liberal? Why do you care about the humiliation of strangers?" than the average sixteenth-century Christian felt to answer the question "Why are you a Christian?" or than most people nowadays feel to answer the question "Are you saved?" Such a person would not need a justification for her sense of human solidarity, for she was not raised to play the language game in which one asks and gets justifications for that sort of belief. Her culture is one in which doubts about the public rhetoric of the culture are met not by Socratic requests for definitions and principles, but by Deweyan requests for concrete alternatives and programs. Such a culture could, as far as I can see, be every bit as self-critical and every bit as devoted to human equality as our own familiar, and still metaphysical, liberal culture—if not more so.

Michel Foucault (1926–1984), near the end of his life, took on a major, four-volume study of the history of sexuality. The selection is from the first volume, a theoretical introduction to the larger project. Published in 1976, it represents an excellent summary of his social theory of power/knowledge in modernity. Soon, however, he had misgivings about the original plan for the sexuality series, leading to a complete revision of his thinking on the subject. At the time of his death in 1984, two of the remaining three volumes were complete (*The Uses of Pleasure* and *The Care of the Soul*), but the project was left open. Throughout his life, Foucault explored the various ways in which political power was subtly invested in the mechanisms of knowledge in the modern world. His studies of sexuality make him a classic source for the history and social theory of sexualities, just as his earlier work had established his importance in other historical fields—penality, medicine, science, madness; and his posthumous writings sketched an enormously important theory of social control and bio-politics which in their way suggestion a convergence with the thinking of his friend Gilles Deleuze whose ideas are represented in Part Six. Yet, at the foundation of all this work there is to be found some reflection of his idea of power-knowledge.

Power as Knowledge[*]
Michel Foucault (1976)

Hence the objective is to analyze a certain form of knowledge regarding sex, not in terms of repression or law, but in terms of power. But the word *power* is apt to lead to a number of misunderstandings—misunderstandings with respect to its nature, its form, and its unity. By power, I do not mean "Power" as a group of institutions and mechanisms that ensure the subservience of the citizens of a given state. By power, I do not mean, either, a mode of subjugation which, in contrast to violence, has the form of the rule. Finally, I do not have in mind a general system of domination exerted by one group over another, a system whose effects, through successive derivations, pervade the entire social body. The analysis, made in terms of power, must not assume that the sovereignty of the state, the form of the law, or the overall unity of a domination are given at the outset; rather, these are only the terminal forms power takes. It seems to me that power must be understood in the first instance as the multiplicity of force relations immanent in the sphere in which they operate and which constitute their own organization; as the process which, through ceaseless struggles and confrontations, transforms, strengthens, or reverses them; as the support which these force relations find in one another, thus forming a chain or a system, or on the contrary, the disjunctions and contradictions which isolate them from one another; and lastly, as the strategies in which they take effect, whose general design or institutional crystallization is embodied in the state apparatus, in the formulation of the law, in the various social hegemonies. Power's condition of possibility, or in any case the viewpoint which permits one to understand its exercise, even in its more "peripheral" effects, and which also makes it possible to use its mechanisms as a grid of intelligibility of the social order, must not be sought in the primary existence of a central power, in a unique source of sovereignty from which secondary and descendent forms would emanate; it is the moving substrate of force relations which, by virtue of their inequality, constantly engender states of power, but the latter are always local and unstable. The omnipresence of power: not because it has the privilege of consolidating everything under its invincible unity, but because

it is produced from one moment to the next, at every point, or rather in every relation from one point to another. Power is everywhere; not because it embraces everything, but because it comes from everywhere. And "Power," insofar as it is permanent, repetitious, inert, and self-reproducing, is simply the over-all effect that emerges from all these mobilities, the concatenation that rests on each of them and seeks in turn to arrest their movement. One needs to be nominalistic, no doubt: power is not an institution, and not a structure; neither is it a certain strength we are endowed with; it is the name that one attributes to a complex strategical situation in a particular society.

Should we turn the expression around, then, and say that politics is war pursued by other means? If we still wish to maintain a separation between war and politics, perhaps we should postulate rather that this multiplicity of force relations can be coded—in part but never totally—either in the form of "war," or in the form of "politics"; this would imply two different strategies (but the one always liable to switch into the other) for integrating these unbalanced, heterogeneous, unstable, and tense force relations.

Continuing this line of discussion, we can advance a certain number of propositions:

Power is not something that is acquired, seized, or shared, something that one holds on to or allows to slip away; power is exercised from innumerable points, in the interplay of nonegalitarian and mobile relations.

Relations of power are not in a position of exteriority with respect to other types of relationships (economic processes, knowledge relationships, sexual relations), but are immanent in the latter; they are the immediate effects of the divisions, inequalities, and disequilibriums which occur in the latter, and conversely they are the internal conditions of these differentiations; relations of power are not in superstructural positions, with merely a role of prohibition or accompaniment; they have a directly productive role, wherever they come into play.

Power comes from below; that is, there is no binary and all-encompassing opposition between rulers and ruled at the root of power relations, and serving as a general matrix—no such duality extending from the top down and reacting on more and more limited groups to the very depths of the social body. One must suppose rather that the manifold relationships of force that take shape and come into play in the machinery of production, in families, limited groups, and institutions, are the basis for

[*]THE HISTORY OF SEXUALITY by Michel Foucault. Originally published in French as *La Volonté du Savoir.* Copyright © 1976 by Editions Gallimard. Reprinted by permission of Georges Borchardt, Inc., for Editions Gallimard.

wide-ranging effects of cleavage that run through the social body as a whole. These then form a general line of force that traverses the local oppositions and links them together; to be sure, they also bring about redistributions, realignments, homogenizations, serial arrangements, and convergences of the force relations. Major dominations are the hegemonic effects that are sustained by all these confrontations.

Power relations are both intentional and nonsubjective. If in fact they are intelligible, this is not because they are the effect of another instance that "explains" them, but rather because they are imbued, through and through, with calculation: there is no power that is exercised without a series of aims and objectives. But this does not mean that it results from the choice or decision of an individual subject; let us not look for the headquarters that presides over its rationality; neither the caste which governs, nor the groups which control the state apparatus, nor those who make the most important economic decisions direct the entire network of power that functions in a society (and makes *it* function); the rationality of power is characterized by tactics that are often quite explicit at the restricted level where they are inscribed (the local cynicism of power), tactics which, becoming connected to one another, attracting and propagating one another, but finding their base of support and their condition elsewhere, end by forming comprehensive systems: the logic is perfectly clear, the aims decipherable, and yet it is often the case that no one is there to have invented them, and few who can be said to have formulated them: an implicit characteristic of the great anonymous, almost unspoken strategies which coordinate the loquacious tactics whose "inventors" or decision-makers are often without hypocrisy.

Where there is power, there is resistance, and yet, or rather consequently, this resistance is never in a position of exteriority in relation to power. Should it be said that one is always "inside" power, there is no "escaping" it, there is no absolute outside where it is concerned, because one is subject to the law in any case? Or that, history being the ruse of reason, power is the ruse of history, always emerging the winner? This would be to misunderstand the strictly relational character of power relationships. Their existence depends on a multiplicity of points of resistance: these play the role of adversary, target, support, or handle in power relations. These points of resistance are present everywhere in the power network. Hence there is no single locus of great

Refusal, no soul of revolt, source of all rebellions, or pure law of the revolutionary. Instead there is a plurality of resistances, each of them a special case: resistances that are possible, necessary, improbable; others that are spontaneous, savage, solitary, concerted, rampant, or violent; still others that are quick to compromise, interested, or sacrificial; by definition, they can only exist in the strategic field of power relations. But this does not mean that they are only a reaction or rebound, forming with respect to the basic domination an underside that is in the end always passive, doomed to perpetual defeat. Resistances do not derive from a few heterogeneous principles; but neither are they a lure or a promise that is of necessity betrayed. They are the odd term in relations of power; they are inscribed in the latter as an irreducible opposite. Hence they too are distributed in irregular fashion; the points, knots, or focuses of resistance are spread over time and space at varying densities, at times mobilizing groups or individuals in a definitive way, inflaming certain points of the body, certain moments in life, certain types of behavior. Are there no great radical ruptures, massive binary divisions, then? Occasionally, yes. But more often one is dealing with mobile and transitory points of resistance, producing cleavages in a society that shift about, fracturing unities and effecting regroupings, furrowing across individuals themselves, cutting them up and remolding them, marking off irreducible regions in them, in their bodies and minds. Just as the network of power relations ends by forming a dense web that passes through apparatuses and institutions, without being exactly localized in them, so too the swarm of points of resistance traverses social stratifications and individual unities. And it is doubtless the strategic codification of these points of resistance that makes a revolution possible, somewhat similar to the way in which the state relies on the institutional integration of power relationships.

It is in this sphere of force relations that we must try to analyze the mechanisms of power. In this way we will escape from the system of Law-and-Sovereign which has captivated political thought for such a long time. And if it is true that Machiavelli was among the few—and this no doubt was the scandal of his "cynicism"—who conceived the power of the Prince in terms of force relationships, perhaps we need to go one step further, do without the persona of the Prince, and decipher power mechanisms on the basis of a strategy that is immanent in force relationships.

To return to sex and the discourses of truth that have taken charge of it, the question that we must address, then, is not: Given a specific state structure, how and why is it that power needs to establish a knowledge of sex? Neither is the question: What over-all domination was served by the concern, evidenced since the eighteenth century, to produce true discourses on sex? Nor is it: What law presided over both the regularity of sexual behavior and the conformity of what was said about it? It is rather: In a specific type of discourse on sex, in a specific form of extortion of truth, appearing historically and in specific places (around the child's body, apropos of women's sex, in connection with practices restricting births, and so on), what were the most immediate, the most local power relations at work? How did they make possible these kinds of discourses, and conversely, how were these discourses used to support power relations: How was the action of these power relations modified by their very exercise, entailing a strengthening of some terms and a weakening of others, with effects of resistance and counterinvestments, so that there has never existed one type of stable subjugation, given once and for all? How were these power relations linked to one another according to the logic of a great strategy, which in retrospect takes on the aspect of a unitary and voluntarist politics of sex? In general terms: rather than referring all the infinitesimal violences that are exerted on sex, all the anxious gazes that are directed at it, and all the hiding places whose discovery is made into an impossible task, to the unique form of a great Power, we must immerse the expanding production of discourses on sex in the field of multiple and mobile power relations.

Which leads us to advance, in a preliminary way, four rules to follow. But these are not intended as methodological imperatives; at most they are cautionary prescriptions.

Rule of Immanence

One must not suppose that there exists a certain sphere of sexuality that would be the legitimate concern of a free and disinterested scientific inquiry were it not the object of mechanisms of prohibition brought to bear by the economic or ideological requirements of power. If sexuality was constituted as an area of investigation, this was only because relations of power had established it as a possible object; and conversely, if power was able to take it as a target, this was because techniques of knowledge and procedures of discourse were capable of investing it. Between techniques of knowledge and strategies of power, there is no exteriority, even if they have specific roles and are linked together on the basis of their difference. We will start, therefore, from what might be called "local centers" of power-knowledge: for example, the relations that obtain between penitents and confessors, or the faithful and their directors of conscience. Here, guided by the theme of the "flesh" that must be mastered, different forms of discourse—self-examination, questionings, admissions, interpretations, interviews—were the vehicle of a kind of incessant back-and-forth movement of forms of subjugation and schemas of knowledge. Similarly, the body of the child, under surveillance, surrounded in his cradle, his bed, or his room by an entire watch-crew of parents, nurses, servants, educators, and doctors, all attentive to the least manifestations of his sex, has constituted, particularly since the eighteenth century, another "local center" of power-knowledge.

Rules of Continual Variations

We must not look for who has the power in the order of sexuality (men, adults, parents, doctors) and who is deprived of it (women, adolescents, children, patients); nor for who has the right to know and who is forced to remain ignorant. We must seek rather the pattern of the modifications which the relationships of force imply by the very nature of their process. The "distributions of power" and the "appropriations of knowledge" never represent only instantaneous slices taken from processes involving, for example, a cumulative reinforcement of the strongest factor, or a reversal of relationship, or again, a simultaneous increase of two terms. Relations of power-knowledge are not static forms of distribution, they are "matrices of transformations." The nineteenth-century grouping made up of the father, the mother, the educator, and the doctor, around the child and his sex, was subjected to constant modifications, continual shifts. One of the more spectacular results of the latter was a strange reversal: whereas to begin with the child's sexuality had been problematized within the relationship established between doctor and parents (in the form of advice, or recommendations to keep the child under observation, or warnings of future dangers), ultimately it was in the relationship of the psychiatrist to the child that the sexuality of adults themselves was called into question.

Rule of Double Conditioning

No "local center," no "pattern of transformation" could function if, through a series of sequences, it did not eventually enter into an over-all strategy. And inversely, no strategy could achieve comprehensive effects if it did not gain support from precise and tenuous relations serving, not as its point of application or final outcome, but as its prop and anchor point. There is no discontinuity between them, as if one were dealing with two different levels (one microscopic and the other macroscopic); but neither is there homogeneity (as if the one were only the enlarged projection or the miniaturization of the other); rather, one must conceive of the double conditioning of a strategy by the specificity of possible tactics, and of tactics by the strategic envelope that makes them work. Thus the father in the family is not the "representative" of the sovereign or the state; and the latter are not projections of the father on a different scale. The family does not duplicate society, just as society does not imitate the family. But the family organization, precisely to the extent that it was insular and heteromorphous with respect to the other power mechanisms, was used to support the great "maneuvers" employed for the Malthusian control of the birthrate, for the populationist incitements, for the medicalization of sex and the psychiatrization of its nongenital forms.

Rule of the Tactical Polyvalence of Discourses

What is said about sex must not be analyzed simply as the surface of projection of these power mechanisms. Indeed, it is in discourse that power and knowledge are joined together. And for this very reason, we must conceive discourse as a series of discontinuous segments whose tactical function is neither uniform nor stable. To be more precise, we must not imagine a world of discourse divided between accepted discourse and excluded discourse, or between the dominant discourse and the dominated one; but as a multiplicity of discursive elements that can come into play in various strategies. It is this distribution that we must reconstruct, with the things said and those concealed, the enunciations required and those forbidden, that it comprises; with the variants and different effects—according to who is speaking, his position of power, the institutional context in which he happens to be situated—that it implies; and with the shifts and reutilizations

of identical formulas for contrary objectives that it also includes. Discourses are not once and for all subservient to power or raised up against it, any more than silences are. We must make allowance for the complex and unstable process whereby discourse can be both an instrument and an effect of power, but also a hindrance, a stumbling-block, a point of resistance and a starting point for an opposing strategy. Discourse transmits and produces power; it reinforces it, but also undermines and exposes it, renders it fragile and makes it possible to thwart it. In like manner, silence and secrecy are a shelter for power, anchoring its prohibitions; but they also loosen its holds and provide for relatively obscure areas of tolerance. Consider for example the history of what was once "the" great sin against nature. The extreme discretion of the texts dealing with sodomy—that utterly confused category—and the nearly universal reticence in talking about it made possible a twofold operation: on the one hand, there was an extreme severity (punishment by fire was meted out well into the eighteenth century, without there being any substantial protest expressed before the middle of the century), and on the other hand, a tolerance that must have been widespread (which one can deduce indirectly from the infrequency of judicial sentences, and which one glimpses more directly through certain statements concerning societies of men that were thought to exist in the army or in the courts). There is no question that the appearance in nineteenth-century psychiatry, jurisprudence, and literature of a whole series of discourses on the species and subspecies of homosexuality, inversion, pederasty, and "psychic hermaphrodism" made possible a strong advance of social controls into this area of "perversity"; but it also made possible the formation of a "reverse" discourse: homosexuality began to speak in its own behalf, to demand that its legitimacy or "naturality" be acknowledged, often in the same vocabulary, using the same categories by which it was medically disqualified. There is not, on the one side, a discourse of power, and opposite it, another discourse that runs counter to it. Discourses are tactical elements or blocks operating in the field of force relations; there can exist different and even contradictory discourses within the same strategy; they can, on the contrary, circulate without changing their form from one strategy to another, opposing strategy. We must not expect the discourses on sex to tell us, above all, what strategy they derive from, or what moral divisions they accompany, or what ideology—dominant or dominated—

they represent; rather we must question them on the two levels of their tactical productivity (what reciprocal effects of power and knowledge they ensure) and their strategical integration (what conjunction and what force relationship make their utilization necessary in a given episode of the various confrontations that occur).

In short, it is a question of orienting ourselves to a conception of power which replaces the privilege of the law with the viewpoint of the objective, the privilege of prohibition with the viewpoint of tactical efficacy, the privilege of sovereignty with the analysis of a multiple and mobile field of force relations, wherein far-reaching, but never completely stable, effects of domination are produced. The strategical model, rather than the model based on law. And this, not out of a speculative choice or theoretical preference, but because in fact it is one of the essential traits of Western societies that the force relationships which for a long time had found expression in war, in every form of warfare, gradually became invested in the order of political power.

Jean Baudrillard (1929–2007) was one of France's most flamboyant social commentators and intellectuals in the fashion that dominated in Paris in the 1960s and 1970s. His explorations of the social reality of simulated worlds, like Disneyland, lead some to dismiss him. Yet his writing, like the selection on simulacra, is deadly serious in an ironic way. Baudrillard, perhaps the most representative of the postmodern cultural leftists, argued (as he does in the selection) that the line between reality and simulation is false. By implication, only modernity maintained the distinction; by inference, today's world has erased it, both in philosophy and, so to speak, in "reality." Baudrillard's early writings, in the years following 1968, were much more in the tradition of Marxism. At that point, Baudrillard was primarily concerned with developing a social theory of mass society based on Marx and Saussure—a critique of political economy and a semiotics. To this day, his *For a Critique of Political Economy* (1972) is rightly considered the most perspicacious interpretation of the close similarity of Marx's and Saussure's theories of social values. In this early period, he also wrote *The System of Objects* (1968) and *Consumer Society* (1970). The selection is obviously from a later period, when Baudrillard had left behind all visible traces of Marxism and his interest in semiotics had been fully transformed into a general, discursive theory of culture. *Cool Memories* (1987) is also from this later phase.

Simulacra and Simulations: Disneyland*
Jean Baudrillard (1983)

> The simulacrum is never that which conceals the truth—it is the truth which conceals that there is none.
> The simulacrum is true.
> —Ecclesiastes

If we were able to take as the finest allegory of simulation the Borges tale where the cartographers of the Empire draw up a map so detailed that it ends up exactly covering the territory (but where, with the decline of the Empire this map becomes frayed and finally ruined, a few shreds still discernible in the deserts—the metaphysical beauty of this ruined abstraction, bearing witness to an imperial pride and rotting like a carcass, returning to the substance of the soil, rather as an aging double ends up being confused with the real thing), this fable would then have come full circle for us, and now has nothing but the discrete charm of second-order simulacra.

Abstraction today is no longer that of the map, the double, the mirror or the concept. Simulation is no longer that of a territory, a referential being or a substance. It is the generation by models of a real without origin or reality: a hyperreal. The territory no longer precedes the map, nor survives it. Henceforth, it is the map that precedes the territory—*precession of simulacra*—it is the map that engenders the territory and if we were to revive the fable today, it would be the territory whose shreds are slowly rotting across the map. It is the real, and not the map, whose vestiges subsist here and there, in the deserts which are no longer those of the Empire, but our own. *The desert of the real itself.*

In fact, even inverted, the fable is useless. Perhaps only the allegory of the Empire remains. For it is with the same imperialism that present-day simulators try to make the real, all the real, coincide with their simulation models. But it is no longer a question of either maps or territory. Something has

*Baudrillard, Jean. *Simulacra and Simulations*. (Brooklyn, NY: Semitotext(e), 1983) pp. 1–13, 23–49. Copyright © 1983 by Semiotext(e). Used by permission of the publisher: http://www.semiotexte.com

disappeared: the sovereign difference between them that was the abstraction's charm. For it is the difference which forms the poetry of the map and the charm of the territory, the magic of the concept and the charm of the real. This representational imaginary, which both culminates in and is engulfed by the cartographer's mad project of an ideal coextensivity between the map and the territory, disappears with simulation, whose operation is nuclear and genetic, and no longer specular and discursive. With it goes all of metaphysics. No more mirror of being and appearances, of the real and its concept; no more imaginary coextensivity: rather, genetic miniaturization is the dimension of simulation. The real is produced from miniaturized units, from matrices, memory banks and command models—and with these it can be reproduced an indefinite number of times. It no longer has to be rational, since it is no longer measured against some ideal or negative instance. It is nothing more than operational. In fact, since it is no longer enveloped by an imaginary, it is no longer real at all. It is a hyperreal: the product of an irradiating synthesis of combinatory models in a hyperspace without atmosphere.

In this passage to a space whose curvature is no longer that of the real, nor of truth, the age of simulation thus begins with a liquidation of all referentials—worse: by their artificial resurrection in systems of signs, which are a more ductile material than meaning, in that they lend themselves to all systems of equivalence, all binary oppositions and all combinatory algebra. It is no longer a question of imitation, nor of reduplication, nor even of parody. It is rather a question of substituting signs of the real for the real itself; that is, an operation to deter every real process by its operational double, a metastable, programmatic, perfect descriptive machine which provides all the signs of the real and short-circuits all its vicissitudes. Never again will the real have to be produced: this is the vital function of the model in a system of death, or rather of anticipated resurrection which no longer leaves any chance even in the event of death. A hyperreal henceforth sheltered from the imaginary, and from any distinction between the real and the imaginary, leaving room only for the orbital recurrence of models and the simulated generation of difference.

The Divine Irreference of Images

To dissimulate is to feign not to have what one has. To simulate is to feign to have what one hasn't. One implies a presence, the other an absence. But the matter is more complicated, since to simulate is not simply to feign: "Someone who feigns an illness can simply go to bed and pretend he is ill. Someone who simulates an illness produces in himself some of the symptoms" (Littré). Thus, feigning or dissimulating leaves the reality principle intact: the difference is always clear, it is only masked; whereas simulation threatens the difference between "true" and "false," between "real" and "imaginary." Since the simulator produces "true" symptoms, is he or she ill or not? The simulator cannot be treated objectively either as ill, or as not ill. Psychology and medicine stop at this point, before a thereafter undiscoverable truth of the illness. For if any symptom can be "produced," and can no longer be accepted as a fact of nature, then every illness may be considered as simulatable and simulated, and medicine loses its meaning since it only knows how to treat "true" illnesses by their objective causes. Psychosomatics evolves in a dubious way on the edge of the illness principle. As for psychoanalysis, it transfers the symptom from the organic to the unconscious order: once again, the latter is held to be real, more real than the former; but why should simulation stop at the portals of the unconscious? Why couldn't the "work" of the unconscious be "produced" in the same way as any other symptom in classical medicine? Dreams already are.

The alienist, of course, claims that "for each form of the mental alienation there is a particular order in the succession of symptoms, of which the simulator is unaware and in the absence of which the alienist is unlikely to be deceived." This (which dates from 1865) in order to save at all cost the truth principle, and to escape the specter raised by simulation: namely that truth, reference and objective causes have ceased to exist. What can medicine do with something which floats on either side of illness, on either side of health, or with the reduplication of illness in a discourse that is no longer true or false? What can psychoanalysis do with the reduplication of the discourse of the unconscious in a discourse of simulation that can never be unmasked, since it isn't false either?

What can the army do with simulators? Traditionally, following a direct principle of identification, it unmasks and punishes them. Today, it can reform an excellent simulator as though he were equivalent to a "real" homosexual, heart-case or lunatic. Even military psychology retreats from the Cartesian clarities and hesitates to draw the distinction between true and false, between the "produced" symptom and the authentic symptom. "If he acts crazy so well, then he must be mad." Nor is it mistaken: in the sense that all lunatics are simulators, and this lack of distinction is the worst form of subversion. Against it, classical reason armed itself with all its categories. But it is this today which again outflanks them, submerging the truth principle.

Outside of medicine and the army, favored terrains of simulation, the affair goes back to religion and the simulacrum of divinity: "I forbade any simulacrum in the temples because the divinity that breathes life into nature cannot be represented." Indeed it can. But what becomes of the divinity when it reveals itself in icons, when it is multiplied in sumulacra? Does it remain the supreme authority, simply incarnated in images as a visible theology? Or is it volatilized into simulacra which alone deploy their pomp and power of fascination—the visible machinery of icons being substituted for the pure and intelligible Idea of God? This is precisely what was feared by the Iconoclasts, whose millennial quarrel is still with us today. Their rage to destroy images rose precisely because they sensed this omnipotence of simulacra, this facility they have of erasing God from the consciousnesses of people, and the overwhelming, destructive truth which they suggest: that ultimately there has never been any God; that only simulacra exist; indeed that God himself has only ever been his own simulacrum. Had they been able to believe that images only occulted or masked the Platonic idea of God, there would have been no reason to destroy them. One can live with the idea of a distorted truth. But their metaphysical despair came from the idea that the images concealed nothing at all, and that in fact they were not images, such as the original model would have made them, but actually perfect simulacra forever radiant with their own fascination. But this death of the divine referential has to be exorcised at all cost.

It can be seen that the iconoclasts, who are often accused of despising and denying images, were in fact the ones who accorded them their actual worth, unlike the iconolaters, who saw in them only reflections and were content to venerate God at one remove. But the converse can also be said, namely that the iconolaters possessed the most modern and adventurous minds, since, underneath the idea of the apparition of God in the mirror of images, they already enacted his death and his disappearance in the epiphany of his representations (which they perhaps knew no longer represented anything, and that they were purely a game, but that this was precisely the greatest game—knowing also that it is dangerous to unmask images, since they dissimulate the fact that there is nothing behind them).

This was the approach of the Jesuits, who based their politics on the virtual disappearance of God and on the worldly and spectacular manipulation of consciences—the evanescence of God in the epiphany of power—the end of transcendence, which no longer serves as alibi for a strategy completely free of influences and signs. Behind the baroque of images hides the grey eminence of politics.

Thus perhaps at stake has always been the murderous capacity of images: murderers of the real; murderers of their own model as the Byzantine icons could murder the divine identity. To this murderous capacity is opposed the dialectical capacity of representations as a visible and intelligible mediation of the real. All of Western faith and good faith was engaged in this wager on representation: that a sign could refer to the depth of meaning, that a sign could *exchange* for meaning and that something could guarantee this exchange—God, of course. But what if God himself can be simulated, that is to say, reduced to the signs which attest his existence? Then the whole system becomes weightless; it is no longer anything but a gigantic simulacrum: not unreal, but a simulacrum, never again exchanging for what is real, but exchanging in itself, in an uninterrupted circuit without reference or circumference.

So it is with simulation, insofar as it is opposed to representation. Representation starts from the principle that the sign and the real are equivalent (even if this equivalence is Utopian, it is a fundamental axiom). Conversely, simulation starts from the Utopia of this principle of equivalence, *from the radical negation of the sign as value*, from the sign as reversion and death sentence of every reference. Whereas representation tries to absorb simulation by interpreting it as false representation, simulation envelops the whole edifice of representation as itself a simulacrum.

These would be the successive phases of the image:

1. It is the reflection of a basic reality.
2. It masks and perverts a basic reality.
3. It masks the *absence* of a basic reality.
4. It bears no relation to any reality whatever: it is its own pure simulacrum.

In the first case, the image is a *good* appearance: the representation is of the order of sacrament. In the second, it is an *evil* appearance: of the order of male-fice. In the third, it *plays at being* an appearance: it is of the order of sorcery. In the fourth, it is no longer in the order of appearance at all, but of simulation.

The transition from signs which dissimulate something to signs which dissimulate that there is nothing, marks the decisive turning point. The first implies a theology of truth and secrecy (to which the notion of ideology still belongs). The second inaugurates an age of simulacra and simulation, in which there is no longer any God to recognize his own, nor any last judgement to separate truth from false, the real from its artificial resurrection, since everything is already dead and risen in advance.

When the real is no longer what it used to be, nostalgia assumes its full meaning. There is a proliferation of myths of origin and signs of reality; of second-hand truth, objectivity and authenticity. There is an escalation of the true, of the lived experience; a resurrection of the figurative where the object and substance have disappeared. And there is a panic-stricken production of the real and the referential, above and parallel to the panic of material production. This is how simulation appears in the phase that concerns us: a strategy of the real, neo-real and hyperreal, whose universal double is a strategy of deterrence.

Hyperreal and Imaginary

Disneyland is a perfect model of all the entangled orders of simulation. To begin with it is a play of illusions and phantasms: pirates, the frontier, future world, etc. This imaginary world is supposed to be what makes the operation successful. But, what draws the crowds is undoubtedly much more the social microcosm, the miniaturized and *religious* revelling in real America, in its delights and drawbacks. You park outside, queue up inside, and are totally abandoned at the exit. In this imaginary world the only phantasmagoria is in the inherent warmth and affection of the crowd, and in that sufficiently excessive number of gadgets used there to specifically maintain the multitudinous affect. The contrast with the absolute solitude of the parking lot—a veritable concentration camp—is total. Or rather: inside, a whole range of gadgets magnetize the crowd into direct flows; outside, solitude is directed onto a single gadget: the automobile. By an extraordinary coincidence (one that undoubtedly belongs to the peculiar enchantment of this universe), this deep-frozen infantile world happens to have been conceived and realized by a man who is himself now cryogenized; Walt Disney, who awaits his resurrection at minus 180 degrees centigrade.

The objective profile of the United States, then, may be traced throughout Disneyland, even down to the morphology of individuals and the crowd. All its values are exalted here, in miniature and comic-strip form. Embalmed and pacified. Whence the possibility of an ideological analysis of Disneyland: . . . digest of the American way of life, panegyric to American values, idealized transposition of a contradictory reality. To be sure. But this conceals something else, and that "ideological" blanket exactly serves to cover over a *third-order simulation*: Disneyland is there to conceal the fact that it is the "real" country, all of "real" America, which *is* Disneyland (just as prisons are there to conceal the fact that it is the social in its entirety, in its banal omnipotence, which is carceral). Disneyland is presented as imaginary in order to make us believe that the rest is real, when in fact all of Los Angeles and the America surrounding it are no longer real, but of the order of the hyperreal and of simulation. It is no longer a question of a false representation of reality (ideology), but of concealing the fact that the real is no longer real, and thus of saving the reality principle.

The Disneyland imaginary is neither true nor false: it is a deterrence machine set up in order to rejuvenate in reverse the fiction of the real. Whence the debility, the infantile degeneration of this imaginary. It is meant to be an infantile world, in order to make us believe that the adults are elsewhere, in the "real" world, and to conceal the fact that real childishness is everywhere, particularly among those adults who go there to act the child in order to foster illusions of their real childishness.

Moreover, Disneyland is not the only one. Enchanted Village, Magic Mountain, Marine World: Los Angeles is encircled by these "imaginary stations" which feed reality, reality-energy, to a town whose mystery is precisely that it is nothing more than a network of endless, unreal circulation: a town of fabulous proportions, but without space or dimensions. As much as electrical and nuclear power stations, as much as film studios, this town, which is nothing more than an immense script and a perpetual motion picture, needs this old imaginary made up of childhood signals and faked phantasms for its sympathetic nervous system.

Arlene Stein (1959–) graduated from Amherst College in 1980 and the University of California Berkeley where she took her PhD in 1993. She taught at the University of Essex and the University of Oregon before joining the Sociology Department at Rutgers. Among her many notable writings are *Stranger Next Door* (2001) and *Shameless* (2006).

Ken Plummer (1946–) was born in London. He is a sociologist who taught for thirty years at the University of Essex from which he retired in 2005 to undergo a liver transplant. He is known the world over for his writings on sexuality, intimate citizenship, and related topics – of which *Sociology: The Basics* (2010) and *Intimate Citizenship* (2003) are among the most recent. "I Can't Even Think Straight" captures a theoretical idea in an unforgettable phrase that today is a commonplace in popular culture. The selection illustrates the degree to which queer theory arose both from Foucault's thinking but also as a theoretical position utterly at ease with the postmodern.

"I Can't Even Think Straight"*
Arlene Stein and Ken Plummer (1994)

.... At its widest, tallest, and Wilde(st), queer theory is a plea for massive transgression of all conventional categorizations and analyses—a Sadean/Nietzschean breaking of boundaries around gender/the erotic/the interpersonal, and a plea for dissidence. More narrowly, it is a political play on the word *queer*, long identified with "homosexuality," and the newest in a series of "reverse affirmations" in which the categories constructed through medicalization are turned against themselves. Often there is overlap between the more narrow (i.e., lesbian and gay) focus and the wider focus on transgression: they are far from separate.

Queer theorists claim that existing gay strategies, and minority group strategies in general, have tended to rely on conceptual dualisms (male/female gender models, natural/artificial ontological systems, or essentialist/constructionist intellectual frameworks)

* Arlene Stein and Ken Plummer. "'I Can't Even Think Straight' 'Queer' Theory and the Missing Sexual Revolution in Sociology." *Sociological Theory*, Vol 12, No. 2 (Jul. 1994), pp. 178-187. Reprinted with the permission of the American Sociological Association and the authors.

that reinforce the notion of min/ create binary oppositions whic. intact. As Teresa de Lauretis has written:

> Homosexuality is no longer to be seen simply as marginal with regard to a dominant, stable form of sexuality (heterosexuality) against which it would be defined ... it is no longer to be seen as transgressive or deviant vis-a-vis a proper, natural sexuality (i.e. institutionalized reproductive sexuality) according to the older, pathological model, or as just another, optional "lifestyle," according to the model of contemporary North American pluralism (1991:iii).

Not content to study the "lesbian community" or the "gay community" as the exclusive site of sexual difference, queer theorists interrogate aspects of social life—the family, intimate relationships—but also look at places not typically thought of as sexualized—the economy, for example.

The homo/hetero divide so artfully assembled in the nineteenth century comes to be a strategy for deconstructing and rereading texts previously assembled through heterosexuality. "The sexual order overlaps with a wide range of institutions and social ideologies," writes Michael Warner (1991:5), so that "to challenge the sexual order is sooner or later to encounter those institutions as problems." Much as feminists began treating gender as a primary lens for understanding problems that did not initially look gender-specific, for queer theorists the personal life is sexualized—and heterosexualized—and so are politics and economics, and just about everything else under the sun.

Queer theorists turn their deconstructive zeal against heterosexuality with a particular vengeance. When lesbian/gay theorists analyzed normative heterosexuality in the past, they envisioned it as a sex/gender system which was largely monolithic. Gayle Rubin (1975), in her classic article "The Traffic in Women," located heterosexuality as central to the reproduction of gender and sexual inequality. Queer theorists, on the other hand, locate within the institution of heterosexuality the seeds of its own demise. As Butler has suggested,

> That heterosexuality is always in the act of elaborating itself is evidence that it is perpetually at risk, that is, that it "knows" its own possibility of being undone (1991:23).

Heterosexuality, in this vision, is a highly unstable system, subject to various slippages, reliant upon carefully constructed individual performances of identity, and dependent upon the exclusion of homosexuality for its very identity. One could say that queer theory normalizes homosexuality by making heterosexuality deviant. Homosexuality ceases to be the exclusive site of sexual difference.

The figure whose influence looms large in this literature is Michel Foucault. His sweeping *History of Sexuality* (1978) details the construction of sexuality through institutional discourses, which come to constitute "regimes of truth." As the result of the Victorian era's "discursive explosion," Foucault argues, sexuality became a mainstay of identity, heterosexual monogamy came to function as a norm, and sexual deviants began to see themselves as distinct persons, possessing particular "natures." Foucault problematizes the belief in a continuous history of homosexuality, arguing that the differences between the homosexuality we know today and previous arrangements of same-sex relations may be so profound as to call into question a defining "essence" of homosexuality. Much the same could be said of sexuality in general. Modern sexuality is a product of modern discourses of sexuality. Knowledge about sexuality can scarcely be a transparent window onto a separate realm of sexuality; rather, it constitutes that sexuality itself.

It has been argued that Foucault's intellectual influence, and certainly the fact that he himself was gay, may be largely responsible for the recent movement of queer theory out of the ghetto (Duggan 1992). It might be argued that lesbians and gay men have long been cultural innovators, but with the influence of Foucault and the rise of postmodernism they emerge, more visibly than ever before, as intellectual innovators and social theorists.

Certainly an affinity between queer culture and postmodernism, which today is perhaps the dominant theoretical approach in the humanities, is clear. Some observers have suggested that the typical postmodernist artifact is playful, self-ironizing, and even schizoid. In much the same way, lesbian/gay culture has often made use of camp, drag, and other cultural strategies to celebrate alienation, distance, and incongruity (Ross 1989). If the goal of the modernist project was to rationally organize social life, postmodernists see rationality as a lie—something which many lesbians and gay men have been saying all along....

Reactions and Alternatives

Jürgen Habermas (1929–) was born in Düsseldorf. After studies at Göttigen and Bonn, he taught at Heidelberg, then Frankfurt. From 1971 to 1983 he was Director of the Max Planck Institute in Frankfurt, thereafter whatever positions he may have held pale before the reality that he become the teacher of Germany, Europe, and the world. He is heir to the titular leadership of the German school of critical theory which is evident in his many writings that engage the continuing question of how the modern world, having survived the terrors of mid-twentieth century, can recover both a deep critical attitude and the better side of the dialectic of Enlightenment. His first book, *The Structural Transformation of the Public Sphere* (1962) suggests the degree to which his thought has always focused on political and public process, while his earliest classic work, *Knowledge and Human Interest* (1968), indicates his affinity for the Frankfurt tradition of rethinking the political and economic undercurrents of scientific knowledge. Yet, few would deny that Habermas's two volume *Theory of Communicative Competence* (1981) is his most enduring theoretical masterpiece. Ever since, he has ceaselessly published on both technical and public subjects. In the latter respect *The European Crisis* (2012) indicates his ability and willingness, well into his ninth decade of life, to engage the most current issues of the day. The selection from the concluding pages of his *Theory of Communicative Action* (1981) summarizes Habermas's astute view of what critical social theory can be.

Critical Theory, the Colonized Lifeworld, and Communicative Competence[*]
Jürgen Habermas (1981)

The work of the Institute for Social Research was essentially dominated by six themes until the early 1940s when the circle of collaborators that had gathered in New York began to break up. These research interests are reflected in the lead theoretical articles that appeared in the main part of the *Zeitschrift für Sozialforschung*. They have to do with (*a*) the forms of integration in postliberal societies, (*b*) family socialization and ego development, (*c*) mass media and mass culture, (*d*) the social psychology behind the cessation of protest, (*e*) the theory of art, and (*f*) the critique of positivism and science. This spectrum of themes reflects Horkheimer's conception of an interdisciplinary social science.

In this phase the central line of inquiry, which I characterized with the catchphrase "rationalization as reification," was to be worked out with the differentiated means of various disciplines. Before the "critique of instrumental reason" contracted the process of reification into a topic for the philosophy of history again, Horkheimer and his circle had made "real abstractions" the object of empirical inquiry. From

* *The Theory of Communicative Action, Volume 2: Lifeworld and Systems, A Critique of Functionalist Reason* by Jürgen Habermas, copyright 1989 by Polity. Originally published as *Theorie des kommunikativen Handelns, Band 2: Zur Kritik der funktionalistischen Vernunft*, Copyright © 1981 by Suhrkamp Verlag, Frankfurt am Main. Reprinted by permission of Polity.

this theoretical standpoint it is not difficult to see the unity in the multiplicity of themes enumerated above....

On our assumption, a considerably rationalized lifeworld is one of the initial conditions for modernization processes. It must be possible to anchor money and power in the lifeworld as media, that is, to institutionalize them by means of positive law. If these conditions are met, economic and administrative systems can be differentiated out, systems that have a complementary relation to one another and enter into interchanges with their environments via steering media. At this level of system differentiation modern societies arise, first capitalist societies, and later—setting themselves off from those—bureaucratic-socialist societies. A capitalist path of modernization opens up as soon as the economic system develops its own intrinsic dynamic of growth and, with its endogenously produced problems, takes the lead, that is, the evolutionary primacy, for society as a whole. The path of modernization runs in another direction when, on the basis of state ownership of most of the means of production and an institutionalized one-party rule, the administrative action system gains a like autonomy in relation to the economic system.

To the extent that these organizational principles are established, there arise interchange relations between the two functionally interlocked subsystems and the societal components of the lifeworld in locked subsystems and the societal components of the lifeworld in which the media are anchored (see Figure 39, p. 320). The lifeworld, more or less relieved of tasks of material reproduction, can in turn become more differentiated in its symbolic structures and can set free the inner logic of development of cultural modernity. At the same time, the private and public spheres are now set off as the environments of the system. According to whether the economic system or the state apparatus attains evolutionary primacy, either private households or politically relevant memberships are the points of entry for crises that are shifted from the subsystems to the lifeworld. In modernized societies disturbances in the material reproduction of the lifeworld take the form of stubborn systemic disequilibria; the latter either take effect directly as *crises* or they call forth *pathologies* in the lifeworld.

Steering crises were first studied in connection with the business cycle of market economies. In bureaucratic socialism, crisis tendencies spring from self-blocking mechanisms in planning administra-

tions, as they do on the other side from endogenous interruptions of accumulation processes. Like the paradoxes of exchange rationality, the paradoxes of planning rationality can be explained by the fact that rational action orientations come into contradiction with themselves through unintended systemic effects. These crisis tendencies are worked through not only in the subsystem in which they arise, but also in the complementary action system into which they can be shifted. Just as the capitalist economy relies on organizational performances of the state, the socialist planning bureaucracy has to rely on self-steering performances of the economy. Developed capitalism swings between the contrary policies of "the market's self-healing powers" and state interventionism. The structural dilemma is even clearer on the other side, where policy oscillates hopelessly between increased central planning and decentralization, between orienting economic programs toward investment and toward consumption.

These *systemic disequilibria* become *crises* only when the performances of economy and state remain manifestly below an established level of aspiration and harm the symbolic reproduction of the lifeworld by calling forth conflicts and reactions of resistance there. It is the societal components of the lifeworld that are directly affected by this. Before such conflicts threaten core domains of social integration, they are pushed to the periphery—before anomic conditions arise there are appearances of withdrawal of legitimation or motivation (see Figure 22, p. 143). But when steering crises—that is, perceived disturbances of material reproduction—are successfully intercepted by having recourse to lifeworld resources, pathologies arise in the lifeworld. These resources appear in Figure 21 (p. 142) as contributions to cultural reproduction, social integration, and socialization. For the continued existence of the economy and the state, it is the resources listed in the middle column as contributing to the maintenance of society that are relevant, for it is here, in the institutional orders of the lifeworld, that subsystems are anchored.

We can represent the replacement of steering crises with lifeworld pathologies as follows: anomic conditions are avoided, and legitimations and motivations important for maintaining institutional orders are secured, at the expense of, and through the ruthless exploitation of, other resources. Culture and personality come under attack for the sake of warding off crises and stabilizing society (first and third columns versus middle column in Figure 21). The consequences of this substitution can be seen in Figure 22: instead of manifestations of anomie (and instead of the withdrawal of legitimation and motivation in place of anomie), phenomena of alienation and the unsettling of collective identity emerge. I have traced such phenomena back to a colonization of the lifeworld and characterized them as a reification of the communicative practice of everyday life.

However, deformations of the lifeworld take the form of a reification of communicative relations only in capitalist societies, that is, only where the private household is the point of incursion for the displacement of crises into the lifeworld. This is not a question of the overextension of a single medium but of the monetarization and bureaucratization of the spheres of action of employees and of consumers, of citizens and of clients of state bureaucracies. Deformations of the lifeworld take a different form in societies in which the points of incursion for the penetration of crises into the lifeworld are politically relevant memberships. There too, in bureaucratic-socialist societies, domains of action that are dependent on social integration are switched over to mechanisms of system integration. But instead of the reification of communicative relations we find the shamming of communicative relations in bureaucratically desiccated, forcibly "humanized" domains of pseudopolitical intercourse in an overextended and administered public sphere. This pseudopoliticization is symmetrical to reifying privatization in certain respects. The lifeworld is not directly assimilated to the system, that is, to legally regulated, formally organized domains of action; rather, systemically self-sufficient organizations are fictively put back into a simulated horizon of the lifeworld. While the system is draped out as the lifeworld, the lifeworld is absorbed by the system….

The test case for a theory of rationality with which the modern understanding of the world is to ascertain its own universality would certainly include throwing light on the opaque figures of mythical thought, clarifying the bizarre expressions of alien cultures, and indeed in such a way that we not only comprehend the learning processes that separate "us" from "them," but also become aware of what we have *unlearned* in the course of this learning. A theory of society that does not close itself off a priori to this possibility of unlearning has to be critical also in relation to the preunderstanding that accrues to it from its own social setting, that is, it has to be open to self-criticism. Processes of unlearning can be

gotten at through a critique of deformations that are rooted in the selective exploitation of a potential for rationality and mutual understanding that was once available but is now buried over.

There is also another reason why the theory of society based on the theory of communicative action cannot stray into foundationalist byways. Insofar as it refers to structures of the lifeworld, it has to explicate a background knowledge over which no one can dispose at will. The lifeworld is at first "given" to the theoretician (as it is to the layperson) as his or her own, and in a paradoxical manner. The mode of preunderstanding or of intuitive knowledge of the lifeworld from within which we live together, act and speak with one another, stands in peculiar contrast, as we have seen, to the explicit knowledge of something. The horizontal knowledge that communicative everyday practice *tacitly* carries with it is paradigmatic for the *certainty* with which the lifeworld background is present; yet it does not satisfy the criterion of knowledge that stands in internal relation to validity claims and can therefore be criticized. That which stands beyond all doubt seems as if it could never become problematic; as what is simply unproblematic, a lifeworld can at most fall apart. It is only under the pressure of approaching problems that relevant components of such background knowledge are torn out of their unquestioned familiarity and brought to consciousness as something in need of being ascertained. It takes an earthquake to make us aware that we had regarded the ground on which we stand everyday as unshakable. Even in situations of this sort, only a small segment of our background knowledge becomes uncertain and is set loose after having been enclosed in complex traditions, in solidaric relations, in competences. If the objective occasion arises for us to arrive at some understanding about a situation that has become problematic, background knowledge is transformed into explicit knowledge only in a piecemeal manner.

This has an important methodological implication for sciences that have to do with cultural tradition, social integration, and the socialization of individuals—an implication that became clear to pragmatism and to hermeneutic philosophy, each in its own way, as they came to doubt the possibility of Cartesian doubt. Alfred Schutz, who so convincingly depicted the lifeworld's mode of unquestioned familiarity, nevertheless missed just this problem: whether a lifeworld, in its opaque take-for-grantedness, eludes the phenomenologist's inquiring gaze or is opened up to it does not depend on just *choosing* to adopt a theoretical attitude. The totality of the background knowledge constitutive for the construction of the lifeworld is no more at his disposition than at that of any social scientist—unless an objective challenge arises, in the face of which the lifeworld as a whole becomes problematic. Thus a theory that wants to ascertain the general structures of the lifeworld cannot adopt a transcendental approach; it can only hope to be equal to the *ratio essendi* of its object when there are grounds for assuming that the objective context of life in which the theoretician finds himself is opening up to him its *ratio cognoscendi*.

This implication accords with the point behind Horkheimer's critique of science in his programmatic essay "Traditional and Critical Theory". "The traditional idea of theory is abstracted from scientific activity as it is carried on within the division of labor at a particular stage in the latter's development. It corresponds to the activity of the scholar which takes place alongside all the other activities of a society, but in no immediately clear connection with them. In this view of theory, therefore, the real social function of science is not made manifest; it conveys not what theory means in human life, but only what it means in the isolated sphere in which, for historical reasons, it comes into existence." As opposed to this, critical social theory is to become conscious of the self-referentiality of its calling; it knows that in and through the very act of knowing it belongs to the objective context of life that it strives to grasp. The context of its emergence does not remain external to the theory, rather, the theory takes this reflectively up into itself: "In this intellectual activity the needs and goals, the experiences and skills, the customs and tendencies of the contemporary form of human existence have all played their part." The same holds true for the context of application: "As the influence of the subject matter on the theory, so also the application of the theory to the subject matter is not only an intrascientific process but a social one as well."

In his famous methodological introduction to his critique of political economy of 1857, Marx applied the type of reflection called for by Horkheimer to one of his central concepts. He explained there why the basic assumptions of political economy rest on a seemingly simple abstraction, which is in fact quite difficult:

It was an immense step forward for Adam Smith to throw out every limiting specification of wealth-creating activity—not only manufacturing, or commercial, or agricultural labor, but one as well as the others, labor in general. With the abstract universality of wealth-creating activity we now have the universality of the object defined as wealth, the product as such or again labor as such, but labor as past objectified labor. How difficult and great this transition was may be seen from how Adam Smith himself from time to time still falls back into the Physiocratic system. Now it might seem that all that had been achieved thereby was to discover the abstract expression for the simplest and most ancient relation in which human beings— in whatever form of society—play the role of producers. This is correct in one respect. Not in another ... Indifference toward specific labors corresponds to a form of society in which individuals can with ease transfer from one labor to another, and where the specific kind is a matter of chance for them, hence of indifference. Not only the category 'labor', but labor in reality has here become the means of creating wealth in general, and has ceased to be organically linked with particular individuals in any specific form. Such a state of affairs is at its most developed in the modern form of existence of bourgeois society—in the United States. Here, then, for the first time, the point of departure of modem economics, namely the abstraction of the category 'labor', 'labor as such', labor pure and simple, becomes true in practice.

Smith was able to lay the foundations of modern economics only after a mode of production arose that, like the capitalist mode with its differentiation of an economic system steered via exchange value, forced a transformation of concrete activities into abstract performances, intruded into the world of work with this real abstraction, and thereby created a problem for the workers themselves: "Thus the simplest abstraction which modem economics places at the head of its discussions and which expresses an immeasurably ancient relation valid in all forms of society, nevertheless achieves practical truth as an abstraction only as a category of the most modern society."

A theory of society that claims universality for its basic concepts, without being allowed simply to bring them to bear upon their object in a conventional manner, remains caught up in the self-referentiality that Marx demonstrated in connection with the concept of abstract labor. As I have argued above, when labor is rendered abstract and indifferent, we have a special case of the transference of communicatively structured domains of action over to media-steered interaction. This interpretation decodes the deformations of the lifeworld with the help of another category, namely, 'communicative action'. What Marx showed to be the case in regard to the category of labor holds true for this as well: "how even the most abstract categories, despite their validity—precisely because of their abstractness—for all epochs, are nevertheless, in the specific character of this abstraction, themselves likewise a product of historical relations, and possess their full validity only for and within these relations." The theory of communicative action can explain why this is so: the development of society must *itself* give rise to the problem situations that *objectively* afford contemporaries a privileged access to the general structures of the lifeworld.

The theory of modernity that I have here sketched in broad strokes permits us to recognize the following: In modern societies there is such an expansion of the scope of contingency for interaction loosed from normative contexts that the inner logic of communicative action "becomes practically true" in the deinstitutionalized forms of intercourse of the familial private sphere as well as in a public sphere stamped by the mass media. At the same time, the systemic imperatives of autonomous subsystems penetrate into the lifeworld and, through monetarization and bureaucratization, force an assimilation of communicative action to formally organized domains of action—even in areas where the action coordinating mechanism of reaching understanding is functionally necessary. It may be that this provocative threat, this challenge that places the symbolic structures of the lifeworld as a whole in question, can account for why they have become accessible to us.

Anthony Giddens (1938–) taught for many years at King's College, Cambridge, where he was professor of sociology in the Faculty of Economics and Politics. He later became director of the London School of Economics. Giddens is also a founder, publisher, and editor of Polity Press, one of the most ambitious and interesting publishers of books in social theory. In 2004 he was elevated to the House of Lords where, as Baron Giddens, he continues to write as a social theoretically informed critique of public issues whilst playing a central role in British political life. Today Giddens is roughly to England what Habermas is to Germany. It would be hard to say which of the two is more prominent in global political debates. Among Giddens's recent books is *The Politics of Climate Change* (2009). His first widely read book was *New Rules of Sociological Methods* (1976). As the title's play on Durkheim suggests, the book is an attempt to reformulate sociological reasoning, in this

instance by reexamining the idea of interpretative, or hermeneutic, sociology. This was Giddens's first statement of structuration theory, which is systematically worked out in *The Constitution of Society* (1984). Giddens has written on many subjects, from war to sexual intimacy. The selection is from *The Consequences of Modernity* (1990), which is his defense of what he calls radicalized modernity. The selection offers a particularly clear illustration of his understanding of the complexity of modern life, stated in his own discursive theoretical style. The tabular presentation of modernity (RM) and post-modernity (PM), though it reflects Giddens's radicalized preferences for RM over PM, offers a useful comparison of theories of the two cultural types. More importantly, the selection presents what is perhaps the crucial idea behind Giddens's structuration theory: that the individual lives in an ongoing recursive relation with the complex structures of modern society. Structures create the individual, while they are being created and held by individuals. Giddens, like others (Gouldner, Bourdieu), views reflexivity as the fundamental feature of modern life arising in the relation of individuals to structures—a relation that creates the series of paradoxes he discusses. In effect, Giddens argues that modernity opens new and different opportunities for human fulfillment. Moderns may be displaced from local communities, but they are reembedded in world culture in ways that can be liberating. This is an example of a reflexive social theory recursively producing a theory of the world as reflexive—a theoretical practice Giddens made concrete through his direct influence on the third way policies of Britain's Labour Party.

Post-Modernity or Radicalized Modernity?[*]
Anthony Giddens (1990)

A Phenomenology of Modernity

Two images of what it feels like to live in the world of modernity have dominated the sociological literature, yet both of them seem less than adequate. One is that of Weber, according to which the bonds of

---

rationality are drawn tighter and tighter, imprisoning us in a featureless cage of bureaucratic routine. Among the three major founders of modern sociology, Weber saw most clearly the significance of expertise in modern social development and used it to outline a phenomenology of modernity. Everyday experience, according to Weber, retains its colour and spontaneity, but only on the perimeter of the "steel-hard" cage of bureaucratic rationality. The image has a great deal of power and has, of course, featured strongly in fictional literature in the twentieth century as well as in more directly sociological discussions. There are many contexts of modern institutions which are marked by bureaucratic fixity. But they are far from all-pervasive, and even in the core settings of its application, namely, large-scale organisations, Weber's characterisation of bureaucracy is inadequate. Rather than tending inevitably towards rigidity, organisations produce areas of autonomy and spontaneity—which are actually often less easy to achieve in smaller groups. We owe this counterinsight to Durkheim, as well as to subsequent empirical study of organisations. The closed climate of opinion within some small groups and the modes of direct sanction available to its members fix the horizons of action much more narrowly and firmly than in larger organisational settings.

The second is the image of Marx—and of many others, whether they regard themselves as Marxist or not. According to this portrayal, modernity is seen as a monster. More limpidly perhaps than any of his contemporaries, Marx perceived how shattering the impact of modernity would be, and how irreversible. At the same time, modernity was for Marx what Habermas has aptly called an "unfinished project." The monster can be tamed, since what human beings have created they can always subject to their own control. Capitalism, simply, is an irrational way to run the modern world, because it substitutes the whims of the market for the controlled fulfilment of human need.

For these images I suggest we should substitute that of the juggernaut**—a runaway engine of enormous power which, collectively as human beings, we can drive to some extent but which also threatens to rush out of our control and which could rend itself asunder. The juggernaut crushes those who resist it,

and while it sometimes seems to have a steady path, there are times when it veers away erratically in directions we cannot foresee. The ride is by no means wholly unpleasant or unrewarding; it can often be exhilarating and charged with hopeful anticipation. But, so long as the institutions of modernity endure, we shall never be able to control completely either the path or the pace of the journey. In turn, we shall never be able to feel entirely secure, because the terrain across which it runs is fraught with risks of high consequence. Feelings of ontological security and existential anxiety will coexist in ambivalence.

The juggernaut of modernity is not all of one piece, and here the imagery lapses, as does any talk of a single path which it runs. It is not an engine made up of integrated machinery, but one in which there is a tensionful, contradictory, push-and-pull of different influences. Any attempt to capture the experience of modernity must begin from this view, which derives ultimately from the dialectics of space and time, as expressed in the time-space constitution of modern institutions. I shall sketch a phenomenology of modernity in terms of four dialectically related frameworks of experience, each of which connects in an integral way with the preceding discussion in this study:

Displacement and reembedding: the intersection of estrangement and familiarity.
Intimacy and impersonality: the intersection of personal trust and impersonal ties.
Expertise and reappropriation: the intersection of abstract systems and day-to-day knowledgeability.
Privatism and engagement: the intersection of pragmatic acceptance and activism.

Modernity "dis-places" in the sense previously analysed—place becomes phantasmagoric. Yet this is a double-layered, or ambivalent, experience rather than simply a loss of community. We can see this clearly only if we keep in mind the contrasts between the pre-modern and the modern described earlier. What happens is not simply that localised influences drain away into the more impersonalised relations of abstract systems. Instead, the very tissue of spatial experience alters, conjoining proximity and distance in ways that have few close parallels in prior ages. There is a complex relation here between familiarity and estrangement. Many aspects of life in local contexts continue to have a familiarity and ease to them, grounded in the day-to-day routines individuals

---

*The term comes from the Hindi Jagannath, "lord of the world," and is a title of Krishna; an idol of this deity was taken each year through the streets on a huge car, which fol- lowers are said to have thrown themselves under, to be crushed beneath the wheels.

follow. But the sense of the familiar is one often mediated by time-space distanciation. It does not derive from the particularities of localised place. And this experience, so far as it seeps into general awareness, is simultaneously disturbing and rewarding. The reassurance of the familiar, so important to a sense of ontological security, is coupled with the realisation that what is comfortable and nearby is actually an expression of distant events and was "placed into" the local environment rather than forming an organic development within it. The local shopping mall is a milieu in which a sense of ease and security is cultivated by the layout of the buildings and the careful planning of public places. Yet everyone who shops there is aware that most of the shops are chain stores, which one might find in any city, and indeed that innumerable shopping malls of similar design exist elsewhere.

A feature of displacement is our insertion into globalised cultural and information settings, which means that familiarity and place are much less consistently connected than hitherto. This is less a phenomenon of estrangement from the local than one of integration within globalised "communities" of shared experience. The boundaries of concealment and disclosure become altered, since many erstwhile quite distinct activities are juxtaposed in unitary public domains. The newspaper and the sequence of television programmes over the day are the most obvious concrete examples of this phenomenon, but it is generic to the time-space organisation of modernity. We are all familiar with events, with actions, and with the visible appearance of physical settings thousands of miles away from where we happen to live. The coming of electronic media has undoubtedly accentuated these aspects of displacement, since they override presence so instantaneously and at such distance. As Joshua Meyrowitz points out, a person on the telephone to another, perhaps on the opposite side of the world, is more closely bound to that distant other than to another individual in the same room (who may be asking, "Who is it? What's she saying?" and so forth).

The counterpart of displacement is reembedding. The disembedding mechanisms lift social relations and the exchange of information out of specific time-space contexts, but at the same time provide new opportunities for their reinsertion. This is another reason why it is a mistake to see the modern world as one in which large, impersonal systems increasingly swallow up most of personal life. The selfsame processes that lead to the destruction of older city neighbourhoods and their replacement by towering office-blocks and skyscrapers often permit the gentrification of other areas and a recreation of locality. Although the picture of tall, impersonal clusters of city-centre buildings is often presented as the epitome of the landscape of modernity, this is a mistake. Equally characteristic is the recreation of places of relative smallness and informality. The very means of transportation which help to dissolve the connection between locality and kinship provide the possibility for reembedding, by making it easy to visit "close" relatives who are far away.

Parallel comments can be made about the intersection of intimacy and impersonality in modern contexts of action. It is simply not true that in conditions of modernity we live increasingly in a "world of strangers." We are not required more and more to exchange intimacy for impersonality in the contacts with others we routinely make in the course of our day-to-day lives. Something much more complex and subtle is involved. Day-to-day contacts with others in pre-modern settings were normally based upon a familiarity stemming in part from the nature of place. Yet contacts with familiar others probably rarely facilitated the level of intimacy we associate with personal and sexual relations today. The "transformation of intimacy" of which I have spoken is contingent upon the very distancing which the disembedding mechanisms bring about, combined with the altered environments of trust which they presuppose. There are some very obvious ways in which intimacy and abstract systems interact. Money, for example, can be spent to purchase the expert services of a psychologist who guides the individual in an exploration of the inner universe of the intimate and the personal.

A person walks the streets of a city and encounters perhaps thousands of people in the course of a day, people she or he has never met before—"strangers" in the modern sense of that term. Or perhaps that individual strolls along less crowded thoroughfares, idly scrutinising passersby and the diversity of products for sale in the shops—Baudelaire's *flâneur*. Who could deny that these experiences are an integral element of modernity? Yet the world "out there"—the world that shades off into indefinite time-space from the familiarity of the home and the local neighbourhood—is not at all a purely impersonal one. On the contrary, intimate relationships can be sustained at distance (regular and sustained contact can be made with other individuals at virtually any point on the earth's surface—as well as some below and above), and personal ties are continually forged with others with whom one was previously unacquainted. We live in a *peopled* world, not merely one of anonymous, blank faces, and the interpolation of abstract systems into our activities is intrinsic to bringing this about.

In relations of intimacy of the modern type, trust is always ambivalent, and the possibility of severance is more or less ever present. Personal ties can be ruptured, and ties of intimacy returned to the sphere of impersonal contacts—in the broken love affair, the intimate suddenly becomes again a stranger. The demand of "opening oneself up" to the other which personal trust relations now presume, the injunction to hide nothing from the other, mix reassurance and deep anxiety. Personal trust demands a level of self-understanding and self-expression which must itself be a source of psychological tension. For mutual self-revelation is combined with the need for reciprocity and support; yet the two are frequently incompatible. Torment and frustration interweave themselves with the need for trust in the other as the provider of care and support.

Deskilling and Reskilling in Everyday Life

Expertise is part of intimacy in conditions of modernity, as is shown not just by the huge variety of forms of psychotherapy and counseling available, but by the plurality of books, articles, and television programmes providing technical information about "relationships." Does this mean that, as Habermas puts it, abstract systems "colonise" a pre-existing "life-world," subordinating personal decisions to technical expertise? It does not. The reasons are twofold. One is that modern institutions do not just implant themselves into a "life-world," the residues of which remain much the same as they always were. Changes in the nature of day-to-day life also affect the disembedding mechanisms, in a dialectical interplay. The second reason is that technical expertise is continuously reappropriated by lay agents as part of their routine dealings with abstract systems. No one can become an expert, in the sense of the possession either of full expert knowledge or of the appropriate formal credentials, in more than a few small sectors of the immensely complicated knowledge systems which now exist. Yet no one can interact with abstract systems without mastering some of the rudiments of the principles upon which they are based.

Sociologists often suppose that, in contrast to the pre-modern era, where many things were mysteries, today we live in a world from which mystery has retreated and where the way "the world works" can (in principle) be exhaustively known. But this is not true for either the lay person or the expert, if we consider their experience as individuals. To all of us living in the modern world things are specifically *opaque*, in a way that was not the case previously. In pre-modern environments the "local knowledge," to adapt a phrase from Clifford Geertz, which individuals possessed was rich, varied, and adapted to the requirements of living in the local milieu. But how many of us today when we switch on the light know much about where the electricity supply comes from or even, in a technical sense, what electricity actually is?

Yet, although "local knowledge" cannot be of the same order as it once was, the sieving off of knowledge and skill from everyday life is not a one-way process. Nor are individuals in modern contexts less knowledgeable about their local milieux than their counterparts in pre-modern cultures. Modern social life is a complex affair, and there are many "filter-back" processes whereby technical knowledge, in one shape or another, is reappropriated by lay persons and routinely applied in the course of their day-to-day activities. As was mentioned earlier, the interaction between expertise and reappropriation is strongly influenced, among other things, by experiences at access points. Economic factors may decide whether a person learns to fix her or his car engine, rewire the electrical system of the house, or fix the roof; but so do the levels of trust that an individual vests in the particular expert systems and known experts involved. Processes of reappropriation relate to all aspects of social life—for example, medical treatment, child-rearing, or sexual pleasure.

For the ordinary individual, all this does not add up to feelings of secure control over day-to-day life circumstances. Modernity expands the arenas of personal fulfilment and of security in respect of large swathes of day-to-day life. But the lay person—and *all* of us are lay persons in respect of the vast majority of expert systems—must ride the juggernaut. The lack of control which many of us feel about some of the circumstances of our lives is real.

It is against this backdrop that we should understand patterns of privatism and engagement. A sense of "survival," in Lasch's use of this term, cannot be absent from our thoughts all of the time in a world in which, for the indefinite future, survival is a real and inescapable issue. On the level of the unconscious—even, and perhaps especially, among those whose attitude is one of pragmatic acceptance towards high-consequence risks—the relation to survival probably exists as existential dread. For basic trust in the continuity of the world must be anchored in the simple conviction that it will continue, and this is something of which we cannot be entirely sure. Saul Bellow remarks in the novel *Herzog*, "The revolution of nuclear terror returns the metaphysical dimension to us. All practical activity has reached this culmination: everything may go now, civilisation, history, nature. Now to recall Mr. Kierkegaard's question . . . " "Mr. Kierkegaard's question" is, how do we avoid the dread of nonexistence, considered not just as individual death but as an existential void? The possibility of global calamity, whether by nuclear war or other means, prevents us from reassuring ourselves with the assumption that the life of the species inevitably surpasses that of the individual.

How remote that possibility is, literally no one knows. So long as there is deterrence, there must be the chance of war, because the notion of deterrence only makes sense if the parties involved are in principle prepared to use the weaponry they hold. Once again, no one, no matter how "expert" about the logistics of weapons and military organisation or about world politics, can say whether deterrence "works," because the most that can be said is that so far there has been no war. Awareness of these inherent uncertainties does not escape the lay population, however vague that awareness might be.

Balanced against the deep anxieties which such circumstances must produce in virtually everyone is the psychological prop of the feeling that "there's nothing that I as an individual can do," and that at any rate the risk must be very slight. Business-as-usual, as I have pointed out, is a prime element in the stabilising of trust and ontological security, and this no doubt applies in respect of high-consequence risks just as it does in other areas of trust relations.

Yet obviously even high-consequence risks are not only remote contingencies, which can be ignored in daily life, albeit at some probable psychological cost. Some such risks, and many others which are potentially life-threatening for individuals or otherwise significantly affect them, intrude right into the core of day-to-day activities. This is true, for example, of any pollution damage which affects the health of adults or children, and anything which produces toxic contents in food or affects its nutritional properties. It is also true of a multitude of technological changes that influence life chances, such as reproductive technologies. The mix of risk and opportunity is so complex in many of the circumstances involved that it is extremely difficult for individuals to know how far to vest trust in particular prescriptions or systems, and how far to suspend it. How can one manage to eat "healthily," for example, when all kinds of food are said to have toxic qualities of one sort or another and when what is held to be "good for you" by nutritional experts varies with the shifting state of scientific knowledge?

Trust and risk, opportunity and danger—these polar, paradoxical features of modernity permeate all aspects of day-to-day life, once more reflecting an extraordinary interpolation of the local and the global. Pragmatic acceptance can be sustained towards most of the abstract systems that impinge on individuals' lives, but by its very nature such an attitude cannot be carried on all the while and in respect of all areas of activity. For incoming expert information is often fragmentary or inconsistent, as is the recycled knowledge which colleagues, friends, and intimates pass on to one another. On a personal level, decisions must be taken and policies forged. Privatism, the avoidance of contestatory engagement—which can be supported by attitudes of basic optimism, pessimism, or pragmatic acceptance—can serve the purposes of day-to-day "survival" in many respects. But it is likely to be interspersed with phases of active engagement, even on the part of those most prone to attitudes of indifference or cynicism. For, to repeat, in respect of the balance of security and danger which modernity introduces into our lives, there are no longer "others"—no one can be completely outside. Conditions of modernity, in many circumstances, provoke activism rather than privatism, because of modernity's inherent reflexivity and because there are many opportunities for collective organisation within the polyarchic systems of modern nation-states.

Objections to Post-Modernity

Let me at this point return briefly to issues raised near the beginning of the book and at the same time look ahead to the closing sections. I have sought to develop an interpretation of the current era which challenges the usual views of the emergence of post-modernity. As ordinarily understood, conceptions of post-modernity—which mostly have their origin in post-structuralist thought—involve a number of distinct strands. I compare this conception of

TABLE [1]   A Comparison of Conceptions
of "Post-Modernity" (PM) and "Radicalised Modernity" (RM)

PM	RM
1. Understands current transitions in epistemological terms or as dissolving epistemology altogether.	1. Identifies the institutional developments which create a sense of fragmentation and dispersal.
2. Focuses upon the centrifugal tendencies of current social transformations and their dislocating character.	2. Sees high modernity as a set of circumstances in which dispersal is dialectically connected to profound tendencies towards global integration.
3. Sees the self as dissolved or dismembered by the fragmenting of experience.	3. Sees the self as more than just a site of intersecting forces; active processes of reflexive self-identity are made possible by modernity.
4. Argues for the contextuality of truth claims or sees them as "historical."	4. Argues that the universal features of truth claims force themselves upon us in an irresistible way given the primacy of problems of a global kind. Systematic knowledge about these developments is not precluded by the reflexivity of modernity.
5. Theorises powerlessness which individuals feel in the face of globalising tendencies.	5. Analyses a dialectic of powerlessness and empowerment, in terms of both experience and action.
6. Sees the "emptying" of day-to-day life as a result of the intrusion of abstract systems.	6. Sees day-to-day life as an active complex of reactions to abstract systems, involving appropriation as well as loss.
7. Regards coordinated political engagement as precluded by the primacy of contextuality and dispersal.	7. Regards coordinated political engagement as both possible and necessary, on a global level as well as locally.
8. Defines post-modernity as the end of epistemology/the individual/ethics.	8. Defines post-modernity as possible transformations moving "beyond" the institutions of modernity.

post-modernity (PM) with my alternative position, which I shall call radicalised modernity (RM), in Table [1].

Nancy Hartsock (1943–) teaches political science and women's studies at the University of Washington. Among her writings is *Money, Sex, and Power: Toward a Feminist Historical Materialism* (1984) and the important article "The Feminist Standpoint: Developing the Ground for a Specifically Feminist Historical Materialism" (1983). The selection is from her essay "Foucault on Power: A Theory for Women?" Here, Hartsock presents a nuanced standpoint response to Foucault, who has been a particularly troubling theorist for feminists.

On the one hand, Foucault's deep critique of modernity and his theory of the diffusion of power throughout the micropolitics of modern society are thought to weaken the basis for informed political action. On the other, few social theorists have done more than Foucault to open consideration of sex and sexuality in social theory and research. Hence, he is sometimes considered a dangerous ally. Another well-known feminist response to Foucault is Nancy Fraser's *Unruly Practices: Power, Discourse and Gender in Contemporary Social Theory* (1989). Hartsock's essay is in Linda Nicholson (ed.), *Feminism/Postmodernism*, which (along with *Feminists Theorize the Political*, edited by Judith Butler and Joan Scott in 1992) is an excellent source for the feminist debate on postmodernism.

A Theory of Power for Women?*

Nancy Hartsock (1987)

To mention the power of women leads immediately to the problem of what is meant by "women." The problem of differences among women has been very prominent in the United States in recent years. We face the task of developing our understanding of difference as part of the theoretical task of developing a theory of power for women. Issues of difference reminds us as well that many of the factors which divide women also unite some women with men—factors such as racial or cultural differences. Perhaps theories of power for women will also be theories of power for other groups as well. We need to develop our understanding of difference by creating a situation in which hitherto marginalized groups can name themselves, speak for themselves, and participate in defining the terms of interaction, a situation in which we can construct an understanding of the world that is sensitive to difference.

What might such a theory look like? Can we develop a general theory, or should we abandon the search for such a theory in favor of making space for a number of heterogeneous voices to be heard? What kinds of common claims can be made about the situations of women and men of color? About those of white women and women and men of color? About the situations of Western peoples and those they have colonized? For example, is it ever legitimate to say "women" without qualification? These kinds of questions make it apparent that the situation we face involves not only substantive claims about the world, but also raises questions about how we come to know the world, about what we can claim for our theories and ultimately about who "we" are. I want to ask what kinds of knowledge claims are required for grounding political action by different groups. Should theories produced by "minorities" rest on different epistemologies than those of the "majority?" Given the fact that the search for theory has been called into question in majority discourse and has been denounced as totalizing, do we want to ask similar questions of minority proposals or set similar standards?

In our efforts to find ways to include the voices of marginalized groups, one might expect helpful guidance from those who have argued against totalizing and universalistic theories such as those of the Enlightenment. Many radical intellectuals have been attracted to a compilation of diverse writings ranging from literary criticism to the social sciences, generally termed postmodern. The writers, among them figures such as Foucault, Derrida, Rorty, and Lyotard, argue against the faith in a universal reason we have inherited from Enlightenment European philosophy. They reject stories that claim to encompass all of human history: As Lyotard puts it, "let us wage war on totality." In its place they propose a social criticism that is *ad hoc*, contextual, plural, and limited. A number of feminist theorists have joined in the criticism of modernity put forward by these writers. They have endorsed their claims about what can and cannot be known or said or read into/from texts.

Despite their apparent congruence with the project I am proposing, I will argue these theories would hinder rather than help its accomplishment. Despite their own desire to avoid universal claims and despite their stated opposition to these claims, some universalistic assumptions creep back into their work. Thus, postmodernism, despite its stated efforts to avoid the problems of European modernism of the eighteenth and nineteenth centuries, at best manages to criticize these theories without putting anything in their place. For those of us who want to understand the world systematically in order to change it, postmodern theories at their best give little guidance. (I should note that I recognize that some postmodernist theorists are committed to ending injustice. But this commitment is not carried through in their theories.) Those of us who are not part of the ruling race, class, or gender, not a part of the minority which controls our world, need to know how it works. Why are we—in all our variousness—systematically excluded and marginalized? What systematic changes would be required to create a more just society? At worst, postmodernist theories can recapitulate the effects of Enlightenment theories which deny the right to participate in defining the terms of interaction. Thus, I contend, in broad terms, that postmodernism represents a dangerous approach for any marginalized group to adopt.

The Construction of the Colonized Other

In thinking about how to think about these issues, I found that the work of Albert Memmi in *The Colonizer and the Colonized* was very useful as a metaphor for understanding both our situation with regard to postmodernist theorists and the situation of some postmodernist theorists themselves: Those of us who have been marginalized enter the discussion from a position analogous to that which the colonized holds in relation to the colonizer. Most fundamentally, I want to argue that the philosophical and historical creation of a devalued "Other" was the necessary precondition for the creation of the transcendental rational subject outside of time and space, the subject who is the speaker in Enlightenment philosophy. Simone de Beauvoir has described the essence of the process in a quite different context: "Evil is necessary to Good, Matter to Idea, and Darkness to Light." While this subject is clearest in the work of bourgeois philosophers such as Kant, one can find echoes of this mode of thought in some of Marx's claims about the proletariat as the universal subject of history.

Memmi described the bond that creates both the colonizer and the colonized as one which destroys both parties, although in different ways. As he draws a portrait of the Other as described by the colonizer, the colonized emerges as the image of everything the colonizer is not. Every negative quality is projected onto her/him. The colonized is said to be lazy, and the colonizer becomes practically lyrical about it. Moreover, the colonized is both wicked and backward, a being who is in some important ways not fully human. As he describes the image of the colonized, feminist readers of de Beauvoir's *Second Sex* cannot avoid a sense of familiarity. We recognize a great deal of this description.

Memmi points to several conclusions drawn about this artificially created Other. First, the Other is always seen as "Not," as a lack, a void, as lacking in the valued qualities of the society, whatever those qualities may be. Second, the humanity of the Other becomes "opaque." Colonizers can frequently be heard making statements such as "you never know what they think. Do they think? Or do they instead operate according to intuition?" (Feminist readers may be reminded of some of the arguments about whether women had souls, or whether they were capable of reason or of learning Latin.) Memmi remarks ironically that the colonized must indeed be very strange, if he remains so mysterious and opaque after years of living with the colonizer. Third, the Others are not seen as fellow individual members of the human community, but rather as part of a chaotic, disorganized, and anonymous collectivity. They carry, Memmi states, "the mark of the plural." In more colloquial terms, they all look alike.

I want to stress once again that I am not claiming that women are a unitary group or that Western white women have the same experiences as women or men of color or as colonized peoples. Rather, I am pointing to a way of looking at the world characteristic of the dominant white, male, Eurocentric ruling class, a way of dividing up the world that puts an omnipotent subject at the center and constructs marginal Others as sets of negative qualities.

What is left of the Other after this effort to dehumanize her or him? She/he is pushed toward becoming an object. As an end, in the colonizer's supreme ambition, she/he should exist only as a function of the needs of the colonizer, that is, be transformed into a pure colonized. An object for himself or herself as well as for the colonizer. The colonized ceases to be a subject of history and becomes only what the colonizer is not. After having shut the colonized out of history and having forbidden him all development, the colonizer asserts his fundamental immobility. Confronted with this image as it is imposed by every institution and in every human contact, the colonized cannot be indifferent to this picture. Its accusations worry the colonized even more because she/he admires and fears the powerful colonizing accuser.

We can expand our understanding of the way this process works by looking briefly at Edward Said's account of the European construction of the Orient. He makes the political dimensions of this ideological move very clear: Said describes the creation of the Orient as an outgrowth of a will to power. "Orientalism," he states, "is a Western style for dominating, restructuring, and having authority over the Orient."

Interestingly enough, in the construction of these power relations, the Orient is often feminized. There is, however, the creation—out of this same process of the opposite of the colonized, the opposite of the Oriental, the opposite of women—of a being who sees himself as located at the center and possessed of all the qualities valued in his society (I use the masculine pronoun here purposely). Memmi describes this process eloquently:

. . . the colonialist stresses those things that keep him separate rather than emphasizing that which might contribute to the foundation of a joint community. In those differences, the colonized is always degraded and the colonialist finds justification for rejecting his subjectivity. But perhaps the most important thing is that once the behavioral feature or historical or geographical factor which characterizes the colonialist and contrasts him with the colonized has been isolated, this gap must be kept from being filled. The colonialist removes the factor from history, time and therefore possible evolution. What is actually a sociological point becomes labeled as being biological, or preferably, metaphysical. It is attached to the colonized's basic nature. Immediately the colonial relationship between colonized and colonizer, founded on the essential outlook of the two protagonists, becomes a definitive category. It is what it is because they are what they are, and neither one nor the other will ever change.

Said points to something very similar. He argues that "European culture gained in strength and identity by setting itself off against the Orient as a sort of surrogate and even underground self." Orientalism is part of the European identity that defines "us" versus the nonEuropeans. To go further, the studied object becomes another being with regard to whom the studying subject becomes transcendent. Why? Because, unlike the Oriental, the European observer is a true human being.

But what does all this have to do with theory and the search for a theory of power for women? I want to suggest that in each of these cases—and the examples could be multiplied—what we see is the construction of the social relations, the power relations, which form the basis of the transcendent subject of Enlightenment theories—he (and I mean *he*) who theorizes. Put slightly differently, the political and social as well as ideological/intellectual creation of the devalued Other was at the same time the creation of the universalizing and totalizing voice postmodernists denounce as the voice of theory. . . .

Toward Theories for Women

Those of us who have been marginalized by the transcendental voice of universalizing theory need to do something other than ignore power relations as Rorty does or resist them as figures such as Foucault and Lyotard suggest. We need to transform them, and to do so, we need a revised and reconstructed theory (indebted to Marx among others) with several important features.

First, rather than getting rid of subjectivity or notions of the subject, as Foucault does and substituting his notion of the individual as an effect of power relations, we need to engage in the historical, political, and theoretical process of constituting ourselves as subjects as well as objects of history. We need to recognize that we can be the makers of history as well as the objects of those who have made history. Our nonbeing was the condition of being of the One, the center, the taken-for-granted ability of one small segment of the population to speak for all; our various efforts to constitute ourselves as subjects (through struggles for colonial independence, racial and sexual liberation struggles, and so on) were fundamental to creating the preconditions for the current questioning of universalist claims. But, I believe, we need to sort out who we really are. Put differently, we need to dissolve the false "we" I have been using into its real multiplicity and variety and out of this concrete multiplicity build an account of the world as seen from the margins, an account which can expose the falseness of the view from the top and can transform the margins as well as the center. The point is to develop an account of the world which treats our perspectives not as subjugated or disruptive knowledges, but as primary and constitutive of a different world. . . .

Second, we must do our work on an epistemological base that indicates that knowledge is possible—not just conversation or a discourse on how it is that power relations work. Conversation as a goal is fine; understanding how power works in oppressive societies is important. But if we are to construct a new society, we need to be assured that some systematic knowledge about our world and ourselves is possible. Those (simply) critical of modernity can call into question whether we ever really knew the world (and a good case can be made that "they" at least did not). They are in fact right that they have not known the world as it is rather than as they wished and needed it to be; they created their world not only in their own image but in the image of their fantasies. To create a world that expresses our own various and diverse images, we need to understand how it works.

Third, we need a theory of power that recognizes that our practical daily activity contains an understanding of the world—subjugated perhaps, but present. Here I am reaffirming Gramsci's argument that everyone is an intellectual and that each of us has an epistemology. The point, then, for "minority" theories is to "read out" the epistemologies in our various practices. I have argued elsewhere for a "standpoint" epistemology—an account of the world with great similarities to Marx's fundamental stance. While I would modify some of what I argued there, I would still insist that we must not give up the claim that material life (class position in Marxist theory) not only structures but sets limits on the understanding of social relations, and that, in systems of domination, the vision available to the rulers will be both partial and will reverse the real order of things.

Fourth, our understanding of power needs to recognize the difficulty of creating alternatives. The ruling class, race, and gender actively structure the material-social relations in which all the parties are forced to participate; their vision, therefore, cannot be dismissed as simply false or misguided. In consequence, the oppressed groups must struggle for their own understandings which will represent achievements requiring both theorizing and the education which grows from political struggle.

Fifth, as an engaged vision, the understanding of the oppressed exposes the relations among people as inhuman and thus contains a call to political action. That is, a theory of power for women, for the oppressed, is not one that leads to a turning away from engagement but rather one that is a call for change and participation in altering power relations.

The critical steps are, first, using what we know about our lives as a basis for critique of the dominant culture and, second, creating alternatives. When the various "minority" experiences have been described and when the significance of these experiences as a ground for critique of the dominant institutions and ideologies of society is better recognized, we will have at least the tools to begin to construct an account of the world sensitive to the realities of race and gender as well as class. To paraphrase Marx, the point is to change the world, not simply to redescribe ourselves or reinterpret the world yet again.

Randall Collins (1941–) was born in Knoxville, Tennessee. His higher education was at Harvard and the University of California at Berkeley where he encountered Erving Goffman. Collins received his PhD in 1969 after which he taught at several prestigious institutions ranging from the University of Virginia and the University of California at Riverside to the University of Pennsylvania. His many honors include serving as President of the American Sociological Association in 2010-11. Collins's books include *Conflict Sociology* (1975), a decidedly non-Marxist study of social conflict; *The Credential Society: An Historical Sociology of Education* (1979), an early venture in social history; *The Sociology of Philosophies* (1998), a magisterial book on the social foundations of philosophy; *Violence: A Microsociological Theory* (2008), which works out the micro-nuances of social violence; among a good many other books and essays. A 2004 book, *Interaction Ritual Chains*—found in the section here—is a later development of the thinking. Still another indication of Randall Collins astonishing range of intellectual and literary accomplishments is the fact that he has published at least one work of fiction.

Interaction Ritual Chains[*]
Randall Collins (1987)

The Microtranslation of Macrostructures

How can macrostructure be composed out of micro events? Clearly it is so composed: What is "empirical" meets us only in the form of micro encounters, and any macrostructure, no matter how large, consists only of the repeated experiences of large numbers of persons in time and space. Our macroconcepts are only words we apply to these aggregations of microencounters. The fact that these words—"nation," "society," "corporation," and so forth—are part of the discourse of everyday life merely presents us with another item of data and does nothing to ensure that the terms correspond accurately to the aggregation of microencounters that actually takes place.

Nevertheless, this gives us the clue to the real dimensions of macrostructures: precisely the lines along which aggregation of microencounters takes place. Macrostructure consists of nothing more than large numbers of microencounters, repeated (or sometimes changing) over time and across space. This gives us exactly the dimensions of macrostructures: the sheer *numbers* of persons and encounters involved; the amount of *time* taken up by encounters of various

* From *The Micro-Macro Link*, edited by Jeffrey C. Alexander, Bernhard Giesen, Richard Munch and Neil J. Smelser © 1987 by the Regents of the University of California. Published by the University of California Press.

kinds and their repetitions; and the configuration they make in physical *space*. Time, space, and number: These are the only macrovariables, and every other macroterminology is metaphorical and ultimately should be translated into these. Everything else in a theory is microprocesses. Moreover, it is at the micro level that the dynamics of any theory must be located. The structures never *do* anything; it is only persons in real situations who act. It is on the micro level that we must show the energizing processes, both those that cause structural change and those that are responsible for maintaining and reproducing the structures from one occasion to another (that is to say, the "glue" that holds structures together).

This may sound as if I am giving a great deal of prominence to the micro. That is true, but we should bear in mind that the theoretical issue is not merely one of showing how macrostructures are composed of aggregations of microencounters, and formulating all laws determining macrostructures in terms of aggregations of microevents in time, space, and number. My own previous writing (1975, 1981*a*, 1981*b*) has tended to stress that goal, but I would now add that this exercise in the "microtranslation of the macrostructure" also has a use in the opposite direction, perhaps even a more immediate use: It shows how microevents, the behavior of individuals in situations, are themselves determined by where they are located in the larger network of microencounters around them in time and space. Macrosociology, seen in a fine-grained way, becomes the key to understanding much of what goes on in the realm of microsociology.

More on this below, when I will discuss the theory of interaction ritual (IR) chains. For the moment I would like to illustrate my point that macrostructures are to be explained by principles that aggregate micro processes in time, space, and number. Here is an example: One principle, which is congruent with a fair amount of data, I have labeled the *principle of social density*, after Durkheim's discussions of this subject (Collins 1975: 75–76). This proposes that the more individuals are exposed to networks of social encounters that are diverse and cosmopolitan, the more their ideas will be abstract, relativistic, and concerned with long-term consequences. Conversely, individuals in localistic and enclosed networks think and speak concretely and particularistically, with a short-term outlook and a "magical" attitude toward forces in the larger world. The distribution of such experiences is one dimension of an explanation of class cultures, if one looks at it from the point of view of a macropattern. The dynamics of this principle result from the ritual nature of interaction, a microprocess (explained in greater detail elsewhere; see Collins 1975: 92–103, 153–154). The principle itself, however, is somewhat more macro than that, for it speaks of the number of encounters of various kinds that one has over a period of time, which is at least a local extension of experience beyond one immediate situation. It does not deal with the entire macrostructure in the largest sense, but it does locate the individual in what might be called the "mesostructure," the network of repeated encounters around him or her.

It should be apparent that the distinction between micro and macro levels is a continuum, not a dichotomy. Microevents are situational; but these can be prolonged, repeated, or aggregated, in time, and the number of encounters spreads out in space, as far as one wishes to look. There is an element of macrostructure in almost any microprocess, in that it is affected by (1) the spatial configuration in which it takes place, such as the sheer physical density of the interactive situation itself, and (2) the number of times such situations (or other types of situations) have been repeated in the past by these individuals. Thus individuals will come into any microsituation with a past history of encounters in other microsituations, and these make up the ingredients of what will happen in that particular situation. This encroaches again on the theory of interaction ritual chains, to be discussed later.

Notice that we can pick out any part of the continuum of time and space upon which to focus theoretically. Thus we have very localistic parts of macrostructure, in the aforementioned "principle of social density" affecting individual outlooks. At the opposite extreme we can deal with the large-scale world arena of states, a large-scale focus in historical time and geographical space. Here again we would expect that explanatory principles would be built around sheer temporal, spatial, and numerical relationships: in this example, among the armed groups and material (spatial) conditions of their supply and communication that make up the state. In fact, I have argued elsewhere (Collins 1981*c*, 1985) that the essence of explaining the power of states is contained in the principles of their *geopolitical* relationships. The growth, contraction, and other structural changes in the military and materially extractive networks that make up states are determined, I have proposed, by certain principles of their long-term spatial relationships and the sheer numerical relationships of their populations and material (in other words, space-occupying) possessions. The social dynamics of the struggle for legitimacy, which makes up the microexperiential reality of the struggle for power, are crucially affected by the rises and falls in military threat based on these geopolitical factors. Thus again at the ultra-macro level, explanatory theory can be resolved into time, space, and number conditions affecting microexperiential events. I could also add as an illustration, in a longer discussion of this topic, an intermediate-sized macrostructure, such as formal organizations, and show how organizational structure is determined by the sheer physical and numerical layout of work, as this sets the stage for struggles for control between organizational authorities and their subordinates (Collins 1975:chap. 6).

I will glide past a fairly complex body of theory at this point and state that the *microtranslation* (as opposed to *microreduction*) of macrostructures is theoretically fruitful; that it is more than a program for the future; that it leads to what I hope are more powerful explanatory generalizations on levels of many sizes of the macrocontinuum.

Interaction Ritual (IR) Chains: The Effect of Macro upon Micro

Let us now consider the opposite issue: the location of individual microexperience within the aggregates of microencounters that make up the macrostructure. This is the model of interaction ritual (IR) chains. The terminology is from Goffman (1967); what it implies is that interactions are not merely instrumental but are procedures that both generate and consume symbols representing group membership. There is nothing particularly mysterious about these symbols; for the most part they are embedded in the cultural codes with which people speak. An interaction typically is the negotiation of a momentarily shared conversational reality. The extent to which some type of conversational reality is created depends upon the motivations and resources of the individuals who come to the encounter. That is, what conversation is produced depends on how much individuals wish to speak to one another in a certain fashion and what stored memories, vocal styles, and the like they bring that will enable them to do so. These motivations and resources come from previous encounters; hence the notion of a *chain* of interaction rituals.

To summarize quickly, every conversation gives some increment to the cultural capital of the indi-

viduals who take part in it. This cultural capital can, in turn, be invested in future conversations. Furthermore, there are various kinds of conversations one may participate in: some more formal, Goffmanian "front-stage"; others more "backstage"; some quite intimate. Some conversational topics are "cheap" and common; they cost little but produce little in the way of distinctive ties among the individuals who take part in them. Other kinds of conversations enact one's membership in a network of power, or create ties in relatively exclusive social circles. Thus underlying the manifest content of conversations is a continual negotiation about one's social memberships. There is a marketlike aspect to the series of conversations that takes place over time as individuals attempt to move toward those symbolic exchanges that bring them the best return on the conversational capital they have accumulated so far. Hence the outcome of any conversation is an "emergent situation," in the sense that it cannot be predicted in advance merely from knowing the past history of only one participant. If we know the past history of all the participants, however, we should be able to judge theoretically who will want to talk with whom about what, and whether the other will reciprocate, and hence what further social ties will be enacted.

One might ask a fundamental question in all such market or market-like models: What is the common denominator among all the different types of conversational exchanges, so that individuals can weigh which type of "good" they would like to attain? How does one decide whether he or she should aim for a conversation that will be entertaining as opposed to one that implies membership in a high-prestige group, or again one that brings intimate ties but in a very small localized connection? There is no conversational equivalent of monetary currency which reduces all these to a common value. Nor, for that matter, do various conversational choices present themselves to individuals with clear and full information of what is available, even from the persons standing immediately in front of them. In general, there are considerable limits simply to translating conventional economic theory into these kinds of social exchanges. Individuals do choose, however, and there seems to be a pattern in how they do so. I argue that the common denominator of conversational choice is emotional rather than cognitive. (This is in keeping with models, both rationalistic and ethnomethodological, that converge on the principle of "bounded rationality," the inability of individuals to weigh complex decisions consciously.)

Let us look at this again from the point of view of a chain of interactions. Each conversation in that chain is a negotiation, which results in the inclusion or exclusion of the individual in some kind of local group membership. One result that the person stores from this, as I have said, is cultural capital: things to talk about in future conversations; another is an increment or decrement in emotional energy. Persons who dominate their conversations acquire more energy, more self-confidence, and a greater tendency to take the initiative in subsequent conversations and to put their cultural capital to use. Similarly, one need not dominate the conversation—as it need not be an authority situation, but possibly an egalitarian, sociable, or even an intimate encounter—in order to gain an energy increment; one need only be fully accepted into group membership. So we have on one hand occasions in which persons gain more emotional energy, which in turn gives them an emotional resource to bring to subsequent conversations. On the other hand, persons who are dominated in conversational situations (which may be as a result of enacting an authority situation as the recipient of orders from another) or who are excluded from informal membership situations lose emotional energy.

In any given encounter, then, all the participants who enter it have both some *cultural capital* and a given degree of *emotional energy* set by their past conversations. There is also a third "resource" that circulates: One's *social reputation* and identity, as circulated not so much in one's own talk as in the network of other people's conversations in which one might figure as a topic. When we come to each new encounter, then, whether that encounter will prove to be attractive to both participants or to one side more than the other, and also who will be able to dominate the interaction, depends on the match among the participants of cultural and emotional resources that are brought to it. Individuals do not have to reflect consciously on these matters[3]; the conversation will run off by a force of its own, will be a success or a perfunctory failure, will be one-sided or two-sided, and so forth, depending on the balance of resources brought into the situation. The emotional energy, in my view, is pivotal in this. It determines what each person will *feel* about the conversation he or she is getting into: how much one wants to talk to the other person, whether it is a high or low priority in comparison to what else each might do, and how successful each will be in bringing off the kind of conversation he or she would like to enact. This is true in various kinds of conversational situations, ranging from a boss trying to control a worker, a boy trying to strike up an acquaintance with a girl, the amount of humor shared by casual acquaintances in the hallway, or a wife feeling whether or not she is in the mood to confide in her husband.

Mustafa Emirbayer describes his profoundly multicultural background in his own words: "I was born in Detroit to parents of Turkish and Crimean Tatar descent. I spent my childhood years in Ann Arbor and then, after my mother remarried, in Santa Barbara. When I was fourteen, we moved to Mexico City, where I attended the American School and, briefly, studied piano at the National Conservatory of Music…. I was the product, however, of a family that placed great stock in a humanistic education, and I was also deeply influenced by their many stories of great historical events seen from up close: the Russian Revolution (when my grandmother was young); Stalin's regime, which only some of my family survived (my grandfather, a prominent Soviet official, perished in the purges); then World War II, at the end of which my mother and others in the family became war refugees in Germany and then Turkey." Such a statement goes a long way toward explaining Emirbayer's inventive approach to social theory. He took his PhD in 1969 at Harvard University where Charles Tilly and Harrison White influenced his core thinking on social networks that, in turn, provides the dynamic to his many books and articles on race, culture, as well as sociological social theory. He teaches at the University of Wisconsin. Among major social theories, Emirbayer is notable for his willingness to write with other theorists, including, of course, **Ann Mische** (1965–), his coauthor of "What is Agency?" Mische took her PhD at the New School for Social Research in 1998 (the very year her essay with Emirbayer was published). She taught at Rutgers before joining the sociology faculty at Notre Dame University. Mische writes in a number of areas, notably peace studies, youth, global development, among other topics. Her work, like her coauthor's, is influential in the interpretation of network or relation studies. "What is Agency?" is of particular importance for its nuanced and original analytic dissection of the nature of social agency—a topic long an ill-explained puzzle to sociologists.

What Is Agency?*

Mustafa Emirbayer and Ann Mische (1998)

The Chordal Triad of Agency

What, then, is human agency? We define it as the temporally constructed engagement by actors of different structural environments—the temporal-relational contexts of action—which, through the interplay of habit, imagination, and judgment, both reproduces and transforms those structures in interactive response to the problems posed by changing historical situations.** This definition encompasses what we shall analytically distinguish below as the different constitutive elements of human agency: iteration, projectivity, and practical evaluation. In broad terms, these correspond to the different temporal orientations of agency, allowing us to examine forms of action that are more oriented (respectively) toward the past, the future, and the present. Such a categorization gives analytical expression to Mead's conception of the positioning of human actors within temporal passage, involving the continual reconstruction of their orientations toward past and future in response to emergent events. In addition, it incorporates Mead's insight that it is the capacity for imaginative distancing, as well as for communicative evaluation, in relation to habitual patterns of social

engagement that drives the development of the reflective intelligence, that is, the capacity of actors to critically shape their own responsiveness to problematic situations.

The iterational element.—The first of these dimensions, which we term the iterational element, has received perhaps the most systematic attention in philosophy and sociological theory, most recently from that tradition of thought that Ortner (1984) describes as theories of practice (see also Turner 1994). It refers to the selective reactivation by actors of past patterns of thought and action, as routinely incorporated in practical activity, thereby giving stability and order to social universes and helping to sustain identities, interactions, and institutions over time.

The projective element.—The second dimension of agency, the projective element, has been largely neglected in recent sociological theory, although it does receive attention in the writings of Alfred Schutz and his followers, and, indirectly, of rational choice theorists. Outside of sociology, concern with projectivity can be found in phenomenological and existential philosophy, psychoanalysis, narrative psychology, and dramaturgic anthropology. Projectivity encompasses the imaginative generation by actors of possible future trajectories of action, in which received structures of thought and action may be creatively reconfigured in relation to actors' hopes, fears, and desires for the future.

The practical-evaluative element.—Finally, the practical-evaluative element of agency has been left strikingly undertheorized by sociological thinkers, although intimations of it can be found in a long tradition of moral philosophy extending from Aristotelian ethics to more recent theories of critical deliberation, as well as certain feminist analyses. It entails the capacity of actors to make practical and normative judgments among alternative possible trajectories of action, in response to the emerging demands, dilemmas, and ambiguities of presently evolving situations.

We should stress from the outset that these are analytical distinctions; all three of these constitutive dimensions of human agency are to be found, in varying degrees, within any concrete empirical instance of action. In this sense, it is possible to speak of a chordal triad of agency within which all three dimensions resonate as separate but not always harmonious tones.*** On the other hand, we also claim that, in any given

---

*Republished with the permission of University of Chicago Press and the authors, from "What is Agency?" by Mustafa Emirbayer and Ann Mische, *The American Journal of Sociology*, Vol. 103, No. 4 (Jan. 1998), pp. 970–974. Copyright 1998, University of Chicago Press; permission conveyed through Copyright Clearance Center, Inc.

**While our principal focus in this article remains the different analytical dimensions of agency rather than action's structural contexts, we follow earlier work (Emirbayer and Goodwin 1996)—along with Sorokin (1947), Parsons and Shils (1951), and, especially, Alexander (1988)—in our disaggregation of the latter. As we conceive of it, the cultural context encompasses those symbolic patterns, structures, and formations (e.g., cultural discourses, narratives, and idioms) that constrain and enable action by structuring actors' normative commitments and their understandings of their world and their possibilities within it. The social-structural context encompasses those network patterns of social ties (see Emirbayer and Goodwin 1994) that comprise interpersonal, interorganizational, or transnational settings of action. Finally, the social-psychological context encompasses those psychical structures that constrain and enable action by channeling actors' flows and investments of emotional energy, including long-lasting durable structures of attachment and emotional solidarity. These interpenetrating (but analytically autonomous) categories crosscut the key institutional sectors of modern social life: the administrative-bureaucratic state, the capitalist economy, and civil society (Emirbayer and Sheller 1996).

***This usage is analogous to Patterson's (1991) discussion of the chordal triad of freedom.

case, one or another of these three aspects might well predominate. It is possible to speak of action that is more (or less) engaged with the past, more (or less) directed toward the future, and more (or less) responsive to the present. In each of the three major sections below, we isolate these various analytical dimensions and examine the internal structure of each. Although it will never be possible to carry out our analytical dissections with surgical precision, we aim to show what agentic processes would entail were one or another of these tones in the chordal triad to be sounded most forcefully.*

Moreover, we also argue that each of the three analytical dimensions can be said to possess its own internal chordal structure. The three dimensions of agency that we describe do not correspond in any simple, exclusive way to past, present, and future as successive stages of action. Rather, empirical social action is constructed through ongoing temporal passage and thus through what Mead calls emergent events, rather than through a sequentiality of discrete acts or stages of one act. Each of our dimensions of agency has itself a simultaneous internal orientation toward past, future, and present, for all forms of agency are temporally embedded in the flow of time. We do claim, however, that for each analytical aspect of agency one temporal orientation is the dominant tone, shaping the way in which actors relate to the other two dimensions of time. Disaggregating the dimensions of agency (and exploring which orientations are dominant within a given situation) allows us to suggest that each primary orientation in the chordal triad encompasses as subtones the other two as well, while also showing how this "chordal composition" can change as actors respond to the diverse and shifting environments around them.**

Several further points of clarification are in order here. First, we must reaffirm that agency as we have

sketched it above is a historically variable phenomenon, embedded in changing theoretical and practical conceptions of time and action. Ours is not a universalistic perspective that assumes that all times, places, and persons are equally iterational, projective, or practical-evaluative. Rather, it is precisely the historical, cultural, and personal variability of agentic orientations that make this framework so compelling. The ways in which people understand their own relationship to the past, future, and present make a difference to their actions; changing conceptions of agentic possibility in relation to structural contexts profoundly influence how actors in different periods and places see their worlds as more or less responsive to human imagination, purpose, and effort.

Second, we follow Mead in arguing that changes in temporal orientation may also involve varying degrees of inventiveness and reflectivity in relation to action and its temporal-relational contexts, although not necessarily, as we shall show later, in simple or straightforward ways. (Such a conception signals our deliberate commitment to a humanistic, normative, and critical perspective upon social life.) While we claim that even habitual action is agentic, since it involves attention and effort, such activity is largely unreflective and taken for granted; as actors encounter problematic situations requiring the exercise of imagination and judgment, they gain a reflective distance from received patterns that may (in some contexts) may allow for greater imagination, choice, and conscious purpose. A disaggregated conception of agency thus allows us to locate more precisely the interplay between the reproductive and transformative dimensions of social action (Hays 1994) and to explain how reflectivity can change in either direction, through the increasing routinization or problematization of experience.

Third, we wish to stress that our conception of agency is intrinsically social and relational (Emirbayer 1997) since it centers around the engagement (and disengagement) by actors of the different contextual environments that constitute their own structured yet flexible social universes. For this reason, and also because of our deep resonance with both classical and contemporary pragmatism, one might characterize our approach as relational pragmatics. Viewed internally, agency entails different ways of experiencing the world, although even here, just as consciousness is always consciousness of something (James 1976; Husserl 1960), so too is agency always agency toward something, by means of which actors enter into relationship with surrounding

---

*We bracket for now the added complication that actors are always embedded within many different temporal-relational contexts at once and thus may exhibit a projective orientation within one context, e.g., even as they exhibit an iterational orientation within another. We return to this issue in the final section of the article.

**Lest we fall into the analytical nightmare of "subsubtones" within "subtones," we wish to stress that the notion of an internal chordal structure is a heuristic device that allows us to analyze variation and change in the composition of agentic orientations; clearly, actors do not dissect experience in such a manner while themselves in the flow of temporal passage. We should also note that what we call chordal structures are not necessarily harmonious; the subtones may be dissonant with one another, creating internal tensions that may spur the recomposition of temporal orientations.

persons, places, meanings, and events. Viewed externally, agency entails actual interactions with its contexts, in something like an ongoing conversation; in this sense, it is "filled with dialogic overtones," as a sort of "link in the chain of speech communication" (Bakhtin 1986, pp. 92, 91). Following Mead and Joas, we highlight the importance of intersubjectivity, social interaction, and communication as critical components of agentic processes: agency is always a dialogical process by and through which actors immersed in temporal passage engage with others within collectively organized contexts of action.

Finally, we ground this capacity for human agency in the structures and processes of the human self, conceived of as an internal conversation possessing analytic autonomy vis-à-vis transpersonal interactions. We conceptualize the self not as a metaphysical substance or entity, such as the "soul" or "will" (see White 1995), but rather as a dialogical structure, itself thoroughly relational. Our perspective, in other words, is relational all the way down.* We cannot begin to explore here the ontology of the self or the full implications for agency of such categories as "desire" (although see Lacan 1977). Nor can we present here a systematic analysis of the components or structures of this self, or elaborate a new philosophical psychology, although we can suggest, following Norbert Wiley (1994, p. 210) in The Semiotic Self, that "the interpretive process [taking place within it] is, within limits, open and free," and that this "in turn allows humans to create as well as to pursue goals."** We maintain that while transpersonal contexts do both constrain and enable the dialogical process, such contexts cannot themselves serve as the point of origin of agentic possibilities, which must reside one level down (so to speak), at the level of self-dynamics.

---

*Such a position does present us with a certain difficulty: namely, that corporate actors such as firms, states, or other organizational entities cannot easily be accommodated within the terms of such a framework unless they are themselves given theoretical status equivalent to that of natural persons or selves (for examples of this mode of reasoning, see Coleman [1990], Luhmann [1990], and White [1992]). While not averse to such a move in principle, we do not pursue all of its many implications in the pages to come, or grapple systematically with the special challenges in translation that it would necessarily entail.

**It is worth noting that Wiley's perspective is itself self-consciously grounded in the pragmatist tradition (see also Wiley 1994, pp. 10, 29, 47); for a similar perspective, see Taylor (1991), Colapietro (1990), and Gergen (1994). More work needs to be done, of course, in theorizing the systematic blockages to such "open and free" intrapsychic communication or dialogue.

New Cultural Theories after Modernity

Cornel West (1953–) was born in Tulsa, Oklahoma. It is said that the two important influences on West in his youth were the Baptist church and the Black Panthers. He studied at Harvard, where he earned magna cum laude honors, then at Princeton, where he encountered Richard Rorty during his doctoral studies. West has taught at Union Theological Seminary in New York City, Princeton, Yale, Harvard, and again at Princeton. His abrupt departure in 2002 from a university professorship at Harvard for a university professorship at Princeton was, in part, inspired by the Harvard president's concerns with West's involvement in popular culture, notably a 2001 rap music album *Sketches of My Culture* with Derek D. A. O. Allen. West also has played cameo cinema roles in sequels to the film *The Matrix*. West's many books include *Prophesy Deliverance! An Afro-American Revolutionary Christianity* (1982), *Prophetic Fragments* (1988), *The American Invasion of Philosophy* (1989), and *Race Matters* (1993). Since then, his life has been a whirlwind of public lectures and media appearances, political and religious commentary, and book publication, including a memoir *Brother West: Living and Loving Out Loud* and *The Rich and the Rest of Us* (2012), with Tavis Smiley with whom he offers a regularly talk radio program. In 2011, West decided to return to his original academic home, The Union Theological Seminary. The selection is from West's contribution to *Out There: Marginalization and Contemporary Cultures* (1990), which he edited with Trinh T. Minh-ha and others.

The New Cultural Politics of Difference[*]
Cornel West (1990)

In these last few years of the twentieth century, there is emerging a significant shift in the sensibilities and outlooks of critics and artists. In fact, I would go so far as to claim that a new kind of cultural worker is in the making, associated with a new politics of difference. These new forms of intellectual consciousness advance reconceptions of the vocation of critic and artist, attempting to undermine the prevailing disciplinary divisions of labor in the academy, museum, mass media and gallery networks, while preserving modes of critique within the ubiquitous commodification of culture in the global village. Distinctive features of the new cultural politics of difference are to trash the monolithic and homogeneous in the name of diversity, multiplicity and heterogeneity; to reject the abstract, general and universal in light of the concrete, specific and particular; and to historicize, contextualize and pluralize by highlighting the contingent, provisional, variable, tentative, shifting and changing. Needless to say, these gestures are not new in the history of criticism or art, yet what makes them novel—along with the cultural politics they produce—is how and what constitutes difference, the weight and gravity it is given in representation and the way in which

[*]Excerpt from Russell Ferguson, Martha Gever Trinh T. Minh-ha, and Cornel West, eds., *Out There: Marginalization and Contemporary Cultures* (Cambridge, MA: MIT Press, 1990), pp. 19–32.

highlighting issues like exterminism, empire, class, race, gender, sexual orientation, age, nation, nature, and region at this historical moment acknowledges some discontinuity and disruption from previous forms of cultural critique. To put it bluntly, the new cultural politics of difference consists of creative responses to the precise circumstances of our present moment—especially those of marginalized First World agents who shun degraded self-representations, articulating instead their sense of the flow of history in light of the contemporary terrors, anxieties and fears of highly commercialized North Atlantic capitalist cultures (with their escalating xenophobias against people of color, Jews, women, gays, lesbians and the elderly). The thawing, yet still rigid, Second World ex-communist cultures (with increasing nationalist revolts against the legacy of hegemonic party henchmen), and the diverse cultures of the majority of inhabitants on the globe smothered by international communication cartels and repressive postcolonial elites (sometimes in the name of communism, as in Ethiopia) or starved by austere World Bank and IMF policies that subordinate them to the North (as in free-market capitalism in Chile) also locate vital areas of analysis in this new cultural terrain.

The new cultural politics of difference are neither simply oppositional in contesting the mainstream (or *male*stream) for inclusion, nor transgressive in the avant-gardist sense of shocking conventional bourgeois audiences. Rather, they are distinct articulations of talented (and usually privileged) contributors to culture who desire to align themselves with demoralized, demobilized, depoliticized and disorganized people in order to empower and enable social action and, if possible, to enlist collective insurgency for the expansion of freedom, democracy and individuality. This perspective impels these cultural critics and artists to reveal, as an integral component of their production, the very operations of power within their immediate work contexts (i.e., academy, museum, gallery, mass media). This strategy, however, also puts them in an inescapable double bind—while linking their activities to the fundamental, structural overhaul of these institutions, they often remain financially dependent on them (so much for "independent" creation). For these critics of culture, theirs is a gesture that is simultaneously progressive *and* co-opted. Yet without social movement or political pressure from outside these institutions (extra-parliamentary and extra-curricular actions like the social movements of the recent past), transfor-

mation degenerates into mere accommodation or sheer stagnation, and the role of the "co-opted progressive"—no matter how fervent one's subversive rhetoric—is rendered more difficult. There can be no artistic breakthrough or social progress without some form of crisis in civilization—a crisis usually generated by organizations or collectivities that convince ordinary people to put their bodies and lives on the line. There is, of course, no guarantee that such pressure will yield the result one wants, but there is a guarantee that the status quo will remain or regress if no pressure is applied at all.

The new cultural politics of difference faces three basic challenges—intellectual, existential and political. The intellectual challenge—usually cast as methodological debate in these days in which academicist forms of expression have a monopoly on intellectual life—is how to think about representational practices in terms of history, culture and society. How does one understand, analyze and enact such practices today? An adequate answer to this question can be attempted only after one comes to terms with the insights and blindnesses of earlier attempts to grapple with the question in light of the evolving crisis in different histories, cultures and societies. I shall sketch a brief genealogy—a history that highlights the contingent origins and often ignoble outcomes—of exemplary critical responses to the question. This genealogy sets forth a historical framework that characterizes the rich yet deeply flawed Eurocentric traditions which the new cultural politics of difference build upon yet go beyond.

An appropriate starting point is the ambiguous legacy of the Age of Europe. Between 1492 and 1945, European breakthroughs in oceanic transportation, agricultural production, state-consolidation, bureaucratization, industrialization, urbanization and imperial dominion shaped the makings of the modern world. Precious ideals like the dignity of persons (individuality) or the popular accountability of institutions (democracy) were unleashed around the world. Powerful critiques of illegitimate authorities—of the Protestant Reformation against the Roman Catholic Church, the Enlightenment against state churches, liberal movements against absolutist states and feudal guild constraints, workers against managerial subordination, people of color and Jews against white and gentile supremacist decrees, gays and lesbians against homophobic sanctions—were fanned and fuelled by these precious ideals refined within the crucible of the Age of Europe. Yet the discrepancy between sterling rhetoric and lived reality, glowing principles and actual practices loomed large.

By the last European century—the last epoch in which European domination of most of the globe was uncontested and unchallenged in a substantive way—a new world seemed to be stirring. At the height of England's reign as the major imperial European power, its exemplary cultural critic, Matthew Arnold, painfully observed in his "Stanzas From the Grand Chartreuse" that he felt some sense of "wandering between two worlds, one dead / the other powerless to be born." Following his Burkean sensibilities of cautious reform and fear of anarchy, Arnold acknowledged that the old glue—religion—that had tenuously and often unsuccessfully held together the ailing European regimes could not do so in the mid-nineteenth century. Like Alexis de Tocqueville in France, Arnold saw that the democratic temper was the wave of the future. So he proposed a new conception of culture—a secular, humanistic one—that could play an integrative role in cementing and stabilizing an emerging bourgeois civil society and imperial state. His famous castigation of the immobilizing materialism of the declining aristocracy, the vulgar philistinism of the emerging middle classes and the latent explosiveness of the working-class majority was motivated by a desire to create new forms of cultural legitimacy, authority and order in a rapidly changing moment in nineteenth century Europe.

For Arnold, (in *Culture and Anarchy*, [1869]) this new conception of culture

> . . . seeks to do away with classes; to make the best that has been thought and known in the world current everywhere; to make all men live in an atmosphere of sweetness and light. . . .
>
> This is the *social idea* and the men of culture are the true apostles of equality. The great men of culture are those who have had a passion for diffusing, for making prevail, for carrying from one end of society to the other, the best knowledge, the best ideas of their time, who have laboured to divest knowledge of all that was harsh, uncouth, difficult, abstract, professional, exclusive; to humanize it, to make it efficient outside the clique of the cultivated and learned, yet still remaining the best knowledge and thought of the time, and a true source, therefore, of sweetness and light.

As an organic intellectual of an emergent middle class—as the inspector of schools in an expanding educational bureaucracy, Professor of Poetry at Oxford (the first non-cleric and the first to lecture in English rather than Latin) and an active participant in a thriving magazine network—Arnold defined and defended a new secular culture of critical discourse. For him, this discursive strategy would be lodged in the educational and periodical apparatuses of modern societies as they contained and incorporated the frightening threats of an arrogant aristocracy and especially of an "anarchic" working-class majority. His ideals of disinterested, dispassionate and objective inquiry would regulate this new secular cultural production, and his justifications for the use of state power to quell any threats to the survival and security of this culture were widely accepted. He aptly noted, "Through culture seems to lie our way, not only to perfection, but even to safety." . . .

Yet Arnold's project was disrupted by the collapse of nineteenth-century Europe—World War I. This unprecedented war brought to the surface the crucial role and violent potential not of the masses Arnold feared but of the state he heralded. Upon the ashes of this wasteland of human carnage—some of it the civilian European population—T. S. Eliot emerged as the grand cultural spokesman. . . .

Eliot's image of Europe as a wasteland, a culture of fragments with no cementing center, predominated in postwar Europe. And though his early poetic practices were more radical, open and international than his Eurocentric criticism, Eliot posed a return to and revision of tradition as the only way of regaining European cultural order and political stability. . . .

The second historical coordinate of my genealogy is the emergence of the USA as *the* world power. The USA was unprepared for world power status. However, with the recovery of Stalin's Russia (after losing 20 million dead), the USA felt compelled to make its presence felt around the globe. Then with the Marshall plan to strengthen Europe against Russian influence (and provide new markets for U.S. products), the 1948 Russian takeover of Czechoslovakia, the 1948 Berlin blockade, the 1950 beginning of the Korean War and the 1952 establishment of NATO forces in Europe, it seemed clear that there was no escape from world power obligations.

The post–World War II era in the USA, or the first decades of what Henry Luce envisioned as "The American Century," was not only a period of incredible economic expansion but of active cultural ferment. In the classical Fordist formula, mass production required mass consumption. With unchallenged hegemony in the capitalist world, the USA took economic growth for granted. Next to exercising its crude, anti-communist, McCarthyist obsessions, buying commodities became the primary act of civic virtue for many American citizens at this time. The creation of a mass middle class—a prosperous working class with a bourgeois identity—was countered by the first major emergence of subcultures of American non-WASP intellectuals: the so-called New York intellectuals in criticism, the Abstract Expressionists in painting and the BeBop artists in jazz music. This emergence signaled a vital challenge to an American male WASP elite loyal to an older and eroding European culture.

The first significant blow was dealt when assimilated Jewish Americans entered the higher echelons of the cultural apparatuses (academy, museums, galleries, mass media). Lionel Trilling is an emblematic figure. This Jewish entree into the anti-Semitic and patriarchal critical discourse of the exclusivistic institutions of American culture initiated the slow but sure undoing of the male WASP cultural hegemony and homogeneity. Lionel Trilling's project was to appropriate Matthew Arnold for his own political and cultural purposes—thereby unraveling the old male WASP consensus, while erecting a new post–World War II liberal academic consensus around cold war, anti-communist renditions of the values of complexity, difficulty, variousness and modulation. In addition, the postwar boom laid the basis for intense professionalization and specialization in expanding institutions of higher education—especially in the natural sciences that were compelled to somehow respond to Russia's successful ventures in space. Humanistic scholars found themselves searching for new methodologies that could buttress self-images of rigor and scientific seriousness. For example, the close reading techniques of New Criticism (severed from their conservative, organicist, anti-industrialist ideological roots), the logical precision of reasoning in analytic philosophy and the jargon of Parsonian structural-functionalism in sociology helped create such self-images. Yet towering cultural critics like C. Wright Mills, W. E. B. Du Bois, Richard Hofstadter, Margaret Mead and Dwight MacDonald bucked the tide. . . .

This threat is partly associated with the third historical coordinate of my genealogy—the decolonization of the Third World. It is crucial to recognize the importance of this world-historical process if one wants to grasp the significance of the end of the Age of Europe and the emergence of the USA as a world power. With the first defeat of a western nation by a non-western nation—in Japan's victory over Russia (1905), revolutions in Persia (1905), Turkey (1908), China (1912), Mexico (1911–12) and much later the independence of India (1947) and China (1948) and the triumph of Ghana (1957)—the actuality of a decolonized globe loomed large. Born of violent struggle, consciousness-raising and the reconstruction of identities, decolonization simultaneously brings with it new perspectives on that long festering underside of the Age of Europe (of which colonial domination represents the *costs* of "progress," "order" and "culture"), as well as requiring new readings of the economic boom in the USA (wherein the Black, Brown, Yellow, Red, female, elderly, gay, lesbian and White working class live the same *costs* as cheap labor at home as well as in U.S.-dominated Latin American and Pacific rim markets).

The impetuous ferocity and moral outrage that motors the decolonization process is best captured by Frantz Fanon in *The Wretched of the Earth* (1961).

Decolonization, which sets out to change the order of the world, is obviously, a program of complete disorder. . . . Decolonization is the meeting of two forces, opposed to each other by their very nature, which in fact owe their originality to that sort of substantification which results from and is nourished by the situation in the colonies. Their first encounter was marked by violence and their existence together—that is to say the exploitation of the native by the settler—was carried on by dint of a great array of bayonets and cannons . . .

In decolonization, there is therefore the need of a complete calling in question of the colonial situation. If we wish to describe it precisely, we might find it in the well-known words: "The last shall be first and the first last." Decolonization is the putting into practice of this sentence.

The naked truth of decolonization evokes for us the searing bullets and bloodstained knives which emanate from it. For if the last shall be first, this will only come to pass after a murderous and decisive struggle between the two protagonists.

Fanon's strong words, though excessively Manichean, still describe the feelings and thoughts between the occupying British Army and colonized Irish in Northern Ireland, the occupying Israeli Army and subjugated Palestinians on the West Bank and Gaza Strip, the South African Army and oppressed Black South Africans in the townships, the Japanese Police and Koreans living in Japan, the Russian Army and subordinated Armenians and others in the Southern and Eastern USSR. His words also partly invoke the sense many Black Americans have toward police departments in urban centers. In other words, Fanon is articulating century-long heartfelt human responses to being degraded and despised, hated and hunted, oppressed and exploited, marginalized and dehumanized at the hands of powerful xenophobic European, American, Russian and Japanese imperial countries.

During the late '50s, '60s and early '70s in the USA, these decolonized sensibilities fanned and fueled the Civil Rights and Black Power movements, as well as the student anti-war, feminist, gray, brown, gay, and lesbian movements. In this period we witnessed the shattering of male WASP cultural homogeneity and the collapse of the short-lived liberal consensus. The inclusion of African Americans, Latino/a Americans, Asian Americans, Native Americans and American women into the culture of critical discourse yielded intense intellectual polemics and inescapable ideological polarization that focused principally on the exclusions, silences and blindnesses of male WASP cultural homogeneity and its concomitant Arnoldian notions of the canon.

In addition, these critiques promoted three crucial processes that affected intellectual life in the country. First is the appropriation of the theories of post-war Europe—especially the work of the Frankfurt school (Marcuse, Adorno, Horkheimer), French/Italian Marxisms (Sartre, Althusser, Lefebvre, Gramsci), structuralisms (Lévi-Strauss, Todorov) and post-structuralisms (Deleuze, Derrida, Foucault). These diverse and disparate theories—all preoccupied with keeping alive radical projects after the end of the Age of Europe—tend to fuse versions of transgressive European modernisms with Marxist or post-Marxist left politics and unanimously shun the term "post-modernism." Second, there is the recovery and revisioning of American history in light of the struggles of white male workers, women, African Americans, Native Americans, Latino/a Americans, gays and lesbians. Third is the impact of forms of popular culture such as television, film, music videos and even sports, on highbrow literate culture. The Black-based hip-hop culture of youth around the world is one grand example.

After 1973, with the crisis in the international world economy, America's slump in productivity, the challenge of OPEC nations to the North Atlantic monopoly of oil production, the increasing competition in hi-tech sectors of the economy from Japan and West Germany and the growing fragility of the international debt structure, the USA entered a period of waning self-confidence (compounded by Watergate) and a nearly contracting economy. As the standards of living for the middle classes declined, owing to runaway inflation, and the quality of living fell for most, due to escalating unemployment, underemployment and crime, religious and secular neo-conservatism emerged with power and potency. This fusion of fervent neo-nationalism, traditional cultural values and "free market" policies served as the ground work for the Reagan-Bush era.

The ambiguous legacies of the European Age, American preeminence and decolonization continue to haunt our postmodern movement as we come to terms with both the European, American, Japanese, Soviet, and Third World *crimes against and contributions to* humanity. The plight of Africans in the New World can be instructive in this regard.

By 1914 European maritime empires had dominion over more than half of the land and a third of the peoples in the world—almost 72 million square kilometers of territory and more than 560 million people under colonial rule. Needless to say, this European control included brutal enslavement, institutional terrorism and cultural degradation of Black diaspora people. The death of roughly seventy-five million Africans during the centuries-long transatlantic slave trade is but one reminder, among others, of the assault on Black humanity. The Black diaspora condition of New World servitude—in which they were viewed as mere commodities with production value, who had no proper legal status, social standing or public worth—can be characterized as, following Orlando Patterson, natal alienation. This state of perpetual and inheritable domination that diaspora Africans had at birth produced the *modern Black diaspora problematic of invisibility and namelessness.* White supremacist practices—enacted under the auspices of the prestigious cultural authorities of the churches, printed media and scientific academics—promoted Black inferiority and constituted the European background against which Black diaspora struggles for identity, dignity (self-confidence, self-respect, self-esteem) and material resources took place.

An inescapable aspect of this struggle was that the Black diaspora peoples' quest for validation and recognition occurred on the ideological, social and cultural terrains of other non-Black peoples. White supremacist assaults on Black intelligence, ability, beauty and character required persistent Black efforts to hold self-doubt, self-contempt and even self-hatred at bay. Selective appropriation, incorporation and re-articulation of European ideologies, cultures and institutions alongside an African heritage—a heritage more or less confined to linguistic innovation in rhetorical practices, stylizations of the body in forms of occupying an alien social space (hair styles, ways of walking, standing, hand expressions, talking) and means of constituting and sustaining comraderie and community (e.g., antiphonal, call-and-response styles, rhythmic repetition, risk-ridden syncopation in spectacular modes in musical and rhetorical expressions)—were some of the strategies employed.

The modern Black diaspora problematic of invisibility and namelessness can be understood as the condition of *relative lack of Black power to represent themselves to themselves and others as complex human beings, and thereby to contest the bombardment of negative, degrading stereotypes put forward by White supremacist ideologies.* The initial Black response to being caught in this whirlwind of Europeanization was to resist the misrepresentation and caricature of the terms set by uncontested non-Black norms and models and fight for self-representation and recognition. Every modern Black person, especially cultural disseminators, encounters this problematic of invisibility and namelessness. The initial Black diaspora response was a mode of resistance that was *moralistic in content* and *communal in character.* That is, the fight for representation and recognition highlighted moral judgments regarding Black "positive" images over and against White supremacist stereotypes. These images "represented" monolithic and homogeneous Black communities, in a way that could displace past misrepresentations of these communities. Stuart Hall has talked about these responses as attempts to change "the relations of representation." . . .

The moralistic and communal aspects of the initial Black diaspora responses to social and psychic erasure were not simply cast into simplistic binary oppositions of positive/negative, good/bad images that privileged the first term in light of a White norm so that Black efforts remained inscribed within the very logic that dehumanized them. They were further complicated by the fact that these responses were also advanced principally by anxiety-ridden, middle-class Black intellectuals, (predominantly male and heterosexual) grappling with their sense of double-consciousness—namely their own crisis of identity, agency and audience—caught between a quest for White approval and acceptance and an endeavor to overcome the internalized association of Blackness with inferiority. . . .

One crucial lesson of this decolonization process remains the manner in which most Third World authoritarian bureaucratic elites deploy essentialist rhetorics about "homogeneous national communities" and "positive images" in order to repress and regiment their diverse and heterogeneous populations. Yet in the diaspora, especially among First World countries, this critique has emerged not so much from the Black male component of the left but rather from the Black women's movement. The decisive push of postmodern Black intellectuals toward a new cultural politics of difference has been made by the powerful critiques and constructive explorations of Black diaspora women (e.g., Toni Morrison). The coffin used to bury the innocent notion of the essential Black subject was nailed shut with the termination of the Black male monopoly on the construction of the Black subject. In this regard, the Black diaspora womanist critique has had a greater impact than the critiques that highlight exclusively class, empire, age, sexual orientation or nature.

This decisive push toward the end of Black innocence—though prefigured in various degrees in the best moments of W. E. B. DuBois, Anna Cooper, C. L. R. James, James Baldwin, Claudia Jones, the later Malcolm X, Frantz Fanon, Amiri Baraka and others—forces Black diaspora cultural workers to encounter what Hall has called the "politics of representation." The main aim now is not simply access to representation in order to produce positive images of homogeneous communities—though broader access remains a practical and political problem. Nor is the primary goal here that of contesting stereotypes—though contestation remains a significant though limited venture. Following the model of the Black diaspora traditions of music, athletics and rhetoric, Black cultural workers must constitute and sustain discursive and institutional networks that deconstruct earlier modern Black strategies for identity-formation, demystify power relations that incorporate class, patriarchal and homophobic biases, and construct more multi-valent and multi-dimensional responses that articulate the complexity and diversity of Black practices in the modern and postmodern world.

Furthermore, Black cultural workers must investigate and interrogate the other of Blackness-Whiteness. One cannot deconstruct the binary oppositional logic of images of Blackness without extending it to the contrary condition of Blackness/ Whiteness itself. However, a mere dismantling will not do—for the very notion of a deconstructive social theory is oxymoronic. Yet social theory is what is needed to examine and *explain* the historically specific ways in which "Whiteness" is a politically constructed category parasitic on "Blackness," and thereby to conceive of the profoundly hybrid character of what we mean by "race," "ethnicity," and "nationality." For instance, European immigrants arrived on American shores perceiving themselves as "Irish," "Sicilian," "Lithuanian," etc. They had to learn that they were "White" principally by adopting an American discourse of positively-valued Whiteness and negatively-charged Blackness. This process by which people define themselves physically, socially, sexually and even politically in terms of Whiteness or Blackness has much bearing not only on constructed notions of race and ethnicity but also on how we understand the changing character of U.S. nationalities. And given the Americanization of the world, especially in the sphere of mass culture, such inquiries—encouraged by the new cultural politics of difference—raise critical issues of "hybridity," "exilic status" and "identity" on an international scale. Needless to say, these inquiries must traverse those of "male/female," "colonizer/colonized," "heterosexual/homosexual," et al., as well.…

Jeffrey C. Alexander (1947–) studied at Harvard College before graduate studies. His PhD in Sociology at the University of California Berkeley was awarded in 1978, after which he taught until 2001 at the University of California Los Angeles. He moved to Yale in 2001 to chair the Department and establish Yale's Center for Cultural Sociology which he today directs with Ron Eyerman and Philip Smith. In 2004 he was became the Lillian Chavenson Saden Professor of Sociology at Yale. Early in his career, Alexander quickly rose to international attention with the publication of his massive four volume work *Theoretical Logic in Sociology* (1982). The parallel between this book and Parsons's *Structural of* *Social Action* (1937) is unmistakable. Some took Alexander's acknowledged goal of reworking the functionalism associated with Parsons as a sign that he was a functionalist, pure and simple.

Yet, even in this first major book, it was evident that Alexander was engaged in a deep epistemological revision of the theoretical logic of Parsons and the classical thinkers. In *Neofunctionalism and After* (1998) he explicitly broke with the functionalist tradition. Thereafter Alexander focused on his already important writings on culture and politics, of which *The Civil Sphere* (2006) is the major work in which he described in historical terms the importance of rethinking democratic politics in respect to a strong theory of culture. Since, he has written and edited, singly and with others, on a wide range of key subjects in cultural sociology, including: *Trauma* (2012) and *The Performance of Politics* (2010). No one has done more to distinguish cultural sociology from the formalizing limitations of an earlier sociology of culture, on the one hand, and, on the other, from varieties of cultural studies that, in his view, lack a strong research program.

Cultural Codes and Democratic Communication*
Jeffrey C. Alexander (2006)

Particular goals and even the most strategic of actions are framed and sometimes bound by commitments to cultural codes. The tradition of Thrasymachus explores the base of politics. But power is also a medium of communication, not simply a goal of interested action or a means of coercion. It has a symbolic code, not only a material base.

It is, in fact, precisely because politics has reference to a symbolic code that it can never be simply situational, for it will always have a generalized dimension as well. This generalized reference makes politics not only contingent and rational but stylized and prescribed. To understand it, we need to employ semiotic theories of binary codes, literary models of rhetoric and narrative, and anthropological concepts of performance and myth. The symbolic medium of politics is a language that political actors themselves do not fully understand. It is not only situationally motivated speech, but deep symbolic structure. In his riposte to functionalist and other equally reductive anthropologies, Lévi-Strauss once insisted that kinship exists "only in human consciousness; it is an arbitrary system of representations, not the spontaneous development of a real situation." This seminal insight is not only anthropological, nor does it apply only to archaic worlds. Wittgenstein placed this notion at the basis of his later, and most profound, language philosophy. In the chapters that follow, it will inform my sociology of the modern civil domain. For I wish to insist on the significance of language in political life, even if I will follow neither structuralism nor Wittgenstein in suggesting we can focus on language alone. As Arlette Farge has written in her investigation of the plebian public sphere in prerevolutionary France, "the words which give opinions—this will do, that will not do—are a reality and show very clearly that the people of Paris did not blindly accept the conditions under which they lived." It is their "speech whose meaning we must strive to discover," she argues, for "words spoken and opinions pronounced could open up distances, cause displacements and organize something which was new to the spheres of saying and doing." It is for this reason, she concludes, that historians "have to cleave to words so as to extract their meanings." So must social theorists and sociologists as well.

Civil society is regulated by an internally complex discourse that allows us to understand the paradox by which its universalistic ideals have so easily been institutionalized in particularistic and anticivil ways. The breadth and scope of a civil community led Kant and other Enlightenment philosophers to identify civil ties by such abstract terms as "reason" and "right." In his discourse ethics, which has done so much to sustain the normative idea of universalism in the present day, Habermas has translated this Enlightenment philosophical vocabulary into a theory of rational speech acts. Making the willingness to cooperate immanent to the efforts that speakers make to gain understanding in conversations, and generalizing from this thought experiment to the macrosociological sphere of civil public life, Habermas has effectively limited analysis of public discourse to such concepts as reasonableness, reciprocity, and fairness. Only such references, he has insisted, can create completely "transparent" communication. As I also mentioned in chapter I, similar strains of abstract universalism permeate Rawls's theory of justice, which rests on the hypothesis that actors can develop solidaristic distributive principles only by denying any actual knowledge of their own particular personal fates. Durkheim's discussion of the growing "abstraction of the collective conscience" and Parsons's of "value generalization" and "instrumental activism" reveal the same effort to tie civil solidarity to an abstract and contentless conception of rationality.

Universalistic ties, however, do not have to be articulated by abstract references to reason or right, to a discourse that transcends the arbitrary in a completely transparent way. Such references do, of course, inform foundational documents like the American *Declaration of Independence* and the French *Declaration of the Rights of Man*. But to limit our thinking about democratic discourse to such symbols alone is to commit what might be called the fallacy of misplaced abstractness. Strange as it may seem, universalism is most often articulated in concrete rather than abstract language. Reworking the narratives and codes of local and particular cultures, normative demands for civility and mutual respect express themselves in figurative images, salty metaphors, hoary myths, and binary oppositions. Universalism anchors itself, in other words, in the everyday lifeworlds within which ordinary people make sense of the world and pass their time. For the French revolutionary *sans-coulettes* and the colonial American patriots, the civil society they fought for was not abstract. For the French, it was the "beloved nation," often portrayed iconically as a woman, Marie, the goddess of liberty. Revolutionary Americans metaphorically inscribed critical reason in the prophetic narratives of the Old Testament and freedom in such icons as the Liberty Tree.

That civil language is symbolic and experiential, not only rational in the moral or strategic sense, that the very effort to speak universalism must always and everywhere take a concrete form, opens our consideration of civil society not only to the particularistic but also the repressive dimensions of modern democratic life. Because meaning is relational and relative, the civility of the self always articulates itself in language about the incivility of the other. This paradox in the very construction of the language of civil society is intensified by the contradictions that inevitably accompany organizational efforts to institutionalize it. There remains the possibility of justice, but it is devilishly difficult to obtain. These are the dilemmas we take up in the chapters that follow.

Henry Louis Gates, Jr. (1950–) was born in Keyser, West Virginia. After completing undergraduate studies at Yale in 1973, Gates studied at Cambridge University, where he received his Ph.D. in 1979. He has taught at Cornell (1985–1990), Duke (1990–1991), and Harvard, where he is director of the W. E. B. Du Bois Institute and professor of humanities. Gates moved to Harvard with the clear intent of rebuilding its African American studies program which today has become one of the most important centers of African American research in the nation. Gates is a prolific author, film producer, and public intellectual. One would not be far wrong to characterize him, relative to Cornel West, as comparably influential if in a more sober and mainstream fashion. For example, he has written regularly for *The New Yorker* magazine and has won numerous awards for not only his scholarly work but his film series *Wonders of the African World and African American Live*s which appeared on American public television. He is the author and editor of numerous books, series, and collections, including *Our Nig: Sketches in the Life of a Free Black* (1983), *Signifying Monkey* (1988*), Loose Canons* (1991), *Colored People* (1994), and the multivolume *Schomburg Library of Nineteenth-Century Black Women Writers*, and, more recently, *Life Upon These Shores: Looking at African American Experience: 1513-2008* (2011). Among other projects, he has edited or co-edited major reference works, including *Africana: Encyclopedia of African and African American Experience* (2008, with Anthony Appiah) and the *Encyclopedia of Africa* (2010, also with Appiah). There is almost no aspect of African world history that his scholarship and filmmaking has not touched in one way or another.

"Race" as the Trope of the World[*]
Henry Louis Gates, Jr. (1986)

Race has become a trope of ultimate, irreducible difference between cultures, linguistic groups, or adherents of specific belief systems which—more often than not—also have fundamentally opposed economic interests. Race is the ultimate trope of difference because it is so very arbitrary in its application.

[*] Gates, Jr., Henry Louis. *Race, Writing, and Difference*. © 1986 The University of Chicago. Reprinted with permission of University of Chicago Press.

The biological criteria used to determine "difference" in sex simply do not hold when applied to "race." Yet we carelessly use language in such a way as to *will* this sense of *natural* difference into our formulations. To do so is to engage in a pernicious act of language, one which exacerbates the complex problem of cultural or ethnic difference, rather than to assuage or redress it.

For literacy, as I hope to demonstrate, is the emblem that links racial alienation with economic alienation. Where better to test this thesis than in the example of the black tradition's first poet in English, the African slave girl Phillis Wheatley. Let us imagine the scene.

One bright morning in the spring of 1772, a young African girl walked demurely into the courthouse at Boston to undergo an oral examination, the results of which would determine the direction of her life and work. Perhaps she was shocked upon entering the appointed room. For there, gathered in a semicircle, sat eighteen of Boston's most notable citizens. Among them was John Erving, a prominent Boston merchant; the Reverend Charles Chauncey, pastor of the Tenth Congregational Church; and John Hancock, who would later gain fame for his signature on the Declaration of Independence. At the center of this group would have sat His Excellency, Thomas Hutchinson, governor of the colony, with Andrew Oliver, his lieutenant governor, close by his side.

Why had this august group been assembled? Why had it seen fit to summon this young African girl, scarcely eighteen years old, before it? This group of "the most respectable characters in *Boston*," as it would later define itself, had assembled to question closely the African adolescent on the slender sheaf of poems that she claimed to have written by herself. We can only speculate on the nature of the questions posed to the fledgling poet. Perhaps they asked her to identify and explain—for all to hear—exactly who were the Greek and Latin gods and poets alluded to so frequently in her work. Perhaps they asked her to conjugate a verb in Latin, or even to translate randomly selected passages from the Latin, which she and her master, John Wheatley, claimed that she "had made some progress in." Or perhaps they asked her to recite from memory key passages from the texts of John Milton and Alexander Pope, the two poets by whom the African claimed to be most directly influenced. We do not know.

We do know, however, that the African poet's responses were more than sufficient to prompt the eighteen august gentlemen to compose, sign, and publish a two-paragraph "Attestation," an open letter "To the Publick" that prefaces Phillis Wheatley's book, and which reads in part:

> We whose Names are underwritten, do assure the World, that the poems specified in the following Page, were (as we veribly believe) written by Phillis, a young Negro Girl, who was but a few Years since, brought an uncultivated Barbarian from *Africa*, and has ever since been, and now is, under the Disadvantage of serving as a Slave in a Family in this Town. She has been examined by some of the best judges, and is thought qualified to write them.

So important was this document in securing a publisher for Phillis Wheatley's poems that it forms the signal element in the prefatory matter printed in the opening pages of her *Poems on Various Subjects, Religious and Moral*, published at London in 1773.

Without the published "Attestation," Phillis Wheatley's publisher claimed, few would believe that an African could possibly have written poetry all by herself. As the eighteen put the matter clearly in their letter, "Numbers would be ready to suspect they were not really the Writings of Phillis." Phillis Wheatley and her master, John Wheatley, had attempted to publish a similar volume in 1770 at Boston, but Boston publishers had been incredulous. Three years later, "Attestation" in hand, Phillis Wheatley and her master's son, Nathaniel Wheatley, sailed for England, where they completed arrangements for the publication of a volume of her poems with the aid of the countess of Huntington and the earl of Dartmouth.

This curious anecdote, surely one of the oddest oral examinations on record, is only a tiny part of a larger, and even more curious, episode in the Enlightenment. Since the beginning of the seventeenth century, Europeans had wondered aloud whether or not the African "species of men," as they most commonly put it, *could* ever create formal literature, could ever master "the arts and sciences." If they could, the argument ran, then the African variety of humanity and the European variety were fundamentally related. If not, then it seemed clear that the African was destined by nature to be a slave.

Why was the creative writing of the African of such importance to the eighteenth century's debate over slavery? I can briefly outline one thesis: after René Descartes, *reason* was privileged, or valorized, above all other human characteristics. Writing, especially after the printing press became so widespread, was taken to be the *visible* sign of reason. Blacks were "reasonable," and hence "men," if—and only if—they demonstrated mastery of "the arts and sciences," the eighteenth century's formula for writing. So, while the Enlightenment is characterized by its foundation on man's ability to reason, it simultaneously used the absence and presence of reason to delimit and circumscribe the very humanity of the cultures and people of color which Europeans had been "discovering" since the Renaissance. The urge toward the systematization of all human knowledge (by which we characterize the Enlightenment) led directly to the relegation of black people to a lower place in the great chain of being, an ancient construct that arranged all of creation on a vertical scale from plants, insects, and animals through man to the angels and God himself.

By 1750, the chain had become minutely calibrated; the human scale rose from "the lowliest Hottentot" (black South Africans) to "glorious Milton and Newton." If blacks could write and publish imaginative literature, then they could, in effect, take a few "giant steps" up the chain of being in an evil game of "Mother, May I?" For example, scores of reviews of Wheatley's book argued that the publication of her poems meant that the African was indeed a human being and should not be enslaved. Indeed, Wheatley herself was manumitted soon after her poems were published. That which was only implicit in Wheatley's case would become explicit fifty years later. George Moses Horton had, by the middle of the 1820s, gained a considerable reputation at Chapel Hill as "the slave-poet." His master printed full-page advertisements in Northern newspapers soliciting subscriptions for a book of Horton's poems and promising to exchange the slave's freedom for a sufficient return on sales of the book. Writing, for these slaves, was not an activity of mind; rather, it was a commodity which they were forced to trade for their humanity.

Blacks and other people of color could not write.

Writing, many Europeans argued, stood alone among the fine arts as the most salient repository of "genius," the visible sign of reason itself. In this subordinate role, however, writing, although secondary to reason, is nevertheless the *medium* of reason's expression. We *know* reason by its writing, by its representations. Such representations could assume spoken or written form. And while several superb scholars give priority to the *spoken* as the privileged of the pair, most Europeans privileged *writing*—in their writings about Africans, at least—as the principal measure of the Africans' humanity, their capacity for progress, their very place in the great chain of being.

The direct correlation between economic and political alienation, on the one hand, and racial alienation, on the other, is epitomized in the following 1740 South Carolina statute that attempted to make it almost impossible for black slaves to acquire, let alone master, literacy:

> *And whereas* the having slaves taught to write, or suffering them to be employed in writing, may be attending with great inconveniences;
>
> *Be it enacted*, that all and every person and persons whatsoever, who shall hereafter teach, or cause any slave or slaves to be taught to write, or shall use or employ any slave as a scribe in any manner of writing whatsoever, hereafter taught to write; every such person or persons shall, for every offense, forfeith the sum of one hundred pounds current money.

Learning to read and to write, then, was not only difficult, it was a violation of a law.

As early as 1705, a Dutch explorer, William Bosman, had encased the commodity function of writing and its relation to racial and economic alienation in a myth which the Africans he "discovered" had purportedly related to him. According to Bosman, the blacks

> tell us, that in the beginning God created Black as well as White men; thereby . . . giving the Blacks the first Election, who chose Gold, and left the Knowledge of Letters to the White. God granted their Request, but being incensed at their Avarice, resolved that the Whites should for ever be their masters, and they obliged to wait on them as their slaves.

Bosman's fabrication, of course, was a claim of origins designed to sanction through mythology a political order created by Europeans. But it was Hume, writing midway through the eighteenth century, who gave to Bosman's myth the sanction of Enlightenment philosophical reasoning.

In a major essay, "Of National Characters" (1748), Hume discusses the "characteristics" of the world's major division of human beings. In a footnote added in 1753 to his original text (the margins

of his discourse), Hume posited with all of the authority of philosophy the fundamental identity of complexion, character, and intellectual capacity:

> I am apt to suspect the negroes, and in general all the other species of men (for there are four or five different kinds) to be naturally inferior to the whites. There never was a civilized nation of any other complexion than white, nor even any individual eminent either in action or speculation. No ingenious manufactures amongst them, *no arts, no sciences* . . . Such a uniform and constant difference could not happen, in so many countries and ages, if *nature* had not made an original distinction betwixt these breeds of men. Not to mention our colonies, there are Negroe slaves dispersed all over Europe, of which none ever discovered any symptoms and ingenuity. . . . In Jamaica indeed they talk of one negroe as a man of parts and learning [Francis Williams, the Cambridge-educated poet who wrote verse in Latin]; but 'tis likely he is admired for very slender accomplishments, like a parrot, who speaks a few words plainly.

Hume's opinion on the subject, as we might expect, became prescriptive.

In his *Observations on the Feeling of the Beautiful and Sublime* (1764), Kant elaborates on Hume's essay in section 4, entitled "Of National Characteristics, So Far as They Depend upon the Distinct Feeling of the Beautiful and Sublime." Kant first claims that "so fundamental is the difference between [the black and white] races of man, . . . it appears to be as great in regard to mental capacities as in color." Kant, moreover, is one of the earliest major European philosophers to conflate color with intelligence, a determining relation he posits with dictatorial surety:

> Father Labat reports that a Negro carpenter, whom he reproached for haughty treatment toward his wives, answered: "You whites are indeed fools, for first you make great concessions to your wives, and afterward you complain when they drive you mad." And it might be that there were something in this which perhaps deserved to be considered; but in short, this fellow was *quite black* from head to foot, a clear proof that what he said was stupid.

The correlation of "black" and "stupid" Kant posits as if it were self-evident.

Hegel, echoing Hume and Kant, claimed that Africans had no history, because they had developed no systems of writing and had not mastered the art of writing in European languages. In judging civilizations, Hegel's strictures with respect to the absence of written history presume a crucial role for *memory*, a collective, cultural memory. Metaphors of the childlike nature of the slaves, of the masked, puppetlike personality of the black, all share this assumption about the absence of memory. Mary Langdon, in her novel *Ida May: A Story of Things Actual and Possible* (1854), writes that "they *are* mere children. . . . You seldom hear them say much about anything that's past, if they only get enough to eat and drink at the present moment." Without writing, no *repeatable* sign of the workings of reason, of mind, could exist. Without memory or mind, no history could exist. Without history, no humanity, as defined consistently from Vico to Hegel, could exist.

Ironically, Anglo-African writing arose as a response to allegations of its absence, Black people responded to these profoundly serious allegations about their "nature" as directly as they could: they wrote books, poetry, autobiographical narratives. Political and philosophical discourse were the predominant forms of writing. Among these, autobiographical "deliverance" narratives were the most common and the most accomplished. Accused of lacking a formal and collective history, blacks published individual histories which, taken together, were intended to narrate in segments the larger yet fragmented history of blacks in Africa, now dispersed throughout a cold New World. The narrated, descriptive "eye" was put into service as a literary form to posit both the individual "I" of the black author as well as the collective "I" of the race. Text created author; and black authors, it was hoped, would create, or re-create, the image of the race in European discourse. The very *face* of the race was contingent upon the recording of the black *voice*. Voice presupposed a face, but also seems to have been thought to determine the very contours of the black face....

California at Santa Cruz where today she is Distinguished Professor Emerita. Haraway lectures widely and is a regular faculty at the European Graduate School. Her writings include *Primate Visions: Gender, Race, and Nature in the World of Modern Science* (1989), *Modest_Witness@Second_Millennium.FemaleMan©_Meets_OncoMouse*™ (1997), and *Simians, Cyborgs, and Women: The Reinvention of Nature* (1991), which is a collection of many of her most important essays in social theory and feminism— all (like "The Cyborg Manifesto") informed by her training in biology. Among her recent books is *When Species Meet* (2008).

The Cyborg Manifesto and Fractured Identities[*]
Donna Haraway (1985)

This chapter is an effort to build an ironic political myth faithful to feminism, socialism, and materialism. Perhaps more faithful as blasphemy is faithful, than as reverent worship and identification. Blasphemy has always seemed to require taking things very seriously. I know no better stance to adopt from within the secular-religious, evangelical traditions of United States politics, including the politics of socialist feminism. Blasphemy protects one from the moral majority within, while still insisting on the need for community. Blasphemy is not apostasy. Irony is about contradictions that do not resolve into larger wholes, even dialectically, about the tension of holding incompatible things together because both or all are necessary and true. Irony is about humour and serious play. It is also a rhetorical strategy and a political method, one I would like to see more honoured within socialist-feminism. At the centre of my ironic faith, my blasphemy, is the image of the cyborg.

A cyborg is a cybernetic organism, a hybrid of machine and organism, a creature of social reality as well as a creature of fiction. Social reality is lived social relations, our most important political construction, a world-changing fiction. The international women's movements have constructed "women's experience," as well as uncovered or discovered this crucial collective object. This experience is a fiction

Donna Haraway (1944–) was trained in the history and philosophy of science. She holds a Ph.D. in biology from Yale. Haraway taught in the History of Consciousness Program at the University of

and fact of the most crucial, political kind. Liberation rests on the construction of the consciousness, the imaginative apprehension, of oppression, and so of possibility. The cyborg is a matter of fiction and lived experience that changes what counts as women's experience in the late twentieth century. This is a struggle over life and death, but the boundary between science fiction and social reality is an optical illusion.

Contemporary science fiction is full of cyborgs—creatures simultaneously animal and machine, who populate worlds ambiguously natural and crafted. Modern medicine is also full of cyborgs, of couplings between organism and machine, each conceived as coded devices, in an intimacy and with a power that was not generated in the history of sexuality. Cyborg "sex" restores some of the lovely replicative baroque of ferns and invertebrates (such nice organic prophylactics against heterosexism). Cyborg replication is uncoupled from organic reproduction. Modern production seems like a dream of cyborg colonization work, a dream that makes the nightmare of Taylorism seem idyllic. And modern war is a cyborg orgy, coded by C^3I, command-control-communication-intelligence, an $84 billion item in 1984's US defence budget. I am making an argument for the cyborg as a fiction mapping our social and bodily reality and as an imaginative resource suggesting some very fruitful couplings. Michel Foucault's biopolitics is a flaccid premonition of cyborg politics, a very open field. . . .

The cyborg is resolutely committed to partiality, irony, intimacy, and perversity. It is oppositional, utopian, and completely without innocence. No longer structured by the polarity of public and private, the cyborg defines a technological polis based partly on a revolution of social relations in the *oikos*, the household. Nature and culture are reworked; the one can no longer be the resource for appropriation or incorporation by the other. The relationships for forming wholes from parts, including those of polarity and hierarchical domination, are at issue in the cyborg world. Unlike the hopes of Frankenstein's monster, the cyborg does not expect its father to save it through a restoration of the garden; that is, through the fabrication of a heterosexual male, through its completion in a finished whole, a city and cosmos. The cyborg does not dream of community on the model of the organic family, this time without the oedipal project. The cyborg would not recognize the Garden of Eden; it is not made of mud and cannot dream of returning to dust. Perhaps that

is why I want to see if cyborgs can subvert the apocalypse of returning to nuclear dust in the manic compulsion to name the Enemy. Cyborgs are not reverent; they do not re-member the cosmos. They are wary of holism, but needy for connection—they seem to have a natural feel for united front politics, but without the vanguard party. The main trouble with cyborgs, of course, is that they are the illegitimate offspring of militarism and patriarchal capitalism, not to mention state socialism. But illegitimate offspring are often exceedingly unfaithful to their origins. Their fathers, after all, are inessential. . . .

So my cyborg myth is about transgressed boundaries, potent fusions, and dangerous possibilities which progressive people might explore as one part of needed political work. One of my premises is that most American socialists and feminists see deepened dualisms of mind and body, animal and machine, idealism and materialism in the social practices, symbolic formulations, and physical artefacts associated with "high technology" and scientific culture. From *One-Dimensional Man* (Marcuse, 1964) to *The Death of Nature* (Merchant, 1980), the analytic resources developed by progressives have insisted on the necessary domination of technics and recalled us to an imagined organic body to integrate our resistance. Another of my premises is that the need for unity of people trying to resist world-wide intensification of domination has never been more acute. But a slightly perverse shift of perspective might better enable us to contest for meanings, as well as for other forms of power and pleasure in technologically mediated societies. . . .

Fractured Identities

It has become difficult to name one's feminism by a single adjective—or even to insist in every circumstance upon the noun. Consciousness of exclusion through naming is acute. Identities seem contradictory, partial, and strategic. With the hard-won recognition of their social and historical constitution, gender, race, and class cannot provide the basis for belief in "essential" unity. There is nothing about being "female" that naturally binds women. There is not even such a state as "being" female, itself a highly complex category constructed in contested sexual scientific discourses and other social practices. Gender, race, or class consciousness is an achievement forced on us by the terrible historical experience of the contradictory social realities of patriarchy, colonialism, and capitalism. And who counts as "us" in my own rhetoric? Which identities are available to ground such a potent political myth called "us," and what could motivate enlistment in this collectivity? Painful fragmentation among feminists (not to mention among women) along every possible fault line has made the concept of woman *elusive*, an excuse for the matrix of women's dominations of each other. For me—and for many who share a similar historical location in white, professional middle-class, female, radical, North American, mid-adult bodies—the sources of a crisis in political identity are legion. The recent history for much of the US left and US feminism has been a response to this kind of crisis by endless splitting and searches for a new essential unity. But there has also been a growing recognition of another response through coalition—affinity, not identity.

Chela Sandoval, from a consideration of specific historical moments in the formation of the new political voice called women of colour, has theorized a hopeful model of political identity called "oppositional consciousness," born of the skills for reading webs of power by those refused stable membership in the social categories of race, sex, or class. "Women of color," a name contested at its origins by those whom it would incorporate, as well as a historical consciousness marking systematic breakdown of all the signs of Man in "Western" traditions, constructs a kind of postmodernist identity out of otherness, difference, and specificity. This postmodernist identity is fully political, whatever might be said about other possible postmodernisms. Sandoval's oppositional consciousness is about contradictory locations and heterochronic calendars, not about relativisms and pluralisms.

Sandoval emphasizes the lack of any essential criterion for identifying who is a woman of colour. She notes that the definition of the group has been by conscious appropriation of negation. For example, a Chicana or US black woman has not been able to speak as a woman or as a black person or as a Chicano. Thus, she was at the bottom of a cascade of negative identities, left out of even the privileged oppressed authorial categories called "women and blacks," who claimed to make the important revolutions. The category "woman" negated all non-white women; "black" negated all non-black people, as well as all black women. But there was also no "she," no singularity, but a sea of differences among US women who have affirmed their historical identity as US women of colour. This identity marks out a self-consciously constructed space that cannot affirm the capacity to act on the basis of natural identification, but only on the basis of conscious coalition, of affinity, of political kinship. Unlike the "woman" of some streams of the white women's movement in the United States, there is no naturalization of the matrix, or at least this is what Sandoval argues is uniquely available through the power of oppositional consciousness.

Sandoval's argument has to be seen as one potent formulation for feminists out of the world-wide development of anti-colonialist discourse; that is to say, discourse dissolving the "West" and its highest product—the one who is not animal, barbarian, or woman; man, that is, the author of a cosmos called history. As orientalism is deconstructed politically and semiotically, the identities of the occident destabilize, including those of feminists. Sandoval argues that "women of colour" have a chance to build an effective unity that does not replicate the imperializing, totalizing revolutionary subjects of previous Marxisms and feminisms which had not faced the consequences of the disorderly polyphony emerging from decolonization. . . .

The theoretical and practical struggle against unity-through-domination or unity-through-incorporation ironically not only undermines the justifications for patriarchy, colonialism, humanism, positivism, essentialism, scientism, and other unlamented -isms, but *all* claims for an organic or natural standpoint. I think that radical and socialist/Marxist-feminisms have also undermined their/our own epistemological strategies and that this is a crucially valuable step in imagining possible unities. It remains to be seen whether all "epistemologies" as Western political people have known them fail us in the task to build effective affinities.

It is important to note that the effort to construct revolutionary standpoints, epistemologies as achievements of people committed to changing the world, has been part of the process showing the limits of identification. The acid tools of postmodernist theory and the constructive tools of ontological discourse about revolutionary subjects might be seen as ironic allies in dissolving Western selves in the interests of survival. We are excruciatingly conscious of what it means to have a historically constituted body. But with the loss of innocence in our origin, there is no expulsion from the Garden either. Our politics lose the indulgence of guilt with the *naïveté* of innocence. But what would another political myth for socialist-feminism look like? What kind of politics could embrace partial, contradictory, permanently unclosed constructions of personal and collective selves and still be faithful, effective—and, ironically, socialist-feminist?

I do not know of any other time in history when there was greater need for political unity to confront effectively the dominations of "race," "gender," "sexuality," and "class." I also do not know of any other time when the kind of unity we might help build could have been possible. None of "us" have any longer the symbolic or material capability of dictating the shape of reality to any of "them." Or at least "we" cannot claim innocence from practising such dominations. White women, including socialist feminists, discovered (that is, were forced kicking and screaming to notice) the non-innocence of the category "woman." That consciousness changes the geography of all previous categories; it denatures them as heat denatures a fragile protein. Cyborg feminists have to argue that "we" do not want any more natural matrix of unity and that no construction is whole. Innocence, and the corollary insistence on victimhood as the only ground for insight, has done enough damage. But the constructed revolutionary subject must give late-twentieth-century people pause as well. In the fraying of identities and in the reflexive strategies for constructing them, the possibility opens up for weaving something other than a shroud for the day after the apocalypse that so prophetically ends salvation history.

Both Marxist/socialist-feminisms and radical feminisms have simultaneously naturalized and denatured the category "woman" and consciousness of the social lives of "women." . . . [N]either Marxist nor radical feminist points of view have tended to embrace the status of a partial explanation; both were regularly constituted as totalities. Western explanation has demanded as much; how else could the "Western" author incorporate its others? Each tried to annex other forms of domination by expanding its basic categories through analogy, simple listing, or addition. Embarrassed silence about race among white radical and socialist feminists was one major, devastating political consequence. History and polyvocality disappear into political taxonomies that try to establish genealogies. There was no structural room for race (or for much else) in theory claiming to reveal the construction of the category woman and social group women as a unified or totalizable whole. The structure of my caricature looks like this:

socialist feminism—structure of class//wage labour//alienation labour, by analogy reproduction, by extension sex, by addition race

radical feminism—structure of gender//sexual appropriation//objectification sex, by analogy labour, by extension reproduction, by addition race

In another context, the French theorist, Julia Kristeva, claimed women appeared as a historical group after the Second World War, along with groups like youth. Her dates are doubtful; but we are now accustomed to remembering that as objects of knowledge and as historical actors, "race" did not always exist, "class" has a historical genesis, and "homosexuals" are quite junior. It is no accident that the symbolic system of the family of man—and so the essence of woman—breaks up at the same moment that networks of connection among people on the planet are unprecedentedly multiple, pregnant, and complex. "Advanced capitalism" is inadequate to convey the structure of this historical moment. In the "Western" sense, the end of man is at stake. It is no accident that woman disintegrates into women in our time. Perhaps socialist feminists were not substantially guilty of producing essentialist theory that suppressed women's particularity and contradictory interests. I think we have been, at least through unreflective participation in the logics, languages, and practices of white humanism and through searching for a single ground of domination to secure our revolutionary voice. Now we have less excuse. But in the consciousness of our failures, we risk lapsing into boundless difference and giving up on the confusing task of making partial, real connection. Some differences are playful; some are poles of world historical systems of domination. "Epistemology" is about knowing the difference.

Trinh T. Minh-ha (1952–) was born in Hanoi where she passed her early years during the French and American wars in Vietnam. She studied music in her native city before migrating to the United States where she earned both her MFA and Ph.D. degrees at the University of Illinois. She is a filmmaker and composer, as well as a social theorist and writer. She is professor of Women's Studies, Film Studies, and Rhetoric at the University of California, Berkeley. Her films include *Reassemblage* (1982), *Naked Spaces—Living Is Round* (1985), and *Surname Viet, Given Name Nam* (1989). The selection is from her best-known written work, *Woman, Native, Other: Writing Postcoloniality and Feminism* (1989). Along with Cornel West and others, she is also editor of *Out There*. Among her recent works are the book *The Digital Film Event* (2005) and the feature-length film *Night Passage* (2004).

Infinite Layers/Third World?[*]
Trinh T. Minh-ha (1989)

Infinite Layers: I am not i can be you and me

A critical difference from myself means that I am not i, am within and without i. I/i can be I or i, you and me both involved. We (with capital W) sometimes include(s), other times exclude(s) me. You and I are close, we intertwine; you may stand on the other side of the hill once in a while, but you may also be me, while remaining what you are and what i am not. The differences made *between* entities comprehended as absolute presences—hence the notions of *pure origin* and *true self*—are an outgrowth of a dualistic system of thought peculiar to the Occident (the "onto-theology" which characterizes Western metaphysics). They should be distinguished from the differences grasped *both between* and *within* entities, each of these being understood as multiple presence. Not One, not two either. "I" is, therefore, not a unified subject, a fixed identity, or that solid mass covered with layers of superficialities one has gradually to peel off before one can see its true face. "I" is, itself, *infinite layers*. Its complexity can hardly be conveyed through such typographic conventions as I, i, or I/i. Thus, I/i am compelled by the will to say/unsay, to resort to the entire gamut of personal pronouns to stay near this fleeing *and* static essence of Not-I. Whether I accept it or not, the natures of *I, i, you, s/he, We, we, they,* and *wo/man* constantly overlap. They all display a necessary ambivalence, for the line dividing *I* and *Not-I, us* and *them,* or *him* and *her* is not (cannot) always (be) as clear as we would like it to be. Despite our desperate, eternal attempt to separate, contain, and mend, categories always leak. Of all the layers that form the open (never finite) totality of "I," which is to be filtered out as superfluous, fake, corrupt, and which is to be called

pure, true, real, genuine, original, authentic? Which, indeed, since all interchange, revolving in an endless process? (According to the context in which they operate, the superfluous can become the real; the authentic can prove fake; and so on.) *Authenticity* as a need to rely on an "undisputed origin," is prey to an obsessive *fear*: that of *losing a connection*. Everything must hold together. In my craving for a logic of being, I cannot help but loathe the threats of interruptions, disseminations, and suspensions. To begin, to develop to a climax, then, to end. To fill, to join, to unify. The order and the links create an illusion of continuity, which I highly prize for fear of nonsense and emptiness. Thus, a clear origin will give me a connection back through time, and I shall, by all means, search for that genuine layer of myself to which I can always cling. To abolish it in such a perspective is to remove the basis, the prop, the overture, or the finale—giving thereby free rein to indeterminacy: the result, forefeared, is either an anarchic succession of climaxes or a de(inex)pressive, uninterrupted monotony—and to enter into the limitless process of interactions and changes that nothing will stop, not even death. In other words, things may be said to be what they are, not exclusively in relation to what was and what will be (they should not solely be seen as clusters chained together by the temporal sequence of cause and effect), but also in relation to each other's immediate presences and to themselves as non/presences. The *real*, nothing else than a *code of representation*, does not (cannot) coincide with the lived or the performed. This is what Vine Deloria, Jr. accounts for when he exclaims: "Not even Indians can relate themselves to this type of creature who, to anthropologists, is the 'real' Indian." A realistic identification with such a code has, therefore, no reality whatsoever: it is like "stopping the ear while trying to steal the bell" (Chinese saying). . . .

The Female Identity Enclosure

Difference as uniqueness or special identity is both limiting and deceiving. If identity refers to the whole pattern of sameness within a human life, the style of a continuing me that permeates all the changes undergone, then difference remains within the boundary of that which distinguishes one identity from another. This means that *at heart*, X must be X, Y must be Y, and Y *cannot* be Y. Those who run around yelling that X is not X and X *can* be Y usually land in a hospital, a "rehabilitation" center, a concentration camp, or a res-er-va-tion. All deviations from the dominant stream of thought, that is to say, the belief in a permanent essence of wo/man and in an invariant but fragile identity, whose "loss" is considered to be a "specifically human danger," can easily fit into the categories of the "mentally ill" or the "mentally underdeveloped." It is probably difficult for a "normal," probing mind to recognize that to seek is to lose, for seeking presupposes a separation between the seeker and the sought, the continuing me and the changes it undergoes. What if the popularized story of the identity crisis proves to be only a story and nothing else? Can identity, indeed, be viewed other than as a by-product of a "manhandling" of life, one that, in fact, refers no more to a consistent "pattern of sameness" than to an inconsequential process of otherness? How am I to lose, maintain, or gain an (fe/male) identity when it is impossible to me to take up a position outside this identity from which I presumably reach in and feel for it? Perhaps a way to portray it is to borrow these verses from the *Cheng-tao-ke*:

You cannot take hold of it,
But you cannot lose it.
In not being able to get it, you get it.
When you are silent, it speaks;
When you speak, it is silent.

Difference in such an insituable context is *that which undermines the very idea of identity*, deferring to infinity the layers whose totality forms "I." It subverts the foundations of any affirmation or vindication of value and cannot, thereby, ever bear in itself an absolute value. The difference (within) between *difference* itself and *identity* has so often been ignored and the use of the two terms so readily confused, that claiming a female/ethnic identity/difference is commonly tantamount to reviving a kind of naive "male-tinted" romanticism. If feminism is set forth as a demystifying force, then it will have to question thoroughly the belief in its own identity. To suppose, like Judith Kegan Gardiner, that "the concept of female identity provides a key to understanding the *special qualities* of contemporary writing by women . . . , the diverse ways in which writing by women *differs* from writing by men," and to "propose the preliminary metaphor 'female identity is a process' for the most fundamental of these differences" does not, obviously, allow us to radically depart from the master's logic. Such a formulation endeavors to "reach a theory of

female identity . . . that *varies from the male model*," and to demonstrate that:

primary identity for women is more flexible and relational *than for men*. Female gender identity is *more* stable *than male gender identity*. Female infantile identifications are *less* predictable *than male ones* . . . the *female counterpart* of the male identity crisis may occur more diffusely, at a different stage, or not at all. (my italics)

It seems quite content with reforms that, at best, contribute to the improvement and/or enlargement of the identity enclosure, but do not, in any way, attempt to remove its fence. The constant need to refer to the "male model" for comparisons unavoidably maintains the subject under tutelage. For the point is not to carve one's space in "identity theories that ignore women" and describe some of the faces of female identity, saying, like Gardiner: "I picture female identity as typically less fixed, less unitary, and more flexible than male individuality, both in its primary core and in the entire maturational complex developed from this core," but patiently to dismantle the very notion of core (be it static or not) and identity.

Woman can never be defined. Bat, dog, chick, mutton, tart. Queen, madam, lady of pleasure. MISTRESS. *Belle-de-nuit*, woman of the streets, fruit-woman, fallen woman. Cow, vixen, bitch. Call girl, joy girl, working girl. Lady and whore are both bred to please. The old Woman image-repertoire says She is a Womb, a mere baby's pouch, or "nothing but sexuality." She is a passive substance, a parasite, an enigma whose mystery proves to be a snare and a delusion. She wallows in night, disorder, and immanence and is at the same time the "disturbing factor (between men)" and the key to the beyond. The further the repertoire unfolds its images, the more entangled it gets in its attempts at capturing Her. "Truth, Beauty, Poetry—she is All: once more all under the form of the Other. All except herself," Simone De Beauvoir wrote. Yet, even with or because of Her capacity to embody All, Woman is the lesser man, and among male athletes, to be called a woman is still resented as the worst of insults. "Wo-" appended to "man" in sexist contexts is not unlike "Third World," "Third," "minority," or "*color*" affixed to *woman* in pseudo-feminist contexts. Yearning for universality, the generic "woman," like its counterpart, the generic "man," tends to efface difference within itself. Not every female is "a real woman," one knows this through hearsay . . . Just as "man" provides an example of how the part played by women has been ignored, undervalued, distorted, or omitted through the use of terminology presumed to be generic, "woman" more often than not reflects the subtle power of linguistic exclusion, for its set of referents rarely includes those relevant to Third World "female persons." "All the Women Are White, All the Blacks are Men, But Some of Us Are Brave" is the title given to an anthology edited by Gloria T. Hull, Patricia Bell Scott, and Barbara Smith. It is, indeed, somehow devious to think that WOMAN also encompasses the Chinese with bound feet, the genitally mutilated Africans, and the one thousand Indians who committed *suttee* for one royal male. Sister Cinderella's foot is also enviably tiny but never crooked! And, European witches were also burnt to purify the body of Christ, but they do not pretend to "self-immolation." "Third World," therefore, belongs to a category apart, a "special" one that is meant to be both complimentary and complementary, for First and Second went out of fashion, leaving a serious Lack behind to be filled.

Third World?

To survive, "Third World" must necessarily have negative *and* positive connotations: negative when viewed in a vertical ranking system—"underdeveloped" compared to over-industrialized, "underprivileged" within the already Second sex—and positive when understood sociopolitically as a subversive, "non-aligned" force. Whether "Third World" sounds negative or positive also depends on *who* uses it. Coming from you Westerners, the word can hardly mean the same as when it comes from Us members of the Third World. Quite predictably, you/we who condemn it most are both we who buy in and they who deny any participation in the bourgeois mentality of the West. For it was in the context of such mentality that "Third World" stood out as a new semantic finding to designate what was known as "the savages" before the Independences. Today, hegemony is much more subtle, much more pernicious than the form of blatant racism once exercised by the colonial West. I/i always find myself asking, in this one-dimension society, where I/i should draw the line between tracking down the oppressive mechanisms of the system and aiding their spread. "Third World" commonly refers to those states in Africa, Asia and Latin America which called themselves "non-aligned," that is to say, affiliated with neither the Western (capitalist) nor the Eastern (communist) power blocs. Thus, if "Third World" is often rejected for its judged-to-be-derogative connotations, it is not so much because of the hierarchical, first-second-third order implied, as some invariably repeat, but because of the growing threat "Third World" consistently presents to the Western bloc the last few decades. The emergence of repressed voices into the worldwide political arena has already prompted her (Julia Kristeva) to ask: "How will the West greet the awakening of the "third world" as the Chinese call it? Can we [Westerners] participate, actively and lucidly, in this awakening when the center of the planet is in the process of moving toward the East?" Exploited, looked down upon, and lumped together in a convenient term that denies their individualities, a group of "poor" (nations), having once sided with neither of the dominating forces, has slowly learned to turn this denial to the best account. "The Third World to Third World peoples" thus becomes an empowering tool, and one which politically includes all non-whites in their solidarist struggle against all forms of Western dominance. And since "Third World" now refers to more than the geographically and economically determined nations of the "South"(versus "North"), since the term comprises such "developed" countries as Japan and those which have opted for socialist reconstruction of their system (China, Cuba, Ethiopia, Angola, Mozambique) as well as those which have favored a capitalist mode of development (Nigeria, India, Brazil), there no longer exists such a thing as a unified unaligned Third World bloc. Moreover, Third World has moved West (or North, depending on where the dividing line falls) and has expanded so as to include even the remote parts of the First World. What is at stake is not only the hegemony of Western cultures, but also their identities as unified cultures. Third World dwells on diversity; so does First World. This is our strength and our misery. The West is painfully made to realize the existence of a Third World in the First World, and vice versa. The Master is bound to recognize that His Culture is not as homogeneous, as monolithic as He believed it to be. He discovers, with much reluctance, He is just another among others.

Thus, whenever it is a question of "Third World women" or, more disquietingly, of "Third World Women in the U.S.," the reaction provoked among many whites almost never fails to be that of annoyance, irritation, or vexation. "Why Third World in the U.S.?" they say angrily; "You mean those who still have relatives in South East Asia?" "Third World! I don't understand how one can use such a term, it doesn't mean anything." Or even better, "Why use such a term to defeat yourself?" Alternatives like "Western" and "non-Western" or "Euro-American" and "non-Euro-American" may sound a bit less charged, but they are certainly neither neutral nor satisfactory, for they still take the dominant group as point of reference, and they reflect well the West's ideology of dominance (it is as if we were to use the term "non-Afro-Asian," for example, to designate all white peoples). More recently, we have been hearing of the Fourth World which, we are told, "is a world populated by indigenous people who still continue to bear a spiritual relationship to their traditional lands." The colonialist creed "Divide and Conquer" is here again, alive and well. Often ill at ease with the outspoken educated natives who represent the Third World in debates and paternalistically scornful of those who remain reserved, the dominant thus decides to weaken this term of solidarity, both by invalidating it as empowering tool and by inciting divisiveness within the Third World—a Third World within the Third World. Aggressive Third World (educated "savages") with its awareness and resistance to domination must therefore be classified apart from gentle Fourth World (uneducated "savages"). Every unaligned voice should necessarily/consequently be either a personal or a minority voice. The (impersonal) majority, as logic dictates, has to be the (aligned) dominant.

> It is, apparently, inconvenient, if not downright mind stretching [notes Alice Walker], for white women scholars to think of black women as women, perhaps because "woman" (like "man" among white males) is a name they are claiming for themselves, and themselves alone. Racism decrees that if they are now women (years ago they were ladies, but fashions change) then black women must, perforce, be something else. (While they were "ladies" black women could be "women" and so on.)

Another revealing example of this separatist majority mentality is the story Walker relates of an exhibit of women painters at the Brooklyn Museum: when asked "Are there no black women painters represented here?" (none of them is, apparently), a white woman feminist simply replies "It's a *women's*

exhibit!" Different historical contexts, different semantic contents. . . .

Gayatri Chakravorty Spivak (1942–) was born in Calcutta, India. After undergraduate studies in English at the University of Calcutta, she did graduate work at Cornell (Ph.D., 1967) in comparative literature. She has taught at many universities, including Iowa, Texas, Wesleyan, Emory, and Pittsburgh, and currently is at Columbia where she cofounded the program in Comparative Literature and holds a distinguished University Professorship. Spivak first came to wide attention with her translation of and remarkable introduction to Derrida's *Of Grammatology* (1976). Her first book was *Myself, Must I Remake: The Life and Poetry of W. B. Yeats* (1974). She has lectured and written on numerous subjects in and around issues in feminism, literary theory, Marxism, deconstructionism, and subaltern studies. Among her many books and collected essays is *In Other Worlds: Essays in Cultural Politics* (1987) and *An Aesthetic Education in the Age of Globalization* (2012). The selection is from Spivak's classic essay, "Can the Subaltern Speak?" which has altered the direction of post-colonial, development, and social theoretical studies by calling attention to the multiple layers of colonial subjugation in relation to the confusion that the subaltern create even for those seeking to understand them.

Can the Subaltern Speak?[*]
Gayatri Chakravorty Spivak (1988)

The first part of my proposition—that the phased development of the subaltern is complicated by the imperialist project—is confronted by a collective of intellectuals who may be called the "Subaltern Studies" group. They *must* ask, Can the subaltern speak? Here we are within Foucault's own discipline of history and with people who acknowledge his influence. Their project is to rethink Indian colonial historiography from the perspective of the discontinuous chain of peasant insurgencies during the colonial occupation. This is indeed the problem of "the

[*] A CRITIQUE OF POSTCOLONIAL REASON: TOWARD A HISTORY OF THE VANISHING PRESENT by Gayatri Chakravorty Spivak, pp. 269–271, 281–290. Copyright © 1999 by the President and Fellows of Harvard College.

permission to narrate" discussed by Said. As Ranajit Guha argues,

> The historiography of Indian nationalism has for a long time been dominated by elitism—colonialist elitism and bourgeois-nationalist elitism . . . shar[ing] the prejudice that the making of the Indian nation and the development of the consciousness—nationalism—which confirmed this process were exclusively or predominantly elite achievements. In the colonialist and neo-colonialist historiographies these achievements are credited to British colonial rulers, administrators, policies, institutions, and culture; in the nationalist and neo-nationalist writings—to Indian elite personalities, institutions, activities and ideas.

Certain varieties of the Indian elite are at best native informants for first-world intellectuals interested in the voice of the Other. But one must nevertheless insist that the colonized subaltern *subject* is irretrievably heterogeneous. . . .

Can the subaltern speak? What must the elite do to watch out for the continuing construction of the subaltern? The question of "woman" seems most problematic in this context. Clearly, if you are poor, black, and female you get it in three ways. If, however, this formulation is moved from the first-world context into the postcolonial (which is not identical with the third-world) context, the description "black" or "of color" loses persuasive significance. The necessary stratification of colonial subject-constitution in the first phase of capitalist imperialism makes "color" useless as an emancipatory signifier. Confronted by the ferocious standardizing benevolence of most U.S. and Western European human-scientific radicalism (recognition by assimilation), the progressive though heterogeneous withdrawal of consumerism in the comprador periphery, and the exclusion of the margins of even the center-periphery articulation (the "true and differential subaltern"), the analogue of class-consciousness rather than race-consciousness in this area seems historically, disciplinarily, and practically forbidden by Right and Left alike. It is not just a question of a *double* displacement, as it is not simply the problem of finding a psychoanalytic allegory that can accommodate the third-world woman with the first.

The cautions I have just expressed are valid only if we are speaking of the subaltern woman's consciousness—or, more acceptably, subject. Reporting on, or better still, participating in, antisexist work among women of color or women in class oppression in the First World or the Third World is undeniably on the agenda. We should also welcome all the information retrieval in these silenced areas that is taking place in anthropology, political science, history, and sociology. Yet the assumption and construction of a consciousness or subject sustains such work and will, in the long run, cohere with the work of imperialist subject-constitution, mingling epistemic violence with the advancement of learning and civilizations. And the subaltern woman will be as mute as ever.

In so fraught a field, it is not easy to ask the question of the consciousness of the subaltern woman; it is thus all the more necessary to remind pragmatic radicals that such a question is not an idealist red herring. Though all feminist or antisexist projects cannot be reduced to this one, to ignore it is an unacknowledged political gesture that has a long history and collaborates with a masculine radicalism that renders the place of the investigator transparent. In seeking to learn to speak to (rather than listen to or speak for) the historically muted subject to the subaltern woman, the postcolonial intellectual *systematically* "unlearns" female privilege. This systematic unlearning involves learning to critique postcolonial discourse with the best tools it can provide and not simply substituting the lost figure of the colonized. Thus, to question the unquestioned muting of the subaltern woman even within the anti-imperialist project of subaltern studies is not, as Jonathan Culler suggests, to "produce difference by differing" or to "appeal . . . to a sexual identity defined as essential and privilege experiences associated with that identity."

Culler's version of the feminist project is possible within what Elizabeth Fox-Genovese has called "the contribution of the bourgeois-democratic revolutions to the social and political individualism of women." Many of us were obliged to understand the feminist project as Culler now describes it when we were still agitating as U.S. academics. It was certainly a necessary stage in my own education in "unlearning" and has consolidated the belief that the mainstream project of Western feminism both continues and displaces the battle over the right to individualism between women and men in situations of upward class mobility. One suspects that the debate between U.S. feminism and European "theory" (as theory is generally represented by women from the

United States or Britain) occupies a significant corner of that very terrain. I am generally sympathetic with the call to make U.S. feminism more "theoretical." It seems, however, that the problem of the muted subject of the subaltern woman, though not solved by an "essentialist" search for lost origins, cannot be served by the call for more theory in Anglo-America either.

That call is often given in the name of a critique of "positivism," which is seen here as identical with "essentialism." Yet Hegel, the modern inaugurator of "the work of the negative," was not a stranger to the notion of essences. For Marx, the curious persistence of essentialism within the dialectic was a profound and productive problem. Thus, the stringent binary opposition between positivism/essentialism (read, U.S.) and "theory" (read, French or Franco-German via Anglo-American) may be spurious. Apart from repressing the ambiguous complicity between essentialism and critiques of positivism (acknowledged by Derrida in "Of Grammatology As a Positive Science"), it also errs by implying that positivism is not a theory. This move allows the emergence of a proper name, a positive essence, Theory. Once again, the position of the investigator remains unquestioned. And, if this territorial debate turns toward the Third World, no change in the question of method is to be discerned. This debate cannot take into account that, in the case of the woman as subaltern, no ingredients for the constitution of the itinerary of the trace of a sexed subject can be gathered to locate the possibility of dissemination.

Yet I remain generally sympathetic in aligning feminism with the critique of positivism and the defetishization of the concrete. I am also far from averse to learning from the work of Western theorists, though I have learned to insist on marking their positionality as investigating subjects. Given these conditions, and as a literary critic, I tactically confronted the immense problem of the consciousness of the woman as subaltern. I reinvented the problem in a sentence and transformed it into the object of a simple semiosis. What does this sentence mean? The analogy here is between the ideological victimization of a Freud and the positionality of the postcolonial intellectual as investigating subject.

As Sarah Kofman has shown, the deep ambiguity of Freud's use of women as a scapegoat is a reaction-formation to an initial and continuing desire to give the hysteric a voice, to transform her into the *subject* of hysteria. The masculine-imperialist ideological formation that shaped that desire into "the daughter's seduction" is part of the same formation that constructs the monolithic "third-world woman." As a postcolonial intellectual, I am influenced by that formation as well. Part of our "unlearning" project is to articulate that ideological formation—by *measuring* silences, if necessary—into the *object* of investigation. Thus, when confronted with the questions, Can the subaltern speak? and Can the subaltern (as woman) speak?, our efforts to give the subaltern a voice in history will be doubly open to the dangers run by Freud's discourse. As a product of these considerations, I have put together the sentence "White men are saving brown women from brown men" in a spirit not unlike the one to be encountered in Freud's investigations of the sentence "A child is being beaten."

The use of Freud here does not imply an isomorphic analogy between subject-formation and the behavior of social collectives, a frequent practice, often accompanied by a reference to Reich, in the conversation between Deleuze and Foucault. So I am not suggesting that "White men are saving brown women from brown men" is a sentence indicating a *collective* fantasy symptomatic of a *collective* itinerary of sadomasochistic repression in a *collective* imperialist enterprise. There is a satisfying symmetry in such an allegory, but I would rather invite the reader to consider it a problem in "wild psychoanalysis" than a clinching solution. Just as Freud's insistence on making the woman the scapegoat in "A child is being beaten" and elsewhere discloses his political interests, however imperfectly, so my insistence on imperialist subject-production as the occasion for this sentence discloses my politics.

Further, I am attempting to borrow the general methodological aura of Freud's strategy toward the sentence he constructed *as a sentence* out of the many similar substantive accounts his patients gave him. This does not mean I will offer a case of transference-in-analysis as an isomorphic model for the transaction between reader and text (my sentence). The analogy between transference and literary criticism or historiography is no more than a productive catachresis. To say that the subject is a text does not authorize the converse pronouncement: the verbal text is a subject.

I am fascinated, rather, by how Freud predicates a *history* of repression that produces the final sentence. It is a history with a double origin, one hidden in the amnesia of the infant, the other lodged in our archaic past, assuming by implication a preoriginary space where human and animal were not yet differentiated. We are driven to impose a homologue of this Freudian strategy on the Marxist narrative to explain the ideological dissimulation of imperialist political economy and outline a history of repression that produces a sentence like the one I have sketched. This history also has a double origin, one hidden in the maneuverings behind the British abolition of widow sacrifice in 1829, the other lodged in the classical and Vedic past of Hindu India, the *Rg-Veda* and the *Dharmasastra*. No doubt there is also an undifferentiated preoriginary space that supports this history.

The sentence I have constructed is one among many displacements describing the relationship between brown and white men (sometimes brown and white women worked in). It takes its place among some sentences of "hyperbolic admiration" or of pious guilt that Derrida speaks of in connection with the "hieroglyphist prejudice." The relationship between the imperialist subject and the subject of imperialism is at least ambiguous.

The Hindu widow ascends the pyre of the dead husband and immolates herself upon it. This is widow sacrifice. (The conventional transcription of the Sanskrit word for the widow would be *sati*. The early colonial British transcribed it *suttee*.) The rite was not practiced universally and was not caste- or class-fixed. The abolition of this rite by the British has been generally understood as a case of "White men saving brown women from brown men." White women—from the nineteenth-century British Missionary Registers to Mary Daly—have not produced an alternative understanding. Against this is the Indian nativist argument, a parody of the nostalgia for lost origins: "The women actually wanted to die."

The two sentences go a long way to legitimize each other. One never encounters the testimony of the women's voice-consciousness. Such a testimony would not be ideology-transcendent or "fully" subjective, of course, but it would have constituted the ingredients for producing a countersentence. As one goes down the grotesquely mistranscribed names of these women, the sacrificed widows, in the police reports included in the records of the East India Company, one cannot put together a "voice." The most one can sense is the immense heterogeneity breaking through even such a skeletal and ignorant account (castes, for example, are regularly described as tribes).

Faced with the dialectically interlocking sentences that are constructible as "White men are saving brown women from brown men" and "The women wanted to die," the postcolonial woman intellectual asks the question of simple semiosis—What does this mean?—and begins to plot a history.

To mark the moment when not only a civil but a good society is born out of domestic confusion, singular events that break the letter of the law to instill its spirit are often invoked. The protection of women by men often provides such an event. If we remember that the British boasted of their absolute equity toward and noninterference with native custom/law, an invocation of this sanctioned transgression of the letter for the sake of the spirit may be read in J. M. Derrett's remark: "The very first legislation upon Hindu Law was carried through without the assent of a single Hindu." The legislation is not named here. The next sentence, where the measure is named, is equally interesting if one considers the implications of the survival of a colonially established "good" society after decolonization: "The recurrence of *sati* in independent India is probably an obscurantist revival which cannot long survive even in a very backward part of the country."

Whether this observation is correct or not, what interests me is that the protection of woman (today the "third-world woman") becomes a signifier for the establishment of a *good* society which must, at such inaugurative moments, transgress mere legality, or equity of legal policy. In this particular case, the process also allowed the redefinition as a crime of what had been tolerated, known, or adulated as ritual. In other words, this one item in Hindu law jumped the frontier between the private and the public domain.

Although Foucault's *historical narrative*, focusing solely on Western Europe, sees merely a tolerance for the criminal antedating the development of criminology in the late eighteenth century, his *theoretical description* of the "episteme" is pertinent here: "The *episteme* is the 'apparatus' which makes possible the separation not of the true from the false, but of what may not be characterized as scientific"—ritual as opposed to crime, the one fixed by superstition, the other by legal science.

The leap of *suttee* from private to public has a clear and complex relationship with the changeover from a mercantile and commercial to a territorial and administrative British presence; it can be followed in correspondence among the police stations, the lower and higher courts, the courts of directors, the prince regent's court, and the like. (It is interesting to note that, from the point of view of the native "colonial subject," also emergent from the feudalism-capitalism transition, *sati* is a signifier with the reverse social charge: "Groups rendered psychologically marginal by their exposure to Western impact . . . had come under pressure to demonstrate, to others as well as to themselves, their ritual purity and allegiance to traditional high culture. To many of them sati became an important proof of their conformity to older norms at a time when these norms had become shaky within.")

Patricia Hill Collins (1948–) is Distinguished University Professor of Sociology at the University Maryland, College Park, after having been chair of African American Studies at the University of Cincinnati. Among her many honors is election as president of the American Sociological Association. Her book *Black Feminist Thought* (1990) has been widely praised for combining a deep personal and historical understanding of African-American women with pathbreaking theoretical analysis. In addition to re-presenting social theory in the tradition of Black feminism, the book is capable of transforming social theoretical analysis generally. The selection, for example, reworks the fractured identity perspective in terms that are more explicitly sociological, thus contributing to feminist theory as well as to sociological theory's concerns with the individual's relation to macrostructures. Her *Black Feminist Thought* (1990) is the first book to integrate the literature of and by African-American women. (The selection necessarily omits Collins's numerous references to those works.) One of her recent books is *From Black Power to Hip Hop: Racism, Nationalism, and Feminism* (2006). Among Collins's many contributions is the theory of intersectionality which is widely used among critical race theorists and derived from her concept of the matrix of domination presented in the selection following.

Black Feminist Thought in the Matrix of Domination[*]
Patricia Hill Collins (1990)

Black feminist thought demonstrates Black women's emerging power as agents of knowledge. By portraying African-American women as self-defined, self-reliant individuals confronting race, gender, and class oppression, Afrocentric feminist thought speaks to the importance that knowledge plays in empowering oppressed people. One distinguishing feature of Black feminist thought is its insistence that both the changed consciousness of individuals and the social transformation of political and economic institutions constitute essential ingredients for social change. New knowledge is important for both dimensions of change.

Knowledge is a vitally important part of the social relations of domination and resistance. By objectifying African-American women and recasting our experiences to serve the interests of elite white men, much of the Eurocentric masculinist worldview fosters Black women's subordination. But placing Black women's experiences at the center of analysis offers fresh insights on the prevailing concepts, paradigms, and epistemologies of this worldview and on its feminist and Afrocentric critiques. Viewing the world through a both/and conceptual lens of the simultaneity of race, class, and gender oppression and of the need for a humanist vision of community creates new possibilities for an empowering Afrocentric feminist knowledge. Many Black feminist intellectuals have long thought about the world in this way because this is the way we experience the world.

Afrocentric feminist thought offers two significant contributions toward furthering our understanding of the important connections among knowledge, consciousness, and the politics of empowerment. First, Black feminist thought fosters a fundamental paradigmatic shift in how we think about oppression. By embracing a paradigm of race, class, and gender as interlocking systems of oppression, Black feminist thought reconceptualizes the social relations of domination and resistance. Second, Black feminist thought addresses ongoing epistemological debates in feminist theory and in the sociology of knowledge concerning ways of assessing "truth." Offering subordinate groups new knowledge about their own experiences can be empowering. But revealing new ways of knowing that allow subordinate groups to define their own reality has far greater implications.

Reconceptualizing Race, Class, and Gender as Interlocking Systems of Oppression

"What *I* really feel is radical is trying to make coalitions with people who are different from you," maintains Barbara Smith. "I feel it is radical to be dealing with race and sex and class and sexual identity all at one time. I think *that* is really radical because it has never been done before." Black feminist thought fosters a fundamental paradigmatic shift that rejects additive approaches to oppression. Instead of starting with gender and then adding in other variables such as age, sexual orientation, race, social class, and religion, Black feminist thought sees these distinctive systems of oppression as being part of one overarching structure of domination. Viewing relations of domination for Black women for any given sociohistorical context as being structured via a system of interlocking race, class, and gender oppression expands the focus of analysis from merely describing the similarities and differences distinguishing these systems of oppression and focuses greater attention on how they interconnect. Assuming that each system needs the others in order to function creates a distinct theoretical stance that stimulates the rethinking of basic social science concepts.

Afrocentric feminist notions of family reflect this reconceptualization process. Black women's experiences as bloodmothers, othermothers, and community othermothers reveal that the mythical norm of a heterosexual, married couple, nuclear family with a nonworking spouse and a husband earning a "family wage" is far from being natural, universal, and preferred but instead is deeply embedded in specific race and class formations. Placing African-American women in the center of analysis not only reveals much-needed information about Black women's experiences but also questions Eurocentric masculinist perspectives on family.

Black women's experiences and the Afrocentric feminist thought rearticulating them also challenge prevailing definitions of community. Black women's actions in the struggle for group survival suggest a vision of community that stands in opposition to that extant in the dominant culture. The definition of community implicit in the market model sees community as arbitrary and fragile, structured fundamentally by competition and domination. In contrast, Afrocentric models of community stress connections, caring, and personal accountability. As cultural workers, African-American women have rejected the generalized ideology of domination advanced by the dominant group in order to conserve Afrocentric conceptualizations of community. Denied access to the podium, Black women have been unable to spend time theorizing about alternative conceptualizations of community. Instead, through daily actions African-American women have *created* alternative communities that empower.

This vision of community sustained by African-American women in conjunction with African-American men addresses the larger issue of reconceptualizing power. The type of Black women's power discussed here does resemble feminist theories of power which emphasize energy and community. However, in contrast to this body of literature whose celebration of women's power is often accompanied by a lack of attention to the importance of power as domination, Black women's experiences as mothers, community othermothers, educators, church leaders, labor union centerwomen, and community leaders seem to suggest that power as energy can be fostered by creative acts of resistance.

The spheres of influence created and sustained by African-American women are not meant solely to provide a respite from oppressive situations or a retreat from their effects. Rather, these Black female spheres of influence constitute potential sanctuaries where individual Black women and men are nurtured in order to confront oppressive social institutions. Power from this perspective is a creative power used for the good of the community, whether that community is conceptualized as one's family, church community, or the next generation of the community's children. By making the community stronger, African-American women become empowered, and that same community can serve as a source of support when Black women encounter race, gender, and class oppression. . . .

Approaches that assume that race, gender, and class are interconnected have immediate practical applications. For example, African-American women continue to be inadequately protected by Title VII of the Civil Rights Act of 1964. The primary purpose of the statute is to eradicate all aspects of discrimination. But judicial treatment of Black women's employment discrimination claims has encouraged Black women to identify race *or* sex as the so-called primary discrimination. "To resolve the inequities that confront Black women," counsels Scarborough, "the courts must first correctly conceptualize them as "Black women," a distinct class protected by Title VII." Such a shift, from protected categories to protected classes of people whose Title VII claims might be based on more than two discriminations, would work to alter the entire basis of current antidiscrimination efforts.

Reconceptualizing phenomena such as the rapid growth of female-headed households in African-American communities would also benefit from a race-, class-, and gender-inclusive analysis. Case studies of Black women heading households must be attentive to racially segmented local labor markets and community patterns, to changes in local political economies specific to a given city or region, and to established racial and gender ideology for a given location. This approach would go far to deconstruct Eurocentric, masculinist analyses that implicitly rely on controlling images of the matriarch or the welfare mother as guiding conceptual premises. . . . Black feminist thought that rearticulates experiences such as these fosters an enhanced theoretical understanding of how race, gender, and class oppression are part of a single, historically created system.

The Matrix of Domination

Additive models of oppression are firmly rooted in the either/or dichotomous thinking of Eurocentric, masculinist thought. One must be either Black or white in such thought systems—persons of ambiguous racial and ethnic identity constantly battle with questions such as "what are you, anyway?" This emphasis on quantification and categorization occurs in conjunction with the belief that either/or categories must be ranked. The search for certainty of this sort requires that one side of a dichotomy be privileged while its other is denigrated. Privilege becomes defined in relation to its other.

Replacing additive models of oppression with interlocking ones creates possibilities for new paradigms. The significance of seeing race, class, and gender as interlocking systems of oppression is that such an approach fosters a paradigmatic shift of thinking inclusively about other oppressions, such as age, sexual orientation, religion, and ethnicity. Race, class, and gender represent the three systems of oppression that most heavily affect African-American women.

But these systems and the economic, political, and ideological conditions that support them may not be the most fundamental oppressions, and they certainly affect many more groups than Black women. Other people of color, Jews, the poor, white women, and gays and lesbians have all had similar ideological justifications offered for their subordination. All categories of humans labeled Others have been equated to one another, to animals, and to nature.

Placing African-American women and other excluded groups in the center of analysis opens up possibilities for a both/and conceptual stance, one in which all groups possess varying amounts of penalty and privilege in one historically created system. In this system, for example, white women are penalized by their gender but privileged by their race. Depending on the context, an individual may be an oppressor, a member of an oppressed group, or simultaneously oppressor and oppressed.

Adhering to a both/and conceptual stance does not mean that race, class, and gender oppression are interchangeable. For example, whereas race, class, and gender oppression operate on the social structural level of institutions, gender oppression seems better able to annex the basic power of the erotic and intrude in personal relationships via family dynamics and within individual consciousness. This may be because racial oppression has fostered historically concrete communities among African-Americans and other racial/ethnic groups. These communities have stimulated cultures of resistance. While these communities segregate Blacks from whites, they simultaneously provide counter-institutional buffers that subordinate groups such as African-Americans use to resist the ideas and institutions of dominant groups. Social class may be similarly structured. Traditionally conceptualized as a relationship of *individual* employees to their employers, social class might be better viewed as a relationship of *communities* to capitalist political economies. Moreover, significant overlap exists between racial and social class oppression when viewing them through the collective lens of family and community. Existing community structures provide a primary line of resistance against racial and class oppression. But because gender crosscuts these structures, it finds fewer comparable institutional bases to foster resistance.

Embracing a both/and conceptual stance moves us from additive, separate systems approaches to oppression and toward what I now see as the more fundamental issue of the social relations of domination. Race, class, and gender constitute axes of oppression that characterize Black women's experiences within a more generalized matrix of domination. Other groups may encounter different dimensions of the matrix, such as sexual orientation, religion, and age, but the overarching relationship is one of domination and the types of activism it generates.

Bell Hooks labels this matrix a "politic of domination" and describes how it operates along interlocking axes of race, class, and gender oppression. This politic of domination

refers to the ideological ground that they share, which is a belief in domination, and a belief in the notions of superior and inferior, which are components of all of those systems. For me it's like a house, they share the foundation, but the foundation is the ideological beliefs around which notions of domination are constructed.

Johnella Butler claims that new methodologies growing from this new paradigm would be "non-hierarchical" and would "refuse primacy to either race, class, gender, or ethnicity, demanding instead a recognition of their matrix-like interaction." Race, class, and gender may not be the most fundamental or important systems of oppression, but they have most profoundly affected African-American women. One significant dimension of Black feminist thought is its potential to reveal insights about the social relations of domination organized along other axes such as religion, ethnicity, sexual orientation, and age. Investigating Black women's particular experiences thus promises to reveal much about the more universal process of domination.

Multiple Levels of Domination

In addition to being structured along axes such as race, gender, and social class, the matrix of domination is structured on several levels. People experience and resist oppression on three levels: the level of personal biography; the group or community level of the cultural context created by race, class, and gender; and the systemic level of social institutions. Black feminist thought emphasizes all three levels as sites of domination and as potential sites of resistance.

Each individual has a unique personal biography made up of concrete experiences, values, motivations, and emotions. No two individuals occupy the same social space; thus no two biographies are identical. Human ties can be freeing and empowering, as is the case with Black women's heterosexual love relationships or in the power of motherhood in African-American families and communities. Human ties

can also be confining and oppressive. Situations of domestic violence and abuse or cases in which controlling images foster Black women's internalized oppression represent domination on the personal level. The same situation can look quite different depending on the consciousness one brings to interpret it.

This level of individual consciousness is a fundamental area where new knowledge can generate change. Traditional accounts assume that power as domination operates from the top down by forcing and controlling unwilling victims to bend to the will of more powerful superiors. But these accounts fail to account for questions concerning why, for example, women stay with abusive men even with ample opportunity to leave or why slaves did not kill their owners more often. The willingness of the victim to collude in her or his own victimization becomes lost. They also fail to account for sustained resistance by victims, even when chances for victory appear remote. By emphasizing the power of self-definition and the necessity of a free mind, Black feminist thought speaks to the importance African-American women thinkers place on consciousness as a sphere of freedom. Black women intellectuals realize that domination operates not only by structuring power from the top down but by simultaneously annexing the power as energy of those on the bottom for its own ends. In their efforts to rearticulate the standpoint of African-American women as a group, Black feminist thinkers offer individual African-American women the conceptual tools to resist oppression.

The cultural context formed by those experiences and ideas that are shared with other members of a group or community which give meaning to individual biographies constitutes a second level at which domination is experienced and resisted. Each individual biography is rooted in several overlapping cultural contexts—for example, groups defined by race, social class, age, gender, religion, and sexual orientation. The cultural component contributes, among other things, the concepts used in thinking and acting, group validation of an individual's interpretation of concepts, the "thought models" used in the acquisition of knowledge, and standards used to evaluate individual thought and behavior. The most cohesive cultural contexts are those with identifiable histories, geographic locations, and social institutions. For Black women African-American communities have provided the location for an Afrocentric group perspective to endure.

Subjugated knowledges, such as a Black women's culture of resistance, develop in cultural contexts controlled by oppressed groups. Dominant groups aim to replace subjugated knowledge with their own specialized thought because they realize that gaining control over this dimension of subordinate groups' lives simplifies control. While efforts to influence this dimension of an oppressed group's experiences can be partially successful, this level is more difficult to control than dominant groups would have us believe. For example, adhering to externally derived standards of beauty leads many African-American women to dislike their skin color or hair texture. Similarly, internalizing Eurocentric gender ideology leads some Black men to abuse Black women. These are cases of the successful infusion of the dominant group's specialized thought into the everyday cultural context of African-Americans. But the long-standing existence of a Black women's culture of resistance as expressed through Black women's relationships with one another, the Black women's blues tradition, and the voices of contemporary African-American women writers all attest to the difficulty of eliminating the cultural context as a fundamental site of resistance.

Domination is also experienced and resisted on the third level of social institutions controlled by the dominant group: namely, schools, churches, the media, and other formal organizations. These institutions expose individuals to the specialized thought representing the dominant group's standpoint and interests. While such institutions offer the promise of both literacy and other skills that can be used for individual empowerment and social transformation, they simultaneously require docility and passivity. Such institutions would have us believe that the theorizing of elites constitutes the whole of theory. The existence of African-American women thinkers such as Maria Stewart, Sojourner Truth, Zora Neale Hurston, and Fannie Lou Hamer who, though excluded from and/or marginalized within such institutions, continued to produce theory effectively opposes this hegemonic view. Moreover, the more recent resurgence of Black feminist thought within these institutions, the case of the outpouring of contemporary Black feminist thought in history and literature, directly challenges the Eurocentric masculinist thought pervading these institutions.

Resisting the Matrix of Domination

Domination operates by seducing, pressuring, or forcing African-American women and members of subordinated groups to replace individual and cultural ways of knowing with the dominant group's specialized thought. As a result, suggests Audre Lorde, "the true focus of revolutionary change is never merely the oppressive situations which we seek to escape, but that piece of the oppressor which is planted deep within each of us." Or as Toni Cade Bambara succinctly states, "revolution begins with the self, in the self."

Lorde and Bambara's suppositions raise an important issue for Black feminist intellectuals and for all scholars and activists working for social change. Although most individuals have little difficulty identifying their own victimization within some major system of oppression—whether it be by race, social class, religion, physical ability, sexual orientation, ethnicity, age or gender—they typically fail to see how their thoughts and actions uphold someone else's subordination. Thus white feminists routinely point with confidence to their oppression as women but resist seeing how much their white skin privileges them. African-Americans who possess eloquent analyses of racism often persist in viewing poor white women as symbols of white power. The radical left fares little better. "If only people of color and women could see their true class interests," they argue, "class solidarity would eliminate racism and sexism." In essence, each group identifies the oppression with which it feels most comfortable as being fundamental and classifies all others as being of lesser importance. Oppression is filled with such contradictions because these approaches fail to recognize that a matrix of domination contains few pure victims or oppressors. Each individual derives varying amounts of penalty and privilege from the multiple systems of oppression which frame everyone's lives.

A broader focus stresses the interlocking nature of oppressions that are structured on multiple levels, from the individual to the social structural, and which are part of a larger matrix of domination. Adhering to this inclusive model provides the conceptual space needed for each individual to see that she or he is *both* a member of multiple dominant groups *and* a member of multiple subordinate groups. Shifting the analysis to investigating how the matrix of domination is structured along certain axes—race, gender, and class being the axes of investigation for African-American women—reveals that different systems of oppression may rely in varying degrees on systemic versus interpersonal mechanisms of domination.

Empowerment involves rejecting the dimensions of knowledge, whether personal, cultural, or institutional, that perpetuate objectification and de-humanization. African-American women and other individuals in subordinate groups become empowered when we understand and use those dimensions of our individual, group, and disciplinary ways of knowing that foster our humanity as fully human subjects. This is the case when Black women value our self-definitions, participate in a Black women's activist tradition, invoke an Afrocentric feminist epistemology as central to our worldview, and view the skills gained in schools as part of a focused education for Black community development. C. Wright Mills identifies this holistic epistemology as the "sociological imagination" and identifies its task and its promise as a way of knowing that enables individuals to grasp the relations between history and biography within society. Using one's standpoint to engage the sociological imagination can empower the individual. "My fullest concentration of energy is available to me," Audre Lorde maintains, "only when I integrate all the parts of who I am, openly, allowing power from particular sources of my living to flow back and forth freely through all my different selves, without the restriction of externally imposed definition."

Black Women as Agents of Knowledge

Living life as an African-American woman is a necessary prerequisite for producing Black feminist thought because within Black women's communities thought is validated and produced with reference to a particular set of historical, material, and epistemological conditions. African-American women who adhere to the idea that claims about Black women must be substantiated by Black women's sense of our own experiences and who anchor our knowledge claims in an Afrocentric feminist epistemology have produced a rich tradition of Black feminist thought.

Traditionally such women were blues singers, poets, autobiographers, storytellers, and orators validated by everyday Black women as experts on a Black women's standpoint. Only a few unusual African-American feminist scholars have been able to defy Eurocentric masculinist epistemologies and explicitly embrace an Afrocentric feminist epistemology. Consider Alice Walker's description of Zora Neale Hurston:

> In my mind, Zora Neale Hurston, Billie Holiday, and Bessie Smith form a sort of unholy trinity. Zora *belongs* in the tradition of black women singers, rather than among "the literati." . . . Like Billie and Bessie she followed her own road, believed in her own gods, pursued her own dreams, and refused to separate herself from "common" people.

Zora Neale Hurston is an exception for prior to 1950, few African-American women earned advanced degrees and most of those who did complied with Eurocentric masculinist epistemologies. Although these women worked on behalf of Black women, they did so within the confines of pervasive race and gender oppression. Black women scholars were in a position to see the exclusion of African-American women from scholarly discourse, and the thematic content of their work often reflected their interest in examining a Black women's standpoint. However, their tenuous status in academic institutions led them to adhere to Eurocentric masculinist epistemologies so that their work would be accepted as scholarly. As a result, while they produced Black feminist thought, those African-American women most likely to gain academic credentials were often least likely to produce Black feminist thought that used an Afrocentric feminist epistemology.

An ongoing tension exists for Black women as agents of knowledge, a tension rooted in the sometimes conflicting demands of Afrocentricity and feminism. Those Black women who are feminists are critical of how Black culture and many of its traditions oppress women. For example, the strong pronatal beliefs in African-American communities that foster early motherhood among adolescent girls, the lack of self-actualization that can accompany the double-day of paid employment and work in the home, and the emotional and physical abuse that many Black women experience from their fathers, lovers, and husbands all reflect practices opposed by African-American women who are feminists. But these same women may have a parallel desire as members of an oppressed racial group to affirm the value of that same culture and traditions. Thus strong Black mothers appear in Black women's literature, Black women's economic contributions to families is lauded, and a curious silence exists concerning domestic abuse.

As more African-American women earn advanced degrees, the range of Black feminist scholarship is expanding. Increasing numbers of African-American women scholars are explicitly choosing to ground their work in Black women's experiences, and, by doing so, they implicitly adhere to an Afrocentric feminist epistemology. Rather than being restrained by their both/and status of marginality, these women make creative use of their outsider-within status and produce innovative Afrocentric feminist thought. The difficulties these women face lie less in demonstrating that they have mastered white male epistemologies than in resisting the hegemonic nature of these patterns of thought in order to see, value, and use existing alternative Afrocentric feminist ways of knowing.

In establishing the legitimacy of their knowledge claims, Black women scholars who want to develop Afrocentric feminist thought may encounter the often conflicting standards of three key groups. First, Black feminist thought must be validated by ordinary African-American women who, in the words of Hannah Nelson, grow to womanhood "in a world where the saner you are, the madder you are made to appear." To be credible in the eyes of this group, scholars must be personal advocates for their material, be accountable for the consequences of their work, have lived or experienced their material in some fashion, and be willing to engage in dialogues about their findings with ordinary, everyday people. Second, Black feminist thought also must be accepted by the community of Black women scholars. These scholars place varying amounts of importance on rearticulating a Black women's standpoint using an Afrocentric feminist epistemology. Third, Afrocentric feminist thought within academia must be prepared to confront Eurocentric masculinist political and epistemological requirements.

The dilemma facing Black women scholars engaged in creating Black feminist thought is that a knowledge claim that meets the criteria of adequacy for one group and thus is judged to be an acceptable knowledge claim may not be translatable into the terms of a different group. Using the example of Black English, June Jordan illustrates the difficulty of moving among epistemologies:

> You cannot "translate" instances of Standard English preoccupied with abstraction or with nothing/nobody evidently alive into Black English. That would warp the language into uses antithetical to the guiding perspective of its community of users. Rather you must first change those Standard English sentences, themselves, into ideas consistent with the person-centered assumptions of Black English.

Although both worldviews share a common vocabulary, the ideas themselves defy direct translation.

For Black women who are agents of knowledge, the marginality that accompanies outsider-within status can be the source of both frustration and creativity. In an attempt to minimize the differences between the cultural context of African-American communities and the expectations of social institutions, some women dichotomize their behavior and become two different people. Over time, the strain of doing this can be enormous. Others reject their cultural context and work against their own best interests by enforcing the dominant group's specialized thought. Still others manage to inhabit both contexts but do so critically, using their outsider-within perspectives as a source of insights and ideas. But while outsiders within can make substantial contributions as agents of knowledge, they rarely do so without substantial personal cost. "Eventually it comes to you," observes Lorraine Hansberry, "the thing that makes you exceptional, if you are at all, is inevitably that which must also make you lonely."

Once Black feminist scholars face the notion that, on certain dimensions of a Black women's standpoint, it may be fruitless to try and translate ideas from an Afrocentric feminist epistemology into a Eurocentric masculinist framework, then other choices emerge. Rather than trying to uncover universal knowledge claims that can withstand the translation from one epistemology to another (initially, at least), Black women intellectuals might find efforts to rearticulate a Black women's standpoint especially fruitful. Rearticulating a Black women's standpoint refashions the concrete and reveals the more universal human dimensions of Black women's everyday lives. "I date all my work," notes Nikki Giovanni, "because I think poetry, or any writing, is but a reflection of the moment. The universal comes from the particular." Bell Hooks maintains, "my goal as a feminist thinker and theorist is to take that abstraction and articulate it in a language that renders it accessible—not less complex or rigorous—but simply more accessible." The complexity exists; interpreting it remains the unfulfilled challenge for Black women intellectuals.

Situated Knowledge, Subjugated Knowledge, and Partial Perspectives

"My life seems to be an increasing revelation of the intimate face of universal struggle," claims June Jordan:

You begin with your family and the kids on the block, and next you open your eyes to what you call your people and that leads you into land reform into Black English into Angola leads you back to your own bed where you lie by yourself, wondering if you deserve to be peaceful, or trusted or desired or left to the freedom of your own unfaltering heart. And the scale shrinks to the use of a skull: your own interior cage.

Lorraine Hansberry expresses a similar idea: "I believe that one of the most sound ideas in dramatic writing is that in order to create the universal, you must pay very great attention to the specific. Universality, I think, emerges from the truthful identity of what is." Jordan and Hansberry's insights that universal struggle and truth may wear a particularistic, intimate face suggest a new epistemological stance concerning how we negotiate competing knowledge claims and identify "truth."

The context in which African-American women's ideas are nurtured or suppressed matters. Understanding the content and epistemology of Black women's ideas as specialized knowledge requires attending to the context from which those ideas emerge. While produced by individuals, Black feminist thought as situated knowledge is embedded in the communities in which African-American women find ourselves.

A Black women's standpoint and those of other oppressed groups is not only embedded in a context but exists in a situation characterized by domination. Because Black women's ideas have been suppressed, this suppression has stimulated African-American women to create knowledge that empowers people to resist domination. Thus Afrocentric feminist thought represents a subjugated knowledge. A Black women's standpoint may provide a preferred stance from which to view the matrix of domination because, in principle, Black feminist thought as specialized thought is less likely than the specialized knowledge produced by dominant groups to deny the connection between ideas and the vested interests of their creators. However, Black feminist thought as subjugated knowledge is not exempt from critical analysis, because subjugation is not grounds for an epistemology.

Despite African-American women's potential power to reveal new insights about the matrix of domination, a Black women's standpoint is only one angle of vision.

Thus Black feminist thought represents a partial perspective. The overarching matrix of domination houses multiple groups, each with varying experiences with penalty and privilege that produce corresponding partial perspectives, situated knowledges, and, for clearly identifiable subordinate groups, subjugated knowledges. No one group has a clear angle of vision. No one group possesses the theory or methodology that allows it to discover the absolute "truth" or, worse yet, proclaim its theories and methodologies as the universal norm evaluating other groups' experiences. Given that groups are unequal in power in making themselves heard, dominant groups have a vested interest in suppressing the knowledge produced by subordinate groups. Given the existence of multiple and competing knowledge claims to "truth" produced by groups with partial perspectives, what epistemological approach offers the most promise?

Dialogue and Empathy

Western social and political thought contains two alternative approaches to ascertaining "truth." The first, reflected in positivist science, has long claimed that absolute truths exist and that the task of scholarship is to develop objective, unbiased tools of science to measure these truths. . . . Relativism, the second approach, has been forwarded as the antithesis of and inevitable outcome of rejecting a positivist science. From a relativist perspective all groups produce specialized thought and each group's thought is equally valid. No group can claim to have a better interpretation of the "truth" than another. In a sense, relativism represents the opposite of scientific ideologies of objectivity. As epistemological stances, both positivist science and relativism minimize the importance of specific location in influencing a group's knowledge claims, the power inequities among groups that produce subjugated knowledges, and the strengths and limitations of partial perspective.

The existence of Black feminist thought suggests another alternative to the ostensibly objective norms of science and to relativism's claims that groups with competing knowledge claims are equal. . . . This approach to Afrocentric feminist thought allows African-American women to bring a Black women's standpoint to larger epistemological dialogues concerning the nature of the matrix of domination. Eventually such dialogues may get us to a point at which, claims Elsa Barkley Brown, "all people can learn to center in another experience, validate it, and judge it by its own standards without need of comparison or need to adopt that framework as their own." In such dialogues, "one has no need to 'decenter' anyone in order to center someone else; one has only to constantly, appropriately, 'pivot the center.'"

Those ideas that are validated as true by African-American women, African-American men, Latina lesbians, Asian-American women, Puerto Rican men, and other groups with distinctive standpoints, with each group using the epistemological approaches growing from its unique standpoint, thus become the most "objective" truths. Each group speaks from its own standpoint and shares its own partial, situated knowledge. But because each group perceives its own truth as partial, its knowledge is unfinished. Each group becomes better able to consider other groups' standpoints without relinquishing the uniqueness of its own standpoint or suppressing other groups' partial perspectives. "What is always needed in the appreciation of art, or life," maintains Alice Walker, "is the larger perspective. Connections made, or at least attempted, where none existed before, the straining to encompass in one's glance at the varied world the common thread, the unifying theme through immense diversity." Partiality and not universality is the condition of being heard; individuals and groups forwarding knowledge claims without owning their position are deemed less credible than those who do.

Dialogue is critical to the success of this epistemological approach, the type of dialogue long extant in the Afrocentric call-and-response tradition whereby power dynamics are fluid, everyone has a voice, but everyone must listen and respond to other voices in order to be allowed to remain in the community. Sharing a common cause fosters dialogue and encourages groups to transcend their differences. . . .

African-American women have been victimized by race, gender, and class oppression. But portraying Black women solely as passive, unfortunate recipients of racial and sexual abuse stifles notions that Black women can actively work to change our circumstances and bring about changes in our lives. Similarly, presenting African-American women solely as heroic figures who easily engage in resisting oppression on all fronts minimizes the very real costs of oppression and can foster the perception that Black women need no help because we can "take it."

Black feminist thought's emphasis on the ongoing interplay between Black women's oppression and Black women's activism presents the matrix of domination as responsive to human agency. Such thought

views the world as a dynamic place where the goal is not merely to survive or to fit in or to cope; rather, it becomes a place where we feel ownership and accountability. The existence of Afrocentric feminist thought suggests that there is always choice, and power to act, no matter how bleak the situation may appear to be. Viewing the world as one in the making raises the issue of individual responsibility for bringing about change. It also shows that while individual empowerment is key, only collective action can effectively generate lasting social transformation of political and economic institutions.

Kimberlé Williams Crenshaw (1959–) was born in Canton, Ohio. She took her bachelor's degree at Cornell in 1981 before studying law at Harvard Law School and the University of Wisconsin. She is professor of law at both UCLA and Columbia University. At Columbia in 2011, she became the founding director of the Center for Intersectionality and Social Policy Studies. Crenshaw is also considered a major figure in Critical Race Studies movement, which, like intersectionality studies, has served as a provocation among legal studies to take racial and other social differences as central to the study and teaching of law. She is a prizewinning teacher, a notable public intellectual, and a leading social theorist whose influence spans most major disciplines. Her books include *On Intersectionality* (2012), *The Race Track: Understanding Structural Racism* (2013), and *Black Girls Matter* (2014). The selection is from her United Nations Background Paper for the 2000 Expert Meeting on the Gender-Related Aspects of Racial Discrimination.

Dimensions of Intersectional Oppression*
Kimberlé Williams Crenshaw (2000)

The conjoining of multiple systems of subordination has been variously described as compound

---

* Kimberlé Williams Crenshaw, "The Structural and Political Dimensions of Intersectional Oppression, as excerpted from *Intersectionality: A Foundations and Frontiers Reader* by Patrick R. Grzanka (Westview Press, 2014), from K. W. Crenshaw, "Background Paper for the Expert Meeting on the Gender-Related Aspects of Race Discrimination" (United Nations, 2000). Reprinted with permission.

discrimination, multiple burdens, or double or triple discrimination. Intersectionality is a conceptualization of the problem that attempts to capture both the structural and dynamic consequences of the interaction between two or more axes of subordination. It specifically addresses the manner in which racism, patriarchy, class oppression and other discriminatory systems create background inequalities that structure the relative positions of women, races, ethnicities, classes—and the like. Moreover, it addresses the way that specific acts and policies create burdens that flow along these axes constituting the dynamic or active aspects of disempowerment.

To use a metaphor of an intersection, we first analogize the various axes of power—i.e., race, ethnicity, gender, or class—as constituting the thoroughfares which structure the social, economic or political terrain. It is through these avenues that disempowering dynamics travel. These thoroughfares are sometimes framed as distinctive and mutually exclusive axes of power, for example racism is distinct from patriarchy which is in turn distinct from class oppression. In fact, the systems often overlap and cross each other, creating complex intersections at which two, three or four of these axes meet. Racialized women are often positioned in the space where racism or xenophobia, class and gender meet. They are consequently subject to injury by the heavy flow of traffic traveling along all these roads. Racialized women and other multiply burdened groups who are located at these intersections by virtue of their specific identities must negotiate the "traffic" that flows through these intersections. This is a particularly dangerous task when the traffic flows simultaneously from many directions. Injuries are sometimes created when the impact from one direction throws victims into the path of oncoming traffic while in other occasions, injuries occur from fully simultaneous collisions. These are the contexts in which intersectional injuries occur—disadvantages or conditions interact with preexisting vulnerabilities to create a distinct dimension of disempowerment.

Categorizing the Intersectional Experience: A Provisional Framework

While it is now widely accepted that women do not always experience sexism

in the same way, and that men and women do not experience racism in the same way, the project of framing the actual circumstances in which experiences of racism and sexism converge is only gradually developing on a global level. Provided below is only a provisional framework intended to assist in cataloging and organizing existing knowledge about the multiple ways that intersectionality might play out in shaping the lives of women around the globe. The objective of these initial topologies is to introduce a language for people to attach to their own experience. It also serves to illustrate the imperative of expanding conceptual parameters of existing treaty discourses. As the topologies show, the intersectional problem is not simply that one discreet form of discrimination is not fully addressed, but that an entire range of human rights violations are obscured by the failure to address fully the intersectional vulnerabilities of marginalized women and occasionally marginalized men, as well.

1. The tragic incidents of racially motivated rape are sometimes preceded by another manifestation of intersectional oppression, the propagation of explicitly raced and gendered propaganda directed against ethnic women in efforts to rationalize sexual aggression against them. This was explicitly deployed in Bosnia and Rwanda, as reported by Human Rights Watch reports from both regions.

2. Women are not the only victims of this intersectional subordination. Racialized gender stereotypes have also been deployed against men to rationalize a sex-inflected form of violence against them. In the US, for example, racist propaganda often preceded and subsequently rationalized the lynching of African American men.

3. Even where sexualized propaganda does not culminate in mass scale sexual violence, there is reason to believe that such targeted propaganda against women is damaging in a host of other ways, and thus forms yet another example of intersectional oppression. Propaganda against poor and racialized women may not only render them likely targets of sexualized violence, it may also contribute to the tendency of many people to doubt their truthfulness when they attempt to seek the protection of authorities. According to Human Rights Watch, Dalit women who attempt to press charges against accused rapists are highly unlikely to have their cases prosecuted, particularly in cases involving higher caste perpetrators. In the US, Black and Latino women are least likely to see the men accused of raping them prosecuted and incarcerated. Studies suggest that the racial identity of the victim plays a significant role in determining such outcomes, and there is evidence that jurors may

be influenced by sexualized propaganda to believe that racialized women were more likely to consent to sex in circumstances that they would find doubtful if the victim were not a racial minority.

4. Sexualized propaganda targeted at racialized women may also contribute to their political subordination, particularly in contexts relating to reproductive policies and social welfare. Justifications for policies that compromise the reproductive rights of poor and minority women such as sterilization, forced birth control, and the imposition of economic penalties and other disincentives for childbearing are sometimes premised on pre-existing images of poor and ethnic women as sexually undisciplined. This might usefully be framed as intersectional discrimination in that the subordinating aspects of these images simultaneously draw upon pre-existing gender stereotypes that draw distinctions between women based on perceived sexual conduct, and also racial or ethnic stereotypes that characterize some race, ethnic or class groups as sexually undisciplined. The consequence for women at the intersection of these stereotypes is that they are particularly vulnerable to punitive measures based largely on who they are.

5. Targeted acts of intentional discrimination are not limited to sexual violence. In employment, education and in other arenas, racialized women are sometimes subject to discriminations and burdens specifically because they are not men and because they are not members of racially or ethnically dominant groups in society. This is in effect compound discrimination: they are excluded on the basis of race from jobs designated for women, and they are excluded from jobs reserved for men on the basis of gender. In effect, they are specifically excluded as minority or ethnic women because there is no role for applicants with their particular ethno-racial and gendered profile.

6. For example, in some workforces, particularly those that are gender and race segregated, racialized women may encounter compound discrimination where as a rule, women are hired for office jobs or positions that involve interaction with the public, while racial or ethnic minorities are hired for industrial work or some other form of gender segregated work. In such instances racialized women experience discrimination because the women's work is not appropriate for racialized women and the work designated for racialized men is deemed inappropriate for women.

7. There are also instances where the overlap between race and gender exclusion also limits the employment or educational opportunities for men.

Where industrial jobs or other male specific modes of employment are limited, and the work that remains is oriented toward women's work, men too might experience compound discrimination: the work that is available to women is not deemed to be appropriate for men, and the work available to more privileged men is not available to racially subordinate men.

8. In education, as well, women of a particular ethno-racial identity may be specifically excluded from educational opportunity, or perhaps undereducated relative to men in their ethno-racial group or more elite women. Recent reports suggest that Albanian girls in Bosnia are specifically excluded from education . . . while in India, Dalit girls are significantly less likely to be educated and sustain extremely high school drop-out rates.

9. A slightly distinct manifestation of intersectional subordination might be framed as structural intersectional subordination. This phenomenon represents a full range of circumstances in which policies intersect with background structures of inequality to create a compounded burden for particularly vulnerable victims. In some instances, a gendered discrimination occurs within a context in which some women are already vulnerable due to race and/or class. In other instances, a policy, practice or individual act on the basis of race, ethnicity or some other factor occurs in a context of a gendered structure that effects women (or sometimes men) in a unique way. The vulnerability of refugee women to sexual violence constitutes an example of an intersectional problem that should be only partially analyzed as ethnic discrimination. As reported by Human Rights Watch, Burundian refugee women in Tanzania report a very high incidence of rape. Their vulnerability to sexual violence is partially structured by gender in that they are often most vulnerable to abuse when they undertake the gender based responsibilities of collecting firewood and other essentials for home. Under prevailing conditions of refugee life, honoring this responsibility requires them to travel alone or in small groups several miles from the refugee camps. Over the course of pursuing these responsibilities, they are often assaulted, sometimes because of their identity as powerless refugee women. Here their condition is the product of ethno-racial disempowerment and patriarchy twice over: because they are women, part of the structure of gender relations requires them to risk their safety to fulfill their responsibilities. As Hutus, they are dislocated aliens in a foreign land; more broadly, the conditions that prevail in their camp,

particularly the lack of bare essentials for survival, are also products of broader patterns of racial power, in particular, the differential resources available to African refugees as opposed to those who are victims of European conflict. Finally, the dynamic nature of their sexual violence is both raced and gendered: the specific abuse to which they are subject is obviously based on their gender while their specific identity as Hutu women renders them particularly vulnerable to racial stereotypes prevalent among Tanzanian men.

10. Another example of structural intersectionality can be captured by the overlapping effects of background structures that interact with a policy or some other decision that create burdens that are disproportionately visited upon marginalized women. What distinguishes this intersectional problem from the examples above is that the policy in question is not in any way targeted toward women or toward any other marginalized people; it simply intersects with other structures to create a subordinating effect. Examples of this kind of subordination might be illustrated in the burdens placed on women by structural adjustment policies within developing economies. The gendered consequences of structural adjustment policies, for example, have already been articulated by a range of critics who note the heavy burden placed on women. It is often women who must pick up the additional burdens created by the retraction of services that were once performed by the state. As the state withdraws resources for the care for the young, infirm and elderly, for example, the consequences of these unmet needs subsequently fall largely on those to whom such responsibilities have been traditionally distributed—women. Yet additional class structures determine which women will physically perform this work, and which women will have this work performed by paying other economically disadvantaged women to do it. Thus poor women must pick up the burden of caring for the families of others as well as their own.

The consequences of structural adjustment—particularly where devaluation of their currencies has reduced their wages—place them in a position in which they are economically forced to take on even more work, often the gendered work that more elite women can turn to the market to secure. The buck stops not at the top but at the bottom, a bottom which is often gendered, classed, and frequently racialized.

Political Intersectionality

The examples set forth above primarily track the material consequences of intersectionality. There is,

however, another aspect of the overlap between race and gender subordination that bears noting. Women who are members of communities that are racially, culturally, or economically marginalized have actively organized in large and small ways to challenge the conditions of their lives. They do so against some of the same obstacles that more elite women face, as well as obstacles that are unique to them. One such obstacle is often framed in terms of their obligation to their social or national group, an obligation that is at times deployed to suppress any critique of such practices or problems that might in some way draw negative attention to the group. Women who insist on pursuing their rights against certain abuses that occur within their communities risk ostracism or other forms of disapproval for allegedly betraying or embarrassing their communities. For example, Anita Hill garnered the world's attention when she accused Clarence Thomas of sexual harassment. Although Hill effectively broke the silence about this widespread problem and raised the level of awareness about sexual harassment in an important way, she was widely regarded by many in the African American community as having betrayed the group's interests. This particular burden is not one that women in racially dominant groups ordinarily face.

Women who challenge discriminatory practices which are defended by others as cultural often find themselves in a particularly precarious position. On one hand, it is sometimes the case that outsiders are all too willing to unleash harsh criticism toward the practices of ethnically or racially different groups even in the face of similarly questionable abuses within their own cultures. On the other hand, when women allow their challenges to patriarchal cultural traditions within their own communities to be silenced, they lose the opportunity to transform practices that are damaging to women.

Gloria Anzaldúa (1942–2004) wrote fiction and nonfiction, including social theory, with intentional reference to her multiple identities—Chicana, *tejana* (Indian), lesbian, feminist, and poet. She taught and lectured at many institutions, including the University of Texas, San Francisco State, and Vermont College. The selection is from *Borderlands/La Frontera: The New Mestiza* (1987), a blend of poetry and autobiography in which the reader can readily discern her social theory. She was the editor of *Making Face, Making Soul/Haciendo*

Cara (1990) and coeditor, with Cherríe Moraga, of *This Bridge Called My Back* (1981), which together are among the best available resources for writings in the women-of-color tradition.

The New Mestiza*
Gloria Anzaldúa (1987)

El otro México que acá hemos construido
el espacio es lo que ha sido
territorio nacional.
Esté el esfuerzo de todos nuestros hermanos
y latinoamericanos que han sabido
progressar.
 —Los Tigres del Norte

"The *Aztecas del norte* . . . compose the largest single tribe or nation of Anishinabeg (Indians) found in the United States today. . . . Some call themselves Chicanos and see themselves as people whose true homeland is Aztlán [the U.S. Southwest]."

Wind tugging at my sleeve
feet sinking into the sand
I stand at the edge where earth touches ocean
where the two overlap
a gentle coming together
at other times and places a violent clash.
Across the border in Mexico
    stark silhouette of houses gutted by waves,
        cliffs crumbling into the sea,
            silver waves marbled with spume
                gashing a hole under the border fence.

 Miro el mar atacar
la cerca en Border Field Park
     con sus buchones de agua,
an Easter Sunday resurrection
of the brown blood in my veins.

Oigo el llorido del mar, el respiro del aire,
    my heart surges to the beat of the sea.
        In the gray haze of the sun
            the gulls' shrill cry of hunger,
                the tangy smell of the sea seeping into me.

I walk   through the hole in the fence
    to the other side.
Under my fingers I feel the gritty wire
rusted by 139 years
    of the salty breath of the sea.

Beneath the iron sky
Mexican children kick their soccer ball across,
run after it, entering the U.S.

    I press my hand to the steel curtain—
        chainlink fence crowned with rolled
            barbed wire
rippling from the sea where Tijuana touches
    San Diego
        unrolling over mountains
            and plains
                and deserts,
this "Tortilla Curtain" turning into *el río Grande*
    flowing down to the flatlands
        of the Magic Valley of South Texas
        its mouth emptying into the Gulf.

1,950 mile-long open wound
            dividing a *pueblo*, a culture,
running down the length of my body,
    staking fence rods in my flesh,
    splits me   splits me
        me raja   me raja

    This is my home
    this thin edge of
        barbwire.
But the skin of the earth is seamless.
The sea cannot be fenced,
el mar does not stop at borders.
To show the white man what she thought of his
                    arrogance.
    Yemaya blew that wire fence down.

    This land was Mexican once,
    was Indian always
        and is.
    And   will be again.

Yo soy un puente tendido
    del mundo gabacho al del mojado,
lo pasado me estirá pa' 'trás
    y lo presente pa' 'delante.
Que la Virgen de Guadalupe me cuide
Ay ay ay, soy mexicana de este lado.

---

*Excerpt from "The Homeland, Aztlan," in *Borderlands/La Frontera*: The New Mestiza, pp. 1–9. © 1987, 1999, 2012 by Aunt Lute Books. www.auntlute.com.

The U.S.-Mexican border *es una herida abierta* where the Third World grates against the first and bleeds. And before a scab forms it hemorrhages again, the lifeblood of two worlds merging to form a third country—a border culture. Borders are set up to define the places that are safe and unsafe, to distinguish *us* from *them*. A border is a dividing line, a narrow strip along a steep edge. A borderland is a vague and undetermined place created by the emotional residue of an unnatural boundary. It is in a constant state of transition. The prohibited and forbidden are its inhabitants. *Los atravesados* live here: the squint-eyed, the perverse, the queer, the troublesome, the mongrel, the mulato, the half-breed, the half dead; in short, those who cross over, pass over, or go through the confines of the "normal." Gringos in the U.S. Southwest consider the inhabitants of the borderlands transgressors, aliens—whether they possess documents or not, whether they're Chicanos, Indians or Blacks. Do not enter, trespassers will be raped, maimed, strangled, gassed, shot. The only "legitimate" inhabitants are those in power, the whites and those who align themselves with whites. Tension grips the inhabitants of the borderlands like a virus. Ambivalence and unrest reside there and death is no stranger.

In the fields, *la migra*. My aunt saying, "*No corran*, don't run. They'll think you're *del otro lao*." In the confusion, Pedro ran, terrified of being caught. He couldn't speak English, couldn't tell them he was fifth generation American. *Sin papeles*—he did not carry his birth certificate to work in the fields. *La migra* took him away while we watched. *Se lo llevaron*. He tried to smile when he looked back at us, to raise his fist. But I saw the shame pushing his head down, I saw the terrible weight of shame hunch his shoulders. They deported him to Guadalajara by plane. The furthest he'd ever been to Mexico was Reynosa, a small border town opposite Hidalgo, Texas, not far from McAllen. Pedro walked all the way to the Valley. *Se lo llevaron sin un centavo al pobre. Se vino andando desde Guadalajara.*

During the original peopling of the Americas, the first inhabitants migrated across the Bering Straits and walked south across the continent. The oldest evidence of humankind in the U.S.—the Chicanos' ancient Indian ancestors—was found in Texas and has been dated to 35,000 b.c. In the Southwest United States archeologists have found 20,000-year-old campsites of the Indians who migrated through, or permanently occupied, the Southwest, Aztlán—land of the herons, land of whiteness, the Edenic place of origin of the Azteca.

In 1000 b.c., descendants of the original Cochise people migrated into what is now Mexico and Central America and became the direct ancestors of many of the Mexican people. (The Cochise culture of the Southwest is the parent culture of the Aztecs. The Uto-Aztecan languages stemmed from the language of the Cochise people.) The Aztecs (the Nahuatl word for people of Aztlán) left the Southwest in 1168 a.d.

> Now let us go.
> > *Tihueque, tihueque,*
> *Vámonos, vámonos.*
> > *Un pájaro cantó.*
> *Con sus ocho tribus salieron*
> > *de la "cueva del origen."*
> *los aztecas siguieron al dios*
> > *Huitzilopochtli.*

Huitzilopochtli, the God of War, guided them to the place (that later became Mexico City) where an eagle with a writhing serpent in its beak perched on a cactus. The eagle symbolizes the spirit (as the sun, the father); the serpent symbolizes the soul (as the earth, the mother). Together, they symbolize the struggle between the spiritual/celestial/male and the underworld/earth/ feminine. The symbolic sacrifice of the serpent to the "higher" masculine powers indicates that the patriarchal order had already vanquished the feminine and matriarchal order in pre-Columbian America.

At the beginning of the 16th century, the Spaniards and Hernán Cortés invaded Mexico and, with the help of tribes that the Aztecs had subjugated, conquered it. Before the Conquest, there were twenty-five million Indian people in Mexico and the Yucatan. Immediately after the Conquest, the Indian population had been reduced to under seven million. By 1650, only one-and-a-half-million pure-blooded Indians remained. The *mestizos* who were genetically equipped to survive small pox, measles, and typhus (Old World diseases to which the natives had no immunity), founded a new hybrid race and inherited Central and South America. *En 1521 nació una nueva raza, el mestizo, el mexicano* (people of mixed Indian and Spanish blood), a race that had never existed before. Chicanos, Mexican-Americans, are the offspring of those first matings.

Our Spanish, Indian, and *mestizo* ancestors explored and settled parts of the U.S. Southwest as early as the sixteenth century. For every gold-hungry *conquistador* and soul-hungry missionary who came north from Mexico, ten to twenty Indians and *mestizos* went along as porters or in other capacities. For the Indians, this constituted a return to the place of origin, Aztlán, thus making Chicanos originally and secondarily indigenous to the Southwest. Indians and *mestizos* from central Mexico intermarried with North American Indians. The continual intermarriage between Mexican and American Indians and Spaniards formed an even greater *mestizaje*. . . .

In the 1800s, Anglos migrated illegally into Texas, which was then part of Mexico, in greater and greater numbers and gradually drove the *tejanos* (native Texans of Mexican descent) from their lands, committing all manner of atrocities against them. Their illegal invasion forced Mexico to fight a war to keep its Texas territory. The Battle of the Alamo, in which the Mexican forces vanquished the whites, became, for the whites, the symbol for the cowardly and villainous character of the Mexicans. It became (and still is) a symbol that legitimized the white imperialist takeover. With the capture of Santa Anna later in 1836, Texas became a republic. *Tejanos* lost their land and, overnight, became the foreigners. . . .

In 1846, the U.S. incited Mexico to war. U.S. troops invaded and occupied Mexico, forcing her to give up almost half of her nation, what is now Texas, New Mexico, Arizona, Colorado and California.

With the victory of the U.S. forces over the Mexican in the U.S.-Mexican War, los *norteamericanos* pushed the Texas border down 100 miles, from *el río Nueces to el río Grande*. South Texas ceased to be part of the Mexican state of Tamaulipas. Separated from Mexico, the Native Mexican-Texan no longer looked toward Mexico as home; the Southwest became our homeland once more. The border fence that divides the Mexican people was born on February 2, 1848 with the signing of the Treaty of Guadalupe-Hidalgo. It left 100,000 Mexican citizens on this side, annexed by conquest along with the land. The land established by the treaty as belonging to Mexicans was soon swindled away from its owners. The treaty was never honored and restitution, to this day, has never been made.

> The justice and benevolence of God
> will forbid that . . . Texas should again
> become a howling wilderness
> trod only by savages, or . . . benighted
> by the ignorance and superstition,
> the anarchy and rapine of Mexican misrule.
> The Anglo-American race are destined
> to be forever the proprietors of
> this land of promise and fulfillment.
> Their laws will govern it,
> their learning will enlighten it,
> their enterprise will improve it.
> Their flocks range its boundless pastures,
> for them its fertile lands will yield . . .
> luxuriant harvests . . .
> The wilderness of Texas has been redeemed
> by Anglo-American blood & enterprise.
> —**William H. Wharton**

The Gringo, locked into the fiction of white superiority, seized complete political power, stripping Indians and Mexicans of their land while their feet were still rooted in it. *Con el destierro y el exilo fuimos desuñados, destroncados, destripados*—we were jerked out by the roots, truncated, disemboweled, dispossessed, and separated from our identity and our history. Many, under the threat of Anglo terrorism, abandoned homes and ranches and went to Mexico. Some stayed and protested. But as the courts, law enforcement officials, and government officials not only ignored their pleas but penalized them for their efforts, *tejanos* had no other recourse but armed retaliation. . . .

Fear of Going Home: Homophobia

For the lesbian of color, the ultimate rebellion she can make against her native culture is through her sexual behavior. She goes against two moral prohibitions: sexuality and homosexuality. Being lesbian and raised Catholic, indoctrinated as straight, I *made the choice to be queer* (for some it is genetically inherent). It's an interesting path, one that continually slips in and out of the white, the Catholic, the Mexican, the indigenous, the instincts. In and out of my head. It makes for *loquería*, the crazies. It is a path of knowledge—one of knowing (and of learning) the history of oppression of our *raza*. It is a way of balancing, of mitigating duality.

In a New England college where I taught, the presence of a few lesbians threw the more conservative heterosexual students and faculty into a panic. The two lesbian students and we two lesbian instructors met with them to discuss their fears. One of the students said, "I thought homophobia meant fear of going home after a residency."

And I thought, how apt. Fear of going home. And of not being taken in. We're afraid of being abandoned by the mother, the culture, *la Raza*, for being unacceptable, faulty, damaged. Most of us unconsciously believe that if we reveal this unacceptable aspect of the self our mother/culture/race will totally reject us. To avoid rejection, some of us conform to the values of the culture, push the unacceptable parts into the shadows. Which leaves only one fear—that we will be found out and that the Shadow-Beast will break out of its cage. Some of us take another route. We try to make ourselves conscious of the Shadow-Beast, stare at the sexual lust and lust for power and destruction we see on its face, discern among its features the undershadow that the reigning order of heterosexual males project on our Beast. Yet still others of us take it another step: we try to waken the Shadow-Beast inside us. Not many jump at the chance to confront the Shadow-Beast in the mirror without flinching at her lidless serpent eyes, her cold clammy moist hand dragging us underground, fangs barred and hissing. How does one put feathers on this particular serpent? But a few of us have been lucky—on the face of the Shadow-Beast we have seen not lust but tenderness; on its face we have uncovered the lie.

Intimate Terrorism: Life in the Borderlands

The world is not a safe place to live in. We shiver in separate cells in enclosed cities, shoulders hunched, barely keeping the panic below the surface of the skin, daily drinking shock along with our morning coffee, fearing the torches being set to our buildings, the attacks on the streets. Shutting down. Woman does not feel safe when her own culture, and white culture, are critical of her; when the males of all races hunt her as prey.

Alienated from her mother culture, "alien" in the dominant culture, the woman of color does not feel safe within the inner life of her Self. Petrified, she can't respond, her face caught between *los intersticios*, the spaces between the different worlds she inhabits.

The ability to respond is what is meant by responsibility, yet our cultures take away our ability to act—shackle us in the name of protection. Blocked, immobilized, we can't move forward, can't move backwards. That writhing serpent movement, the very movement of life, swifter than lightning, frozen.

We do not engage fully. We do not make full use of our faculties. We abnegate. And there in front of us is the crossroads therefore responsible and to blame (being a victim and transferring the blame on culture, mother, father, ex-lover, friend, absolves me of responsibility), or to feel strong, and, for the most part, in control.

My Chicana identity is grounded in the Indian woman's history of resistance. The Aztec female rites of mourning were rites of defiance protesting the cultural changes which disrupted the equality and balance between female and male, and protesting their demotion to a lesser status, their denigration. Like *la Llorona*, the Indian woman's only means of protest was wailing.

So *mamá, Raza*, how wonderful, *no tener que rendir cuentas a nadie*. I feel perfectly free to rebel and to rail against my culture. I fear no betrayal on my part because, unlike Chicanas and other women of color who grew up white or who have only recently returned to their native cultural roots, I was totally immersed in mine. It wasn't until I went to high school that I "saw" whites. Until I worked on my master's degree I had not gotten within an arm's distance of them. I was totally immersed *en lo mexicano*, a rural, peasant, isolated, *mexicanismo*. To separate from my culture (as from my family) I had to feel competent enough on the outside and secure enough inside to live life on my own. Yet in leaving home I did not lose touch with my origins because *lo mexicano* is in my system. I am a turtle, wherever I go I carry "home" on my back.

Not me sold out my people but they me. So yes, though "home" permeates every sinew and cartilage in my body, I too am afraid of going home. Though I'll defend my race and culture when they are attacked by non-*mexicanos, conosco el malestar de mi cultura*. I abhor some of my culture's ways, how it cripples its women, *como burras*, our strengths used against us, lowly *burras* bearing humility with dignity. The ability to serve, claim the males, is our highest virtue. I abhor how my culture makes *macho* caricatures of its men. No, I do not buy all the myths of the tribe into which I was born. I can understand why the more tinged with Anglo blood, the more adamantly my colored and colorless sisters glorify their colored culture's values—to offset the extreme devaluation of it by the white culture. It's a legitimate reaction. But I will not glorify those aspects of my culture which have injured me and which have injured me in the name of protecting me.

So, don't give me your tenets and your laws. Don't give me your lukewarm gods. What I want is an accounting with all three cultures—white, Mexican,

Indian. I want the freedom to carve and chisel my own face, to stanch the bleeding with ashes, to fashion my own gods out of my entrails. And if going home is denied me then I will have to stand and claim my space, making a new culture—*una cultura mestiza*—with my own lumber, my own bricks and mortar and my own feminist architecture.

Judith Butler (1956–) is Maxine Elliot Professor of Rhetoric and Composition at Berkeley and Hannah Arendt Professor of Philosophy at the European Graduate School. She is the author of *Gender Trouble: Feminism and the Subversion of Identity* (1990). The selection is from her contribution to *Inside/Out: Lesbian Theories, Gay Theories* (edited by Diana Fuss, 1991), an excellent and important collection of the writings of gay and lesbian social theorists. She is a prolific author and lecturer. Her many books include *Precarious Life* (2004) and *Power of Religion in Public Life* (2011). The range of her intellectual and academic contributions is so broad as to make formal classification impossible except to say that her thinking is invariably original and deep.

Imitation and Gender Insubordination[*]
Judith Butler (1991)

To Theorize as a Lesbian?

At first I considered writing a different sort of essay, one with a philosophical tone: the "being" of being homosexual. The prospect of *being* anything, even for pay, has always produced in me a certain anxiety, for "to be" gay, "to be" lesbian seems to be more than a simple injunction to become who or what I already am. And in no way does it settle the anxiety for me to say that this is "part" of what I am. To write or speak *as a lesbian* appears a paradoxical appearance of this "I," one which feels neither true nor false. For it is a production, usually in response to a request, to come out or write in the name of an identity which, once produced, sometimes func-

---

[*] Reproduced by permission of Taylor and Francis Group, LLC, a division of Informa plc, from *Inside/Out: Lesbian Theories, Gay Theories*, edited by Diana Fuss, pp. 13-29. Copyright 1991, Routledge; permission conveyed through Copyright Clearance Center, Inc.

tions as a politically efficacious phantasm. I'm not at ease with "lesbian theories, gay theories," for as I've argued elsewhere, identity categories tend to be instruments of regulatory regimes, whether as the normalizing categories of oppressive structures or as the rallying points for a liberatory contestation of that very oppression. This is not to say that I will not appear at political occasions under the sign of lesbian, but that I would like to have it permanently unclear what precisely that sign signifies. So it is unclear how it is that I can contribute to this book and appear under its title, for it announces a set of terms that I propose to contest. One risk I take is to be recolonized by the sign under which I write, and so it is this risk that I seek to thematize. To propose that the invocation of identity is always a risk does not imply that resistance to it is always or only symptomatic of a self-inflicted homophobia. Indeed, a Foucaultian perspective might argue that the affirmation of "homosexuality" is itself an extension of a homophobic discourse. And yet "discourse," he writes on the same page, "can be both an instrument and an effect of power, but also a hindrance, a stumbling-block, a point of resistance and a starting point for an opposing strategy."

So I am skeptical about how the "I" is determined as it operates under the title of the lesbian sign, and I am no more comfortable with its homophobic determination than with those normative definitions offered by other members of the "gay or lesbian community." I'm permanently troubled by identity categories, consider them to be invariable stumbling-blocks, and understand them, even promote them, as sites of necessary trouble. In fact, if the category were to offer no trouble, it would cease to be interesting to me: it is precisely the *pleasure* produced by the instability of those categories which sustains the various erotic practices that make me a candidate for the category to begin with. To install myself within the terms of an identity category would be to turn against the sexuality that the category purports to describe; and this might be true for any identity category which seeks to control the very eroticism that it claims to describe and authorize, much less "liberate."

And what's worse, I do not understand the notion of "theory," and am hardly interested in being cast as its defender, much less in being signified as part of an elite gay/lesbian theory crowd that seeks to establish the legitimacy and domestication of gay/lesbian studies within the academy. Is there a pregiven distinction between theory, politics, culture, media?

How do those divisions operate to quell a certain intertextual writing that might well generate wholly different epistemic maps? But I am writing here now: is it too late? Can this writing, can any writing, refuse the terms by which it is appropriated even as, to some extent, that very colonizing discourse enables or produces this stumbling block, this resistance? How do I relate the paradoxical situation of this dependency and refusal?

If the political task is to show that theory is never merely *theoria*, in the sense of disengaged contemplation, and to insist that it is fully political (*phronesis* or even *praxis*), then why not simply call this operation *politics*, or some necessary permutation of it?

I have begun with confessions of trepidation and a series of disclaimers, but perhaps it will become clear that *disclaiming*, which is no simple activity, will be what I have to offer as a form of affirmative resistance to a certain regulatory operation of homophobia. The discourse of "coming out" has clearly served its purposes, but what are its risks? And here I am not speaking of unemployment or public attack or violence, which are quite clearly and widely on the increase against those who are perceived as "out" whether or not of their own design. Is the "subject" who is "out" free of its subjection and finally in the clear? Or could it be that the subjection that subjectivates the gay or lesbian subject in some ways continues to oppress, or oppresses most insidiously, once "outness" is claimed? What or who is it that is "out," made manifest and fully disclosed, when and if I reveal myself as lesbian? What is it that is now known, anything? What remains permanently concealed by the very linguistic act that offers up the promise of a transparent revelation of sexuality? Can sexuality even remain sexuality once it submits to a criterion of transparency and disclosure, or does it perhaps cease to be sexuality precisely when the semblance of full explicitness is achieved? Is sexuality of any kind even possible without that opacity designated by the unconscious, which means simply that the conscious "I" who would reveal its sexuality is perhaps the last to know the meaning of what it says?

To claim that this is what I *am* is to suggest a provisional totalization of this "I." But if the I can so determine itself, then that which it excludes in order to make that determination remains constitutive of the determination itself. In other words, such a statement presupposes that the "I" exceeds its determination, and even produces that very excess in and by the act which seeks to exhaust the semantic field of

that "I." In the act which would disclose the true and full content of that "I," a certain radical *concealment* is thereby produced. For it is always finally unclear what is meant by invoking the lesbian-signifier, since its signification is always to some degree out of one's control, but also because its *specificity* can only be demarcated by exclusions that return to disrupt its claim to coherence. What, if anything, can lesbians be said to share? And who will decide this question, and in the name of whom? If I claim to be a lesbian, I "come out" only to produce a new and different "closet." The "you" to whom I come out now has access to a different region of opacity. Indeed, the locus of opacity has simply shifted: before, you did not know whether I "am," but now you do not know what that means, which is to say that the copula is empty, that it cannot be substituted for with a set of descriptions. And perhaps that is a situation to be valued. Conventionally, one comes out *of* the closet (and yet, how often is it the case that we are "outed" when we are young and without resources?); so we are out of the closet, but into what? what new unbounded spatiality? the room, the den, the attic, the basement, the house, the bar, the university, some new enclosure whose door, like Kafka's door, produces the expectation of a fresh air and a light of illumination that never arrives? Curiously, it is the figure of the closet that produces this expectation, and which guarantees its dissatisfaction. For being "out" always depends to some extent on being "in"; it gains its meaning only within that polarity. Hence, being "out" must produce the closet again and again in order to maintain itself as "out." In this sense, *outness* can only produce a new opacity; and *the closet* produces the promise of a disclosure that can, by definition, never come. Is this infinite postponement of the disclosure of "gayness," produced by the very act of "coming out," to be lamented? Or is this very deferral of the signified *to be valued*, a site for the production of values, precisely because the term now takes on a life that cannot be, can never be, permanently controlled?

It is possible to argue that whereas no transparent or full revelation is afforded by "lesbian" and "gay," there remains a political imperative to use these necessary errors or category mistakes, as it were (what Gayatri Spivak might call "catachrestic" operations: to use a proper name improperly), to rally and represent an oppressed political constituency. Clearly, I am not legislating against the use of the term. My question is simply: which use will be legislated, and what play will there be between legislation and use such that the instrumental uses of "identity" do not become regulatory imperatives? If it is already true that "lesbians" and "gay men" have been traditionally designated as impossible identities, errors of classification, unnatural disasters within juridico-medical discourses, or, what perhaps amounts to the same, the very paradigm of what calls to be classified, regulated, and controlled, then perhaps these sites of disruption, error, confusion, and trouble can be the very rallying points for a certain resistance to classification and to identity as such.

The question is not one of *avowing* or *disavowing* the category of lesbian or gay, but, rather, why it is that the category becomes the site of this "ethical" choice? What does it mean to *avow* a category that can only maintain its specificity and coherence by performing a prior set of *disavowals*? Does this make "coming out" into the avowal of disavowal, that is, a return to the closet under the guise of an escape? And it is not something like heterosexuality or bisexuality that is disavowed by the category, but a set of identificatory and practical crossings between these categories that renders the discreteness of each equally suspect. Is it not possible to maintain and pursue heterosexual identifications and aims within homosexual practice, and homosexual identifications and aims within heterosexual practices? If a sexuality is to be disclosed, what will be taken as the true determinant of its meaning: the phantasy structure, the act, the orifice, the gender, the anatomy? And if the practice engages a complex interplay of all of those, which one of these erotic dimensions will come to stand for the sexuality that requires them all? Is it the *specificity* of a lesbian experience or lesbian desire or lesbian sexuality that lesbian theory needs to elucidate? Those efforts have only and always produced a set of contests and refusals which should by now make it clear that there is no necessarily common element among lesbians, except perhaps that we all know something about how homophobia works against women—although, even then, the language and the analysis we use will differ.

To argue that there might be a *specificity* to lesbian sexuality has seemed a necessary counterpoint to the claim that lesbian sexuality is just heterosexuality once removed, or that it is derived, or that it does not exist. But perhaps the claim of specificity, on the one hand, and the claim of derivativeness or non-existence, on the other, are not as contradictory as they seem. Is it not possible that lesbian sexuality is a process that reinscribes the power domains that it resists, that it is constituted in part from the very heterosexual matrix that it seeks to displace, and that its specificity is to be established, not *outside* or *beyond* that reinscription or reiteration, but in the very modality and effects of that reinscription. In other words, the negative constructions of lesbianism as a fake or a bad copy can be occupied and reworked to call into question the claims of heterosexual priority. In a sense I hope to make clear in what follows, lesbian sexuality can be understood to redeploy its "derivativeness" in the service of displacing hegemonic heterosexual norms. Understood in this way, the political problem is not to establish the specificity of lesbian sexuality over and against its derivativeness, but to turn the homophobic construction of the bad copy against the framework that privileges heterosexuality as origin, and so "derive" the former from the latter. This description requires a reconsideration of imitation, drag, and other forms of sexual crossing that affirm the internal complexity of a lesbian sexuality constituted in part within the very matrix of power that it is compelled both to reiterate and to oppose.

On the Being of Gayness as Necessary Drag

The professionalization of gayness requires a certain performance and production of a "self" which is the *constituted effect* of a discourse that nevertheless claims to "represent" that self as a prior truth. When I spoke at the conference on homosexuality in 1989, I found myself telling my friends beforehand that I was off to Yale to be a lesbian, which of course didn't mean that I wasn't one before, but that somehow then, as I spoke in that context, I *was* one in some more thorough and totalizing way, at least for the time being. So I *am* one, and my qualifications are even fairly unambiguous. Since I was sixteen, being a lesbian is what I've been. So what's the anxiety, the discomfort? Well, it has something to do with that redoubling, the way I can say, I'm going to Yale to be a lesbian; a lesbian is what I've been being for so long. How is it that I can both "be" one, and yet endeavor to be one at the same time? When and where does my being a lesbian come into play, when and where does this playing a lesbian constitute something like what I am? To say that I "play" at being one is not to say that I am not one "really"; rather, how and where I play at being one is the way in which that "being" gets established, instituted, circulated, and confirmed. This is not a performance from which I can take radical distance, for this is deep-seated play, psychically entrenched play, *and this "I" does not play its lesbianism as a role*. Rather, it is through the repeated play of this sexuality that the "I" is insistently reconstituted as a lesbian "I"; paradoxically, it is precisely the repetition of that play that establishes as well the *instability* of the very category that it constitutes. For if the "I" is a site of repetition, that is, if the "I" only achieves the semblance of identity through a certain repetition of itself, then the I is always displaced by the very repetition that sustains it. In other words, does or can the "I" ever repeat itself, cite itself, faithfully, or is there always a displacement from its former moment that establishes the permanently non-self-identical status of that "I" or its "being lesbian"? What "performs" does not exhaust the "I"; it does not lay out in visible terms the comprehensive content of that "I," for if the performance is "repeated," there is always the question of what differentiates from each other the moments of identity that are repeated. And if the "I" is the effect of a certain repetition, one which produces the semblance of a continuity or coherence, then there is no "I" that precedes the gender that it is said to perform; the repetition, and the failure to repeat, produce a string of performances that constitute and contest the coherence of that "I."

But *politically*, we might argue, isn't it quite crucial to insist on lesbian and gay identities precisely because they are being threatened with erasure and obliteration from homophobic quarters? Isn't the above theory *complicitous* with those political forces that would obliterate the possibility of gay and lesbian identity? Isn't it "no accident" that such theoretical contestations of identity emerge within a political climate that is performing a set of similar obliterations of homosexual identities through legal and political means?

The question I want to raise in return is this: ought such threats of obliteration dictate the terms of the political resistance to them, and if they do, do such homophobic efforts to that extent win the battle from the start? There is no question that gays and lesbians are threatened by the violence of public erasure, but the decision to counter that violence must be careful not to reinstall another in its place. Which version of lesbian or gay ought to be rendered visible, and which internal exclusions will that rendering visible institute? Can the visibility of identity *suffice* as a political strategy, or can it only be the starting point for a strategic intervention which calls for a transformation of policy? Is it not a sign of despair over public politics when identity becomes its own policy, bringing with it those who would "police" it from various sides? And this is not a call to return to silence or invisibility, but, rather, to make use of a category that can be called into question, made to account for what it excludes. That any consolidation of identity requires some set of differentiations and exclusions seems clear. But which ones ought to be valorized? That the identity-sign I use now has its purposes seems right, but there is no way to predict or control the political uses to which that sign will be put in the future. And perhaps this is a kind of openness, regardless of its risks, that ought to be safeguarded for political reasons. If the rendering visible of lesbian/gay identity now presupposes a set of exclusions, then perhaps part of what is necessarily excluded is *the future uses of the sign*. There is a political necessity to use some sign now, and we do, but how to use it in such a way that its futural significations are not *foreclosed*? How to use the sign and avow its temporal contingency at once?

In avowing the sign's strategic provisionality (rather than its strategic essentialism), that identity can become a site of contest and revision, indeed, take on a future set of significations that those of us who use it now may not be able to foresee. It is in the safeguarding of the future of the political signifiers—preserving the signifier as a site of rearticulation—that LaClau and Mouffe discern its democratic promise.

Within contemporary U.S. politics, there are a vast number of ways in which lesbianism in particular is understood as precisely that which cannot or dare not *be*. In a sense, Jesse Helms's attack on the NEA for sanctioning representations of "homoeroticism" focuses various homophobic fantasies of what gay men are and do on the work of Robert Mapplethorpe. In a sense, for Helms, gay men exist as objects of prohibition; they are, in his twisted fantasy, sadomasochistic exploiters of children, the paradigmatic exemplars of "obscenity"; in a sense, the lesbian is not even produced within this discourse as a prohibited object. Here it becomes important to recognize that oppression works not merely through acts of overt prohibition, but covertly, through the constitution of viable subjects and through the corollary constitution of a domain of unviable (un)subjects—*abjects*, we might call them—who are neither named nor prohibited within the economy of the law. Here oppression works through the production of a domain of unthinkability and unnameability. Lesbianism is not explicitly prohibited in part because it has not even made its way into the thinkable, the imaginable, that grid of cultural intelligibility that regulates the real and the nameable. How, then, to "be" a lesbian in a political context in which the lesbian does not exist? That is, in a political discourse that wages its violence against lesbianism in part by excluding lesbianism from discourse itself? To be prohibited explicitly is to occupy a discursive site from which something like a reverse-discourse can be articulated; to be implicitly proscribed is not even to qualify as an object of prohibition. And though homosexualities of all kinds in this present climate are being erased, reduced, and (then) reconstituted as sites of radical homophobic fantasy, it is important to retrace the different routes by which the unthinkability of homosexuality is being constituted time and again.

It is one thing to be erased from discourse, and yet another to be present within discourse as an abiding falsehood. Hence, there is a political imperative to render lesbianism visible, but how is that to be done outside or through existing regulatory regimes? Can the exclusion from ontology itself become a rallying point for resistance?

Here is something like a confession which is meant merely to thematize the impossibility of confession: As a young person, I suffered for a long time, and I suspect many people have, from being told, explicitly or implicitly, that what I "am" is a copy, an imitation, a derivative example, a shadow of the real. Compulsory heterosexuality sets itself up as the original, the true, the authentic; the norm that determines the real implies that "being" lesbian is always a kind of miming, a vain effort to participate in the phantasmatic plenitude of naturalized heterosexuality which will always and only fail. And yet, I remember quite distinctly when I first read in Esther Newton's *Mother Camp: Female Impersonators in America* that drag is not an imitation or a copy of some prior and true gender; according to Newton, drag enacts the very structure of impersonation by which *any gender* is assumed. Drag is not the putting on of a gender that belongs properly to some other group, i.e. an act of *ex*propriation or *ap*propriation that assumes that gender is the rightful property of sex, that "masculine" belongs to "male" and "feminine" belongs to "female." There is no "proper" gender, a gender proper to one sex rather than another, which is in some sense that sex's cultural property. Where that notion of the "proper" operates, it is always only *improperly* installed as the effect of a compulsory system. Drag constitutes the mundane way in which genders are appropriated, theatricalized,

worn, and done; it implies that all gendering is a kind of impersonation and approximation. If this is true, it seems, there is no original or primary gender that drag imitates, but *gender is a kind of imitation for which there is no original*; in fact, it is a kind of imitation that produces the very notion of the original as an *effect* and consequence of the imitation itself. In other words, the naturalistic effects of heterosexualized genders are produced through imitative strategies; what they imitate is a phantasmatic ideal of heterosexual identity, one that is produced by the imitation as its effect. In this sense, the "reality" of heterosexual identities is performatively constituted through an imitation that sets itself up as the origin and the ground of all imitations. In other words, heterosexuality is always in the process of imitating and approximating its own phantasmatic idealization of itself—*and failing*. Precisely because it is bound to fail, and yet endeavors to succeed, the project of heterosexual identity is propelled into an endless repetition of itself. Indeed, in its efforts to naturalize itself as the original, heterosexuality must be understood as a compulsive and compulsory repetition that can only produce the *effect* of its own originality; in other words, compulsory heterosexual identities, those ontologically consolidated phantasms of "man" and "woman," are theatrically produced effects that posture as grounds, origins, the normative measure of the real.

Reconsider then the homophobic charge that queens and butches and femmes are imitations of the heterosexual real. Here "imitation" carries the meaning of "derivative" or "secondary," a copy of an origin which is itself the ground of all copies, but which is itself a copy of nothing. Logically, this notion of an "origin" is suspect, for how can something operate as an origin if there are no secondary consequences which retrospectively confirm the originality of that origin? The origin requires its derivatives in order to affirm itself as an origin, for origins only make sense to the extent that they are differentiated from that which they produce as derivatives. Hence, if it were not for the notion of the homosexual *as* copy, there would be no construct of heterosexuality *as* origin. Heterosexuality here presupposes homosexuality. And if the homosexual *as copy precedes* the heterosexual as *origin*, then it seems only fair to concede that the copy comes before the origin, and that homosexuality is thus the origin, and heterosexuality the copy.

But simple inversions are not really possible. For it is only *as* a copy that homosexuality can be argued to *precede* heterosexuality as the origin. In other words, the entire framework of copy and origin proves radically unstable as each position inverts into the other and confounds the possibility of any stable way to locate the temporal or logical priority of either term.

But let us then consider this problematic inversion from a psychic/political perspective. If the structure of gender imitation is such that the imita*ted* is to some degree produced—or, rather, *repro*-duced—by imitation (see again Derrida's inversion and displacement of mimesis in "The Double Session"), then to claim that gay and lesbian identities are implicated in heterosexual norms or in hegemonic culture generally is not to *derive* gayness from straightness. On the contrary, *imitation* does not copy that which is prior, but produces and *inverts* the very terms of priority and derivativeness. Hence, if gay identities are implicated in heterosexuality, that is not the same as claiming that they are determined or derived from heterosexuality, and it is not the same as claiming that that heterosexuality is the only cultural network in which they are implicated. These are, quite literally, *inverted* imitations, ones which invert the order of imitated and imitation, and which, in the process, expose the fundamental dependency of "the origin" on that which it claims to produce as its secondary effect.

What follows if we concede from the start that gay identities as derivative inversions are in part defined in terms of the very heterosexual identities from which they are differentiated? If heterosexuality is an impossible imitation of itself, an imitation that performatively constitutes itself as the original, then the imitative parody of "heterosexuality"—when and where it exists in gay cultures—is always and only an imitation of an imitation, a copy of a copy, for which there is no original. Put in yet a different way, the parodic or imitative effect of gay identities works neither to copy nor to emulate heterosexuality, but rather, to expose heterosexuality as an incessant and *panicked* imitation of its own naturalized idealization. That heterosexuality is always in the act of elaborating itself is evidence that it is perpetually at risk, that is, that it "knows" its own possibility of becoming undone: hence, its compulsion to repeat which is at once a foreclosure of that which threatens its coherence. That it can never eradicate that risk attests to its profound dependency upon the homosexuality that it seeks fully to eradicate and never can or that it seeks to make second, but which is always already there as a prior possibility. Although this failure of

naturalized heterosexuality might constitute a source of pathos for heterosexuality itself—what its theorists often refer to as its constitutive malaise—it can become an occasion for a subversive and proliferating parody of gender norms in which the very claim to originality and to the real is shown to be the effect of a certain kind of naturalized gender mime.

It is important to recognize the ways in which heterosexual norms reappear within gay identities, to affirm that gay and lesbian identities are not only structured in part by dominant heterosexual frames, but that they are *not* for that reason *determined* by them. They are running commentaries on those naturalized positions as well, parodic replays and resignifications of precisely those heterosexual structures that would consign gay life to discursive domains of unreality and unthinkability. But to be constituted or structured in part by the very heterosexual norms by which gay people are oppressed is not, I repeat, to be claimed or determined by those structures. And it is not necessary to think of such heterosexual constructs as the pernicious intrusion of "the straight mind," one that must be rooted out in its entirety. In a way, the presence of heterosexual constructs and positionalities in whatever form in gay and lesbian identities presupposes that there is a gay and lesbian repetition of straightness, a recapitulation of straightness—which is itself a repetition and recapitulation of its own ideality—within its own terms, a site in which all sorts of resignifying and parodic repetitions become possible. The parodic replication and resignification of heterosexual constructs within non-heterosexual frames brings into relief the utterly constructed status of the so-called original, but it shows that heterosexuality only constitutes itself as the original through a convincing act of repetition. The more that "act" is expropriated, the more the heterosexual claim to originality is exposed as illusory.

Although I have concentrated in the above on the reality-effects of gender practices, performances, repetitions, and mimes, I do not mean to suggest that drag is a "role" that can be taken on or taken off at will. There is no volitional subject behind the mime who decides, as it were, which gender it will be today. On the contrary, the very possibility of becoming a viable subject requires that a certain gender mime be already underway. The "being" of the subject is no more self-identical than the "being" of any gender; in fact, coherent gender, achieved through an apparent repetition of the same, produces as its *effect* the illusion of a prior and volitional subject. In this sense, gender is not a performance that a prior subject elects to do, but gender is *performative* in the sense that it constitutes as an effect the very subject it appears to express. It is a *compulsory* performance in the sense that acting out of line with heterosexual norms brings with it ostracism, punishment, and violence, not to mention the transgressive pleasures produced by those very prohibitions.

To claim that there is no performer prior to the performed, that the performance is performative, that the performance constitutes the appearance of a "subject" as its effect is difficult to accept. This difficulty is the result of a predisposition to think of sexuality and gender as "expressing" in some indirect or direct way a psychic reality that precedes it. The denial of the *priority* of the subject, however, is not the denial of the subject; in fact, the refusal to conflate the subject with the psyche marks the psychic as that which exceeds the domain of the conscious subject. This psychic excess is precisely what is being systematically denied by the notion of a volitional "subject" who elects at will which gender and/or sexuality to be at any given time and place. It is this excess which erupts within the intervals of those repeated gestures and acts that construct the apparent uniformity of heterosexual positionalities, indeed which compels the repetition itself, and which guarantees its perpetual failure. In this sense, it is this excess which, within the heterosexual economy, implicitly includes homosexuality, that perpetual threat of a disruption which is quelled through a reenforced repetition of the same. And yet, if repetition is the way in which power works to construct the illusion of a seamless heterosexual identity, if heterosexuality is compelled to *repeat itself* in order to establish the illusion of its own uniformity and identity, then this is an identity permanently at risk, for what if it fails to repeat, or if the very exercise of repetition is redeployed for a very different performative purpose? If there is, as it were, always a compulsion to repeat, repetition never fully accomplishes identity. That there is a need for a repetition at all is a sign that identity is not self-identical. It requires to be instituted again and again, which is to say that it runs the risk of becoming *de*-instituted at every interval.

So what is this psychic excess, and what will constitute a subversive or *de*-instituting repetition? First, it is necessary to consider that sexuality always exceeds any given performance, presentation, or narrative which is why it is not possible to derive or read off a sexuality from any given gender presentation. And sexuality may be said to exceed any definitive narrativization.

Sexuality is never fully "expressed" in a performance or practice; there will be passive and butchy femmes, femmy and aggressive butches, and both of those, and more, will turn out to describe more or less anatomically stable "males" and "females." There are no direct expressive or causal lines between sex, gender, gender presentation, sexual practice, fantasy and sexuality. None of those terms captures or determines the rest. Part of what constitutes sexuality is precisely that which does not appear and that which, to some degree, can never appear. This is perhaps the most fundamental reason why sexuality is to some degree always closeted, especially to the one who would express it through acts of self-disclosure. That which is excluded for a given gender presentation to "succeed" may be precisely what is played out sexually, that is, an "inverted" relation, as it were, between gender and gender presentation, and gender presentation and sexuality. On the other hand, both gender presentation and sexual practices may corollate such that it appears that the former "expresses" the latter, and yet both are jointly constituted by the very sexual possibilities that they exclude.

This logic of inversion gets played out interestingly in versions of lesbian butch and femme gender stylization. For a butch can present herself as capable, forceful, and all-providing, and a stone butch may well seek to constitute her lover as the exclusive site of erotic attention and pleasure. And yet, this "providing" butch who seems *at first* to replicate a certain husband-like role, can find herself caught in a logic of inversion whereby that "providingness" turns to a self-sacrifice, which implicates her in the most ancient trap of feminine self-abnegation. She may well find herself in a situation of radical need, which is precisely what she sought to locate, find, and fulfill in her femme lover. In effect, the butch inverts into the femme or remains caught up in the specter of that inversion, or takes pleasure in it. On the other hand, the femme who, as Amber Hollibaugh has argued, "orchestrates" sexual exchange, may well eroticize a certain dependency only to learn that the very power to orchestrate that dependency exposes her own incontrovertible power, at which point she inverts into a butch or becomes caught up in the specter of that inversion, or perhaps delights in it.

Psychic Mimesis

Whether loss or mimetism is primary (perhaps an undecidable problem), the psychic subject is nevertheless constituted internally by differentially gendered Others and is, therefore, never, as a gender, self-identical.

In my view, the self only becomes a self on the condition that it has suffered a separation (grammar fails us here, for the "it" only becomes differentiated through that separation), a loss which is suspended and provisionally resolved through a melancholic incorporation of some "Other." That "Other" installed in the self thus establishes the permanent incapacity of that "self" to achieve self-identity; it is as it were always already disrupted by that Other; the disruption of the Other at the heart of the self is the very condition of that self's possibility.

Such a consideration of psychic identification would vitiate the possibility of any stable set of typologies that explain or describe something like gay or lesbian identities. And any effort to supply one—as evidenced in Kaja Silverman's recent inquiries into male homosexuality—suffer from simplification, and conform, with alarming ease, to the regulatory requirements of diagnostic epistemic regimes. If incorporation in Freud's sense in 1914 is an effort to *preserve* a lost and loved object and to refuse or postpone the recognition of loss and, hence, of grief, then to become *like* one's mother or father or sibling or other early "lovers" may be an act of love and/or a hateful effort to replace or displace. How would we "typologize" the ambivalence at the heart of mimetic incorporations such as these?

How does this consideration of psychic identification return us to the question, what constitutes a subversive repetition? How are troublesome identifications apparent in cultural practices? Well, consider the way in which heterosexuality naturalizes itself through setting up certain illusions of continuity between sex, gender, and desire. When Aretha Franklin sings, "you make me feel like a natural woman," she seems at first to suggest that some natural potential of her biological sex is actualized by her participation in the cultural position of "woman" as object of heterosexual recognition. Something in her "sex" is thus expressed by her "gender" which is then fully known and consecrated within the heterosexual scene. There is no breakage, no discontinuity between "sex" as biological facticity and essence, or between gender and sexuality. Although Aretha appears to be all too glad to have her naturalness confirmed, she also seems fully and paradoxically mindful that that confirmation is never guaranteed, that the effect of naturalness is only achieved as a consequence of that moment of hetero-

sexual recognition. After all, Aretha sings, you make me feel *like* a natural woman, suggesting that this is a kind of metaphorical substitution, an act of imposture, a kind of sublime and momentary participation in an ontological illusion produced by the mundane operation of heterosexual drag.

But what if Aretha were singing to me? Or what if she were singing to a drag queen whose performance somehow confirmed her own?

How do we take account of these kinds of identifications? It's not that there is some kind of *sex* that exists in hazy biological form that is somehow *expressed* in the gait, the posture, the gesture; and that some sexuality then expresses both that apparent gender or that more or less magical sex. If gender is drag, and if it is an imitation that regularly produces the ideal it attempts to approximate, then gender is a performance that *produces* the illusion of an inner sex or essence or psychic gender core; it *produces* on the skin, through the gesture, the move, the gait (that array of corporeal theatrics understood as gender presentation), the illusion of an inner depth. In effect, one way that gender gets naturalized is through being constructed as an inner psychic or physical *necessity*. And yet, it is always a surface sign, a signification on and with the public body that produces this illusion of an inner depth, necessity or essence that is somehow magically, causally expressed.

To dispute the psyche as *inner depth*, however, is not to refuse the psyche altogether. On the contrary, the psyche calls to be rethought precisely as a compulsive repetition, as that which conditions and disables the repetitive performance of identity. If every performance repeats itself to institute the effect of identity, then every repetition requires an interval between the acts, as it were, in which risk and excess threaten to disrupt the identity being constituted. The unconscious is this excess that enables and contests every performance, and which never fully appears within the performance itself. The psyche is not "in" the body, but in the very signifying process through which that body comes to appear; it is the lapse in repetition as well as its compulsion, precisely what the performance seeks to deny, and that which compels it from the start.

To locate the psyche within this signifying chain as the instability of all iterability is not the same as claiming that it is inner core that is awaiting its full and liberatory expression. On the contrary, the psyche is the permanent failure of expression, a failure that has its values, for it impels repetition and so reinstates the possibility of disruption. What then does it mean to pursue disruptive repetition within compulsory heterosexuality?

Although compulsory heterosexuality often presumes that there is first a sex that is expressed through a gender and then through a sexuality, it may now be necessary fully to invert and displace that operation of thought. If a regime of sexuality mandates a compulsory performance of sex, then it may be only through that performance that the binary system of gender and the binary system of sex come to have intelligibility at all. It may be that the very categories of sex, of sexual identity, of gender are produced or maintained in the *effects* of this compulsory performance, effects which are disingenuously renamed as causes, origins, disingenuously lined up within a causal or expressive sequence that the heterosexual norm produces to legitimate itself as the origin of all sex. How then to expose the causal lines as retrospectively and performatively produced fabrications, and to engage gender itself as an inevitable fabrication, to fabricate gender in terms which reveal every claim to the origin, the inner, the true, and the real as nothing other than the effects of *drag*, whose subversive possibilities ought to be played and replayed to make the "sex" of gender into site of insistent political play? Perhaps this will be a matter of working sexuality *against* identity, even against gender, and of letting that which cannot fully appear in any performance persist in its disruptive promise.

Paula Gunn Allen (1939–2008) was born on the Cubero land grant in New Mexico into Laguna, Sioux, Pueblo, and Chicano family cultures. Although she held a Ph.D. and taught at Berkeley, Allen is principally known for her many writings about Native American life. Among her five books of poetry are *The Blind Lion* (1974), *A Cannon Between My Knees* (1981), and *Shadow Country* (1982). Her fiction includes *The Woman Who Owns the Shadows* (1983), and her principal nonfiction publications are *The Sacred Hoop: Recovering the Feminine in American Indian Traditions* (1986) and *Grandmothers of the Light: A Medicine Woman's Source Book* (1991).

Who Is Your Mother? Red Roots of White Feminism*
Paula Gunn Allen (1986)

At Laguna Pueblo in New Mexico, "Who is your mother?" is an important question. At Laguna, one of several of the ancient Keres gynocratic societies of the region, your mother's identity is the key to your own identity. Among the Keres, every individual has a place within the universe—human and nonhuman—and that place is defined by clan membership. In turn, clan membership is dependent on matrilineal descent. Of course, your mother is not only that woman whose womb formed and released you—the term refers in every individual case to an entire generation of women whose psychic, and consequently physical, "shape" made the psychic existence of the following generation possible. But naming your own mother (or her equivalent) enables people to place you precisely within the universal web of your life, in each of its dimensions: cultural, spiritual, personal, and historical.

Among the Keres, "context" and "matrix" are equivalent terms, and both refer to approximately the same thing as knowing your derivation and place. Failure to know your mother, that is, your position and its attendant traditions, history, and place in the scheme of things, is failure to remember your significance, your reality, your right relationship to earth and society. It is the same thing as being lost—isolated, abandoned, self-estranged, and alienated from your own life. This importance of tradition in the life of every member of the community is not confined to Keres Indians; all American Indian Nations place great value on traditionalism.

The Native American sense of the importance of continuity with one's cultural origins runs counter to contemporary American ideas: in many instances, the immigrants to America have been eager to cast off cultural ties, often seeing their antecedents as backward, restrictive, even shameful. Rejection of tradition constitutes one of the major features of American life, an attitude that reaches far back into American colonial history and that now is validated by virtually every cultural institution in the country. Feminist practice, at least in the cultural artifacts the community values most, follows this cultural trend as well.

---

*From "The Sacred Hoop" by Paula Gunn Allen. Copyright © 1986, 1992 by Paula Gunn Allen. Reprinted by permission of Beacon Press, Boston.

The American idea that the best and the brightest should willingly reject and repudiate their origins leads to an allied idea—that history, like everything in the past, is of little value and should be forgotten as quickly as possible. This all too often causes us to reinvent the wheel continually. We find ourselves discovering our collective pasts over and over, having to retake ground already covered by women in the preceding decades and centuries. The Native American view, which highly values maintenance of traditional customs, values, and perspectives, might result in slower societal change and in quite a bit less social upheaval, but it has the advantage of providing a solid sense of identity and lowered levels of psychological and interpersonal conflict.

Contemporary Indian communities value individual members who are deeply connected to the traditional ways of their people, even after centuries of concerted and brutal effort on the part of the American government, the churches, and the corporate system to break the connections between individuals and their tribal world. In fact, in the view of the traditionals, rejection of one's culture—one's traditions, language, people—is the result of colonial oppression and is hardly to be applauded. They believe that the roots of oppression are to be found in the loss of tradition and memory because that loss is always accompanied by a loss of positive sense of self. In short, Indians think it is important to remember, while Americans believe it is important to forget.

The traditional Indians' view can have a significant impact if it is expanded to mean that the sources of social, political, and philosophical thought in the Americas not only should be recognized and honored by Native Americans but should be embraced by American society. If American society judiciously modeled the traditions of the various Native Nations, the place of women in society would become central, the distribution of goods and power would be egalitarian, the elderly would be respected, honored, and protected as a primary social and cultural resource, the ideals of physical beauty would be considerably enlarged (to include "fat," strong-featured women, gray-haired, and wrinkled individuals, and others who in contemporary American culture are viewed as "ugly"). Additionally, the destruction of the biota, the life sphere, and the natural resources of the planet would be curtailed, and the spiritual nature of human and nonhuman life would become a primary organizing principle of human society. And if the traditional tribal systems that are emulated included pacifist ones, war would cease to be a major method of human problem solving.

Remembering Connections and Histories

The belief that rejection of tradition and of history is a useful response to life is reflected in America's amazing loss of memory concerning its origins in the matrix and context of Native America. America does not seem to remember that it derived its wealth, its values, its food, much of its medicine, and a large part of its "dream" from Native America. It is ignorant of the genesis of its culture in this Native American land, and that ignorance helps to perpetuate the long-standing European and Middle Eastern monotheistic, hierarchical, patriarchal cultures' oppression of women, gays, and lesbians, people of color, working class, unemployed people, and the elderly. Hardly anyone in America speculates that the constitutional system of government might be as much a product of American Indian ideas and practices as of colonial American and Anglo-European revolutionary fervor.

Even though Indians are officially and informally ignored as intellectual movers and shapers in the United States, Britain, and Europe, they are peoples with ancient tenure on this soil. During the ages when tribal societies existed in the Americas largely untouched by patriarchal oppression, they developed elaborate systems of thought that included science, philosophy, and government based on a belief in the central importance of female energies, autonomy of individuals, cooperation, human dignity, human freedom, and egalitarian distribution of status, goods, and services. Respect for others, reverence for life, and as a by-product, pacifism as a way of life; importance of kinship ties in the customary ordering social interaction; a sense of the sacredness and mystery of existence; balance and harmony in relationships both sacred and secular were all features of life among the tribal confederacies and nations. And in those that lived by the largest number of these principles, gynarchy was the norm rather than the exception. Those systems are as yet unmatched in any contemporary industrial, agrarian, or postindustrial society on earth.

There are many female gods recognized and honored by the tribes and Nations. Femaleness was highly valued, both respected and feared, and all social institutions reflected this attitude. Even modern sayings, such as the Cheyenne statement that a people is not conquered until the hearts of the women are on the ground, express the Indians' understanding that without the power of woman the people will not live, but with it, they will endure and prosper.

Indians did not confine this belief in the central importance of female energy to matters of worship. Among many of the tribes (perhaps as many as 70 percent of them in North America alone), this belief was reflected in all of their social institutions. The Iroquois Constitution or White Roots of Peace, also called the Great Law of the Iroquois, codified the Matrons' decision-making and economic power:

> The lineal descent of the people of the Five Fires (the Iroquois Nations) shall run in the female line. Women shall be considered the progenitors of the Nation. They shall own the land and the soil. Men and women shall follow the status of their mothers. (Article 44)

> The women heirs of the chieftainship titles of the League shall be called Oiner or Otinner [Noble] for all time to come. (Article 45)

> If a disobedient chief persists in his disobedience after three warnings [by his female relatives, by his male relatives, and by one of his fellow council members, in that order], the matter shall go to the council of War Chiefs. The Chiefs shall then take away the title of the erring chief *by order of the women in whom the title is vested.* When the chief is deposed, the women shall notify the chiefs of the League . . . and the chiefs of the League shall sanction the act. The women will then select another of their sons as a candidate and the chiefs shall elect him. (Article 19) (Emphasis mine)

The Matrons held so much policy-making power traditionally that once, when their position was threatened they demanded its return, and consequently the power of women was fundamental in shaping the Iroquois Confederation sometime in the sixteenth or early seventeenth century. It was women

> who fought what may have been the first successful feminist rebellion in the New World. The year was 1600, or thereabouts, when these tribal feminists decided that they had had enough of unregulated warfare by their

men. Lysistratas among the Indian women proclaimed a boycott on lovemaking and childbearing. Until the men conceded to them the power to decide upon war and peace, there would be no more warriors. Since the men believed that the women alone knew the secret of childbirth, the rebellion was instantly successful.

> In the Constitution of Deganawidah the founder of the Iroquois Confederation of Nations had said: "He caused the body of our mother, the woman, to be of great worth and honor. He purposed that she shall be endowed and entrusted with the birth and upbringing of men, and that she shall have the care of all that is planted by which life is sustained and supported and the power to breathe is fortified: *and moreover that the warriors shall be her assistants.*"

> The footnote of history was curiously supplied when Susan B. Anthony began her "Votes for Women" movement two and a half centuries later. Unknowingly the feminists chose to hold their founding convention of latter-day suffragettes in the town of Seneca [Falls], New York. The site was just a stone's throw from the old council house where the Iroquois women had plotted their feminist rebellion. (Emphasis mine)

Beliefs, attitudes, and laws such as these became part of the vision of American feminists and of other human liberation movements around the world. Yet feminists too often believe that no one has ever experienced the kind of society that empowered women and made that empowerment the basis of its rules of civilization. The price the feminist community must pay because it is not aware of the recent presence of gynarchical societies on this continent is unnecessary confusion, division, and much lost time.

The Root of Oppression Is Loss of Memory

An odd thing occurs in the minds of Americans when Indian civilization is mentioned: little or nothing. As I write this, I am aware of how far removed my version of the roots of American feminism must seem to those steeped in either mainstream or radical versions of feminism's history. I am keenly aware of the lack of image Americans have about our continent's recent past. I am intensely conscious of popular notions of Indian women as beasts of burden, squaws, traitors, or, at best, vanished denizens of a long-lost wilderness. How odd, then, must my contention seem that the gynocratic tribes of the American continent provided the basis for all the dreams of liberation that characterize the modern world.

We as feminists must be aware of our history on this continent. We need to recognize that the same forces that devastated the gynarchies of Britain and the Continent also devastated the ancient African civilizations, and we must know that those same materialistic, antispiritual forces are presently engaged in wiping out the same gynarchical values, along with the peoples who adhere to them, in Latin America. I am convinced that those wars were and continue to be about the imposition of patriarchal civilization over the holistic, pacifist, and spirit-based gynarchies they supplant. To that end the wars of imperial conquest have not been solely or even mostly waged over the land and its resources, but they have been fought within the bodies, minds, and hearts of the people of the earth for dominion over them. I think this is the reason traditionals say we must remember our origins, our cultures, our histories, our mothers and grandmothers, for without that memory, which implies continuance rather than nostalgia, we are doomed to engulfment by a paradigm that is fundamentally inimical to the vitality, autonomy, and self-empowerment essential for satisfying, high-quality life.

Eve Kosofsky Sedgwick (1950–2009) was born in Dayton, Ohio, and educated at Yale and Columbia. She taught at Hamilton and Amherst colleges, Boston University, then at Duke where she was the Newman Ivy White Professor of English before accepting a Distinguished Professorship in English at the Graduate Center of the City University of New York. Her 1990 book, *Epistemology of the Closet*, is considered a classic in the tradition of gay theory. Sedgwick is also the author of *Between Men: English Literature and Male Homosocial Desire* (1985), *A Dialogue in Love* (1999), as well as a collection of poetry, *Fat Art, Thin Art* (1994).

Epistemology of the Closet[*]
Eve Kosofsky Sedgwick (1990)

Epistemology of the Closet proposes that many of the major nodes of thought and knowledge in twentieth-century Western culture as a whole are structured—indeed, fractured—by a chronic, now endemic crisis of homo/heterosexual definition, indicatively male, dating from the end of the nineteenth century. The book will argue that an understanding of virtually any aspect of modern Western culture must be, not merely incomplete, but damaged in its central substance to the degree that it does not incorporate a critical analysis of modern homo/heterosexual definition; and it will assume that the appropriate place for that critical analysis to begin is from the relatively decentered perspective of modern gay and antihomophobic theory. . . .

The word "homosexual" entered Euro-American discourse during the last third of the nineteenth century—its popularization preceding, as it happens, even that of the word "heterosexual." It seems clear that the sexual behaviors, and even for some people the conscious identities, denoted by the new term "homosexual" and its contemporary variants already had a long, rich history. So, indeed, did a wide range of other sexual behaviors and behavioral clusters. What *was* new from the turn of the [20th] century was the world-mapping by which every given person, just as he or she was necessarily assignable to a male or a female gender, was now considered necessarily assignable as well to a homo- or a hetero-sexuality, a binarized identity that was full of implications, however confusing, for even the ostensibly least sexual aspects of personal existence. It was this new development that left no space in the culture exempt from the potent incoherences of homo/heterosexual definition.

New, institutionalized taxonomic discourses—medical, legal, literary, psychological—centering on homo/heterosexual definition proliferated and crystallized with exceptional rapidity in the decades around the turn of the century, decades in which so many of the other critical nodes of the culture were being, if less suddenly and newly, nonetheless also definitively reshaped. Both the power relations between the genders and the relations of nationalism and imperialism, for instance, were in highly visible

---

[*] From *Epistemology of the Closet* by Eve Kosofsky Sedgwick © 2008 by the Regents of the University of California. Published by the University of California Press.

crisis. For this reason, and because the structuring of same-sex bonds can't, in any historical situation marked by inequality and contest *between* genders, fail to be a site of intensive regulation that intersects virtually every issue of power and gender, lines can never be drawn to circumscribe within some proper domain of sexuality (whatever that might be) the consequences of a shift in sexual discourse. Furthermore, in accord with Foucault's demonstration, whose results I will take to be axiomatic, that modern Western culture has placed what it calls sexuality in a more and more distinctively privileged relation to our most prized constructs of individual identity, truth, and, knowledge, it becomes truer and truer that the language of sexuality not only intersects with but transforms the other languages and relations by which we know. . . .

But, in the vicinity of the closet, even what *counts* as a speech act is problematized on a perfectly routine basis. As Foucault says: "there is no binary division to be made between what one says and what one does not say; we must try to determine the different ways of not saying such things . . . There is not one but many silences, and they are an integral part of the strategies that underlie and permeate discourses." "Closetedness" itself is a performance initiated as such by the speech act of a silence—not a particular silence, but a silence that accrues particularity by fits and starts, in relation to the discourse that surrounds and differentially constitutes it. The speech acts that coming out, in turn, can comprise are as strangely specific. And they may have nothing to do with the acquisition of new information. I think of a man and a woman I know, best friends, who for years canvassed freely the emotional complications of each other's erotic lives—the man's eroticism happening to focus exclusively on men. But it was only after one particular conversational moment, fully a decade into this relationship, that it seemed to either of these friends that permission had been given to the woman to refer to the man, in their conversation together, as *a gay man*. Discussing it much later, both agreed they had felt at the time that this one moment had constituted a clear-cut act of coming out, even in the context of years and years beforehand of exchange predicated on the man's being gay. What was said to make this difference? Not a version of "I am gay," which could only have been bathetic between them. What constituted coming out for this man, in this situation, was to use about

himself the phrase "coming out"—to mention, as if casually, having come out to someone else. (Similarly, a T-shirt that ACT UP sells in New York bearing the text, "I am out, therefore I am," is meant to do for the wearer, not the constative work of reporting that s/he *is* out, but the performative work of coming out in the first place.) . . . The fact that silence is rendered as pointed and performative as speech, in relations around the closet, depends on and highlights more broadly the fact that ignorance is as potent and as multiple a thing there as is knowledge. . . .

Historically, the framing of *Epistemology of the Closet* begins with a puzzle. It is a rather amazing fact that, of the very many dimensions along which the genital activity of one person can be differentiated from that of another (dimensions that include preference for certain acts, certain zones or sensations, certain physical types, a certain frequency, certain symbolic investments, certain relations of age or power, a certain species, a certain number of participants, etc. etc. etc.), precisely one, the gender of object choice, emerged from the turn of the century, and has remained, as *the* dimension denoted by the now ubiquitous category of "sexual orientation." This is not a development that would have been foreseen from the viewpoint of the fin de siècle itself, where a rich stew of male algolagnia, child-love, and autoeroticism, to mention no more of its components, seemed to have as indicative a relation as did homosexuality to the whole, obsessively entertained problematic of sexual "perversion" or, more broadly, "decadence." Foucault, for instance, mentions the hysterical woman and the masturbating child, along with "entomologized" sexological categories such as zoophiles, zooerasts, auto-monosexuals, and gynecomasts, as typifying the new sexual taxonomies, the *"specification of individuals"* that facilitated the modern freighting of sexual definition with epistemological and power relations. True as his notation is, it suggests without beginning to answer the further question: why the category of "the masturbator," to choose only one example, should by now have entirely lost its diacritical potential for specifying a particular kind of person, an identity, at the same time as it continues to be true becomes increasingly true—that, for a crucial strain of Western discourse, in Foucault's words "the homosexual was now a species." So, as a result, is the heterosexual, and between *these* species the human species has come more and more to be divided. . . .

These deconstructive contestations can occur, moreover, only in the context of an entire cultural network of normative definitions, definitions themselves equally unstable but responding to different sets of contiguities and often at a different rate. The master terms of a particular historical moment will be those that are so situated as to entangle most inextricably and at the same time most differentially the filaments of other important definitional nexuses. In arguing that homo/heterosexual definition has been a presiding master term of the past century, one that has the same, primary importance for all modern Western identity and social organization (and not merely for homosexual identity and culture) as do the more traditionally visible cruxes of gender, class, and race, I'll argue that the now chronic modern crisis of homo/heterosexual definition has affected our culture through its ineffaceable marking particularly of the categories secrecy/disclosure, knowledge/ignorance, private/public, masculine/feminine, majority/minority, innocence/initiation, natural/artificial, new/old, discipline/terrorism, canonic/noncanonic, wholeness/decadence, urbane/provincial, domestic/foreign, health/illness, same/different, active/passive, in/out, cognition/paranoia, art/kitsch, utopia/apocalypse, sincerity/sentimentality, and voluntarity/addiction. And rather than embrace an idealist faith in the necessarily, immanently self-corrosive efficacy of the contradictions inherent to these definitional binarisms, I will suggest instead that contests for discursive power can be specified as competitions for the material or rhetorical leverage required to set the terms of, and to profit in some way from, the operations of such an incoherence of definition. ...

PART SIX

Global Realities in an
Uncertain Century

Early in the twenty-first century, it soon became clear that something fundamental had changed in the world at large. The attacks on the United States on September 11, 2001 quickly became a symbol of that change. On the day itself the collapsing buildings in New York City were a sight people the world over had never before seen. Some said it was comparable to Pearl Harbor. But, as awful as the Japanese attack on Hawaii on December 7, 1941 was, Japan was then already well understood to be building toward war with the Americans. However, with 9/11, no one knew exactly who was behind it, save for the vague suggestion of foreign terrorists. Even after their identities were known, only the foreign policy experts knew who Osama Bin Laden was, and even they weren't sure at first where he was and how he sent the signal. The general population knew nothing of this and least of all could they understand, as time went by, why those of his religious culture might want to kill Americans. The shock of it all grew out of a long-held innocence of the American people and, to a lesser degree, of all common people of the so-called West. The West had been a world colonizer but, for the most part, its people knew very little about the realities of life around the globe.

But the surprise was not the only way changing global realities dawned on the innocent. The very visual effect of 9/11 was unique in human history. In 1941, it was not possible to watch the raid at Pearl Harbor as it happened. President Franklin Delano Roosevelt in Washington DC only heard of it after the fact by telephone. Then, there were no televisual media and certainly no satellite communications as today. September 11 was horrible because we watched the World Trade Towers collapse. Today we see movies of Pearl Harbor, but that is not the same as being there as the world was on 9/11. The death of thousands of people is horrifying however knowledge of it is conveyed. But somehow, seeing victims falling from the sky to the ground before the dust of the fallen towers covered them over forever, makes a lasting impression even (perhaps especially) when one watches the collapse as it happens.

Even those who were in or near the towers as they were burning could not see the coming disaster full screen. The dust blinded them. They knew, to be sure, that the scene was deadly, but, running for their lives, they could not have had the distance to feel it as the widescreen event it was or even to reach out for the dead as their bodies crashed to earth. I have held people as they lay dying, but those experiences were nothing like the remote intimacy of death and suffering that a powerful medium brought into my home, my bones, my memory. To speak of remote intimacy is strange, but there are few better ways to put it. When the worst catastrophes come to us in all their High Density pixilated panorama, we are shaken differently from those at ground zero, perhaps more deeply. We saw it all as it happened for what it meant for time to come. 9/11 was unthinkable, an unspeakable horror that, until then, only those left standing on the fields of savage warfare or amid the devastation of mass annihilation after saturation or atomic bombings can be supposed to have experienced. We who live in the twenty-first century experience things

Timeline: 1995–2014

Social Theory

		Wider World

Social Theory

Edward Said, *Intellectual Exile: Expatriates and Marginals* 1994

Manuel Castells, *The Network Society* 1996

Charles Tilly, *Roads From Past to Future: The Invisible Elbow* 1997

Julia Kristeva, *Portable Kristeva: Women's Time* 1997

Avery Gordon, *Ghostly Matters* 1997

Giorgio Agamben, *Homo Sacer: Sovereign Power and Bare Life* 1998

Mustafa Emirbayer and Anne Mische, *What is Agency?* 1998

Saskia Sassen, *Globalization and its Discontents: Toward a Feminist Analytics* 1999

William Julius Wilson, *Bridge Over the Racial Divide: The Limits of Race* 1999

Ulrich Beck, *World Risk Society* 1999

Kimberlé Williams Crenshaw, *Dimensions of Intersectional Oppression*, 2000

Zygmunt Bauman, *Liquid Modernity* 2001

Stanley Hoffman, *The Clash of Globalizations* 2002

Achille Mbembe, *Necropolitics: Late Modern Colonial Occupation* 2003

Robert Pogue Harrison, *Dominion of the Dead*, 2003

Immanuel Wallerstein, *World-Systems Analysis: The Modern World-System in Crisis* 2004

David Harvey, *Brief History of Neo-Liberalism: Neo-liberalism on Trial* 2005

Wider World

1995

Bosnian Serbs massacre Muslins in Bosnia **1995**

Peace talks in Dayton, Ohio on civil war in Bosnia **1995**

Bill Clinton reelected US president **1996**

Microsoft's Bill Gates world's richest person **1996**

Desmond Tutu heads Truth and Reconciliation Commission in SA **1996**

Stuart Hall, *Modernity: The Global, the Local, and the Return of Ethnicity* **1996**

Spice Girls first million dollar album **1996**

Deng dies in Beijing **1997**

Tony Blair leads Labor Party to electoral triumph **1997**

James Cameron's *Titanic* **1997**

Hong Kong returned to China **1997**

J.K. Rowling's first Harry Potter novel **1997**

Viagra **1998**

Civil War in Congo **1998**

Attack on US embassy in Kenya linked to al-Qaeda **1998**

Serbian genocide in Albania **1998**

US Senate Republicans fail to impeach Bill Clinton **1999**

Nelson Mandela retires **1999**

Russian army in Chechnya **1999**

Macau returned to China by Portugal **1999**

Yelstin resigns Russia **1999**

2000

Michael Hardt and Antonio Negri, *Empire: The Multitude Against the Empire* **2000**

Vladimir Putin elected president of Russia **2000**

Dot.com market collapses **2000**

George W. Bush elected US president **2000**

Osama bin Laden orders 9/11 attack on US **2001**

Wikipedia **2001** starts

US war in Afghanistan begins **2001**

Apple iPod **2001**

Speed of Personal Computers leaps **2001**

Euro currency **2002**

iMac 4G **2002**

US invades Iraq **2002**

Human Genome complete **2003**

MySpace **2003**

Web 2.0 **2004**

George W. Bush reelected **2004**

Rovers explore Mars **2004**

One gigabyte data storage chip achieved **2004**

Facebook starts **2004**

YouTube **2004**

Flash drives replace floppy discs **2004**

2005

Angela Merkel chancellor of Germany **2005**

Katrina devastates New Orleans **2005**

Suicide bombings in London **2005**

Social Theory

Jeffrey Alexander, *Civil Sphere: Cultural Codes and Democratic Communication* 2006

Raewyn Connell, *Southern Theory: Gender and Violence* 2007

Bruno Latour, *Spheres and Networks: The Spaces of Material Life* 2009

Elijah Anderson, *Cosmopolitan Canopy: The "Nigger Moment"* 2011

Thomas Piketty, *Central Contradictions of, Capital in the Twenty-First Century*, 2014

Waverly Duck, *Benita's Story: No Way Out*, 2015

Oliver Sacks, *Urge* 2015

Ta-Nehisi Coates, *Prison and the Gray Wastes*, 2015

Eula Biss, *White Debt* 2015

Owen Fiss, *The Perils of Constitutional Minimalism*, 2015

Marianne Robinson, *Fear* 2015

Wider World

2006

Twitter **2006**

Pluto no longer planet **2006**

Saddam Hussein executed **2006**

World-wide economic downturn **2007**

Kindle appears **2007**

Benazir Bhutto assassinated Pakistan **2007**

Nicolas Sarkozy elected French president **2008**

Barak Obama elected US president **2008**

Dmitry Medvedev elected Russian president **2008**

Beijing Olympic Games **2008**

Portable PC market surges **2009**

Evidence of water on local moon **2009**

2010

Earthquake devastates Haiti **2010**

Oil spill devastates Gulf of Mexico waters **2010**

Tea Party dominates US Congress **2010**

Tsunami and earthquake shakes Japan **2011**

China's Three Gorges Damn opens **2011**

7 million Facebook users **2011**

Osama bin Laden killed **2011**

World population 7 billion **2012**

Barak Obama reelected US president **2012**

2014

US troops may leave Afghanistan **2014**

Ebola Pandemic, **2014**

Russia annexes Crimea **2014**

Islamic States begins offensive in Syria and Iraq **2014**

US normalizes relations with Cuba **2015**

A global climate change pact is agreed to in Paris by 147 nations **2015**

Iran's dismantling of nuclear program certified by UN **2016**

Boko Haram leaves 6,500 malnourished children in Nigeria **2016**

few, if any, others before us experienced. When the unthinkable happens, we must feel it and think it even when it terrifies the mind and heart. There is no pure "we" of this or any other world, but when information technologies invite people the world over to feel and think about some embracing event, the differences among us are oddly softened.

Social theory, most fundamentally, is about thinking the *unthinkable*. When a child asks a hard question, a code of silence is being broken by the sheer innocence of the question. Why, asked Noah—then a child, now quite grown—do schools require small boys and girls to walk in sex-segregated lines? Why, asked Lafeyette—when he too was still young, wondering about the violence and misery of his home in Chicago's worst corner—are there no children here? The why may be suppressed. The question may be put by anyone of whatever age or experience. But when and wherever anyone asks such a question, and asks it from experience with any of social life's riddles, she is performing social theory. Social theory begins in rude awakenings—in a shock of sudden realization that the worlds one shares with others are not what you were taught to believe they should be.

One of the elegant contradictions of social theory—especially in our day when much of it seems so complicated—is that even the most academic social theories have their start in the questions more often asked by those on the raw social margins. Social theories begin, that is, among those whose living is a constant struggle to deal with realities decrepit by contrast to the ideals they hear preached at the soup kitchens or see on whatever televisual glimpses they may catch in their migrations to and from refugee camps or trailer parks. The contradiction, therefore, is that social theory, whether practical or academic, is about social life's most inscrutably big questions, yet the nasty soil from which it grows is spoiled by social failure to provide for the common good.

But today, early still in a new century, the problem social theories of all kinds must face is that one hardly knows what is meant by the "social" in social theory. The truth is that this adjective, "social," and the substantive noun from which it is derived, "society," have always been rather spongy terms. When, for example, one says that sociology is the study of society—or that social theory is the unthinkable theory of social things—it is far from clear what is meant. What, specifically, is "society"—or, for that matter, any sphere of social things small or grand? For a good many years since early in the nineteenth century when "society" no longer referred simply to "high society," there was always a ready-made, if unsatisfying, answer. In the modern era, especially in the nineteenth and twentieth centuries, a society was, more or less, a term corresponding to some specific social order associated with a nation.

When Marx wrote his critique of modern capitalism, he hardly ever made reference to a specific society in which the evils of capitalism were at play. Yet, we know for a fact that he wrote his great book *Capital* after many years of research in the British Museum and was well informed by Friedrich Engels's studies of the factory system in England. Marx may not have dwelt on British society, but it was modern, industrial England that he had in mind. In the mid-nineteenth century, the factory system of which he and others like Charles Dickens wrote was usually Great Britain's—the world's most advanced industrial economy. It was, thus, that system which impressed itself on Marx's theory of the workings of capitalism in modern society. And this was what most social theorists since did as well. They took for their idea of what a society was the national society they knew best. Well into the twentieth century, social theorists began to write about *modern* societies. When they did, they usually still had in mind European and North American societies because these were the societies in which modern institutions were most advanced. Anthropologists, it is true, studied pre-modern societies and often their studies were used as models for the concept of society. But even then, so-called "primitive" societies were imagined to be radically different from modern ones. For the early social theories, society was modern and modern society was exemplified by the advanced societies of the modern West.

Yet, most obviously, after the two world wars of the twentieth century, even Europeans and Americans had to come face-to-face with other societies. In the second of these wars, it was not all that surprising that Germany was capable of developing a mighty military machine from its own advanced industrial system, but when Japan, a tiny East Asian island state, did the same and was able to challenge the European and American powers—*that* was something different in the popular imagination. In the average Euro-American's way of thinking, Asia was another world. Of course, we know today that traditional Asian societies, like the Chinese, the Indian, and the Japanese, as well as many others of the ancient Euro-Asian regions, were great powers with scientific and cultural achievements that rivaled those of Europe. Scholars knew this, as did missionaries and businessmen who followed the colonial pathways to invest in the East Indies and China and other so-called foreign places. During World War II, I was a small boy in a highly educated family in the Midwest. But when my father was sent off to fight in Asia, I had not the least idea who the Japanese really were and, so far as I could tell, no one else I knew, including my mother, did either. On the other hand, we knew plenty about the Germans because German immigrants largely populated our city. Had we lived in California, it might have been different, save for the fact that there the Japanese immigrants were rounded up and sent to concentration camps. No one ever asked why the Germans in my town weren't sent away.

Still, after the world wars ended in 1945, it became clear that the West had been forced to acknowledge the wider world. After, even Americans had to think about the world, if only because its economy meant rebuilding Europe and Asia. It is one thing to *have* an enemy. It is another to join a former enemy in nation rebuilding. Eventually the Japanese gave us cars and electronics; we gave them baseball and pop music. In Europe, former colonies followed India's struggle for independence from Britain in 1947. Soon enough, all of Europe's overseas colonies began to throw off the yoke of the colonial system. With new relations to their former colonies, Europeans had to get down to the business of understanding them. Euro-Americans had to think about the world in a different way. The sun was indeed setting on the British Empire, as it was on all of the West's colonial territories. In the years from India's independence in 1947 to 1968, the hottest year of the revolutionary 1960s, decolonization became a near universal accomplishment. By 1968, the aftereffects of the collapse of the long-enduring colonial system menacingly crept into the powerful nations of the West. In the United States the civil rights and Black power movements were, by 1968, but two of many movements for, in effect, the decolonization of women, gays, poor people, students, as well as Blacks and many others. In Europe during the same period, many of the same movements took hold with the one notable difference that, in the place of former slaves seeking civil rights, there were immigrants from Europe's former colonies in Asia, the Caribbean, and Africa demanding both cultural as well as civil rights.

The example of the rebellious colonized peoples inspired rebellion among people who had been virtually colonized in North America and Europe. The lasting effect of what at the time seemed to be a short-term series of internal crises in the European and North American states, turned out to be quite a long term crisis that led, by the end of the twentieth century, to a structural attack on the comfortable and privileged in affluent countries of the world. Multiculturalism was in many ways the first wave of their demands for recognition of real social and cultural differences. But as time went by, mere recognition was not sufficient. By the beginning of the twenty-first century the globally excluded was so pervasive as to include those trapped in the affluent nations. Everywhere the most poor had begun to press their demands. This global resistance movement came at the very time when the Euro-American societies were facing real limits on their already miserly ability to develop social programs for the poor. The curve of cross purposes between the well-established and the marginal created a structural inversion not only within and among the powerful nation-states but also between them and the world at large. The structural strains at once created a false sense of connection between the parts of world and an aggravation of their differences. Where the Internet allowed the parts to sense a connection, the global economic crisis, then only faintly felt, made real the differences.

This structural change was commonly called, not always accurately, globalization. The main thing wrong with the term "globalization" is that it suggests a clearly defined, historical process whereby history moves from one stage to another, just as, centuries before, the traditional mutated into the modern. The problem with thinking of globalization in this way is that it is too early to tell what will become of the world of the future. More importantly, the changes now occurring seem to be *fundamental* in the true sense of the word—that is, global changes that may well be shaking the *foundations* of the world as we knew it causing, at least, the idealism of modernity to expose the reality of its hind parts. Economic inequalities will always in the long run soil even the best of moral intentions, especially when the intentions are held to be at the heart of modern culture.

If it is remotely possible that the changes are as deep in the structures of the world as I think (and I am not alone), then, when deep structural changes are combined with new experience-altering information technologies, social theory may no longer simply be *social*. Somehow, sooner or later, what for so long we thought of as social theory may have to be known by some other name. Classical assumptions that the social aspect of societies are neatly lodged within the borders of a given nation-state—neither American nor British; neither Chinese or Japanese; nor even any one ethnic, religious, or national cultural—just don't work any longer. The world is still multicultural, but now it is also global. Nation states are still powerful institutions but they, even the strongest ones, are now embedded in a set of global economic and political forces than none can control by itself. Whether it makes sense to rename social theory *global theory* or, as some suggest, cyber-theory, is far from apparent. But at least we need to think deeply about what social theory is.

Whatever social theory does in and along the time of the twenty-first century it must do no fewer than two things at once: One is to take the measure of global realities; the other is to rethink its past history in order to assess which of the old ideas and realities are still alive to today's encompassing global ones. Together these are salient among the forces that conjure up twenty-first century social theory's unthinkable riddle. *How amid uncertain global realities are we to think about the ghosts of societies past in which we still must live, for better or worse?*

Uncertain Global Realities

Whatever comes to pass as the years of this century unfold, what we can say for certain about the present situation is that global realities impose a deep structural uncertainty on nearly everything our ancestors took for granted. To describe as simply uncertain the present state of the world is a modest alternative to the many grand prophecies about the end of this world or, as some (myself included) once did, postmodern. In times of certain change but uncertain futures it is always better practical sociological sense to be alert to all the clues that present themselves but cautious before jumping to conclusion as to what they mean. One could say that a social theorist of global uncertainties must be patient but diligent crime scene investigators. All we have are clues, even when they seem to converge on the prospect of a radical, if not total, change in the worlds about.

This is especially so for we who are heirs to all the economic, cultural, political, and other of the benefits *and* costs of a modern world that began as long ago as the first European voyages of discovery around 1500. Karl Marx, once again, provides a strikingly apt characterization of that world as it had come to be under fully blown industrial capitalism in the 1800s:

All fixed, fast-frozen relations, with their train of ancient and venerable prejudices and opinions, are swept away, all new-formed ones become antiquated before they can ossify. All that is solid melts into air, all that is holy is profaned, and man is at last compelled to face with sober senses, his real conditions of life, and his relations with his kind.

In this famous line from the *Manifesto of the Communist Party*, Marx claims that the steady progress toward a better life that modernity promised was always based not just on shaky foundations but on ones that melted away. "All that is solid melts into air" is a figure of speech that expressed Marx's view that capitalism is constantly revolutionizing the world it exploits in order to extract its wealth. The factory system destroyed agrarian and rural life. The industrial and commercial centers of capitalism were, literally, built on the exhausted bodies of workers. Factories themselves reduced the need for human labor by imposing new assembly techniques and technologies that, in turn, undercut the access of workers to decent income. Now, the globalizing world villages in Africa, like small company towns in the United States, are emptying out as the young seek a life in cities from which, in time, their children flee as jobs are outsourced to the poorer regions of the world where labor is cheaper, until it is not. The vast landscape of human progress covers over the trash and debris of buildings torn down, lives ruined, communities, in effect, vaporized.

Zygmunt Bauman is one of the latest and most astute to pick up on Marx's theme of the unstable, destructive, structural features of modern capitalist societies built on porous foundations. He writes of liquid modernity as the torrent of melted and liquefied human hopes that lay hidden behind the apparent solidity of industrial capitalism. Even today, we know that sheets of steel are mixed, smelted, and rolled in order to be fashioned into fast-moving cars or sturdy cellphone towers. In them and such like we may think we see the genius of the modern world's capacity to produce new and wonderful conveniences—faster transportation, better cell phones, and all the rest. But, if we are honest, we soon enough realize that those fancy cars end up as junk to be melted down for some other use. The cell phones lose their signals only to be replaced with more advanced models while we dump the old ones in basements or attics; in time they, too, are sent off to be stripped and melted. And so on. To say that the modern is always changing is not to say that it is changing for the good. Many if not most of us travel on bridges or live in apartments and houses built on the bones of ancestors we never knew—individuals who died along the way to feed the insatiable appetite of modern greed. "All fixed, fast-frozen relations ... are swept away."

If this, then so, too, the modern world itself. Immanuel Wallerstein, more than any social theorist, was the first to analyze the historical facts that tell the story of the modern world-system. Since the first book in his work appeared in 1974, Wallerstein has carefully traced the history of the early beginnings in the colonization of the Americas in the sixteenth century through its development in the expansion of the colonial system to Asia, then to the rise of the powerful modern nation states culminating in the global British system in the nineteenth century followed by America supremacy after World War II. The most striking of his arguments is that after five hundred years, from roughly 1490 to 1990, the modern world-system fell into paralyzing structural crisis. In his "Modern World-System in Crisis" (2004) Wallerstein summarizes that history now identifies its crucial year as 1968. It was in that period that the ability of Western powers, not even the United States, systematically to control the world-system crashed. The crisis was not due to a failure of nerve, or a lack of economic or military power, but due to the dynamics of the system itself. The global costs of production grew too extreme. In what Wallerstein calls the world revolution of 1968 (an approximate date to be sure) the mounting costs of labor and resources combined with the declining ability of states to extract taxes began to pull the system apart. Taxation could no longer cover the hidden costs of the industrial degradations of the environment that corporations had passed on to the state that, in turn, passed them to tax payers. As capitalism moved to exploit rich and cheap labor regions, there too surplus values met the increasing costs of human and natural destruction wrought by industrial capitalism.

Today, the United States is the world's largest economy by volume and its military is unquestionably superior by far. Yet, in the United States, as elsewhere, ordinary citizens experience the harsh reality of a fragile global economy that cannot sustain the rate of growth that led a series of nations to become the global economic power. Growth is slowing now even in China. Jobs and capital flow around the world. The US borrows from China but is unable on its own to produce goods that sell in China well enough to pay back the debt. China and the European Community (the third major global economy) have grown rapidly in part because they did not bear the costs of maintaining a global military that protects, among much else, international capital interests in natural and labor resources. Since World War II the Americans paid for capitalism's military security. Still, to this day, 60 percent of US tax revenues go to support its military, while the society is humbled by high unemployment and limited social services. At the same time, all the major economic powers and a good many second-tier wealthy nations must import petroleum and gas resources from Africa, the Middle East, and the far north. No nation, except Russia, has enough energy within its own borders; yet Russia is economically crippled in other ways. Only Brazil has made some progress toward self-sufficiency by investing in energy-conserving programs. All this makes even the most powerful nations vulnerable to global forces. Their borders are breached by immigrants but also by the outflow of capital, including technologies and other information resources that pay for their reliance on imports. No border guard can control borders like these. Capital wealth is welcomed in China, which spends from its treasury to gain international advantages, especially in Africa. China wants to control its population's access to global information. But not even North Korea has been able to do that perfectly. Social media and other cyber technologies make it nearly impossible to control what people think and with whom they associate. Osama Bin Laden sent his signal to bomb the towers by cell phone from across the world.

How did this come to pass in the years between 1968 and, for example, 2001? A reasonable, if sketchy, outline of Wallerstein's idea would go something like this: The melting towers on September, 11, 2001 were a long-range effect of the decolonizing movements in Africa, the Caribbean, and Asia in the 1950s through the 1960s—of which the world revolutions of 1968 (Wallerstein's phrase) were an evident outcome; which in turn led, in part, to America's withdrawal from Vietnam and, in a bizarre mimicry of the American failure, to the Soviets' arrogant attempt to colonize Afghanistan; which led, in some weird way, to the economic and political collapse of the Soviet Union and of its client states in and around 1991; which in turn strengthened the American hand as the only truly powerful nation-state on the globe; which led to the invasion of Iraq in 1992; which failed, we now know, in spite of its apparent success; which may have set the Americans up ever more as the Evil Beast of the other world that came out of its caves in Afghanistan; which, the decade before, the Americans had abandoned after they had joined forces with the Taliban to chase the Soviets away; which abandonment led the Taliban to harbor the Islamic fringe that sent the men to crash the planes that felled the World Trade Center; which led the Americans back to Afghanistan, then back once again to Iraq; which thereafter led who knows where and why? A sketch is but a sketch; still lines like these can be drawn to at least suggest connections over the last half of the twentieth century that came to a turning point in 1968 toward the events that led to the fall of the Cold War system, then to 9/11, now to our time. Wallerstein, the careful scholar as well social critic, is careful to say that the global situation is now in a state of uncertainty that will last for sometime. He is clear that the traditional capitalist system has come undone. Whether some other global system will emerge to replace it remains to be seen.

Still, anyone willing to look can see that, in spite of the uncertainty, capitalism remains the dominant economic system the world over. In "Neoliberalism on Trial," David Harvey explains that one of the ways capitalism has adapted to the new world is by taking over a classical liberal theory that free markets are the hope of mankind to invent a neoliberalism that takes account of global economic realities by advocating a global marketplace of labor, resources, and goods. In the end, as is apparent, neoliberal ideology now dominates the economic world under the unproven theory that free trade in labor, goods, and capital will benefit the world as a whole. Harvey warns that, like the free market ideology that Marx criticized in the nineteenth century, today's free markets merely extend the regime of control over individuals. "To live under neoliberalism," Harvey said, "also means to accept or submit to [the] bundle of rights necessary for capital accumulation." Capitalism wins, or so it seems, in these days when the shrinking number of obscenely rich get richer as the rest of the world gets poorer.

The term "globalization" had become commonplace by the end of the 1990s. Wallerstein conveyed his disdain for the concept by almost never using it. His view is that the modern world-system always has been global since the sixteenth century. At the other extreme, there are many who, variously, consider globalization a process whereby humankind would fully achieve its dream of a better world. By contrast, there are still skeptics who believe either that nothing has changed or, if it has, that the world is changing for the worse by abandoning its classic values.

Stanley Hoffman, in "The Clash of Globalizations" (2002), took the quite different view that, simply, there is no one globalization. There are, instead, no fewer than three types of globalization: cultural, political, and economic. The clashes among them create the true state of global realities. Those who glorified the cultural promise of new technologies must contend, as they seldom do, with the negative reality of new technologies capable of initiating terrible political events. Terrorists use cell phones to blow themselves and others away. No less, the very speed of cash transfers allow rich speculators to gain unheard of personal wealth while some of their selfish system sucks the value out of banks, financial companies, and real estate to the point of causing economic distress (the crash of 2008, for example). Hoffman pulled no punches. He took account, of terrorism, among other global realities, while at the same examining the realities and myths of the good and bad of the new global world.

In studying the writings of Wallerstein, Bauman, Harvey, and Hoffman, it is possible to construct an outline of the several structural features that shape the challenges facing any social theory of globalization or whatever one wants to call it. Some, like Stuart Hall, writing in 1996, had already explored the important features of the late modern world. In "Narrating the Nation: An Imagined Community," Hall analyzed the question of the actual underlying nature of the modern nation by advancing a concept already well known from Benedict Anderson's *Imagined Communities* (1983). The main theoretical claim is that at the originating core of a nation-state lies a series of cultural aspects that appeal to the imagination of its people. These include the diffusion of stories, myths of origins, invented traditions, and folk wisdom—all of which conspire to give a nation's people a sense of national identity.

Americans, even now, are repeatedly taught the myth that they are the greatest nation on earth. This of course is at best exaggeration and at worst nonsense. Though, in different ways, others took on the question of whether globalization was eroding the power and character of the nation-state, Hall was one of the first to treat to the question of the cultural power of the nation skeptically. The theoretical conclusion of his argument is that identity is no one thing; in fact, far from being primarily a nation's gift to its people, a national identity is ultimately less important than local, ethnic, and other group-defined experiences. Who is to say that a Turkish citizen of Germany is more German than Turkish or, even, Kurdish, perhaps Armenian? Only the individuals themselves, of course.

While Hall emphasized a key cultural feature of global realities, Manuel Castells, writing about the same time, developed what is recognized to be one of the most important social theories on the subject of the global effects of information technology. Castells argued that the world has become a network society in which different regions, nations, and locales are linked, to varying degrees, in a vast global network. His 1996 book, *Rise of the Network Society*, is still the most instructive discussion of the ways a network (a figure that calls to mind the Internet) is not just a technological phenomenon but also a general global fact of life. People and groups, regardless of their local or national affinities, are linked in new social institutions that cross national boundaries. Castells is at once analytic and critical of the new world system of networks.

Other social theorists see the dynamics of global assaults on national authority as an opportunity for the formerly, if virtually, colonized. Saskia Sassen, in "Toward a Feminist Analytics of the Global Economy" (1998), makes a strong case that feminist theories and practices emerge under globalization as part of a new regime of human rights. As the old order declines, national sovereignty loses its grip on its citizens who, in turn, step into the void to assert their previously illegitimate rights. Sassen's thinking is a sophisticated global application of earlier theories of social movements. Social changes occur when an old order is split and rendered incapable of enforcing its control over formerly excluded peoples.

Amartya Sen's discussion of Asian values would not normally be classified as a theory of globalization. In fact, in many ways, the book from which the selection is taken, *Development as Freedom* (1999), is a general philosophical defense of the economic theories for which he was awarded the Nobel Prize in Economics in 1998. Since the 1960s, theories of economic development had been derived from the very Western claim that the economic history of the world passed through necessary stages. The least-developed areas are considered primitive and pre-modern by contrast to the more developed thus truly modern. Sen was born in India. He knows from experience what the realities are. Although he has never, to my knowledge, said it this way, Sen had every reason to take offense at the ideology that his native West Bengal was nothing more than a failed Norway. The essay "Asian Values and the West's Claim to Uniqueness" (1999), while evidently part of a general revision of modernization theory, is, at the same time, a subtle but clear rebuke of the modern West's cultural and economic ignorance of Asia and its values.

If Sen retains a clear sense of respect for the prospect that economic development based on Western wealth and ideas might promote freedom among the world's poor, Ulrich Beck's theory of this new world as a risk society is daring in the way it exposes the dangers facing nearly everyone. "As the bipolar world fades away," Beck notes, "we are moving from a world of enemies to one of dangers and risks." At first glance, one might think this is a half-baked statement—a soft way to say that, in the absence of global enemies, the world itself is risky. So who is it that *is* not familiar with the risks of this life? But on closer inspection, what Beck is arguing is that the disappearance of nation-based enemies, such the rival Cold War powers, cuts individuals (in the broadest sense, including perhaps even nations) loose to face dangers on all sides but also to remake themselves—as individuals, groups, even nations. It is one thing to be infused with a sense of American identity as the nation most opposed to communism; it is quite another to be freed from the limits of being a good society opposed to a bad one, thus to face the world as it is with dangers on all sides. In a certain sense, the fear associated with terrorism is a fear that one never knows when a bomb will blow things up. At the same time vigilance is not a bad quality of character. Beck thus is largely optimistic that a cosmopolitan democracy based on shared global concerns can come together. Still, he is cautious because "we must reflect on the dark side, on the ways [the idea of global democracy] can be used politically as a front for old style imperial adventures." The new realities are dangerous, in part, because they put us at risk of turning back to the old forms in the name of something new. Beck may not convince everyone, but he certainly represents the general position (of which there are many iterations) that, though the world is changing, many of the traditional values of the modern era can be renewed under new global values like cosmopolitanism.

On the other hand, Achille Mbembe, in "Necropolitics" (2003), defends a theoretical attitude so bold as to be truly, deeply unthinkable. Mbembe's concept "necropolitics" literally means that all politics lead to deadly outcomes; at their origin, modern politics are, according to Michael Foucault (whom Mbembe cites), what has control over life and death. This, of course, is a direct contradiction of liberal, life-promising Euro-American values. Mbembe is from South Africa. What makes Mbembe's theory so disturbing is that his necropolitics is more than a theory. He provides ample empirical grounding for the idea. Among them is the case of the former African colonies and, controversially, the Palestinian territories. He argues that the old colonial system, deadly as it was, has transformed itself today into a newer and subtler, if just as deadly, system. Now virtually, if not actually, colonized people are imprisoned in territorial zones of exclusion, their lands bulldozed, their movements regulated, their means of cultural communication jammed, ultimately their rights, thus their lives, ruined. One could say that Mbembe took Bauman's idea of liquid modernity one giant step further by suggesting that the aim of the modern politics of control is, in the end, to kill the human spirit by methods of confinement and surveillance that first crush the life out of the excluded, and then the population itself.

Taken together, any representative sample of theoretical attempts to explain the full range of global realities cannot but create an uneasy sense of uncertainty. Whether one uses the word "uncertainty" in the relatively analytic manner of Immanuel Wallerstein or in the harsher forms of Ulrich Beck's risk society or Achille Mbembe's necropolitics, a fair sense of the range of possibilities converges on a telling point. Social theory, whatever it is called, must somehow rethink the world's past to account for the new. This is not so simple as one might assume because whenever there is a new world, the ghosts of its past remain.

Rethinking the Past that Haunts the Future

Anyone who has forced herself to read through social theories proclaiming or justifying a new *something* will have the impression that social theories are destined to be inscrutable and edgy. Yet, even in cases like Beck and Mbembe what stands out is that the authors studiously embed their new theories in systematic and appreciative references to those that came before. In this respect, social theory is like any and all attempts to come to terms with whatever is new. A serious thinker, whether academic or practical, whether an author of serious books or a scribbler of Facebook messages, cannot avoid using the tools, including the languages and concepts, available. Even Marx, always a good classical example, wrote his radical interpretation of the flaws of capital accumulation by borrowing from and deeply criticizing classical, early modern political economy. So, too, early users of the first iPhone may have thought they had in their hands another type of telephone, when, as things turned out, smart phones become something else again, at least a tiny but powerful computer. The new never appears to be completely new, if only because whatever it becomes we who buy or use it come to it only with the language and knowledge we already possess. The old, in effect, teaches us how to think about the new.

Not only this, but what needs to be said is that social theories of uncertain worlds cannot ride the forward curve of the fresh wave. Some may even appear to be more of the same old thing tweaked. Hence, a general rule of any and all, academic or practical, attempts to rethink a changing world: New ideas about new realities are just like new tastes in style or new brands of music or new telephones and so on. They enter the world as it is under the cover of being a version of the familiar. There is a good reason for this. Human beings are like salmon that always return to the same Alaskan river to spawn or be eaten by hungry bears. Nature is not radical; otherwise it would not be natural. Human beings are, first and foremost, part of nature. Rarely do we enjoy stuff that is too new. This is why, commercially, there are museums to products that were too new to sell—Edsels, snake oils, Studebakers, Smurfs, bell-bottom jeans, and millions of other things lost in a Smithsonian warehouse somewhere. Some things sell for a while, but the majority drop from sight. Where are those Cadillac fins? Why is Elvis really dead? The new eventually drops away because, more times than not, the fashionable stuff was too different. I'll admit it: I once "sold" postmodernism, a mindset for which, now, there are no takers other than naïve cheapskates looking for an easy laugh. In this respect, social theories tend to be like Smurfs—once a rage, then not so much, soon enough gone. Smurfs came from Belgium, mutated into toys kids wanted, but this season they are relegated to the back shelves of Toys-R-Us. In social theory, August Comte and Herbert Spencer are Smurfs. Karl Marx and Max Weber still sell, much to the everlasting irritation of right-wingers who, for some reason, still hate Marx, and sociology students who still find Weber hard to read.

Above all else, social theories are human things. As a result, some of the theories that have attempted to come to terms with the uncertain new worlds are old hat. Neoliberalism is classical liberalism dusted off and rebranded. David Harvey's critique of neoliberalism is a fancy (if compelling) new version of Marx's criticism of liberal political economy. Social theory, like toy marketing, *always* must understand old markets for ideas even as it seeks to sell the new.

In this sense, the new is always haunted by the past. Or, like Charles Dickens's story of the ghosts of Christmas past, there is always a ghost somewhere haunting our selfish and ungenerous minds. We really don't want to give something away even to poor, crippled children. We do, but only when we are spooked by a reminder that what we give away at holiday time always comes out of our treasury of memories—of the habits we have or the terrible things we have done. Social theory is, in another sense, the guilty mind of collective life coming to terms with what has been repressed over the years.

When Avery Gordon, in *Ghostly Matters* (1997), says that "haunting is a constituent feature of modern social life," she is claiming not only that ghosts are real but that they are particularly real in the modern world. Another way to put this startling idea is to reconsider the idea that it, as so many things do, goes back to Marx. The modern world is, inherently, a world of destruction, one, in the phrase Bauman picks up, in which everything melts away or, better, a world in which everything vaporizes into a ghost. If you find this a bit of a stretch, then just think back to any ghost story you may have read in childhood in school, and ask what in stories like Shakespeare's *Hamlet* is a ghost meant to represent? Is not a ghost the frightening apparition of one who is thought to be dead and gone who appears in the present? Ghosts stories around campfires are child's play at frightening themselves about the very real fact the child is away from the home she misses especially at night. The fun of camp life is always haunted by the reality that any one away from home misses it, even if what she is escaping is an abusive father or brother. And is this not, in effect, what Hamlet's dreadful vision of its murdered father's spirit reminds? "I am thy father's spirit/ doom'd for a certain term to walk the night."

If a social theory of the modern world is a theory of a deadly world, then its destructive forces are hidden from view as if they were gone or had never lived. Avery Gordon, thereby, invokes the concept of the ghost. "The ghost is not simply dead," she writes, "but a social figure, and investigating it can lead to that dense site where history and subjectivity make social life." We who now live in an uncertain world can only think of what global realities are becoming by turning more than before to the ghostly remains of the worlds as we knew them or as they were known to those who came before us, there to find the concepts and language by which we can think the new we hardly understand.

Edward Said in his essay on the intellectual exile draws on his experience of having become a world-famous literary theorist teaching at Columbia University in New York City—a city in which he came to make a new life after having been born in Egypt and growing up in the Middle East before his father sent him to the United States for education. In time, he returned to explore his roots in the troubled Middle East. He became a spokesman for the Palestinian cause, even when writing, as an exile, on the ways modern literary fiction told the stories of a world fabricated on the exclusion of its colonial subjects. The nineteenth century British novel is nothing if not, in the central hidden figure of Charlotte Bronte's *Jane Eyre,* the story of Rochester's insane wife of his colonizing past—the mad woman in the attic.

Said, the exile from the torn colonized Middle Eastern past, unembarrassedly assumes his exilic status to be the critical theorist who can see what he has lost because he was once there. "It is a popular but mistaken assumption that being exiled is to be totally cut off, isolated, hopelessly separated from your place of origins." The problem of being an exile, he says, is "in living with the many reminders that you are in exile." The new global realities can thus be seen as living in the indefinite pose of an exile. If the worlds are becoming global, then people, rich and poor, must live away from home, in effect both stateless and homeless. We are cut off, even as we remember from whence we came. Said is a model for the social theorist whose vocation is determined and enhanced by assuming the position of the exile. To think the problems of this world requires that we move out of it.

Chief among the exiles in this world are the living ghosts of the colonial and slaveholding pasts. Whites in the Euro-American world dominated the nonwhite colonial worlds to create a global economic system that is, in Fanon's language, a world cut in two—and a world cut by racial evil. No nation today is more haunted by race than the United States—the land of the free and the home of the brave that refused to give up slavery until the issue split the nation in two with brother fighting brother. The North forced the issue in the South where the tobacco and cotton economies depended on slave labor of forced exiles from Africa. Exile is not always a choice; more often it is imposed and, when it is, the exile is subjugated. Slavery is now gone, so, too, is Jim Crow, but racism remains in the often-unconscious ways whites treat Blacks who are in every respect their equal or superior except for skin color. Elijah Anderson may shock white readers with the truth of his 2011 essay on the "Nigger Moment." Civil whites would never use the word "nigger" with a conscious intent to injure, but they reveal the ghosts of their uncivil racist past when they occasionally slip by using expressions like "your people" or, worse, express surprise that a Black plays golf. In the story Anderson reports here, Nathan, a Black school child, asks his mother "Why is it that the black kids cause all the trouble?"—an attitude about himself that he learned from a series of nigger moments on the play ground and in the classroom. Nigger moments are everywhere. I live in a predominantly white neighborhood near a poorer one. The nervous white folk in the district have organized a crime watch program that organizes email reports of suspicious people in the neighborhood. One summer morning, a group of kids were walking aimlessly along one of the streets. A resident reported that he had confronted them and shouted, "You don't belong here." The kids were Black. The righteous resident was not. Think of it in this day and age.

The ghosts of racism are more than the unwitting and witless things said to nonwhite people. William Julius Wilson has long been known for his influential studies of the plight of poor blacks in American cities. Wilson's 1978 book, *Declining Significance of Race: Blacks and Changing American Institutions,* is now a classic but at first it was greeted with considerable rage. Many, both white and Black, thought the book dismissed the importance of race as a factor in the high rates of poverty among urban Blacks. On the contrary, he argued that class was as important as race, especially as the modern economy began to falter. Wilson continued to write on the subject. By 1999, in *Bridge Over the Racial Divide* he continued to insist that the evidence was irrefutable that *When Work Disappears* (the title of his 1996 book) it is Blacks who suffer disproportionately. More than twenty years after *Declining Significance of Race,* Wilson had won the argument. Only the most backward of political ideologues would today claim that race is not still one of the major ghosts of American economic culture.

Wilson, it should be said, thinks of himself as a theorist, even though his research is rigorously empirical and quantitative. He makes this assertion because he is among those who have always worked with sociology's basic categories while setting a high a standard for seeking evidence that support or refute what some theorists merely claim to be so. Similarly, Charles Tilly's 1996 essay, "Invisible Elbow," challenges one of modern social thought's earliest theories of economic markets—that they are governed by what Adam Smith, in 1759, called the "invisible hand of the market." This idea was one of the classic concepts from the Scottish Enlightenment that, apart from its influence on economic theory, was also an early model of rational thought. The world, including the economic world, is reasonable—from which Smith and other classical political economists deduced a general principle of moral action: *behave sensibly and the invisible hand of the market will reward you.* Tilly's essay introduced the concept of the invisible elbow to argue that, in social science, as in daily life, however much we would like to think of the world as orderly in fact nations and individuals are not. We knock the milk from the counter with our awkward elbows just as nations stumble into wars they cannot win. The social may be rational in some ways, but it is also a series of accidents.

In social theory as it is practiced outside academic social sciences, there are writers who earnestly rethink the concepts that are usually taken as given in the nature of things. Julia Kristeva has done this in "Women's Time" (1979) just as Raewyn Connell has in *Southern Theory* (2007). Neither time nor geography is the property of a given group. It may seem strange for a feminist like Kristeva even to use the concept of "women's time," but in doing so, she is setting the terms for moving away from time's traditions wherein men set the clocks. Though writing on a very different subject, Raewyn Connell, Australia's leading social theorist, exposed the underlying fact that social theory has largely been a Northern enterprise, with Euro-Americans criticizing their Northern politics with Northern ways of thinking. Connell's idea of Southern theory may seem odd coming from someone native to such a European, if Southern, culture as Australia, yet she made the case that the South actually does think differently—an unsurprising claim in light of her astute interpretations of postcolonial histories and theories.

Though many find it disconcerting, thinkers once dismissed as passing fads continue to influence social theory. Gilles Deleuze and Félix Guattari are notorious for their difficult books, including *Thousand Plateaus* (1980). Their writing is sprawling and seemingly disconnected. But this is for a reason. Their basic idea (if there is a single basic one) is that thought itself, and therefore social thought, as well as culture and politics, were formed in the classical age around an unexpressed but pervasive axiom: all thought is like a tree with a single rap root that reaches down for the deep, nourishing truth. Against this, they pose the rhizome. "Unlike trees or their roots, the rhizome connects any point to any other point, and its traits are not necessarily linked to traits of the same nature." Among many other influences, Deleuze and Guattari were important sources for rethinking the theory global political power, notably in a sensational 2000 book *Empire* by Michael Hardt and Antonio Negri. The most unsettling but still plausible line in their book is simply "Empire has no limits." Compare this claim Castells's theory of networks, and you can begin to see a trend. There is, in fact, a decided way in which the pathways of economic, political, and military communications create new connections in the world at large. The Internet began in a serious way in 1962 when the United States Department of Defense was mandated to create a network that linked all of its mainframe computers wherever they were located. From their beginnings as military instruments, information technologies have developed into tools everyone uses. There would be no email without satellites and no satellites without military and government interests in the surveillance of populations. The networks of information that thrill and entertain us also make us vulnerable to hackers and observers of all kinds, most of them up to no good. Governments and their police track what we do and say on the Internet as does Google and its corporate clients who look for trends in what books and music we buy, what words we use in notes to friends, and what mischief we make for ourselves late at night when clicking on a nasty site that appeals to our most prurient appetites.

"We know what we are doing, but we continue to do it." This is a paraphrase of the line Slavoj Žižek borrows from Peter Sloterdijk to characterize the way people enter into accord with the cultures they know, even when they know they are as silly and stupid as Herbert Marcuse first argued years ago in *One Dimension Man* (1964). Popular media are self-conscious attempts to defuse our critical thinking about the world as it is. Who has not watched, even if for a while, some canned sitcom or game show on television in order, as it is often said, "to relax"? What is being relaxed by this intoxicating stuff is our minds. We know it, but we do it. Cynicism is a way of life, implies Žižek, because few are they who don't know that their habits are not, in certain evident ways, ignorant and self-destructive, yet we do it.

With writers like Žižek and Deleuze, social theory enters into a world of strange language and odd literary forms that mean to shock us into awareness that the old assumptions about how to think and act haunt us still as the world becomes something radically new. Yet, even as some social theorists embark on new and different methods and terms, some turn back to the most ancient of ideas. Among these would be Giorgio Agamben whose 1998 book, *Homo Sacer: Sovereign Power and Bare Life,* begins with an interpretation of the ancient Greek concepts of life. His theoretical purpose is to radicalize the idea of human life as sacred (*homo sacer*). Agamben, a classicist by training, points out that one of the classic Greek terms for life, *bios*, or political, life is in our time a cover for the fact that in the modern world of allegedly life-giving democratic politics, even the *democratic* state reserves unto itself the right to suspend the political rights in the name of a national crisis. This is what Hitler did, and this is also, shockingly, what Abraham Lincoln did in the worst moments of the American Civil War. "The sacredness of life," writes Agamben, "which is invoked today as an absolutely fundamental right in opposition to sovereign power, in fact, originally expresses precisely both life's subjection to a power over death and life's irreplaceable exposure in the relation of abandonment." Is this not true? It is not just former slaves, like their ancestors, who were exposed to lynching or indigenous people who were cast out of their lands but even in the world as it is there are millions of hungry people who seek no more than a chance to survive who are sent away by the militia or the border patrols. Sovereign power, says Agamben, like Mbembe, is at the heart of the modern system of political control. We with leisure to read a book may say this is not our problem, but who among us has any idea who is monitoring our movements on the computer to look for a reason to cut us off and even, in some cases, to imprison us. I don't smoke pot, but many of my friends do. Most of them, like many students, do along with other drugs. Not one of them supposes they will be arrested, if only because they may not live in Singapore or Texas. Still, some are, and some of them, if their skin color is of a certain kind, suffer imprisonment. Prisons are filled with lives ruined by police surveillance. One need not be indifferent to the dangers of drug use to be aware that among those captured and sent away the line distinguishing them from us is uncertain.

Social Theory at the Limits of the Social

It is all too easy to suggest that the strange effect of the writings of some new global thinkers like Deleuze and Žižek, of Agamben and Mbembe, is nothing more than a deliberate obfuscation. Yet, when one considers that they are addressing very serious issues, it becomes clear that something else is at play. Those who struggle with such problems are attempting to think through what hitherto had been unthinkable—that the social worlds are not, after all, straightforwardly accessible to the modern mind. If social theory began and developed as theories of societal structures and events, then what becomes of the *social* in social theory when the emergent reality is *global*. Once it is granted that societies are no longer the only, nor even the most important, reality in and around which social orders are formed, then a reality that is more than merely new is challenging the possibility of a *social* theory. Global things are, clearly, social. People, communities, even nations organize themselves according to the effects of forces greater than the social power of any given society—the costs of energy, the disappearance of jobs, the migrations of the many to find a better life, the pending disaster of climate change, and much more of the sort. Global realities may, to be sure, remain more or less friendly to traditional social habits and structures but they also can, and do, force habits and structures to adapt to worlds that are, it seems, different in kind. Global things are not just bigger and perhaps more potent that social things; they are very likely things of quite a different nature.

We are far from knowing just how and to what extent global things will change how we live with others. Global forces are already, well into the twenty-first century, challenging deep human and social assumptions and, thereby, how we think the social. As a result, social theory must work not only at the limit of prior theories about societies, but also well beyond prior limits of the traditional idea of the social.

To make matters even more complicated, we must remember that the term "global" has two meanings. One, of course, refers to the world as a whole or, more precisely, what happens on our globe. The other meaning of global refers to all that takes places in any given sphere of human conduct—as in, everywhere at once. In respect to social theory, the second meaning implicitly challenges the methods, one might say, by which we attempt to come to terms with things that once were merely social but now are also global. This second meaning of the term suggests that when it becomes necessary to study the social as a global thing, then it also becomes necessary to discover new methods beyond those that were formulated when it was common to consider social theory the theory of bounded, even local, societies.

Or to put it differently, thinking the global is a vastly more challenging proposition. Analytic statistics, for one example, are at best imperfectly applied to global realities, if only because basic data are collected differently from place to place, and in some places they are not collected at all. Likewise, such well-honored methods as ethnography or participant observation are, almost by definition, impossible when it comes to global things. Just as the demographic data on far mountain villages of Kyrgyzstan are difficult to collect, there can be no such thing as an ethnography of a global village (so to speak).

As a consequence, the stubborn reality of global things forces social theory to work and think at the limits of the social where no one method is possible. Social theories of the natural world of things cannot be quantified any more than can ordinary human experiences of fear, guilt, death, illegal wars and incarcerations. Similarly, consider so global a social thing as capitalism, which is obviously global even as it is so apparently social in the sense of affecting ordinary life. The theoretical conundrum here is that even rigorous quantitative methods, like those of Thomas Piketty's study of capitalism in the 21st century, result in the troubling conclusion that capital wealth over time has not, and will not, encourage social progress for ordinary people and institutions. But, otherwise, there are theoretical outliers in public writings that address social issues without regard to any standard empirical method. Thus, at the limits of the social where fear, urges, fears, death, irrational imprisonment, and legal contradictions reside, social theories can be found in essays and stories, even fictions that once seemed anything but conventional for theoretical study of social things.

Among sociologists, for example, none has been more daring in challenging the nature of the social that Bruno Latour, a French sociologist of science. Latour takes up a classic concept as ancient as life itself. In "Spheres and Networks," a widely circulated public lecture given in 2009 at Harvard, Latour advances a theory that redefines the place of nature in human life. It is well known, he argues, that modern thought was founded on the distinction between the social and natural. Social things are considered superior to nature. Latour draws on his own studies of scientific laboratories and natural history, as well as social theory, to insist that the human or social sphere is not superior to the natural. All things of this world—human, animal, natural, and material—are just that, things. All elements of the world are, in effect, on the same level of existence. The human is no more superior to nature than the wealthy are to the poor. We are organized (when we are) into networks, a term he uses differently from Castells. Networks for Latour are assemblages of things of all kinds—water, people, animals, winds—that come together as "actants" (not actors) to form communal arrangements. A tsunami is wind and fire and water, all of which flood the shorelines, gathering up animals and people into a network of survival. Like so many other social ideas, this may strike the reader as absurd, especially when Latour writes, as he has, about the democracy of all things. But, pause for a second to consider that we humans with all our pride of place are, like our dogs and the trees about, natural beings. We sniff and do our business and shed our lives when the wind blows hard. Our bodies live and die according to the rules of nature. When they live, we walk the earth to get our new clothes dirty. When they die, we return to the air or the ground according to local practices for the disposal of the dead. Alive or dead, we living things are destined to become material dust. If you doubt it, just ponder the last time a flood or a quake, a wind or ice storm, a drought or tsunami hit near to home. Those who survive do so because they learn to live like the plants and animals—without light or heat, scratching about for food and water, figuring out by their natural senses where to flee for safer ground or to dig out from under the waves of sand and dirt.

The French economist Thomas Piketty, in "The Central Contradictions of Capitalism," challenged not only economic science but also all the social sciences to rethink the very nature of the social and its limits in relation to economic forces. In particular he questions the long-held belief that social progress is closely bound to economic growth. In a magisterial historical study, Piketty argues that if social progress depends on enhanced levels of household income, then, in the three centuries of middle and late capitalism, the evidence is that growth in the aggregate level of capital wealth has always far exceeded income—and unless something changes, he adds, social progress will continue to recede as capital wealth grows more and more.

In respect to a seemingly quite different domain, Owen Fiss, an American legal scholar, in "The Perils of Constitutional Minimalism," has written of how the wars against terrorism have bred a relaxation of constitutional principles. As the United States pursues its war against global terrorism by the administrative imprisonment of terrorists, legal arguments have ignored constitutional principles by falling back on minimal statutory precedents. Incarceration without trial of alleged terrorists in Guantánamo, itself a legally questionable military base in Cuba, is sustained on legally questionable grounds. Also, in respect to the troubling illegitimacies of incarceration, in "Prison and Gray Wastes," Ta-Nehisi Coates, a senior editor at *The Atlantic*, revives the controversial sociological issue of what in 1965 Daniel Patrick Moynihan called the tangle of pathology of the Black family. But in his 2015 essay Coates revises white liberal thinking by analyzing the Black family has part of what he calls the gray waste produced and reproduced in America's carceral society—a society that controls its racial minorities by imprisonment.

Though it may seem a stretch to say so, the rapid emergence of neurosciences in their many forms are challenging us to think anew about the relation between mental life and society. In "Urge," the neurologist Oliver Sacks describes the plight of Walter, who was afflicted by a neurological disorder that caused him to experience uncontrollable urges—among them a sexual impulse that led him to download child pornography. Walter never touched any one sexually except for his wife. Once treated medically, Walter's urge disappeared. Yet, he was sentenced to twenty-six months in prison, followed by twenty-five months of what can only be called home incarceration. Once again confinement is imposed on an individual who was labeled deviant in spite of a perfectly treatable neurological condition.

Eula Biss's "White Debt" has become a contemporary classic of sorts because she so powerfully deploys her literary elegance to cut through the thickets of white racial guilt—a phrase almost universally deployed but just as commonly ill-considered. In "Fear," Marilynne Robinson, one of America's most acclaimed storytellers, examines the complex cultural and emotional issues behind her country's incoherent fear that stands behind a completely irrational denial of the realities of gun violence and the controls that would limit it.

The final limit on social theory is death—a topic that social theorists have, for the most part, ignored. *Social Theory* concludes with a selection from Robert Pogue Harrison's *The Dominion of Dead.* Harrison is a professor of Italian literature at Stanford, thus not even remotely a social theorist in the common sense of the term. Yet, he convincingly resurrects the land of the dead as central to social life in his description of "some of the manifold relations the living maintain with the giant family of the dead, both in past and present times." To consider the dead is ultimately to put social life hard up against its limits imposed by the global reality that the fundamental truth of nature is that none escapes the dominion of the dead, which in life reminds us of how little we are and in death absorbs us into a giant family of those who have gone before. Social things amid the global realities are increasingly forced to contend with nature's whims—environmental whims that we humanoids, in our arrogance, may have caused but when they flood upon us, they do as if we were no different in kind from our drowned pets or collapsed homes.

C.L.

Global Uncertainties

Immanuel Wallerstein (1930–) was among the first to understand the global implications of the collapse of the Soviet Union and its client states in 1990–1991. Soon after, he began publishing a steady stream of essays and books that predicted global trouble for American power, which, at the time, seemed invincible. Among the books from this period of his work are *Geopolitics and Geoculture* (1991), *After Liberalism* (1995), *Utopistics* (1998), *The End of the World as We Knew It* (1999) and *The Decline of American Power* (2003). Since, Wallerstein published the fourth volume of his magisterial work, *The Modern World System* (2011) which covers the early modern liberal period after the 1848 revolution. Here as in other of his works, the reader can appreciate the nuanced historical detail in respect to which Wallerstein has portrayed the long enduring history of the modern world-system as at once stable yet at times caught in periods of uncertainty. The selection is from *World-Systems Analysis: An Introduction* (2004), which succinctly summarizes the analytic history and concepts of his analytic method, culminating in a sharp examination of the present period of uncertainty that threatens the future prospects of a capitalist world-system.

The Modern World-System in Crisis[*]
Immanuel Wallerstein (2004)

....The modern world-system in which we are living, which is that of a capitalist world-economy, is currently in precisely such a crisis, and has been for a while now. This crisis may go on another twenty-five to fifty years. Since one central feature of such a transitional period is that we face wild oscillations of all those structures and processes we have come to know as an inherent part of the existing world-system, we find that our short-term expectations are necessarily quite unstable. This instability can lead to considerable anxiety and therefore violence as people try to preserve acquired privileges and hierarchical rank in a very unstable situation. In general, this process can lead to social conflicts that take a quite unpleasant form.

When did this crisis start? Geneses of phenomena are always the most debatable topic in scientific discourse. For one can always find forerunners and forebodings of almost anything in the near past, but also of course in the very far past. One plausible moment at which to start the story of this contemporary systemic crisis is the world revolution of 1968, which unsettled the structures of the world-system considerably. This world revolution marked the end of a long period of liberal supremacy, thereby dislocating the geoculture that had kept the political institutions of the world-system intact. And dislocating this geoculture unhinged the underpinnings of the capitalist world-economy and exposed it to the full force of political and cultural shocks to which it had always been subject, but from which it had previously been somewhat sheltered.…

.…[T]he three costs of production—remuneration, inputs, and taxation—have all been rising steadily over the past five hundred years and particularly over the past fifty years. On the other hand, the sales prices have not been able to keep pace, despite increased effective demand, because of a steady expansion in the number of producers and hence of their recurring inability to maintain oligopolistic conditions. This is what one means by a squeeze on profits. To be sure, producers seek to reverse these conditions constantly, and are doing so at present. To appreciate the limits of their ability to do so, we must return to the cultural shock of 1968.

The world-economy in the years after 1945 saw the largest expansion of productive structures in the history of the modern world-system. All the structural trends of which we have been speaking—costs of remuneration, costs of inputs, taxation—took a sharp upward turn as a result. At the same time, the antisystemic movements, which we previously discussed, made extraordinary progress in realizing their immediate objective—coming to power in the state structures. In all parts of the world, these movements seemed to be achieving step one of the two-step program. In a vast northern area from central Europe to East Asia (from the Elbe to the Yalu Rivers), Communist parties governed. In the pan-European world (western Europe, North America, and Australasia), social democratic parties (or their equivalents) were in power, or at least in alternating power. In the rest of Asia and most of Africa, national liberation movements had come to power. And in Latin America, nationalist/populist movements gained control.

The years after 1945 thus became a period of great optimism. The economic future seemed bright, and popular movements of all kinds seemed to he achieving their objectives. And in Vietnam, a little country struggling for its independence seemed to be holding the hegemonic power, the United States, in check. The modern world-system had never looked so good to so many people, a sentiment that had an exhilarating effect, but in many ways also a very stabilizing effect.

Nonetheless, there was an underlying and growing disillusion with precisely the popular movements in power. The second step of the two-step formula—change the world—seemed in practice much further from realization than most people had anticipated. Despite the overall economic growth of the world-system, the gap between core and periphery had become greater than ever. And despite the coming to power of the antisystemic movements, the great participatory élan of the period of mobilization seemed to die out once the antisystemic movements came to power in any given state. New privileged strata emerged. Ordinary people were now being asked not to make militant demands on what was asserted to be a government that represented them. When the future became the present, many previously ardent militants of the movements began to have second thoughts, and eventually began to dissent.

It was the combination of long-existing anger about the workings of the world-system and disappointment with the capacity of the antisystemic movements to transform the world that led to the world revolution of 1968. The explosions of 1968 contained two themes repeated virtually everywhere, whatever the local context. One was the rejection of U.S. hegemonic power, simultaneously with a complaint that the Soviet Union, the presumed antagonist of the United States, was actually colluding in the world order that the United States had established. And the second was that the traditional antisystemic movements had not fulfilled their promises once in power. The combination of these complaints, so widely repeated, constituted a cultural earthquake. The many uprisings were like a phoenix and did not put the multiple revolutionaries of 1968 in power, or not for very long. But they legitimated and strengthened the sense of disillusionment not only with the old antisystemic movements but also with the state structures these movements had been fortifying. The long-term certainties of evolutionary hope had become transformed into fears that the world-system might be unchanging.

This shift in worldwide sentiment, far from reinforcing the status quo, actually pulled the political and cultural supports from under the capitalist world-economy. No longer would oppressed people be sure that history was on their side. No longer could they therefore be satisfied with creeping improvements, in the belief that these would see fruition in the lives of their children and grandchildren. No longer could they be persuaded to postpone present complaints in the name of a beneficent future. In short, the multiple producers of the capitalist world-economy had lost the main hidden stabilizer of the system, the optimism of the oppressed. And this of course came at the very worst moment, when the squeeze on profits was beginning to be felt in a serious way.

The cultural shock of 1968 unhinged the automatic dominance of the liberal center, which had prevailed in the world-system since the prior world revolution of 1848. The right and the left were liberated from their role as avatars of centrist liberalism and were able to assert, or rather reassert, their more radical values. The world-system had entered into the period of transition, and both right and left were determined to take advantage of the increasing chaos to ensure that their values would prevail in the new system (or systems) that would eventually emerge from the crisis....

Stanley Hoffman (1928–2015) is the Paul and Catherine Buttenwieser University Professor at Harvard where, also, he had long been the chairman of the Minda de Gunzburg Center for European Studies. Hoffman was born in Vienna, studied and taught in Paris, and, after his move to Harvard in 1955, became one of the leading intellectual forces in the Atlantic community of nations. His books include *Gulliver's Troubles, or the Setting of American Foreign Policy* (1968), *Decline or Renewal? France Since the Thirties* (1974), and *World Disorders: Troubled Peace in the Post–Cold War Era* (1998). The selection is from an essay that appeared in *Foreign Affairs* in 2002, immediately becoming one of the most controversial and influential essays in the globalization debate among diplomats and foreign policy experts as well as social scientists.

The Clash of Globalizations*
Stanley Hoffman (2002)

A New Paradigm?

What is the state of international relations today? In the 1990s, specialists concentrated on the partial disintegration of the global order's traditional foundations: states. During that decade, many countries, often those born of decolonization, revealed themselves to be no more than pseudostates, without solid institutions, internal cohesion, or national consciousness. The end of communist coercion in the former Soviet Union and in the former Yugoslavia also revealed long-hidden ethnic tensions. Minorities that were or considered themselves oppressed demanded independence. In Iraq, Sudan, Afghanistan, and Haiti, rulers waged open warfare against their subjects. These wars increased the importance of humanitarian interventions, which came at the expense of the hallowed principles of national sovereignty and nonintervention. Thus the dominant tension of the decade was the clash between the fragmentation of states (and the state system) and the progress of economic, cultural, and political integration—in other words, globalization.

Everybody has understood the events of September 11 as the beginning of a new era. But what does this break mean? In the conventional approach to international relations, war took place among states. But in September, poorly armed individuals suddenly challenged, surprised, and wounded the world's dominant superpower. The attacks also showed that, for all its accomplishments, globalization makes an awful form of violence easily accessible to hopeless fanatics. Terrorism is the bloody link between interstate relations and global society. As countless individuals and groups are becoming global actors along with states, insecurity and vulnerability are rising. To assess today's bleak state of affairs, therefore, several questions are necessary. What concepts help explain the new global order? What is the condition of the interstate part of international relations? And what does the emerging global civil society contribute to world order?

Sound and Fury

Two models made a great deal of noise in the 1990s. The first one—Francis Fukuyama's "End of History" thesis—was not vindicated by events. To be sure, his argument predicted the end of ideological conflicts, not history itself, and the triumph of political and economic liberalism. That point is correct in a narrow sense: the "secular religions" that fought each other so bloodily in the last century are now dead. But Fukuyama failed to note that nationalism remains very much alive. Moreover, he ignored the explosive potential of religious wars that has extended to a large part of the Islamic world.

Fukuyama's academic mentor, the political scientist Samuel Huntington, provided a few years later a gloomier account that saw a very different world. Huntington predicted that violence resulting from international anarchy and the absence of common values and institutions would erupt among civilizations rather than among states or ideologies. But Huntington's conception of what constitutes a civilization was hazy. He failed to take into account sufficiently conflicts within each so-called civilization, and he overestimated the importance of religion in the behavior of non-Western elites, who are often secularized and Westernized. Hence he could not clearly define the link between a civilization and the foreign policies of its member states.

Other, less sensational models still have adherents. The "realist" orthodoxy insists that nothing has changed in international relations since Thucydides and Machiavelli: a state's military and economic power determines its fate; interdependence and international institutions are secondary and fragile phenomena; and states' objectives are imposed by the threats to their survival or security. Such is the world described by Henry Kissinger. Unfortunately, this venerable model has trouble integrating change, especially globalization and the rise of nonstate actors. Moreover, it overlooks the need for international cooperation that results from such new threats as the proliferation of weapons of mass destruction (WMD). And it ignores what the scholar Raymond Aron called the "germ of a universal consciousness": the liberal, promarket norms that developed states have come to hold in common.

Taking Aron's point, many scholars today interpret the world in terms of a triumphant globalization that submerges borders through new means of information and communication. In this universe, a state choosing to stay closed invariably faces decline and growing discontent among its subjects, who are eager for material progress. But if it opens up, it must accept a reduced role that is mainly limited to social protection, physical protection against aggression or civil war, and maintaining national identity. The champion of this epic without heroes is *The New York Times* columnist Thomas Friedman. He contrasts barriers with open vistas, obsolescence with modernity, state control with free markets. He sees in globalization the light of dawn, the "golden straitjacket" that will force contentious publics to understand that the logic of globalization is that of peace (since war would interrupt globalization and therefore progress) and democracy (because new technologies increase individual autonomy and encourage initiative).

Back to Reality

These models come up hard against three realities. First, rivalries among great powers (and the capacity of smaller states to exploit such tensions) have most certainly not disappeared. For a while now, however, the existence of nuclear weapons has produced a certain degree of prudence among the powers that have them. The risk of destruction that these weapons hold has moderated the game and turned nuclear arms into instruments of last resort. But the game could heat up as more states seek other WMD as a way of narrowing the gap between the nuclear club and the other powers. The sale of such weapons thus becomes a hugely contentious issue, and efforts to slow down the spread of all WMD, especially to dangerous "rogue" states, can paradoxically become new causes of violence.

Second, if wars between states are becoming less common, wars within them are on the rise—as seen in the former Yugoslavia, Iraq, much of Africa, and Sri Lanka. Uninvolved states first tend to hesitate to get engaged in these complex conflicts, but they then (sometimes) intervene to prevent these conflicts from turning into regional catastrophes. The interveners, in turn, seek the help of the United Nations or regional organizations to rebuild these states, promote stability, and prevent future fragmentation and misery.

Third, states' foreign policies are shaped not only by realist geopolitical factors such as economics and military power but by domestic politics. Even in undemocratic regimes, forces such as xenophobic passions, economic grievances, and transnational ethnic solidarity can make policymaking far more complex and less predictable. Many states—especially the United States—have to grapple with the frequent interplay of competing government branches. And the importance of individual leaders and their personalities is often underestimated in the study of international affairs.

For realists, then, transnational terrorism creates a formidable dilemma. If a state is the victim of private actors such as terrorists, it will try to eliminate these groups by depriving them of sanctuaries and punishing the states that harbor them. The national interest of the attacked state will therefore require either armed interventions against governments supporting terrorists or a course of prudence and discreet pressure on other governments to bring these terrorists to justice. Either option requires a questioning of sovereignty—the holy concept of realist theories. The classical realist universe of Hans Morgenthau and Aron may therefore still be very much alive in a world of states, but it has increasingly hazy contours and offers only difficult choices when it faces the threat of terrorism.

At the same time, the real universe of globalization does not resemble the one that Friedman celebrates. In fact, globalization has three forms, each with its own problems. First is economic globalization, which results from recent revolutions in technology, information, trade, foreign investment, and international business. The main actors are companies, investors, banks, and private services industries, as well as states and international organizations. This present form of capitalism, ironically foreseen by Karl Marx and Friedrich Engels, poses a central dilemma between efficiency and fairness. The specialization and integration of firms make it possible to increase aggregate wealth, but the logic of pure capitalism does not favor social justice. Economic globalization has thus become a formidable cause of inequality among and within states, and the concern for global competitiveness limits the aptitude of states and other actors to address this problem.

Next comes cultural globalization. It stems from the technological revolution and economic globalization, which together foster the flow of cultural goods. Here the key choice is between uniformization (often termed "Americanization") and diversity. The result is both a "disenchantment of the world" (in Max Weber's words) and a reaction against uniformity. The latter takes form in a renaissance of local cultures and languages as well as assaults against Western culture, which is denounced as an arrogant bearer of a secular, revolutionary ideology and a mask for U.S. hegemony.

Finally there is political globalization, a product of the other two. It is characterized by the preponderance of the United States and its political institutions and by a vast array of international and regional organizations and transgovernmental networks (specializing in areas such as policing or migration or justice). It is also marked by private institutions that are neither governmental nor purely national—say, Doctors Without Borders or Amnesty International. But many of these agencies lack democratic accountability and are weak in scope, power, and authority. Furthermore, much uncertainty hangs over the fate of American hegemony, which faces significant resistance abroad and is affected by America's own oscillation between the temptations of domination and isolation.

The benefits of globalization are undeniable. But Friedmanlike optimism rests on very fragile foundations. For one thing, globalization is neither inevitable nor irresistible. Rather, it is largely an American creation, rooted in the period after World War II and based on U.S. economic might. By extension, then, a deep and protracted economic crisis in the United States could have as devastating an effect on globalization as did the Great Depression.

Second, globalization's reach remains limited because it excludes many poor countries, and the states that it does transform react in different ways. This fact stems from the diversity of economic and social conditions at home as well as from partisan politics. The world is far away from a perfect integration of markets, services, and factors of production. Sometimes the simple existence of borders slows down and can even paralyze this integration; at other times it gives integration the flavors and colors of the dominant state (as in the case of the Internet).

Third, international civil society remains embryonic. Many nongovernmental organizations reflect only a tiny segment of the populations of their members' states. They largely represent only modernized countries, or those in which the weight of the state is not too heavy. Often, NGOs have little independence from governments.

Fourth, the individual emancipation so dear to Friedman does not quickly succeed in democratizing regimes, as one can see today in China. Nor does emancipation prevent public institutions such as the International Monetary Fund, the World Bank, or the World Trade Organization from remaining opaque in their activities and often arbitrary and unfair in their rulings.

Fifth, the attractive idea of improving the human condition through the abolition of barriers is dubious. Globalization is in fact only a sum of techniques (audio and videocassettes, the Internet, instantaneous communications) that are at the disposal of states or private actors. Self-interest and ideology, not humanitarian reasons, are what drive these actors. Their behavior is quite different from the vision of globalization as an Enlightenment-based utopia that is simultaneously scientific, rational, and universal. For many reasons—misery, injustice, humiliation, attachment to traditions, aspiration to more than just a better standard of living—this "Enlightenment" stereotype of globalization thus provokes revolt and dissatisfaction.

Another contradiction is also at work. On the one hand, international and transnational cooperation is necessary to ensure that globalization will not be undermined by the inequalities resulting from market fluctuations, weak statesponsored protections, and the incapacity of many states to improve their fates by themselves. On the other hand, cooperation presupposes that many states and rich private players operate altruistically—which is certainly not the essence of international relations—or practice a remarkably generous conception of their long-term interests. But the fact remains that most rich states still refuse to provide sufficient development aid or to intervene in crisis situations such as the genocide in Rwanda. That reluctance compares poorly with the American enthusiasm to pursue the fight against al Qaeda and the Taliban. What is wrong here is not patriotic enthusiasm as such, but the weakness of the humanitarian impulse when the national interest in saving non-American victims is not self-evident.

Imagined Communities

Among the many effects of globalization on international politics, three hold particular importance. The first concerns institutions. Contrary to realist predictions, most states are not perpetually at war with each other. Many regions and countries live in peace; in other cases, violence is internal rather than state-to-state. And since no government can do everything by itself, interstate organisms have emerged. The result, which can be termed "global society," seeks to reduce the potentially destructive effects of national regulations on the forces of integration. But it also seeks to ensure fairness in the world market and create international regulatory regimes in such areas as trade, communications, human rights, migration,

and refugees. The main obstacle to this effort is the reluctance of states to accept global directives that might constrain the market or further reduce their sovereignty. Thus the UN's powers remain limited and sometimes only purely theoretical. International criminal justice is still only a spotty and contested last resort. In the world economy—where the market, not global governance, has been the main beneficiary of the state's retreat—the network of global institutions is fragmented and incomplete. Foreign investment remains ruled by bilateral agreements. Environmental protection is badly ensured, and issues such as migration and population growth are largely ignored. Institutional networks are not powerful enough to address unfettered short-term capital movements, the lack of international regulation on bankruptcy and competition, and primitive coordination among rich countries. In turn, the global "governance" that does exist is partial and weak at a time when economic globalization deprives many states of independent monetary and fiscal policies, or it obliges them to make cruel choices between economic competitiveness and the preservation of social safety nets. All the while, the United States displays an increasing impatience toward institutions that weigh on American freedom of action. Movement toward a world state looks increasingly unlikely. The more state sovereignty crumbles under the blows of globalization or such recent developments as humanitarian intervention and the fight against terrorism, the more states cling to what is left to them.

Second, globalization has not profoundly challenged the enduring national nature of citizenship. Economic life takes place on a global scale, but human identity remains national hence the strong resistance to cultural homogenization. Over the centuries, increasingly centralized states have expanded their functions and tried to forge a sense of common identity for their subjects. But no central power in the world can do the same thing today, even in the European Union. There, a single currency and advanced economic coordination have not yet produced a unified economy or strong central institutions endowed with legal autonomy, nor have they resulted in a sense of postnational citizenship. The march from national identity to one that would be both national and European has only just begun. A world very partially unified by technology still has no collective consciousness or collective solidarity. What states are unwilling to do the world market cannot do all by itself, especially in engendering sense of world citizenship.

Third, there is the relationship between globalization and violence. The traditional state of war, even if it is limited in scope, still persists. There are high risks of regional explosions in the Middle East and in East Asia, and these could seriously affect relations between the major powers. Because of this threat, and because modern arms are increasingly costly, the "anarchical society" of states lacks the resources to correct some of globalization's most flagrant flaws. These very costs, combined with the classic distrust among international actors who prefer to try to preserve their security alone or through traditional alliances, prevent a more satisfactory institutionalization of world politics—for example, an increase of the UN's powers. This step could happen if global society were provided with sufficient forces to prevent a conflict or restore peace—but it is not.

Globalization, far from spreading peace, thus seems to foster conflicts and resentments. The lowering of various barriers celebrated by Friedman, especially the spread of global media, makes it possible for the most deprived or oppressed to compare their fate with that of the free and well-off. These dispossessed then ask for help from others with common resentments, ethnic origin, or religious faith. Insofar as globalization enriches some and uproots many, those who are both poor and uprooted may seek revenge and self-esteem in terrorism.

Globalization and Terror

Terrorism is the poisoned fruit of several forces. It can be the weapon of the weak in a classic conflict among states or within a state, as in Kashmir or the Palestinian territories. But it can also be seen as a product of globalization. Transnational terrorism is made possible by the vast array of communication tools. Islamic terrorism, for example, is not only based on support for the Palestinian struggle and opposition to an invasive American presence. It is also fueled by a resistance to "unjust" economic globalization and to a Western culture deemed threatening to local religions and cultures.

If globalization often facilitates terrorist violence, the fight against this war without borders is potentially disastrous for both economic development and globalization. Antiterrorist measures restrict mobility and financial flows, while new terrorist attacks could lead the way for an antiglobalist reaction comparable to the chauvinistic paroxysms of the 1930s.

Global terrorism is not the simple extension of war among states to nonstates. It is the subversion of traditional ways of war because it does not care about the sovereignty of either its enemies or the allies who shelter them. It provokes its victims to take measures that, in the name of legitimate defense, violate knowingly the sovereignty of those states accused of encouraging terror. . . .

But all those trespasses against the sacred principles of sovereignty do not constitute progress toward global society, which has yet to agree on a common definition of terrorism or on a common policy against it. Indeed, the beneficiaries of the antiterrorist "war" have been the illiberal, poorer states that have lost so much of their sovereignty of late. Now the crackdown on terror allows them to tighten their controls on their own people, products, and money. They can give themselves new reasons to violate individual rights in the name of common defense against insecurity—and thus stop the slow, hesitant march toward international criminal justice.

Zygmunt Bauman (1925–) was born in Poznan, Poland, from which, during World War II, his family fled for the Soviet Union. As a young man of eighteen years, Bauman fought with the Free Polish Army against the Nazi occupation. He rose to the rank of captain, but after the war he was purged from the army by the Communists. Still, he remained in Poland through his graduate studies and began his academic career as a lecturer in social sciences at the University of Warsaw. In 1971, he emigrated to England for a professorship at the University of Leeds, which he held until retirement in 2001. Since, Bauman has only increased the range and number of his books on a dazzling range of subjects. More than all but a few sociologists, Bauman writes with an authentic literary voice and reliable political conviction that stems in some part from his youthful experiences in Eastern Europe. Among his books are *Legislators and Interpreters* (1987), *Modernity and the Holocaust* (1989), *Postmodern Ethics* (1993), and *Thinking Sociologically* (1990). The selection is from *Liquid Modernity* (2001), an extended meditation on modernity that, perhaps, only an intellectual nomad like Bauman could write with such assurance.

Liquid Modernity[*]
Zygmunt Bauman (2001)

Liquids, unlike solids, cannot easily hold their shape. Fluids, so to speak, neither fix space nor bind time. While solids have clear spatial dimensions but neutralize the impact, and thus downgrade the significance, of time (effectively resist its flow or render it irrelevant), fluids do not keep to any shape for long and are constantly ready (and prone) to change it; and so for them it is the flow of time that counts, more than the space they happen to occupy: that space, after all, they fill "but for a moment." In a sense, solids cancel time; for liquids, on the contrary, it is mostly time that matters. When describing solids, one may ignore time altogether; in describing fluids, to leave time out of account would be a grievous mistake. Descriptions of fluids are all snapshots, and they need a date at the bottom of the picture.

Fluids travel easily. They "flow," "spill," "run out," "splash," "pour over," "leak," "flood," "spray," "drip," "seep," "ooze"; unlike solids, they are not easily stopped—they pass around some obstacles, dissolve some others and bore or soak their way through others still. From the meeting with solids they emerge unscathed, while the solids they have met, if they stay solid, are changed—get moist or drenched. The extraordinary mobility of fluids is what associates them with the idea of "lightness." There are liquids which, cubic inch for cubic inch, are heavier than many solids, but we are inclined nonetheless to visualize them all as lighter, less "weighty" than everything solid. We associate "lightness" or "weightlessness" with mobility and inconstancy: we know from practice that the lighter we travel the easier and faster we move.

These are reasons to consider "fluidity" or "liquidity" as fitting metaphors when we wish to grasp the nature of the present, in many ways *novel*, phase in the history of modernity.

I readily agree that such a proposition may give a pause to anyone at home in the "modernity discourse" and familiar with the vocabulary commonly used to narrate modern history. Was not modernity a process of "liquefaction" from the start? Was not "melting the solids" its major pastime and prime accomplishment all along? In other words, has modernity not been "fluid" since its inception?

These and similar objections are well justified, and will seem more so once we recall that the famous phrase "melting the solids", when coined a century and a half ago by the authors of *The Communist Manifesto*, referred to the treatment which the self-confident and exuberant modern spirit awarded the society it found much too stagnant for its taste and much too resistant to shift and mould for its ambitions—since it was frozen in its habitual ways. If the "spirit" was "modern," it was so indeed in so far as it was determined that reality should be emancipated from the "dead hand" of its own history—and this could only be done by melting the solids (that is, by definition, dissolving whatever persists over time and is negligent of its passage or immune to its flow). That intention called in turn for the "profaning of the sacred": for disavowing and dethroning the past, and first and foremost "tradition"—to wit, the sediment and residue of the past in the present; it thereby called for the smashing of the protective armour forged of the beliefs and loyalties which allowed the solids to resist the "liquefaction."

Let us remember, however, that all this was to be done not in order to do away with the solids once and for all and make the brave new world free of them for ever, but to clear the site for *new and improved solids*; to replace the inherited set of deficient and defective solids with another set, which was much improved and preferably perfect, and for that reason no longer alterable. When reading de Tocqueville's *Ancien Régime*, one might wonder in addition to what extent the "found solids" were resented, condemned and earmarked for liquefaction for the reason that they were already rusty, mushy, coming apart at the seams and altogether unreliable. Modern times found the pre-modern solids in a fairly advanced state of disintegration; and one of the most powerful motives behind the urge to melt them was the wish to discover or invent solids of—for a change—*lasting* solidity, a solidity which one could trust and rely upon and which would make the world predictable and therefore manageable.

The first solids to be melted and the first sacreds to be profaned were traditional loyalties, customary rights and obligations which bound hands and feet, hindered moves and cramped the enterprise. To set earnestly about the task of building a new (truly solid!) order, it was necessary to get rid of the ballast with which the old order burdened the builders. "Melting the solids" meant first and foremost shedding the "irrelevan

---

[*]Bauman, Zygmunt. *Liquid Modernity*. Polity Press, 2001. © 2001 Polity Press. Reprinted with permission of Polity Press.

obligations standing in the way of rational calculation of effects; as Max Weber put it, liberating business enterprise from the shackles of the family-household duties and from the dense tissue of ethical obligations; or, as Thomas Carlyle would have it, leaving solely the "cash nexus" of the many bonds underlying human mutuality and mutual responsibilities. By the same token, that kind of "melting the solids" left the whole complex network of social relations unstuck—bare, unprotected, unarmed and exposed, impotent to resist the business-inspired rules of action and business-shaped criteria of rationality, let alone to compete with them effectively.

That fateful departure laid the field open to the invasion and domination of (as Weber put it) instrumental rationality, or (as Karl Marx articulated it) the determining role of economy: now the "basis" of social life gave all life's other realms the status of "superstructure"—to wit, an artefact of the "basis" whose sole function was to service its smooth and continuing operation. The melting of solids led to the progressive untying of economy from its traditional political, ethical and cultural entanglements. It sedimented a new order, defined primarily in economic terms. That new order was to be more "solid" than the orders it replaced, because—unlike them—it was immune to the challenge from noneconomic action. Most political or moral levers capable of shifting or reforming the new order have been broken or rendered too short, weak or otherwise inadequate for the task. Not that the economic order, once entrenched, will have colonized, re-educated and converted to its ways the rest of social life; that order came to dominate the totality of human life because whatever else might have happened in that life has been rendered irrelevant and ineffective as far as the relentless and continuous reproduction of that order was concerned. . . .

The task of constructing a new and better order to replace the old and defective one is not presently on the agenda—at least not on the agenda of that realm where political action is supposed to reside. The "melting of solids," the permanent feature of modernity, has therefore acquired a new meaning, and above all has been redirected to a new target—one of the paramount effects of that redirection ·ing the dissolution of forces which could keep the ·stion of order and system on the political agenda.

·olids whose turn has come to be thrown into ·lting pot and which are in the process of ·lted at the present time, the time of fluid ·are the bonds which interlock individual

choices in collective projects and actions—the patterns of communication and co-ordination between individually conducted life policies on the one hand and political actions of human collectivities on the other. . . .

Modernity means many things, and its arrival and progress can be traced using many and different markers. One feature of modern life and its modern setting stands out, however, as perhaps that "difference which make[s] the difference"; as the crucial attribute from which all other characteristics follow. That attribute is the changing relationship between space and time.

Modernity starts when space and time are separated from living practice and from each other and so become ready to be theorized as distinct and mutually independent categories of strategy and action, when they cease to be, as they used to be in long premodern centuries, the intertwined and so barely distinguishable aspects of living experience, locked in a stable and apparently invulnerable one-to-one correspondence. In modernity, time has *history*, it has history because of the perpetually expanding "carrying capacity" of time—the lengthening of the stretches of space which units of time allow to "pass," "cross," "cover"—or *conquer*. Time acquires history once the speed of movement through space (unlike the eminently inflexible space, which cannot be stretched and would not shrink) becomes a matter of human ingenuity, imagination and resourcefulness.

The very idea of speed (even more conspicuously, that of acceleration), when referring to the relationship between time and space, *assumes* its variability, and it would hardly have any meaning at all were not that relation truly changeable, were it an attribute of inhuman and pre-human reality rather than a matter of human inventiveness and resolve, and were it not reaching far beyond the narrow range of variations to which the natural tools of mobility—human or equine legs—used to confine the movements of premodern bodies. Once the distance passed in a unit of time came to be dependent on technology, on artificial means of transportation, all extant, inherited limits to the speed of movement could be in principle transgressed. Only the sky (or, as it transpired later, the speed of light) was now the limit, and modernity was one continuous, unstoppable and fast accelerating effort to reach it.

Thanks to its newly acquired flexibility and expansiveness, modern time has become, first and foremost, the weapon in the conquest of space. In the modern struggle between time and space, space was the solid and stolid, unwieldy and inert side, capable of waging only a defensive, trench war—being an obstacle to the resilient advances of time. Time was the active and dynamic side in the battle, the side always on the offensive: the invading, conquering and colonizing force. Velocity of movement and access to faster means of mobility steadily rose in modern times to the position of the principal tool of power and domination. . . .

Throughout the solid stage of the modern era, nomadic habits remained out of favour. Citizenship went hand in hand with settlement, and the absence of "fixed address" and "statelessness" meant exclusion from the law-abiding and law-protected community and more often than not brought upon the culprits legal discrimination, if not active prosecution. While this still applies to the homeless and shifty "underclass," which is subject to the old techniques of panoptical control (techniques largely abandoned as the prime vehicle of integrating and disciplining the bulk of the population), the era of unconditional superiority of sedentarism over nomadism and the domination of the settled over the mobile is on the whole grinding fast to a halt. We are witnessing the revenge of nomadism over the principle of territoriality and settlement. In the fluid stage of modernity, the settled majority is ruled by the nomadic and exterritorial elite. Keeping the roads free for nomadic traffic and phasing out the remaining check-points has now become the meta-purpose of politics, and also of wars, which, as Clausewitz originally declared, are but "extension of politics by other means."

The contemporary global elite is shaped after the pattern of the old-style "absentee landlords". It can rule without burdening itself with the chores of administration, management, welfare concerns, or, for that matter, with the mission of "bringing light," "reforming the ways," morally uplifting, "civilizing" and cultural crusades. Active engagement in the life of subordinate populations is no longer needed (on the contrary, it is actively avoided as unnecessarily costly and ineffective)—and so the "bigger" is not just not "better" any more, but devoid of rational sense. It is now the smaller, the lighter, the more portable that signifies improvement and "progress." Travelling light, rather than holding tightly to things deemed attractive for their reliability and solidity—that is, for their heavy weight, substantiality and unyielding power of resistance—is now the asset of power.

Holding to the ground is not that important if the ground can be reached and abandoned at whim, in a short time or in no time. On the other hand, holding too fast, burdening one's bond with mutually binding commitments, may prove positively harmful and the new chances crop up elsewhere. Rockefeller might have wished to make his factories, railroads and oil-rigs big and bulky and own them for a long, long time to come (for eternity, if one measures time by the duration of human or human family life). Bill Gates, however, feels no regret when parting with possessions in which he took pride yesterday; it is the mind-boggling speed of circulation, of recycling, ageing, dumping and replacement which brings profit today—not the durability and lasting reliability of the product. In a remarkable reversal of the millennia-long tradition, it is the high and mighty of the day who resent and shun the durable and cherish the transient, while it is those at the bottom of the heap who—against all odds—desperately struggle to force their flimsy and paltry, transient possessions to last longer and render durable service. The two meet nowadays mostly on opposite sides of the jumbo-sales or used-car auction counters.

David Harvey (1935–) was born in Kent, England. He has long been one of the most influential and cited writers in the general field of social theory. Harvey is now Distinguished Professor of Anthropology and Geography—a title that begins to suggest the range of his interests. Formerly, he taught at Johns Hopkins University and, before that, as Halford Mackinder Professor of Geography at Oxford. His writings on social and urban spaces have enjoyed a considerable influence the world over—especially among those seeking to retain a Marxian edge against the confusions wrought by debates over the postmodern and globalization. His books include *Social Justice and the City* (1973), *Limits to Capital* (1983), *The Condition of Postmodernity* (1989), *Justice, Nature and the Geography of Difference* (1996), and *The New Imperialism* (2003). The selection is one of his many critical discussions of global phenomena. In this case of the attempt of a liberal political economy to maintain its control of global political economy by reshaping the relations of state and regional institutions with respect to an implicit theory of a global market. Harvey is merciless in his criticism that this allegedly new form of liberal economics is more destructive even than the traditional one it purports to replace.

Neoliberalism on Trial[*]
David Harvey (2005)

....Neoliberalism is in the first instance a theory of political economic practices that proposes that human well-being can best be advanced by liberating individual entrepreneurial freedoms and skills within an institutional framework characterized by strong private property rights, free markets, and free trade. The role of the state is to create and preserve an institutional framework appropriate to such practices. The state has to guarantee, for example, the quality and integrity of money. It must also set up those military, defence, police, and legal structures and functions required to secure private property rights and to guarantee, by force if need be, the proper functioning of markets. Furthermore, if markets do not exist (in areas such as land, water, education, health care, social security, or environmental pollution) then they must be created, by state action if necessary. But beyond these tasks the state should not venture. State interventions in markets (once created) must be kept to a bare minimum because, according to the theory, the state cannot possibly possess enough information to second-guess market signals (prices) and because powerful interest groups will inevitably distort and bias state interventions (particularly in democracies) for their own benefit.

There has everywhere been an emphatic turn towards neoliberalism in political-economic practices and thinking since the 1970s. Deregulation, privatization, and withdrawal of the state from many areas of social provision have been all too common. Almost all states, from those newly minted after the collapse of the Soviet Union to old-style social democracies and welfare states such as New Zealand and Sweden, have embraced, sometimes voluntarily and in other instances in response to coercive pressures, some version of neoliberal theory and adjusted at least some policies and practices accordingly. Post-apartheid South Africa quickly embraced neoliberalism, and even contemporary China, as we shall see, appears to be headed in this direction. Furthermore, the advocates of the neoliberal way now occupy positions of considerable influence in education (the universities and many 'think tanks'), in the media, in corporate boardrooms and financial insti-

tutions, in key state institutions (treasury departments, the central banks), and also in those international institutions such as the International Monetary Fund (IMF), the World Bank, and the World Trade Organization (WTO) that regulate global finance and trade. Neoliberalism has, in short, become hegemonic as a mode of discourse. It has pervasive effects on ways of thought to the point where it has become incorporated into the common-sense way many of us interpret, live in, and understand the world.

The process of neoliberalization has, however, entailed much 'creative destruction', not only of prior institutional frameworks and powers (even challenging traditional forms of state sovereignty) but also of divisions of labour, social relations, welfare provisions, technological mixes, ways of life and thought, reproductive activities, attachments to the land and habits of the heart. In so far as neoliberalism values market exchange as 'an ethic in itself, capable of acting as a guide to all human action, and substituting for all previously held ethical beliefs', it emphasizes the significance of contractual relations in the marketplace. It holds that the social good will be maximized by maximizing the reach and frequency of market transactions, and it seeks to bring all human action into the domain of the market. This requires technologies of information creation and capacities to accumulate, store, transfer, analyse, and use massive databases to guide decisions in the global marketplace. Hence neoliberalism's intense interest in and pursuit of information technologies (leading some to proclaim the emergence of a new kind of 'information society'). These technologies have compressed the rising density of market transactions in both space and time. They have produced a particularly intensive burst of what I have elsewhere called 'time-space compression'. The greater the geographical range (hence the emphasis on 'globalization') and the shorter the term of market contracts the better. This latter preference parallels Lyotard's famous description of the postmodern condition as one where 'the temporary contract' supplants 'permanent institutions in the professional, emotional, sexual, cultural, family and international domains, as well as in political affairs'. The cultural consequences of the dominance of such a market ethic are legion....

The positive sense of justice as a right has, for example, been a powerful provocateur in political movements: struggles against injustice have often animated movements for social change. The inspir-

[*]A BRIEF HISTORY OF NEOLIBERALISM by Harvey (2005) 1371w from pp. 2-4, 180-181© 1988 by Oxford University Press, Inc. By permission of Oxford University Press, USA.

ing history of the civil rights movement in the US is a case in point. The problem, of course, is that there are innumerable concepts of justice to which we may appeal. But analysis shows that certain dominant social processes throw up and rest upon certain conceptions of justice and of rights. To challenge those particular rights is to challenge the social process in which they inhere. Conversely, it proves impossible to wean society away from some dominant social process (such as that of capital accumulation through market exchange) to another (such as political democracy and collective action) without simultaneously shifting allegiance from one dominant conception of rights and of justice to another. The difficulty with all idealist specifications of rights and of justice is that they hide this connection. Only when they come to earth in relation to some social process do they find social meaning.

[In the case of neoliberalism,] rights cluster around two dominant logics of power—that of the territorial state and that of capital. However much we might wish rights to be universal, it is the state that has to enforce them. If political power is not willing, then notions of rights remain empty. Rights are, therefore, derivative of and conditional upon citizenship. The territoriality of jurisdiction then becomes an issue. This cuts both ways. Difficult questions arise because of stateless persons, illegal immigrants, and the like. Who is or is not a 'citizen' becomes a serious issue defining principles of inclusion and exclusion within the territorial specification of the state. How the state exercises sovereignty with respect to rights is itself a contested issue, but there are limits placed on that sovereignty (as China is discovering) by the global rules embedded in neoliberal capital accumulation. Nevertheless, the nation-state, with its monopoly over legitimate forms of violence, can in Hobbesian fashion define its own bundle of rights and be only loosely bound by international conventions. The US, for one, insists on its right not to be held accountable for crimes against humanity as defined in the international arena at the same time as it insists that war criminals from elsewhere must be brought to justice before the very same courts whose authority it denies in relation to its own citizens.

To live under neoliberalism also means to accept or submit to that bundle of rights necessary for capital accumulation. We live, therefore, in a society in which the inalienable rights of individuals (and, recall, corporations are defined as individuals before the law) to private property and the profit rate trump any other conception of inalienable rights you can think of. Defenders of this regime of rights plausibly argue that it encourages 'bourgeois virtues', without which everyone in the world would be far worse off. These include individual responsibility and liability; independence from state interference (which often places this regime of rights in severe opposition to those defined within the state); equality of opportunity in the market and before the law; rewards for initiative and entrepreneurial endeavour; care for oneself and one's own; and an open marketplace that allows for wide-ranging freedoms of choice of both contract and exchange. This system of rights appears even more persuasive when extended to the right of private property in one's own body (which underpins the right of the person to freely contract to sell his or her labour power as well as to be treated with dignity and respect and to be free from bodily coercions such as slavery) and the right to freedom of thought, expression, and speech. These derivative rights are appealing. Many of us rely heavily upon them. But we do so much as beggars live off the crumbs from the rich man's table....

Manuel Castells (1942–) was born in Spain but lived in exile, mostly in France, during the last years of the repressive Franco regime in his native land. He has taught in universities in every part of the world, including Paris, Madrid, Hong Kong, Singapore, Moscow, and throughout Latin America. He was professor of sociology and urban planning at the University of California at Berkeley until retirement when he became University Professor at the University of Southern California. Since 1979 he has been professor of sociology and urban planning at the University of California at Berkeley. He has written numerous books, including *The Economic Crisis and American Society* (1980), *The Information City* (1989), and *The Rise of the Network Society* (1996), which is the first book in a trilogy, *The Information Age: Economy, Society and* Culture.

Informationalism and Networks[*]
Manuel Castells (2008)

I have conceptualized as the network society the social structure resulting from the interaction between the new technological paradigm and social organization at large.

Often, the emerging society has been characterized as information society or knowledge society. I take exception with this terminology—not because knowledge and information are not central in our society, but because they have always been so, in all historically known societies. What is new is the microelectronics-based, networking technologies that provide new capabilities to an old form of social organization: networks. Networks throughout history had a major advantage and a major problem vis-a-vis other forms of social organization. On the one hand, they are the most adaptable and flexible organizational forms, so following very efficiently the evolutionary path of human social arrangements. On the other hand, in the past they could not master and coordinate the resources needed to accomplish a given task or fulfill a project beyond a certain size and complexity of the organization required to perform the task. Thus, in the historical record, networks were the domain of the private life, while the world of production, power, and war was occupied by large, vertical organizations, such as states, churches, armies, and corporations that could marshall vast pools of resources around the purpose defined by a central authority. Digital networking technologies enable networks to overcome their historical limits. They can, at the same time, be flexible and adaptive thanks to their capacity to decentralize performance along a network of autonomous components, while still being able to coordinate all this decentralized activity on a shared purpose of decision making. Digital communication networks are the backbone of the network society, as power networks (meaning energy networks) were the infrastructure on which the industrial society was built, as it was demonstrated by historian Thomas Hughes. To be sure, the network society manifests itself in many different forms, according to the culture, institutions, and historical trajectory of each society, as the industrial society

encompassed realities as different as the United States, and the Soviet Union, England or Japan, while still sharing some fundamental features that were recognized as defining industrialism as a distinct form of human organization—not determined by the industrial technologies, but unthinkable without these technologies.

Furthermore, because the network society is based on networks, and communication networks transcend boundaries, the network society is global, it is based on global networks. So, it is pervasive throughout the planet, its logic transforms extends to every country in the planet, as it is diffused by the power embedded in global networks of capital, goods, services, labor, communication, information, science, and technology. So, what we call globalization is another way to refer to the network society, although more descriptive and less analytical than what the concept of network society implies. Yet, because networks are selective according to their specific programs, because they can simultaneously communicate and incommunicate, the network society diffuses in the entire world, but does not include all people. In fact, in this early 21st century, it excludes most of humankind, although all of humankind is affected by its logic, and by the power relationships that interact in the global networks of social organization...

The network society, in the simplest terms, is a social structure based on networks operated by information and communication technologies based in microelectronics and digital computer networks that generate, process, and distribute information on the basis of the knowledge accumulated in the nodes of the networks. A network is a formal structure... It is a system of interconnected nodes. Nodes are, formally speaking, the points where the curve intersects itself. Networks are open structures that evolve by adding or removing nodes according to the changing requirements of the programs that assign performance goals to the networks. Naturally, these programs are decided socially from outside the network. But once they are inscripted in the logic of the network, the network will follow efficiently these instructions, adding, deleting, and reconfigurating, until a new program replaces or modifies the codes that command its operational system....

There is an even deeper transformation of political institutions in the network society: the rise of a new

---

[*]From Mannuel Castells and Gustavo Cardoso, "The Network Society: From Knowledge to Policy," Washington DC, Johns Hopkins Center for Transatlantic Relations, pp. 3-5, 7, 15-16. © 2005, Center for Transatlantic Relations. Reprinted with permission.

form of state that gradually replaces the nation-states of the industrial era. This is related to globalization, that is the formation of a network of global networks than link selectively across the planet all functional dimensions of societies. Because the network society is global, the state of the network society cannot operate only or primarily in the national context. It has to engage in a process of global governance but without a global government. The reasons why there is not a global government, and it is unlikely it will be one in the foreseeable future, are rooted in the historical inertia of institutions, and of the social interests and values embedded in these institutions. Simply put, neither current political actors nor people at large want a world government, so it will not happen. But since global governance of some sort is a functional need, nation-states are finding ways to co-manage the global processes that affect most of the issues related to their governing practice. To do so, they increasingly share sovereignty while still proudly branding their flags. They form networks of nation-states, the most integrated and significant of which is the European Union. But they are around the world a number of state associations more or less integrated in their institutions and their practice that structure specific processed of transnational governance. In addition, nation-states have spurred a number of formal and informal international and supranational institutions that actually govern the world. Not only the United Nations, and various military alliances, but also the International Monetary Fund and its ancillary agency, the World Bank, the G-8 club of leading countries in the world (with the permission of China), and a number of ad hoc groupings.

Furthermore, to connect the global and the local, nation-states have asserted or fostered a process of decentralization that reaches out to regional and local governments, and even to NGOs, often associated to political management. Thus, the actual system of governance in our world is not centered around the nation-state, although nationstates are not disappearing by any means. Governance is operated in a network of political institutions that shares sovereignty in various degrees and reconfigurates itself in a variable geopolitical geometry. This is what I have conceptualized as **the network state.** It is not the result of technological change, but the response to the structural contradiction between a global system and a national state. However, globalization is the form that takes the diffusion of the network society in its planetary reach, and new communication and transportation technologies provide the necessary infrastructure for the process of globalization. New communication technologies also help the actual operation of a complex network state, but this is a tool of performance rather than a determining factor. The transition from the nation-state to the network state is an organizational and political process prompted by the transformation of political management, representation and domination in the conditions of the network society.

Saskia Sassen (1949–) is the Robert S. Lynd Professor of Sociology at Columbia University. Previously, she was Ralph Lewis Professor of Sociology at the University of Chicago. She was born in Holland, brought up in Argentina, and today studies the globalizing world. The selection is from one of Sassen's most widely read books, *Globalization and Its Discontents* (1999). She is also the author of *Guests and Aliens* (1999), *The Global City* (2001, revised), *Denationalization: Economy and Polity in a Global Digital Age* (2003), and other books. She is, amid much else, chair of the Information Technology, International Cooperation and Global Security Committee of the Social Science Research Council.

Toward a Feminist Analytics of the Global Economy[*]
Saskia Sassen (1999)

The current phase of the world economy is characterized by significant discontinuities with the preceding periods and radically new arrangements. This becomes particularly evident when one examines the impact of globalization on the territorial organization of economic activity and on the organization of political power. Economic globalization has reconfigured fundamental properties of the nation–state, notably exclusive territoriality and sovereignty. There is an incipient unbundling of the exclusive territoriality we have long associated with the nation–state. The most strategic instantiation of

[*] Sassen, Saskia. *Globalization and Its Discontents*. New York: The New Press, 1998. Print. © 1998. Reprinted with permission of the author.

this unbundling is the global city, which operates as a partly denationalized platform for global capital. At a lower order of complexity, the transnational corporation and global finance markets can also be seen as having this effect through their cross-border activities and the new legal regimes that frame these activities. Sovereignty is also being unbundled by these economic practices, noneconomic practices, and new legal regimes. At the limit this means the state is no longer the only site of sovereignty and the normativity that accompanies it. Further, the state is no longer the exclusive subject for international law. Other actors, from NGOs and first-nation people to supranational organizations, are increasingly emerging as subjects of international law and actors in international relations.

Developing a feminist analytics of today's global economy will require us to factor in these transformations if we are to go beyond merely updating the economic conditions of women and men in different countries. . . .

The purpose here is to contribute to a feminist analytics that allows us to re-read and reconceptualize major features of today's global economy in a manner that captures strategic instantiations of gendering as well as formal and operational openings that make women visible and lead to greater presence and participation. This re-reading differs markedly from mainstream accounts of the global economy. Such mainstream accounts emphasize only technical and abstract economic dynamics and proceed as if these dynamics are inevitably gender-neutral yet rarely, if ever, address this matter. . . .

Valorization and Devalorization Processes: A First Step Toward Locating Gendering

A central assumption in much of my work has been that we learn something about power through its absence and by moving through or negotiating the borders and terrains that connect powerlessness to power. Powerlessness is not a silence at the bottom; its absence is present and has consequences. The terms and language of the engagement force particular positions and preempt others.

In the day-to-day work of the leading services complex dominated by finance, a large share of the jobs involved are low pay and manual, many held by women and immigrants. Although these types of workers and jobs are never represented as part of the global economy, they are in fact part of the infrastructure of jobs involved in running and implementing the global economic system, including such an advanced form of it, as international finance. The top end of the corporate economy—the corporate towers that project engineering expertise, precision, "techne"—is far easier to mark as necessary for an advanced economic system than are truckers and other industrial service workers, even though these are necessary ingredients. We see here a dynamic of valorization that has sharply increased the distance between the devalorized and the valorized, indeed overvalorized, sectors of the economy.

Immigrant work environments in large cities, often subsumed under the notion of the ethnic economy and the informal economy are rarely recognized as possibly part of the global information economy. Much of what we still narrate in the language of immigration and ethnicity is actually a series of processes having to do with: 1) the globalization of economic activity, cultural activity, and of identity formation; and 2) the increasingly marked racialization of labormarket segmentation so that the components of the production process in the advanced global information economy that take place in immigrant work environments are components not recognized as part of that global information economy.

What we see at work here is a series of processes that valorize and overvalorize certain types of outputs, workers, firms and sectors, and devalorize others. Does the fact of gendering, for example, the devaluing of female-typed jobs, facilitate these processes of devalorization? We cannot take devalorization as a given: devalorization is a produced outcome. . . .

There is, to some extent, a joining of two different dynamics in the condition of women. On the one hand, they are constituted as an invisible and disempowered class of workers in the service of the strategic sectors constituting the global economy. This invisibility keeps them from emerging as whatever would be the contemporary equivalent of the "labor aristocracy" of earlier economic organizational forms, when workers' positions in leading sectors had the effect of empowering them—a dynamic articulating the corporate and the labor sector in a manner radically different from today's. On the other hand, the access to wages and salaries (even if low), the growing feminization of the job supply, and the growing feminization of business opportunities brought about with informalization alter the gender hierarchies in which they find themselves.

This is particularly striking in the case of immigrant women. There is a large literature showing that immigrant women's regular wage work and improved access to other public realms have an impact on their gender relations. Women gain greater personal autonomy and independence while men lose ground. Women gain more control over budgeting and other domestic decisions and greater leverage in requesting help from men in domestic chores. Also, their access to public services and other public resources gives them a chance to become incorporated in the mainstream society—they are often the ones in the household who mediate in this process. It is likely that some women benefit more than others from these circumstances; we need more research to establish the impact of class, education, and income on these gendered outcomes. . . .

The Unbundling of Sovereignty: Implications for a Feminist Analysis

Economic globalization represents a major transformation, not only in the territorial organization of economic activity, but also in the organization of political power, notably sovereignty as we have known it. Today the major dynamics at work in the global economy have the capacity to undo the intersection of sovereignty and territory embedded in the modern state and the modern inter-state system. As with the discussion earlier, the main concern in this section is to capture strategic instantiations, in this case, the transformation of political power.

Along with the unbundling of territoriality, represented in the discussion earlier by the ascendance of global cities, there is an unbundling of sovereignty. We are seeing the relocation of various components of sovereignty onto supranational, nongovernmental, or private institutions. This brings with it a potential strengthening of alternative subjects of international law and actors in international relations, for example, the growing voice of nongovernmental organizations and minorities in international fora. It also carries implications for conceptions of membership. Both can facilitate the ascendance of women, whether individuals or collectives, as subjects of international law and the formation of cross-border feminist solidarities. . . .

Why does it matter that we develop a feminist critique of sovereignty today in the context of globalization? It matters because globalization is creating new operational and formal openings for the participation of nonstate actors and subjects. Once the sovereign state is no longer viewed as the exclusive representative of its population in the international arena, women and other nonstate actors can gain more representation in international law; contribute to the making of international law; and give new meaning to older forms of international participation, such as women's long-standing work in international peace efforts. Beyond these issues of participation and representation is a question about the implications of feminist theory for alternative conceptions of sovereignty. It seems to me that at this point a feminist theory of the state would have to factor in the major transformations of the state brought about by globalization, most particularly, what I think of as the decentralization of sovereignty onto nonstate actors and the corresponding formation of other sites for normativity beyond that embedded in the nation–state.

Here I will confine myself to a brief examination of the transformation of sovereignty under the impact of globalization. This effort parallels that of the first part of this paper—to expand the analytic terrain within which we conceptualize key properties, in this case sovereignty. I see this as one step in the broader agenda of specifying a feminist analytics for understanding the global economy today. But, the major task clearly lies ahead and is collective and cross-border in character.

Two kinds of developments in this new transnational, social, and economic order matter for my discussion of sovereignty. One is the emergence of what I will call new sites of normativity, and the other, at a more operational level, is the formation of new transnational legal regimes and regulatory institutions that are either private or supranational and have taken over functions until recently located in governmental institutions. I argue that two institutional arenas have emerged as new sites for normativity alongside the more traditional normative order represented by the nation–state: the global capital market and the international human rights regime. The global capital market now concentrates sufficient power *and legitimacy* to command accountability from governments regarding their economic policies, as was illustrated by the recent crisis in Mexico. So does the international human rights regime, as is particularly evident in matters involving immigration and refugees, where courts have invoked international human rights instruments even when this overrides decisions taken by their national legislatures.

What matters for the purpose of the discussion here is that both contain a de facto transnationalizing of state policy which in turn creates practical and formal openings for the participation of nonstate actors. This represents a transformation of sovereignty as we have known and formalized it. . . .

International Human Rights and State Sovereignty

International human rights, while rooted in the founding documents of nation–states, are today a force that can undermine the exclusive authority of the state over its nationals and thereby contribute to transform the interstate system and international legal order. Membership in nation–states ceases to be the only ground for the realization of rights. All residents, whether citizens or not, can claim their human rights. Human rights begin to impinge on the principle of nation-based citizenship and the boundaries of the nation. . . .

In both Western Europe and the United States it is interesting to note that immigrants and refugees have been key claimants, and in that sense, mechanisms for the expansion of the human rights regime. Several court cases show how undocumented immigration creates legal voids which are increasingly filled by invoking human rights covenants. In many of these cases, we can see the individual or nonstate actors bringing the claims based on international human rights codes as expanding international law. The state, in this case the judiciary, "mediates between these agents and the international legal order." Courts have emerged as central institutions for a whole series of changes.

The fact that individuals and nonstate actors can make claims on states under the rule of law based on international human rights codes, signals a development that goes beyond the expansion of human rights within the framework of nation–states. It can redefine notions of nationality and membership. Under human rights regimes states must increasingly take account of *persons qua persons*, rather than *qua* citizens. The individual is now an object of law and a site for rights regardless of whether a citizen or an alien, a man or a woman where there are gendered legal regimes.

The as yet small but growing ability of nongovernmental organizations and individuals to make claims on the basis of international human rights instruments has implications beyond the boundaries of individual states. It affects the configuration of the international order and strengthens the international civil arena. The concept of nationality is being partly displaced from a principle that reinforces state sovereignty and self-determination (through the state's right/power to define its nationals), to a concept which emphasizes that the state is accountable to all its residents on the basis of international human rights law. The individual emerges as an object of international law and institutions. International law still protects state sovereignty and has in the state its main subject; but it is no longer the case that the state is the only such subject. . . .

There is a larger theoretico-political question underlying some of these issues that has to do with which actors gain the legitimacy for governance of the global economy and the legitimacy to take over rules and authorities hitherto encased in the nation-state. It also raises a question about the condition of international public law. Do the new systems for governance that are emerging, and the confinement of the role of nation–states in the global economy to furthering deregulations, markets, and privatization, indicate a decline of international public law?

The ascendance of an international human rights regime and of a large variety of nonstate actors in the international arena signals the expansion of an international civil society. This is clearly a contested space, particularly when we consider the logic of the capital market—profitability at all costs—against that of the human rights regime. But it does represent a space where women can gain visibility as individuals and as collective actors, and come out of the invisibility of aggregate membership in a nation-state exclusively represented by the sovereign. The practices and claims enacted by nonstate actors in this international space may well contribute to creating international law, as is most clearly the case with both the international human rights regime and the demands for rights made by firms and markets with global operations. For women, this means at least partly working outside the state, through nonstate groups and networks. The needs and agendas of women are not necessarily defined exclusively by state borders. We are seeing the formation of cross-border solidarities and notions of membership rooted in gender, sexuality, and feminism, as well as in questions of class and country status, i.e., First versus Third World, which cut across all of these membership notions.

Amartya Sen (1933–) was born in Santinkiketan, West Bengal , to a family with roots in Dhaka, now the capital of Bangladesh. As a child, Sen witnessed the human miseries wrought by the 1943 famine in Bengal in which some two million people lost their lives. The experience so profoundly affected him as to shape his future as an economist and social philosopher known for arguing with great persuasiveness the liberating power of economic development for the world's poor. Sen studied at Presidency College in Calcutta before attending Trinity College in Cambridge. Over the years since, he has taught at Presidency, Trinity, Delhi University, the London School of Economics, Oxford, MIT, and Harvard. Sen was awarded the 1988 Nobel Prize in Economics. His books include *On Economic Inequality* (1973), *Poverty and Famines: An Essay on Entitlement and Depression* (1981), *On Ethics and Economics* (1987), and *Rationality and Freedom* (2003). The selection is from Sen's *Development as Freedom* (1999).

Asian Values and the West's Claims to Uniqueness*
Amartya Sen (1999)

The nature of Asian values has often been invoked in recent years to provide justification for authoritarian political arrangements in Asia. These justifications of authoritarianism have typically come not from independent historians but from the authorities themselves (such as governmental officers or their spokesmen) or those close to people in power, but their views are obviously consequential in governing the states and also in influencing the relation between different countries.

Are Asian values opposed—or indifferent—to basic political rights? Such generalizations are often made, but are they well grounded? In fact, generalizations about Asia are not easy, given its size. Asia is

where about 60 percent of the total world population live. What can we take to be the values of so vast a region, with such diversity? There are no quintessential values that apply to this immensely large and heterogeneous population, none that separate them out as a group from people in the rest of the world.

Sometimes the advocates of "Asian values" have tended to look primarily at East Asia as the region of particular applicability. The generalization about the contrast between the West and Asia often concentrates on the land to the east of Thailand, even though there is a more ambitious claim that the rest of Asia is also rather "similar." For example, Lee Kuan Yew outlines "the fundamental difference between Western concepts of society and government and East Asian concepts" by explaining, "when I say East Asians, I mean Korea, Japan, China, Vietnam, as distinct from Southeast Asia, which is a mix between the Sinic and the Indian, though Indian culture itself emphasizes similar values."

In fact, however, even East Asia itself has much diversity, and there are many variations to be found among Japan and China and Korea and other parts of East Asia. Various cultural influences from within and outside the region have affected human lives over the history of this rather large territory. These influences still survive in a variety of ways. To illustrate, my copy of Houghton Mifflin's international *Almanac* describes the religion of the 124 million Japanese in the following way: 112 million Shintoist and 93 million Buddhist. Different cultural influences still color aspects of the identity of the contemporary Japanese, and the same person can be *both* Shintoist and Buddhist.

Cultures and traditions overlap over regions such as East Asia and even within countries such as Japan or China or Korea, and attempts at generalization about "Asian values" (with forceful—and often brutal—implications for masses of people in this region with diverse faiths, convictions and commitments) cannot but be extremely crude. Even the 2.8 million people of Singapore have vast variations of cultural and historical traditions. Indeed, Singapore has an admirable record in fostering intercommunity amity and friendly coexistence.

The Contemporary West and Claims to Uniqueness

Authoritarian lines of reasoning in Asia—and more generally in non-Western societies—often receive indirect backing from modes of thought in the West itself. There is clearly a tendency in America and Europe to assume, if only implicitly, the primacy of political freedom and democracy as a fundamental and ancient feature of Western culture—one not to be easily found in Asia. It is, as it were, a contrast between the authoritarianism allegedly implicit in, say, Confucianism vis-à-vis the respect for individual liberty and autonomy allegedly deeply rooted in Western liberal culture. Western promoters of personal and political liberty in the non-Western world often see this as bringing Occidental values to Asia and Africa. The world is invited to join the club of "Western democracy" and to admire and endorse traditional "Western values."

In all this, there is a substantial tendency to extrapolate *backward* from the present. Values that European Enlightenment and other relatively recent developments have made common and widespread cannot really be seen as part of the long-run Western heritage—experienced in the West over millennia. What we do find in the writings by particular Western classical authors (for example, Aristotle) is support for selected *components* of the comprehensive notion that makes up the contemporary idea of political liberty. But support for such components can be found in many writings in Asian traditions as well.

To illustrate this point, consider the idea that personal freedom for all is important for a good society. This claim can be seen as being composed of two distinct components, to wit, (1) *the value of personal freedom*: that personal freedom is important and should be guaranteed for those who "matter" in a good society, and (2) *equality of freedom*: everyone matters and the freedom that is guaranteed for one must be guaranteed for all. The two together entail that personal freedom should be guaranteed, on a shared basis, for all. Aristotle wrote much in support of the former proposition, but in his exclusion of women and slaves did little to defend the latter. Indeed, the championing of equality in this form is of quite recent origin. Even in a society stratified according to class and caste, freedom could be seen to be of great value for the privileged few (such as the Mandarins or the Brahmins), in much the same way freedom is valued for nonslave men in corresponding Greek conceptions of a good society.

Another useful distinction is between (1) *the value of toleration*: that there must be toleration of diverse beliefs, commitments, and actions of different people; and (2) *equality of tolerance*: the toleration that is offered to some must be reasonably offered to all (except when tolerance of some will lead to intolerance for others). Again, arguments for some tolerance can be seen plentifully in earlier Western writings, without that tolerance being supplemented by equality of tolerance. The roots of modern democratic and liberal ideas can be sought in terms of *constitutive* elements, rather than as a whole.

In doing a comparative scrutiny, the question has to be asked whether these constitutive components can be seen in Asian writings in the way they can be found in Western thought. The presence of these components must not be confused with the absence of the opposite, viz., of ideas and doctrines that clearly *do not* emphasize freedom and tolerance. Championing of order and discipline can be found in Western classics as well. Indeed, it is by no means clear to me that Confucius is more authoritarian in this respect than, say, Plato or St. Augustine. The real issue is not whether these non-freedom perspectives are *present* in Asian traditions, but whether the freedom-oriented perspectives are *absent* there.

This is where the diversity of Asian value systems—which incorporates but transcends regional diversity—becomes quite central. An obvious example is the role of Buddhism as a form of thought. In Buddhist tradition, great importance is attached to freedom, and the part of the earlier Indian theorizing to which Buddhist thoughts relate has much room for volition and free choice. Nobility of conduct has to be achieved in freedom, and even the ideas of liberation (such as *moksha*) have this feature. The presence of these elements in Buddhist thought does not obliterate the importance for Asia of ordered discipline emphasized by Confucianism, but it would be a mistake to take Confucianism to be the only tradition in Asia—indeed even in China. Since so much of the contemporary authoritarian interpretation of Asian values concentrates on Confucianism, this diversity is particularly worth emphasizing.

Interpretations of Confucius

Indeed, the reading of Confucianism that is now standard among authoritarian champions of Asian values does less than justice to the variety within Confucius's own teachings. Confucius did not recommend blind allegiance to the state. When Zilu asks him "how to serve a prince," Confucius replies,

"Tell him the truth even if it offends him." Those in charge of censorship in Singapore or Beijing might take a very different view. Confucius is not averse to practical caution and tact, but does not forgo the recommendation to oppose a bad government. "When the [good] way prevails in the state, speak boldly and act boldly. When the state has lost the way, act boldly and speak softly."

Indeed, Confucius provides a clear pointer to the fact that the two pillars of the imagined edifice of Asian values, namely loyalty to family and obedience to the state, can be in severe conflict with each other. Many advocates of the power of "Asian values" see the role of the state as an extension of the role of the family, but as Confucius noted, there can be tension between the two. The Governor of She told Confucius, "Among my people, there is a man of unbending integrity: when his father stole a sheep, he denounced him." To this Confucius replied, "Among my people, men of integrity do things differently: a father covers up for his son, a son covers up for his father—and there is integrity in what they do."

Ashoka and Kautilya

Confucius's ideas were altogether more complex and sophisticated than the maxims that are frequently championed in his name. There is also a tendency to neglect other authors in the Chinese culture and to ignore other Asian cultures. If we turn to Indian traditions, we can, in fact, find a variety of views on freedom, tolerance, and equality. In many ways, the most interesting articulation of the need for tolerance on an egalitarian basis can be found in the writings of Emperor Ashoka, who in the third century b.c. commanded a larger Indian empire than any other Indian king (including the Mughals, and even the Raj, if we leave out the native states that the British let be). He turned his attention to public ethics and enlightened politics in a big way after being horrified by the carnage he saw in his own victorious battle against the kingdom of Kalinga (what is now Orissa). He converted to Buddhism, and not only helped to make it a world religion by sending emissaries abroad with the Buddhist message to east and west, but also covered the country with stone inscriptions describing forms of good life and the nature of good government.

The inscriptions give a special importance to tolerance of diversity. For example, the edict (now numbered XII) at Erragudi puts the issue thus:

. . . a man must not do reverence to his own sect or disparage that of another man without reason. Depreciation should be for specific reason only, because the sects of other people all deserve reverence for one reason or another.

By thus acting, a man exalts his own sect, and at the same time does service to the sects of other people. By acting contrariwise, a man hurts his own sect, and does disservice to the sects of other people. For he who does reverence to his own sect while disparaging the sects of others wholly from attachment to his own, with intent to enhance the splendour of his own sect, in reality by such conduct inflicts the severest injury on his own sect.

The importance of tolerance is emphasized in these edicts from the third century b.c., both for public policy by the government and as advice for behavior of citizens to one another.

On the domain and coverage of tolerance, Ashoka was a universalist, and demanded this for all, including those whom he described as "forest people," the tribal population living in preagricultural economic formations. Ashoka's championing of egalitarian and universal tolerance may appear un-Asian to some commentators, but his views are firmly rooted in lines of analysis already in vogue in intellectual circles in India in the preceding centuries. . . .

Islamic Tolerance

Because of the experience of contemporary political battles, especially in the Middle East, Islamic civilization is often portrayed as being fundamentally intolerant and hostile to individual freedom. But the presence of diversity and variety *within* a tradition applies very much to Islam as well. In India, Akbar and most of the other Moghuls provide good examples of both theory and practice of political and religious tolerance. Similar examples can be found in other parts of the Islamic culture. The Turkish emperors were often more tolerant than their European contemporaries. Abundant examples of this can be found also in Cairo and Baghdad. Indeed, even the great Jewish scholar Maimonides, in the twelfth century, had to run away from an intolerant Europe (where he was born) and from its persecution of Jews, to the security of a tolerant and urbane Cairo and the patronage of Sultan Saladin.

Similarly, Alberuni, the Iranian mathematician, who wrote the first general book on India in the early eleventh century (aside from translating Indian mathematical treatises into Arabic), was among the earliest of anthropological theorists in the world. He noted—and protested against—the fact that "depreciation of foreigners . . . is common to all nations towards each other." He devoted much of his life to fostering mutual understanding and tolerance in his eleventh-century world.

It is easy to multiply examples. The point to be seized is that the modern advocates of the authoritarian view of "Asian values" base their reading on very arbitrary interpretations and extremely narrow selections of authors and traditions. The valuing of freedom is not confined to one culture only, and the Western traditions are not the only ones that prepare us for a freedom-based approach to social understanding.

Globalization: Economics, Culture and Rights

The issue of democracy also has a close bearing on another cultural matter that has received some justified attention recently. This concerns the overwhelming power of Western culture and lifestyle in undermining traditional modes of living and social mores. For anyone concerned about the value of tradition and of indigenous cultural modes this is indeed a serious threat.

The contemporary world is dominated by the West, and even though the imperial authority of the erstwhile rulers of the world has declined, the dominance of the West remains as strong as ever—in some ways stronger than before, especially in cultural matters. The sun does not set on the empire of Coca-Cola or MTV.

The threat to native cultures in the globalizing world of today is, to a considerable extent, inescapable. The one solution that is not available is that of stopping globalization of trade and economies, since the forces of economic exchange and division of labor are hard to resist in a competitive world fueled by massive technological evolution that gives modern technology an economically competitive edge.

This is a problem, but not just a problem, since global trade and commerce can bring with it—as Adam Smith foresaw—greater economic prosperity for each nation. But there can be losers as well as gainers, even if in the net the aggregate figures move up rather than down. In the context of economic disparities, the appropriate response has to include concerted efforts to make the form of globalization less destructive of employment and traditional livelihood, and to achieve gradual transition. For smoothing the process of transition, there also have to be opportunities for retraining and acquiring of new skills (for people who would otherwise be displaced), in addition to providing social safety nets (in the form of social security and other supportive arrangements) for those whose interests are harmed—at least in the short run—by the globalizing changes.

This class of responses will to some extent work for the cultural side as well. Skill in computer use and the harvesting of Internet and similar facilities transform not only economic possibilities, but also the lives of the people influenced by such technical change. Again, this is not necessarily regrettable. There remain, however, two problems—one shared with the world of economics and another quite different.

First, the world of modern communication and interchange requires basic education and training. While some poor countries in the world have made excellent progress in this area (countries in East Asia and Southeast Asia are good examples of that), others (such as those in South Asia and Africa) have tended to lag behind. Equity in cultural as well as economic opportunities can be profoundly important in a globalizing world. This is a shared challenge for the economic and the cultural world.

The second issue is quite different and distances the cultural problem from the economic predicament. When an economic adjustment takes place, few tears are shed for the superseded methods of production and for the overtaken technology. There may be some nostalgia for specialized and elegant objects (such as an ancient steam engine or an old-fashioned clock), but in general old and discarded machinery is not particularly wanted. In the case of culture, however, lost traditions may be greatly missed. The demise of old ways of living can cause anguish, and a deep sense of loss. It is a little like the extinction of older species of animals. The elimination of old species in favor of "fitter" species that are "better" able to cope and multiply can be a source of regret, and the fact that the new species are "better" in the Darwinian system of comparison need not be seen as consolation enough.

This is an issue of some seriousness, but it is up to the society to determine what, if anything, it wants to do to preserve old forms of living, perhaps even at significant economic cost. Ways of life can be preserved if the society decides to do just that, and it is a question of balancing the costs of such preservation with the value that the society attaches to the objects and the lifestyles preserved. There is, of course, no ready formula for this cost-benefit analysis, but what is crucial for a rational assessment of such choices is the ability of the people to participate in public discussions on the subject. We come back again to the perspective of capabilities: that different sections of the society (and not just the socially privileged) should be able to be active in the decisions regarding what to preserve and what to let go. There is no compulsion to preserve every departing lifestyle even at heavy cost, but there is a real need—for social justice—for people to be able to take part in these social decisions, if they so choose. This gives further reason for attaching importance to such elementary capabilities as reading and writing (through basic education), being well informed and well briefed (through free media), and having realistic chances of participating freely (through elections, referendums and the general use of civil rights). Human rights in the broadest sense are involved in this exercise as well. . . .

As it happens, the view that Asian values are quintessentially authoritarian has tended to come, in Asia, almost exclusively from spokesmen of those in power (sometimes supplemented—and reinforced—by Western statements demanding that people endorse what are seen as specifically "Western liberal values"). But foreign ministers, or government officials, or religious leaders, do not have a monopoly in interpreting local culture and values. It is important to listen to the voices of dissent in each society. Aung San Sun Kyi has no less legitimacy—indeed clearly has rather more—in interpreting what the Burmese want than have the military rulers of Myanmar, whose candidates she had defeated in open elections before being put in jail by the defeated military junta.

The recognition of diversity within different cultures is extremely important in the contemporary world. Our understanding of the presence of diversity tends to be somewhat undermined by constant bombardment with oversimple generalizations about "Western civilization," "Asian values," "African cultures" and so on. Many of these readings of history and civilization are not only intellectually shallow, they also add to the divisiveness of the world in which we live. The fact is that in any culture, people seem to like to argue with one another, and frequently do exactly that—given the chance. The presence of dissidents makes it problematic to take an unambiguous view of the "true nature" of local values. In fact, dissidents tend to exist in every society—often quite plentifully—and they are frequently willing to take very great risks regarding their own security. Indeed, had the dissidents not been so tenaciously present, authoritarian polities would not have had to undertake such repressive measures in practice, to supplement their intolerant beliefs. The presence of dissidents *tempts* the authoritarian ruling groups to take a repressive view of local culture and, at the same time, that presence itself *undermines* the intellectual basis of such univocal interpretation of local beliefs as homogenous thought.

Western discussion of non-Western societies is often too respectful of authority—the governor, the minister, the military junta, the religious leader. This "authoritarian bias" receives support from the fact that Western countries themselves are often represented, in international gatherings, by governmental officials and spokesmen, and they in turn seek the views of their opposite numbers from other countries. An adequate approach of development cannot really be so centered only on those in power. The reach has to be broader, and the need for popular participation is not just sanctimonious rubbish. Indeed, the idea of development cannot be dissociated from it.

As far as the authoritarian claims about "Asian values" are concerned, it has to be recognized that values that have been championed in the past of Asian countries—in East Asia as well as elsewhere in Asia—include an enormous variety. Indeed, in many ways they are similar to substantial variations that are often seen in the history of ideas in the West also. To see Asian history in terms of a narrow category of authoritarian values does little justice to the rich varieties of thought in Asian intellectual traditions. Dubious history does nothing to vindicate dubious politics.

Ulrich Beck (1944–) was born in Stolp, Germany (now Stupsk in Poland). He studied at Munich University from which he finished his doctorate in 1972. Today Beck is professor at the University of Munich and the British Journal of Sociology Professor at the London School of Economics. His 1992 book, *Risk*

Society, quickly became one of the most widely read and discussed books among social scientists in Europe. The influence of Beck's ideas led subsequently to a Distinguished Research Professorship at the University of Cardiff, an honorary degree from the University of Jyvaskyla in Finland, and membership on the Future Commission of the German Government. The affinities among his ideas to those of the British social theorists of reflexive modernity (most notably Anthony Giddens) are witness not only to the emerging unity of European social thought, but also to its independence from the once dominant influence of American sociology. Beck's books include *Reflexive Modernization* (with Anthony Giddens and Scott Lash; 1994), *Ecological Politics in an Age of Risk* (1995), and *Brave New World of Work* (2000). This selection is from Beck's *World Risk Society* (1999),

World Risk Society*
Ulrich Beck (1999)

All around the world, contemporary society is undergoing radical change that poses a challenge to Enlightenment-based modernity and opens a field where people *choose* new and unexpected forms of the social and the political. Sociological debates of the nineties have sought to grasp and conceptualize this reconfiguration. Some authors lay great stress on the openness of the human project amid new contingencies, complexities and uncertainties, whether their main operative term is "postmodernity" (Bauman, Lyotard, Harvey, Haraway), "late modernity" (Giddens), the "global age" (Albrow) or "reflexive modernization" (Beck, Giddens, Lash). Others have prioritized research into new forms of experimental identity (Melucci) and sociality (Maffesoli), the relationship between individualization and political culture (Touraine), the "post-national constellation" (Habermas) or the preconditions of "cosmopolitan democracy" (Held). Others still have contributed a wave of books on the "politics of nature" (Vandana Shiva, Gernot Bohme, Maarten Hajer, John S. Dryzek, Tim Hayward, Andrew Dobson, Barbara Adam, Robin Grove-White and Brian Wynne). All agree that in the decades ahead we will confront profound contradictions and perplexing paradoxes; and experience hope embedded in despair.

In an attempt to summarize and systematize these transformations, I have for some time been working with a distinction between first modernity and second modernity. The former term I use to describe the modernity based on nation–state societies, where social relations, networks and communities are essentially understood in a territorial sense. The collective patterns of life, progress and controllability, full employment and exploitation of nature that were typical of this first modernity have now been undermined by five interlinked processes: globalization, individualization, gender revolution, underemployment and global risks (as ecological crisis and the crash of global financial markets). The real theoretical and political challenge of the second modernity is the fact that society must respond to all these challenges *simultaneously*.

If the five processes are considered more closely, it becomes clear what they have in common: namely, they are all unforeseen consequences of the victory of the first, simple, linear, industrial modernization based on the national state (the focus of classical sociology from Durkheim, Weber and Marx to Parsons and Luhmann). This is what I mean by talking of "reflexive modernization". Radicalized modernization undermines the foundations of the first modernity and changes its frame of reference, often in a way that is neither desired nor anticipated. Or, in the terms of system theory: the unforeseen consequences of functional differentiation can no longer be controlled by further functional differentiation. In fact, the very idea of controllability, certainty or security—which is so fundamental in the first modernity—collapses. A new kind of capitalism, a new kind of economy, a new kind of global order, a new kind of society and a new kind of personal life are coming into being, all of which differ from earlier phases of social development. Thus, sociologically and politically, we need a paradigm-shift, a new frame of reference. This is not "postmodernity" but a second modernity, and the task that faces us is to reform sociology so that it can provide a new framework for the reinvention of society and politics. Research work on reflexive modernization does not deal only with the *decline* of the Western model. The key question is how that model relates to the *different modernities* in other parts of the world. Which new and unexpected forms of the social are emerging? Which new social and political forces, and which lines of conflict, are appearing on the horizon?

In world risk society, non-Western societies share with the West not only the same space and time but also—more importantly—the same basic challenges of the second modernity (in different places and with different cultural perceptions). To stress this aspect of sameness—and not otherness—is already an important step in revising the evolutionary bias that afflicts much of Western social science to this day, a bias whereby contemporary non-Western societies are relegated to the category of "traditional" or "pre-modern" and thus defined not in their own terms, but as the opposite or the absence of modernity. (Many even believe that the study of pre-modern Western societies can help us understand the characteristics of non-Western societies today!) To situate the non-Western world firmly within the ambit of a second modernity, rather than of tradition, allows a *pluralization of modernity,* for it opens up space for the conceptualization of divergent trajectories of modernities in different parts of the world. This idea of multiple modernities recalls Nehru's image of a "garb of modernity" that can be worn in a number of ingeniously different ways.

The increasing speed, intensity and significance of processes of transnational interdependence, and the growth in discourses of economic, cultural, political and societal "globalization," suggest not only that non-Western societies should be included in any analysis of the challenges of the second modernity, but also that the specific refractions and reflections of the global need to be examined in these different sites of the emerging global society. . . .

As the bipolar world fades away, we are moving from a world of enemies to one of dangers and risks. But what does "risk" mean? Risk is the modern approach to foresee and control the future consequences of human action, the various unintended consequences of radicalized modernization. It is an (institutionalized) attempt, a cognitive map, to colonize the future. Every society has, of course, experienced dangers. But the risk regime is a function of a new order: it is not national, but global. It is rather intimately connected with an administrative and technical decision-making process. Risks presuppose decision. These decisions were previously undertaken with fixed norms of calculability, connecting means and ends or causes and effects. These norms are precisely what "world risk society" has rendered invalid. All of this becomes very evident with private insurance, perhaps the greatest symbol of calculation and alternative security—which does not cover nuclear disaster, nor climate change and its consequences, nor the breakdown of Asian economies, nor the low-probability high consequences risk of various forms of future technology. In fact, most controversial technologies, like genetic engineering, are not privately insured. . . .

In world risk society the politics and subpolitics of risk definition become extremely important. Risks have become a major force of political mobilization, often replacing references to, for example, inequalities associated with class, race and gender. This highlights the new *power game* of risk and its meta-norms: who is to define the riskiness of a product, a technology, and on what grounds in an age of manufactured uncertainties? When, in 1998, the Greens entered Gerhard Schroder's government in Germany, they began to act upon and change some of those power relations of risk definition by, for example, a strategy of pluralization of experts, calling counter-experts into governmental commissions for security who had previously been excluded; or by raising the level of acceptable insurance; or by enforcing legal norms which so far have not really been taken seriously; and so on. This, within the common framework, looks of minor, negligible importance. But this is exactly the point: in risk society seemingly unimportant areas of political intervention and action are becoming extremely important and seemingly "minor" changes do induce basic long-term transformations in the power game of risk politics.

Thus the framework of risk society again connects what have been strictly discrete areas: the question of nature, the democratization of democracy and the future role of the state. Much political debate over the last twenty years has centred on the decline in the power and legitimacy of government and the need to renew the culture of democracy. Risk society demands an opening up of the decision-making process, not only of the state but of private corporations and the sciences as well. It calls for institutional reform of those "relations of definition," the hidden power-structure of risk conflicts. This could encourage environmental innovations and help to construct a better developed public sphere in which the crucial questions of value that underpin risk conflicts can be debated and judged.

But at the same time new prominence of risk connects, on the one hand, individual autonomy and insecurity in the labour market and in gender relations, and, on the other hand, the sweeping influence of scientific and technological change. World risk society opens public discourse and social science to the challenges of ecological crisis, which, as we now know, are global, local and personal at one and the same time. Nor is this all. In the "global age," the theme of risk unites many otherwise disparate areas of new transnational politics with the question of cosmopolitan democracy: with the new political economy of uncertainty, financial markets, transcultural conflicts over food and other products (BSE), emerging "risk communities," and, last but not least, the anarchy of international relations. Personal biographies as well as world politics are getting "risky" in the global world of manufactured uncertainties.

But the globality of risk does not, of course, mean a global equality of risk. The opposite is true: the first law of environmental risks is: *pollution follows the poor.* In the last decade poverty has intensified everywhere. The UN says more than 2,400 million people now live without sanitation, a considerable increase on a decade ago; 1,200 million have no safe drinking water; similar numbers have inadequate housing, health and education services; more than 1,500 million are now undernourished, not because there is no food, or there is too much drought, but because of the increasing marginalization and exclusion of the poor.

Not only has the gap between rich and poor grown, but more people are falling into the poverty trap. Free-market economic policies, imposed on indebted countries by the West, worsen the situation by forcing countries to develop expert industry to supply the rich, rather than to protect, educate or care for the weakest. The poorest countries now spend more servicing their debt to the richest countries than they do on health and education in their own countries.

The past decade has shown that the dogmatic free-market economics imposed throughout the 1980s—and to which every world and nation forum has since signed up—has exacerbated environmental risks and problems just as much as central planning from Moscow ever did. Indeed free-market ideology has increased the sum of human misery. On the back of crucial free-trade pacts like the WTO and NAFTA, for example, consumption is now virtually out of control in the richest countries. It has multiplied six times in less than twenty-five years, according to the UN. The richest 20 percent of the people are consuming roughly six times more food, energy, water, transportation, oil and minerals than their parents were.

Risk and *responsibility* are intrinsically connected, as are risk and *trust*, risk and *security* (insurance and safety). To whom can responsibility (and therefore costs) be attributed? Or do we live in a context of "organized irresponsibility"? This is one of the major issues in most of the political conflicts of our time. Some believe that risk induces control, so that the greater the risk the greater the need for controllabil-

ity. The concept of "world risk society," however, draws attention to the *limited* controllability of the dangers we have created for ourselves. The main question is how to take decisions under conditions of manufactured uncertainty, where not only is the knowledgebase incomplete, but more and better knowledge often means more uncertainty. . . .

We live in an age of risk that is global, individualistic and more moral than we suppose. The ethic of individual self-fulfilment and achievement is the most powerful current in modern Western society. Choosing, deciding, shaping individuals who aspire to be the authors of their lives, the creators of their identities, are the central characters of our time.

This "me-first" generation has been much criticized, but I believe its individualism is moral and political in a new sense. In many ways this is a more moral time than the 1950s and 1960s. Freedom's children feel more passionately and morally than people used to do about a wide range of issues—from our treatment of the environment and animals, to gender, race and human rights around the world.

It could be that this provides the basis for a new cosmopolitanism, by placing globality at the heart of political imagination, action and organization. But any attempt to create a new sense of social cohesion has to start from the recognition that individualization, diversity and scepticism are written into our culture.

Let us be clear what "individualization" means. It does *not* mean individualism. It does *not* mean individuation—how to become a unique person. It is *not* Thatcherism, not market individualism, not atomization. On the contrary, individualization is a *structural* concept, related to the welfare state; it means "*institutionalized* individualism." Most of the rights and entitlements of the welfare state, for example, are designed for individuals rather than for families. In many cases they presuppose employment. Employment in turn implies education, and both of these presuppose mobility. By all these requirements people are invited to constitute themselves as individuals: to plan, understand, design themselves as individuals and, should they fail, to blame themselves. Individualization thus implies, paradoxically, a collective lifestyle.

When this is coupled with the language of ethical globalization, I am convinced that a cosmopolitan democracy is a realistic, if utopian, project—though in an age of side-effects, we must also reflect on the dark side, on the ways it can be used politically as a front for oldstyle imperial adventures.

Are we a "me-first" society? One might think so from the catchphrases that dominate public debate: the dissolving of solidarity, the decline of values, the culture of narcissism, entitlement-oriented hedonism, and so on. On this view, modern society lives off moral resources it is unable to renew; the transcendental "value ecology," in which community, solidarity, justice and ultimately democracy are "rooted," is decaying; modernity is undermining its own indispensable moral prerequisites.

Achille Mbembe (1957–) was born in French Cameroon. He studied in France, achieving a PhD in History from the Sorbonne in 1989. He has taught or lectured throughout Africa and in the United States as well as Europe and has held faculty positions at Columbia, Pennsylvania, Berkeley, and Yale. He is currently professor at the Wits Institute for Social and Economic Research at the University of Witwatersrand, South Africa. The selection is from his 2003 essay, "Necropolitics," which upon publication immediately became a source of debate world-wide for its clearly stated, but philosophically grounded, idea that in the modern world as it is politics are above all the politics of death.

Necropower and the Late Modern Colonial Occupation[*]
Achille Mbembe (2003)

It might be thought that the ideas developed above relate to a distant past. In the past, indeed, imperial wars did have the objective of destroying local powers, installing troops, and instituting new models of military control over civil populations. A group of local auxiliaries could assist in the management of conquered territories annexed to the empire. Within the empire, the vanquished populations were given a status that enshrined their despoilment. In these configurations, violence constituted the original form of the right, and exception provided the structure of sovereignty. Each stage of imperialism also involved certain key technologies (the gunboat, quinine, steamship lines, submarine telegraph cables, and colonial railroads).

Colonial occupation itself was a matter of seizing, delimiting, and asserting control over a physical geographical area — of writing on the ground a new set of social and spatial relations. The writing of new spatial relations (territorialization) was, ultimately, tantamount to the production of boundaries and hierarchies, zones and enclaves; the subversion of existing property arrangements; the classification of people according to different categories; resource extraction; and, finally, the manufacturing of a large reservoir of cultural imaginaries. These imaginaries gave meaning to the enactment of differential rights to differing categories of people for different purposes within the same space; in brief, the exercise of sovereignty. Space was therefore the raw material of sovereignty and the violence it carried with it. Sovereignty meant occupation, and occupation meant relegating the colonized into a third zone between subjecthood and objecthood.

Such was the case of the apartheid regime in South Africa. Here, the *township* was the structural form and the *homelands* became the reserves (rural bases) whereby the flow of migrant labor could be regulated and African urbanization held in check. As Belinda Bozzoli has shown, the township in particular was a place where "severe oppression and poverty were experienced on a racial and class basis." A sociopolitical, cultural, and economic formation, the township was a peculiar spatial institution scientifically planned for the purposes of control. The functioning of the homelands and townships entailed severe restrictions on production for the market by blacks in white areas, the terminating of land ownership by blacks except in reserved areas, the illegalization of black residence on white farms (except as servants in the employ of whites), the control of urban influx, and later, the denial of citizenship to Africans.

Frantz Fanon describes the spatialization of colonial occupation in vivid terms. For him, colonial occupation entails first and foremost a division of space into compartments. It involves the setting of boundaries and internal frontiers epitomized by barracks and police stations; it is regulated by the language of pure force, immediate presence, and frequent and direct action; and it is premised on the principle of reciprocal exclusivity. But more important, it is the very way in which necropower operates: "The town belonging to the colonized people ... is a place of ill fame, peopled by men of evil repute. They are born there, it matters little where or how; they die there, it matters not where, nor how. It is a world without spaciousness; men live there on top of each other. The native town is a hungry town, starved of bread, of meat, of shoes, of coal, of light. The native town is a crouching village, a town on its knees." In this case, sovereignty means the capacity to define who matters and who does not, who is *disposable* and who is not.

Late-modern colonial occupation differs in many ways from early-modern occupation, particularly in its combining of the disciplinary, the biopolitical, and the necropolitical. The most accomplished form of necropower is the contemporary colonial occupation of Palestine.

Here, the colonial state derives its fundamental claim of sovereignty and legitimacy from the authority of its own particular narrative of history and identity. This narrative is itself underpinned by the idea that the state has a divine right to exist; the narrative competes with another for the same sacred space. Because the two narratives are incompatible and the two populations are inextricably intertwined, any demarcation of the territory on the basis of pure identity is quasi-impossible. Violence and sovereignty, in this case, claim a divine foundation: peoplehood itself is forged by the worship of one deity, and national identity is imagined as an identity against the Other, other deities. History, geography, cartography, and archaeology are supposed to back these claims, thereby closely binding identity and topography. As a consequence, colonial violence and occupation are profoundly underwritten by the sacred terror of truth and exclusivity (mass expulsions, resettlement of "stateless" people in refugee camps, settlement of new colonies). Lying beneath the terror of the sacred is the constant excavation of missing bones; the permanent remembrance of a torn body hewn in a thousand pieces and never self-same; the limits, or better, the impossibility of representing for oneself an "original crime," an unspeakable death: the terror of the Holocaust.

To return to Fanon's spatial reading of colonial occupation, the late-modern colonial occupation in Gaza and the West Bank presents three major characteristics in relation to the working of the specific terror formation I have called necropower. First is the dynamics of territorial fragmentation, the sealing off and expansion of settlements. The objective of this process is twofold: to render any movement impossible and to implement separation along the model of the apartheid state. The occupied territories are therefore divided into a web of intricate internal borders and various isolated cells. According to Eyal Weizman,

by departing from a planar division of a territory and embracing a principle of creation of three-dimensional boundaries across sovereign bulks, this dispersal and segmentation clearly redefines the relationship between sovereignty and space.

For Weizman, these actions constitute "the politics of verticality." The resultant form of sovereignty might be called "vertical sovereignty." Under a regime of vertical sovereignty, colonial occupation operates through schemes of over- and underpasses, a separation of the airspace from the ground. The ground itself is divided between its crust and the subterrain. Colonial occupation is also dictated by the very nature of the terrain and its topographical variations (hilltops and valleys, mountains and bodies of water). Thus, high ground offers strategic assets not found in the valleys (effectiveness of sight, self-protection, panoptic fortification that generates gazes to many different ends). Says Weizman: "Settlements could be seen as urban optical devices for surveillance and the exercise of power." Under conditions of late-modern colonial occupation, surveillance is both inward- and outward-oriented, the eye acting as weapon and vice versa. Instead of the conclusive division between two nations across a boundary line, "the organization of the West Bank's particular terrain has created multiple separations, provisional boundaries, which relate to each other through surveillance and control," according to Weizman. Under these circumstances, colonial occupation is not only akin to control, surveillance, and separation, it is also tantamount to seclusion. It is a *splintering occupation*, along the lines of the splintering urbanism characteristic of late modernity (suburban enclaves or gated communities).

From an infrastructural point of view, a splintering form of colonial occupation is characterized by a network of fast bypass roads, bridges, and tunnels that weave over and under one another in an attempt at maintaining the Fanonian "principle of reciprocal exclusivity." According to Weizman, "the bypass roads attempt to separate Israeli traffic networks from Palestinian ones, preferably without allowing them ever to cross. They therefore emphasize the overlapping of two separate geographies that inhabit the same landscape. At points where the networks do cross, a makeshift separation is created. Most often, small dust roads are dug out to allow Palestinians to cross under the fast, wide highways on which Israeli vans and military vehicles rush between settlements."

Under conditions of vertical sovereignty and splintering colonial occupation, communities are separated across a y-axis. This leads to a proliferation of the sites of violence. The battlegrounds are not located solely at the surface of the earth. The underground as well as the airspace are transformed into conflict zones. There is no continuity between the ground and the sky. Even the boundaries in airspace are divided between lower and upper layers. Everywhere, the symbolics of the *top* (who is on top) is reiterated. Occupation of the skies therefore acquires a critical importance, since most of the policing is done from the air. Various other technologies are mobilized to this effect: sensors aboard unmanned air vehicles (UAVs), aerial reconnaissance jets, early warning Hawkeye planes, assault helicopters, an Earth-observation satellite, techniques of "hologrammatization." Killing becomes precisely targeted.

Such precision is combined with the tactics of medieval siege warfare adapted to the networked sprawl of urban refugee camps. An orchestrated and systematic sabotage of the enemy's societal and urban infrastructure network complements the appropriation of land, water, and airspace resources. Critical to these techniques of disabling the enemy is *bulldozing*: demolishing houses and cities; uprooting olive trees; riddling water tanks with bullets; bombing and jamming electronic communications; digging up roads; destroying electricity transformers; tearing up airport runways; disabling television and radio transmitters; smashing computers; ransacking cultural and politico-bureaucratic symbols of the proto-Palestinian state; looting medical equipment. In other words, *infrastructural warfare*. While the Apache helicopter gunship is used to police the air and to kill from overhead, the armored bulldozer (the Caterpillar D-9) is used on the ground as a weapon of war and intimidation. In contrast to early-modern colonial occupation, these two weapons establish the superiority of high-tech tools of late-modern terror.

As the Palestinian case illustrates, late-modern colonial occupation is a concatenation of multiple powers: disciplinary, biopolitical, and necropolitical. The combination of the three allocates to the colonial power an absolute domination over the inhabitants of the occupied territory. The *state of siege* is itself a military institution. It allows a modality of killing that does not distinguish between the external and the internal enemy. Entire populations are the target of the sovereign. The besieged villages and towns are sealed off and cut off from the world. Daily life is militarized. Freedom is given to local military commanders to use their discretion as to when and whom to shoot. Movement between the territorial cells requires formal permits. Local civil institutions are systematically destroyed. The besieged population is deprived of their means of income. Invisible killing is added to outright executions....

Rethinking the Past that Haunts the Future

Avery Gordon (1958–) is professor of Sociology at the University of California at Santa Barbara and visiting professor at the Centre for Research Architecture of Goldsmith's College, University of London. She is highly regarded for her brilliance as a writer, social critic, cultural theorist, radio producer, and art critic—a range of talents foreshadowed by the variety of her educational experiences: a B.A. in history from Warwick, a B.S. in foreign service and an M.A. in women's studies from Georgetown, and a Ph.D. in sociology from Boston College. Her *Ghostly Matters: Haunting and the Sociological Imagination* (1997), from which the selection is taken, is read by scholars and students in many fields, not to mention by the general public (notably by at least one group of prisoners). The reach of her work is due to Gordon's ability to uncover the hidden realities so often disguised; here the role of haunting in the long traditions of social thought as well as in the literature of the marginalized. She is co-host (with Elizabeth Robinson) of a weekly public affairs radio show originating from KCSB, Santa Barbara. Gordon's latest book is *Keeping Good Time* (2004).

Ghostly Matters*
Avery Gordon (1997)

That life is complicated may seem a banal expression of the obvious, but it is nonetheless a profound theoretical statement—perhaps the most important theoretical statement of our time. Yet despite the best intentions of sociologists and other social analysts, this theoretical statement has not been grasped in its widest significance. There are at least two dimensions to such a theoretical statement. The first is that the power relations that characterize any historically embedded society are never as transparently clear as the names we give to them imply. Power can be invisible, it can be fantastic, it can be dull and routine. It can be obvious, it can reach you by the baton of the police, it can speak the language of your thoughts and desires. It can feel like remote control, it can exhilarate like liberation, it can travel through time, and it can drown you in the present. It is dense and superficial, it can cause bodily injury, and it can harm you without seeming ever to touch you. It is systematic and it is particularistic and it is often both at the same time. It causes dreams to live and dreams to die. We can and must call it by recognizable names, but so too we need to remember that power arrives in forms that can range from blatant white

* Gordon, Avery. *Ghostly Matters: Haunting and the Sociological Imagination.* (University of Minnesota Press, 1997) pp. 3–8, 12–13, and 17. English translation and Foreword © 1997 by the University of Minnesota Press. Original French edition copyright by Les Editions de Minuit.

supremacy and state terror to "furniture without memories."

One day, the students in my undergraduate course on American culture and I made a thorough list of every possible explanation Toni Morrison gives in *The Bluest Eye* (1970) for why dreams die. These ranged from explicit externally imposed and internalized white supremacist standards of value, *the nature of white man's work*, and the dialectics of violence and hatred to *disappointment, to folding up inside*, to *being put outdoors*, to *the weather*, to *deformed feet and lost teeth*, to *nobody pays attention*, to *it's too late, to total damage, to furniture without memories*, to *the unyielding soil*, and to what Morrison sometimes just calls *the thing*, the sedimented conditions that constitute what is in place in the first place. This turns out to be not a random list at all, but a way of conceptualizing the complicated workings of race, class, and gender, the names we give to the ensemble of social relations that create inequalities, situated interpretive codes, particular kinds of subjects, and the possible and impossible themselves. Such a conceptualization asks that we constantly move within and between *furniture without memories* and Racism and Capitalism. It asks us to move analytically between that sad and sunken couch that sags in just that place where an unrememberable past and an unimaginable future force us to sit day after day and the conceptual abstractions because everything of significance happens there among the inert furniture and the monumental social architecture.

But this list also reminds us that even those who live in the most dire circumstances possess a complex and oftentimes contradictory humanity and subjectivity that is never adequately glimpsed by viewing them as victims or, on the other hand, as superhuman agents. It has always baffled me why those most interested in understanding and changing the barbaric domination that characterizes our modernity often—not always—withhold from the very people they are most concerned with the right to complex personhood. Complex personhood is the second dimension of the theoretical statement that life is complicated. Complex personhood means that all people (albeit in specific forms whose specificity is sometimes everything) remember and forget, are beset by contradiction, and recognize and misrecognize themselves and others. Complex personhood means that people suffer graciously and selfishly too, get stuck in the symptoms of their troubles, and also transform themselves. Complex personhood means that even those called "Other" are never never that.

Complex personhood means that the stories people tell about themselves, about their troubles, about their social worlds, and about their society's problems are entangled and weave between what is immediately available as a story and what their imaginations are reaching toward. Complex personhood means that people get tired and some are just plain lazy. Complex personhood means that groups of people will act together, that they will vehemently disagree with and sometimes harm each other, and that they will do both at the same time and expect the rest of us to figure it out for ourselves, intervening and withdrawing as the situation requires. Complex personhood means that even those who haunt our dominant institutions and their systems of value are haunted too by things they sometimes have names for and sometimes do not. At the very least, complex personhood is about conferring the respect on others that comes from presuming that life and people's lives are simultaneously straightforward and full of enormously subtle meaning.

That life is complicated is a theoretical statement that guides efforts to treat race, class, and gender dynamics and consciousness as more dense and delicate than those categorical terms often imply. It is a theoretical statement that might guide a critique of privately purchased rights, of various forms of blindness and sanctioned denial; that might guide an attempt to drive a wedge into lives and visions of freedom ruled by the nexus of market exchange. It is a theoretical statement that invites us to see with portentous clarity into the heart and soul of American life and culture, to track events, stories, anonymous and history-making actions to their density, to the point where we might catch a glimpse of what Patricia Williams calls the "vast networking of our society" and imagine otherwise. You could say this is a folk theoretical statement. We need to know where we live in order to imagine living elsewhere. We need to imagine living elsewhere before we can live there.

The Alchemy of Race and Rights by Patricia Williams (1991) is a book that captured my attention because, among other things, here is a woman who does not know if she is crazy or not, who sees ghosts and polar bears and has conversations with her sister about haunted houses and writes all of it down for us while she is sitting in her bathrobe with disheveled hair. Patricia Williams is a commercial lawyer and a professor of contract and property law. Her great-great grandmother was a slave, property. Her great-great grandmother's owner and the father of her children was Austin Miller, a well-known Tennessee lawyer and jurist. What is Patricia Williams looking for?

I track meticulously the dimension of meaning in my great-great-grandmother as chattel: the meaning of money; the power of consumerist world view, the deaths of those we label the unassertive and the inefficient. I try to imagine where and who she would be today. I am engaged in a long-term project of tracking his [Austin Miller's] words—through his letters and opinions—and those of his sons who were also lawyers and judges, of finding the shape described by her absence in all this.

I see her shape and his hand in the vast networking of our society, and in the evils and oversights that plague our lives and laws. The control he had over her body. The force he was in her life, in the shape of my life today. The power he exercised in the choice to breed her or not. The choice to breed slaves in his image, to choose her mate and be that mate. In his attempt to own what no man can own, the habit of his power and the absence of her choice.

I look for her shape and his hand.

I look for her shape and his hand; this is a massive project, very treacherous, very fragile. This is a project in which haunting and phantoms play a central part. This is a project where *finding the shape described by her absence* captures perfectly the paradox of tracking through time and across all those forces that which makes its mark by being there and not there at the same time. Cajoling us to reconsider (if only to get some peace), and because cajoling is in the nature of the ghost, the very distinctions between there and not there, past and present, force and shape. From force to hand to her ghostly presence in the register of history and back again, this is a particular kind of social alchemy that eludes us as often as it makes us look for it. Patricia Williams is not alone in the search for the shape of force and lost hands; there is company for the keeping. Wahneema Lubiano (1992, 1993), too, is looking for the haunting presence of the state in the cultural zones where it seemingly excuses itself. Kimberlé Crenshaw (1991) is trying to raise the specter of the ghostly violence of law's regime of objects, its objectivity. Catherine Clément has for some time been trying to *"remember today"* the "zone" that "somewhere every culture has . . . for what it excludes" (Cixous and

Clément 1986). Norma Alarcón (1990) is following the barely visible tracks of the Native Woman across the U.S.–Mexico border, as she shadows the making of the liberal citizen-subject. Hortense Spillers (1987a) is reconstructing the American grammatology that lost some subjects in one passage and found others in a phantasmatic family of bad mothers and absent fathers. Maxine Hong Kingston (1977) is mapping the trans-Pacific travel of ghostly ancestors and their incessant demands on the living. Gayatri Spivak (1987, 1989a, 1993) keeps vigilant watch over the dialectic of presence and absence that characterizes "our" benevolent metropolitan relationship to the subaltern women "over there." *I look for her shape and his hand.*

Ghostly Matters is about haunting, a paradigmatic way in which life is more complicated than those of us who study it have usually granted. Haunting is a constituent element of modern social life. It is neither premodern superstition nor individual psychosis; it is a generalizable social phenomenon of great import. To study social life one must confront the ghostly aspects of it. This confrontation requires (or produces) a fundamental change in the way we know and make knowledge, in our mode of production.

Ghosts are a somewhat unusual topic of inquiry for a social analyst (much less a degreed sociologist). It may seem foreign and alien, marginal to the field that conventionally counts as living social reality, the field we observe, measure, and interpret, the field that takes the measure of us as much as we take the measure of it. And foreign and alien it is, for reasons that are both obvious and stubbornly oblique. . . .

I came to write about ghostly matters not because I was interested in the occult or in parapsychology, but because ghostly things kept cropping up and messing up other tasks I was trying to accomplish. Call it grounded theory: in one field another emerged to literally capture my attention and become the field work. The persistent and troubling ghosts in the house highlighted the limitations of many of our prevalent modes of inquiry and the assumptions they make about the social world, the people who inhabit these worlds, and what is required to study them. The available critical vocabularies were failing (me) to communicate the depth, density, and intricacies of the dialectic of subjection and subjectivity (or what in my business we call structure and agency), of domination and freedom, of critique and utopian longing. Of course, it is not simply the vocabularies themselves that are at fault, but the constellation of effects, historical and institutional, that make a vocabulary a social practice of producing knowledge. A vocabulary and a practice were missing while demanding their due. Haunted and, I admit, sometimes desperate, sociology certainly—but also the human sciences at large—seemed to provide few tools for understanding how social institutions and people are haunted, for capturing enchantment in a disenchanted world.

If haunting describes how that which appears to be not there is often a seething presence, acting on and often meddling with taken-for granted realities, the ghost is just the sign, or the empirical evidence if you like, that tells you a haunting is taking place. The ghost is not simply a dead or a missing person, but a social figure, and investigating it can lead to that dense site where history and subjectivity make social life. The ghost or the apparition is one form by which something lost, or barely visible, or seemingly not there to our supposedly well-trained eyes, makes itself known or apparent to us, in its own way, of course. The way of the ghost is haunting, and haunting is a very particular way of knowing what has happened or is happening. Being haunted draws us affectively, sometimes against our will and always a bit magically, into the structure of feeling of a reality we come to experience, not as cold knowledge, but as a transformative recognition. . . .

To say that sociology or social analysis more broadly must retain a double structure of thought that links the epistemological and the social, or, in other words, to say that sociology has to respond *methodologically* and not only as if from an autonomous distance begs the question of what exactly the novel postmodern social conditions to which we ought to respond are. Difficult diagnostic issues are at stake here, exacerbated by "the effort to take the temperature of the age without instruments and in a situation in which we are not even sure there is so coherent a thing as an "age," or zeitgeist or "system" or "current situation" any longer" (Jameson 1991: xi). It is no doubt true that some of the central characteristics of the modern systems of capitalism, state and subject formation, and knowledge production are undergoing significant modifications, and many are working to describe these changes and their implications (see Bauman [1988] 1994; Haraway 1985; Harvey 1989; Jameson 1991; Lash 1990). An equally powerful argument could be made, as Derrick Bell (1992) does in one of the more moving examples of Antonio Gramsci's maxim—optimism of the will, pessimism of the intellect—that things have hardly changed at all. I am simply not in a position

to adjudicate the degree of continuity or discontinuity at such a grand scale and am inclined to consider most conclusions premature at this point, and perhaps at any point. In my own limited view, therefore, we are not "post" modern yet, although it is arguably the case that the fundamental contradictions at the heart of modernity are more exposed and much is up for grabs in the way we conceive the possibilities for knowledge, for freedom, and for subject-hood in the wake of this exposure. It is also arguably the case that the strong sense of living in "a strange new landscape . . . the sense that something has changed, that things are different, that we have gone through a transformation of the life world which is somehow decisive but incomparable with the older convulsions of modernization and industrialization" (Jameson 1991: xxi) so pervasive in many quarters is an influential and itself motivating social and cultural fact.

Of one thing I am sure: *it's not that the ghosts don't exist.* The postmodern, late-capitalist, postcolonial world represses and projects its ghosts or phantoms in similar intensities, if not entirely in the same forms, as the older world did. Indeed, the concentration on haunting and ghosts is a way of maintaining the salience of social analysis as bounded by its social context, as in history, which is anything but dead and over, while avoiding simple reflectionism. Yet, in one particularly prominent framing of postmodernism, an overweening and overstated emphasis on new electronic technologies of communication, on consumerism, and on the spectacular world of commodities has, despite the rhetoric of exposing the new machinery, replaced conventional positivism with a postmodernist version that promotes the telecommunicative visibility of all codings and decodings. Crudely put, when postmodernism means that everything is on view, that everything can be described, that all "tacitly present means . . . [become] conscious object[s] of self-perfection," it displays an antighost side that resembles modernity's positivities more than it concedes. . . .

In a 1981 introduction to *Invisible Man*, Ralph Ellison wrote: "despite the bland assertions of sociologists, [the] 'high visibility' [of the African-American man] actually rendered one *un*-visible" (xii). Hypervisibility is a persistent alibi for the mechanisms that render one *un*-visible: "His darkness . . . glow[ing] . . . within the American conscience with such intensity that most whites feigned moral blindness toward his predicament." The difficulty for us now, as it was for Ellison when he published *Invisible Man* in 1952, is the extent to which the mediums of public image making and visibility are inextricably wedded to the co-joined mechanisms that systematically rendered certain groups of people apparently *privately* poor, uneducated, ill, and disenfranchised.

Ellison's *Invisible Man* gives double reference both to the unvisibility of the hypervisible African-American man and to the invisibility of "the Man" who persistently needs an alibi for the blindness of his vision. As a strategy of analysis, Ellison's insight underscores the need to conceptualize visibility as a *complex system of permission and prohibition, punctuated alternately by apparitions and hysterical blindness*. If Ellison's argument encourages us to interrogate the mechanisms by which the highly visible can actually be a type of invisibility, Toni Morrison's (1989) argument that "invisible things are not necessarily not-there" encourages the complementary gesture of investigating how that which appears absent can indeed be a seething presence. Both these positions are about how to write ghost stories—about how to write about *permissions and prohibitions, presence and absence, about apparitions and hysterical blindness*. To write stories concerning exclusions and invisibilities is to write ghost stories. To write ghost stories implies that ghosts are real, that is to say, that they produce material effects. To impute a kind of objectivity to ghosts implies that, from certain standpoints, the dialectics of visibility and invisibility involve a constant negotiation between what can be seen and what is in the shadows.

Edward Said (1935–2003) was born a Palestinian in Jerusalem. His early education was in Cairo, before studying at Princeton, then Harvard. His academic home for many years until his death was Columbia University in New York City, where he taught Comparative Literature. His most famous book is *Orientalism* (1978), in which he gave the world the term for and concept of Western culture's systematic prejudice against Islamic culture, and by extension all non-Western cultures. Said was among the world's most important literary critics. He was also an accomplished musician. Even more, Said was known and respected (if begrudgingly by those who opposed his politics) as an intellectual and political representative of the Palestinian people. The sheer range of his writing suggests the sort of nomadic genius he was: *Joseph Conrad and the Fiction of Autobiography* (1966), *The Question of Palestine*

(1979), *Covering Islam* (1981), *Parallels and Paradoxes: Explorations in Music and Society* (with Daniel Barenboim; 2002), among many other titles.

Intellectual Exile: Expatriates and Marginals[*]
Edward Said (1994)

Exile is one of the saddest fates. In premodern times banishment was a particularly dreadful punishment since it not only meant years of aimless wandering away from family and familiar places, but also meant being a sort of permanent outcast, someone who never felt at home, and was always at odds with the environment, inconsolable about the past, bitter about the present and the future. There has always been an association between the idea of exile and the terrors of being a leper, a social and moral untouchable. During the twentieth century, exile has been transformed from the exquisite, and sometimes exclusive, punishment of special individuals—like the great Latin poet Ovid, who was banished from Rome to a remote town on the Black Sea—into a cruel punishment of whole communities and peoples, often the inadvertent result of impersonal forces such as war, famine, and disease.

In this category are the Armenians, a gifted but frequently displaced people who lived in large numbers throughout the eastern Mediterranean (Anatolia especially) but who after genocidal attacks on them by the Turks flooded nearby Beirut, Aleppo, Jerusalem and Cairo, only to be dislocated again during the revolutionary upheavals of the post–World War Two period. I have long been deeply drawn to those large expatriate or exile communities who peopled the landscape of my youth in Palestine and Egypt. There were many Armenians of course, but also Jews, Italians, and Greeks who, once settled in the Levant, had grown productive roots there—these communities after all produced prominent writers like Edmond Jabes, Giuseppe Ungaretti, Constantine Cavafy—that were to be brutally torn up after the establishment of Israel in 1948 and after the Suez

---

war of 1956. To new nationalist governments in Egypt and Iraq and elsewhere in the Arab world, foreigners who symbolized the new aggression of European postwar imperialism were forced to leave, and for many old communities this was a particularly nasty fate. Some of these were acclimatized to new places of residence, but many were, in a manner of speaking, re-exiled.

There is a popular but wholly mistaken assumption that being exiled is to be totally cut off, isolated, hopelessly separated from your place of origin. Would that surgically clean separation were true, because then at least you could have the consolation of knowing that what you have left behind is, in a sense, unthinkable and completely irrecoverable. The fact is that for most exiles the difficulty consists not simply in being forced to live away from home, but rather, given today's world, in living with the many reminders that you are in exile, that your home is not in fact so far away, and that the normal traffic of everyday contemporary life keeps you in constant but tantalizing and unfulfilled touch with the old place. The exile therefore exists in a median state, neither completely at one with the new setting nor fully disencumbered of the old, beset with half-involvements and half-detachments, nostalgic and sentimental on one level, an adept mimic or a secret outcast on another. Being skilled at survival becomes the main imperative, with the danger of getting too comfortable and secure constituting a threat that is constantly to be guarded against. . . .

The widespread territorial rearrangements of the post–World War Two period produced huge demographic movements, for example, the Indian Muslims who moved to Pakistan after the 1947 partition, or the Palestinians who were largely dispersed during Israel's establishment to accommodate incoming European and Asian Jews; and these transformations in turn gave rise to hybrid political forms. In Israel's political life there has been not only a politics of the Jewish diaspora but also an intertwining and competing politics of the Palestinian people in exile. In the newly founded countries of Pakistan and Israel the recent immigrants were seen as part of an exchange of populations, but politically they were also regarded as formerly oppressed minorities enabled to live in their new states as members of the majority. Yet far from settling sectarian issues, partition and the separatist ideology of new statehood have rekindled and often inflamed them. My concern here is more with the largely unaccommodated exiles, like Palestinians or the new Muslim immigrants in

continental Europe, or the West Indian and African blacks in England, whose presence complicates the presumed homogeneity of the new societies in which they live. The intellectual who considers him- or herself to be a part of a more general condition affecting the displaced national community is therefore likely to be a source not of acculturation and adjustment, but rather of volatility and instability.

This is by no means to say that exile doesn't also produce marvels of adjustment . . . here I want to focus on its opposite, the intellectual who because of exile cannot, or, more to the point, will not make the adjustment, preferring instead to remain outside the mainstream, unaccommodated, unco-opted, resistant: but first I need to make some preliminary points.

One is that while it is an *actual* condition, exile is also for my purposes a *metaphorical* condition. By that I mean that my diagnosis of the intellectual in exile derives from the social and political history of dislocation and migration with which I began this lecture, but is not limited to it. Even intellectuals who are lifelong members of a society can, in a manner of speaking, be divided into insiders and outsiders: those on the one hand who belong fully to the society as it is, who flourish in it without an overwhelming sense of dissonance or dissent, those who can be called yea-sayers; and on the other hand, the nay-sayers, the individuals at odds with their society and therefore outsiders and exiles so far as privileges, power, and honors are concerned. The pattern that sets the course for the intellectual as outsider is best exemplified by the condition of exile, the state of never being fully adjusted, always feeling outside the chatty, familiar world inhabited by natives, so to speak, tending to avoid and even dislike the trappings of accommodation and national well-being. Exile for the intellectual in this metaphysical sense is restlessness, movement, constantly being unsettled, and unsettling others. You cannot go back to some earlier and perhaps more stable condition of being at home; and, alas, you can never fully arrive, be at one with your new home or situation.

Secondly—and I find myself somewhat surprised by this observation even as I make it—the intellectual as exile tends to be happy with the idea of unhappiness, so that dissatisfaction bordering on dyspepsia, a kind of curmudgeonly disagreeableness, can become not only a style of thought, but also a new, if temporary, habitation. The intellectual as ranting Thersites perhaps. A great historical prototype for what I have in mind is a powerful eighteenth-century figure, Jonathan Swift, who never got over his fall from influence and prestige in England after the Tories left office in 1714, and spent the rest of his life as an exile in Ireland. An almost legendary figure of bitterness and anger—*saeve indignatio* he said of himself in his own epitaph—Swift was furious at Ireland, and yet its defender against British tyranny, a man whose towering Irish works *Gulliver's Travels* and *The Drapier's Letters* show a mind flourishing, not to say benefiting, from such productive anguish.

To some degree the early V. S. Naipaul, the essayist and travel writer, resident off and on in England, yet always on the move, revisiting his Caribbean and Indian roots, sifting through the debris of colonialism and post-colonialism, remorselessly judging the illusions and cruelties of independent states and the new true believers, was a figure of modern intellectual exile.

Even more rigorous, more determinedly the exile than Naipaul, is Theodor Wiesengrund Adorno. He was a forbidding but endlessly fascinating man, and for me, the dominating intellectual conscience of the middle twentieth century, whose entire career skirted and fought the dangers of fascism, communism and Western mass consumerism. Unlike Naipaul, who has wandered in and out of former homes in the Third World, Adorno was completely European, a man entirely made up of the highest of high cultures that included astonishing professional competence in philosophy, music (he was a student and admirer of Berg and Schoenberg), sociology, literature, history, and cultural analysis. Of partially Jewish background, he left his native Germany in the mid-1930s shortly after the Nazi seizure of power: he went first to read philosophy at Oxford, which is where he wrote an extremely difficult book on Husserl. He seems to have been miserable there, surrounded as he was by ordinary language and positivist philosophers, he with his Spenglerian gloom and metaphysical dialectics in the best Hegelian manner. He returned to Germany for a while but, as a member of the University of Frankfurt Institute of Social Research, reluctantly decamped for the safety of the United States, where he lived for a time first in New York (1938–41) and then in southern California.

Although Adorno returned to Frankfurt in 1949 to take up his old professorship there, his years in America stamped him with the marks of exile forever. He detested jazz and everything about popular culture; he had no affection for the landscape at all; he seems to have remained studiously mandarin in his ways; and therefore, because he was brought up in a Marxist-Hegelian philosophical tradition, everything about the worldwide influence of American films, industry, habits of daily life, fact-based learning, and pragmatism raised his hackles. Naturally Adorno was very predisposed to being a metaphysical exile before he came to the United States: he was already extremely critical of what passed for bourgeois taste in Europe, and his standards of what, for instance, music ought to have been were set by the extraordinarily difficult works of Schoenberg, works which Adorno averred were honorably destined to remain unheard and impossible to listen to. Paradoxical, ironic, mercilessly critical: Adorno was the quintessential intellectual, hating *all* systems, whether on our side or theirs, with equal distaste. For him life was at its most false in the aggregate—the whole is always the untrue, he once said—and this, he continued, placed an even greater premium on subjectivity, on the individual's consciousness, on what could not be regimented in the totally administered society.

But it was his American exile that produced Adorno's great masterpiece, the *Minima Moralia*, a set of 153 fragments published in 1953, and subtitled "Reflections from Damaged Life." . . . The core of Adorno's representation of the intellectual as a permanent exile, dodging both the old and the new with equal dexterity, is a writing style that is mannered and worked over in the extreme. It is fragmentary first of all, jerky, discontinuous; there is no plot or predetermined order to follow. It represents the intellectual's consciousness as unable to be at rest anywhere, constantly on guard against the blandishments of success, which, for the perversely inclined Adorno, means trying consciously *not* to be understood easily and immediately. Nor is it possible to retreat into complete privacy, since as Adorno says much later in his career, the hope of the intellectual is not that he will have an effect on the world, but that someday, somewhere, someone will read what he wrote exactly as he wrote it.

One fragment, number 18 in *Minima Moralia*, captures the significance of exile quite perfectly. "Dwelling, in the proper sense," says Adorno, "is now impossible. The traditional residences we have grown up in have grown intolerable: each trait of comfort in them is paid for with a betrayal of knowledge, each vestige of shelter with the musty pact of family interests." So much for the prewar life of people who grew up before Nazism. Socialism and American consumerism are no better: there "people live if not in slums, in bungalows that by tomorrow may be leaf-huts, trailers, cars, camps, or the open air." Thus, Adorno states, "the house is past [i.e. over]. . . . The best mode of conduct, in face of all this, still seems an uncommitted, suspended one. . . . *It is part of morality not to be at home in one's home.*"

William Julius Wilson (1935–) was professor of Sociology at the University of Chicago until 1996, when he became the Malcolm Wiener Professor of Social Policy at Harvard University. In the Chicago years he did much of the empirical work for his three controversial books—*The Declining Significance of Race* (1980), *The Truly Disadvantaged: The Inner City, the Underclass, and Public Policy* (1987), and *When Work Disappears: The World of the New Urban Poor* (1996). By focusing attention on the urban underclass, Wilson has forcibly altered both the academic and public debates over the respective roles of race and class in urban poverty. He has been widely honored for his work, including election as president of the American Sociological Association, as member of the National Academy of Science, and as recipient of a MacArthur Foundation fellowship.

Global Economic Changes and the Limits of the Race Relations Vision*
William Julius Wilson (1999)

Despite African Americans' strong focus on the effects of racial discrimination in domestic U.S. employment, their economic fate is inextricably connected with the structure and functioning of a much broader, globally influenced modern economy. Racial bias continues to be an important factor that aggravates black employment problems. Nonetheless, it is important to be aware of the *nonracial* economic forces that have sharply increased joblessness and declining real wages among many African Americans in the last several decades. As the black economist Vivian Henderson argued over two decades ago, racism put blacks in their economic place, but changes in the modern economy have disrupted

* From *The Bridge over the Racial Divide: Rising Inequality and Coalition Politics* by William Julius Wilson © 2001 by the Regents of the University of California. Published by the University of California Press.

that place and further restricted opportunities. In this chapter I underline the importance of understanding race neutral economic forces that create profound effects within all American communities, forces that represent changes in the new economy. I give special attention to the impact of these changes on the African American community to further stimulate thought on coalition building in pursuit of a broad-based economic agenda for ordinary families. Because the economic problems in the black community are often perceived primarily or solely in terms of race—as if they are independent of the race-neutral economic trends affecting families and neighborhoods across the nation—the idea of multiracial coalition building on issues that do not ostensibly involve race is difficult for many to fathom. The remaining sections of this chapter reveal the limits of this vision of race relations.

In recent years a "twist" in the demand for different types of labor has occurred. The wedding of emerging technologies and international competition has eroded the basic institutions of the mass production system. In the last several decades, almost all of the improvements in productivity have been associated with technology and human capital, thereby drastically reducing the importance of physical capital and natural resources. The changes in technology that are producing new jobs make many others obsolete.

The workplace has been revolutionized by technological changes that range from the development of robotics to the information highway. Whereas educated workers are at least keeping pace with the increased use of information-based technologies and microcomputers, less sophisticated workers face the growing threat of job displacement in certain industries. Between 1979 and 1994 the employment-to-population ratio increased by 1 percent for college graduates but declined by 3 percent for high school graduates and by 10 percent for high school dropouts. In the new global economy, highly educated, well-trained men and women are in demand. This may be seen most dramatically in the sharp differences in employment experiences among American males. Unlike men with lower levels of education, college-educated men are working more, not less.

The shift in the demand for labor has been especially devastating for those low-skilled workers whose incorporation into the mainstream economy has been marginal or recent. Even before the economic restructuring of the nation's economy, low-skilled

African Americans were at the end of the employment line, often the last to be hired and the first to be let go. The economic situation for many blacks has now been further weakened because they tend not only to reside in communities that have higher jobless rates and lower employment growth, but also to lack access to areas of higher employment and job growth.

Of all the changes in the economy that have adversely affected low-skilled African American workers, perhaps the most significant have been those in the manufacturing sector. One study revealed that in the 1970s "up to half of the huge employment declines for less-educated blacks might be explained by industrial shifts away from manufacturing toward other sectors." The manufacturing losses in some northern cities have been staggering. In the twenty-year period from 1967 to 1987, Philadelphia lost 64 percent of its manufacturing jobs; Chicago lost 60 percent; New York City, 58 percent; and Detroit, 51 percent. In absolute numbers, these percentages represent the loss of 160,000 jobs in Philadelphia, 326,000 in Chicago, 520,000—over half a million, in New York, and 108,000 in Detroit. . . .

The structural shift in the distribution of industrial job opportunities is not the only reason for declining earnings among young black male workers. Important changes in the patterns of occupational staffing within firms and industries, including those in manufacturing, are also to blame. Substantial numbers of new professional, technical, and managerial positions have been created that primarily benefit those with higher levels of formal education. Because such jobs require at least some education beyond high school, young dropouts and even high school graduates "have faced a dwindling supply of career jobs offering the real earnings opportunities available to them in the 1960s and early 1970s."

Most of the new jobs for workers with limited training and education are in the service sector and are disproportionately held by women. This is even truer for those who work in social services, which include the industries of health, education, and welfare. Within central cities the number of jobs for less educated workers has declined precipitously. However, many workers stayed afloat thanks to jobs in the expanding social service sector, especially black women who had some years of high school but no diploma. . . .

The computer revolution is a major reason for the shift in the demand for skilled workers. Whereas only one-quarter of American workers directly used a computer in their jobs in 1983, by 1993 that figure had risen to almost half the workforce. According to the economist Alan Krueger, "The expansion of computer use can account for one-third to two-thirds of the increase in the payoff to education between 1984 and 1993 [in the United States]. Two reasons for this increased payoff are cited: first, even after a number of background factors, such as experience and education, are taken into account, those who use computers at work tend to be paid more than those who do not; second, the industries with the greatest shift in employment toward more highly skilled workers are those in which computer technology is more intensively used. . . . The share of workers with college degrees increased most sharply in the industries with the most rapid expansion of computer use.

Early studies of the diffusion of computer technology have revealed a strong positive relationship between computer ownership and income and education. And although systematic research is lacking, it is clear that in jobless ghetto areas and depressed rural areas computerization and telecommunications are severely underdeveloped.

A recent study illustrates how lack of access to key technological resources can be predicted along race and class lines, specifically in relation to ownership of home computers. In this study 73 percent of white students lived in households with a home computer, whereas only 32 percent of black students did so. Overall, 44.2 percent of the white respondents owned a computer at home, compared with 29 percent of black respondents. The authors found, however, that household income rather than race explained home computer ownership—levels of income correspond to the probability of owning a computer at home, regardless of race. . . .

The shift in demand for skilled versus low-skilled workers can also be related to the growing internationalization of economic activity, including increased trade with countries that have large numbers of low-skilled, low-wage workers. Two developments facilitated the growth in global economic activity: (1) advances in information and communications technologies, which significantly lowered transportation and communication costs and thereby encouraged companies to shift work to low-wage areas around the world; and (2) the expansion of free trade, which reduced the price of imports and raised the output of export industries.

The increased output of export industries aids skilled workers, simply because skilled workers are heavily represented in export industries. But increasing imports that compete with labor-intensive industries (for example, apparel, textile, toys, footwear, and some manufacturing) hurt unskilled labor. "As a share of the U.S. economy, trade has been expanding since the late 1960s," asserts the economist James K. Galbraith, "and imports of manufacturing from developing countries, in particular, grew dramatically in the early 1980s." According to economic theory, the expansion of trade with countries that have a large proportion of relatively unskilled labor will result in downward pressure on the wages of low-skilled American workers because it will lower the prices of the goods they produce. . . .

It is important to note that in the United States the sharp decline in the relative demand for low-skilled labor has had a more adverse effect on blacks than on whites because a substantially larger proportion of African Americans is unskilled. Although the number of skilled blacks (including managers, professionals, and technicians) has increased sharply in the last several years, the proportion of those who are unskilled remains large. This is because the black population, burdened by cumulative experiences of racial restrictions, was overwhelmingly unskilled just several decades ago.

Although racial discrimination and segregation exacerbate the labor market problems of low-skilled African Americans, we must not lose sight of the fact that many of these problems are currently driven by fundamental changes in the new global economy. Nonetheless, there is a tendency among policy makers, scholars, and black leaders to view economic problems in the black community separately from the national and international trends affecting American families and neighborhoods. If the economic problems of the African American community are defined solely in racial terms, they can be isolated and viewed as requiring only race-based solutions, such as those proposed by the Left, or narrow political solutions with subtle racial connotations, such as welfare reform, as proposed by the Right. If leaders in the African American community perceive the economic problems of black people as separate from the national and international trends affecting ordinary American families, they will be less likely to see the need to join forces with other groups seeking economic reform.

University of Indiana, the University of Chicago, and Northwestern University. During graduate studies in sociology, he worked self-consciously in the Chicago tradition of ethnographical studies of the urban poor with Gerald Suttles and Howard Becker. Upon publication of *A Place on the Corner: A Study of Black Street Corner Men* (1978) his doctoral thesis became a classic in the study of Black men on the economic margins of urban life. Since, Anderson has published other path breaking books on the social realities of Blacks living in the changing considerations of economic and racial inequalities. Among these are *Streetwise* (1990), *Code of the Street* (1998) and, most recently, *The Cosmopolitan Canopy: Race and Civility in Everyday Life* (2011). After teaching at Swarthmore and the University of Pennsylvania for many years, in 2007 he became the William K. Lanman, Jr. Professor of Sociology at Yale University, where he directs Yale's Urban Ethnography Project. He is currently at work on a major new work, *The Iconic Ghetto*. For the nervous politically correct, it should be noted that the expression "The Nigger Moment" is meant by Anderson to call attention to the lingering ordinary life experiences of racial stereotyping Blacks of all social strata encountered.

=====

The "Nigger Moment" in the Cosmopolitan Canopy[*]
Elijah Anderson (2011)

Nathan said to me, "Mom, why is it that the black kids start all the trouble?" I asked him what he meant. He described how this one young man was always starting trouble in school; he sounded like a bully. I tried to explain that sometimes people have difficult home lives and that he probably brought some of that tension to school. But I said, "Nathan, I want you to understand that ignorance comes in any color." So we began to talk about race. As I was driving him to Arthur Ashe [Youth Tennis Center] in Roxborough, the conversation got kind of heated. He said, "Mommy, I think you're a racist." I said, "No, I'm not a racist, I'm a realist." Because I was pointing out what blacks

---

Elijah Anderson (1943–) was born of modest circumstances in Arkansas. He was educated at the

had gone through. I was really advocating the black experience. Maybe he thought I was putting down white people, I don't know. But I just wanted him to know that ignorance comes in any color. "You'll see this as you grow up." I just remember what he called me. I was really just trying to give him a sense of our history.

I don't know how long it was after that, but it was very close in my mind, and he could remember this discussion very clearly, he had this confrontation at tennis. A group of students was bussed in to play. They were all white. It was kind of strange. I had never seen this before. The coach had grouped Nathan and this other young fellow to play doubles in the little tennis match. He was quite good, so the coach put them together. Then Nathan missed the ball, and this Caucasian young man called him a bunch a nasty, dirty words. I couldn't hear it because I was up in [the stands]. But I could tell by his body language, and I could tell by my son's face. He was just stunned that these words were coming out of this young man's mouth. He looks up at me up on the platform, and I just looked at him to say, "You handle it—I'm not gonna handle it!" He then looks at the coach to handle it, but the coach didn't handle it. So it was left that way. If you know my son, he shows everything on his face. He was just stunned. He was paralyzed. As he came up the steps, I just looked at him. And my words [to him] were, "Ignorance comes in any color." He began to tell me what the young man said. It was incredible. He was cursing Nathan, calling him dumb, a lot of crazy adjectives—I don't even know [them all]. That began to open his eyes. It was clearly racial. The boy just thought he could run over him. My son was the only black person, and this was what came out. About a month later, when they were playing, this kid came with this same kind of aggressiveness. This is when Nathan began to be exposed. He had learned what was expected of him. He learned who he was at that time.

Nathan was on his way to becoming cosmopolitan, but this experience gave rise to doubts and second thoughts.

If a young person once disregarded the entreaties of more ethnocentric black people, he or she may now listen to their opinions. A youth who had doubted the warnings of the old heads—mature black men and women who pass on their painfully accumulated wisdom to the next generation—may give their advice more respect. In his imagination, these voices all chime in, "We told you so." In the heat of this moment, he must recalculate both the consonant and the discordant sounds. A few simple messages begin to resonate for him: "Don't trust white people"; "Choose white friends and associates with care." Not only does he begin to give ethnocentric arguments more weight, but he also develops a certain black consciousness. His wariness around whites may begin to show, and his white friends may now discern a certain swagger in his step and a chip on his shoulder.

In such tense circumstances, the most unsophisticated young brothers are ready to blow up whenever they perceive a slight. Many a life has been turned upside down or ruined by such haste. The young brother risks calling forth the stereotype of the angry black man, all too easily dismissed by his white counterparts. The old heads caution him to "suck it up" and to learn from and build on this traumatic experience. They say, "Pick your battles" or "All races have good and bad people." He listens and tries to learn patience.

It is very difficult for many people to come to terms with what has happened to them. It is equally difficult to normalize it, seeking out a universalistic explanation, denying the role of racism, and asserting that blacks and whites are really equal. "No, this would not have happened to a white man in a similar situation," he argues. These are the lessons of the brothers and sisters who have survived a succession of "nigger moments" and have developed the insight and strength to carry on.

The victim in a "nigger moment" may, in turn, identify his or her abuser as a racist—the most powerful verbal weapon in the black person's arsenal. This label is a potent epithet that can be irreparably damaging. In turn, the labeler may be accused of "playing the race card," a phrase that has become a rival epithet directed at blacks. Blacks and whites continue to parry one another as public spaces and relationships are perpetually renegotiated.

While avoiding the "nigger moment" is foremost in the minds of many African Americans and keeps them from fully trusting white people, the potential use of the epithet "racist" makes many whites apprehensive about having closer relations with blacks. These concerns are at the heart of the anxiety and insecurity experienced on both sides of the color line. In today's professional work settings that involve interracial interaction, no one wants to be accused of racism or of acting in ways that are racially motivated. Conservatives as well as liberals seek to avoid this appellation, which all acknowledge is seriously damaging. The term "racist" possesses immense power.

When this label is applied, a degradation ceremony begins immediately, whether or not the party is guilty or his conduct has even been investigated. The person on the receiving end of the epithet is being called out on a charge many are prepared to believe. Although a contest may ensue, the label is so powerful that accusations alone may destroy the person's reputation. Media commentators have lost their jobs and managers of large organizations have had to forfeit their positions.

Whether institutional racism is due to sins of commission or to those of omission does not matter, for the result is the same. From the ghetto wastelands in urban centers to the pervasive racial disparities in income, wealth, health, and educational achievement, the bitter fruits of white privilege and black disinheritance are visible. The beneficiaries of this weighty history are also in plain sight. White persons, no matter how humble their origins, are still favored by the legacy of slavery and segregation that pervades contemporary society. Some observers have called this American apartheid.

In the past, the color line in most American cities was painfully clear. Black people "knew their place"—and they did their best to adapt and work around this reality. Over the past forty years, as the racial incorporation process has led to the emergence of a large black middle class, the color line has begun to blur. In some places, at some times, it seems nonexistent. Yet it can still be drawn at any moment. As blacks and whites interact in public, each takes the other's reaction into his calculation of what he expects and can get away with. Navigating the unstable terrain demands unusual poise and forbearance, as assumptions of equality and inclusiveness can suddenly be called into question.

All these dilemmas and contradictions of status figure into race relations today. In our pluralistic society, most Americans have attained a degree of cosmopolitanism. Yet everyone has a mixture of cosmo and ethno elements in his worldview. The public space of the cosmopolitan canopy encourages us to express our better selves and reminds us to keep our ethnocentric feelings in check. Ethno-leaning people can practice acting cosmopolitan, even if they need to put on gloss to give a convincing performance. When ethnocentrically oriented people are in the company of like-minded others, they may drop their pretenses of tolerance and reveal their ethnocentric sides.

The cosmopolitan canopies of the city can be likened to little islands of civility, peaceful settings in which denizens of the urban environment can call time-out from the hustle and bustle of city life. Usually these are settings of utter diversity, and visitors are attracted here in part because these settings are open to everyone. And when people visit, they are inclined to study and observe one another and the goings-on around them—and they generally strive to get along. But they can also be defensive here, becoming engaged in a kind of social reconnaissance, checking out the other, scrutinizing interesting but unknown others—people they otherwise would never encounter up close—in circumstances uniquely afforded by the canopy, and, at times, holding one another accountable. Social life is not always about comity and goodwill under the canopy, but most often it is a pleasant environment, and civility is the usual order of the day.

Stigma underlies the "nigger moment" for blacks under the canopy; in sociological terms, "nigger" can be taken as a metaphor for outcaste status, but this is subject to negotiation depending on situations and social context. At times older people, poor people, white women (as well as white men on occasion), Jews, Muslims, Indians, Latinos, and other people of color are, unfortunately, negatively impacted by this dynamic. Virtually anyone with provisional status may experience a "nigger moment" at any time because issues such as sexual preference, poverty, gender, age, and skin color can and do tear the canopy from time to time.

Of these threats to the canopy, "nigger moments" are the most dangerous and potentially destabilizing. As I've indicated, the canopy is ordinarily an amazing place that privileges diversity by encouraging its denizens to express their more cosmopolitan sides, while encouraging people to keep their ethnocentric feelings in check. In those circumstances in which the canopy is torn, when there is such an interactional crisis of sorts, prevailing conditions most often, but not always, deter people from responding to others in a truly hostile manner. Individuals like Shawn, Jesse, and Nathan will forever be scarred by their "moments," and there is no escaping the harm that these moments inflicted on them and, by implication, their communities.

Such moments represent points of profound tension, when the scales fall from the victim's eyes and he realizes that his racial assumptions about his immediate environment are untrue. There is often a shock of recognition and a painful personal crisis.

Meanwhile, everyone observing the incident is interested in what will happen next; all stakeholders are intently focused on what has happened and what then will be done about it. No one takes more interest in such transactions than young people, as they appear eager to learn by example and precedent, waiting in the wings to succeed their elders. The outcome of the incident naturally weakens or strengthens the canopy, determining its ultimate health and integrity.

But the canopy is an ongoing concern, and, as Everett Hughes, the great University of Chicago sociologist, would have appreciated, a unique urban institution whose hallmark is a certain resilience and change as it goes about meeting the exigencies of its everyday environment. As parties recover and regroup, come together, continue to model civility in public, and are constantly exposed to one another's humanity, life goes on. For better or worse, people's observations, and the folk ethnography in which they engage, serve as a cognitive and cultural base for new modes of behavior, as they adopt appropriate interactional glosses that help them through emergent conditions, situations, and circumstances. Differences in race, ethnicity, gender, or sexual preference may surface to upset the social balance found there, but they never rend the canopy beyond repair. The simple provocations, revelations, and pleasures diverse people find in one another's company induce them to return to the cosmopolitan canopy again and again. It is through such ongoing activity, the goings-on of everyday life in public, that the canopy renews itself....

Waverly Duck (1976–) was born in Detroit to a family of modest economic means. He began his higher education at Connecticut College, before transferring to Wayne State University in Detroit where, in 2004, he completed his PhD. He has been a visiting scholar at the University of Pennsylvania before postdoctoral work at Yale where he became the associate director of Yale's Urban Ethnography Project. He has been visiting professor and research fellow at the University of Wisconsin, Madison where he was also affiliated with the Waisman Center for research on childhood psychopathology. Professor Duck currently teaches sociology at the University of Pittsburg. The selection is drawn from his book, *No Way Out: Precarious Living in the Shadow of Poverty and Drug Dealing*

(2015). No Way Out appeared in the wake of a storm of controversy over ethnography methods occasioned by Alice Goffman's now famous (or, some think, notorious) book *On the Run: Fugitive Life in an American City.* As important as *On the Run* is, *No Way Out* promises to stand up to those who complain that the ethnographic method is vulnerable to partial and personal interpretation of life on the streets. The selection, "Benita's Story: Coping with Poverty" is just one of the many instances in which Duck draws on his years experience in impoverished neighborhoods to draw a clean but powerful story of the multiple ways that life in the shadows of poverty, while precarious, can also be orderly and dignified.

Benita's Story: Coping with Poverty[*]
Waverly Duck (2015)

In the subsequent weeks, I met Benita, my name for the mother of Ali and one other boy who participated in the camp (her two other children did not attend). From her I learned about the daily realities these boys faced. It took me over a year to get to know Benita before I formally interviewed her. At that point she was twenty-six years old. She had dropped out of high school in the tenth grade and left home at seventeen to live with the father of her two oldest children; they lived together for five years. She later earned her GED at age twenty-four.

Her smile was stunning, and I found her extremely disarming. At five feet five, with a medium-brown complexion, high cheekbones, and thick black shoulder-length hair, Benita reminded me immediately of a young Janet Jackson. Her voice was low and soft but rose when she was excited or upset. She constantly smiled when we talked, and she had a tendency to take deep breaths when she tried to explain things to me. Yet, with her face at rest when she listened intently, she looked sad and melancholy. Her eyes seemed to water as if she were constantly on the verge of tears.

Benita had a wonderful sense of humor, and at times when I didn't get a joke, she would explain to me why her comments were funny. For example, when her six-year-old son Joaquin came home from

---

[*] Republished with permission of University of Chicago Press, from *No Way Out: Precarious Living in the Shadow of Poverty.* Copyright 2015, University of Chicago Press; permission conveyed through Copyright Clearance Center, Inc.

his first day of first grade and asked her to buy him boxers instead of briefs, she laughed and looked at Joaquin and joked with him, saying, "Aw, my baby want to look sexy for those first-grade girls." Embarrassed, Joaquin threw his hand up and ran upstairs to his bedroom. I joked with her, stating that it was the first time that I had ever heard the words "sexy" and "first grade" in the same sentence. We laughed, but she explained that Joaquin wanted to start sagging his pants like the older boys, for whom boxers, not briefs, were the underwear of choice. I admired her sense of humor, which I soon recognized was a coping mechanism.

Benita and I talked weekly on the phone, and I would sometimes visit her at home and take her grocery shopping, to her nurse's aide job, or to pick up her kids from school. Our relationship was something of an equal exchange. I shared as much information about my life as she shared about hers. Our most intense conversation was about how the crack cocaine epidemic had changed cities all over the country. She told me:

> Crack was something else. I had family sold crack. My cousin use to sell crack in the late eighties. He was killed when I was in the second or third grade. To this day nobody knows who did it. They found his body in a vacant lot in another city, shot up. My mother and my aunt had a falling out because my cousin tried to get my brother to sell. Crack was crazy, man; I mean people were, like, leaving their babies at our house, coming back days later. Didn't make any sense. The robbing, the raids, family members stealing from you. . . . Crack was something else.

She raised similar concerns regarding her oldest children's father, who battled heroin addiction. While she expressed disappointment that he was unable to help her with child care and her finances, she preferred to limit his contact with their children because of his addiction. Benita explained that her children usually interacted with their father while the grandparents were present. While his family helped her sporadically, disagreements over the way she parented often created long periods with limited or no communication. On numerous occasions I tried to get Benita to discuss the father's limited involvement, but she refused. She blamed his addiction as the problem, not him, reminding me that "he still the father" of

her children and that she was "not going to bad-mouth their dad."

The family resources available to Benita were tenuous. She understood the limitations of those around her but was equally concerned about the negative influences that certain people might have on her children and the judgments of others regarding her own parenting abilities. Her investment in these relationships appeared to depend on her freedom to parent as she saw fit. Benita reported losing some access to her female kin networks over time, but she was quick to point out that a crisis (such as a threat of imprisonment) or a celebration (such as her daughter graduating from high school) could alleviate strained relationships. While these networks were not permanently harmed, they could become compromised for long periods of time.

Local churches and religious organizations have been a constant and vitally important resource in communities such as Bristol Hill. The availability of space and the philosophy of unconditional opportunities for membership within such institutions have saved many families by providing numerous resources, such as after-school programs. Yet these community resources are often secondary to the elaborate and intertwined kin networks that form the fragile safety net that such families so desperately need when things go wrong. Families under extreme stress and facing great uncertainly heavily relied on their relatives, friends, and religious institutions for sustainability in their day-to-day lives.

Even when Benita had seemingly exhausted her options, these networks together created a buffer that often led to acts of goodwill from both relatives and strangers alike. For example, when Benita was arrested, both sets of her in-laws contributed to her bail, and a paternal aunt watched all four of her children for a few days upon her release; in addition, all of her siblings sent her money. After this crisis, her father came from another state to move in with her and help pay her rent and bills and care for her children. Benita had also lived with her mother during her first pregnancy; her father's insurance paid for costs associated with the birth.

But this kinship network could "tap out." Her brother, who lived out of state, refused to accept her calls after not hearing from her for four years. (Their estrangement appeared to be related to a violent incident that she declined to discuss in depth, simply stating that she refused to let any man put his hands on her.) Her sister, who also lived out of state, was cautious about contacting Benita because of her previous relationships with drug dealers and her constant relocations. In addition, Benita's father complained when she failed to repay a series of loans. Benita's mother, who lived the closest to her, avoided her because she didn't like being used for child care.

This limited contact was partially her choice as well. "My family is too judgmental, so I try to keep them out of my business," she said. Her children continued to visit her mother and her sister occasionally; Benita's mother even had primary custody of her two older children for a time, cementing a significant relationship with them. Benita pointed out that she was hesitant to ask her parents for help because they were both living on fixed incomes. Even though she received their help in the past, she now had only limited contact with them because, as she put it, her mother and sister viewed her as "too needy."

While Benita criticized her children's paternal relatives, their fathers' siblings and extended kin nonetheless offered various opportunities to her children, even while she and their fathers rarely communicated. In Benita's children's teenage years, they took a more active approach to their relationships with their fathers but also a more critical view of them, as they worked to establish and nurture relationships with cousins, aunts, uncles, and even former spouses of their fathers.

Although her children's fathers' kin might have served as an additional support system, their animosity toward Benita for getting pregnant and taking resources (profits from the drug trade) from his immediate family made them less willing to help. As with her own family, she was, at times, reluctant to engage with the children's paternal grandparents because she wanted to keep her life private. The parents of her two older children's father called on child protective services on multiple occasions to have her children removed from her home. The charges ranged from abandonment to poor living conditions, and in the end each case was closed with no findings of abuse or neglect. While these grandparents said that they did not want custody, Benita complained that they seized every opportunity to have her children taken away. Her two youngest children's paternal relatives will only see them when their father is present.

As I came to know Benita better, I realized that her access to familial assistance varied with the severity of the crisis and, importantly, how it might affect her children. While the long-term child care and loans that she had received in the past were now unavailable, her family's concern for the wellbeing of the children and their desire to come together for special events such as birthdays and holiday celebrations was still very apparent.

The kinship network on which so many poor black women rely has been severely compromised in Benita's case, and she has few places to turn to for support. Violence, addiction, and state involvement have limited her contact with kin. Her own frequent moves, previous intimate relationships, consistent debt, and child care needs have also compromised familial relationships. This analysis of the material and interpersonal resources on which black mothers living in poverty rely is inspired by Carol Stack's *All Our Kin* (1974), which described the networks that mothers formed within their neighborhoods based mostly on their own relatives and, depending on the circumstances, the families of their children's fathers. Benita's story shows not only the devastating consequences of recent changes in welfare policy on poor families' financial situation but also their corrosive effects of deepening impoverishment on their interpersonal support networks.

Charles Tilly (1929–2008) was born in Lombard, Illinois, and educated at Harvard, where he earned his Ph.D. in 1958. He was the Joseph L. Buttenwieser Professor of Social Science at Columbia University, after a number of years as Distinguished University Professor at the New School, and professor at Michigan and Harvard before that. Tilly has been honored the world over for his historically subtle research in the political sociology of modern societies. His books include *The Vendee* (1964), *Strikes in France: 1930–1964* (1974, with Edward Shorter), *From Mobilization to Revolution* (1978), *The Contentious French* (1986), *Popular Contention in Great Britain, 1758–1838* (1995), *Durable Inequality* (1998), and *The Politics of Collective Violence* (2003). The selection is from *Roads from Past to Future* (1997). Tilly was a member of the National Academy of Sciences, fellow of the American Academy of Arts and Sciences, and a Chevalier de L'Ordre des Palmes Académiques.

Future Social Science and the Invisible Elbow[*]
Charles Tilly (1996)

For the Invisible Hand, let's substitute the Invisible Elbow. Coming home from the grocery store, arms overflowing with food-filled bags, you wedge yourself against the doorjamb, somehow free a hand to open the kitchen door, enter the house, then nudge the door closed with your elbow. Because elbows are not prehensile and, in this situation, not visible either, you sometimes slam the door smartly, sometimes swing the door halfway closed, sometimes miss completely on the first pass, sometimes bruise your arm on the wood, sometimes shatter the glass, and sometimes—responding to one of these earlier calamities—spill groceries all over the kitchen floor.

You, your elbow, the groceries, and the kitchen have systematic properties that strongly limit the likely consequences of your attempted nudge. Over many trips to the grocery store, which of these outcomes occurs forms a frequency distribution with stable probabilities modified by learning. With practice, you may get your door-closing average up to .900. After a calamitous elbow shot, however, you tell a story not of frequency distributions, but of good intentions frustrated by bad circumstances: the floor was wet, children left toys just inside the door, the grocery bagger put heavy items on top, or something of the sort. Thus we . . . save the belief in rational action, at least our own.

Don't hear my analysis as an irrationalist model of social life. Despite the fact that batters rationally aim to hit safely on almost every swing, over the long run, few major-league baseball players ever maintain batting averages even a third of the way to .900. As Herbert Simon has taught us to understand, instead of true maximizing, most of us mostly "satisfice" by settling for the first outcome of our efforts that falls within an acceptable zone. Despite the appeal of solipsism to postmodernists and paranoids, faulty everyday talk contains enough redundancy and error correction to convey meanings from one person to another. Even great dancers make constant adjustments to their own and their partners' almost imperceptible deviations from choreographed movements. Life is like that. The big differences among persons and groups lie not in the frequency with which they make mistakes, but in the speed, frequency, and manner of their correction. Smart people correct their many errors fast and well.

All life, I am claiming, fills with erroneous interactions, therefore with unanticipated consequences. But life also teems with error correction and responses, sometimes almost instantaneous, to unexpected outcomes. In conversation, we incessantly utter mistakes, receive signals from ourselves or others that mark our errors, then repair them so quickly and well that no one notices unless a witness replays the tape. Erving Goffman delighted in collecting errors and repairs in radio announcing, for example:

Disk Jockey: "And now a record by Little Willie John . . . here's 'Sleep-Sleep-Sleep' . . . By the way, did you get any last night? . . . *(pause)* . . . sleep, that is!"

Or the more subtle:

So all you do when you are on your way home is, stop by at Korvette's and leave your odor . . . order!!!

Only transcription of the text, or replay of the tape, captures the odor of the disorder. . . .

When working in Toronto, I asked my three eldest children to draw maps of the city from memory. Seven-year-old Laura drew an area bounded on the west (left) and the north (up) by the closest major thoroughfares to our house, placed the block containing our house prominently in the lower left (southwest) corner, displayed two more adjacent blocks (one with major areas marked "playground," "grass," and "working"), and sketched in a few other schematic streets, both vertical and horizontal. Nine-year-old Kit bounded her map vertically with the southward-flowing Humber and Don Rivers, placed the McDonald-Cartier Freeway at the northern limits, and limned in a gridwork of vertical and horizontal streets centering almost precisely on our home block. Chris, then eleven, produced a wondrously detailed map of the metropolis, complete with north, east, south, and west compass points. In Lake Ontario, he placed a presentable outline of Toronto Island, then next to it a blob labeled "this represents all other islands." All three children innovated delightfully. But all three also followed conventions of mapmaking they had somehow absorbed from schooling and everyday practice: north to the top, streets horizontal and vertical within that frame, major boundaries defined by waterways and big thoroughfares.

Of course, my children were responding not just to convention, but to verifiable features of the Toronto cityscape, all of which they had observed

---

[*]Tilly, Charles. *Roads from Past to Future*, Lanham, MD: Rowman & Littlefield, 1997. Print. Reprinted with permission of Rowman & Littlefield.

piecemeal even if they had never regarded all of them simultaneously. Indeed, their maps identified common features of Toronto, Cleveland, Chicago, Milwaukee, and other lakeside cities—features that themselves resulted from the interplay of topography, city-building conventions, and the incremental error-filled interactions of local residents. At all these levels, innovation, error, and conformity alike operate within constraints set by previous understandings and practices; they thereby produce intelligible structure.

Here, we encounter another paradox, for those very regularities define possibilities that could occur, but do not—at least not yet. Sound social science concerns counterfactuals: explaining what actually occurs, which ironically requires specifying what did *not* occur but could have occurred, then comparing factual with counterfactual. The central work of social science consists of specifying nonexistent social structures and processes that were possible, that are now possible, that under specifiable circumstances will be possible. Strong explanations do just that, comparing observed states with other possible states, using known causes to account for the differences. Game theory and Markov processes gain some of their intuitive appeal as representations of social life because they explicitly represent choice points, hence counterfactuals.

Counterfactual explanation makes social science a powerful complement to ethics and politics. In his renowned lecture "Science as a Vocation," Max Weber touched on this realization, but reduced it to the observation that if you choose a certain end, scientific experience can teach "you have to use such and such a *means* in order to carry out your conviction practically." If actors could actually anticipate consequences of their chosen actions and then produce the actions without error, we would indeed only need to sort intentions and preferences.

Much more, however, lies beyond that point. Every ethical or political proposal imports, however covertly, a theory of the possible, a selection among alternative actions that theory names as possible, and causal arguments relating actions to outcomes. To advocate turning away aspiring immigrants in order to protect your country's existing workers against unfair competition invokes a theory of competition, an argument concerning the probable effects of immigration and suppositions about the efficacy of anti-migration controls.

Even short of adjudicating fairness, social scientists have much to say about ethically implicated theories of possibility, selections among possible actions, and causal arguments. However one comes down on the question, to the extent that it generates reliable knowledge of causes and possibilities, social science obviously bears on ethical and political choices. For that very reason, assertions of social science's explanatory power regularly stir passions rarely seen in discussions of astronomy and geology: they constitute claims to pronounce on the possibility assumptions of religious, moral, and political doctrines.

Incessant error intersects with counterfactual explanation at two different points. First, the order-producing imbrication of error-filled interaction in shared understandings and interpersonal networks constitutes a causal domain requiring explanation of what actually happens along with what else might have happened. Second, the implicit computation of possible interaction and their possible outcomes that inheres in every initiation of interaction, erroneous or otherwise, takes place within limits set by the actor's social location and the previous history of the interaction in question. That constraint on decision-making itself requires counterfactual explanation. Any explanation of social processes worth its salt must account both for social interaction and for its consequences in the face of omnipresent constraint and error. . . .

Responses to error, in any case, are neither instinctual nor random; they draw on historically accumulated shared understandings, on culture. They also take place within constraining webs of previously established social relations and, in the process, alter those webs incrementally. Culture and social relations, however, do not alter unpredictably; they interact, and they obey strong constraints as they interact.

Julia Kristeva (1941–) was born in Bulgaria. In 1965, she emigrated to Paris for graduate studies and immediately associated herself with the famous *Tel Quel* group of revolutionary culture theorists commonly known as the poststructuralists. Kristeva is a Lacanian psychoanalyst, feminist theorist, literary and social critic, and novelist, as well as one of the world's most prominent cultural and literary theorists. Her books include *Desire in Language: A Semiotic Approach to Literature and Art* (1980), as well as *Revolution in Poetic Language* (1980; her 1974 doctoral thesis).

Women's Time*

Julia Kristeva (1977, 1997)

The nation, which was the dream and the reality of the nineteenth century, seems to have reached both its peak and its limit with the 1929 crash and the National Socialist apocalypse. We have witnessed the destruction of its very foundation—economic homogeneity, historical tradition, and linguistic unity. World War II, which was fought in the name of national values, brought an end to the reality of the nation, which it turned into a mere illusion that has been preserved for ideological or strictly political purposes ever since. Even if the resurgence of nations and nationalists may warrant hope or fear, the social and philosophical coherence of the nation has already reached its limit.

The search for economic *homogeneity* has given way to *interdependence* when it has not yielded to the economic superpowers of the world. In like manner, historical tradition and linguistic unity have been molded into a broader and deeper denominator that we might call a symbolic denominator: a cultural and religious memory shaped by a combination of historical and geographical influences. This memory generates national territories determined by the ever diminishing but still widespread conflicts between political parties. At the same time, this common "symbolic denominator" is a means not only to globalization and economic standardization but also to entities that are greater than any one nation and that *sometimes* embrace the boundaries of an entire continent.

In this way, a "common symbolic denominator" can lead to a new social grouping that is greater than the nation, though it enables the nation to retain and build upon its characteristics instead of losing them. This transformation occurs, however, within a paradoxical temporal structure, a sort of "future perfect" in which the most deeply repressed and transnational past gives a distinctive character to programmed uniformity. For the memory in question (the common symbolic denominator) is linked to the solution that spatially and temporally united human groupings have offered less for the problems of the *production* of material goods (which is the domain of economics, human relations, and politics) than of *reproduction*—the survival of the species, life and death, the body, sex, and the symbol. If it is true, for instance, that Europe represents this sort of

sociocultural grouping, its existence stems more from its "symbolic denominator" of art, philosophy, and religion than from its economic profile. Of course, economics is a function of collective memory, but its characteristics are easily modified by pressures from one's partners in the world.

Therefore, we see that this sort of social grouping is endowed with a *solidity* rooted in the various modes of reproduction and its representations by which the biological species is placed within a temporally determined humanity. Yet, it is also tainted with a certain *fragility*, for the symbolic denominator can no longer aspire to universality and endure the influences and assaults inflicted by other sociocultural memories. Hence, Europe, which is still fairly inconstant, is obliged to identify with the cultural, artistic, philosophical, and religious manifestations of other supranational groupings. Such identifications are of no surprise when the entities in question share a historical connection, like Europe and North America, or Europe and Latin America. They also occur, however, when the universality of this symbolic denominator juxtaposes two modes of production and reproduction that may seem incongruous, like those of Europe and the Arab world, Europe and India, Europe and China, and so forth.

In short, when dealing with the sociocultural groupings of the "European" type, we are forever faced with two major issues: first, that of *identity*, which is brought about by historical sedimentation, and second, the *loss of identity*, which is caused by memory links that bypass history in favor of anthropology. In other words, we are confronted with two temporal dimensions: the time of linear, cursive history, and the time of another history, that is, another time, a *monumental* time (the nomenclature comes from Nietzsche) that incorporates these supranational sociocultural groupings within even larger entities.

I would like to draw attention to certain formations that seem to embody the dynamics of this sort of sociocultural organism. I am speaking of groups we call "sociocultural" because they are defined by their role in production, but also (and especially) because of their role in the mode of reproduction and its representations. Although these groups share all the traits of the sociocultural formation in question, they *transcend* it and link it to other sociocultural formations. I am thinking specifically of sociocultural groups that we summarily define according to age categories (for instance, "European youth"), or

---

*From *New Maladies of the Soul*, by Julia Kristeva, translated by Ross Guberman. © 1995 Columbia University Press.

gender divisions (for instance, "European women"), and so forth. Clearly, European youth and European women have a particularity of their own, and it is no less obvious that what defines them as "youth" or "women" is concomitant with their "European" origin and shared by their counterparts in North America and China, among others. Insofar as they participate in "monumental history," they are not merely European "youth" or "women." In a most specific way, they will mirror the universal features of their structural position with regard to reproduction and its representations. . . .

Which Time?

Joyce said "Father's time, mother's species," and it seems indeed that the evocation of women's name and fate privileges the *space* that *generates* the human species more than it does *time*, destiny, or history. Modern studies of subjectivity—of its genealogy or its accidents—have reaffirmed this separation, which may result from sociohistorical circumstances. After listening to his patients' dreams and fantasies, Freud grew to believe that "hysteria was linked to place." Subsequent studies on children's acquisition of the symbolic function have shown that the permanency and quality of maternal love pave the way for the earliest spatial references, which give rise to childhood laughter and then prepare the whole array of symbolic manifestations that permit sign and syntax.

Before endowing the patient with a capacity for transference and communication, do not both anti-psychiatry and applied psychoanalysis (when applied to the treatment of psychoses) purport to mark out new places that serve as gratifying and healing substitutes for long-standing deficiencies of maternal space? The examples of this are many, but they all converge upon the problematics of space, which so many religions with a matriarchal bent attribute to "the woman" and which Plato, who echoed the atomists of antiquity within his own system, referred to as the aporia of the *chora*, a matrixlike space that is nourishing, unnameable, prior to the One and to God, and that thus defies metaphysics.

As for time, female subjectivity seems to offer it a specific concept of measurement that essentially retains *repetition* and *eternity* out of the many modalities that appear throughout the history of civilization. On the one hand, this measure preserves cycles, gestation, and the eternal return of biological rhythm that is similar to the rhythm of nature. Its predictability can be shocking, but its simultaneity with

what is experienced as extra-subjective and cosmic time is a source of resplendent visions and unnameable jouissance. On the other hand, it preserves a solid temporality that is faultless and impenetrable, one that has so little to do with linear time that the very term "temporality" seems inappropriate. All-encompassing and infinite, like imaginary space, it reminds us of Hesiod's Kronos, the incestuous son who smothered Gaea with his entire being in order to take her away from Ouranos the father. It also recalls the myths of resurrection in the various traditions that have perpetuated the trace of a maternal cult through its most recent manifestation within Christianity. In Christianity, the body of the Virgin Mother does not die, but travels from one space to another within the same time frame, whether by dormition (according to the Orthodox faith) or assumption (according to Catholicism).

These two types of temporality—cyclical and monumental—are traditionally associated with female subjectivity, when female subjectivity is considered to be innately maternal. We must not forget, however, that repetition and eternity serve as fundamental conceptions of time in numerous experiences, notably mystical ones. That the modern feminist movement has identified with these experiences suggests that it is not intrinsically incompatible with "masculine" values.

On the other hand, female subjectivity poses a problem only with respect to a certain conception of time, that of time as planning, as teleology, as linear and prospective development—the time of departure, of transport and arrival, that is, the time of history. It has been amply demonstrated that this sort of temporality is inherent in the logical and ontological values of any given civilization. We can assume that it explains a rupture, a waiting period, or an anxiety that other temporalities hide from our view. This sort of time is that of language, of the enunciation of sentences (noun phrase and verb phrase, linguistic topic and comment, beginning and end), and it is maintained through its outer limit—death. A psychoanalyst would call it obsessional time, for the very structure of the slave can be found within the mastery of this time. A male or female hysteric (who suffers from reminiscences, according to Freud) would identify, rather, with prior temporal modalities—the cyclical, the monumental.

Within the bounds of a given civilization, however, this antinomy of psychic structures becomes an antinomy among social groups and ideologies. Indeed, the radical viewpoints of certain feminists are akin to the discourse of marginal spiritual or mystic groups, as well as, interestingly enough, to the concerns of modern science. Is it not true that the problematics of a time indissociable from space—of a space-time placed in an infinite expansion or articulated by accidents and catastrophes—are of great interest to space science as well as genetics? And in a different way, is it not true that the media revolution that has manifested itself as the information age suggests that time is frozen or exploded according to the fortuity of demand? Is it a time that returns to its source but cannot be mastered, that inexorably overwhelms its subject and restricts those who assimilate it to only two concerns: who will wield power over the origin (its programming) and the end (its use)?

The reader may be struck by these fluctuating points of reference—mother, woman, hysteric. Although the seemingly coherent use of the word "woman" in current ideology may have a "popular" or "shock" effect, it eradicates the differences among the various functions and structures that operate beneath this word. The time may have come, in fact, to celebrate the *multiplicity* of female perspectives and preoccupations. In a more accurate, honest, and less self-serving way, we must guarantee that the *fundamental difference* between the sexes arises out of the network of these differences. Feminism has accomplished a formidable task by making this difference a *painful* one, which means it is able to generate contingency and symbolic life in a civilization that has nothing to do besides playing the stock market and waging war.

We cannot speak about Europe or about "women in Europe" without defining the history that encompasses this sociocultural reality. It is true that a feminine sensibility has been in existence for more than a century now, but it is likely that by introducing its notion of time, it clashes with the idea of an "Eternal Europe," or perhaps even a "Modern Europe." Feminine sensibility, rather, would look for its own trans-European temporality by way of the European past and present as well as the European "ensemble," defined as the storehouse of memory. We can contend, however, that European feminist movements have displayed three attitudes toward this conception of linear temporality—a temporality that we readily deem to be masculine, and that is as "civilizational" as it is obsessional.

When the women's movement began as the struggle of suffragists and existential feminists, it sought to stake out its place in the linear time of planning and history. As a result, although the movement was universalist from the start, it was deeply rooted in the sociopolitical life of nations. The political demands of women, their struggles for equal pay for equal work and for the right to the same opportunities that men have, as well as the rejection of feminine or maternal traits considered incompatible with participation in such a history all stem from the *logic of identification* with values that are not ideological (such values have been rightly criticized as too reactionary) but logical and ontological with regard to the dominant rationality of the nation and the state.

It is unnecessary to enumerate all the benefits that this logic of identification and spirited protest have offered and still offer to women (abortion rights, contraception, equal pay, professional recognition, and more). These benefits have had or will soon prove to have even more significant effects than those of the Industrial Revolution. This current of feminism, which is universalist in scope, *globalizes* the problems of women of various social categories, ages, civilizations, or simply psychic structures under the banner of Universal Woman. In this world, a reflection about *generations* of women could only be conceived of as a succession, a progression that sought to implement the program set out by its founding members.

A second phase is associated with women who have come to feminism since May 1968 and who have brought their aesthetic or psychoanalytic experiences with them. This phase is characterized by a quasi-universal rejection of linear temporality and by a highly pronounced mistrust of political life. Although it is true that this current of feminism still has an allegiance to its founding members and still focuses (by necessity) on the struggle for the sociocultural recognition of women, in a *qualitative* sense, it sees itself in a different light from the prior generation of feminists.

The "second phase" women, who are primarily interested in the specificity of feminine psychology and its symbolic manifestations, seek a language for their corporeal and inter-subjective experiences, which have been silenced by the cultures of the past. As artists or writers, they have undertaken a veritable exploration of the *dynamics of signs*. At least on the level of its intentions, their exploration is comparable to the most ambitious projects for religious and artistic upheaval. Attributing this experience to a new generation does not merely imply that new concerns have been added to the earlier demands of sociopolitical identity, for it also means that by requiring that we recognize an irreducible and self-sufficient singularity that is multifaceted, flowing, and in some ways non-identical, feminism is currently situated outside the linear time of identities that communicate through projections and demands. Today, feminism is returning to an archaic (mythic) memory as well as to the cyclical or monumental temporality of marginal movements. It is clearly not by chance that the European and trans-European problem has manifested itself at the same time as this new phase of feminism.

What sociopolitical processes or events have led to this mutation? What are its problems, its contributions, its limits?

Raewyn Connell (1944–) is University Professor at the University of Sydney. She formerly taught at Harvard, the University of California at Santa Cruz, and Macquarie University where she achieved the distinction of having been the youngest scholar to be appointed Professor (a status that in Australia is usually reserved only for the most distinguished member of a faculty). Her 1988 book, *Gender and Power*, is considered the *locus classicus* in the study of masculinities and as one of the most sophisticated social theorists of gender and politics. Her other books include *Gender* (2002), *Masculinities* (1995), and *The Men and Boys* (2000). Connell is the 1995 winner of the American Sociological Association's Sex and Gender Section Award for Distinguished Scholarship and a Fellow of the Australian Academy of Social Sciences. Connell's *Southern Theory* (2007), from which the selection is taken, is a startling criticism of the Northern bias of sociology and social theory.

Southern Theory: Gender and Violence[*]
Raewyn Connell (2007)

Among the criticisms of *Subaltern Studies* was that it had little to say about caste, and little to say (despite the involvement of a well-known feminist, Gayatri Spivak) about gender relations. These criticisms are broadly correct, for the early issues. The narratives of peasant risings talk a lot about local leaderships, but

[*]Connell, Raewyn. *Southern Theory.* Malden, MA: Polity Press, 2007. © 2007 Polity Press. Reprinted with permission of Polity Press. Also reproduced by permission of Allen & Unwin Pty Ltd.

hardly notice that the leaders are exclusively men. However, gender issues do creep in. In the fifth volume, Guha (1987) himself wrote a superb paper, 'Chandra's Death,' about a peasant family in mid-nineteenth century Bengal. In this he worked from tiny fragments of evidence to build a picture of the gender order in rural society and the responses rural women made to patriarchal power.

Of course, Guha was not the first man to concern himself with the oppression of women. As Chatterjee (1993: Chs 6-7) notes, gender justice had been a major issue in mid-nineteenth century Bengal. Claims about the barbarous Indian treatment of women were part of the British justification of colonial rule; but the issue was also addressed by indigenous intellectuals. Iswarchandra Vidyasagar, an educational reformer and a central figure in the 'Calcutta renaissance' of the mid-nineteenth century, sharply criticized the patriarchal kinship system of his day, including polygamy, child marriage and the ban on widows remarrying. He wrote the scathing lines:

> Let not the unfortunate weaker sex be born in a country where the men have no pity, no dharma, no sense of right and wrong, no ability to discriminate between beneficial and harmful, where preservation of what has been customary is considered the only duty, the only *dharma*...By what sin do women come to be born Bharatvarsha at all? (Quoted in Sarkar 1997: 267)

In the next generation, Bankimchandra Chatterjee [Chattopadhyay], the best-known Indian novelist before Tagore, and famous as the author of the hymn *Bande Mataram* (Hail to the Mother), which became a national song, took an even more radical position. In an essay on 'Equality', he denounced the fact that 'in all countries women are the slaves of men.' He argued not only for widow remarriage and women's property rights, but also for women's right to move in public space, and the need for *men* to share childcare and housework, a position still radical a hundred years later (Chatterjee 1986). Chatterjee later returned from this view, but other men in the Indian intelligentsia also took up the cause of women's rights, including Sayyid Ahmad Khan, as mentioned in Chapter 6.

The development of a *women's* politics around gender justice was a slow and complex process. Women were present in the nationalist movement in considerable numbers, and not just elite women. Gandhi's mass action campaigns depended on women's support. But mainstream nationalism, as Partha Chatterjee (1993) argues, did not articulate a gender politics in the public realm. A diverse group of women's organisations set up an umbrella organisation, the All India Women's Conference, in the 1920s. This body did articulate an equal-rights perspective, but lost influence after independence. Those women's organisations which had a mass reach were mainly the affiliated groups set up by male-controlled political parties.

Their effect is illuminated by Raka Ray's (1999) study of feminist politics in Kolkata and Mumbai, which looks closely at Paschim Banga Ganatantrik Mahila Samiti, the women's wing of West Bengal's governing Communist Party of India (Marxist). The Samiti functioned mainly to implement the official line coming down from the male leadership, and that line insisted on solidarity between working-class women and men. The women of the Samiti, while working for women's economic and educational advancement, therefore shied away from any direct challenge to the interests of men—for instance, from making a public issue of domestic violence.

Violence against women was, however, the galvanizing issue in other parts of India. Some feminist groups formed in the early 1970s. In the years immediately after Indira Gandhi's temporary dictatorship, the 'Emergency' of 1975–1977, feminist organising spread rapidly. A wide range of autonomous women's groups came into existence, periodicals were launched—the best-known, *Manushi*, began publication in 1979—research and teaching began, and public campaigns were undertaken (Kumar 1999).

A few years later, Nandita Gandhi and Nandita Shah (1992) conducted an interview survey of women's groups across the country, and were impressed by the range and diversity of activism. There were campaigns around domestic violence, dowry murders, rape, women's health, women in the workplace, legal reform, and more. But for all this diversity, it was the continuing fact of men's violence—the sense of threat under which women lived—that was central to the movement. As the editorial in the first issue of *Manushi* put it:

To live as a woman is to live in fear—of molestation, rape, of social stigma in almost every action of ours. We have to be afraid to do so many things—to be outside after dark, to travel alone, to step outside the home, to be alone in the home, to be with others, to ac-

knowledge even to ourselves our own desires—to love, to laugh, to live (Kishwar and Vanita 1984: 243).

We might therefore expect Indian feminism to generate distinctive theories about violence and the nature of a gender system that produced such pervasive fear. But Gandhi and Shah, who subtitled their book *Theory and Practice in the Contemporary Women's Movement in India*, found little theoretical work going on. Women's movement conferences, on their account, focused on empirical documentation of the position of women and on debating problems of activism. And of one occasion when there was a conscious attempt to promote theory, the report ruefully: 'A study circle formed by Shakti, a Bombay based resource centre, to discuss analytical concepts such as patriarchy, feminism and its various streams, had to close down for want of people' (Gandhi and Shah 1992: 288).

Can an energetic, diverse and creative movement, which is grappling with issues about state power, caste inequalities and cultural definitions of women's bodies, function without theory? Perhaps not, because several kinds of theory were soon imported. One was a body of ideas long familiar on the Indian left, Marxist political economy. Indian feminists became involved in the debates, also familiar in the metropole, about productive and unproductive labour, wages for housework, women as a reserve army of labour, Engels on the family, and so on. For instance, Gabriele Dietrich (1992), a participant for fourteen years, devoted a heavyweight chapter of her *Reflections on the Women's Movement in India* to these ideas. She concludes, unsurprisingly, that the women's question cannot be solved within capitalism, but also that an autonomous women's movement is necessary.

Other Indian feminists read the literature of radical feminism produced, mainly in the United States, in the 1970s. The concept of 'patriarchy' as a system of domination was articulated by Women's Liberation at the start of that decade. Not long afterwards, Mary Daly, Susan Griffin, Carolyn Merchant and others reworked this idea into a dichotomous vision of gender in which females are peaceful, cooperative and close to nature while males are aggressive, competitive and hostile to nature. This model was picked up by the woman who, after Spivak, became India's best-known feminist outside India, Vandana Shiva.

In *Staying Alive: Women, Ecology and Development*, Shiva (1989) applies this model, her immediate sources being Merchant and Griffin, to environmental struggles in India. The strengths of the book include a narrative of the Chipko forest protection movement in North India since 1972, in which Shiva emphasizes, in a way *Subaltern Studies* never did, the importance of women in local leadership. The book sharply criticizes 'Green Revolution' agriculture, on the basis of village-level research on sorghum, and development programs that harvest water. Both are criticised for disrupting village women's labour and the reproduction of local communities and environments.

These analyses, however, are embedded in a righteous rhetoric in which women are always good, ecologically knowledgeable, embedded in nature, caring, quiet and committed to the production of life. Men are mostly bad and noisy, and white Western men are extremely bad and exceptionally noisy, being hell-bent on markets, profits and development. Development is always destructive, always against women's interests, and always resisted by 'women, peasants and tribals.' These good folk, according to Shiva, are involved in the traditional worship of nature as Mother, and support the creative 'feminine principle' known in Indian tradition as 'Prakriti'.

Well. A quarter of the peasants on the Indian subcontinent are Muslim and extremely unlikely to be into nature worship. (It is specifically rejected in the *Qur'an*, see e.g. Sura 13.) The other peasants are divided among hundreds of dialects, castes and religious communities. As Bina Agarwal (1992) observes in a judicious critique, Shiva ignores social, religious, regional and national diversity in constructing an idealised picture of women; she ignores processes of gender change; and she misses the importance of local class power in economic processes.

The arbitrary character of Shiva's text is curiously revealed, for an Australian reader, by her discussion of eucalyptus trees. Here Shiva (1989: 78-82) converts a perfectly valid argument against monoculture of exotics in India into a denunciation of eucalyptus trees themselves, which seem to epitomise the grasping, masculine, anti-life forces that Shiva hates. She does not seem to know that eucalyptus is not a 'single species,' but a very large genus with more than 500 varied species, beautifully adapted to the different environments across Australia, and much loved in their native places. (For their career as exotics under British and French colonialism, see Zacharin 1976.)

Yet a third style of metropolitan feminism is invoked in a later issue of *Subaltern Studies*. Susie Tharu and Tejaswini Niranjana (1996) are concerned about the rise of women's activism in right-wing Hindu nationalist agitations, and about how the empowerment of women can be misused by marketers of contraceptive chemicals and misrepresented in discussions of the anti-alcohol movement among village women. What is the theoretical problem here? To Tharu and Niranjana, it is feminism's supposed complicity with humanism and failure to break with the 'humanist subject.' The diagnosis is taken straight from the manual of North American feminist postmodernism.

These texts bring to a head a major problem about theory in the global South. No intellectuals working outside the metropole can ignore the intellectual production of the metropole. For many purposes, it is feasible and labour-saving to import metropolitan theory and simply give it a local gloss. That is understandable where an activist movement faces huge practical problems, which is true for the Indian women's movement. It is also understandable—though the dynamics are different—where a large part of the audience is located in the metropole, which is true for the later *Subaltern Studies* and for Shiva's environmentalism.

The question of Southern theory has, of course, been considered by Indian intellectuals. Chatterjee (1993), for instance, argues for 'an Indian history of peasant struggle' rather than an application of European models. He offers some interesting ideas about how European thought about modernity became a universal model and led to misreadings of colonial society....

Slavoj Žižek (1949–) was born in Ljubljana, Slovenia. He studied philosophy in his native city before going to Paris to study psychoanalysis. Žižek is surely one of the most uncommonly brilliant and baffling thinkers of our time. His lectures and writings are remarkable for their surprising juxtapositions of subtle theoretical analysis to references from popular culture, cinema, and religion. He is a professor in the European Graduate School and senior researcher at the Institute of Sociology, University of Ljubljana. He has taught also at Columbia, Princeton, and the New School, Michigan, to name a few. His books include *The Fragile Absolute: or Why the Christian Legacy Is Worth*

Fighting For (2000), *Enjoy Your Symptom!: Jacques Lacan in Hollywood and Out* (2000), and *The Ticklish Subject: The Absent Centre of Political Ontology (Wo Es War)* (1999). The selection is from his first book, *The Sublime Object of Ideology (Phronesis)* (1989), which, while more accessible than some of the later ones, contains the core of his continuing effort to rethink (or, better, *replay*) cultural theory.

Cynicism as a Form of Ideology*
Slavoj Žižek (1989–2001 & after)

The Social Symptom

How, then, call we define the Marxian symptom? Marx "invented the symptom" (Lacan) by means of detecting a certain fissure, an asymmetry, a certain "pathological" imbalance which belies the universalism of the bourgeois "rights and duties". This imbalance, far from announcing the "imperfect realization" of these universal principles—that is, an insufficiency to be abolished by further development—functions as their constitutive moment: the "symptom" is, strictly speaking, a particular element which subverts its own universal foundation, a species subverting its own genus. In this sense, we can say that the elementary Marxian procedure of "criticism of ideology" is already "symptomatic": it consists in detecting a point of breakdown *heterogenous* to a given ideological field and at the same time *necessary* for that field to achieve its closure, its accomplished form.

This procedure thus implies a certain logic of exception: every ideological Universal—for example freedom, equality—is "false" in so far as it necessarily includes a specific case which breaks its unity, lays open its falsity. Freedom, for example: a universal notion comprising a number of species (freedom of speech and press, freedom of consciousness, freedom of commerce, political freedom, and so on) but also, by means of a structural necessity, a specific freedom (that of the worker to sell freely his own labour on the market) which subverts the universal notion. That is to say, this freedom is the very opposite of effective freedom: by selling his labour "freely," the worker *loses* his freedom—the real content of this free act of sale is the worker's enslavement to capital. The crucial point is, of course, that it is precisely this

paradoxical freedom, the form of its opposite, which closes the circle of "bourgeois freedoms." . . .

In his attribution of the discovery of symptom to Marx, Lacan is, however, more distinct: he locates this discovery in the way Marx conceived the *passage* from feudalism to capitalism: "One has to look for the origins of the notion of symptom not in Hippocrates but in Marx, in the connection he was first to establish between capitalism and what?—the good old times, what we call the feudal times" (Lacan, 1975a, p. 106). To grasp the logic of this passage from feudalism to capitalism we have first to elucidate its theoretical background, the Marxian notion of commodity fetishism.

In a first approach, commodity fetishism is "a definite social relation between men, that assumes, in their eyes, the fantastic form of a relation between things." The *value* of a certain commodity, which is effectively an insignia of a network of social relations between producers of diverse commodities, assumes the form of a quasi-"natural" property of another thing-commodity, money: we say that the value of a certain commodity is such-and-such amount of money. Consequently, the essential feature of commodity fetishism does not consist of the famous replacement of men with things ("a relation between men assumes the form of a relation between things"); rather, it consists of a certain misrecognition which concerns the relation between a structured network and one of its elements: what is really a structural effect, an effect of the network of relations between elements, appears as an immediate property of one of the elements, as if this property also belongs to it outside its relation with other elements.

Such a misrecognition can take place in a "relation between things" as well as in a "relation between men"—Marx states this explicitly apropos of the simple form of the value-expression. The commodity A can express its value only by referring itself to another commodity, B, which thus becomes its equivalent: in the value relationship, the natural form of the commodity B (its use-value, its positive, empirical properties) functions as a form of value of the commodity A; in other words, the body of B becomes for A the mirror of its value. To these reflections, Marx added the following note [*Capital* I]:

> In a sort of way, it is with man as with commodities. Since he comes into the world neither with a looking-glass in his hand, nor as a Fichtian philosopher, to whom "I am I" is sufficient, man first sees and recognizes

* Žižek, Slavoj. *The Sublime Object of Ideology*. London: Verso, 1989. Print. Reprinted with permission of Verso.

himself in other men. Peter only establishes his own identity as a man by first comparing himself with Paul as being of like kind. And thereby Paul, just as he stands in his Pauline personality, becomes to Peter the type of the genus homo.

This short note anticipates in a way the Lacanian theory of the mirror stage: only by being reflected in another man—that is, in so far as this other man offers it an image of its unity—can the ego arrive at its self-identity; identity and alienation are thus strictly correlative. . . .

The most elementary definition of ideology is probably the well-known phrase from Marx's Capital: *"Sie wissen das nicht, aber sie tun es"*—*"they do not know it, but they are doing it"*. The very concept of ideology implies a kind of basic, constitutive *naïveté*: the misrecognition of its own presuppositions, of its own effective conditions, a distance, a divergence between so-called social reality and our distorted representation, our take consciousness of it. That is why such a "naïve consciousness" can be submitted to a critical-ideological procedure. The aim of this procedure is to lead the naïve ideological consciousness to a point at which it can recognize its own effective conditions, the social reality that it is distorting, and through this very act dissolve itself. In the more sophisticated versions of the critics of ideology—that developed by the Frankfurt School, for example—it is not just a question of seeing things (that is, social reality) as they "really are," of throwing away the distorting spectacles of ideology; the main point is to see how the reality itself cannot reproduce itself without this so-called ideological mystification. The mask is not simply hiding the real state of things; the ideological distortion is written into its very essence.

We find, then, the paradox of a being which can reproduce itself only in so far as it is misrecognized and overlooked: the moment we see it "as it really is," this being dissolves itself into nothingness or, more precisely, it changes into another kind of reality. That is why we must avoid the simple metaphors of de-masking, of throwing away the veils which are supposed to hide the naked reality. We can see why Lacan, in his Seminar on *The Ethic of Psychoanalysis*, distances himself from the liberating gesture of saying finally that "the emperor has no clothes." The point is, as Lacan puts it, that the emperor is naked only beneath his clothes, so if there is an unmasking gesture of psychoanalysis, it is closer to Alphonse

Allais's well-known joke, quoted by Lacan: somebody points at a woman and utters a horrified cry, "Look at her, what a shame, under her clothes, she is totally naked" (Lacan, 1986, p. 231).

But all this is already well known: it is the classic concept of ideology as "false consciousness," misrecognition of the social reality which is part of this reality itself. Our question is: Does this concept of ideology as a naïve consciousness still apply to today's world? Is it still operating today? In the *Critique of Cynical Reason*, a great bestseller in Germany (Sloterdijk, 1983), Peter Sloterdijk puts forward the thesis that ideology's dominant mode of functioning is cynical, which renders impossible—or, more precisely, vain—the classic critical-ideological procedure. The cynical subject is quite aware of the distance between the ideological mask and the social reality, but he none the less still insists upon the mask. The formula, as proposed by Sloterdijk, would then be: "they know very well what they are doing, but still, they are doing it." Cynical reason is no longer naïve, but is a paradox of an enlightened false consciousness: one knows the falsehood very well, one is well aware of a particular interest hidden behind an ideological universality, but still one does not renounce it. . . .

If we want to grasp this dimension of fantasy, we must return to the Marxian formula "they do not know it, but they are doing it," and pose ourselves a very simple question: Where is the place of ideological illusion, in the "*knowing*" or its "*doing*" in the reality itself? At first sight, the answer seems obvious: ideological illusion lies in the "knowing." It is a matter of a discordance between what people are effectively doing and what they think they are doing—ideology consists in the very fact that the people "do not know what they are really doing," that they have a false representation of the social reality to which they belong (the distortion produced, of course, by the same reality). Let us take again the classic Marxian example of so-called commodity fetishists: money is in reality just an embodiment, a condensation, a materialization of a network of social relations—the fact that it functions as a universal equivalent of all commodities is conditioned by its position in the texture of social relations. But to the individuals themselves, this function of money—to be the embodiment of wealth—appears as an immediate, natural property of a thing called "money," as if money is already in itself, in its immediate material reality, the embodiment of wealth. Here, we have touched upon the classic Marxist motive of "reification": behind the things, the relation between things, we must detect the social relations, the relations between human subjects.

Gilles Deleuze (1925–1995) began his academic career as a philosopher and author of works so original that Michel Foucault once wrote, "perhaps one day this century will be called Deleuzian." Like many of the philosophers of the 1960s in Paris, Foucault included, Deleuze's writing went far beyond philosophy to embrace politics, literature, and psychoanalysis as well as social theory. He committed suicide in 1995.

Félix Guattari (1930–1992) combined much the same formation and trajectory as Deleuze's. If anything, he was the more active politically and the more directly concerned with the politics of the anti-psychiatry movement of the 1960s. Deleuze and Guattari met at the University of Vincennes, a hotbed of revolutionary activity in Paris during the events of May 1968. Then began their collaboration that issued, first, in *Anti-Oedipus* (1972), then *A Thousand Plateaus* (1980). The selection is from the latter work, which was extremely slow to gain recognition in the Anglophone world, in large part due to its extreme difficulty and perverse originality. Yet, its most famous concept—that of the rhizome as a figure in the service of a profound rethinking of culture and politics as rooted in obscure, underground connections without beginning or end—has come to be a decisive tool for reconsideration of global realities in the aftermath of 2001 and the uncertainties it represents.

The Rhizome/A Thousand Plateaus[*]
Gilles Deleuze and Félix Guattari (1980–2001)

Let us summarize the principal characteristics of a rhizome: unlike trees or their roots, the rhizome connects any point to any other point, and its traits are not necessarily linked to traits of the same nature; it brings into play very different regimes of signs, and

[*]Deleuze, Gilles and Félix Guattari. Brain Massumi, trans. *A Thousand Plateaus: Capitalism and Schizophrenia.* University of Minnesota Press, 1987. Print. Copyright 1987 by the University of Minnesota Press. © 1988 Athlone Press. Reprinted with permission of The Athlone Press, an imprint of Bloomsbury Publishing Plc. Originally published as *Mille Plateaux,* volume 2 of *Capitalisme et Schizoprhénie* © 1980 by Les Editions de Minuit, Paris.

even nonsign states. The rhizome is reducible neither to the One nor the multiple. It is not the One that becomes Two or even directly three, four, five, etc. It is not a multiple derived from the One, or to which One is added ($n + 1$). It is composed not of units but of dimensions, or rather directions in motion. It has neither beginning nor end, but always a middle (*milieu*) from which it grows and which it overspills. It constitutes linear multiplicities with n dimensions having neither subject nor object, which can be laid out on a plane of consistency, and from which the One is always subtracted ($n - 1$). When a multiplicity of this kind changes dimension, it necessarily changes in nature as well, undergoes a metamorphosis. Unlike a structure, which is defined by a set of points and positions, with binary relations between the points and biunivocal relationships between the positions, the rhizome is made only of lines: lines of segmentarity and stratification as its dimensions, and the line of flight or deterritorialization as the maximum dimension after which the multiplicity undergoes metamorphosis, changes in nature. These lines, or lineaments, should not be confused with lineages of the arborescent type, which are merely localizable linkages between points and positions. Unlike the tree, the rhizome is not the object of reproduction: neither external reproduction as image-tree nor internal reproduction as tree-structure. The rhizome is an antigenealogy. It is a short-term memory, or anti-memory. The rhizome operates by variation, expansion, conquest, capture, offshoots. Unlike the graphic arts, drawing, or photography, unlike tracings, the rhizome pertains to a map that must be produced, constructed, a map that is always detachable, connectable, reversible, modifiable, and has multiple entryways and exits and its own lines of flight. It is tracings that must be put on the map, not the opposite. In contrast to centered (even polycentric) systems with hierarchical modes of communication and preestablished paths, the rhizome is an acentered, nonhierarchical, nonsignifying system without a General and without an organizing memory or central automaton, defined solely by a circulation of states. What is at question in the rhizome is a relation to sexuality—but also to the animal, the vegetal, the world, politics, the book, things natural and artificial—that is totally different from the arborescent relation: all manner of "becomings."

A plateau is always in the middle, not at the beginning or the end. A rhizome is made of plateaus. Gregory Bateson uses the word "plateau" to designate something very special: a continuous, self-vibrating region of intensities whose development avoids any orientation toward a culmination point or external end. Bateson cites Balinese culture as an example: mother-child sexual games, and even quarrels among men, undergo this bizarre intensive stabilization. "Some sort of continuing plateau of intensity is substituted for [sexual] climax," war, or a culmination point. It is a regrettable characteristic of the Western mind to relate expressions and actions to exterior or transcendent ends, instead of evaluating them on a plane of consistency on the basis of their intrinsic value. For example, a book composed of chapters has culmination and termination points. What takes place in a book composed instead of plateaus that communicate with one another across microfissures, as in a brain? We call a "plateau" any multiplicity connected to other multiplicities by superficial underground stems in such a way as to form or extend a rhizome. We are writing this book as a rhizome. It is composed of plateaus. We have given it a circular form, but only for laughs. Each morning we would wake up, and each of us would ask himself what plateau he was going to tackle, writing five lines here, ten there. We had hallucinatory experiences, we watched lines leave one plateau and proceed to another like columns of tiny ants. We made circles of convergence. Each plateau can be read starting anywhere and can be related to any other plateau. To attain the multiple, one must have a method that effectively constructs it; no typographical cleverness, no lexical agility, no blending or creation of words, no syntactical boldness, can substitute for it. In fact, these are more often than not merely mimetic procedures used to disseminate or disperse a unity that is retained in a different dimension for an image-book. Technonarcissism. Typographical, lexical, or syntactic creations are necessary only when they no longer belong to the form of expression of a hidden unity, becoming themselves dimensions of the multiplicity under consideration; we only know of rare successes in this. We ourselves were unable to do it. We just used words that in turn function for us as plateaus. RHIZOMATICS = SCHIZO-ANALYSIS = STRATOANALYSIS = PRAGMATICS = MICROPOLITICS. These words are concepts, but concepts are lines, which is to say, number systems attached to a particular dimension of the multiplicities (strata, molecular chains, lines of flight or rupture, circles of convergence, etc.). Nowhere do we claim for our concepts the title of a science. We are no more familiar with scientificity than we are with ideology; all we know are assemblages. And the only assemblages are machinic assemblages of desire and collective assemblages of enunciation. No significance, no subjectification: writing to the nth power (all individuated enunciation remains trapped within the dominant significations, all signifying desire is associated with dominated subjects). An assemblage, in its multiplicity, necessarily acts on semiotic flows, material flows, and social flows simultaneously (independently of any recapitulation that may be made of it in a scientific or theoretical corpus). There is no longer a tripartite division between a field of reality (the world) and a field of representation (the book) and a field of subjectivity (the author). Rather, an assemblage establishes connections between certain multiplicities drawn from each of these orders, so that a book has no sequel nor the world as its object nor one or several authors as its subject. In short, we think that one cannot write sufficiently in the name of an outside. The outside has no image, no signification, no subjectivity. The book as assemblage with the outside, against the book as image of the world. A rhizome-book, not a dichotomous, pivotal, or fascicular book. Never send down roots, or plant them, however difficult it may be to avoid reverting to the old procedures. "Those things which occur to me, occur to me not from the root up but rather only from somewhere about their middle. Let someone then attempt to seize them, let someone attempt to seize a blade of grass and hold fast to it when it begins to grow only from the middle." Why is this so difficult? The question is directly one of perceptual semiotics. It's not easy to see things in the middle, rather than looking down on them from above or up at them from below, or from left to right or right to left: try it, you'll see that everything changes. It's not easy to see the grass in things and in words (similarly, Nietzsche said that an aphorism had to be "ruminated"; never is a plateau separable from the cows that populate it, which are also the clouds in the sky).

History is always written from the sedentary point of view and in the name of a unitary State apparatus, at least a possible one, even when the topic is nomads. What is lacking is a Nomadology, the opposite of a history.

Giorgio Agamben (1942–) has become Italy's best-known contemporary philosopher. His books and lectures are translated and read with astonishing frequency. He teaches philosophy at Università

Iuav di Venezia and lectures regularly in France and the United States, among other places. The selection is from his most famous book *Homo Sacer: Sovereign Power and Bare Life* in which he deftly interprets classical and modern philosophical ideas to the end of challenging the modern world to recognize the foundational deceptions of the liberal state in its presumed right to suspend its own laws in order to create exceptions that have the effect of forcing groups of people onto the conditions of bare life—the extreme of exclusion at the margins of biological survival.

Sovereign Power and Bare Life[*]
Giorgio Agamben (1998)

The Greeks had no single term to express what we mean by the word "life." They used two terms that, although traceable to a common etymological root, are semantically and morphologically distinct: zoē, which expressed the simple fact of living common to all living beings (animals, men, or gods), and *bios*, which indicated the form or way of living proper to an individual or a group. When Plato mentions three kinds of life in the *Philebus*, and when Aristotle distinguishes the contemplative life of the philosopher (*bios theôrçtikos*) from the life of pleasure (*bios apolaustikos*) and the political life (*bios politikos*) in the *Nichomachean* Ethics, neither philosopher would ever have used the term zoē (which in Greek, significantly enough, lacks a plural). This follows from the simple fact that what was at issue for both thinkers was not at all simple natural life but rather a qualified life, a particular way of life. Concerning God, Aristotle can certainly speak of a *zoē aristē kai aidios*, a more noble and eternal life (*Metaphysics*, 1072b, 28), but only insofar as he means to underline the significant truth that even God is a living being (similarly, Aristotle uses the term *zoē* in the same context—and in a way that is just as meaningful—to define the act of thinking). But to speak of a *zoē politikē* of the citizens of Athens would have made no sense. Not that the classical world had no familiarity with the idea that natural life, simple *zoē* as such, could be a good in itself. In a passage of the *Politics*, after noting that the end of the city is life according to the good, Aristotle expresses his awareness of that idea with the most perfect lucidity:

> This [life according to the good] is the greatest end both in common for all men and for each man separately. But men also come together and maintain the political community in view of simple living, because there is probably some kind of good in the mere fact of living itself [*kata to zēn auto monon*]. If there is no great difficulty as to the way of life [*kata ton bion*], clearly most men will tolerate much suffering and hold on to life [*zoē*] as if it were a kind of serenity [*euēmeria*, beautiful day] and a natural sweetness. (1278b, 23–31)

In the classical world, however, simple natural life is excluded from the *polis* in the strict sense, and remains confined—as merely reproductive life—to the sphere of the *oikos*, "home" (*Politics*, 1252a, 26–35). At the beginning of the *Politics*, Aristotle takes the greatest care to distinguish the *oikonomos* (the head of an estate) and the *despotçs* (the head of the family), both of whom are concerned with the reproduction and the subsistence of life, from the politician, and he scorns those who think the difference between the two is one of quantity and not of kind. And when Aristotle defined the end of the perfect community in a passage that was to become canonical for the political tradition of the West (1252b, 30), he did so precisely by opposing the simple fact of living (to *zēn*) to politically qualified life (*to eu zēn*): *ginomenē men oun tou zēn heneken, ousa de tou eu zēn*, "born with regard to life, but existing essentially with regard to the good life" (in the Latin translation of William of Moerbeke, which both Aquinas and Marsilius of Padua had before them: *facta quidem igitur vivendi gratia, existens autem gratia bene vivendi*).

It is true that in a famous passage of the same work, Aristotle defines man as a *politikon zôon* (*Politics*, 1253a, 4). But here (aside from the fact that in Attic Greek the verb *bionai* is practically never used in the present tense), "political" is not an attribute of the living being as such, but rather a specific difference that determines the genus *zôon*. (Only a little later, after all, human politics is distinguished from that of other living beings in that it is founded, through a supplement of politicity [*policità*] tied to language, on a community not simply of the pleasant and the painful but of the good and the evil and of the just and the unjust.)

Michel Foucault refers to this very definition when, at the end of the first volume of The *History of Sexuality*, he summarizes the process by which, at the threshold of the modern era, natural life begins to be included in the mechanisms and calculations of State power, and politics turn into *biopolitics*. "For millennia," he writes, "man remained what he was for Aristotle: a living animal with the additional capacity for political existence; modern man is an animal whose politics calls his existence as a living being into question" (*La volonté*, p. 188).

According to Foucault, a society's "threshold of biological modernity" is situated at the point at which the species and the individual as a simple living body become what is at stake in a society's political strategies. After 1977, the courses at the Collège de France start to focus on the passage from the "territorial State" to the "State of population" and on the resulting increase in importance of the nation's health and biological life as a problem of sovereign power, which is then gradually transformed into a "government of men" (*Dits et écrits*, 3:719). "What follows is a kind of bestialization of man achieved through the most sophisticated political techniques. For the first time in history, the possibilities of the social sciences are made known, and at once it becomes possible both to protect life and to authorize a holocaust." In particular, the development and triumph of capitalism would not have been possible, from this perspective, without the disciplinary control achieved by the new biopower, which, through a series of appropriate technologies, so to speak created the "docile bodies" that it needed.

Almost twenty years before *The History of Sexuality*, Hannah Arendt had already analyzed the process that brings *homo laborans*—and, with it, biological life as such—gradually to occupy the very center of the political scene of modernity. In *The Human Condition*, Arendt attributes the transformation and decadence of the political realm in modern societies to this very primacy of natural life over political action. That Foucault was able to begin his study of biopolitics with no reference to Arendt's work (which remains, even today, practically without continuation) bears witness to the difficulties and resistances that thinking had to encounter in this area. And it is most likely these very difficulties that account for the curious fact that Arendt establishes no connection between her research in *The Human Condition* and the penetrating analyses she had previously devoted to totalitarian power (in which a biopolitical

perspective is altogether lacking), and that Foucault, in just as striking a fashion, never dwelt on the exemplary places of modern biopolitics: the concentration camp and the structure of the great totalitarian states of the twentieth century.

Foucault's death kept him from showing how he would have developed the concept and study of biopolitics. In any case, however, the entry of *zoē* into the sphere of the *polis*—the politicization of bare life as such—constitutes the decisive event of modernity and signals a radical transformation of the political-philosophical categories of classical thought. It is even likely that if politics today seems to be passing through a lasting eclipse, this is because politics has failed to reckon with this foundational event of modernity. The "enigmas" (Furet, *L'Allemagne nazi*, p. 7) that our century has proposed to historical reason and that remain with us (Nazism is only the most disquieting among them) will be solved only on the terrain—biopolitics—on which they were formed. Only within a biopolitical horizon will it be possible to decide whether the categories whose opposition founded modern politics (right/left, private/public, absolutism/democracy, etc.)—and which have been steadily dissolving, to the point of entering today into a real zone of indistinction—will have to be abandoned or will, instead, eventually regain the meaning they lost in that very horizon. And only a reflection that, taking up Foucault's and Benjamin's suggestion, thematically interrogates the link between bare life and politics, a link that secretly governs the modern ideologies seemingly most distant from one another, will be able to bring the political out of its concealment and, at the same time, return thought to its practical calling. . . .

What defines the status of *homo sacer* is therefore not the originary ambivalence of the sacredness that is assumed to belong to him, but rather both the particular character of the double exclusion into which he is taken and the violence to which he finds himself exposed. This violence—the unsanctionable killing that, in his case, anyone may commit—is classifiable neither as sacrifice nor as homicide, neither as the execution of a condemnation to death nor as sacrilege. Subtracting itself from the sanctioned forms of both human and divine law, this violence opens a sphere of human action that is neither the sphere of *sacrum facere* nor that of profane action. This sphere is precisely what we are trying to understand here.

We have already encountered a limit sphere of human action that is only ever maintained in a relation of exception. This sphere is that of the sovereign decision, which suspends law in the state of exception and thus implicates bare life within it. We must therefore ask ourselves if the structure of sovereignty and the structure of *sacratio* might be connected, and if they might, from this perspective, be shown to illuminate each other. We may even then advance a hypothesis: once brought back to his proper place beyond both penal law and sacrifice, *homo sacer* presents the originary figure of life taken into the sovereign ban and preserves the memory of the originary exclusion through which the political dimension was first constituted. The political sphere of sovereignty was thus constituted through a double exclusion, as an excrescence of the profane in the religious and of the religious in the profane, which takes the form of a zone of indistinction between sacrifice and homicide. *The sovereign sphere is the sphere in which it is permitted to kill without committing homicide and without celebrating a sacrifice, and sacred life—that is, life that may be killed but not sacrificed—is the life that has been captured in this sphere.*

It is therefore possible to give a first answer to the question we put to ourselves when we delineated the formal structure of the exception. What is captured in the sovereign ban is a human victim who may be killed but not sacrificed: *homo sacer.* If we give the name bare life or sacred life to the life that constitutes the first content of sovereign power, then we may also arrive at an answer to the Benjaminian query concerning "the origin of the dogma of the sacredness of life." The life caught in the sovereign ban is the life that is originarily sacred—that is, that may be killed but not sacrificed—and, in this sense, the production of bare life is the originary activity of sovereignty. The sacredness of life, which is invoked today as an absolutely fundamental right in opposition to sovereign power, in fact originally expresses precisely both life's subjection to a power over death and life's irreparable exposure in the relation of abandonment.

Social Theory at the Limits of the Social

Bruno Latour (1947–) was born in Beaune, Burgundy, to the well-known wine-growing family. His education was in France, initially in philosophy, then anthropology. From 1982 to 2006 he was professor at the Centre de Sociologie de l'Innovation at the Ecole Nationale Supérieure des Mines in Paris. Over the years down to the present he has held positions at Sciences Po in France, University of California at San Diego, the London School of Economics, and Harvard. He broke into world notice with the 1979 book (with Steve Woolgar), *Laboratory Life: The Social Construction of Scientific Facts*—a book that challenged and revolutionized science studies for its daring central claim that scientific discovery is bound by necessity to the material conditions of the scientific laboratory, including its equipment, machinery, and other material things. Since *Laboratory Life*, Latour has written countless articles and books, including *We Have Never Been Modern* (1991), *Pandora's Hope* (1999), and *Reassembling the Social* (2005). The last mentioned could be thought of as an attempt to revise social theory by decomposing the classical assumption that the sphere of social life is somehow different in kind from nature. Here and in other writings, including the text here presented, Latour pursues the idea that social things operate of the same level of reality as natural ones. This notion offers the original, if counterintuitive, notion that reality is purely and simply a network of material things without distinction save for the ways social, natural, and material things similarly organize themselves into what

he calls "networks of actants." The selection is from a 2009 article called "Spheres and Networks: Two Ways to reinterpret Globalization."

Spheres and Networks: The Spaces of Material Life[*]
Bruno Latour (2009)

The opposite strategies of naturalization and socialization are able to stupefy the mind only because they are always thought of separately. But as soon as you combine the two moves, you realize that nature and society are two perfectly happy bedfellows whose opposition is a farce, and that what Peter [Sloterdijk] and I did was, in our own ways, to kick *both* of them out of their beds, and then to attempt something just as foreign to naturalization as it is to socialization—or, even worse, to "social construction." Spheres and networks allow, in our view, a reclaiming of the little beings that make up the life supports without the superficial gloss the philosophy of natural sciences has provided them: The re-localization and re-embodiment of science allows us to extract, so to speak, the epistemological poison out of the sweet honey of scientific objectivity. You may throw *Dasein* into the world by redistributing its *properties*

[*]Excerpt from Bruno Latour, "Spheres and Networks: Two Ways to Reinterpret Globalization." © 2012 Bruno Latour/President and Fellows of Harvard College. Text originally appeared in *Harvard Design Magazine*, number 30, Spring/Summer 2009. Reprinted with permission.

(a word, by the way, more easily connected to the verb "to have" than the verb "to be"), only if the world into which it is thrown is not that of "nature." And the only way this world can be real, objective, and material without being "natural" is first to have redistributed and re-localized science. As the *alter-mondialistes* and antiglobalization folks chant so rightly: "Another world is possible." Maybe, but on the condition that we are no longer restricted to the meager combat rations of nature and society.

When we ponder how the global world could be made habitable—a question especially important for architects and designers—we now mean habitable for billions of humans and trillions of other creatures that no longer form a nature or, of course, a society, but rather, to use my term, a possible *collective* (contrary to the dual notions of nature-and-society, the collective is *not* collected *yet*, and no one has the slightest idea of what it is to be composed of, how it is to be assembled, or even if it should be assembled into one piece). But why has the world been made uninhabitable in the first place? More precisely, why has it not been conceived as if the question of its habitability was the only question worth asking?

I am more and more convinced that the answer lies in this extremely short formula: *lack of space*. Paradoxically, the whole enterprise around spheres and networks—which superficially looks like a reduction, a limitation, to tiny local scenes—is in effect a search for space, for a vastly more comfortably inhabitable space. When we speak of the global, of globalization, we always tend to exaggerate the extent to which we access this global sphere: In effect, we do nothing more than gesture with a hand that [has] never been much bigger than a reasonably sized pumpkin. Peter has a version even more radical than my pumpkin argument: There is no access to the global for the simple reason that you always move from one place to the next through narrow corridors without ever being outside. Outside you would as certainly die as would a cosmonaut who, much like the famed Capitaine Haddock, simply decides to leave the space station without a spacesuit. Global talks are at best tiny topics inside well-heated hotel rooms in Davos.

The great paradox of our two enterprises is that spheres and networks are ways first to localize the global so as, in a second move, to provide more space in the end than the mythical "outside" that had been devised by the nature-and-society mythology.

An anthropologist of the Moderns like myself cannot but be continually struck by how implausi-ble, uncomfortable, and cramped have been the places that the architects of the Moderns have devised for them—and here I am not thinking only of card-carrying architects but also of people like John Locke or Immanuel Kant or Martin Heidegger. It is ironic that so many people on the Left, at least in Europe, complain that we live in a time when the wretched of the world are no longer longing for any utopia. For me, it is the whole history of the Moderns that offers up a most radical utopia in the etymological sense: The Moderns have no place, no topos, no locus to sit and stay. The view from nowhere, so prevalent in the old scientific imagination, also means that there is nowhere for those who hold it to realistically reside. Could you survive a minute as a brain in a vat separated by a huge gap from "reality"? And yet this is the posture you are supposed to hold in order to think logically. Could you survive much longer by having your mind turned into a computer-like brain? Modernists have no place, no hookup, no plugs-in for harnessing in any plausible way the revelations of science about what it is to be material and objective. I learned from Marshall Sahlins this joke: "Reality is a nice place to visit, but no one ever lives there"—Without doubt a Modernists' joke: Realism is not their forte.

How can we account, as historians and anthropologists and philosophers, for this lack of space, a lack of space so radical that Modernists had to migrate into a continuously renewed utopia? One distinct possibility is the confusion of space with paper. Architects are especially familiar with the manipulation of drawings, and this manipulation is now at the fingertips of any dumb-downed user of CAD design software or even Google maps. Manipulation of geometric forms is so intoxicating that it can lead some—notably my compatriot René Descartes—to imagine that this is also the way in which material things navigate and reside *in space*. My argument is that *res extensa*—taken for the "material world" and considered until recently as the stuff out of which "nature" is made— is an unfortunate confusion of the properties of geometrical forms on white paper with the ways material beings *stand*.

Let us be careful here: I am not saying that *human* intentional embodied mind and spirit never really look at the material world according to the laws of geometry. (The critique has been made often enough; the whole of phenomenology has explored this avenue already.) I am saying that even the material physical objects making up the world do not stand in the world according to what would be expected of them if they were thrown into *res extensa*. In other words, the "scientific world view" is unfair to human intentionality, spiritual values, and ethical dimensions does not bother me too much: I am much more concerned if it is even more unfair to the peculiar ways electrons, rocks, amoebas, lice, rats, plants, buildings, locomotives, computers, mobiles, and pills have a hold and a standing in this world. Nothing, absolutely nothing, ever resided in *res extensa*—not even a worm, a tick, or a speck of dust—but masses of beings have been exquisitely *drawn* on white paper, engraved on copper, photographed on silver salt-coated plates, modeled on the computer, etc.—including worms, ticks, and grains of dust. *Res extensa* pertains to art history, to the history of the publishing press, to the history of computers, to the history of perspective, to the history of projective geometry, and to a host of other disciplines, but it is definitely *not* part of natural history. Among the most puzzling features of the Moderns is how extremely difficult it is for them to be materialist: What they call matter remains even today a highly idealist projection.

What would be amusing, if it had not been such a waste of time, is that "spiritualists" have exerted themselves for three centuries trying to save from the diluvium the little arch of the human soul floating on the vast ocean of the ever-mounting *res extensa*, without realizing that this ocean was but a trickle of highly localized techniques to allow on paper—and later on screen—the manipulation of figures by conserving a certain number of constants. The achievements of what I have called *inscription* and *immutable and combinable mobiles* are admirable, but they should not be confused either with a catastrophic diluvium or with the magnificent advent of Reason on earth. Far from being what the world is made of—and thus out of which the *res cogitans* should flee as far as possible—they are no more than a few of the many components *contained* inside the world of spheres and networks. The global is a form of circulation inside those sites, not what could contain them. The Latin etymology of the *res extensa* contains, to be sure, an *extensibility* that borders on the infectious, but this is no reason for sound minds to let it trespass beyond the narrow confines of inscription practices—and even less to imagine that it is such a mimetic description of the world that the whole real world of living organisms should migrate out of the *res extensa*, now construed as "space," as the only thing that really stands. This absurdly extensive definition of the *res extensa* is probably the

most hidden but the most potent source of nihilism. Imagine that—the real world confused with the white expanse of a piece of paper!

There is probably no more decisive difference among thinkers than the position they are inclined to take on space: Is space what *inside which* reside objects and subjects? Or is space *one* of the many connections made by objects and subjects? In the first tradition, if you empty the space of all entities there is something left: space. In the second, since entities engender their space (or rather their spaces) as they trudge along, if you take the entities out, nothing is left, especially space. Tell me what your position on space is, and I'll tell you who you are: I suspect such a touchstone is equally discriminating for philosophers, architects, art historians, and others.

In the case of Peter and me, I hope it's clear that we belong to the same side of the divide: Spheres and networks have been devised to suck in the *res extensa*, to bring it back to specific places, trades, instruments, and media, and to let it circulate again but without losing a moment of what in the industry is called its traceability. Peter has even succeeded in devoting a whole volume of his trilogy, *Sphären*, to the rematerialization and relocalization of the global itself, so that thanks to his painstaking redescription, even the famous "view from nowhere" has found a place, a specific architecture, generally that of Domes and Halls and frescoes, a specific lighting, a specific posture. History of thought is now being made part of the history of art, of architecture, of design, of intellectual technologies—in brief a branch of spherology. The global is part of local histories.

Such an important turn in the history of rationality should not be overlooked: Whereas in earlier periods, the advent of Reason was predicated on the nonlocal, nonsituated, nonmaterial utopia of mind and matter, it is now possible to dissipate those phantoms and to observe them move inside specific spheres and networks. At any rate, we might now be slightly more realistic about what it is to be thrown into the world and attached to objects. "The Sleep of Reason" may "Produce Monsters" but also sweet dreams: It has taken some time for Reason to finally wake up from those as well.

I recognize that at first this could seem like a bizarre contradiction: How could we claim that spheres and networks provide more space when their first effect is to shrink everything that was outside and un-situated inside precisely delineated arenas? To be sure the critical effect is clearly visible: The global is accompanied back to the rooms in which it is produced; the laws of nature are situated inside the quasi-"parliaments" where they are voted on, and no one is allowed to jump outside as if there existed a room of no room. But how could we keep pretending that this shrinking enterprise provides in the end *more* space for a more comfortably habitable world, that it is not just a critical move, a clever but in the end only negative mean of humiliating the arrogance of materialists and spiritualists alike?

Well, to understand why it is not a contradiction or a paradox, or even a critical move, you have to consider the alternative: a vast outside that is so un-situated as to be totally implausible, where the only choice offered to its inhabitants is between two forms of inhumanity: one provided by naturalization (a human made up of idealized bits extracted from all the scientific disciplines parading as matter), the other provided by socialization (a human extracted from the life supports and air-conditioning that allow it to survive).

The choice is not between nature and society—two ways of being inhuman. The real choice is between two utterly different distributions of spatial conditions: one in which there is a vast outside and infinite space but where every organism is cramped and unable to deploy its life forms; the other in which there are only tiny insides, networks and spheres, but where the artificial conditions for the deployment of life forms are fully provided and paid for.

Does it make a difference? You bet. Do you realize that organisms are still homeless in the strictures of Modernism? That we are still unable to define what a tool, a technique, and a technology are, without alternating between hype and nostalgia? That there is still no space for making sense of the billions of migrations that define the "global" but in effect not-so-global world? That, as it became pretty clear last fall, we still don't have, after two centuries of economics, a remotely realistic portrait of what an economy is, of the simple phenomenon of confidence, trust, and credit? That we are unable to find space for gods except by putting them into the cesspool of the mind? That psychology is still a tramp looking for a plausible shelter?

Every winter in France we are faced with the same *crise du logement*, the same building crunch. Well, there is a *crise du logement* of truly gigantic proportion in our total inability to find rooms for the homeless of Modernism. Indeed, Modernism itself is homeless, forcing its inhabitants to dream of a place to live that is uninhabitable—dare I say it?—by construction. What we need is more room for a new type of *real* or *realist* estate. (In a strange sense and in spite of so much work on Modernist architecture, the links to be made between Modernism and architecture have not even begun yet—and this might be the reason why, strangely enough, so many intellectual enterprises, after a detour through Romance language departments in the 1980s, have recently migrated from deserted philosophy departments to design and architecture schools.)

There is some urgency in concluding the thought experiment I invited you to make, because the outside is in short supply today anyway. It is not by coincidence that spheres and networks have been proposed as an alternative to the nature-and-society quandary just at the moment when the ecological crisis began to throw the very notion of an outside in doubt. As is now well known, the notion of "environment" began to occupy public consciousness precisely when it was realized that no human action could count on an outside environment any more: There is no reserve outside which the unwanted consequences of our collective actions could be allowed to linger and disappear from view. Literally there is no outside, no *décharge* where we could discharge the refuse of our activity. What I said earlier, rather philosophically, that the problem was "lack of space," now takes a much more radical, practical, literal, and urgent meaning: No outside is left. As usual, Peter has a striking way to bring this up when he says that the earth is finally round: Of course we knew that before, and yet the earth's rotundity was still theoretical, geographical, at best aesthetic. Today it takes a new meaning because the consequences of our actions travel around the blue planet and come back to haunt us: It is not only Magellan's ship that is back but also our refuse, our toxic wastes and toxic loans, after several turns. Now, we sense, we suffer from it: The earth is round for good. What the churches had never managed to make us feel—that our sins will never disappear—has taken a new meaning: There is no way to escape our deeds. And it burns like hell! ...

Thomas Piketty (1941–) was born in Clichy, France. He was educated at the Ecole normale supérieure where he studied mathematics. In 1993 he took his PhD in Economics at the Ecole des Hautes Etudes en Sciences Sociales (EHESS) in conjunction with the European Doctoral Programme in Economics. He has taught economics at the Massachusetts Institute of Technology and has been a research fellow in France's National Centre for Scientific Research (CNRS). He is now professor at the Paris School of Economics and Directeur d'Etudes at the Ecole des Hautes Etudes en Sciences Sociales. Upon publication in 2014 of his magisterial book *Capital in the Twenty-First Century*, Piketty immediately became globally famous. The book radically challenged previous methods for the study of capital wealth to the end of establishing r>g as the social scientific equivalent of $E=mc^2$. In this tidy formula he summarizes his detailed historical research that capital wealth will always outrun personal and family income unless there is a radical taxation on wealth.

The Central Contradictions of Capitalism: r > g[*]
Thomas Piketty (2014)

The overall conclusion of this study is that a market economy based on private property, if left to itself, contains powerful forces of convergence, associated in particular with the diffusion of knowledge and skills; but it also contains powerful forces of divergence, which are potentially threatening to democratic societies and to the values of social justice on which they are based. The principal destabilizing force has to do with the fact that the private rate of return on capital, r, can be significantly higher for long periods of time than the rate of growth of income and output, g. The inequality r > g implies that wealth accumulated in the past grows more rapidly than output and wages. This inequality expresses a fundamental logical contradiction. The entrepreneur inevitably tends to become a rentier, more and more dominant over those who own nothing but their labor. Once constituted, capital reproduces itself faster than output increases. The past devours the future. The consequences for the long-term dynamics of the wealth distribution are potentially terrifying, especially when one adds that the return on capital varies directly with the size of the initial stake and that the divergence in the wealth distribution is occurring on a global scale. The problem is enormous,

and there is no simple solution. Growth can of course be encouraged by investing in education, knowledge, and nonpolluting technologies. But none of these will raise the growth rate to 4 or 5 percent a year. History shows that only countries that are catching up with more advanced economies—such as Europe during the three decades after World War II or China and other emerging countries today—can grow at such rates. For countries at the world technological frontier— and thus ultimately for the planet as a whole—there is ample reason to believe that the growth rate will not exceed 1–1.5 percent in the long run, no matter what economic policies are adopted. With an average return on capital of 4–5 percent, it is therefore likely that r > g will again become the norm in the twenty-first century, as it had been throughout history until the eve of World War I. In the twentieth century, it took two world wars to wipe away the past and significantly reduce the return on capital, thereby creating the illusion that the fundamental structural contradiction of capitalism (r > g) had been overcome. To be sure, one could tax capital income heavily enough to reduce the private return on capital to 1 less than the growth rate. But if one did that indiscriminately and heavy-handedly, one would risk killing the motor of accumulation and thus further reducing the growth rate. Entrepreneurs would then no longer have the time to turn into rentiers, since there would be no more entrepreneurs. The right solution is a progressive annual tax on capital. This will make it possible to avoid an endless inegalitarian spiral while preserving competition and incentives for new instances of primitive accumulation. For example, I earlier discussed the possibility of a capital tax schedule with rates of 0.1 or 0.5 percent on fortunes under 1 million euros, 1 percent on fortunes between 1 and 5 million euros, 2 percent between 5 and 10 million euros, and as high as 5 or 10 percent for fortunes of several hundred million or several billion euros. This would contain the unlimited growth of global inequality of wealth, which is currently increasing at a rate that cannot be sustained in the long run and that ought to worry even the most fervent champions of the self-regulated market. Historical experience shows, moreover, that such immense inequalities of wealth have little to do with the entrepreneurial spirit and are of no use in promoting growth. Nor are they of any "common utility," to borrow the nice expression from the 1789 Declaration of the Rights of Man and the Citizen with which I began this book. The difficulty is that this

---

[*]CAPITAL IN THE TWENTY-FIRST CENTURY by Thomas Piketty, translated by Arthur Goldhammer, Copyright © 2014 by the President and Fellows of Harvard College.

solution, the progressive tax on capital, requires a high level of international cooperation and regional political integration. It is not within the reach of the nationstates in which earlier social compromises were hammered out. Many people worry that moving toward greater cooperation and political integration within, say, the European Union only undermines existing achievements (starting with the social states that the various countries of Europe constructed in response to the shocks of the twentieth century) without constructing anything new other than a vast market predicated on ever purer and more perfect competition. Yet pure and perfect competition cannot alter the inequality r > g, which is not the consequence of any market "imperfection." On the contrary. Although the risk is real, I do not see any genuine alternative: if we are to regain control of capitalism, we must bet everything on democracy—and in Europe, democracy on a European scale. Larger political communities such as the United States and China have a wider range of options, but for the small countries of Europe, which will soon look very small indeed in relation to the global economy, national withdrawal can only lead to even worse frustration and disappointment than currently exists with the European Union. The nation-state is still the right level at which to modernize any number of social and fiscal policies and to develop new forms of governance and shared ownership intermediate between public and private ownership, which is one of the major challenges for the century ahead. But only regional political integration can lead to effective regulation of the globalized patrimonial capitalism of the twenty-first century.

For a Political and Historical Economics

I would like to conclude with a few words about economics and social science. As I made clear in the introduction, I see economics as a subdiscipline of the social sciences, alongside history, sociology, anthropology, and political science. I hope that this book has given the reader an idea of what I mean by that. I dislike the expression "economic science," which strikes me as terribly arrogant because it suggests that economics has attained a higher scientific status than the other social sciences. I much prefer the expression "political economy," which may seem rather old-fashioned but to my mind conveys the only thing that sets economics apart from the other social sciences: its political, normative, and moral purpose. From the outset, political economy sought to study

scientifically, or at any rate rationally, systematically, and methodically, the ideal role of the state in the economic and social organization of a country. The question it asked was: What public policies and institutions bring us closer to an ideal society? This unabashed aspiration to study good and evil, about which every citizen is an expert, may make some readers smile. To be sure, it is an aspiration that often goes unfulfilled. But it is also a necessary, indeed indispensable, goal, because it is all too easy for social scientists to remove themselves from public debate and political confrontation and content themselves with the role of commentators on or demolishers of the views and data of others. Social scientists, like all intellectuals and all citizens, ought to participate in public debate. They cannot be content to invoke grand but abstract principles such as justice, democracy, and world peace. They must make choices and take stands in regard to specific institutions and policies, whether it be the social state, the tax system, or the public debt. Everyone is political in his or her own way. The world is not divided between a political elite on one side and, on the other, an army of commentators and spectators whose only responsibility is to drop a ballot in a ballot box once every four or five years. It is illusory, I believe, to think that the scholar and the citizen live in separate moral universes, the former concerned with means and the latter with ends. Although comprehensible, this view ultimately strikes me as dangerous. For far too long economists have sought to define themselves in terms of their supposedly scientific methods. In fact, those methods rely on an immoderate use of mathematical models, which are frequently no more than an excuse for occupying the terrain and masking the vacuity of the content. Too much energy has been and still is being wasted on pure theoretical speculation without a clear specification of the economic facts one is trying to explain or the social and political problems one is trying to resolve. Economists today are full of enthusiasm for empirical methods based on controlled experiments. When used with moderation, these methods can be useful, and they deserve credit for turning some economists toward concrete questions and firsthand knowledge of the terrain (a long overdue development). But these new approaches themselves succumb at times to a certain scientistic illusion. It is possible, for instance, to spend a great deal of time proving the existence of a pure and true causal relation while forgetting that the question itself is of limited interest. The new methods often lead to a neglect of history and of the fact that historical experience remains our principal source of knowledge. We cannot replay the history of the twentieth century as if World War I never happened or as if the income tax and PAYGO pensions were never created. To be sure, historical causality is always difficult to prove beyond a shadow of a doubt. Are we really certain that a particular policy had a particular effect, or was the effect perhaps due to some other cause? Nevertheless, the imperfect lessons that we can draw from history, and in particular from the study of the last century, are of inestimable, irreplaceable value, and no controlled experiment will ever be able to equal them. To be useful, economists must above all learn to be more pragmatic in their methodological choices, to make use of whatever tools are available, and thus to work more closely with other social science disciplines.

Owen Fiss (1938–) was born in the Bronx, New York. He was educated at Dartmouth, Oxford, and Harvard Law School, after which he clerked for US Court of Appeals Judge Thurgood Marshall and for Supreme Court Justice William J. Brennan, Jr. Fiss also served in the Civil Rights Division of the United States Department of Justice. Today he is Sterling Professor Emeritus of Law at Yale University and has been called by Yale Law School dean Robert Post "one of the truly magisterial figures in contemporary American legal academics." His primary domain of research and writing is American constitutional law, and he is among the most frequently cited scholars in the field, as a result of which he is honored the world over. The selection "The Perils of Constitutional Minimalism" is from his recent book, *A War Like No Other: The Constitution in a Time of Terror,* the very title of which suggests the range of Fiss's intellectual work.

The Perils of Constitutional Minimalism[*]
Owen Fiss (2015)

Cuba is an island 112 miles off the coast of Florida. The United States freed it of Spanish dominion in the Spanish-American War of 1898 but did not take possession of Cuba as spoils of war. Rather, it

[*] Fiss, Owen. "The Perils of Constitutional Minimalism," from *A War Like No Other.* © 2015, The New Press.

contented itself with a 45-square-mile area on the southeastern corner of the island, known as Guantánamo Bay, which has been an American naval station ever since.

As a purely formal matter, the United States occupies Guantánamo under a lease, which was first executed in 1903 and modified in 1934. The lease reserves "ultimate sovereignty" in Cuba, but it has no term. The United States possesses the unilateral power to terminate the lease, and has occupied and maintained exclusive control of the territory for more than a century.

Each year the United States tenders the rent—approximately $4,000—but for decades, the Castro government has refused to accept it. The Guantánamo Naval Station has its own residences and stores, some of which are well-known American franchises, and it is separated from the rest of Cuba by an extensive fencing system. There is no exchange between the rest of the island and the U.S.-run naval station, with the exception of a handful of elderly Cuban employees. Cuban law, such as it is, does not reach Guantánamo.

In January 2002, as the initial phase of the war in Afghanistan still raged, the Bush administration decided to open a prison in Guantánamo, and it has interned hundreds of men there who were captured in that war. Over the years, it has been used to detain al-Qaeda suspects seized in a wide number of countries—including Bosnia, Thailand, and Zambia—but Guantánamo remains first and foremost a prison for men captured in Afghanistan or near the border in Pakistan. None of the Guantánamo prisoners is an American citizen. At its height, between six hundred and eight hundred men were imprisoned at Guantánamo.

The United States invaded Afghanistan in October 2001 and ousted the Taliban in less than six months. Under the oversight of the United States and its allies, by the end of 2004 the Afghan people adopted a constitution and held democratic elections. At that point, the war in Afghanistan appeared at an end. Even though there is a growing insurgency in parts of that country, all claims of military exigency that might have justified the initial detention policy at Guantánamo today seem stale. It is important to remember, however, that the United States invaded Afghanistan not simply to oust the Taliban regime for supporting and protecting al-Qaeda but also, and perhaps more important, to vanquish al-Qaeda itself. This objective has not been achieved, and it is this larger conflict between al-Qaeda and the United States that has been used to justify the continuing detention of the Guantánamo prisoners.

The basic constitutional question posed by Guantánamo is whether the prisoners held there have any constitutional rights that might be protected by the courts and, if so, what those rights might be. This may not seem much of a question in many democracies throughout the world, including Israel, because they view their constitutions in universalistic terms. The guarantee of human dignity, for example, controls the actions of Israeli officers wherever they act and against whomever they act.[1] The U.S. Supreme Court moved toward such a cosmopolitan conception of the U.S. Constitution during the Warren Court era, but starting in 1990 it headed in a different direction.

The issue arose in a case involving a search of the home—in Mexico—of a Mexican citizen who had been seized—also in Mexico—by agents of the United States and who was then taken for trial to the United States.[2] The search had been conducted by American officials and was challenged as a violation of the Fourth Amendment. Chief Justice William Rehnquist, purporting to speak for a majority, wrote an opinion that espoused a more nationalist conception of the Constitution. According to him, the Constitution protected American citizens from the actions of U.S. officials no matter where they were located. It also protected foreign nationals when they were living in the United States and were part of the American political community, but the Constitution, reasoned Rehnquist, afforded no protection to foreign nationals abroad. The Bush administration's decision to transform Guantánamo into a prison rests on the assumption that it, like Mexico, is not part of the United States and that the prisoners, since they are all aliens, cannot claim the protection of the Constitution and the various legal procedures, such as habeas corpus, that could secure that protection.

For their part, the Guantánamo prisoners and their lawyers challenged the legality of their detention and thus contested the scope and force of Rehnquist's 1990 ruling. Rehnquist had emphasized the special wording of the Fourth Amendment, which speaks of "the right of the people," and thus it was not at all clear that the 1990 case applied to provisions such as the Due Process Clause of the Fifth Amendment, which protects the life, liberty, and property of "any person." A question could also be raised as to whether Rehnquist's opinion had the backing of a majority and thus governed. The crucial fifth vote came from Justice Anthony Kennedy, then a recent appointee, who said that he joined Rehnquist's opinion, but then went on to express the view that "the Government may act only as the Constitution authorizes, whether the actions in question are foreign or domestic."[3] He implied that the government might be obliged to respect certain basic rights even when acting overseas, though constitutional norms would have to be adjusted to take account of the different contexts. Kennedy thought the phrase "the right of the people" appearing in the Fourth Amendment was not a term of limitation but more a rhetorical flourish to emphasize the rights being conferred.

On two separate occasions, once in June 2004 and then again in June 2006, the Supreme Court addressed the claims of the Guantánamo prisoners. Both decisions rebuffed the Bush administration and received banner headlines in the press. Such results were indeed remarkable because a majority of the justices seemed to cut through a tradition in American history of judicial deference to the executive on military matters. Yet, on closer inspection, these victories for the Guantánamo prisoners were less momentous than they first appeared. Rather than resolving the basic constitutional claims of the prisoners, the Court based these decisions entirely on statutory grounds.

In fashioning the opinions in this way, Justice Stevens, who wrote for the Court in both instances, seemed to be pursuing a methodology—widely referred to as minimalism—that has gained currency in recent years in some corners of the liberal establishment in the United States.[4] One tenet of minimalism directs the judiciary to resolve cases on statutory grounds if at all possible, and to turn to the constitutional issues only if necessary. Those who defend this method of decision making argue that minimalism lets judges reduce the potential costs of wrong decisions. Constitutional decisions are for all time, the apostles of minimalism note, while a statutory interpretation can easily be corrected. Perhaps more important, minimalists also say that relying on statutory grounds encourages—nay, requires—the president to work with Congress to further his objectives, thereby promoting the democratic values of the nation.

To the surprise of no one, after each of the Court's decisions the Bush administration turned to Congress and quickly obtained the necessary legislative warrant for its detention program in Guantánamo.

As a consequence, Congress became a full partner of the president in this front of the War on Terror. This turn of events has led me to ponder the wisdom of minimalism as a decisional strategy.

Part of my concern with minimalism is specific to the Guantánamo detainees. For years on end, they have been unable to obtain a satisfactory response to their constitutional claims. Their continued imprisonment has been the subject of a series of judicial rulings and congressional enactments, and the Court's initial decisions, couched in statutory terms that virtually invited legislative intervention, made it more difficult—not impossible, but considerably more difficult—for the Court to reach a satisfactory resolution of the ultimate constitutional issues. In this respect, the decision to proceed in two steps, as minimalism dictates, already has had enormous costs, even if the Court eventually affords the detainees all that the Constitution promises.

My concern, however, is not confined to the Guantánamo prisoners and their hardships. Minimalism can be faulted not just for the hardship it imposed upon the prisoners and government institutions but also because it is based on two theoretical misunderstandings. One relates to the Court's function. To my eyes, the Court sits not to resolve the dispute before it, which may leave the Court free to choose the narrowest ground that would serve that purpose, but rather to nourish and protect the basic values of the Constitution. The duty of the Court is to act—not minimally nor even maximally but responsibly—so as to be mindful of its role within the political system as the guardian of the Constitution.

A second failing of minimalism arises from its supposition of a necessary antagonism between constitutional pronouncements and democratic values. I maintain that democracy should not be understood as simple majoritarianism ("let the political branches have their say") but as a deep and broad-based deliberative process in which we—all of us—give content to the values that define us as a nation. Constitutional pronouncements by the Court do not prevent or even stifle such deliberations but give them a certain vitality by fully revealing the threat that is posed to our basic commitments.

Oliver Sacks (1933–2015) was born in Willesden, London into a Jewish family. His parents were both accomplished physicians. During the bombing of London in the World War, Oliver and his brother were sent off to a boarding school in the Midlands where they were starved and otherwise treated with cruelty. Still, Sacks survived the sadism of the place to attend St. Paul's School, London, then The Queen's College, Oxford, where he studied physiology and biology and earned his medical degree. Since then he came to devote himself to neurology. By the 1970s Sacks came to pubic attention for writings like *Awakenings* (1973), which became a motion picture starring Robin Williams. Other of his better known books are *The Man Who Mistook His Wife for a Hat* (1985), *Seeing Voices* (1989), *Musicophilia: Tales of Music and the Brain* (2007), and *Hallucinations* (2012). Oliver Sacks taught at the Albert Einstein College of Medicine and New York University School of Medicine before joining the Columbia University Medical Center in 2007, where he was also the first Columbia University Artist. Early in 2015 he learned that ocular cancer would take his life in a matter months. In those months he published a series of essays on his coming to terms with his life and death. "Urge" was his last essay, published just after his death in August.

Urge[*]
Oliver Sacks (2015, posthumous)

Walter B., an affable, outgoing man of forty-nine, came to see me in 2006. As a teenager, following a head injury, he had developed epileptic seizures—these first took the form of attacks of déjà vu that might occur dozens of times a day. Sometimes he would hear music that no one else could hear. He had no idea what was happening to him and, fearing ridicule or worse, kept his strange experiences to himself.

Finally he consulted a physician who made a diagnosis of temporal lobe epilepsy and started him on a succession of antiepileptic drugs. But his seizures—both grand mal and temporal lobe seizures—became more frequent. After a decade of trying different antiepileptic drugs, Walter consulted another neurologist, an expert in the treatment of "intractable" epilepsy, who suggested a more radical approach—surgery to remove the seizure focus in his right temporal lobe. This helped a little, but a few years later, a second, more extensive operation was needed. The second surgery, along with medication, controlled his seizures more effectively but almost immediately led to some singular problems.

Walter, previously a moderate eater, developed a ravenous appetite. "He started to gain weight," his wife later told me, "and his pants changed three sizes in six months. His appetite was out of control. He would get up in the middle of the night and eat an entire bag of cookies, or a block of cheese with a large box of crackers."

"I ate everything in sight," Walter said. "If you put a car on the table, I would have eaten it." He became very irritable, too, he told me:

I raged for hours at inappropriate things at home (no socks, no rye bread, perceived criticisms). Driving home from work a driver squeezed me on a merge. I accelerated and cut him off. I rolled my window down, gave him the finger, and began screaming at him, and threw a metal coffee mug and hit his car. He called the police from his cell. I was pulled over and ticketed.

Walter's attention assumed an all-or-none quality. "I became distracted so easily," he said, "that I couldn't get anything started or done." Yet he was also prone to getting "stuck" in various activities—playing the piano, for example, for eight or nine hours at a time.

Even more disquieting was the development of an insatiable sexual appetite. "He wanted to have sex all the time," his wife said.

He went from being a very compassionate and warm partner to just going through the motions. He didn't remember having just been intimate.... He wanted sex constantly after his surgery...at least five or six times a day. He also gave up on foreplay. He would always want to get right to it.

There were only fleeting moments of satiety, and within seconds of orgasm, he wanted intercourse again and again. When his wife became exhausted, he turned to other outlets. Walter had always been a devoted and thoughtful husband, but now his sexual desires, his urges, spread beyond the monogamous heterosexual relationship he had enjoyed with his wife.

It was morally inconceivable for him to force his sexual attentions on a man, woman, or child—Internet pornography, he felt, was the least harmful answer; it could provide some sort of release and satisfaction, even if only in fantasy. He spent hours masturbating in front of his computer screen while his wife slept.

After he started viewing adult pornography, various websites solicited him to purchase and download child pornography, and he did. He became curious, too, about other forms of sexual stimulation—with men, with animals, with fetishes. Alarmed and ashamed of these new compulsions, so alien to his previous sexual nature, Walter found himself engaged in a grim struggle for control. He continued to go to work, to go out socially, to meet his friends for meals or movies. During these times he was able to keep his compulsions in check, but at night, alone, he gave in to his urges. Deeply ashamed, he told no one of his predicament, living a double life for more than nine years.

Then the inevitable happened, and federal agents came to Walter's house to arrest him for possession of child pornography. This was terrifying, but it was also a relief, because he no longer had to hide or dissimulate—he called it "coming out of the shadows." His secret was exposed now to his wife and his children, and to his physicians, who immediately put him on a combination of drugs that diminished—indeed, virtually abolished—his sexual drive, so that he went from insatiable libido to almost no libido at all. His wife told me that his behavior instantly "reverted back to loving and compassionate." It was, she said, as if "a faulty switch was turned off"—a switch that had no middle position between on and off.

I saw Walter on several occasions in the time between his arrest and his prosecution, and he expressed fear—mostly of the reactions of his friends, colleagues, and neighbors. ("I thought they would point fingers or throw eggs at me.") But he thought it unlikely that a court would view his conduct as criminal, in view of his neurological condition.

On this point, Walter was wrong. Fifteen months after his arrest, his case finally came to court, and he was prosecuted for downloading child pornography. The prosecutor insisted that his so-called neurological condition was of no relevance, a red herring. Walter, he argued, was a lifelong pervert, a menace to the public, and should be put away for the maximum term of twenty years.

The neurologist who had originally suggested temporal lobe surgery and had treated Walter for almost twenty years appeared in court as an expert witness, and I submitted a letter to be read in court, explaining the effects of his brain surgery. We both pointed out that Walter's condition was a rare but well-recognized one called Klüver-Bucy syndrome, which manifests itself as insatiable eating and sexual drive, sometimes combined with irritability and distractibility, all on a purely physiological basis. (The syndrome had first been recognized in the 1880s, in lobectomized monkeys, and subsequently described in human beings.)

The all-or-none reactions that Walter had shown were characteristic of impaired central control systems; they may occur, for example, in parkinsonian patients on L-dopa. Normal control systems have a middle ground and respond in a modulated fashion, but Walter's appetitive systems were continually on "go"—there was scarcely any sense of consummation, only the drive for more and more. Once his physicians became aware of the problem, medication readily brought it under control—albeit at the cost of a sort of chemical castration.

In court, his neurologist emphasized that Walter was no longer subject to his sexual urges, and that he had never actually laid hands on anyone other than his wife. (He also noted that, among more than thirty-five cases on record of pedophilia associated with neurological disorders, only two had been arrested and charged with criminal behavior.) In my own letter to the court, I wrote:

Mr. B. is a man of superior intelligence and a real moral delicacy and sensibility, who at one point was driven to act out of character under the spur of an irresistible physiological compulsion.... He is strictly monogamous.... There is nothing in his history or his current ideation to suggest that [he] is a pedophile. He poses no risk to children or to anyone else.

At the end of the trial, the judge agreed that Walter could not be held accountable for having Klüver-Bucy syndrome. But he *was* culpable, she said, for not speaking sooner about the problem to his doctors, who could have helped, and for persisting for many years in behavior that, by supporting a criminal industry, was injurious to others; "yours is not a victimless crime," she emphasized.

She sentenced him to twenty-six months in prison, followed by twenty-five months of home confinement and then a further five-year period of supervision. Walter accepted his sentence with a remarkable degree of equanimity. He managed to survive prison life with relatively little trauma and made good use of his time in jail, establishing a musical band with some fellow inmates, reading voraciously, and writing long letters (he often wrote to me about the neuroscience books he was reading).

His seizures and his Klüver-Bucy syndrome remained well controlled by medication, and his wife stood by him throughout his years of prison and home confinement. Now that he is a free man, they have largely resumed their previous lives. They still go to the church where they were married many years ago, and he is active in his community.

When I saw him recently, he was clearly enjoying life, relieved that he had no more secrets to hide. He radiated an ease I had never seen in him before.

"I'm in a real good place," he said.

Ta-Nehisi Coates (1975–) was born in Baltimore, Maryland. His father was a Black Panther, and later the founder and publisher of Black Classic Press; his mother was a schoolteacher. The family experience clearly shaped is interested in a literary career. Coates studied at Howard University, where the experience of living in an all but totally Black institution further encouraged a writing career that was to yield major works that today challenge his readers to rethink all too casual attitudes toward an allegedly post-racial society in the Obama era. After a number of years early in the 2000s writing for local and national newspaper and magazines, Coates joined the editorial staff of *The Atlantic* magazine where, in time, he published articles directed at white America, including "The Fear of a Black President" (2012) and "The Case for Reparations" (2014). Then in 2015 his book *Between the World and Me* established Coates as a literary figure and (in a term he would not likely welcome) race theorist with whom any responsible thinker must contend. *Between the World and Me* led quickly to a National Book Award for Non-fiction and a MacArthur Foundation genius grant. The selection "Prison and the Gray Wastes" is from a 2015 *Atlantic* cover essay, "The Black Family in the Age of Mass Incarceration."

Prison and Gray Wastes[*]

Ta-Nehisi Coates (2015)

Our carceral state banishes American citizens to a gray wasteland far beyond the promises and protections the government grants its other citizens. Banishment continues long after one's actual time behind bars has ended, making housing and employment hard to secure. And banishment was not simply a well-intended response to rising crime. It was the method by which we chose to address the problems that preoccupied Moynihan, problems resulting from "three centuries of sometimes unimaginable mistreatment." At a cost of $80 billion a year, American correctional facilities are a social-service program—providing health care, meals, and shelter for a whole class of people.

As the civil-rights movement wound down, Moynihan looked out and saw a black population reeling under the effects of 350 years of bondage and plunder. He believed that these effects could be addressed through state action. They were—through the mass incarceration of millions of black people.

"We Are Incarcerating Too Few Criminals."

The Gray Wastes—our carceral state, a sprawling netherworld of prisons and jails—are a relatively recent invention. Through the middle of the 20th century, America's imprisonment rate hovered at about 110 people per 100,000. Presently, America's incarceration rate (which accounts for people in prisons *and* jails) is roughly 12 times the rate in Sweden, eight times the rate in Italy, seven times the rate in Canada, five times the rate in Australia, and four times the rate in Poland. America's closest to-scale competitor is Russia—and with an autocratic Vladimir Putin locking up about 450 people per 100,000, compared with our 700 or so, it isn't much of a competition. China has about four times America's population, but American jails and prisons hold half a million more people. "In short," an authoritative report issued last year by the National Research Council concluded, "the current U.S. rate of incarceration is unprecedented by both historical and comparative standards."

What caused this? Crime would seem the obvious culprit: Between 1963 and 1993, the murder rate doubled, the robbery rate quadrupled, and the aggravated-assault rate nearly quintupled. But the

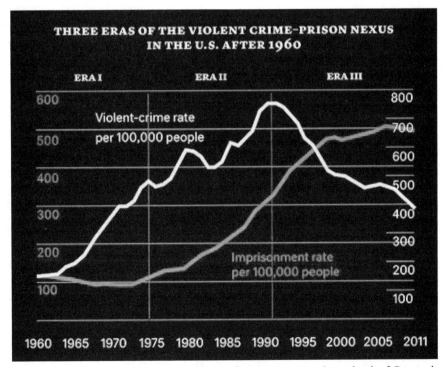

Credit: Robert Sampson. Data from: Bureau of Justice Statistics; Sourcebook of Criminal Justice Statistics; Uniform Crime Reporting System.

relationship between crime and incarceration is more discordant than it appears. Imprisonment rates actually fell from the 1960s through the early '70s, even as violent crime increased. From the mid-'70s to the late '80s, both imprisonment rates and violent-crime rates rose. Then, from the early '90s to the present, violent-crime rates fell while imprisonment rates increased.

The incarceration rate rose independent of crime—but not of criminal-justice policy. Derek Neal, an economist at the University of Chicago, has found that by the early 2000s, a suite of tough-on-crime laws had made prison sentences much more likely than in the past. Examining a sample of states, Neal found that from 1985 to 2000, the likelihood of a long prison sentence nearly doubled for drug possession, tripled for drug trafficking, and quintupled for nonaggravated assault.

That explosion in rates and duration of imprisonment might be justified on grounds of cold pragmatism if a policy of mass incarceration actually caused crime to decline. Which is precisely what some politicians and policy makers of the tough-on-crime '90s were claiming. "Ask many politicians, newspaper editors, or criminal justice 'experts' about our prisons, and you will hear that our problem is that we put too many people in prison," a 1992 Justice Department report read. "The truth, however, is to the contrary; we are incarcerating too *few* criminals, and the public is suffering as a result."

History has not been kind to this conclusion. The rise and fall in crime in the late 20th century was an international phenomenon. Crime rates rose and fell in the United States and Canada at roughly the same clip—but in Canada, imprisonment rates held steady. "If greatly increased severity of punishment and higher imprisonment rates caused American crime rates to fall after 1990," the researchers Michael Tonry and David P. Farrington have written, then "what caused the Canadian rates to fall?" The riddle is not particular to North America. In the latter half of the 20th century, crime rose and then fell in Nordic countries as well. During the period of rising crime, incarceration rates held steady in Denmark, Norway, and Sweden—but declined in Finland. "If punishment affects crime, Finland's crime rate should have shot up," Tonry and Farrington write, but it did not. After studying California's tough "Three Strikes and You're Out" law—which mandated at least a 25-year sentence for a third "strikeable offense," such as murder or robbery—researchers at UC Berkeley and the University of Syd-

ney, in Australia, determined in 2001 that the law had reduced the rate of felony crime by no more than 2 percent. Bruce Western, a sociologist at Harvard and one of the leading academic experts on American incarceration, looked at the growth in state prisons in recent years and concluded that a 66 percent increase in the state prison population between 1993 and 2001 had reduced the rate of serious crime by a modest 2 to 5 percent—at a cost to taxpayers of $53 billion.

From the mid-1970s to the mid-'80s, America's incarceration rate doubled. From the mid-'80s to the mid-'90s, it doubled again. Then it went still higher.

This bloating of the prison population may not have reduced crime much, but it increased misery among the group that so concerned Moynihan. Among all black males born since the late 1970s, one in four went to prison by their mid-'30s; among those who dropped out of high school, seven in 10 did. "Prison is no longer a rare or extreme event among our nation's most marginalized groups," Devah Pager, a sociologist at Harvard, has written. "Rather it has now become a normal and anticipated marker in the transition to adulthood."

The emergence of the carceral state has had far-reaching consequences for the economic viability of black families. Employment and poverty statistics traditionally omit the incarcerated from the official numbers. When Western recalculated the jobless rates for the year 2000 to include incarcerated young black men, he found that joblessness among all young black men went from 24 to 32 percent; among those who never went to college, it went from 30 to 42 percent. The upshot is stark. Even in the booming '90s, when nearly every American demographic group improved its economic position, black men were left out. The illusion of wage and employment progress among African American males was made possible only through the erasure of the most vulnerable among them from the official statistics.

These consequences for black men have radiated out to their families. By 2000, more than 1 million black children had a father in jail or prison—and roughly half of those fathers were living in the same household as their kids when they were locked up. Paternal incarceration is associated with behavior problems and delinquency, especially among boys.

"More than half of fathers in state prison report being the primary breadwinner in their family," the National Research Council report noted. Should the family attempt to stay together through incarceration, the loss of income only increases, as the mother must pay for phone time, travel costs for visits, and legal fees. The burden continues after the father returns home, because a criminal record tends to injure employment prospects. Through it all, the children suffer.

Many fathers simply fall through the cracks after they're released. It is estimated that between 30 and 50 percent of all parolees in Los Angeles and San Francisco are homeless. In that context—employment prospects diminished, cut off from one's children, nowhere to live—one can readily see the difficulty of eluding the ever-present grasp of incarceration, even once an individual is physically out of prison. Many do not elude its grasp. In 1984, 70 percent of all parolees successfully completed their term without arrest and were granted full freedom. In 1996, only 44 percent did. As of 2013, 33 percent do.

The Gray Wastes differ in both size and mission from the penal systems of earlier eras. As African Americans began filling cells in the 1970s, rehabilitation was largely abandoned in favor of retribution—the idea that prison should not reform convicts but punish them. For instance, in the 1990s, South Carolina cut back on in-prison education, banned air conditioners, jettisoned televisions, and discontinued intramural sports. Over the next 10 years, Congress repeatedly attempted to pass a No Frills Prison Act, which would have granted extra funds to state correctional systems working to "prevent luxurious conditions in prisons." A goal of this "penal harm" movement, one criminal-justice researcher wrote at the time, was to find "creative strategies to make offenders suffer."

Eula Biss (1977–) studied at Hampshire College, a school noted for the relative flexibility of its culture and curriculum. After college she earned an M.F.A. from the University of Iowa. Currently she is an artist-in-residence in the English Department at Northwestern University. Though a relatively young and decidedly new non-fiction author, Biss has made a considerable mark with her first books—*Balloonists Hanging Loose* (2002), *Notes From No Man's Land* (2009), and *On Immunity: An Inoculation* (2014), which was a finalist for the National Book Critics Circle Award (a prize she won in 2010 for *Notes From No Man's Land*). When her essay "White Debt" appeared in the *New York*

Times Magazine in 2015, it created an immediate sensation among readers, including academics, concerned with the maze of issues surrounding whiteness and reparations for racial injustice—a subject on which Ta-Nehisi Coates has written to comparable public effect. "White Debt" remains a key theoretical text, written honestly from within the white world about the complicated truth of white guilt. Social theory, it should be remembered, is itself a type of non-fiction writing, but in the hands of academics it is seldom written with the verve and straightforward insight that Biss exemplifies.

White Debt[*]
Eula Biss (2015)

Whiteness is not a kinship or a culture. White people are no more closely related to one another, genetically, than we are to black people. American definitions of race allow for a white woman to give birth to black children, which should serve as a reminder that white people are not a family. What binds us is that we share a system of social advantages that can be traced back to the advent of slavery in the colonies that became the United States. "There is, in fact, no white community," as Baldwin writes. Whiteness is not who you are. Which is why it is entirely possible to despise whiteness without disliking yourself.

When he was 4, my son brought home a library book about the slaves who built the White House. I didn't tell him that slaves once accounted for more wealth than all the industry in this country combined, or that slaves were, as Ta-Nehisi Coates writes, "the down payment" on this country's independence, or that freed slaves became, after the Civil War, "this country's second mortgage." Nonetheless, my overview of slavery and Jim Crow left my son worried about what it meant to be white, what legacy he had inherited. "I don't want to be on this team," he said, with his head in his hands. "You might be stuck on this team," I told him, "but you don't have to play by its rules." Even as I said this, I

---

knew that he would be encouraged, at every juncture in his life, to believe wholeheartedly in the power of his own hard work and deservedness, to ignore inequity, to accept that his sense of security mattered more than other people's freedom and to agree, against all evidence, that a system that afforded him better housing, better education, better work and better pay than other people was inherently fair.

My son's first week in kindergarten was devoted entirely to learning rules. At his school, obedience is rewarded with fake money that can be used, at the end of the week, to buy worthless toys that break immediately. Welcome to capitalism, I thought when I learned of this system, which produced, that week, a yo-yo that remained stuck at the bottom of its string. The principal asked all the parents to submit a signed form acknowledging that they had discussed the Code of Conduct with their children, but I didn't sign the form. Instead, my son and I discussed the civil rights movement, and I reminded him that not all rules are good rules and that unjust rules must be broken. This was, I now see, a somewhat unhinged response to the first week of kindergarten. I know that schools need rules, and I am a teacher who makes rules, but I still want my son to know the difference between compliance and complicity.

For me, whiteness is not an identity but a moral problem. Becoming black is not the answer to the problem of whiteness, though I sympathize with the impulse, as does Noel. "Imagine the loneliness of those who, born to a group they regard as unjust and oppressive and not wanting to be part of that group, are left on their own to figure their way out," Noel wrote recently in his own narrative, "Passing," the story of how he left a lower-middle-class family and a college education to work in factories for the next 23 years.

I met Noel after he left the factories for Harvard, when he was the editor, with John Garvey, of a journal called Race Traitor. In it, I read about groups of volunteers who worked in shifts using video cameras to record police misconduct in their cities. I read about the school-board member who challenged the selection practices that had produced, in a district where only 22 percent of the students were white, a gifted program in which 81 percent of the students were white. Race Traitor articulated for me the possibility that a person who looks white can refuse to act white, meaning refuse to collude with the injustices of the law-enforcement system and the educational system, among other things. This is what Noel called "new abolitionism." John Brown was his

model, and the institution he was intent on abolishing was whiteness.

It was because I read Race Traitor in my 20s that I stopped, in my 30s, when I saw a black man being handcuffed by his car on an empty stretch of road next to a cemetery in Chicago. I was carrying my son, who was 2, on the back of my bicycle. "What do you want?" the police officer yelled at me, already irritated, as soon as I stopped. "I'm just watching," I said. "Just being a witness." I didn't yet own a phone that could record video. He took a few threatening steps toward me, yelling about what I would do differently in his situation if I was so smart. My son was scared and began to cry. The officer kept barking at me. When my son broke into a loud wail, I memorized the number on the back of the police van and left. I now wonder what I thought I was going to do with that number: report the police to the police? By the time I got back to my apartment, my hands were still shaking, I had forgotten the number and I was dismayed with myself.

Refusing to collude in injustice is, I've found, easier said than done. Collusion is written onto our way of life, and nearly every interaction among white people is an invitation to collusion. Being white is easy, in that nobody is expected to think about being white, but this is exactly what makes me uneasy about it. Without thinking, I would say that believing I am white doesn't cost me anything, that it's pure profit, but I suspect that isn't true. I suspect whiteness is costing me, as Baldwin would say, my moral life.

And whiteness is costing me my community. It is the wedge driven between me and my neighbors, between me and other mothers, between me and other workers. I know there's more too. I have written and erased a hundred sentences here, trying and failing to articulate something that I can sense but not yet speak. Like a bad loan, the kind in which the payments increase over time, the price of whiteness remains hidden behind its promises....

The moral concept of *Schuld* ("guilt"), Nietzsche wrote, "descends from the very material concept of *Schulden* ('debts')." Material debt predates moral debt. The point he is making is that guilt has its source not in some innate sense of justice, not in God, but in something as base as commerce. Nietzsche has the kind of disdain for guilt that many people now reserve for "white guilt" in particular. We seem to believe that the crime is not investing in whiteness but feeling badly about it.

Even before I started reading Nietzsche, I had the uncomfortable suspicion that my good life, my house and my garden and the "good" public school my son attends, might not be entirely good. Even as I painted my walls and planted my tomatoes and attended parent-teacher conferences last year, I was pestered by the possibility that all this was built on a bedrock of evil and that evil was running through our groundwater. But I didn't think in exactly those terms because the word "evil" is not usually part of my vocabulary—I picked it up from Nietzsche.

"Evil" is how slaves describe their masters. In Nietzsche's telling, Roman nobles called their way of life "good," while their Jewish slaves called the same way of life "evil." The invention of the concept of evil was, according to Nietzsche, a kind of power grab. It was an attempt by the powerless to undermine the powerful. More power to them, I think. But Nietzsche and I disagree on this, among other things. Like many white people, he regards guilt as a means of manipulation, a killjoy. Those who resent the powerful, he writes, use guilt to undermine their power and rob them of their pleasure in life. And this, I believe, is what makes guilt potentially redemptive.

Guilt is what makes a good life built on evil no longer good. I have a memory of the writer Sherman Alexie cautioning me against this way of thinking. I remember him saying, "White people do crazy [expletive] when they feel guilty." That I can't dispute. Guilty white people try to save other people who don't want or need to be saved, they make grandiose, empty gestures, they sling blame, they police the speech of other white people and they dedicate themselves to the fruitless project of their own exoneration. But I'm not sure any of that is worse than what white people do in denial. Especially when that denial depends on a constant erasure of both the past and the present.

Once you've been living in a house for a while, you tend to begin to believe that it's yours, even though you don't own it yet. When those of us who are convinced of our own whiteness deny our debt, this may be an inevitable result of having lived for so long in a house bought on credit but never paid off. We ourselves have never owned slaves, we insist, and we never say the n-word. "It is as though we have run up a credit-card bill," Coates writes of Americans, "and, having pledged to charge no more, remain befuddled that the balance does not disappear." A guilty white person is usually imagined as someone made impotent by guilt, someone rendered powerless. But why not imagine guilt as a prod, a goad, an impetus to action? Isn't guilt an essential cog in the machinery of the conscience? When I search back through my correspondence with Sherman Alexie, I find him insisting that we can't afford to disempower white people because we need them to empower the rest of us. White people, he proposes, have the political power to make change exactly because they are white.

What is the condition of white life? We are moral debtors who act as material creditors. Our banks make bad loans. Our police, like Nietzsche's creditors, act out their power on black bodies. And, as I see in my own language, we confuse whiteness with ownership. For most of us, the police aren't "ours" any more than the banks are. When we buy into whiteness, we entertain the delusion that we're business partners with power, not its minions. And we forget our debt to ourselves.

Marilynne Robinson (1943–) spent her youth in the small town of her birth, Sandpoint, Idaho. She was educated at Pembroke College (once the sister school of Brown University) and Washington University's doctoral program in English. Though acquainted with the wider world, Robinson's literary fiction is rooted in rural, small town America. Her four novels—*Housekeeping* (1980), *Gilead* (2004), *Home* (2008), and *Lila* (2014)—unflinchingly probe the common grace with which unassuming characters confront ordinary human troubles. Robinson's fiction has been nominated for virtually every important literary prize. Gilead won the 2004 Pulitzer Prize for Fiction and the National Book Critics Circle Award. In 2015 *The New York Review of Books* published an extended conversation between President Barack Obama and Robinson. A constant theme of her fiction and non-fiction is the importance of Christian religious values. Yet, the selection here, demonstrates, those values serve not to proselytize but to illuminate the human condition, as in effect a kind of soft analytic tool. "Fear" may not seem to be social theory in the usual sense of the word. Yet the essay conveys a fresh interpretation of complex interplay of American religious ideas, fear, and gun violence. "Fear" thus stands as one of the more important pubic discussions of the central role that fear plays in American and global societies.

Fear[*]

Marilynne Robinson (2015)

America is a Christian country. This is true in a number of senses. Most people, if asked, will identify themselves as Christian, which may mean only that they aren't something else. Non-Christians will say America is Christian, meaning that they feel somewhat apart from the majority culture. There are a large number of demographic Christians in North America because of our history of immigration from countries that are or were also Christian. We are identified in the world at large with this religion because some of us espouse it not only publicly but also vociferously. As a consequence, we carry a considerable responsibility for its good name in the world, though we seem not much inclined to consider the implications of this fact. If we did, some of us might think a little longer about associating the precious Lord with ignorance, intolerance, and belligerent nationalism. These few simple precautions would also make it more attractive to the growing numbers among our people who have begun to reject it as ignorant, intolerant, and belligerently nationalistic, as they might reasonably conclude that it is, if they hear only the loudest voices.

There is something I have felt the need to say, that I have spoken about in various settings, extemporaneously, because my thoughts on the subject have not been entirely formed, and because it is painful to me to have to express them. However, my thesis is always the same, and it is very simply stated, though it has two parts: first, contemporary America is full of fear. And second, fear is not a Christian habit of mind. As children we learn to say, "Yea, though I walk through the valley of the shadow of death, I will fear no evil, for Thou art with me." We learn that, after his resurrection, Jesus told his disciples, "Lo, I am with you always, to the close of the age." Christ is a gracious, abiding presence in all reality, and in him history will finally be resolved....

Granting the perils of the world, it is potentially a very costly indulgence to fear indiscriminately, and to try to stimulate fear in others, just for the excitement of it, or because to do so channels anxiety or loneliness or prejudice or resentment into an emotion that can seem to those who indulge it like shrewdness or courage or patriotism. But no one

seems to have an unkind word to say about fear these days, un-Christian as it surely is.

We who are students of Calvin's tradition know that our ancestors in the tradition did not spare their lives or their fortunes. They were loyal to the will of God as they understood it at the most extreme cost to themselves—in worldly terms, that is. They also defended their faith militarily, with intelligence and great courage, but without ultimate success, except in the Low Countries. Therefore the migration of Pilgrims and Puritans, and Huguenots as well, and the great flourishing of Calvinist civilization in the New World. We might say that the oppressors meant it for evil, but God meant it for good, except this might lead us to forget a crucial thing, a factor not present in the story of Joseph and his brothers. Those oppressors were motivated by fear of us. We were heretics by their lights, and therefore a threat to the church, to Christian civilization, to every soul who felt our influence. We filled more or less the same place in the European imagination that Islam does now, one difference being that the Christianity now assumed to be under threat on that most secular continent is merely sociological and cultural, in effect racial, and another difference being that there was no ideal of tolerance and little concept of due process to mitigate the violence the presence of our ancestors inspired. Quite the opposite. To suppress our tradition however viciously was a pious act.

The terrible massacres of Protestants in France in the sixteenth century, whether official or popular in their origins, reflect the fear that is engendered by the thought that someone really might destroy one's soul, plunge one into eternal fire by corrupting true belief even inadvertently. If someone had asked a citizen of Lyon, on his way to help exterminate the Calvinists, to explain what he and his friends were doing, he would no doubt have said that he was taking back his city, taking back his culture, taking back his country, fighting for the soul of France. This kind of language was not invented in order to be used against Calvinists—Europe had been purging itself of heretics since the thirteenth century, so the pattern was already well established. These same terms had been used centuries before by the Roman emperor Julian, called the Apostate, when he tried to return Rome from its emerging Christianity to the old classical paganism. But it was applied to our case with notable rigor and persistence, and with great effect....

It is difficult for any number of reasons to define a religion, to establish an essence and a circumference,

[*] Robinson, Marilynne. "No Fear" from THE GIVENNESS OF THINGS by Marilynne Robinson. © 2015, Farrar, Straus and Giroux.

and this is true not least because it always has its supernumeraries, often legions of them.

Calvin had his supernumeraries, great French lords who were more than ready to take up arms in his cause, which was under severe persecution. He managed to restrain them while he lived, saying that the first drop of blood they shed would become a torrent that drowned France. And, after he died, Europe was indeed drenched in blood. So there is every reason to suppose that Calvin would have thought his movement had lost at least as much as it gained in these efforts to defend it, as he anticipated it would. Specifically, in some degree it lost its Christian character, as Christianity, or any branch of it, always does when its self-proclaimed supporters outnumber and outshout its actual adherents. What is true when there is warfare is just as true when the bonding around religious identity is militantly cultural or political.

Robert Pogue Harrison (1954–) was born in Izmir, Turkey. His official home page offers the following succinct and telling summary of his career: "Professor Harrison received his doctorate in romance studies from Cornell University in 1984, with a dissertation on Dante's Vita Nuova. In 1985 he accepted a visiting assistant professorship in the Department of French and Italian at Stanford. In 1986 he joined the faculty as an assistant professor. He was granted tenure in 1992 and was promoted to full professor in 1995. In 1997 Stanford offered him the Rosina Pierotti Chair. In 2002, he was named chair of the Department of French and Italian. He is also lead guitarist for the cerebral rock band Glass Wave." In short, Harrison rose rapidly to the top of his profession without sacrificing his outside interest in music and performance. Readers of his books cannot help but add that his richly informed scholarship comes forth as itself a performance of shear intellectual brilliance across a number of subjects. His first book, *The Body of Beatrice* (1988), is a revision of his doctoral thesis on Dante's *Vita Nuova*. His second, *Forests: the Shadow of Civilization* (1992), is a study of the role of forests in Western cultural imagination and is no doubt a precursor to *Gardens: An Essay on the Human Condition* (2008). The selection is from the Preface to Harrison's 2003 book, *The Dominion of the Dead*, in which (as he does in other writings) Harrison probes deeply in the cultural traditions of the West

to discover compelling facts of human existence, notably, here, in the bond that can be ignored but not denied between the living the dead.

The Dominion of the Dead[*]
Robert Pogue Harrison (2003)

Whatever the rift that separates their regimes, nature and culture have at least this much in common: both compel the living to serve the interests of the unborn. Yet they differ in their strategies in one decisive respect: culture perpetuates itself through the power of the dead, while nature, as far as we know, makes no use of this resource except in a strictly organic sense. In the human realm the dead and the unborn are native allies, so much so that from their posthumous abode—wherever it be—the former hound the living with guilt, dread, and a sense of responsibility, obliging us, by whatever means necessary, to take the unborn into our care and to keep the story going, even if we never quite figure out what the story is about, what our part in it is, the end toward which it's progressing, or the moral it contains. One day the science of genetics may decode the secrets of this custodianship, but meanwhile we may rest assured that there exists an allegiance between the dead and the unborn of which we the living are merely the ligature.

Our basic human institutions—religion, matrimony, and burial, if one goes along with the Giambattista Vico, but also law, language, literature, and whatever else relies on the transmission of legacy—are authored, always and from the very start, by those who came before. The awareness of death that defines human nature is inseparable from—indeed, it arises from—our awareness that we are not self-authored, that we follow in the footsteps of the dead. Everywhere one looks across the spectrum of human cultures one finds the foundational authority of the predecessor. Nonhuman species obey only the law of vitality, but humanity in its distinctive features is through and through necrocratic. Whether we are conscious of it or not we do the will of the ancestors: our commandments come to us from their realm; their precedents are our law; we submit to their dictates, even when we rebel against them. Our diligence, hardihood, rectitude, and heroism, but also our folly, spite, rancor, and pathologies, are so many signatures of the dead on the contracts that seal our identities. We inherit their obsessions; assume their burdens; carry on their causes; promote their mentalities, ideologies, and very often their superstitions; and often we die trying to vindicate their humiliations. Why this servitude? We have no choice. Only the dead can grant us legitimacy. Left to ourselves we are all bastards. In exchange for legitimacy, we humans need and crave more than anything else, we surrender ourselves to their dominion. We may, in our modern modes, ignore or reject their ancient authority; yet, if we are to gain a margin of real freedom—if we are to become "absolutely modern," as Rimbaud put it—we must begin by first acknowledging the traditional claims that such authority has on us.

This book offers some broad perspectives on only *some* of the manifold relations the living maintain with the giant family of the dead in Western culture, both in past and present times. In themselves these relations are so vast, profound, and numerous that no book could hope to deal with their topics except fractionally and selectively. I use the word *topics* advisedly here, for in the following pages I seek out places or topoi in our midst where the dead exert their power, press their demands, grant or deny their blessing, become loquacious, and in general co-habit our worlds. Such places where the dead carry on a secular afterlife (I have little to say about any other, nonsecular afterlife they may or may not enjoy) include graves, homes, laws, words, images, dreams, rituals, monuments, and the archives of literature, whose voices always have a posthumous character of sorts. Like human dwelling, the afterlife needs places to take place *in*. If humans dwell, the dead, as it were, indwell—and very often in the same space. I am interested here above all in nature and modes of this indwelling of the dead in the worlds of the living.

My main objective in investigating these places is not to pursue an anthropology, even less a psychology, but to uncover what I call the humic foundations of our life worlds. A humic foundation is one whose contents have been buried so that they may be reclaimed by the future. The humic holds in its conserving element the unfinished story of what has come to pass. If it is true that we move forward into the future only by retrieving the past, it is because through burial, we consign the future of our legacies into this humic element, with its vast, diversely populated underworlds. Thus burial does not mean only the laying of bodies to rest in the ground (although religion and matrimony are more likely to disappear among humans than burial customs are). In a broader sense it means to store, preserve, and put the past on hold. Dead etymons, latent meanings, and lateral connotations lie buried in the roots and phonemes of our living words, where they carry on an active afterlife. Our psyches are the graveyards of impressions, traumas, desires, and archetypes that confound the law of obsolescence. Vico, who devoted his career to "unearthing" it, believed that all the poetic wisdom of the ancients lies buried in the Homeric epics. In some instances the buried is indeed consigned to oblivion; in others it is in fact given up to repetition and reinheritance.

If I were to try to phrase the principal thesis of this study—a hazardous proposition, to be sure, since a number of diverse theses come together here—I would say that humans bury not simply to achieve closure and effect a separation from the dead but also and above all to humanize the ground on which they build their worlds and found their histories. And since I will be referring to the human rather often in these pages, let me put forward a premise here to the effect that humanity is not a species (*Homo sapiens* is a species); it is a way of being mortal and relating to the dead. To be human means above all to bury. Vico suggests as much when he reminds us that "*humanitas* in Latin comes first and properly from *humando*, burying" (*New Science* 12). By *properly* he means essentially and irreducibly. And if I have mentioned Vico more than once already it is because his *New Science* (1744) is the major inspiration for this study. Certainly it was Vico who first helped me understand how the human is bound up with the humus and why burial figures as the generative institution of human nature, taking the word *nature* in its full etymological sense (from *nasci*, "to be born"). As *Homo sapiens* we are born of our biological parents. As human beings we are born of the dead—of the regional ground they occupy, of the languages they inhabited, of the worlds they brought into being, of the many institutional, legal, cultural, and psychological legacies that, through us, connect them to the unborn.

Name Index

Notes to Accompany "The New Mestiza" (Gloria Anzaldúa, 1987)

1. Los Tigres del Norte is a *conjunto* band.

2. Jack D. Forbes, *Aztecas del Norte: The Chicanos of Aztlán.* (Greenwich, CT: Fawcett Publications, Premier Books, 1973), 13, 183; Eric R. Wolf, *Sons of Shaking Earth* (Chicago, IL: University of Chicago Press, Phoenix Books, 1959), 32.

3. John R. Chávez, *The Lost Land: The Chicano Images of the Southwest* (Albuquerque, NM: University of New Mexico Press, 1984), 9.

4. Chávez, 9. Besides the Aztecs, the Ute, Gabrillino of California, Pima of Arizona, some Pueblo of New Mexico, Comanche of Texas, Opata of Sonora, Tarahumara of Sinaloa and Durango, and the Huichol of Jalisco speak Uto-Aztecan languages and are descended from the Cochise people.

5. Reay Tannahill, *Sex In History* (Briarcliff Manor, NY: Stein and Day/Publishers/Scarborough House, 1980), 308.

6. Chávez, 21.

7. Isabel Parra, *El Libro Mayor de Violeta Parra* (Madrid, España: Ediciones Michay, S.A., 1985), 156-7.

8. From the Mexican *corrido, "Del peligro de la. Intervención"* Vicente T. Mendoza, *El Corrido Mexicano* (México. D.E: Fondo De Cultura Económica, 1954), 42.

9. Arnoldo De León, *They Called Them Greasers: Anglo Attitudes Toward Mexicans in Texas, 1821-1900* (Austin:, TX: University of Texas Press, 1983), 2-3.